CASES

Cases Following Chapter 15

Services Marketing

People, Technology, Strategy

SIXTH EDITION

Christopher Lovelock
Yale University

Jochen Wirtz
National University of Singapore

PEARSON

Prentice
Hall

Upper Saddle River, New Jersey 07458

Library of Congress Cataloging-in-Publication Data

Lovelock, Christopher H.
    Services marketing : people, technology, strategy / Christopher Lovelock,
Jochen Wirtz.—6th ed.
        p. cm.
    Includes bibliographical references and index.
    ISBN 0-13-187552-3 (alk. paper)
    1. Marketing—Management.   2. Professions—Marketing.   3. Service industries—
Marketing.   4. Customer services—Marketing.   I. Wirtz, Jochen.   II. Title.

HF5415.13.L5883 2007
658.8—dc22

2006024219

Senior Acquisitions Editor: Katie Stevens
VP/Editorial Director: Jeff Shelstad
Product Development Manager: Ashley Santora
Project Manager: Melissa Pellerano
Editorial Assistant: Christine Ietto
Marketing Assistant: Laura Cirigliano
Associate Director, Production Editorial: Judy Leale
Managing Editor: Renata Butera
Permissions Coordinator: Charles Morris
Associate Director, Manufacturing: Vinnie Scelta
Manufacturing Buyer: Michelle Klein
Design/Composition Manager: Christy Mahon
Composition Liaison: Suzanne Duda
Art Director: Jayne Conte
Manager, Cover Visual Research & Permissions: Karen Sanatar
Composition: Techbooks
Full-Service Project Management: Techbooks
Printer/Binder: Courier Westford
Typeface: 10/12 Palatino

Credits and acknowledgments borrowed from other sources and reproduced, with permission, in this textbook appear on page 633.

Pearson Education LTD.
Pearson Education Singapore, Pte. Ltd.
Pearson Education, Canada, Ltd.
Pearson Education–Japan

Pearson Education Australia PTY, Limited
Pearson Education North Asia Ltd.
Pearson Educación de Mexico, S.A. de C.V.
Pearson Education Malaysia, Pte. Ltd.

10 9 8 7 6 5 4 3 2 1
ISBN: 0-13-187552-3

To my brothers, Roger and Jeremy, and my
sister, Rachel, with love

—CHL

To Jeannette, the light of my life and wonderful mother
of our three children, Lorraine, Stefanie, and Alexander, with love

—JW

ABOUT THE AUTHORS

As a team, Christopher Lovelock and Jochen Wirtz provide a blend of skills and experience that's ideally suited to writing an authoritative and engaging services marketing text. This book marks their second collaboration on an edition of *Services Marketing*. Since first meeting in 1992, they've worked together on a variety of projects, including cases, articles, conference papers, two Asian adaptations of earlier editions of *Services Marketing*, and *Services Marketing in Asia: A Case Book*. In 2005, both were actively involved in planning the American Marketing Association's biennial Service Research Conference, hosted that year by the National University of Singapore and attended by participants from 22 countries on five continents.

Christopher Lovelock is one of the pioneers of services marketing. Based in Massachusetts, he consults and gives seminars and workshops for managers around the world, with a particular focus on strategic planning in services and managing the customer experience. Since 2001, he has been an adjunct professor at the Yale School of Management, where he teaches an MBA services marketing course.

After obtaining a BCom and an MA in economics from the University of Edinburgh, he worked in advertising with the London office of J. Walter Thompson Co. and then in corporate planning with Canadian Industries Ltd. in Montreal. Later, he obtained an MBA from Harvard and a Ph.D. from Stanford, where he was also a postdoctoral fellow.

Professor Lovelock's distinguished academic career has included 11 years on the faculty of the Harvard Business School and two years as a visiting professor at IMD in Switzerland. He has also held faculty appointments at Berkeley, Stanford, and the Sloan School at MIT, as well as visiting professorships at INSEAD in France and The University of Queensland in Australia.

Author or co-author of over 60 articles, more than 100 teaching cases, and 21 books, Dr. Lovelock has also seen his work translated into 10 languages. He serves on the editorial review boards of the *International Journal of Service Industry Management, Journal of Service Research, Service Industries Journal, Cornell Hotel and Restaurant Administration Quarterly,* and *Marketing Management,* and is also an ad-hoc reviewer for the *Journal of Marketing*.

Widely acknowledged as a thought leader in services, Christopher Lovelock has been honored by the American Marketing Association's prestigious Award for Career Contributions in the Services Discipline. In 2005 his article with Evert Gummesson, "Whither Services Marketing? In Search of a New Paradigm and Fresh Perspectives," won the AMA's Best Services Article Award and was a finalist for the IBM award for the best article in the *Journal of Service Research*. Earlier, he received a best article award from the *Journal of Marketing*. Recognized many times for excellence in case writing, he has twice won top honors in the *BusinessWeek* "European Case of the Year" Award.

Jochen Wirtz has worked in the field of services for more than 18 years, and holds a Ph.D. in services marketing from the London Business School. He is an associate professor at the National University of Singapore (NUS), where he teaches services marketing in executive, MBA, and undergraduate programs and is co-director of the dual-degree UCLA–NUS Executive MBA Program.

Professor Wirtz's research focuses on service management topics, including customer satisfaction, service guarantees, and revenue management. He has published over 60 academic articles, 80 conference papers, and some 50 book chapters, and is co-author of 10 books, including his latest book, *Flying High in a Competitive Industry—Cost-Effective Service Excellence at Singapore Airlines* (Singapore: McGraw-Hill, 2006).

Professor Wirtz has received seven awards for outstanding teaching at the NUS Business School and in 2003 was honored by the prestigious, university-wide "Outstanding Educator Award." His six research awards include the Emerald Literati Club 2003 Award for Excellence for the year's most outstanding article in the *International Journal of Service Industry Management*. He serves on the editorial review boards of seven academic journals, including the *International Journal of Service Industry Management*, *Journal of Service Research*, and *Cornell Hotel and Restaurant Administration Quarterly*, and is also an ad-hoc reviewer for the *Journal of Consumer Research* and *Journal of Marketing*. Professor Wirtz chaired the American Marketing Association's biennial Service Research Conference in 2005, and in 2006 he was the chair for the Services Marketing Track at the Academy of Marketing Science Annual Conference.

Dr. Wirtz has been an active management consultant, working with international consulting firms, including Accenture, Arthur D. Little, and KPMG, and major service firms in the areas of strategy, business development, and customer feedback systems. Originally from Germany, Jochen Wirtz spent seven years in London before moving to Asia.

About the Contributors of the Readings and Cases

Leonard L. Berry is Distinguished Professor of Marketing and holds the M.B. Zale Chair in Retailing and Marketing Leadership at the Mays Business School, Texas A&M University.

Diane Brady writes for *BusinessWeek.*

Susan Cadwallader is an assistant professor at the Mays Business School, Texas A&M University.

Lewis P. Carbone is founder, president, and CEO of Experience Engineering.

Phil Chap, MBA '05, was formerly a research assistant at the Yale School of Management.

Richard B. Chase is Justin B. Dart Professor of Operations Management and director of the Center for Service Excellence, University of Southern California.

Prosenjit Datta writes for *Businessworld*, India.

John Deighton is Harold M. Brierley Professor of Business Administration at Harvard Business School.

Thomas Dotzel is a doctoral candidate at the Mays Business School, Texas A&M University.

Lorelle Frazer is an associate professor at Griffith University, Australia.

Leonardo R. Garcia is Dean, School of Professional and Continuing Education, De La Salle College of St. Benilde, Philippines.

Keith A. Gilson is an associate principal, McKinsey & Company, Toronto, Canada.

Stephan H. Haeckel is founder of Adaptive Business Systems and past chairman of the Marketing Science Institute.

Roger Hallowell is managing partner, The Center for Executive Development.

Loizos Heracleous is a fellow in strategy and organization, Templeton College, Oxford University, UK.

James L. Heskett is Baker Foundation Professor at Harvard Business School.

Kate Scorza Ingram, MBA '05, was formerly a research assistant at the Yale School of Management.

Robert Johnston is a professor at Warwick Business School, University of Warwick, UK.

Deepak A. Khandelwal is a principal at McKinsey & Company, Toronto, Canada.

Sheryl E. Kimes is a professor at the School of Hotel Administration, Cornell University.

Jill Klein is an associate professor of marketing at INSEAD, France.

Gina S. Krishnan writes for *Businessworld,* India.

Youngme Moon is an associate professor at Harvard Business School.

Janet Turner Parish is an assistant professor at the Mays Business School, Texas A&M University.

John A. Quelch is Senior Associate Dean and Lincoln Filene Professor of Business Administration at Harvard Business School.

Frederick F. Reichheld is a director emeritus of Bain & Company and a Bain Fellow.

John H. Roberts is a marketing professor with joint appointments at the Australian Graduate School of Management and the London Business School.

Venkatesh Shanker holds the Coleman Chair in Marketing at the Mays Business School, Texas A&M University.

Emily Thornton writes for *BusinessWeek.*

Nick Wingfield is a staff reporter at *The Wall Street Journal.*

Lauren Wright is a professor of marketing at California State College, Chico.

BRIEF CONTENTS

CONTENTS

PART IV: IMPLEMENTING PROFITABLE SERVICE STRATEGIES   356

PREFACE

Services dominate the expanding world economy as never before, and nothing stands still. Technology continues to evolve in dramatic ways. Established industries evolve or sink into decline. Famous old companies merge or disappear, as new industries emerge and rising stars seize the business headlines. Competitive activity is fierce, with firms often employing new strategies and tactics in response to customers' ever-changing needs, expectations, and behavior. Customers themselves are being forced to confront change, which some see as presenting opportunities and others as an inconvenience or even a threat. If one thing is clear, it's that skills in marketing and managing services have never been more important!

As the field of services marketing has evolved so, too, has this book, with each successive edition representing a significant revision over its predecessor. This new, Sixth Edition, is no exception. Readers can be confident that it reflects the reality of today's world, incorporates recent academic and managerial thinking, and illustrates cutting-edge service concepts.

You'll find that this text takes a strongly managerial perspective, yet is rooted in solid academic research, complemented by memorable frameworks. Our goal is to bridge the all-too-frequent gap between theory and the real world. Practical management applications are reinforced by numerous examples within the 15 chapters. Complementing the text are 11 interesting, up-to-date readings and 18 outstanding, classroom-tested cases.

Preparing this new edition has been an exciting challenge. Services marketing, once a tiny academic niche championed by just a handful of pioneering professors, has become a thriving area of activity for both research and teaching. There's growing student interest in taking courses in this field, which makes good sense from a career standpoint, because most business school graduates will be going to work in service industries, and managers report that manufacturing-based models of business practice are not always useful to them.

WHAT'S NEW IN THIS EDITION?

This Sixth Edition represents a significant revision. Its contents reflect ongoing developments in the service economy, new research findings, and enhancements to the structure and presentation of the book in response to feedback from reviewers and adopters.

New Topics, New Structure

- The chapter text is now organized around a new framework for developing effective service marketing strategies that emphasizes the value exchange between suppliers and their customers. This framework, which allows for a flexible approach to teaching, is depicted in Figure 1.11 (p. 28) and forms the structure of the book, enabling students to see how different chapter topics relate to each other.
- Parts I and II have been restructured to improve the logical sequencing of topics. In particular, discussion of positioning strategy (Chapter 7) now follows rather than precedes chapters addressing such strategic elements as product elements, service delivery, communications, and pricing.

Figure A Four-Part Structure of the Book

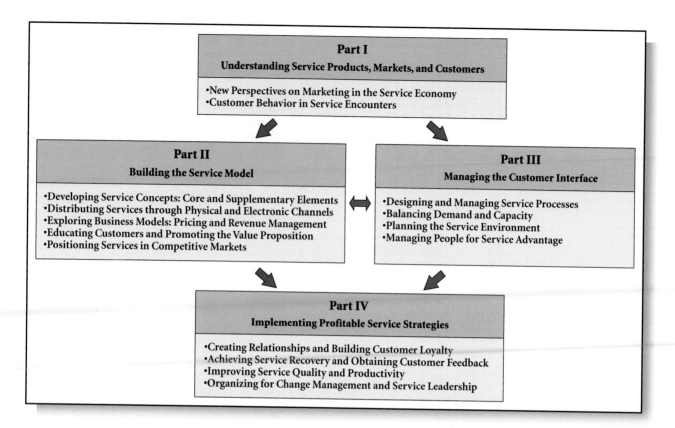

- Each of the 15 chapters has been revised. All chapters incorporate new examples and references to recent research, and some have been retitled to reflect important changes in emphasis. **Figure A** displays the four-part structure of the book, showing how chapter topics are sequenced.
- Chapter 1, "New Perspectives on Marketing in the Service Economy," has been completely rewritten. It explores the nature of the modern service economy, and presents a clear new conceptualization of the nature of services, based on award-winning research by one of the authors. In addition, this chapter offers a compelling discussion of the distinctive challenges facing service marketers but explicitly avoids sweeping generalizations. It introduces the eight key elements of the services marketing mix (referred to collectively as the 8 Ps), and presents the organizing framework for the book.
- Chapter 2, "Customer Behavior in Service Encounters," has also been substantially revised and is now organized around a three-stage model of service consumption that distinguishes, where necessary, between high- and low-contact services. At each stage, this model presents relevant insights from different concepts that are central to understanding, analyzing, and managing customer behavior.
- New applications of technology—from Internet-based strategies to biometrics—and the opportunities and challenges they pose, for customers and service marketers alike, are woven into the text at relevant points across virtually all chapters, as well as being illustrated in boxed inserts.
- Among the significant enhancements to other chapters, you'll find: a new treatment of service pricing, including expanded coverage of revenue management and thought-provoking coverage of abusive and confusing pricing practices; an overview of recent developments in electronic communications such as iTV, blogs, and Internet advertising; the latest thinking on cost-effective service excellence; an expanded section on the "wheel of loyalty" and customer relationship

management (CRM); and discussion of current thinking on change management and service leadership.

- In rewriting and restructuring the chapters, we worked hard to create a text that is clear, readable, and focused. Boxed inserts within the chapters are designed to capture student interest and provide opportunities for in-class discussion. They describe significant research findings, illustrate practical applications of important service marketing concepts, and describe best practices by innovative service organizations from the United States and other countries. Most of these inserts are either new to the Sixth Edition or have been updated.

New Readings

- Eight of the 11 readings are new to this edition. In response to reviewers' suggestions, we selected readings that are relatively short, well written, and appealing to both undergraduates and MBA students.
- These readings, drawn from such respected publications as *Harvard Business Review, BusinessWeek, Journal of Service Research, MIT Sloan Management Review, The Wall Street Journal,* and *The McKinsey Quarterly,* complement the text and offer students a chance to explore key issues in greater depth, as well as to examine interesting and even provocative market trends.
- Among the authors of these readings are leading professors and management consultants from around the world, as well as journalists writing for noted business publications.

New Cases

- *Services Marketing,* Sixth Edition, features an exceptional selection of 18 up-to-date, classroom-tested cases of varying lengths and levels of difficulty. We wrote a majority of the cases ourselves. Others are drawn from the case collections of Harvard, INSEAD, and Yale.
- Ten of the 18 cases are new to this edition. Four of the cases carried over from the previous edition have been revised or updated. Copyright dates range from 2000 to 2007.
- Responding to reviewer and adopter requests, we've increased the proportion of short and medium-length cases.
- The new selection provides even broader coverage of service marketing issues and application areas, with cases featuring a wide array of industries and organizations, ranging in size from multinational giants to small entrepreneurial start-ups. Two nonprofit organizations are included.

WHAT AIDS ARE AVAILABLE FOR INSTRUCTORS?

We've developed the following new and improved pedagogical aids to help instructors develop and teach courses built around this book and to create stimulating learning experiences for students both in and out of the classroom.

Teaching Aids Within the Text

- An introduction to each chapter highlights the key issues and questions addressed.
- Three types of boxed inserts are found throughout the chapters and often lend themselves well to in-class discussions:

    Best Practice in Action (illustrations of the application of best practices)

    Research Insights (summaries of relevant and often provocative academic research)

    Service Perspectives (examples that illustrate key concepts)

- Interesting graphics, photographs, and reproductions of advertisements enhance student learning, provide opportunities for discussion, and add visual appeal.
- Review Questions and Application Exercises are located at the end of each chapter.

Pedagogical Materials Available from the Publisher

An exceptional instructor's resource manual features:

- Detailed course design and teaching hints, plus two sample course outlines.
- Chapter-by-chapter teaching suggestions, plus discussion of learning objectives and sample responses to study questions and exercises.
- An overview of each reading, with suggestions for how to use it and the most appropriate chapter(s) with which to assign it.
- A description of 16 suggested student exercises and five comprehensive projects (designed for either individual or team work).
- Detailed teaching notes for each case, including teaching objectives, suggested study questions, in-depth analysis of each question, and helpful hints on teaching strategy designed to aid student learning, create stimulating class discussions, and help instructors create end-of-class wrap-ups and "takeaways."
- Tables suggesting which cases and readings to pair with which chapters.
- Two alternative notes—one shorter, one longer—offering advice to students on case preparation and written analysis of cases.
- A brand-new test bank for use in quizzes and exams.
- Additional cases, available online, including several popular cases featured in previous editions of *Services Marketing* and a selection of cases on marketing non-profit services.
- More than 300 PowerPoint slides, keyed to each chapter and featuring both "word" slides and graphics. All slides have been redesigned to be clear, comprehensible, and easily readable.

FOR WHAT TYPES OF COURSES CAN THIS BOOK BE USED?

This text is equally suitable for courses directed at advanced undergraduates or MBA and EMBA students. *Services Marketing,* Sixth Edition, places marketing issues within a broader general management context. The book will appeal both to full-time students headed for a career in management and to EMBAs and executive program participants who are combining their studies with ongoing work in managerial positions.

Whatever a manager's specific job may be, we argue that he or she has to understand and acknowledge the close ties that link the marketing, operations, and human resource functions. With that perspective in mind, we've designed this book so that instructors can make selective use of chapters, readings, and cases to teach courses of different lengths and formats in either services marketing or service management.

WHAT ARE THE BOOK'S DISTINGUISHING FEATURES?

Key features of this highly readable book include:

- A strong managerial orientation and strategic focus that address the need for service marketers not only to understand customer needs and behavior but also how to use these insights to develop strategies for competing effectively in the marketplace
- Use of memorable conceptual frameworks that have been classroom-tested for relevance among both undergraduates and MBA students

- Incorporation of key academic research findings
- Use of interesting examples to link theory to practice
- Inclusion of carefully selected readings and cases to accompany the text chapters
- Extensive and up-to-date references at the end of each chapter
- An international perspective

We've designed *Services Marketing*, Sixth Edition, to complement the materials found in traditional marketing principles texts. Recognizing that the service sector of the economy can best be characterized by its diversity, we believe that no single conceptual model suffices to cover marketing-relevant issues among organizations ranging from huge international corporations (in fields such as airlines, banking, insurance, telecommunications, freight transportation, and professional services) to locally owned and operated small businesses, such as restaurants, laundries, taxi services, dental offices, and many business-to-business services. In response, the book offers a carefully-designed "toolbox" for service managers, teaching students how different concepts, frameworks, and analytical procedures can best be used to examine and resolve the varied challenges faced by managers in different situations.

ACKNOWLEDGMENTS

Over the years, many colleagues in both the academic and business worlds have provided us with valued insights into the management and marketing of services through their publications, in conference or seminar discussions, and stimulating individual conversations. Both of us have benefited enormously from in-class and after-class discussions with our students and executive program participants.

We're much indebted to those researchers and teachers who helped to pioneer the study of services marketing and management, and from whose work we continue to draw inspiration. Among them are John Bateson of SHL Group; Leonard Berry of Texas A&M University; Mary Jo Bitner and Stephen Brown of Arizona State University; Richard Chase of the University of Southern California; Pierre Eiglier of IAE, Université d'Aix-Marseille III; Raymond Fisk of the University of New Orleans; Christian Grönroos of the Swedish School of Economics in Finland; Stephen Grove of Clemson University; Evert Gummesson of Stockholm University; James Heskett and Earl Sasser of Harvard University; Benjamin Schneider, emeritus of the University of Maryland; and Valarie Zeithaml of the University of North Carolina. We salute, too, the contributions of the late Eric Langeard, Theodore Levitt, and Daryl Wyckoff.

A particular acknowledgment is due to five individuals who have made exceptional contributions to the field, not only in their roles as researchers and teachers but also as journal editors, in which capacity they facilitated publication of many of the important articles cited in this book. They are Bo Edvardsson, University of Karlstad and editor, *International Journal of Service Industry Research (IJSIM)*; Robert Johnston, University of Warwick and founding editor of *IJSIM*; Jos Lemmink, Maastricht University and former editor, *IJSIM*; A. "Parsu" Parasuraman, University of Miami and editor, *Journal of Service Research (JSR)*, and Roland Rust of the University of Maryland, editor, *Journal of Marketing* and founding editor, *JSR*.

Although it's impossible to mention everyone who has influenced our thinking, we particularly want to express our appreciation to the following: Tor Andreassen, Norwegian School of Management; David Bowen, Thunderbird Graduate School of Management; John Deighton and Leonard Schlesinger, currently or formerly of Harvard Business School; Loizos Heracleous, Oxford University; Douglas Hoffmann, Colorado State University; Sheryl Kimes, Cornell University; Jean-Claude Larréché, INSEAD; David Maister, Maister Associates; Anna Mattila, Pennsylvania State University; Anat Rafaeli, Technion–Israeli Institute of Technology; Frederick Reichheld, Bain & Co; Bernd Stauss, Katholische Universität Eichstät; Charles Weinberg, University of British Columbia; Lauren Wright, California State University, Chico; and George Yip, London Business School.

We've also gained important insights from our co-authors on international adaptations of *Services Marketing*, and are grateful for the friendship and collaboration of Guillermo D'Andrea of IAE, Universidad Austral, Argentina; Luis Huete of IESE, Spain; Keh Hean Tat of Peking University, China; Denis Lapert of INT–Management, France; Barbara Lewis, formerly of Manchester School of Management, UK; Lu Xiongwen of Fudan University, China; Jayanta Chatterjee of Indian Institute of Technology at Kanpur, India; Javier Reynoso of Tec de Monterrey, Mexico; Paul Patterson of the University of New South Wales, Australia; Sandra Vandermerwe of Imperial College, London; and Rhett Walker of LaTrobe University, Australia.

It's a pleasure to acknowledge the insightful and helpful comments of reviewers of this and previous editions: Anna S. Mattila of Pennsylvania State University; Robert P. Lambert of Belmont University; Terri Rittenburg of the University of Wyoming; Ben Judd of the University of New Haven; Harry Domicone of California Lutheran University; Lisa Simon of California Polytechnic State University; Bill Hess of Golden Gate University; P. Sergius Koku of Florida Atlantic University; Martin J. Lattman of Johns Hopkins University; Daryl McKee of Louisiana State University; Cynthia Rodriguez Cano of Augusta State University; and Frederick Crane of the University of New Hampshire. They challenged our thinking and encouraged us to include many substantial changes. In addition, we benefited from the valued advice of Sharon Beatty of the University of Alabama and Karen Fox of Santa Clara University, who provided numerous thoughtful suggestions for improvement.

It takes more than authors to create a book and its supplements. Warm thanks are due to our research assistants, who helped us with various aspects of the cases, the text, or the instructor's resource manual. They are Chen Zhaohui, Patricia Chew, Kate Ingram, Phil Chap, and Lou Seng Lee. Tim Lovelock has provided valued assistance over the course of several editions. And we're very appreciative of all the hard work put in by the editing and production staff who worked to transform our manuscript into a handsome published text. They include Katie Stevens, acquisitions editor; Melissa Pellerano, project manager; Christine Ietto, editorial assistant; and Renata Butera, production and managing editor.

Christopher Lovelock

Jochen Wirtz

Services Marketing

People, Technology, Strategy

Part

I

Understanding Service Markets, Products, and Customers

*P*art I lays out the building blocks for studying services and learning how you can become an effective service marketer. In Chapter 1, we define the nature of services and how they create value for customers without transfer of ownership. Highlighting some of the distinctive challenges involved in marketing services, we present a framework for developing a services marketing strategy that forms the basis for each of the chapters in Parts II, III, and IV of the book.

Chapter 2 provides a foundation for understanding consumer needs and behavior in both high-contact and low-contact service environments. We employ practical concepts to help you analyze and interpret the roles that customers play in the creation and delivery of different types of services, including those involving self-service technologies. In particular, we present a three-stage model of service consumption that explores how customers make decisions, respond to service encounters, and evaluate service performance.

UNDERSTANDING CUSTOMER NEEDS, DECISION-MAKING AND BEHAVIOR IN SERVICE ENCOUNTERS

Differences among Services Affect Customer Behavior

Three-Stage Model of Service Consumption
- Prepurchase Stage: Search, evaluation of alternatives, decision
- Service Encounter Stage: Role in high-contact vs. low-contact delivery
- Post-Encounter Stage: Evaluation against expectations, future intentions

(Chapter 2)

Building the Service Model
- Develop service concept: Core and supplementary elements
- Select physical and electronic channels for service delivery
- Set prices with reference to costs, competition, and value
- Educate customers and promote the value proposition
- Position the value proposition against competing alternatives

Managing the Customer Interface
- Design and manage service processes
- Balance demand against productive capacity
- Plan the service environment
- Manage service employees for competitive advantage

Implementing Profitable Service Strategies
- Create customer relationships and build loyalty
- Plan for service recovery and create customer feedback systems
- Continuously improve service quality and productivity
- Organize for change management and service leadership

Chapter 1

New Perspectives on Marketing in the Service Economy

> *Ours is a service economy and has been for some time.*
>
> —KARL ALBRECHT AND RON ZEMKE

> *In today's marketplace, consumers have the power to pick and choose as never before.*
>
> —THE ECONOMIST

Like every reader of this book, you're an experienced service consumer. You use an array of services every day—although some, like talking on the phone, using a credit card, riding a bus, or withdrawing money from an ATM, may be so routine that you hardly notice them unless something goes wrong. Other service purchases may involve more thought and be more memorable—for instance, getting your hair cut or styled, booking a cruise vacation, getting financial advice, or having a medical examination. Enrolling in college or graduate school may be one of the biggest service purchases you will ever make. The typical university is a complex service organization that offers not only educational services, but also libraries, student accommodation, health care, athletic facilities, museums, security, counseling and career services. On campus you may find a bookstore, post office, photocopying services, Internet access, bank, food, entertainment, and more. Your use of these services are examples of service consumption at the individual, or B2C (business-to-consumer) level.

Companies and not-for-profit organizations use a wide array of B2B (business-to-business) services, varying to some degree according to the nature of their industry, but usually involving purchases on a much larger scale than those made by individuals or households. Nowadays, business customers are outsourcing more and more tasks to external service suppliers in order to focus on their core business. Without these needed services, offering them needed solutions and good value at a price they can afford, their companies can't hope to succeed.

Unfortunately, customers are not always happy with the quality and value of the services they receive. Sometimes you may be delighted with your service experiences, but there have probably been times when you were very disappointed. Both individual and corporate purchasers complain about broken promises, poor value for money, lack of understanding of their needs, rude or incompetent personnel, inconvenient service hours, bureaucratic procedures, wasted time, malfunctioning self-service machines, complicated web sites, and a host of other problems.

Suppliers of services, who often face stiff competition, sometimes appear to have a very different set of concerns. Many owners and managers complain about how difficult it is to keep costs down and make a profit, to find skilled and motivated employees, or to satisfy customers who, they sometimes grumble, have become unreasonably demanding. Fortunately, there are service companies that know how to please their customers while also running a productive, profitable operation, staffed by pleasant and competent employees, and accessible through user-friendly self-service technology.

You probably have some favorite services that you like to patronize. Have you ever stopped to think about how these organizations succeed in delivering service that meets your needs and even exceeds your expectations? This book will teach you how service businesses should be managed to achieve customer satisfaction and profitable performance. In addition to studying the key concepts, organizing frameworks, and tools of services marketing, you'll also be introduced to a wide array of examples from across the United States and around the world. From their experiences you can draw important lessons on how to succeed in service markets that are becoming increasingly competitive.

In this opening chapter, we present an overview of today's dynamic service economy and invite you to explore the following questions:

1. Why study services?
2. How important is the service sector in our economy, and what are its principal industries?
3. What exactly *is* a service, and how should it be conceptualized and defined?
4. What distinctive marketing challenges do services present relative to goods?
5. Why do services need an expanded marketing mix, comprising 8 Ps rather than 4 Ps?

We conclude the chapter by presenting a framework for developing and implementing service marketing strategies. This framework provides the structure for the book.

Here's a paradox: We live in a service economy, but at most business schools the academic study and teaching of marketing is still dominated by a manufacturing perspective. If you have previously taken a marketing course, you most likely learned more about marketing manufactured products, especially consumer goods, than about marketing services. Fortunately, a growing and enthusiastic group of scholars, consultants, and teachers, including the authors of this text, have chosen to focus on services marketing and to build on the extensive research that has been conducted in this field over the past three decades. You can be confident that this book will provide you with information and skills that are highly relevant in today's business climate.

Services Dominate the Economy in Most Nations

The size of the service sector is increasing around the world, in both developed and emerging countries. Figure 1.1 displays the composition of the U.S. economy, in which private service industries account for more than two-thirds of the value of the gross domestic product (GDP). This figure includes services offered by nonprofits, sometimes referred to as charities or nongovernmental organizations (NGOs). These organizations, involved in arts, education, health care, human services, and faith-based activities, collectively contribute more than 6 percent of economic activity. When we add the output of federal, state, and local governments—which are involved primarily in service delivery—the total for services reaches almost 80 percent of the value of GDP.

For-profit and not-for-profit services differ in their underlying goals, although both want to create value for their various stakeholders. For-profit businesses seek to achieve *financial* profits subject to *social* constraints, whereas not-for-profit service suppliers seek to achieve *social* profits subject to *financial* constraints.[1] Many public agencies and nonprofit organizations charge a price for their services that partially covers their costs, but they often depend on donations, grants, or tax-based subsidies to cover the rest. (For simplicity, we will use the terms *business, company, corporation,*

Figure 1.1
Contribution of Service Industries to U.S. Gross Domestic Product, 2004

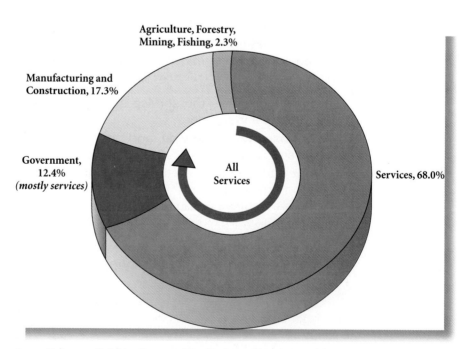

Agriculture, Forestry, Mining, Fishing, 2.3%

Manufacturing and Construction, 17.3%

Government, 12.4% *(mostly services)*

All Services

Services, 68.0%

Source: Data compiled from Bureau of Economic Analysis, *Survey of Current Business,* May 2005, Table 2, p. 14.

Figure 1.2 Estimated Size of Service Sector in Selected Countries as a Percentage of Gross Domestic Product

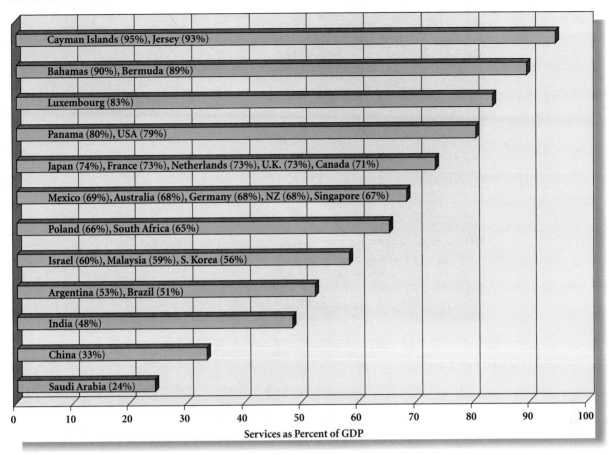

(Note: Estimates are from different years and may not be compiled from directly comparable measures; figures are rounded to the nearest whole percentage.)

Source: The World Factbook 2005, Central Intelligence Agency, www.odci.gov/cia/publications/factbook.

firm, and *organization* in this book to apply generically to all types of service providers.)

As in the United States, most emerging and developed countries have seen their service economies grow rapidly. Figure 1.2 shows the relative size of the service sector in an array of both large and very small economies. In most of the more highly developed nations, services typically account for between two-thirds and three-fourths of GDP, although manufacturing-oriented South Korea (56 percent) is an exception. Which is the world's most service-dominated economy? It's probably the Cayman Islands (95 percent), a group of small, British-administered islands in the western Caribbean, known for both tourism and offshore financial and insurance services. Jersey, the Bahamas, and Bermuda, all small islands with a similar economic mix, are not far behind. Luxembourg (83 percent) has the most service-dominated economy in the European Union. Panama's strong showing (80 percent) reflects not only the operation of the Panama Canal—widely used by cruise ships as well as freight vessels—but also such related services as container ports, flagship registry, and a free port zone, as well as financial services, insurance, and tourism (Figure 1.3).

Near the opposite end of the scale is China (33 percent), whose emerging economy is dominated by a substantial agricultural sector and booming manufacturing and construction industries. However, China's economic growth is now leading to increased demand for business and consumer services. China's government is investing heavily in service infrastructure, including shipping facilities and new airport

Figure 1.3 The Panama Canal Forms the Backbone of This Country's Service Economy

terminals. Shanghai, the country's major commercial center, even boasts the world's fastest airport train service, featuring German-designed vehicles powered by magnetic levitation and capable of speeds of up to 260 mph (420 km/h). Last among relatively affluent countries is Saudi Arabia, with its oil-dominated economy to which services contribute only 24 percent of GDP.

Classifying Service Industries

What industries make up the service sector, and which are the biggest? The latter may not be the ones you first imagine, because this diverse sector includes many services targeted at business customers, some of which are not highly visible unless you happen to work in that industry. National economic statistics are a useful starting point. To provide a better understanding of today's service-dominated economy, government statistical agencies have developed new ways to classify industries. In the United States, the manufacturing-oriented Standard Industrial Classification (SIC) system, developed in the 1930s, is being replaced by the new North American Industry Classification System (NAICS).[2] Canada and Mexico are adopting it, too. (For details, see Research Insights 1.1).

Contribution to Gross Domestic Product

To see how much value each of the major service industry groups contributes to the U.S. gross domestic product, take a look at Figure 1.4. Would you have guessed that real estate and rental and leasing would be the largest service industry sector in the United States, accounting for $1,451 billion in 2004, almost one-eighth of GDP? Over 90 percent of this figure comes from such activities as renting residential or commercial property; managing properties on behalf of their owners; providing realty services to facilitate purchases, sales, and rentals; and appraising property to determine its condition and value. The balance is accounted for by renting or leasing a wide variety of other manufactured products, ranging from heavy construction equipment (with or without operators) to office furniture, tents, and party supplies. Another large cluster of services provides for distribution of physical products. Wholesale and retail trade, plus freight transportation and warehousing, collectively account for about 15 percent of GDP.

The North American Industry Classification System—developed jointly by the statistical agencies of Canada, Mexico, and the United States—offers a new approach to classifying industries in the economic statistics of the three North American Free Trade Agreement (NAFTA) countries. It replaces previous national systems, such as the SIC codes formerly used in the United States.

NAICS (pronounced "nakes") includes many new service industries that have emerged in recent decades and also reclassifies as services "auxiliary" establishments that provide services to manufacturing industries—examples include accounting, food service, and transportation. Every sector of the economy has been restructured and redefined. NAICS includes 358 new industries that the SIC did not identify, 390 that are revised from their SIC counterparts, and 422 that continue substantially unchanged. These industries are grouped into sectors and further subdivided into subsectors, industry groups, and establishments.

Among the new sectors and subsectors devoted to services are *Information*, which recognizes the emergence and uniqueness of businesses in the "information economy"; *Health Care and Social Assistance; Professional, Scientific and Business Services; Educational Services; Accommodation and Food Services;* and *Arts, Entertainment and Recreation* (which includes most businesses engaged in meeting consumers' cultural, leisure, or entertainment interests).

NAICS uses a consistent principle for classification, grouping together businesses that use similar production processes. Its goal is to make economic statistics more useful and to capture developments that encompass applications of high technology (e.g., cellular telecommunications), new businesses that previously did not exist (e.g., environmental consulting), and changes in the way business is done (e.g., warehouse clubs).

The NAICS codes are set up in such a way that researchers can drill down within broad industry sectors to obtain information on tightly defined types of service establishments. For instance, NAICS code 71 designates arts, entertainment and recreation. Code 7112 designates spectator sports, and code 711211 designates sports teams and clubs. By looking at changes over time in current dollars (adjusted for inflation), it's possible to determine which industries have been growing and which have not. The NAICS codes are also being used to categorize employment statistics and numbers of establishments within a particular industry. And a new North American Product Classification System (NAPCS) defines thousands of service products. If you want to research service industries and service products, NAICS data is a great place to start.

Sources: Economic Classification Policy Committee, *NAICS—North American Industry Classification System: New Data for a New Economy*, Washington, DC: Bureau of the Census, October 1998; North American Industry Classification System, *United States 2002* [Official NAICS manual], Washington, DC: National Technical Information Service, PB2002101430*SS, 2002. See also www.census.gov/epcd/www/naics.html.

Other substantial industry sectors or subsectors are professional and business services (11.4 percent), finance and insurance (8.3 percent), health care and social assistance (6.9 percent), and information (4.9 percent)—a category that includes broadcasting, telecommunications, publishing, and the sound-recording industry. Accommodation and food services constitute only 2.6 percent, while the arts, entertainment, and recreation subsector—which includes such high-profile consumer services as spectator sports, fitness centers, skiing facilities, museums and zoos, performing arts, casinos, golf courses, marinas, and theme parks—collectively represents a mere 1.0 percent of GDP. Nevertheless, in an economy with an output of over $11.7 trillion, this last group of services was still valued at an impressive $119 billion in 2004.

Most New Jobs Are Generated by Services

Employment is predicted to continue shrinking in manufacturing, mining, and agriculture in the United States, although there will be some growth in the number of construction jobs. Like most developed economies, the United States will look to service industries for new job creation. And, contrary to popular impressions, many new service jobs are likely to be well-paid positions that require a good educational

Figure 1.4
Value Added by
Service Industry
Categories to
U.S. Gross Domestic
Product, 2004
(in $ billions)

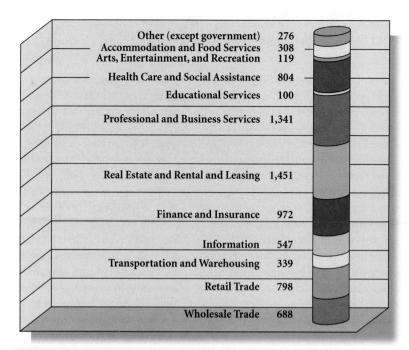

Other (except government)	276
Accommodation and Food Services	308
Arts, Entertainment, and Recreation	119
Health Care and Social Assistance	804
Educational Services	100
Professional and Business Services	1,341
Real Estate and Rental and Leasing	1,451
Finance and Insurance	972
Information	547
Transportation and Warehousing	339
Retail Trade	798
Wholesale Trade	688

Source: Data compiled from Bureau of Economic Analysis, *Survey of Current Business,* May 2005, Table 1, p. 13.

foundation. Some of the fastest growth is expected in knowledge-based industries—such as professional and business services, education, and health services. Many jobs in these industries demand significant training and educational qualifications, and employees are often highly compensated.[3]

Will service jobs be lost to lower-cost countries? New communications technology means that some service work can be carried out far from where customers are located. A study by the international consulting firm McKinsey & Co. estimated that 11 percent of service jobs around the world could be carried out remotely. In practice, however, McKinsey predicts that the percentage of service jobs actually "offshored" will prove much more limited, reaching only 1 percent of all service employment in the developed countries by 2008.[4] Of course, loss of even that small percentage will still affect a large number of workers, including some well-paid professionals whose work can be performed much less expensively by, say, highly qualified engineers working in India.

Powerful Forces Are Transforming Service Markets

Service markets are shaped by government policies, social changes, business trends, advances in information technology, and internationalization (Figure 1.5). Collectively, these forces are reshaping demand, supply, the competitive landscape, and even customers' styles of decision making. *The Economist* argues that the Internet is transferring power from suppliers to customers, especially in consumer markets.[5] Deregulation and advances in technology have broken the rigid structure of the financial services industry. The travel industry will never be the same again now that travelers can easily research alternatives and make their own bookings. Electronic distribution is changing relationships and roles among suppliers, intermediaries, and customers as traditional channel members (such as local travel agencies) are replaced by innovative newcomers such as Orbitz, Travelocity, and Priceline.[6]

From one industry to another, competition is stimulating innovation, especially through application of new and improved technologies. Competition occurs not only among firms within the *same* industry, but also among firms from *other* industries that can offer customers new solutions to their needs through alternative

Figure 1.5
Factors Stimulating
the Transformation of
the Service Economy

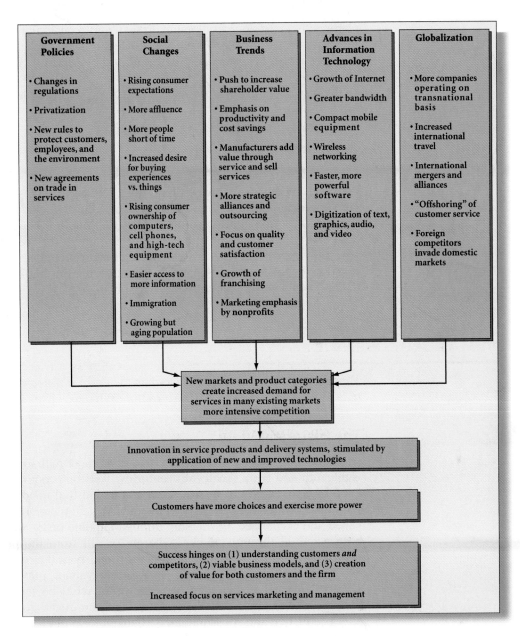

Government Policies	Social Changes	Business Trends	Advances in Information Technology	Globalization
• Changes in regulations • Privatization • New rules to protect customers, employees, and the environment • New agreements on trade in services	• Rising consumer expectations • More affluence • More people short of time • Increased desire for buying experiences vs. things • Rising consumer ownership of computers, cell phones, and high-tech equipment • Easier access to more information • Immigration • Growing but aging population	• Push to increase shareholder value • Emphasis on productivity and cost savings • Manufacturers add value through service and sell services • More strategic alliances and outsourcing • Focus on quality and customer satisfaction • Growth of franchising • Marketing emphasis by nonprofits	• Growth of Internet • Greater bandwidth • Compact mobile equipment • Wireless networking • Faster, more powerful software • Digitization of text, graphics, audio, and video	• More companies operating on transnational basis • Increased international travel • International mergers and alliances • "Offshoring" of customer service • Foreign competitors invade domestic markets

New markets and product categories create increased demand for services in many existing markets more intensive competition

Innovation in service products and delivery systems, stimulated by application of new and improved technologies

Customers have more choices and exercise more power

Success hinges on (1) understanding customers *and* competitors, (2) viable business models, and (3) creation of value for both customers and the firm

Increased focus on services marketing and management

approaches.[7] Think for a moment about person-to-person communications. Voice telephone has long competed with first-class letter mail, then Internet-based email emerged to compete with both voice telephone and letter mail, and more recently, text messaging (primarily on mobile [cell] phones) has emerged to compete with all of them. Which of these options are you currently using more, and which less, than you did a few years ago? In the past few years, you've been able to watch how the Internet and mobile telephony have evolved, adding new services and features. Consider what you can download to your cell phone (mobile handset) today that you couldn't have done a few years ago!

Customer needs and behavior are evolving, in response to changing demographics and lifestyles. The implications? Managers of service organizations need to focus more sharply on marketing strategy if they hope to meet—or even anticipate—these needs with services that customers see as offering value.

Customers are a vital source of ideas, not only for new products but also for improvements to existing ones.[8] Even established, traditional services such as hotels need enhancement. By working with experts in research and development, and with operations and human resource managers, marketers may be able to create new service features that customers will value. Research into customer needs and priorities can provide vital insights into what specific features to emphasize and how much they might be worth to customers. The Courtyard by Marriott chain boasts that its hotels were "designed by business travelers for business travelers," with rooms containing all the services and amenities they require to be comfortable and productive.

Understanding Services Offers Personal Competitive Advantage

Learning about the distinctive characteristics of services and how they affect both customer behavior and marketing strategy will give you important insights—and perhaps create a competitive advantage for your own career. Unless you're predestined to work in a family manufacturing or agricultural business, the probability is high that you'll spend most of your working life in service organizations. You may also find yourself serving as a volunteer or board member for a nonprofit organization. Maybe the knowledge gained from studying this book will even stimulate you to think about starting your own service business!

WHAT ARE SERVICES?

Thus far, our discussion of services has focused on different types of service industries. But now it's time to ask the question: What exactly is a *service*?

The Historical View

Attempts to describe and define services go back more than two centuries. In the late eighteenth and early nineteenth centuries, classical economists focused on the creation and possession of wealth. They contended that goods (initially referred to as "commodities") were objects of value over which ownership rights could be established and exchanged. Ownership implied tangible possession of an object that had been acquired through purchase, barter, or gift from the producer or a previous owner, and was legally identifiable as the property of the current owner.

Adam Smith's famous book, *The Wealth of Nations,* published in Great Britain in 1776, distinguished between the outputs of what he termed "productive" and "unproductive" labor.[9] The former, he stated, produced goods that could be stored after production and subsequently exchanged for money or other items of value. But unproductive labor, however "honourable, … useful, or … necessary," created services that *perished* at the time of production and therefore didn't contribute to wealth. Building on this theme, the French economist, Jean-Baptiste Say, argued that production and consumption were inseparable in services, coining the term "immaterial products" to describe them.[10]

Today, we know that production and consumption are indeed *separable* for many services (think of dry cleaning, lawn mowing, and weather forecasting), and that not all service performances are perishable (consider audio or video recordings of concert performances and sports events). Very significantly, many services are designed to create *durable value* for their recipients (your own education being a case in point). But the distinction between ownership and *nonownership* remains a valid one, emphasized by several leading service marketing scholars.[11]

A Fresh Perspective: Benefits Without Ownership

Consider this: You didn't acquire ownership of the hotel room in which you stayed last weekend, nor of the physical therapist who worked on your injured knee, nor of the concert you just attended. But if you and other customers didn't receive a transfer of ownership the last time you purchased a service, then what exactly did you buy? What have you got to show for your money, as well as the time and effort involved? What are, or were, the benefits? What problems did the service help you solve? In short: Where's the value?

Christopher Lovelock and Evert Gummesson contend that services involve a form of *rental*. Service customers obtain benefits by renting the right to use a physical object, to hire the labor and expertise of personnel, or to pay for access to facilities and networks.[12] (Many services involve all three elements.) Value is created when customers benefit from obtaining desired experiences and solutions. We use the word *rent* here as a generic term to denote the payment made for using or accessing something—typically for a defined period of time—instead of buying it outright. You can't own people—slavery has been outlawed—but you can rent their labor and expertise.

Paying for temporary use of an object or for access to a physical facility is a way for customers to enjoy use of things that they cannot afford to buy, cannot justify purchasing, or prefer not to retain and store after use. In addition, renting—in the form of access and usage fees—offers customers a means to participate in network systems that individuals and most organizations couldn't possibly afford to own and operate themselves.

We can identify five broad categories within the nonownership framework:

- *Rented goods services.* These services enable customers to obtain the temporary right to exclusive use a physical good that they prefer not to own. Examples include boats, power tools, combine harvesters, and formal clothing worn only for weddings and proms.
- *Defined space and place rentals.* Here, customers obtain use of a defined portion of a larger space in a building, vehicle, or other area, sharing its use with other customers under varying levels of privacy. A seat ("my place") is the most individual unit of rental for a person. Examples of this type of rental include a hotel room, a seat in an aircraft, a suite in an office building, a table and chairs in a restaurant, or a storage container in a warehouse. The space is typically designated by location, but the purpose to which it is put may vary widely, ranging from a place in which to perform business activities to one where a meal may be enjoyed. In other words, renting the space may be either an end in itself or simply a means to an end. Some spaces may be physically identical but carry higher value because of location, such as a room with a view or a seat closer to the theater stage.
- *Labor and expertise rentals.* Customers hire other people to perform work that they either choose not to do for themselves (for instance, cleaning a house), or are unable to do because they lack the necessary expertise, tools, or skills. In many instances, customers may effectively rent the services of an entire team, as in car repair, surgery, and management consulting.
- *Access to shared physical environments.* These environments may be located indoors or outdoors—or a combination of both. Examples include museums, theme parks, trade shows, gyms, zoos, ski resorts, golf courses, and toll roads. In return for a fee, customers rent the right to share use of the environment in question with other customers. Which of these have you used or visited lately?
- *Systems and networks: access and usage.* Here, customers rent the right to participate in a specified network such as telecommunications, utilities, banking, insurance, or specialized information services. Service providers often create a veritable menu of terms for access and use in response to varying customer needs and differing abilities to pay.

In many instances, two or more of these categories may be combined. When you take a taxi, you're hiring both a driver and a vehicle. If you undergo surgery, you are, in essence, hiring a skilled team of medical personnel, led by the surgeon, as well as renting temporary (but exclusive) use of specialized equipment in a dedicated operating theater at a hospital or clinic.

How does the distinction between ownership and nonownership affect the nature of marketing tasks and strategy? Service Perspectives 1.1 highlights six important implications.

1. *There's a market for renting durable goods instead of selling them.* Solutions to temporary needs can often be better met by renting than by owning. Among the most widely rented products are vehicles, construction and excavation equipment, generators, tents, party supplies, power tools, furniture, formal wear, and sporting goods, such as skis. For longer-term use, there may be financial advantages to making rental/lease payments instead of capital investments. Marketers can add further value through such services as delivery and pickup, cleaning, insurance, and maintenance. They can even supply trained personnel to operate rented equipment.

2. *Renting portions of a larger physical entity can form the basis for services.* You can think of some types of service facility as "sausages" from which customers rent "slices"—such as seats in a movie theater or aircraft, rooms in a hotel, or suites in an office building—for defined periods of time. Renting "my apartment" or "our office suite" conveys the right to exclusive but temporary use of a unit within a larger building. Customers benefit from economies of scale by sharing a large facility with many users, while enjoying varying degrees of separation and even privacy.

3. *Customers need to be more closely engaged with service suppliers.* When buyers acquire ownership of a product, they are free to use it where, when, and as they wish (within reason). In services, however, suppliers need to exercise some control over how customers use equipment and facilities, interact with service personnel, and interface with systems and networks. Many services involve a division of labor between suppliers and customers, with the latter expected to know and obey the "rules." And most rented goods also require formalized return procedures at designated times and locations.

4. *Time plays a central role in most services.* Ownership is for as long as the object lasts or until the owner chooses to dispose of it. Rental or access is most typically defined in terms of specified time periods, with pricing often related to units of time. A key marketing challenge for service suppliers is to make sure that the objects, facilities, and labor they offer are "rented out" over time as fully as possible at the most favorable rates—that's the route to creating value through higher revenues and profits. Achieving this objective places a premium on developing strategies to bring supply and demand into balance. Customers, too, are concerned with time. In order to improve the convenience and appeal of their service offerings, marketers must understand the role that time plays in customers' lifestyles, and how different people perceive, value, and budget time.

5. *Customer choice criteria may differ between rentals and outright purchases.* Marketing a rental car for a few days to a couple vacationing in Hawaii is a very different task from a local dealer's attempts to sell a car to these same people back in their hometown. Renters usually reserve a particular class or category of vehicle rather than a specific brand and model. Instead of worrying about physical characteristics such as color, upholstery, and number of cup holders, customers will focus on rental location and hours, insurance coverage, cleanliness and maintenance of vehicles, ease of using reservation systems, the quality of service provided by customer-contact personnel, and loyalty rewards such as miles for airline travel.

6. *Services offer opportunities for resource sharing.* In developing countries, improving the quality of life among poor consumers requires finding creative ways of sharing access to goods, physical facilities, systems, and expertise to bring prices down to affordable levels. And in a world in which many resources are believed to be finite, replacing ownership by rental may be the best way in both emerging and developed economies to avoid waste by sharing use of products that incorporate these scarce resources.

Source: Adapted from Christopher Lovelock and Evert Gummesson, "Whither Services Marketing? In Search of a New Paradigm and Fresh Perspectives," *Journal of Service Research,* 7, August 2004, 20–41.

Defining Services

Already it will be clear to you that services cover a vast array of different and often very complex activities. The word *service* was originally associated with the work that servants did for their masters. In time, a broader association emerged, captured in the dictionary definition of "the action of serving, helping, or benefiting; conduct tending to the welfare or advantage of another."[13] Early marketing definitions of services contrasted them against goods. John Rathmell defined services in broad terms as "acts, deeds, performances, or efforts" and argued that they had different characteristics from goods—defined as "articles, devices, materials, objects, or things."[14]

We believe, however, that services need to be defined in their own right, not in relation to goods. A short and snappy definition, such as the oft-repeated "something that can be bought and sold but that cannot be dropped on your foot,"[15] may be amusing and memorable, but unfortunately it's not particularly helpful as a guide to marketing strategy. Instead, we offer the comprehensive definition shown above.

Note that we define services as *economic activities* between two parties, implying an exchange of value between seller and buyer in the marketplace. We describe services as *performances* that are most commonly *time-based*. We emphasize that purchasers buy services because they are looking for *desired results*. In fact, many firms explicitly market their services as "solutions" to prospective customers' needs. And finally, our definition emphasizes that while customers *expect to obtain value* from their service purchases *in exchange for their money, time, and effort*, this value comes from *access to a variety of value-creating elements rather than from transfer of ownership.* (Spare parts installed during repairs and restaurant-prepared food and beverages are among the few exceptions, but the value added by these items is usually less than that of the accompanying service elements.)

Service Products Versus Customer Service and After-Sales Service

With the growth of the service economy, and emphasis on adding value-enhancing services to manufactured goods, the line between services and manufacturing sometimes becomes blurred. Many manufacturing firms—from auto manufacturers Ford and Fiat to aerospace engine producers GE and Rolls Royce, and high-tech equipment manufacturers IBM and Xerox—are moving aggressively into service businesses.[17] Theodore Levitt, respected as one of the world's leading marketing experts, long ago observed: "There are no such things as service industries. There are only industries whose service components are greater or less than those of other industries. Everybody is in service."[18] More recently, Roland Rust suggested that manufacturing firms had gotten this message when he noted that "most goods businesses now view themselves primarily as services."[19] Nevertheless, it's important to clarify the distinction between *service products* and what is often termed *customer service* (or customer support). Every business should have a customer service orientation, but not every business markets what NAICS data categorizes as a service product.

In this book we describe a firm's market offerings as being divided into *core product* elements and *supplementary service* elements—those activities or amenities that facilitate and enhance use of the core offering. We draw a clear distinction between *marketing of services*—in which a service itself is the core product—and *marketing through services*. Certainly, great service often helps to sell a physical good and even make it more useful—and thereby valuable—to the buyer. Many firms in manufacturing, agricultural, natural resource, or construction industries now base their marketing strategies on a philosophy of serving customers well and adding supplementary service elements to the core product. However, that core product is still a physical good (a term we use here to include structures and commodities) when marketing's goal is to sell the item and transfer ownership. Supplementary services may include consultation, finance, shipping, installation, maintenance, upgrades, and, finally, removal and environmentally responsible disposal. These services may be offered "free" (meaning effectively that their cost is bundled with the price of the initial product purchase) or charged for separately.

Many manufacturing firms have transitioned from simply bundling supplementary services with their physical products to reformulating and enhancing certain elements so that they can be marketed as stand-alone services. At that point, the firm may target new customers who haven't previously purchased its manufactured products—and may even have no interest in doing so. As the organization's expertise builds, it may add new service products that it never offered before. IBM, once known only as a manufacturer of computers and business machines, today offers four main groups of services: strategic outsourcing, business consulting, integrated technology services, and maintenance. Collectively, these services generated $46.2 billion in service revenues in 2004—almost half of IBM's total revenues—and contributed a gross profit of $11.6 billion.[20]

You'll find that the same distinction between customer service and service products exists for consumer goods, especially durables. Purchasers of luxury cars, such as those marketed under Toyota's Lexus brand, receive not only excellent warranty coverage but also an exceptional level of service from the Lexus-trained dealer, a franchisee who is running a service business. However, these cars are still manufactured products, and we must distinguish between marketing that product at the time of sale and marketing services that customers will pay for to maintain their car in good working order for several years after the sale. Lexus dealers don't compete with Jaguar or BMW for service sales; instead, they compete with the best independent repair garages, which not only offer excellent repair and maintenance service, but may also be more conveniently located relative to many Lexus owners' homes or offices.

SERVICES POSE DISTINCTIVE MARKETING CHALLENGES

Are the marketing concepts and practices developed in manufacturing companies directly transferable to service organizations in which no transfer of ownership takes place? The answer is often "no." In particular, when customers rent goods rather than buying them, their expectations and decision criteria are different—and so will be the nature of their experiences, including how they interact with the service firm that "loans" them the physical product. As a result, marketing management tasks in the service sector tend to differ from those in the manufacturing sector in several important respects. Table 1.1 lists eight common differences between services and goods, and highlights key managerial implications that will form the basis for analysis and discussion in this and later chapters. It's important to recognize that these differences, though they are useful generalizations, *do not apply equally to all services.*

Most Service Products Cannot Be Inventoried

Because services involve actions or performances, they are *ephemeral*—transitory and perishable—and so can't usually be stocked as inventory following production. (Exceptions are found among those service activities that can be recorded for later use in electronic or printed form.) Although facilities, equipment, and labor can be held in readiness to create the service, each represents productive capacity, not the product itself. If there's no demand, unused capacity is wasted and the firm loses the chance to create value from these assets. During periods when demand exceeds capacity, customers may be sent away disappointed or asked to wait until later. A key task for service marketers, therefore, is to find ways of smoothing demand levels to match available capacity through promotions, reservations, and dynamic pricing strategies.

Intangible Elements Usually Dominate Value Creation

Many services include important physical elements, such as hotel beds, theater interiors, spare parts installed during repairs, and bank cards and checkbooks. However,

Table 1.1 Marketing Implications of Eight Common Differences Between Services and Goods

DIFFERENCE	IMPLICATIONS	MARKETING-RELATED TASKS
Most service products cannot be inventoried	• Customers may be turned away or have to wait	• Smooth demand through promotions, dynamic pricing, and reservations • Work with operations to adjust capacity
Intangible elements usually dominate value creation	• Customers can't taste, smell, or touch these elements and may not be able to see or hear them • Harder to evaluate service and distinguish from competitors	• Make services tangible through emphasis on physical clues • Employ concrete metaphors and vivid images in advertising, branding
Services are often difficult to visualize and understand	• Customers perceive greater risk and uncertainty	• Educate customers to make good choices, explain what to look for, document performance, offer guarantees
Customers may be involved in co-production	• Customers interact with provider's equipment, facilities, and systems • Poor task execution by customers may hurt productivity, spoil service experience, curtail benefits	• Develop user-friendly equipment, facilities, and systems • Train customers to perform effectively; provide customer support
People may be part of the service experience	• Appearance, attitude, and behavior of service personnel and other customers can shape the experience and affect satisfaction	• Recruit, train, and reward employees to reinforce the planned service concept • Target the right customers at the right times, shape their behavior
Operational inputs and outputs tend to vary more widely	• Harder to maintain consistency, reliability, and service quality or to lower costs through higher productivity • Difficult to shield customers from results of service failures	• Set quality standards based on customer expectations; redesign product elements for simplicity and failure-proofing • Institute good service recovery procedures • Automate customer–provider interactions; perform work while customers are absent
The time factor often assumes great importance	• Customers see time as a scarce resource to be spent wisely; dislike wasting time waiting, want service at times that are convenient	• Find ways to compete on speed of delivery, minimize burden of waiting, offer extended service hours
Distribution may take place through nonphysical channels	• Information-based services can be delivered through electronic channels such as the Internet or voice telecommunications, but core products involving physical activities or products cannot	• Seek to create user-friendly, secure web sites and free access by telephone • Ensure that all information-based service elements can be downloaded from site

often it is the intangible elements—such as processes, Internet-based transactions, and the expertise and attitudes of service personnel—that create the most value in service performances. Customers can't taste, smell, or touch these elements, and they may not be able to see or hear them. That makes it more difficult to assess important service features in advance of use and to evaluate the quality of the performance itself. Similarly, the lack of easy reference points can make it hard for customers to distinguish among competing suppliers.

A useful way to distinguish between goods and services, first suggested by Lynn Shostack, is to place them on a spectrum from tangible-dominant to intangible-dominant

Figure 1.6
Relative Value Added
by Physical Versus
Intangible Elements in
Goods and Services

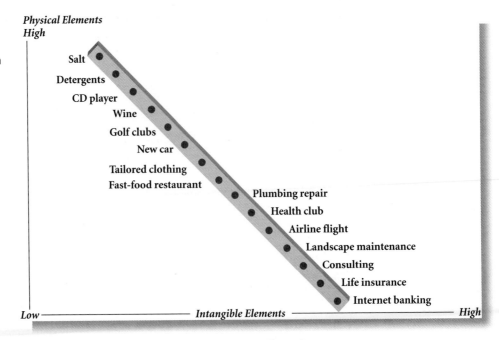

Source: Adapted from an earlier schematic by G. Lynn Shostack.

(see Figure 1.6 for a hypothesized scale presenting an array of examples).[21] Clearly, there are some potentially ambiguous products in the middle. Are custom tailors, plumbers, and fast-food restaurants delivering goods or services? One suggested economic test of whether a product should be regarded as a good or a service is whether more than half the value comes from intangible service elements.[22] At full-service restaurants, for example, the cost of the food itself may account for as little as 20 to 30 percent of the price of the meal. Most of the value added comes from food preparation and cooking, table service, the restaurant environment, and facilities such as parking, toilets, and coatroom.

When there are few physical elements, marketers often employ physical images and metaphors to highlight service benefits and demonstrate the firm's competencies. Creating physical clues and strong brand associations helps to make services more "tangible."[23]

Services Are Often Difficult to Visualize and Understand

Many services can be described as "mentally intangible," meaning that it's difficult for customers to visualize the experience in advance of purchase and to understand what they will be getting. This situation can make service purchases seem risky.

Mental intangibility is most likely to present a problem (and thus a perceived risk) for first-time customers who lack prior exposure to a particular type of service. Frequent users have the advantage of past experiences that can serve as benchmarks, so they know what clues to look for. Based on a study of a British police department, Paul Flanagan, Robert Johnston, and Derek Talbot argue that infrequently used service organizations, especially those in the public sector, need to build *confidence* in their abilities in advance of use and then justify that confidence by actions that create lasting trust.[24] An important point to remember is that any memorable experience can build trust—or destroy it.

Well-trained salespeople or customer service representatives can reduce the perceived risk of purchase by helping prospective customers to make good choices—such as identifying the specific service features that will be useful for certain types of people—and by educating them on what to expect both during and after service delivery. Documenting performance, explaining what was done and why, and offering guarantees are additional ways to reassure customers and reduce anxiety. Confidence can be created in advance by emphasizing the firm's experience or the credentials and expertise of individual service providers.

Customers May Be Involved in Co-production

Some services require customers to participate actively in co-producing the service product. For instance, you're expected to cooperate with service personnel in settings such as hair salons, hotels, quick-service restaurants, and libraries, even doing some of the work yourself rather than being waited on. In fact, service scholars argue that customers often function as *partial employees*.[25] (How do you feel about being described that way?) Increasingly, your involvement takes the form of self-service, often using the technology of smart machines, telecommunications, and the Internet.[26] Simple examples include withdrawing money from an ATM, using an automated kiosk to check yourself in for a flight at an airport, and reserving seats for the "Big Game" via a web site. Access to self-service technologies (SSTs) is important, too, for customers using B2B and professional services. [27] A key issue for marketers is how satisfied customers are with the quality of service delivered by SSTs. Do customers see electronic channels that require them to do more work as better or worse than face-to-face alternatives? What needs do SSTs meet that traditional alternatives can't? What are their strong and weak attributes? Good research can help us to learn the answers, and we'll be examining the impact of technology-driven services on customers—and how to manage them well—throughout this book.[28]

In many industries you now have a choice. You can do your banking through multiple channels, shop at a retail store or order goods online, attend classes in a lecture hall or watch a cable or satellite-based transmission of that same class.[29] You'll even find choices within the same physical site. For instance, at your local gym or health club, you can choose between getting the benefits you want by working out independently on the equipment or obtaining knowledgeable advice and feedback from a personal trainer as she supervises your efforts (Figure 1.7).

Service firms have much to gain from helping customers to become more competent and productive.[30] And so do customers. After all, if you do a poor job of performing the tasks for which you're responsible, that may spoil your service experience and curtail the benefits you hope to receive. By contrast, if things are made easy for you, not

Figure 1.7
Co-producing the Service: Working out at the Gym Under the Direction of a Personal Trainer

only will you have a better experience and outcome, your greater efficiency may boost the firm's productivity, lower its costs, and even enable it to reduce the price you pay. This means that service marketers should work with specialists from different departments to develop web sites, equipment, facilities, and systems that are user-friendly. They should ensure that customers get the training they need to use these options well, and they should ensure that operations personnel can offer real-time support.

People May Be Part of the Service Experience

You have probably noted that the difference between one service supplier and another often lies in the attitude and skills of their employees. Well-managed firms devote special care to selecting, training, and motivating the people who will be responsible for serving customers directly. In addition to possessing the technical skills required by the job, these individuals also need to possess good interpersonal skills and to display positive attitudes.

When you encounter other customers at a service facility, you know that they, too, can affect your satisfaction. How they are dressed, how many are present, who they are, and how they behave can all serve to reinforce or negate the image that a firm is trying to project and the experience it's trying to create. Were you annoyed by the customer at the next table talking loudly on her phone about problems at work, or angered by the fellow seated beside you in the theater who spilled his sticky soda on your clothes? Alternatively, were you grateful to the friendly traveler who showed you how to operate the complicated ticketing machine? At a play or circus or sporting event, the enthusiasm of the audience fans can add to the excitement. However, if some members become too rowdy and abusive, it may detract from your enjoyment. Customer *misbehavior* presents a marketing problem.

The marketing implications are clear: In addition to managing their own employees effectively to ensure good service delivery, firms must also manage and shape customer behavior. In a shared service setting, other customers should enhance the experience, not detract from its value. In some instances, service marketers need to think carefully about whether it's a good idea to mix several segments together in the same service facility at the same time. One of the authors has never forgotten staying at a hotel where half the guests were attending an academic conference and the rest were football fans from out of town who had come for the weekend to support their team. We differed sharply in our expectations of what constituted a good experience!

Operational Inputs and Outputs Tend to Vary More Widely

Unlike many services, manufactured goods can be produced at a distant factory, under controlled conditions, and checked for conformance with quality standards long before they reach the customer. However, when a service is delivered directly and consumed as it's produced, final "assembly" must take place in real time. You've probably noticed that service execution often differs among employees, between the same employee and different customers, and even from one time of day to another. Attitudes, transaction speed, and quality of performance can vary widely, and it's hard, sometimes even impossible, to shield customers from the results of service failures. These factors can make it difficult for service organizations to improve productivity, control quality, and ensure reliable delivery. As a former packaged goods marketer once observed after moving to a new position with Holiday Inn:

> We can't control the quality of our product as well as a Procter and Gamble control engineer on a production line can. . . . When you buy a box of Tide, you can reasonably be 99 and 44/100ths percent sure that this stuff will work to get your clothes clean. When you buy a Holiday Inn room, you're sure at some lesser percentage that it will work to give you a good night's sleep without any hassle, or people banging on the walls and all the bad things that can happen in a hotel.[31]

Nevertheless, the best service firms have made significant progress in reducing variability by adopting standardized procedures, implementing rigorous management of service quality, training employees carefully, and automating tasks previously performed by human beings. They also make sure that employees are well trained in service recovery procedures in case things do go wrong.

The Time Factor Often Assumes Great Importance

Many services are delivered in real time while customers are physically present. Today's customers are the most time-sensitive in history, are in more of a hurry, and see wasted time as a cost to avoid.[32] You probably do, too. Customers may be willing to pay extra to save time, such as taking a taxi when a city bus serves the same route, or to get a needed task performed faster. Increasingly, busy customers expect service to be available when it suits them, rather than when it suits the supplier. If one firm responds by offering extended hours, its competitors often feel obliged to follow suit. Nowadays, a growing number of services are available 24/7.

Another concern of customers is how much time elapses between making a request for service and receiving the finished output. If you've used a particular type of service previously, you're likely to have expectations about how long a certain task—whether it involves repairing a car, cleaning a suit, or documenting health insurance—should take to complete. Successful service marketers understand customers' time constraints and priorities. They collaborate with operations managers to find new ways to compete on speed. They strive to minimize customer waiting times, and they seek to make waiting itself less burdensome.

Distribution May Take Place Through Nonphysical Channels

Manufacturers require physical distribution channels to move their products from the factory to customers, either directly or through wholesale and retail intermediaries. Some service businesses are able to use electronic channels to deliver all (or at least some) of their service elements. Today's banks offer customers a choice of distribution channels, including visiting a branch, using a network of ATMs, doing business by telephone (including text messaging), or conducting banking transactions on the Internet. Many information-based services can be delivered almost instantaneously to any location in the world that has Internet access.

The Internet and its key component, the World Wide Web (www), is reshaping distribution strategy for a broad array of industries.[33] However, we need to distinguish between the potential for delivering information-based *core products* (those that respond to customers' primary requirements) and simply providing *supplementary services* that facilitate purchase and use of physical goods. Examples of such core products include the online educational programs offered by the University of Phoenix and automobile insurance coverage from Progressive Casualty Insurance Co.

Contrast these two web-enabled services with the web site of REI, a renowned supplier of specialty outdoor gear and clothing, which has 78 retail stores across the United States. By visiting www.rei.com, you can learn about the pros and cons of (say) different camping gear, obtain online live help, place orders for specific products, and pay for them online. Similarly, without leaving your home, let alone the country, you can review British Airways' worldwide schedules at www.ba.com, check out how fares vary according to time of day and day of week (you'll find huge variations in economy fares on some routes within Europe), make a reservation, indicate any special needs, and pay for the electronic ticket. In both cases, however, delivery of the core product itself must take place through physical channels. The tent and sleeping bag that you bought from REI will be delivered to your home by UPS, FedEx, or the US Postal Service (your choice). You'll have to go to the airport in person to board your British Airways flight. Much e-commerce activity concerns supplementary services that are based on *transfer of information* and *payments relating to the product*, as opposed to downloading the core product itself. Figure 1.8 displays examples of both types of web site.

Figure 1.8 Two Types of Web Sites

Web sites can deliver Progressive Insurance's services directly, but . . .

Courtesy of Progressive Insurance.

SERVICES REQUIRE AN EXPANDED MARKETING MIX

Marketing can be viewed in several ways. You can look at it as a strategic and competitive thrust pursued by top management, as a set of functional activities performed by line managers, or as a customer-driven orientation for the entire organization. In this book, we seek to integrate all three perspectives. We use the term marketing in its broadest sense to include all customer-facing actitivities. In our teaching and consulting, we like to emphasize to senior managers that *marketing is the only function that acts to bring operating revenues into a business.* All other functions, however important they may be, are effectively cost centers. Sometimes that news comes as a shock!

The 8 Ps of Services Marketing

When they are developing strategies to market manufactured goods, marketers usually address four basic strategic elements: product, price, place (or distribution), and promotion (or communication). As a group, these are often referred to as the "4 Ps" of the marketing mix.[34] This concept is one of the staples of almost any introductory marketing course. But to capture the distinctive nature of service performances, we need to modify the original terminology and speak instead of *product elements, place and time, price and other user outlays,* and *promotion and education.* We then extend the mix by adding four elements associated with service delivery: *physical environment, process, people,* and *productivity and quality.*[35] Collectively, these eight elements, which we refer to as the "8 Ps" of services marketing, represent the ingredients required to create viable strategies for meeting customer needs profitably in a competitive marketplace. You can think of these elements as the eight strategic levers of services marketing.

Our visual metaphor for the 8 Ps is the racing "eight," a lightweight boat or "shell" powered by eight rowers, made famous by the Oxford-versus-Cambridge boat race that

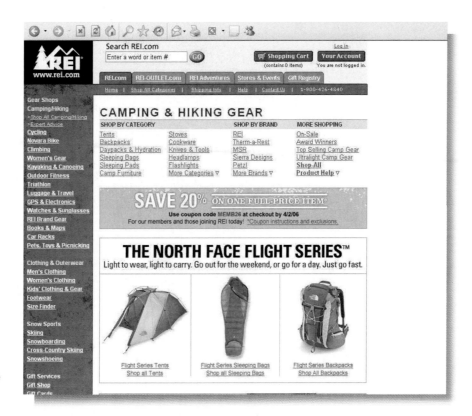

Recreational Equipment, Inc. (REI). Kent, Washington.

REI's Camping Gear Requires a Physical Channel to Reach the Customer

has taken place annually on the River Thames near London for over 150 years. Today, similar races involving multiple teams are a staple of rowing competitions around the world and a featured sport in the Summer Olympics. Speed comes not only from the rowers' physical strength, but also from their harmony and cohesion as a team. To achieve full effectiveness, each of the eight rowers must pull on his or her oar in unison with the others, following the direction of the coxswain, who sits in the stern. A similar synergy and integration among the 8 Ps is required for success in any competitive service business. The "cox"—who steers the boat, sets the pace, motivates the crew, and keeps a close eye on competing boats in the race—is a metaphor for management (Figure 1.9).

Now, let's look briefly at each of the 8 Ps in turn. We'll be covering each one in depth later in the book, as indicated by the chapter numbers following each subhead below.

Product Elements (Chapter 3)
Service products lie at the heart of a firm's marketing strategy. If a product is poorly designed, it won't create meaningful value for customers, even if the rest of the 8 Ps are well executed. Planning the marketing mix begins with creating a service concept that will offer value to target customers and satisfy their needs better than competing alternatives. Working to transform this concept into reality involves design of a cluster of different but mutually reinforcing elements. Service products consist of a core product that responds to the customers' primary need and an array of supplementary service elements that help customers to use the core product effectively as well as adding value through welcomed enhancements.

Place and Time (Chapter 4)
Delivering product elements to customers involves decisions on where and when the former are delivered to the latter, as well as the methods and channels employed. Delivery may involve use of physical or electronic channels (or both), depending on the nature of the service. Use of messaging services and the Internet allows information-based services to be delivered in cyberspace for retrieval, wherever and whenever it suits customers. Firms may deliver service directly to end users or through intermediary

Figure 1.9 Working in Unison: The 8 Ps of Services Marketing

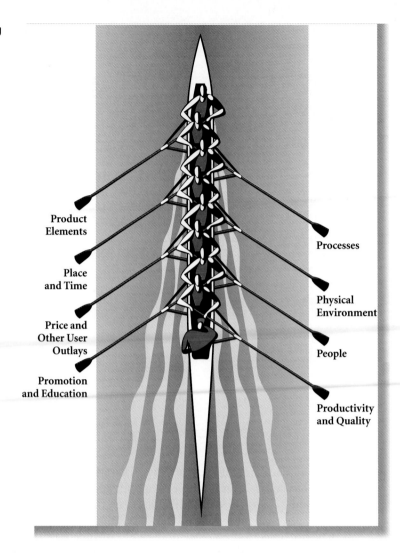

Product Elements

Place and Time

Price and Other User Outlays

Promotion and Education

Processes

Physical Environment

People

Productivity and Quality

organizations, such as retail outlets that receive a fee or commission, to perform certain tasks associated with sales, service, and customer contact. Speed and convenience of place and time have become important determinants of effective service delivery.

Price and Other User Outlays (Chapter 5)

This component must address the twin perspectives of the service firm and its customers. Like product value, the value inherent in payments is central to marketing's role in facilitating a value exchange between the firm and its customers. For suppliers, pricing strategy is the financial mechanism though which income is generated to offset the costs of providing service and create a surplus for profits. Pricing strategy is often highly dynamic, with price levels being adjusted over time according to such factors as type of customer, time and place of delivery, level of demand, and available capacity. Customers, by contrast, see price as a key part of the costs they must incur to obtain wanted benefits. To calculate whether a particular service is "worth it," they may go beyond just money and also assess the outlays of their time and effort. Service marketers, therefore, must not only set prices that target customers are willing and able to pay, but also understand—and seek to minimize, where possible—other burdensome outlays that customers incur in using the service. These outlays may include additional monetary costs (such as travel expenses to a service location), time expenditures, unwanted mental and physical effort, and exposure to negative sensory experiences.

Promotion and Education (Chapter 6)

What should we tell customers and prospects about our services? No marketing program can succeed without effective communications. This component plays three vital roles: providing needed information and advice, persuading target customers of the merits of a specific brand or service product, and encouraging them to take action at specific times. In services marketing, much communication is educational in nature, especially for new customers. Suppliers need to teach these customers about the benefits of the service, where and when to obtain it, and how to participate in service processes to get the best results. Communications may be delivered by individuals, such as salespeople and front-line staff; at web sites; on display screens in self-service equipment; and through a wide array of advertising media. Promotional activities—which may include a monetary incentive—are often designed to stimulate immediate trial purchases or to encourage consumption when demand is low.

Process (Chapter 8)

Smart managers know that, where services are concerned, *how* a firm does things—the underlying processes—is often as important as *what* it does, particularly if the product is a rather mundane one offered by many competitors. So, creating and delivering product elements requires design and implementation of effective processes. Customers are often actively involved in these processes, especially when acting as co-producers. Badly designed processes lead to slow, bureaucratic, and ineffective service delivery, wasted time, and a disappointing experience. They also make it difficult for front-line staff to do their jobs well, resulting in low productivity and increased likelihood of service failure.

Physical Environment (Chapter 10)

The appearance of buildings, landscaping, vehicles, interior furnishing, equipment, staff members' uniforms, signs, printed materials, and other visible cues all provide tangible evidence of a firm's service quality. Service firms need to manage physical evidence carefully, because it can have a profound impact on customers' impressions.

People (Chapter 11)

Despite technology advances, many services will always require direct interaction between customers and contact personnel. The nature of these interactions strongly influences how customers perceive service quality.[36] Knowing that (dis)satisfaction with service quality often reflects customers' assessments of front-line staff, successful service firms devote significant effort to recruiting, training, and motivating employees. And recognizing that customers may themselves contribute (positively or negatively) to how others experience service performances, proactive marketers try to shape customers' roles and manage their behavior.

Productivity and Quality (Chapter 14)

Though they are often treated separately, productivity and quality should be seen as two sides of the same coin. No service organization can afford to address one in isolation from the other. Improving *productivity* is essential to any strategy for reducing costs, but managers must beware of making inappropriate cuts in service that will be resented by customers (and perhaps by employees, too). Improving *quality*, which should be defined from a customer perspective, is essential for product differentiation and for building customer satisfaction and loyalty. However, it's unwise to invest in service quality improvements without understanding the trade-off between the incremental costs involved and the incremental revenues anticipated from offering better quality on specific dimensions. If customers aren't willing to pay extra for more quality, then the firm will lose money. The strategies with the biggest potential payoffs may be those that seek to improve productivity and quality simultaneously. Advances in technology sometimes offer promising opportunities, but innovations must be user-friendly and deliver benefits that customers will value.

Marketing Must Be Integrated with Other Management Functions

Earlier, we described the 8 Ps as the strategic levers of services marketing. As you think about these different elements, it should quickly become clear that marketers

Figure 1.10
Marketing,
Operations, and
Human Resources
Functions Must
Collaborate to Serve
the Customer

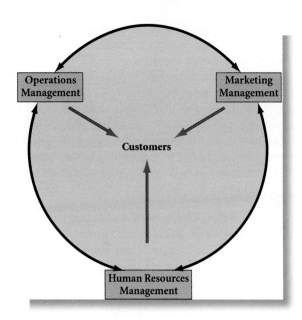

working in a service business can't expect to operate successfully in isolation from managers in other functions. In fact, three management functions play central and interrelated roles in meeting the needs of service customers: marketing, operations, and human resources (HR). Figure 1.10 illustrates this interdependency. One of top management's responsibilities is to ensure that managers and other employees in each of these three functions don't isolate themselves in departmental silos.

Operations is the primary line function in a service business, responsible for managing service delivery through equipment, facilities, systems, and many tasks performed by customer contact employees. In most service organizations, you can also expect to see operations managers actively involved in product and process design, many aspects of the physical environment, and implementation of productivity and quality improvement programs. HR is often seen as a staff function, responsible for job definition, recruitment, training, reward systems, and quality of work life—all of which are, of course, central to the people element. But in a well-managed service business, HR managers view these activities from a strategic perspective, engaging in design and monitoring of all service delivery processes that involve employees, in working with marketers to ensure that employees have the skills and training to deliver promotional messages and educate customers, and in designing those aspects of the physical environment that directly feature employees—including uniforms, personal appearance, and stage-managed behavior.

For these reasons, we don't limit our coverage exclusively to marketing in this book. In many of the chapters you'll also find us referring to service operations and human resource management. Some firms deliberately rotate their managers among different job functions, especially between marketing and operations positions, precisely so that they will be able to appreciate different perspectives. Your own career in services might follow a similar path.

Imagine yourself as the manager of a small hotel. Or, if you like, think big and picture yourself as the chief executive officer (CEO) of a major bank. In both instances, you need to be concerned about satisfying your customers on a daily basis, about operational systems running smoothly and efficiently, and about making sure that your employees are not only working productively, but are also delivering good service. In short, integration of activities among functions is the name of the game in services. Problems in any one of these three areas can negatively affect execution of tasks in the other functions and result in dissatisfied customers. Only a minority of people who work in a service firm are employed in formal marketing positions. However, argues Evert Gummesson, all those whose work affects the customer in some way—either through direct contact or through design of processes and policies that shape customers' experiences—need to think of themselves as *part-time marketers*.[37]

A Framework for Developing Effective Service Marketing Strategies

To help you understand what is involved in developing marketing strategies that will be appropriate for different types of services, Figure 1.11 presents a framework that outlines the key steps. It shows how each of the chapters in this book fits together with the others as they address related topics and issues. Note the arrows linking the different boxes in the diagram: They make it clear that the process of creating a strategy is not like stopping at a series of points along a one-way street. Instead, it's an iterative process; that is, one whose components may have to be revisited more than once because they are interdependent. Decisions in one area must be consistent with those taken in another, so that each strategic element will mutually reinforce the remainder. A sound services marketing strategy is based on a solid knowledge of the market, customers, and the competition. It is actionable—that is, the firm possesses the necessary resources. And it sets realistic goals toward which progress can readily be measured.

Understanding the Customer

Now it's time to put you in the driver's seat, thinking like a manager rather than a student, as you negotiate the different steps. Our framework begins with—and will continually involve—your ability to understand customers' needs and how they behave in service environments (Chapter 2). Important concerns for you and your colleagues will include how people search for information, how they establish expectations, and how they choose among alternative suppliers. You should also be monitoring *service encounters*, those moments of truth when customers interact with the firm and the proverbial rubber meets the road. Are their expectations being met or missed? As a result, are they satisfied or disappointed? And do they plan to use your firm's services again, or switch to a competitor?

Building the Service Model

This task (addressed in Part II of the book) requires you and other members of the management team to create a meaningful *value proposition*—a specified package of benefits and solutions, emphasizing key points of difference relative to competing alternatives and how it proposes to deliver them to target customers.[38] You'll need to develop a distinctive *service concept* that responds to specific customer needs and market opportunities, as opposed to proposing a generic, "me too" offering. Transforming this concept into a service product means developing a specific package of core and supplementary product elements, and then distributing each element of this package to customers at appropriate places and times. Depending on the nature of the product, you may be selecting a variety of both physical and electronic channels to deliver all the different product elements to customers. More and more, "place" is no longer a geographic location, open during only limited hours, but somewhere in cyberspace that customers can access at will, 24/7.

To ensure that your strategy will be financially viable, you must create a *business model* that will allow the costs of creating and delivering the service (plus a margin for profits) to be recovered through realistic pricing strategies. Of course, you know that customers won't buy unless they perceive that the benefits obtained from this *value exchange* will exceed the financial and other costs they incur, including their time and effort. So, your value proposition must be actively promoted through effective communications and there must be a strategy for educating customers—especially first-time users—about how to make good choices and use the service to their best advantage. And finally, to ensure that this value proposition will be commercially viable, your strategy must stake out a distinctive and defensible *position* in the market against competing alternatives, so that your company can attract a sufficient volume of business from the types of customers that it is targeting.

Managing the Customer Interface

Your task continues with development of strategies for managing the customer interface—embracing all points at which customers interact with your company. It will

Figure 1.11 A Framework for Developing a Services Marketing Strategy

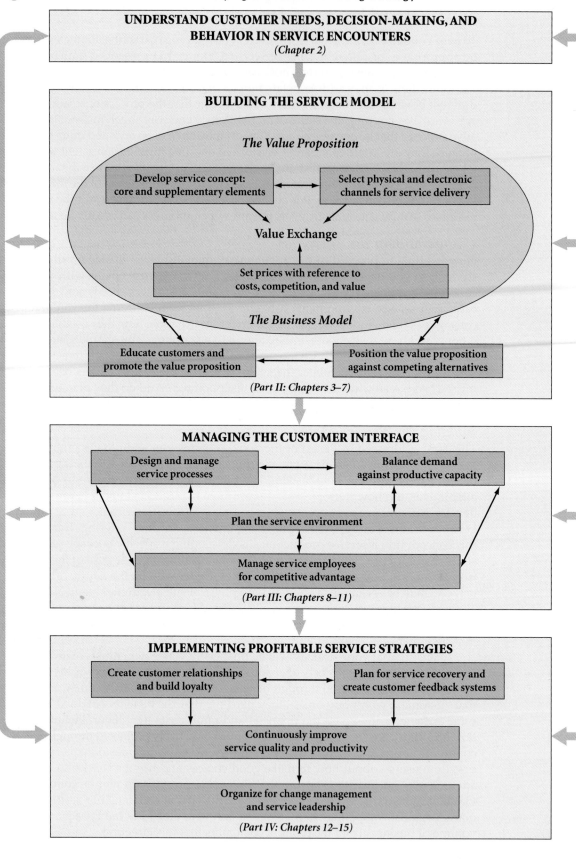

UNDERSTAND CUSTOMER NEEDS, DECISION-MAKING, AND
BEHAVIOR IN SERVICE ENCOUNTERS
(Chapter 2)

BUILDING THE SERVICE MODEL

The Value Proposition

Develop service concept:
core and supplementary elements

Select physical and electronic
channels for service delivery

Value Exchange

Set prices with reference to
costs, competition, and value

The Business Model

Educate customers and
promote the value proposition

Position the value proposition
against competing alternatives

(Part II: Chapters 3–7)

MANAGING THE CUSTOMER INTERFACE

Design and manage
service processes

Balance demand
against productive capacity

Plan the service environment

Manage service employees
for competitive advantage

(Part III: Chapters 8–11)

IMPLEMENTING PROFITABLE SERVICE STRATEGIES

Create customer relationships
and build loyalty

Plan for service recovery and
create customer feedback systems

Continuously improve
service quality and productivity

Organize for change management
and service leadership

(Part IV: Chapters 12–15)

involve working with your colleagues in operations and HR to design effective service processes—with your own particular focus, as a marketer, being on the role played by customers and the experiences you wish to engineer for them as they move through each step of the process toward a desired outcome. Closely related to the task is the question of how best to balance demand for the service (which in some markets may fluctuate widely over time) against the organization's productive capacity. If your job is in a service business that requires customers to enter the service factory, you'll also have to spend time thinking about design of the physical environment or *servicescape*.[39] And if the service involves contact between customers and service personnel, you'll need to work with your colleagues in HR to develop strategies for managing employees in ways that will enable them to deliver outstanding performances. HR managers who think strategically recognize that loyal, skilled, motivated employees who can work well independently or together in teams represent a key competitive advantage.

Implementing Service Strategies

Next, it's time to focus on some of the activities involved in implementing service marketing strategies. Achieving profitability will require creating relationships with customers from the right market segments and finding ways to build and reinforce their loyalty. When things go wrong (as they do from time to time, even in the best-run service businesses), your goal must be to achieve service recovery and retain customers; an important task will be to obtain customer feedback to help the firm avoid failures and better meet customers' needs and expectations in the future. Developing strategies for improving service quality and productivity will provide the necessary leverage for financial success: Unless your customers are satisfied with the quality of the service they receive, the company's revenues will decline as these customers take their business to competitors; and unless your firm can continually improve productivity, it may lose control of its costs and fail to create value for its owners. Long-term planning requires you to consider how the organization should evolve in response to emerging customer needs, market trends, competitive dynamics, and technologies. What needs to change if your firm is to achieve and maintain service leadership? And how should the process of change be led and managed? Consider this: Eventually, you may be in charge of such an initiative yourself!

CONCLUSION

Why study services? Because modern economies are driven by individual service businesses operating within a remarkable array of industries. Collectively, they're responsible for the creation of a substantial majority of all new jobs, both skilled and unskilled, around the world. Many of these industries are undergoing dramatic transformations, driven by advances in technology, globalization, changes in government policies, and evolving consumer needs and lifestyles. Important business trends include outsourcing and strategic alliances. In such an environment, effective marketing plays a vital role in determining whether an individual organization survives and thrives or declines and fails.

In this chapter, we've demonstrated that services require a distinctive approach to marketing, because the context and the tasks often differ in important respects from those in the manufacturing sector. To succeed as a marketing manager in a service business requires that you not only understand key marketing concepts and tools, but also know how to use them effectively. Each of the 8 Ps—the strategic levers of services marketing—potentially has a role to play, but it's how well you tie them together that will make the difference. As you study this book, attend classes, and undertake projects, remember that the winners in today's highly competitive service markets progress by continually rethinking the way they do business, by looking for innovative ways to serve their customers better, by taking advantage of new developments in technology, and by embracing a disciplined and well-organized approach to creating and implementing marketing strategy.

REVIEW QUESTIONS

1. Is it possible for an economy to be based entirely on services? Is it a sign of weakness if a national economy manufactures few of the goods that it consumes?
2. What are the main reasons for the growing share of the service sector in all the major economies of the world?
3. What is so distinctive about services marketing that it requires a special approach, set of concepts, and body of knowledge?
4. "The 4 Ps are all a marketing manager needs to create a marketing strategy for a service business." Prepare a

response that argues the contrary, and justify your conclusions.

5. What types of services do you think are (a) most affected and (b) least affected by the problem of variable inputs and outputs. Why?

6. Why is time so important in services?

7. Explain each of the following terms, provide examples, and explain their importance for services marketing: (a) partial employee; (b) part-time marketer; (c) value proposition.

8. How has the development of self-service technologies affected services marketing strategy? What factors determine whether customers make use of them or not?

9. Why do marketing, operations, and human resources have to be more closely linked in services than in manufacturing? Give examples.

10. The term "marketing mix" could suggest that marketing managers are mixers of ingredients. Is that perspective a recipe for success when employing the 8 Ps to develop a services marketing strategy?

APPLICATION EXERCISES

1. Visit the web sites of the following national statistical bureaus: U.S. Bureau of Economic Analysis (www.bea.gov); Statistics Canada (www.statcan.ca); British Office of National Statistics (www.statistics.gov.uk); and Singapore (www.singstat.gov.sg). In each instance, obtain data on the latest trends in services as (a) a percentage of gross domestic product; (b) the percentage of employment accounted for by services; (c) breakdowns of these two statistics by type of industry; and (d) service exports and imports.

2. Review IBM's annual report, www.ibm.com/annual-report, recent quarterly reports, www.ibm.com/

investor, and other information on its web site describing its different businesses. What conclusions do you draw about future opportunities in different markets? What do you see as competitive threats?

3. Give examples of how Internet and telecommunications technologies (e.g., Interactive Voice Response Systems [IVRs] and mobile commerce [M-commerce]) have changed some of the services that you use.

4. Choose a service company with which you are familiar and show how each of the eight elements (8 Ps) of services marketing applies to a specific product.

ENDNOTES

1. Christopher H. Lovelock and Charles B. Weinberg, *Public and Nonprofit Marketing,* 2nd ed. Redwood City, CA: The Scientific Press, 1989; Paul Flanagan, Robert Johnston, and Derek Talbot, "Customer Confidence: The Development of 'Pre-Experience' Concept." *International Journal of Service Industry Management,* 16, no. 4 (2005): 373–384.

2. U.S. Department of Commerce, *North American Industry Classification System—United States.* Washington, DC: National Technical Information Service PB 2002-101430, 2002.

3. "The Great Jobs Switch." *The Economist* (October 1, 2005): 11, 14.

4. Diana Farrell, Martha A. Laboissière, and Jaeson Rosenfeld, "Sizing the Emerging Global Labor Market." *The McKinsey Quarterly,* no. 3 (2005): 93–103.

5. "Crowned at Last." *The Economist* (April 2, 2005): 3–6.

6. Bill Carroll and Judy Siguaw, "The Evolution of Electronic Distribution: Effects on Hotels and Intermediaries." *Cornell Hotel and Restaurant Administration Quarterly,* 44 (August 2003): 38–51.

7. Michael D. Johnson and Anders Gustafsson, *Competing in a Service Economy.* San Franciso: Jossey-Bass, 2003.

8. Jonas Matthing, Bodil Sandén, and Bo Edvardsson, "New Service Development: Learning from and with Customers." *International Journal of Service Industry Management,* 15, no. 5 (2004): 479–459.

9. Adam Smith, (1776), *The Wealth of Nations, Books I–III,* with an Introduction by A. Skinner. London: Penguin Books, 1969.

10. Jean Baptiste Say (1803), *A Treatise on Political Economy.* Reprints of Economic Classics. New York: Augustus M. Kelly, 1964.

11. Robert C. Judd, "The Case for Redefining Services." *Journal of Marketing,* 28 (January 1964): 59; John M. Rathmell, *Marketing in the Service Sector.* Cambridge, MA: Winthrop, 1974; Christopher H. Lovelock and Evert Gummesson, "Whither Services Marketing? In Search of a New Paradigm and Fresh Perspectives." *Journal of Service Research,* 7 (August 2004): 20–41.

12. Lovelock and Gummeson, "Whither Services Marketing."

13. William R. Trumble and Angus Stevenson (eds.) *Shorter Oxford English Dictionary,* 5th ed. Oxford, UK: Oxford University Press, 2002: 2768.

14. John M. Rathmell, "What Is Meant by Services?" *Journal of Marketing,* 30 (October 1966): 32–36.

15. Evert Gummesson (citing an unknown source), "Lip Service: A Neglected Area in Services Marketing." *Journal of Consumer Services,* no. 1 (Summer 1987): 19–22.

16. Adapted from a definition by Christopher Lovelock (identified anonymously as Expert 6, Table II, p. 112) in Bo Edvardsson, Anders Gustafsson, and Inger Roos, "Service Portraits in Service Research: A Critical Review." *International Journal of Service Industry Management,* 16, no. 1 (2005): 107–121.

17. Rogelio Oliva and Robert L. Kallenberg, "Managing the Transition from Products to Services." *International Journal of Service Industry Management,* 14, no. 2 (2003): 160–172; Jeremy Howells, "Innovation, Consumption

and Services: Encapsulation and the Combinatorial Role of Services." *The Service Industries Journal,* 24 (January 2004): 19–36; Mohanbir Sawhney, Sridhar Balasubramanian, and Vish V. Krishnan, "Creating Growth with Services." *MIT Sloan Management Review,* 45 (Winter 2004): 34–43; Sara Brax, "A Manufacturer Becoming Service Provider—Challenges and a Paradox." *Managing Service Quality,* 15, no. 2 (2005): 142–155; Wayne A. Neu and Stephen A. Brown, "Forming Successful Business-to-Business Services in Goods-Dominant Firms." *Journal of Service Research,* 8 (August 2005), 3–17; Morris A. Cohen, Narendra Agrawal, and Vipul Agrawal, "Winning in the Aftermarket." *Harvard Business Review,* 84 (May 2006): 1–4.

18. Theodore Levitt, *Marketing for Business Growth.* New York: McGraw-Hill, 1974, p. 5.

19. Roland Rust, "What Is the Domain of Service Research?" (editorial). *Journal of Service Research,* 1 (November 1998): 107.

20. *IBM Annual Report.* Armonk, NY: International Business Machines Corporation, 2005 (available online at ftp://ftp.software.ibm.com/annualreport/2004/2004_ibm_annual.pdf).

21. G. Lynn Shostack, "Breaking Free from Product Marketing." *Journal of Marketing,* 41 (April 1977): 73–80.

22. W. Earl Sasser, R. Paul Olsen, and D. Daryl Wyckoff, *Management of Service Operations: Text, Cases, and Readings.* Boston: Allyn & Bacon, 1978.

23. William R. George and Leonard L. Berry, "Guidelines for the Advertising of Services." Business Horizons (July–August 1981): 52–56; Banwari Mittal, "The Advertising of Services: Meeting the Challenge of Intangibility." *Journal of Service Research,* 2 (August 1999): 98–116; Banwari Mittal and Julie Baker, "Advertising Strategies for Hospitality Services." *Cornell Hotel and Restaurant Administration Quarterly,* 43 (April 2002): 51–63.

24. Flanagan, Johnston, and Talbot, "Customer Confidence."

25. The term "partial employee" was coined by P. K. Mills and D. J. Moberg, "Perspectives on the Technology of Service Operations." *Academy of Management Review,* 7, no. 3, (1982): 467–478. For recent research on this topic, see Karthik Namasivayam, "The Consumer as Transient Employee: Consumer Satisfaction Through the Lens of Job-Performance Models." *International Journal of Service Industry Management,* 14, no. 4 (2004): 420–435; An-Tien Hsieh, Chang-Hua Yen, and Ko-Chien Chin, "Participative Customers as Partial Employees and Service Provider Workload." *International Journal of Service Industry Management,* 15, no. 2 (2004): 187–200.

26. Matthew L. Meuter, Mary Jo Bitner, Amy L. Ostrom, and Stephen W. Brown, "Choosing Among Alternative Delivery Modes: An Investigation of Customer Trial of Self Service Technologies." *Journal of Marketing,* 69 (April 2005): 61–84.

27. Devashish Pujari, "Self-Service with a Smile: Self-Service Technology (SST) Encounters Among Canadian Business-to-Business." *International Journal of Service Industry Management,* 15, no. 2 (2004): 200–219; Angus Laing, Gillian Hogg, and Dan Winkelman, "The Impact of the Internet on Professional Relationships: The Case of Health Care." *The Service Industries Journal,* 25 (July 2005): 675–688.

28. Matthew L. Meuter, Amy Ostrom, Robert Roundtree, and Mary Jo Bitner, "Self-Service Technologies: Understanding Customer Satisfaction with Technology-Based Service Encounters." *Journal of Marketing,* 64 (July 2000): 50–64; A. Parasuraman, Valarie Zeithaml, and Arvind Malhotra, "E-S-QUAL: A Multiple Item Scale for Assessing Electronic Service Quality." *Journal of Service Research,* 7 (February 2005): 213–233.

29. Philip J. Coelho and Chris Easingwood, "Multiple Channel Systems in Services: Pros, Cons, and Issues." *The Service Industries Journal,* 24 (September 2004): 1–30.

30. Bonnie Farber Canziani, "Leveraging Customer Competency in Service Firms." *International Journal of Service Industry Management,* 8, no. 1 (1997): 5–25.

31. Gary Knisely, "Greater Marketing Emphasis by Holiday Inns Breaks Mold." *Advertising Age* (January 15, 1979).

32. Gary Stix, "Real Time." *Scientific American* (September 2002): 36–39.

33. Coelho and Easingwood, "Multiple Channel Systems in Services."

34. The 4 Ps classification of marketing decision variables was created by E. Jerome McCarthy, *Basic Marketing: A Managerial Approach.* Homewood, IL: Richard D. Irwin, 1960. It was a refinement of the long list of ingredients included in the marketing mix concept, created by Professor Neil Borden at Harvard Business School in the 1950s. Borden got the idea from a colleague who described the marketing manager's job as being a "mixer of ingredients."

35. An expanded 7 Ps marketing mix was first proposed by Bernard H. Booms and Mary J. Bitner, "Marketing Strategies and Organization Structures for Service Firms," in J. H. Donnelly and W. R. George, *Marketing of Services.* Chicago: American Marketing Association, 1981, pp. 47–51. The eighth P, productivity and quality, was added by Christopher Lovelock and Lauren Wright, *Principles of Service Marketing and Management.* Upper Saddle River, NJ: Prentice Hall, 1999.

36. For a review of the literature on this topic, see Michael D. Hartline and O. C. Ferrell, "The Management of Customer Contact Service Employees." *Journal of Marketing,* 60, no. 4 (October 1996): 52–70.

37. The term "part-time marketer" was created by Evert Gummesson, "The New Marketing: Developing Long-Term Interactive Relationships." *Long Range Planning,* 4 (1987). See also Christian Grönroos, *Service Management and Marketing,* 2nd ed. Chichester, UK: John Wiley & Sons, 2001; and Evert Gummesson, *Total Relationship Marketing,* 2nd ed. Oxford, UK: Butterworth Heinemann, 2002.

38. James C. Anderson, James C. Narus, and Wouter van Russom, "Customer Value Propositions in Business Markets." *Harvard Business Review,* 84 (March 2006): 1–4.

39. The term "servicescape" was coined by Mary Jo Bitner, "Servicescapes: The Impact of Physical Surroundings on Customers and Employees." *Journal of Marketing,* 56 (April 1992): 57–71.

Chapter

2

Customer Behavior in Service Encounters

I can't get no satisfaction.

MICK JAGGER

An individual who seeks out the necessary information and chooses wisely has a better chance of getting satisfaction than Mick Jagger.

CLAES FORNELL

All the world's a stage and all the men and women merely players; they have their exits and their entrances and one man in his time plays many parts.

WILLIAM SHAKESPEARE, *AS YOU LIKE IT*

*U*nderstanding customer behavior lies at the heart of marketing. Without this understanding, no organization can hope to create and deliver services that will result in satisfied customers.

In order to develop effective marketing strategies, we need, first, to understand why customers use services and how they choose among competing service suppliers. Our interest then shifts to examining the nature of the encounters that customers have with their chosen service provider during service delivery and consumption. How are customers interacting with service facilities, service personnel, and even other customers? What are their expectations at each step in service delivery? Finally, of course, we should determine whether the experience of using the service and receiving its benefits has met customers' expectations and left them satisfied and ready to repurchase in the future.

An important theme in this chapter is that not all services are alike and that differences among services have important implications for customer behavior. In particular, "high-contact" encounters between customers and service organizations differ sharply from "low-contact" encounters. The nature of some services, such as restaurants, hospitals, and airlines, requires customers to visit these facilities and engage in face-to-face interactions with employees. By contrast, customers of service industries such as insurance and cable TV rarely, if ever, visit the supplier's offices; even if something goes wrong or they wish to make changes, they will generally speak to a representative by phone, mail a letter, or send an email.

In this chapter, we analyze the nature of service consumption and consider how firms should manage encounters to create satisfied customers and desirable outcomes for the business itself. We introduce four categories of services and show how the extent of customer contact and the nature of the underlying delivery processes affect both the nature of the service encounter and customer behavior.

We explore the following questions:

1. What are the four broad categories of services? And why does each pose such distinctive service management challenges?
2. What is the three-stage model of service consumption? And which perspectives help us to understand and better manage consumer behavior at each stage?
3. What perceived risks do customers face in selecting, purchasing, and using services? And how can firms reduce consumer risk perceptions?
4. How do customers form expectations of service?
5. How do role theory and script theory help us to understand consumer behavior during the service encounter?
6. What insights can be gained from viewing service delivery as a form of theater?

DIFFERENCES AMONG SERVICES AFFECT CUSTOMER BEHAVIOR

Important marketing-relevant differences exist among services. These differences include whether service is targeted at customers in person or at their possessions, whether service actions and output are tangible or intangible in nature, whether customers need to be involved in service production; and how much contact (if any) they need to have with service facilities, employees, and other customers. We turn to the most fundamental of the 8 Ps (introduced in Chapter 1), the *processes* by which service products are created and delivered, to categorize services in ways that help us understand how these differences arise and what they mean for customer behavior.

Four Broad Categories of Services

Marketers don't usually need to know the specifics of how physical goods are manufactured—that responsibility belongs to the people who run the factory. However, the situation is different in services. Because their customers are often involved in service production and may have preferences for certain methods of service delivery, marketers must understand the nature of the processes through which services are created and delivered. As you learned in Chapter 1, a *process* is a particular method of operation or a series of actions, typically involving multiple steps that often need to take place in a defined sequence.

Think about the steps a customer goes through at a hair salon: phoning in advance to make an appointment, arriving at the salon, waiting, having a shampoo, discussing options with the cutter, having her hair cut and styled, tipping, paying, and finally leaving. Service processes range from relatively simple procedures involving only a few steps—such as filling a car's tank with fuel—to highly complex activities such as transporting passengers on an international flight.

From an operational perspective, a process involves taking inputs and transforming them into output. But what is each service organization actually processing, and how does it perform this task? Three broad categories of things are processed in services: people, physical objects, and data. In many cases, ranging from health clubs to education, customers themselves are the principal input to the service process. In other instances, the key input is an object such as a defective machine or a piece of financial data. In some services, as in all manufacturing, the process is physical and something tangible takes place. But where data are concerned, as in services such as insurance or research, the process can be almost entirely intangible.

Viewing services from this perspective, we can categorize them into four broad groups, based on tangible actions to either people's bodies or to their physical possessions, and intangible actions to either people's minds or to their intangible assets Figure 2.1.[1]

We refer to these categories as *people processing, possession processing, mental stimulus processing,* and *information processing.* Although the industries within each category may appear at first sight to be very different, analysis will show that they do, in fact, share important process-related characteristics. As a result, managers from different industries may obtain valued insights by studying another industry within the same category and then create useful innovations for their own organization. Let's

Figure 2.1 Four Categories of Services

What Is the Nature of the Service Act?	Who or What Is the Direct Recipient of the Service?	
	People	**Possessions**
Tangible Actions	**People processing** (services directed at people's bodies): Passenger transportation Health care Lodging Beauty salons Physical therapy Fitness centers Restaurants/bars Barbers Funeral services	**Possession processing** (services directed at physical possessions): Freight transportation Repair and maintenance Warehousing/storage Office cleaning services Retail distribution Laundry and dry cleaning Refueling Landscaping/gardening Disposal/recycling
Intangible Actions	**Mental stimulus processing** (services directed at people's minds): Advertising/PR Arts and entertainment Broadcasting/cable Management consulting Education Information services Music concerts Psychotherapy Religion Voice telephone	**Information processing** (services directed at intangible assets): Accounting Banking Data processing Data transmission Insurance Legal services Programming Research Securities investment Software consulting

examine why these four different types of processes often have distinctive implications for marketing, operations, and human resource strategies.

People Processing

From ancient times, people have sought out services directed at themselves—being transported, fed, lodged, restored to health, or made more beautiful. To receive these types of services, customers must physically enter the service system. Why? Because they are an integral part of the process and cannot obtain the desired benefits by dealing at arm's length with service suppliers. In short, they must enter the *service factory*, a physical location where people or machines (or both) create and deliver service benefits to customers. Sometimes, of course, service providers are willing to come to customers, bringing the necessary tools of their trade to create the desired benefits at the customers' preferred locations.

If you, as a customer, want the benefits that a people processing service has to offer, you must be prepared to cooperate actively with the service operation. For example, if you want a manicure, you have to cooperate with the manicurist by specifying what you want, sitting still, and presenting each hand for treatment when requested. If you need an eye exam, the optometrist will ask you to submit to a number of tests and, for those that check the acuity of your vision, to report what you see on the chart or other display.

The amount of time required of customers in people processing services varies widely, ranging from boarding a city bus for a short ride to undergoing a lengthy course of treatments at a hospital. In between these extremes are such activities as ordering and eating a meal; having your hair washed, cut, and styled; or spending several nights in a hotel room. The output from these services (after a period of time that can vary from minutes to months) is a customer who has reached her destination or satisfied his hunger or is now sporting clean and stylishly cut hair or has had a good night's sleep away from home or is now in physically better health.

Managers should be thinking about process and output from the standpoint of what happens to the customer (or the physical object being processed). Reflecting on the service process helps to identify not only what benefits are being created at each point in the process but also the nonfinancial costs incurred by the customer in terms of time, mental and physical effort, and even fear and pain.

Possession Processing

Often, customers ask a service organization to provide tangible treatment for some physical possession—a house that has been invaded by insects, a hedge that has grown too high, a malfunctioning elevator, a package that needs to be sent to another city, dirty clothes, or a sick pet.

Many such activities are quasi-manufacturing operations and do not involve simultaneous production and consumption. Examples include cleaning, maintaining, storing, improving, or repairing physical objects—both living and inanimate—that belong to the customer in order to extend their usefulness. Additional possession processing services include transport and storage of goods; wholesale and retail distribution; and installation, removal, and disposal of equipment—in short, the entire value-adding chain of activities that may take place during the lifetime of the object in question. The actual service process might involve applying insecticide to a house to get rid of ants, trimming a hedge at an office park, repairing a car, installing new software in a computer, cleaning a jacket, or giving an injection to the family dog. In each instance, the output should be a satisfactory solution to the customer's problem.

Customers are less physically involved with this type of service than with people processing services. Consider the difference between passenger and package transportation. In the former case you have to go along for the ride to obtain the benefit of traveling from one location to another. With packages, however, you drop your parcel off at a mailbox or post office counter (or request a courier to collect it from your home or office) and wait for it to be delivered to the recipient.

In most possession processing services, the customer's involvement is usually limited to dropping off the item that needs treatment, requesting the service, explaining the problem, and later returning to pick up the item and pay the bill. In such instances, production and consumption can be described as *separable*. Sometimes, however, customers choose to be present during service delivery, perhaps wishing to supervise cutting of the hedge or comfort the family dog while it receives treatment at the veterinary clinic.

Mental Stimulus Processing

Services directed at people's minds include education, news and information, professional advice, psychotherapy, entertainment, and certain religious activities. Anything touching people's minds has the power to shape attitudes and influence behavior. So, when customers are in a position of dependency or there is potential for manipulation, strong ethical standards and careful oversight are required. Obtaining the full benefit of such services requires an investment of time and a degree of mental effort on the customer's part. However, recipients don't necessarily have to be physically present in a service factory—just mentally in communication with the information being presented. There's an interesting contrast here with people processing services. Passengers can sleep through a flight and still arrive at their desired destination. But if you fall asleep in class or during an educational TV broadcast, you won't be any wiser at the end than at the beginning!

Services such as entertainment and education are often created in one place and transmitted by television, radio, or the Internet to individual customers in distant locations. However, they can also be delivered to groups of customers at the originating location in a facility such as a theater or lecture hall. As you know, watching a live concert on television is not the same experience as watching it in a concert hall (or other performance center) in the company of hundreds or even thousands of other people. Managers of concert halls face many of the same challenges as their colleagues in people processing services. Similarly, the experience of participating in a discussion-based class through interactive cable television lacks the intimacy of people debating one another in the same room.

Because the core content of services in this category is information based (whether music, voice, or visual images), it can be converted to digital bits or analog signals; recorded for posterity; and transformed into a manufactured product, such as a CD or DVD, which may then be packaged and marketed much like any other physical good. For instance, the Boston Symphony Orchestra's concerts can be attended live, viewed live or prerecorded on TV, heard live or prerecorded on the radio, or purchased as digital recordings (Figure 2.2). Services in this category can thus be "inventoried," for consumption at a later date than their production. In fact, the same performance can be consumed repeatedly. For some customers, purchasing an educational video to play at home may be a better solution than taking a class. Increasingly, customers can download electronic content on demand through their computers or cell phones from a supplier such as Apple's music/video online shop.

Information Processing

Information processing has been revolutionized by computers, but not all information is processed by machines. Professionals in a wide variety of fields also use their brains to perform information processing and packaging. Information is the most intangible form of service output, but it may be transformed into more enduring, tangible forms such as letters, reports, books, CD-ROMs, or DVDs. Among the services that are highly dependent on the effective collection and processing of information

Figure 2.2
Attending a Live Concert Is Only One of the Several Ways to Consume a Performance by the Boston Symphony Orchestra

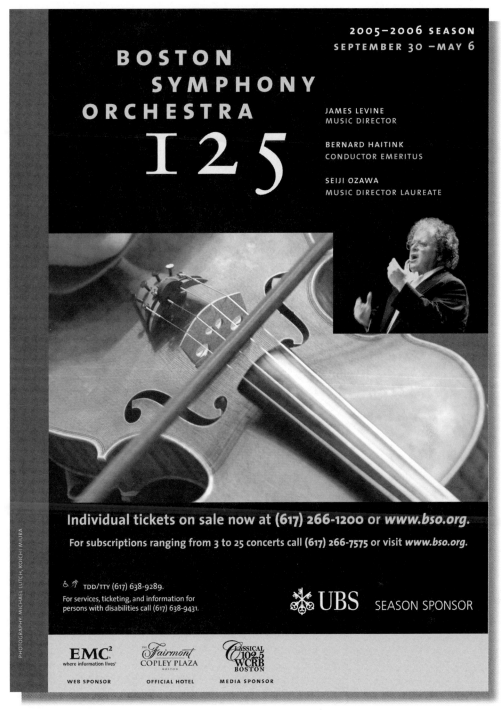

Reprinted by permission of Boston Symphony Orchestra and Michael J. Lutch.

are financial services and professional services such as accounting, law, marketing research, management consulting, and medical diagnosis.

The line between information processing and mental stimulus processing may be blurred. For instance, a stockbroker may use an analysis of client's brokerage transactions to recommend the most appropriate type of investment strategy for the future. An attorney in a corporate law firm may spot patterns that pose legal risks for clients and advise them accordingly. And market researchers may see opportunities to publish useful insights that they have gained from reviewing trends over time. For simplicity, we will periodically combine our coverage of mental stimulus processing services and information processing services under the umbrella term *information-based services*.

Insights and Implications

The differences among these four categories show how unwise it is to overgeneralize about services. At the same time, managers in a particular service industry shouldn't fall into the trap of believing that their situation is unique and they have nothing to learn from any other service industry.

As customers, the nature of our involvement in service production varies widely and also changes rapidly. We have to visit the service factory for people processing but not for the other types of services—although tradition and personal preferences may still lead us to do so. Our choices may reflect such factors as whether we like to be served by employees face to face or prefer to engage in self-service, whether we're willing to travel to a service facility or prefer to obtain service from a remote location such as our home or office, how sociable we are, and how tightly we budget our time for conducting service transactions. Consumption activities range from predominantly tangible activities to almost entirely intangible ones. Information-based service output can be recorded and stored for later use, thus offering customers greater convenience and more control over how they use their time.

The extent of customer involvement in both information and mental stimulus processing is often determined more by tradition and a personal desire to meet the supplier face to face than by the needs of the operational process. Strictly speaking, face-to-face contact is quite unnecessary in industries such as banking or insurance. As a customer, why go to the service factory when there's no compelling need to do so? Habit and tradition often lie at the root of existing service delivery systems and consumption patterns. Professionals and their clients may say they prefer to meet face to face because they learn more about each other's needs, capabilities, and personalities. However, experience shows that successful personal relationships, built on trust, can be created and maintained purely through telephone and email contact.

CUSTOMER DECISION MAKING: THE THREE-STAGE MODEL OF SERVICE CONSUMPTION

Consumption of any type of product involves purchase and use. To develop effective marketing strategies, we must understand how people make decisions about buying and using a service, what the experience of service delivery and consumption is like for customers, and how they evaluate that experience.

Service consumption can be divided into three principal stages: prepurchase, service encounter, and post-encounter. As shown in Figure 2.3, each stage in the three-stage model of service consumption contains two or more steps. However, as noted on the left-hand side of the diagram, the nature of these steps often varies between high- and low-contact services. Furthermore, at each stage, different concepts offer insights that can help us to understand, analyze, and manage what is taking place. On the right-hand side of the diagram, you will find the key concepts discussed in this chapter.

Prepurchase Stage

A person's decision to buy and use a service reflects arousal of an underlying need. Are there dirt marks on the suit that you're planning to wear for that important interview next week? Is a health problem causing you discomfort? Are you feeling hungry? Do you need help preparing your tax return? Are you looking for something fun to do over the holidays? Once you recognize a need, you start to look for a solution, and that requires searching for information and sometimes advice. Organizations, too, have needs. Corporate purchasing decisions, though often more complex than those of individuals and households, also require finding appropriate solutions.

Figure 2.3 The Three Stage Model of Service Consumption

High Contact Services	Low Contact Services		Key Concepts
		1. PREPURCHASE STAGE	
Can visit physical sites, observe	Surf Web, phone calls visit library	**Awareness of Need**	*Need arousal*
		Information search	
(+ low-contact options)		• Clarify needs	*Evoked set*
		• Explore solutions	
		• Identify alternative service products and suppliers	*Search, experience, and credence attributes*
		Evaluation of alternatives (solutions and suppliers)	*Perceived risk*
		• Review supplier information (e.g., advertising, brochures, websites, etc.)	*Formation of expectations*
		• Review information from third parties (e.g., published reviews, ratings, comments on web, blogs, complaints to public agencies satisfaction ratings, awards)	*- desired service level*
Can visit in person and observe (possibly test) facilities, equipment, operation in action; meet personnel, see customers (+ remote options)	Primarily remote contact (websites, blogs, phone, email, publications, etc.)	• Discuss options with service personnel	*- predicted service level*
		• Get advice and feedback from third party advisors, other customers	*- adequate service level*
			- zone of tolerance
		Make decision on service purchase	
		2. SERVICE ENCOUNTER STAGE	
At physical site (or remote reservation)	Remote	**Request service from chosen supplier or initiate self-service (payment may be upfront or billed later)**	*Moments of truth*
			Service encounters
At physical site *only*	Remote	**Service delivery by personnel or self-service**	*Servuction system*
			Role and script theories
			Theater as metaphor
		3. POST-ENCOUNTER STAGE	
		Evaluation of service performance	*Confirmation/disconfirmation of expectations*
		Future intentions	*Dissatisfaction, satisfaction, and delight*

If your purchase is routine and relatively low-risk, you may move quickly to selecting and using a specific service provider. Indeed, many decisions involve simply repeating previous usage behavior. But in situations where more is at stake or you're using a service for the first time, you may be willing to invest time and effort to figure out your requirements more precisely, learn about the pros and cons of possible courses of action, and identify and evaluate alternative suppliers. Contrast how you approached the process of applying to college versus deciding where to go for an inexpensive meal. The next step is to identify potential suppliers and then weigh the benefits and risks of each option before making a final decision. By this point, you have developed some expectations about the nature of your forthcoming service experience and the benefits that you anticipate.

Service Encounter Stage

After making a purchase decision, customers move on to the core of the service experience: the service encounter stage, which usually includes a series of contacts with the chosen service provider (or its designated agents). This stage often begins with placing an order, requesting a reservation, or even submitting an application (consider the process of obtaining a loan, seeking insurance coverage, or getting into college or graduate school). Contacts may take the form of personal exchanges between customers and service employees, or impersonal interactions with machines or computers. During service delivery, many customers start evaluating the quality of service they are receiving and deciding whether it meets their expectations. High-contact services usually supply a greater array of clues to service quality than do low-contact services.

Post-encounter Stage

During the post-encounter stage, customers continue the ongoing evaluation of service quality that they began earlier. Depending on whether their expectations were met, this evaluation may lead them to feel satisfaction or dissatisfaction with the service experience—an outcome that will affect their future intentions, such as whether to remain loyal to the provider that delivered service and whether to make positive or negative recommendations to family members and other associates.

THE PREPURCHASE STAGE

The prepurchase stage begins with *need arousal*—the prospective customer's awareness of a need—and continues through information search and evaluation of alternatives to a decision on whether to make a service purchase.

Customers Seek Solutions to Aroused Needs

People buy goods and services to meet specific needs or wants. Some needs are often deeply rooted in people's unconscious minds and may concern issues relating to personal identity and aspirations. Other needs, such as alleviating hunger (a short-term issue but one that arises several times daily) or dealing with, say, chronic back pain (a long-term problem), are more overt because they're based on the customer's physical condition. External sources, including marketing activities, may also stimulate awareness of a need. As shown in Figure 2.4, Prudential Financial uses advertising to urge people to start thinking about their retirement needs, encouraging them to visit a web site where they can learn more about their options. When people recognize a need, they are more likely to be motivated to take action to resolve it.

In developed economies, increased spending on more elaborate vacations, sports, entertainment, restaurant meals, and other service experiences is assuming greater priority for consumers, even at the expense of spending slightly less on physical goods. This shift in consumer behavior and attitudes provides opportunities for those service companies that understand and meet changing needs. For example,

Figure 2.4
Prudential Financial's Advertising Stimulates Thinking About Retirement Needs

Courtesy of Masterfile Corporation.

some astute service providers have capitalized on the increased interest in extreme sports by offering such services as guided mountain climbs, paragliding, white-water rafting trips, and mountain biking adventures. The notion of service experiences also extend to business and industrial situations; consider the example of modern trade shows, where exhibitors, including manufacturers, set out to engage customers' interest through interactive presentations and even entertainment.[2]

As consumers review and clarify their needs, they can start to explore potential solutions and suppliers. Alternative solutions might involve deciding among different approaches to addressing the same basic problem, such as hiring a landscaping firm to cut down a dying tree in your yard as opposed to buying a chainsaw and doing it yourself. Or choosing between going out to a movie theater, renting a video to play at home,

some astute service providers have capitalized on the increased interest in extreme sports by offering such services as guided mountain climbs, paragliding, white-water rafting trips, and mountain biking adventures. The notion of service experiences also extend to business and industrial situations; consider the example of modern trade shows, where exhibitors, including manufacturers, set out to engage customers' interest through interactive presentations and even entertainment.[2]

As consumers review and clarify their needs, they can start to explore potential solutions and suppliers. Alternative solutions might involve deciding among different approaches to addressing the same basic problem, such as hiring a landscaping firm to cut down a dying tree in your yard as opposed to buying a chainsaw and doing it yourself. Or choosing between going out to a movie theater, renting a video to play at home, or downloading an on-demand movie from your cable service company. And, of course, there's always the alternative of doing nothing—at least for the time being. The alternatives that consumers consider actively are known as the *evoked set*, which is derived from options that consumers remember from past experience and exposure, plus new options that are highlighted by external sources, including advertising, retail displays, news stories, and recommendations from both service personnel and other customers.

Evaluating a Service May Be Difficult

Many services—especially those that provide few tangible clues—can be difficult to evaluate before purchase. As a result, customers may worry about the risk of making a purchase that subsequently proves to be disappointing. If you buy a physical good that proves unsatisfactory, you can usually return or replace it—although it may take extra effort on your part to do so. These options are not as readily available with services. Although some services can be repeated, such as recleaning clothes that have not been laundered satisfactorily, this is not a practical solution in the case of a poorly performed play or a badly taught course (do you really want to take "Principles of Cost Accounting" again next semester?).

Ease or difficulty of evaluation in advance of purchase is a function of product attributes. Many goods and some services are relatively high in *search attributes*—tangible characteristics that customers can evaluate before purchase. More complex goods and most services, by contrast, emphasize *experience attributes* such as reliability, ease of use, and customer support, that inexperienced purchasers can discern only during delivery and consumption. Finally, there are *credence attributes*, characteristics that customers find hard to evaluate even after consumption—often relating to the benefits actually delivered.[3] When discussing these three dimensions, we should be careful not to overgeneralize. In particular, there may be big differences between an experienced customer's ability to evaluate a service and that of a first-time user.

Search Attributes

Search attributes help customers evaluate a product before purchasing it. Style, color, texture, taste, and sound are features that allow prospective consumers to try out, taste test, or "test drive" a product before purchasing it. These tangible characteristics help customers understand and evaluate what they will get in exchange for their money and reduce the sense of uncertainty or risk associated with the purchase occasion. Clothing, furniture, cars, electronic equipment, and foods are among the manufactured products that are high in search attributes. Search attributes are found in many service environments as well. For example, you can assess some attributes before you visit a particular restaurant, including the type of food, the location and availability of parking, the "positioning" of the restaurant (fine dining, casual, family-type restaurant, etc.), and the price level. At a hotel, you can ask a room clerk to let you see alternative rooms; you can check out a golf course without actually playing a round, or take a tour of a health club and try out one or two pieces of equipment.

Experience Attributes

When attributes can't be evaluated before purchase, customers must "experience" the service to know what they are getting. In our restaurant example, you won't know how much you actually like the food, the service provided by your waiter, and the atmosphere in the restaurant on that particular evening until you are actually consuming the service.

Vacations, live entertainment performances, sporting events, and even many medical procedures fall into this category. Although people can examine brochures, scroll through web sites describing a specific holiday destination, view travel films, or read reviews by travel experts, they can't really evaluate or feel the dramatic beauty associated with, say, hiking in the Canadian Rockies or snorkeling in the Caribbean until they experience these activities. Nor can customers always rely on information from friends, family, or other personal sources when evaluating these

and similar services, because different people may interpret or respond to the same stimuli in different ways. Consider your own experiences in following up on recommendations from friends to see a particular movie. Perhaps you can recall an occasion when you walked into the theater with high expectations, but felt disappointed after viewing the film because you didn't like it as much as your friends had.

Credence Attributes

Product characteristics that customers find impossible to evaluate confidently even after purchase and consumption are known as credence attributes, because the customer is forced to trust that certain tasks have been performed from which benefits will result. In our restaurant example, credence attributes include the hygiene conditions of the kitchen, and the healthiness of the cooking ingredients.

It's not easy for a customer to determine the quality of repair and maintenance work performed on a car, household appliance, or a piece of industrial machinery. Patients can't usually evaluate how well their dentists have performed complex dental procedures. And consider the purchase of professional services. People seek such assistance precisely because they lack the necessary training and expertise themselves—think about counseling, surgery, legal advice, and consulting services. How can you really be sure after the fact that the best possible job was done? Sometimes it comes down to a matter of having confidence in the provider's skills (Figure 2.5).

Uncertainty About the Outcomes Increases Perceived Risk

Perceived risk is especially relevant for services that are difficult to evaluate before purchase and consumption. First-time users are likely to face greater uncertainty. Think about how you felt the first time you had to make decisions about choosing and using an unfamiliar service, especially one with important consequences. It's likely that you worried about the probability of a negative outcome. The worse the possible outcome and the more likely it is to occur, the higher is the perception of risk. Table 2.1 outlines seven categories of perceived risks.

How Might Consumers Handle Perceived Risk?

People who feel uncomfortable with perceived risks during the prepurchase stage can use a variety of methods to reduce them. In fact, you've probably tried some

Table 2.1   Perceived Risks in Purchasing and Using Services

TYPE OF RISK	EXAMPLES OF CUSTOMER CONCERNS
Functional (unsatisfactory performance outcomes)	• Will this training course give me the skills I need to get a better job? • Will this credit card be accepted wherever and whenever I want to make a purchase? • Will the dry cleaner be able to remove the stains from this jacket?
Financial (monetary loss, unexpected costs)	• Will I lose money if I make the investment recommended by my stockbroker? • Could my identity be stolen if I make this purchase on the Internet? • Will I incur a lot of unanticipated expenses if I go on this vacation? • Will repairing my car cost more than the original estimate?
Temporal (wasting time, consequences of delays)	• Will I have to wait in line before entering the exhibition? • Will service at this restaurant be so slow that I will be late for my afternoon meeting? • Will the renovations to our bathroom be completed before our friends come to stay with us?
Physical (personal injury or damage to possessions)	• Will I get hurt if I go skiing at this resort? • Will the contents of this package get damaged in the mail? • Will I fall sick if I travel abroad on vacation?
Psychological (personal fears and emotions)	• How can I be sure that this aircraft won't crash? • Will the consultant make me feel stupid? • Will the doctor's diagnosis upset me?
Social (how others think and react)	• What will my friends think of me if they learn that I stayed at this cheap motel? • Will my relatives approve of the restaurant I have chosen for the family reunion dinner? • Will my business colleagues disapprove of my selection of an unknown law firm?
Sensory (unwanted effects on any of the five senses)	• Will I get a view of the parking lot rather than the beach from my restaurant table? • Will the hotel bed be uncomfortable? • Will I be kept awake by noise from the guests in the room next door? • Will my room smell of stale cigarette smoke? • Will the coffee at breakfast taste disgusting?

of the following risk-reduction strategies yourself before deciding to purchase a service:

- Seeking information from respected personal sources (family, friends, peers)
- Relying on a firm that has a good reputation
- Looking for guarantees and warranties
- Visiting service facilities or trying aspects of the service before purchasing
- Asking knowledgeable employees about competing services
- Examining tangible cues or other physical evidence
- Using the Internet to compare service offerings and to search for independent reviews and ratings

What Risk Reduction Strategies Can Service Suppliers Develop?

Well-managed firms work hard to reduce the perceived risk of purchasing their services, especially when these services are expensive and have durable outcomes. Strategies vary according to the nature of the service. They may include all or some of the following:

- Offering performance warranties
- Money-back (or repeat the service) guarantees
- Enabling prospective customers to preview the service through brochures, web sites, and videos
- Encouraging prospects to visit the service facilities in advance of purchase
- Instituting visible safety procedures
- Training staff members to be respectful and empathetic in their dealings with customers
- Providing 24/7 access by a toll-free telephone call to a customer service center or informative web site
- Delivering automated messages about anticipated problems to a designated cell phone (e.g., an airline that updates customers about flight delays)

- Giving customers access to online information about the status of an order or procedure.

Perhaps you've had the experience of tracking the progress of an important package sent by FedEx, DHL, UPS, or another logistics firm. Knowing that you will be able to follow your package as it moves through the system can be very reassuring. So is dealing with a service representative who takes time to put you at your ease and answer all your questions in a helpful and straightforward manner. It gives you confidence that you'll make the right decisions, get solutions that are relevant for your situation, and feel afterwards that you obtained fair value in exchange for your money, time, and effort.

Strategic Responses to Managing Customer Perceptions of Risk

Among the factors that cause services to be high in experience and credence attributes are that performances are transitory, many intangible elements are involved, and the variability of inputs and outputs often leads to quality control problems. These characteristics present special challenges for service marketers, requiring them to find ways to reassure customers and reduce the perceived risks associated with buying and using services whose performance and value can't easily be predicted and may even be difficult to ascertain after consumption.

Marketers whose products are high in experience characteristics often try to create more search attributes to assist prospective customers. One approach is to offer a free trial. Some providers of online computer services have adopted this strategy. For example, AOL (America Online) offers potential users free software and the chance to try its services without charge for a limited period. This strategy reduces customers' concerns about entering into a paid contract without first being able to test the service. AOL hopes that consumers will be "hooked" on its web services by the end of the free trial period. One approach used by AOL has been to distribute a CD in a package bundled within local newspapers delivered to home subscribers (Figure 2.6).

Advertising is another way to help customers visualize service benefits. For instance, the only tangible thing credit card customers get directly from the company is a small plastic card, followed at monthly intervals by an account statement. But that's hardly the essence of the benefits provided by this low-contact service. Think about the credit card advertisements you've seen recently. Did they promote

Figure 2.6 AOL Offers Free Trial Software to Attract Prospective Customers

Figure 2.7 XL Capital Promotes Its Strengths in Insuring Large Risks

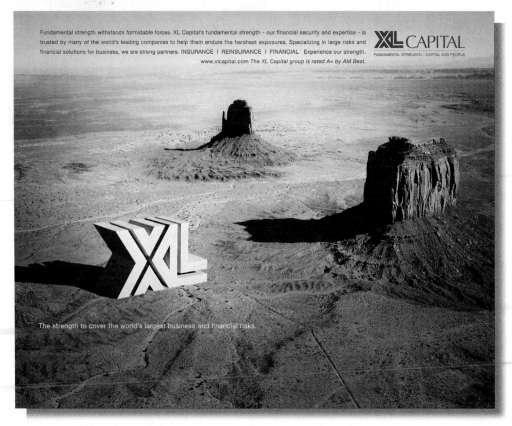

Fundamental strength withstands formidable forces. XL Capital's fundamental strength - our financial security and expertise - is trusted by many of the world's leading companies to help them endure the harshest exposures. Specializing in large risks and financial solutions for business, we are strong partners. INSURANCE | REINSURANCE | FINANCIAL Experience our strength. www.xlcapital.com *The XL Capital group is rated A+ by AM Best.*

XL CAPITAL
FUNDAMENTAL STRENGTH - CAPITAL AND PEOPLE

The strength to cover the world's largest business and financial risks.

the card itself, or did they feature exciting products you could purchase and exotic places to which you could travel by using your card? Such advertisements stimulate consumer interest by showing physical evidence of the benefits of credit card use.

Insurance companies often use metaphors in their advertising. To demonstrate its size and fundamental strengths in helping protect companies from large risks, including those resulting from climatic or environmental factors (such as hurricanes), the financial firm XL Capital displays its logo in the form of a giant obelisk, located between cliffs and a lighthouse (Figure 2.7), as well as in other dramatic settings.

Providers of services that are high in credence characteristics have an even greater challenge. Professionals such as doctors, architects, and lawyers often display their degrees and other certifications—they want customers to "see" the credentials that qualify them to provide expert service. Many professional firms have developed web sites to inform prospective clients about their services, highlight their expertise, and even showcase successful past engagements.

Evaluations of such services may be affected by customers' interactions with the physical setting of the business, employees, and even other customers. For example, your experience of a haircut may combine your impression of the hair salon, how well you can describe what you want to the stylist, the stylist's ability to understand and do what you've requested, and the appearance of the other customers and employees in the salon. Savvy organizations that have multiple points of contact with customers engage in *evidence management,* an organized and explicit approach to presenting customers with coherent evidence of their abilities in the form of clues emitted by their employees' dress and behavior and the appearance of furnishings, equipment, and facilities.[4]

Understanding Customers' Service Expectations

Customers evaluate service quality by comparing what they expected with what they perceive they received from a particular supplier. If their expectations are met or exceeded, customers believe they have received high-quality service. Provided that the price/quality relationship is acceptable and other situational and personal factors are positive, customers are likely to be satisfied and are therefore more likely to make repeat purchases and remain loyal to that supplier. However, if the service experience does not meet their expectations, customers may complain about poor service quality, suffer in silence, or switch providers in the future.[5] In highly competitive service markets, customers increasingly expect service providers to anticipate their needs and deliver on them.[6]

Customers' expectations about what constitutes good service vary from one business to another. For example, although accounting and veterinary surgery are both professional services, the experience of meeting an accountant to talk about your tax returns is very different from visiting a vet to get treatment for your sick pet. Expectations are also likely to vary in relation to differently positioned service providers in the same industry. Although travelers may expect no-frills service for a short domestic flight on a discount carrier, they would undoubtedly be very dissatisfied with that same level of service if they encountered it in economy class on a full-service airline flying long-haul international routes. When individual or corporate purchasers evaluate the quality of a service, they may be judging it against an internal standard that existed before the service experience.[7] Perceived service quality results from comparing the service you perceived you obtained against what you expected to receive. People's expectations about services are influenced by prior experiences with a particular service provider, competing services in the same industry, or related services in different industries. If you have no relevant prior experience, you may base your prepurchase expectations on word-of-mouth comments, news stories, or the firm's own marketing efforts. Smart firms manage customers' expectations at each step in the service encounter so that they expect what the firm can deliver.[8]

Expectations change over time, too, being influenced by both supplier-controlled factors such as advertising, pricing, new technologies, and service innovation, as well as social trends, advocacy by consumer organizations, and increased access to information through the media and the Internet. For instance, health care consumers are now better informed and often seek a more participative role in decisions relating to medical treatment. Service Perspectives 2.1 describes a new assertiveness among parents of children with serious illnesses.

The Components of Customer Expectations

Expectations embrace several elements, including desired service, adequate service, predicted service, and a zone of tolerance that falls between the desired and adequate service levels. The model shown in Figure 2.8, originated by Profs. A. Parasuraman, Leonard Berry, and Valarie Zeithaml, shows how expectations for desired service and adequate service are formed.[10]

Desired and Adequate Service Levels

The type of service customers hope to receive is termed *desired service*. It's a "wished for" level—a combination of what customers believe can and should be delivered in the context of their personal needs. However, most customers are realistic. Recognizing that a firm can't always deliver the level of their preferred level of service, they also have a threshold level of expectations, termed *adequate service,* defined as the minimum level of service customers will accept without being dissatisfied. The levels of both desired and adequate service expectations may reflect explicit and implicit promises by the provider, word-of-mouth comments, and the customer's past experience (if any) with this organization.[11]

Predicted Service Level

The level of service that customers actually anticipate receiving is known as *predicted service,* which directly affects how they define "adequate service" on that occasion. If good service is predicted, the adequate level will be higher than if poorer service is

SERVICE PERSPECTIVES 2.1
Parents Seek Involvement in Medical Decisions Affecting Their Children

Many parents want to participate actively in decisions relating to their children's medical treatment. Thanks in part to in-depth media coverage of medical advances and health-related issues, as well as the educational efforts of consumer advocates, parents are better informed and more assertive than in previous generations, no longer willing simply to accept the recommendations of medical specialists. In particular, parents whose child has been born with congenital defects or has developed a life-threatening illness are often willing to invest immense amounts of time and energy to learn everything they can about their child's condition. Some have even founded nonprofit organizations centered on a specific disease to bring together other families facing the same problems and to help raise money for research and treatment.

The Internet has made it much easier to access health care information and research findings. A study by the Texas-based Heart Center of 160 parents who had Internet access and children with cardiac problems found that 58 percent obtained information related to their child's diagnosis. Four out of five users searching for cardiology-related information stated that locating the information was easy; of those, half could name a favorite cardiology web site. Almost all felt that the information was helpful in understanding their child's condition. The study reported that six parents even created interactive personal web sites related specifically to their child's congenital heart defect.[9]

Commenting on the phenomenon of highly informed parents, Norman J. Siegel, MD, former chair of pediatrics at Yale New Haven Children's Hospital, observed:

> It's a different practice today. The old days of "trust me, I'm going to take care of this" are completely gone. I see many patients who come in carrying a folder with printouts from the Internet and they want to know why Dr. So-and-So wrote this. They go to chat rooms, too. They want to know about the disease process, if it's chronic. Some parents are almost as well informed as a young medical student or house officer.

Dr. Siegel said he welcomed the trend and enjoyed the discussions but admitted that some physicians found it hard to adapt.

Source: Christopher Lovelock and Jeff Gregory, "Yale New Haven Children's Hospital," New Haven, CT: Yale School of Management, 2003 (case).

predicted. Customer predictions of service may be situation-specific. From past experience, for example, customers visiting a museum on a summer day may expect to see larger crowds if the weather is poor than if the sun is shining. So a 10-minute wait to buy tickets on a cool, rainy day in summer might not fall below their adequate service level. Another factor that may set this expectation is the service level anticipated from other suppliers.

Figure 2.8
Factors Influencing Customer Expectations of Service

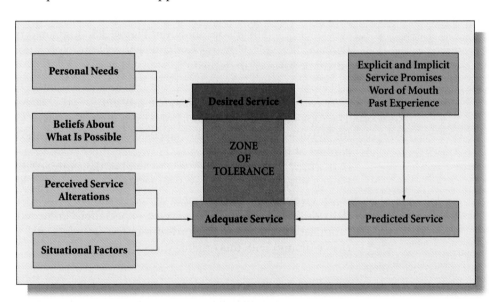

Source: Adapted from Valarie A. Zeithaml, Leonard A. Berry, and A. Parasuraman, "The Nature and Determinants of Customer Expectations of Service," *Journal of the Academy of Marketing Science* 21, no. 1 (1993): 1–12.

Zone of Tolerance

It can be hard to for firms to achieve consistent delivery by all employees in the same company and even by the same service employee from one time of day and one day to another. The extent to which customers are willing to accept this variation is called the *zone of tolerance* (see Figure 2.3) Performing too low causes frustration and dissatisfaction, whereas exceeding the desired service level should please and surprise customers. Another way of looking at the zone of tolerance is to think of it as the range of service within which customers don't pay explicit attention to service performance.[12] When service falls outside this range, customers will react, either positively or negatively.

The size of the zone of tolerance can be larger or smaller for individual customers, depending on such factors as competition, price, or importance of specific service attributes, each of which can influence the level of adequate service. By contrast, desired service levels tend to move up very slowly in response to accumulated customer experiences. Consider a small business owner who needs some advice from her accountant. Her ideal level of professional service may be a thoughtful response by the following day. However, if she makes her request at the time of year when all accountants are busy preparing corporate and individual tax returns, she will probably know from experience not to expect a fast response. Although her ideal service level probably won't change, her zone of tolerance for response time may be broader because she has a lower adequate service threshold at busy times of year.

It's important for firms to understand how wide customers' zone of tolerance is. In a study of guests at four-star, five-star, and resort hotels in Northern Cyprus (located in the eastern Mediterrean), Halil Nadiri and Kashif Hussain found a relatively narrow zone of tolerance between desired and adequate service levels.[13] Examination of individual attributes showed that customers were more sensitive about intangibles such as prompt service, employee courtesy, and convenience of operating hours than about tangibles such as physical facilities and modern-looking equipment.

Making a Service Purchase Decision

Having evaluated possible alternatives, the consumer may now be ready to make a decision, selecting one option in preference to the others. Many purchase decisions are quite simple and can be made quickly, without too much thought—the perceived risks are low, the alternatives are clear, and, because they have been used before, their characteristics are easily understood. If the consumer already has a favorite supplier, he or she will probably choose it again, in the absence of a compelling reason to do otherwise.

In many instances, however, decisions involve trade-offs. Price is often the key variable: Is it worth paying more for faster service, as in choosing between a taxi and a bus? Or for a better seat in a theater so that you can be located closer to the performers? Or for a larger rental car that will give family members more room on a long vacation drive? For more complex decisions, trade-offs can involve multiple attributes: In choosing an airline, convenience of schedules, reliability, seat comfort, attentiveness of cabin crew, and availability of meals may well vary among different carriers, even at the same fares. Once the decision has been made, the consumer is ready to move to the service encounter stage. This next step may take place immediately, as in deciding to hail a taxi or enter a fast-food outlet, or may first involve an advance reservation, as usually happens when planning a flight or attending a live theater performance.

THE SERVICE ENCOUNTER STAGE

Your experience of purchasing and consuming a service typically takes the form of a series of encounters. A *service encounter* is a period of time during which you, as a customer, interact directly with a service provider.[14] Although some of these encounters are very brief and consist of just a few steps—consider what is involved in a taxi ride or a phone call—others may extend over a longer time frame and involve multiple actions of varying degrees of complexity. A leisurely restaurant meal might stretch over a couple of hours; a visit to a theme park might last all day. If you use a service that requires advance reservation, that first step might have been taken days or even weeks before arriving at the service facility.

Service Encounters as "Moments of Truth"

Richard Normann borrowed the metaphor "moment of truth" from bullfighting to show the importance of contact points with customers:

> [W]e could say that the perceived quality is realized at the moment of truth, when the service provider and the service customer confront one another in the arena. At that moment they are very much on their own. . . . It is the skill, the motivation, and the tools employed by the firm's representative and the expectations and behavior of the client which together will create the service delivery process.[15]

In bullfighting, what is at stake is the life of either the bull or the matador (or possibly both). The moment of truth is the instant at which the matador deftly slays the bull with his sword—hardly a comfortable analogy for a service organization intent on building long-term relationships with its customers! Normann's point, of course, is that it's the life of the relationship that is at stake. Contrary to bullfighting, the goal of relationship marketing—which we explore in depth in Chapter 12—is to prevent one unfortunate (mis)encounter from destroying what is already, or has the potential to become, a mutually valued, long-term relationship.

Jan Carlzon, the former chief executive of Scandinavian Airlines System (SAS), used the "moment of truth" metaphor as a reference point for transforming SAS from an operations-driven business into a customer-driven airline. Carlzon made the following comments about his airline:

> Last year, each of our 10 million customers came into contact with approximately five SAS employees, and this contact lasted an average of 15 seconds each time. Thus, SAS is "created" 50 million times a year, 15 seconds at a time. These 50 million "moments of truth" are the moments that ultimately determine whether SAS will succeed or fail as a company. They are the moments when we must prove to our customers that SAS is their best alternative.[16]

Each service business faces similar challenges in defining and managing the moments of truth that its customers will encounter in that particular industry.

Service Encounters Range from High-Contact to Low-Contact

Each of the four categories of services described at the beginning of the chapter involves different levels of contact with the service operation. In Figure 2.9, we group services into three levels of customer contact, representing the extent of interaction with service personnel, physical service elements, or both. You'll notice that traditional retail banking, person-to-person telephone banking, and Internet banking are each located in very different parts of that chart. While recognizing that level of customer contact covers a spectrum, it's useful to examine the differences between organizations at the high and low ends, respectively.

High-Contact Services

Using a high-contact service entails interactions throughout service delivery between customers and the organization. The customer's exposure to the service provider takes on a physical and tangible nature. When customers visit the facility where service is delivered, they enter a service "factory"—something that rarely happens in a manufacturing environment. Viewed from this perspective, a motel is a lodging factory, a

Figure 2.9
Levels of Customer
Contact with Service
Organizations

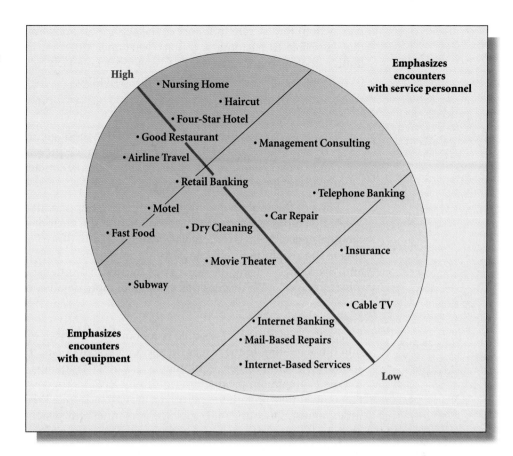

hospital is a health treatment factory, an airliner is a flying transportation factory, and a restaurant is a food service factory. Because each of these industries focuses on "processing" people rather than inanimate objects, the marketing challenge is to make the experience an appealing one for customers in terms of both the physical environment and their interactions with service personnel. During the course of service delivery, customers are usually exposed to many physical clues about the organization—the exterior and interior of its buildings, equipment and furnishings, appearance and behavior of service personnel, and even other customers.

Low-Contact Services

At the opposite end of the spectrum, low-contact services involve little, if any, physical contact between customers and service providers. Instead, contact takes place at arm's length through the medium of electronic or physical distribution channels—a fast-growing trend in today's convenience-oriented society. Many high-contact and medium-contact services are being transformed into low-contact services as customers undertake more self-service; conduct their insurance and banking transactions by mail, telephone, and the Internet; or research and purchase a host of information-based services by visiting web sites rather than bricks-and-mortar facilities. As highlighted in Figure 2.9, some service industries offer customers a choice of delivery systems featuring different levels of contact.

If you're like many people, you may alternate between high-contact and low-contact delivery channels in your use of retail banking services. The nature of your encounters with the bank varies accordingly.

The Servuction System

French researchers Pierre Eiglier and Eric Langeard were the first to conceptualize the service business as a system that integrated marketing, operations, and customers themselves. They coined the term *servuction system* (combining the terms service and production) to describe that part of the service organization's physical environment that is visible to customers, contact personnel, other customers and—very importantly—the customer in person.[17] Christopher Lovelock subsequently expanded this conceptual framework to embrace three overlapping elements:

- *Service operations,* where inputs are processed and the elements of the service product are created
- *Service delivery,* where final "assembly" of these elements takes place and the product is delivered to the customer, often in the presence of other customers
- *Other contact points,* which embraces all points of contact with customers, including advertising, billing, and market research.

Parts of this system are visible (or otherwise apparent) to customers; other parts are hidden and, as Richard Chase points out, the customer may not even know of their existence.[18] Some writers use the terms "front office" and "back office" in referring to the visible and invisible parts of the operation. Others talk about "front stage" and "backstage," using the analogy of theater to dramatize the notion that service is a performance.[19] We discuss this analogy in more detail later in the chapter.

Service Operations

Like a theatrical play, the visible components of service operations can be divided into those relating to the actors (or service personnel) and those relating to the stage set (or physical facilities, equipment, and other tangibles). Like any audience, customers evaluate the production on those elements they actually experience during their encounters and on the perceived service outcome. What goes on backstage is of little interest. Of course, if backstage personnel and systems (e.g., billing, ordering, account keeping) fail to perform their support tasks properly in ways that affect the quality of front-stage activities, customers will notice. For instance, restaurant patrons will be disappointed if they order fish from the menu but are told it is unavailable or find that their food is overcooked.

The proportion of the overall service operation that is visible to customers varies according to the level of contact. Because high-contact services involve the physical person of the customer, the visible component of the service operations element tends to be substantial.

Low-contact services usually strive to minimize customer contact with the service provider, so most of the service operations element is confined to a remotely located backstage (sometimes referred to as a technical core); front-stage elements are often limited to mail and telecommunications. Think for a moment about the telephone company that you use. Do you have any idea where its offices are located? If you have a credit card, it's likely that your transactions are processed far from where you live.

Service Delivery

Service delivery is concerned with where, when, and how the service product is delivered to the customer. This subsystem embraces not only the visible elements of the service operating system—buildings, equipment, and personnel—but may also involve exposure to other customers. Using the theater analogy, the distinction between high-contact and low-contact services can be likened to the differences between live theater on a stage and a drama created for television or even for radio. That's because customers of low-contact services normally never see the "factory" where the work is performed; at most, they will talk with a service provider (or problem solver) by telephone. Without buildings and furnishings or even the appearance of employees to provide tangible clues, customers must make judgments about service quality based on ease of telephone access, followed by the voice and responsiveness of a telephone-based customer service representative. That's like old-fashioned radio theater.

When service is delivered through impersonal electronic channels, such as self-service machines, interactive voice response (IVR) systems, or via the customer's own computer, there is very little traditional "theater" left to the performance. Some firms compensate for this by giving their machines names, playing recorded music, or installing moving color graphics on video screens, adding sounds, and creating computer-based interactive capabilities to give the experience a more human feeling. Responsibility for designing and managing service delivery systems has traditionally fallen to operations managers. However, marketing needs to be involved, too, to research how consumers behave during service delivery and ensure that the system is designed with their needs and concerns in mind.

Other Contact Points

In addition to the service delivery system, other elements that contribute to the customer's overall view of a service business include communication efforts by the advertising and sales departments, telephone calls and letters from service personnel, billings from the accounting department, random exposures to service personnel and facilities, news stories and editorials in the mass media, word-of-mouth comments from current or former customers, and even participation in market research studies.

Service Marketing Systems for High- and Low-Contact Services

Collectively, the visible part of service operations, service delivery, and other contact points add up to what we call the *service marketing system*. This represents all the many different ways the customer may learn about and encounter the organization in question. Because services are experiential, each of these many elements offers clues about the nature and quality of the service product. Inconsistency among various elements may weaken the organization's credibility in the customers' eyes. Figure 2.10 depicts the service marketing system for a high-contact service such as a hotel, health club, or full-service restaurant.

Figure 2.11 shows how things change when customers deal with a low-contact service, such as a credit card account or Internet-based insurance firm, where, by definition, service encounters are unlikely to involve visits to company sites or meetings with service personnel. Instead, access to the service will be made through self-service equipment, either a card reader in a store, a kiosk at a remote location, or perhaps the customer's own computer. Additional contact will come through mailings or emailings from the company. The list of other contact points is also shorter. As a result, customers have fewer encounters in each service transaction, and a failure at one "moment of truth" may take on greater significance than in a high-contact environment.

An individual's behavior often reflects personal attitudes and beliefs. Research by A. Parasuraman shows that certain personal characteristics are associated with customer readiness to accept new self-service technologies (SSTs), factors of critical importance for companies seeking to persuade customers to use low-contact forms

Figure 2.10
The Service Marketing System for a High-Contact Service

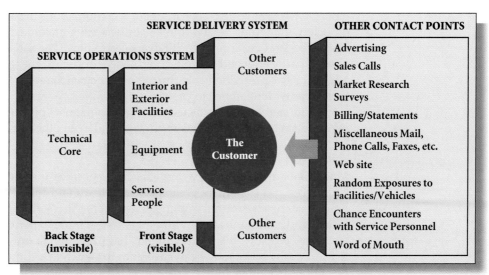

Figure 2.11
The Service Marketing
System for a Low-
Contact Service

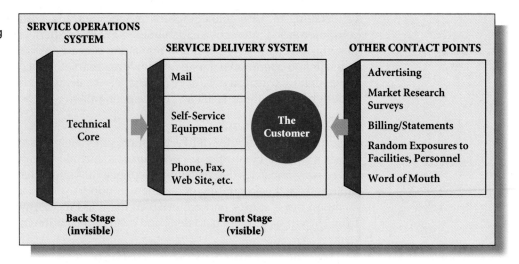

of service delivery. These attributes include innovativeness, a positive view of technology, and a belief that technology offers increased control, flexibility, and efficiency in people's lives.[20] Factors that are negatively associated with the adoption of technology include distrust, a perceived lack of control, feelings of being overwhelmed by technology, and skepticism about whether the technology will perform satisfactorily. Service providers must consider these factors before implementing new technologies that may negatively affect customers' evaluations of the service experience.

Role and Script Theories

The servuction model is static and describes a single service encounter or moment of truth. Service processes, however, usually consist of a series of encounters, such as your experiences with a flight, from making a reservation to checking in, taking the flight, and retrieving your bags on arrival. A knowledge of role and script theories can help us to understand, design, and manage both customer behavior and employee behavior during in those encounters.

Roles

If we view service delivery from a theatrical perspective, then both employees and customers act out their parts in the performance according to predetermined roles. Stephen Grove and Ray Fisk define a *role* as "a set of behavior patterns learned through experience and communication, to be performed by an individual in a certain social interaction in order to attain maximum effectiveness in goal accomplishment."[21] Roles have also been defined as combinations of social cues, or expectations of society, that guide behavior in a specific setting or context.[22] In service encounters, employees and customers each have roles to play. The satisfaction and productivity of both parties depend on role congruence, or the extent to which each person acts out his or her prescribed role during a service encounter. Employees must perform their roles with reference to customer expectations or risk dissatisfying or losing customers altogether. And as a customer you, too, must "play by the rules," or risk causing problems for the firm, its employees, and even other customers.

Scripts

Much like a movie script, a service script specifies the sequences of behavior that employees and customers are expected to learn and follow during service delivery. Employees receive formal training. Customers learn scripts through experience, education, and communication with others.[23] The more experience a customer has with a service company, the more familiar that particular script becomes. Unwillingness to learn a new script may be a reason not to switch to a competing organization. Any deviations from this known script may frustrate both customers and employees and

Not all service providers require customers to attend performances at the company's "theater," especially in a business-to-business context. In many instances, the customer's own facilities provide the stage where the service employees perform with their props. For example, outside accountants are often hired to provide specialized services at a client's site. (Although this may be convenient for the client, it isn't always very appealing for the visiting accountants, who have sometimes found themselves housed in rat-infested basements or inventorying frozen food for hours in a cold storage locker.[25]) Telecommunication linkages offer an alternative performance environment, allowing customers to be involved in the drama from a remote location—a delivery option long awaited by those traveling accountants, who would probably much prefer to work for their clients from the comfort of their own offices via the Internet.

Front-stage personnel are members of a cast, playing roles as *actors* in a drama, and supported by a backstage production team. In some instances, they are expected to wear special costumes when on stage (such as the protective clothing—traditionally white but now increasingly colored and patterned—worn by dental professionals, the fanciful uniforms often worn by hotel doormen, or the more basic brown ones worn by UPS drivers). When service employees wear distinctive apparel, they stand out from personnel at other firms, providing physical evidence of brand identity. In many service companies, the choice of uniform design and colors is carefully integrated with other corporate design elements. Front-stage employees are often required to conform to both a dress code and grooming standards (such as Disney's rule that employees can't wear beards, except as required in costumed roles).

Depending on the nature of their work, employees may be have to learn and repeat specific lines, ranging from announcements in several languages in a location attracting a diverse audience to a sing-song sales spiel (think of the last telemarketer who called you) to a parting salutation of "Have a nice day!" And just as in theater, companies often use scripting to define actors' behavior as well as their lines. Eye contact, smiles, and handshakes may be required in addition to a spoken greeting. Other rules of conduct, welcomed by many customers, may include bans on smoking, eating, drinking, chewing gum, or using cell phones for personal conversations while on duty.

Implications of Customer Participation in Service Creation and Delivery

The more work that customers are expected to do in their role as co-producers, the greater is their need for information about how to perform for best results. The necessary education can be provided in many different ways. Advertising for new services often contains significant educational content. Brochures, posted instructions, and web sites are also widely used approaches. During a service encounter, customers are more likely to engage in self-service when automated machines provide user-friendly operating instructions (Figure 2.13). Thoughtful banks place a telephone beside their ATMs so that customers can call a "real person" for help and advice at any time if the machine malfunctions or they are confused about the on-screen instructions. Increasingly, machines are programmed to provide information and instructions in several languages—a marketing advantage when serving a multilingual population.

In many businesses, customers look to employees for advice and assistance and are frustrated if they can't obtain it. Service providers, ranging from sales assistants and customer service representatives to flight attendants and nurses, must be trained to help them improve their own teaching skills. As a last resort, people may turn to other customers for help. Think about your experiences in unfamiliar surroundings when you were grateful for the friendly advice or assistance provided by a fellow customer. And you've probably reached out yourself to assist someone who seemed to be having difficulties in a service setting where you already knew the ropes.

Figure 2.13
Tourists Appreciate
Easy-to-Understand
Instructions When
Traveling Abroad

Benjamin Schneider and David Bowen recommend giving customers a realistic service preview in advance of service delivery, so that they have a clear picture of the role they're expected to play in co-production.[26] For example, a company might show a video presentation to help customers understand their role in the service encounter. This technique is used by some dentists to help patients understand the surgical processes they are about to experience and indicate how they should cooperate to help make things go as smoothly as possible. Bo Edvardsson, Bo Enquist, and Robert Johnson propose creation of what they term a "hyperreal prepurchase service experience, involving active customer participation in a physical setting.[27] This approach involves active customer development of an experience room in which prospective customers are exposed in groups to both physical and intangible artifacts.

THE POST-ENCOUNTER STAGE

During the post-encounter stage, customers evaluate the service performance they have received and compare it with their prior expectations. Let's explore how expectations relate to customer satisfaction and future intentions.

How Confirmation or Disconfirmation of Expectations Relates to Satisfaction and Delight

The terms "quality" and "satisfaction" are sometimes used interchangeably. Some researchers believe, however, that perceived service quality is just one component of customer satisfaction, which also reflects price/quality trade-offs, and personal and situational factors.[28]

Satisfaction can be defined as an attitude-like judgment following a purchase act or a series of consumer product interactions.[29] Most studies are based on the theory that the confirmation/disconfirmation of preconsumption expectations is the essential determinant of satisfaction.[30] This means that customers have certain service standards in mind before consumption (their expectations), observe service performance and compare it to their standards, and then form satisfaction judgments based on this comparison. The resulting judgment is labeled *negative disconfirmation* if the service is worse than expected, *positive disconfirmation* if it is better than expected, and simple *confirmation* if it is as expected.[31] When there is substantial positive disconfirmation, plus pleasure and an element of surprise, then customers are likely to be delighted.

Customer Delight

Findings from a research project by Richard Oliver, Roland Rust, and Sajeev Varki suggest that delight is a function of three components: (1) unexpectedly high levels of performance, arousal (e.g., surprise, excitement), and positive affect (e.g., pleasure, joy, or happiness).[32] By contrast, satisfaction alone is a function of positively disconfirmed expectations (better than expected) and positive affect. The researchers asked: "If delight is a function of surprisingly unexpected pleasure, is it possible for delight to be manifest in truly mundane services and products, such as newspaper delivery or trash collecting?" Certainly, it's possible in seemingly mundane fields such as insurance (see Best Practice in Action 2.1). However, once customers have been delighted, their expectations are raised. They will be dissatisfied if service levels return to previous levels, and it may take more effort to "delight" them in the future.[33] So, achieving delight requires focusing on what is currently unknown or unexpected by the customer. It's more than just avoiding problems—the "zero defects" strategy.

Based on analysis of 10 years of data from the American Customer Satisfaction Index (ACSI), Claes Fornell and his colleagues caution against trying to exceed customer expectations on a continual basis, arguing that reaching for unobtainable objectives may backfire. They note that such efforts often come close to the point of diminishing returns.[34]

BEST PRACTICE IN ACTION 2.1
Progressive Insurance Delights Its Customers

Progressive Casualty Insurance Co. prides itself on providing extraordinary customer service—and its accomplishments in the area of claims processing are particularly impressive. To lower its costs and simultaneously improve customer satisfaction and retention, the company introduced its Immediate Response service, offering customers 24/7 access to claims handling. Adjusters work out of mobile claims vans rather than offices, and Progressive has a target of 9 hours for an adjuster to inspect a damaged vehicle. In many instances, claims representatives actually arrive at the scene of an accident while the evidence is still fresh. Consider the following scenario. The crash site in Tampa, Florida, is chaotic and tense. Two cars are damaged, and although the passengers aren't bleeding, they are shaken up and scared. Lance Edgy, a senior claim representative for Progressive, arrives on the scene just minutes after the collision. He calms the victims and advises them on medical care, repair shops, police reports, and legal procedures. Edgy invites William McAllister, Progressive's policy holder, into an air-conditioned van equipped with comfortable chairs, a desk, and two cell phones. Even before the tow trucks have cleared away the wreckage,

Edgy is able to offer his client a settlement for the market value of his totaled Mercury. McAllister, who did not appear to have been at fault in this accident, later stated in amazement: "This is great—someone coming right out here and taking charge. I didn't expect it at all."

The shortened time cycle has advantages for Progressive, too. Costs are reduced, there's less likelihood that lawyers will become involved when settlement offers are made promptly, and it's easier to prevent fraud. Progressive continues to find new ways to delight its customers. Its web site, www.progressive.com, has been consistently been rated as the top overall among Internet-based insurance carriers by Gómez.com (an Internet quality measurement firm), which places a priority on a site's educational, purchasing, and servicing capabilities. Progressive has also been cited for pleasantly surprising its customers with consumer-friendly innovations and extraordinary customer service.

Sources: Ronald Henkoff, "Service Is Everybody's Business," *Fortune,* June 27, 1994, p. 50; Michael Hammer, "Deep Change: How Operational Innovation Can Transform Your Company," *Harvard Business Review,* 82 (April 2004): 84–95; www.progressive.com, accessed December 12, 2005.

Strategic Links Between Customer Satisfaction and Corporate Performance

Why is satisfaction important to service managers? There's convincing evidence of strategic links between the level of customer satisfaction achieved for a company's services and that firm's overall performance. Researchers from the University of Michigan found that, on average, every 1 percent increase in customer satisfaction is associated with a 2.37 percent increase in a firm's return on investment (ROI).[35] And analysis of companies' scores on the American Customer Satisfaction Index (ACSI) shows that, on average, among publicly traded firms, a 5 percent change in ACSI score is associated with a 19 percent change in the market value of common equity.[36] In other words, by creating more value for the customer, as measured by increased satisfaction, the firm creates more value for its owners.

Susan Fournier and David Mick state:

> Customer satisfaction is central to the marketing concept. . . . [I]t is now common to find mission statements designed around the satisfaction notion, marketing plans and incentive programs that target satisfaction as a goal, and consumer communications that trumpet awards for satisfaction achievements in the marketplace.[37]

Most service providers wait until after service delivery has been completed before asking customers to complete satisfaction surveys (if they even bother to do this). In extended, high-contact encounters, however, this approach inevitably misses opportunities to address problems while the customer is still engaged in the process—or before they have even made a decision to purchase. If customers are uneasy with the prospect of using a particular service, they may decide against purchasing it. And if they feel uncomfortable with some aspect of a service encounter, they may decide to quit before completing a transaction, especially if they haven't yet had to pay for it.

Getting Feedback During Service Delivery

Although it's not always practical to administer formal surveys in mid-encounter, managers can train service personnel to be more observant, so that they can identify customers who appear to be having difficulties, look frustrated, or seem otherwise ill at ease, and then ask if they need assistance. If experience shows that customers are continually discomforted by a particular aspect of the service encounter, this indicates a need for redesign and improvement.

Deborah Spake and her colleagues have developed a methodology for measuring a consumer's comfort level, which can be applied at each stage from prepurchase to post-encounter and is particularly applicable to high-contact services.[38] In surveying consumers, they found that respondents associated an increased comfort level with reduced perceived risk. Words and phrases such as safety, security, being worry-free, and having assurance of the quality of the service provided were mentioned, as were having peace of mind, being at ease with the service provider, and trusting them.

The importance of getting feedback during service delivery is that when things are going badly for the customer, there may still be an opportunity to practice service recovery so that the customer leaves feeling satisfied. Such an outcome improves the likelihood that the customer will remain loyal. The importance of customer loyalty is discussed in depth in Chapter 12.

CONCLUSION

Customer behavior in a service environment is affected by the nature of the service being used. Services vary widely and can be categorized according to the nature of the underlying process: Is the service directed at customers in person or their possessions? And are service actions tangible or intangible in nature? Each of the resulting four categories of services tends to involve different types of encounters between customers and the organization.

The three-stage model of service consumption helps us to understand how individuals recognize their needs, address perceived risks, search for alternative solutions, choose and use services, and then evaluate their experiences against their prior expectations. Service consumption places the customer in the servuction system, which in a high-contact environment combines the visible physical aspects of the service operation—facilities, equipment, and service personnel—plus other customers. The higher the level of contact, the greater the number of touch points between the customer and the service business. In a low-contact environment, by contrast, the customer may never see the company's facilities nor deal face to face with its employees. A knowledge of role and script theories can help us to understand and manage both customer behavior and employee behavior during those encounters. During the post-encounter stage, customers evaluate the service performance they have received, compare it to their prior expectations, and start to make decisions about future intentions.

In all types of services, managing service encounters effectively is central to creating satisfied customers who will be willing to enter into long-term relationships with the service provider. Whether customers are satisfied will depend on how well (if at all) their expectations were met. Gaining a better understanding of how customers evaluate, select, and use services should lie at the heart of strategies for designing and delivering service products, which we discuss in the next chapter.

REVIEW QUESTIONS

1. Clarify the differences among the four broad categories of services, provide examples for each, and explain the service management challenges related to each of the four categories.
2. Explain the three-stage model of service consumption.
3. Describe search, experience, and credence attributes and give examples of each.
4. Explain why services tend to be harder for customers to evaluate than goods.
5. Why does consumer perception of risk constitute an important aspect in selecting, purchasing, and using services? How can firms reduce consumer risk perceptions?
6. How are customers' expectations formed? Explain the difference between desired service and adequate service with reference to a service experience you've had recently.
7. Choose a service with which you are familiar and create a diagram that represents the servuction system. Define the front-stage and backstage activities.
8. Describe the difference between high-contact and low-contact servuction systems, and explain how the nature of the customer's experience may differ between the two.
9. What are "moments of truth"?
10. How do the concepts of role theory, script theory, and theatrical perspective help to provide insights into consumer behavior during the service encounter?
11. Describe the relationship between customer expectations and customer satisfaction.

APPLICATION EXERCISES

1. Develop two different customer scripts, one for a standardized service and one for a customized service. Map all key customer steps of this script across all three stages of service consumption. What are the key differences between the standardized and customized services?
2. Select three services, one high in search attributes, one high in experience attributes, and one high in credence attributes. Specify what product characteristics make them easy or difficult for consumers to evaluate and suggest specific strategies that marketers can adopt in each case to facilitate evaluation and reduce perceived risk.
3. Develop a simple questionnaire designed to measure the key components of customer expectations (i.e., desired, adequate, and predicted service, and the zone of tolerance). Conduct 10 interviews with key target customers of a service of your choice to understand the structure of their expectations.
4. What are the backstage elements of (a) a car repair facility, (b) an airline, (c) a university, and (d) a consulting firm? Under what circumstances would it be appropriate to allow customers to see some of these backstage elements, and how would you do it?
5. What roles are played by front-stage service personnel in low-contact organizations? Are these roles more or less important to customer satisfaction than in high-contact services?
6. What actions could a bank take to encourage more customers to bank by phone, mail, the Internet, or through ATMs rather than visiting a branch?
7. Visit the facilities of two competing service firms in the same industry (e.g., two retailers, restaurants, or gas stations) that you believe have different approaches to service. Compare and contrast, using suitable frameworks from this chapter.
8. Apply the script theory and role theory concepts to a common service of your choice. What insights can you give that would be useful for management?
9. Describe a low-contact service encounter via email or mail, a low-contact encounter via phone, and a high-contact, face-to-face encounter that you have had recently. How satisfied were you with each of the encounters? What were the key drivers of your overall satisfaction with these encounter? In each instance, what could the service provider have done to improve the situation?

1. These classifications are derived from Christopher H. Lovelock, "Classifying Services to Gain Strategic Marketing Insights," *Journal of Marketing,* 47 (Summer 1983): 9–20.

2. B. Joseph Pine and James H. Gilmore, "Welcome to the Experience Economy," *Harvard Business Review,* 76 (July–August 1998): 97–108.

3. Valarie A. Zeithaml, "How Consumer Evaluation Processes Differ Between Goods and Services," in J. A. Donnelly and W. R. George (eds.), *Marketing of Services.* Chicago: American Marketing Association, 1981, pp. 186–190.

4. Leonard L. Berry and Neeli Bendapudi, "Clueing in Customers," *Harvard Business Review,* 81 (February 2003): 100–107.

5. Jaishankar Ganesh, Mark J. Arnold, and Kristy E. Reynolds, "Understanding the Customer Base of Service Providers: An Examination of the Differences Between Switchers and Slayers," *Journal of Marketing,* 64, no. 3 (2000): 65–87.

6. Uday Karmarkar, "Will You Survive the Service Revolution?" *Harvard Business Review,* 82 (June 2004): 101–108.

7. See Benjamin Schneider and David E. Bowen, *Winning the Service Game.* Boston: Harvard Business School Press, 1995; Valarie A. Zeithaml, Leonard L. Berry, and A. Parasuraman, "The Nature and Determinants of Customer Expectations of Services," *Journal of the Academy of Marketing Science,* 21, 1993,

8. Ray W. Coye, "Managing Customer Expectations in the Service Encounter," *International Journal of Service Industry Management,* 15, no. 4 (2004): 54–71.

9. C. M. Ikemba et al., "Internet Use in Families with Children Requiring Cardiac Surgery for Congenital Heart Disease," *Pediatrics,* 109, no. 3 (2002): 419–422.

10. Valarie A. Zeithaml, Leonard L. Berry, and A. Parasuraman, "The Behavioral Consequences of Service Quality," *Journal of Marketing,* 60 (Apil 1996): 31–46; R. Kenneth Teas and Thomas E. DeCarlo, "An Examination and Extension of the Zone-of-Tolerance Model: A Comparison to Performance-Based Models on Perceived Quality," *Journal of Service Research,* 6, no. 3 (2004): 272–286.

11. Cathy Johnson and Brian P. Mathews, "The Influence of Experience on Service Expectations," *International Journal of Service Industry Management,* 8, no. 4 (1997): 46–61.

12. Robert Johnston, "The Zone of Tolerance: Exploring the Relationship Between Service Transactions and Satisfaction with the Overall Service," *International Journal of Service Industry Management,* 6, no. 5 (1995): 46–61.

13. Halil Nadiri and Kashif Hussain, "Diagnosing the Zone of Tolerance for Hotel Services," *Managing Service Quality,* 15, no. 5 (2005): 259–277.

14. Lynn Shostack, "Planning the Service Encounter," in J. A. Czepiel, M. R. Solomon, and C. F. Surprenant (eds.), *The Service Encounter.* Lexington, MA: Lexington Books, 1985, pp. 243–254.

15. Normann first used the term "moments of truth" in a Swedish study in 1978; subsequently it appeared in English in Richard Normann, *Service Management: Strategy and Leadership in Service Businesses,* 2nd ed. Chichester, UK: John Wiley & Sons, 1991, pp. 16–17.

16. Jan Carlzon, *Moments of Truth.* Cambridge, MA: Ballinger, 1987, p. 3.

17. Pierre Eiglier and Eric Langeard, "Services as Systems: Marketing Implications," in Pierre Eiglier, Eric Langeard, Christopher H. Lovelock, John E.G. Bateson, and Robert F. Young, *Marketing Consumer Services: New Insights.* Cambridge, MA: Marketing Science Institute, Report #77-115, November 1977, pp. 83–103; Eric Langeard, John E. Bateson, Christopher H. Lovelock, and Pierre Eiglier, *Services Marketing: New Insights from Consumers and Managers.* Marketing Science Institute, Report #81-104, August 1981.

18. Richard B. Chase, "Where Does the Customer Fit in a Service Organization?" *Harvard Business Review,* 6 (November–December 1978): 137–142.

19. Stephen J. Grove, Raymond P. Fisk, and Joby John, "Services as Theater: Guidelines and Implications," in Teresa A. Schwartz and Dawn Iacobucci (eds.), *Handbook of Services Marketing and Management.* Thousand Oaks, CA: Sage, 2000, pp. 21–36.

20. A. Parasuraman, "Technology Readiness Index [TRI]: A Multiple-Item Scale to Measure Readiness to Embrace New Technologies," *Journal of Service Research,* 2 (2000): 307–320.

21. Stephen J. Grove and Raymond P. Fisk, "The Dramaturgy of Services Exchange: An Analytical Framework for Services Marketing," in L. L. Berry, G. L. Shostack, and G. D. Upah (eds.), *Emerging Perspectives on Services Marketing.* Chicago: American Marketing Association, 1983, pp. 45–49.

22. Michael R. Solomon, Carol Suprenant, John A. Czepiel, and Evelyn G. Gutman, "A Role Theory Perspective on Dyadic Interactions: The Service Encounter," *Journal of Marketing,* 49 (Winter 1985): 99–111.

23. See R. P. Abelson, "Script Processing in Attitude Formation and Decision-Making," in J. S. Carrol and J. W. Payne (eds.), *Cognitive and Social Behavior.* Hillsdale, NJ: Erlbaum, 1976, pp. 33–45; Ronald H. Humphrey and Blake E. Ashforth, "Cognitive Scripts and Prototypes in Service Encounters," in *Advances in Service Marketing and Management.* Greenwich, CT: JAI Press, 1994, pp. 175–199; Richard Harris, Kim Harris, and Steve Baron, "Theatrical Service Experiences: Dramatic Script Development with Employees," *International Journal of Service Industry Management,* 14, no. 2 (2003): 184–199.

24. Grove, Fisk, and John, "Services as Theater"; Steve Baron, Kim Harris, and Richard Harris, "Retail Theater: The 'Intended Effect' of the Performance," *Journal of Service Research,* 4 (May 2003): 316–332; Richard Harris, Kim Harris, and Steve Baron, "Theatrical Service Experiences: Dramatic Script Development with Employees," *International Journal of Service Industry Management* 14, no. 2 (2003): 184–199.

25. Elizabeth MacDonald, "Oh, the Horrors of Being a Visiting Accountant," *The Wall Street Journal*, March 10, 1997, p. B1.

26. Benjamin Schneider and David E. Bowen, *Winning the Service Game*. Boston: Harvard Business School Press, 1995, p. 92.

27. Bo Edvardsson, Bo Enquist, and Robert Johnson, "Cocreating Customer Value in the Prepurchase Service Experience," *Journal of Service Research*, 8 (November 2005): 149–161.

28. Valarie A. Zeithaml, Mary Jo Bitner, and Dwayne D. Gremler, *Services Marketing: Integrating Customer Focus Across the Firm*, 4th ed. Burr Ridge, IL: Irwin-McGraw-Hill, 2006.

29. Youjae Yi, "A Critical Review of Customer Satisfaction," in V. A. Zeithaml (ed.), *Review of Marketing 1990*. Chicago: American Marketing Association, 1990.

30. Richard L. Oliver, "Customer Satisfaction with Service," in Teresa A. Schwartz and Dawn Iacobucci (eds.), *Handbook of Service Marketing and Management*. Thousand Oaks, CA: Sage, 2000, pp. 247–254; Jochen Wirtz and Anna S. Mattila, "Exploring the Role of Alternative Perceived Performance Measures and Needs-Congruency in the Consumer Satisfaction Process," *Journal of Consumer Psychology*, 11, no. 3 (2001): 181–192.

31. Richard L. Oliver, *Satisfaction: A Behavioral Perspective on the Consumer*. New York: McGraw-Hill, 1997.

32. Richard L. Oliver, Roland T. Rust, and Sajeev Varki, "Customer Delight: Foundations, Findings, and Managerial Insight," *Journal of Retailing*, 73 (Fall 1997): 311–336.

33. Roland T. Rust and Richard L. Oliver, "Should We Delight the Customer?" *Journal of the Academy of Marketing Science*, 28, no. 1 (2000): 86–94.

34. Claes Fornell, David VanAmburg, Forrest Morgeson, Eugene W. Anderson, Barbara Everitt Bryant, and Michael D. Johnson, *The American Customer Satisfaction Index at Ten Years—A Summary of Findings: Implications for the Economy, Stock Returns and Management*. Ann Arbor, MI: National Quality Research Center, University of Michigan, 2005, p. 54.

35. Eugene W. Anderson and Vikas Mittal, "Strengthening the Satisfaction-Profit Chain," *Journal of Service Research*, 3 (November 2000): 107–120.

36. Fornell et al., *The American Customer Satisfaction Index at Ten Years*, p. 40.

37. Susan Fournier and David Glen Mick, "Rediscovering Satisfaction," *Journal of Marketing*, 63 (October 1999): 5–23.

38. Deborah F. Spake, Sharon E. Beatty, Beverly K. Brockman, and Tammy Neal Crutchfield, "Development of the Consumer Comfort Scale: A Multi-Study Investigation of Service Relationships," *Journal of Service Research*, 5, no. 4 (May 2003): 316–332.

In a Dizzying World, One Way to Keep Up: Renting Possessions

DVDS, MUSIC AND HANDBAGS LOSE THRILL OF OWNERSHIP; "BUY IT, LOVE IT, SELL IT"

BY NICK WINGFIELD

Developing trends in consumer behavior offer opportunities for service entrepreneurs. In a search for new benefits, some consumers are moving away from extended ownership of durable goods. Instead they are choosing to rent products, to resell goods on eBay after brief use, or to quickly trade in relatively new goods for the latest model. The products involved range from consumer electronics and music to handbags and sporting goods.

Karl Marx thought private property needed to be abolished before society could perfect itself. Then again, he never saw Mark Rosa flip golf clubs.

The 45-year-old high-school teacher from Antlers, Okla., used to buy new clubs every 10 years or so. Thanks to a program set up by Callaway Golf Co., he now upgrades virtually every year. Mr. Rosa buys his new gear online, which Callaway ships by mail. He sends back the old clubs in the same box, typically getting a trade-in price of about $300 for a set that originally cost $500.

"I play with a guy at a local club—he's 70 years old, and he's still playing on a 1950s set" of golf clubs, says Mr. Rosa. "There are people like me, the newer generation, who trade up technology, looking for an edge."

All over the consumer marketplace, people who used to buy things for keeps are renting, flipping, or instantly upgrading. These shoppers care less about whether things are truly theirs and more about whether they can get the latest and best. Whereas once they could only shop this way in niche areas such as car leases, now they can also try handbags, consumer electronics, movies and music.

The best-known model is Netflix Inc. Since it started in 1999, the Los Gatos, Calif., company has signed up more than 3.5 million subscribers who typically pay $18 a month to rent DVD movies that are sent to them in the mail. Users send them back in pre-paid envelopes.

In recent years, companies like Jiggerbug and GameFly have taken the Netflix approach to audio books and videogames. RealNetworks Inc. rents access to music online. Encyclopaedia Britannica Inc.'s fastest-growing business isn't books or CD-ROMs, but selling access to its encyclopedia online, for a fee. Customers "don't think about owning that kind of product in perpetuity anymore," says Patti Ginnis, a Britannica marketing executive.

Technology both creates and satisfies this desire. Hot products are now rendered obsolete or unfashionable at a dizzying rate. At the same time, the Internet has created a huge and efficient market for ordering new goods and selling them fast on sites such as eBay.

Paul Archambault, a Waterford, N.Y., computer programmer, buys and sells on eBay the way some people check out books from the library. At 3 a.m. one recent morning, on his way to the Albany airport, Mr. Archambault popped into a Wal-Mart and paid nearly $200 for a Nintendo DS videogame console and two games to keep him busy on a trip to Des Moines, Iowa.

While waiting to board his flight, Mr. Archambault photographed the device, which was still in its box, and sent the images to an eBay auction from his laptop through the terminal's wireless connection. His ad mentioned that he planned to use the game for just the weekend. The auction closed the day after Mr. Archambault returned and fetched slightly more than the $200 he paid.

"I love to have the latest and greatest," he explains.

Several years ago. eBay Inc. of San Jose, Calif., began sending emails to users suggesting a price at which the item they just acquired might be resold. The response was strong from people wanting to flip cellphones, iPods, PCs and sporting equipment, says Michael Dearing, senior vice president and general merchandise manager at eBay, "The duration for which [those items are] considered good or leading or appealing is getting shorter and shorter over time," he says. To encourage these new virtual renters, eBay has begun using the slogan; "Buy It, Love It, Sell It."

David Wasmund, an office manager in Sterling Heights, Mich., recently sold one type of iPod on eBay so he could buy another, newer model. He's used the same tactic to flip cellphones. He says the resale price is typically 25% to 30% below what he paid if he unloads the product within a year. "I know even if I buy something and I don't like it, I can turn around and put it on" eBay, he says.

Matt Morgan has stopped buying music altogether. A 29-year-old recruiter in San Francisco, he rents music through RealNetwork's Rhapsody service for $10 a month, which gives him unlimited access to more than a million music tracks. The catch: If he stops paying, he won't be able to listen to the music. Mr. Morgan says he "can't remember the last time I went into a store and bought a CD."

Nicole Mazzola Ferrer, a 30-year-old project manager for a Kirkland, Wash., technology company, pays $50 a month to rent handbags from a Web service called Bag Borrow or Steal. One at a time, she checks out bags that sell for up to $500 in retail stores. Ms. Mazzola Ferrer uses a bag anywhere from a few days to a month, before mailing it back in exchange for a fresh one when novelty fades or a special occasion arises.

One hitch: Some women might be reluctant to borrow used bags. Adam Dell, a venture capitalist in New York, who invested in Bag Borrow or Steal, says all the company's bags are delivered in excellent condition, after being inspected and cleaned. Mr. Dell compares the process to certified pre-owned vehicle programs.

Carrying a used bag doesn't bother Ms. Mazzola Ferrer, who figures she used to spend more than $100 a month buying handbags she would "get sick" of quickly. By renting, she can carry around nicer bags than she could afford at retail. And, she says, "my husband appreciates that half the closet isn't consumed by handbags."

Part

Building the Service Model

*P*art II of the book shows how to build a service model, a central aspect of our strategic marketing framework. We stress the importance of creating a meaningful *value proposition*—a specified package of benefits and solutions that highlights key points of difference relative to competing alternatives. This value proposition must address and integrate two components: creation of a *service concept* and delivery of its different elements through physical and electronic channels.

The next step involves developing a *business model* for recovering all costs (plus a margin for profits) through realistic pricing strategies. To ensure that target customers perceive the benefits from this *value exchange* as exceeding the financial costs, time, and effort that they incur, the value proposition must be communicated in ways that help customers to make good choices and use the service to best advantage. Finally, the strategy must stake out a distinctive and defensible *position* in the market against competing alternatives.

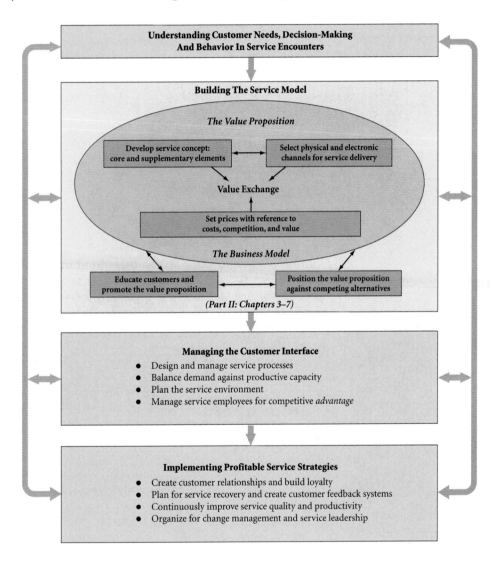

Chapter 3

Developing Service Concepts: Core and Supplementary Elements

> *Each and every one of you will make or break the promise that our brand makes to customers.*

AN AMERICAN EXPRESS MANAGER, SPEAKING TO HIS EMPLOYEES.

Creating a service concept is the initial step in building an overall service model. This task focuses our attention on the first of the 8 Ps, *Product elements.* All service organizations face choices concerning the types of products to offer and how to deliver them to customers. To better understand the nature of services, it's useful to distinguish between the core product and the supplementary elements that facilitate its use and enhance its value for customers. By flowcharting the sequence of encounters that customers have with a service organization, we can gain valuable insights into the nature of an existing service.

Recognizing that a value proposition may embrace all or part of the whole cluster of benefits that a firm offers to deliver to the target market, service marketers need to create a coherent offering in which each element is compatible with the others and all are mutually reinforcing.

In competitive environments, service marketers need to focus on innovation, seeking to develop new services or enhance existing ones. New service development may involve either the product itself or the processes used to create it. In fact, the availability of new delivery processes for existing services often changes the nature of the service experience and may even create new benefits.

In this chapter, we consider the nature of service products, how to add value to them, and how to design them. We explore such questions as:

1. What do we mean by a service product?
2. What insights can we obtain from flowcharting service usage?
3. How can we categorize the supplementary services that surround core products, and how do they add value for customers?

4. Why should service firms create separate brand names for their different products?

5. What are the main approaches to designing new services?

PLANNING AND CREATING SERVICES

What do we mean by a service "product"? When customers purchase a manufactured good such as a camera, a commodity such as diesel fuel, or an agricultural product such as a bag of potatoes, they take title to physical objects. Service performances, however, are experienced rather than owned. Even when there are physical elements to which the customer does take title—such as a cooked meal (which is promptly consumed), a surgically implanted pacemaker, or a replacement part for a car—a significant portion of the price paid by customers is for the value added by the service elements, including expert labor and the use of specialized equipment. A service product comprises all the elements of the service performance, both tangible and intangible, that create value for customers.

Augmenting the Core Product

Services are usually defined with reference to a particular industry—for instance, health care or transportation—based on the core set of benefits and solutions delivered to customers. However, delivery of this *core product* is typically accompanied by a variety of other service-related activities that we refer to collectively as *supplementary services,* which facilitate use of the core product and add value and differentiation to the customer's overall experience. Core products tend to become commodities as an industry matures and competition increases, so the search for competitive advantage often emphasizes performance on supplementary services.

The core-and-supplementary combination represents the *service concept* (sometimes referred to in a manufacturing context as the augmented product). Lynn Shostack developed a molecular model (Figure 3.1) that uses a chemical analogy to help

Figure 3.1
Shostack's Molecular Model: Passenger Airline Service

Source: G. Lynn Shostack, "Breaking Free from Product Marketing," *Journal of Marketing,* 44 (April 1977): 73–80, published by the American Marketing Association. Reprinted with permission.

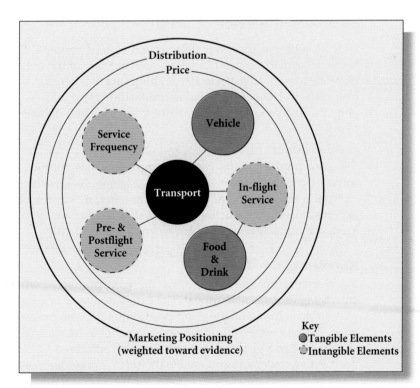

marketers visualize and manage what she termed a "total market entity."[1] Her model can be applied to either goods or services. At the center is the core benefit, addressing the basic customer need, which is linked to a series of other service characteristics. She argues that, as in chemical formulations, a change in one element may completely alter the nature of the entity. Surrounding the molecules are a series of bands representing price, distribution, and market positioning (communication messages).

The molecular model can help you to identify the tangible and intangible elements involved in service delivery. For an airline, for example, the intangible elements include transportation itself; service frequency; and preflight, in-flight, and postflight service. However, the aircraft and the food and drinks that are served are all tangible. The greater the proportion of intangible elements, the more necessary it is to provide tangible clues about the features and quality of the service.

Pierre Eiglier and Eric Langeard proposed a model in which the core service is surrounded by an array of supplementary services that are specific to that particular product.[2] Their approach, like Shostack's, emphasizes the interdependence of the various components. They distinguish between those elements needed to facilitate use of the core service (such as the reception desk at a hotel) and those that enhance the appeal of the core service (such as a fitness center and business services at a hotel).

Both models offer useful insights. Shostack wants us to determine which service elements are tangible and which are intangible in order to help formulate product policy and communication programs. Eiglier and Langeard ask us to think about two issues: first, whether supplementary services are needed to facilitate use of the core service or simply to add extra appeal; and second, whether customers should be charged separately for each service element or whether all elements should be bundled under a single price tag. Further insight is provided by Christian Grönroos, who clarifies the different roles ascribed to supplementary services by describing them as either facilitating services (or goods), which facilitate use of the core product, and supporting services (or goods), which increase the value of the service and/or help to differentiate it.[3] (For greater clarity, we will refer to the latter as enhancing services.)

Designing a Service Concept

How should you go about designing a service concept? Experienced service marketers recognize the need to take a holistic view of the entire performance that they want customers to experience, highlighting the specific dimensions on which the firm plans to compete. The value proposition must address and integrate three components: core product, supplementary services, and delivery processes.

Core Product

The core product is the central component that supplies the principal, problem-solving benefits customers seek. Thus, transport solves the need to move a person or a physical object from one location to another; management consulting should yield expert advice on what actions a client should take; and repair services restore a damaged or malfunctioning machine to good working order.

Supplementary Services

Supplementary services augment the core product, both facilitating its use and enhancing its value and appeal. The extent and level of supplementary services often play a role in differentiating and positioning the core product against competing services. Adding more supplementary elements or increasing the level of performance should be done in ways that enhance the perceived value of the core product for prospective customers and enable the service provider to charge a higher price.

Delivery Processes

The third component concerns the processes used to deliver both the core product and each of the supplementary services. The design of the service offering must address the following issues:

- How the different service components are delivered to the customer
- The nature of the customer's role in those processes
- How long delivery lasts
- The prescribed level and style of service to be offered.

Each of the four categories of processes introduced in Chapter 2—people processing, possessing processing, mental stimulus processing, and information processing—has different implications for operational procedures, the degree of customer contact with service personnel and facilities, and requirements for supplementary services. As you might anticipate, people processing services typically involve more supplementary elements than the other categories, because customers must come to the service factory and spend time there during service delivery.

The integration of the core product, supplementary services, and delivery processes is captured in Figure 3.2, which illustrates the components of the service offering for an overnight stay at a luxury hotel—which not only offers more services than a motel, but also a delivers higher level of performance on those tangible and intangible elements that are common to both types of accommodation.

The core product—overnight rental of a bedroom—is dimensioned by service level, scheduling (how long the room may be used before another payment becomes due), the nature of the process (in this instance, people processing), and the role of

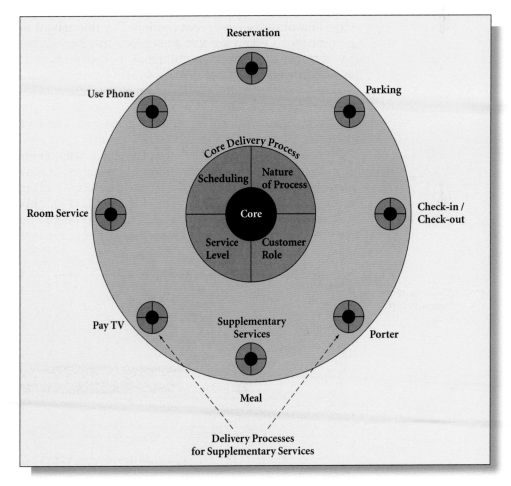

Figure 3.2
Depicting the Service Offering for an Overnight Hotel Stay

the customers in terms of what they are expected to do for themselves and what the hotel will do for them, such as making the bed, supplying bathroom towels, and cleaning the room.

Surrounding the core is an array of supplementary services, ranging from reservations to meals and in-room service elements. As with the core product, delivery processes must be specified for each of these elements. The more expensive the hotel, the higher should be the level of service on each element (for example, covered parking with valet assistance, better food, and a broader array of movies on Pay TV). Additional services might also be offered, such as a business center, a bar, a pool, and a health club. One of the characteristics of a top-of-the line hotel is doing things for customers that they might otherwise have to do for themselves and providing an extended schedule for service delivery, including 24-hour room service.

Documenting the Delivery Sequence over Time

The next task in designing a service concept requires you to address the sequence in which customers will use each of the core and supplementary services and to determine the approximate length of time required in each instance. This information, which should reflect a good understanding of customer needs, habits, and expectations, is necessary not only for marketing purposes but also for facilities planning, operations management, and allocation of personnel. In some instances, as in the script for teeth cleaning services at the dentist, discussed in Chapter 2 (see Figure 2.11), certain service elements must be delivered in a prescribed sequence. In other instances, there may be some flexibility.

Time plays a key role in services, not only from an operational standpoint as it relates to allocating and scheduling purposes, but also from the perspective of customers themselves. In the hotel industry, neither the core service nor its supplementary elements are all delivered continuously throughout the duration of the service performance. Certain services must necessarily be used before others. In this industry, as in many services, consumption of the core product is sandwiched between use of supplementary services that are needed earlier or later in the delivery sequence. Figure 3.3 adds a temporal dimension to the different elements of the luxury hotel service concept (as depicted in Figure 3.2), identifying when and for how long they are likely to be consumed by a typical guest from a given segment. Not every guest uses every service, of course, and schedules may vary.

An important aspect of service planning is determining the amount of time that customers may spend on different service elements. In some instances, research may show that customers from a given segment expect to budget a specific amount of time for a given activity that has value for them and will not wish to be rushed (for instance, eight hours for sleeping, an hour and a half for a business dinner, 20 minutes for breakfast). In other instances, such as making a reservation, checking in and out,

Figure 3.3
Temporal Dimension to Augmented Hotel Product

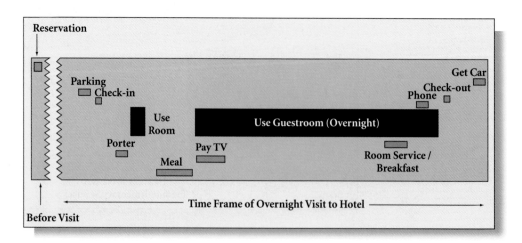

A laboratory study is one that simulates real-world events in a controlled setting. One such study explored how respondents judged hypothetical service encounters in three different service categories—a weekend car rental, an international flight, and a retail purchase (Hansen and Danaher, 1999). Within each category, one of three scenarios was presented to participants. In the first, the initial service events were performed well, the core service adequately, and the concluding steps poorly, thus creating a deteriorating trend; in the second, the situation was reversed, to create an improving trend; and in the third, a consistently adequate service was delivered from start to finish. The findings showed that a weak start that built toward a strong finish received more favorable judgments than did the other scenarios. A conclusion to be drawn from this research is that managers who are not immediately able to raise all elements of the service encounter should begin by focusing on improving the concluding events in the process rather than the opening steps.

Another laboratory study simulated a visit to a restaurant (Hamer et al., 1999). Respondents were presented with two scenarios in which they were going out to eat with a group of friends and were given information at certain key steps during the service

encounter. The findings showed that respondents continuously updated their expectations during service delivery and that these evolving expectations had a larger effect on their perceptions of service quality than did perceived service performance. A key managerial insight from this study is that it's very important for managers to shape and control customers' expectations as service delivery proceeds.

An exploratory study of sequential service encounters in a real-world setting was conducted by Verhoef et al. (2004). It examined telephone calls by customers to the call center of a large financial service provider. The findings suggested that customer satisfaction was not created solely by the average quality of the events in the service process but could be enhanced by a positive peak experience at some point in the process.

Sources: David E. Hansen and Peter J. Danaher, "Inconsistent Performance During the Service Encounter," *Journal of Service Research*, 1 (February 1999): 227–235; Lawrence O. Hamer, Ben Shaw-Ching Liu, and D. Sudharshan, "The Effects of Intraencounter Changes in Expectations on Perceived Service Quality Models," *Journal of Service Research*, 1 (February 1999): 275–289; Peter C. Verhoef, Gerrit Antonides, and Arnoud N. de Hoog, "Service Encounters as a Sequence of Events: The Importance of Peak Experiences," *Journal of Service Research*, 7 (August 2004): 53–64.

or waiting for a car to be retrieved from valet parking, customers may wish to minimize or even eliminate time spent on what they perceive as nonproductive activities.

Do customers' expectations change during the course of service delivery in light of the perceived quality of each sequential encounter? In many cases, the answer is yes. Ideally, service firms should try to provide consistently high performance at each step; in reality, many service performances are inconsistent. Arguing that it's even more important to end on a strong note than to begin on one, a principle that applies to low-contact services as well as high-contact ones, Richard Chase and Sriram Dasu note that many commercial web sites are designed with attractive home pages that create high expectations, but that become progressively less appealing and even problematic to use as customers move toward conclusion of a purchase.[4] This situation can lead customers to abandon their electronic shopping carts in midtransaction. Research Insights 3.1 provides some additional food for thought.

Flowcharting Service Delivery Helps to Clarify Product Elements

Flowcharting, a technique for displaying the nature and sequence of the different steps involved in delivering service to customers, offers a way to understand the totality of the customer's service experience. Marketers find that creating a flowchart for a specific service is particularly useful for distinguishing between those steps at which customers use the core service and those involving service elements that supplement the core product. For instance, for restaurants, food and beverages constitute the core product, but supplementary services may include reservations, valet parking, a coat room, being escorted to a table, ordering from the menu, billing, payment, and use of restrooms. If you prepare flowcharts for a variety of

Figure 3.4 Simple Flowcharts for Delivery of Various Types of Services

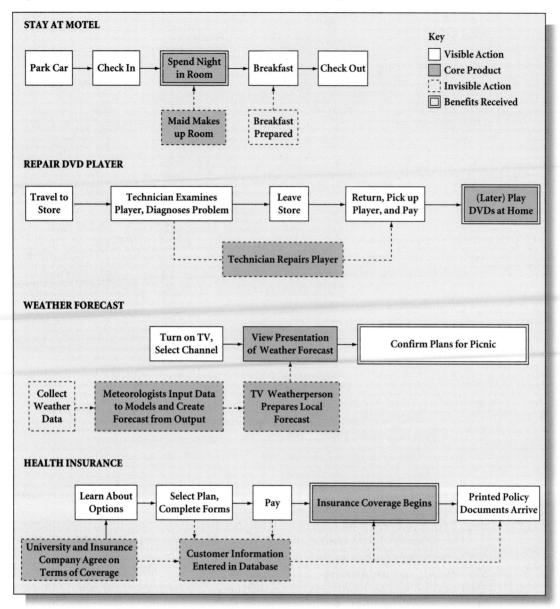

services, you will soon notice that although the core products may differ widely, common supplementary elements—from information to billing and from reservations/order taking to problem resolution—keep recurring.

Using this approach will help you to see how the nature of the customer's involvement with the service organization varies among each of the four categories of services—people processing, possession processing, mental stimulus processing, and information processing. Let's take one example of each category—staying in a motel, getting a DVD player repaired, obtaining a weather forecast, and purchasing health insurance. Figure 3.4 displays a simple flowchart that demonstrates what's involved in each of four scenarios. Imagine that you are the customer in each instance, and think about the extent and nature of your involvement in the service delivery process and the types of encounters with the organization that take place.

- *Stay at a motel (people processing).* It's late evening. You're driving on a long trip and are getting tired. Spotting a motel displaying a vacancy sign, you decide it's time to stop for the night; on closer inspection, however, the building exterior looks run down, there are weeds growing through cracks in the asphalt parking lot, and the grass needs cutting. You decide to continue and soon come to another motel, which, in addition to a vacancy sign, also displays a price that seems very reasonable. You park your car, noting that the grounds are clean and that the buildings seem freshly painted. On entering the reception area, you're greeted by a friendly clerk, who checks you in and gives you the key to a room. You move your car to the space in front of your assigned unit and let yourself in. After undressing and using the bathroom, you go to bed. Following a good night's sleep, you rise the next morning, shower, dress, and pack. Then you walk to reception, where you take advantage of the free coffee, juice, and donuts, return your key to a different clerk, pay, and drive away.

- *Repair a DVD player (possession processing).* When you use your DVD player, the picture quality on the TV screen is poor. Fed up with the situation, you search the Yellow Pages to find an appliance repair store in your area. At the store, the neatly dressed technician checks your machine carefully but quickly and declares that it needs to be adjusted and cleaned. His professional manner inspires confidence. The estimated price seems realistic and you're reassured to learn that repairs are guaranteed for three months, so you agree to the work and are told that the player will be ready in three days' time. The technician disappears into the back office with your machine and you leave the store. On the appointed day, you return to pick up the product; the technician explains the work that he did and demonstrates that the machine is now working well. You pay the agreed price and leave the store with your machine. Back home, you plug in the player, insert a DVD, and find that the picture is much improved.

- *Weather forecast (mental stimulus processing).* You're planning a picnic trip to the lake, but one of your friends says she's heard that it's going to be really cold this weekend. Back home that evening, you check the weather forecast on TV. The meteorologist shows animated charts indicating the probable path of a cold front over the next 72 hours and states that the latest National Weather Service computer projections suggest the front will remain well to the north of your area (Figure 3.5). Armed with this information, you call your friends to tell them that the picnic is on.

Figure 3.5
Weather Forecasting Is a Service Directed at Customers' Minds

- *Health insurance (information processing).* Your university mails you a package of information before the beginning of the new semester. This package includes a student health service brochure describing the several different health insurance options available to students. You can also get further information from a web site or by telephone. Although you consider yourself very healthy, except for seasonal allergies, you remember the unfortunate experience of a friend who recently incurred heavy hospital bills for treatment of a badly fractured ankle. Because he had no health insurance, he was forced to liquidate his modest savings to pay the bills. You don't want to pay for more coverage than you need, so you telephone and ask for information and advice from a counselor. At Registration, you select an option that will cover the cost of hospital treatment, as well as visits to the student health center. You fill in a printed form that includes some standard questions about your medical history and then sign it. The cost of the insurance is added to your bill for the semester. A few weeks later, you receive printed confirmation of your coverage in the mail. Now you no longer have to worry about the risk of unexpected medical expenses.

Insights from Flowcharting

As you can see from these flowcharts, your role as a customer for each of these service products varies sharply from one category to another. The first two examples involve physical processes and the latter two are information-based. At the two motels, you made advance judgments about service quality based on the physical appearance of the buildings and grounds, deciding not to stay at the first motel because of negative clues. At the second motel, you rent use of a bedroom, bathroom, and other physical facilities for the night. Parking is included, too. The management has added value by offering a simple breakfast as part of the package.

Your role at the appliance repair store, however, is limited to briefly explaining the symptoms, leaving the machine, and returning several days later to pick it up. You have to trust the technician's competence and honesty in executing the service in your absence. However, inclusion of a guarantee lowers the risk. You enjoy the benefits later, when you use the repaired machine.

The other two services, weather forecasting and health insurance, involve intangible actions and a less active role for you as consumer. The TV station you watch competes with other stations (and with radio stations, newspapers, and the Internet) for an audience, so it must appeal on the design of its graphics, the personality and presentation skills of its meteorologist, convenience of its schedule, and a reputation for accuracy. You incur no financial cost to obtain the forecast, but you may have to watch some ads first, because advertising revenues constitute the business model that funds the station's operations. Delivery of the information you need takes only a couple of minutes, and you can act on it immediately. Obtaining health insurance, by contrast, takes more time and mental effort, because you have to evaluate several options and complete a detailed application. Then you may have to wait for the policy to be issued and coverage to begin. Your choice of health plan will reflect the cost relative to the benefits offered. How clearly these benefits are explained may influence your decision. If their brand names are familiar, you may also be influenced by the reputation of the companies providing the insurance.

Each of the flowcharts in Figure 3.4 features a core product, of course, and three of the four (motel, repair, insurance) include several supplementary services. We now take an in-depth look at the role played by different types of supplementary services, demonstrating the importance of designing a service concept in which both core and supplementary service elements meet consistent standards and mutually reinforce each other.

Figure 3.7 Credit Card Companies Join Forces to Educate Consumers

Courtesy of Your Credit Card Companies.

Banks, insurance companies, and utilities require prospective customers to go through an application process designed to gather relevant information and to screen out those who do not meet basic enrollment criteria (such as a bad credit record or serious health problems). Universities also require prospective students to apply for admission. Reservations (including appointments and check-in) represent a special type of order taking that entitles customers to a specified unit of service—for example, an airline seat, a restaurant table, a hotel room, time with a qualified professional, or admission to a facility such as a theater or sports arena with designated seating. Accuracy in scheduling is vital—reserving seats for the wrong day is likely to be unpopular with customers.

Ticketless systems, based on telephone or web-site reservations, provide enormous cost savings for airlines, because there are no travel agent commissions to pay—customers book directly—and administrative effort is drastically reduced. A paper ticket at an airline may be handled 15 times, whereas an electronic ticket requires just one step. Customers receive a confirmation number when they make

Table 3.2
Examples of Order-Taking Elements

Applications
- Membership in clubs or programs
- Subscription services (e.g., utilities)
- Prerequisite-based services (e.g., financial credit, college enrollment)

Order Entry
- On-site order fulfillment
- Mail/telephone order placement
- email/web site order placement

Reservations and Check-in
- Seats/tables/rooms
- Vehicles or equipment rental
- Professional appointments
- Admission to restricted facilities (e.g., museums, aquariums)

the reservation and need only show identification at the airport to claim their seats and receive a boarding pass.

Billing

Billing is common to almost all services (unless the service is provided free of charge). Inaccurate, illegible, or incomplete bills risk disappointing customers who may, up to that point, have been quite satisfied with their experience. Such failures add insult to injury if the customer is already dissatisfied. Billing should also be timely, because it stimulates faster payment. Procedures range from verbal statements to a machine-displayed price, and from handwritten invoices to elaborate monthly statements of account activity and fees (Table 3.3). Perhaps the simplest approach is self-billing, by which the customer tallies up the amount of an order and authorizes a card payment or writes a check. In such instances, billing and payment are combined into a single act, although the seller may still need to check for accuracy.

Customers usually expect bills to be clear and informative, and itemized in ways that make it clear how the total was computed. Unexplained, arcane symbols that have all the meaning of hieroglyphics on an Egyptian monument (and are decipherable only by the high priests of accounting and data processing) do not create a favorable impression of the supplier. Nor does fuzzy printing or illegible handwriting. Laser printers, with their ability to switch fonts and typefaces, to box and to highlight, can produce statements that are not only more legible but also organize information in more useful ways. Marketing research can help here, by asking customers what information they want and how they would like it to be organized.

Busy customers hate to be kept waiting for a bill to be prepared in a hotel, restaurant, or rental car lot. Many hotels and rental car firms have now created express check-out options, taking customers' credit card details in advance and documenting charges later by mail. However, accuracy is essential. Customers use the express check-outs to save time; they certainly don't want to waste time later seeking corrections and refunds. An alternative express check-out procedure is used by some car rental companies. An agent meets customers as they return their cars, checks the

Table 3.3
Examples of Billing Elements

- Periodic statements of account activity
- Invoices for individual transactions
- Verbal statements of amount due
- Machine display of amount due
- Self-billing (computed by customer)

Table 3.4
Examples of Payment
Elements

> **Self-Service**
> - Insert card, cash, or token in machine
> - Electronic funds transfer
> - Mail a check
> - Enter credit card number online
>
> **Direct to Payee or Intermediary**
> - Cash handling and change giving
> - Check handling
> - Credit/charge/debit card handling
> - Coupon redemption
> - Tokens, vouchers, etc.
>
> **Automatic Deduction from Financial Deposits (e.g., bank charges) Control and Verification**
> - Automated systems (e.g., machine-readable tickets that operate entry gates)
> - Human systems (e.g., toll collectors, ticket inspectors)

mileage/kilometrage and fuel gauge readings, and then prints a bill on the spot using a portable wireless terminal. Many hotels push bills under guestroom doors on the morning of departure showing charges to date; others offer customers the option of previewing their bills before checkout on the TV monitor in their room.

Payment

In most cases, a bill requires the customer to take action on payment (and such action may be very slow in coming!). One exception is bank statements, which detail charges that have already been deducted from the customer's account. Increasingly, customers expect ease and convenience of payment, including credit, when they make purchases in their own countries and while traveling abroad.

A variety of options exist for customers to make payment. (Table 3.4). Self-service payment systems, for instance, require insertion of coins, banknotes, tokens, or cards in machines. Equipment breakdowns will destroy the whole purpose of such a system, so good maintenance and rapid-response troubleshooting are essential. Much payment still takes place through hand-to-hand transfers of cash and checks, but credit and debit cards are growing in importance as more and more establishments accept them. Other alternatives include vouchers, coupons, or prepaid tickets. Firms benefit from prompt payment, because that reduces the amount of accounts receivable. To reinforce good behavior, NStar, a Massachusetts electrical utility, periodically sends "thank you" notes to customers who have consistently paid on time.

To ensure that people actually pay what is due, some service businesses have instituted control systems, such as ticket checks before entering a movie theater or on board a train. However, inspectors and security officers must be trained to combine politeness with firmness in performing their jobs, so that honest customers do not feel harassed.

Consultation

Now we move to enhancing supplementary services, led by consultation. In contrast to information, which suggests a simple response to customers' questions (or printed information that anticipates their needs), consultation involves a dialog to probe customer requirements and then develop a tailored solution. Table 3.5 provides examples of several supplementary services in the consultation category. At its simplest, consultation consists of immediate advice from a knowledgeable service person in response to the request, "What do you suggest?" (For example, you might ask the person who cuts your hair for advice on hairstyles and hair products.) Effective consultation requires an understanding of each customer's current situation, before

Table 3.5
Examples of
Consultation Elements

- Customized advice
- Personal counseling
- Tutoring/training in product use
- Management or technical consulting

suggesting a suitable course of action. Good customer records can be a great help in this respect, particularly if relevant data can be retrieved easily from a remote terminal.

Counseling represents a more subtle approach to consultation because it involves helping customers better understand their situations so that they can come up with their "own" solutions and action programs. This approach can be a particularly valuable supplement to services such as health treatment, in which part of the challenge is to get customers to take a long-term view of their personal situation and to adopt more healthful behaviors, often involving significant lifestyle changes. For example, diet centers such as Weight Watchers use counseling to help customers change behaviors so that weight loss can be sustained after the initial diet is completed.

More formalized efforts to provide management and technical consulting for corporate customers include the "solution selling" associated with expensive industrial equipment and services. The sales engineer researches the customer's situation and then offers objective advice about what particular package of equipment and systems will yield the best results for the customer. Some consulting services are offered free of charge, in the hope of making a sale. In other instances, however, the service is "unbundled" and customers are expected to pay for it. Advice can also be offered through tutorials, group training programs, and public demonstrations.

Hospitality

Hospitality-related services should, ideally, reflect pleasure at meeting new customers and greeting old ones when they return. Well-managed businesses try, at least in small ways, to ensure that their employees treat customers as guests. Courtesy and consideration for customers' needs apply to both face-to-face encounters and telephone interactions (Table 3.6). Hospitality finds its fullest expression in face-to-face encounters. In some cases, it starts (and ends) with an offer of transport to and from the service site, as with courtesy shuttle buses. If customers must wait outdoors before the service can be delivered, then a thoughtful service provider will offer weather protection; if customers wait indoors, then a waiting area with seating and even entertainment (TV, newspapers or magazines) to pass the time may be provided. Recruiting employees who are naturally warm, welcoming, and considerate for customer-contact jobs helps to create a hospitable atmosphere.

The quality of the hospitality services offered by a firm plays an important role in determining your satisfaction (or dissatisfaction) with the core product. This is especially

Table 3.6
Examples of Hospitality
Elements

Greeting
Food and beverages
Toilets and washrooms
Waiting facilities and amenities
- Lounges, waiting areas, seating
- Weather protection
- Magazines, entertainment, newspapers
Transport
Security

true for people processing services, because you cannot easily leave the service facility until delivery of the core service is completed. Strategies for improving customer satisfaction often center on looking for ways to add or improve supplementary services. For instance, a hospital may seek to enhance its appeal by providing the level of room service, including meals, that might be expected in a good hotel. Some airlines seek to differentiate themselves from their competitors with better meals and more attentive cabin crew; Singapore Airlines is well recognized on both counts.[6]

Although preflight and in-flight hospitality is important, an airline journey doesn't really end until passengers reach their final destination. Air travelers have come to expect departure lounges, but British Airways (BA) came up with the novel idea of an arrivals lounge for its terminals at London's Heathrow and Gatwick airports, to serve passengers arriving early in the morning after long, overnight flights from the Americas, Asia, Africa, and Australia. It offers holders of first and business class tickets or a BA Executive Club gold card (awarded to the airline's most frequent flyers) the opportunity to use a special lounge where they can take a shower, change, use a spa, have breakfast, and make phone calls and check their email before continuing to their final destination feeling a lot fresher. It's a nice competitive advantage, which BA actively promotes. Other airlines have felt obliged to copy this innovation, although few can match the array of services offered by BA.

Failures in hospitality may extend to the physical design of the areas where customers wait before receiving service. A survey found that unappealing offices and lack of creature comforts can drive away patients of cosmetic surgeons (Research Insights 3.2).

Safekeeping

When customers are visiting a service site, they often want assistance with their personal possessions. In fact, unless certain safekeeping services are provided (such as

---

RESEARCH INSIGHTS 3.2
Cosmetic Surgeons' Offices Turn Off Patients

It appears that plastic surgeons could use some service marketing training along with their other courses in medical school. That's the diagnosis of two experts, Kate Altork and Douglas Dedo, who did a study of patients' reactions to doctors' offices. They found that many patients will cancel a surgery, change doctors, or refuse to consider future elective surgery if they feel uneasy in the doctor's office. The study results suggested that patients don't usually "doctor-jump" because they don't like the doctor but because they don't like the context of the service experience. The list of common patient dislikes includes: graphic posters of moles and skin cancers decorating office walls; uncomfortable plastic identification bracelets for patients; claustrophobic examining rooms with no windows or current reading material; bathrooms that aren't clearly marked; and not enough wastebaskets and water coolers in the waiting room.

What do patients want? Most requests are surprisingly simple and involve creature comforts such as tissues, water coolers, telephones, plants, and bowls of candy in the waiting room and live flower arrangements in the lobby. Patients also want windows in the examining rooms and gowns that wrap around the entire body. They would like to sit on a real chair when they talk to a doctor instead of perching on a stool or examining table. Finally, preoperative patients prefer to be separated from postoperative patients, because they don't want to be disturbed by sitting next to someone in the waiting room whose head is wrapped in bandages.

These study results suggest that cosmetic surgery patients would rather visit an office that looks like a more like a health spa than a hospital ward. By thinking like service marketers, savvy surgeons could use this information to create patient-friendly environments that will complement rather than counteract their technical expertise.

Source: Adapted from Lisa Bannon, "Plastic Surgeons Are Told to Pay More Attention to Appearances," *The Wall Street Journal*, March 15, 1997, p. B1.

Table 3.7
Examples of Safekeeping
Elements

Caring for Possessions Customers Bring with Them
- Child care
- Pet care
- Parking facilities for vehicles
- Valet parking
- Coat rooms
- Baggage handling
- Storage space
- Safe deposit boxes
- Security personnel

Caring for Goods Purchased (or Rented) by Customers
- Packaging
- Pickup
- Transportation and delivery
- Installation
- Inspection and diagnosis
- Cleaning
- Refueling
- Preventive maintenance
- Repairs and renovation
- Upgrade

safe and convenient parking for their cars), some customers may not come at all. On-site safekeeping services includes coatrooms; baggage transport, handling, and storage; safekeeping of valuables; and even child care and pet care (Table 3.7) Responsible businesses pay close attention to safety and security issues for customers who are visiting the firm's premises. Wells Fargo Bank mails a brochure with its bank statements containing information about using its ATM machines safely, educating its customers about how to protect both their ATM cards and themselves from theft and personal injury. And the bank makes sure that its machines are in brightly lit, highly visible locations.

Additional safekeeping services may involve physical products that customers buy or rent. They may include packaging, pickup and delivery, assembly, installation, cleaning, and inspection. These services may be offered free or for an additional fee.

Exceptions

Exceptions involve supplementary services that fall outside the routine of normal service delivery (Table 3.8). Astute businesses anticipate exceptions and develop contingency plans and guidelines in advance. That way, employees will not appear helpless and surprised when customers ask for special assistance. Well-defined procedures make it easier for employees to respond promptly and effectively. There are several types of exceptions:

1. *Special requests.* A customer may request service that requires a departure from normal operating procedures. Advance requests often relate to personal needs, including care of children, dietary requirements, medical needs, religious observance, and personal disabilities. Such requests are particularly common in the travel and hospitality industries.
2. *Problem solving.* Sometimes, normal service delivery (or product performance) fails to run smoothly as a result of an accident, delay, equipment failure, or a customer having difficulty using a product.
3. *Handling of complaints/suggestions/compliments.* This activity requires well-defined procedures. It should be easy for customers to express dissatisfaction, offer suggestions for improvement, or pass on compliments; and service providers should be able to make an appropriate response quickly.

Table 3.8
Examples of
Exceptions Elements

Special Requests in Advance of Service Delivery
- Children's needs
- Dietary requirements
- Medical or disability needs
- Religious observances
- Deviations from standard operating procedures

Handling Special Communications
- Complaints
- Compliments
- Suggestions

Problem Solving
- Warranties and guarantees against product malfunction
- Resolving difficulties that arise from using the product
- Resolving difficulties caused by accidents, service failures, and problems with staff or other customers
- Assisting customers who have suffered an accident or medical emergency

Restitution
- Refunds
- Compensation in kind for unsatisfactory goods and services
- Free repair of defective goods

4. *Restitution.* Many customers expect to be compensated for serious performance failures. Compensation may take the form of repairs under warranty, legal settlements, refunds, an offer of free service, or another form of payment-in-kind.

Managers need to keep an eye on the level of exception requests. Too many requests may indicate that standard procedures need revamping. For instance, if a restaurant frequently receives requests for special vegetarian meals because there are none on the menu, it may be time to revise the menu to include at least one such dish. A flexible approach to exceptions is generally a good idea, because it reflects responsiveness to customer needs. On the other hand, too many exceptions may compromise safety, negatively impact other customers, and overburden employees.

Managerial Implications

The eight categories of supplementary services that form the "flower of service" collectively provide many options for enhancing core products, both goods and services. Most supplementary services do (or should) represent responses to customer needs. As we noted earlier, some are facilitating services—such as information and reservations—that enable customers to use the core product more effectively. Others are "extras" that enhance the core or even reduce its nonfinancial costs (for example, meals, magazines, and entertainment are hospitality elements that help pass the time). Some elements—notably billing and payment—are, in effect, imposed by the service provider. Even if they are not actively desired by the customer, they still form part of the overall service experience. Any badly handled element may negatively affect customers' perceptions of service quality. The "information" and "consultation" petals illustrate the emphasis in this book on the need for education as well as promotion in communicating with service customers.

Not every core product is surrounded by a large number of supplementary services from all eight petals. People processing services tend to be the most demanding in terms of supplementary elements—especially hospitality—because they involve close (and often extended) interactions with customers. When customers don't visit the service factory, the need for hospitality may be limited to simple courtesies in letters and telecommunications. Possession processing services sometimes place heavy demands on safekeeping elements, but there may be no need for this particular petal when providing information processing services in which customers and suppliers deal entirely at arm's length. Financial services that are provided electronically are an exception, however—companies must ensure that their customers' intangible financial assets and their privacy are carefully safeguarded in transactions that occur via phone or the Web.

A study of Japanese, American, and European firms serving business-to-business markets found that most companies simply added layer upon layer of services to their core offerings without knowing what customers really valued.[7] Managers surveyed in the study indicated that they did not understand which services should be offered to customers as a standard package accompanying the core, and which could be offered as options for an extra charge. Without this knowledge, developing effective pricing policies can be tricky. There are no simple rules governing pricing decisions for core products and supplementary services, but managers should continually review their own policies and those of competitors to make sure they are in line with both market practice and customer needs. We'll discuss these and other pricing issues in more detail in Chapter 5.

In summary, Tables 3.1 through 3.8 can serve as a checklist in the continuing search for new ways to augment existing core products and to design new offerings. The lists provided in these eight tables do not claim to be all-encompassing, because some products may require specialized supplementary elements. In general, a firm that competes on a low-cost, no-frills basis needs fewer supplementary elements than one marketing an expensive, high-value-added product. Offering progressively higher levels of supplementary services around a common core may offer the basis for a product line of differentiated offerings, similar to the various classes of travel offered by airlines. Regardless of which supplementary services a firm decides to offer, all of the elements in each petal should receive the care and attention needed to consistently meet defined service standards. That way the resulting "flower" will always have a fresh and appealing appearance—rather than looking wilted or disfigured by neglect.

PLANNING AND BRANDING SERVICE PRODUCTS

In recent years, more and more service businesses have started talking about their *products*—a term previously associated with manufactured goods. Some even speak of their "products and services," an expression also used by service-driven manufacturing firms. What is the distinction between these two terms in today's business environment?

A *product* implies a defined and consistent "bundle of output" and also the ability to differentiate one bundle of output from another. In a manufacturing context, the concept is easy to understand and visualize. Service firms can also differentiate their products in a fashion similar to the various "models" offered by manufacturers. Fast-food restaurants are sometimes described as "quasi-manufacturing" operations because they produce a physical output combined with value-added service. At each site, they display a menu of their products, which are of course highly tangible. If you are a burger connoisseur, you can easily distinguish Burger King's Whopper from a Whopper with Cheese, as well as a Whopper from a Big Mac. The service comes from speedy delivery of a freshly prepared food item, the ability (in some instances) to order and pick up freshly cooked food from a drive-in location without leaving one's car, the availability within the restaurant of self-service drinks, condiments, and napkins, and the opportunity to sit down and eat one's meal at a table.

Providers of more intangible services also offer a "menu" of products, representing an assembly of carefully prescribed elements built around the core product, and may bundle in certain value-added supplementary services. For instance, banks offer a variety of accounts, insurance providers offer different types of policies, and universities offer different degree programs, each composed of a mix of required

Figure 3.8 The Spectrum of Branding Alternatives

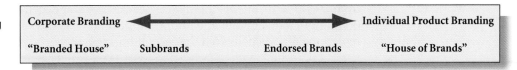

and elective courses. Let's look at some more examples, considering hotels, a computer support service, and an international airline.

Product Lines and Brands

Most service organizations offer a line of products rather than just a single product. As a result, they must choose among three broad alternatives: using a single brand to cover all products and services, a separate stand-alone brand for each offering, or some combination of these two extremes.[8] These alternatives are represented as a spectrum in Figure 3.8. David Aaker and E. Joachimsthaler use the term *branded house* to describe a company, such as the Virgin Group, that applies its brand name to multiple offerings in often unrelated fields.[9] Next on this spectrum are *subbrands*, for which the master brand is the primary frame of reference but the product itself also has a distinctive name (Singapore Airlines Raffles Class, denoting the company's business class service, is an example). Subbrands are followed by *endorsed brands*, for which the product brand dominates but the corporate name is still featured (many hotel corporations adopt this approach). At the far end of the spectrum is the *house of brands* strategy, exemplified by Procter and Gamble, which makes some 80 packaged goods products, each of which is actively promoted under its own brand name.

Hotel Branding

The United States has more than 200 hotel brands competing for business, more than any other product category. Many hotel chains offer a family of subbrands/endorsed brands. For instance, Hilton Hotels Corporation, Intercontinental, and Starwood each has seven subbrands, whereas Marriott International has 12 (plus the wholly owned Ritz-Carlton chain, which, to protect its exclusive image, is not normally identified for marketing purposes as part of the Marriott Group).

For a multibrand strategy to succeed, each brand must promise a distinctive value proposition, targeted at a different customer segment. Because accommodations vary by service level (and thus price), room configurations and amenities also vary. Certain brands are targeted at guests who are making an extended stay, and there are resort brands that primarily target vacationers. In some instances, segmentation is situation-based: The same individual may have different needs (and willingness to pay) under differing circumstances, such as when traveling with family or traveling on business. A strategy of brand extension is aimed at encouraging customers to continue patronizing units within the brand family and may be reinforced by loyalty programs. A study of the brand-switching behavior of some 5,400 hotel customers found that brand extensions do seem to encourage customer retention, but that the strategy may be less effective in discouraging switching when the number of brands reaches four or more.[10]

Sun Microsystems Hardware and Software Support

As an example of branding a high-tech, business-to-business product line, consider Sun Microsystems. The company offers a comprehensive hardware and software support program branded as "SunSpectrum Support."[11] Four different levels of support are available, subbranded from platinum to bronze. The objective is to give buyers the flexibility to choose a level of support consistent with their own organization's needs (and willingness to pay), ranging from expensive, mission-critical support at the enterprise level (Platinum Service Plan) to relatively inexpensive assistance with self-service maintenance support (Bronze Service Plan). Service availability ranges from 24/7, with on-site hardware service coverage delivered within two hours (Platinum), to telephone and online support on weekdays from 8 a.m. to 5 p.m. and replacement parts delivered the second business day.

British Airways Subbrands

A comprehensive example of strong subbranding in the airline industry comes from British Airways (BA), which offers seven distinct air travel products. There are four intercontinental offerings—First (deluxe service), Club World (business class), World Traveller Plus (premium economy class), and World Traveller (economy class); two intra-European subbrands—Club Europe (business class) and Euro-Traveller (economy class); and, within the United Kingdom, Shuttle, offering frequent, economy-class service between London and other major British cities. Each BA subbrand represents a specific service concept and a set of clearly stated product specifications for preflight, in-flight, and on-arrival service elements.

To provide additional focus on product, pricing, and marketing communications, responsibility for managing and developing each service is assigned to a separate management team. Through internal training and external communications, staff and passengers alike are kept informed of the characteristics of each service. Except for domestic services, most aircraft in BA's fleet are configured in several classes. For instance, the airline's intercontinental fleet of Boeing 747s and 777s is equipped to serve First, Club World, World Traveller Plus, and World Traveller passengers.

On any given route, all passengers traveling on a particular flight receive the same core product—say, a 10-hour journey from Los Angeles to London—but the nature and extent of most of the supplementary elements differ widely, both on the ground and in the air. Passengers in Club World, for instance, not only benefit from better tangible elements—such as more comfortable seats that fold into beds, upscale food, and the use of an airport lounge before the flight, they also receive more personalized service from airline employees and benefit from faster service on the ground at check-in, passport control in London (special lines), and baggage retrieval (priority handling). First Class passengers are even more pampered. The higher the service level, of course, the higher the price!

Offering a Branded Experience

Branding can be employed at both the corporate and product levels by almost any service business. In a well-managed firm the corporate brand is not only easily recognized but also has meaning for customers, standing for a particular way of doing business. Applying distinctive brand names to individual products enables the firm to communicate to the target market the distinctive experiences and benefits associated with a specific service concept. In short, it helps marketers to establish a mental picture of the service in customers' minds and to clarify the nature of the value proposition.

The Forum Corporation, a consulting firm, differentiates between (1) a random customer experience with high variability, (2) a generic branded experience by suppliers who offer a consistently similar experience, differentiated only by the presence of the brand name (ATMs are a good example), and (3) a "branded customer experience," in which the customer's experience is shaped in specific and meaningful ways.[12] (See Service Perspectives 3.1 for Forum's recommendations on how to achieve this.)

Around the world, many financial service firms continue to create and register brand names to distinguish the different accounts and service packages that they offer. Their objective is to transform a series of service elements and processes into a consistent and recognizable service experience, offering a definable and predictable output at a specified price. Unfortunately, there's often little discernible difference—other than name—between one bank's branded offering and another's, and their value propositions may be unclear. Don Shultz emphasizes that "The brand promise or value proposition is not a tag line, an icon, or a color or a graphic element, although all of these may contribute. It is, instead, the heart and soul of the brand. . . ."[13]

Forum Corporation identifies six basic steps to develop and deliver the "branded customer experience":

1. Target profitable customers, employing behavior segmentation rather than demographics.
2. Achieve a superior understanding of what your targeted customers value.
3. Create a brand promise—an articulation of what target customers can expect from their experience with your organization—that is of value to customers, addresses a need, is actionable and can be incorporated into standards, and provides focus for the organization and its employees.
4. Apply that understanding to shape a truly differentiated customer experience.
5. Give employees the skills, tools, and supporting processes needed to deliver the defined customer experience.
6. Make everyone a brand manager.
7. Make promises that your processes can exceed.
8. Measure and monitor: Consistency of delivery is paramount.

Sources: Forum Issues #17. Boston: The Forum Corporation, 1997; Joe Wheeler and Shaun Smith, "Loyalty by Design," Forum Corporation, 2003, www.forum.com/publications, accessed March 2003.

An important role for service marketers is to become "brand champions," familiar with and responsible for shaping every aspect of the customer's experience. We can relate the notion of a branded service experience to the "flower of service" metaphor by emphasizing the need for consistency in the color and texture of each petal. Unfortunately, many service experiences remain haphazard and create the impression of a flower stitched together with petals drawn from many different plants.

We return to a discussion of branding in the context of marketing communications strategy in Chapter 6.

DEVELOPMENT OF NEW SERVICES

Competitive intensity and customer expectations are increasing in nearly all service industries. Thus, success lies not only in providing existing services well, but also in creating new approaches to service. Because the outcome and process aspects of a service often combine to create the experience and benefits received by customers, both aspects must be addressed in development of new services.

A Hierarchy of New Service Categories

There are many different ways for a service provider to innovate. Below we identify seven categories of new services, ranging from major innovations to simple style changes.

1. *Major service innovations* are new core products for markets that have not been previously defined. They usually include both new service characteristics and radical new processes. Examples include FedEx's introduction of overnight, nationwide, express package delivery in 1971 and eBay's launch of online auction services.
2. *Major process innovations* consist of using new processes to deliver existing core products in new ways with additional benefits. For example, the University of Phoenix competes with other universities by delivering undergraduate and graduate degree programs in a nontraditional way. It has no permanent central campus, but offers courses either online or in rented facilities. Its students get most of the benefits of a college degree in half the time and at a much lower price than at other universities.[14] In recent years, the growth of the Internet has led to creation of many new start-up businesses employing new retailing models that

don't use traditional stores but do save customers time and travel. Often, these models add new, information-based benefits such as greater customization, the opportunity to visit chat rooms with fellow customers, and suggestions for additional products that match well with what has already been purchased.

3. *Product-line extensions* are additions to current product lines by existing firms. The first company in a market to offer such a product may be seen as an innovator; the others are merely followers, often acting defensively. These new services may be targeted at existing customers to serve a broader array of needs or designed to attract new customers with different needs (or both). Delta Airlines is one of several major carriers to attempt the launch of a separate low-cost operation designed to compete with discount carriers such as Jet Blue and Southwest Airlines, but none of these ventures has been successful. Telephone companies have introduced numerous value-added services such as call waiting and call forwarding. In banking, many banks now retail insurance products in the hope of increasing the number of profitable relationships with existing customers.

4. *Process-line extensions* are less innovative than process innovations, but often represent distinctive new ways of delivering existing products, either with the intent of offering more convenience and a different experience for existing customers or of attracting new customers who find the traditional approach unappealing. Most commonly, they involve adding a lower-contact distribution channel to an existing high-contact channel, such as creating telephone-based or Internet-based banking services. Barnes and Noble, the leading bookstore chain in the United States, added Internet retailing through BarnesandNoble.com, to help it compete with Amazon.com. Such dual-track approaches are sometimes referred to as "clicks and mortar." Creating self-service options to complement delivery by service employees is another form of process-line extension.

5. *Supplementary service innovations* take the form of adding new facilitating or enhancing service elements to an existing core service, or of significantly improving an existing supplementary service. FedEx Kinkos now offers customers high-speed Internet access round-the-clock, seven days a week, at most of its locations in the United States and Canada. Low-tech innovations for an existing service can be as simple as adding parking at a retail site or agreeing to accept credit cards for payment. Multiple improvements may have the effect of creating what customers perceive as an entirely new experience, even though it is built around the same core. Theme restaurants such as the Rainforest Café enhance the core food service with new experiences. These cafés are designed to keep customers entertained with aquariums, live parrots, waterfalls, fiberglass monkeys, talking trees that spout environmentally related information, and regularly timed thunderstorms, complete with lightning.[15]

6. *Service improvements* are the most common type of innovation. They involve modest changes in the performance of current products, including improvements to either the core product or to existing supplementary services.

7. *Style changes* represent the simplest type of innovation, typically involving no changes in either processes or performance. However, they are often highly visible, create excitement, and may serve to motivate employees. Examples include repainting retail branches and vehicles in new color schemes, outfitting service employees in new uniforms, introducing a new bank check design, or minor changes in service scripts for employees.

As the above typology suggests, service innovation can occur at many different levels, and not every type of innovation has an impact on the characteristics of the service product or is experienced by the customer.

Reengineering Service Processes

The design of service processes has implications not only for customers but also for the cost, speed, and productivity with which the desired outcome is achieved. Improving productivity in services often requires speeding up the overall process (or

Figure 3.9 Alternative Service Concepts for Meal Delivery

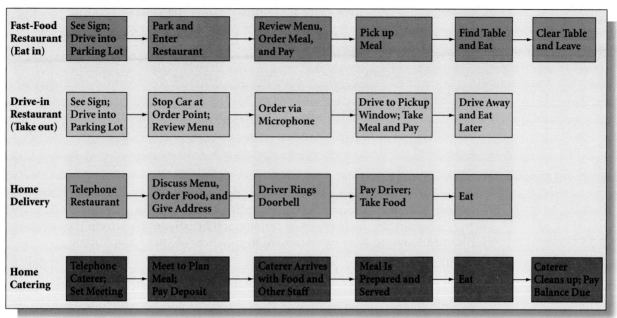

cycle time), because the cost of creating a service is usually related to how long it takes to deliver each step in the process, plus any dead time between each step. *Reengineering* involves analyzing and redesigning processes to achieve faster and better performance.[16] To reduce overall process time, analysts must identify each step, measure how long it takes, look for opportunities to speed it up (or even eliminate it altogether), and cut out dead time. Running tasks in parallel rather than in sequence is a well-established approach to speeding up processes (a simple household example is to cook the vegetables for a meal while the main dish is in the oven, rather than waiting to cook them until after the main dish is removed). Service companies can use blueprinting (discussed in Chapter 8) to diagram these aspects of service operations in a systematic way.

Examination of processes may also lead to creation of alternative delivery methods that are so radically different as to constitute entirely new service concepts. Options may include eliminating certain supplementary services, adding new ones, instituting self-service procedures, and rethinking where and when service is delivered. Figure 3.9 illustrates this principle with simple flowcharts of four alternative ways to deliver meal service, as compared to a full-service restaurant. Take a look and contrast what happens front-stage at a fast-food restaurant, a drive-in restaurant, home delivery, and home catering. From the customer's perspective, what has been added to or deleted from the scenario at a full-service restaurant? And in each instance, how do these changes affect backstage activities?

Physical Goods as a Source of New Service Ideas

Goods and services may be competitive substitutes when they offer the same key benefits. For example, if your lawn needs mowing, you could buy a lawn mower and do it yourself or you could contract with a lawn maintenance service to take care of the chore, effectively avoiding ownership and renting both labor and machines. Such decisions may be shaped by the customer's skills, physical capabilities, and time budget, as well as such factors as cost comparisons between purchase price (plus operating costs) and service fees, storage space for purchased products, and anticipateed frequency of need.

Many services can be built around providing an alternative to owning a physical good and enabling customers to do the work themselves. Figure 3.10 shows four possible delivery alternatives each for car travel and word processing, respectively.

Figure 3.10
Services as
Substitutes for Goods
Ownership and
Personal Task
Performance

	OWN A PHYSICAL GOOD	RENT THE USE OF A PHYSICAL GOOD
PERFORM THE WORK ONESELF	• Drive Own Car • Type on Own Word Processor	• Rent a Car and Drive It • Rent a Word Processor and Type on It
HIRE SOMEONE TO DO THE WORK	• Hire a Chauffeur to Drive Car • Hire a Typist to Use Word Processor	• Hire a Taxi or Limousine • Send Work Out to a Secretarial Service

Three of these alternatives present service opportunities. Each alternative is based on choosing between ownership and rental of the necessary physical goods, and between performing self-service or hiring another person to perform the necessary tasks. Additional services can be added to enhance the value proposition.

Any new physical product has the potential to create a need for related possession processing services (particularly if the product is a high-value, durable item.) Industrial equipment may require servicing throughout its lifespan, beginning with financing and insurance, then shipping (and possibly installation), and continuing with maintenance, cleaning, repair, consulting advice and problem solving, upgrading, and ultimate disposal. Historically, such after-sales services have generated important revenue streams for many years after the initial sale for products such as trucks, factory machinery, locomotives, computers, and jet engines.

Caterpillar, the well-known manufacturer of heavy-duty earthmoving and construction equipment, has developed a portfolio of service businesses (Figure 3.11) to complement its highly cyclical manufacturing business.[17] These services include:

- *Cat Financial*, which extends credit for three-quarters of all Caterpillar sales
- *Cat Insurance*, which serves both dealers and customers, protecting equipment against physical damage and also offering extended warranty coverage

Figure 3.11
Caterpillar Promotes
Its Service Businesses

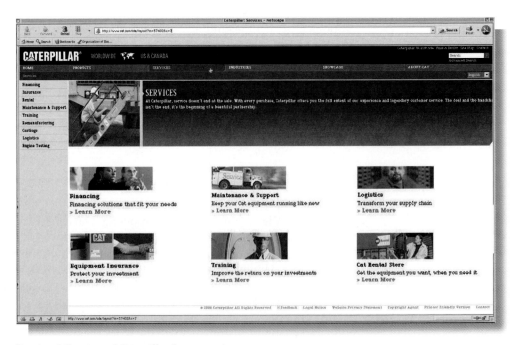

Reprinted Courtesy of Caterpillar, Inc.

- *Cat Rental Stores,* a network of dealer-owned facilities that offer daily, weekly, and monthly rentals of Caterpillar products and related equipment
- *Cat Logistics,* which undertakes supply chain management for customers around the world, offering both planning and program management
- *Equipment Training Solutions Group,* which offers courses for operators to help them select the right equipment for the job and use it skillfully to improve productivity, decrease downtime, reduce operating costs, and enhance safety
- *Maintenance and Support,* which creates individualized customer support agreements that are tailored to each customer's specific needs and can range from simple preventive maintenance kits to sophisticated total cost performance guarantees
- *Remanufacturing,* which uses proprietary technologies to salvage, clean, restore, and rebuild used equipment from both Caterpillar and other original equipment manaufacturers

Using Research to Design New Services

If a company is designing a new service from scratch, how can it figure out what features and price will create the best value for target customers? It's hard to know without asking these customers—hence the need for research. Research Insights 3.3 presents a classic example of how the Marriott Corporation used market research experts to help with new service development in the hotel industry.

Marriott was sufficiently encouraged by the findings to build three prototype Courtyard by Marriott hotels. After testing the concept under real-world conditions and making some refinements, the company developed a large chain whose advertising slogan became "Courtyard by Marriott—the hotel designed by business travelers." Marriott continues to use this theme, with recent advertising for Courtyard headlined "Architects Design Most Hotels, Road Warriors Designed Ours," and promoting free high-speed Internet access and 24-hour business services (Figure 3.13).

The new service concept filled a gap in the market with a product that represented the best balance between the price customers were prepared to pay and the physical and service features they most desired. The success of the Courtyard concept led Marriott to use the same research methodology to develop additional customer-driven products. These include Fairfield Inn, a moderately-priced chain whose rooms are supported by only limited hotel services, and SpringHill Suites, a moderately priced all-suites hotel targeted at both business and pleasure travelers and offering separate working, sleeping, and eating areas, including a pantry with sink, microwave, and coffee maker.

Achieving Success in Developing New Services

Consumer goods are notorious for their high failure rates: More than 90 percent of the 30,000 new products introduced each year fail.[18] Services are not immune to the high failure rates that plague new manufactured products. The advent of the Internet stimulated entrepreneurs to create numerous new "dot.com" companies to deliver Internet-based services, but the vast majority failed within just a few years. The reasons for failure ranged widely, including not meeting a demonstrable consumer need, inability to cover costs from revenues, and poor execution. In the restaurant business, H. T. Parsa and his colleagues found a failure rare of about 26 percent during the first year, rising to close to 60 percent within three years. Interestingly, the rate varied widely by type of food served, ranging from 33 percent for seafood and burger restaurants to 76 percent for sub shops and bakeries and 86 percent for restaurants serving Mexican food.[19]

Chris Storey and Christopher Easingwood argue that in developing new services, the core product is of secondary importance. It's the quality of the total service offering, and also of the marketing support that goes with this, that are vital. Underlying success

When Marriott was designing a new chain of hotels for business travelers (which eventually became known as Courtyard by Marriott), it hired marketing research experts to help establish an optimal design concept. Because there are limits to how much service and how many amenities can be offered at any given price, Marriott needed to know how customers would make trade-offs in order to arrive at the most satisfactory compromise in terms of value for money. The intent of the research was to get respondents to trade off different hotel service features to see which ones they valued most. Marriott's goal was to determine if a niche existed between full-service hotels and inexpensive motels, especially in locations where demand was not high enough to justify a large full-service hotel. If such a niche existed, executives wanted to develop a product to fill that gap.

A sample of 601 consumers in four metropolitan areas participated in the study. Researchers used a sophisticated technique known as conjoint analysis, which asks survey respondents to make trade-offs among different groupings of attributes. The objective was to determine which mix of attributes at specific prices offered them the highest degree of utility. The 50 attributes in the Marriott study were divided into the following seven factors (or sets of attributes), each containing a variety of different features based on detailed studies of competing offerings:

1. *External factors*—building shape, landscaping, pool type and location, hotel size
2. *Room features*—room size and décor, climate control, location and type of bathroom, entertainment systems, other amenities
3. *Food-related services*—type and location of restaurants, menus, room service, vending machines, guest shop, in-room kitchen
4. *Lounge facilities*—location, atmosphere, type of guests
5. *Services*—reservations, registration, check-out, airport limousine, bell desk (baggage service), message center, secretarial services, car rental, laundry, valet
6. *Leisure facilities*—sauna, whirlpool, exercise room, racquetball and tennis courts, game room, children's playground
7. *Security*—guards, smoke detectors, 24-hour video camera

For each of these seven factors, respondents were presented with a series of stimulus cards displaying different levels of performance for each attribute. For instance, the "Rooms" stimulus card displayed nine attributes, each of which had three to five different levels. Thus, *amenities* ranged from "small bar of soap" to "large soap, shampoo packet, shoeshine mitt" to "large soap, bath gel, shower cap, sewing kit, shampoo, special soap" and then to the highest level, "large soap, bath gel, shower cap, sewing kit, special soap, toothpaste, etc."

In the second phase of the analysis, respondents were shown a number of alternative hotel profiles, each featuring different levels of performance on the various attributes. They were asked to indicate on a 5-point scale how likely they would be to stay at a hotel with these features, given a specific room price per night. Fifty different profiles were developed for this research, with each respondent being asked to evaluate five of them.

The research yielded detailed guidelines for the selection of almost 200 features and service elements, representing those attributes that provided the highest utility for the customers in the target segments, at prices they were willing to pay. An important aspect of the study was that it focused not only on what business travelers wanted, but also identified what they liked but weren't prepared to pay for (there's a difference, after all, between wanting something and being willing to pay for it). Using these inputs, the design team was able to meet the specified price while retaining the features most desired by the target market.

Sources: Jerry Wind, Paul E. Green, Douglas Shifflet, and Marsha Scarbrough, "Courtyard by Marriott: Designing a Hotel Facility with Customer Based Marketing Models," *Interfaces,* 19 (January–February 1989): 25–47; Paul E. Green, Abba M. Krieger, and Yoram (Jerry) Wind, "Thirty Years of Conjoint Analysis: Reflections and Prospects," *Interfaces,* 31 (May–June 2001): S56–S73.

in these areas, they emphasize, is market knowledge: "Without an understanding of the marketplace, knowledge about customers, and knowledge about competitors, it is very unlikely that a new product will be a success."[20] Stephen Tax and Ian Stuart contend that new services should be defined in terms of the extent of change required to the existing service system, relative to the interactions among participants (people), processes, and physical elements (e.g., facilities and equipment).[21] They propose a seven-step planning cycle to evaluation the feasibility and associated risks of integrating a new service development into a firm's existing service system.

To what extent can rigorously conducted and controlled development processes for new services enhance their success rate? A study by Scott Edgett and Steven Parkinson focused on discriminating between successful and unsuccessful new financial services.[22] They found that the three factors that contributed most to success were, in order of importance:

1. *Market synergy.* The new product fit well with the existing image of the firm, provided a superior advantage to competing products in terms of meeting customers' known needs, and received strong support during and after the launch from the firm and its branches; further, the firm had a good understanding of its customers' purchase decision behavior.
2. *Organizational factors.* There was strong interfunctional cooperation and coordination; development personnel were fully aware of why they were involved and of the importance of new products to the company.
3. *Market research factors.* Detailed and scientifically designed market research studies were conducted early in the development process, with a clear idea of the type of information to be obtained; a good definition of the product concept was developed before field surveys were undertaken.

Another survey of financial service firms to determine what distinguished successful from unsuccessful products yielded similar findings.[23] In this instance, the key factors underlying success were determined as *synergy* (the fit between the product and the firm in terms of needed expertise and resources being present) and *internal marketing* (the support given to staff prior to launch to help them understand the new product and its underlying systems, plus details about direct competitors, and support).

Courtyard by Marriott's success in a very different industry—a people processing service with many tangible components—supports the notion that a highly structured development process will increase the chances of success for a complex service innovation. However, it's worth noting that there may be limits to the degree of structure that can and should be imposed. Swedish researchers Bo Edwardsson, Lars Haglund, and and Jan Mattson reviewed new service development in telecommunications, transport, and financial services. They concluded that:

> [C]omplex processes like the development of new services cannot be formally planned altogether. Creativity and innovation cannot only rely on planning and control. There must be some elements of improvization, anarchy, and internal competition in the development of new services. . . . We believe that a contingency approach is needed and that creativity on the one hand and formal planning and control on the other can be balanced, with successful new services as the outcome.[24]

An important conclusion from subsequent research in Sweden concerns the role of customers in service innovation. Researchers found that at the idea-generation stage, the quality of ideas submitted differed significantly depending on whether they were created by professional service developers or by the users themselves. Users' ideas were judged to be more original and and to have a higher perceived value to customers. However, on average, these ideas were harder to convert into commercial services.[25]

CONCLUSION

A service concept consists of a core product bundled with a variety of supplementary service elements. The core product responds to the customer's need for a basic benefit, such as transportation to a specific location, resolution of a specific health problem, or repair of malfunctioning equipment. Supplementary services are those elements that facilitate and enhance use of the core service. They range from provision of needed information and advice to taking a reservation, offering hospitality to customers, and billing.

Designing a service concept is a complex task that requires an understanding of how the core and supplementary services should be combined, sequenced, delivered, and scheduled to create a value proposition that meets the needs of target market segments. Flowcharting, a technique for displaying the nature and sequence of the different steps involved in delivering service to customers, offers a way to understand the totality of the customer's service experience.

Different types of core products often share use of similar supplementary elements. The "flower of service" concept categorizes supplementary services into eight groups (each represented as a petal surrounding the core). The eight groups are information, consultation, order taking, hospitality, safekeeping, exceptions, billing, and payment. The flower analogy can help us to understand the need for consistent performance on all supplementary elements, so that a weakness in one element doesn't spoil the overall impression. Because supplementary elements are often common to several industries, managers should be studying businesses outside their own industries in a search for "best-in-class" performers on specific supplementary services.

Many firms create several service concepts with different performance attributes and brand each package with a distinctive name. However, unless each of these subbrands offers and fulfills a meaningful value proposition, this strategy is not likely to be effective against the competition.

Although innovation is central to effective marketing, major service innovations are relatively rare. More common is the use of new technologies, such as the Internet, to deliver existing services in new ways. In mature industries, in which the core service may become a commodity, the search for competitive advantage often centers on creating new supplementary services or significantly improving performance on existing ones. The chances of success for a new service concept increase when it fits well with the firm's expertise, resources, and existing image; provides a superior advantage over competing services in terms of meeting customers' needs; and is well supported by coordinated efforts among the different functional areas.

REVIEW QUESTIONS

1. Explain the role of supplementary services. Can they be applied to goods as well as services? If so, how might they relate to marketing strategy?
2. How does flowcharting help us to understand:
   (a) The differences between people processing services, possession processing services, mental stimulus processing services, and information processing services?
   (b) The nature and role of the supplementary services accompanying a core product?
3. Explain the distinction between enhancing and facilitating supplementary services. Give several examples of each, citing services that you have used recently.
4. How is branding used in services marketing? What is the distinction between a corporate brand such as

Marriott and the names of its various inn and hotel chains?
5. What does British Airways gain from using such subbrand names as Club World or Euro Traveller? What not just use business class and economy class?
6. Explain the "flower of service" concept and identify each of the petals. What insights does this concept provide for service marketers?
7. What is the purpose of techniques such as conjoint analysis in designing new services?
8. Why do new services often fail? What factors are associated with successful development of new services?

APPLICATION EXERCISES

1. Identify some real-world examples of branding in financial services, such as specific types of retail bank accounts or insurance policies, and define their characteristics. How meaningful are these brands likely to be to customers?

2. Choose a service with which you are familiar and create a simple flowchart for it. Define the front-stage and backstage activities.

ENDNOTES

1. G. Lynn Shostack, "Breaking Free from Product Marketing." *Journal of Marketing*, 44 (April 1977): 73–80.
2. Pierre Eiglier and Eric Langeard, "Services as Systems: Marketing Implications," in P. Eiglier, E. Langeard, C. H. Lovelock, J. E. G. Bateson, and R. F. Young, *Marketing Consumer Services: New Insights.* Cambridge, MA: Marketing Science Institute, 1977,

pp. 83–103. Note: An earlier version of this article was published in French in *Révue Française de Gestion* (March–April 1977): 72–84.
3. Christian Grönroos, *Service Management and Marketing.* Lexington, MA: Lexington Books, 1990, p. 74.
4. Richard B. Chase and Sriram Dasu, "Want to Perfect Your Company's Service? Use Behavioral Science." *Harvard Business Review,* 79 (June 2001): 79–84.

5. The "flower of service" concept presented in this section was first introduced in Christopher H. Lovelock, "Cultivating the Flower of Service: New Ways of Looking at Core and Supplementary Services," in P. Eiglier and E. Langeard (eds.), *Marketing, Operations, and Human Resources: Insights into Services.* Aix-en-Provence, France: IAE, Université d'Aix-Marseille III, 1992, pp. 296–316.

6. Loizos Heracleous, Jochen Wirtz, and Nitin Pangarkar, *Flying High: Cost Effective Service Excellence—Lessons from Singapore Airlines.* Singapore: McGraw Hill, 2006.

7. James C. Anderson and James A. Narus, "Capturing the Value of Supplementary Services," Harvard Business Review, 73 (January–February 1995): 75–83.

8. James Devlin, "Brand Architecture in Services: The Example of Retail Financial Services." *Journal of Marketing Management,* 19 (2003): 1043–1065.

9. David Aaker and E. Joachimsthaler, "The Brand Relationship Spectrum: The Key to the Brand Challenge." *California Management Review,* 42, no. 4 (2000), 8-23.

10. Weizhong Jiang, Chekitan S. Dev, and Vithala R. Rao, "Brand Extension and Customer Loyalty: Evidence from the Lodging Industry." *Cornell Hotel and Restaurant Administration Quarterly,* (August 2002): 5–16.

11. www.sun.com/service/support/sunspectrum, accessed Janaury 2, 2006.

12. Joe Wheeler and Shaun Smith, *Managing the Experience.* Upper Saddle River, NJ: Prentice Hall, 2003.

13. Don E. Shultz, "Getting to the Heart of the Brand." *Marketing Management,* (September–October 2001): 8–9.

14. See James Traub, "Drive-Thru U." *The New Yorker,* October 20 and 27, 1997; and Joshua Macht, "Virtual You." *Inc. Magazine,* January 1998, pp. 84–87.

15. Chad Rubel, "New Menu for Restaurants: Talking Trees and Blackjack." *Marketing News,* July 29, 1996, p. 1.

16. See, for example, Michael Hammer and James Champy, *Reengineering the Corporation.* New York: HarperBusiness, 1993.

17. Michael Arndt, "Cat Sinks Its Claws into Services" *Business Week,* December 5, 2005, pp. 56–58.

18. Clayton M. Christenson, Scott Cook, and Taddy Hall, "Marketing Malpractice: The Cause and the Cure." *Harvard Business Review,* (December 2005): 4–12.

19. H. T. Parsa, John T. Self, David Njite, and Tiffany King, "Why Restaurants Fail." *Cornell Hotel and Restaurant Administration Quarterly,* 46 (August 2005): 304–322.

20. Chris D. Storey and Christopher J. Easingwood, "The Augmented Service Offering: A Conceptualization and Study of Its Impact on New Service Success." *Journal of Product Innovation Management,* 15 (1998): 335–351.

21. Stephen S. Tax and Ian Stuart, "Designing and Implementing New Services: The Challenges of Integrating Service Systems." *Journal of Retailing,* 73, no. 1 (1997): 105–134.

22. Scott Edgett and Steven Parkinson, "The Development of New Financial Services: Identifying Determinants of Success and Failure." *International Journal of Service Industry Management,* 5, no. 4 (1994): 24–38.

23. Christopher Storey and Christopher Easingwood, "The Impact of the New Product Development Project on the Success of Financial Services." *Service Industries Journal,* 13, no. 3 (July 1993): 40–54.

24. Bo Edvardsson, Lars Haglund, and Jan Mattsson, "Analysis, Planning, Improvisation and Control in the Development of New Services." *International Journal of Service Industry Management,* 6, no. 2 (1995): 24–35 (at page 34). See also Bo Edvardsson and Jan Olsson, "Key Concepts for New Service Development." *The Service Industries Journal,* 16 (April 1996): 14–164.

25. Peter R. Magnusson, Jonas Matthing, and Per Kristensson, "Managing User Involvement in Service Innovation: Experiments with Innovating End Users." *Journal of Service Research,* 6 (November 2003): 111–124; Jonas Matthing, Bodil Sandén, and Bo Edvardsson, "New Service Development: Learning from and with Customers." *International Journal of Service Industry Management,* 15, no. 5 (2004): 479–498.

Chapter 4

Distributing Services Through Physical and Electronic Channels

Companies best equipped for the twenty-first century will consider investment in real time systems as essential to maintaining their competitive edge and keeping their customers.

REGIS MCKENNA

Think globally, act locally.

JOHN NAISBITT

An important part of the service model is the distribution of core and supplementary service elements through selected physical and electronic channels. Delivering a service to customers involves decisions about where, when, and how. The rapid growth of the Internet and broadband mobile communications means that service marketing strategies must address issues of *Place and time*, paying at least as much attention to speed, scheduling, and electronic access as to the more traditional notion of physical location. Furthermore, in the heat of globalization, important questions are being raised concerning the design and implementation of international service marketing strategies.

In this chapter, we discuss the role that delivery plays in service marketing strategies both locally and globally, and explore the following questions:

1. How can services be distributed? What are the main modes of distribution?
2. What are the distinctive challenges of distributing people processing services, possession processing services, and information-based services?

3. What are the implications for a firm of delivering through both physical and electronic channels?
4. What roles should intermediaries play in distributing services?
5. What are the drivers of globalization of services and their distribution?

DISTRIBUTION IN A SERVICES CONTEXT

If you mention distribution, many people are likely to think of moving boxes through physical channels to distributors and retailers for sale to end users. In services, though, there's often nothing to move. Experiences, performances, and solutions are not physically shipped and stored. Meanwhile, informational transactions are increasingly conducted via electronic channels. How, then, does distribution work in a services context? In a typical sales cycle, distribution embraces three interrelated elements:

- *Information and promotion flow:* distribution of information and promotion materials relating to the service offer. The objective is to get the customer interested in buying the service.
- *Negotiation flow:* reaching an agreement on the service features and configuration, and the terms of the offer, so that a purchase contract can be closed. The objective is to sell the *right* to use a service (e.g., sell a reservation or a ticket).
- *Product flow:* Many services, especially those involving people processing or possession processing, require physical facilities for delivery. Here, distribution strategy requires development of a network of local sites. For information-processing services, such as Internet banking, distance learning, broadcast news, and entertainment, the product flow can be undertaken via electronic channels, employing one or more centralized sites.

Distinguishing Between Distribution of Supplementary and Core Services

Distribution can relate to the core service as well to supplementary services. That's an important distinction, as many core services require a physical location, which severely restricts distribution For instance, you can only consume Club Med holidays at Club Med Villages, and a live performance of a Broadway show must take place at a theater in Manhattan (until it goes on tour). However, many supplementary services are informational in nature and can be distributed widely and cost-effectively via other means. Prospective Club Med customers can get information and consultation from a travel agent, either face to face, online, by phone, or even by mail, and then make a booking through one of these same channels. In similar fashion, you can purchase theater tickets through an agency without the need for an advance trip to the physical facility itself.

When you look at the eight petals of the "flower of service," you can see that no fewer than five supplementary services are information-based (Figure 4.1). Information, consultation, order taking, billing, and payment (e.g., via credit card) can all be transmitted using the digital language of computers. Even service businesses that involve physical core products, such as retailing and repair, are shifting delivery of many supplementary services to the Internet, closing physical branches, and relying on speedy business logistics to enable a new strategy of arm's-length transactions with their customers.

The distribution of information, consultation, and order taking (or reservations and ticket sales) has reached extremely sophisticated levels in some global service industries, requiring a number of carefully integrated channels targeted at key customer segments. For instance, Starwood Hotels & Resorts Worldwide—whose 725 hotels include such brands as Sheraton, Westin, and St. Regis—has more than 30

Figure 4.1
Information and Physical Processes of the Augmented Service Product

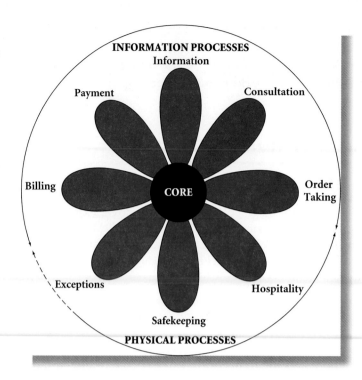

global sales offices (GSOs) around the world to manage customer relationships with key global accounts, offering a one-stop solution to corporate travel planners, wholesalers, meeting planners, incentive houses, and major travel organizations.[1] The company has also set up 12 customer servicing centers (CSCs) around the world to provide one-stop customer service for its guests, covering worldwide hotel reservations, enrolment and redemption of Starwood's loyalty program, and general customer service. You only need to call one toll-free number to book any Starwood hotel. Alternatively, you can reserve rooms through electronic channels, including the Westin and Sheraton web sites.

DETERMINING THE TYPE OF CONTACT: OPTIONS FOR SERVICE DELIVERY

Decisions on where, when, and how to deliver service have important effects on the nature of customers' service experiences. They determine the types of encounters (if any) with service personnel, and the price and other costs incurred to obtain the service.

Several factors shape distribution and delivery strategies. A key question is whether the nature of the service or the firm's positioning strategy requires customers to be in direct physical contact with its personnel, equipment, and facilities. (As we saw in Chapter 2, this is inevitable for people processing services, but optional for other categories.) If so, do customers have to visit the facilities of the service organization, or will the latter send personnel and equipment to customers' own sites? Alternatively, can transactions between provider and customer be completed at arm's length through the use of either telecommunications or physical channels of distribution?

Distribution Options for Serving Customers

Another issue concerns the firm's strategy in terms of distribution sites. As shown in Table 4.1, there are six possible options. Should it expect customers to come to a company site? Or should service personnel go to visit customers at their own locations? Alternatively, can service be delivered remotely, without either side having to meet?

Table 4.1
Six Options for
Service Delivery

NATURE OF INTERACTION BETWEEN CUSTOMER AND SERVICE ORGANIZATION	AVAILABILITY OF SERVICE OUTLETS	
	SINGLE SITE	MULTIPLE SITES
Customer goes to service organization	Theater Barbershop	Bus service Fast-food chain
Service organization comes to customer	House painting Mobile car wash	Mail delivery Auto club road service
Customer and service organization transact remotely (mail or electronic communications)	Credit card company Local TV station	Broadcast network Telephone company

And for each of these three options, should the firm maintain just a single outlet or offer to serve customers through multiple outlets at different locations?

Customers Visit the Service Site

The convenience of service factory locations and operational schedules assume great importance when a customer has to be physically present—either throughout service delivery or even just to initiate and terminate the transaction. Elaborate statistical analysis, in the form of retail gravity models, is sometimes used to aid decisions on where to locate supermarkets and similar large stores relative to prospective customers' homes and workplaces. Traffic counts and pedestrian counts help to establish how many prospective customers pass by certain locations in a day. Construction of an expressway or the introduction of a new bus or rail service may have a significant effect on travel patterns and, in turn, determine which sites are now more desirable and which are less so.

The tradition of having customers visit the service site for services that don't involve people processing is now being challenged by advances in telecommunications and business logistics. The result is increased availability of services delivered at arm's length.

Service Providers Go to Their Customers

For some types of services, the supplier visits the customer. Aramark, which provides food services to a wide array of customers, from schools and hospitals to sports stadiums and prisons, must necessarily bring its equipment, food products, and personnel to the customer's site, because the need is location-specific. In fact, going to the customer's site is unavoidable whenever the object of the service is some immovable physical item, such as a tree to be pruned, installed machinery to be repaired, or a house that requires pest control treatment.

In other instances, going to the customer is optional. Because it's more expensive and time-consuming for the service provider to send personnel and their equipment to the customer than vice versa, the trend has been toward requiring customers to come to the service provider instead (few doctors make house calls nowadays!). In remote areas such as Alaska or Canada's Northwest Territories, service providers often fly to visit their customers, because the latter find it so difficult to travel. Australia is famous for its Royal Flying Doctor Service, whose physicians fly into farms and sheep stations in the Outback.

In general, service providers are more likely to visit corporate customers at their premises than to visit individuals in their homes, reflecting the larger volume associated with business-to-business transactions. However, there may be a profitable niche in serving individuals who are willing to pay a premium for the convenience of receiving personal visits. One young veterinarian has built her business around making house calls to sick pets. She has found that customers are glad to pay extra for a service that not only saves them time, but is also less stressful for their pets than waiting in a crowded veterinary clinic, full of other nervous animals and their worried owners.

Other consumer services of this nature include mobile car washing, office and in-home catering, and made-to-measure tailoring services for business people.

A growing category of services involves the rental of both equipment and labor for special occasions or in response to customers who need to expand their productive capacity during busy periods. Service Perspectives 4.1 describes the business-to-business services of Aggreko, an international company that rents generating and cooling equipment around the world.

SERVICE PERSPECTIVES 4.1
Power and Temperature Control for Rent

You probably think of electricity as coming from a distant power station and of air conditioning and heating as fixed installations. So how would you deal with the following challenges?

- Luciano Pavarotti, the famous tenor, is giving an open-air concert in Münster, Germany, and the organizers require an uninterruptible source of electrical power for the duration of the concert, independent of the local electricity supply.

- A tropical cyclone has devastated the small mining town of Pannawonica in Western Australia, destroying everything in its path, including power lines, and electrical power must be restored as soon as possible so that the town and its infrastructure can be rebuilt.

- In Amsterdam, organizers of the World Championship Indoor Windsurfing competition need to power 27 wind turbines that will be installed along the length of a huge indoor pool to create winds of 20 to 30 mph (32 to 48 km/h).

- A U.S. Navy submarine needs a shore-based source of power when when it is docked at a remote Norwegian port.

- Sri Lanka faces an acute shortage of electricity-generating capability after water levels fall dangerously low at major hydroelectric dams, a result of insufficient monsoon rains two years in a row.

- Hotels in Florida need to be dried out following water damage during a hurricane.

- A large power-generating plant in Oklahoma urgently seeks temporary capacity to replace one of its cooling towers, destroyed in a tornado the previous day.

- The Caribbean island of Bonaire requires a temporary power station to stabilize its grid after fire damages the main power plant and results in widespread blackouts.

These are all challenges that have been faced and met by a company called Aggreko, which describes itself as "The World Leader in Temporary Utility Rental Solutions." Aggreko operates from more than 100 depots in 28 countries worldwide, using more than $1 billion of rental equipment to serve customers in 60 countries. It rents a "fleet" of mobile electricity generators, oil-free air compressors, and temperature-control devices ranging from water chillers and industrial air conditioners to giant heaters and dehumidifiers.

Aggreko's customer base is dominated by large companies and government agencies. Although much of its business comes from predicted needs, such as backup operations during planned factory maintenance or the filming of a James Bond movie, the firm is poised to resolve problems that arise unexpectedly from emergencies or natural disasters.

Much of the firm's rental equipment is contained in soundproofed, boxlike structures that can be shipped anywhere in the world to create the specific type and level of electrical power output or climate-control capability required by the client. Consultation, installation, and ongoing technical support add value to the core service. Emphasis is placed on solving customer problems rather than just renting equipment. Some customers have a clear idea of their needs in advance, others require advice on how to develop innovative and cost-effective solutions to what may be unique problems, and still others are desperate to restore power that has been lost because of an unexpected disaster. In the last-mentioned instance, speed is essential, because downtime can be extremely expensive and lives may depend on the promptness of Aggreko's response.

Delivering service requires Aggreko to ship its equipment to the customer's site. Following the Pannawonica cyclone, Aggreko's West Australian team swung into action, rapidly dispatching some 30 generators ranging in size from 60 to 750 kVA, plus cabling, refueling tankers, and other equipment. The generators were transported by means of four "road trains," each comprising a giant tractor unit hauling three 40-ft (13-m) trailers. Technicians and additional equipment were flown in on two Hercules aircraft. The Aggreko technicians remained on site for six weeks, providing 24/7 service while the town was being rebuilt.

Sources: Adapted from Aggreko's "International Magazine," 1997, www.aggreko.com, accessed May 2006.

The Service Transaction Is Conducted Remotely

When you deal with a service firm through remote transactions, you may never see the service facilities or meet service personnel face to face. There tend to be fewer service encounters, and those encounters that you do have with service personnel are more likely to be made via a call center or, even more remotely, by mail or email.

Repair services for small pieces of equipment sometimes require customers to ship the product to a maintenance facility, where it is serviced and then returned. Many service providers offer solutions with the help of integrated logistics firms such as FedEx or UPS. These solutions range from storage and express delivery of spare parts for aircraft (B2B delivery) to pickup of defective mobile phones from customers' homes and subsequent return of the repaired phone to the customer (B2C pickup and delivery). Any information-based product can be delivered almost instantaneously through the Internet to almost any point in the world. As a result, physical logistics services are now competing with telecommunications services.

Channel Preferences Vary Among Consumers

The use of different channels to deliver the same service not only has different cost implications for a service organization; it also dramatically affects the nature of the service experience for the customer—banking services, for instance, can be delivered remotely via computer or mobile phone, a voice response system, a call center, and automatic teller machines; or face to face in a branch, or, in the case of private banking. through a direct visit to a wealthy customer's home. Recent research has explored how customers choose among personal, impersonal and self-service channels and has identified the following key drivers:[2]

- For complex and high-perceived-risk services, people tend to rely on personal channels. For example, customers are happy to apply for credit cards using remote channels, but prefer a face-to-face transaction when obtaining a mortgage.
- Individuals with greater confidence and knowledge about a service and/or the channel are more likely to use impersonal and self-service channels.
- Customers who look for the instrumental aspects of a transaction prefer more convenience, and this often means the use of impersonal and self-service channels. Customers with social motives tend to use personal channels.
- Convenience is a key driver of channel choice for the majority of consumers. Service convenience means saving time and effort rather than saving money. A customer's search for convenience is not just confined to the purchase of core products but also extends to convenient times and places. People want easy access to supplementary services, too—especially information, reservations, and problem solving.

Service providers have to be careful when channels are priced differently—increasingly, sophisticated customers take advantage of price variations among channels and markets, a strategy known as arbritraging.[3] For example, customers can ask the expensive full-service broker for advice (and perhaps place a small order) and then conduct the bulk of their trades via the much lower-priced discount broker. Service providers need to develop effective strategies that will enable them to deliver value and capture it through the appropriate channel.

PLACE AND TIME DECISIONS

How should service managers make decisions on the places where service is delivered and the times when it is available? The answer: Start by understanding customer needs and expectations, competitive activity, and the nature of the service operation. As we noted earlier, the distribution strategies employed for some supplementary service elements may differ from those used to deliver the core product itself. For instance, as a customer, you're probably willing to go to a particular location at a specific time to attend a sporting or entertainment event. But you probably want greater flexibility and convenience when reserving a seat in advance, so you may expect the reservations service to be open for extended hours, to offer booking and credit card payment by phone or the Web, and to deliver tickets through postal or electronic channels.

Where Should Service Be Delivered in a Bricks-and-Mortar Context?

Deciding where to locate a service facility for customers involves very different considerations from locating the backstage elements, where cost, productivity and access to labor are often key determinants. In the first instance, customer convenience and preference are key. Firms should make it should be easy for people to access frequently purchased services facing active competition.[4] Examples include retail banks and fast-food restaurants. However, customers may be willing to travel farther from their homes or workplaces to reach specialty services.

Locational Constraints

Although customer convenience is important, operational requirements set tight constraints for some services. Airports, for instance, are often inconveniently located relative to travelers' homes, offices, or destinations. Because of noise and environmental

People Get Upset When Electronic Distribution Systems Let Them Down

Reprinted from Christopher Lovelock, *Product Plus* (New York: McGraw-Hill, 1994), 283. Copyright © Christopher H. Lovelock 1994.

factors, finding suitable sites for construction of new airports or expansion of existing ones is a very difficult task. (A governor of Massachusetts was once asked what would be an acceptable location for a second airport to serve Boston; he thought for a moment and then responded, "Nebraska!") One way to make airport access more convenient is to install fast rail links, such as San Francisco's BART service, London's Heathrow Express, or the futuristic 260-mph (420-km/h) service to Shanghai's new airport, the first in the world to use magnetic levitation technology. A different type of location constraint is imposed by other geographic factors, such as terrain and climate. By definition, ski resorts have to be in the mountains and ocean beach resorts on the coast.

The need for economies of scale is another operational issue that may restrict choice of locations. Major hospitals offer many different health care services at a single location, requiring a very large facility. Customers requiring complex, in-patient treatment must go to the service factory, rather than be treated at home. However, an ambulance—or even a helicopter—can be sent to pick them up. Medical specialists, as opposed to general practitioners, often find it convenient to locate their offices close to a hospital because it saves them time when they need to treat their patients.

Ministores

An interesting innovation among multisite service businesses involves creating numerous small service factories to maximize geographic coverage. Automated kiosks represent one approach. ATMs offer many of the functions of a bank branch within a compact, self-service machine that can be located within stores, hospitals, colleges, airports, and office buildings. Another approach results from separating the front and back stages of the operation. Taco Bell's innovative K-Minus strategy involves restaurants without kitchens.[5] Food preparation takes place in a central commissary from which meals are shipped to restaurants (which can now devote more of their expensive floor-area to customer use) and to other "points of access" (such as mobile food carts), where the food can be reheated before serving.

Increasingly, firms offering one type of service business are purchasing space from another provider in a complementary field. Perhaps you've noticed small bank branches inside supermarkets, and food outlets such as Dunkin' Donuts and Subway sharing space with a fast-food restaurant such as Burger King.

Locating in Multipurpose Facilities

The most obvious locations for consumer services are close to where customers live or work. Modern buildings are often designed to be multipurpose, featuring not only office or production space but also such services as a bank (or at least an ATM), a restaurant, a hair salon, several stores, and maybe a health club. Some companies even include a children's day care facility to make life easier for busy working parents.

Interest is growing in siting retail and other services on transportation routes and in bus, rail, and air terminals. With many domestic airlines in the United States either abandoning on-board food service on short flights or charging for meals on longer flights, entrepreneurs now staff small retail stands in airport concourses, selling passengers packaged salads, sandwiches, and beverages before they board their flights. Most major oil companies have developed chains of retail stores to complement the fuel pumps at their service stations, thus offering customers the convenience of one-stop shopping for fuel, vehicle supplies, food, and a selection of basic household products. Truckstops on major highways often include laundry centers, toilets, ATMs, Internet access, restaurants, and inexpensive accommodation, in addition to a variety of vehicle maintenance and repair services. In one of the most interesting new retailing developments, airport terminals—designed as part of the infrastructure for

Large airports used to be places where thousands of people spent time waiting with little to keep them occupied. Airports were often bound by contract to a single food operator, which translated into low-quality food at high prices. Other than visiting stores selling newspapers, magazines, and paperback books, there wasn't much opportunity for travelers to shop unless they wanted to spend money on expensive (and often tawdry) souvenirs. The one exception was the tax-free shop at international airports, where opportunities to save money created a brisk trade in alcohol, perfumes, tobacco, and consumer products such as cameras. Today, however, some airports have terminals that have been transformed into shopping malls. London's Heathrow Airport even has a branch of Harrods, the famous department store.

Three factors make investments in airport retailing very appealing. One is the upscale demographics of airline passengers, whose numbers continue to grow rapidly. A second is that many passengers have time to spare while waiting for their flights. Tighter security requirements mean that passengers must now check in very early for their flights. Finally, many existing terminal interiors have free space that can be put to profitable use. As terminals are expanded, new retail sites can be included as an integral part of the design.

The first (and still the most successful) custom-built airport retail complex in the United States is the Pittsburgh AIRMALL, created as part of a new airport terminal and operated under a 15-year contract by BAA International, the largest global airport operator. Pittsburgh is an important hub airport serving more than 14 million passengers a year, most whom are domestic travelers. Goods and services available in the AIRMALL's more than 100 stores and restaurants range from tasty take-out sandwiches for passengers who don't expect a meal on their discount-priced flight to $15 massages for tired travelers with aching backs. Perhaps the most striking statistic is that sales per square foot are four to five times those of typical U.S. regional shopping centers.

BAA also operates long-term retail contracts at Baltimore-Washington and Boston's Logan Airport in the United States as well as at seven airports in the United Kingdom. It has equity investments in six Australian airports and one in Naples, Italy.

Source: BAA International, www.baa.com, accessed May 2006.

air transportation services—are being transformed into vibrant shopping malls—a big change from the nondescript areas where passengers and their bags used to be processed (see Service Perspectives 4.2).

When Should Service Be Delivered?

In the past, most retail and professional services in industrialized countries followed a traditional schedule of being available about 40 or 50 hours a week. In large measure, this routine reflected social norms (and even legal requirements or union agreements) as to what were appropriate hours for people to work and for enterprises to sell things. The situation inconvenienced working people, who had to shop either during their lunch break or on Saturdays. Historically, Sunday opening was strongly discouraged in most Christian cultures and was often prohibited by law, reflecting a long tradition based on religious practice.

Today, the situation has changed. For some highly responsive service operations, the standard has become 24/7 service—24 hours a day, 7 days a week, around the world. (For an overview of the factors behind the move to more extended hours, see Service Perspective 4.3.) Some firms, however, have resisted the trend to seven-day operations. Atlanta-based Chick-fil-A, a highly successful restaurant chain, declares that "being closed on Sunday is part of our value proposition" and claims that giving managers and crews a day off is a factor in the firm's extremely low turnover rate.

At least five factors are driving the move toward extended operating hours and seven-day operations. This trend, which originated in the United States, has since spread to many other countries around the world.

- **Economic pressure from consumers.** The growing number of two-income families and single wage earners who live alone need time outside normal working hours to shop and use other services. Once one store or firm in any given area extends its hours to meet the needs of these market segments, competitors often feel obliged to follow. Chain stores have often led the way.

- **Changes in legislation.** Support has declined for the traditional religious view that a specific day (Sunday in predominantly Christian cultures) should be legislated as a day of rest for one and all, regardless of religious affiliation. In a multicultural society, of course, it's a moot point which day should be designated as special—for observant Jews and Seventh Day Adventists, Saturday is the Sabbath; for Muslims, Friday is the holy day; and agnostics or atheists are presumably indifferent. There has been a gradual erosion of such legislation in Western nations in recent years.

- **Economic incentives to improve asset utilization.** A great deal of capital is often tied up in service facilities. The incremental cost of extending hours is often relatively modest, and if it reduces crowding and increases revenues, then it is economically attractive. There are costs involved in shutting down and reopening a facility such as a supermarket, yet climate control and some lighting must be left running all night, and security personnel must be paid 24/7. So, even if the number of extra customers served is minimal, there are both operational and marketing advantages to remaining open 24 hours a day.

- **Availability of employees to work during "unsocial" hours.** Changing lifestyles and a desire for part-time employment have created a growing labor pool of people who are willing to work evenings and nights. They include students looking for part-time work outside classroom hours, people working a second job, parents juggling child care responsibilities, and others who simply prefer to work by night and relax or sleep by day.

- **Automated self-service facilities.** Self-service equipment has become increasingly reliable and user-friendly. Many machines now accept card-based payments in addition to coins and banknotes. Installing unattended machines may be economically feasible alternative for locations that cannot support a staffed facility. Unless a machine requires frequent servicing or is particularly vulnerable to vandalism, the incremental cost of going from limited hours to 24-hour operation is minimal. In fact, it may be simpler to leave machines running continuously than to turn them on and off.

DELIVERING SERVICES IN CYBERSPACE

Developments in telecommunications and computer technology have spurred many new approaches to service delivery. In the hospitality industry, for instance, reservations are increasingly handled via firms' web sites. For example, Swissôtel Hotels & Resorts executed an entire campaign to increase online bookings, especially among the important business traveler segment. Within seven months of launch in early 2005, its revamped web site (www.swissotel.com) more than doubled online revenues.[6] Apart from the enhanced express reservation functions (with fewer "clicks"), user-friendly navigation, and online promotions and incentives, the hotel company's "Best Rate Guarantee" was a key driver of its success. Guests booking via its web site were guaranteed the best rate for their booking. If they found another web site with a lower rate, Swissôtel not only matched this rate, it also offered an additional 50 percent discount on the first night of the guest's stay. The guarantee gave customers peace of mind. Swissôtel's logo (see Figure 4.2) now includes its web site address to drive its guests toward online reservations and services.

Of course, not all customers like to use self-service equipment, so migration of customers to new electronic channels may require different strategies for different segments,[7] as well as recognition that some proportion of customers will never shift voluntarily from their preferred high-contact delivery environments. An alternative that appeals to many people, perhaps because it uses a familiar technology, is conducting

Figure 4.2
Swissôtel's Logo
Incorporates Its Web
Site Address.

Courtesy of Swissôtel.

banking and other service transactions by voice telephone. However, automated phone services can be another matter. How do you feel about voicemail transactions, with their sometimes lengthy messages promoting other services, trying to drive you to the company's web site, and then, if you persist, requiring you to "press 1" for this and "press 7" for that several times before you finally reach the transaction you actually want to make?

Service Delivery Innovations Facilitated by Technology

More recently, entrepreneurs have taken advantage of the Internet to create new services. Four innovations of particular interest are

- Development of "smart" mobile telephones and PDAs (personal digital assistants), and Wi-Fi high-speed Internet technology that can link users to the Internet wherever they may be.
- Usage of voice-recognition technology that allows customers to give information and request service simply by speaking into a phone or microphone.
- Creation of web sites that provide information, take orders, and even serve as a delivery channel for information-based services.
- Commercialization of "smart cards" containing a microchip that can store detailed information about the customer and act as an electronic purse containing digital money. The ultimate in self-service banking will be when you can not only use a smart card as an electronic wallet for a wide array of transactions, but also refill it from a special card reader connected to your PC.

Singly or in combination, electronic channels offer a complement or alternative to traditional physical channels for delivering information-based services. Best Practice in Action 4.1 describes a multichannel application for electronic banking.

e-Commerce: The Move to Cyberspace

As a distribution channel, the Internet facilitates five categories of "flow": *information, negotiation, service, transactions,* and *promotion.* Compared to traditional channels, it's better able to help researchers collect data on consumer information-seeking and search behaviors, obtain feedback quickly from consumers, and create online communities to help market goods and services.[8]

Amazon.com pioneered the concept of the virtual store, but now there are thousands of them all over the world. Among the factors luring customers into virtual stores are convenience, ease of search (obtaining information and searching for desired items or services), a broader selection, and the potential for better prices. Enjoying 24/7 service with prompt delivery is particularly appealing to customers whose busy lives leave them short of time (see Service Perspectives 4.4). Think about the products that you, your family, and friends have purchased lately through the Internet. Why did you select this channel in preference to alternative forms of service delivery?

Many retailers, such as the giant bookstore chain Barnes and Noble, have developed a strong Internet presence to complement their physical stores, in an effort to

First Direct, a division of HSBC, a large global bank, has become famous as the originator of the concept of a retail bank without branches. By mid-2006, it was serving more than 1.2 million customers throughout the United Kingdom (and abroad) through call centers located far from the financial powerhouses of London, a web site, text messaging on mobile phones, and access to HSBC's large network of ATMs.

In January 2000, First Direct—by that time describing itself as "the largest virtual bank in the world"—announced that it would transform itself into an e-bank and set the standard for e-banking. At the heart of the strategy is a multichannel approach to banking that combines First Direct's telephone banking experience with the strengths of the Internet and the versatility of mobile phone technologies to deliver a superior service at fiercely competitive prices. As noted by chief executive Alan Hughes: "We are the first bank in the world to reengineer our entire business for the e-age. The scale of the initiative creates a new category of e-banking and sets a benchmark for the industry around the globe. More than a bank, first-direct.com will be the first Internet banking store."

By 2006, three-fourths of all customer contact with First Direct was electronic and 40 percent of sales were via e-channels. Some 840,000 customers were using Internet banking and 460,000 used SMS (short message service) text messaging. The bank sent out some 3.5 million text messages a month.

A central element in this strategy is to offer Britain's most comprehensive mobile phone banking service, recognizing that almost all adults in the UK either own or use a mobile phone. Through SMS text messages, First Direct customers have access to ministatements on up to three accounts and can be advised when credits or debits enter or leave the account. In addition, they are alerted automatically if their accounts go into the red.

Although person-to-person voice telephone still remains the backbone of the bank's relationship with its customers, in August 2005 the bank launched a new Webchat service, enabling customers to "talk" with banking reps through a keyboard and mouse rather than by phone. It promotes this service as offering the immediacy of a phone conversation with the convenience of email.

Is this nontraditional strategy working? The evidence suggests a resounding "yes." In 2002, an independent global survey of 25,000 customers of financial organizations worldwide found that, among all banks surveyed, First Direct had the greatest proportion of customers prepared to recommend their own bank. Despite intense competition among British banks and the costs of continued investment in technology, First Direct has been profitable since 1995. Every year since 1993, it has been both the most recommended bank in the United Kingdom and, by a very wide margin, the one with the most satisfied customers.

Source: Anne-Marie Cagna and Jean-Claude Larréché, "First Direct 2005: The Most Recommended Bank in the World." Fontainebleau, France: INSEAD, 2005; press releases distributed on www.firstdirect.com/press/key, accessed May 2006.

counter competition from "cyberspace retailers" such as Amazon.com, which has no stores. However, adding an Internet channel to an established physical channel is a double-edged strategy. It requires high capital setup costs, and no one can be sure whether the investment will lead to long-term profits and high growth.[9]

Web sites are becoming increasingly sophisticated, but also more user-friendly. They often simulate the services of a well-informed sales assistant in steering customers toward items that are likely to be of interest. Some even provide the opportunity for "live" email dialog with helpful customer service personnel. Facilitating searches is another useful service on many sites, ranging from looking at what books are available by a particular author to finding schedules of flights between two cities on a specific date.

Particularly exciting are recent developments that link web sites, customer relationship management (CRM) systems, and mobile telephony. Integrating mobile devices into the service delivery infrastructure can be used as a means to (1) *access* services, (2) *alert* customers to opportunities or problems by delivering the right information or interaction at the right time, and (3) *update* information in real time to ensure that it is continuously accurate and relevant.[10] For example, customers can set stock alerts on their broker's web site and get an email or SMS alert when a certain price level is reached (or breached), or a particular transaction has been conducted, or they can obtain real-time information on stock prices. Customers can respond by accessing the brokerage and trade directly by voice or via an SMS interface, as they prefer.

In a test of comparative shopping speed, *The Wall Street Journal* sent two reporters on a mission on America's busiest shopping day of the year, the day after Thanksgiving (retailers call it Black Friday, because it puts them in the black for the year!). Each had a budget of $2,000 and an identical list of 12 gifts to purchase—ranging from a variety of unbranded items (a cashmere sweater for sister, a sport watch for husband) to a Barbie Magic Pegasus for a 4-year-old girl and the hard-to-find new Microsoft Xbox 360 videogame system for an 11-year-old boy. Their goal was to see how quickly they could complete the assignment and who could get the best gifts for the least money.

One reporter went to the huge Mall at Short Hills, in New Jersey, which includes five anchor stores; the second stayed home, shopped online, and ordered items for overnight delivery. In a parallel race, a professional shopper at the same mall and a Web expert were given the same assignment. The results? The Web expert completed the task in just under 3 hours and $800 under budget (but a couple of the items he purchased were deemed as inferior in quality to those obtained at the mall). The personal shopper came in second, with a total bill $500 under budget but having taken 7 hours and 15 minutes. Third was the reporter shopping online, who spent $1,906 (including shipping costs) and took 7 hours and 40 minutes, but admitted he had become distracted and wasted time surfing the Web. Meantime, the reporter shopping at the mall took 8 hours and spent $1,836. However, neither reporter succeeded in buying the Xbox 360.

Source: Ellen Gamermann and Reed Albergotti, "The Great Holiday Shopping Race," *The Wall Street Journal* (December 3–4, 2005): P6–P7.

THE ROLE OF INTERMEDIARIES

Many service organizations find it cost-effective to outsource certain tasks. Most frequently, this delegation concerns supplementary service elements. For instance, despite their increased use of telephone call centers and the Internet, cruise lines and resort hotels still rely on travel agents to handle a significant portion of their customer interactions, such as giving out information, taking reservations, accepting payment, and ticketing. Of course, many manufacturers rely on the services of distributors or retailers to stock and sell their physical products to end users, and also to take responsibility for supplementary services such as information, advice, order taking, delivery, installation, billing and payment, and certain types of problem solving. In some cases, they may also handle certain types of repairs and upgrades.

How should a service provider work in partnership with one or more intermediaries to deliver a complete service package to customers? In Figure 4.3 we use the "flower of service" framework (introduced in Chapter 3) to show an example in which the core product is delivered by the originating supplier, together with certain

Figure 4.3 Splitting Responsibilities for Supplementary Service Elements

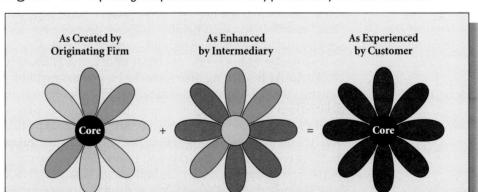

As Created by Originating Firm + As Enhanced by Intermediary = As Experienced by Customer

supplementary elements in the informational, consultation, and exceptions categories, but delivery of other supplementary services is delegated to an intermediary to complete the offering as experienced by the customer. In other instances, several specialist outsourcers might be involved as intermediaries for specific elements. The challenge for the original supplier is to act as guardian of the overall process, ensuring that each element offered by intermediaries fits the overall service concept to create a consistent and seamless branded service experience.

Franchising

Even delivery of the core product can be outsourced to an intermediary. Franchising has become a popular way to expand delivery of an effective service concept, embracing all of the 8 Ps (see Chapter 1), to multiple sites, without the level of investment capital that would be needed for rapid expansion of company-owned and -managed sites.[11] It's an appealing strategy for growth-oriented service firms because franchisees are highly motivated to ensure customer orientation and high-quality service operations.[12] Although franchising is most commonly associated with fast-food outlets (for an example, see Figure 4.4), the concept has been applied to a very wide array of both consumer and business-to-business services and now spans some 75 different product categories. In your own role as a consumer, you are probably patronizing more franchises than you realize. New types of franchises are being created and commercialized all the time in countries around the world.[13]

According to the International Franchise Association, some 760,000 franchise businesses in the United States provide jobs for more than 18 million people and create over $1.5 trillion in economic activity—about 9.5 percent of the private sector's total output.[14] Among the cases featured in this book is "Aussie Pooch Mobile," which describes a successful Australian-based franchised dog-washing service (see pages 520–531).

Nevertheless, there is a significant attrition rate among franchisors in the early years of a new franchise system, with one-third of all systems failing within the first four years and no less than three-quarters of all franchisors ceasing to exist after 12 years.[15] Success factors for franchisors include being able to achieve a larger size with a more recognizable brand name, offering franchisees fewer supporting services but longer-term contracts, and having fewer headquarters staff per outlet. Because growth is very important to achieve an efficient scale, some franchisors adopt a strategy known as "master franchising," which involves delegating the responsibility for recruiting, training, and supporting franchisees within a given geographic area. Master franchisees are often individuals who have already succeeded as operators of an individual franchise outlet.

A franchisor recruits entrepreneurs who are willing to invest their own time and equity in managing a previously developed service concept. In return, the franchisor

Figure 4.4
Dunkin' Brands Uses Franchising to Distribute Its Branded Service Concepts, Dunkin' Donuts (Coffee and Baked Goods), Baskin-Robbins (Ice Cream) and Togo's (Sandwiches)

provides training in how to operate and market the business, sells necessary supplies, and provides promotional support at a national or regional level to augment local marketing activities (which are paid for by the franchisee, but must adhere to copy and media guidelines prescribed by the franchisor).

A disadvantage of delegating activities to franchisees is that it entails some loss of control over the delivery system and, thereby, over how customers experience the actual service. Ensuring that an intermediary adopts exactly the same priorities and procedures as prescribed by the franchisor is difficult, yet it's vital to effective quality control. Franchisors usually seek to exercise control over all aspects of the service performance through a contract that specifies adherence to tightly defined service standards, procedures, scripts, and physical presentation. Franchisors control not only output specifications, but also the appearance of the servicescape, employee performance, and such elements as service timetables.

An ongoing problem is that as franchisees gain experience, they may start to resent the various fees they pay the franchisor and believe that they can operate the business better without the constraints imposed by the agreement. The resulting disputes often lead to legal fights between the two parties.

An alternative to franchising is licensing another supplier to act on the original supplier's behalf to deliver the core product. Trucking companies regularly make use of independent agents, instead of locating company-owned branches in each of the different cities they serve. They may also choose to contract with independent "owner-operators," who drive their own trucks, rather than buy their own trucks and employ full-time drivers.[16]

Other service distribution agreements include financial services. Banks seeking to move into investment services often act as the distributor for mutual fund products created by an investment firm that lacks extensive distribution channels of its own. Many banks also sell insurance products underwritten by an insurance company. They collect a commission on the sale but normally are not involved in handling claims.

The Challenge of Distribution in Large Domestic Markets

There are important differences between marketing services within a limited geographic area and marketing services in a federal nation covering a large geographic area, such as Canada, Australia, or the United States. In these cases, physical logistics immediately become more challenging for many types of services, because of the distances involved and the existence of multiple time zones. Multiculturalism is also an issue, because of the growing proportion of immigrants and the presence of indigenous peoples. Firms that market across Canada have to work in two official languages, English and French (the latter is spoken throughout Quebec, where it is the only official language; in parts of New Brunswick, which is officially bilingual; and in northeastern Ontario). Finally, there are differences within each country between the laws and tax rates of the various states or provinces and those of the respective federal governments. The challenges in Australia and Canada, however, pale in comparison to those facing service marketers in the mega-economy of the United States.

Visitors from overseas who tour the United States are often overwhelmed by the immense size of the country, surprised by the diversity of its people, astonished by the climatic and topographic variety of the landscape, and impressed by the scale and scope of some of its business undertakings. Consider some of the statistics. Marketing at a national level in the "lower 48" states involves dealing with a population of some 300 million people and transcontinental distances that exceed 2,500 miles (4,000 km). If Hawaii and Alaska are included, the market embraces even greater distances, covering six time zones, incredible topographic variety, and all climatic zones from arctic to tropical. From a logistical standpoint, serving customers in all 50 states might seem at least as complex as serving customers throughout, say, Europe, North Africa, and the Middle East, were it not for the fact that the United States has an exceptionally well developed communications, transportation, and distribution infrastructure.

The United States is less homogeneous than national stereotypes might suggest. As a federal nation, the country has a diverse patchwork of government practices. In addition to observing federal laws and paying federal taxes, service businesses operating nationwide may also need to conform to relevant state and municipal laws and plan for variations in tax policies from one state to another. However U.S. firms operating in multiple states may find this exposure an advantage when expanding overseas (see Figure 4.5). Because cities, counties, and special districts (such as regional transit authorities) have taxing authority in many states, there are also thousands of variations

Figure 4.5 The Giant U.S. Law Firm Wilmer Cutler Pickering Hale and Dorr LLP Now Operates in Five Countries on Three Continents

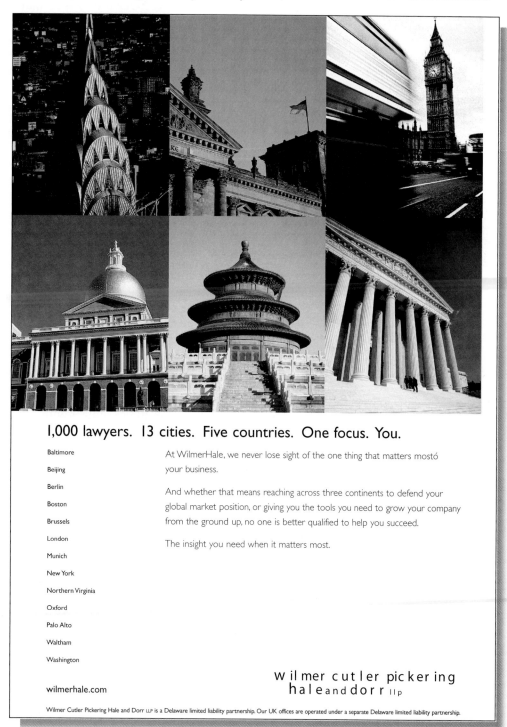

1,000 lawyers. 13 cities. Five countries. One focus. You.

Baltimore
Beijing
Berlin
Boston
Brussels
London
Munich
New York
Northern Virginia
Oxford
Palo Alto
Waltham
Washington

wilmerhale.com

At WilmerHale, we never lose sight of the one thing that matters most—your business.

And whether that means reaching across three continents to defend your global market position, or giving you the tools you need to grow your company from the ground up, no one is better qualified to help you succeed.

The insight you need when it matters most.

wilmer cutler pickering
hale and dorr llp

Wilmer Cutler Pickering Hale and Dorr LLP is a Delaware limited liability partnership. Our UK offices are operated under a separate Delaware limited liability partnership.

Courtesy of WilmerHale.

in sales tax across the United States Some states deliberately seek out new business investments by promoting their lower tax rates or offering tax incentives to encourage firms to establish or relocate factories, call centers, or back-office operations.

As the U.S. population has becomes increasingly mobile and multicultural, market segmentation issues have become more complex for U.S. service marketers operating on a national scale as they encounter growing populations of immigrants (as well as visiting tourists) who speak many languages, led by Spanish. U.S. economic statistics show a wider range of household incomes and personal wealth (or lack thereof) than almost anywhere else on earth. Corporate customers, too, present considerable diversity, although the relevant variables may be different.

Faced with an enormous and diverse domestic marketplace, most large U.S. service companies simplify their marketing and management tasks by targeting specific market segments (see Chapter 7). Some firms segment on a geographic basis. Others target certain groups based on demographics, lifestyle, needs, or—in a corporate context—industry type and company size. Smaller firms wishing to operate nationally usually choose to seek out narrow market niches, a task made easier today by the growing use of web sites and email. However, the largest national service operations face tremendous challenges as they seek to serve multiple segments across a huge geographic area. They must strike a balance between standardization of strategies across all the elements embraced by the 8 Ps and adaptation to different segments and local market conditions—decisions that are especially challenging when they concern high-contact services in which customers visit the delivery site in person.

DISTRIBUTING SERVICES INTERNATIONALLY

What are the alternative ways a service company can tap the potential of international markets? They depend in part on the nature of the underlying processes and delivery system. People, possession, and information processing services have vastly different requirements in an international distribution strategy.

How Service Processes Affect International Market Entry

People Processing Services

People processing services require direct contact with the customer. There are three options:

- *Export the service concept.* Acting alone or in partnership with local suppliers, the firm establishes a service factory in another country. The objective may be to reach out to new customers, or to follow existing corporate or individual customers to new locations (or both). This approach is commonly used by chain restaurants, hotels, car rental firms, and weight-reduction clinics, for which a local presence is essential in order to be able to compete. For corporate customers, the industries are likely to be in fields such as banking, professional services, and business logistics (among others).
- *Import customers.*[17] Customers from other countries are invited to come to a service factory with distinctive appeal or competences in the firm's home country. People travel from abroad to ski at outstanding North American resorts, such as Whistler-Blackholm in British Columbia or Vail in Colorado. If they can afford it, they may also travel for specialized medical treatment at famous U.S. hospitals and clinics, such as the Massachusetts General Hospital or the Mayo Clinic. Increasingly, a two-way traffic is developing in health care, with a growing number of patients from North America, Europe, and Australasia traveling to custom-built modern hospitals in Asian countries for an array of medical interventions by Western-trained specialists, ranging from hip replacements to cosmetic surgery. Even after paying for travel and accommodation, the total cost usually amounts

to far less than patients would pay in their home countries, with the added attraction of recuperating under vacation-like conditions at an often exotic location. Prosenjit Datta and Gina Krishnan's article, "The Health Travellers" (reproduced on pp. 207–210), provides a fascinating perspective on these developments.
- *Transport customers to new locations.* In the case of passenger transportation, embarking on international service takes the form of opening new routes to desired destinations. This strategy is generally used to attract new customers, in addition to expanding choices for existing customers.

Best Practice in Action 4.2 describes some of the ways in which Groupe Accor, a major international hotel chain, has developed a global presence.

Possession Processing Services

Possession processing involves services to the customer's physical possessions and includes repair and maintenance, freight transport, cleaning, and warehousing. Most services in this category require an ongoing local presence, regardless of whether customers drop off items at a service facility or personnel visit the customer's site. Sometimes, however, expert personnel may be flown in from a base in another country. In a few instances, a transportable item of equipment may be shipped to a foreign service center for repair, maintenance, or upgrade. Like passenger carriers, operators of freight transport services enter new markets by opening new routes.

Information-Based Services

Information-based services includes two categories, *mental processing services* (services to the customer's mind, such as news and entertainment) and *information processing services* (services to customers' intangible assets, such as banking and insurance). Information-based services can be distributed internationally in one of three ways:

- *Export the service to a local service factory.* The service can be made available in a local facility that customers visit. For instance, a film made in Hollywood can be shown in movie theaters around the world, or a college course can be designed in one country and then be offered by approved teachers elsewhere.
- *Import customers.* Customers may travel abroad to visit a specialist facility, in which case the service takes on the characteristics of a people processing service. For instance, large numbers of foreign students study at U.S. and Canadian universities.
- *Export the information via telecommunications and transform it locally.* Rather than ship object-based services stored on physical media such as CDs or DVDs from their country of origin, the data can be downloaded from that country for physical production in local markets (even by customers themselves).

In theory, none of these information-based services requires face-to-face contact with customers, because all can potentially be delivered at arm's length through telecommunications or mail. Banking, insurance, and news are good examples of services that can be delivered from other countries. Bank customers requiring cash in another country need only visit a local ATM connected to a global network such as VISA. In practice, however, a local presence may be necessary to build personal relationships, conduct on-site research (as in consulting or auditing), or even to fulfill legal requirements.

Barriers to International Trade in Services

The marketing of services internationally has been the fastest-growing segment of international trade.[18] Transnational strategy involves the integration of strategy formulation and its implementation across all the countries in which the company elects to do business. Barriers to entry, historically a serious problem for foreign firms wishing to do business abroad, are slowly diminishing. The passage of free-trade legislation in recent years has been an important facilitator of transnational operations. Notable developments include NAFTA (linking Canada, Mexico, and the United States), Latin

Paris-based Groupe Accor is one of the world's leaders in the lodging industry. It has recently sold its investments in the travel agency and contract food service businesses in order to focus on its core activities. According to experts, Accor is one of a few truly global hotel companies, with some 4,000 hotels containing some 470,000 rooms in 92 countries. Over the years, the group has proved itself to be a highly innovative service provider, as reflected by its in-depth market opportunity analysis, integrated offerings, and international growth strategies.

Accor has gone from being the first truly European hotel chain to being one of the largest hotel chains in the world. It operates brands in several distinct categories of hotels, including the four/five-star Sofitel brand, three/four-star Novotel, three/four-star Mercure, and two/three-star Ibis. Accor has also pioneered an easily prefabricated, replicable budget hotel concept known as the Formule 1 chain. In the United States, Accor operates the Motel 6 chain of budget motels and Red Roof Inns, and has plans for other acquisitions. Care is given to maintaining the distinctive identities of each of its hotel brands. Some 1,000 hotels, including 700 in Europe, are operated by franchisees. Accor plans to invest some €2.3 billion ($2.9 billion) between 2006 and 2010 as it adds 200,000 new hotel rooms, primarily in the economy and budget hotel categories. Two-thirds of these new rooms will be opened in emerging markets.

Accor's former chairman, Jean-Marc Espalioux, sought to give the company the integrated structure it needed to operate and compete on a global basis. Under his leadership, hotel activities were restructured into three strategic segments, reflecting their market positioning. There are also two functional divisions. The first, a global services division, was created to spearhead the major functions common to all hotel activities: information systems, reservation systems, maintenance and technical assistance, purchasing, key accounts, and partnerships and synergy between the hotel and other activities. The second, the hotel development division, is structured by brand and by region and is responsible for working with the management of each hotel to develop marketing, service development, and growth strategies. Espalioux was a strong believer in economies of scale:

> In view of the revolution in the service sector which is now taking place, I do not see any future for purely national hotel chains—except for very specific niche markets with special architecture and locations, such as Raffles in Singapore or the Ritz in Paris. National chains can't invest enough money.

The group is continuing its internationalization drive, focusing on further consolidating and integrating its network, as well as building a presence in such emerging markets as Poland, Hungary, and other ex-Soviet bloc countries. Espalioux was very aware that the underlying obstacle to successful globalization in services was—and continues to be—people:

> Globalization brings considerable challenges which are often underestimated. The principal difficulty is getting our local management to adhere to the values of the group. [They] must understand our market and culture, for example, and we have to learn about theirs.

Because international cooperation, communication, and teamwork are integral to achieving global consistency, Accor has eliminated, as much as possible, hierarchy, rigid job descriptions and titles, and even organizational charts. Its 168,000 associates are encouraged to interact as much as possible both with their colleagues and with guests. They define the limits of their jobs within the context of the overall "customer experience," and are recognized and rewarded on how well they meet these definitions. In addition to these structural and organizational initiatives, video conferencing and other technologies are used extensively to create and reinforce a common, global culture among Accor employees around the world. All of the group's European hotels are linked together through a sophisticated IT network, and Accor hotels worldwide are linked to a 24/7 global reservation system.

Sources: Andrew Jack, "The Global Company: Why There Is No Future for National Hotel Chains," *Financial Times* (October 10, 1997); W. Chan Kim and Renee Mauborgne, "Value Innovation: The Strategic Logic of High Growth," *Harvard Business Review* (January–February 1997): 121–123; and the firm's web site, www.accor.com/gb/groupe/accueil.asp, accessed May 2006.

American economic blocs such as Mercosur and Pacto Andino, and the European Union, now 25 countries strong, which is expected to expand its membership further in the coming years (see Service Perspectives 4.5).

However, operating successfully in international markets remains difficult for some services. Despite the efforts of the World Trade Organization (WTO) and its predecessor, GATT (General Agreement on Trade and Tariffs), there are many hurdles to overcome. Airline access is a sore point. Many countries require bilateral

Many of the challenging strategic decisions facing service marketers in pan-European markets are extensions of decisions already faced by firms operating on a national basis in the United States. Although it is geographically more compact than the United States, the 25-country European Union (EU) has an even larger population (460 million versus 300 million) and is culturally and politically more diverse, with more distinct variations in tastes and lifestyles, plus the added complication of 21 official national languages and a variety of regional tongues, from Catalan to Welsh. As new countries join the EU, the "single market" will become even larger. The anticipated admission of several more Eastern European countries in the next few years, led by Romania and Bulgaria, and the possibility of a formal link to Turkey (whose land area straddles Europe and Asia) will add further cultural diversity and bring the EU market closer to Russia and the countries of Central Asia.

Within the EU, the European Commission has made huge progress in harmonizing standards and regulations to level the competitive playing field and discourage efforts by individual member countries to protect their own service and manufacturing industries. The results are already evident, with many service firms operating across Europe (as well as overseas).

Another important economic step facilitating transnational marketing on a pan-European basis is monetary union. In January 1999, the exchange values of 11 national European currencies were linked to a new currency, the euro, which completely replaced all European currencies in 2002. Today, services are priced in euros from Finland to Portugal. Other European countries, including Britain and Sweden, may eventually decide to switch to euros, although this issue remains contentious.

However, although the potential for freer trade in services within the EU continues to increase, you should recognize that "Greater Europe," ranging from Iceland to Russia west of the Ural Mountains, includes many countries that are likely to remain outside the Union for some years to come. Some of these countries, such as Switzerland and Norway (which both rejected membership), tend to enjoy much closer trading relations with the EU than others. Whether there will ever be full political union—a "United States of Europe"—remains a hotly debated and contested issue. However, from a services marketing standpoint, the EU is certainly moving toward the U.S. model in terms of both scale and freedom of movement. See http://europa.eu.int for more information on the EU.

(two-country) agreements on establishing new routes. If one country is willing to allow entry by a new carrier but the other is not, then access is blocked. Compounding government restrictions of this nature are capacity limits at certain major airports, which lead to denial of new or additional landing rights for foreign airlines. Both passenger and freight transport are affected by such restrictions.

Other constraints may include administrative delays, refusals by immigration offices to provide work permit applications for foreign managers and workers, heavy taxes on foreign firms, domestic preference policies designed to protect local suppliers, legal restrictions on operational and marketing procedures (including international data flows), and the lack of broadly agreed accounting standards for services. Different languages and cultural norms may require expensive changes in the nature of a service and how it is delivered and promoted. The cultural issue has been particularly significant for the entertainment industry. Many nations are wary of seeing their own culture swamped by U.S. imports.

Factors Favoring Adoption of Transnational Strategies

Several forces or *industry drivers* influence the trend toward globalization and the creation of transnationally integrated strategy.[19] As applied to services, these forces are market drivers, competition drivers, technology drivers, cost drivers, and government drivers. Their relative significance may vary by type of service.

Market Drivers

Market factors that stimulate the move toward transnational strategies include common customer needs across many countries, global customers who demand

Figure 4.6 DHL Combines Multiple Transport Modes to Create Integrated Logistics Solutions for Its Global Customer Base

Courtesy of DHL International Ltd.

consistent service from suppliers around the world, and the availability of international channels in the form of efficient physical supply chains or electronic networks.

As large corporate customers become global, they seek to standardize and simplify the suppliers used in different countries for a wide array of business-to-business services. For instance, they may seek to minimize the number of auditors they use around the world, expressing a preference for "Big Four" accounting firms that can apply a consistent approach (within the context of the national rules prevailing within each country of operation). Use of globalized corporate banking, insurance, and management consulting services are further examples. Similarly, the development of global logistics and supply chain management capabilities among such firms as DHL, FedEx, and UPS has encouraged many manufacturers to outsource responsibility for their logistics function to a single firm (Figure 4.6). In each instance, there are real advantages in consistency, ease of access, consolidation of information, and accountability. Similarly, international business travelers and tourists often feel more comfortable with predictable standards of performance for such travel-related services as airlines and hotels.

Competition Drivers

The presence of competitors from different countries, interdependence of countries, and the transnational policies of competitors themselves are among the key competition drivers that exercise a powerful force in many service industries. Firms may be obliged to follow their competitors into new markets in order to protect their positions elsewhere. Similarly, once a major player moves into a new foreign market, a scramble for territory among competing firms may ensue.

Technology Drivers

Technology drivers tend to center around advances in information technology—such as enhanced performance and capabilities in telecommunications, computerization, and software; miniaturization of equipment; and the digitization of voice, video, and text so that all can be stored, manipulated, and transmitted in the digital language of computers. For information-based services, the growing availability of broadband telecommunication channels, capable of moving vast amounts of data at great speed, is playing a major role in opening up new markets.[20] Access to the Internet is accelerating around the world. Significant economies may be gained by centralizing "information hubs" on a continent-wide or even global basis. Firms can take advantage of favorable labor costs and exchange rates by consolidating operations of supplementary services (such as reservations) or back-office functions (such as accounting) in just one or a few selected countries.

Cost Drivers

Big is sometimes beautiful from a cost standpoint. There may be economies of scale to be gained from operating on an international or even global basis, plus sourcing efficiencies as a result of favorable logistics and lower costs in certain countries. Lower operating costs for telecommunications and transportation, accompanied by improved performance, facilitate entry into international markets. The effects of these drivers vary according to the level of fixed costs required to enter an industry and the potential for cost savings. Barriers to entry caused by the upfront cost of equipment and facilities may be reduced by such strategies as equipment leasing (as many airlines do), seeking investor-owned facilities such as hotels and then obtaining management contracts, or awarding franchises to local entrepreneurs. However, cost drivers may be less applicable for services that are primarily people-based. When most elements of the service factory are replicated in multiple locations, scale economies tend to be lower and experience curves flatter.

Government Drivers

Government policies can serve to encourage or discourage development of a transnationally integrated strategy. Among these drivers are favorable trade policies, compatible technical standards, and common marketing regulations. For instance, the actions taken by the European Commission to create a single market throughout the EU are a stimulus to creation of pan-European service strategies in numerous industries.

Furthermore, the World Trade Organization (WTO) and its focus on the internationalization of services has pushed governments around to world to create more favorable regulatory environments for transnational service strategies. The power of the drivers for internationalization can be seen in the case of the Qantas airliner arriving in Hong Kong described in Service Perspectives 4.6.

Many of the factors driving internationalization and the adoption of transnational strategies also promote the trend to have nationwide operations. The market, cost, technological, and competitive forces that encourage creation of nationwide service businesses or franchise chains are often the same as those that subsequently drive some of the same firms to operate transnationally.

How the Nature of Service Processes Affects Opportunities for Internationalization

Are some types of services easier to internationalize than others? Our analysis suggests that this is indeed the case. Table 4.2 summarizes important variations in the impact of each of the five groups of drivers on three broad categories of services: people processing services, possession processing services; and information-based services.

People Processing Services

The service provider needs to maintain a local geographic presence, stationing the necessary personnel, buildings, equipment, vehicles, and supplies within reasonably easy reach of target customers. If the customers are themselves mobile, as in the case of business travelers and tourists, then the same customers may patronize a company's offerings in many different locations, and make comparisons between them. Times are changing in health care. Diagnosis and monitoring of patients can be conducted at a distance through electronic sensors. A growing number of highly specialized surgical procedures can be performed robotically by skilled practitioners located far away. However, to receive such surgery, the patient will still need to visit a local health care facility that has the necessary equipment, and be cared for by locally based personnel.

A white-and-red Boeing 747, sporting the flying kangaroo of Qantas, banks low over Hong Kong's dramatic harbor, crowded with merchant vessels, as it nears the end of its 10-hour flight from Australia. Once it has landed, the aircraft taxis past a kaleidoscope of tailfins representing airlines from more than a dozen different countries on several continents—just a sample of all the carriers that offer service to this remarkable city.

The passengers include business travelers and tourists, as well as returning residents. After passing through immigration and customs at the striking modern airport, most visitors will be heading first for their hotels, many of which belong to global chains (some of them, Hong Kong-based). Some travelers will be picking up cars, reserved earlier from Hertz or one of the other well-known rental car companies with facilities at the airport. Others will take the fast train into the city. Tourists on packaged vacations are actively looking forward to enjoying Hong Kong's renowned Cantonese cuisine. Parents, however, are resigned to having their children demand to eat at the same fast-food chains that can be found back home. Many of the more affluent tourists are planning to go shopping, not only in distinctive Chinese jewelry and antiques stores, but also in the internationally branded luxury stores that can be found in most world-class cities.

What brings the business travelers to this SAR ("special administrative region") of China? Many are negotiating supply contracts for manufactured goods ranging from clothing to toys to computer components, whereas others have come to market their own goods and services. Some are in the shipping or construction businesses, others in an array of service industries ranging from telecommunications to entertainment and international law. The owner of a large Australian tourism operation has come to negotiate a deal for package vacations on Queensland's famous Gold Coast. The Brussels-based, Canadian senior partner of a Big Four accounting firm is halfway through a grueling round-the-world trip to persuade the offices of an international conglomerate to consolidate all its auditing business on a global basis with his firm alone. An American executive and her British colleague, both working for a large telecom company, are hoping to achieve similar goals by selling a multinational corporation on the concept of employing their firm to manage all of its telecommunications activities worldwide. And more than a few of the passengers either work for international banking and financial service firms or have come to Hong Kong, one of the world's most dynamic financial centers, to seek financing for their own ventures.

In the Boeing's freight hold can be found not only passengers' bags, but also cargo for delivery to Hong Kong and other Chinese destinations. The freight includes mail, Australian wine, some vital spare parts for an Australian-built high-speed ferry operating out of Hong Kong, a container full of brochures and display materials about the Australian tourism industry for an upcoming trade promotion, and a variety of other high-value merchandise. Waiting at the airport for the aircraft's arrival are local Qantas personnel, baggage handlers, cleaners, mechanics, and other technical staff, customs and immigration officials, and, of course, people who have come to greet individual passengers. A few are Australians, but the great majority are local Hong Kong Chinese, many of whom have never traveled very far afield. Yet in their daily lives, they patronize banks, fast-food outlets, retail stores, and insurance companies whose brand names—promoted by global advertising campaigns—may be equally familiar to their expatriate relatives living in countries such as Australia, Britain, Canada, Singapore, and the United States. They can watch CNN on cable TV, listen to the BBC World Service on the radio, make phone calls through Hong Kong Telecom (itself part of a worldwide operation), and watch movies from Hollywood either in English or dubbed into the Cantonese dialect of Chinese. Welcome to the world of global services marketing!

Possession Processing Services

Possession processing services may also be geographically constrained in many instances. A local presence is still required when the supplier must come to repair or maintain objects in a fixed location. However, smaller, transportable items can be shipped to distant centers for repair, cleaning, and maintenance. Certain types of service processes can be applied to physical products through electronic diagnostics and transmission of so-called remote fixes.

Information-Based Services

Information-based services are perhaps the most interesting category of services from the standpoint of global strategy development, because they depend on the

Table 4.2
Impact of Globalization Drivers on Various Service Categories

Globalization Drivers	People Processing	Possession Processing	Information Based
Competition	Simultaneity of production and consumption limits leverage of foreign-based competitive advantage in front stage of service factory, but advantage in management systems can be basis for globalization.	Lead role of technology creates driver for globalization of competitors with technical edge (e.g., Singapore Airlines' technical servicing for other carriers' aircraft).	Highly vulnerable to global dominance by competitors with monopoly or competitive advantage in information (e.g., BBC, Hollywood, CNN), unless restricted by governments.
Market	People differ economically and culturally, so needs for service and ability to pay may vary. Culture and education may affect willingness to do self-service.	Less variation for service to corporate possessions, but level of economic development affects demand for services to individually owned goods.	Demand for many services is derived to a significant degree from economic and educational levels. Cultural issues may affect demand for entertainment.
Technology	Use of IT for delivery of supplementary services may be a function of ownership and familiarity with technology, including telecommunications and intelligent terminals.	Need for technology-based service delivery systems is a function of the types of possessions requiring service and the cost trade-offs in labor substitution.	Ability to deliver core services through remote terminals may be a function of investments in computerization, quality of telecommunications infrastructure, and education levels.
Cost	Variable labor rates may affect pricing in labor-intensive services (consider self-service in high-cost locations).	Variable labor rates may favor low-cost locations if not offset by shipment costs. Consider substituting equipment for labor.	Major cost elements can be centralized and minor cost elements localized.
Government	Social policies (e.g., health care) vary widely and may affect labor costs, role of women in front-stage jobs, and hours/days on which work can be performed.	Tax laws, environmental regulations, and technical standards may decrease/increase costs and encourage/discourage certain types of activity.	Policies on education, censorship, public ownership of communications, and infrastructure standards may affect demand and supply and distort pricing.

transmission or manipulation of data in order to create value. The advent of modern global telecommunications, linking intelligent machines to powerful databases, makes it increasingly easy to deliver information-based services around the world.

In addition to such industries as financial services, insurance, news, and entertainment, education is becoming a likely candidate for globalized distribution. Many universities already have international campuses, extension courses delivered by both local and traveling faculty, and long-established correspondence programs. On a national basis, the University of Phoenix in the United States and the Open University in the United Kingdom are among the national leaders in electronically distributed programs. A truly globalized service is the next logical step. Local-presence requirements may be limited to a terminal, ranging from a simple telephone or fax machine to a computer or more specialized equipment, connected to a reliable telecommunications infrastructure. If the local infrastructure is not of sufficiently high quality, then the use of mobile or satellite communications may solve the problem in some instances.

CONCLUSION

"Where? When? How?" Responses to these three questions form the foundation of service delivery strategy. The customer's service experience is a function of both service performance and delivery characteristics.

"Where?" relates, of course, to the places where customers can obtain delivery of the core product, one or more supplementary services, or a complete package. In this chapter, we presented a categorization scheme for thinking about alternative place-related strategies, ranging from customers coming to the service site, to service personnel visiting the customer, and finally a variety of options for remote transactions, including delivery through both physical and electronic channels, both nationally and globally. "When?" involves decisions on scheduling of service delivery. Customer demands for greater convenience are leading many firms to extend their hours and days of service, with the ultimate flexibility being offered by 24/7 service every day of the year.

"How?" concerns channels and procedures for delivering the core and supplementary service elements to customers. Advances in technology are having a major impact on the alternatives available and on the economics of those alternatives. Responding to customer needs for flexibility, many firms now offer several alternative choices of delivery channels.

Although service firms are much more likely than manufacturers to control their own delivery systems, there is also a role for intermediaries to deliver either the core services, as is the case for franchisees, or supplementary services, such as travel agents.

More and more service firms are marketing across national borders. Stimulating (or constraining) the move to transnational strategies are five key industry drivers: market factors, costs, technology, government policies, and competitive forces. However, significant differences exist in the extent to which the various drivers apply to people processing, possession processing, and information-based services.

REVIEW QUESTIONS

1. What is meant by "distributing services?" How can an experience or something intangible be distributed?
2. Why is it important to consider the distribution of core and supplementary services both separately and jointly?
3. What risks and opportunities are entailed for a retail service firm in adding electronic channels of delivery by (a) paralleling an existing channel involving physical stores, or (b) replacing the physical stores with a combined Internet and call center channel? Give examples.
4. Why should service marketers be concerned with new developments in mobile communications?
5. What can service marketers who are planning transnational strategies learn from studying existing practices within the United States?
6. What marketing and management challenges are raised by the use of intermediaries in a service setting?
7. What are the key drivers for increasing globalization of services?
8. How does the nature of the service affect the opportunities for globalization?

APPLICATION EXERCISES

1. Identify three situations in which you use self-service delivery. For each situation, what is your motivation for using this approach to delivery, rather than having service personnel do it for you?
2. Think of three services that you buy or use either mostly or exclusively via the Internet. What is the value proposition of this channel to you over alternative channels (e.g., phone, mail, or branch network)?
3. Select two business format franchises other than food service, choosing one targeted primarily at consumer markets and the other targeted primarily at business-to-business markets. Develop a profile of each, examining its strategy across each of the 8 Ps and also evaluating its competitive positioning.
4. Select three different service industries. For each, what do you see as being the most significant of the five industry drivers as forces for globalization and why?
5. Obtain recent statistics for international trade in services for the United States and another country of your choice. What are the dominant categories of service exports and imports? What factors do you think are driving trade in specific service categories? What differences do you see between the countries?

1. Jochen Wirtz and Jeannette P. T. Ho, "Westin in Asia: Distributing Hotel Rooms Globally." In Jochen Wirtz and Christopher H. Lovelock (eds.). *Services Marketing in Asia—A Case Book* (Singapore: Prentice Hall, 2005): 253–259.

2. The section is based on the following sources: Nancy Jo Black, Andy Lockett, Christine Ennew, Heidi Winklhofer, and Sally McKechnie, "Modelling Consumer Choice of Distribution Channels: An Illustration from Financial Services." *International Journal of Bank Marketing,* 20, no. 4 (2002): 161–173; Jinkook Lee, "A Key to Marketing Financial Services: The Right Mix of Products, Services, Channels and Customers." *Journal of Services Marketing,* 16, no. 3 (2002): 238–258; and Leonard L Berry, Kathleen Seiders, and Dhruv Grewal, "Understanding Service Convenience," *Journal of Marketing,* 66, no. 3 (July 2002): 1–17.

3. Paul F. Nunes and Frank V. Cespedes, "The Customer Has Escaped." *Harvard Business Review,* 81, no. 11 (2003): 96–105.

4. Michael A. Jones, David L. Mothersbaugh, and Sharon E. Beatty, "The Effects of Locational Convenience on Customer Repurchase Intentions Across Service Types." *Journal of Services Marketing,* 17, no. 7 (2004): 701–712.

5. James L. Heskett, W. Earl Sasser, Jr., and Leonard A. Schlesinger, *The Service Profit Chain* (New York: The Free Press, 1997): 218–220.

6. www.swissotel.com and www.eyefortravel.com, accessed November 2005.

7. Recent research on the adoption of self-service technologies includes: Matthew L. Meuter, Mary Jo Bitner, Amy L. Ostrom, and Stephen W. Brown, "Choosing Among Alternative Service Delivery Modes: An Investigation of Customer Trial of Self-Service Technologies." *Journal of Marketing,* 69 (April 2005): 61–83; James M. Curran and Matthew L. Meuter, "Self-Service Technology Adoption: Comparing Three Technologies." *Journal of Services Marketing,* 19, no. 2 (2005): 103–113.

8. P. K. Kannan, "Introduction to the Special Issue: Marketing in the E-Channel." *International Journal of Electronic Commerce,* 5, no. 3 (2001): 3–6; Customer satisfaction and loyalty can be built with electronic channels that build "digital proximity"; see Sonja M. Salmen and Andrew Muir, "Electronic Customer Care: The Innovative Path to E-Loyalty." *Journal of Financial Services Marketing,* 8, no. 2 (2003): 133–144.

9. Inge Geyskens, Katrijn Gielens, and Marnik G Dekimpe, "The Market Valuation of Internet Channel Additions." *Journal of Marketing,* 66, no. 2 (April 2002): 102–119. For a study showing that customer perception of greater integration of physical and online channels is important in a multichannel strategy and is associated with higher loyalty, see Elliot Bendoly, James D. Blocher, Kurt M. Bretthauer, Shanker Krishnan, and M. A. Venkataramanan, "Online/In-Store Integration and Customer Retention." *Journal of Service Research,* 7, no. 4 (2005): 313–327.

10. Katherine N. Lemon, Frederick B. Newell, and Loren J. Lemon, "The Wireless Rules for e-Service." In Roland T. Rust and P. K. Kannan (eds.), *New Directions in Theory and Practice* (Armonk, NY: M. E. Sharpe, 2002): 200–232.

11. Richard C. Hoffman and John F. Preble, "Global Franchising: Current Status and Future Challenges." *Journal of Services Marketing,* 18, no. 2 (2004): 101–113.

12. James Cross and Bruce J. Walker, "Addressing Service Marketing Challenges Through Franchising." In Teresa A. Swartz and Dawn Iacobucci (eds.), *Handbook of Services Marketing & Management* (Thousand Oaks, CA: Sage Publications, 2000): 473–484; Lavent Altinay, "Implementing International Franchising: The Role of Intrapreunership." *International Journal of Service Industry Management,* 15, no. 5 (2004): 426–443.

13. Richard C. Hoffman and John F. Preble, "Global Franchising: Current Status and Future Challenges." *Journal of Services Marketing,* 18, no. 2 (2004): 101–113.

14. "Extending the Front Lines of Franchising." *Business Week Online,* accessed September 19, 2005.

15. Scott Shane and Chester Spell, "Factors for New Franchise Success." *Sloan Management Review* (Spring 1998): 43–50.

16. For a discussion on what to watch for when parts of the service are outsourced, see Lauren Keller Johnson, "Outsourcing Postsale Service: Is Your Brand Protected? Before You Spin Off Repairs, or Parts Distribution, or Customer Call Centers, Consider the Cons as well as the Pros." *Harvard Business Review Supply Chain Strategy* (July 2005): 3–5.

17. This term was coined by Curtis P. McLauglin and James A. Fitzsimmons, "e-Service: Strategies for Globalizing Service Operations." *International Journal of Service Industry Management,* 7, no. 4 (1996): 43–57.

18. Rajshkhar G. Javalgi and D. Steven White, "Strategic Challenges for the Marketing of Services Internationally." *International Marketing Review* 19, no. 6 (2002): 563–581.

19. John K. Johansson and George S. Yip, "Exploiting Globalization Potential: US and Japanese Strategies." *Strategic Management Journal* (October 1994): 579–601; Christopher H. Lovelock and George S. Yip, "Developing Global Strategies for Service Businesses." *California Management Review,* 38 (Winter 1996): 64–86; May Aung and Roger Heeler, "Core Competencies of Service Firms: A Framework for Strategic Decisions in International Markets." *Journal of Marketing Management,* 17 (2001): 619–643; Rajshkhar G. Javalgi and D. Steven White, "Strategic Challenges for the Marketing of Services Internationally." *International Marketing Review,* 19, no. 6 (2002): 563–581.

20. Rajshekhar G. Javalgi, Charles L. Martin, and Patricia R. Todd, "The Export of E-Services in the Age of Technology Transformation: Challenges and Implications for International Service Providers." *Journal of Services Marketing,* 18, no. 7 (2004): 560–573.

Chapter 5

Exploring Business Models: Pricing and Revenue Management

Creating a viable service requires a business model that allows the costs of creating and delivering the service, plus a margin for profits, to be recovered through realistic pricing and revenue management strategies.

Pricing of services, however, is complicated. Consider the bewildering fee schedules of many consumer banks or mobile phone service providers, or try to understand the fluctuating fare structure of a full-service airline. Service organizations even use different terms to describe the prices they set. Universities talk about tuition, professional firms collect fees, banks impose interest and service charges, brokers charge commissions, some expressways impose tolls, utilities set tariffs, and insurance companies determine premiums—and the list goes on.

A key goal of effective pricing strategy is to manage revenues in ways that support the firm's profitability objectives. Doing so requires a good understanding of costs, competitors' pricing, and the value created for customers. This sounds straightforward, but it is a real challenge for service firms, for whom unit costs may be difficult to determine and fixed costs difficult to allocate appropriately across multiple service offerings. Competitors' pricing cannot be compared dollar for dollar as services are often location- and time-specific, and customer's switching costs can be significant. Increasingly, customers complain of pricing schedules that they perceive as confusing and unfair. Finally, value to customers usually varies widely among segments and even within the same segment across time. And customers won't buy unless they perceive that the benefits they are obtaining in this value exchange exceed the financial and other costs—notably time and effort—that they incur. That's why we refer to this element of the 8 Ps as *Price and other user outlays.*

In this chapter, we review the role of pricing in services marketing and provide some guidelines on how to develop an effective pricing strategy. Specifically, we address the following questions:

1. What are the three main foundations to pricing a service?
2. Why is cost-based pricing so challenging for many service firms, and how can activity-based costing improve costing of services?
3. How do customers perceive the nonmonetary costs of obtaining service, and what might service providers do to reduce them?
4. How does revenue management improve profitability?
5. Why are some key ethical concerns today about service pricing strategies?
6. What are the seven questions marketers need to answer before designing an effective pricing schedule?

EFFECTIVE PRICING IS CENTRAL TO FINANCIAL SUCCESS

Marketing is the only function that brings operating revenues into the organization. All other management functions incur costs. A *business model* is the mechanism whereby, through effective pricing, sales are transformed into revenues, costs are covered, and value is created for the owners of the business. As noted by Joan Magretta:

> A good business model answers Peter Drucker's age-old questions: Who is the customer? And what does the customer value? It also answers the fundamental questions that every manager must ask: How do we make money in this business? What is the underlying economic logic that explains how we can deliver value to customers at an appropriate cost?[1]

In many service industries, pricing was traditionally driven by a financial and accounting perspective, which often used cost-plus pricing. Price schedules were often tightly constrained by government regulatory agencies—and some still are. Today, however, most service businesses enjoy significant freedom in setting prices, and have a good understanding of value-based and competitive pricing. These developments have led to creative pricing schedules and sophisticated revenue management systems.

In this chapter we focus on business models that require end users to pay a price that covers the financial costs of receiving service. However, there are many instances when all or part of the cost is covered by third parties. Thus, advertising revenues pay the cost of supplying most broadcast radio and TV services, health insurers pay much of the cost of medical care for patients who carry such insurance, donations enable museums to set admission prices lower than they would otherwise, and tax revenues allow public schools to offer free education.

Pricing is typically more complex in services than it is in manufacturing. Because there's no ownership of services, it's usually harder for managers to determine the financial costs of creating a process or performance for a customer, compared to identifying the costs associated with creating and distributing a physical good. The inability to inventory services places a premium on bringing demand and supply into balance, a task in which pricing plays a key role. The importance of the time factor in service delivery means that speed of delivery and avoidance of waiting time often increase value. With the increase in value, customers may be prepared to pay a higher price for the service.

What does a marketing perspective bring to pricing? Effective pricing strategies seek to enhance (or even maximize) the level of revenues, often by discriminating among different market segments based on their value perceptions and ability to pay, and among different time periods based on variations in demand levels over time.

Consumers often find service pricing difficult to understand (e.g., insurance products or hospital bills), risky (when you make a hotel reservation on three different days, you may be offered three different prices), and sometimes even unethical (e.g., many bank customers complain about an array of fees and charges they perceive as unfair). Examine your own purchasing behavior: How did you feel the last time you had to decide on booking a vacation, reserving a rental car, or opening a new bank account? In this chapter, you will learn how to set an effective pricing and revenue management strategy that fulfills the promise of the value proposition so that a value exchange takes place (i.e., the consumer decides to buy your service).

Objectives for Establishing Prices

Any pricing strategy must be based on a clear understanding of a company's pricing objectives. The most common pricing objectives are related to revenue and profits, building demand, and developing a user base (Table 5.1).

Generating Revenues and Profits

Within certain limits, profit-seeking firms aim to maximize long-term revenue, contributions, and profits. Perhaps top management is eager to reach a particular financial target or seeks a specific percentage return on investment. Revenue targets may be broken down by division, geographic unit, type of service, and even by key customer segments. This practice requires prices to be set based on a good knowledge of costing, competition, and price elasticity of the market and value perceptions, all of which we will discuss later in this chapter.

Table 5.1
Alternative Objectives for Pricing

Revenue and Profit Objectives

Seek Profit
- Make the largest possible contribution or profit.
- Achieve a specific target level, but do not seek to maximize profits.
- Maximize revenue from a fixed capacity by varying prices and target segments over time, typically using a yield or revenue management system.

Cover Costs
- Cover fully allocated costs, including institutional overhead.
- Cover costs of providing one particular service, excluding overhead.
- Cover incremental costs of selling one extra unit or to one extra customer.

Patronage and User Base-Related Objectives

Build Demand
- Maximize demand (when capacity is not a constraint), subject to achieving a certain minimum level of revenues.
- Achieve full capacity utilization, especially when high capacity utilization adds to the value created for all customers (e.g., a "full house" adds excitement to a play or a basketball game).

Build a User Base
- Stimulate trial and adoption of a service. This is especially important for new services with high infrastructure costs and for membership-type services that generate significant revenues from their continued use after adoption (e.g., mobile phone service subscriptions, or life insurance plans).
- Build market share and/or a large user base, especially if there are significant economies of scale that can lead to a competitive cost advantage (e.g., if development or fixed costs are high).

In capacity-constrained organizations, financial success is often a function of ensuring optimal use of productive capacity at any given time. Hotels, for instance, seek to fill their rooms, because an empty room is an unproductive asset. Similarly, professional firms want to keep their staff members occupied. Thus, when demand is low, such organizations may offer special discounts to attract additional business. Conversely, when demand exceeds capacity, these types of businesses may increase their prices, and focus on segments that are willing to pay higher amounts. We'll discuss these practices in detail in the section on revenue management.

Building Demand

In some instances, maximizing patronage, subject to achieving a certain minimum level of profits, may be more important than maximizing profit. Getting a full house in a theater, sports stadium, or race track usually creates excitement that enhances customers' experience. It also creates an image of success that attracts new patrons.

Developing a User Base

New services, in particular, often have trouble attracting customers. Yet, in order to create the impression of a successful launch, and to enhance the image of the firm, it's important that the firm is seen to be attracting a good volume of business from the right types of customers. Introductory price discounts are often used to stimulate trial and sign up customers, sometimes in combination with promotional activities such as contests and giveaways. For example, to compete with rival UPS and build sales for its network of more than 1,300 FedEx Kinko's Office and Print Center locations in the United States, FedEx promoted savings of up to 30 percent on express shipments from these stores.

In those industries that require large investments in infrastructure (e.g., mobile phone or broadband service), it's important to build a critical mass of users quickly. Market leadership often means low cost per user, so volume is necessary to generate sufficient revenue for future investments such as upgrading technology and infrastructure. As a result, penetration pricing is often used in such industries.

PRICING STRATEGY STANDS ON THREE LEGS

The foundation underlying pricing strategy can be described as a tripod, with costs to the provider, competition, and value to the customer as the three legs (Figure 5.1). The costs that a firm needs to recover usually impose a minimum price, or floor, for a specific service offering, and the customer's perceived value of the offering sets a maximum, or ceiling. The price charged by competitors for similar or substitute services typically determines where, within the floor-to-ceiling range, the price can be

Figure 5.1 The Pricing Tripod

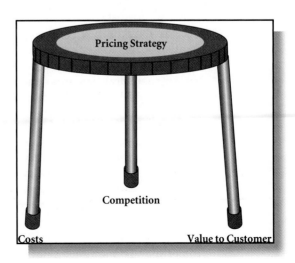

set. The pricing objectives of the organization then determine where actual prices should be set given the feasible range provided by the pricing tripod analysis. Let's look at each leg of the pricing tripod in more detail.

Cost-Based Pricing

It's usually harder to establish the costs involved in producing an intangible performance than it is to identify the labor, materials, machine time, storage, and shipping costs associated with producing a physical good. Yet without a good understanding of costs, how can managers price at levels sufficient to yield a desired profit margin? Because of the labor and infrastructure needed to create performances, many service organizations have a much higher ratio of fixed costs to variable costs than is typical in manufacturing firms.

Establishing the Costs of Providing Service

Even if you have already taken a marketing course, you may find it helpful to review how service costs can be estimated, using fixed, semivariable, and variable costs, as well as how the notions of contribution and break-even analysis can help in pricing decisions (see Marketing Review box on page 129). These traditional cost accounting approaches work well for service firms with significant variable costs and/or semivariable costs (e.g., many professional services). For complex product lines with shared infrastructure (e.g., retail banking products), it may be worthwhile to consider the more complex activity-based costing (ABC) approach.

Activity-Based Costing

A growing number of organizations have reduced their dependence on traditional cost accounting systems and developed activity-based cost management systems, which recognize that virtually all activities taking place within a firm directly or indirectly support the production, marketing, and delivery of goods and services. Moreover, ABC systems link resource expenses to the variety and complexity of goods and services produced—not just to the physical volume. A set of activities is combined that comprise the processes needed to create and deliver the service. Each step in a flowchart constitutes an activity with which costs can be associated. This approach makes ABC ideally suited for use in a service organization.

If it is implemented well, the ABC approach yields reasonably accurate cost information about service business activities and processes—and about the costs of creating specific types of services, performing activities in different locations (even different countries), or serving specific customers.[2] The net result is a management tool that can help companies pinpoint the profitability of different services, channels, market segments, and individual customers.[3]

It's essential to distinguish between those activities that are mandatory for operation of a particular service business and those that are discretionary. The traditional approach to cost control often results in reducing the value generated for customers, because the activity that is pruned is, in fact, mandatory to provide a certain level and quality of service. For instance, many firms have created marketing problems for themselves by firing large numbers of customer service employees, in an attempt to save money. However, this strategy often boomeranged, resulting in a rapid decline in service levels that spurred discontented customers to take their business elsewhere.

Pricing Implications of Cost Analysis

To make a profit, a firm must set its price high enough to recover the full costs of producing and marketing the service, and add a sufficient margin to yield the desired profit margin at the predicted sales volume. Service businesses with high fixed costs include those with expensive physical facilities (such as hospitals or colleges), or a fleet of vehicles (such as airlines or trucking companies), or a network (such as telecommunications companies, railroads, or gas pipeline companies).

In some of these services, however, the variable costs of serving an extra customer may be minimal. Under such conditions, managers may feel that they have

MARKETING REVIEW
UNDERSTANDING COSTS, CONTRIBUTION, AND BREAK-EVEN ANALYSIS

Fixed costs—sometimes referred to as overheads—are those economic costs that a supplier would continue to incur (at least in the short run) even if no services were sold. These costs are likely to include rent, depreciation, utilities, taxes, insurance, salaries and wages for managers and long-term employees, security, and interest payments.

Variable costs refer to the economic costs associated with serving an additional customer, such as making an additional bank transaction or selling an additional seat on a flight. In many services, such costs are very low. For instance, very little labor or fuel cost involved in transporting an extra passenger on a flight. In a theater, the cost of seating an extra patron is close to zero. More significant variable costs are associated with such activities as serving food and beverages, or installing new parts when undertaking repairs, because they include providing often costly physical products in addition to labor. Just because a firm has sold a service at a price that exceeds its variable cost doesn't mean that the firm is now profitable, for there are still fixed and semivariable costs to be recouped.

Semivariable costs fall in between fixed and variable costs. They represent expenses that rise or fall in a stepwise fashion as the volume of business increases or decreases. Examples include adding an extra flight to meet increased demand on a specific air route or hiring a part-time employee to work in a restaurant on busy weekends.

Contribution is the difference between the variable cost of selling an extra unit of service and the money received from the buyer of that service. It goes to cover fixed and semivariable costs before creating profits.

Determining and allocating economic costs can be a challenging task in some service operations because of the difficulty of deciding how to assign fixed costs in a multiservice facility, such as a hospital. For instance, there are certain fixed costs associated with running the emergency department in a hospital. Beyond that, there are fixed costs of running the hospital of which the emergency department is a part. How much of the hospital's fixed costs should be allocated to the emergency department? A hospital manager might use one of several approaches to calculate the emergency department's share of overheads. These might include (1) the percentage of total floor space that it occupies, (2) the percentage of employee hours or payroll that it accounts for, or (3) the percentage of total patient contact hours involved. Each method is likely to yield a totally different fixed-cost allocation: One method might show the emergency department to be very profitable, while the other might make it seem like a big loss-producing operation.

Break-even analysis: Managers need to know at what sales volume level a service will become profitable. This is called the break-even point. The necessary analysis involves dividing the total fixed and semivariable costs by the contribution received on each unit of service. For instance, if a 100-room hotel needs to cover fixed and semivariable costs of $2 million a year, and the average contribution per room-night is $100, then the hotel needs to sell 20,000 room-nights per year out of a total annual capacity of 36,500. If prices are cut by an average of $20 per room-night (*or* variable costs rise by $20), then the contribution will drop to $80 and the hotel's break-even volume will rise to 25,000 room-nights. The required sales volume needs to be related to *price sensitivity* (Will customers be willing to pay this much?), *market size* (Is the market large enough to support this level of patronage after taking competition into account?), *maximum capacity* (the hotel in our example has a capacity of 36,500 room-nights per year, assuming no rooms are taken out of service for maintenance or renovation).

tremendous pricing flexibility and be tempted to set a very low price to boost sales. Some firms promote *loss leaders,* which are services sold at less than full cost to attract customers, who (it is hoped) will then be tempted to buy profitable service offerings from the same organization in the future. However, there will be no profit at the end of the year unless all relevant costs have been recovered. Many service businesses have gone bankrupt because they ignored this fact. Hence, firms that compete on the basis of low prices need to have a very good understanding of their cost structure and of the sales volume needed to break even at particular prices.

One advantage of outsourcing is that the cost of service provision becomes more explicit, with outsourced services such as customer contact centers, ownership and operation of equipment or software often being priced on a per-use, per-transaction, per-call, or per-minute basis, thereby avoiding the misperception that variable costs are negligible.

As a service marketer, you will need to move beyond seeing costs just from an accounting perspective. Rather, you should them as an integral part of the company's efforts to create value for its customers. Antonella Carù and Antonella Cugini clarify the limitations of traditional cost measurement systems, and recommend relating the costs of any given activity to the value generated:

> Costs have nothing to do with value, which is established by the market and, in the final analysis, by the degree of customer acceptance. The customer is not interested a priori in the cost of a product . . . but in its value and price. . . .
>
> Management control which limits itself to cost monitoring without interesting itself in value is completely one-sided. . . . The problem of businesses is not so much that of cost control as it is the separation of value activities from other activities. The market only pays for the former. Businesses which carry out unnecessary activities are destined to find themselves being overtaken by competitors which have already eliminated these.[4]

Competition-Based Pricing

Firms with relatively undifferentiated services need to monitor what competitors are charging and should try to price accordingly. When customers see little or no difference between competing offerings, they may just choose what they perceive to be the cheapest. In such a situation, the firm with the lowest cost per unit of service enjoys an enviable market advantage, and often assumes *price leadership*. Here, one firm acts as the price leader, with others taking their cue from this company. You can sometimes see this phenomenon at the local level when several gas stations within a short distance of one another compete. As soon as one station raises or lowers its prices, the others follow suit.

Price competition intensifies with (1) increasing number of competitors, (2) increasing number of substituting offers, (3) wider distribution of competitor and/or substitution offers, and (4) increasing surplus capacity in the industry. Although some service industries can be fiercely competitive (e.g., the airline industry or online banking), not all are, especially when one or more the following circumstances reduce price competition:

- *Non-price-related costs of using competing alternatives are high.* When saving time and effort are of equal or greater importance to customers than price in selecting a supplier, the intensity of price competition is reduced.
- *Personal relationships matter.* For services that are highly personalized and customized, such as hair styling or family medical care, relationships with individual providers are often very important to customers, thus discouraging them from responding to competitive offers.
- *Switching costs are high.* When it takes time, money, and effort to switch providers, customers are less likely to take advantage of competing offers. Cellular phone providers often require a one- or two-year contract from their subscribers, and specifying significant financial penalties for early cancellation of service.
- *Time and location specificity reduce choice.* When people want to use a service at a specific location or at a particular time (or perhaps both, simultaneously), they usually find they have fewer options.[5]

Firms that are always reacting to competitors' price changes run the risk of pricing *lower* than might really be necessary. Managers should beware of falling into the trap of comparing competitors' prices dollar for dollar, and then seeking to match them. A better strategy is to take into account the entire cost to customers of each competitive offering, including all related financial and nonmonetary costs, plus potential switching costs, and then compare this total with that of the provider's own service. Managers should also assess the effect of distribution, time, and location factors, as well as estimating competitors' available capacity, before deciding what response is appropriate.

Value-Based Pricing

No customer will pay more for a service than he or she thinks it is worth (although people are often disappointed when they review the value of the service they actually received). So marketers need to understand how customers perceive service value in order to set an appropriate price. Gerald Smith and Thomas Nagle emphasize the importance of understanding the monetary worth of the incremental value created by a service, a task that often requires extensive marketing research, especially in business-to-business markets.[6]

Understanding Net Value

When customers purchase a service, they are weighing the perceived benefits of the service against the perceived costs they will incur. As we saw in Chapter 3, companies sometimes create several tiers of service, recognizing the various trade-offs that customers are willing to make among these various costs. Customer definitions of value may be highly personal and idiosyncratic. Valarie Zeithaml proposes four broad expressions of value:

- Value is low price.
- Value is whatever I want in a product.
- Value is the quality I get for the price I pay.
- Value is what I get for what I give.[7]

In this book, we focus on the fourth category and use the term *net value*, which is the sum of all perceived benefits (gross value) minus the sum of all perceived costs of service. The greater the positive difference between the two, the greater is the net value. Economists use the term *consumer surplus* to define the difference between the price customers pay and the amount they would actually have been willing to pay to obtain the desired benefits (or "utility") offered by a specific product.

If the perceived costs of a service are greater than the perceived benefits, then the service in question will possess negative net value, and the consumer will not buy. You can think of calculations that customers make in their minds as being similar to weighing materials on a pair of old-fashioned scales, with product benefits in one tray and the costs associated with obtaining those benefits in the other tray (Figure 5.2). When customers evaluate competing services, they are basically comparing the relative net values.

Enhancing Gross Value

Hermann Simon, an international consultant, argues that service pricing strategies are often unsuccessful because they lack a clear association between price and value.[8] As we discussed in Chapter 3, a marketer can increase the gross value of a service by adding benefits to the core product and by enhancing supplementary services. There are four distinct but related strategies for capturing and communicating the value of a service: uncertainty reduction, relationship enhancement, low cost leadership, and value perception management.[9]

Reducing Uncertainty

If customers are unsure about how much value they will receive from a particular service, they may remain with a supplier they already know or not purchase at all. Possible ways, individually or in combination, to reduce this uncertainty, include benefit-driven pricing, and flat-rate pricing.

- *Benefit-driven pricing* involves pricing that aspect of the service that benefits customers directly (requiring marketers to research what aspects of the service their customers value most and what aspects they value least.) For instance, prices for online information services are often based on log-on time, but what customers really value is the information that is browsed and retrieved. Poorly designed web sites often waste customers' time because they are difficult to navigate and make it hard for users to find what they're looking for. The result is that pricing and value creation are out of sync.

Figure 5.2 Net Value equals Benefits minus Costs

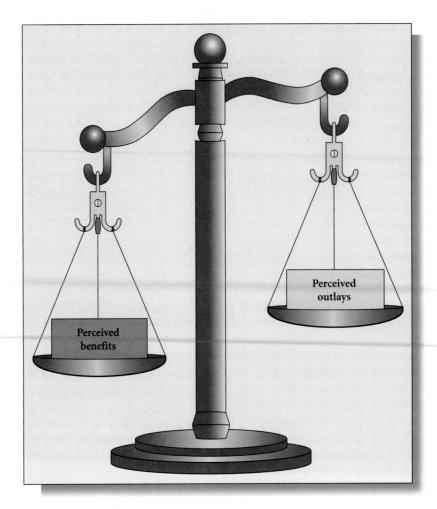

- *Flat-rate pricing* involves quoting a fixed price in advance of service delivery so as to avoid surprises for users. In essence, the risk is transferred from the customer to the supplier in the event that the service takes longer to deliver or costs were underestimated. Flat-rate pricing can be effective in situations where service prices are unpredictable, suppliers are poor at cost control, or competitors make low estimates to win business but subsequently claim that they were not making a firm pricing commitment.

Relationship Pricing

Discounting to win new business is not the best approach if a firm is seeking to attract customers who will remain loyal. Research indicates that those who are attracted by cut-price offers are easily enticed away by another offer from a competitor.[10] More creative strategies focus on giving customers both price and nonprice incentives to consolidate their business with a single supplier. A strategy of discounting prices for large purchases can often be profitable for both parties, because the customer benefits from lower prices, while the supplier may enjoy lower variable costs resulting from economies of scale. An alternative to volume discounting on a single service is to offer discounts when two or more services are purchased together. The greater the number of different services a customer purchases from a single supplier, the closer the relationship is likely to be.

Cost Leadership

Low-priced services appeal to customers on tight financial budgets and may also stimulate larger purchases. One challenge when pricing low is to convince customers that they shouldn't equate price with quality but instead feel they're getting good value. A second challenge is to ensure that economic costs are kept low enough to enable profits. Some service businesses have built their entire strategy around being

Figure 5.3 Blondie Seeks Her Money's Worth from the Plumber

the cost leader. A classic U.S. example of a cost leader in the airline business is Southwest Airlines, whose low fares often compete with the price of bus, train, or car travel. Southwest's low-cost operations strategy has been studied by airlines all over the world and now has many imitators, including Ryanair and easyJet in Europe, and WestJet in Canada, as well as JetBlue and others in the United States.

Managing the Perception of Value

Value is subjective, and not all customers have the expertise to assess the quality and value they receive. This is true in particular for credence services (discussed in Chapter 2), for which customers cannot assess the quality of a service even after consumption.[11] Marketers of services such as strategy consulting and specialized hospitals must find ways to communicate the time, research, professional expertise, and attention to detail that go into, for example, completing a best-practice consulting project. Why? Because the invisibility of backstage facilities and labor makes it hard for customers to see what they're getting for their money.

Consider a homeowner who calls an electrician to repair a defective circuit. The electrician arrives, carrying a small bag of tools. He disappears into the closet where the circuit board is located, soon locates the problem, replaces a defective circuit breaker, and presto! Everything works. A mere 20 minutes has elapsed. A few days later, the homeowner is horrified to receive a bill for $90, most of it for labor charges. Just think what the couple could have bought for that amount of money—new clothes, several compact discs, a nice dinner. Not surprisingly, customers are often left feeling that they have been exploited—take a look at Blondie's reaction to the plumber in Figure 5.3.

Effective communications and even personal explanations are needed to help customers understand the value they receive. What they often fail to recognize are the fixed costs that business owners need to recoup: the office, telephone, insurance, vehicles, tools, fuel, and office support staff. The variable costs of a home visit are also higher than they appear. To the 20 minutes spent at the house might be added 15 minutes of driving each way, plus 5 minutes each to unload and reload needed tools and supplies from the van, thus effectively tripling the labor time to a total of 60 minutes devoted to this call. And the firm still has to add a margin in order to make a profit.

More recently, auctions and dynamic pricing have become increasingly popular as a way to price according to value perceptions of customers—see Service Perspectives 5.1.

Reducing Related Monetary and Nonmonetary Costs

From a customer's standpoint, the price charged by a supplier is only part of the costs involved in purchasing and using a service. Users incur other outlays, comprising both *incremental financial outlays* and a variety of *nonmonetary* costs.

Incremental Financial Outlays

Customers often incur significant financial costs in searching for, purchasing, and using the service, above and beyond the purchase price paid to the supplier. For instance, the cost of an evening at the theater for a couple with young children usually

Dynamic pricing—also known as customized or personalized pricing—is a new version of the age-old practice of price discrimination and is popular with service suppliers because of its potential to increase profits. Retailing over the internet, or e-tailing, lends itself well to this strategy because changing prices electronically is a simple procedure. Dynamic pricing enables e-tailers to charge different customers different prices for the same product based on information collected about their purchase history, preferences, price sensitivity, and so on. Tickets.com gained up to 45% more revenue per event when pricing of concerts and events was adjusted to meet demand and supply.

E-tailers are often uncomfortable about admitting to use of dynamic pricing because of the ethical and legal issues associated with price discrimination. Customers of Amazon.com were upset when they learned that the online megastore was not charging everyone the same price for the same movie DVDs. A study of online consumers by the University of Pennsylvania's Annenberg Public Policy Center found that 87 percent of respondents did not think dynamic pricing was acceptable.

Reverse Auctions

Travel e-tailers such Priceline.com, Hotwire.com, and Lowestfare.com follow a customer-driven pricing strategy known as a *reverse auction*. Each firm acts as an intermediary between prospective buyers, who request quotations for a product or service, and multiple suppliers, who quote the best price they're willing to offer. Buyers can then review the offers and select the supplier that best meets their needs. Although the offer usually describes product attributes, it often doesn't provide brand information. Priceline has moved to correct this deficiency. Says a spokesperson, "Customers can now choose the exact brand name and product from a published list price, whereas before they could only use our name-your-own-price [service]. As a result, people were never sure what hotel they would get until they made their purchase, so if you were traveling with friends, you wouldn't know if you'd get the same hotel."

Different business models underlie these services. Although some are provided free to end users, most e-tailers either receive a commission from the supplier or do not pass on the whole savings. Others charge customers either a fixed fee or one based on a percentage of the savings.

Traditional Auctions

Other e-tailers, such as eBay and Yahoo! Auctions, follow the traditional online auction model in which bidders place bids for an item and compete with each other to determine who buys it. Marketers of both consumer and industrial products use such auctions to sell obsolete or overstock items, collectibles, rare items, and second-hand merchandise. This form of retailing has become immensely successful since eBay first launched it in 1995.

Shopbots Help Consumers to Benefit from Dynamic Pricing

Consumers now have tools of their own to combat the potentially exploitive practices of dynamic pricing. One approach involves using shopbots to track competitive prices. *Shopbots*, or shopping robots, are basically intelligent agents that automatically collect price and product information from multiple online vendors. A customer has only to visit a shopbot site, such as Dealtime.com, and run a search for the desired item. The shopbot instantly queries all the associated retailers to check availability, features, and price, then presents the results in a comparison table.

There's little doubt that dynamic pricing is here to stay. With further advances in technology and wider applications, it is extending its reach to more and more service categories.

Sources: Stephan Biller, Lap Mui Ann Chan, David Simchi-Levi, and Julie Swann, "Dynamic Pricing and Direct-to-Customer Model in the Automotive Industry," *Electronic Commerce Research*, 5, no. 2 (April 2005): 309–334; Melissa Campanelli, "Getting Personal: Will Engaging in Dynamic Pricing Help or Hurt Your Business?" *Entrepreneur*, 33, issue 10 (October 2005): 44–46; Mikhail I. Melnik, and James Alm, "Seller Reputation, Information Signals, and Prices for Heterogeneous Coins on eBay." *Southern Economic Journal*, 72, issue 2 (2005): 305–328.

far exceeds the price of the two tickets, because it can include such expenses as hiring a babysitter, travel, parking, food, and beverages.

Nonmonetary Costs

Nonmonetary costs reflect the time, effort, and discomfort associated with search, purchase, and use of a service. Like many customers, you may refer to them collectively as "effort" or "hassle." Nonmonetary costs tend to be higher when customers are involved in production (which is particularly important in people processing services and in self-service) and must travel to the service site. Services that are high in experience and credence attributes may also create psychological costs, such as anxiety. There are four distinct categories of nonmonetary costs: time, physical, psychological, and sensory costs.

- *Time costs* are inherent in service delivery. Today's customers are often time-constrained and may use similar terms to define time usage as they do for money, speaking of budgeting, spending, investing, wasting, losing, and saving time. Time spent on one activity represents an opportunity cost because it could be spent more profitably in other ways. Internet users are often frustrated by the amount of time they spend to find information on a web site. Many people loathe visiting government offices to obtain passports, driving licenses, or permits, not because of the fees involved, but because of the time "wasted."
- *Physical costs* (such as fatigue and discomfort) may be incurred in obtaining services, especially if customers must go to the service factory, if queuing is involved, and if delivery entails self-service.
- *Psychological costs* such as mental effort, perceived risk, cognitive dissonance, feelings of inadequacy, or fear are sometimes attached to buying and using a particular service.
- *Sensory costs* relate to unpleasant sensations affecting any of the five senses. In a service environment, these costs may include putting up with noise, unpleasant smells, drafts, excessive heat or cold, uncomfortable seating, visually unappealing environments, and even nasty tastes.

As shown in Figure 5.4, service users can incur costs during any of the three stages of the service consumption model introduced in Chapter 2. Consequently, firms have to consider (1) *search costs,* (2) *purchase and service encounter costs,* and (3) *postconsumption* or *aftercosts.* When you were looking at colleges and universities, how much money, time, and effort did you spend before deciding where to apply? How much time and effort would you put into selecting a new mobile phone service provider or a bank, or planning a vacation?

A strategy of minimizing those nonmonetary and related monetary costs to increase consumer value can create competitive advantage for a firm. Possible approaches include:

- Working with operations experts to reduce the time required to complete service purchase, delivery, and consumption

Figure 5.4
Defining Total User Costs

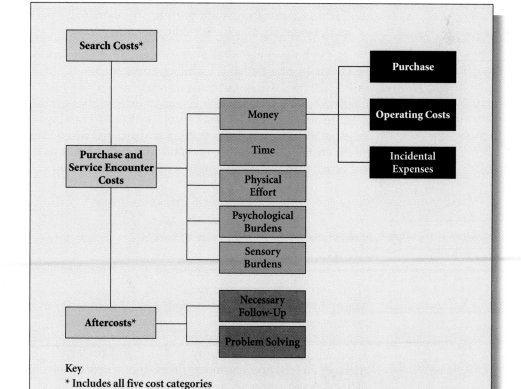

Figure 5.5
Trading Off Monetary
and Nonmonetary
Costs

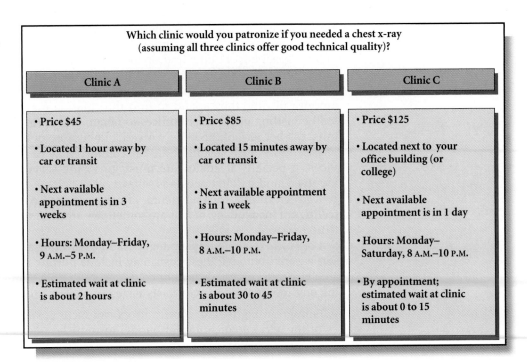

**Which clinic would you patronize if you needed a chest x-ray
(assuming all three clinics offer good technical quality)?**

Clinic A	Clinic B	Clinic C
• Price $45	• Price $85	• Price $125
• Located 1 hour away by car or transit	• Located 15 minutes away by car or transit	• Located next to your office building (or college)
• Next available appointment is in 3 weeks	• Next available appointment is in 1 week	• Next available appointment is in 1 day
• Hours: Monday–Friday, 9 A.M.–5 P.M.	• Hours: Monday–Friday, 8 A.M.–10 P.M.	• Hours: Monday–Saturday, 8 A.M.–10 P.M.
• Estimated wait at clinic is about 2 hours	• Estimated wait at clinic is about 30 to 45 minutes	• By appointment; estimated wait at clinic is about 0 to 15 minutes

- Minimizing unwanted psychological costs of service at each stage by eliminating or redesigning unpleasant or inconvenient procedures, educating customers on what to expect,. and retraining staff to be friendlier and more helpful
- Eliminating or minimizing unwanted physical effort, notably during search and delivery processes
- Decreasing unpleasant sensory costs of service by creating more attractive visual environments, reducing noise, installing more comfortable furniture and equipment, curtailing offensive smells, and the like
- Suggesting ways in which customers can reduce associated monetary costs, including discounts with partner suppliers (e.g., parking) or offering mail or online delivery of activities that previously required a personal visit.

Perceptions of net value may vary widely among customers and from one situation to another for the same customer. Service markets can often be segmented by sensitivity to time savings and convenience versus sensitivity to price savings.[12] Consider Figure 5.5, which identifies a choice of three clinics available to an individual who needs to obtain a routine chest x-ray. In addition to varying dollar prices for the service, there are different time and effort costs associated with using each service. Depending on the customer's priorities, nonmonetary costs may be as important as, or even more important than, the price charged by the service providers.

REVENUE MANAGEMENT: WHAT IT IS AND HOW IT WORKS

Many service businesses now focus on strategies to maximize the revenue (or contribution) that can be derived from available capacity at any given time. Revenue management is important in value creation, as it ensures better capacity utilization and reserves available capacity for higher-paying segments. It's a sophisticated approach to managing supply and demand under varying degrees of constraint. Airlines, hotels, and car rental firms, in particular, have become adept at varying their prices in response to the price sensitivity and needs of different market segments at different times of the day, week, or season.

Reserving Capacity for High-Yield Customers

In practice, revenue management (also known as yield management) involves setting prices according to predicted demand levels among different market segments. The least price-sensitive segment is the first to be allocated capacity, paying the highest price; other segments follow at progressively lower prices. Because higher-paying segments often book closer to the time of actual consumption, firms need a disciplined approach to save capacity for them instead of simply selling on a first-come, first-served basis. For example, business travelers often reserve airline seats, hotel rooms, and rental cars at short notice, but vacationers may book leisure travel months in advance, and convention organizers often block hotel space years in advance of a big event.

A well-designed revenue management system can predict with reasonable accuracy how many customers will use a given service at a specific time at each of several different price levels, and then block the relevant amount of capacity at each level (known as a *price bucket*). Sophisticated firms use complex mathematical models for this purpose and employ revenue managers to make decisions about inventory allocation.

In the case of airlines, these models integrate massive historical databases on past passenger travel and can forecast demand up to one year in advance for each individual departure. At fixed intervals, the revenue manager—who may be assigned specific routes at a large airline—checks the actual pace of bookings (i.e., sales at a given time before departure) and compares it with the forecasted pace. If there are significant deviations between actual and forecasted demand, the manager adjusts the size of the inventory buckets. For example, if the booking pace for a higher-paying segment is stronger than expected, additional capacity is allocated to this segment and taken from the lowest-paying segment. The objective is to maximize the revenues from the flight. Best Practice in Action 5.1 shows how revenue management has been implemented at American Airlines, long an industry leader in this field.

BEST PRACTICE IN ACTION 5.1
Pricing Seats on Flight AA 2015

Revenue management departments use sophisticated yield management software and powerful computers to forecast, track, and manage each flight on a given date separately. Let's look at American Airlines flight 2015, a popular flight from Chicago to Phoenix, Arizona, which departs daily at 5:30 p.m. on the 1,370-mi (2,200-km) journey.

The 125 seats in coach (economy class) are divided into seven fare categories, called "buckets" by yield management specialists. There is an enormous variation in ticket prices among these seats: Round-trip fares range from $238 for a bargain excursion ticket (with various restrictions and a cancellation penalty) all the way to $1,404 for an unrestricted fare. Seats are also available in the small first-class section, at an even higher price. Scott McCartney tells how ongoing analysis by the computer program changes the allocation of seats among the seven buckets in economy class:

> In the weeks before each Chicago–Phoenix flight, American's yield management computers constantly adjust the number of seats in each bucket, taking into account tickets sold, historical ridership patterns, and connecting passengers likely to use the route as one leg of a longer trip.

If advance bookings are slim, American adds seats to low-fare buckets. If business customers buy unrestricted fares earlier than expected, the yield management computer takes seats out of the discount buckets and preserves them for last-minute bookings that the database predicts will still show up.

With 69 of 125 coach seats already sold four weeks before one recent departure of Flight 2015, American's computer began to limit the number of seats in lower-priced buckets. A week later, it totally shut off sales for the bottom three buckets, priced $300 or less. To a Chicago customer looking for a cheap seat, the flight was "sold out.". . .

One day before departure, with 130 passengers booked for the 125-seat flight, American still offered five seats at full fare because its computer database indicated 10 passengers were likely not to show up or take other flights. Flight 2015 departed full and no one was bumped.

Although AA 2015 for that date is now history, it has not been forgotten. The booking experience for this flight was saved in the memory of the yield management program to help the airline do an even better job of forecasting in the future.

Source: Adapted from Scott McCartney, "Ticket Shock: Business Fares Increase Even as Leisure Travel Keeps Getting Cheaper." *The Wall Street Journal,* (November 3, 1997): A1, A10.

(Q) What is your role as a revenue manager?

(A) When I started in 1993, the primary focus was on forecasting, inventory control, pricing, market segment and geographic mix, and allotment control. The Internet changed the scene significantly and several global giants, like Expedia and Travelocity, emerged after 9/11 when travel bookings plummeted and the industry realized the power of the Internet to help them sell distressed inventory. But airlines and hotels want to control their own inventory and pricing to cut costs and reduce reliance on intermediaries, so there's increasing focus on driving bookings via direct channels such as their own branded websites, building online brands, and implementing CRM programs. My role has also broadened to include revenue management of secondary income sources such as restaurants, golf courses and spa, as well as mainstream hotel rooms.

(Q) What differences do you see between revenue management for airlines and hotels?

(A) Fundamentally, the techniques of forecasting and optimizing pricing and inventory controls are the same. However, some key differences exist. Airlines have a larger ability to use pricing to expand travel demand from the home market. By contrast, pricing practices in hotels can shift market share within a location but, as a rule, not overall market size. Although consumers see many pricing practices—such as advance purchase restrictions and discounts—as fair practice for the airline industry, they see them as less fair when applied by the hotel industry.

Organizational structure also tends to be different. The airlines adopt central revenue management control for all flights and revenue managers have little interaction with the reservations and sales teams in the field. A more precise and statistical application of pricing and inventory control is thus the focus. In the hotel industry, revenue management is decentralized to every hotel, requiring daily interaction with reservations and sales. The human element is key for successful implementation in hotels, requiring acceptance of pricing and inventory decisions not only by consumers but also by internal departments such as reservations, sales and even front office.

(Q) What skills do you need to succeed as a revenue manager?

(A) Strong statistical and analytical skills are essential, but to be really successful, revenue managers need to have equally strong interpersonal and influencing skills in order for their decisions to be accepted by other departments. Traditional ways of segmenting customers via their transactional characteristics such as booking lead time, channel of reservation and type of promotion are insufficient. Both behavioral characteristics (such as motive for travel, products sought, spending pattern and degree of autonomy) and emotional characteristics (such as self-image, conspicuous consumer or reluctant traveler, impulse or planned) need to be incorporated into revenue management considerations.

(Q) How are revenue management practices perceived by customers?

(A) The art of implementation is not to let the customers feel that your pricing and inventory control practices are unfair and meant primarily to increase the top and bottom line of the company. Intelligent and meaningful rate fences have to be used to allow customers to self-segment so that they retain a feeling of choice.

(Q) What is the daily nature of the job?

(A) The market presents a lot of demand changes and you need to monitor your competitors' price as it fluctuates daily across the various distribution changes. It's definitely a pre-requisite to be quick in analysis and decisive. One needs to feel comfortable taking calculated risks and choose from a plethora of revenue management and pricing tools to decide on the best fit for the situation.

We thank Jeannette Ho, Vice President Distribution Marketing & Revenue Management at Raffles International Limited, for this interview, conducted January 6, 2006. Jeannette has been responsible for spearheading and implementing the revenue management initiatives for the Group since February 2005. Her team drives the company's global distribution strategy and oversees its e-commerce channels and Central Reservations System. Over the past 12 years, Jeannette has been working in revenue management with various international companies such as Singapore Airlines, Banyan Tree, and the Westin Stamford & Westin Plaza Hotels.

How Does Competitors' Pricing Affect Revenue Management?

Because revenue management systems monitor booking pace, they indirectly pick up the effect of competitors' pricing. If a firm prices too low, it will experience a higher booking pace, and its cheaper seats will fill up quickly. That is generally not good, as it means a higher share of late-booking but high-fare-paying customers will not be able to get their seats confirmed, and will therefore fly on competing airlines. If the initial pricing is too high, the firm will get too low a share of early-booking segments (which still tend to offer a reasonable yield) and may later have to offer deeply discounted "last-minute" prices to sell excess capacity and thus obtain some contribution toward fixed costs. Some of these sales may take place through reverse auctions, using intermediaries such as Priceline.com.

Revenue management has been most effective when applied to operations characterized by relatively fixed capacity, a high fixed cost structure, perishable inventory, variable and uncertain demand, and varying customer price sensitivity. Industries that have implemented revenue management successfully include airlines, car rentals, hotels, and, more recently, hospitals, restaurants, golf courses, on-demand IT services, data processing centers, and even nonprofit organizations.[13] Service Perspectives 5.2 gives insights to the work and thinking of a revenue manager.

Price Elasticity

Revenue management requires two or more segments that attach different value to the service and have different price elasticities. To allocate and price capacity effectively, the revenue manager needs to determine how sensitive demand is to price and what net revenues will be generated at different prices for each target segment. The concept of elasticity describes how sensitive demand is to changes in price, and is computed as follows:

$$\text{Price elasticity} = \frac{\text{percentage change in demand}}{\text{percentage change in price}}$$

When price elasticity is at "unity," sales of a service rise (or fall) by the same percentage that price falls (or rises). If a small change in price has a big effect on sales, demand for that product is said to be price-elastic. If a change in price has little effect on sales, demand is described as price-inelastic. The concept is illustrated in the simple chart presented in Figure 5.6, which shows the price elasticity for two segments, one with a highly elastic demand (a small change in price results in a big change in

Figure 5.6
Illustration of Price Elasticity

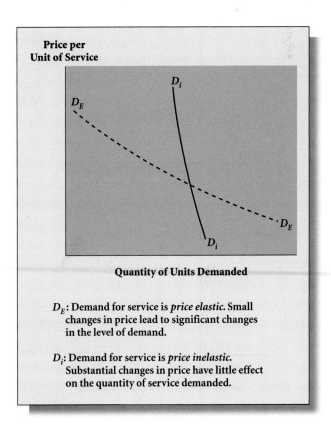

D_E: Demand for service is *price elastic.* Small changes in price lead to significant changes in the level of demand.

D_i: Demand for service is *price inelastic.* Substantial changes in price have little effect on the quantity of service demanded.

the amount demanded), and the other with a highly inelastic demand (even big changes in price have little effect on the amount demanded).

Designing Rate Fences

Inherent in revenue management is the concept of *price customization*—charging different customers different prices for what is, in effect, the same product. As noted by Hermann Simon and Robert Dolan,

> The basic idea of price customization is simple: Have people pay prices based on the value they put on the product. Obviously you can't just hang out a sign saying "Pay me what it's worth to you" or "It's $80 if you value it that much but only $40 if you don't." You have to find a way to segment customers by their valuations. In a sense, you have to "build a fence" between high-value customers and low-value customers so the "high" buyers can't take advantage of the low price.[14]

How can a firm ensure that customers for whom the service offers high value are unable to take advantage of lower price buckets? Properly designed rate fences allow customers to self-segment on the basis of service characteristics and willingness to

Table 5.2
Key Categories of
Rate Fences

RATE FENCES	EXAMPLES
Physical (product-related) Fences	
Basic product	• Class of travel (business/economy class)
	• Size and furnishing of a hotel room
	• Seat location in a theater
Amenities	• Free breakfast at a hotel, airport pick up, etc.
	• Free golf cart at a golf course
Service level	• Priority wait listing, separate check-in counters with no or only short lines
	• Increase in baggage allowance
	• Dedicated service hotlines
	• Dedicated account management team
Nonphysical Fences	
Transaction Characteristics	
Time of booking or reservation	• Requirements for advance purchase
	• Must pay full fare 2 weeks before departure
Location of booking or reservation	• Passengers booking air tickets for same route in different countries charged different prices
Flexibility of ticket use	• Fees/penalties for canceling or changing a reservation (up to loss of entire ticket price)
	• Nonrefundable reservations fees
Consumption Characteristics	
Time or duration of use	• Early-bird special in a restaurant before 6:00 p.m.
	• Must stay over a Saturday night for an airline, hotel, or car rental booking.
	• Must stay at least for 5 nights
Location of consumption	• Price based on departure location, especially in international travel
	• Prices vary by location (between cities, city center versus edges of the city)
Buyer Characteristics	
Frequency or volume of consumption	• Member of certain loyalty tier with the firm (e.g., Platinum member) gets priority pricing, discounts, or loyalty benefits
Group membership	• Child, student, senior citizen discounts
	• Affiliation with certain groups (e.g., alumni)
Size of customer group	• Group discounts based on size of group

pay, and help companies to restrict lower prices to customers who are willing to accept certain restrictions on their purchase and consumption experiences.

Fences can be either physical or nonphysical. *Physical fences* refer to tangible product differences related to the different prices, such as the seat location in a theater, or the size and furnishing of a hotel room. *Nonphysical fences* refer to consumption, transaction, or buyer characteristics. For example, they include staying a certain length of time in a hotel, playing golf on a weekday afternoon, cancellation or change penalties, or booking a certain length of time ahead. Examples of common rate fences are shown in Table 5.2.

Physical fences reflect tangible differences in the actual service (e.g., first class is better than economy class), whereas nonphysical services actually refer to the same basic service (e.g., there is no difference in economy class service whether a person bought a ticket really cheaply or paid full fare for it).

In summary, using a detailed understanding of customer needs, preferences, and willingness to pay, product and revenue managers can jointly design effective products comprising the core service, physical product features (physical fences), and nonphysical product features (nonphysical fences). A good understanding of the demand curve is needed so that "buckets" of inventory can be assigned to the various products and price categories. An example from the airline industry is shown in Figure 5.7. And lastly, the design of revenue management systems needs to incorporate safeguards for

Figure 5.7
Relating Price Buckets to the Demand Curve

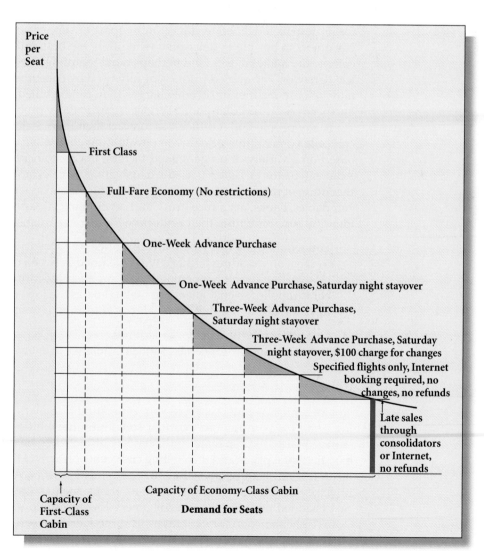

Note: Dark shaded areas denote amount of consumer surplus (goal of segmented pricing is to minimize this).

consumers. For additional insights into revenue management strategies, see the reading by Sheryl E. Kimes and Richard B. Chase, "The Strategic Levers of Yield Management," on pages 211–219.

ETHICAL CONCERNS IN SERVICE PRICING

Do you sometimes have difficulty understanding how much it's going to cost you to use a service? Do you believe that many prices are unfair? If so, you're not alone.[15] The fact is, service users can't always be sure in advance what they will receive in return for their payments. There's an implicit assumption among many customers that a higher-priced service should offer more benefits and better quality than a lower-priced one. For example, a professional—say, a lawyer—who charges very high fees is assumed to be more skilled than one who is relatively inexpensive. Although price can serve as a surrogate for quality, it is sometimes hard to be sure whether the extra value is really there.

Are Service Pricing Schedules Too Complex?

Pricing schedules for services tend to be complex and hard to understand. Comparison across providers may even require complex spreadsheets or even mathematical formulas. Consumer advocates sometimes charge that this complexity represents a deliberate choice on the part of service suppliers, who don't want customers to be able to determine who offers the best value for the money. In fact, complexity makes it easy (and perhaps more tempting) for firms to engage in unethical behavior. The quoted prices typically used by consumers for price comparisons may be only the first of several charges they can be billed. As described in Service Perspectives 5.3, cellular phone service is particularly problematic in this respect.

Many people find it difficult to forecast their own usage, which makes it hard to compute comparative prices when evaluating competing suppliers whose fees are based on a variety of usage-related factors. It's no coincidence that humorist Scott Adams (creator of *Dilbert*), used exclusively service examples when he "branded" the future of pricing as "confusiology." Noting that firms such as telecommunication companies, banks, insurance firms, and other financial service providers offer nearly identical services within their respective industries, Adams remarked:

> You would think this would create a price war and drive prices down to the cost of providing it (that's what I learned between naps in my economic classes), but it isn't happening. The companies are forming efficient confusopolies so customers can't tell who has the lowest prices. Companies have learned to use the complexities of life as an economic tool.[16]

One of the roles of effective government regulation, says Adams, should be to discourage this tendency for certain service industries to evolve into "confusopolies."

Piling on the Fees

Not all business models are based on generating income from sales. There is a growing trend today to impose fees that sometimes have little to do with usage. In the United States, the car rental industry has attracted some notoriety for advertising bargain rental prices and then telling customers on arrival that other fees such as collision insurance and personal insurance are compulsory. Also, staff sometimes fails to clarify certain "small-print" contract terms such as (say) a high-mileage charge that is added once the car exceeds a very low threshold of free miles. The "hidden extras" phenomenon for car rentals in some Florida resort towns got so bad at one point that people were joking, "The car is free, the keys are extra." A not uncommon practice when the car is returned is to charge a fee for refueling a partially empty tank that far exceeds what the driver would pay at the pump.[17]

Recent years have seen a rapid expansion in the availability of cellular (mobile) telephone services. Significant technological improvements have expanded the capability of these services, including the ability to transmit photos and download music. Not surprisingly, demand has exploded and competition has become intense.

In tailoring their services to the widely varying needs and calling patterns of different market segments, cell phone companies have developed a bewildering array of plans that defy easy comparison across suppliers. Plans can be national, regional, or purely local in scope. Monthly fees vary according to the number of minutes selected in advance, which typically include separate allowances for peak and off-peak minutes. Overtime minutes and "roaming minutes" on other carriers are charged at higher rates. Some plans allow unlimited off-peak calling; others allow free incoming calls. Some providers charge calls per second, per 6-second block, or even per-minute block, resulting in vastly different costs per call. Family plans let parents and children pool their monthly minutes for use on several phones as long as the total for everyone's calling doesn't exceed the monthly quota.

In addition, baffling new fees have started to appear on bills, ranging from a "paper bill fee" to pay for the bill itself to obscure-sounding fees such as "property tax allotment," "single bill fee," and "carrier cost recovery fee." Bundled plans that include mobile, landline, and Internet services compound the confusion further, in that the various surcharges can increase the total bill by up to 25 percent. Phone bills of course include real taxes (e.g., sales tax), but on many bills the majority of surcharges, which users often misread as taxes, go directly to the phone company. For instance, the "property tax allotment" is nothing more than a factor for the property taxes the carrier pays, the "single bill fee" charges for consolidated billing of the mobile and landline services, and the "carrier cost recovery fee" is a catch-all for all sorts of operating expenses.

Research by Consumers Union (CU) found high levels of customer dissatisfaction with cell phone service. In addition to poor-quality reception, dropped calls, and inaccessible service, many concerns related to billing and pricing, with complaints about overcharges, billing mistakes, and bills padded with extra charges. Compounding the problem is the fact that companies make it hard to switch. Typically, subscribers have to sign a one- or two-year contract that imposes significant penalties, often in the range $100 to $200, for early termination. In an editorial entitled "Cell Hell," Jim Guest, CU's president, observed:

> In the 10 years since *Consumer Reports* started rating cell phones and calling plans, we've never found an easy way to compare actual costs. From what our readers tell us, they haven't either. Each carrier presents its rates, extra charges, and calling areas differently. Deciphering one company's plan is hard enough, but comparing plans from various carries is nearly impossible.

CU advocates stronger regulation of the industry to protect consumers from confusing and abusive practices, including a government-mandated standard format for presenting calling plan features and charges. According to David Bergmann of the Office of the Ohio Consumers' Council and chairman of the telecommunications committee at the National Association of State Utility Consumer Advocates, all these extra and confusing charges should be included in the advertised prices of calling plans. He said, "I don't pay a health and safety fee to restaurants. If they want to raise the price of a meal, that's fine. But customers shouldn't order something and not know what is going into the bill."

Source: Jim Guest, "Cell Hell" (p. 3) and "Complete Cell-Phone Guide," *Consumer Reports* (February 2003): 11–27; and Ken Belson, "A Monthly Mystery." *The New York Times* (August 27, 2005).

There has also been a trend toward adding (or increasing) fines and penalties. Banks have been heavily criticized for using penalties as an important revenue-generating tool as opposed to using them merely to educate customers and achieve compliance with payment deadlines. Chris Keeley, a New York University student, used his debit card to buy $230 worth of Christmas gifts. His holiday mood soured when he received a notice from his bank that he had overdrawn his checking account. Although his bank authorized each of his seven transactions, it charged him $31 per payment, totaling $217 for only $230 in purchases. Keeley maintained that he had never requested the so-called overdraft protection on his account and wished his bank had rejected the transactions, because he would then simply have paid by credit card. He fumed, "I can't help but think they wanted me to keep spending money so that they could collect these fees."[18]

The importance of fees as a proportion of profits has increased dramatically—for some banks they now exceed earnings from mortgages, credit cards, and all other lending combined. None of the fees is more controversial than "bounce protection" (i.e., allowing you to overdraw your account beyond an agreed credit line), which generates some $8 billion in income for banks and making up almost 30 percent of all their service fees. Critics feel that some banks market bounce protection too aggressively. Regulators are particularly worried about bounce protection being offered via ATMs. For example, a customer with a balance of $300 in his account, but a $500 bounce protection, could be told at the ATM that he has $800 available. If he withdrew $400, the ATM would still show available funds of $370 (after charging a fee of, for example, $30 for using the bounce protection balance).

Some banks don't charge for overdraft protection. Said Dennis DiFlorio, president for retail banking at Commerce Bancorp Inc. in Cherry Hill, New Jersey: "It's outrageous. It's not about customer convenience. It's just a way for banks to make money off customers." Commerce and other banks offer services that cover overdrafts automatically from savings accounts, other accounts, or even the customer's credit card, and don't charge fees for doing so.[19] (For further thoughts on this topic, see the reading by Emily Thornton, "Fees! Fees! Fees!" on pages 220–229.)

It's possible to design penalties that do not seem unfair to customers. Research Insights 5.1 describes what drives customers' fairness perceptions about service fees and penalties.

Designing Fairness into Revenue Management

A well-implemented revenue management strategy does not mean blind pursuit of short-term yield maximization. The following specific approaches can help to reconcile yield management practices with customer satisfaction, trust, and goodwill:[20]

- *Design price schedules and fences that are clear, logical, and fair.* Firms should proactively spell out all fees and expenses (e.g., no-show or cancellation charges) clearly in advance, so that there are no surprises. A related approach is to develop a simple fee structure so that customers can more easily understand the financial implications of a specific usage situation. For a rate fence to be perceived as fair, customers must be easily able to understand them (i.e., fences have to be transparent and upfront), see the logic in them, and be convinced that they are difficult to circumvent and therefore fair.
- *Use high published prices and frame fences as discounts.* Rate fences framed as customer gains (i.e., discounts) are generally perceived as more fair than those framed as customer losses (i.e., surcharges), even if the situations are economically equivalent. For example, a customer who patronizes her hair salon on Saturdays may perceive the salon as profiteering if she finds herself facing a weekend surcharge. However, she is likely to find the higher weekend price more acceptable if the hair salon advertises its peak weekend price as the published price, and offers a $5 discount for weekday haircuts. Furthermore, having a high published price also helps to increase the reference price and potentially quality perceptions, in addition to the feeling of being rewarded for the weekday patronage.
- *Communicate consumer benefits of revenue management.* Marketing communications should position revenue management as a win–win practice. Providing different price and value balances allows a broader spectrum of customers to self-segment and enjoy the service. It allows each customer to find the price and benefits (value) balance that best satisfies his or her needs. For example, charging a higher price for the best seats in the theater recognizes that some people are willing and able to pay more for a better location and makes it possible to sell other seats at a lower price.
- *Use bundling to "hide" discounts.* Bundling a service into a package effectively obscures the discounted price. When a cruise line includes the price of air travel or ground transportation in the cruise package, the customer knows only the total price, not the cost of the individual components. Bundling usually makes price comparisons between the bundles and its components impossible, and

Various types of "penalties" are part and parcel of many pricing schedules, ranging from late fees for DVD rentals to cancellation charges for hotel bookings and charges for late credit card payments. Customer responses to penalties can be very negative, and can lead to switching providers and poor "word of mouth." Young Kim and Amy Smith conducted an online survey using the critical incident technique (CIT), in which the 201 respondents were asked to recall a recent penalty incident, describe the situation, and then complete a set of structured questions based on how the respondents felt and how they responded to that incident. Their findings showed that negative consumer responses can be reduced significantly by following these three guidelines:

1. *Make Penalties Relative to the Crime Committed.* The survey showed that customers' negative reaction to a penalty increased drastically when they perceived that the penalty was out of proportion to the "crime" committed. Customers' negative feelings were further aggravated if they were "surprised" by the penalty being suddenly charged to them and they had not been aware of the fee or the magnitude of the fee. These findings suggest that firms can reduce negative customer responses significantly by exploring which amounts are seen as reasonable or fair for a given "customer lapse," and the fines/fees are communicated effectively even before a chargeable incident occurs (e.g., in a banking context, through a clearly explained fee schedule, and through front-line staff that explain at the time of opening an account or purchase of a bank service the potential fines or fees associated with various "violations," such as overdrawing beyond the authorized limits, bounced checks, or late payments.

2. *Consider Causal Factors and Customize Penalties.* The study showed that customers' perceptions of fairness were lower and negative responses were higher when they perceived the causes that led to the penalty to be out of their control ("I mailed the check on time—it must have been delayed in the mail"), rather than when they felt it was within their control and really their fault ("I forgot to mail the check"). To increase the perception of fairness, firms may want to identify common penalty causes that are typically out of the control of the customer, and allow the frontline to waive or reduce such fees.

In addition, it was found that customers who generally observe all the rules, and therefore have not paid fines in the past, react particularly negatively if they are fined. One respondent said, "I have always made timely payments and have never been late with a payment—they should have considered this and waived the fee." Service firms should take into account customers' penalties history in dealing with penalties, and offer differential treatments based on past behavior—perhaps waiving the fine for a first incident while at the same time communicating that the next time the fee will be charged.

3. *Focus on Fairness and Manage Emotions During Penalty Situations.* Consumers' responses are heavily driven by their perception of fairness. Customers are likely to perceived penalties as excessive and respond negatively if they find that a penalty is out of proportion compared to the damage or extra work created by the incident. One consumer complained, "I thought this particular penalty [credit card late payment] was excessive. You are already paying high interest; the penalty should have been more in line with the payment. The penalty was more than the payment!" Considering customers' perceptions of fairness might mean, for example, that the late fee for keeping a DVD too long should not exceed the potentially lost rental fees during that period.

Service companies can also make penalties seem more fair by providing adequate explanations and justifications for the penalty. Ideally, penalties should be imposed for the good of other customers (e.g., "We kept the room for you, though we could have given it to a guest on our waiting list") or the community, but not as a means for generating significant profit. Finally, the font line should to be trained in how handle customers who have become angry or distressed and who complain about penalties. (See Chapter 13 for some recommendations on how to deal with such situations.)

In sum, this study shows how firms can reduce customer unhappiness related to penalties.

Source: Adapted from Young "Sally" K. Kim and Amy K. Smith, "Crime and Punishment: Examining Customers' Responses to Service Organizations' Penalties." *Journal of Service Research,* 8, no. 2 (2005): 162–180.

thereby sidesteps potential perceptions of unfairness and reductions in reference prices.

- *Take care of loyal customers.* Firms should build in strategies for retaining valued customers, even to the extent of not charging the maximum feasible amount on a given transaction. After all, customer perceptions of price gouging do not build trust. Yield management systems can be programmed to incorporate "loyalty multipliers" for regular customers, so that reservations systems can give them "special treatment" status at peak times, even when they are not paying premium rates.

- *Use service recovery to compensate for overbooking.* Many service firms over-book to compensate for anticipated cancellations and no-shows. Profits increase, but so, too, does the incidence of being unable to honor reservations. Being "bumped" by an airline or "walked" by a hotel can lead to a loss of customer loyalty and adversely affect a firm's reputation. So it's important to back up over-booking programs with well-designed service recovery procedures, such as:

1. Give customers a choice between retaining their reservation and receiving compensation.
2. Provide sufficient advance notice that customers are able to make alternative arrangements.
3. If possible, offer a substitute service that will delight customers.

A Westin beach resort has found that it can free up capacity by offering guests who are departing the next day the option of spending their last night in a luxury hotel near the airport or in the city at no cost. Guest feedback on the free room, upgraded service, and a night in the city after a beach holiday has been very positive. From the hotel's perspective, this practice trades the cost of securing a one-night stay in another hotel against that of turning away a multiple-night guest arriving that same day.

PUTTING SERVICE PRICING INTO PRACTICE

Although the main decision in pricing is usually seen as how much to charge, there are also other decisions to be made. Table 5.3 summarizes the questions that service marketers need to ask themselves as they prepare to create and implement a well-thought-out pricing strategy. Let's look at each in turn.

How Much to Charge?

Realistic decisions on pricing are critical for financial solvency. The pricing tripod model, discussed earlier (Figure 5.2), provides a useful departure point. The three elements involve determining the relevant economic costs to be recovered at different sales volumes and setting the relevant floor price; assessing the elasticity of demand of the service from both the providers' and customers' perspectives, as it helps to set a "ceiling" price for any given market segment; and analyzing the intensity of price competition among the providers.

A specific figure must be set for the price itself. This task involves several considerations, including the need to consider the pros and cons of setting a rounded price and the ethical issues involved in setting a price exclusive of taxes, service charges, and other extras.

What Should Be the Specified Basis for Pricing?

It's not always easy to define a unit of service as the specified basis for pricing. There may be many options. For instance, should price be based on completing a promised service task—such as repairing a piece of equipment, or cleaning a jacket? Should it be based on admission to a service performance—such as an educational program, a concert, or a sports event? Should it be time-based—for instance, using an hour of a lawyer's time, or occupying a hotel room for a night? Alternatively, should it be related to a monetary value associated with service delivery, as when an insurance company scales its premiums to reflect the amount of coverage provided, or a realtor takes a commission that is a percentage of the selling price of a house?

Some service prices are tied to the consumption of physical resources, such as food, drinks, water, or natural gas. In the hospitality industry, rather than charging customers an hourly rate for occupying a table and chairs, restaurants put a sizable markup on the food and drink items consumed. Recognizing the fixed cost of table service—such as a clean tablecloth for each party—restaurants in some countries impose a fixed cover

Table 5.3
Some Pricing Issues

---

1. How much should be charged for this service?
- What costs are the organization attempting to recover? Is the organization trying to achieve a specific profit margin or return on investment by selling this service?
- How sensitive are customers to various prices?
- What prices are charged by competitors?
- What discount(s) should be offered from basic prices?
- Are psychological pricing points (e.g., $4.95 versus $5.00) customarily used?

2. What should be the basis of pricing?
- Execution of a specific task
- Admission to a service facility
- Units of time (hour, week, month, year)
- Percentage commission on the value of the transaction
- Physical resources consumed
- Geographic distance covered
- Weight or size of object serviced
- Should each service element be billed independently?
- Should a single price be charged for a bundled package?

3. Who should collect payment?
- The organization that provides the service
- A specialist intermediary (travel or ticket agent, bank, retailer, etc.)
- How should the intermediary be compensated for this work—flat fee or percentage commission?

4. Where should payment be made?
- The location at which the service is delivered
- A convenient retail outlet or financial intermediary (e.g., bank)
- The purchaser's home (by mail or phone)

5. When should payment be made?
- Before or after delivery of the service
- At which times of day
- On which days of the week

6. How should payment be made?
- Cash (exact change or not?)
- Token (where can these be purchased?)
- Stored value card
- Check (how to verify?)
- Electronic funds transfer
- Charge card (credit or debit)
- Credit account with service provider
- Vouchers
- Third-party payment (e.g., insurance company or government agency)?

7. How should prices be communicated to the target market?
- Through what communication medium? (advertising, signage, electronic display, salespeople, customer service personnel)
- What message content (how much emphasis should be placed on price?)

---

charge that is added to the cost of the meal. Others may establish a minimum meal charge per person. Transport firms have traditionally charged by distance, with freight companies using a combination of weight or cubic volume and distance to set their rates. Such a policy has the virtue of consistency and reflects calculation of an average cost per mile (or kilometer). However, it ignores relative market strength on different routes, which should be included when a yield management system is used. Simplicity may suggest a flat rate, as with postal charges for domestic letters below a certain weight, or a rate for packages that groups geographic distances into broad zones.

For some services, prices may include separate charges for access and for usage. Recent research suggests that access or subscription fees are an important driver of adoption and customer retention, whereas usage fees are much more important drivers of actual usage.[21]

Price Bundling

As we emphasize throughout this book, many services unite a core product with a variety of supplementary services. Meals and bar service on a cruise ship offer one example, baggage service on a train or aircraft another. Should such service packages be priced as a whole (referred to as a "bundle"), or should each element be priced separately? To the extent that people prefer to avoid making many small payments, bundled pricing may be preferable, and it is certainly simpler to administer. But if customers dislike feeling that they have been charged for product elements they did not use, itemized pricing may be preferable.

Bundled prices offer firms a certain guaranteed revenue from each customer, while giving the latter a clear idea in advance how much the bill will be. Unbundled pricing provides customers with flexibility in what they choose to acquire and pay for.[22] However, they may be angered if they discover that the actual price of what they consume, inflated by all the "extras," is substantially higher than the advertised base price that attracted them in the first place.

Discounting

Selective price discounting targeted at specific market segments can offer important opportunities to attract new customers and fill capacity that would otherwise go unused. However, unless it is used with effective rate fences that allow a clean targeting of specific segments, a strategy of discounting should be approached cautiously. It reduces the average price and contribution received, and may attract customers whose only loyalty is to the firm that can offer the lowest price on the next transaction. Volume discounts are sometimes used to cement the loyalty of large corporate customers who might otherwise spread their purchases among several different suppliers.

Who Should Collect Payment?

As discussed in Chapter 3, supplementary services include information, order taking, billing, and payment. Customers appreciate it when a firm makes it easy to obtain price information and make reservations. They also expect well-presented billing and convenient procedures for making payment. Sometimes, firms delegate these tasks to intermediaries, such as travel agents who make hotel and transport bookings and collect payment from customers, and ticket agents who sell seats for theaters, concert halls, and sports stadiums. Although the original supplier pays a commission, the intermediary is usually able to offer customers greater convenience in terms of where, when, and how payment can be made. Using intermediaries may also result in a net savings in administrative costs. Nowadays, however, many service firms are promoting their web sites as direct channels for customer self-service, thus bypassing traditional intermediaries and avoiding payment of commissions.

Where Should Payment Be Made?

Service delivery sites are not always conveniently located. Airports, theaters, and stadiums, for instance, are often situated some distance from where potential patrons live or work. When consumers have to purchase a service before using it, there are obvious benefits to using intermediaries that are more conveniently located, or allowing payment by mail or bank transfer. A growing number of organizations now accept Internet, telephone, and fax bookings with payment by credit card.

When Should Payment Be Made?

Two basic options are to ask customers to pay in advance (as with an admission charge, airline ticket, or postage stamps), or to bill them once service delivery has been completed, as with restaurant bills and repair charges. Occasionally, a service provider may ask for an initial payment in advance of service delivery, with the balance being due later. This approach is quite common for expensive repair and maintenance jobs, when the firm—often a small business with limited working capital—must buy materials up front.

Asking customers to pay in advance means that the buyer is paying before the benefits are received. However, prepayments may be advantageous to the customer as well as to the provider. Sometimes it is inconvenient to pay each time a regularly patronized service—such as the Postal Service or public transport—is used. To save time and effort, customers may prefer the convenience of buying a book of stamps or a monthly travel pass. Performing arts organizations with heavy up-front financing requirements offer discounted subscription tickets in order to bring in money before the season begins.

Finally, the timing of payment can determine usage patterns. From an analysis of the payment and attendance records of a Colorado-based health club, John Gourville and Dilip Soman found that members' usage patterns were closely related to their payment schedules. When members made payments annually, their use of the club was highest during the months immediately following payment and then declined steadily until the next payment; members with monthly payment plans used the health club much more consistently and were more likely to renew, perhaps because each month's payment encouraged them to use what they were paying for.

Gourville and Soman conclude that the timing of payment can be used more strategically to manage capacity utilization. For instance, if a golf club wants to reduce demand during its busiest time, it can bill its fees long before the season begins (e.g., in January rather than in May or June), as the member's pain of payment will have faded by the time the peak summer months come, and thereby reduce the need to get his or her "money's worth." A reduction in demand during the peak period would then allow the club to increase its membership.[23]

How Should Payment Be Made?

As shown earlier in Table 5.3, there are many different forms of payment. Cash may appear to be the simplest method, but it raises security problems and is inconvenient when exact change is required (e.g., to operate machines). Accepting payment by check for all but the smallest purchases is now fairly widespread and offers customer benefits, although it may require controls to discourage bad checks, such as a hefty charge for returned checks ($15 to $20 on top of any bank charges is not uncommon at retail stores).

Credit and debit cards can be used around the world. As their acceptance has become almost universal, businesses that refuse to accept them increasingly find themselves at a competitive disadvantage. Many companies also offer customers the convenience of a credit account, which generates a membership relationship between the customer and the firm. Other payment procedures include tokens or vouchers as supplements to (or instead of) cash. Tokens with a predefined value can simplify the process of paying road and bridge tolls, or public transit fares. Vouchers are sometimes provided by social service agencies to elderly or low-income people. Such a policy achieves the same benefits as discounting, but avoids the need to publicize different prices and to require cashiers to check eligibility.

Now coming into broader usage are prepayment systems based on cards that store value on a magnetic strip or in a microchip embedded within the card. Service firms that want to accept payment in this form, however, must first install card readers. Service marketers should remember that the simplicity and speed with which payment is made may influence the customer's perception of overall service quality. To save its customers time and effort, Chase bank has introduced credit cards with what it calls "blink," an embedded technology that can be read by a point-of-sale terminal without physically touching it (Figure 5.8).

Interestingly, a recent study found that the payment mechanism has an effect on the total spending of customers, especially for discretionary consumption items such as spending in cafes.[24] The less tangible or immediate the payment mechanism, the more consumers tend to spend. Cash is the most tangible (i.e., consumers will be

Figure 5.8 Chase Advertises Its Fast New Credit Card Scanning Service, "blink"

Courtesy JP Morgan Chase & Company.

more careful and spend less), followed by credit cards, prepayment cards, and finally, more sophisticated and even less tangible and immediate mechanisms such as payment via one's mobile phone bill.

How Should Prices Be Communicated to the Target Markets?

The final task, once each of the other issues has been addressed, is to decide how the organization's pricing policies can best be communicated to its target market(s). People need to know the price for some product offerings well in advance of purchase. They may also need to know how, where, and when that price is payable. This information must be presented in ways that are intelligible and unambiguous, so that customers will not be misled and question the ethical standards of the firm. Dismayed by the complexity of cell-phone calling plans in the United States, Consumers Union has called for a simple, standardized summary of the features of each calling plan that would simplify the process for consumers to compare competing offers. This would be similar in style to the government-mandated box printed on all credit card solicitations that lays out, in standard format and readable type, the offer's essential rates and terms.[25]

Managers must decide whether to include information on pricing in advertising for the service. It may be appropriate to relate the price to the costs of competing products. Certainly, salespeople and customer service representatives should be able to give prompt, accurate responses to customer queries about pricing, payment, and credit. Good signage at retail points of sale will save staff members from having to answer basic questions about prices.

Finally, when the price is presented in the form of an itemized bill, marketers should ensure that it is both accurate and intelligible. Hospital bills, which may run to multiple pages and contain dozens or even hundreds of items, have been much criticized for inaccuracy. Hotel bills, despite containing fewer entries, are also notoriously inaccurate. One study estimated that business travelers in the United States may be overpaying for their hotel rooms by half-a-billion dollars a year, with 11.6 percent of all bills incorrect, resulting in an average overpayment of $11.36.[26]

CONCLUSION

To determine an effective pricing strategy, a firm has to have a good understanding of its costs, the value created for customers, and competitor pricing. Defining costs tends to be more difficult in a service business than in a manufacturing operation. Without a good understanding of costs, managers cannot be sure that the prices set are, in fact, sufficient to recover all costs.

Another challenge is to relate the value that customers perceive in a service to the price they are willing to pay for it. This step requires an understanding of other costs that the customer may be incurring in purchase and use, including outlays of a nonfinancial nature, such as time and effort. Managers also need to recognize that the same service may not be valued in the same way by all customers, offering the potential to set different prices for different market segments.

Competitor pricing cannot be compared dollar for dollar. Services tend to be location- and time-specific, and competitor services have their own set of related monetary and nonmonetary costs, sometimes to the extent that the actual prices charged become secondary for competitive comparisons. Competitive pricing needs to take all those factors into account.

Revenue management is a powerful tool that helps to manage demand and price different segments closer to their perceived values. Well-designed physical and nonphysical rate fences help to define "products" for each target segment. However, great care has to be taken in the way revenue management is implemented, to ensure that customer satisfaction and perceived fairness are not compromised.

A pricing strategy must address the central issue of what price to charge for selling a given unit of service at a particular point in time (however that unit may be defined). Because services often combine multiple elements, pricing strategies need to be highly creative.

Finally, firms need to be careful lest pricing schedules become so complex and hard to compare that they simply confuse customers. A policy of deliberately creating confusing price schedules, including hiding certain costs that only become apparent to customers after usage, is likely to lead to accusations of unethical behavior, loss of trust, and customer dissatisfaction.

REVIEW QUESTIONS

1. What is the role of service pricing and revenue management in a business model?
2. How can the three main approaches to service pricing be integrated to arrive at a good pricing point for a particular service?
3. How can a service firm compute its unit costs for pricing purposes? How does predicted and actual capacity utilization affect unit costs and profitability?
4. Why can't we compare competitor prices dollar for dollar in a service context?
5. Why is the price charged by the firm only one, and often not the most important, component of the total cost to the consumer? When should we cut non-price-related costs to the bone, even if that incurs higher costs and a higher price to be charged?
6. What is the role of nonmonetary costs in a business model, and how do they relate to the consumer's perception of the offered value exchange?
7. What is revenue management, how does it work, and what type of service operations benefit most

from good revenue management systems and why?

8. Why are ethical concerns and fairness perception important issues when designing service fee schedules and revenue management strategies? What are potential consumer responses to service pricing schedules or policies that are perceived as being unfair?

9. How can we improve the perceived fairness of pricing schedules, and what are the implications of these rec-ommendations? How can perceptions of unfairness be mitigated and perceptions of fairness created?

10. How can we charge different prices to different segments without customers feeling cheated? How can we even charge the same customer different prices at different times, contexts, and/or occasions, and at the same time be seen as fair?

11. What are the seven key decisions managers need to make when designing an effective pricing schedule?

APPLICATION EXERCISES

1. Select a service organization of your choice and find out what its pricing policies and methods are. In what respects are they similar to or different from what has been discussed in this chapter?

2. From a customer perspective, what serves to define value in the following services: (a) a hairdressing salon; (b) a legal firm specializing in business and taxation law; and (c) a nightclub?

3. Explore two highly successful business models that are based on innovative service pricing and/or revenue management strategies, and identify two business models that failed because of major issues in their pricing or revenue management strategy. What lessons can you learn from your analysis of these successful and unsuccessful pricing and revenue management strategies?

4. Review recent bills that you have received from service businesses, such as those for telephone, car repair, cable TV, and credit cards. Evaluate each one against the following criteria: (a) general appearance and clarity of presentation; (b) easily understood terms of payment; (c) avoidance of confusing terms and definitions; (d) appropriate level of detail; (e) unanticipated ("hidden") charges; (f) accuracy; (g) ease of access to customer service in case of problems or disputes.

5. How might revenue management be applied to (a) a professional firm (e.g., consulting); (b) a restaurant; and (c) a golf course? What rate fences would you use and why?

6. Collect the pricing schedules of three leading mobile phone service providers. Identify all the pricing dimensions (e.g., airtime, subscription fees, free minutes, per-second/6-seconds/per-minute billing, airtime rollover, etc.) and pricing levels for each dimension (i.e., the range that is offered by the players in the market). Determine the usage profile for a particular target segment (e.g., a young executive who uses the phone mostly for personal calls, or a full-time student). Based on the usage profile, determine the lowest-cost provider. Next, measure the pricing schedule preferences of your target segment (e.g., via conjoint analysis). Finally, advise the smallest of the three providers how to redesign its pricing schedule to make it more attractive to your target segment.

7. Consider a service of your choice, and develop a comprehensive pricing schedule. Apply the seven questions marketers need to answer to design an effective pricing schedule.

ENDNOTES

1. Joan Magretta, "Why Business Models Matter." *Harvard Business Review,* 80 (May 2002): 86–92.

2. Daniel J. Goebel, Greg W. Marshall, and William B. Locander, "Activity Based Costing: Accounting for a Marketing Orientation." *Industrial Marketing Management,* 27, no. 6 (1998): 497–510; Thomas H. Stevenson and David W. E. Cabell, "Integrating Transfer Pricing Policy and Activity-Based Costing." *Journal of International Marketing,* 10, no. 4 (2002): 77–88.

3. Robin Cooper and Robert S. Kaplan, "Profit Priorities from Activity-Based Costing." *Harvard Business Review,* 69, no. 3 (May–June 1991): 130–135.

4. Antonella Carù and Antonella Cugini, "Profitability and Customer Satisfaction in Services: An Integrated Perspective Between Marketing and Cost Management Analysis." *International Journal of Service Industry Management,* 10, no. 2 (1999): 132–156.

5. Kristina Heinonen, "Reconceptualizing Customer Perceived Value: The Value of Time and Place." *Managing Service Quality,* 14, no. 3 (2004): 205–215.

6. Gerald E. Smith and Thomas T. Nagle, "How Much Are Customers Willing to Pay?" *Marketing Research* (Winter 2002): 20–25.

7. Valarie A. Zeithaml, "Consumer Perceptions of Price, Quality, and Value: A Means-End Model and Synthesis of Evidence." *Journal of Marketing,* 52 (July 1988): 2–21;. A recent paper exploring alternative conceptualizations of value is Chien-Hsin Lin, Peter J. Sher, and Hsin-Yu Shih, "Past Progress and Future Directions in Conceptualizing Customer Perceived Value." *International Journal of Service Industry Management,* 16, no 4 (2005): 318–336.

8. Hermann Simon, "Pricing Opportunities and How to Exploit Them." *Sloan Management Review,* 33 (Winter 1992): 71–84.

9. This discussion is based primarily on Leonard L. Berry and Manjit S. Yadav, "Capture and Communicate Value in the Pricing of Services." *Sloan Management Review,* 37 (Summer 1996): 41–51.

10. Frederick F. Reichheld, *The Loyalty Effect* (Boston: Harvard Business School Press, 1996): 82–84.

11. Anna S. Mattila and Jochen Wirtz, "The Impact of Knowledge Types on the Consumer Search Process—An Investigation in the Context of Credence Services." *International Journal of Service Industry Management,* 13, no. 3 (2002): 214–230.

12. Leonard L. Berry, Kathleen Seiders, and Dhruv Grewal, "Understanding Service Convenience." *Journal of Marketing,* 66 (July 2002): 1–17.

13. For application of yield management to industries beyond the traditional airline, hotel, and car rental contexts, see Anthony Ingold, Una McMahon-Beattie, and Ian Yeoman (eds.), *Yield Management Strategies for the Service Industries,* 2nd ed. (London: Continuum, 2000); Sheryl E. Kimes and Jochen Wirtz, "Perceived Fairness of Revenue Management in the US Golf Industry." *Journal of Revenue and Pricing Management,* 1, no. 4 (2003): 332–344; Sheryl E. Kimes and Jochen Wirtz, "Has Revenue Management Become Acceptable? Findings from an International Study and the Perceived Fairness of Rate Fences." *Journal of Service Research,* 6 (November 2003): 125–135; Richard Metters and Vicente Vargas, "Yield Management for the Nonprofit Sector." *Journal of Service Research,* 1 (February 1999): 215–226; Sunmee Choi and Anna S. Mattila, "Hotel Revenue Management and Its Impact on Customers' Perception of Fairness." *Journal of Revenue and Pricing Management,* 2, no 4 (2004): 303–314; Alex M. Susskind, Dennis Reynolds, and Eriko Tsuchiya, "An Evaluation of Guests' Preferred Incentives to Shift Time-Variable Demand in Restaurants." *Cornell Hotel and Restaurant Administration Quarterly,* 44, no. 1 (2004): 68–84; Parijat Dube, Yezekael Hayel, and Laura Wynter, "Yield Management for IT Resources on Demand: Analysis and Validation of a New Paradigm for Managing Computing Centres." *Journal of Revenue and Pricing Management,* 4, no 1 (2005): 24–38.

14. Hermann Simon and Robert J. Dolan, "Price Customization." *Marketing Management* (Fall 1998): 11–17.

15. Lisa E. Bolton, Luk Warlop, and Joseph W. Alba, "Consumer Perceptions of Price (Un)Fairness." *Journal of Consumer Research,* 29, no. 4 (2003): 474–491; Lan Xia, Kent B. Monroe, and Jennifer L. Cox, "The Price is Unfair! A Conceptual Framework of Price Fairness Perceptions." *Journal of Marketing,* 68 (October 2004): 1–15. Christian Homburg, Wayne D. Hoyer, and Nicole Koschate, "Customer's Reactions to Price Increases: Do Customer Satisfaction and Perceived Motive Fairness Matter?" *Journal of the Academy of Marketing Science,* 33, no. 1 (2005): 36–49.

16. Scott Adams, *The Dilbert™ Future—Thriving on Business Stupidities in the 21st Century* (New York: HarperBusiness, 1997): 160.

17. Ian Ayres and Barry Nalebuff, "In Praise of Honest Pricing." *Sloan Management Review* (Fall 2003): 24–28.

18. Dean Foust, "Protection Racket? As Overdraft and Other Fees Become Huge Profit Sources for Banks, Critics See Abuses." *Business Week* (February 5, 2005): 68–89.

19. The banking examples and data in this section are from Dean Foust, "Protection Racket? As Overdraft and Other Fees Become Huge Profit Sources for Banks, Critics See Abuses." *Business Week* (February 5, 2005): 68–89.

20. Parts of this section are based on Jochen Wirtz, Sheryl E. Kimes, Jeannette P. T. Ho, and Paul Patterson, "Revenue Management: Resolving Potential Customer Conflicts." *Journal of Revenue and Pricing Management,* 2, no. 3 (2003): 216–228.

21. Peter J. Danaher, "Optimal Pricing of New Subscription Services: An Analysis of a Market Experiment." *Marketing Science,* 21 (Spring 2002): 119–129; Gilia E. Fruchter and Ram C. Rao, "Optimal Membership Fee and Usage Price over Time for a Network Service." *Journal of Services Research,* 4 (2001): 3–15.

22. Avery Johnson, "Northwest to Charge Passengers in Coach for Meals." *The Wall Street Journal* (February 16, 2005).

23. John Gourville and Dilip Soman, "Pricing and the Psychology of Consumption." *Harvard Business Review,* 80 (September 2002): 90–96.

24. Dilip Soman, "The Effect of Payment Transparency on Consumption: Quasi-Experiments from the Field." *Marketing Letters,* 14, no. 3 (2003): 173–183.

25. "Needed: Straight Talk About Cellphone Calling Plans." *Consumer Reports* (February 2003): 18.

26. See, for example, Anita Sharpe, "The Operation Was a Success; The Bill Was Quite a Mess." *The Wall Street Journal* (September 17, 1997): 1; Gary Stoller, "Hotel Bill Mistakes Mean Many Pay Too Much." *USA Today* (July 12, 2005), accessed at www.news.yahoo.com/s/usatoday.

Chapter 6

Educating Customers and Promoting the Value Proposition

> *Life is for one generation; a good name is forever.*
>
> —JAPANESE PROVERB

> *Education costs money, but then so does ignorance.*
>
> —SIR CLAUS MOSER

*C*ommunication is the most visible or audible—some would say intrusive—of marketing activities, but its value is limited unless it is used intelligently in conjunction with other marketing efforts. An old marketing axiom says that the fastest way to kill a poor product is to advertise it heavily. By the same token, an otherwise well-researched and well-planned marketing strategy, designed to deliver, say, new Web-based services at a reasonable price, is likely to fail if people lack knowledge of the service, how to access it, and how to use it to best advantage. It's for good reason that we define the marketing communication element of the 8 Ps as *Promotion and education*.

Through communication, marketers explain and promote the value proposition that their firm is offering. They inform existing or prospective customers in the target segments about service features and benefits, price and other costs, the channels through which service is delivered, and when and where it is available. Where appropriate, they marshal persuasive arguments for using a particular service and seek to create preference for selecting their firm's brand. And through both personal instructions from customer contact employees and use of educational tools, marketers seek to help customers make well-informed choices and become effective participants in service delivery processes.

Much confusion surrounds the scope of marketing communication. Some people still define this element of the services marketing mix too narrowly. Communications must be viewed more broadly than as just

154

the use of paid media advertising, public relations, and professional salespeople. Today, there are many other ways for a service business to communicate with current and prospective customers. The location and atmosphere of a service delivery facility, corporate design features such as the consistent use of colors and graphic elements, the appearance and behavior of employees, the design of a web site—all contribute to an impression in the customer's mind that reinforces or contradicts the specific content of formal communication messages. The past few years have seen the emergence of new and exciting opportunities for reaching prospects through the Internet, with degrees of targeting and message specificity that were previously unimaginable, especially in consumer markets.

In this chapter we explore the following questions:

1. What is distinctive about the nature of marketing communications for services?
2. What are the elements of the marketing communications mix and what are the strengths and weaknesses of each major element in a services context?
3. How does the level of customer contact affect communication strategy?
4. How should marketing communication objectives be defined?
5. What is the potential value of the Internet, cellular, and other new electronic media as communication channels?

THE ROLE OF MARKETING COMMUNICATION

In a service setting, marketing communications tools are especially important because they help create powerful images and a sense of credibility, confidence, and reassurance. Marketing communications, in one form or another, are essential to a company's success. Without effective communications, prospects may never learn of a service firm's existence, what it has to offer them, the value proposition of each of its products, and how to use them to best advantage. Customers might be more easily lured away by competitors and competitive offerings, and there would be no proactive management and control of the firm's identity. Let's look at some specific tasks that can be performed by marketing communication.

Adding Value Through Communication Content

Information and consultation represent important ways to add value to a product. Prospective customers may need information and advice about what service options are available to them, where and when these services are available, how much they cost, and what specific features, functions, and service benefits there are. Companies also use marketing communications to persuade target customers that their service product offers the best solution to meet those customers' needs, relative to the offerings of competing firms. See Figure 6.1 for an advertisement about how Wausau conveys this, building on its in-depth expertise in preventing and managing accidents in the workplace.

Communication efforts serve not only to attract new users but also to maintain contact with an organization's existing customers and build relationships with them. Nurturing customer relationships depends on a comprehensive and up-to-date customer database, and the ability to make use of this in a personalized way.

Techniques for keeping in touch with customers and building their loyalty include direct mail and contacts by telephone or other forms of telecommunication, including email, web sites, and even text messages sent via mobile phone. Doctors, dentists, and household maintenance services often post annual checkup reminders to their customers. Some businesses even send birthday and anniversary cards to

Figure 6.1
Wausau Promotes
Its Innovative
"people@work"
Program, Targeted at
Employees

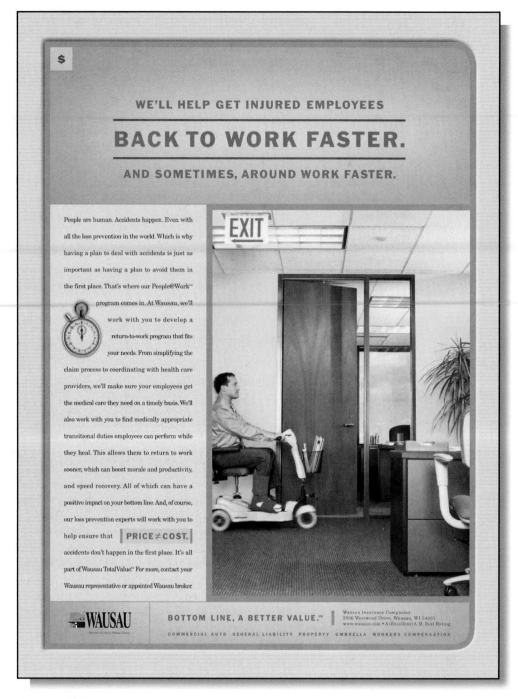

Courtesy of Wausau Insurance.

valued customers. Banks and utility companies often include a brief newsletter with their account statements or print customized information on each statement in an effort to cross-sell additional services.

COMMUNICATING SERVICES PRESENTS BOTH CHALLENGES AND OPPORTUNITIES

Traditional marketing communication strategies were shaped largely by the needs and practices associated with marketing manufactured goods. However, several of the differences that distinguish services from goods have a significant effect on the ways we approach the design of marketing communication programs in service

Table 6.1
Advertising Strategies for Overcoming Intangibility

INTANGIBILITY PROBLEM	ADVERTISING STRATEGY	DESCRIPTION
INCORPOREAL EXISTENCE	PHYSICAL REPRESENTATION	SHOW PHYSICAL COMPONENTS OF SERVICE
Generality:		
• For objective claims	System documentation	Objectively document physical system capacity
	Performance documentation	Document and cite past performance statistics
• For subjective claims	Service performance episode	Present an actual service delivery incident
Nonsearchability	Consumption documentation	Obtain and present customer testimonials
	Reputation documentation	Cite independently audited performance
Abstractness	Service consumption episode	Capture and display typical customers benefiting from the service
Impalpability	Service process episode	Present a vivid documentary on the step-by-step service process
	Case history episode	Present an actual case history of what the firm did for a specific client
	Service consumption episode	An articulate narration or depiction of a customer's subjective experience

Source: Banwari Mittal and Julie Baker, "Advertising Strategies for Hospitality Services." *Cornell Hotel and Restaurant Administration Quarterly,* 43 (April 2002): 53. Copyright Cornell Unversity. All rights reserved. Used by permission.

businesses.[1] In particular, we need to consider the implications of intangibility in service performance, customer involvement in production, the role of customer contact personnel, the difficulty of evaluating many services, and the need to bring demand and supply into balance.

Overcoming the Problems of Intangibility

Because services are performances rather than objects, their benefits can be difficult to communicate to customers, especially when the service in question does not involve any tangible actions to customers or their possessions.[2] Banwari Mittal suggests that intangibility creates four problems for marketers seeking to promote its attributes or benefits: abstractness, generality, nonsearchability, and mental impalpability.[3] Emphasizing that service marketers need to create messages that clearly communicate intangible service attributes and benefits to potential consumers, he and Julie Baker discuss the implications of each of these problems[4] and propose specific communications strategies for dealing with them (see Table 6.1).

Abstractness. Because abstract concepts such as financial security, expert advice, or safe transportation do not have one-to-one correspondence with physical objects, it can be challenging for marketers to connect their services to those concepts.

Generality. Generality refers to items that comprise a class of objects, persons, or events—for instance, airline seats, flight attendants, and cabin service. These general classes do have physical analogs, and most consumers of the service know what they are, but a key task for marketers seeking to create a distinctive value proposition is to communicate what makes a specific offering meaningfully different from (and superior to) competing offerings.

Nonsearchability. Nonsearchability refers to the fact that intangibles cannot be searched or inspected before they are purchased. Physical service attributes, such as the appearance of a health club and the type of equipment installed, can be checked in advance, but the experience of working with a trainer can only be determined through extended personal involvement. And, as we noted in Chapter 2, credence attributes, such as a surgeon's expertise, must be taken on faith.

Mental impalpability. Many services are sufficiently complex, multidimensional, or novel that it is difficult for consumers—especially new prospects—to understand what the experience of using them will be like and what benefits will result.

Commonly used strategies in advertising include the use of tangible cues whenever possible, especially for low-contact services that involve few tangible elements. It's also helpful to include "vivid information" that catches the audience's attention and produces a strong, clear impression on the senses, especially for services that are complex and highly intangible.[5] Consider the advertising campaign created by Accenture, the international consulting firm, to dramatize the abstract notion of helping clients capitalize on innovative ideas in a fast-moving world. It features the champion golfer, Tiger Woods, in eye-catching situations to highlight the firm's ability to help clients "develop the reflexes of a high-performance business" (Figure 6.2).

Figure 6.2
Accenture Promotes Its Ability to Turn Innovative Ideas into Results

Courtesy of Accenture.

Experts often recommend using visual stimuli and documentation in order to overcome service intangibility and better communicate a firm's value proposition,. To test the effectiveness of visualization and documentations strategies for hedonic and utilitarian services, academic researchers conducted a laboratory experiment.

They showed 160 student subjects one print advertisement each, and then measured their responses. An ad for a spring-break travel service was used as the hedonic service in the study, and one for a bank with specific student offers was used for the utilitarian service. In the visualization condition, one picture of the hotel and one of young adults in an ocean-side pool were added to the text for the hedonic service. For the bank, photos of the exterior of the bank building and an ATM were shown. The study then compared the text-only condition with the ad that contained the pictures. Documentation was operationalized using an indirect comparative advertising copy stating the high performance of the service provider along the three most important attributes for the respective two services.

The findings showed that for both types of services, ads based on a visualization strategy were perceived as being more informative than text-only ads. Participants who viewed the visualization ads perceived the services to be of higher quality and were more likely to say they intended to use these services. By contrast, documentation worked well for the hedonic service but not the utilitarian one (further research is needed to explain why).

The study has two important managerial implications.

1. *Use pictures to tangibilize the value proposition.* Whether you market a hedonic or a utilitarian service, show pictures and photos to communicate the potential benefits of your service. For example, Hilton Hotels Corp. started using photos to market its Chef's Signature Catering Collection, replacing its more traditional method of sending text-only menu information to clients who wanted to plan a dinner at the hotel. One Hilton executive noted, "people eat with their eyes, and when they see something they can relate to, something they can recognize, it develops a level of confidence and comfort level for the customer."

2. *Comparative data help readers to visualize hedonic services.* The study indicated that hedonic services can benefit from adding comparative information into their ads. For example, if Six Flags Great America advertises that its Déjà vu roller coaster is 196 ft (60 m) tall compared to only 120 ft of other top roller coasters, and that its speed is up to 65 mph (104 km/h), compared to only 50 to 60 mph for other roller coasters, then one should expect readers to better visualize the Déjà vu as one of the tallest and fastest roller coasters in the world. Simply listing the height and speed alone wouldn't be as effective—readers need the benchmarking provided by the comparative information.

Source: Adapted from Donna J. Hill, Jeff Blodgett, Robert Baer, and Kirk Wakefield, "An Investigation of Visualization and Documentation Strategies in Service Advertising." *Journal of Service Research,* 7, no. 2 (2004): 155–166.

As another example, an ad for a large law firm showed a picture of empty jurors' chairs to draw attention to its trial lawyers' skills in presenting complex cases to juries, which must then withdraw from the courtroom to deliberate on the verdict. Similarly, MasterCard's TV and print advertisements emphasize the tangible things that can be purchased with its credit card—complete with a listing of the price of each item. In each ad, all of the items purchased with the card lead to a "priceless" experience (a clever and memorable reference to the concept of intangibility). Research Insights 6.1 shows how visualization and comparative advertising affect consumer perceptions of both hedonic services (those that bring pleasure and enjoyment) and utilitarian services (those that are consumed for practical or functional purposes).

Using Methaphors to Communicate the Value Proposition

Some companies have created metaphors that are tangible in nature to help communicate the benefits of their service offerings. Insurance companies often use this approach to market their very intangible products. Thus Allstate advertises that "You're in Good Hands," and Prudential uses the Rock of Gibraltar as a symbol of corporate strength. Professional service firms sometimes use metaphors to communicate their value propositions more dramatically and to emphasize key points of difference relative to competing alternatives.[6] When possible, advertising metaphors

Figure 6.3 AT Kearney Uses Bear Traps as a Metaphor for Problems

WHAT DID YOUR CONSULTANTS LEAVE BEHIND?

When a consultancy works only with the senior executives, they often leave you with more problems than they solved. A.T. Kearney, however, collaborates with your entire team. So you not only get big ideas, but an organization prepared to implement them—and deliver even more.

ATKEARNEY IDEAS THAT LAST.

"What Did Your Consultants Leave Behind," Copyright A. T. Kearney. All rights reserved. Reprinted with permission.

should highlight *how* service benefits are actually provided.[7] AT Kearney emphasizes that it includes all management levels in seeking solutions, not just higher-level management. Its clever advertisement, showing bear traps across the office floor, draws attention to the way in which the company differentiates its service through careful work with all levels in its client organizations, thus avoiding the problems left behind by other consultants who work only with top management (Figure 6.3).

A challenge facing DHL, the international logistics and delivery firm, was to promote the efficiency of its import express service. Its advertising agency's clever solution was to use the easily grasped metaphor of a heavily knotted string to repre-

Figure 6.4 DHL Uses a Clever Metaphor to Communicate Its Value Proposition

Imports

DHL Import Express

We make importing smooth.

We know how the complexities of importing can tie your supply chain up in knots. DHL Import Express smoothens the whole process with just one phone call, whether you're shipping between countries or importing from a choice of over 200. What's more, you get one invoice billed in your local currency from one company, making shipments convenient, hassle-free and fast. So you can rest assured that your shipments will be delivered door-to-door with no hidden costs and you can track them every step of the way. Call DHL today or visit us at **www.importexpress.dhl.com**

Deutsche Post World Net
MAIL EXPRESS LOGISTICS FINANCE

DHL

Courtesy of DHL Express Singapore.

sent how complex importing can be, and a straight string to show how easy it would be using DHL's service (Figure 6.4).

Facilitate Customer Involvement in Production

When customers are actively involved in service production, they need training to help them perform well—just as employees do. Improving productivity often involves making innovations in service delivery. However, the desired benefits won't be achieved if customers resist new, technologically based systems or avoid self-service alternatives.

One approach to training customers, recommended by advertising experts, is to show service delivery in action. Television and videos are good media, because of

Chapter 6 Educating Customers and Promoting the Value Proposition **161** their ability to engage the viewer as filmed or animated material displays a seamless sequence of events in visual form. Some dentists show their patients videos of surgical procedures before the surgery takes place. Shouldice Hospital in Toronto, featured in Case 16 on pages 592–601, specializes in hernia repair. It offers prospective patients an opportunity to view an online simulation and explains the hospital experience with hernia repair on its web site (see www.shouldice.com). This educational technique helps patients prepare mentally for the experience and shows them what role they need to play in service delivery to ensure a successful surgery and a satisfying experience.

Advertising and publicity can make customers aware of changes in service features and delivery systems. Marketers often use sales promotions to motivate customers, offering them incentives to make the necessary changes in their behavior. Publicizing price discounts is one way to encourage self-service on an ongoing basis. At self-service gas pumps, for instance, the price difference versus full-service is often substantial. Other incentives to change include promotions that offer a chance to win a reward. And, if necessary, well-trained customer contact personnel can provide one-to-one tutoring to help customers adapt to new procedures.

Help Customers to Evaluate Service Offerings

Even if customers understand what a service is supposed to do, they may have difficulty distinguishing one firm from another and knowing what level of performance to expect from a particular supplier. Possible solutions include providing tangible clues related to service performance, highlighting the quality of equipment and facilities, and emphasizing employee characteristics such as their qualifications, experience, commitment, and professionalism.

Some performance attributes lend themselves better to advertising than others. When an airline wants to boast about its punctuality, reporting favorable statistics collected by a government agency offers credible support for this claim. However, airlines don't like to talk overtly about safety, because even the admission that things might go wrong makes many passengers nervous. Instead, they approach this ongoing customer concern indirectly, advertising the expertise of their pilots, the newness of their aircraft, and the skills and training of their mechanics. To document the superior quality and reliability of its small-package delivery services, a FedEx advertisement showed the awards it received for being rated as highest in customer satisfaction for air, ground, and international delivery from J. D. Power and Associates, widely known and respected for its customer satisfaction research in numerous industries. Its Consumer Center web site includes ratings of service providers in finance and insurance, health care, telecommunications, and travel, plus useful information and advice.[8]

In low-contact services for which much of the firm's expertise is hidden, firms may need to illustrate equipment, procedures, and employee activities that take place backstage. For instance, how do prospective buyers know whether they are getting the best value from insurance services? One approach is to show how the firm is trying to reduce losses due to accidents or to reduce costs. Liberty Mutual has run ads using attention-getting headlines such as "Wake up, you're dead," which shows a grim-looking auto safety expert who is researching how to prevent highway accidents caused by driver fatigue. The company's "I love dissecting humans" ad includes an amusing photo of one of the company's field investigators, who describes her work in detecting and preventing insurance fraud. The fraud prevention ad shows just how serious the problem is for the insurance industry, in which fraudulent claims amount to an estimated $25 billion a year.

Stimulate or Dampen Demand to Match Capacity

Many live service performances—a seat at the theater for Friday evening's performance, or a haircut at Supercuts on Tuesday morning—are time-specific and can't be stored for resale at a later date. Advertising and sales promotions can help to change the timing of customer use and thus help to match demand with the capacity available at a given time.

Demand management strategies include reducing usage during peak demand periods and stimulating it during off-peak periods. Low demand outside peak periods poses a serious problem for service industries with high fixed costs, such as hotels. One strategy is to run promotions that offer extra value—such as a room upgrade and a free breakfast—in an attempt to stimulate demand without decreasing price. When demand increases, the number of promotions can be reduced or eliminated.

Promote the Contribution of Service Personnel

In high-contact services, front-line personnel are central to service delivery. Their presence makes the service more tangible and, in many cases, more personalized. An ad that shows employees at work helps prospective customers understand the nature of the service encounter and implies a promise of the personalized attention that they can expect to receive.

Advertising, brochures, and web sites can also show customers the work that goes on behind the scenes to ensure good service delivery. Highlighting the expertise and commitment of employees whom customers normally never encounter may enhance trust in the organization's competence and commitment to service quality.

Advertisers must be reasonably realistic in their depictions of service personnel, because their messages help set customers' expectations. If a firm's communications show friendly, smiling workers but, in reality, most employees turn out to be glum, frazzled, or rude, customers will most certainly be disappointed. At a minimum, service personnel should be informed about the content of new advertising campaigns or brochures.

SETTING COMMUNICATION OBJECTIVES

What role should communication play in helping a service firm achieve its marketing goals? A useful checklist for marketing communications planning is provided by the "5 Ws" model:

Who is our target audience?

What do we need to communicate and achieve?

How should we communicate this?

Where should we communicate this?

When do the communications need to take place?

Let's consider the issues of defining the target audience and specifying communication objectives. Then we'll review the wide array of communication tools available to service marketers. Issues relating to the location and scheduling of communication activities tend to be situation-specific, and so we won't address them here.

Target Audience

Prospects, users, and employees represent three broad target audiences, each of which can be further divided. Because marketers of consumer services do not usually know prospects in advance, they usually need to employ a traditional communications mix, comprising such elements as media advertising, public relations, and use of purchased lists for direct mail or telemarketing. By contrast, more cost-effective channels may be available to reach existing users, including selling efforts by customer contact personnel, point-of-sale promotions, and other information distributed during service encounters. If the firm has a membership relationship with its customers and has a database containing contact information, it can distribute highly targeted information through direct mail, email, or telephone. These channels

- Create memorable images of specific companies and their brands.
- Build awareness of and interest in an unfamiliar service or brand.
- Build preference by communicating the strengths and benefits of a specific brand.
- Compare a service with competitors' offerings and counter competitive claims.
- Reposition a service relative to competing offerings.
- Stimulate demand in low-demand periods and discourage demand during peak periods.
- Encourage trial by offering promotional incentives.
- Reduce uncertainty and perceived risk by providing useful information and advice.
- Provide reassurance, such as by promoting service guarantees.
- Familiarize customers with service processes in advance of use.
- Teach customers how to use a service to their own best advantage.
- Recognize and reward valued customers and employees.

may serve to complement and reinforce broader communications channels or simply replace them.

Employees serve as a secondary audience for communication campaigns through public media. A well-designed campaign targeted at users, nonusers, or both can also be motivating for employees, especially those play front-stage roles. In particular, it may help to shape employees' behavior if the advertising content shows them what is being promised to customers. However, there's a risk of generating cynicism among employees and actively demotivating them if the communication in question promotes levels of performance that employees regard as unrealistic or even impossible to achieve. Communications directed specifically at staff are normally part of an internal marketing campaign, using company-specific channels, and so are not accessible to customers. We will discuss internal communications in Chapter 11.

Specifying Communication Objectives

Marketers need to be clear about their goals; otherwise it will be difficult to formulate specific communications objectives and select the most appropriate messages and communication tools to achieve them. Table 6.2 presents a list of common educational and promotional objectives for service businesses. Objectives may include shaping and managing customer behavior in any of the three stages of the purchase and consumption process that we discussed in Chapter 2: the prepurchase stage, the service encounter stage, and the postconsumption stage.

Key Planning Considerations

Planning of a marketing communications campaign should reflect a good understanding of the service product and how well prospective buyers can evaluate its characteristics in advance of purchase. It's essential to understand target market segments and their exposure to different media, as well as consumers' awareness of the product and their attitudes toward it. Decisions include determining the content, structure, and style of the message to be communicated; its manner of presentation; and the media most suited to reaching the intended audience. Additional considerations include the budget available for execution, time frames (as defined by such factors as seasonality, market opportunities, and anticipated competitive activities), and methods of measuring and evaluating performance.

THE MARKETING COMMUNICATIONS MIX

Most service marketers have access to numerous forms of communication, referred to collectively as the *marketing communications mix*. Different communication elements have distinctive capabilities relative to the types of messages they can convey

Figure 6.5 The Marketing Communications Mix for Services

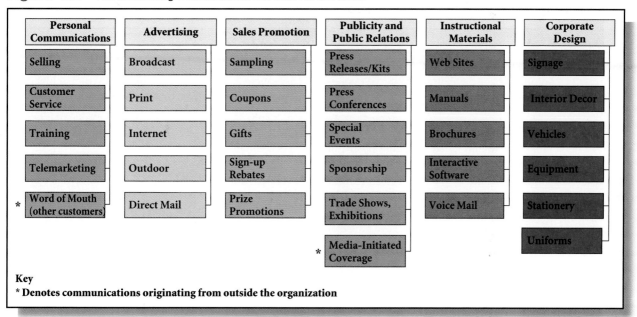

and the market segments most likely to be exposed to them. As shown in Figure 6.5, the mix includes personal contact, advertising, publicity and public relations, sales promotion, instructional materials, and corporate design.

Experts draw a broad division between *personal communications* (those in the left-hand column of boxes in Figure 6.5), which involve personalized messages that move in both directions between the two parties—such as personal selling, telemarketing, customer training, customer service, and word of mouth—and *impersonal communications* (a much larger group of possibilities depicted in all the other columns), in which messages move in only one direction and are generally targeted at a large group of customers and prospects rather than at a single individual.

However, technology has created a gray area between personal and impersonal communications. For instance, firms often combine word processing technology with information from a database to create an impression of personalization. Think about the direct mail and email messages that you've received, containing a personal salutation and perhaps some reference to your specific situation or past use of a particular product. Similarly, interactive software, voice recognition technology, and computer-generated voice prompts and responses can simulate a two-way conversation. A few firms are beginning to experiment with Web-based agents—on-screen simulations that move, speak, and even change expression.

New Opportunities for Highly Targeted Communications

With the advances of on-demand technologies, consumers are increasingly empowered to decide how and when they like to be reached. This development is transforming marketing communications on TV, radio, and the Internet (see Service Perspectives 6.1).

Communications Originate from Different Sources

As shown in Figure 6.6, not all communications messages received by the target audience originate from the service provider. Specifically, word-of-mouth and media stories or editorials originate from outside the organization and are not under its direct control. Messages from an internal source can be divided into those received through production channels and those transmitted through marketing channels. Let's look at the options within each of these three originating sources.

Technology has created some exciting new communications channels that offer important opportunities for targeting. Among the key developments are TiVo, podcasting, and pop-ups.

TIVO

TiVo (also known as digital video recording [DVR] or personal video) can record programs digitally on its hard disk very much like a video cassette recorder (VCR). Unlike a VCR, however, TiVo is "always on" and continuously stores up to some 30 minutes of TV programming. This means that TiVo users can pause or rewind live TV. In fact, many users begin watching a TV program after the broadcast has started so that they can fast-forward and skip the commercials.

According to Kagan Research, about 38 million (32 percent) of U.S. households will own DVRs (digital video recorders) by 2009. Marketers will have to respond quickly by experimenting with options beyond their traditional 30- or 60-second spots.

TiVo has been courting marketers with the promise of interactivity, measurability, and long-form advertising. In June 2004, Charles Schwab & Co. became the first financial services company to use TiVo's new interactive technology, employing a 30-second spot featuring golfer Phil Mickelson. The spot allowed viewers to move from the commercial into a 4-minute video to watch three segments hosted by the golf pro. Viewers could also order information on Schwab's golf-rewards program at the same time. The effectiveness of ads can be immediately measured based on viewer responses.

PODCASTING

The term *podcasting* comes from the words "iPod" and "broadcasting." It refers to a group of technologies for distributing audio or video programs over the Internet using a publisher/subscriber model. Podcasting enables independent producers to create self-published, syndicated "shows," and gives broadcast radio or television programs a new distribution method. Subscribing to podcasts allows users to collect individual programs from a variety of sources for replay at the user's convenience. Initially, podcasting spread rapidly through word of mouth via the already-popular weblogs of early podcasters and podcast listeners. Blogger and

technology columnist Doc Searls kept track of how many "hits" Google found for the word "podcasts." There were 24 hits on September 28, 2004, 526 hits on September 30, then 2,750 hits three days later. The number doubled every few days, passing 100,000 by October 18, 2004, and a year later, Google recorded over 100 million hits!

While podcasters took advantage of the sound-file synchronization feature of Apple Computer's iPod and iTunes software, the technology had always been compatible with other players and programs.

Some traditional broadcasters were quick to adopt the podcasting format. The syndicated radio show *Web Talk Radio* became the first to do so in September 2004 and was followed quickly by other stations.

POP-UPS

Pop-ups refer to a form of ads that launch automatically in a new browser window when a web page is loaded. The problem with pop-ups is that they are often regarded as annoying and intrusive, distracting Web users with unrequested commercial messages. Recent research findings by Chan, Dodd and Stevens suggest that many people have a strong and intense dislike for pop-up ads, which results in a negative attitude toward the advertiser and even the web site from which the pop-up is launched. Pop-ups cause damage if they create a poor online experience, and viewers have learned to ignore such ads in their various forms—often closing the pop-ups before the message can be seen or read, or using pop-up blockers to prevent their appearance in the first place. Service companies need to think carefully before employing this tool.

Sources: Kenneth C. Wilbur, 2004. "Modeling the Effects of Advertisement-Avoidance Technology on Advertisement-Supported Media: The Case of Digital Video Recorders." Working Paper, Mimeo, University of Virginia; Sean Silverthorne, "TiVo Ready to Fast Forward?" *HBS Working Knowledge,* November 15, 2004; Doc Searls, "DIY Radio with PODcasting," *Doc Searls' IT Garage,* September 28, 2004, accessed December 20, 2005, downloaded from www.itgarage.com; Anne Chan, Jon Dodd, and Robert Stevens, "The Efficacy of Pop-ups and the Resulting Effect on Brands," White Paper by Bunnyfoot Universality, January 1, 2004, accessed December 20, 2005, downloaded from www.bunnyfoot.com.

Messages Transmitted Through Production Channels

Messages transmitted through production channels comprises communications developed within the organization and transmitted through the production channels that deliver the service itself—primarily service outlets and front-line staff. A further

Figure 6.6 Sources of Messages Received by a Target Audience

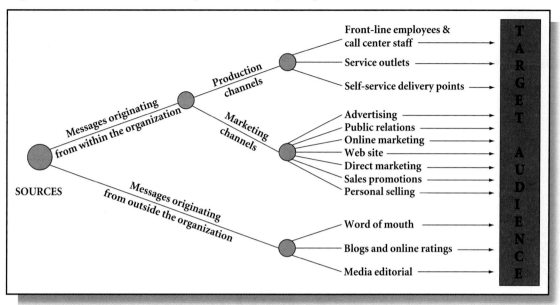

Source: Adapted from a diagram by Adrian Palmer, *Principles of Services Marketing,* 4th ed. London: McGraw-Hill, 2005: 397.

subdivision exists when the originating service firm employs intermediaries to deliver service.

Customer Service from Front-Line Staff

Employees in front-line positions may serve customers face to face or by telephone. Customers' perceptions of the firm are shaped by how they view these individuals.[9] For example, customers of Enterprise Rent-A-Car are pleasantly surprised by the professional appearance of its customer contact personnel. In contrast to other rental car firms, male employees wear suits and females wear dresses or smart skirts. In short, they dress for differentiation.[10] Those responsible for delivering the core service may also be responsible for delivery of a variety of supplementary services, such as providing information, taking reservations, receiving payments, and solving problems. New customers, in particular, often rely on customer service personnel for assistance in learning how to use a service effectively and how to resolve problems.

When several different products are available from the same supplier, firms encourage their customer service staff to cross-sell additional services. However, this approach is likely to fail if strategies are not planned and executed properly.[11] In the banking industry, for example, a highly competitive marketplace and new technologies have forced banks to add more services in an attempt to increase their profitability. In many banks, tellers who traditionally provided customer service are now expected to promote new services to their customers as well. Despite training, many employees feel uncomfortable in this role and don't perform as effectively as salespeople. (This issue is raised in Case 12 about Menton Bank, on pp. 569–576.)

Customer Training

Some companies, especially those that sell complex business-to-business services, offer formal training courses to familiarize their customers with the service product and teach them how to use it to their best advantage. Alternatively (or additionally), this task may be assigned to the same front-line personnel who handle service delivery.

In the telecommunications industry, many firms offer customer education training programs to personal users to stimulate adoption and increased use of their services. Customers learn how to use and benefit from the full potential of service offerings. Mid-River Telephone Cooperative, based in Circle, Montana, holds customer appreciation days and Internet workshops, at which it provides free food and high-speed

Internet connections. Customer service representatives (CSRs) then interact with customers and answer any questions. The firm's member service coordinator, Dick Melvin, elaborated, "More tech-savvy customers generally ask more advanced questions, about Web design, for example. They have been very receptive to this type of training because of the individual attention they receive." He added that the CSRs not only teach Internet usage from basic to advanced levels, they even explain the features that customers encounter on their monthly bills.[12]

Service Outlets

Both planned and unintended messages reach customers through the medium of the service delivery environment itself. Impersonal messages can be distributed in the form of banners, posters, signage, brochures, video screens, and audio. As noted in other chapters, the physical design of the service outlet—what we call the *servicescape*—also sends a message to customers.[13] Corporate design consultants are sometimes asked to advise on servicescape design, to coordinate the visual elements of both interiors and exteriors so that they may complement and reinforce the positioning of the firm and shape the nature of the customers' service experiences in desired ways.

Messages Transmitted Through Marketing Channels

As shown earlier in Figure 6.5, service marketers have a wide array of communication tools at their disposal. We briefly review the principal elements.

Personal Selling

Interpersonal encounters in which efforts are made to educate customers and promote preference for a particular brand or product are referred to as *personal selling*. Many firms, especially those marketing business-to-business services, maintain dedicated sales forces or employ agents and distributors to undertake personal selling efforts on their behalf. For infrequently purchased services such as property, insurance, and funeral services, the firm's representative may act as a consultant to help buyers make appropriate decisions.

Relationship marketing strategies are often based on account management programs, under which customers are assigned a designated account manager who acts as an interface between the customer and the supplier. Account management is commonly practiced by industrial and professional firms that sell relatively complex services, resulting in an ongoing need for advice, education, and consultation. Examples of account management for individual consumers can be found in insurance, investment management, and medical services.

However, face-to-face selling to new prospects is expensive. A lower-cost alternative is *telemarketing*, involving use of the telephone to reach prospective customers. At the consumer level, there is growing frustration with the intrusive nature of telemarketing, which is often timed to reach people when they are home in the evening or at weekends.

Trade Shows

In the business-to-business marketplace, trade shows are a popular form of publicity that also includes important personal selling opportunities.[14] In many industries, trade shows stimulate extensive media coverage and offer business customers an opportunity to find out about the latest offerings from a wide array of suppliers in the field. Service vendors provide physical evidence in the form of exhibits, samples, and demonstrations, and brochures to educate and impress these potential customers. Trade shows can be very productive promotional tools, because they are among the few opportunities in which large numbers of prospective buyers come to the marketer rather than the other way around. A sales representative who usually reaches no more than four to five prospective clients per day in the field may be able to generate five qualified leads per hour at a show.

Consumers often face a bewildering array of choices when purchasing goods and services from online vendors. One way in which "e-tailers" try to assist consumers is to offer electronic recommendation agents as part of their service. Recommendation agents are relatively low-cost "virtual salespeople" designed to help consumers make their selections among large numbers of competing offerings by generating rank-ordered alternative lists based on consumer preferences.

However, research by Lerzan Aksoy for her doctoral dissertation showed that many existing online agents rank options in different ways than the consumers they are designed to help. First, they weight product attributes differently from consumers; second, they may use alternative decision strategies that do not match the simple rules of thumb used by consumers themselves.

The research simulated selection of a cellular phone from among 32 alternatives, described on a web site as each having differing features relating to price, weight, talk time, and standby time. The study results demonstrated that it helps consumers to use a recommendation agent that thinks like them, either in terms of attribute weights or decision strategies. When the ways in which agents work are completely dissimilar, then consumers may be no better off—and sometimes worse served—than if they simply used a randomly ordered list of options. Even though the subjects in this research tended to defer to the agent's recommendations, those who felt it had a dissimilar decision strategy and dissimilar attribute weights from their own were less likely to come back to the website, recommend it to friends, or believe that the site had met their expectations well.

Source: Lerzan Aksoy, Paul N. Bloom, Nicholas H. Lurie, and Bruce Cooil, "Should Recommendation Agents Think Like People?" *Journal of Service Research,* 8 (May 2006): 297–315.

Advertising

As the dominant form of communication in consumer marketing, advertising is often the first point of contact between service marketers and their customers, serving to build awareness, inform, persuade, and remind. It plays a vital role in providing factual information about services and educating customers about product features and capabilities. To demonstrate this role, Grove, Pickett and Laband carried out a study comparing newspaper and TV advertising for goods and services.[15] Based on a review of 11,543 TV advertisements over a 10-month period and of 30,940 newspaper display advertisements that appeared over a 12-month period, they found that ads for services were significantly more likely than those for goods to contain factual information on price, guarantees/warranties, documentation of performance, and availability (where, when, and how to acquire products).

Another option, used increasingly by online vendors, is to use electronic recommendation agents as part of the service to consumers.[16] Recent academic research suggests ways to make them more effective (Research Insights 6.2).

One of the challenges facing advertisers is how to get their messages noticed. In general, people are tiring of ads in all their forms. A recent study by Yankelovich Inc., a U.S. marketing services consulting firm that provides innovative, solutions-oriented consulting and research across a broad range of industries, says that consumer resistance to the growing intrusiveness of advertising has reached an all-time high. The study found that 65 percent of people feel "constantly bombarded" by ad messages and that 59 percent feel that ads have very little relevance to them.[17] Television and radio broadcasts are cluttered with commercials, while newspapers and magazines sometimes seem to contain more ads than news and features. How can a firm hope to stand out from the crowd? Longer, louder commercials and larger-format ads are not necessarily the answer. Some advertisers stand out by employing striking designs or a distinctively different format. Others, such as Comcast, seek to catch the audience's attention through use of humor, as it seeks to show how slow competing services are compared to its own high-speed cable Internet access.

A wide array of paid advertising media is available, including broadcast (TV and radio), print (magazines and newspapers), movie theaters, and many types of outdoor media (posters, billboards, electronic message boards, and the exteriors of buses or bicycles). Some media are more focused than others, targeting specific geographic areas or audiences with a particular interest. Advertising messages delivered through mass media are often reinforced by direct marketing tools such as mailings, telemarketing, or email.

Despite being the dominant form of communication in consumer marketing, the effectiveness of advertising remains hugely controversial. Conventional wisdom in the industry is that sales may well increase for a certain period even after the end of the advertising campaign. However, there comes a point when sales start to decline and it becomes extremely expensive to rebuild the brand. Robert Shaw, of the Cranfield School of Management, runs a forum in which large companies try to monitor the "marketing payback" from advertising. According to Shaw, the results were "never terribly good," with less than half of the ads generating a positive return on their investment.[18]

Direct Marketing

Direct marketing embraces such tools as mailings, recorded telephone messages, faxes, and email. These channels offer the potential to send personalized messages to highly targeted microsegments. Direct strategies are most likely to be successful when marketers possess a detailed database of information about customers and prospects.

Advances in on-demand technologies such as email spam filters, TiVo, podcasting, and pop-up blockers empower consumers to decide how and when they prefer to be reached and by whom. Because a 30-second TV spot interrupts a viewer's favorite program and a telemarketing call interrupts a meal, customers increasingly use such technologies to protect their time, thereby reducing the effectiveness of mass media. These developments give rise to *permission marketing*, where customers are encouraged to "raise their hands" and agree to learn more about a company and its products in anticipation of receiving useful marketing information or something else of value. Instead of annoying prospects by interrupting their personal time, permission marketing allows customers to self-select into the target segments.

In the permission marketing model, the goal is to persuade consumers to volunteer their attention. By reaching out only to individuals who have expressed prior interest in receiving a certain type of message, permission marketing enables service firms to build stronger relationships with their customers. In particular, email in combination with web sites can be integrated into a one-to-one permission-based medium.[19] For instance, people can be invited to register at the firm's web site and can specify what type of information they would like to receive via email. These emails can be designed as the start of a more interactive, multilayered communication process, in which customers can request regular information about topics of their interest, and if they are particularly excited about a new service or piece of information, they can click through a URL link embedded in the email to more in-depth information and even video materials, and finally to subscribe online to additional services, or recommend their friends, and the like.

The greater effectiveness of permission-based communications combined with the falling prices and improving quality of customer relationship management (CRM) and online technology, which together power permission-based marketing, has led many service firms to increasing their focus on permission-based marketing strategies. To see how some firms have implemented excellent permission-based marketing strategies, just go to Amazon.com or Hallmark.com and register at these web sites.

Sales Promotion

A useful way of looking at sales promotions is as a communication attached to an incentive. Sales promotions are usually specific to a time period, price, or customer group—sometimes all three. Typically, the objective is to accelerate the purchasing decision or motivate customers to use a specific service sooner, in greater volume with each purchase, or more frequently.[20] Sales promotions for service firms may take such forms as samples, coupons and other discounts, gifts, and competitions with prizes. Used in these forms, sales promotions add value, provide a "competitive edge," boost sales during periods when demand would otherwise be weak, speed the introduction and acceptance of new services, and generally get customers to act faster than they would in the absence of any promotional incentive.[21]

Some years ago, SAS International Hotels devised an interesting sales promotion targeted at older customers. If a hotel had vacant rooms, guests over 65 years of age could get a discount equivalent to their years (e.g., a 75-year-old could save 75 percent of the normal room price). All went well until a Swedish guest checked into one of the SAS chain's hotels in Vienna, announced his age as 102, and asked to be paid 2 percent of the room rate in return for staying the night. This request was granted, whereupon the spry centenarian challenged the general manager to a game of tennis—and got that, too (the results of the game were not disclosed). Events like these are the stuff of dreams for public relations people. In this case, a clever promotion led to a humorous, widely reported story that showed the hotel chain in a favorable light.

Public Relations

Public relations (PR) involves efforts to stimulate positive interest in an organization and its products by sending out news releases, holding press conferences, staging special events, and sponsoring newsworthy activities put on by third parties. A basic element in public relations strategy is the preparation and distribution of press releases (including photos and/or videos) that feature stories about the company, its products, and its employees. PR executives also arrange press conferences and distribute press kits when they feel a story is especially newsworthy. A key task performed by corporate PR specialists at many service organizations involves teaching senior managers how to present themselves well at news conferences or in radio and TV interviews, especially at times of crisis or when faced with hostile questioning.

Other widely used PR techniques include recognition and reward programs, obtaining testimonials from public figures, community involvement and support, fundraising, and obtaining favorable publicity for the organization through special events and *pro bono* work. These tools can help a service organization build its reputation and credibility, form strong relationships with its employees, customers, and the community, and secure an image conducive to business success.

Firms can also win wide exposure through sponsorship of sporting events and other high-profile activities where banners, decals, and other visual displays provide continuing repetition of the corporate name and symbol. For instance, all the yachting syndicates participating in the America's Cup races have relied on corporate sponsorship to help cover the huge costs of participating in this event. Most syndicates have multiple sponsors, whose names or logos appear prominently on the yacht's sails and hulls. All sponsors gain significant media exposure during the extended racing season, although there's always the risk the yacht may perform badly or even capsize and sink. The winning yacht generates prestige for its sponsors, which may incorporate this success into subsequent advertising campaigns for an extended period after the races.

Unusual activities can present an opportunity to promote a company's expertise. FedEx gained significant favorable publicity when it safely transported two giant pandas from Chengdu, China, to the National Zoo in Washington, D.C. The pandas flew in specially designed containers aboard a FedEx aircraft renamed *FedEx PandaOne*. In addition to press releases, the company also featured information about the unusual shipment on a special page in its web site.

Messages Originating from Outside the Organization

Some of the most powerful messages about a company and its products come from outside the organization and are not controlled by the marketer.

Word of Mouth

Recommendations from other customers are generally viewed as more credible than firm-initiated promotional activities and can have a powerful influence on people's decisions to use (or avoid using) a service. In fact, the greater the risk that customers perceive in purchasing a service, the more actively they will seek and rely on word of mouth (WOM) to guide their decision making.[22] Customers who are less knowledgeable about a service rely more on WOM than do expert consumers.[23] WOM even takes place during service encounters. When customers talk with each other about some aspect of service, this information can influence both their behavior and their satisfaction with the service.[24] Frederick Reichheld argues that whether or not customers are willing to give positive WOM for a firm is the single most important predictor of top-line growth.[25]

Because WOM can act as such a powerful and highly credible selling agent, some marketers employ a variety of strategies to stimulate positive and persuasive comments from existing customers.[26] These include:

- Referencing other purchasers and knowledgeable individuals (for instance, "We have done a great job for ABC Corp., and if you wish, feel free to talk to Mr. Cabral, their MIS manager, who oversaw the implementation of our project").
- Creating exciting promotions that get people talking about the great service the firm provides.
- Developing referral incentive schemes, such as offering an existing customer some units of free or discounted service in return for introducing new customers to the firm.
- Offering promotions that encourage customers to persuade others to join them in using the service (for instance, "Bring two friends, and the third eats for free," or "Subscribe to two mobile service plans, and we'll waive the monthly subscription fee for all subsequent family members").
- Presenting and publicizing testimonials that simulate WOM. Advertising and brochures sometimes feature comments from satisfied customers.

Research shows that the extent and content of word of mouth is related to satisfaction levels. Customers who hold strong views are likely to tell more people about their experiences than those with milder views. And extremely dissatisfied customers tell more people than those who are highly satisfied.[27] Noting the important role that service employees play in customer satisfaction, Dwayne Gremler and his colleagues suggest that measures to improve the quality of customer–employee interactions may be a an appropriate strategy for stimulating positive WOM.[28] Interestingly, even customers who were initially dissatisfied with a service can end up spreading positive WOM if they are delighted with the way the firm handled service recovery.[29] The ubiquity of the Internet has accelerated the spread of personal influence, causing it to evolve into a "viral marketing" phenomenon that businesses can ill afford to ignore.[30] Research Insights 6.2 discusses recent research on why and how people pass on emails. In fact, viral marketing, which takes advantage of networks among customers and prospects to influence attitudes and behaviors, has now become an industry in itself. One of the early success stories of viral marketing was the Hotmail free email service, which grew from zero to 12 million users in 18 months on a miniscule advertising budget, thanks mostly to the inclusion of a promotional message including the Hotmail URL in every email sent by its users.[31] eBay and other firms that engage in electronic auctions rely on users to rate sellers and buyers in order to build trust in the items offered on their web sites and thereby facilitate transactions between strangers who, without access to such peer ratings, might be reluctant to transact on these sites.

Blogs—A New Type of Online WOM[32]

Weblogs, commonly referred to as blogs, are becoming increasingly popular. Blogs are frequently modified web pages in which entries are listed in reverse chronological

How can firms make better use of pass-along emails and viral marketing? First, managers need to understand how consumers respond when they receive pass-along emails, what senders write in such messages, and what motivates recipients to forward them. The following three studies sought answers to these questions.

Study 1 explored how recipients responded to pass-along emails and how these communications differed from undesirable spam. Eight focus groups were conducted, involving a total of 66 individuals. Respondents considered emails as spam when the sender wasn't known. By contrast, recipients typically knew who had sent them a pass-along email. When questioned about the types of viral messages they receive, there was consistent mention of jokes, followed by virus alerts, inspirational stories, religious messages, requests to vote on certain issues, lost children, chain letters, poems, animated clips, links to specific web sites, and urban legends.

The positive emotions that recipients experienced when receiving what they viewed as meaningful messages ranged from simply good (e.g., "someone is thinking about me"), and brightens my day ("when it's someone I haven't heard from in a while"), to excited ("it's like seeing a letter in the mail") and rewarded ("when I get something from the church"). Negative emotions included irritation (e.g., when the message seemed irrelevant, felt like a waste of time, or when an individual sent too many messages), anger (e.g., when an individual had asked to be taken off a list), disappointment (e.g., when a person wanted a more personal note from someone), to skeptical (if an offer looked too good to be true), burdened (e.g., when the recipient had too much work, felt overwhelmed or obligated to answer).

In *Study 2*, the researchers conducted a content analysis of 1,259 pass-along messages sent by 34 focus group participants in order to better understand what types of messages were forwarded. The analysis revealed that 40 percent of messages were actually forwarded to others. The main reasons for not doing so involved messages that were perceived to be out of date, uninteresting, or inappropriate. Alternatively, respondents were in a rush and did not have time to forward messages. About one-third of the forwarded emails were sent with a personalized note, mostly to motivate the recipient to read the message. When recipients forwarded pass-along emails, the great majority did not change the subject line. Only a few of the forwarded emails concerned products, services, or companies, suggesting that either firms are not making much use of pass-along emails or that they are not using them effectively.

Study 3 focused on the reasons why people forward pass-along emails. The six top-rated reasons centered on enjoyment and entertainment (e.g., "it's fun," "I enjoy it," and "it's entertaining"), and social motivations (e.g., "to help others," and "to let others know I care about their feelings"). The findings also showed that for a message to be forwarded it must be important or contain something the sender believes the recipient will like.

This research demonstrates that there is untapped potential for service marketers to use pass-along emails in their communications efforts. However, the findings also suggest that (1) firms need to be careful in crafting messages their target segments will find relevant enough to forward; (2) the message content should spark emotion (e.g., humor, fear, or inspiration) and appeal to the desire for fun, entertainment, and social connection; and (3) firms should think carefully about the wording of the subject line, as it is likely to be forwarded unchanged.

Source: Adapted from Joseph E. Phelps, Regina Lewis, Lynne Mobilio, David Perry, and Niranjan Raman, "Viral Marketing or Electronic Word-of-Mouth Advertising: Examining Consumer Responses and Motivations to Pass Along Emails." *Journal of Advertising Research* (December 2004): 333–348.

sequence. They can be best described as online journals, diaries, or news listings, where people can post anything, about whatever they like. Their authors, known as bloggers, usually focus on narrow topics, and quite a few have become *de facto* watchdogs and self-proclaimed experts in certain fields. Blogs can be about anything, ranging from baseball and sex to karate and financial engineering. There are a growing number of travel-oriented sites, ranging from Hotel.chatter.com (focused on boutique hotels) to CruiseDiva.com (reporting on the cruise industry) and pestiside.hu ("the daily dish of cosmopolitan Budapest"). Some sites, such as the travel-focused tripadvisor.com, allow users to post their own reviews or ask questions that more experienced travelers may be able to answer.[33]

Marketers are interested in the way that blogs have evolved into a new form of social interaction on the Web: a massively distributed but completely connected conversation covering every imaginable topic, including consumers' experiences with service firms and their recommendations on avoiding or patronizing certain firms. A by-product of this online communication is the set of hyperlinks made between weblogs in the exchange of dialog. These links allows customers to share information with others and influence opinions of a brand or product—just google the terms "Citibank and blog," or "Charles Schwab and blog" and you will see an entire list of blogs or blog entries relating to these service firms. A few savvy service firms have started to monitor blogs, viewing them as a form of immediate market research and feedback. Some service companies have even started their own blogs; see, for example, Google's blog at http://googleblog.blogspot.com.

Editorial Coverage

Although some media coverage of firms and their services is stimulated by public relations activity, broadcasters and publishers often initiate their own coverage. In addition to news stories about a company and its services, editorial coverage can take several other forms. Investigative reporters might conduct an in-depth study of a company, especially if they believe it is putting customers at risk, cheating them, employing deceptive advertising, or otherwise exploiting them. Some columnists specialize in helping customers who have been unable to get complaints resolved.

Journalists responsible for consumer affairs often contrast and compare service offerings from competing organizations, identifying their strong and weak points, and offering advice on "best buys." In a more specialized context, *Consumer Reports,* the monthly publication of Consumers' Union, periodically evaluates services that are offered on a national basis, including financial services and telecommunications. It recently undertook an in-depth analysis of the cellular telephone industry, commenting on the strengths and weaknesses of different service providers and seeking to determine the true cost of their often confusingly priced plans.[34]

Ethical Issues in Communication

Few aspects of marketing lend themselves so easily to misuse (and even abuse) as advertising, selling, and sales promotion. The fact that customers often find it hard to evaluate services makes them more dependent on marketing communication for information and advice. Communication messages often include promises about the benefits that customers will receive and the quality of service delivery. When promises are made and then broken, customers are disappointed because their expectations have not been met.[35] Their disappointment and even anger will be even greater if they have wasted money, time, and effort and have no benefits to show in return or have actually suffered a negative effect. Employees, too, may feel disappointed and frustrated as they listen to customers' complaints about unfulfilled expectations.

Some unrealistic service promises result from poor internal communications between operations and marketing personnel concerning the level of service performance that customers can reasonably expect. In other instances, unethical advertisers and salespeople deliberately make exaggerated promises to secure sales. Finally, there are deceptive promotions that lead people to think that they have a much higher chance of winning prizes or awards than is really the case. Fortunately, there are many consumer watchdogs on the lookout for these deceptive marketing practices. They include consumer protection agencies, trade associations within specific industries, and journalists who investigate customer complaints and seek to expose fraud and misrepresentation.

A different type of ethical issue concerns unwanted intrusion by aggressive marketers into people's personal lives. The increase in telemarketing, direct mail, and email is frustrating for those who receive unwanted sales communications. How do you feel when your evening meal at home is interrupted by a telephone call from a stranger trying to interest you in buying services in which you have no interest? Even if you are interested, you may feel, as many do, that your privacy has been violated. To address growing hostility toward these practices, both government agencies and trade associations have acted to protect consumers. In the United States, the Federal Trade Commission's National Do Not Call Registry enables consumers to remove their home and mobile numbers from telemarketing lists for a five-year period. People who continue to receive unauthorized calls from commercial telemarketers can file a complaint, and the telemarketing firm may be subject to heavy fines for such violations.[36] Similarly, the Direct Marketing Association helps consumers remove their names from mailing, telemarketing, and email lists.[37]

THE ROLE OF CORPORATE DESIGN

Have you noticed how some firms stick out in your mind because of the colors that they use, the widespread application of their logos, the uniforms worn by their personnel, and the design of their physical facilities? Many service firms employ a unified and distinctive visual appearance for all tangible elements, to facilitate recognition and reinforce a desired brand image. Corporate design strategies are usually created by external consulting firms and include such features as stationery and promotional literature, retail signage, uniforms, and color schemes for painting vehicles, equipment, and building interiors. The objective is to provide a recognizable theme linking all the firm's operations in a branded service experience through the strategic use of physical evidence.

Corporate design is particularly important for companies that operate in competitive markets in which it's necessary to stand out from the crowd and to be instantly recognizable in different locations. For example, gasoline retailing provides striking contrasts in corporate designs, from BP's bright green-and-yellow service stations to Texaco's red, black, and white and Sunoco's blue, maroon, and yellow.

Companies in the highly competitive express delivery industry tend to use their names as a central element in their corporate designs. When Federal Express changed its trading name to the more modern FedEx, it also changed its logo to feature the new name in a distinctive logo. Consistent applications of this design were developed for use in settings ranging from business cards to boxes and from employee caps to aircraft exteriors. When the company decided to rebrand a ground delivery service it had purchased, it chose the name FedEx Ground and developed an alternative color treatment of the standard logo (purple and green rather than purple and orange). Its goal was to transfer the positive image of reliable, on-time service associated with its air services to its less expensive small-package ground service. The well-known air service was then rebranded as FedEx Express. Other subbrands in what the firm refers to as "the FedEx family of companies" include FedEx Home Delivery (delivers to U.S. residential addresses), FedEx Freight (regional, less-than-truckload transportation for heavyweight freight), FedEx Custom Critical (nonstop, door-to-door delivery of time-critical shipments), FedEx Trade networks (customs brokerage, international freight forwarding, and trade facilitation), Fedex Supply Chain Services (a comprehensive suite of solutions that synchronize the movement of goods), and Fedex Kinko's (office and printing services, technology services, shipping supplies, and packing services, located in both city and suburban retail stores).

Many companies use a trademarked symbol, rather than a name, as their primary logo.[38] Shell makes a pun of its English name by displaying a yellow scallop shell on a red background, which has the advantage of making its vehicles and service stations instantly recognizable. McDonald's "Golden Arches" is said to be the most widely recognized corporate symbol in the world and is featured not only at its restaurants and on employee uniforms but also in the company's advertising. However, international companies operating in many countries need to select their designs carefully to avoid conveying a culturally inappropriate message through unfortunate choices of names, colors, or images.

At a basic level, some companies have succeeded in creating tangible, recognizable symbols to associate with their corporate brand names. Animal motifs are common physical symbols for services. Examples include the eagles of the US Postal Service, AeroMexico and Eagle Star Insurance, the lions of ING Bank and the Royal Bank of Canada, the ram of the investment firm T. Rowe Price, and the Chinese dragon of Hong Kong's Dragonair. Merrill Lynch, the global financial services company, derived its corporate symbol, a bull, from its famous slogan, "We're Bullish on America." Easily recognizable corporate symbols are especially important when services are offered in markets where the local language is not written in Roman script or where a significant proportion of the population is functionally illiterate.

MARKETING COMMUNICATIONS AND THE INTERNET

The Internet is now an integral part of marketing communications strategy. Perhaps its most remarkable aspect is its ubiquity: A web site hosted in one country can be accessed from almost anywhere in the world, offering the simplest form of international market entry available—in fact, as Christian Grönroos points out, "the firm cannot avoid creating interest in its offerings outside its local or national market."[39] However, creating international access and developing an international strategy are two very different things.

Internet Marketing Offers Powerful Opportunities for Interactivity

Marketers use the Internet for a variety of communications tasks. These tasks include promoting consumer awareness and interest, providing information and consultation, facilitating two-way communications with customers through email and chat rooms, stimulating product trial, enabling customers to place orders, and measuring the effectiveness of specific advertising or promotional campaigns. Not only can firms market through their own web sites, they can place advertising on a variety of other sites. Advertising on the Web allows companies to supplement conventional communications channels at a reasonable cost. However, like any of the elements of the marketing communications mix, Internet advertising should be part of an integrated, well-designed communications strategy.[40]

Enabling marketers to communicate and establish a rapport with individual customers is one of the Web's greatest strengths. The interactive nature of the Internet has the potential to increase customer involvement dramatically. In addition to facilitating email-based permission marketing as discussed earlier in this chapter, the Internet enables "self-service" marketing, in which individual customers control the nature and extent of their contact with those web sites that they choose to visit. Many banks allow customers to pay bills electronically, apply for loans over the Internet, and check their account balances online. Whistler/Blackholm ski resort in British Columbia uses its web site to promote advance online purchase of lift tickets at a discount. This site also offers instructions on how the online ticket window works, describes where to pick up the tickets, and provides responses to frequently asked questions (FAQs).

Web Site Design Considerations

From a communication standpoint, a web site should contain information that a company's target customers will find useful and interesting. Internet users expect speedy access, easy navigation, and content that is both relevant and up to date.

Service firms should set explicit communication goals for their web sites. Is the site to be a promotional channel, a self-service option that diverts customers away from contact with service personnel, an automated news room that disseminates information about the company and its products, as well as offering an archive of past press releases; or even all of these?

Some firms choose to emphasize promotional content, seeking to present the firm and its products in a favorable light and to stimulate purchase; others view their sites as educational and encourage visitors to search for needed information, even providing links to related sites.

Innovative companies are continually looking for ways to improve the appeal and usefulness of their sites. The appropriate communication content varies widely from one type of service to another. A B2B site may offer visitors access to a library of technical information (e.g., Siebel or SAP both provide substantial information on their customer relationship management solutions at their respective web sites, www.siebel.com and www.sap.com). By contrast, a web site for an MBA program might include attractive photographs featuring the location, the facilities, and past students, and short videos showing the university, its professors and facilities, student testimonials, and even the graduation ceremony.

Marketers must also address other attributes such as downloading speed that affect web site "stickiness" (that is, whether site visitors are willing to spend time on the site and will revisit it in the future). A sticky site is

- *High in content quality.* Relevant and useful content is king. A site needs to contain what visitors are looking for on the site.
- *Easy to use.* Ease of use means good navigation, and a site structure that is neither overcomplicated nor too big, and is well signposted. Customers do not get lost in good sites.
- *Quick to download.* Viewers don't want to wait and will often give up if it takes too long for pages to download from a site. Good sites download quickly, and bad sites are slow.
- *Updated frequently.* Good sites look fresh and up to date. They include recently posted information that visitors find relevant and timely.[41]

A memorable Web address helps to attract visitors to a site. Ideally, they are based on the company's name (e.g., www.citibank.com or www.aol.com), although sometimes an alternative must be found if the simple form of the name has already been taken by a similarly named company in another industry. Ensuring that people are aware of the address requires displaying it prominently on business cards, letterhead stationery, email templates, brochures, advertising, promotional materials and even vehicles. One of the largest of the European discount airlines, easyJet, has painted its address in huge orange letters on each of its aircraft (Figure 6.7).

Effective Advertising on the Internet

Internet advertising, also called *Webvertising,* has become an important part of the communications mix for most service firms. There are two main options, banner advertising and search engine advertising. In each case, advertisers can include moving images and create links to more extended video presentations.

Banner Advertising

Many firms pay to place advertising banners and buttons on portals such as Yahoo or Netscape, as well as on other firms' web sites. The usual goal is to draw online traffic to the advertiser's own site. In many instances, web sites include advertising messages from other marketers with related but noncompeting services. Yahoo's stock quotes page, for example, features a sequence of advertisements for various financial service providers. Similarly, many web pages devoted to a specific topic feature a small message from Amazon.com, inviting the reader to identify books on these same topics by clicking the accompanying hyperlink button to the Internet retailer's book

Figure 6.7
easyJet Paints Its Web Site Address on Each of Its More than 200 Aircraft

Source: www.easyjet.com/EN/Abut/photgallery.html. © easyJet airline company limited.

site. In such cases, it's easy for the advertiser to measure how many visits to its own site are generated by click-throughs.

Simply obtaining a large number of exposures ("eyeballs") to a banner (a thin horizontal ad running across all or part of a web page), a skyscraper (a long skinny ad running vertically down one side of a web site), or a button doesn't necessarily lead to increases in awareness, preference, or sales for the advertiser. One consequence is that the practice of paying a flat monthly rate for banner advertising is falling out of favor. Even when visitors click through to the advertiser's site, this action doesn't necessarily result in sales. Consequently, there's now more emphasis on advertising contracts that tie fees to marketing-relevant behavior by these visitors, such as providing the advertiser with some information about themselves or making a purchase. Today, Internet advertisers usually pay only if a visitor to the host site clicks through on the link to the advertisers' site. This is the equivalent of paying for the delivery of junk mail only to households that read it.[42]

Search Engine Advertising

Search engines are a form of a reverse broadcast network. Instead of advertisers broadcasting their messages to consumers, search engines let advertisers know exactly what consumers want through their keyword search, and advertisers can then target relevant marketing communications directly at these consumers.[43] One of the phenomenal success stories of Internet advertising has been Google (see Service Perspectives 6.2), with firms such as Yahoo!, AOL, and MSN also seeking to become major players in this field.

Advertisers have several options. They can pay for the targeted placement of ads to keyword searches relevant to the advertising firm, they can sponsor a short text message with a click-through link, located parallel to the search results, or they can buy top rankings in the display of search results through a "pay-for-placement" option. This last-mentioned approach is somewhat controversial because it conflicts with users' expectations that the rankings will reflect the best fit with the keywords employed in the search. Google's policy is to shade paid listings that appear at the top of the rankings column and identify them as "sponsored links." Pricing for these ads and placements can be based on either number of impressions (i.e., eyeballs) or

Graduate students Larry Page and Sergey Brin, who were both fascinated by mathematics, computers, and programming from an early age, founded Google in 1998. Seven years later, following Google's successful public offering, they had become billionaires and Google itself had become one of the world's most valuable companies.

The company has the grand vision: "To organize the world's information and make it universally accessible and useful." The utility and ease of its search engine has made it immensely successful, almost entirely through word of mouth from satisfied users. Few company names become verbs, but "to google" has now entered common use in English.

Its popularity has enabled Google to become a new and highly targeted advertising medium, selling advertisements that appear next to its search results. Branded as Google AdWords, its service allows businesses to connect with potential customers at the precise moment when the latter are looking at related topics or even specific product categories. Specifically, firms buy the opportunity to be associated with particular search categories or terms. To explore Google's advertising business model, just "google" a few words and observe what appears on your screen in addition to the search results.

Google prices its "sponsored links" service as "cost per click." This price depends on the popularity of the search terms with which the advertiser wants to be associated. Heavily used terms such as "MBA" are more expensive than less popular terms such as "MSc in Business." Advertisers can easily keep track of their ad performance using the reports in Google's online account Control Center.

Advertisers can also display their ads at web sites that are part of the Google content network. Google calls them "site targeted ads." Advertisers can specify either individual web sites or web site content (e.g., about travel or baseball). Site targeting allows advertisers to handpick their target audiences, which can be really large (e.g., all baseball fans in the United States, or even in the world) or small and focused (e.g., people interested in fine dining in the Boston area). When an advertiser designs a site-targeted campaign, it can either name the sites where it would like to advertise or simply give Google a list of key words that describes the site. The Google AdWords matching system then analyzes the terms and creates a list of available content network sites.

Google has also created a separate service called Google AdSense. It's a fast and convenient service targeted at web site publishers of all sizes. In return for displaying relevant Google ads on their web site's content pages, publishers receive a share of the advertising revenue generated.

The company's ability to deliver an advertising medium that is highly targeted, contextual, and results-based has been extremely attractive to advertisers and has led to rapid revenue growth and profits. It's no surprise that Google's success is frightening other advertising media.

Sources: Roben Farzad and Ben Elgin, "Googling for Gold." *BusinessWeek* (December 5, 2005): 60–70; www.google.com, accessed January 3, 2006.

click-throughs, both of which are achieved by placing sponsored links at the top of search results.

Developing an Integrated Marketing Communications Strategy

Many service firms initially organized their web site and online marketing activities into separate groups that were mostly isolated from other marketing activities. However, if it is isolated this way, a firm's online communications—or for that matter any other market communications channel—may deliver conflicting messages and result in confused consumers who will not have a clear picture of a firm's positioning and value proposition.

Have you ever seen a new, exciting service promotion being touted at a firm's web site, only to find when you then visited a branch office that the counter staff was not aware of this promotion and couldn't sell it to you? What went wrong? In many service firms, different departments look after different aspects of a firms market communications. For example, the marketing department is in charge of advertising, the PR department of public relations, functional specialists look after a company's web site and its direct marketing and promotions activities, operations of customer service, and human resources of training. The service failure described above is a consequence of these various departments not coordinating their efforts effectively.

With so many channels delivering messages to customers and prospects, it becomes more and more important for firms to adopt the concept of integrated marketing communications (IMC). IMC ties together and reinforces all communications to deliver a strong brand identity. It means that a firm's various media deliver the same messages and have the sae look and feel, and the communications from the different media and communications approaches all become part of a single, overall message about the service firm and its products. Firms can achieve this by giving ownership of IMC to a single department (e.g., marketing), or by appointing a marketing communications director who has overall responsibility for all of the firm's market communications.

CONCLUSION

The *Promotion and education* element of the 8 Ps requires a somewhat different emphasis from the communications strategy used to market goods. The communication tasks facing service marketers include emphasizing tangible clues for services that are difficult to evaluate, clarifying the nature and sequence of the service performance, highlighting the performance of customer contact personnel, and educating the customer about how to participate effectively in service delivery.

Many different communication elements are available to help companies create a distinctive position in the market and reach prospective customers. The options in the marketing communication mix include personal communications such as personal selling and customer service, as well as impersonal communications such as advertising, sales promotions, public relations, corporate design, and

the physical evidence offered by the servicescape of the service delivery site. Instructional materials, from brochures to web sites, often play an important role in educating customers on how to make good choices and obtain the best use from the services they have purchased. Developments in technology, especially the Internet, are changing the face of marketing communications, driving innovations such as permission marketing and exciting possibilities for highly targeted online advertising.

A key point for you to take away from this chapter is that effective service marketers are good educators who can use a variety of communication media in cost-efficient ways, not only to promote their firm's value propositions but also to teach prospects and customers what they need to know about selecting and using these services.

REVIEW QUESTIONS

1. In what ways do the objectives of services communications differ substantially from those of goods marketing?
2. Which elements of the marketing communications mix you would use for each of the following scenarios? Explain your answers.
   - A newly established hair salon in a suburban shopping center
   - An established restaurant facing declining patronage because of new competitors
   - A large, single-office accounting firm in a major city that serves primarily business clients
3. What roles do personal selling, advertising, and public relations play in (a) attracting new customers to visit a service outlet, and (b) retaining existing customers?
4. Discuss the relative effectiveness of brochures and web sites for promoting (a) a ski resort, (b) a business school, (c) a fitness center, and (d) an online broker.

5. Why is word of mouth considered so important for the marketing of services? How can a service firm that is the quality leader in its industry induce and manage word of mouth?
6. Why is permission-based marketing gaining so much focus in service firms' communications strategies?
7. What do you see as important opportunities and threats of viral marketing. How can service firms leverage viral marketing, and how can they overcome its potential challenges?
8. Explain why weblogs are potentially powerful influencers in market spaces with a high proportion of technologically savvy consumers.
9. What are the different forms of online marketing? Which do you think would be the most effective online marketing strategies for an online broker, a new discotheque in Los Angeles, and a fine-dining restaurant in New York?

APPLICATION EXERCISES

1. Describe four common educational and promotional objectives in service settings and provide a specific example for each of the objectives you list.

2. Identify one advertisement (or other means of communication) each that aims mainly at managing consumer behavior in the (a) choice, (b) consumption, and (c) postconsumption stages. Explain how they try to achieve their objectives and discuss how effective they may be.

3. Discuss the significance of search, experience, and credence attributes for the communications strategy of a service provider. Assume that the objective of the communications strategy is to attract new customers.

4. If you were exploring your current university or researching the degree program you are now in, what could you learn from blogs and any other online word of mouth you can find? How would that information influence the decision of a prospective new applicant to your university? Given that you are an expert about the school and degree you are taking, how accurate do you think is the information you found online?

5. Identify an advertisement that runs the risk of attracting mixed segments to a service business. Explain why this may happen and state what negative consequences, if any, there are likely to be.

6. Describe and evaluate recent public relations efforts made by service organizations in connection with three or more of the following: (a) launching a new offering; (b) opening a new facility; (c) promoting an expansion of existing services; (d) announcing an upcoming event; or (e) responding to a negative situation that has arisen. (Pick a different organization for each category.)

7. What tangible cues could a scuba diving school or a dentistry office use to position itself as appealing to upscale customers?

8. Explore the web sites of a management consulting firm, an Internet retailer, and an insurance company. Critique them for ease of navigation, content, and visual design. What, if anything, would you change about each site?

9. Register at Amazon.com and Hallmark.com, and analyze their permission-based communications strategy. What are their marketing objectives? Evaluate their permission-based marketing for a specific customer segment of your choice—what is excellent, what is good, and what could be further improved?

10. Conduct a Google search for (a) MBA programs, and (b) holiday resorts. Examine two or three contextual ads that are triggered by your searches. Critique these contextual ads—what are they doing right, and what can be improved?

ENDNOTES

1. For a useful review, see Kathleen Mortimer and Brian P. Mathews, "The Advertising of Services: Consumer Views v. Normative Dimensions." *The Service Industries Journal*, 18 (July 1998): 14–19.

2. James F. Devlin and Sarwar Azhar, "Life Would Be a Lot Easier if We Were a Kit Kat: Practitioners' Views on the Challenges of Branding Financial Services Successfully." *Brand Management*, 12, no. 1 (2004): 12–30.

3. Banwari Mittal, "The Advertising of Services: Meeting the Challenge of Intangibility." *Journal of Service Research*, 2 (August 1999): 98–116.

4. Banwari Mittal and Julie Baker, "Advertising Strategies for Hospitality Services." *Cornell Hotel and Restaurant Administration Quarterly*, 43 (April 2002): 51–63.

5. Donna Legg and Julie Baker, "Advertising Strategies for Service Firms," in C. Surprenant (ed.), *Add Value to Your Service*. Chicago: American Marketing Association, 1987: 163–168. See also Donna J. Hill, Jeff Blodgett, Robert Baer, and Kirk Wakefield, "An Investigation of Visualization and Documentation Strategies in Service Advertising." *Journal of Service Research*, 7 (November 2004): 155–166; Debra Grace and Aron O'Cass, "Service Branding: Consumer Verdicts on Service Brands." *Journal of Retailing and Consumer Services*, 12 (2005): 125–139.

6. James C. Anderson, James C. Narus, and Wouter van Russom, "Customer Value Propositions in Business Markets." *Harvard Business Review*, 84 (March 2006): 1–4.

7. Banwari Mittal, "The Advertising of Services: Meeting the Challenge of Intangibility." *Journal of Service Research*, 2 (August 1999): 98–116.

8. http://consumercenter.jdpower.com/cc/rd/cc/index.asp, accessed May 2006.

9. For a framework and checklist to identify and sustain service brand values, see Leslie De Chernatony and Susan Drury, "Identifying and Sustaining Service Brands' Values." *Journal of Marketing Communications*, 10 (June 2004): 73–93.

10. Leonard L. Berry, "Cultivating Service Brand Equity." *Journal of the Academy of Marketing Science*, 28, no. 1 (2000): 128–137.

11. David H. Maister, "Why Cross Selling Hasn't Worked." In *True Professionalism*, New York: The Free Press, 1997: 178–184.

12. Megan O'Donnell, "What Type of Training or Education Do You Provide to Customers for New Technology Offerings?" *Rural Communications* (July–August 2005): 12.

13. Mary Jo Bitner, "Servicescapes: The Impact of Physical Surroundings on Customers and Employees." *Journal of Marketing*, 56 (April 1992): 57–71.

14. Dana James, "Move Cautiously in Trade Show Launch." *Marketing News* (November 20, 2000: 4, 6; Elizabeth Light, "Tradeshows and Expos—Putting Your Business on Show." *Her Business* (March–April 1998): 14–18; Susan Greco, "Trade Shows Versus Face-to-Face Selling." *Inc.* (May 1992): 142.

15. Stephen J. Grove, Gregory M. Pickett, and David N. Laband, "An Empirical Examination of Factual Information Content Among Service Advertisements." *The Service Industries Journal*, 15 (April 1995): 216–233.

16. Gerard Haübl and Kyle B. Murray, "Preference Construction and Persistence in Digital Marketplaces: The Role of Electronic Recommendation Agents." *Journal of Consumer Psychology*, 13 no. 1 (2003): 75–91; Lerzan Aksoy, Paul N. Bloom, Nicholas H. Lurie, and Bruce Cooil, "Should Recommendation Agents Think Like People?" *Journal of Service Research*, 8 (May 2006): 297–315.

17. "The Future of Advertising—The Harder Hard Sell." *The Economist* (June 24, 2004).

18. Ibid.

19. Seth Godin and Don Peppers, *Permission Marketing: Turning Strangers into Friends and Friends into Customers.* New York: Simon & Schuster, 1999; Ray Kent and Hege Brandal, "Improving Email Response in a Permission Marketing Context." *International Journal of Market Research*, 45, quarter 4 (2003): 489–503.

20. Gila E. Fruchter and Z. John Zhang, "Dynamic Targeted Promotions: A Customer Retention and Acquisition Perspective." *Journal of Service Research*, 7 (August 2004): 3–19.

21. Ken Peattie and Sue Peattie, "Sales Promotion—A Missed Opportunity for Service Marketers." *International Journal of Service Industry Management*, 5, no. 1 (1995): 6–21.

22. Harvir S. Bansal and Peter A. Voyer, "Word-of-Mouth Processes Within a Services Purchase Decision Context." *Journal of Service Research*, 3, no. 2 (November 2000): 166–177.

23. Anna S. Mattila and Jochen Wirtz, "The Impact of Knowledge Types on the Consumer Search Process—An Investigation in the Context of Credence Services," *International Journal of Research in Service Industry Management*, 13, no. 3 (2002): 214–230.

24. Kim Harris and Steve Baron, "Consumer-to-Consumer Conversations in Service Settings." *Journal of Service Research*, 6, no. 3 (2004): 287–303.

25. Frederick F. Reichheld, "The One Number You Need to Grow." *Harvard Business Review*, 81, no. 12 (2003): 46–55. For an explanation of how different types of epidemics, including word-of-mouth epidemics, develop, see Malcom Gladwell, *The Tipping Point*. New York: Little, Brown and Company, 2000, p. 32.

26. Jochen Wirtz and Patricia Chew, "The Effects of Incentives, Deal Proneness, Satisfaction and Tie Strength on Word-of-Mouth Behaviour." *International Journal of Service Industry Management*, 13, no. 2 (2002): 141–162. Tom J. Brown, Thomas E. Barry, Peter A. Dacin, and Richard F. Gunst, "Spreading the Word: Investigating Antecedents of Consumers' Positive Word-of-Mouth Intentions and Behaviors in a Retailing Context." *Journal of the Academy of Marketing Science*, 33, no. 2 (2005): 123–138; John E. Hogan, Katherine N. Lemon, and Barak Libai, "Quantifying the Ripple: Word-of-Mouth and Advertising Effectiveness." *Journal of Advertising Research* (September 2004): 271–280.

27. Eugene W. Anderson, "Customer Satisfaction and Word of Mouth." *Journal of Service Research*, 1 (August 1998): 5–17. Magnus Söderlund, "Customer Satisfaction and Its Consequences on Customer Behaviour Revisited: The Impact of Different Levels of Satisfaction on Word of Mouth, Feedback to the Supplier, and Loyalty. *International Journal of Service Industry Management*, 9, no. 2 (1998): 169–188. Srini S. Srinivasan, Rolph Anderson, and Kishore Ponnavolu, "Customer Loyalty in e-Commerce: An Exploration of Its Antecedents and Consequences." *Journal of Retailing*, 78, no. 1 (2002): 41–50.

28. Dwayne D. Gremler, Kevin P. Gwinner, and Stephen W. Brown, "Generating Positive Word-of-Mouth Communication Through Customer-Employee Relationships." *International Journal of Service Industry Management*, 12, no. 1 (2000): 44–59.

29. Jeffrey G. Blodgett, Kirk L. Wakefield, and James H. Barnes, "The Effects of Customer Service on Consumers Complaining Behavior." *Journal of Services Marketing*, 9, no. 4 (1995): 31–42; Jeffrey G. Blodgett and Ronald D. Anderson, "A Bayesian Network Model of the Consumer Complaint Process." *Journal of Service Research*, 2, no. 4 (May 2000): 321–338; Stefan Michel, "Analyzing Service Failures and Recoveries: A Process Approach." *International Journal of Service Industry Management*, 12, no. 1 (2001): 20–33; James G Maxham III and Richard G Netemeyer, "A Longitudinal Study of Complaining Customers' Evaluations of Multiple Service Failures and Recovery Efforts." *Journal of Marketing*, 66, no. 4 (2002): 57–72.

30. Renee Dye, "The Buzz on Buzz." *Harvard Business Review*, (November–December 2000): 139–146. Sandeep Krishnarmurthy, "Viral Marketing: What Is It and Why Should Every Service Marketer Care?" *Journal of Services Marketing*, 15 (2001); Joseph E. Phelps, Regina Lewis, Lynne Mobilio, David Perry, and Niranjan Raman, "Viral Marketing or Electronic Word-of-Mouth Advertising: Examining Consumer Responses and Motivations to Pass Along Emails." *Journal of Advertising Research* (December 2004): 333–348

31. Steve Jurvetson, "What Exactly Is Viral Marketing?" *Red Herring*, 78 (2000): 110–112.

32. This section draws from Lev Grossman, "Meet Joe Blog." Time (June 21, 2004): 65; S. C. Herring, L. A. Scheidt, E. Wright, and S. Bonus, "Weblogs as a Bridging Genre." *Information, Technology & People*, 18, no. 2 (2005): 142–171; C. Marlow, "Audience, Structure and Authority in the Weblog Community." Paper presented at International Communication Association Conference, New Orleans, LA, 2004, web.media.mit.edu/~cameron/cv/pubs/04-01.pdf, accessed December 19, 2005; Ericka Menchen Trevino, "Blogger Motivations: Power, Pull, and Positive Feedback." Paper Presented at AoIR 6.0, October 9, 2005, http://blog.erickamenchen.net/MenchenBlogMotivations.pdf, accessed December 19, 2005.

33. Steven Kurutz, "For Travelers, Blogs Level the Playing Field." *The New York Times* (August 7, 2005): TR-3.

34. "Three Steps to Better Cellular." *Consumer Reports* (February 2003): 15–27.

35. Louis Fabien, "Making Promises: The Power of Engagement." *Journal of Services Marketing*, 11, no. 3 (1997): 206–214.

36. www.donotcall.gov/default.aspx, accessed May 2006.
37. www.dmaconsumers.org/consumerassistance.html, accessed May 2006.
38. Abbie Griffith, "Product Decisions and Marketing's Role in New Product Development." In *Marketing Best Practices*, Orlando, FL: The Dryden Press, 2000: 253.
39. Christian Grönroos, "Internationalization Strategies for Services." *The Journal of Services Marketing*, 13, no. 4/5 (1999): 290–297.

40. Stefan Lagrosen, "Effects of the Internet on the Marketing Communication of Service Companies." *Journal of Services Marketing*, 19, no. 2 (2005): 63–69.
41. Paul Smith and Dave Chaffey, *eMarketing Excellence*. Oxford, UK: Elsevier Butterworth-Heinemann, 2005: 173
42. "The Future of Advertising—The Harder Hard Sell." *The Economist* (June 24. 2004).
43. Catherine Seda, "Search Engine Advertising: Buying Your Way to the Top to Increase Sales (Voices That Matter)." Indianapolis, IN: New Riders Press, 2004: 4–5.

Chapter 7

Positioning Services in Competitive Markets

To succeed in our overcommunicated society, a company must create a position in the prospect's mind, a position that takes into consideration not only a company's own strengths and weaknesses, but those of its competitors as well.

—AL REIS AND JACK TROUT

The essence of strategy is choosing to perform activities differently than rivals do.

—MICHAEL PORTER

Ask a group of managers in different service businesses how they compete, and the chances are high that many will say simply, "on service." Press them a little further, and they may add words or phrases such as "value for money," "service quality," "our people," or "convenience." None of this is very helpful to a marketing specialist who is trying to develop a meaningful value proposition and a viable business model for a service product that will enable it to compete profitably in the marketplace.

At issue is what makes consumers or institutional buyers select—and remain loyal to—one supplier over another. Terms such as "service" typically subsume a variety of specific characteristics, ranging from the speed with which a service is delivered to the quality of interactions between customers and service personnel; and from avoiding errors to providing desirable "extras" to supplement the core service. Likewise, "convenience" could refer to a service that's delivered at a convenient location, available at convenient times, or easy to use. Without knowing which product features are of specific interest to customers, it's hard for managers to develop an appropriate strategy. In a highly competitive environment, there's a risk that customers will perceive little real difference between competing alternatives and so make their choices based on who offers the lowest price.

Positioning strategy is concerned with creating, communicating, and maintaining distinctive differences that will be noticed and valued by those customers with whom the firm would most like to develop a long-term relationship. Successful positioning requires managers to understand their target customers' preferences, their conceptions of value, and the characteristics of their competitors' offerings. *Price* and *Product* attributes are the two elements of the 8 P marketing variables that are most commonly associated with positioning strategy, but delivery systems, service schedules, and locations (*Place and time*) also play a role for many services.

In this chapter, we examine the need for focus in a competitive environment, and review the issues involved in developing a positioning strategy. Specifically, we explore the following questions:

1. Why is it so important for service firms to adopt focused strategies in their choice of markets and products?
2. What is the distinction between important and determinant attributes in consumer decision making?
3. What are the key concepts underlying competitive positioning strategy for services?
4. When is it appropriate to reposition an existing service offering?
5. How can positioning maps help us to understand and respond better to competitive dynamics?

FOCUS UNDERLIES THE SEARCH FOR COMPETITIVE ADVANTAGE

As competition intensifies in the service sector, it's becoming ever more important for service organizations to differentiate their products in ways that are meaningful to customers. In highly developed economies, growth is slowing in mature consumer service industries such as banking, insurance, hospitality, and education. So, for a firm to grow, it has to take share from domestic competitors or expand into international markets. In each instance, firms should be selective in targeting customers and seek to be distinctive in the way they present themselves. A market niche that may seem too narrow to offer sufficient sales within one country may represent a substantial market when viewed from an international or even global perspective.

Competitive strategy can take many different routes. George Day observes:

The diversity of ways a business can achieve a competitive advantage quickly defeats any generalizations or facile prescriptions. . . . First and foremost, a business must set itself apart from its competition. To be successful, it must identify and promote itself as the best provider of attributes that are important to target customers.[1]

What this means is that managers need to think systematically about all facets of the service package and to emphasize competitive advantage on those attributes that will be valued by customers in the target segment(s).

Four Focus Strategies

It's usually not realistic for a firm to try to appeal to all potential buyers in a market, because customers are varied in their needs, purchasing behavior, and consumption

Figure 7.1
Basic Focus Strategies
for Services

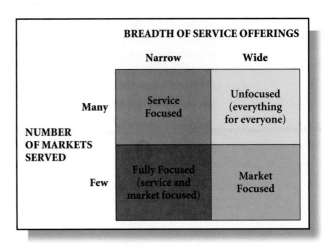

		BREADTH OF SERVICE OFFERINGS	
		Narrow	**Wide**
NUMBER OF MARKETS SERVED	**Many**	Service Focused	Unfocused (everything for everyone)
	Few	Fully Focused (service and market focused)	Market Focused

Source: Robert Johnston, "Achieving Focus in Service Organizations." *The Service Industries Journal,* 16 (January 1996): 10–20.

patterns, and often are too numerous and geographically widely spread. Service firms also vary widely in their abilities to serve different types of customers. So, rather than attempting to compete in an entire market, each company needs to focus its efforts on those customers it can serve best. In marketing terms, *focus* means providing a relatively narrow product mix for a particular market segment—a group of buyers who share common characteristics, needs, purchasing behavior, or consumption patterns. This concept is at the heart of virtually all successful service strategies among firms, which have identified the strategically important elements in their service operations and have concentrated their resources on them.

The extent of a company's focus can be described along two dimensions: market focus and service focus.[2] *Market focus* is the extent to which a firm serves few or many markets, whereas *service focus* describes the extent to which it offers few or many services. These two dimensions define the four basic focus strategies shown in Figure 7.1.

A *fully focused* organization provides a limited range of services (perhaps just a single core product) to a narrow and specific market segment. A *market-focused* company concentrates on a narrow market segment but offers a wide range of services. *Service-focused* firms offer a narrow range of services to a fairly broad market. Finally, many service providers fall into the *unfocused* category, because they try to serve broad markets and provide a wide range of services. In general, that's not a good idea, although public utilities and government agencies may be obliged to do so.

How should you decide which of the three alternative "focused" strategies to pursue? Adopting a fully focused strategy presents both risks and opportunities. Developing recognized expertise in a well-defined niche may provide protection against would-be competitors and allows a firm to charge premium prices. The biggest risk is that the market may be too small to generate the volume of business needed for financial success. Other risks include the danger that demand for the service may be displaced by generic competition from alternative products, or that purchasers in the chosen segment may be very susceptible to an economic downturn.

One reason why firms with a narrow product line elect to serve multiple segments (a service-focused strategy) is to create a portfolio of customers that hedges against such a risk. However, as new segments are added, the firm needs to develop expertise in serving each segment, which may require a broader sales effort and greater investment in marketing communication—particularly in B2B markets.

Offering a broad product line to a narrowly defined target segment often looks attractive, because it offers the potential of selling multiple services to a single purchaser. However, before adopting a market focused strategy, managers need to be sure that their firms have the operational capability to do an excellent job of delivering each of the different services selected. They also need to understand customer purchasing practices and preferences. In a business-to-business context, when trying to cross-sell additional services to the same client, many firms have been disappointed to find that decisions on purchasing the new service are made by an entirely different group within the client company.

MARKET SEGMENTATION FORMS THE BASIS FOR FOCUSED STRATEGIES

Service firms vary widely in their abilities to serve different types of customers. Hence, rather than trying to compete in an entire market, perhaps against superior competitors, each firm should adopt a strategy of market segmentation, identifying those parts, or segments, of the market that it can serve best. Firms that are in tune with customer requirements may choose to employ a needs-based segmentation approach, focusing on those customers whom research shows to value specific attributes.[3]

Market and Micro-Segmentation

Because each person or corporate purchaser has distinctive (even unique) characteristics and needs, any prospective buyer is potentially a separate target segment. Traditionally, firms have sought to achieve economies of scale by marketing to all customers within a specific market segment and serving each in a similar fashion. A strategy of *mass customization*—offering a service with some individualized product elements to a large number of customers at a relatively low price—may be achieved by offering a standardized core product but tailoring supplementary service elements to fit the requirements of individual buyers.[4]

The creation of customer databases and sophisticated analytical software makes it now possible for firms to adopt *micro-segmentation* strategies targeted at small groups of customers that share certain relevant characteristics at a specific point in time (note the strategy employed by the Royal Bank of Canada, as described in Best Practice in Action 7.1).

Identifying and Selecting Target Segments

A *market segment* is composed of a group of buyers who share common characteristics, needs, purchasing behavior, or consumption patterns. Effective segmentation should group buyers into segments in ways that result in as much similarity as possible on the relevant characteristics within each segment, but dissimilarity on those same characteristics between segments.

A *target segment* is one that a firm has selected from among those in the broader market and may be defined on the basis of several variables. For instance, a department store in a particular city might target residents of the metropolitan area (geographic segmentation), who have incomes within a certain range (demographic segmentation), value personal service from knowledgeable staff, and are not highly price-sensitive (both reflecting segmentation according to expressed attitudes and behavioral intentions). Because at least some competing retailers in the city will be targeting the same customers, the department store has to create a distinctive appeal (appropriate characteristics to highlight might include a wide array of merchandise categories, breadth of selection within each product category, and the availability of such supplementary services as advice and home delivery). Service firms that are developing strategies based on use of technology recognize that customers can also be segmented according to their degree of competence and comfort in using technology-based delivery systems.

Some market segments offer better opportunities than others. Marketers should select target segments not only on the basis of their sales and profit potential, but also with reference to the firm's ability to match or exceed competing offerings directed at the same segment. Sometimes research will show that certain market segments are

At least once a month, Toronto-based analysts at the Royal Bank of Canada (the country's largest bank) use data modeling to segment its base of 10 million customers. The segmentation variables include credit risk profile, current and projected profitability, life stage, likelihood of leaving the bank, channel preference (i.e., whether customers like to use a branch, self-service machines, the call center, or online banking), product activation (how quickly customers actually use a product they have bought), and propensity to purchase another product (i.e., cross-selling potential). Says a senior vice president, "Gone are the days when we had mass buckets of customers that would receive the same treatment or same offer on a monthly basis. Our marketing strategy is [now] much more personalized. Of course, it's the technology that allows us to do that."

The main source of data is the marketing information file, which records what products customers hold with the bank, the channels they use, their responses to past campaigns, transactional data, and details of any restrictions on soliciting customers. Another source is the enterprise data warehouse, which stores billing records and information from every document a new or existing customer fills out.

Royal Bank analysts run models based on complex algorithms that can slice the bank's massive customer database into tightly profiled micro-segments that are based on simultaneous use of several variables, including the probability that target customers will respond positively to a particular offer. Customized marketing programs can then be developed for each of these micro-segments, giving the appearance of a highly personalized offer. The data can also be used to improve the bank's performance on unprofitable accounts by identifying these customers and offering them incentives to use lower-cost channels.

An important goal of Royal Bank's segmentation analysis is to maintain and enhance profitable relationships. The bank has found that customers who hold packages of several services are more profitable than those who don't. These customers also stay with the bank an average of three years longer. As a result of the sophisticated segmentation practices at Royal Bank, the response rates to its direct marketing programs have jumped from an industry average of only 3 percent to as high as 30 percent.

Source: Adapted from Meredith Levinson, "Slices of Lives." *CIO Magazine* (August 15, 2000).

"underserved," meaning that their needs are not well met by existing suppliers. Such markets are often surprisingly large.

In many emerging-market economies, huge numbers of consumers have incomes that are too small to attract the interest of service businesses accustomed to focus on the needs of more affluent customers. Collectively, however, small wage earners represent a very big market and may offer even greater potential for the future, as many of them move up toward middle-class status. Service Perspectives 7.1 describes an innovative approach to providing financial services to lower-income households in Mexico.

SERVICE ATTRIBUTES AND LEVELS

How can you best develop the right service concept for a particular target segment? Formal research is often needed to identify what attributes of a given service are important to specific market segments and how well prospective customers perceive competing organizations as performing against these attributes. However, it's dangerous to overgeneralize. You should recognize that the same individuals may set different priorities for attributes according to:

- The purpose for using the service
- Who makes the decision
- The timing of use (time of day/week/season)
- Whether the individual is using the service alone or with a group
- The composition of that group

Banco Azteca, which opened in 2002, is Mexico's first new bank in nearly a decade. It targets the 16 million households in the nation who earn the equivalent of $250 to $1,300 a month, working as taxi drivers, factory hands, and teachers, among others. Despite their combined income of $120 billion, these individuals are of little interest to most banks, which consider small accounts a nuisance. Not surprisingly, only one in 12 of these households has a savings account.

Banco Azteca was the brainchild of Ricardo Salinas Pliego, head of a retail–media–telecommunications empire that includes Grupo Elektra, Mexico's largest appliance retailer. Its branches, located within the more than 900 Elektra stores, are decorated in the green, white, and red colors of the Mexican flag. They seek to create a welcoming atmosphere and feature posters with the Azteca slogan, which translates as "A bank that's friendly and treats you well."

Azteca's relationship with Elektra seeks to take advantage of the retailer's 50-year track record in consumer finance and the fact that some 70 percent of its merchandise is sold on credit. Elektra has an excellent record in credit sales, with a 97 percent repayment rate, and a rich database of customers' credit histories. So top management felt it made sense to convert Elektra credit departments in each store into Azteca branches with an expanded line of services.

The new bank has invested heavily in information technology, including high-tech fingerprint readers that eliminate the need for customers to present printed identification or passbooks. It also takes its services to the people through a 3,000-strong force of loan agents on motorcycles. The bank offers personal loans and time deposits and is rolling out used-car loans, mortgages for low-income buyers, and debit cards. Loans may often use customers' previously purchased possessions as collateral.

In 2003, Grupo Elektra received authorization from the Ministry of Finance to purchase a private insurance company, which it renamed Seguros Azteca. This firm offers basic insurance products at very low prices to a population segment that has historically been ignored by the Mexican insurance industry. Policies are distributed through Banco Azteca's branch network. The following year, the bank expanded its activities to finance individuals who wished to start or expand small businesses

Sources: Geri Smith, "Buy a Toaster, Open a Banking Account." *Business Week* (January 13, 2003): 54; www.gruposalinas.com/companies/banco.shtml, accessed May 2006.

Consider the criteria that you might use when choosing a restaurant for lunch when (1) on vacation with friends or family, (2) meeting with a prospective business client, or (3) going for a quick meal with a co-worker. Given a reasonable selection of alternatives, it's unlikely that you would choose the same type of restaurant in each instance, let alone the same one. It's possible, too, that if you left the decision to another person in the party, he or she would make a different choice.

Important Versus Determinant Attributes

Consumers usually make their choices among alternative service offerings on the basis of perceived differences among them. However, the attributes that distinguish competing services from one another are not always the most important ones. For instance, many travelers rank "safety" as their number-one consideration in air travel. They may avoid traveling on unknown carriers or on an airline that has a poor safety reputation, but after eliminating such alternatives from consideration, a traveler flying on major routes is still likely to have several choices of carrier that are perceived as equally safe. Hence, safety is not usually an attribute that influences the customer's choice at this point.

Determinant attributes (i.e., those that actually determine buyers' choices among competing alternatives) are often some way down the list of service characteristics that are important to purchasers, but they are the attributes on which customers see significant differences among competing alternatives. For example, convenience of departure and arrival times, availability of frequent-flyer miles and related loyalty privileges, quality of food and drinks service on board the aircraft, or the ease of making reservations, might be determinant characteristics for business travelers when selecting an airline. For budget-conscious vacation travelers, on the other hand, price might assume primary importance.

The marketing researchers' task, of course, is to survey customers in the target segment, identify the relative importance of various attributes, and then ask which ones have been determinant during recent decisions involving a choice of service suppliers. Researchers also need to be aware how well each competing service is perceived by customers as performing on these attributes. Findings from such research form the necessary basis for developing a positioning (or repositioning) campaign.[5]

Establishing Service Levels and Tiers

Creating a positioning strategy requires more than just identifying those attributes that are important to customers in the target segment. You also need to make decisions on *service levels*, that is, the level of performance you plan to offer on each attribute. Establishing standards for such levels is simpler for attributes that are easily quantified. Examples include vehicle speed (as in express trains and buses), hours of service, and physical dimensions, such as the size of rooms in hotels. Each of these variables is easy to understand and measure; therefore, all are generalizable. However, characteristics such as the quality of personal service, or a hotel's degree of luxury, are more qualitative and therefore are subject to individual interpretation. To clarify the situation and facilitate both service design and performance measurement, you need to operationalize each attribute and establish unambiguous standards. For instance, if customers say they value physical comfort, what does that mean for a hotel versus an airline, beyond the size of the room or the seat? In a hotel context, does it refer to ambient conditions, such as temperature and absence of noise? Or to visible, tangible elements such as the bed? In practice, hotel managers need to address both ambient conditions and tangible elements.

You can often segment customers according to their willingness to trade off price versus service level across a broad array of attributes within the service concept. Price-insensitive customers are willing to pay a relatively high price to obtain a high level of service on each of the attributes that are important to them. By contrast, price-sensitive customers will look for an inexpensive service that offers a relatively low level of performance on many key attributes—although there may be others, such as safety, on which they are unwilling to compromise.

In a number of service industries, the most explicit form of positioning strategy is based on offering several price-based classes of service concept, each based on packaging a distinctive level of service performance across many attributes. This phenomenon, known as *service tiering*, is particularly evident in industries such as hotels, airlines, car rentals, and computer hardware and software support. Table 7.1 displays examples of the key tiers within each of these industries. Other examples of tiering include health care insurance, cable television, and credit/charge cards.

In the hotel industry, the tiers are created by external rating agencies. For instance, hotels and motels are rated by independent organizations, such as the Mobil Guide, Yahoo, automobile associations, or (in some countries) government agencies on a one-to-five rating system, often expressed by stars or diamonds. Hotels and motels are inspected at periodic intervals and evaluated against an array of specific criteria. New hotels are designed with a specific tier in mind, although five-star status cannot usually be obtained in the United States until the hotel has been operational for some time and thus has demonstrated its ability (and particularly that of its staff) to deliver consistently high levels of performance. An existing lodging establishment may be upgraded or downgraded, based on whether the inspectors find that service levels have been improved or have slipped.

In the car rental industry, the size and type of car forms the primary basis of tiering. Obtaining higher levels of performance on other service attributes usually requires participation in membership programs. In the airline industry, individual carriers decide what levels of performance should be included with each class of service. Pressures to save money often result in a financially troubled airline reducing

Table 7.1
Examples of Service
Tiering

Industry	Tiers	Key Service Attributes and Physical Elements Used in Tiering
Lodging	Star or diamond ratings (5 to 1)	Architecture; landscaping; room size, furnishings, and décor; restaurant facilities and menus; room service hours; array of services and physical amenities; staffing levels; caliber and attitudes of employees
Airline	Classes (intercontinental): first, business, premium economy, economy[a]	Seat pitch (distance between rows), seat width, and reclining capability; meal and beverage service; staffing ratios; check-in speed; departure and arrival lounges; baggage retrieval speed
Car rental	Class of vehicle[b]	Based on vehicle size (from subcompact to full size), degree of luxury, plus special vehicle types (minivan, SUV, convertible)
Hardware and software support	Support levels[c]	Hours and days of service; speed of response; speed of delivering replacement parts; technician-delivered service versus advice on self-service; availability of additional services

[a]Only a few airlines offer as many as four classes of intercontinental service; domestic services usually feature one or two classes.

[b]Avis and Hertz offer seven classes based on size and luxury, plus several special vehicle types.

[c]Sun Microsystems offers four support levels.

its service-level standards. However, innovative carriers, such as British Airways, Singapore Airlines, and Virgin Atlantic, are continually trying to add new service features—particularly in business class—that will create a competitive advantage and enable them to sell more seats at full fare. Unlike these three carriers, each of which offers business class seats that fold flat into beds for overnight travel, many airlines have not yet matched this feature. As a result, there is inconsistency within tiers among competing airlines. In other industries, tiering often reflects an individual firm's strategy of bundling service elements into a limited number of packages, rather than offering a broad *à la carte* menu of options, each priced separately.

Not every player in an industry chooses to compete within each tier. Discount airlines, for instance, offer only a stripped-down version of economy class. Similarly, luxury hotel chains choose not to offer options below the four-star level. New entrants to an industry often do best to seek a niche position within a single tier, rather than trying to serve customers with a me-too product in every tier, which is a very expensive proposition. Thus, MAXjet launched an all-business-class airline in November 2005, featuring New York–London service at much lower prices than most major carriers charge for business class travel. This airline's value proposition is based on providing "international business class to and from London for the price of economy."[6]

POSITIONING DISTINGUISHES A BRAND FROM ITS COMPETITORS

Competitive positioning strategy is based on establishing and maintaining a distinctive place in the market for an organization and/or its individual product offerings. Jack Trout has distilled the essence of positioning into the following four principles:[7]

1. A company must establish a position in the minds of its targeted customers.
2. The position should be singular, providing one simple and consistent message.

3. The position must set a company apart from its competitors.
4. A company cannot be all things to all people—it must focus its efforts.

These principles apply to any type of organization that competes for customers. Understanding the principles of positioning is key to developing an effective competitive posture. The concept of positioning is certainly not limited to services—indeed, it had its origins in packaged-goods marketing—but it offers valuable insights by forcing service managers to analyze their firm's existing offerings and to provide specific answers to the following questions:

- What does our firm currently stand for in the minds of current and prospective customers?
- What customers do we serve now, and which ones would we like to target for the future?
- What is the value proposition for each of our current service offerings (core products and their accompanying supplementary service elements), and what market segments is each one targeted at?
- In each instance, how do our service offerings differ from those of our competitors?
- How well do customers in the chosen target segments perceive our service offerings as meeting their needs?
- What changes do we need to make to our offerings in order to strengthen our competitive position within our target segment(s)?

One of the challenges in developing a viable positioning strategy is to avoid the trap of investing too heavily in points of difference that can easily be copied. As researchers Kevin Keller, Brian Sternthal, and Alice Tybout note: "Positioning needs to keep competitors out, not draw them in."[8] When Roger Brown and Linda Mason, founders of the Bright Horizons chain of child care centers, were developing their service concept and business model, they took a long, hard look at the industry.[9] Discovering that for-profit child care companies had adopted low-cost strategies and were running their centers as a commodity business, the Browns selected a different approach that competitors would find very difficult to copy (Best Practice in Action 7.2).

Product Positioning Versus Copy Positioning

Customers' brand choices reflect which brands they know and remember, and then, how each of these brands is positioned within each customer's mind. These positions are perceptual. You need to remember that people make their decisions based on their perceptions of reality, rather than on an expert's definition of that reality.

Many marketers associate positioning primarily with the communication elements of the marketing mix, notably advertising, promotions, and public relations. This view reflects the widespread use of advertising in packaged-goods marketing to create images and associations for broadly similar branded products so as to give them a special distinction in the customer's mind—an approach sometimes known as *copy positioning*. A classic example is the rugged Western cowboy—the "Marlboro man"—created for a major cigarette brand. Note, however, that this imagery has nothing to do with the physical qualities of the tobacco; it is just a means of differentiating and adding glamour to what is essentially a commodity. Vijay Mahajan and Jerry Wind maintain that consumers who derive emotional satisfaction from a brand are likely to be less price-sensitive.[10]

Examples of how imagery may be used for positioning purposes in services are found in McDonald's efforts to appear "kid friendly" (including its emphasis on Ronald McDonald, the clown), humorous advertising by Geico featuring a gecko lizard, or the gracious service offered by Singapore Airlines' distinctively uniformed female flight attendants (the company's advertising never features their male cabin staff).

Roger Brown and Linda Mason met at business school, following previous experience as management consultants. After graduation, they operated programs for refugee children in Cambodia and then ran a Save the Children relief program in East Africa. Returning to the United States in 1986, they saw a need for child care centers that would provide caring, educational environments and give parents confidence in their children's well-being. So they set out to create a profitable chain of child care centers that would be differentiated from the commoditized services offered by existing chains and many independent centers.

Their analysis showed an industry with many unappealing characteristics: no barriers to entry, chronically low margins, high labor intensity, no proprietary technology, low economies of scale, weak brand distinctions, and heavy regulatory oversight. So Brown and Mason developed and evolved a service concept that would allow them to turn these industry weaknesses into strengths for their own company, Bright Horizons (BH). Instead of marketing their services directly to parents—a one-customer-at-a-time sale—BH formed partnerships with companies seeking to offer an on-site day care center for employees with small children. The advantages included:

- A powerful, low-cost marketing channel
- A partner/customer who supplied the capital to build and outfit the center and would have a vested interest in helping BH achieve its goal of delivering high-quality care
- Benefits for parents, who would be attracted to a BH center (rather than competing alternatives) because of its proximity to their own workplace, thus reducing commuting times and offering greater peace of mind

To achieve differentiation based on higher quality, Bright Horizons offered a premium pay and benefits package, to attract the best staff. Determining that traditional approaches to child care either lacked curricular guidance or mandated strict, cookie-cutter lesson plans, BH developed a flexible curriculum, "World at

Their Fingertips," which outlined a course of study but gave teachers control over daily lesson plans.

Going beyond variable state and local licensing requirements, the company sought accreditation for its centers from the National Association for the Education of Young Children (NAEYC) and actively promoted this credential. BH's emphasis on quality meant that it could meet or exceed the highest local/state government licensing standards. As a result, heavy regulatory oversight represents an opportunity, not a threat, for BH and gives it a source of competitive advantage.

With the support and expertise of its clients, which include many hi-tech firms, BH has developed innovative technologies such as streaming video of its classrooms to the parents' desktops; digitally scanned or photographed artwork; electronic posting of menus, calendars, and student assessments; and online student assessment capabilities. All serve to differentiate BH and help it to stay ahead of the competition.

BH sees labor as a competitive advantage, not a commodity, seeks to recruit and retain the best people, and has achieved "employer of choice" status in the child care industry. It has been named seven times to *Fortune* magazine's list of "The 100 Best Companies to Work For." Clients want to hire BH as a partner because they know they can trust the staff.

Brown believes that traditional child care chains get little value from their brands, despite expensive brand-building advertising campaigns directed at parents. Parents don't look for a national brand, he says, they want a great local program and are indifferent to whether it's part of a national network. By contrast, employers are aware of and value BH's strong brand reputation.

By mid-2006, Bright Horizons was operating more than 600 centers in the United States, Canada, and Europe for over 400 of the world's leading employers, including corporations, hospitals, universities, and government offices.

Sources: Roger Brown, "How We Built a Strong Company in a Weak Industry." *Harvard Business Review* (February 2001): 51–57; www.brighthorizons.com, accessed May 2006.

Markets are constantly changing, however, creating both threats and opportunities among competing firms. For instance, it used to be that when large companies were looking for auditing services, they typically turned to one of the Big Four accounting firms, prestigious players offering global coverage. A growing number of clients, however, are now switching to "Tier Two" accounting firms in a search for better service, a lower bill, or both.[11] Grant Thornton, the fifth largest firm in the industry, has successfully positioned itself as offering easy access to partners and having "a passion for the business of accounting." Its advertising promotes an award

When you have a passion for accounting...
it shows!

There is a select group of individuals in this world who have a passion for the business of accounting. Yes, that's right, accounting. And that group happens to be the accountants at Grant Thornton.

Recently, J.D. Power and Associates ranked Grant Thornton "Highest Performance Among Audit Firms Serving Companies with up to $1 Billion in Annual Revenue" in a U.S. study that looked at understanding client operations and industry, responding to requests and questions, and trustworthiness.

With Grant Thornton you get easy access to partners that's been the hallmark of Grant Thornton in the U.S. for 80 years. And you get the benefit of Grant Thornton International member firms in 110 countries that fast-growth companies look for in today's global markets. Why not give our CEO, **Ed Nusbaum**, a call at **312.602.8003** or contact our partners at www.GrantThornton.com?

Find out how it feels to work with people who love what they do!

Grant Thornton
A passion for the business of accounting®

Kim Nunley
Office Managing Partner

J.D. Power and Associates 2004 Audit Firm Performance Study℠. Study based on responses from 1,007 audit committee chairs and 944 chief financial officers. www.jdpower.com
Grant Thornton LLP is the U.S. member firm of Grant Thornton International.

Courtesy Grant Thornton, LLP.

from J. D. Powers ranking it as achieving "Highest Performance Among Audit Firms Serving Companies with up to $12 billion in Annual Revenue" (Figure 7.2).

Some slogans promise a specific benefit, designed to make the company stand out from its competitors, such as Verizon's "We never stop working for you," Prudential Financial's "Growing and protecting your wealth," FedEx Ground's "Relax, It's FedEx," T. Rowe Price's "Invest with Confidence," or Lands' End's "Shopping online beats standing in line," However, as Sally Dibb and Lyndon Simkin point out:

> Evidence of strong branding in the service sector does not end with such catch phrases. [The leading organizations in different fields] already have a strong brand image in the sense that customers generally know exactly what they stand for. They are, already, clearly positioned in the customers' minds.[12]

Positioning strategy is becoming more sophisticated as growing numbers of firms engage in co-branding.[13] This endeavor can take several forms, including shared facilities, joint promotions, and even co-branded products. In New England, the Stop & Shop supermarket chain has reached an agreement with Citizens Bank to install small branches of that bank inside all its stores. To obtain financial support and promotional leverage, Boston's Museum of Fine Arts seeks a prominent corporate sponsor for each of its major exhibitions. And American Airlines, Citibank, and Visa jointly offer a credit card. In each case, the imagery associated with one brand has the potential to influence consumer perceptions of the other(s).

Our primary concern in this chapter is the role of positioning in guiding marketing strategy development for services that compete on more than just imagery or vague promises. This entails decisions on substantive attributes that are important to customers, relating to product performance, price, and service availability. To improve a product's appeal to a specific target segment, you may need to change its performance on certain attributes, to reduce its price, or to alter the times and locations when it is available or the forms of delivery that are offered. In such instances, the primary task of communication—advertising, personal selling, and public relations—is to ensure that prospective customers accurately perceive the position of the service on dimensions that are important to them in making choice decisions. Additional excitement and interest may be created by evoking certain images and associations in the advertising, but these are likely to play only a secondary role in customer choice decisions unless competing services are perceived as virtually identical on performance, price, and availability.

The Role of Positioning in Marketing Strategy

Positioning plays a pivotal role in marketing strategy, because it links market analysis and competitive analysis to internal corporate analysis. From these three, a position statement can be developed that enables the service organization to answer the questions, "What is our product (or service concept), what do we want it to become, and what actions must we take to get there?" Table 7.2 summarizes the principal uses of positioning analysis as a diagnostic tool, providing input to decisions relating to product development, service delivery, pricing, and communication strategy.

Developing a positioning strategy can take place at several different levels, depending on the nature of the business in question. Among multisite, multiproduct service businesses, a position might be established for the entire organization, for a given service outlet, or for a specific service offered at that outlet. There must be consistency among the positioning of different services offered at the same location, because the image of one may spill over onto the others, especially if they are perceived to be related. For instance, if a hospital has an excellent reputation for warm and competent obstetrical services, that may enhance perceptions of its services in gynecology and pediatrics. By contrast, it may be detrimental to all three services if their positioning is conflicting.

Because of the intangible, experiential nature of many services, an explicit positioning strategy is valuable in helping prospective customers to get a mental "fix" on what to expect. Failure to select a desired position in the marketplace—and to develop a marketing action plan designed to achieve and hold this position—may result in one of several possible outcomes, all undesirable:

1. The organization (or one of its products) is pushed into a position in which it faces head-on competition from a stronger competitor.
2. The organization (product) is pushed into a position that nobody else wants, because there is little customer demand.
3. The organization's (product's) position is so blurred that nobody knows what its distinctive competence really is.

Table 7.2
Principal Uses of
Positioning Analysis
as a Diagnostic Tool

1. Provide a useful diagnostic tool for defining and understanding the relationships between products and markets:
   - How does the product compare with competitive offerings on specific attributes?
   - How well does product performance meet consumer needs and expectations on specific performance criteria?
   - What is the predicted consumption level for a product with a given set of performance characteristics offered at a given price?
2. Identify market opportunities for
   a. Introducing new products
      - What segments to target?
      - What attributes to offer relative to the competition?
   b. Redesigning (repositioning) existing products
      - Appeal to the same segments or to new ones?
      - What attributes to add, drop, or change?
      - What attributes to emphasize in advertising?
   c. Eliminating products that
      - Do not satisfy consumer needs
      - Face excessive competition
3. Make other marketing mix decisions to preempt or respond to competitive moves:
   a. Distribution strategies
      - Where to offer the product (locations, types of outlet)?
      - When to make the product available?
   b. Pricing strategies
      - How much to charge?
      - What billing and payment procedures to use?
   c. Communication strategies
      - What target audience(s) are most easily convinced that the product offers a competitive advantage on attributes that are important to them?
      - What message(s)? Which attributes should be emphasized and which competitors, if any, should be mentioned as the basis for comparison on those attributes?
      - Which communication channels: personal selling versus different advertising media? (Selected for their ability not only to convey the chosen message(s) to the target audience(s) but also to reinforce the desired image of the product.)

INTERNAL, MARKET, AND COMPETITOR ANALYSES

The research and analysis that underlie development of an effective positioning strategy are designed to highlight both opportunities and threats to the firm in the competitive marketplace, including the presence of generic competition and competition from substitute products. Figure 7.3 identifies the basic steps involved in identifying a suitable market position and developing a strategy to reach it.

Market Analysis

Market analysis addresses such factors as the overall level and trend of demand, and the geographic location of this demand. Is demand for the benefits offered by this type of service increasing or decreasing? Are there regional or international variations in the level of demand? Alternative ways of segmenting the market should be considered and an appraisal made of the size and potential of different market segments. Research may be needed to gain a better understanding not only of customer needs and preferences within each of the different segments, but also of how each perceives the competition.

Internal Corporate Analysis

In internal corporate analysis, the objective is to identify the organization's resources (financial, labor and know-how, and physical assets), any limitations or constraints, its goals (profitability, growth, professional preferences, etc.), and how its values shape the way it does business. Using insights from this analysis, management

Figure 7.3
Developing a Market
Positioning Strategy

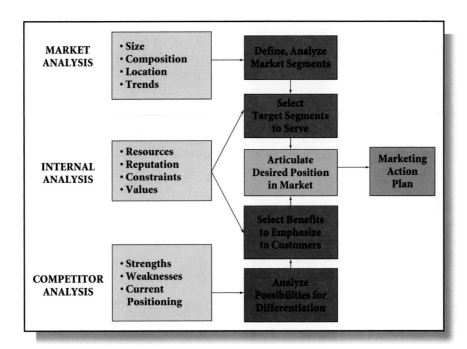

MARKET ANALYSIS
- Size
- Composition
- Location
- Trends

Define, Analyze Market Segments

Select Target Segments to Serve

INTERNAL ANALYSIS
- Resources
- Reputation
- Constraints
- Values

Articulate Desired Position in Market

Marketing Action Plan

Select Benefits to Emphasize to Customers

COMPETITOR ANALYSIS
- Strengths
- Weaknesses
- Current Positioning

Analyze Possibilities for Differentiation

Source: Adapted from an earlier schematic by Michael R. Pearce.

should be able to select a limited number of target market segments that can be served with either new or existing services.

Competitor Analysis

Identification and analysis of competitors can provide a marketing strategist with a sense of their strengths and weaknesses, which, in turn, may suggest opportunities for differentiation. Relating these insights back to the internal corporate analysis should suggest what might be viable opportunities for differentiation and competitive advantage, and thereby enable managers to decide which benefits should be emphasized to which target segments. This analysis should consider both direct and indirect competition.

Position Statement

The outcome of integrating these three forms of analysis is a statement that articulates the desired position of the organization in the marketplace (and, if desired, that of each of the component services that it offers). Armed with this understanding, marketers should be able to develop a specific plan of action. The cost of implementing this plan must, of course, be related to the expected payoff.

Anticipating Competitive Response

Before embarking on a specific plan of action, you should consider the possibility that one or more competitors might pursue the same market position. Perhaps another service organization has independently conducted the same positioning analysis and arrived at similar conclusions? Or an existing competitor may feel threatened by the new strategy and take steps to reposition its own service to compete more effectively. Alternatively, a new entrant to the market may decide to play "follow the leader," yet be able to offer customers a higher service level on one or more attributes and/or a lower price.

The best way to anticipate possible competitive responses is to identify all current or potential competitors and to put yourself in their own management's shoes by conducting an internal corporate analysis for each of these competitors.[14]

Coupling the insights from the analysis with data from existing market and competitive analysis (with your own firm cast in the role of competitor) should provide a good sense of how competitors may be likely to act. If chances seem high that a stronger competitor will move to occupy the same niche with a superior service concept, then it may be wise to reconsider the situation.

Some firms develop sophisticated simulation models to analyze the effects of alternative competitive moves. How would a price cut affect demand, market share, and profits? Based on past experience, how might customers in different segments respond to increases or decreases in the level of quality on specific service attributes?

BEST PRACTICE IN ACTION 7.3
Positioning a Brand Across Multiple Services at Rentokil Initial

With sales of $2 billion in 2005, Rentokil Initial is one of the world's largest business services companies. The UK-based firm operates in 43 countries, including the United States and Canada, where it employs the Initial brand name. It has evolved substantially from its origins as a manufacturer of rat poison and a pesticide for killing wood-destroying beetles. When the firm determined that it could make more money by providing a service to kill rodents than by selling products that customers would use themselves to target these pests, it shifted to pest control and extermination services.

Through organic growth and acquisition, Rentokil Initial has developed an extensive product range that includes testing and safety services; security; parcels delivery; interior plants landscaping (including sale or rental of tropical plants); specialized cleaning services; pest control; clinical waste collection and disposal; personnel services; and a washroom solutions service that supplies and maintains a full array of equipment, dispensers, and consumables.

The firm sees its core competence as "the ability to carry out high quality services on other people's premises through well-recruited, well-trained, and motivated staff." In the United States and Canada, Chicago-headquartered Initial Tropical Plants serves 25,000 customers coast to coast. Its 1,400 co-workers manage 1.6 million plants, producing revenues of $112 million. It is the only national supplier of such services in a highly fragmented industry in which competition is local in character.

Promoting use of additional services to existing customers is an important aspect of the firm's strategy. Initial Integrated Services offers clients the opportunity to move beyond the established concept of "bundling" services—bringing together several free-standing support services contracts from one provider—to full integration of services. Clients purchase sector-specific solutions delivering multiple services but featuring just "one invoice, one account manager, one helpdesk, one contract and one motivated service team."

According to former chief executive Sir Clive Thomson:

> Our objective has been to create a virtuous circle. We provide a quality service in industrial and commercial activities under the same brand-name, so that a customer satisfied with one Rentokil Initial Service is potentially a satisfied customer for another. . . . Although it was considered somewhat odd at the time, one of the reasons we moved into [providing and maintaining] tropical plants [for building interiors] was in fact to put the brand in front of decision makers. Our service people maintaining the plants go in through the front door and are visible to the customer. This contrasts with pest control where no one really notices unless we fail. . . . The brand stands for honesty, reliability, consistency, integrity and technical leadership.

Rentokil Initial's success lies in its ability to position each of its many business and commercial services in terms of the company's core brand values, which include providing superior standards of customer care and utilizing the most technically advanced services and products. The brand image is reinforced through physical evidence in terms of distinctive uniforms, vehicle color schemes, and use of the corporate logo.

Investment in R&D ensures constant improvement. In December 2005, the company announced its latest achievement, the RADAR intelligent rodent trap. RADAR attracts rats and mice into a sealable chamber and kills them humanely by injecting carbon dioxide. Using Rentokil's unique "pestconnect" technology, the trap causes emails to be sent to the customer and the local branch when a rodent is caught; a Rentokil technician receives a text message identifying which unit has been activated at which customer's premises, and its precise location. Pestconnect checks each individual RADAR unit every 10 minutes, 24/7. Getting information in real time enables technicians to remove dead rodents promptly and to control future infestation better.

Sources: Clive Thompson, "Rentokil Initial: Building a Strong Corporate Brand for Growth and Diversity." in F. Gilmore (ed.), *Brand Warriors* (London: HarperCollinsBusiness, 1997), pp. 123–124; TXT Technology 4 Pest Control, press release, December 6, 2005, www.rentokil-initial.com, accessed May 2006.

How long would it take before customers responded to a new advertising campaign designed to change perceptions?

Evolutionary Positioning

Positions are rarely static: They need to evolve over time in response to changing market structures, technology, competitive activity, and the evolution of the firm itself. Many types of business lend themselves to evolutionary repositioning by adding or deleting services and target segments. Some companies have shrunk their offerings and divested certain lines of business in order to be more focused. Others have expanded their offerings in the expectation of increasing sales to existing customers and attracting new ones. Thus service stations have added small convenience stores offering extended hours of service, while supermarkets and other retailers have added banking and pharmacy services. New developments in technology provide many opportunities for introducing not only new services but also new delivery systems for existing products.

When a company has a trusted and successful brand, it may be possible to extend a position based on perceived quality in one type of service to a variety of related services under the same umbrella brand. Best Practice in Action 7.3 features the example of Rentokil Initial, a provider of business-to-business services, which has profited from the growing trend toward outsourcing of services related to facilities maintenance.

USING POSITIONING MAPS TO PLOT COMPETITIVE STRATEGY

Developing a positioning "map"—a task sometimes referred to as perceptual mapping—is a useful way of representing consumers' perceptions of alternative products graphically. A map is usually confined to two attributes (although three-dimensional models can be used to portray three of these attributes). When more than three dimensions are needed to describe product performance in a given market, then a series of separate charts needs to be drawn for visual presentation purposes. A computer model, of course, can handle as many attributes as are relevant.[15]

Information about a product (or a company's position relative to any one attribute) can be inferred from market data, derived from ratings by representative consumers, or both. If consumer perceptions of service characteristics differ sharply from "reality" as defined by management, then marketing efforts may be needed to change these perceptions.

An Example of Applying Positioning Maps to the Hotel Industry

The hotel business is highly competitive, especially during seasons when the supply of rooms exceeds demand. Within each class of hotels, customers visiting a large city may find that they have several alternatives from among which to select a place to stay. The degree of luxury and comfort in physical amenities will be one choice criterion; research shows that business travelers are concerned not only with the comfort and facilities offered by their rooms (where they may wish to work as well as sleep), but also with the characteristics of other physical spaces, ranging from the reception area to meeting rooms, a business center, restaurants, a swimming pool, and exercise facilities.

The quality and range of services offered by hotel staff is another key criterion: Can a guest get 24-hour room service? Can clothes be laundered and pressed? Is there a knowledgeable concierge on duty? Are staff available to offer professional business services? There are other choice criteria, too, perhaps relating to the ambiance of the hotel (modern architecture and decor are favored by some customers, others may prefer "Old World" charm and antique furniture). Additional attributes include factors such as quietness, safety, cleanliness, and special rewards programs for frequent guests.

Let's look at an example, based on a real-world situation, of how developing a positioning map of their own and competing hotels helped managers of the Palace, a successful four-star hotel, develop a better understanding of future threats to their established market position in a large city that we will call Belleville.

The Palace, located on the edge of the booming financial district, was an elegant old hotel that had been extensively renovated and modernized a few years earlier. Its competitors included eight four-star establishments and the Grand, one of the city's oldest hotels, which had a five-star rating. The Palace had been very profitable for its owners in recent years and boasted an above-average occupancy rate. For many months of the year, it was sold out on weekdays, reflecting its strong appeal to business travelers, who were very attractive to the hotel because of their willingness to pay a higher room rate than tourists or convention goers. However, the general manager and his staff saw problems on the horizon. Planning board permission had recently been granted for four large new hotels in the city, and the Grand had just started a major renovation and expansion project, which included construction of a new wing. There was a risk that customers might see the Palace as falling behind.

To understand better the nature of the competitive threat, the hotel's management team worked with a consultant to prepare charts that displayed the Palace's position in the business traveler market both before and after the advent of new competition. Four attributes were selected for study: room price, level of physical luxury, level of personal service, and location. In this instance, management did not conduct new consumer research; instead they inferred customer perceptions based on published information, data from past surveys, and reports from travel agents and knowledgeable hotel staff members who interacted frequently with customers. Information on competing hotels was not difficult to obtain, because the locations were known, the physical structures were relatively easy to visit and evaluate, and the sales staff kept themselves informed on pricing policies and discounts. A convenient surrogate measure for service level was the ratio of rooms per employee, easily calculated from the published number of rooms and employment data provided to the city authorities. Data from surveys of travel agents conducted by the Palace provided additional insights on the quality of personal service at each competitor.

Scales were then created for each attribute. Price was simple, because the average price charged to business travelers for a standard single room at each hotel was already quantified. The rooms-per-employee ratio formed the basis for a service-level scale, with low ratios being equated with high service. This scale was then modified slightly in the light of what was known about the quality of service actually delivered by each major competitor. Level of physical luxury was more subjective. The management team identified the hotel that members agreed was the most luxurious (the Grand) and then the four-star hotel that they viewed as having the least luxurious physical facilities (the Airport Plaza). All the other four-star hotels were then rated on this attribute relative to these two benchmarks.

Location was defined with reference to the stock exchange building in the heart of the financial district, because past research had shown that a majority of the Palace's business guests were visiting destinations in this area. The location scale plotted each hotel in terms of its distance from the stock exchange. The competitive set of 10 hotels lay within a four-mile, fan-shaped radius, extending from the exchange through the city's principal retail area (where the convention center was also located) to the inner suburbs and the nearby airport. Two positioning maps were created to portray the existing competitive situation. The first (Figure 7.4) showed the 10 hotels

Figure 7.4
Positioning Map of
Belleville's Principal
Business Hotels:
Service Level Versus
Price Level (Before
New Competition)

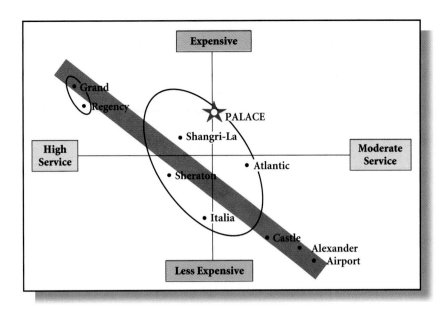

Figure 7.5
Positioning Map of
Belleville's Principal
Business Hotels:
Location Versus
Physical Luxury
(Before New
Competition)

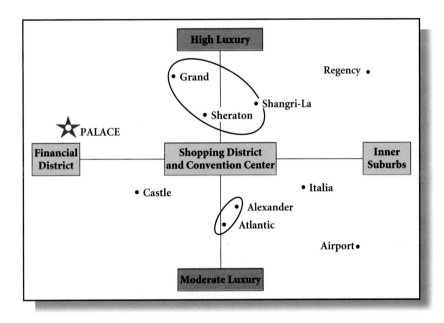

on the dimensions of price and service level; the second (Figure 7.5) displayed them on location and degree of physical luxury.

A quick glance at Figure 7.4 shows a clear correlation between the attributes of price and service: Hotels that offer higher levels of service are relatively more expensive. The shaded bar running from the upper left to the lower right highlights this relationship, which is not a surprising one (and can be expected to continue diagonally downwards for three-star and lesser-rated establishments). Further analysis shows that there appear to be three clusters of hotels within what is already an upscale market category. At the top end, the four-star Regency is close to the five-star Grand; in the middle, the Palace is clustered with four other hotels; and at the lower end, there is another cluster of three hotels. One surprising insight from this map is that the Palace appears to be charging significantly more (on a relative basis) than its service level seems to justify. Because its occupancy rate is very high, guests are evidently willing to pay the going rate.

In Figure 7.5 you can see how the Palace is positioned relative to the competition on location and degree of luxury. We don't expect these two variables to be related, and they don't appear to be. A key insight here is that the Palace occupies a relatively empty portion of the map. It is the only hotel in the financial district—a fact that probably explains its ability to charge more than its service level (or degree of physical luxury) seems to justify. There are two clusters of hotels in the vicinity of the shopping district and convention center: a relatively luxurious group of three, led by the Grand, and a second group of two, offering a moderate level of luxury.

Mapping Future Scenarios to Identify Potential Competitive Responses

What of the future? The Palace's management team next sought to anticipate the positions of the four new hotels being constructed in Belleville, as well as the probable repositioning of the Grand (see Figures 7.6 and 7.7). The construction sites were already known: Two would be in the financial district and two in the vicinity of the convention center, itself under expansion. Press releases distributed by the Grand had already declared its management's intentions: The "New" Grand would be not only larger, the renovations would be designed to make it even more luxurious, and there were plans to add new service features.

Predicting the positions of the four new hotels was not difficult for experts in the field; however, they recognized that customers might initially have more difficulty in predicting each hotel's level of performance on different attributes, especially if they were unfamiliar with the chain that would be operating the hotel in question. Preliminary details of the new hotels had already been released to city planners and the business community. The owners of two of the hotels had declared their intentions to seek five-star status, although this might take a few years to achieve. Three of the newcomers would be affiliated with international chains and their strategies could be guessed by examining recent hotels opened in other cities by these same chains.

Pricing was also easy to project. New hotels use a formula for setting posted room prices (the prices typically charged to individuals staying on a week night in high season). This price is linked to the average construction cost per room at the rate of $1 per night for every $1,000 of construction costs. Thus, a 200-room hotel that costs $40 million to build (including land costs) would have an average room cost of $200,000 and would need to set a price of $200 per room night. Using this formula, Palace managers concluded that the four new hotels would have to charge significantly more than the Grand or Regency, in effect establishing what marketers call a *price umbrella* above existing price levels and thereby giving competitors the option of raising their own prices. To justify their high prices, the new hotels would have to offer customers very high standards of service and luxury. At the same time, the New Grand would need to raise its own prices to recover the costs of renovation, new construction, and enhanced service offerings (see Figure 7.6).

Assuming no changes by either the Palace or other existing hotels, the effect of the new competition in the market clearly posed a significant threat to the Palace, which would lose its unique location advantage and in future be one of three hotels in the immediate vicinity of the financial district (Figure 7.7). The sales staff believed that many of the Palace's existing business customers would be attracted to the Continental and the Mandarin and willing to pay their higher rates in order to obtain the superior benefits offered. The other two newcomers were seen as more of a threat to the Shangri-La, Sheraton, and New Grand in the shopping district/convention center cluster. Meantime, the New Grand and the newcomers would create a high-price/high-service (and high-luxury) cluster at the top end of the market, leaving the Regency in what might prove to be a distinctive—and therefore defensible—space of its own.

Positioning Charts Help Executives Visualize Strategy

The Palace Hotel example demonstrates the insights that come from visualizing competitive situations. One of the challenges that strategic planners face is to ensure that all executives have a clear understanding of the firm's current situation before moving to discuss changes in strategy. Chan Kim and Renée Mauborgne argue that

Figure 7.6
Future Positioning
Map of Belleville's
Business Hotels:
Service Level Versus
Price Level

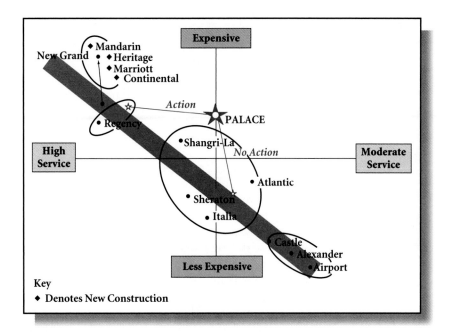

Figure 7.7
Future Positioning
Map of Belleville's
Business Hotels:
Location Versus
Physical Luxury

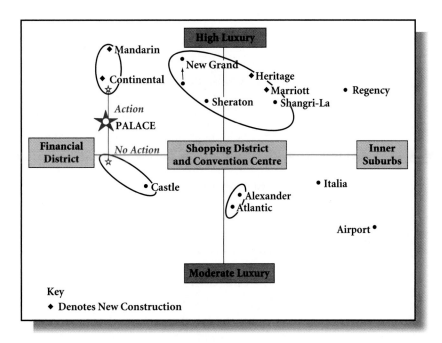

graphic representations of a firm's strategic profile and product positions are much easier to grasp than tables of quantitative data or paragraphs of prose. Charts and maps can facilitate what they call a "visual awakening." By enabling senior managers to compare their business with that of competitors and understand the nature of competitive threats and opportunities, visual presentations can highlight gaps between how customers (or prospects) see the organization and how management sees it, and thus help confirm or dispel beliefs that a service or a firm occupies a unique niche in the marketplace.[16]

By examining how anticipated changes in the competitive environment would literally redraw the current positioning map, the management team at the Palace could see that the hotel could not hope to remain in its current market position once it lost its location advantage. Unless they moved proactively to enhance its level of service and physical luxury, raising its prices to pay for such improvements, the hotel was likely to find itself being pushed into a lower price bracket that might even make it difficult to maintain current standards of service and physical upkeep.

Sometimes firms have to make a significant change in an existing position. Such a strategy, known as *repositioning*, might mean revising service characteristics or redefining target market segments. At the firm level, repositioning may entail abandoning certain products and withdrawing completely from some market segments.

Changing Perceptions Through Advertising

Improving negative brand perceptions may require extensive redesign of the core product and/or supplementary services. However, weaknesses are sometimes perceptual rather than real. Ries and Trout describe the case of Long Island Trust, historically the leading bank serving this large suburban area to the east of New York City.[17]

After laws were passed to permit unrestricted branch banking throughout New York State, many of the big banks from neighboring Manhattan began invading Long Island. Research showed that Long Island Trust was rated below banks such as Chase Manhattan and Citibank on such key selection criteria as branch availability, full range of services offerings, service quality, and capital resources. However, Long Island Trust ranked first on helping Long Island residents and the Long Island economy.

The bank's advertising agency developed a campaign promoting the "Long Island position," playing to its perceived strengths rather than seeking to improve perceptions on attributes on which it was perceived less favorably. The tenor of the campaign can be gauged from the following extract from a print ad:

> Why send your money to the city if you live on the Island? It makes sense to keep your money close to home. Not at a city bank but at Long Island Trust. Where it can work for Long Island. After all, we concentrate on developing Long Island. Not Manhattan Island or some island off Kuwait. . . .

Other advertisements in the campaign promoted similar themes, such as "The city is a great place to visit, but would you want to bank there?"

When identical research was repeated 15 months later, Long Island Trust's position had improved on every attribute. The campaign had succeeded in reframing its brand image by changing its customers' frame of reference from a global to a local perspective. Although the firm had not changed any of its core or supplementary services, the perceived strength of being a Long Island bank for Long Islanders now had a strongly positive "halo" effect on all other attributes.

Innovation in Positioning

Most companies focus on matching and beating their rivals, with the result that their strategies tend to emphasize the same basic dimensions of competition. However, one way to compete is to introduce new dimensions into the positioning equation that other firms cannot immediately match.

James Heskett frames the issue nicely:

> The most successful service firms separate themselves from "the pack" to achieve a distinctive position in relation to their competition. They differentiate themselves . . . by altering typical characteristics of their respective industries to their competitive advantage.[18]

CONCLUSION

Most service businesses face active competition. Marketers need to find ways of creating meaningful value propositions for their products that stake out a distinctive and defensible *position* in the marketplace against competing alternatives. Ideally, a firm should target segments that it can serve better than other providers, offering and promoting a higher level of performance than competitors on those attributes that are particularly valued by customers in the target segment. The nature of services introduces a number of distinctive possibilities for competitive differentiation, going beyond price and physical product features to include: location and scheduling; performance levels such as speed of service delivery and the caliber of service personnel; and a range of options for customer involvement in the production process.

The concept of positioning is valuable because it forces explicit recognition of the different attributes comprising the overall service concept and emphasizes the need for marketers to understand which attributes determine customer choice behavior. Positioning maps provide a visual way of summarizing research data and display how different firms are perceived as performing relative to each other on key attributes. When combined with information on the preferences of different segments, including the level of demand that might be anticipated from such segments, positioning maps may suggest opportunities for creating new services or repositioning existing ones to take advantage of unserved market needs.

REVIEW QUESTIONS

1. Why should service firms focus their efforts? Describe the basic focus options, and illustrate them with examples.
2. What is the distinction between important and determinant attributes in consumer choice decisions? How can research can help you to understand which is which?
3. Describe what is meant by positioning strategy and the marketing concepts that underlie it.
4. Identify the circumstances under which it is appropriate to reposition an existing service offering.
5. How can positioning maps help managers better understand and respond to competitive dynamics?

APPLICATION EXERCISES

1. Find examples of companies that illustrate each of the four focus strategies discussed in this chapter.
2. Choose an industry you are familiar with (such as fast-food restaurants, TV networks, or grocery stores) and create a perceptual map showing the competitive positions of different competitors in the industry, using attributes that you consider represent key consumer choice criteria.
3. The travel agency business is losing business to online bookings offered to passengers by airline web sites. Identify some possible focus options open to travel agencies wishing to develop new lines of business that would compensate for this loss of airline ticket sales.
4. Provide two examples of service tiering other than airlines, hotels, car rentals, and hardware/software support services. For each example, what key attributes are employed to differentiate one tier from another?
5. Imagine that you are a consultant to the Palace Hotel. Consider the options facing the hotel based on the four attributes in the positioning charts (Figures 7.6 and 7.7). What actions do you recommend the Palace take in these circumstances? Justify your recommendations.

ENDNOTES

1. George S. Day, *Market Driven Strategy*. New York: The Free Press, 1990, p. 164.
2. Robert Johnston, "Achieving Focus in Service Organizations." *The Service Industries Journal*, 16 (January 1996): 10–20.
3. A best-practice example in a B2B context is discussed in Ernest Waaser, Marshall Dahneke, Michael Pekkarinen, and Michael Weissel, "How You Slice It: Smarter Segmentation for Your Sales Force." *Harvard Business Review*, 82, no. 3 (2004): 105–111.
4. James Gilmore and B. Joseph Pine, II, *Markets of One: Creating Customer-Unique Value Through Mass Customization*. Boston: Harvard Business School Press, 2000.
5. For further insights into multiattribute modeling, see William D. Wells and David Prensky, *Consumer Behavior*. New York: John Wiley & Sons, 1996), pp. 321–325.
6. www.maxjet.com, accessed July 2006.
7. Jack Trout, *The New Positioning: The Latest on the World's #1 Business Strategy*. New York: McGraw-Hill, 1997.
8. Kevin Lane Keller, Brian Sternthal, and Alice Tybout, "Three Questions You Need to Ask About Your Brand." *Harvard Business Review*, 80 (September 2002): 84.
9. Roger Brown, "How We Built a Strong Company in a Weak Industry." *Harvard Business Review*, 79 (February 2001): 51–57.
10. Vijay Mahajan and Yoram (Jerry) Wind, "Got Emotional Product Positioning?" *Marketing Management* (May–June 2002): 36–41.
11. Nanette Byrnes, "The Little Guys Doing Large Audits." *BusinessWeek* (August 22/29, 2005): 39.
12. Sally Dibb and Lyndon Simkin, "The Strength of Branding and Positioning in Services." *International Journal of Service Industry Management*, 4, no. 1 (1993): 25–35.

13. Chris Lederer and Sam Hill, "See Your Brands Through Your Customers' Eyes." *Harvard Business Review,* 79 (June 2001): 125–133.

14. For a detailed approach, see Michael E. Porter, "A Framework for Competitor Analysis," in *Competitive Strategy.* New York: The Free Press, 1980, pp. 47–74.

15. For examples of developing research data for perceptual mapping purposes, see Glen L. Urban and John M. Hauser, *Design and Marketing of New Products,* 2nd ed. Englewood Cliffs, NJ: Prentice Hall, 1993.

16. W. Chan Kim and Renée Mauborgne, "Charting Your Company's Future." *Harvard Business Review,* 80 (June 2002): 77–83.

17. Al Ries and Jack Trout, *Positioning: The Battle for Your Mind,* 1st ed., rev. New York: Warner Books, 1986.

18. James L. Heskett, *Managing in the Service Economy.* Boston: Harvard Business School Press, 1984, p. 45.

The Health Travellers

PROSENJIT DATTA AND GINA S. KRISHNAN

As international trade builds, one alternative to exporting services is to import customers. Cross-border travel for medical services is a growing market in health care delivery, stimulated by demand from aging consumers in affluent nations. Countries that can offer inexpensive but high-quality treatment in modern hospitals are creating a boom in health care tourism. Patients seeking joint replacements, cardiac care, organ transplants, dental care, facelifts, and laser eye surgery find they can get needed treatments faster and more cheaply by traveling to Asia, South Africa, or Eastern Europe. They can even combine treatment and recuperation with a vacation.

Cyril Parry waited for a very long time for his turn to come. The 59-year-old retiree from Birmingham, UK, was suffering from rheumatoid-arthritis. He needed a hip replacement operation urgently He waited patiently though his pain was getting worse and his movements increasingly restricted. Unfortunately, Parry was stuck at the end of a very long queue. The overburdened National Health Service orthopaedic surgeons in the UK were booked solid—for several years. Finally, Parry was told that his turn would come four years and nine months down the line.

That was when Parry started surfing the Net to see if he could get his hip surgery done elsewhere in the world. After a full year of research, he shortlisted two destinations: a hospital in Thailand and Apollo Speciality Hospital, Chennai. In November this year, Parry opted for the latter because, at £4,000 (excluding airfare but inclusive of a 10-day stay, post-operative care and a full health check-up), it was almost £5,000 cheaper than the Thai option.

It was ironic that Parry needed to travel abroad for his treatment He was, after all, undergoing a procedure called the 'Birmingham Hip Resurfacing'—a new technique considered as a superior alternative to the full-hip replacement surgery, and named after the city it was pioneered in. It was perfected at the Royal Orthopedic Hospital in Birmingham as recently as 1998.

Cyril Parry needed to travel because of the health-care system followed in the UK which is creating long waiting lists of patients in that country. More on that later. But long waiting lists are not the only reason that there's been a huge surge in medical travel globally in recent years. Patients from rich countries in the Middle East travel to the US when they need top notch medical care. Residents of poor developing nations such as Nigeria or Bangladesh travel to their more developed neighbours for medical treatment because there aren't enough good facilities available in their own countries. Thousands of Japanese citizens seeking medical treatment fly abroad because of the prohibitive costs of treatment in their home country. Americans seeking cosmetic surgery often fly to South Africa for face tucks and breast augmentation because their insurance coverage doesn't pay for those—and it is cheaper to get them done in South Africa than back home.

AN OVERVIEW OF HEALTH TOURISM

COUNTRY	NO OF FOREIGNERS TREATED LAST YEAR	FROM	MONEY EARNED	STRENGTHS
Thailand	60,000	US, UK	$470 m	Cosmetic surgery, organ transplants dental treatment, joint replacements
Jordan	126,000	Middle East	$600 m	Organ transplants, fertility treatment, cardiac care
India	100,000	Middle East Bangladesh, UK, developing countries	N.A.	Cardiac care, joint replacements, Lasik
Malaysia	85,000	US, Japan, developing countries	$40 m	Cosmetic surgery
South Africa	50,000	US, UK	N.A.	Cosmetic surgery, Lasik, dental treatment
Cuba	N.A.	Latin America, US	$25 m–50 m	Specialist niche treatment: Vitiligo [skin], night blindness; cosmetic surgery

Nobody has collated the complete worldwide statistics about how many people travel abroad for health and medical care-related reasons every year or how much they spend. But a Saudi Arabian report pointed out that in 2000, medical travellers from the Gulf region alone spent over $27 billion seeking treatment in various nations around the world. If the medical travellers from around the world spent even half as much that year, the total business in 2000 alone would have been in excess of $40 billion. And even that could be an underestimate.

"The estimate is that the healthcare market in the Organisation of Economic Cooperation and Development countries alone is worth about $3 trillion, and expected to go up to $4 trillion in 2005," says Rupa Chanda, professor at the Indian Institute of Management—Bangalore, and who was part of a working group led by Isher Ahluwalia of ICRIER which prepared a report for the World Trade Organization on the potential for trade in health services. Chanda refuses to hazard a guess on how much of this is actually cross-border medical traffic, just saying that the opportunity is huge.

More importantly, it is growing rapidly and turning out to be an immense business opportunity for nations that are positioning themselves correctly. Last year, just five countries in Asia—Thailand, Malaysia, Jordan, Singapore and India—pulled in over 1.3 million medical travellers and earned over $1 billion (in treatment costs alone). In each of these nations, medical travel spends are growing at 20%-plus year-on-year.

Elsewhere around the world, Hong Kong, Lithuania and South Africa are emerging as big medical/healthcare destinations. And a dozen other nations including Croatia and Greece plan to make themselves attractive healthcare destinations.

By itself, travelling abroad for health is not a new phenomenon—even in ancient times, there were examples of people travelling abroad to spas or famous medical centres for health treatment. But in the past five years or so, the movement has accelerated sharply. It has developed a massive momentum for two critical reasons.

The first is, of course, the demographics of the developed nations and also the problems that are cropping up in their healthcare systems. In the US, the UK, Japan and many European nations, the proportion of the elderly (60 years and above) vis-à-vis the total population is increasing rapidly. In the US, the baby boomers—the biggest chunk of the population—have either hit retirement age or are heading towards it. The number of people aged 65 years and above is expected to double in the next 15 years. In the UK, the people aged 60 years and above will form 25% of the population in the next 30 years—up from 16% now. Similar trends are being seen in almost all nations in Western Europe. Meanwhile, life expectancy here has risen steadily over the years. Add the two up and you get a big surge in demand for healthcare.

The big problem is that as their health needs increase exponentially, the healthcare systems in these countries are beginning to creak under the pressure. The number of doctors and nurses joining the workforce in both the UK and the US is not keeping pace with all the demands of the ageing population. This is creating the push factor.

Meanwhile, there is a pull factor being created by a handful of developing countries like Thailand and Malaysia that have good doctors and excellent facilities, and which are positioning themselves as medical destinations in order to boost their economies. Both Thailand and Malaysia see this developing into a multi-billion dollars-a-year business. There is also the other factor—like people from the least developed countries who find affordable sophisticated medical care facilities in developing countries like India and Malaysia. "The competence and skills of Indian doctors is accepted internationally and people are coming from all over the world to our hospital to get treatment," says Prathap C. Reddy, chairman, Apollo hospital group. Curt Schroeder, CEO of Thailand's Bumrungrad Hospital, echoes that sentiment about his country's healthcare facilities.

Cross-border travel for healthcare reasons is still a highly disorganised movement, but nations are slowly waking up to its potential. In some places the governments have taken a lead. In others, like South Africa and Lithuania, travel agents specialising in medical tourism are driving the trend. In India, private hospitals like Apollo and Escorts Heart Institute and Research Centre are trying to attract patients on their own.

Though the movement can still be considered to be in its infancy, medical travel has come under the radar of both the World Health Organisation (WHO) and the World Trade Organization (WTO). As far back as the early 1990s, the WHO commissioned the Social Sector Development Strategies, Inc. (SSDS, Inc.), a Boston-based non-profit organisation specialising in global healthcare systems, to see whether the English-speaking Caribbean islands could become a significant healthcare destination

TREATMENT COSTS ($)

PROCEDURE	US	INDIA	SOUTH AFRICA	THAILAND
Facelift	6,000–20,000	10,000–20,000	1,252	2,882
Hip replacement	17,000	2,500	9,671	N.A
Open heart Surgery	150,000	5,000–10,000	13,333	7,500
Eye (Lasik)	3,100	7,000	2,166	730

for travellers from the US, the UK and Canada. The study took a hard look at both the advantages and the disadvantages of these nations before reluctantly coming to the conclusion that they would be uncompetitive in most of the areas. The WHO'S interest is simple—it realises that medical travel can help boost the medical facilities (and the medical economy) in developing countries while also taking care of some of the problems of rich nations. The WTO sees medical travel as one of the four modes . . . that will help boost trade in healthcare services worldwide. Both WHO and WTO understand that medical travel could ameliorate much of the demand-supply imbalance in global healthcare. Developed nations benefit as costs or waiting time—or both—come down for a significant chunk of their population. Developing countries benefit as it brings in revenues—and provides the right spur to improve their overall healthcare sector, apart from reducing brain drain in their medical fraternities. Least developed countries, too, benefit as they lack facilities for cutting-edge treatment.

THE TRAVELLERS

You could divide the world's medical travellers into four distinct geographical groups who travel for distinctly different reasons. The first is made up of the Americans. Indeed, countries like Thailand, Malaysia and South Africa, which were the first to try and tap 'medical tourists', all geared their systems to attract the growing American clientele.

Why would the Americans travel abroad when their own country boasts of the best medical facilities in the world? And especially as they don't have to wait in queue like the British? The two Es: ego and economy. The US healthcare system is predominantly insurance-driven. But health insurance covers critical care—not cosmetic care. And there are vast numbers of Americans today who are looking for cosmetic surgery—whether it involves a facelift, a liposuction or dental treatment for a brighter smile.

According to the American Society of Aesthetic Plastic Surgery, in 2002, 6.6 million Americans went in for cosmetic surgery in the US itself. They were also the biggest chunk of foreign customers for cosmetic surgeons in Thailand, Malaysia and South Africa. These three countries, between them, pulled in over 100,000 Americans seeking cosmetic surgery.

As the baby boomers—those 76 million Americans born between 1946 and 1964—age, they are increasingly going in for facelifts, botox treatments, tummy tucks, et al. And since cosmetic surgery is mostly not covered by medical insurance, many Americans prefer to travel abroad. A full facelift costs $8,000–20,000 in the US and only $1,252 in South Africa. Thailand is slightly more expensive at $2,682. Best of all, going abroad means a vacation as well after the surgery is over.

Vanity isn't the only reason why Americans seek treatment abroad though. Lack of insurance cover is another. Last year, 15.2% of the US population—some 43.6 million people—had no health insurance coverage. And a significant proportion of even the 84% with insurance were under-insured.

Many of these people weren't poor—at least according to developing country standards. Some of them were people between jobs who didn't have insurance simply because they were earlier covered by their employers. Given the increasing cost of medical treatment in the US, it made sound economic sense to seek treatment abroad.

If cosmetic surgery and costs were the factors driving the Americans to travel abroad, the second major group—the British—were being forced to seek medical treatment in other countries by the sheer waiting lists caused by the National Health Service (NHS). Unlike in the US, the British healthcare system ensures free treatment to all its citizens. The only problem is that the NHS, which was set up in 1948, is struggling to cope because of a shortage of both doctors and hospital beds. (Private medical facilities are available in the UK, but they are prohibitively expensive and also relatively fewer in number.) In 2001, more than 1 million British citizens were waiting for inpatient treatment and half-a-million for outpatient treatment according to a study by the Vienna University of Economics and Business Administration. At least 40% of the people requiring inpatient care needed to wait over three months for their turn to come. Hip replacement and eyecare had the longest waiting periods.

The situation is so bad that in 2002, the NHS started a pilot scheme 'overseas treatment' to see if surgery services abroad could be bought to shorten the waiting lists. The project focussed mainly on facilities available in the European Union—in countries like Austria and Germany. Meanwhile, many thousands of British patients take the initiative to seek their own treatment abroad without waiting for the NHS to sort out its problems.

The third big group of medical travellers comes from the Middle East. These are citizens of the oil rich nations flying abroad to seek medical facilities that are either unavailable or in short supply in their own countries. An agency in Saudi Arabia estimated that every year, more than 500,000 people from the Middle East travel seeking medical treatment for everything from open heart surgery to infertility treatments. They travel everywhere—to Jordan, Saudi Arabia and Bahrain; to the US; to India, Thailand and Malaysia. By some estimates, India itself attracted 70,000-plus medical travellers from the Middle East last year.

Finally, the last group of medical travellers form a motley lot. They are from the least developed countries and countries with generally poor medical infrastructure, who usually seek treatment facilities at some neighbouring country with better infrastructure. Last year, it was estimated that at least 50,000 people from Bangladesh and Nepal came for medical treatment to India. A significant majority of the 126,000 medical travellers to Jordan came from neighbours with poor medical infrastructure facilities.

TAPPING THE BIG MARKET

A $40-billion-plus market growing at over 20% a year throws up huge opportunities for anyone smart enough to tap into it. The SSDS, Inc. study for the WHO pointed out that business opportunities covered a big spectrum—from retirement homes and spas, to cosmetic and dental surgery, to critical but non-emergency surgery needs like hip replacements, organ transplants, angioplasty and vision correction. Other studies show even alternative healthcare could be a significant niche opportunity.

In the initial years, most countries that tapped into the medical destination opportunity essentially focussed either on spas or on the 'vanity' and the 'exotic' surgery requirements. In South Africa a number of outfits (travel agents with hospital connections) sprang up to tap into the market for facelifts, tummy lucks and cosmetic dental surgery. Thailand initially had a somewhat dubious reputation as an excellent country to go to for sex change operations. India's primary claim to fame was its ayurvedic treatment centers. "Beauty, youth and wellness is a huge area for growth and we need to promote it aggressively," says Apollo's Reddy.

Over the past few years, though, many countries have realised that an equally big opportunity lies in promoting the more conventional treatments. Some of this, of course, was always happening in the background—like people from Mauritius, Bangladesh and the Gulf coming to India for conventional surgeries and people from Japan flying to Singapore, Malaysia or Thailand for similar reasons. Only now, the nations have started pitching themselves as world-class but inexpensive destinations for almost all health requirements.

They might be getting some unexpected help soon—from insurance giants. Healthcare insurers in the developed countries are not blind to the fact that the option of medical treatment in countries like Thailand and Malaysia could help them reduce premiums and offer options to people who are currently uninsured. Over the next few years, insurance firms are expected to provide a fillip to the medical travel business.

Most insurance companies in the US and the UK have already accredited hospitals worldover where Western visitors can seek emergency medical treatment. Now a few hospitals in Thailand are going a step further—they are getting themselves accredited by the Joint Commission Accreditation of Healthcare Organizations (JCAHO). A full accreditation from this organisation allows a hospital to pitch for the insurance traffic too. Travelling has never been so healthy before.

The Strategic Levers of Yield Management

SHERYL E. KIMES AND RICHARD B. CHASE

Yield management, controlling customer demand through the use of variable pricing and capacity management to enhance profitability, has been examined extensively in the services literature. Most of this work has been tactical and mathematical rather than managerial. In this article, the authors suggest that a broader view of yield management is valuable to both traditional and nontraditional users of the approach. Central to this broader view is the recognition of how different combinations of pricing and duration can be used as strategic levers to position service firms in their markets and the identification of tactics by which management can deploy these strategic levers. The authors also propose that further development of yield management requires that when the service is delivered should be treated as a design variable that should be as carefully managed as the service process itself.

Although commonly associated with marketing as a revenue management tool, yield management has significant impacts on other service business functions. It affects operations in capacity planning, human resource management in worker selection and training, and business strategy through the way the service firm positions itself in the market. Despite this widespread impact and the considerable attention it has received, formal yield management is still viewed primarily as a pricing/inventory management tool. What is lacking is a broader theory of yield management that would permit other service industries to gain the benefits of yield management-type thinking and provide insights into new areas in which experienced companies might further apply the concept. Our objective in this article is to develop the groundwork for such a theory. Our focus will be on the strategic levers available for yield management, how they have been applied in traditional yield management settings, and how they, along with some tactical tools, can be applied to other service settings.

A MODIFIED DEFINITION OF YIELD MANAGEMENT

A common definition of yield management is the application of information systems and pricing strategies to "sell the right capacity to the right customers at the right prices" (Smith, Leimkuhler, and Darrow 1992). Implicit in this definition is the notion of time-perishable capacity and, by extension, the notion of segmentation of capacity according to when it is booked, when and how long it is to be used, and according to the customer who uses it. In other words, "an hour is not an hour is not an hour" when it comes to customer preferences or capacity management. In light of this subtle point, we offer a slightly modified definition of the term. That is, yield management may be defined as managing the four Cs of perishable service: calendar (how far in advance reservations are made), clock (the time of day service is offered), capacity (the inventory of service resources), and cost (the price of the service) to manage a fifth C, customer demand, in such a way as to maximize profitability.

Strategic Levers

A successful yield management strategy is predicated on effective control of customer demand. Businesses have two interrelated strategic levers with which to accomplish this: pricing and duration of customer use. Prices can be fixed (one price for the same service for all customers for all times) or variable (different prices for different times or for different customer segments), and duration can be predictable or unpredictable.

Variable pricing to control demand is conceptually a straightforward process. It can take the form of discount prices at off-peak hours for all customers, such as low weekday rates for movies, or it can be in the form of price discounts for certain classes of customers, such as senior discounts at restaurants.

Duration control presents a more complicated decision problem but at the same time represents an area that would improve the effectiveness of yield management. By implementing duration controls, companies maximize overall revenue across all time periods rather than just during high-demand periods. If managers want to increase control over duration, they can refine their definition of duration, reduce the uncertainty of arrival, reduce the uncertainty of the duration, or reduce the amount of time between customers. We will discuss each of these tactics later.

Different industries use different combinations of variable pricing and duration control (Figure 1). Industries

Figure 1 Typical Pricing and Duration Positioning of Selected Services Industries

		Price	
		Fixed	**Variable**
Duration	**Predictable**	**Quadrant 1:** Movies Stadiums/Arenas Convention Centers	**Quadrant 2:** Hotels Airlines Rental Cars Cruise Lines
	Unpredictable	**Quadrant 3:** Restaurants Golf Courses Internet Service Providers	**Quadrant 4:** Continuing Care Hospitals

traditionally associated with yield management (hotel, airline, rental car, and cruise line) tend to use variable pricing and a specified or predictable duration (Quadrant 2). Movie theaters, performing arts centers, arenas, and convention centers use a fixed price for a predictable duration (Quadrant 1), whereas restaurants, golf courses, and Internet service providers use a fixed price with unpredictable customer duration (Quadrant 3). Many health care industries charge variable prices (Medicare or private pay) but do not know the duration of patient use (Quadrant 4). There is no fixed demarcation point between quadrants, so an industry may lie partially in one quadrant and partially in another. The intent of this classification method is to help industries not currently using yield management develop a strategic framework for developing yield management. More specifically, what we are trying to show is which quadrant industries are in and what they can do to move to Quadrant 2. For example, restaurant management does not have control of duration; they need to pursue some duration management approach. Or, if hotel management does not adequately control length of stay, they may want to modify their forecasting system from room nights to arrivals to enhance their reservation system.

As indicated above, successful yield management applications are generally found in Quadrant 2 industries. The reason is that a predictable duration enables clear delineation of the service portfolio, and variable pricing enables generating maximum revenue from each service offering within the portfolio. We hasten to point out that even those industries that are listed in this quadrant have structural features that inhibit them from achieving their full profit potential. A brief review of the development of yield management in the airline and hotel industries will help illustrate these points.

Airline Industry

Deregulation of the American airline industry was the major impetus for the development of yield management. Before deregulation in 1978, major carriers offered one-price service between cities. Essentially, most airlines were operating in Quadrant 1: Their flight durations were extremely predictable, and their price was fixed (Figure 2).

Immediately after deregulation, many new airlines emerged, and one airline, People's Express, developed an aggressive low-cost strategy. The People's Express story is well known: Their airfares were considerably lower than those of the major carriers, and customers were attracted to the limited service that People's Express flights offered. The major carriers such as American Airlines, United Airlines, and Delta Airlines, aided by new computerized reservation systems, employed variable pricing on a flight-by-flight basis to match or undercut fares offered by People's Express. Cost-conscious passengers then switched to the major carriers, and People's Express was eventually forced out of business. Donald Burr, the former CEO of People's Express, attributes his airline's failure to the lack of good information technology and the subsequent inability to practice yield management (Anonymous 1992; Cross 1997).

Seeing the benefits of differential pricing, most major North American carriers instituted yield management and moved into Quadrant 2. Yield management allowed airlines to determine the minimum fare (of a set mix of fares) that should be available for a specific flight. Differential pricing, in combination with the predictability of flight duration, gave them the enviable position of variable pricing with predictable duration.

Another trend that emerged after deregulation was the hub-and-spoke system. Previously, airlines operated on an origin-destination basis, and although connecting flights

Figure 2 The Airline Industry

		Price	
		Fixed	**Variable**
Duration	**Predictable**	Quadrant 1: Before De-regulation	Quadrant 2: Immediately after De-regulation
	Unpredictable	Quadrant 3: None Identified	Quadrant 4: Hub-and-Spoke System

existed, the concept of a hub city did not. Most major airlines now operate with a hub-and-spoke system, and their forecasting and yield management systems are based around the associated flight legs (Skwarek 1996). Leg-based solutions have inherent problems and may lead to suboptimal solutions. Although the revenue on each flight leg may be optimized, revenue over the entire airline network may not. In an attempt to circumvent this problem, some airlines (notably American Airlines) developed virtual nesting systems (Smith, Leimkuhler, and Darrow 1992), in which different origin-destination pairs were classified by revenue generated. Unfortunately, current origin-destination forecasting and yield management systems have a high forecast error that results in an unreliable solution.

The lack of origin-destination forecasting may seem like a minor point, but it prevents airlines from truly managing the predictability of their duration. In a sense, the hub-and-spoke system has caused the airline industry to move into the bottom half of Quadrant 2 or the top half of Quadrant 4. The hub-and-spoke system, in combination with airline pricing systems, has created problems such as passengers attempting to obtain a lower fare by completing only one leg of their multileg flight (a "hidden city"). The empty seat on the remaining flight leg represents lost revenue to the airlines so safeguards have been instituted to avoid this problem. Only one major carrier, Southwest Airlines, has resisted the temptation of the hub-and-spoke system. This represents a competitive advantage for their yield management system because they are better able to manage the predictability of their flight durations (Anonymous 1994b).

Hotel Industry

Unlike the airline industry, traditional hotels are usually located in Quadrant 3. Although group and tour operators have multiple negotiated rates (Hoyle, Dorf, and Jones 1991; Vallen and Vallen 1991), most traditional hotels charge essentially one room rate (or perhaps a low-season and

high-season rate) for transient guests. Length of stay is not explicitly considered, and forecasts are designed to predict nightly occupancy (Figure 3). Typically, the goal of the traditional hotel is to maximize occupancy for a given night, and managers seldom look at long-term revenue generation.

After the airlines started using yield management, many hotel managers were impressed with the increased revenue claimed by the airlines and applied the concept of variable pricing to the hotel industry. When hotels started using variable pricing, they did not apply the concept of qualified rates, in which customers had to meet certain requirements to obtain a lower room rate. They instead relied on top-down pricing, in which reservation agents quoted the highest rate first and, if faced with resistance, offered the next of several lower rates until the customers acquiesced or they reached a minimum level previously established by management. Many major hotel chains still use this pricing method. Although short-term revenue gains may result from top-down pricing, customers view this practice unfavorably (Kimes 1994). Most hotels using this approach forecast room nights and use the forecasted nightly occupancy rate to develop pricing recommendations (Kimes 1989). Length-of-stay issues are not considered, and occupancy and rates are managed for one night at a time.

Some hotel chains, notably Marriott and Forte Hotels, saw the benefits associated with predictable durations (Anonymous 1994a). To reap the benefits associated with duration controls, they switched from forecasting room nights to forecasting arrivals by length of stay and/or room rate. Forte charged only one rate and concentrated solely on length of stay. Guests requesting a 2-night stay might be accepted, whereas those requesting a 1-night stay might be rejected depending on the projected demand. Marriott forecasted by arrival day, length of stay, and room rate and was able to determine the best set of reservation requests to accept. Still other hotel chains tried to implement length-of-stay controls without changing their forecasting system from room nights to arrivals. Without arrival information, they had no way of knowing

Figure 3 The Hotel Industry

		Price	
		Fixed	**Variable**
Duration	**Predictable**	Quadrant 1: Forte	Quadrant 2: Marriott Sheraton Holiday Inn
	Unpredictable	Quadrant 3: Traditional Hotels	Quadrant 4: Initial Yield Management Attempts

if their restrictions made sense or if they were unnecessarily turning away potential customers.

The focus on length of stay not only changed the forecasting systems in place at leading hotels but also changed the mathematical methods used to develop yield management recommendations. Many hotel chains (e.g., Holiday Inn, Hilton, Sheraton, and Hyatt) have instituted linear-programming-based systems in which length of stay and room rate are explicitly considered (Hensdill 1998; Vinod 1995).

USING THE STRATEGIC LEVERS

Industries in Quadrants 1, 3, and 4 can move into Quadrant 2 to achieve some of the revenue gains associated with yield management by manipulating duration and price.

Although there are still problems facing the hotel and airline industries, their experience provides a rich context from which to understand the tactical tools needed to improve revenue generation. Specific tools associated with each strategic yield management lever can allow managers to move their company into a better revenue-generating position.

Duration Methods

If managers want to increase control over duration, they can refine their definition of duration, reduce the uncertainty of arrival, reduce the uncertainty of the duration, or reduce the amount of time between customers (Figure 4).

Figure 4 Methods of Managing Duration

	Possible Approaches
Refine Definition	Time Event
Uncertainty of Arrival: **Internal Measures**	Forecasting Overbooking
Uncertainty of Arrival: **External Measures**	Penalties Deposits
Uncertainty of Duration: **Internal Measures**	Forecasting by Time of Arrival, Length of Stay, and Customer Characteristics
Uncertainty of Duration **External Measures**	Penalties Restrictions Process Analysis
Reduce Time Between **Customers**	Process Analysis

Refining the Definition of Duration

Duration is how long customers use a service and is measured either in terms of time (i.e., the number of nights or number of hours) or by event (i.e., a meal or a round of golf). When duration is defined as an event rather than time, forecasting the length of duration generally becomes more difficult. Thus, if duration for an industry could be defined in time rather than events, better forecasting, and hence control of duration, would likely result.

Even industries that use time-based duration definitions can refine this definition and thereby enhance their operations. Most hotels sell rooms by the day, or more specifically, they sell rooms from 3 p.m. (check-in) to noon (check-out). Sheraton Hotels and The Peninsula Hotel in Beverly Hills allow customers to check in at any time of the day and check out at any time without penalty (Anonymous 1997; Barker 1998). By refining their definition of duration, they have improved customer satisfaction, made better use of capacity, and increased revenue.

Uncertainty of Arrival

Because many capacity-constrained firms have perishable inventory, they must protect themselves from no-shows or late arrivals. Firms can use both internal (not involving customers) and external (involving customers) approaches to decrease uncertainty of arrival.

Internal Approaches   Most capacity-constrained service firms use overbooking to protect themselves against no-shows. Published overbooking models often use Markovian decision processes or simulation approaches (for example, Lieberman and Yechialli 1978; Rothstein 1971, 1985; Schlifer and Vardi 1975), but in practice many companies use service-level approaches. (Anonymous 1993; Smith, Leimkuhler, and Darrow 1992) or the critical fractile method (as suggested by Sasser, Olsen, and Wyckoff 1978). The key to a successful overbooking policy is to obtain accurate no-show and cancellation information and to develop overbooking levels that will maintain an acceptable level of customer service.

Once an overbooking policy is implemented, companies must develop good internal methods for handling displaced customers. The frontline personnel who must assist displaced customers should receive appropriate training and compensation for dealing with potentially angry consumers. Companies can choose to select which customers to displace on either a voluntary or involuntary manner. The airline industry, with its voluntary displacement system, has increased customer goodwill while increasing long-term profit (Anonymous 1993; Rothstein 1985). Other industries base their displacement decision on time of arrival (if customers are late, their reservation is no longer honored), frequency of use (regular customers are never displaced), or perceived importance (important customers are never displaced).

External Approaches   External approaches to reduce arrival uncertainty shift the responsibility of arriving to the customer. The deposit policies used at many capacity-constrained service firms such as cruise lines and resorts are excellent examples of external approaches. In addition, the cancellation penalties imposed by these companies represent an attempt to make customers more responsible for arriving. Restaurants are experimenting with cancellation penalties and ask customers for their credit card numbers when taking reservations (Brehaus 1998). If patrons do not arrive within 15 minutes of the reservation time, a penalty fee is charged to their credit cards. Interestingly, the car rental industry, which has considerable yield management experience, makes very limited use of external approaches. With the exception of specialty cars and vans, customers are not asked to guarantee their rental and have no responsibility for showing up. With no incentives for customers to arrive, it is not surprising that in busy tourist markets such as Florida, no-shows can account for as much as 70 percent of the reservations (Stern and Miller 1995). Besides these negative incentives, some companies use service guarantees to encourage people to show up on time. American Golf, for example, offers discounted or free play to golfers whose actual tee-off time is delayed by more than 10 minutes of their reservation time.

Uncertainty of Duration

Reducing duration uncertainty enables management to better gauge capacity requirements and hence make better decisions as to which reservation requests to accept. As in the case of arrival uncertainty, both internal and external approaches can be used for this purpose.

Internal Approaches   Internal approaches include accurate forecasting of the length of use and the number of early and late arrivals and departures and improving the consistency of service delivery. By knowing how long customers plan to use the service, managers can make better decisions as to which reservation requests to accept. If a restaurant manager knows that parties of two take approximately 45 minutes to dine and parties of four take about 75 minutes, he or she can make better allocation decisions. Likewise, knowing how many customers will change their planned duration of use enhances capacity decisions. For example, in a hotel, accurately forecasting how many customers book for 4 nights but leave after 3, or request additional nights, facilitates room and staff allocations. Similarly, if a rental car company knows that 20 percent of its week-long rentals are returned after 5 days, the fleet supply requirement can be adjusted accordingly.

Early research and practice in yield management focused on single flight legs or room nights and did not consider duration. Expected marginal seat revenue (EMSR) based models (Belobaba 1987; Littlewood 1972) are widely used in the airline industry (Williamson 1992) and result in allocation decisions for flight legs at various days before departure. Early hotel yield management systems based minimum rate decisions on forecasted occupancy but did not consider the impact of length of stay (Kimes 1989). Some airlines have tried to compensate for the lack of duration control by using actual nesting (Smith, Leimkuhler, and Darrow 1992; Vinod 1995; Williamson 1992) but still have not achieved the goal of full origin-destination control (Vinod 1995).

Linear programming has been used to help make better duration and pricing allocation decisions (Kimes 1989; Weatherford 1995; Williamson 1992). The bid price, defined as the shadow price of the capacity constraint, can be used to determine the marginal value of an additional seat, room, or other inventory unit (Phillips 1994; Vinod 1995; Williamson 1992). This value can then be used to determine the minimum price available for different durations. Dynamic programming (Bitran and Mondschein 1995) has also been suggested as a possible method for considering hotel length of stay.

The accuracy of the forecast affects the effectiveness of the yield management system. Lee (1990), in his study of airline forecasting, found that a 10 percent improvement in forecast accuracy resulted in a 3 percent to 5 percent increase in revenue on high-demand flights.

If duration is to be explicitly addressed, forecasts of customer duration must be developed. Airlines typically forecast demand by flight leg (Lee 1990; Vinod 1995), but to truly practice duration control, airlines must forecast demand by all possible origin-destination pairs. As previously mentioned, the hub-and-spoke system has increased the number of forecasts required and the subsequent accuracy of those forecasts. Some airlines have tried to reduce the number of forecasts needed by using virtual nesting (Smith, Leimkuhler, and Darrow 1992; Vinod 1995). Preliminary research on airline-forecasting accuracy (Weatherford 1998) shows that an increase in the number of daily forecasts required increases the forecast error.

When hotels forecast customer duration, they must forecast by day of arrival, length of stay, and possible rate class (Kimes, O'Sullivan, and Scott 1998). Hotels using linear programming and bid-price approaches forecast at this level of detail, and some have developed even more detailed forecasts. The magnitude of this problem becomes apparent when you consider that for each day of arrival, a hotel might consider 10 different lengths of stay and 10 different rate classes. If room type is included, a hotel may have 200 to 300 different forecasts per day.

Consistency of duration (i.e., most customers using the service for about the same length of time) is typically achieved through internal process changes. For example, TGI Fridays redesigned their restaurant menus and service delivery systems to make dining time more consistent as well as faster. Some restaurants in the theater district of New York City have placed an hourglass on the table of each party. When the sand in the hourglass is gone, patrons have a visual cue to finish dinner and leave so they will not be late to the theater. Or, in a much different context, if a prison warden knows that 25 percent of prisoners sentenced to 10 years serve only 4, additional prisoners may be incarcerated.

External Approaches   External approaches for handling uncertainty of duration generally reach the customer in the form of deposits or penalties. Some hotels have instituted early and late departure fees (Miller 1995), and airlines have penalized passengers who purchase tickets through hidden cities. Although penalties may work in the short term, they risk incurring customer wrath and hurting the company in the long run. For this reason, internal approaches are generally preferable.

Reduce Time Between Customers

Reducing the amount of time between customers (changeover time reduction), by definition, means that more customers can be served in the same or a shorter period of time. Although changeover time reduction is not normally considered a tool of yield management, it is a tactic that can be used to increase revenue per available inventory unit. Such tactics play an important role in the yield management strategy. Changeover time reduction has become a common strategy for airlines. Southwest Airlines and Shuttle by United both boast of 20-minute ground turnarounds of their aircraft (compared to the average of 45 minutes at most airlines) and have been able to increase the utilization of their planes (Kimes and Young 1997). Many restaurants have instituted computerized table management systems that track tables in use, the progress of the meal, and when the bill is paid. When customers leave, the table management system notifies bussers, and the table is cleared and reset (Liddle 1996). The result is an increase in table utilization and, hence, revenue per table.

Price

Industries actively practicing yield management use differential pricing—charging customers using the same service at the same time different prices, depending on customer and demand characteristics. Passengers in the economy section of a flight from New York City to Los Angeles may pay from nothing (for those using frequent-flyer vouchers) to more than $1,500. The fares vary according to the time of reservation, the restrictions imposed, or the group or company affiliation. In contrast to such Quadrant 2 pricing, Quadrant 1 and 3 industries use relatively fixed pricing and charge customers using the same service at the same time the same price.

Customers tend to develop reference prices for various transactions. If companies change price, they must do so carefully to avoid upsetting their customers (Kahneman, Knetsch, and Thaler 1986). Although it is possible to charge more solely based on high demand, customers may resent being charged different prices for essentially the same service. Two mechanisms—proper price mix and rate fences—

Figure 5 Methods of Managing Price

	Possible Approaches
Proper Price Mix	**Price Elasticities** **Competitive Pricing** **Optimal Pricing Policies**
Rate Fences: Physical	**Type of Inventory** **Amenities**
Rate Fences: Nonphysical	**Restrictions** **Time of Usage** **Time of Reservation** **Group Membership**

provide opportunities to alter price while maintaining goodwill (Figure 5).

Proper Price Mix

Companies must be sure that they offer a logical mix of prices from which to choose. If customers do not see much distinction between the different prices being quoted, a differential-pricing strategy may not work. Determining the best mix of prices is difficult because management often has little information on price elasticities. This, in turn, often results in pricing decisions based solely on competitive pressures. It should be noted, however, that airlines such as American Airlines have been working hard on the issues of elasticity and of multiple legs and have made some progress.

Optimal pricing policies, in which customers are asked to name the prices that they would consider to be cheap, expensive, too cheap to be of reasonable quality, and too expensive to be considered, have been developed by Taco Bell and have been tested for use with meeting planners (Lewis and Shoemaker 1997). Optimal pricing policies represent a relatively simple way of determining price sensitivity and acceptable price ranges.

Although not widely publicized, some restaurant companies are experimenting with menu pricing based on price elasticities. Large chain restaurant companies analyze the price elasticities of various menu items and make appropriate pricing changes (Kelly, Kiefer, and Burdett 1994).

Rate Fences

The possession of a good pricing structure does not ensure the success of a variable pricing strategy. Companies must also have a logical rationale or, in industry terms, rate fences that can be used to justify price discrimination. (Or, as one somewhat cynical hotel executive states, "We want something we can say out loud without laughing.")

Quadrant 2 industries often use rate fences such as when the reservation is booked or when the service is consumed, to determine the price a customer will pay. Rate fences refer to qualifications that must be met to receive a discount (Hanks, Cross, and Noland 1992). Rate fences can be physical or nonphysical in nature and represent a rationale for why some customers pay different prices for the same service.

Physical rate fences include tangible features such as room type or view for hotels, seat type or location for airlines, or table location for restaurants. Other physical rate fences are the presence or absence of certain amenities (free golf cart use with a higher price, free breakfast with a higher price, or free soft drinks at a movie theater).

Nonphysical rate fences can be developed that can help shift demand to slower periods, reward regular customers, or reward reliable customers. Nonphysical rate fences include cancellation or change penalties and benefits based on when the reservation was booked, desired service duration, group membership or affiliation, and time of use.

Even today, it is common practice for companies to adopt differential pricing schemes without rate fences. Hotels use top-down pricing in which reservation agents quote the rack rate (generally the highest rate) and only quote lower rates if customers ask for them. Knowledgeable customers may know to ask for the lower rate, but inexperienced customers may not. Customers view this practice highly unfavorably (Kimes 1994).

MOVING TO A MORE PROFITABLE QUADRANT

The strategic levers described above can be used to help companies move into more profitable quadrants by making duration more predictable and/or by varying prices. Generally, companies try to manipulate one strategic lever at a time, but it is possible, although difficult, for a company to try to simultaneously adjust price and duration. The following examples of potential moves show the possibilities for various industries.

Differential Pricing: Quadrant 1 to Quadrant 2

Movie Theaters

Although reservation systems and differential pricing have been used in Europe for many years, American movie theaters usually charge the same price for all seats and offer discounted seats only for matinees or for senior citizens. However, things are changing rapidly, and some new movie houses are now offering differential pricing based on seat location, time of show, and access to amenities. For example, the 70-seat Premium Cinema in Lombard, Illinois, has been booked solid since its opening April 3, 1998. Guests willing to pay $15 for access to a separate entrance with valet parking are admitted to a private lounge, where they can purchase champagne at $12 per glass and buy prime-rib sandwiches at the same price. They offer free popcorn (all you can eat) and have a full-time concierge to get it for the customers. As of yet, they have not gone to the next step of developing an overbooking strategy.

Control Duration: Quadrant 3 to Quadrant 1

Golf Courses

Golf courses seem to be in the worst possible position—they charge a fixed price for an event of unknown duration. Much of the problem stems from the definition of duration as an event, typically 18 holes of golf played during daylight hours. Alternative definitions of duration abound. The golf course could sell 9-hole rounds; it could institute shotgun golf, in which different groups start simultaneously at multiple holes; or it could use express golf, in which golfers run between holes and receive two scores, elapsed time and stroke count, at the end of each round. (The latter perhaps becoming a new Olympic event.) None of these modifications reduce variability in and of themselves; however, they do provide ways of redefining duration for more creative applications of yield management.

Arrival uncertainty could be reduced by instituting deposit policies or by developing good overbooking policies. Duration uncertainty could be reduced by adding marshals to help move golfers along on the course, by provision of free golf carts to speed the time between holes, and by more accurately forecasting play length based on time of day, week, and party size. More golfers could be accommodated if tee-time intervals were reduced or if party size were better regulated.

Control Duration: Quadrant 4 to Quadrant 2

Health Care

Health care organizations use differential pricing (often government mandated) but have difficulties managing duration. If hospital or nursing home managers do not know how long patients will be using beds or rooms, it is difficult to effectively plan and manage capacity. In a nursing home, the health of potential patients could be evaluated and actuarial tables used to estimate the duration of patient stay. In private and nonprofit facilities, attempts could be made to select the best mix of private-pay and Medicare patients with a bias toward private-pay patients with a long duration.

The issue of duration control of health care has caused political controversy. During the mid-1990s, insurance companies in New York reduced the maximum length of insurable hospital stay for childbirth to 1 day. After intensive lobbying pressure from hospitals and medical associations, the state legislature outlawed this practice and guaranteed all new mothers a minimum length of stay of 48 hours.

Differential Pricing: Quadrant 3 to Quadrant 4

Internet Service Providers (ISPs)

ISPs offer Internet bandwidth to customers. Because not all customers use their full allotment of bandwidth at the same time, the ISP overbooks the bandwidth. If too many customers try to access the Internet at once, service deteriorates.

ISPs operate at 100 percent capacity during certain times of the day and at other times have available bandwidth. Currently, most ISPs charge a flat monthly rate for Internet access, and there is no off-peak discount. Some customers are heavy users during the day, whereas others are heavy nighttime users. ISPs must maintain a mix of these customers to operate effectively. By identifying common demographic characteristics within each segment, ISPs could target specific types of users to add to the mix (M. Freimer, personal communication, 1998).

CONCLUSION

Effective use of the strategic levers of pricing and duration control can help capacity-constrained firms make more profitable use of their resources. Real potential exists for novel use of these tools in industries not typically associated with yield management. Even companies with yield management experience can improve performance by refining their deployment of these levers. The research challenge is to help managers identify yield management opportunities and to develop appropriate pricing and duration control approaches.

Beyond where to apply yield management, there are the questions of how to develop a yield management strategy, how to train people in the tools to implement it, and how to maintain and improve customer satisfaction while applying yield management practices. In the long run, achieving the full potential from yield management lies in management's ability to market and manage every available moment as a unique product. This, in turn, requires that we treat when the service is provided as a design variable that should be as carefully managed as the service process itself. Such a reformulation presents an exciting conceptual challenge to the emerging field of service research.

REFERENCES

"Adding to Forte's Fortune," (1994a), *Scorecard*, Second Quarter, 4–5.

Barker, J. (1998), "Flexible Check-in Expands," *Successful Meetings* 47 (January): 32.

Belobaba, P. P. (1987), "Air Travel Demand and Airline Seat Inventory Management," Ph.D. thesis, Massachusetts Institute of Technology.

Bitran, G. R. and S. V. Mondschein (1995), "An Application of Yield Management to the Hotel Industry Considering Multiple Day Stays," *Operations Research*, 43, 427–43.

Brehaus, B. (1998), "Handling No-Shows: Operators React to Reservation Plan," *Restaurant Business Magazine* 1 (16): 13.

"A Conversation with Don Burr," (1992), *Scorecard*, Fourth Quarter, 6–7.

Cross, R. G. (1997), *Revenue Management: Hard-Core Tactics for Market Domination*. New York: Broadway Books.

"Flying High with Herb Kelleher," (1994b), *Scorecard*, Third Quarter, 1–3.

Freimer, M. (1998), personal communication.

Hanks, R. D., R. G. Cross, and R. P. Noland. (1992), "Discounting in the Hotel Industry: A New Approach," *Cornell Hotel and Restaurant Administration Quarterly* 33 (3): 40–45.

Hensdill, C. (1998), "The Culture of Revenue Management," *Hotels* (March): 83–86.

"Hotel Adopts 24-Hour Check-in Policy," (1997), *Hospitality Law* 12 (1): 7.

Hoyle, L. H., D. C. Dorf, and T. J. A. Jones. (1991), *Managing Conventions and Group Business*, Washington, DC: The Educational Institute of the American Hotel and Motel Association.

Kahneman, D., J. Knetsch, and R. Thaler. (1986), "Fairness as a Constraint on Profit Seeking: Entitlements in the Market," *American Economic Review* 76 (4): 728–41.

Kelly, T. J., N. M. Kiefer, and K. Burdett. (1994), "A Demand-Based Approach to Menu Pricing," *Cornell Hotel and Restaurant Administration Quarterly* 34 (3): 40–45.

Kimes, S. E. (1989), "Yield Management: A Tool for Capacity-Constrained Service Firms," *Journal of Operations Management* 8 (4): 348–63.

———. (1994), "Perceived Fairness of Yield Management," *Cornell Hotel and Restaurant Administration Quarterly* 34 (1): 22–29.

Kimes, S. E. and Franklin Young. (1997), "Shuttle by United," *Interfaces* 27 (3): 1–13.

Kimes, S. E., M. O'Sullivan and D. Scott. (1998), "Hotel Forecasting Methods," working paper. Cornell University School of Hotel Administration.

Lee, A. O. (1990), "Airline Reservations Forecasting: Probabilistic and Statistical Models of the Booking Process," Ph.D. thesis, Massachusetts Institute of Technology.

Lewis, R. C and S. Shoemaker (1997), "Price Sensitivity Measurement: A Tool for the Hospitality Industry," *Cornell Hotel and Restaurant Administration Quarterly* 38 (2): 44–54.

Liddle, A. (1996), "New Computerized Table Management Reduces Guests' Waits, Empty Seats," *Nation's Restaurant News* (August 5): 22.

Lieberman, V. and U. Yechialli (1978), "On the Hotel Overlooking Problem: An Inventory Problem with Stochastic Cancellations," *Management Science* 24, 1117–26.

Littlewood, K. (1972), "Forecasting and Control of Passenger Bookings," *AGIFORS Symposium Proceedings* 12, 95–117.

Miller, L. (1995), "Check-Out Made Pricier," *Wall Street Journal*, October 20, B6.

Phillips, R. L. (1994), "A Marginal Value Approach to Airline Origin and Destination Revenue Management," in *Proceedings of the 16th Conference on System Modeling and Optimization*, J. Henry and P. Yvon, eds. New York: Springer-Verlag, 907–17.

Rothstein, M. (1971), "An Airline Overbooking Model," *Transportation Science* 5, 180–92.

———. (1985), "OR and the Airline Overbooking Problem," *Operations Research* 33 (2): 237–48.

Sasser, W. E., R. P. Olsen, and D. D. Wyckoff (1978), *Management of Service Operations*. Boston: Allyn and Bacon.

Schlifer E. and Y. Vardi. (1975), "An Airline Overbooking Policy," *Transportation Sciences* 9, 101–14.

"Simon Says," (1993), *Scorecard*, First Quarter, 10–12.

Skwarek, D. K. (1996), "Competitive Impacts of Yield Management System Components: Forecasting and Sell-Up Models," MIT Flight Transportation Lab Report No. R96–6. Cambridge, MA: Massachusetts Institute of Technology.

Smith, B. C., J. F. Leimkuhler, and R. M. Darrow. (1992), "Yield Management at American Airlines," *Interfaces* 22 (1): 8–31.

Stern, G. and L. Miller (1995), "Rental Car Companies Set to Impose Cancellation Penalties for No-Shows," *The Wall Street Journal*, December 26, A3.

Vallen, J. J. and G. K. Vallen (1991), *Check-in, Check-Out*, Dubuque, IA: William C. Brown.

Vinod, B. (1995), "Origin-and-Destination Yield Management," in *Handbook of Airline Economics*, D. Jenkins, ed. New York: McGraw-Hill, 459–68.

Weatherford, L. R. (1995), "Length of Stay Heuristics: Do They Really Make a Difference?" *Cornell Hotel and Restaurant Administration Quarterly* 36 (6): 47–56.

———(1998), "Forecasting Issues in Revenue Management," INFORMS conference presentation, Montreal, Canada, May.

Williamson, E. L. (1992), "Airline Network Seat Control," Ph.D. thesis, Massachusetts Institute of Technology.

FEES! FEES! FEES!

EMILY THORNTON

> *Companies can't raise price, so they're socking consumers with hundreds of hidden charges—and that's creating stealth inflation and fueling a popular backlash*

America used to be the land of the free. Now, it's the land of the fee. Companies, hard-pressed for money, are taking every possible opportunity to nickel-and-dime people to death. Need a monthly brokerage account statement mailed to you? Ameritrade may charge you $2 per statement. Want your hotel room cleaned? The Alexander Hotel in Miami Beach, Fla., will bill you an extra $2.50 daily for housekeeping. Have to return a new camcorder? Best Buy Co. will dock you 15% as a "restocking fee." Want to buy a season ticket for pro football? The New York Jets will make you pay $50 for the privilege of getting on their waiting list.

I GOTTA PAY WHAT?

> *People will pay billions of dollars more in fees this year. Here are some examples:*

Financial Services

$50 Billion

for banks and credit-card issuers   Nobody beats the banks and other financial services companies when it comes to adding on the fees. Banks will get **$30 billion** this year from customers paying extra for bounced checks, using automated teller machines, and other added charges. Credit-card issuers will rake in an estimated **$20 billon** in extra charges such as late-payment fees, which have been rising. And that doesn't even include fees that online brokers charge small-time investors.

State Governments

$40 Billion

from various legislative acts   Politicians don't like to raise taxes—so they're hiking fees instead. To close budget gaps, states levied **$2.6 billion** in new charges this year, on top of **$37 billion** they were already collecting. The new fees include higher penalties for driving without carrying a license, court filing fees, late bar-closing fees, and such absurdities as in Alaska, where anyone who wants to drive on new tires now has to pay the government $2.50 per tire.

Telecom

$33 Billion

for wireless, long-distance, and cable   Setup fees. Change-of-service fees. Service-termination fees. Directory-assistance fees. Regulatory assessment fees. Number-portability fees. Cable hookup and equipment fees. Telecom and cable companies have been adding on numerous extra charges to boost revenues and cover expenses. All told, fees add **20%** to the cost of wireless service, **15%** to the cost of long distance, and at least **5%** to cable and satellite service.

Travel

$17 Billion

for hotels and airlines   That advertised $200 flight could cost a lot more, once you pay airport-security fees, landing fees, and fuel surcharges. Changing your reservation could cost $100. Some airlines now charge even for food on certain flights. Such fees bring the industry **$16 billon**. Once you reach your destination, don't be surprised if your hotel tacks on extra for using the exercise room, accepting packages, or cleaning your room. Total hotel fee revenues: **$1 billion.**

Other Industries

Varies

More and more industries are getting in on the fee racket. Some examples: Retailers such as Target and Best Buy force shoppers to shell out **15%** of a product's price for the privilege of returning expensive electronic items. Package-delivery companies charge extra for delivery to remote areas, for customers mislabeling or using the wrong packaging, and even for the gas used by the companies' trains, trucks, and airplanes. Approximate cost to customers: **$4 billion.**

Data: National Conference of State Legislatures, PricewaterhouseCoopers, Saveonphone.com, companies, local officials, AFMS Transportation Management Group, UBS Warburg, Air Transport Assn., SJ Consulting Group, Consumer Federation of America, Wireless Consumers Alliance, R.K. Hammer, *BusinessWeek*

Reprinted from 09/23/03 issue of *Business Week* by special permission, Copyright © 2003 by the McGraw-Hill Companies, Inc.

The U.S. economy has become sneaky. Inflation is officially low, but Americans face an ever-growing mountain of extra charges that are pushing up the true cost of purchases. No area is safe, from retail to finance to travel to sports. "You have companies charging fees for things that were free on an unprecedented scale," says Claes G. Fornell, marketing professor at the University of Michigan Business School.

The extra hits—each one typically small by itself—add up to big money. . . . AT&T could bring in as much as $475 million by charging its long-distance customers a new 99¢ monthly "regulatory assessment fee." Fresh fees for services such as housekeeping will generate $100 million for hotels this year, according to PriceWaterhouseCoopers. Fees on consumers who pay bills online bring banks an estimated $2 billion. And credit-card late-payment fees—up by 11% over the past year, on average—could reach an astonishing $11 billion this year, estimates investment bank R. K. Hammer.

The fee frenzy is mainly an attempt by Corporate America to escape the brutal price wars of the past few years. Companies can't raise list prices without losing business, so they are burying higher charges in the fine print instead. "It's much easier to raise a price through obscure fees and surcharges than it is to raise a sales price," says Stephen Brobeck, executive director of the Consumer Federation of America.

The plethora of stealth charges makes it much harder for consumers to use the Internet to do comparison shopping, as they started to do in the late 1990s. The result is that apparently simple buying decisions are turning into a hopeless and discouraging labyrinth. In response, frustrated consumers are fueling a backlash, including the creation of new vigilante organizations to pressure companies to roll back fees. . . .

The growing significance of extra fees means that inflation is understated. Surprisingly many add-on charges are not reflected in the Bureau of Labor Statistics consumer price index. One reason is that many companies, especially in airlines and telecom, haven't provided the BLS with a full breakdown of their charges. In addition, fees for such things as credit-card late payments and airline-ticket changes—both rising—are not included in the government's figures. The implication: Fears of deflation may be overblown. Instead, the true rate of inflation, so important for setting monetary policy, is probably higher than the 2% or so that the BLS is reporting.

State and local governments are also willing participants in the fee game. Rather than hike taxes, politicians are hitting up Americans with a bewildering array of fees, fines, and penalties. Cash-strapped states will pull in $2.6 billion in new revenues this year by raising more than 200 different fees on everything from fishing licenses to fingerprint processing to driving with new tires. On Aug. 15, the fine for driving without possession of a driver's license in New Jersey jumped to $173, up from $44. Some of the charges are ridiculous: With some exceptions, blind Massachusetts residents will now have to shell out $10 once, and $15 every five years, for certification that proves they are legally blind.

> It's not just Big Business. Government plays the game, too. This year, states brought in new revenues by jacking up 200 different fees.

Already, the new wave of consumer outrage is having serious consequences for politicians. One reason California Governor Gray Davis lost so much support was the popular outrage after he hiked car-registration fees that he had cut several years ago. They will triple this year, to an average of $234 annually, up from $76.

Corporations are feeling the heat as well. A string of suits involving fee abuses filed by class-action lawyers, state attorneys general, and private groups like the AARP are under way. New York State Attorney General Eliot Spitzer made Sears, Roebuck & Co. and EchoStar Communications Corp. pay millions of dollars to settle claims of excessive surcharges on recycling car batteries and undisclosed satellite-service termination fees. "We were not aware New York had a law capping the fee, and once we knew we changed it almost immediately," says Sears spokesman Bill Masterson. Echostar points out that there was no finding of wrongdoing and that it settled to avoid costly litigation. And a California Superior Court judge has ordered MasterCard and Visa to refund $800 million to customers for charging hidden fees on purchases made in foreign currencies. Visa denies the charges and is fighting the ruling. MasterCard plans to appeal the suggested restitution procedures.

There are other signs that popular dissatisfaction with fees may finally be having an impact. Fees for using ATMs have been a bane of consumers for years. On Sept. 3, Washington Mutual, one of the most aggressive retail

---

FEE FRENZY: THE HIDDEN ECONOMIC COSTS

Price Transparency Makes it difficult to compare prices on the Internet because many charges aren't reflected

Confusion Frustrates consumers by creating an opaque labyrinth of seemingly arbitrary charges

Policy Creates stealth inflation, which potentially distorts economic policymaking

Waste Diverts corporate resources into coming up with new, more complicated ways to charge fees

Data: *BusinessWeek*

HOW TO STAND UP TO THE NICKEL-AND-DIMERS

In a world of fees gone wild, what's a consumer to do? In some industries, such as banking, complaining customers can sometimes get fees rolled back. In others, such as telecom, it may be best to seek out competitors without fees. When a charge seems especially underhanded, an individual may want to join a consumer-action group.

In retail banking, consumers can get around certain fees if they're willing to give up some services. The first step is to get educated: Ask about the pricing and fee structure before signing up for a service. It may be possible, for example, to avoid checking-account fees, which can be as high as $20 a month, by signing up for direct deposit or forgoing the return of canceled checks.

But don't stop there. Given industry competition, banks are often willing to reduce other fees when faced with a determined customer. Call to question unreasonable or inflated charges. "In a marketplace where prices are increasingly negotiable, complaining consumers have a fair chance of persuading sellers to reduce or eliminate individual fees," says Stephen Brobeck, executive director of the Consumer Federation of America.

Credit-card companies often will waive late fees for longtime cardholders in good standing when requested. You also have some clout when it comes to annual credit-card fees: Call the company and ask about the costs of other cards it offers. You may get a better deal by switching.

An effective option, of course, is to change companies when dissatisfied with fees. "The must successful consumers are the ones willing to walk away," says Matthew Smith, founder of complaints.com, an online databank of consumer gripws. Major long-distance phone carriers AT&T, Sprint, and MCI introduced new fees this summer and may be faced with a customer exodus once people discover that low-priced long-distance carriers such as TCI and ZoneLD are just as good—and they "don't have the same fees," says Bill Hardekopf, CEO of SaveOnPhone.com, a consumer Web site. SaveOnPhone.com is one of the many vigilantes that have popped up all over the Web to police extra charges. This site helps consumers shop for cheap long-distance service by comparing carrier plans, providing a rate calculator, and offering consumer tips. Phone-bill-alert.com asks consumers to watch their phone bill and report any fee increases to the site. If the phone companies have violated any regulations, the site will alert the appropriate agencies. Consumers can also earn up to $20 if they are the first to report a rate or fee increase not already listed on the site.

Two more general Web sites, ripoffreport.com and complaints.com, give consumers a place to report and vent their frustration with companies that charge excessive fees.

Finally, outraged individuals can look for help from consumer groups such as Consumers Union or the U.S. Public Interest Research Group. These knowledgeable, politically savvy organizations know how to effect change. Consumers Union, for example, took on Barnes & Noble Inc. and Blockbuster Inc. for the monthly service fees they charged on unused balances on electronic gift cards and certificates. "It's your money; you [or someone] paid in advance, so you shouldn't have to pay a fee," argues Gail K. Hillebrand, an attorney at Consumers Union in San Francisco. The group helped get a law passed in California in July that bans nearly all fees on gift cards and certificates.

Such action may well become more common as frustration with fees grows. If it does, corporations might back off from nickel-and-diming those they are supposed to serve.

By Toddi Gutner in New York

Fed Up with Fees?

Five Steps to Fight Back

1. Call the company's customer-service number and speak with a supervisor. Ask for a description of the company policy.

2. Complain to the supervisor if you're still dissatisfied. Keep good notes on whom you speak with and when. Be persistent.

3. Switch companies if your complaint isn't met with a rollback of fees.

4. If a fee seems particularly unfair, send a complaint to the attorney general, who may sue if there are enough complaints.

5. Join forces with organized groups such as Consumers Union or U.S. PIRG.

banks in the country, stopped levying such charges on users of its ATMS in the New York area, even ones with accounts at other banks. Meanwhile, Congress is weighing tougher disclosure requirements for mutual-fund fees and for mortgage closing costs, which can be hundreds of dollars. "There are incredible abuses out there," says Housing & Urban Development Dept. Secretary Mel Martinez.

Fees have long been a fact of life in some industries, such as financial services and travel. Car renters, for example, are used to having their bills inflated by extra charges, such as gas-tank refill penalties.

But the urge to raise fees has gotten out of hand. One of the worst offenders is the telecom industry, which advertises cheap wireless and long-distance calling plans and then lards on extra charges that add 20% to consumers' cell-phone bills, on average. Many wireless-service providers are charging extra to help pay for new technology to enable customers to switch companies without giving up their phone numbers. Sprint PCS, for example, is charging 18 million customers $1.10 a month, which would amount to $238 million annually. Sprint refuses to confirm or deny the total. AT&T'S regulatory assessment fee, charged to its long-distance customers, covers such items as property taxes and expenses associated with regulatory proceedings.

Phone companies justify their extra fees as the only way to cover expenses without losing customers. "Sprint's recovery of these costs via the surcharges will end when these costs are recovered as permitted by law," says spokesman Dan Wilinsky. Adds AT&T spokesman Bob Nersesian: "If you're advertising a higher rate based on your expenses, and your competitors are advertising a lower rate but adding various fees at the bottom of the line, what are you supposed to do?"

Other companies use charges to weed out unprofitable customers or to change their behavior. Some airlines have recently started charging passengers $50 for paper tickets and $25 for every bag over 50 pounds. Ameritrade's $2 fee for monthly statements encourages people to wait for free quarterly statements or to get updates on their accounts online. And most online brokerages impose an extra fee on small-time investors who do not make a minimum number of trades. E*Trade Group Inc. and TD Waterhouse introduced in 2001 "maintenance" fees on brokerage accounts. "Our customers have access to streaming quotes, a rich set of research tools," says Connie Dotson, E*Trade's chief communications officer. "If the account itself doesn't generate the revenues to offset the cost, then for that value we charge a maintenance fee."

Package-delivery companies such as United Parcel Service Inc. and FedEx Corp. have offset increased expenses by adding on fee after fee over the past few years. Starting in 1999, package-delivery companies charged $1 per package for deliveries to remote areas. Now, they tack on "fuel surcharges" for the gas in the planes, trains, and trucks used to deliver packages. These fees are broken out on bills for regular customers, though not always for infrequent ones. Indeed, Airborne Inc. has listed a 25¢ charge for handwritten airbills on its Web site even though the company says it doesn't charge it. "It covers us in case we do decide to charge the fee in the future," says spokesman Robert Mintz.

In the retail sector, fees take a different form. Target Corp. and Best Buy Co. make customers pay a "restocking fee" of 15% for the privilege of returning electronics items such as camcorders, laptops, and radar detectors. Although neither Target nor Best Buy will disclose how much they earn from such fees, it's not small change for consumers. Best Buy justifies the penalty as a way to discourage people who would take the camcorder, say, and return it after using it once. Target did not return repeated calls.

So many people have asked about these restocking fees that Massachusetts' consumer-affairs department posted an alert about the practices on the Web in August. It warned that some retailers made people pay such fees even when they bought a defective product. "That's illegal," says Tatum Zuckerman, at the state's consumer hotline.

Not to be outdone, the original leader in fees, financial services, is finding new ways to raise revenue from customers. The growing dependence of banks on fee income has spawned a new breed of consulting, such as at Houston-based Strunk & Associates LLP, which helps banks find new sources of revenue. One example: offering protection against bouncing checks, for a fee. Strunk justifies such fees as a way to improve customer service.

No one can beat the credit-card industry for its fee inventiveness. Deadlines for paying bills have been shortened to as little as two weeks, and they're strictly enforced, producing more late fees. Not coincidentally, the number of credit-card issuers with $35 late fees doubled last year, says Consumer Action. People can avoid late fees by paying their bills over the phone or online. But some banks and credit-card companies charge for that, too. Washington Mutual charges virtually all of its customers a total of $60 a year to pay their bills online. And it costs $15 to pay bills at the last minute over the phone at MBNA Corp. and Providian Financial Corp. MBNA and Providian say it takes staff time to process these payments by phone and that customers can pay online for free.

It does make sense to charge a premium for added services that cost more to provide, rather than force all customers to pay the same amount, whether or not they use the extra services. Splitting out such fees helps keep basic costs low. One example: charging extra for airline food. United Airlines Inc. has been trying out making passengers on certain flights pay $10 for chicken sandwiches supplied by TGI Friday's and meals from Eli's Cheesecake. Northwest Airlines and US Airways Group Inc. have also started to charge for food. "It's proven to be extremely popular," says US Airways spokesman David Castelveter. "Customers have a choice."

But many fees have no such justification, and ultimately, the niggling could cost companies their customers. Consider Natalie Armstrong in Gorham, Me. She and her husband have been back to Sears only once since her husband Lester was ambushed in January by $29 in late-payment fees along with a $1 "service" charge from a Sears credit card for a $14 part for his saw. After he convinced one clerk that his payment was actually on time, the company hit him with $30 more in fees. In the end, he handed over $60 in cash to a salesperson. After being contacted by *Business Week*, Sears pledged to refund the late-fee charges.

> *Consumers are voting with their feet: Add-on charges that have no justification are increasingly driving them away.*

Some banks are backing down after a barrage of criticism. Bank of America stopped charging customers to pay bills online last May when it discovered it could get more of their business if it offered the service for free. Last December, Bank One Corp. ditched a $3 charge for no-frills checking-account customers to use a branch teller when it discovered that irate customers were bolting to rivals. "Imagine if you are a retail store and your goal is to sell sweaters, and you're charging admission," says Charles W. Scharf, president and CEO of retail banking, who changed the policy after he got his job in May, 2002 "It's counterproductive."

Still, many businesses are holding firm. The New York Jets responded to fans outraged over the waiting-list fee by announcing that people lucky enough to get season tickets could deduct the $50 they paid for waiting for them. The goal of the fee, says the Jets, is to prune the list to fans who are genuinely interested in buying tickets, "Some people aren't even alive who are on the list," says spokesman Ron Colangelo.

Nobody figures fees will be eliminated entirely. But as the country recovers from an era of corporate scandal, it's not too much to ask that companies keep prices easy to understand. That way people will know they're getting what they pay for.

With Michael Arndt in Chicago

Best Practice: Defensive Marketing

How a Strong Incumbent Can Protect Its Position

JOHN H. ROBERTS

> *Facing deregulation, the Australian telephone company Telstra developed a marketing strategy that blunted the attack of a potentially powerful new rival.*

Marketing is typically seen as a tool for growth. A company can use it to successfully launch a product, make inroads into a new market, or gain share with existing products in its current market. But for nearly every new product launch, market entrant, or industry upstart grabbing market share, there is an incumbent that must defend its position. If the defender can't hang on to what it has, it loses the foundation on which to build its own growth.

While there has been much research on marketing as an offensive tactic, there has been remarkably little on how strong incumbents can use marketing to preemptively respond to new or anticipated threats, whether they arise because of deregulation, patent expiration, changing technology, or rivals' shifting competitive advantage. And that's a shame, because many of the marketing challenges defenders face have distinct characteristics. For example, an incumbent usually has an installed base of customers, which means the company has detailed information about the customers it wants to keep and how it might keep them. But a new entrant has the advantage of being able to cherry-pick valuable customers, raiding the most fertile segments in the market, while the incumbent has to defend across its entire customer base.

When the Australian telecommunications market was fully deregulated in the late-1990s, state-owned Telstra faced competition for the first time. And its new rival, a joint subsidiary of American company BellSouth and UK company Cable & Wireless, promised to be a formidable contender. Telstra knew it was going to lose significant market share to the newcomer, called Optus; its goal was to both minimize and slow the rate of that loss while retaining its valuable customers.

Telstra adopted a defensive marketing method that allowed it to do just that. Using a model to predict consumers' responses to the rival service (a model that marketing analyst Charles Nelson, marketing professor Pamela Morrison, and I helped develop as consultants to Telstra), the company was able to select from a variety of strategies that ultimately helped to blunt Optus's attack. Telstra's defense was particularly effective because the company initiated it even before Optus began doing business.

In some cases, the method led Telstra to make sharp changes in strategic direction. The company rethought its pricing strategy, for instance, to counter an Optus strength that the customer response model unexpectedly revealed, helping Telstra to retain several points of market share it otherwise would have lost. The strategies described here, though specific to Telstra's situation, offer lessons for any company facing new and potentially damaging competition.

DECIDING WHAT TO FIGHT WITH

Defensive marketing begins with an assessment of the weapons you have available to protect your market position. These include your brand identity, or how customers perceive you; the mix of products and services supporting that identity, including their pricing; and the means of communicating your identity, such as advertising.

The effectiveness of these weapons will depend on several factors, including your status as an incumbent For example, you may decide that your brand identity needs to be modified if you are to retain customers or delay their defection. But this may prove difficult While consumers' perceptions of a new entrant are likely to be malleable, their image of an incumbent is likely to be well formed. The defender may own the perception of "heritage" in the customer's mind—but may also be stuck with that label despite massive advertising outlays aimed at changing it Meanwhile, a new entrant can relatively quickly and easily adopt an image—say, "breath of fresh air"—from an array of branding alternatives.

In other cases, a weapon such as advertising may be *more* effective in the hands of a defender because of the incumbent's size. For example, if the incumbent has ten times the revenue of the new entrant and each puts the same percentage of revenue into advertising, the defender will be able to outshout the newcomer by an order of magnitude, giving it an obvious advantage—at least when communicating messages that aren't intended to entirely reposition a well-established brand.

An assessment of the strengths and weaknesses of your arsenal with help you choose from four types of defensive marketing strategies. A customer defects when the benefits of staying with an incumbent are outweighed by those of switching to a new entrant. And that doesn't necessarily happen right away; an incumbent may be able to delay a customer's switch. Consequently, to hold on to customers, the incumbent can try to increase its perceived advantages in their eyes (a *positive strategy*). In the case of customers who will ultimately switch, the incumbent can try to at least slow the rate of their departure (an *inertia strategy*). Similarly, the incumbent can try to reduce its perceived drawbacks relative to the new rival, again either to retain customers (a *parity strategy*) or to decelerate the loss of them (a *retarding strategy*). With the first two types of strategies, you establish and communicate your points of superiority relative to the new entrant; with the second two, you establish and communicate strategic points of comparability with your rival. (See the exhibit "Choosing the Right Defensive Strategy.")

Telstra identified its areas of superiority and weakness relative to Optus by conducting an economic analysis of the competitive landscape and by using the model for predicting customer responses to both companies' moves. Take the issue of pricing. Telstra had originally planned to meet an anticipated Optus pricing challenge head-on, relying on its greater financial resources to weather a price war. But an economic analysis suggested that pricing was in fact likely to be a source of weakness for Telstra because it had a cost disadvantage. While government regulations stipulated that Telstra charge Optus only the marginal cost of providing capacity to the newcomer on the Telstra network, the incumbent had to bear the entire fixed costs of maintaining the network. Despite Telstra's deep financial resources, a price war clearly wouldn't be a good way to retain customers.

If Telstra had gone ahead and decided, despite its cost disadvantage, to compete with Optus on price, the strategy would have been doubly flawed, as the customer response model revealed. The model allows an incumbent to accurately gauge consumer reactions to both its and the new entrant's marketing actions—and thereby focus its efforts on areas that will be most effective in minimizing the level and rate of market share loss to the new entrant (For a detailed description of the model, go to www.agsm.edu.au/cam-defence.)

In the area of pricing, the model revealed that Telstra's customers, although likely to respond favorably to Optus's low prices, didn't view lower Telstra prices as a strong incentive to stay with the company—possibly because a Telstra price decrease would only raise questions in consumers' minds about why the company hadn't dropped its prices before it had competition.

CHOOSING THE RIGHT DEFENSIVE STRATEGY

Defensive marketing strategies can be categorized by their aims—that is, whether a strategy is designed to retain customers or merely to slow the rate of their switching to a new rival. They can also be categorized by the means to achieve those aims—that is, whether a strategy focuses on the incumbent's strengths or on the rival's perceived strengths.

	Leverage your strengths	Mitigate your rival's strengths
Retain customers	**Positive strategies:** Hold on to customers by emphasizing the perceived advantages of your product, service, or company.	**Parity strategies:** Hold on to customers by matching, neutralizing, or blunting the perceived advantages of the new entrant's product, service, or company.
Slow the rate of customer loss	**Inertial strategies:** Acknowledge that some customers will leave despite your strengths, but offer product or service enhancements that will delay their defection. Emphasize that benefits lost in the switch may be major ones.	**Retarding strategies:** Acknowledge that some customers will leave because of the new entrant's perceived advantages, but offer product or service enhancements that will delay their defection. Emphasize that benefits gained in the switch may be only minor ones.

Realizing its dual weaknesses in this area—hindered from offering better pricing because of its higher cost structure and now realizing that its customers wouldn't value its price cuts as much as Optus's—Telstra adopted a parity strategy in which it created strategically chosen, but quite limited, points of price superiority over Optus. That is, while Optus on average offered lower prices, Telstra's prices were lower on some routes and at certain times of day. This meant that the lower-priced carrier for a given customer depended on that individual's specific calling patterns—a muddied situation in which consumers were less likely to take the big step of switching phone companies on the basis of price.

The success of Telstra's pricing strategy, supported by aggressive advertising, was evident in survey results—when asked whether Telstra or Optus offered cheaper service, many people said they didn't know or "it depends"—and in an assessment by the Australian Consumers' Association, publisher of *Choice* magazine, which declined to recommend either Telstra or Optus as the outright cheapest provider.

Another area of weakness that Telstra needed to counter, this one with a retarding strategy, concerned what might be called the "punishment factor." The model suggested that people would switch more quickly to Optus if they were angry with Telstra and wanted to "teach Telstra a lesson." Telstra moved swiftly to assuage these people with a television advertising campaign that implicitly acknowledged the company's service shortcomings but emphasized its vow to improve. The anthemic jingle proclaimed, "Good, better, best. We will never rest. Until our good is better. And our better best." In mounting this campaign, Telstra leveraged the incumbent's typical advantage of advertising clout. Six months after Optus entered the market, Telstra still had a market share 12 times that of its rival and could afford a major advertising effort.

But this retarding strategy wouldn't have worked if Telstra hadn't backed up its message with improved service. The customer response model indicated that nearly 60% of customers thought that "most people had a major service problem with Telstra." (Interestingly, only 19% reported having experienced a problem themselves—an indication that Telstra, while disappointing a significant number of customers, was actually doing a better job of providing service than it was in communicating its record to customers.) Consequently, Telstra launched a high-profile effort to upgrade and publicize its service efforts—particularly in the area of billing, a hot spot for criticism—as a way to improve customers' experiences and perceptions.

Telstra considered and rejected one inertial strategy. The customer data suggested that consumers' perceptions of reliability were an important driver in the rate of share loss: "Using Optus might be risky" was one of the strongest factors in people's decisions about whether to switch quickly to the new provider. Telstra wondered if it could leverage this risk aversion, as well as its long-established reputation for dependability, to slow customers' defections to Optus. But the market research also showed that customers felt they could easily switch back to Telstra if Optus did not live up to its promise, so Telstra decided not to make any marketing moves based on customers' differing perceptions of reliability.

An inertial strategy that the company did use is one available, in some form, to many incumbents. Based on consumers' positive perceptions of Telstra as a home-grown company, the incumbent (in its advertising copy, press releases, and product support) played up its Australian roots—and, by implication, Optus's foreign owners and recent arrival in the Australian market. This, combined with the established relationship consumers had with Telstra, allowed a somewhat nostalgic feeling of "better the devil you know" to influence consumers' judgments.

DECIDING WHOM TO FIGHT FOR

After having looked at the marketing strategies you can adopt and the weapons you can wield to defend your share, you need to take a closer look at your customers. Individual consumers will differ both in the likelihood that they'll switch to a rival and in the reasons that would prompt them to do so. Furthermore, there are clearly some customers you'd hate to lose more than others.

Therefore, you need to segment your customers based on two variables: their value to you and their vulnerability to being poached by the new entrant (See the exhibit "Value and Vulnerability.") You can identify the customers you are at greatest risk of losing, or the *vulnerables*, by using the customer response model. You can identify the customers you would most like to retain, or the *valuables*, by assessing their direct and indirect effect on your profitability. In Telstra's case, this included, for example, the degree to which customers used the network during nonpeak hours, when there was plenty of system capacity. Incumbents have the advantage of knowing which customers they want to keep because of existing data—for Telstra, its current customers' calling patterns. (At the same time, however, Telstra couldn't easily walk away from the mass market. Unlike Optus, it couldn't select only the most profitable customers, the ones it had identified as valuables.)

So what challenges do you face with each of these customer segments? In the case of customers who are vulnerable but not valuable, none at all: In fact, you *hope* they switch to the new entrant For customers who are not vulnerable and not valuable, you try to make them more valuable by reducing the cost of serving them or getting them to increase their purchase of higher-margin products or services. If that isn't successful, you may actually try to increase their vulnerability to the blandishments of your rival by, say, reducing the services you currently offer that

	Vulnerable	**Not Vulnerable**
Valuable	These profitable customers are unhappy with your company. Work vigorously to *retain them.*	These loyal, profitable customers are currently happy with your company. *Maintain their margins.*
Not Valuable	These unprofitable customers are likely to defect from your company. Let them go, or even *encourage their departure.*	These unprofitable customers are happy with your company. Try to *make them valuable or vulnerable.*

are unprofitable for you. For example, deregulation typically permits companies to eliminate such practices as rate averaging, which in effect subsidizes certain customers at the expense of others through discounts and concessions like extended payment plans.

The big challenge comes with your valuable customers, whether they're vulnerable or not. The goal is to give the valuable-vulnerables a reason to stay without offering the valuable-not vulnerables a benefit that isn't needed to ensure their loyalty. Telstra had to figure out how to price its services in a way that would defend the valuable-vulnerables against efforts by Optus to lure them away without cutting the rates of the valuable-not vulnerables, customers perfectly happy with the current services at the current prices. It is unethical, and sometimes illegal, to offer different deals to different customers, unless the pricing discrepancy is based on the different costs of serving them. But what if Telstra could get the two groups to self-select the desired pricing plan?

To do this, Telstra analyzed the traits of the two segments. One important finding: The valuable-vulnerables were particularly knowledgeable about the services they were paying for, and they were more likely than the valuable-not vulnerables to research alternatives in order to get a good deal. With this in mind, Telstra launched Flexiplans, add-on services costing between $2 and $10 per month, which allowed customers to, say, extend the hours in which they could make calls at the low weekend rate. The packages targeted particular Optus price plans,

as well as times of the day and days of the week that were desired calling times for consumers and times of spare capacity for Telstra. This way, Telstra would always have some routes and times of day in which its services were cheaper than Optus's.

The typical reaction of the inquisitive valuable-vulnerables was to do the math and say, "Yes, I'll be a lot better off even after paying the additional monthly charge." The reaction of the valuable-not vulnerables was to say, "I'm paying enough already, and I don't need any extra services"—even if they would have saved money overall with one of the plans. The extra charge didn't generate much additional revenue for Telstra. What it did do was get only those keen on saving money to apply for the Flexiplan packages—and thereby give them a reason to stick with Telstra.

THE SPOILS OF WAR

Telstra's defensive analyses and strategies helped the company better prepare for Optus's assault by providing accurate estimates of Telstra's potential market share loss. The customer response model indicated that, even given Telstra's use of several defensive strategies, share loss after six months would be more than twice what Telstra's management had originally planned for—nearly 9% rather than the anticipated 4%. The forecast helped the company better allocate its human and capital resources.

For example, Telstra reduced its engineering expenditures so they were in line with the lower physical plant requirements resulting from the reduced market share.

More important, the defensive strategies Telstra employed prevented the share loss from being even worse and helped the company contain any losses to strategic areas it had deemed less important The company's analysis found that the Flexiplan pricing strategy helped Telstra hold on to roughly 4% of the market—representing $28 million in annual revenue—that the company otherwise would have lost. Telstra's "Good, better, best" advertising campaign, designed to prevent the rapid flight of customers angry with the company's past performance, helped it hold on, at least initially, to an additional 3.5% of the market Changes in the way the company managed its large corporate accounts, the cell phone market, and its international calling services also produced significant savings.

Viewing marketing through a defensive lens helped turn what might have been a rout by Optus into a closely fought battle that left Telstra with some losses but the lion's share of the market. Telstra was ready to fight another day. Its preemptive strategy, implemented prior to Optus's launch, had blunted Optus's initial momentum. And once that happened, it was a lot easier for Telstra to defend its customer base in the long, slow trench warfare that followed.

The defender may own the perception of "heritage" in the customer's mind—but may also be stuck with that label despite massive advertising outlays aimed at changing it.

Part 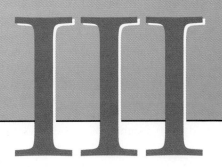III

Managing the Customer Interface

*P*art III of the book focuses on managing the interface between customers and the service organization. It begins with design of an effective service delivery *Process,* specifying how operating and delivery systems link together to create the promised value proposition. Customers are often actively involved in service creation, especially if they are acting as co-producers, and the process becomes their experience. A related task in markets with widely fluctuating demand levels is to balance the level and timing of customer demand against available productive capacity.

The next steps involve two elements of the 8 Ps that are particularly important in high-contact services. *Physical service environments* help to engineer customers' service experiences and provide clues to positioning strategy and service quality. *People* are a defining element of many services. Effective management of frontline employees is key to delivering customer satisfaction, productivity, and competitive advantage.

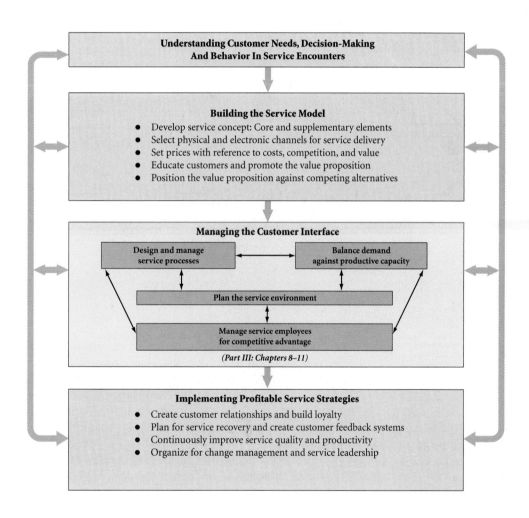

Chapter 8

Designing and Managing Service Processes

> *The new frontier of competitive advantage is the customer interface. Making yours a winner will require the right people and, increasingly, the right machines—on the front lines.*
>
> JEFFREY RAYPORT AND BERNARD JAWORSKI

> *Ultimately, only one thing really matters in service encounters—the customer's perceptions of what occurred.*
>
> RICHARD B. CHASE AND SRIRAM DASU

Processes are the architecture of services. They describe the method and sequence in which service operating systems work, specifying how they link together to create the value proposition that has been promised to customers. In high-contact services, customers themselves are an integral part of the operation and the process becomes their experience. Badly designed processes are likely to annoy customers because they often result in slow, frustrating, and poor-quality service delivery. Similarly, poor processes make it difficult for front-line staff to do their jobs well, result in low productivity, and increase the risk of service failures.

One of the distinctive characteristics of many services is the way in which the customer is involved in their creation and delivery. All too often, however, service design and operational execution seems to ignore the customer perspective, with each step in the process being handled as a discrete event rather than being integrated into a seamless process.

In this chapter, we emphasize the importance for service marketers of understanding how service processes work and where customers fit within the operation. Specifically, we address the following questions:

1. How can service blueprinting be used to design a service and create a satisfying experience for customers?

2. What can be done to reduce the likelihood of failures during service delivery?
3. How can service redesign improve both quality and productivity?
4. Under what circumstances should customers be viewed as co-producers of service, and what are the implications?
5. What factors lead customers to embrace or reject new self-service technologies?
6. What should managers do to control uncooperative or abusive customers?

BLUEPRINTING SERVICES TO CREATE VALUED EXPERIENCES AND PRODUCTIVE OPERATIONS

It's no easy task to create a service, especially one that must be delivered in real time with customers present in the service factory. To design services that are both satisfying for customers and operationally efficient, marketers and operations specialists need to work together. In high-contact services in which employees interact directly with customers, it may also be appropriate to involve human resource experts.

A key tool that we use to design new services (or redesign existing ones) is known as *blueprinting*. It's a more sophisticated version of *flowcharting*, which we introduced in Chapter 3. As we distinguish between these terms in a service context, a flowchart describes an existing process, often in fairly simple form, but a blueprint specifies in some detail how a service process should be constructed.

Perhaps you're wondering where the term *blueprinting* comes from and why we're using it here. The design for a new building or a ship is usually captured on architectural drawings called blueprints, so-called because reproductions have traditionally been printed on special paper and on which all the drawings and annotations appear in blue. These blueprints show what the product should look like and detail the specifications to which it should conform. In contrast to the physical architecture of a building or a piece of equipment, service processes have a largely intangible structure. That makes them all the more difficult to visualize. As Lynn Shostack has pointed out, the same is true of processes such as logistics, industrial engineering, decision theory, and computer systems analysis, each of which employs blueprintlike techniques to describe processes involving flows, sequences, relationships, and dependencies.[1]

Developing a Blueprint

How should you get started on developing a service blueprint? First, you need to identify all the key activities involved in creating and delivering the service in question and then specify the linkages between these activities.[2] Initially, it's best to keep activities relatively aggregated in order to define the "big picture." You can later refine any given activity by "drilling down" to obtain a higher level of detail. In an airline context, for instance, the passenger activity of "boards aircraft" actually represents a series of actions and can be decomposed into such steps as "wait for seat rows to be announced, give agent boarding pass for verification, walk down jetway, enter aircraft, let flight attendant verify boarding pass, find seat, stow carry-on bag, sit down."

A key characteristic of service blueprinting is that it distinguishes between what customers experience "front-stage" and the activities of employees and support processes "backstage," where customers can't see them. Between the two lies what is called the *line of visibility*. Operationally oriented businesses are sometimes so focused on managing backstage activities that they neglect the customer's purely front-stage perspective. Accounting firms, for instance, often have elaborately documented procedures and standards for how to conduct an audit, but may lack clear standards for hosting a meeting with clients or how staff members should answer the telephone.

Service blueprints clarify the interactions between customers and employees, and how these are supported by backstage activities and systems. By clarifying interrelationships among employee roles, operational processes, information technology, and customer interactions, blueprints can facilitate the integration of marketing, operations, and human resource management within a firm. Although there's no single, required way to prepare a service blueprint, we recommended that a consistent approach be used within any one organization. To illustrate blueprinting later in this chapter, we adapt and simplify an approach proposed by Jane Kingman-Brundage.[3]

Blueprinting also gives managers the opportunity to identify potential *fail points* in the process, points where there is a significant risk of things going wrong and diminishing service quality. When managers are aware of these fail points, they are better able to take preventive measures, prepare contingency plans, or both. They can also pinpoint stages in the process at which customers commonly have to wait. Armed with this knowledge, marketing and operational specialists can then develop standards for execution of each activity, including times for completion of a task, maximum wait times between tasks, and scripts to guide interactions between staff members and customers.

Creating a Script for Employees and Customers

A well-planned script should provide a full description of the service encounter and can itself help to identify potential or existing problems in a specific service process. Recall from Chapter 2 the script for teeth cleaning and a simple dental examination involving three players—the patient, the receptionist, and the dental hygienist. Each of these players may be invited to review the script and to identify either missing or superfluous steps, to suggest changes in sequence, or to highlight ways in which developments in either information technology or dental equipment and treatment might require changes in the procedures.

By examining existing scripts, service managers may discover ways to modify the nature of customer and employee roles in order to improve service delivery, increase productivity, and enhance the nature of the customer's experience. As service delivery procedures evolve in response to new technology or other factors, revised scripts may need to be developed.

Blueprinting the Restaurant Experience: A Three-Act Performance

To illustrate blueprinting of a high-contact, people processing service, we examine the experience of dinner for two at Chez Jean, an upscale restaurant that enhances its core food service with a variety of supplementary services (see Figure 8.1, pp. 236–239). A typical rule of thumb in full-service restaurants is that the cost of purchasing the food ingredients represents about 20 to 30 percent of the price of the meal. The balance can be seen as the fees that customers are willing to pay for "renting" a table and chairs in a pleasant setting, the services of food preparation experts and their kitchen equipment, and serving staff to wait on them in the dining room.

The key components of the blueprint, reading from top to bottom, are

1. Definition of standards for each front-stage activity (only a few examples are actually specified in the figure)
2. Physical and other evidence for front-stage activities (specified for all steps)
3. Principal customer actions (illustrated by pictures)
4. Line of interaction
5. Front-stage actions by customer-contact personnel
6. Line of visibility

7. Backstage actions by customer-contact personnel
8. Support processes involving other service personnel
9. Support processes involving information technology

Reading from left to right, the blueprint prescribes the sequence of actions over time. In Chapter 2, we likened service performances to theater. To emphasize the involvement of human actors in service delivery, we've followed the practice adopted by some service organizations of using pictures to illustrate each of the 14 principal steps involving our two customers (there are other steps not shown), beginning with making a reservation and concluding with departure from the restaurant after the meal. Like many high-contact services involving discrete transactions—as opposed to the continuous delivery found in, say, utility or insurance services—the "restaurant drama" can be divided into three "acts," representing activities that take place before the core product is encountered, delivery of the core product (in this case, the meal), and subsequent activities while still involved with the service provider.

The "stage" or *servicescape* includes both the exterior and interior of the restaurant. Front-stage actions take place in a very visual environment; restaurants are often quite theatrical in their use of physical evidence (such as furnishings, décor, uniforms, lighting, and table settings) and may also employ background music in their efforts to create a themed environment that matches their market positioning.

Act I—Prologue and Introductory Scenes

In this particular drama, Act I begins with a customer making a reservation by telephone with an unseen employee. This action could take place hours or even days in advance of visiting the restaurant. In theatrical terms, the telephone conversation can be likened to a radio drama, with impressions being created by the nature of the respondent's voice, speed of response, and style of the conversation. When our customers arrive at the restaurant, a valet parks their car, they leave their coats in the coatroom, and enjoy a drink in the bar area while waiting for their table. The act concludes with their being escorted to a table and seated.

These five steps constitute the couple's initial experience of the restaurant performance, with each involving an interaction with an employee —by phone or face to face. By the time the two of them reach their table in the dining room, they've been exposed to several supplementary services and have also encountered a sizable cast of characters, including five or more contact personnel, as well as many other customers.

Standards can be set for each service activity, but should be based on a good understanding of guest expectations (remember our discussion in Chapter 2 of how expectations are formed). Below the line of visibility, the blueprint identifies key actions to ensure that each front-stage step is performed in a manner that meets or exceeds those expectations. These actions include recording reservations, handling customers' coats, preparing and delivering food, maintenance of facilities and equipment, training and assignment of staff for each task, and use of information technology to access, input, store, and transfer relevant data.

Act II—Delivery of the Core Product

As the curtain rises on Act II, our customers are finally about to experience the core service they came for. For simplicity, we've condensed the meal into just four scenes. In practice, reviewing the menu and placing the order are two separate activities; meantime, meal service proceeds on a course-by-course basis. If you were actually running a restaurant yourself, you'd need to go into greater detail to identify each of the many steps involved in what is often a tightly scripted drama. Assuming that all goes well, the two guests will have an excellent meal, nicely served in a pleasant atmosphere, and perhaps a fine wine to enhance it. But if the restaurant fails to satisfy their expectations (and those of its many other guests) during Act II, it's going to be in serious trouble. There are numerous potential fail points. Is the menu information complete? Is it intelligible? Is everything listed on the menu actually available

Figure 8.1 Blueprinting a Full-Service Restaurant Experience

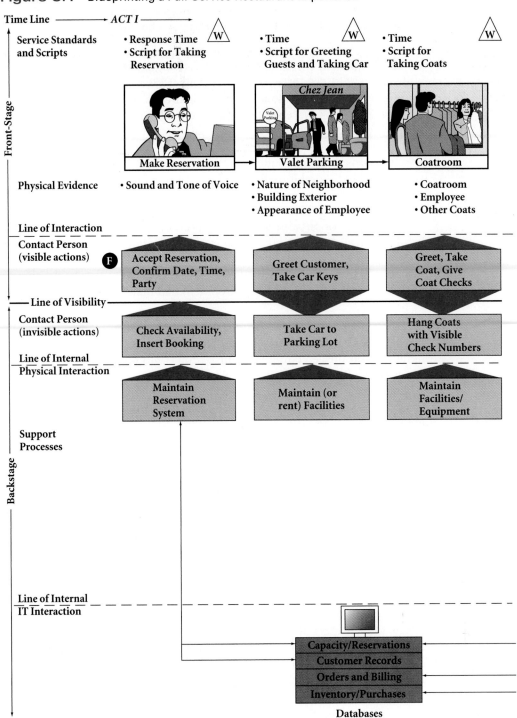

Figure 8.1 (Continued)

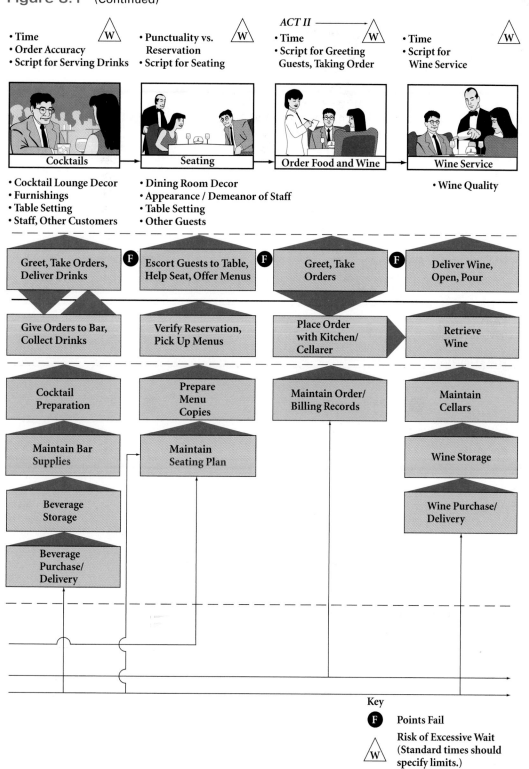

Cocktails

• Time
• Order Accuracy
• Script for Serving Drinks

Seating

• Punctuality vs.
  Reservation
• Script for Seating

ACT II

Order Food and Wine

• Time
• Script for Greeting
  Guests, Taking Order

Wine Service

• Time
• Script for
  Wine Service

• Cocktail Lounge Decor
• Furnishings
• Table Setting
• Staff, Other Customers

• Dining Room Decor
• Appearance / Demeanor of Staff
• Table Setting
• Other Guests

• Wine Quality

Greet, Take Orders,
Deliver Drinks   **F**

Escort Guests to Table,
Help Seat, Offer Menus   **F**

Greet, Take
Orders   **F**

Deliver Wine,
Open, Pour

Give Orders to Bar,
Collect Drinks

Verify Reservation,
Pick Up Menus

Place Order
with Kitchen/
Cellarer

Retrieve
Wine

Cocktail
Preparation

Prepare
Menu
Copies

Maintain Order/
Billing Records

Maintain
Cellars

Maintain Bar
Supplies

Maintain
Seating Plan

Wine Storage

Beverage
Storage

Wine Purchase/
Delivery

Beverage
Purchase/
Delivery

Key

F Points Fail

/W\ Risk of Excessive Wait
(Standard times should
specify limits.)

Figure 8.1 (Continued)

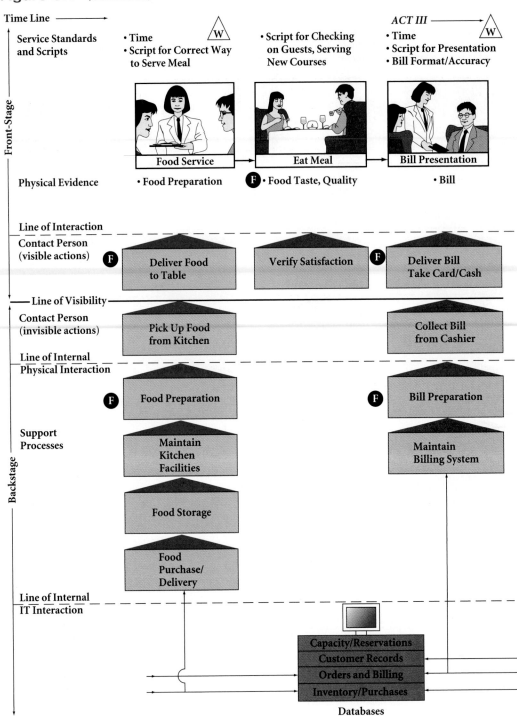

Figure 8.1 (Continued)

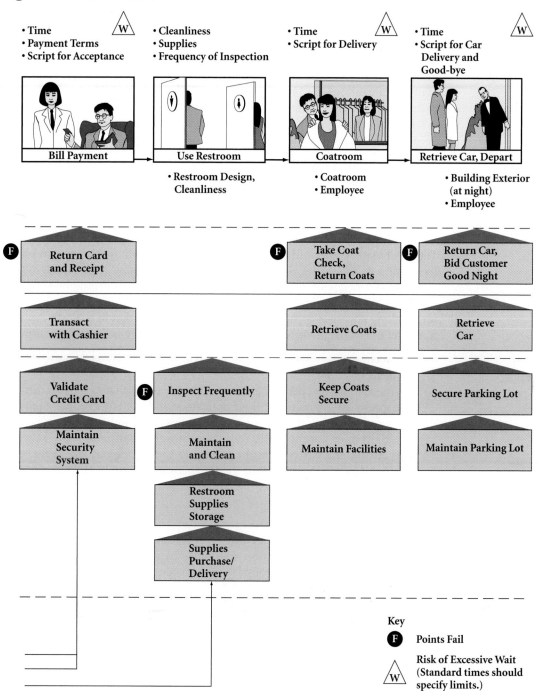

• Time /W\
• Payment Terms
• Script for Acceptance

• Cleanliness
• Supplies
• Frequency of Inspection

• Time /W\
• Script for Delivery

• Time /W\
• Script for Car
  Delivery and
  Good-bye

Bill Payment → **Use Restroom** → **Coatroom** → **Retrieve Car, Depart**

• Restroom Design,
  Cleanliness

• Coatroom
• Employee

• Building Exterior
  (at night)
• Employee

F Return Card and Receipt

F Take Coat Check, Return Coats

F Return Car, Bid Customer Good Night

Transact with Cashier

Retrieve Coats

Retrieve Car

Validate Credit Card

F Inspect Frequently

Keep Coats Secure

Secure Parking Lot

Maintain Security System

Maintain and Clean

Maintain Facilities

Maintain Parking Lot

Restroom Supplies Storage

Supplies Purchase/ Delivery

Key

F Points Fail

/W\ Risk of Excessive Wait
(Standard times should
specify limits.)

this evening? Will explanations and advice be given in a friendly and noncondescending manner for guests who have questions about specific menu items or are unsure about which wine to order?

After our customers decide on their meals, they place their orders with the server, who must then pass on the details to personnel in the kitchen, bar, and billing desk. Mistakes in transmitting information are a frequent cause of quality failures in many organizations. Bad handwriting or unclear verbal requests can lead to delivery of the wrong items altogether—or of the right items incorrectly prepared.

In subsequent scenes of Act II, our customers may evaluate not only the quality of food and drink—the most important dimension of all—but also how promptly it is served (not too promptly, for that might suggest frozen foods cooked by microwave!), and the style of service. A technically correct performance by the server can still be spoiled by such human failures as a disinterested, cold, or ingratiating manner, or by displaying overly casual behavior.

Act III—The Drama Concludes

The meal may be over, but much is still taking place both front-stage and backstage as the drama moves to its close. The core service has now been delivered, and we'll assume that our customers are happily digesting it. Act III should be short. The action in each of the remaining scenes should move smoothly, quickly, and pleasantly, with no shocking surprises at the end. We can hypothesize that in a North American environment, most customers' expectations would probably include the following:

- An accurate, intelligible bill is presented promptly, as soon as the customer requests it.
- Payment is handled politely and expeditiously (with all major credit cards accepted).
- The guests are thanked for their patronage and invited to come again.
- Customers visiting the restrooms find them clean and properly supplied.
- The right coats are promptly retrieved from the coatroom.
- The customer's car is brought promptly to the door in the same condition as when it was left; the attendant thanks them again and bids them a good evening.

Identifying Fail Points

Running a good restaurant is a complex business, and much can go wrong. A good blueprint should draw attention to points in service delivery where things are particularly at risk of going wrong. From a customer perspective, the most serious fail points, marked in our blueprint by **F**, are those that will result in failure to access or enjoy the core product. They involve the reservation (could the customer get through by phone? Was a table available at the desired time and date? Was the reservation recorded accurately?) and seating (Was a table available when promised?).

Since service delivery takes place over time, there is also the possibility of delays between specific actions, requiring the customers to wait. Common locations for such waits are identified on the blueprint by ⚠. Excessive waits will annoy customers. In practice, every step in the process—both front-stage and backstage—has some potential for failures and delays. In fact, failures often lead directly to delays, reflecting orders that were never passed on, or time spent correcting mistakes.

David Maister coined the acronym OTSU ("opportunity to screw up") to highlight the importance of thinking about all the things that might go wrong in delivering a particular type of service.[4] OTSUs are funny when you talk about them. John Cleese made millions of people laugh with his portrayal of an inept hotel manager in the television series *Fawlty Towers*. And Chevy Chase entertained movie audiences for years by playing a customer tortured by inept, rude, or downright cruel service employees. But customers don't always see the humor when the joke is on them. It's only by identifying all the possible OTSUs associated with a particular task that service managers can put together a delivery system that's explicitly designed to avoid such problems.

Setting Service Standards

Through both formal research and on-the-job experience, service managers can learn the nature of customer expectations at each step in the process. As outlined in Chapter 2, customers' expectations range across a spectrum—referred to as the *zone of tolerance*—from desired service (an ideal) to a threshold level of merely adequate service (refer back to Chapter 2, Figure 2.4). Service providers should design standards for each step that are sufficiently high to satisfy and even delight customers; if that's not possible, they will need to modify customer expectations. These standards might include time parameters, the script for a technically correct performance, and prescriptions for appropriate style and demeanor. Standards must be expressed in ways that permit objective measurement.

The opening scenes of a service drama are particularly important, because customers' first impressions can affect their evaluations of quality during later stages of service delivery. Perceptions of service experiences tend to be cumulative.[5] If a couple of things go badly wrong at the outset, customers may simply walk out. Even if they stay, they may now be looking for other things that aren't quite right. On the other hand, if the first steps go really well, customers' zones of tolerance may increase so that they are more willing to overlook minor mistakes later in the service performance. Research by Marriott Hotels indicates that four of the five top factors contributing to customer loyalty come into play during the first 10 minutes of service delivery.[6] And research into the design of doctors' offices and medical procedures suggests that unfavorable initial impressions can lead patients to cancel surgery or even change doctors.[7] However, performance standards should not be allowed to fall off toward the end of service delivery. Other research findings point to the importance of a strong finish and suggest that a service encounter that is perceived to start poorly but then builds in quality will be better rated than one that starts well but declines to end poorly.[8]

Just how often do failures intervene to ruin customers' experience and spoil their good humor? Think back to your own experience. Can you remember occasions on which the experience of a nice meal in Act II was completely spoiled by one or more failures in Act III? Our own informal research among participants in dozens of executive programs has found that the most commonly cited source of dissatisfaction with restaurants is an inability to get the bill quickly at lunchtime, after customers have finished their meal and are ready to leave. This seemingly minor failing, unrelated to the core product, can nevertheless leave a bad taste in a customer's mouth that taints the overall dining experience, even if everything else has gone well. When customers are on a tight time budget, making them wait unnecessarily at any point in the process is akin to stealing their time.

Our restaurant example was deliberately chosen to illustrate a high-contact, people processing service with which you and other readers are likely to be familiar. However, many possession processing services (such as repair or maintenance) and information processing services (such as insurance or accounting) involve far less contact with customers, because much of the action takes place backstage. In these situations, a failure committed front-stage is likely to represent a higher proportion of the customer's service encounters with a company and may therefore be viewed even more seriously, because there are fewer subsequent opportunities to create a favorable impression.

Failure Proofing Can Improve Reliability of Service Processes[9]

Careful analysis of the reasons for failure in service processes often reveals opportunities for "failure proofing" certain activities in order to reduce or even eliminate the risk of errors. Fail-safe methods need to be designed not only for employees but also for customers, especially in services in which the latter participate actively in creation and delivery processes. Service Perspectives 8.1 describes the poka-yoke technique that is widely used to fail-safe service processes.

One of the most useful Total Quality Management (TQM) methods in manufacturing is the application of poka-yoke, or fail-safe methods to prevent errors in manufacturing processes. Richard Chase and Douglas Stewart introduced this concept to fail-safe service processes.

Part of the challenge of implementing poka-yokes in service context is the need to address not only server errors, but also customer errors. Server poka-yokes ensure that service staff do things correctly, as requested, in the right order and at the right speed. Examples include surgeons whose surgical instrument trays have indentations for each instrument. For a given operation, all of the instruments are nested in the tray so it is clear if the surgeon has not removed all instruments from the patient before closing the incision.

Some service firms use poka-yokes to ensure that certain steps or standards in the customer–staff interaction are adhered to. A bank ensures eye contact by requiring tellers to record the customer's eye color on a checklist at the start of a transaction. Some firms place mirrors at the exits of staff areas to foster a neat appearance. Front-line staff can then automatically check their appearance before greeting a customer. At one restaurant, servers place round coasters in front of those diners who have ordered decaffeinated coffee and square coasters in front of the others.

Customer poka-yokes usually focus on preparing customers for the encounter (including getting them to bring the right materials for the transaction and to arrive on time, if applicable), understanding and anticipating their role in the service transaction, and selecting the correct service or transaction. Examples that prepare customers for the encounter include printing dress-code requests on invitations, sending reminders of dental appointments, and printing guidelines on customer cards (e.g., "Please have your account and pin number ready before calling our service reps"). Poka-yokes that address customer errors during the encounter include beepers at automated teller machines (ATMs) so that customers do not forget to take their card, and locks on aircraft lavatory doors that must be engaged in order to switch on the lights.

Designing poka-yokes is part art and part science. Most of the procedures seem trivial, but this is actually a key advantage of this method. It can be used to design frequently occurring service failures out of service processes, and to ensure adherence to certain service standards or service steps.

Source: Adapted from Richard B. Chase and Douglas M. Stewart, "Make Your Service Fail-Safe." *Sloan Management Review* (Spring 1994): 35–44.

SERVICE PROCESS REDESIGN

Service process redesign revitalizes processes that have become outdated. However, that doesn't necessarily mean that the processes were poorly designed in the first place. Rather, changes in technology, customer needs, added service features, and new offerings may have made existing processes crack and creak.[10] Mitchell T. Rabkin, M.D., formerly president of Boston's Beth Israel Hospital (now Beth Israel-Deaconess Medical Center), characterized the problem as "institutional rust" and declared: "Institutions are like steel beams—they tend to rust. What was once smooth and shiny and nice tends to become rusty."[11] He suggested that there were two main reasons for this situation. The first involves changes in the external environment that make existing practices obsolete and require redesign of the underlying processes—or even creation of brand-new processes—in order for the organization to remain relevant and responsive. In health care, such changes may reflect new forms of competition, legislation, technology, health insurance policies, and evolving customer needs.

The second reason for institutional rusting occurs internally. Often, it reflects a natural deterioration of internal processes, creeping bureaucracy, or the evolution of spurious, unofficial standards (see Best Practice in Action 8.1). Symptoms such as extensive information exchange, data redundancy, a high ratio of checking or control activities to value-adding activities, increased exception processing, and growing numbers of customer complaints about inconvenient and unnecessary procedures often indicate that a process is not working well and requires redesign.

One of the distinctive characteristics of Mitchell T. Rabkin's 30-year tenure as president of Boston's Beth Israel Hospital was his policy of routinely visiting all areas of the hospital. He usually did so unannounced and in a low-key fashion. No one working at the hospital was surprised to see Dr. Rabkin drop by at almost any time of the day or night. His natural curiosity gave him unparallel insights into how effectively service procedures were working and the subtle ways in which things could go wrong. As the following story reveals, he discovered that there is often a natural deterioration of messages over time.

> One day, I was in the EU [emergency unit], chatting with a house officer [physician] who was treating a patient with asthma. He was giving her medication through an intravenous drip. I looked at the formula for the medication and asked him, "Why are you using this particular cocktail?" "Oh," he replied, "that's hospital policy." Since I was certain that there was no such policy, I decided to investigate.

What had happened went something like this. A few months earlier, Resident [physician] A says to Intern B, who is observing her treat a patient: "This is what I use for asthma." On the next month's rotation, Intern B says to new Resident C: "This is what Dr. A uses for asthma." The following month, Resident C says to Intern D, "This is what we use for asthma." And finally, within another month, Intern D is telling Resident E, "It's hospital policy to use this medication."

As a result of conversations like these, well-intentioned but unofficial standards keep cropping up. It's a particular problem in a place like this, which isn't burdened by an inhuman policy manual where you must look up the policy for everything you do. We prefer to rely on people's intelligence and judgment and limit written policies to overall, more general issues. One always has to be aware of the growth of institutional rust and to be clear about what is being done and why it is being done.

Source: Christopher Lovelock, *Product Plus*. New York: McGraw-Hill, 1994, p. 355.

Examining blueprints of existing services may suggest opportunities for product improvement that might be achieved by reconfiguring delivery systems, adding or deleting specific elements, or repositioning the service to appeal to other segments. Each year, Avis determines a set of factors that car renters care about the most. The company breaks down the car rental process into more than 100 incremental steps, including making reservations, finding the pickup counter, getting to the car, driving it, returning it, paying the bill, and so forth.[12] Because Avis knows customers' key concerns, it claims it can quickly identify ways to improve their satisfaction. What travelers most desire is to get their rental car quickly and drive away, so the firm has designed its processes to achieve that goal. "We're constantly making little enhancements around the edges," says Scott Deaver, the company's executive vice president—marketing. Obviously, Avis is living up to its tagline, "We Try Harder," which the company has employed for some 40 years. "It's not a slogan," says Deaver. "It's in the DNA of the place."

Managers in charge of service process redesign projects should look for opportunities to achieve a quantum leap in both productivity and service quality at the same time. Restructuring or reengineering the ways in which tasks are performed has significant potential to increase output, especially in many backstage jobs.[13] Redesign efforts typically focus on achieving the following key performance measures: (1) reduced number of service failures, (2) reduced cycle time from customer initiation of a service process to its completion, (3) enhanced productivity, and (4) increased customer satisfaction. Ideally, redesign efforts should achieve all of the four measures simultaneously.

Service process redesign encompasses reconstitution, rearrangement, or substitution of service processes.[14] These efforts can be categorized into a number of types, including:

- *Eliminating non–value-adding steps.* Often, activities at the front-end and back-end processes of services can be streamlined with the goal of focusing on the benefit-producing part of the service encounter. For example, a customer wanting to rent a car is not interested in filling out forms, or processing payment and check of the returned car. Service redesign streamlines these tasks by trying to eliminate non–value-adding steps. The outcomes are typically increased productivity and customer satisfaction.

- *Shifting to self-service.* Significant productivity and sometimes even service quality gains can be achieved by increasing self-service when redesigning services. For example, FedEx succeeded in shifting more than 50 percent of its transactions from its call centers to its web site, thus reducing the number of employees in its call centers by some 20,000 persons.
- *Delivering direct service.* This type of redesign involves bringing the service to the customer instead of bringing the customer to the service firm. This is often done to improve convenience for the customer, but can also result in productivity gains if companies can do away with expensive locations.
- *Bundling services.* Bundling services involves bundling, or grouping, multiple services into one offer, focusing on a well-defined customer group. Bundling can help increase productivity (the bundle is already tailored for a particular segment, making the transaction faster, and the marketing costs of each service are often reduced), while at the same time adding value to the customer through lower transaction costs. It often has a better fit to the needs of the target segment.
- *Redesigning the physical aspects of service processes.* Physical service redesign focuses on the tangible elements of a service process, and includes changes to the service facilities and equipment to improve the service experience. This leads to convenience, and productivity, and often also enhances the satisfaction and productivity of front-line staff.

Table 8.1 summarizes five types of service redesign, provides an overview of their potential benefits for the firm and its customers, and highlights potential challenges

Table 8.1 Five Types of Service Redesign

Approach and Concept	Potential Company Benefits	Potential Customer Benefits	Challenges/Limitations
Elimination of non–value-added steps (streamlines process)	• Improves efficiency • Increases productivity • Increases ability to customize service • Differentiates company	• Improves efficiency, speed • Shifts tasks from customer to service firm • Separates service activation from delivery • Customizes service	• Requires customer education and employee training to implement smoothly and effectively
Self-service (customer assumes role of producer)	• Lowers cost • Improves productivity • Enhances technology reputation • Differentiates company	• Increases speed of service • Improves access • Saves money • Increases perception of control	• Must prepare customers for the role • Limits face-to-face interaction and opportunities to build relationships • Harder to get customer feedback
Direct service (service delivered to the customer's location)	• Eliminates store location limitations • Expands customer base • Differentiates company	• Increases convenience • Improves access	• Imposes logistical burdens • May be costly • Needs credibility and trust
Bundled service (combines multiple services into a package)	• Differentiates company • Aids customer retention • Increases per-capita service use	• Increases convenience • Customizes service	• Requires extensive knowledge of targeted customers • May be perceived as wasteful
Physical service (manipulation of tangibles associated with the service)	• Improves employee satisfaction • Increases productivity • Differentiates company	• Increases convenience • Enhances function • Generates interest	• Easily imitated • Requires expense to effect and maintain • Raises customer expectations for the industry

Source: Adapted from Leonard L. Berry and Sandra K. Lampo, "Teaching an Old Service New Tricks: The Promise of Service Redesign." *Journal of Service Research,* 2, no. 3 (2000): 265–275.

or limitations. You should note that these redesigns are often used in combination. For example, central to Amazon.com's success is the combined appeal of self-service, direct service, and minimization of non–value-added steps through the effective capture of customer preferences, plus shipping and payment data.

Another dimension of service redesign concerns decisions on who should be responsible for delivery of each of the component elements in the blueprint. Increasingly, companies are outsourcing noncore activities to specialist suppliers. IBM employs the term *componentization* to describe the deconstruction (or unbundling) of a company's activities and subsequent reconstruction into *value nets* (as opposed to a value chain), in which value is created by businesses and their suppliers, buyers, and partners by combining and enhancing the component services collectively provided by participants.[15] "Businesses," argue Luba Cherbakov and her colleagues at IBM, "should view themselves as a federation of capabilities that collaborate with other enterprises within a business ecosystem."[16]

THE CUSTOMER AS CO-PRODUCER

Blueprinting helps to specify the role of customers in service delivery and to identify the extent of contact between them and service providers. Blueprinting also clarifies whether the customer's role in a given service process is primarily that of passive recipient or entails active involvement in creating and producing the service.

Levels of Customer Participation

Customer participation refers to the actions and resources supplied by customers during service production and/or delivery, including mental, physical, and even emotional inputs.[17] Some degree of customer participation in service delivery is inevitable in people processing services and in many other services involving real-time contact between customers and providers. However, as Mary Jo Bitner and her colleagues show, the extent of such participation varies widely and can be divided into three broad levels.[18]

Low Participation Level
With a low participation level, employees and systems do all the work. Products tend to be standardized. Payment may be the only required customer input. In situations in which customers come to the service factory, all that is required is the customers' physical presence. Visiting a movie theater or taking a bus are examples. In possession processing services such as routine cleaning or maintenance, customers can remain entirely uninvolved with the process other than providing access to service providers and making payment.

Moderate Participation Level
With a moderate participation level, customer inputs are required to assist the firm in creating and delivering service and in providing a degree of customization. These inputs may include provision of information, personal effort, or even physical possessions. When getting their hair washed and cut, customers must let the cutter know what they want and cooperate during the various steps in the process. If a client wants an accountant to prepare a tax return, she must first pull together information and physical documentation that the accountant can use to prepare the return correctly and then be prepared to respond to any questions that the latter may have.

High Participation level
With a high participation level, customers work actively with the provider to co-produce the service. Service cannot be created apart from the customer's purchase

and active participation. In fact, if customers fail to assume this role effectively and don't perform certain mandatory production tasks, they will jeopardize the quality of the service outcome. Marriage counseling and some health-related services fall into this category, especially those related to improvement of the patient's physical condition, such as rehabilitation or weight loss, in which customers work under professional supervision. Successful delivery of many business-to-business services requires customers and providers to work closely together as members of a team, such as for management consulting and supply chain management services.

Self-Service Technologies

The ultimate form of involvement in service production is for customers to undertake a specific activity themselves, using facilities or systems provider by the service supplier. In effect, the customer's time and effort replaces that of a service employee. In the case of telephone and Internet-based service, customers even provide their own terminals.

Consumers are faced with an array of self-service technologies (SSTs) that allow them to produce a service independent of direct service employee involvement.[19] SSTs include automated banking terminals, self-service scanning at supermarket checkouts and self-service gasoline pumps, automated telephone systems such as phone banking, automated hotel check-out, and numerous Internet-based services.

Information-based services lend themselves particularly well to use of SSTs and include not only such supplementary services as getting information, placing orders and reservations, and making payment, but also delivery of core products in fields such as banking, research, entertainment, and self-paced education. One of the most significant innovations of the Internet era has been the development of online auctions, led by eBay. No human auctioneer is needed as an intermediary between buyers and sellers. Many companies have developed strategies designed to encourage customers to undertake self-service through the World Wide Web. They hope to divert customers from using more expensive alternatives such as direct contact with employees, use of intermediaries such as brokers and travel agents, or voice-to-voice telephone.

Nevertheless, not all customers take advantage of SSTs. Matthew Meuter and his colleagues observe: "For many firms, often the challenge is not managing the technology but rather getting consumers to try the technology."[20]

Psychological Factors in Customer Co-production

The logic of self-service historically relied on an economic rationale, emphasizing the productivity gains and cost savings that result when customers take over work previously performed by employees. In many instances, a portion of the resulting savings is shared with customers in the form of lower prices as an inducement for them to change their behavior.

Given the significant investment in time and money required for firms to design, implement, and manage SSTs, it's critical for service marketers to understand how consumers decide between using an SST option and relying on a human provider. We need to recognize that SSTs present both advantages and disadvantages. In addition to benefiting from time and cost savings, flexibility, convenience of location, greater control over service delivery, and a higher perceived level of customization, customers may also derive fun, enjoyment, and even spontaneous delight from SST usage.[21] However, there's evidence that some consumers see the introduction of SSTs into the service encounters as something of a threat, causing anxiety and stress among those who are uncomfortable using them.[22] Some consumers view service encounters as social experiences and prefer to deal with people, others purposely try to avoid such contact—especially if they have a poor perception of a firm's employees.

Research by James Curran, Matthew Meuter, and Carol Surprenant found that multiple attitudes drive customer intentions to use a specific SST, including global attitudes toward related service technologies, global attitudes toward the specific service firm, and attitudes toward its employees.[23]

What Aspects of SSTs Please or Annoy Customers?

Research suggests that customers both love and hate SSTs.[24] They love SSTs when SSTs bail them out of difficult situations, often because SST machines are conveniently located and accessible 24/7. And of course, as Figure 8.2 shows, a web site is as close as the nearest computer, making this option much more accessible than the company's physical sites. Customers also love SSTs when they perform better than the alternative of being served by a service employee, enabling users to get detailed information and complete transactions faster than they could through face-to-face or telephone contact. Experienced travelers rely on SSTs to save time and effort at airports, rental car facilities, and hotels. As a *Wall Street Journal* article summarized the trend, "Have a Pleasant Trip: Eliminate Human Contact."[25] Consultants Jeffrey Rayport and Bernard Jaworski argue that success at the customer interface requires an understanding of what target customers want from an interaction. Sometimes a well-designed SST can deliver better service than a human being. Said one customer about the experience of purchasing convenience store items from a new model of automated vending machine, "A guy in the store can make a mistake or give you a hard time, but not the machine. I definitely prefer the machine."[26] In short, many customers are still in awe of technology and what it can do for them—when it works well.

However, customers hate SSTs when they fail. Users get angry when they find that machines are out of service, their pin numbers are not accepted, web sites are down, or tracking numbers do not work. Even when SSTs do work, customers are frustrated by poorly designed technologies that make service processes difficult to understand and use. A common complaint is difficulty in navigating one's way around a web site (perhaps you've been frustrated by that problem). Users also get frustrated when they themselves mess up, due to such errors as forgetting their passwords, failing to

Figure 8.2
HSBC, "The World's Local Bank," Brings Its Global Site to Your Local Computer

Courtesy HSBC.

provide information as requested, or simply hitting the wrong button. Self-service logically implies that customers can cause their own dissatisfaction. However, Neeli Bendapudi and Robert Leone note that even when it is the customers' own fault, they may still blame the service provider for not providing a simpler and more user-friendly system, and then, on the next occasion, revert to the traditional human-based system.[27]

Designing a web site to be virtually failure-proof is no easy task and can be very expensive, but it is through such investments that companies create loyal users and active word of mouth. Best Practice in Action 8.2 describes the emphasis on user-friendliness of TLContact's CarePages service. (Note: this innovative company is profiled in depth in the case that appears on pp. 616–625).

A key problem with SSTs is that so few of them incorporate service recovery systems. In too many instances, when the process fails, there is no simple way to recover on the spot. Typically, customers are forced to telephone or make a personal visit to

BEST PRACTICE IN ACTION 8.2
TLContact Creates an Exceptional User Experience with Its CarePages Service

When his sister Sharon's five-day old baby underwent surgery at the University of Michigan Medical Center in early 1998 to correct a life-threatening heart defect, Mark Day was more than a thousand miles away at Stanford, studying for a Ph.D. in engineering. Feeling isolated, knowing nothing about the heart, and wanting to do something useful, Mark turned for medical information to the Internet, which was just beginning to hit its stride. Within a few weeks, he had created a simple web site that family and friends could access. He edited the information he had gathered and loaded it on the site, together with bulletins on Matthew's condition and how the baby was responding to treatment. "It was a very simple site," Mark declared later. "If I had paid somebody else to do it for me, it probably wouldn't have cost more than a few hundred dollars." To minimize the need for emailing, Mark added a bulletin board so that people could send messages to Sharon and her husband, Eric.

To everyone's surprise, the site proved exceptionally popular. News spread by word of mouth and the site recorded hundreds of daily visitors, with more than 200 different people leaving messages for the family. People who confessed that they had never before used the Internet found a way to access the site, follow baby Matthew's progress, and send messages.

Two years and three operations later, Matthew was a happy, healthy toddler. His parents, Eric and Sharon Langshur, decided to create a company, TLContact.com, to commercialize Mark's concept as a service for patients and their families. They invited Mark to join the company as chief technology officer. To ensure quality control and retain intellectual capital, Mark decided to build the necessary software systems in-house, rather than subcontracting the task to outside vendors. He hired a skilled technical team, including programmers and graphic designers.

Recognizing that TLC's patient sites, known as CarePages, would be accessed by a wide array of individuals, many of whom would be under stress and even having their first experience using the Internet, Mark and his team placed a premium on ease of use. He commented, "It's very difficult to create a piece of software that's really user-friendly. It takes an incredible amount of skill, effort, and time to develop something that's usable, functional, and scalable—meaning that it can be expanded and built upon without failing." The total cost of creating the initial functioning web site was close to half a million dollars.

As the company grew, continued investments were made to expand the functionality of the service for patients, visitors, and sponsoring hospitals, to eliminate any problems that users had reported, and to further improve user-friendliness. Enhancements included an option for user feedback, addition of an email notification tool to announce updated news on a CarePage, and the ability to access CarePages through a hospital's own web site. Receiving feedback that users encountered problems when they mistyped a CarePage name and then failed to gain access, TLC added software logic to fix common mistakes, thereby reducing the volume of customer service enquiries. By 2006, TLC had turned the corner financially and was growing rapidly. Heartwarming tributes from satisfied users were pouring in. But work continued to enhance the CarePage experience, with software changes and improvements being made every six to eight weeks.

Source: Christopher Lovelock, "CarePages.com (A)." 2006 (case 18 reproduced on pp. 616–625), www.carepages.com/home.jsp, accessed May 2006.

resolve the problem, which may be exactly what they were trying to avoid in the first place. Mary Jo Bitner suggests that managers should put their firms' SSTs to the test by asking the following basic questions:[28]

- *Does the SST work reliably?* Firms must ensure that SSTs work as dependably as promised and that the design is user friendly for customers. Southwest Airlines' online ticketing services have set a high standard for simplicity and reliability. It boasts the highest percentage of online ticket sales of any airline—clear evidence of customer acceptance.
- *Is the SST better than the interpersonal alternative?* If it doesn't save time or provide ease of access, cost savings, or some other benefit, then customers will continue to use familiar conventional processes. Amazon.com's success reflects its efforts to create a highly personalized, efficient alternative to visiting a retail store.
- *If it fails, what systems are in place to recover?* It's critical for firms to provide systems, structures, and recovery technologies that will enable prompt service recovery when things go wrong. Some banks have a phone beside each ATM, giving customers direct access to a 24-hour customer service center if they have questions or run into difficulties. Supermarkets that have installed self-service check-out lanes usually assign one employee to monitor the lanes; this practice combines security with customer assistance. In telephone-based service systems, well-designed voicemail menus include an option for customers to reach a customer service representative.

Customers as Partial Employees

Some researchers argue that firms should view customers as "partial employees," who can influence the productivity and quality of service processes and outputs.[29] This perspective requires a change in management mindset, as Schneider and Bowen make clear:

> If you think of customers as partial employees, you begin to think very differently about what you hope customers will bring to the service encounter. Now they must bring not only expectations and needs but also relevant service production competencies that will enable them to fill the role of partial employees. The service management challenge deepens accordingly.[30]

They suggest that customers who are offered an opportunity to participate at an active level are more likely to be satisfied—regardless of whether they actually choose the more active role—because they like to be offered a choice.

However, as documented by Stephen Tax, Mark Colgate, and David Bowen, customers cause about one-third of all service problems.[31] Recovering from instances of customer failure, they argue, is difficult—not least because customers and the company may have different views of what caused the problem. Instead, they recommend that firms focus on preventing customer failures by collecting data on problem occurrence, analyzing the root causes, and establishing preventive solutions.

Managing customers effectively as partial employees is another way to avoid such failures. This task requires using the same human resource strategy as managing a firm's paid employees and should follow these four steps:

1. Conduct a "job analysis" of customers' present roles in the business and compare it against the roles that the firm would like them to play.
2. Determine if customers are aware of how they are expected to perform and have the skills needed to perform as required. The more work that customers are expected to do, the greater their need for education on how to perform their roles for best results. The necessary education can be provided in many different ways. Brochures and posted instructions are two widely used approaches. Automated machines often contain detailed operating instructions and diagrams. Many web

sites include an FAQ (frequently asked questions) section. eBay's web site provides detailed instructions for getting started, including on how to submit an item for auction and how to bid for items you might want to buy. See also Chapter 14, pp. 435–441, on how to manage customer reluctance to adopt new service processes.

3. Motivate customers by ensuring that they will be rewarded for performing well (e.g., satisfaction from better quality and more customized output, enjoyment of participating in the actual *process*, a belief that their own productivity speeds the *process* and keeps costs down).

4. Appraise customers' performance regularly. If it is unsatisfactory, seek to change their roles and the procedures in which they are involved. Alternatively, consider "terminating" these customers (nicely, of course) and look for new ones.

Effective human resource management starts with recruitment and selection. The same approach should hold true for "partial employees." So if co-production requires specific skills, firms should target their marketing efforts to recruit new customers who have the competency to perform the necessary tasks.[32] (Many colleges do just this in their student selection process.) When the relationship is not working out, termination remains an option of last resort. Physicians have a legal and ethical duty to help their patients, but the relationship will succeed only if it is mutually cooperative. Sooner or later, most doctors encounter a patient so abusive, noncompliant (in terms of following a prescribed treatment), dishonest, or troublesome that the physician simply has to ask that individual to seek care elsewhere.[33]

DYSFUNCTIONAL CUSTOMER BEHAVIOR DISRUPTS SERVICE PROCESSES

Other customers often form an important element in service encounters. In many people processing services, we expect to find other customers present and to share service facilities with them. Their behavior can contribute positively or negatively to the functioning of specific service delivery processes and may even affect the outcome.

Customers who act in uncooperative or abusive ways are a problem for any organization. However, they have even more potential for mischief in service businesses, particularly those in which many other customers are present in the service factory. As you know from your own experience, other people's behavior can affect your enjoyment of a service. If you like classical music and attend symphony concerts, you expect audience members to remain quiet during the performance, not spoiling the experience for others by talking, coughing loudly, or failing to turn off their cell phones. By contrast, a silent audience would be deadly during a rock concert or team sports event, where active audience participation adds to the excitement. There's a fine line, however, between spectator enthusiasm and abusive behavior by supporters of rival sports teams. Firms that fail to deal effectively with customer misbehavior risk damaging their relationships with all the other customers they'd like to keep.

Addressing the Challenge of Jaycustomers[34]

Visitors to North America from other English-speaking countries are often puzzled by the term *jaywalker*, a distinctively American word used to describe people who cross streets at unauthorized places or in a dangerous manner. The prefix "jay" comes from a nineteenth-century slang term for a stupid person. We can create a whole vocabulary of derogatory terms by adding the prefix "jay" to existing nouns and verbs. How about *jaycustomer*, for example, to denote someone who "jayuses" a service or "jayconsumes" a physical product (and then "jaydisposes" of it afterwards)? We define a *jaycustomer* as one who acts in a thoughtless or abusive way, causing problems for the firm, its employees, and other customers.

Every service has its share of jaycustomers, but opinions on this topic seem to polarize around two opposing views of the situation. One is denial: "The customer is king and can do no wrong." The other view sees the marketplace of customers as positively overpopulated with nasty people who cannot be trusted to behave in ways that self-respecting service providers should expect and require. The first viewpoint has received wide publicity in gung-ho management books and in motivational presentations to captive groups of employees. However, the second view often appears to be dominant among cynical managers and employees who have been burned at some point by customer misbehavior. As with so many opposing viewpoints in life, there are important grains of truth in both perspectives. What is clear, however, is that no self-respecting firm wants an ongoing relationship with an abusive customer.

Six Types of Jaycustomers

Jaycustomers are undesirable. At worst, a firm needs to control or prevent their abusive behavior. At best, it would like to avoid attracting them in the first place. Defining the problem is the first step in resolving it, so let's start by considering the different segments of jaycustomers who prey on providers of both goods and services. We've identified six broad categories and given them generic names, but many customer contact personnel have come up with their own special terms. As you reflect on these categories, you may be temped to add a few more of your own.

The Thief

The thief jaycustomer has no intention of paying and sets out to steal goods and services (or to pay less than full price by switching price tickets, or contesting bills on baseless grounds). Shoplifting is a major problem in retail stores. What retailers euphemistically call "shrinkage" is estimated to cost them huge sums of money in annual revenues. Many services lend themselves to clever schemes for avoiding payment. For those with technical skills, it's sometimes possible to bypass electricity meters, access telephone lines free of charge, or circumvent normal cable TV feeds. Riding free on public transportation, sneaking into movie theaters, or not paying for restaurant meals are also popular. And we mustn't forget the use of fraudulent forms of payment such as stolen credit cards or checks drawn on accounts without any funds. Finding out how people steal a service is the first step in preventing theft or catching thieves and, where appropriate, prosecuting them. However, managers should try not to alienate honest customers by degrading their service experiences. And provision must be made for honest but absent-minded customers who forget to pay.

The Rulebreaker

Just as highways need safety regulations (including "Don't Jaywalk"), many service businesses need to establish rules of behavior for employees and customers to guide them safely through the various steps of the service encounter. Some of these rules are imposed by government agencies for health and safety reasons. The sign found in many restaurants that states "No shirt, no shoes—no service" demonstrates a health-related regulation. And air travel provides one of the best of examples of rules designed to ensure safety—there are few other environments outside prison where healthy, mentally competent, adult customers are quite so constrained (albeit with good reason).

In addition to enforcing government regulations, suppliers often impose their own rules to facilitate smooth operations, avoid unreasonable demands on employees, prevent misuse of products and facilities, protect themselves legally, and discourage individual customers from misbehaving. Ski resorts, for instance, are getting tough on careless skiers who pose risks to both themselves and others. Collisions can cause serious injury and even kill. So ski patrol members must be safety-oriented and sometimes take on a policing role. Just as dangerous drivers can lose their licenses, so dangerous skiers can lose their lift tickers.

At Vail and Beaver Creek in Colorado, ski patrollers once revoked nearly 400 lift tickets in just a single weekend. At Winter Park near Denver, skiers who lose their passes for dangerous behavior may have to attend a 45-minute safety class before they can get their passes back. Ski patrollers at Vermont's Okemo Mountain may issue warnings to reckless skiers by attaching a bright orange sticker to their lift tickets. If they are pulled over again for inappropriate behavior, such skiers may be escorted off the mountain and banned for a day or more. "We're not trying to be Gestapos on the slopes," says the resort's marketing director, "just trying to educate people."

How should a firm deal with rulebreakers? Much depends on which rules have been broken. In the case of legally enforceable ones—theft, bad debts, trying to take guns on aircraft—the courses of action need to be laid down explicitly to protect employees and to punish or discourage wrongdoing by customers. Company rules are a little more ambiguous. Are they really necessary in the first place? If not, the firm should get rid of them. Do they deal with health and safety? If so, educating customers about the rules should reduce the need for taking corrective action. The same is true for rules designed to protect the comfort and enjoyment of all customers. There are also unwritten social norms such as "thou shalt not cut in line" (although this is a much stronger cultural expectation in the United States or Canada than in many countries, as any visitor to Paris Disneyland can attest). Other customers can often be relied on to help service personnel enforce rules that affect everybody else; they may even take the initiative in doing so.

There are risks attached to making lots of rules. They can make an organization appear bureaucratic and overbearing. And they can transform employees, whose orientation should be service to customers, into police officers who see (or are told to see) their most important task as enforcing all the rules. The fewer the rules, the more explicit the important ones can be.

The Belligerent

You've probably seen him (or her) in a store, at the airport, in a hotel or restaurant—red in the face and shouting angrily, or perhaps icily calm and mouthing off insults, threats, and obscenities. Things don't always work as they should: Machines break down, service is clumsy, customers are ignored, a flight is delayed, an order is delivered incorrectly, staff are unhelpful, a promise is broken. Or perhaps the customer in question is expressing resentment at being told to abide by the rules. Service personnel are often abused, even when they are not to blame. If an employee lacks authority to resolve the problem, the belligerent may become madder still, even to the point of physical attack. Unfortunately, when angry customers rant at service personnel, the latter sometimes respond in kind, thus escalating the confrontation and reducing the likelihood of resolution (Figure 8.3).

Drunkenness and drug abuse add extra layers of complication. Organizations that care about their employees go to great efforts to develop skills in dealing with these difficult situations. Training exercises that involve role-playing help employees develop the self-confidence and assertiveness that they need to deal with upset, belligerent customers (sometimes referred to as "irates"). Employees also need to learn how to defuse anger, calm anxiety, and comfort distress (particularly when there is good reason for the customer to be upset with the organization's performance).

"We seem to live in an age of rage," declare Stephen Grove, Raymond Fisk, and Joby John, noting a general decline in civility.[35] They suggest that rage behaviors are learned via socialization as appropriate responses to certain situations. Research by Roger Bougie and his colleagues determined that anger and dissatisfaction are qualitatively different emotions. Whereas dissatisfied customers had a feeling of unfulfillment or "missing out" and wanted to find out who or what was responsible for the event, angry customers were thinking how unfair the situation was, sought to get back at the organization, and wanted to hurt someone.[36]

Figure 8.3
Confrontations Between Customers and Service Employees Can Easily Escalate

The problem of "air rage" has attracted particular attention in recent years because of the risks that it poses to innocent people (see Service Perspectives 8.2). Blair Berkley and Mohammad Ala note that even before the events of September 11, 2001, violent passengers were considered to be the number-one security concern in the airline industry.[37]

What should an employee do when an aggressive customer brushes off attempts to defuse the situation? In a public environment, one priority should be to move the person away from other customers. Sometimes supervisors may have to arbitrate disputes between customers and staff members; at other times, they need to stand behind the employee's actions. If a customer has physically assaulted an employee, it may be necessary to summon security officers or the police. Some firms try to conceal such events, fearing bad publicity. Others, however, feel obliged to make a public stand on behalf of their employees, such as the Body Shop manager who ordered an ill-tempered customer out of the store, telling her, "I won't stand for your rudeness to my staff."

Telephone rudeness poses a different challenge. Service personnel have been known to hang up on angry customers, but that action doesn't resolve the problem. Bank customers, for instance, tend to get upset upon learning that checks have been returned because the account is overdrawn (which means they've broken the rules) or that a request for a loan has been denied. One approach for handling customers who continue to berate a telephone-based employee is for the latter to say firmly, "This conversation isn't getting us anywhere. Why don't I call you back in a few minutes when you've had time to digest the information?" In many cases, a break for reflection is exactly what's needed.

Joining the term "road rage"—coined in 1988 to describe angry, aggressive drivers who threaten other road users—is "air rage," describing the behavior of violent, unruly passengers who endanger flight attendants, pilots, and other passengers. Incidents of air rage are perpetrated by only a tiny fraction of all airline passengers—reportedly about 5,000 times a year—but each incident in the air may affect the comfort and safety of hundreds of other people.

Although terrorism is an ongoing concern, out-of-control passengers pose a serious threat to safety, too. On a flight from Orlando, Florida, to London, a drunken passenger smashed a video screen and began ramming a window, telling fellow passengers they were about to "get sucked out and die." The crew strapped him down and the aircraft made an unscheduled landing in Bangor, Maine, where U.S. marshals arrested him. Another unscheduled stop in Bangor involved a drug smuggler flying from Jamaica to the Netherlands. When a balloon filled with cocaine ruptured in his stomach, he went berserk, pounding a bathroom door to pieces and grabbing a female passenger by the throat.

On a flight from London to Spain, a passenger who was already drunk at the time of boarding became angry when a flight attendant told him not to smoke in the lavatory and then refused to serve him another drink. Later, he smashed her over the head with a duty-free vodka bottle before being restrained by other passengers (she required 18 stitches to close the wound). Other dangerous incidents have included throwing hot coffee at flight attendants, head-butting a co-pilot, trying to break into the cockpit, throwing a flight attendant across three rows of seats, and attempting to open an emergency door in flight. On a U.S. domestic flight with a tragic outcome, a violent passenger was restrained and ultimately suffocated by other passengers after he kicked through the cockpit door of an airliner 20 minutes before it was scheduled to land in Salt Lake City, Utah.

A growing number of carriers are taking air rage perpetrators to court. Northwest Airlines permanently blacklisted three violent travelers from flying on its aircraft. British Airways gives out "warning cards" to any passenger who gets dangerously out of control. Celebrities are not immune to air rage. Rock star Courtney Love blamed her "potty mouth" after being arrested on arrival in London for disruptive behavior on board a flight from Los Angeles. Some airlines carry physical restraints to subdue out-of-control passengers until they can be handed over to airport authorities.

In April 2000, the U.S. Congress increased the civil penalty for air rage from $1,100 to $25,000 in an attempt to discourage passengers from misbehaving. Criminal penalties—a $10,000 fine and up to 20 years in jail—can also be imposed for the most serious incidents. Some airlines have been reluctant to publicize this information for fear of appearing confrontational or intimidating. However, the visible implementation of antiterrorist security precautions has made it more acceptable to tighten enforcement of procedures designed to control and punish air rage.

What causes air rage? Psychological feelings of a loss of control, or problems with authority figures may be causal factors for angry behavior in many service settings. Researchers suggest that air travel, in particular, has become increasingly stressful as a result of crowding and longer flights; the airlines themselves may have contributed to the problem by squeezing rows of seats more tightly together and failing to explain delays. Findings suggest that risk factors for air travel stress include anxiety and an anger-prone personality; they also show that traveling on unfamiliar routes is more stressful than traveling on a familiar one. Another factor may be restrictions on smoking. However, alcohol abuse underlies a majority of incidents.

Airlines are training their employees to handle violent individuals and to spot problem passengers before they start causing serious problems. Some carriers offer travelers specific suggestions on how to relax during long flights. And some airlines have considered offering nicotine patches to passengers who are desperate for a smoke but are no longer allowed to light up. Increased security in the air may be curtailing rage behavior on board flights, but concern continues to grow about passenger rage on the ground. An Australian survey of airport employees found that 96 percent of airport staff had experienced air rage at work: 31 percent of agents experienced some form of air rage daily and another 35 percent witnessed it weekly, 70 percent had witnessed a passenger threaten an agent or fellow passenger, 32 percent had seen a passenger physically assault a fellow agent or passenger, and 15 percent of agents reported that they had been physically touched or assaulted by a passenger.

Sources: Based on information from multiple sources, including: Daniel Eisenberg, "Acting Up in the Air." *Time,* December 21, 1998; "Air Rage Capital: Bangor Becomes Nation's Flight Problem Drop Point." *The Baltimore Sun,* syndicated article, September 1999; Melanie Trottman and Chip Cummins, "Passenger's Death Prompts Calls for Improved 'Air Rage' Procedures." *The Wall Street Journal,* September 26, 2000; Blair J. Berkley and Mohammad Ala, "Identifying and Controlling Threatening Airline Passengers." *Cornell Hotel and Restaurant Administration Quarterly,* 42 (August–September 2001): 6–24; www.airsafe.com/issues/rage.htm, accessed January 16, 2006; Australian Services Union, www.asu.asn.au/media/airlines_general/20031021_airrage.html, accessed January 16, 2006.

The Family Feuders

People who get into arguments (or worse) with other customers—often members of their own family—make up a subcategory of belligerents we call "family feuders." Employee intervention may calm the situation or may actually make it worse. Some situations require detailed analysis and a carefully measured response. Others, such as customers starting a food fight in a nice restaurant (yes, such things do happen), require almost instantaneous response. Service managers in these situations need to be prepared to think on their feet and act fast.

The Vandal

The level of physical abuse to which service facilities and equipment can be subjected is truly astonishing. Soft drinks are poured into bank cash machines; graffiti are scrawled on both interior and exterior surfaces; burn holes from cigarettes scar carpets, tablecloths, and bedcovers; bus seats are slashed and hotel furniture broken; telephone handsets are torn off; customers' cars are vandalized; glass is smashed and fabrics are torn. The list is almost endless. Customers don't cause all of the damage, of course. Bored or drunk young people are the source of much exterior vandalism. And disgruntled employees have been known to commit sabotage. But much of the problem does originate with paying customers who choose to misbehave. Alcohol and drugs are sometimes the cause, psychological problems may contribute, and carelessness can play a role. There are also occasions when unhappy customers, feeling mistreated by the service provider, try to take revenge in some way.

The best cure for vandalism is prevention. Improved security discourages some vandals. Good lighting helps, as does open design of public areas. Companies can choose pleasing yet vandal-resistant surfaces, protective coverings for equipment, and rugged furnishings. Educating customers on how to use equipment properly (rather than fighting with it) and providing warnings about fragile objects can reduce the likelihood of abuse or careless handling. And there are economic sanctions: security deposits or signed agreements in which customers agree to pay for any damage they cause.

What should managers do if prevention fails and damage is done? If the perpetrator is caught, they should first clarify whether there are any extenuating circumstances (because accidents do happen). Sanctions for deliberate damage can range from a warning to prosecution. As far as the physical damage itself is concerned, it's best to fix it fast (within any constraints imposed by legal or insurance considerations). The general manager of a bus company had the right idea when he said, "If one of our buses is vandalized, whether it's a broken window, a slashed seat, or graffiti on the ceiling, we take it out of service immediately, so nobody sees it. Otherwise you just give the same idea to five other characters who were too dumb to think of it in the first place!"

The Deadbeat

Leaving aside those individuals who never intended to pay in the first place (our term for them is "the thief"), there are many reasons why customers fail to pay for services they have received. Once again, preventive action is better than a cure. A growing number of firms insist on prepayment. Any form of ticket sale is a good example of this. Direct marketing organizations ask for your credit card number as they take your order, as do most hotels when you make a reservation. The next best thing is to present the customer with a bill immediately upon completion of service. If the bill is to be sent by mail, the firm should send it fast, while the service is still fresh in the customer's mind.

Not every apparent delinquent is a hopeless deadbeat. Perhaps there's good reason for the delay, and acceptable payment arrangements can be worked out. A key question is whether such a personalized approach can be cost-justified, relative to the results obtained by purchasing the services of a collection agency. There may be other considerations, too. If the client's problems are only temporary, what is the long-term value of maintaining the relationship? Will it create positive goodwill and

To learn more about dysfunctional customer behavior in the hospitality industry, Lloyd Harris and Kate Reynolds of Cardiff University in Wales developed a research project to identify and categorize different types of misconduct. Open-ended interviews, typically lasting one hour (but sometimes longer) were conducted with 31 managers, 46 front-line employees, and 29 customers. These interviews took place in 19 hotels (all of which had restaurants and bars), 13 restaurants, and 16 bars. A purposive sampling plan was employed, with the goal of selecting informants with extensive participation in and insights of service encounters. All informants had encountered—or had perpetrated—what could be considered as jaycustomer behavior and were invited to give details of specific incidents. In total, the 106 respondents generated 417 critical incidents.

Based on analysis of these incidents, Harris and Reynolds codified eight types of behavior:

1. *Compensation letter writers*, who deliberately and fraudulently write to centralized customer service departments with largely unjustified complaints in anticipation of receiving a check or gift voucher

2. *Undesirable customers*, whose behavior falls into three subgroups: (a) irritating behavior by "jaykids" and "jayfamilies"; (b) criminal behavior, typically involving drug sales or prostitution; and (c) homeless individuals who use an organization's facilities and steal other customers' refreshments.

3. *Property abusers*, who vandalized facilities and stole items—most often to keep as souvenirs

4. *[Off-duty] service workers*, who know how to work the system to their own advantage as customers and deliberately disrupt service encounters, either for financial gain or simply to cause problems for front-line staff

5. *Vindictive customers*, who are violent toward people or property, possibly because of some perceived injustice

6. *Oral abusers*, including professional complainers seeking compensation and "ego hunters" who take pleasure from offending front-line staff and other customers

7. *Physical abusers*, who physically harm front-line staff

8. *Sexual predators*—often acting in groups—who engage in sexual harassment of front-line personnel either verbally or behaviorally

Some of these behaviors, such as letter writing and property abuse, are covert in nature (that is, not evident to others at the time they are committed). Certain underlying causes assert themselves across multiple categories; they include desire for personal gain, drunkenness, personal psychological problems, and negative group dynamics.

Table A shows the percentage of employees and customers reporting incidents within each category. Rather remarkably, with the exception of the "undesirable customers" category, the incidents in the customer column are all self-reports of the respondents' own misbehavior.

Table A Percentage of Respondents Reporting Incidents by Category

CATEGORY	EMPLOYEES	CUSTOMERS
Compensation letter writers	30%	20%
Undesirable customers	39	47
Property abusers	51	20
[Off-duty] service workers	11	11
Vindictive customers	30	22
Oral abusers	92	70
Physical abusers	49	20
Sexual predators	38	0

The verbatim reports of jaycustomer behavior recorded in this study make somber—even scary—reading. In particular, they demonstrate especially the challenges posed to management and staff by manipulative customers seeking personal financial gain and by the abusive behavior of individuals, sometimes acting in groups and fueled by alcohol, who appear to be unconstrained by traditional societal norms.

Source: Adapted from Lloyd C. Harris and Kate L. Reynolds, "Jaycustomer Behavior: An Exploration of Types and Motives in the Hospitality Industry." *Journal of Services Marketing*, 18, no. 5 (2004): 339–357.

word of mouth to help the customer work things out? These decisions are judgment calls, but if creating and maintaining long-term relationships is the firm's ultimate goal, they bear exploration.

Consequences of Dysfunctional Customer Behavior

Lloyd Harris and Kate Reynolds emphasize that dysfunctional customer behavior has consequences for staff working front-stage, for other customers, and for the organization itself.[38] Employees who are abused may not only find their mood or temper negatively affected in the short run; they may eventually suffer long-term psychological damage. Their own behavior, too, may take on negative dimensions, such as taking revenge on abusive customers. Staff morale can be hurt, with implications for both productivity and quality.

The consequences for customers can take both positive and negative forms. Other customers may rally to the support of an employee whom they perceive as having been abused; however, bad behavior can also be contagious, leading a bad situation to escalate as others join in. More broadly, being exposed to negative incidents can spoil the consumption experience for many customers, even leading them to terminate their use of the service in question. Companies suffer financially when demotivated employees no longer work as efficiently and effectively as before, or when employees are forced to take medical leave. There may also be direct financial losses from restoring stolen or damaged property, legal costs, and paying fraudulent claims.

As suggested by the earlier discussion of air rage, the nature of jaycustomer behavior is likely to be shaped by the characteristics of the service industry in which it occurs. Research Insights 8.1 reports on a study of jaycustomers in the hospitality industry.

Implications for Service Design and Management

When customers come to the service factory and interact with service personnel and facilities, how they behave may have crucial implications for the effectiveness and profitability of the organization. The stakes are raised further in a high-contact environment in which many other customers are present simultaneously. Some jaycustomer behavior is premeditated, but some is situational. Designing a process that minimizes the risk of failure, eliminates steps that add no value for customers, avoids undesired waits, and maintains a comfortable physical environment may help reduce some of the factors that generate customer anger and frustration.

CONCLUSION

In this chapter, we emphasized the importance of designing and managing service processes, which are central in creating the service product and significantly shape the customer experience. We covered in-depth blueprinting as a powerful to understand, document, analyze, and improve service processes. Blueprinting helps to identify and reduce service fail points, and provides important insights for service process redesign.

An important part of process design is to define the roles customers should play in the production of services. Their level of desired participation needs to be determined and customers need to be motivated and taught to play their part in the service delivery.

REVIEW QUESTIONS

1. What is the role of blueprinting in designing, managing, and redesigning service processes?
2. How can fail-safe procedures be used to reduce service failures?
3. Describe how blueprinting helps to identify the relationship between core and supplementary services.
4. How does creation and evaluation of a service blueprint help managers understand the role of time in service delivery?

5. Why is periodic process redesign necessary, and what are the main types of service process redesign?
6. Why does the customer's role as a co-producer need to be designed into service processes? What are the implications of considering customers as partial employees?
7. Explain what factors make customers like and dislike self-service technologies.
8. What are the different types of jaycustomers, and how can a service firm deal with the behavior of such customers?

APPLICATION EXERCISES

1. Review the blueprint of the restaurant visit in Figure 8.1. Identify several possible OTSUs for each step in the front-stage process. Consider possible causes underlying each potential failure and suggest ways to eliminate or minimize these problems.

2. Prepare a blueprint for a service with which you are familiar. Upon completion, consider (a) what are the tangible cues or indicators of quality from the customer's perspective considering the line of visibility; (b) whether all steps in the process are necessary; (c) the extent to which standardization is possible and advisable throughout the process; (d) the location of potential fail points and how they could be designed out of the process, or what service recovery procedures could be introduced; and (e) what are potential measures of process performance.

3. Observe supermarket shoppers who use self-service check-out lanes and compare them to those who use the services of a checker. What differences do you observe? How many of those conducting self-service scanning appear to run into difficulties, and how do they resolve their problems?

4. Identify one web site that is exceptionally user-friendly and another that is not. What are the factors that make for a satisfying user experience in the first instance and a frustrating one in the second? Specify recommendations for improvements in the second web site.

5. Identify the potential behavior of jaycustomers for a service of your choice. What type of misbehavior(s) are they committing, and what are the implications for (a) the service provider and (b) other customers? How can the service process be designed to minimize or control the specific jaycustomer misbehavior(s) that you have identified?

ENDNOTES

1. See G. Lynn Shostack, "Understanding Services Through Blueprinting." In T. Schwartz et al., *Advances in Services Marketing and Management, 1992.* Greenwich, CT: JAI Press, 1992, pp. 75–90.

2. G. Lynn Shostack, "Designing Services That Deliver." *Harvard Business Review* (January–February 1984): 133–139.

3. Jane Kingman-Brundage, "The ABCs of Service System Blueprinting." In M. J. Bitner and L. A. Crosby (eds.), *Designing a Winning Service Strategy.* Chicago: American Marketing Association, 1989.

4. David Maister, now president of Maister Associates, coined the term OTSU while teaching at Harvard Business School in the 1980s.

5. See for example, Eric J. Arnould and Linda L. Price, "River Magic: Extraordinary Experience and the Extended Service Encounter." *Journal of Consumer Research*, 20 (June 1993): 24–25; Arnould and Price, "Collaring the Cheshire Cat: Studying Customers' Services Experience Through Metaphors." *The Service Industries Journal*, 16 (October 1996): 421–442; Nick Johns and Phil Tyas, "Customer Perceptions of Service Operations: Gestalt, Incident or Mythology?" *The Service Industries Journal*, 17 (July 1997): 474–488.

6. "How Marriott Makes a Great First Impression." *The Service Edge*, 6 (May 1993): 5.

7. Lisa Bannon, "Plastic Surgeons Are Told to Pay More Attention to Appearances." *The Wall Street Journal*, March 15, 1997, p. B1.

8. David E. Hansen and Peter J. Danaher, "Inconsistent Performance During the Service Encounter: What's a Good Start Worth?" *Journal of Service Research*, 1 (Feburary 1999): 227–235; Richard B. Chase and Sriram Dasu, "Want to Perfect Your Company's Service? Use Behavioral Science." *Harvard Business Review*, 79 (June 2001): 78–85.

9. Based in part on Richard B. Chase and Douglas M. Stewart, "Make Your Service Fail-Safe." *Sloan Management Review* (Spring 1994): 35–44.

10. Jochen Wirtz and Monica Tomlin, "Institutionalizing Customer-Driven Learning Through Fully Integrated Customer Feedback Systems." *Managing Service Quality*, 10, no. 4 (2000): 205–215.

11. Mitchell T. Rabkin, cited in Christopher H. Lovelock, *Product Plus.* New York: McGraw-Hill, 1994, pp. 354–355.

12. Thomas Mucha, "The Payoff for Trying Harder." *Business 2.0* (July 2002): 84–86.

13. See, for example, Michael Hammer and James Champy, *Reeingineering the Corporation.* New York: Harper Business, 1993.

14. This section is partially based on Leonard L. Berry and Sandra K. Lampo, "Teaching an Old Service New Tricks—The Promise of Service Redesign." *Journal of Service Research*, 2, no. 3 (February 2000): 265–275. Berry and Lampo identified the following five service redesign concepts: self-service, direct service, preservice, bundled service, and physical service. We expanded some of these concepts in this section to embrace more of the productivity-enhancing aspects of process redesign such as eliminating non–value-adding work steps in all stages of service delivery.

15. D. Bovet and J. Martha, *Breaking the Supply Chain to Unlock Hidden Profits.* New York: John Wiley & Sons, 2000.

16. L. Cherbakov, G. Galambos, R. Harishankar, S. Kalyana, and G. Rackham, "Impact of Service Orientation at the Business Level." *IBM Systems Journal*, 44, no. 4 (2005): 653–668.

17. Amy Risch Rodie and Susan Schultz Klein, "Customer Participation in Services Production and Delivery." In T. A. Schwartz and D. Iacobucci (eds.), *Handbook of Service Marketing and Management.* Thousand Oaks, CA: Sage Publications, 2000, pp. 111–125.

18. Mary Jo Bitner, William T. Faranda, Amy R. Hubbert, and Valarie A. Zeithaml, "Customer Contributions and Roles in Service Delivery." *International Journal of Service Industry Management*, 8, no. 3 (1997): 193–205.

19. Matthew L. Meuter, Amy L. Ostrom, Robert I. Roundtree, and Mary Jo Bitner, "Self-Service Technologies: Understanding Customer Satisfaction with Technology-Based Service Encounters." *Journal of Marketing,* 64 (July 2000): 50–64.

20. Matthew L. Meuter, Mary Jo Bitner, Amy L. Ostrom, and Stephen W. Brown, "Choosing Among Alternative Service Delivery Modes: An Investigation of Customer Trial of Self-Service Technologies." *Journal of Marketing,* 69 (April 2005): 61–83.

21. Pratibha A. Dabholkar, "Consumer Evaluations of New Technology-Based Self-Service Options: An Investigation of Alternative Models of Service Quality." *International Journal of Research in Marketing*, 13 (1996): 29–51; Mary Jo. Bitner, Stephen W. Brown, and Matthew L. Meuter, "Technology Infusion in Service Encounters." *Journal of the Academy of Marketing Science,* 28, no. 1 (2000): 138–149; Pratibha A. Dabholkar, L. Michelle Bobbitt, and Eun-Ju Lee, "Understanding Consumer Motivation and Behavior Related to Self-Scanning in Retailing." *International Journal of Service Industry Management,* 14, no. 1 (2003): 59–95.

22. David G. Mick and Susan Fournier, "Paradoxes of Technology: Consumer Cognizance, Emotions, and Coping Strategies." *Journal of Consumer Research,* 25 (September 1998): 123–143.

23. James M. Curran, Matthew L. Meuter, and Carol G. Surprenant, "Intentions to Use Self-Service Technologies: A Confluence of Multiple Attitudes." *Journal of Service Research,* 5 (February 2003): 209–224.

24. Meuter et al., "Self-Service Technologies" (2000); Mary Jo Bitner, "Self-Service Technologies: What Do Customers Expect?" *Marketing Management* (Spring 2001): 10–11.

25. Kortney Stringer, "Have a Pleasant Trip: Eliminate All Human Contact." *The Wall Street Journal,* October 31, 2002.

26. Jeffrey F. Rayport and Bernard J. Jaworski, "Best Face Forward." *Harvard Business Review,* 82 (December 2004).

27. Neeli Bendapudi and Robert P. Leone, "Psychological Implications of Customer Participation in Co-production." *Journal of Marketing,* 67 (January 2003): 14–28.

28. Bitner, "Self-Service Technologies" (2001).

29. David E. Bowen, "Managing Customers as Human Resources in Service Organizations." *Human Resources Management,* 25, no. 3 (1986): 371–383.

30. Benjamin Schneider and David E. Bowen, *Winning the Service Game.* Boston: Harvard Business School Press, 1995, p. 85.

31. Stephen S. Tax, Mark Colgate, and David E. Bowen, "How to Prevent Customers from Failing." *MIT Sloan Management Review,* 47 (Spring 2006): 30–38.

32. Bonnie Farber Canziani, "Leveraging Customer Competency in Service Firms." *International Journal of Service Industry Management,* 8. no. 1 (1997): 5–25.

33. Kim Painter, "Cutting Ties to Vexing Patients." *USA Today,* January 14, 2003, p. 8D.

34. This section is adapted from Christopher Lovelock, *Product Plus.* New York: McGraw-Hill, 1994, chap. 15.

35. Stephen J. Grove, Raymond P. Fisk, and Joby John, "Surviving in the Age of Rage," *Marketing Management* (March/April 2004): 41–46.

36. Roger Bougie, Rik Pieters, and Marcel Zeelenberg, "Angry Customers Don't Come Back, They Get Back: The Experience and Behavioral Implications of Anger and Dissatisfaction in Services." *Journal of the Academy of Marketing Science,* 31, no. 4 (2003): 377–393.

37. Blair J. Berkley and Mohammad Ala, "Identifying and Controlling Threatening Airline Passengers." *Cornell Hotel and Restaurant Administration Quarterly,* 42 (August–September 2001): 6–24.

38. Lloyd C. Harris and Kate L. Reynolds, "The Consequences of Dysfunctional Customer Behavior." *Journal of Service Research,* 6 (November 2003): 144–161; Lloyd C. Harris and Kate L. Reynolds, "Jaycustomer Behavior: An Exploration of Types and Motives in the Hospitality Industry." *Journal of Services Marketing,* 18, no. 5 (2004): 339–357.

Chapter 9

Balancing Demand and Productive Capacity

> *Balancing the supply and demand sides of a service industry is not easy, and whether a manager does it well or not makes all the difference.*

EARL SASSER

> *They also serve who only stand and wait.*

JOHN MILTON

*F*luctuating demand is a major challenge for many types of capacity-constrained service organizations, including airlines, restaurants, vacation resorts, courier services, consulting firms, theaters, and call centers. These demand fluctuations, which may range in frequency from as long as a season of the year to as short as an hour, play havoc with efficient use of productive assets, thus eroding profitability. By working collaboratively with managers in operations and human resources, service marketers may be able to develop strategies to bring demand and capacity into balance in ways that create benefits for customers as well as improving financial returns for the business.

In this chapter, we consider the nature of demand and supply in services and explore the following questions:

1. What is meant by "capacity" in a service context, and how is it measured?
2. Can variations in demand be predicted and their causes identified?
3. How can capacity management techniques be employed to match variations in demand?
4. What marketing strategies are available to smooth out fluctuations in demand?
5. If customers must wait for service, how can this activity be made less burdensome for them?
6. What is involved in designing an effective reservations system?

Most services are perishable and normally cannot be stockpiled for sale at a later date, posing a challenge for any capacity-constrained service that faces wide swings in demand. The problem is most acute among services that process people or physical possessions—such as transportation, lodging, food service, repair and maintenance, entertainment, and health care. It also affects labor-intensive, information-processing services that face cyclical shifts in demand. Accounting and tax preparation are cases in point.

Effective use of productive capacity is one of the secrets of success in such businesses. The goal should not be to utilize staff, labor, equipment, and facilities as much as possible, but rather to use them as *productively* as possible. At the same time, the search for productivity must not be allowed to undermine service quality and degrade the customer experience.

From Excess Demand to Excess Capacity

The problem is a familiar one. "It's either feast or famine for us!" sighs the manager. "In peak periods, we're disappointing prospective customers by turning them away. And in low periods, our facilities are idle, our employees are standing around looking bored, and we're losing money."

At any given moment, a fixed-capacity service may face one of four conditions (see Figure 9.1):

- *Excess demand.* The level of demand exceeds maximum available capacity, with the result that some customers are denied service and business is lost.
- *Demand exceeds optimum capacity.* No one is turned away, but conditions are crowded and customers are likely to perceive a deterioration in service quality and may feel dissatisfied.
- *Demand and supply are well balanced at the level of optimum capacity.* Staff and facilities are busy without being overworked, and customers receive good service without delays.
- *Excess capacity.* Demand is below optimum capacity and productive resources are underutilized, resulting in low productivity. Low usage also poses a risk that customers may find the experience disappointing or have doubts about the viability of the service.

Figure 9.1
Implications of
Variations in Demand
Relative to Capacity

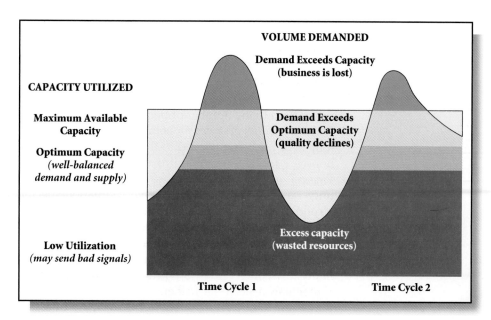

Sometimes optimum and maximum capacities are one and the same. At a live theater or sports performance, a full house is grand, because it stimulates the players and creates a sense of excitement and audience participation. The net result? A more satisfying experience for all. With most other services, however, you probably feel that you get better service if the facility is not operating at full capacity. The quality of restaurant service, for instance, often deteriorates when every table is occupied, because the staff is rushed and there is a greater likelihood of errors or delays. And if you are traveling alone in an aircraft with high-density seating, you tend to feel more comfortable if the seat next to you is empty. When repair and maintenance shops are fully scheduled, delays may result if there is no slack in the system to allow for unexpected problems in completing particular jobs.

There are two basic approaches to the problem of fluctuating demand. One is to adjust the level of capacity to meet variations in demand. This approach requires an understanding of what constitutes productive capacity and how it may be increased or decreased on an incremental basis. The second approach is to manage the level of demand, using marketing strategies to smooth out the peaks and fill in the valleys so as to generate a more consistent flow of requests for service. Many firms use a mix of both approaches.[1]

MANY SERVICE ORGANIZATIONS ARE CAPACITY-CONSTRAINED

There are often limits to a firm's capacity to serve additional customers at any particular time. Service firms may also be constrained in terms of being unable to reduce their productive capacity during periods of low demand. In general, organizations that engage in physical processes such as people or possession processing are more likely to face capacity constraints than those that engage in information-based processes. A radio station, for instance, may be constrained in its geographic reach by the strength of its signal, but within that radius, any number of listeners can tune in to a broadcast.

Defining Productive Capacity

What do we mean by *productive capacity*? The term refers to the resources or assets that a firm can employ to create goods and services. In a service context, productive capacity can take several forms:

1. *Physical facilities designed to contain customers* and used for delivering people processing services or mental stimulus-processing services. Examples include medical clinics, hotels, passenger aircraft, and college classrooms. The primary capacity constraint is likely to be defined in terms of such furnishings as beds, rooms, or seats. In some cases, for health or safety reasons, local regulations may set an upper limit to the number of people allowed in.
2. *Physical facilities designed for storing or processing goods* that either belong to customers or are being offered to them for sale. Examples include pipelines, warehouses, parking lots, and railroad freight wagons.
3. *Physical equipment used to process people, possessions, or information* may embrace a huge range of items and may be very situation-specific—diagnostic equipment, airport security detectors, toll gates, bank ATMs, and "seats" in a call center are among the many items whose absence in sufficient numbers for a given level of demand can bring service to a crawl (or a complete stop).
4. *Labor* is a key element of productive capacity in all high-contact services and many low-contact ones. Staffing levels for restaurant servers, nurses, and call center staff need to be sufficient to meet anticipated demand—otherwise customers are kept waiting or service is rushed. Professional services are especially

dependent on highly skilled staff to create high-value-added, information-based output. Abraham Lincoln captured it well when he remarked that "A lawyer's time and expertise are his stock in trade."

5. *Infrastructure.* Many organizations are dependent on access to sufficient capacity in the public or private infrastructure to be able to deliver quality service to their own customers. Capacity problems of this nature may include congested airways that lead to air traffic restrictions on flights, traffic jams on major highways, and power failures (or "brown-outs" caused by reduced voltage).

Measures of capacity utilization include the number of hours (or percentage of total available time) that facilities, labor, and equipment are productively employed in revenue operation, and the units or percentage of available space (e.g., seats, cubic freight capacity, telecommunications bandwidth) that is utilized in revenue operations. Human beings tend to be far more variable than equipment in their ability to sustain consistent levels of output over time. One tired or poorly trained employee staffing a single station in an assembly-line service operation such as a cafeteria restaurant or a motor vehicle license bureau can slow the entire service to a crawl.

Many services, such as health care or repair and maintenance, involve multiple actions delivered sequentially. What this means is that a service organization's capacity to satisfy demand is constrained by one or more of its physical facilities, equipment, personnel, and the number and sequence of services provided. In a well-planned, well-managed service operation, the capacity of the facility, supporting equipment, and service personnel will be in balance. Similarly, sequential operations will be designed to minimize the likelihood of bottlenecks at any point in the process. Best Practice in Action 9.1 describes how one airline sought to improve its capacity to serve at the check-in stage.

Financial success in capacity-constrained businesses is, in large measure, a function of management's ability to use productive capacity—staff, labor, equipment, and facilities—as efficiently and as profitably as possible. In practice, however, it's difficult to achieve this ideal all the time. Not only do demand levels vary, often randomly, the time and effort required to process each person or thing may vary widely at any point in the process. In general, processing times for people are more variable than for objects or things, reflecting varying levels of preparedness ("I've lost my credit card"), argumentative versus cooperative personalities ("If you won't give me a table with a view, I'll have to ask for your supervisor"), and so forth. However, service tasks are not necessarily homogeneous. In both professional services and repair jobs, diagnosis and treatment times vary according to the nature of the customers' problems.

BEST PRACTICE IN ACTION 9.1
Improving Check-in Service at Logan Airport

To streamline its check-in service at Boston's Logan International Airport, a major airline turned to MIT Professor Richard Larson, who heads a consulting firm called QED. Technicians from QED installed pressure-sensitive rubber mats on the floor in front of the ticket counters. Pressure from each customer's foot upon approaching or leaving the counter recorded the exact time on an electronic device embedded in the mats. From these data, Larson was able to profile the waiting situation at the airline's counters, including average waiting times, how long each transaction took, how many customers waited longer than a given length of time (and at what hours on what days), and even how many bailed out of a long line. Analysis of these data, collected over a long period, yielded information that helped the airline to plan its staffing levels to match more closely the demand levels projected at different times.

Source: Richard Saltus, "Lines, Lines, Lines, Lines. . . The Experts Are Trying to Ease the Wait." *The Boston Globe,* October 5, 1992, pp. 39, 42.

Capacity Levels Can Sometimes Be Stretched or Shrunk

Some capacity is elastic in its ability to absorb extra demand. A subway car, for instance, may offer 40 seats and allow standing room for another 60 passengers with adequate handrail and floor space for all. Yet at rush hours perhaps up to 200 standees can be accommodated under sardine-like conditions. Similarly, the capacity of service personnel can be stretched and may be able to work at high levels of efficiency for short periods of time. However, staff would quickly tire and begin providing inferior service if they had to work that fast all day long.

Even when capacity appears to be fixed, as when it is based on the number of seats, there may still be opportunities to accept extra business at busy times. Some airlines, for instance, increase the capacity of their aircraft by switching to a higher-capacity aircraft on a certain route on a busy day. Similarly, a restaurant may add extra tables and chairs. Upper limits to such practices are often set by safety standards or by the capacity of supporting services, such as the kitchen.

Another strategy for stretching capacity is to utilize the facilities for longer periods. One example is universities that offer evening classes and weekend programs. Alternatively, the average amount of time that customers (or their possessions) spend in process may be reduced. Sometimes this is achieved by minimizing slack time, as when the bill is presented promptly to a group of diners relaxing at the table after a meal. In other instances, it may be achieved by cutting back the level of service—say, offering a simpler menu at busy times of day.

Adjusting Capacity to Match Demand

Another set of options involves tailoring the overall level of capacity to match variations in demand—a strategy that is also known as *chasing demand* There are several actions that managers can take to adjust capacity as needed.[2]

- *Schedule downtime during periods of low demand.* To ensure that 100 percent of capacity is available during peak periods, repair and renovations should be conducted when demand is expected to be low. Employee holidays should also be taken during such periods.
- *Use part-time employees.* Many organizations hire extra workers during their busiest periods. Examples include temporary postal workers and retail store associates during the Christmas season, extra staff for tax-preparation service firms in the spring, and additional hotel employees during holiday periods and major conventions.
- *Rent or share extra facilities and equipment.* To limit investment in fixed assets, a service business may be able to rent extra space or machines at peak times. Firms with complementary demand patterns may enter into formal sharing agreements.
- *Ask customers to share.* Capacity can be stretched by asking customers to share a unit of capacity that is normally dedicated to one individual. For instance, at busy airports and train stations, where the supply of taxis is sometimes insufficient to meet demand, travelers going in the same direction may be given the option of sharing a ride at a reduced rate.
- *Invite customers to perform self-service.* If the number of employees is limited, capacity can be increased by involving customers in co-production of certain tasks. One way to do this is by adding self-service technologies, such as electronic kiosks at airports for airline ticketing and check-in (Figure 9.2) or automated check-out stations at supermarkets.
- *Cross-train employees.* Even when the service delivery system appears to be operating at full capacity, certain physical elements—and their attendant employees—may be underutilized. If employees can be cross-trained to perform a variety of tasks, they can be shifted to bottleneck points as needed,

Figure 9.2
Continental Airlines Boosts Check-in Capacity by Installing Self-Service Ticketing Machines at the Airport

thereby increasing total system capacity. In supermarkets, for instance, the manager may call on stockers to operate cash registers when check-out lines become too long. Likewise, during slow periods, cashiers may be asked to help stock shelves.

Creating Flexible Capacity

Sometimes, the problem lies not in the overall capacity but in the mix that's available to serve the needs of different market segments. For instance, on a given flight, an airline may have too few seats in economy even though there are empty seats in the business class cabin; or a hotel may find itself short of suites one day when standard rooms are still available. One solution lies in designing physical facilities to be flexible. Some hotels build rooms with connecting doors. With the door between two rooms locked, the hotel can sell two bedrooms; with the door unlocked and one of the bedrooms converted into a sitting room, the hotel can now offer a suite.

Boeing, facing stiff competition from Airbus, received what were described, tongue-in-cheek, as "outrageous demands" from prospective customers when it was designing its 777 airliner. The airlines wanted an aircraft in which galleys and lavatories could be relocated, plumbing and all, almost anywhere in the cabin within a matter of hours. Boeing gulped but solved this challenging problem. Airlines can rearrange the passenger cabin of the "Triple Seven" within hours, reconfiguring it with varying numbers of seats allocated among different classes.

Not all unsold productive capacity is wasted. Many firms take a strategic approach to disposition of anticipated surplus capacity, allocating it in advance to build relationships with customers, suppliers, employees, and intermediaries.[3] Possible applications include free trials for prospective customers and for intermediaries who sell to end customers, employee rewards, and bartering with the firm's own suppliers. Among the most widely bartered services are advertising space or airtime, airline seats, and hotel rooms.

Now let's look at the other side of the equation. To control variations in demand for a particular service, managers need to determine what factors govern that demand.

Understanding Patterns of Demand

Research should begin by getting some answers to a series of important questions about the patterns of demand and their underlying causes[4] (Table 9.1).

As you think about some of the seemingly "random" causes, consider how rain and cold affect the use of indoor and outdoor recreational or entertainment services. Then reflect on how heart attacks and births affect the demand for hospital services. Imagine what it is like to be a police officer, firefighter, or ambulance driver—you never know exactly where your next call will come from, nor what the nature of the emergency will be. Finally, consider the impact of natural disasters, such as earthquakes, tornadoes, and hurricanes, not only on emergency services but also for disaster recovery specialists and insurance firms.

Most periodic cycles influencing demand for a particular service vary in length from one day to 12 months. The impact of seasonal cycles is well known and affects demand for a broad array of services. Low demand in the off-season poses significant problems for tourism promoters.

In many instances, multiple cycles may operate simultaneously. For example, demand levels for public transport may vary by time of day (highest during commute hours), day of week (less travel to work on weekends but more leisure travel), and season of year (more travel by tourists in summer). The demand for service during the peak period on a Monday in summer is likely to be very different from the level during the peak period on a Saturday in winter, reflecting day-of-week and seasonal variations jointly.

Table 9.1
Questions About Demand Patterns and Their Underlying Causes

---

1. *Do demand levels follow a predictable cycle?*
   If so, is the duration of the **demand cycle**
   - One *day* (varies by hour)
   - One *week* (varies by day)
   - One *month* (varies by day or by week)
   - One *year* (varies by month or by season or reflects annual public holidays)
   - Another period
2. *What are the underlying causes of these cyclical variations?*
   - Employment schedules
   - Billing and tax payment/refund cycles
   - Wage and salary payment dates
   - School hours and vacations
   - Seasonal changes in climate
   - Occurrence of public or religious holidays
   - Natural cycles, such as coastal tides
3. *Do demand levels seem to change randomly?*
   If so, could the underlying causes be
   - Day-to-day changes in the weather
   - Health events whose occurrence cannot be pinpointed exactly
   - Accidents, fires, and certain criminal activities
   - Natural disasters (e.g., earthquakes, storms, mudslides, and volcanic eruptions)
4. *Can demand for a particular service over time be disaggregated by market segment to reflect such components as*
   - Use patterns by a particular type of customer or for a particular purpose
   - Variations in the net profitability of each completed transaction

---

Analyzing Drivers of Demand

No strategy for smoothing demand is likely to succeed unless it is based on an understanding of why customers from a specific market segment choose to use the service when they do. It's difficult for hotels to convince business travelers to remain on Saturday nights, because few executives do business over the weekend. Instead, hotel managers may do better to promote weekend use of their facilities for conferences or pleasure travel. Attempts to get commuters to shift their travel to off-peak periods will probably fail, because such travel is determined by people's employment hours. Instead, efforts should be directed at employers to persuade them to adopt flextime or staggered working hours. These firms recognize that no amount of price discounting is likely to develop business out of season. However, summer resort areas such as Cape Cod may have good opportunities to build business during the "shoulder seasons" of spring and fall (which some consider the most attractive times to visit the Cape) by promoting different attractions—such as hiking, birdwatching, visiting museums, and looking for bargains in antique stores—and altering the mix and focus of services to target a different type of clientele.

Keeping good records of each transaction helps enormously when it comes to analyzing demand patterns based on past experience. Best-practice queuing systems supported by sophisticated software can track customer consumption patterns by date and time of day automatically. Where it is relevant, it's also useful to record weather conditions and other special factors (a strike, an accident, a big convention in town, a price change, launch of a competing service, etc.) that might have influenced demand.

Dividing up Demand by Market Segment

Random fluctuations are usually caused by factors beyond management's control. However, analysis will sometimes reveal that a predictable demand cycle for one segment is concealed within a broader, seemingly random pattern. This fact illustrates the importance of breaking down demand on a segment-by-segment basis. For instance, a repair and maintenance shop that services industrial electrical equipment may already know that a certain proportion of its work consists of regularly scheduled contracts to perform preventive maintenance. The balance may come from "walk-in" business and emergency repairs. Although it might seem hard to predict or control the timing and volume of such work, further analysis might show that walk-in business was more prevalent on some days of the week than others, and that emergency repairs were frequently requested following damage sustained during thunderstorms (which tend to be seasonal in nature and can often be forecast a day or two in advance).

Not all demand is desirable. In fact, some requests for service are inappropriate and make it difficult for the organization to respond to the legitimate needs of its target customers. As discussed in Best Practice in Action 9.2, many calls to emergency numbers such as 911 are not really problems that fire, police, or ambulance services should be dispatched to solve. Discouraging undesirable demand such as this through marketing campaigns or screening procedures will not, of course, eliminate random fluctuations in the remaining demand. It may, however, help to keep peak demand levels within the service capacity of the organization.

Can marketing efforts smooth out random fluctuations in demand? The answer is generally no, because these fluctuations are usually caused by factors beyond the organization's control. However, detailed market analysis may sometimes reveal that a predictable demand cycle for one segment is concealed within a broader, seemingly random pattern. For example, a retail store might experience wide swings in daily patronage, but note that a core group of customers visit every weekday to buy staple items such as newspapers and candy.

The ease with which total demand can be broken down into smaller components depends on the nature of the records kept by management. If each customer transaction

Have you ever wondered what it's like to be a dispatcher for an emergency telephone service such as 911? People differ widely in what they consider to be an emergency.

Imagine yourself in the huge communications room at Police Headquarters in New York. A gray-haired sergeant is talking patiently by phone to a woman who has dialed 911 because her cat has run up a tree and she's afraid it's stuck there. "Ma'am, have you ever seen a cat skeleton in a tree?" the sergeant asks her. "All those cats get down somehow, don't they?" After the woman has hung up, the sergeant turns to a visitor and shrugs. "These kinds of calls keep pouring in," he says. "What can you do?" The trouble is, when people call an emergency number with complaints about noisy parties next door, pleas to rescue cats, or requests to turn off leaking fire hydrants, they may be slowing response times to fires, heart attacks, or violent crimes.

At one point, the situation in New York City got so bad that officials were forced to develop a marketing campaign to discourage people from making inappropriate requests for emergency assistance through the 911 number. The problem was that what might seem like an emergency to the caller—a beloved cat stuck up a tree, a noisy party that was preventing a tired person from getting needed sleep—was not a life (or property)-threatening situation of the type that the city's emergency services were poised to resolve. So a communications campaign, using a variety of media, was developed to urge people not to call 911 unless they were reporting a *dangerous emergency*. For help in resolving other problems, they were asked to call their local police station or other city agencies. The ad shown below appeared on New York City buses and subways.

Figure 9-A   Ad Discouraging Nonemergency Calls to 911

is recorded separately, and backed up by detailed notes (as in a medical or dental visit, or an accountant's audit), then the task of understanding demand is greatly simplified. In subscription and charge account services, when each customer's identity is known and itemized monthly bills are sent, managers can gain some immediate insights into usage patterns. Some services, such as telephone and electricity, even have the ability to track subscriber consumption patterns by time of day. Although these data may not always yield specific information on the purpose for which the service is being used, it is often possible to make informed judgments about the volume of sales generated by different user groups.

DEMAND LEVELS CAN BE MANAGED

There are five basic approaches to managing demand. The first, which has the virtue of simplicity but little else, involves *taking no action and leaving demand to find its own level*. Eventually, customers learn from experience or word of mouth when they can expect to stand in line to use the service and when it will be available without delay. The trouble is, they may also learn to find a competitor who is more responsive, and

Table 9.2
Alternative Demand-
Management
Strategies for Various
Capacity Situations

	CAPACITY SITUATION RELATIVE TO DEMAND	
APPROACH USED TO MANAGE DEMAND	INSUFFICIENT CAPACITY (EXCESS DEMAND)	EXCESS CAPACITY (INSUFFICIENT DEMAND)
Take no action	Unorganized queuing results (may irritate customers and discourage future use)	Capacity is wasted (customers may have a disappointing experience for services such as theater)
Reduce demand	Higher prices will increase profits; communication can encourage use in other time slots (can this effort be focused on less profitable and desirable segments?)	Take no action (but see preceding)
Increase demand	Take no action unless opportunities exist to stimulate (and give priority to) more profitable segments	Lower prices selectively (try to avoid cannibalizing existing business; ensure that all relevant costs are covered); use communications and variation in products and distribution (but recognize extra costs, if any, and make sure that appropriate trade-offs are made between profitability and use levels)
Inventory demand by reservation system	Consider priority system for most desirable segments; make other customers shift to off-peak period or to future peak	Clarify that space is available and that no reservations are needed
Inventory demand by formalized queuing	Consider override for most desirable segments; try to keep waiting customers occupied and comfortable; try to predict wait period accurately	Not applicable

low off-peak utilization cannot be improved unless action is taken. More interventionist approaches involve influencing the level of demand at any given time, by taking active steps to *reduce demand in peak periods* and to *increase demand when there is excess capacity.*

Two more approaches both involve *inventorying demand until capacity becomes available.* A firm can accomplish this either by introducing a booking or *reservations system* that promises customers access to capacity at specified times, or by *creating formalized queuing systems* (or by a combination of the two).

Table 9.2 links these five approaches to the two problem situations of excess demand and excess capacity, and provides a brief strategic commentary on each. Many service businesses face both situations at different points in the cycle of demand, and should consider use of the interventionist strategies described.

Marketing Strategies Can Reshape Some Demand Patterns

Several marketing-mix variables have roles to play in stimulating demand during periods of excess capacity, and in decreasing or shifting demand during periods of insufficient capacity. Price is often the first variable to be proposed for bringing demand and supply into balance, but changes in product, distribution strategy, and communication efforts can also play important roles. Although each element is discussed separately, effective demand management efforts often require changes in two or more elements jointly.

Figure 9.3 Hotel Demand Curves by Segment and by Season

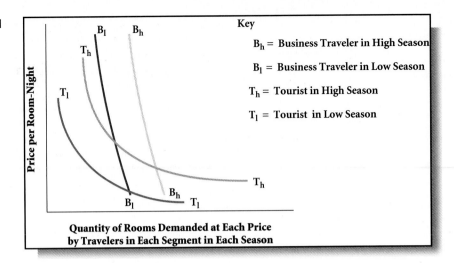

Key

B$_h$ = Business Traveler in High Season

B$_l$ = Business Traveler in Low Season

T$_h$ = Tourist in High Season

T$_l$ = Tourist in Low Season

Price per Room-Night

Quantity of Rooms Demanded at Each Price by Travelers in Each Segment in Each Season

Use Price and Other Costs to Manage Demand

One of the most direct ways of reducing excess demand at peak periods is to charge customers more money to use the service during those periods. Other costs, too, may have a similar effect. For instance, if customers learn that they are likely to face increased time and effort costs during peak periods, this information may lead those who dislike spending time waiting in crowded and unpleasant conditions to try later. Similarly, the lure of cheaper prices and an expectation of no waiting may encourage at least some people to change the timing of their behavior, whether it be shopping, travel, or visiting a museum.

Some firms use pricing strategy to balance supply and demand. For the monetary price of a service to be effective as a demand-management tool, managers must have some sense of the shape and slope of a product's demand curve—that is, how the quantity of service demanded responds to increases or decreases in the price per unit at a particular time (Figure 9.3 shows a sample demand curve). It's important to determine whether the demand curve for a specific service varies sharply from one time period to another. For instance, will the same person be willing to pay more for a weekend stay in a hotel on Cape Cod in summer than in winter (when the weather can be freezing)? The answer is probably "yes." If so, significantly different pricing schemes may be needed to fill capacity in each time period.

Complicating matters further, there may be separate demand curves for different segments within each time period (business travelers are usually less price-sensitive than tourists). One of the most difficult tasks facing service marketers is to determine the nature of all these different demand curves. Research, trial and error, and analysis of parallel situations in other locations or in comparable services are all ways of obtaining an understanding of the situation. Many service businesses explicitly recognize the existence of different demand curves by establishing distinct classes of service, each priced at levels appropriate to the demand curve of a particular segment. In essence, each segment receives a variation of the basic product, with value being added to the core service through supplementary services to appeal to higher-paying segments. For instance, in computer and printing service firms, product enhancement takes the form of faster turnaround and more specialized services; and in hotels, a distinction is made among rooms of different size and amenities, and with different views.

In each case, the objective is to maximize the revenues received from each segment. When capacity is constrained, however, the goal in a profit-seeking business should be to ensure that as much capacity as possible is utilized by the most profitable segments available at any given time. Airlines, for instance, hold a certain number of seats for business passengers paying full fare and place restrictive conditions on excursion fares for tourists (such as requiring advance purchase and a Saturday night stay) in order to prevent business travelers from taking advantage of cheap fares designed to attract tourists who can help fill the aircraft. Pricing strategies of this nature are known as *revenue management* and are discussed in Chapter 5.

Change Product Elements

Although pricing is often a commonly advocated method of balancing supply and demand, it is not quite as universally feasible for services as for goods. A rather obvious example is provided by the respective problems of a ski manufacturer and a ski slope operator during the summer. The former can either produce for inventory or try to sell skis in the summer at a discount. If the skis are sufficiently discounted, some customers will buy before the ski season in order to save money. However, in the absence of skiing opportunities, no skiers would buy lift tickets for use on a midsummer day at any price. So, to encourage summer use of the lifts, the operator has to change the service product offering (see Best Practice in Action 9.3).

Similar thinking prevails at a variety of other seasonal businesses. Thus, tax preparation firms offer bookkeeping and consulting services to small businesses in slack months, educational institutions offer weekend and summer programs for adults and senior citizens, and small pleasure boats offer cruises in the summer and a dockside venue for private functions in winter months. These firms recognize that no amount of price discounting is likely to develop business out of season and that new value propositions targeted at different segments are needed.

Many service offerings remain unchanged throughout the year, but others undergo significant modifications according to the season. Hospitals, for example, usually offer the same array of services throughout the year. By contrast, resort hotels sharply alter the mix and focus of their peripheral services, such as dining, entertainment, and sports, to reflect customer preferences in different seasons.

There can be variations in the product offering even during the course of a 24-hour period. Some restaurants provide a good example of this, marking the passage of the hours with changing menus and levels of service, variations in lighting and decor, opening and closing of the bar, and the presence or absence of entertainment. The goal is to appeal to different needs within the same group of customers, to reach out to different customer segments, or to do both, according to the time of day.

Modify the Place and Time of Delivery

Rather than seeking to modify demand for a service that continues to be offered at the same time in the same place, some firms respond to market needs by modifying the time and place of delivery. Three basic options are available.

The first represents a strategy of *no change*: regardless of the level of demand, the service continues to be offered in the same location at the same times. By contrast, a second strategy involves *varying the times when the service is available*, to reflect changes in customer preference by day of week, by season, and so forth. Theaters and cinema complexes often offer matinees on weekends, when people have more leisure time throughout the day; during the summer, cafes and restaurants may stay open later because of the general inclination of people to enjoy the longer, balmier evenings outdoors; and shops may extend their hours in the lead-up to Christmas or during school holiday periods.

A third strategy involves *offering the service to customers at a new location*. One approach is to operate mobile units that take the service to customers, rather than requiring them to visit fixed-site service locations. Traveling libraries, mobile car wash services, in-office tailoring services, home-delivered meals and catering services, and vans equipped with primary care medical facilities are examples of this. A cleaning and repair firm that wishes to generate business during low-demand periods might offer free pickup and delivery of portable items that need servicing.

It used to be that ski resorts shut down once the snow melted and the slopes became unskiable. The chairlifts stopped operating, the restaurants closed, and the lodges were locked and shuttered until winter approached and the snows fell again. In time, however, some ski operators recognized that a mountain offers summer pleasures, too, and kept lodging and restaurants open for hikers and picnickers. Some even built Alpine Slides—curving tracks in which wheeled toboggans could run from the summit to the base—and thus created demand for tickets on the ski lifts. With the construction of condominiums for sale, demand increased for warm-weather activities as the owners flocked to the mountains in summer and early fall.

The arrival of the mountain biking craze created opportunities for equipment rentals as well as chairlift rides. Killington Resort in Vermont has long encouraged summer visitors to ride to the summit, see the view, and eat at the mountaintop restaurant. But now it also enjoys a booking business in renting mountain bikes and related equipment (such as helmets). Beside the base lodge, where in winter skiers would find rack after rack of skis for rent, the summer visitor can now choose from rows of mountain bikes. Bikers transport their vehicles up to the summit on specially equipped chairlifts, and then ride them down designated trails. Serious hikers reverse the process—climbing to the summit via trails that seek to avoid descending bikes, getting refreshments at the restaurant, and then taking the chairlift back down to the base. Once in a while, a biker will actually choose to ride his or her bike up the mountain, but such gluttons for punishment are few and far between.

Most large ski resorts look for a variety of additional ways to attract guests to their hotels and rental homes during the summer. Mont Tremblant, Quebec, for instance, is located beside an attractive lake. In addition to swimming and other water sports on the lake, the resort offers visitors such activities as a championship golf course, tennis, rollerblading, and a children's day camp. And hikers and mountain bikers come to ride the lifts up the mountain.

Figure 9-B Riding the Chairlift up Mont Tremblant to Hike and Bike Rather Than Ski

Alternatively, service firms whose productive assets are mobile may choose to follow the market when that, too, is mobile. For instance, some car rental firms establish seasonal branch offices in resort communities. In these new locations, they often change the schedule of service hours (as well as certain product features) to conform to local needs and preferences.

Promotion and Education

Even if the other variables of the marketing mix remain unchanged, communication efforts alone may be able to help smooth demand. Signage, advertising, publicity, and sales messages can be used to educate customers about the timing of peak periods and encourage them to avail themselves of the service at off-peak times when there will be fewer delays.[5] Examples include U.S. Postal Service requests to "Mail Early for Christmas," public transport messages urging noncommuters—such as shoppers or tourists—to avoid the crush conditions of the commute hours, and communications from sales reps for industrial maintenance firms advising customers of periods when preventive maintenance work can be done quickly. In addition, management can ask service personnel (or intermediaries such as travel agents) to encourage customers with discretionary schedules to favor off-peak periods.

Changes in pricing, product characteristics, and distribution must be communicated clearly. If a firm wants to obtain a specific response to variations in marketing-mix elements, it must, of course, inform customers fully about their options. As discussed in Chapter 5, short-term promotions, combining both pricing and communication elements as well as other incentives, may provide customers with attractive incentives to shift the timing of service usage.

INVENTORY DEMAND THROUGH WAITING LINES AND RESERVATIONS

One of the challenges of services is that, being performances, they cannot normally be stored for later use. A haircutter cannot prepackage a haircut for the following day: the haircut must be provided in real time. In an ideal world, nobody would ever have to wait to conduct a service transaction. However, firms cannot afford to provide extensive extra capacity that will go unutilized most of the time. As we have seen, there are a variety of procedures for bringing demand and supply into balance. But what's a manager to do when the possibilities for shaping demand and adjusting capacity have been exhausted and yet supply and demand are still out of balance? Not taking any action and leaving customers to sort things out is no recipe for customer satisfaction. Rather than allowing matters to degenerate into a random free-for-all, customer-oriented firms try to develop strategies for ensuring order, predictability, and fairness.

In businesses in which demand regularly exceeds supply, managers can often take steps to inventory demand. This task can be achieved in one of two ways: (1) by asking customers to wait in line (queuing), usually on a first-come, first-served basis; or (2) by offering them the opportunity of reserving or booking space in advance.

Waiting Is a Universal Phenomenon

It's estimated that Americans spend 37 billion hours a year (an average of almost 150 hours each) waiting in lines, "during which time they fret, fidget, and scowl," according to the *Washington Post*.[6] Similar (or worse) situations seem to prevail around the world. Nobody likes to be kept waiting (Figure 9.4). It's boring, time-wasting, and sometimes physically uncomfortable, especially if there is nowhere to sit or you are outdoors. And yet waiting for a service process is an almost universal phenomenon: Almost every organization faces the problem of waiting lines somewhere in its operation. People are kept waiting on the phone, listening to recorded messages that "your call is important to us"; they line up with their supermarket carts to check out their grocery purchases; and they wait for their bills after a restaurant meal. They sit in their cars waiting to enter drive-in car washes, and to pay at toll booths.

Figure 9.4 Hertz Helps Its Customers to Avoid the Time and Hassle of Waiting in Line

A 2005 national survey of 1,000 adults in the United States revealed that the waiting lines most dreaded by Americans are those in doctors' offices (cited by 27 percent) and in government departments that issue motor vehicle registrations and drivers' licenses (26 percent), followed by grocery stores (18 percent) and airports (14 percent).[7] Situations that make it even worse at retail check-outs include slow or inefficient cashiers, someone changing their mind about an item that has already been rung up, and a person who leaves the line to run back for an item. It doesn't take long before people start to lose their cool: One-third of Americans say they get frustrated after waiting in line for 10 minutes or less (although women report more patience than men and are more likely to chat with others to pass the time while waiting).

Physical and inanimate objects wait for processing, too. Customers' emails sit in customer service staff's inboxes, appliances wait to be repaired, and checks wait to be cleared at a bank. In each instance, a customer may be waiting for the outcome of that work—an answer to an email, an appliance that is working again, or a check credited to the customer's balance.

Why Waiting Lines Occur

Waiting lines—known to operations researchers as *queues*—occur whenever the number of arrivals at a facility exceeds the capacity of the system to process them. In a very real sense, queues are basically a symptom of unresolved capacity management problems. Analysis and modeling of queues is a well-established branch of operations management. Queuing theory has been traced back to 1917, when a Danish telephone engineer was charged with determining how large the switching unit in a telephone system had to be to keep the number of busy signals within reason.[8]

As the telephone example suggests, not all queues take the form of a physical waiting line in a single location. When customers deal with a service supplier at arm's length, as in information processing services, they call from home, office, or college using telecommunication channels such as voice telephone or the Internet. Typically, calls are answered in the order received, often requiring customers to wait their turn in a virtual line. Some physical queues are geographically dispersed. Travelers wait at many different locations for the taxis they have ordered by phone to arrive and pick them up.

Many web sites now allow people to do things for themselves, such as obtaining information or making reservations, that formerly required making telephone calls or visiting a service facility in person. Companies often promote the time savings that can be achieved. Although accessing the Web can be slow sometimes, at least the wait is conducted while the customer is comfortably seated and able to attend to other matters while waiting.

For some services, the problem of reducing customer waiting time requires a multipronged strategy, as evidenced by the approach taken by a Chicago bank (Best Practice in Action 9.4). Increasing capacity simply by adding more space or more staff is not always the optimal solution in situations in which customer satisfaction must be balanced against cost considerations. Like that bank, managers should consider a variety of alternatives, such as

- Rethinking the design of the queuing system
- Redesigning processes to shorten the time of each transaction
- Managing customers' behavior and their perceptions of the wait
- Installing a reservations system

Different Queue Configurations

There are a variety of different types of queues, and the challenge for managers is to select the most appropriate procedure. Figure 9.5 shows diagrams of several types that you have probably experienced yourself. In single-line, sequential stages, customers proceed through several serving operations, as in a cafeteria. Bottlenecks may occur at any stage at which the process takes longer to execute than at previous stages. Many cafeterias have lines at the cash register because the cashier takes longer to calculate how much you owe and to make change than the servers take to slap food on your plate.

Parallel lines to multiple servers offer more than one serving station, allowing customers to select one of several lines in which to wait. Banks and ticket windows are common examples. Fast-food restaurants usually have several serving lines in operation at busy times of day, with each offering the full menu. A parallel system can have either a single stage or multiple stages. The disadvantage of this design is that lines may

How should a big retail bank respond to increased competition from new financial service providers? A large bank in Chicago decided that enhancing service to its customers would be an important element in its strategy. One opportunity for improvement was to reduce the amount of time that customers spent waiting in line for service in the bank's retail branches—a frequent source of complaints. Recognizing that no single action could resolve the problem satisfactorily, the bank adopted a three-pronged approach.

First, technological improvements were made to the service operation, starting with introduction of an electronic queuing system that not only routed customers to the next available teller station but also provided supervisors with online information to help match staffing to customer demand. Meantime, computer enhancements provided tellers with more information about their customers, enabling them to handle more requests without leaving their stations. And new cash machines for tellers saved them from selecting bills and counting them twice (yielding a time savings of 30 seconds for each cash withdrawal transaction).

Second, changes were made to human resource strategies. The bank adopted a new job description for teller managers that made them responsible for customer queuing times and for expediting transactions. It created an officer-of-the-day program, under which a designated officer was equipped with a beeper and assigned to help staff with complicated transactions that might otherwise slow them down. A new job category of peak-time teller was introduced, paying premium wages for 12 to 18 hours of work a week. Existing full-time tellers were given cash incentives and recognition to reward improved productivity on predicted high-volume days. Lastly, management reorganized meal arrangements. On busy days, lunch breaks were reduced to half-hour periods and staff received catered meals; meantime, the bank cafeteria was opened earlier to serve peak-time tellers.

A third set of changes centered on customer-oriented improvements to the delivery system. Quick-drop desks were established on busy days to handle deposits and simple requests, while newly created express teller stations were reserved for deposits and check cashing. Lobby hours were expanded from 38 to 56 hours a week, including Sundays. A customer brochure, *How to Lose Wait*, alerted customers to busy periods and suggested ways of avoiding delays.

Subsequently, internal measures and customer surveys showed that the improvements had not only reduced customer wait times but also increased customer perceptions that this bank was "the best" bank in the region for minimal waits in teller lines. The bank also found that adoption of extended hours had deflected some of the "noon rush" to before-work and after-work periods.

Source: Adapted from Leonard L. Berry and Linda R. Cooper, "Competing with Time-Saving Service." *Business,* 40, no. 2 (1990): 3–7.

not move at equal speed. How many times have you chosen what looked like the shortest line, only to watch in frustration as the lines on either side of you moved at twice the speed of yours, because someone in your line had a complicated transaction? A common solution here is to create a *single line to multiple servers* (commonly known as a "snake"). This approach is encountered frequently at post offices and airport check-ins.

Designated lines involve assigning different lines to specific categories of customer. Examples include express lines (for instance, 12 items or less) and regular lines at supermarket check-outs, and different check-in stations for first-class, business-class, and economy-class airline passengers. *Take a number* saves customers the need to stand in a queue, because they know they will be called in sequence. This procedure allows customers to sit down and relax (if seating is available) or to guess how long the wait will be and do something else in the meantime—but at the risk losing their place if earlier customers are served more quickly than expected. Users of this approach include large travel agents and supermarket departments, such as the deli counter or the bakery.

Hybrid approaches to queue configuration also exist. For instance, a cafeteria with a single serving line might offer two cash register stations at the final stage. Similarly, patients at a small medical clinic might visit a single receptionist for registration; proceed sequentially through multiple channels for testing, diagnosis, and treatment; and conclude by returning to a single line for payment at the receptionist's

Figure 9.5
Alternative Queue
Configurations

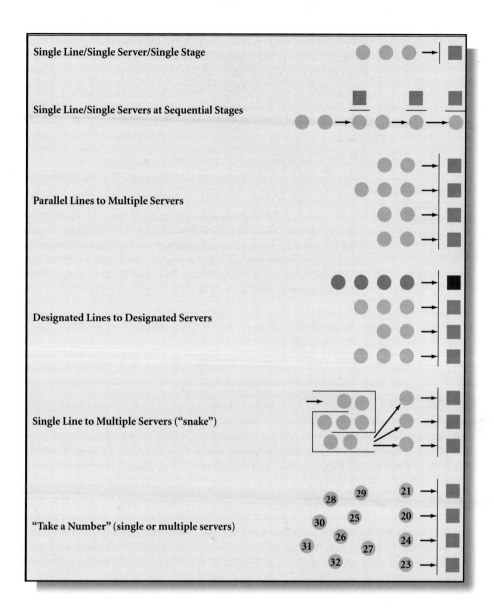

desk. Research suggests that selecting the most appropriate type of queue is important to customer satisfaction. Anat Rafaeli and her colleagues found that the way a waiting area is structured can produce feelings of injustice and unfairness in customers. Customers who waited in parallel lines to multiple servers reported significantly higher agitation and greater dissatisfaction with the fairness of the service delivery process than customers who waited in a single line ("snake") to access multiple servers, even though both groups of customers waited an identical amount of time and were involved in completely fair service processes.[9]

The issue of perceived fairness also arises in establishing waitlist strategies in restaurants, especially those that do not take reservations for small groups. Waiting customers are often very conscious of their own progress toward getting a table. Perhaps you've watched resentfully as other diners who arrived at a busy restaurant later than you were given priority and leapfrogged the line. It doesn't seem fair—especially when you are hungry.

Four common waitlist policies are party size seating, which involves matching the number of people to the size of the table; VIP seating, which gives priority to favored customers; call-ahead seating, which allows people to telephone in advance of arrival to hold a place on the waitlist; and large-party reservations. Kelly McGuire and Sheryl Kimes studied customer perceptions of these policies and found that although seating by party size and call-ahead seating were considered relatively fair by respondents, the greater the familiarity with these waitlisting techniques, the fairer customers perceived them to be. However, taking reservations only for large parties was perceived as slightly unfair (suggesting that reservations should be extended to all) and VIP seating as relatively unfair (suggesting that preferential treatment of VIPs should be handled discreetly so that other diners are unaware of it).[10]

Virtual Waits

One of the problems associated with waiting in line is the waste of time this involves for customers. When two or more people are waiting together, it's sometimes possible for one to remain and the others to go off and do something else for a while. The "virtual queue" strategy is an innovative way to take the physical waiting out of the wait altogether. Instead, customers register their place in line on a computer, which estimates the time at which they will reach the front of the virtual line and should return to claim their place.[11] Best Practice in Action 9.5 describes the virtual queuing systems used at Disney and Six Flags theme parks.

BEST PRACTICE IN ACTION 9.5
Waiting in a Virtual Queue for Theme Park Attractions

Disney is well known for its efforts to give visitors to its theme parks information on how long they may have to wait to ride a particular attraction and for entertaining guests while they are waiting in line. However, the company found that the long waits at its most popular attractions still represented a major source of dissatisfaction, and so created an innovative solution.

The concept of the virtual queue was first tested at Disney World. At the most popular attractions there, guests were able to register their place in line with a computer and were then free to use the wait time visiting other places in the park. Surveys showed that guests who used the new system spent more money, saw more attractions, and had significantly higher satisfaction. After further refinement, the system—now named FASTPASS—was introduced at the five most popular attractions at Disney World and subsequently extended to all Disney parks worldwide. It is now used by more than 50 million guests a year.

FASTPASS is easy to use. When guests approach a FASTPASS attraction, they are given two clear choices: Obtain a FASTPASS ticket there and return at a designated time, or wait in a standby line. Signs indicate how long the wait is in each instance. The wait time for each line tends to be self-regulating, because a large difference between the two will lead to increasing numbers of people choosing the shorter line. In practice, the virtual wait tends to be slightly longer than the physical one. To use the FASTPASS option, guests insert their park admission ticket into a special turnstile and receive a FASTPASS ticket specifying a return time. Guests have some flexibility because the system allows them a 60-minute window beyond the printed return time.

The Six Flags chain of theme parks has developed its own approach, called FastLane, which involves an extra fee. At five of the parks, you can rent a palm-sized device called a Q-bot. At the Texas and St. Louis parks, the fee is $10 for the Q-bot plus an additional $10 for each person in the group who wishes to use FastLane. At the other three parks, guests can choose between standard and gold service, which costs $25 per Q-bot and per guest at the New England and Georgia parks; at the Great America park near Philadelphia, standard service costs $15 and gold costs $33.

At each ride you wish to use, you insert the Q-bot into a slot at the FastLane sign. The device calculates how long the current wait is, then schedules a reservation that allows a 10-minute window, after which you lose your place. For purchasers of standard service, the FastLane virtual wait is the same as the physical wait; for gold service purchasers, however, the wait is reduced by up to 75 percent. A few minutes before your scheduled time, the Q-bot will vibrate, beep, and display a messag saying, "Next Ride Soon," reminding you to go to the ride, where you enter through a special FastLane channel. The Q-bot will also display messages notifying you in the event that a ride malfunction has caused delays and giving you a new return time.

Sources: Duncan Dickson, Robert C. Ford, and Bruce Laval, "Managing Real and Virtual Waits in Hospitality and Service Organizations." *Cornell Hotel and Restaurant Administration Quarterly*, 46 (February 2005): 52–68; Arthur Levine, "Six Flags Guests Get Out of Line." About.com Travel, http://themeparks.about.com/cs/sixflagsparks/a/blfastlanea.htm, accessed December 20, 2005; Lo-Q Virtual Queuing Inc., www.lo-qusa.com/fastlane/pricing.htm, accessed December 20, 2005.

The concept of virtual waiting has many potential applications. Like theme parks, operations such as cruise ships and all-inclusive resorts offer multiple activities for their guests, but capacity is usually limited and so waiting is inevitable at popular times. A similar phenomenon occurs in health clubs, where certain items of equipment are more popular than others and usage is often rationed by limiting the amount of time that any one client may use that equipment. Restaurants can use a virtual queue strategy if customers are willing to remain within buzzing range of a pager system. In fact, it could be employed by any free-standing visitor attraction where waiting lines are regularly encountered.

Queuing Systems Can Be Tailored to Market Segments

Although the basic rule in most queuing systems is "first come, first served," not all queuing systems are organized on this basis. Market segmentation is sometimes used to design queuing strategies that set different priorities for different types of customers. Allocation to separate queuing areas may be based on any of the following.

- *Urgency of the job.* At many hospital emergency units, a triage nurse is assigned to greet incoming patients and decide who requires priority medical treatment and who can safely be asked to register and then sit down while they wait their turn.
- *Duration of service transaction.* Banks, supermarkets, and other retail services often institute "express lanes" for shorter, less complicated tasks.
- *Payment of a premium price.* Airlines usually offer separate check-in lines for first-class and economy-class passengers, with a higher ratio of personnel to passengers in the first-class line, resulting in reduced waits for those who have paid more for their tickets. At some airports, premium passengers may use faster lanes for the security check.
- *Importance of the customer.* A special area may be reserved for members of frequent user clubs. Airlines often provide lounges, offering newspapers and free refreshments, where frequent flyers can wait for their flights in greater comfort.

MINIMIZE PERCEPTIONS OF WAITING TIME

Research shows that people often think they have waited longer for a service than they actually did. Studies of public transportation use, for instance, have shown that travelers perceive time spent waiting for a bus or train as passing one and a half to seven times more slowly than the time actually spent traveling in the vehicle.[12] People don't like wasting their time on unproductive activities, any more than they like wasting money. Customer dissatisfaction with delays in receiving service can often stimulate strong emotions, even anger.[13]

The Psychology of Waiting Time

The noted philosopher William James observed, "Boredom results from being attentive to the passage of time itself." Savvy service marketers recognize that customers experience waiting time in differing ways, depending on the circumstances. Table 9.3 highlights 10 propositions on the psychology of waiting lines.

When increasing capacity is simply not feasible, service providers should try to be creative and look for ways to make waiting more palatable for customers. Doctors and dentists stock their waiting rooms with piles of magazines for people to read while waiting. Car repair facilities may have a television for customers to watch. One tire dealer goes even further, providing customers with free popcorn, soft drinks, coffee, and ice cream while they wait for their cars to be serviced.

Table 9.3
Ten Propositions on the Psychology of Waiting Lines

1. *Unoccupied time feels longer than occupied time.* When you're sitting around with nothing to do, time seems to crawl. The challenge for service organizations is to give customers something to do or to distract them while waiting.
2. *Pre- and postprocess waits feel longer than in-process waits.* Waiting to buy a ticket to enter a theme park is different from waiting to ride on a roller coaster once you're in the park. There's also a difference between waiting for coffee to arrive near the end of a restaurant meal and waiting for the server to bring you the check once you're ready to leave.
3. *Anxiety makes waits seem longer.* Can you remember waiting for someone to show at a rendezvous and worrying about whether you had got the time or the location correct? While waiting in unfamiliar locations, especially outdoors and after dark, people often worry about their personal safety.
4. *Uncertain waits are longer than known, finite waits.* Although any wait may be frustrating, we can usually adjust mentally to a wait of known length. It's the unknown that keeps us on edge. Imagine waiting for a delayed flight and not being told how long the delay is going to be. You don't know whether you have the time to get up and walk around the terminal or whether to stay at the gate in case the flight is called any minute.
5. *Unexplained waits are longer than explained waits.* Have you ever been in a subway or an elevator that has stopped for no apparent reason, without anyone telling you why? In addition to uncertainty about the length of the wait, there's added worry about what is going to happen. Has there been an accident on the line? Will you have to leave the train in the tunnel? Is the elevator broken? Will you be stuck for hours in close proximity with strangers?
6. *Unfair waits are longer than equitable waits.* Expectations about what is fair or unfair sometimes vary from one culture or country to another. In the United States, Canada, or Britain, for example, people expect everybody to wait their turn in line and are likely to get irritated if they see others jumping ahead or being given priority for no apparently good reason.
7. *The more valuable the service, the longer people will wait.* People will queue overnight under uncomfortable conditions to get good seats at a major concert or sports event that is expected to sell out.
8. *Solo waits feel longer than group waits.* Waiting with one or more people you know is reassuring. Conversation with friends can help to pass the time, but not everyone is comfortable talking to a stranger.
9. *Physically uncomfortable waits feel longer than comfortable waits.* "My feet are killing me!" is one of the most frequently heard comments when people are forced to stand in line for a long time. And they are whether seated or unseated, waiting seems more burdensome if the temperature is too hot or too cold, if it's drafty or windy, and if there is no protection from rain or snow.
10. *Unfamiliar waits seem longer than familiar ones.* Frequent users of a service know what to expect and are less likely to worry while waiting. New or occasional users of a service, by contrast, are often nervous, wondering not only about the probable length of the wait but also about what happens next.

Source: (items 1–8) David H. Maister, "The Psychology of Waiting Lines." In J. A. Czepiel, M. R. Solomon, and C. F. Surprenant, *The Service Encounter.* Lexington, MA: Lexington Books/D.C. Heath, 1986, pp. 113–123; *(item 9)* M. M. Davis and J. Heineke, "Understanding the Roles of the Customer and the Operation for Better Queue Management." *International Journal of Service Industry Management,* 7, no. 5 (1994): 21–34; *(item 10)* Peter Jones and Emma Peppiat, "Managing Perceptions of Waiting Times in Service Queues." *International Journal of Service Industry Management,* 7, no. 5 (1996): 47–61.

An experiment at a large bank in Boston found that installing an electronic news display in the lobby led to greater customer satisfaction, but it didn't reduce the perceived time spent waiting for teller service.[14] In some locations, transit operators erect heated shelters equipped with seats to make it less unpleasant for travelers to wait for a bus or train in cold weather. Restaurants solve the waiting problem by inviting dinner guests to have a drink in the bar until their table is ready (that approach makes money for the house as well as keeping the customer occupied). In similar fashion, guests waiting in line for a show at a casino may find themselves queuing in a corridor lined with slot machines.

The doorman at one Marriott Hotel has taken it on himself to bring a combination barometer/thermometer to work each day, hanging it on a pillar at the hotel entrance where guests waiting can spend a moment or two examining it while they wait for a taxi or for their car to be delivered from the valet parking.[15] Theme park operators cleverly design their waiting areas to make the wait look shorter than it really is, finding ways to give customers in line the impression of constant progress, and make time seem to pass more quickly by keeping customers amused or diverted while they wait. Recognizing that customers don't want to waste time on either preprocess or postprocess waits, rental car firms try to minimize customer waiting when the car is returned, employing agents with wireless, hand-held terminals to meet customers in the parking area, enter fuel and mileage, and then compute and print bills on the spot.

Give Customers Information on Waits

Does it help to tell people how long they are likely to have to wait for service? Common sense suggests that this is useful information for customers, because it allows them to make decisions as to whether they can afford to take the time to wait now or should come back later. It also enables them to plan the use of their time while waiting.

An experimental study in Canada looked at how students responded to waits while conducting transactions by computer—a situation similar to waiting on hold on the telephone, in that there are no visual clues as to the probable wait time.[16] The study examined dissatisfaction with waits of 5, 10, or 15 minutes under three conditions: (1) the student subjects were told nothing, (2) they were told how long the wait was likely to be, or (3) they were told what their place in line was. The results suggested that for 5-minute waits, it was not necessary to provide information to improve satisfaction. For waits of 10 or 15 minutes, offering information appeared to improve customers' evaluations of service. However, for longer waits, the researchers suggest that it may be more positive to let people know how their place in line is changing than to let them know how much time remains before they will be served. One conclusion we might draw is that people prefer to see (or sense) that the line is moving, rather than to watch the clock.

CREATE AN EFFECTIVE RESERVATIONS SYSTEM

Ask someone what services come to mind when you talk about reservations and most likely they will cite airlines, hotels, restaurants, car rentals, and theater seats. Use synonyms such as "bookings" or "appointments" and they may add haircuts, visits to professionals such as doctors and consultants, vacation rentals, and service calls to fix anything from a broken refrigerator to a neurotic computer.

Reservations are intended to guarantee that service will be available when the customer wants it. They are commonly used by many people processing services, including restaurants, hotels, airlines, doctors, dentists, and hairdressing salons (Figure 9.6). The presence of such systems enables demand to be controlled and smoothed out in a more manageable way. By capturing data, reservation systems also help organizations to prepare operational and financial projections for future periods. Systems vary from a simple appointments book for a doctor's office, using handwritten entries, to a central, computerized data bank for an airline's worldwide operations.

When goods require servicing, their owners may not wish to be parted from them for long, so it's important to be able to promise a particular time when the item should be dropped off and to guarantee prompt completion of the needed work. Households with only one car, for example, or factories with a vital piece of equipment often cannot afford to be without such items for more than a day or two.

Figure 9.6
Reservations Are
Required at Most Hair
Salons

Reservations systems serve the interests of both customers and the business. By requiring reservations for routine repair and maintenance, management can ensure that some time will be kept free for handling emergency jobs which, because they are unpredictable and carry a premium price, generate a much higher margin.

Taking reservations also serves to presell a service, to inform customers and to educate them about what to expect. Customers who hold reservations should be able to count on avoiding a queue, because they have been guaranteed service at a specific time. A well-organized reservations system allows the organization to deflect demand for service from a first-choice time to earlier or later times, from one class of service to another ("upgrades" and "downgrades"), and even from first-choice locations to alternative ones. However, problems arise when customers fail to show or when service firms overbook. Marketing strategies for dealing with these operational problems include requiring a deposit, canceling non-paid reservations after a certain time, and providing compensation to victims of overbooking.

The challenge in designing reservation systems is to make them fast and user-friendly for both staff and customers. Many firms now allow customers to make their own reservations on a self-service basis by web site—a trend that seems certain to grow. Customers also appreciate it when the system can provide detailed information about the type of service they are reserving. For instance, can a hotel assign a specific room on request? Or at least, can it assign a room with a view of the lake rather than one with a view of the parking lot and the nearby power station?

Reservations Strategies Should Focus on Yield

Service organizations often use percentage of capacity sold as a measure of operational efficiency. Transport services talk of the "load factor" achieved, hotels of their "occupancy rate," and hospitals of their "census." Similarly, professional firms can calculate what proportion of a partner's or an employee's time is classified as billable hours, and repair shops can look at utilization of both equipment and labor. By themselves, however, these percentage figures tell us little of the relative profitability of the business attracted, because high utilization rates may be obtained at the expense of heavy discounting—or even outright giveaways.

More and more, service firms are looking at their *yield*—that is, the average revenue received per unit of capacity. The aim is to maximize this yield in order to improve profitability. As noted in Chapter 5, revenue management strategies designed to achieve this goal are widely used in such capacity-constrained industries as passenger airlines, hotels, and car rentals. Revenue management systems based on mathematical modeling are of greatest value for service firms that find it expensive to modify their capacity but incur relatively low costs when they sell another unit of available capacity.[17] Other characteristics encouraging use of such programs include fluctuating demand levels, ability to segment markets by extent of price sensitivity, and sale of services well in advance of usage.

Yield analysis forces managers to recognize the opportunity cost of selling capacity for a given date to a customer from one market segment when another might subsequently yield a higher rate. Consider the following problems facing sales managers for different types of capacity-constrained service organizations.

- Should a hotel accept an advance booking from a tour group of 200 room nights at $80 each when some of these same room nights might possible be sold later at short notice to business travelers at the full posted rate of $140?
- Should a railroad with 30 empty freight cars at its disposal accept an immediate request for a shipment worth $900 per car or hold the cars idle for a few more days in the hope of getting a priority shipment that would be twice as valuable?
- How many seats on a particular flight should an airline sell in advance to tour groups and passengers traveling at special excursion rates?
- Should an industrial repair and maintenance shop reserve a certain proportion of productive capacity each day for emergency repair jobs that offer a high contribution margin and the potential to build long-term customer loyalty, or should it simply follow a strategy of making sure that there are sufficient jobs, mostly involving routine maintenance, to keep its employees fully occupied?
- Should a printing shop process all jobs on a first-come, first-served basis, with a guaranteed delivery time for each job, or should it charge a premium rate for "rush" work, and tell customers with "standard" jobs to expect some variability in completion dates?

Decisions on problems such as these deserve to be handled with a little more sophistication than just resorting to the "bird in the hand is worth two in the bush" formula. Good information, based on detailed record keeping of past usage and supported by current market intelligence, is the key to allocating the inventory of capacity among different segments. The decision to accept or reject business should be based on realistic estimates of the probabilities of obtaining higher-rated business and awareness of the need to maintain established (and desirable) customer relationships. Managers who decide on the basis of guesswork and "gut feel" are little better than gamblers who bet on rolls of the dice.

Figure 9.7 illustrates capacity allocation in a hotel setting, in which demand from different types of customers varies not only by day of the week but also by season. These allocation decisions by segment, captured in reservation databases that are accessible worldwide, tell reservations personnel when to stop accepting reservations at certain prices, even though many rooms may still remain unbooked. Loyalty program members, who are primarily business travelers, are obviously a particularly desirable segment.

Similar charts can be constructed for most capacity-constrained businesses. In some instances, capacity is measured in terms of seats for a given performance, seat-miles, or room-nights; in others it may be in terms of machine time, labor time, billable professional hours, vehicle miles, or storage volume—whichever is the scarce resource. Unless it's easy to divert business from one facility to a similar alternative, allocation planning decisions will have to be made at the level of geographic operating units. So each hotel, repair and maintenance center, or computer service bureau may need its own plan. On the other hand, transport vehicles represent a mobile

Figure 9.7
Setting Capacity
Allocation Targets by
Segment for a Hotel

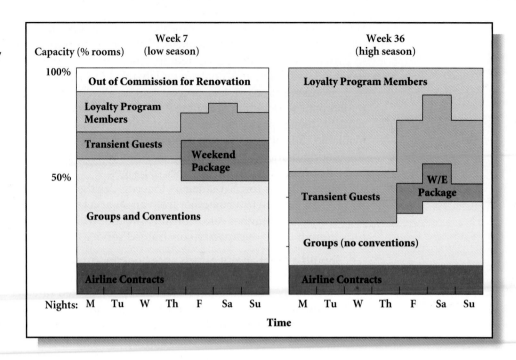

capacity that can be allocated across any geographic area the vehicles are able to serve.

In large organizations, such as major airlines or hotel chains, the market is very dynamic, because the situation is constantly changing. For instance, the demand for both business and pleasure travel reflects current or anticipated economic conditions. Although many business travelers are not price-sensitive, some companies insist that employees shop for the best travel bargains they can find within the constraints of their business travel needs. Pleasure travelers are often very price-sensitive; a special promotion, involving discounted fares and room rates, may encourage people to undertake a trip that they would not otherwise make.

Viewed from the perspective of the individual hotel or airline, competitive activity has the potential to play havoc with demand forecasts. Imagine that you are a hotel owner and a new hotel opens across the street with a special discount offer. How will it affect you? Alternatively, consider the effect if an existing competitor burns down. The airline business is notoriously changeable. Fares can be slashed overnight. A competitor may introduce a new nonstop service between two cities or cut back its existing schedule on another route. Travel intermediaries and savvy customers watch these movements like hawks and may be quick to cancel one reservation (even if it involves paying a penalty) in order to take advantage of a better price or a more convenient schedule that can be obtained elsewhere.

Effective Demand and Capacity Management Requires Information

Managers require substantial information to help them develop effective strategies to manage demand and capacity and then monitor subsequent performance in the marketplace. Following are some important categories of information for this purpose.

- *Historical data* on the level and composition of demand over time, including responses to changes in price or other marketing variables
- *Forecasts* of the level of demand for each major segment under specified conditions
- *Segment-by-segment data* to help management evaluate the effect of periodic cycles and random demand fluctuations

- *Cost data* to enable the organization to distinguish between fixed and variable costs and to determine the relative profitability of incremental unit sales to different segments and at different prices
- *Meaningful variations in demand levels and composition* on a location-by-location basis (in multisite organizations)
- *Customer attitudes* toward queuing under varying conditions
- *Customer opinions* on whether the quality of service delivered varies with different levels of capacity utilization

Where might all this information come from? Many large organizations with expensive fixed capacity have implemented revenue management systems (discussed in Chapter 5). For organizations without such systems, much of the needed data are probably already being collected within the organization—not necessarily by marketers—and new studies can be conducted to obtain additional data. A stream of information comes into most service businesses, notably concerning individual customer transactions. Sales receipts alone often contain vast detail. Service businesses need to collect detailed information for operational and accounting purposes and can frequently associate specific customers with specific transactions.

Unfortunately, the marketing value of such data is often overlooked, and they are not always stored in ways that permit easy retrieval and analysis by marketers. Nevertheless, collection and storage of customer transaction data can often be reformatted to provide at least some of the desired information, including how existing segments have responded to past changes in marketing variables.

Other information may have to be collected through special studies, such as customer surveys, or reviews of analogous situations. It may also be necessary to collect information on competitive performance, because changes in the capacity or strategy of competitors may require corrective action.

When new strategies are under consideration, operations researchers can often contribute useful insights by developing simulation models of the effect of changes in different variables. Such an approach is particularly useful in service "network" environments, such as theme parks and ski resorts, where customers can choose among multiple activities at the same site. Madeleine Pullman and Gary Thompson modeled customer behavior at a ski resort, where skiers can choose among different lifts and ski runs of varying lengths and levels of difficulty. Through analysis, they were able to determine the potential future effect of lift-capacity upgrades (bigger or faster chairlifts), capacity expansion in the form of extended skiing terrain, industry growth, day-to-day price variations, customer response to information about wait times at different lifts, and changes in the customer mix.[18]

CONCLUSION

Because many capacity-constrained service organizations have heavy fixed costs, even modest improvements in capacity utilization can have a significant effect on the bottom line. In this chapter we have also shown how managers can transform fixed costs into variable costs through such strategies as using rented facilities or part-time labor. Creating a more flexible approach to productive capacity allows a firm to adopt strategy to match capacity to demand (also called "chase demand" strategy), thereby improving productivity.

Decisions on *Place and time* are closely associated with balancing demand and capacity. Demand is often a function of where the service is located and when it's offered. As we saw with the example of the mountain resorts, the appeal of many destinations varies with the seasons.

Marketing strategies involving use of *Product elements, Price,* and *Promotion and education* are often useful in managing demand for a service at a particular place and time.

The time-bound nature of services is a critical management issue today, especially with customers becoming more time-sensitive and more conscious of their personal time constraints and availability. People processing services are particularly likely to impose the burden of unwanted waiting on their customers, because the latter cannot avoid coming to the "factory" for service. Reservations can shape the timing of arrivals, but sometimes queuing is inevitable. Managers who can act to save customers more time (or at least make time pass more pleasantly) are often able to create a competitive advantage for their organizations.

STUDY QUESTIONS

1. Why is capacity management particularly significant for service firms?
2. What is meant by "chasing demand"?
3. What does "inventory" mean for service firms, and why is it perishable?
4. How does optimum capacity utilization differ from maximum capacity utilization? Give examples of situations in which the two may be the same and of ones in which they differ.
5. Select a service organization of your choice and identify its particular patterns of demand with reference to the checklist provided in Figure 9.1.

(a) What is the nature of this service organization's approach to capacity and demand management?
(b) What changes would you recommend in relation to its management of capacity and demand and why?
6. Why should service marketers be concerned about the amount of time that customers spend in (a) pre-process waits, (b) in-process waits, and (c) post-process waits?
7. What do you see as the advantages and disadvantages of the different types of queues for an organization serving large numbers of customers?

APPLICATION EXERCISES

1. Identify some specific examples of companies in your community (or region) that significantly change their product and/or marketing mix variables in order to encourage patronage during periods of low demand.
2. Give examples, based on your own experience, of a reservation system that worked really well, and of one that worked really badly. Identify and evaluate the reasons for the success and failure of these two

systems. What recommendations would you make to both firms to improve (or further improve in case of the good example) their reservation systems?
3. Review the 10 propositions on the psychology of waiting lines. Which are the most relevant at (a) a city bus stop on a cold, dark evening, (b) check-in for a flight at the airport, (c) a doctor's office where patients are seated, and (d) a ticket line for a football game that is expected to be a sell-out?

ENDNOTES

1. Kenneth J. Klassen and Thomas R. Rohleder, "Combining Operations and Marketing to Manage Capacity and Demand in Services." *The Service Industries Journal*, 21 (April 2001): 1–30.
2. Based on material in James A. Fitzsimmons and M. J. Fitzsimmons, *Service Management: Operations, Strategy, and Information Technology*, 3rd ed. New York: Irwin McGraw-Hill, 2000; and W. Earl Sasser, Jr., "Match Supply and Demand in Service Industries." *Harvard Business Review*, 54 (November–December 1976): 133–140.
3. Irene C. L. Ng, Jochen Wirtz, and Khai Sheang Lee, "The Strategic Role of Unused Service Capacity." *International Journal of Service Industry Management*, 10, no. 2 (1999): 211–238.
4. Christopher H. Lovelock, "Strategies for Managing Capacity-Constrained Service Organisations." *Service Industries Journal*, 3 (November 1984): 12–30.
5. Kenneth J. Klassen and Thomas R. Rohleder, "Using Customer Motivations to Reduce Peak Demand: Does It Work?" *Service Industries Journal*, 24 (September 2004): 53–70.
6. Malcolm Galdwell, "The Bottom Line for Lots of Time Spent in America." *The Washington Post* (syndicated article, February 1993).
7. Chase "Just in the Blink of Time" Index—National Results. Chase Bank News Release, May 19, 2005, www.chaseblink.com, accessed January 5, 2006.
8. Richard Saltus, "Lines, Lines, Lines, Lines. . . The Experts Are Trying to Ease the Wait." *The Boston Globe*, October 5, 1992, pp. 39, 42.
9. Anat Rafaeli, G. Barron, and K. Haber, "The Effects of Queue Structure on Attitudes." *Journal of Service Research*, 5 (November 2002): 125–139.
10. Kelly A. McGuire and Sheryl E. Kimes, "The Perceived Fairness of Waitlist-Management Techniques for Restaurants." *Cornell Hotel and Restaurant Administration Quarterly*, 47 (May 2006): 121–134.
11. Duncan Dickson, Robert C. Ford, and Bruce Laval, "Managing Real and Virtual Waits in Hospitality and Service Organizations." *Cornell Hotel and Restaurant Administration Quarterly*, 46 (February 2005): 52–68.
12. Jay R. Chernow, "Measuring the Values of Travel Time Savings." *Journal of Consumer Research*, 7 (March 1981): 360–371. (*Note:* This entire issue was devoted to the consumption of time.)
13. Ana B. Casado Diaz, and Francisco J. Más Ruiz, "The Consumer's Reaction to Delays in Service." *International Journal of Service Industry Management*, 13, no. 2 (2002): 118–140.

14. Karen L. Katz, Blaire M. Larson, and Richard C. Larson, "Prescription for the Waiting-in-Line Blues: Entertain, Enlighten, and Engage." *Sloan Management Review,* 31 (Winter 1991): 44–53

15. Bill Fromm and Len Schlesinger, *The Real Heroes of Business and Not a CEO Among Them.* New York: Currency Doubleday, 1994, p. 7.

16. Michael K. Hui and David K. Tse, "What to Tell Customers in Waits of Different Lengths: An Integrative Model of Service Evaluation." *Journal of Marketing,* 80, no. 2 (April 1996): 81–90.

17. Sheryl E. Kimes and Richard B. Chase, "The Strategic Levers of Yield Management." *Journal of Service Research,* 1 (November 1998): 156–166; Anthony Ingold, Una McMahon-Beattie, and Ian Yeoman, eds., *Yield Management Strategies for the Service Industries,* 2nd ed., London: Continuum, 2000.

18. Madeleine E. Pullman and Gary M. Thompson, "Evaluating Capacity- and Demand-Management Decisions at a Ski Resort." *Cornell Hotel and Restaurant Administration Quarterly,* 43 (December 2002): 25–36; Madeleine E. Pullman and Gary Thompson, "Strategies for Integrating Capacity with Demand in Service Networks." *Journal of Service Research,* 5 (February 2003): 169–183.

Chapter 10

Crafting the Service Environment

> *Managers... need to develop a better understanding of the interface between the resources they manipulate in atmospherics and the experience they want to create for the customer.*

JEAN-CHARLES CHEBAT AND LAURETTE DUBÉ

> *Restaurant design has become as compelling an element as menu, food and wine... in determining a restaurant's success.*

DANNY MEYER

The physical service environment that customers experience is the endpoint of the service delivery system captured in the *Place and time* element of the 8 Ps. In high-contact services, it plays a key role in shaping the service experience and enhancing (or undermining) customer satisfaction. Disney theme parks are often cited as vivid examples of service environments that make every customer feel comfortable and highly satisfied, and leave a long-lasting impression. In fact, organizations from hospitals to hotels and from restaurants to professional firms have come to recognize that the service environment is an important component of their marketing mix and overall value proposition.

Service environments communicate and determine the positioning of the service, shape employee as well as customer productivity, guide customers through the delivery system, and may represent a core component of a firm's search for competitive advantage.

In this chapter, we look at the importance of designing service environments to help engineer customer experiences, convey the planned image of the firm, solicit the desired responses from customers and employees, support service operations, and enhance both quality and productivity. Specifically, we explore the following questions:

1. What is the purpose of the service environment?
2. What are the various effects that the service environment can have on people?
3. What are the theories behind people's responses?
4. What are the dimensions of the service environment?
5. How can we design a servicescape to achieve the desired effects?

WHAT IS THE PURPOSE OF SERVICE ENVIRONMENTS?

Service environments, also called *servicescapes*, relate to the style and appearance of the physical surroundings and other experiential elements encountered by customers at service delivery sites.[1] Designing the service environment is an art that takes considerable time and effort, and can be expensive to implement. Once they are designed and built, service environments are not easy to change. Let's examine why many service firms take so much trouble to shape the environment in which their customers and service personnel will interact.

Shaping Customers' Experiences and Behavior

For organizations that deliver high-contact services, the design of the physical environment and the way in which tasks are performed by customer-contact personnel jointly play a vital role in creating a particular corporate identity and shaping the nature of customers' experiences. This environment and its accompanying atmosphere affect buyer behavior in three important ways:

1. *As a message-creating medium,* using symbolic cues to communicate to the intended audience about the distinctive nature and quality of the service experience
2. *As an attention-creating medium,* to make the servicescape stand out from that of competing establishments, and to attract customers from target segments
3. *As an affect-creating medium,* employing colors, textures, sounds, scents, and spatial design to enhance the desired service experience, and/or to heighten an appetite for certain goods, services, or experiences.

Image, Positioning, and Differentiation

Services are often intangible, and customers cannot assess their quality well. So customers use the service environment as an important proxy for quality, and firms take great pains to signal quality and portray the desired image. Perhaps you've seen the reception areas of successful professional firms, such as investment banks or management consulting firms, where the decor and furnishings tend to be elegant and designed to impress. In retailing, the store environment affects how customers perceive the quality of the merchandise. Like other people, you probably infer higher merchandise quality if the goods are displayed in an environment with a prestige image rather than in one that creates a discount image.[2] Consider Figure 10.1, which shows the lobbies of the Orbit Hotel and Hostel in Los Angeles and the St. Regis Grand Hotel in Rome, two different types of hotel that cater to two very different target segments. The Orbit caters to younger guests who love fun but have low budgets, and the St. Regis to a more mature, affluent, and prestigious clientele that includes upscale business travelers. Each of these two servicescapes clearly communicates and reinforces its hotel's respective positioning and sets service expectations as guests arrive.

Many servicescapes are purely functional. Firms seeking to convey the impression of low-price service do so by locating in inexpensive neighborhoods, occupying buildings

Figure 10.1 Comparison of Hotel Lobbies

with a simple appearance, minimizing wasteful use of space, and dressing their employees in practical, inexpensive uniforms. However, servicescapes do not always shape customer perceptions and behavior in ways intended by their creators. Veronique Aubert-Gamet notes that customers often make creative use of physical spaces and objects for different purposes. For instance, business people may set aside a restaurant table for use as a temporary office desk, with papers spread around and a laptop computer and mobile phone positioned on its surface, competing for space with the food and beverages.[3] Students meeting for a study date in a restaurant or coffee shop often do the same with their textbooks and notepads. Smart designers keep an eye open for such trends—they may even lead to the creation of a new service concept.

The Servicescape as Part of the Value Proposition

Physical surroundings help to shape appropriate feelings and reactions in customers and employees.[4] Consider how effectively many amusement parks use the servicescape concept to enhance their service offerings. The clean environment of Disneyland or Denmark's Legoland, plus employees in colorful costumes, all contribute to the sense of fun and excitement that visitors encounter on arrival and throughout their visit.

Resort hotels illustrate how servicescapes form a core part of the value proposition. Club Med's villages, designed to create a totally carefree atmosphere, may have provided the original inspiration for "getaway" holiday environments. New destination resorts are not only far more luxurious than Club Med, but also draw inspiration from theme parks to create fantasy environments, both inside and outside. Perhaps the most extreme examples can be found in Las Vegas. Facing competition from numerous casinos in other locations, Las Vegas has repositioned itself away from being a somewhat unsavory adult destination—once described in a London newspaper as "the electric Sodom and Gomorrah"—to a somewhat more wholesome fun resort where families, too, can have fun. The gambling is still there, of course, but many of the huge hotels recently built (or rebuilt) have been transformed into visually striking entertainment centers that feature such attractions as erupting "volcanoes," mock sea battles, and striking reproductions of Paris, the Pyramids, and Venice and its canals.

Even movie theaters are discovering the power of servicescapes. Attendance at movies has been falling in the United States, and some of the big chains are hurting. However, a few upstart boutique chains are trying a different approach. By building extravagant theaters and offering plush amenities, including lavishly decorated bars and restaurants and supervised playrooms for children, chains such as Florida-based Muvico are successfully enticing moviegoers to abandon their home entertainment centers—despite sharply higher admission prices. Says Muvico's CEO, Hamid Hashemi, of his competitors: "At the end of the day, you all get the same 35-mm tape. . . . What sets you apart is how you package it."[5] At one Egyptian-themed Muvico cinema, moviegoers follow a purple-tiled pattern representing the Nile into the lobby, passing between hieroglyph-covered pillars. Inside the auditorium, they find wide aisles and seats upholstered in red velvet. It's a very different experience from the megaplex at the local mall.

Facilitate the Service Encounter and Enhance Productivity

Service environments are often designed to facilitate the service encounter and to increase productivity. Richard Chase and Douglas Stewart highlighted ways in which fail-safe methods embodied in the service environment can help reduce service failures and support a fast and smooth service delivery process.[6] For example, color-coded keys on cash registers allow cashiers to identify the numerical figures and product codes that each button stands for. To foster a neat appearance of frontline staff, mirrors can be placed where staff can automatically check their appearance before going "on stage" to meet customers. Child care centers use toy outlines on walls and floors to show where toys should be placed after use. In fast-food restaurants and school cafeterias, strategically located tray-return stands and notices on walls remind customers to return their trays.

UNDERSTANDING CONSUMER RESPONSES TO SERVICE ENVIRONMENTS

Environmental psychology studies how people respond to specific environments. We can apply theories from this field to better understand and manage how customers behave in different service settings.

Figure 10.2 Model of Environmental Responses

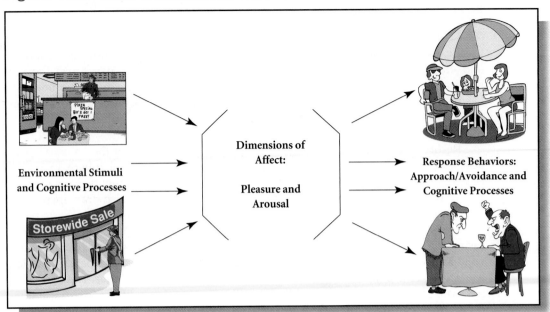

Feelings are a Key Driver of Customer Responses to Service Environments

Two important models help us better understand consumer responses to service environments: the Mehrabian-Russell stimulus–response model and Russell's model of affect.

The Mehrabian-Russell Stimulus–Response Model

Figure 10.2 displays a simple yet fundamental model of how people respond to environments. The model holds that the environment, its conscious and unconscious perception and interpretation, influence how people feel in that environment.[7] People's feelings in turn drive their responses to that environment. Feelings are central to the model, which posits that feelings, rather than perceptions or thoughts, drive behavior. For example, we don't avoid an environment simply because there are a lot of people around us; rather we are deterred by the unpleasant feeling of crowding, of people being in our way, of lacking perceived control, and of not being able to get what we want as fast as we wish to. If we had all the time in the world, felt excited about being part of the crowd during seasonal festivities, then exposure to the same number of people might lead to feelings of pleasure and excitement that would lead us to want to stay and explore that environment.

In environmental psychology, the typical outcome variable is "approach" or "avoidance" of an environment. Of course, in services marketing, we can add a long list of additional outcomes that a firm might want to manage, including how much money people spend and how satisfied they are with the service experience after they have left the firm's premises.

The Russell Model of Affect

Given that affect or feelings are central to how people respond to an environment, we need to understand those feelings better. Russell's model of affect Figure 10.3 is widely used to help understand feelings in service environments and suggests that emotional responses to environments can be described along two main dimensions, pleasure and arousal.[8] Pleasure is a direct, subjective response to the environment, depending on how much the individual likes or dislikes the environment. Arousal refers to how stimulated the individual feels, ranging from deep sleep (lowest level

Figure 10.3
The Russell Model of Affect

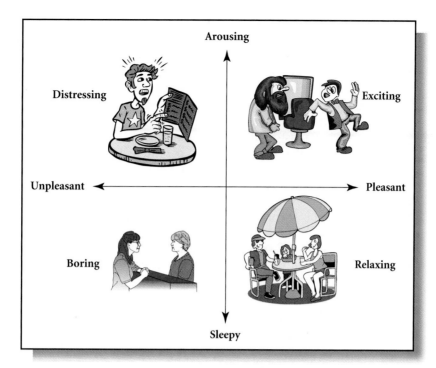

of internal activity) to highest levels of adrenaline in the bloodstream—for example, when bungee jumping (highest level of internal activity). The arousal quality is much less subjective than its pleasure quality. Arousal quality depends largely on the information rate or load of an environment. For example, environments are stimulating (i.e., have a high information rate) when they are complex, include motion or change, and have novel and surprising elements. A low-rate, relaxing environment has the opposite characteristics.

You may ask how can all your feelings and emotions be explained by only two dimensions? Russell separated the cognitive or thinking part of emotions from these two basic underlying emotional dimensions. Thus, the emotion of anger about a service failure could be modeled as high arousal, and high displeasure, which would locate it in the distressing region in our model, combined with a cognitive attribution process. When a customer attributes a service failure to the firm (i.e., he thinks it is the firm's fault that this has happened, that it is under the firm's control, and that the firm is not doing much to avoid it happening again), then this powerful cognitive attribution process feeds directly into high arousal and displeasure. Similarly, most other emotions can be dissected into their cognitive and affective components.

The advantage of Russell's model of affect is its simplicity, as it allows a direct assessment of how customers feel while they are in the service environment. Firms can set targets for affective states. For example, the operator of a bungee-jumping business or a roller-coaster might want its customers to feel aroused (assuming that there is little pleasure in having to gather all one's courage before jumping). A disco or theme park operator may want customers to feel excited (a relatively high-arousal environment combined with pleasure); a bank may want its customers to feel confident. A spa may want customers to feel relaxed, and so on. Later in this chapter, we discuss how service environments can be designed to deliver the types of service experiences desired by customers.

Drivers of Affect

Affect can be caused by perceptions and cognitive processes of any degree of complexity. However, the more complex a cognitive process becomes, the more powerful is its potential impact on affect. For example, a customer's disappointment with service level and food quality in a restaurant (a complex cognitive process, in which perceived quality is compared to previously held service expectations) cannot be compensated by a simple cognitive process such as the subconscious perception of pleasant background music. Yet this doesn't mean that such simple processes are unimportant.

In practice, the large majority of people's service encounters are routine, with little high-level cognitive processing. We tend to function on "autopilot" and follow our service scripts when doing routine transactions such as using a bus or subway, or entering a fast-food restaurant or a bank. Most of the time, it's the simple cognitive processes that determine how people feel in the service setting. Those include the conscious and even unconscious perceptions of space, colors, scents, and so on. However, should higher levels of cognitive processes be triggered—for instance, through something surprising in the service environment—then it's the interpretation of this surprise that determine people's feelings.[9]

Behavioral Consequences of Affect

At the most basic level, pleasant environments tend to draw people in, whereas unpleasant ones result in avoidance behaviors. Arousal acts as an amplifier of the basic effect of pleasure on behavior. If the environment is pleasant, increasing arousal can generate excitement, leading to a stronger positive consumer response. Conversely, if a service environment is inherently unpleasant, managers should avoid increasing arousal levels, as this would move customers into the "distressed" region. For example, loud, fast-beat music would increase the stress levels of shoppers when they are trying to make their way through crowded aisles on a pre-Christmas Friday evening. In such situations, managers need to find ways to lower the information load of the environment.

Customers have strong affective expectations of some services. Think of such experiences as a romantic candle-lit dinner in a restaurant, a relaxing spa visit, or an exciting time at the stadium or the disco. When customers have strong affective expectations, it is important that the environment be designed to match those expectations.[10]

Finally, how customers feel during the service encounter is an important driver of loyalty. Research has shown that positive affect drives hedonic shopping value, which in turn increases repeat purchasing behavior, whereas negative affect mostly reduces utilitarian shopping value and thereby lowers customer share.[11]

The Servicescapes Model—An Integrative Framework of Consumer Responses to Service Environments

Building on the basic models in environmental psychology, Mary Jo Bitner has developed a comprehensive model that she has named the servicescape.[12] Figure 10.4 shows the main dimensions that she identified in service environments, which include ambient conditions, space/functionality, and signs, symbols, and artifacts. Because individuals tend to perceive these dimensions holistically, the key to effective design is how well each individual dimension fits together with everything else.

Next, the model shows that there are customer and employee-response moderators. This means that the same service environment can have different effects on different customers, depending on who that customer is and what she or he likes—beauty lies in the eyes of the beholder, and is subjective. Rap music may be sheer pleasure to some customer segments, and sheer torture to others.

One important contribution of Bitner's model is inclusion of employee responses to the service environment. After all, employees spend much more time there than do customers, and it's crucially important that designers become aware of how a particular environment enhances (or at least does not reduce) the productivity of front-line personnel and the quality of service that they deliver.

Internal customer and employee responses can be categorized into cognitive responses (e.g., quality perceptions and beliefs), emotional responses (e.g., feelings

Figure 10.4 The Servicescapes Model

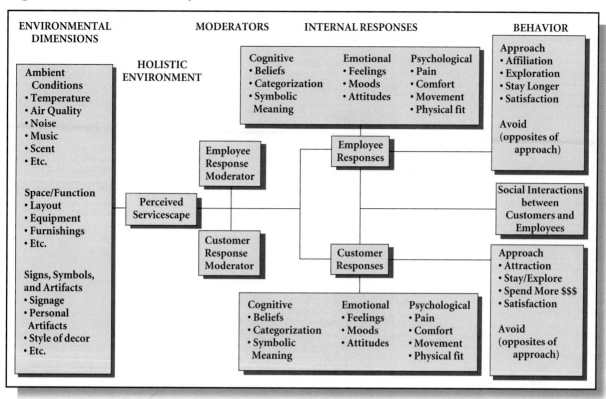

Source: Mary Jo Bitner, "Servicescapes: The Impact of Physical Surroundings on Customers and Employees," *Journal of Marketing* 56 (April 1992): 57–71. American Marketing Association.

and moods), and psychological responses (e.g., pain and comfort). These internal responses lead to overt behavioral responses such as avoiding a crowded department store or responding positively to a relaxing environment by remaining there longer and spending extra money on impulse purchases

DIMENSIONS OF THE SERVICE ENVIRONMENT

Service environments are complex and have many design elements. In Table 10.1, for example, you can see an overview of all the design elements that might be encountered in a retail outlet. In this section, we focus on the main dimensions of the service environment in the servicescape model, which are the ambient conditions, space and functionality, and signs, symbols and artifacts.[13]

The Effect of Ambient Conditions

Ambient conditions refer to those characteristics of the environment that pertain to your five senses. Even when they're not noted consciously, they may still affect your emotional well-being, perceptions, and even attitudes and behaviors. They are composed of literally hundreds of design elements and details that must work together if they are to create the desired service environment.[14] The resulting atmosphere creates a mood that is perceived and interpreted by customers.[15] Ambient conditions are perceived both separately and holistically, and include lighting and color schemes, size and shape perceptions, sounds such as noise and music, temperature, and scents or smells. Clever design of these conditions can elicit desired behavioral responses among consumers. Consider the innovative thinking underlying the new

Table 10.1
Design Elements of a
Retail Store
Environment

DIMENSIONS	DESIGN ELEMENTS	
Exterior facilities	• Architectural style • Height of building • Size of building • Color of building • Exterior walls and exterior signs • Storefront • Marquee • Lawns and gardens	• Window displays • Entrances • Visibility • Uniqueness • Surrounding stores • Surrounding areas • Parking and accessibility • Congestion
General interior	• Flooring and carpeting • Color schemes • Lighting • Scents • Odors (e.g., tobacco smoke) • Sounds and music • Fixtures • Wall composition • Wall textures (paint, wallpaper) • Ceiling composition	• Temperature • Cleanliness • Width of aisles • Dressing facilities • Vertical transportation • Dead areas • Merchandise layout and displays • Price levels and displays • Cash register placement • Technology/modernization
Store layout	• Allocation of floor space for selling, merchandise, personnel, and customers • Placement of merchandise • Grouping of merchandise • Workstation placement • Placement of equipment • Placement of cash register	• Waiting areas • Traffic flow • Waiting queues • Furniture • Dead areas • Department locations • Arrangements within departments
Interior displays	• Point-of-purchase displays • Posters, signs, and cards • Pictures and artwork • Wall decorations • Themesetting • Ensemble	• Racks and cases • Product display • Price display • Cut cases and dump bins • Mobiles
Social dimensions	• Personnel characteristics • Employee uniforms • Crowding	• Customer characteristics • Privacy • Self-service

Source: Adapted from Barry Berman and Joel R. Evans, *Retail Management—A Strategic Approach*, 8th ed. Upper Saddle River, NJ: Prentice-Hall, 2001, p. 604; L. W. Turley and Ronald E. Milliman, "Atmospheric Effects on Shopping Behavior: A Review of the Experimental Literature." *Journal of Business Research*, 49 (2000): 193–211.

trend to transform dental clinics into relaxing dental spas, as described in Best Practice in Action 10.1.

Music

In service settings, music can have a powerful effect on perceptions and behaviors, even if it's played at barely audible volumes. As shown in the servicescape model in Figure 10.4, the various structural characteristics of music such as tempo, volume, and harmony are perceived holistically.[16] Numerous research studies have found that fast-tempo music and high-volume music increases arousal levels,[17] which can then lead customers to increase their pace of various behaviors. People tend to adjust their pace, either voluntarily or involuntarily, to match the tempo of music as shown in Research Insights 10.1.

Does it surprise you to learn that music can also be used to deter the wrong type of customers? Many service environments, including subway systems, supermarkets, and other publicly accessible locations, attract individuals who are not bona-fide customers. Some are jaycustomers (see Chapter 8), whose behavior causes problems for management and customers alike. In the United Kingdom, an increasingly popular strategy for driving such individuals away is to play classical music,

Dentistry is not a service that most people look forward to. Some patients simply find it uncomfortable, especially if they have to remain in a dental chair for an extended period. Many are afraid of the pain associated with certain procedures. And others risk their health by avoiding going to the dentist altogether. Now however, some practitioners are embracing "spa dentistry," in which juice bars, neck rubs, foot massages, and even scented candles and the sound of wind chimes are used to pamper patients and distract them from necessarily invasive treatments inside their mouths.

"It's not about gimmicks," says Timothy Dotson, owner of the Perfect Teeth Dental Spa in Chicago, as a patient breathed strawberry-scented nitrous oxide. "It's treating people the way they want to be treated. It helps a lot of people overcome fear." His patients seem to agree. "Nobody likes coming to the dentist, but this makes it so much easier," remarked one woman as she waited for a crown while a heated massage pad was kneading her back.

Amenities such as hot towels, massages, aromatherapy, coffee, fresh cranberry-orange bread, and white wine spritzers reflect dentists' efforts to meet changing consumer expectations, especially at a time when there is growing consumer demand for esthetic care to whiten and reshape teeth to create a perfect smile. The goal is to entice patients who might otherwise find visiting the dentist a stressful situation. Many dentists who offer spa services do not charge extra for them, arguing that their cost is more than covered by repeat business and patient referrals.

In Houston, Max Greenfield has embellished his Image Max Dental Spa with fountains and modern art. Patients can change into a robe, sample eight different aromas of oxygen, and meditate in a relaxation room decorated like a Japanese garden. The actual dental area features lambskin leather chairs, hot aromatherapy towels, and a procedure known as "bubble gum jet massage" that uses air and water to clean teeth.

Although dental offices from Los Angeles to New York are adopting spa techniques, some question whether this touchy-feely approach is good dentistry or just a passing fad. "I just can't see mingling the two businesses together," remarked the dean of one university dental school.

Source: Adapted from "Dentists Offer New Services to Cut the Fear Factor," *Chicago Tribune* syndicated article, February 2003.

which is apparently painful to vandals' and loiterers' ears! Co-op, a UK grocery chain, has been experimenting with playing music outside its outlets to stop teenagers from hanging around and intimidating customers. Its staff have a remote control and, as reported by Steve Broughton of Co-op, "can turn the music on if there's a situation developing and they need to disperse people."

A number of field experiments have shown the dramatic effects music can have on customers. For example, a restaurant study conducted over eight weeks showed that beverage revenue increased substantially when slow-beat rather than fast-beat music was played. Customers who dined in a slow-music environment spent longer in the restaurant than individuals in a fast-music condition. Likewise, shoppers walked less rapidly when slow music was played and increased their level of impulse purchases. Playing familiar music in a store was shown to stimulate shoppers, and thereby reduce their browsing time, whereas playing unfamiliar music induced shoppers to spend more time there.

In situations that require waiting for service, effective use of music may shorten perceived waiting time and increase customer satisfaction. Relaxing music proved effective in lowering stress levels in a hospital's surgery waiting room. And pleasant music has even been shown to enhance customers' perceptions of, and attitude toward, service personnel.

Sources: Laurette Dubé and Sylvie Morin, "Background Music Pleasure and Store Evaluation Intensity Effects and Psychological Mechanisms." *Journal of Business Research,* 54 (2001): 107–113; Clare Caldwell and Sally A. Hibbert, "The Influence of Music Tempo and Musical Preference on Restaurant Patrons' Behavior." *Psychology and Marketing,* 19, no. 11 (2002): 895–917.

Figure 10.5
Classical Music Can
Be Used to Deter
Vandals and Loiterers

The London Underground (subway) system has made extensive use of classical music as a deterrent. Thirty stations pump out Mozart and Haydn to discourage loitering and vandalism. A London Underground spokesperson reports that the most effective deterrents are anything written by Mozart or sung by Pavarotti. According to Adrian North, a psychologist researching the link between music and behavior at Leicester University, unfamiliarity is a key factor in driving people away. When the target individuals are not used to strings and woodwinds, Mozart will do (Figure 10.5). However, for the more musically literate loiterer, an atonal barrage is likely to work better. For instance, North tormented Leicester's students in the student union bar with what he describes as "computer-game music." It cleared the place!

Scent

An ambient smell is one that pervades an environment, may or may not be consciously perceived by customers, and is not related to any particular product. We are experiencing the power of smell when we are hungry and get a whiff of freshly baked croissants long before we pass a Delifrance Café. This smell makes us aware of our hunger and points us to the solution (i.e., walk into Delifrance and get some food). Other examples include the smell of freshly baked cookies on Main Street in Disney's Magic Kingdom to relax customers and provide a feeling of warmth, or the smell of potpourri in Victoria's Secret stores to create the ambiance of a lingerie closet.[18] Olfaction researcher Alan R. Hirsch, M.D., of the Smell & Taste Treatment and Research Foundation in Chicago, is convinced that in a few years we will understand scents so well that we will be able to use them to manage people's behaviors.[19] Service marketers will be interested in how to make you hungry and thirsty in a restaurant, relax you in a dentist's waiting room, and energize you to work out harder in a gym.

In aromatherapy, it is generally accepted that scents have distinct characteristics and can be used to solicit certain emotional, physiological, and behavioral responses. Table 10.2 shows the generally assumed effects of specific scents on people as prescribed by aromatherapy. In service settings, research has shown that scents can have significant effect on customer perceptions, attitudes, and behaviors. For example:

- Gamblers plunked 45 percent more quarters into slot machines when a Las Vegas casino was scented with a pleasant artificial smell. When the intensity of the scent was increased, spending jumped by 53 percent.[20]

Table 10.2
Aromatherapy—The Effects of Selected Fragrances on People

FRAGRANCE	AROMA TYPE	AROMATHERAPY CLASS	TRADITIONAL USE	POTENTIAL PSYCHOLOGICAL EFFECT ON PEOPLE
Eucalyptus	Camphoraceous	Toning, stimulating	Deodorant, antiseptic, soothing agent; helps remove odor and can be used to cleanse skin	Stimulating and energizing; helps to create balance and the feeling of cleanliness and hygiene
Lavender	Herbaceous	Calming, balancing, soothing	Muscle relaxant, soothing agent, astringent, skin conditioner	Relaxing and calming; helps to create a homely and comfortable feel
Lemon	Citrus	Energizing, uplifting	Antiseptic, soothing agent	Boosts energy levels and helps to make people feel happy and rejuvenated
Black pepper	Spicy	Balancing, soothing	Muscle relaxant, aphrodisiac	Helps to balance people's emotions and enables people to feel sexually aroused

Sources: www.fragrant.demon.co.uk, and www.naha.org/WhatisAromatherapy; Dana Butcher, "Aromatherapy—Its Past and Future." *Drug and Cosmetic Industry,* 16, no. 3 (1998): 22—24; Shirley Price and Len Price, *Aromatherapy for Health Professionals,* 2nd ed. New York: Churchill Livingstone, 1999, pp. 145–160; Anna S. Mattila and Jochen Wirtz, "Congruency of Scent and Music as a Driver of In-Store Evaluations and Behavior." *Journal of Retailing,* 77 (2001): 273–289.

- People were more willing to buy Nike sneakers and pay more for them—an average of US$10.33 more per pair—when they tried on the shoes in a floral-scented room. The same effect was found even when the scent was so faint that people could not detect it—that is, the scent was perceived unconsciously.[21]

Color

Color "is stimulating, calming, expressive, disturbing, impressional, cultural, exuberant, symbolic. It pervades every aspect of our lives, embellishes the ordinary, and gives beauty and drama to everyday objects."[22] Researchers have found that colors have a strong effect on people's feelings.[23]

The de-facto system used in psychological research is the Munsell system, which defines colors in the three dimensions of hue, value, and chroma.[24] *Hue* is the pigment of the color (i.e., the name of the color: red, orange, yellow, green, blue, or violet). *Value* is the degree of lightness or darkness of the color, relative to a scale that extends from pure black to pure white. *Chroma* refers to hue intensity, saturation, or brilliance; high-chroma colors have a high intensity of pigmentation in them and are perceived as rich and vivid, whereas low-chroma colors are perceived as dull. Hues are classified into warm colors (red, orange, and yellow hues) and cold colors (blue and green), with orange (a mix of red and yellow) being the warmest and blue being the coldest of the colors. These colors can be used to manage the warmth of an environment. For example, if a violet is too warm, you can cool it off by reducing the amount of red. Or if a red is too cold, warm it up by giving it a shot of orange.[25] Warm colors are associated with elated mood states, and arousal, but also heightened anxiety, whereas cool colors reduce arousal levels and can elicit emotions such as peacefulness, calmness, love, and happiness.[26] Table 10.3 summarizes common associations and responses to colors.

Research in a service environment context has shown that despite differing color preferences, people are generally drawn to warm-color environments. However,

Table 10.3
Common Associations and Human Responses to Colors

Color	Degree of Warmth	Nature Symbol	Common Associations and Human Responses to Colors
Red	Warm	Earth	High energy and passion; can excite, stimulate, and increase arousal levels and blood pressure
Orange	Warmest	Sunset	Emotions, expression, and warmth; noted for its ability to encourage verbal expression of emotions
Yellow	Warm	Sun	Optimism, clarity, and intellect; bright yellow often noted for its mood-enhancing ability
Green	Cool	Growth, grass, and trees	Nurturing, healing, and unconditional love
Blue	Coolest	Sky and ocean	Relaxation, serenity, and loyalty; lowers blood pressure; is a healing color for nervous disorders and for relieving headaches, because of its cooling and calming nature
Indigo	Cool	Sunset	Meditation and spirituality
Violet	Cool	Violet flower	Spirituality; reduces stress and can create an inner feeling of calm

Sources: Sara O. Marberry and Laurie Zagon, *The Power of Color—Creating Healthy Interior Spaces.* New York: John Wiley, 1995, p. 18; Sarah Lynch, *Bold Colors for Modern Rooms: Bright Ideas for People Who Love Color.* Gloucester, MA: Rockport Publishers, 2001, pp. 24–29.

paradoxically, finding show that red-hued retail environments are seen as negative, tense, and less attractive than cool-color environments.[27] Warm colors encourage fast decision making and in service situations are best suited for low-involvement decisions or impulse purchases. Cool colors are favored when consumers need time to make high-involvement purchases.[28]

Although we have an understanding of the general effects of colors, their use in any specific context needs to be approached with caution. For example, a transportation company in Israel decided to paint its buses green as part of an environmentalism public relations campaign. Reactions to this seemingly simple act from multiple groups of people were unexpectedly negative. Some customers found the green color hampering service performance (because the green buses blended in with the environment and were more difficult to see), or as representing undesirable notions such as terrorism or enemy sports teams, and as esthetically unappealing and inappropriate.[29]

A good example of using color schemes to enhance the service experience is provided by the HealthPark Medical Center in Fort Meyers, Florida, which has combined full-spectrum color in its lobby with unusual lighting to achieve a dreamlike setting. The lobby walls are washed with rainbow colors by an arrangement of high intensity blue, green, violet, red, orange, and yellow lamps. Craig Roeder, the lighting designer for the hospital, explained, "It's a hospital. People walk into it worried and sick. I tried to design an entrance space that provides them with light and energy—to 'beam them up' a little bit before they get to the patient rooms."[30]

Spatial Layout and Functionality

As service environments have to fulfill specific purposes and customer needs, spatial layout and functionality are particularly important. *Spatial layout* refers to the floorplan, size and shape of furnishings, counters, and potential machinery and equipment, and the ways in which they are arranged. *Functionality* refers to the ability of those items to facilitate the performance of service transactions. Spatial layout and functionality create the visual as well as functional servicescape for delivery and consumption to take place. They determine the user-friendliness and the ability of the facility to service customers well, and they not only affect the

Figure 10.6
The Spacious Kuala Lumpur International Airport in Malaysia Is Designed to Help Travelers Find Their Way

efficiency of the service operation, they also shape the customer experience (Figure 10.6). Tables that are too close in a café, counters in a bank that lack privacy, uncomfortable chairs in a lecture theater, and lack of car parking space can all leave negative impressions on customers, affect their service experience and buying behavior, and consequently the business performance of the facility.

Signs, Symbols, and Artifacts

Many things in the service environment act as explicit or implicit signals to communicate the firm's image, help customers find their way (e.g., to certain service counters, or the exit), and to convey the service script (e.g., queuing systems). In particular, first-time customers will automatically try to draw meaning from the environment to guide them through the service processes.

Examples of explicit signals include signs, which can be used as labels (e.g., to indicate the name of the department or counter), for giving directions (e.g., entrance, exit, the way to elevators and toilets), for communicating the service script (e.g., take a number and watch for your number to be called, or clear the tray after your meal), and behavioral rules (e.g., switch off or turn your mobile devices to silent mode during the performance, or smoking/no-smoking areas). Signs are frequently used to teach and reinforce behavioral rules in service settings. Singapore, which strictly enforces rules in many service settings, especially in public buildings and public transport, is sometimes referred to ironically as a "fine" city (Figure 10.7).

The challenge for servicescape designers is to use signs, symbols, and artifacts to guide customers clearly through the process of service delivery and to teach the service process in as intuitive a manner as possible. This task assumes particular importance in situations in which there is a high proportion of new or infrequent customers, and/or a high degree of self-service, especially when few service staff are available to help guide customers through the process.

Customers become disoriented when they cannot derive clear signals from a servicescape, leading to anxiety and uncertainty about how to proceed and how to obtain the desired service. Customers can easily feel lost in a confusing environment and experience anger and frustration as a result. Think about the last time you were in a hurry and tried to find your way through an unfamiliar hospital, shopping

Figure 10.7
Signs Are Frequently
Used to Teach and
Reinforce Behavioral
Rules in Service
Settings

Note: Fines are in
Singapore dollars (equivalent to roughly US$300).

center, or airport, where the signs and other directional cues were not intuitive to you. At many service facilities, customers' first point of contact is likely to be the location where they park their cars. As emphasized in Best Practice in Action 10.2, the principles of effective environment design apply even in this very mundane environment.

People Are Part of the Service Environment, Too

The appearance and behavior of both service personnel and customers can reinforce or detract from the impression created by a service environment. Within the constraints imposed by legal obligations and skill requirements, service firms may seek to recruit staff to fill specific roles, costume them in uniforms that are consistent with the servicescape in which they will be working, and script their speech and movements. Dennis Nickson and his colleagues use the term "aesthetic labor" to capture the impor-

BEST PRACTICE IN ACTION 10.2
Guidelines for Parking Design

Car parks play an important role at many service facilities. Effective use of signs, symbols, and artifacts in a parking lot or garage helps customers find their way, manages their behavior, and portrays a positive image for the sponsoring organization.

- **Friendly warnings.** All warning signs should communicate a customer benefit. For instance, "Fire lane—for everyone's safety we ask you not to park in the fire lane."

- **Fresh paint.** Curbs, crosswalks, and lot lines should be repainted regularly, before any cracking, peeling, or disrepair become evident. Proactive and frequent repainting give positive cleanliness cues and projects a positive image.

- **Safety lighting.** Good lighting that penetrates all areas makes life easier for customers and enhances safety. Firms may want to draw attention to this feature with notices stating that "Parking lots have been specially lit for your safety."

- **Maternity parking.** Handicapped spaces are often required by law but require special stickers on

the vehicle. A few thoughtful organizations have designated "expectant mother" parking spaces, painted with a blue/pink stork. This strategy demonstrates a sense of caring and understanding of customer needs.[31]

- **Help customers remember where they left their vehicle.** Forgetting where one left the family car in a huge lot or parking structure can be a nightmare. Many parking garages have adopted color-coded floors to help customers remember which level they parked on. Boston's Logan Airport goes two steps further. Each level has been assigned a theme associated with Massachusetts, such as Paul Revere's Ride, Cape Cod, or the Boston Marathon. An image is attached to each theme—a male figure on horseback, a lighthouse, or a woman runner. And while waiting for the elevator, travelers hear a few bars of music that are tied to the theme for that level; in the case of the Boston Marathon floor, it's the theme music from *Chariots of Fire*, an Oscar-winning movie about an Olympic runner.

tance of the physical imagery conveyed by customer-facing staff.[32] Likewise, marketing communications may seek to attract customers who will not only appreciate the ambience created by the service provider but will actively enhance it by their appearance and behavior. In hospitality and retail settings, newcomers often survey the array of existing customers before deciding whether to patronize the establishment.

Consider Figure 10.8, which shows the interior of two restaurants. Imagine that you have just entered each of these two dining rooms. How is each positioning itself within the restaurant industry? What sort of meal experience can you expect? And what are the clues that you employ to make your judgments? In particular, what inferences do you draw from looking at the customers who are already seated in each restaurant?

Figure 10.8
Distinctive Servicescapes—From Table Settings to Furniture and Room Design—Create Different Customer Expectations of These Two Restaurants

Although individuals often perceive particular aspects or individual design features of an environment, it is the total configuration of all those design features that determines consumer responses. Consumers perceive service environments holistically.[33]

Design with a Holistic View

Whether a dark, glossy wooden floor is the perfect flooring depends on everything else in that service environment, including the type, color scheme, and materials of the furniture, the lighting, the promotional materials, to the overall brand perception and positioning of the firm. Servicescapes have to be seen holistically, which means no dimension of the design can be optimized in isolation, because everything depends on everything else. Research Insights 10.2 shows that even the arousal elements of scent and music interact and need to be considered in conjunction to elicit the desired consumer responses.

The holistic characteristic of environments makes designing service environments an art, so much so that professional designers tend to focus on specific types of servicescapes. For example, a handful of famous interior designers do nothing but create hotel lobbies around the world. Similarly, there are design experts who focus exclusively on restaurants, bars, clubs, cafés and bistros, or retail outlets, or health care facilities, and so forth.[34]

Design from a Customer's Perspective

Many service environments are built with an emphasis on esthetic values, and designers sometimes forget the most important factor to consider when designing service environments—the customers who will be using them. Ron Kaufman, a consultant and trainer on service excellence, experienced the following design flaws in two new high-profile service environments.

- "A new Sheraton Hotel just had opened in Jordan without clear signage that would guide guests from the ballrooms to the restrooms. The signs that did exist were etched in muted gold on dark marble pillars. More 'obvious' signs were apparently inappropriate amidst such elegant décor. Very swish, very chic, but who were they designing it for?"
- "At the Dragon Air lounge in Hong Kong's new airport, a partition of colorful glass hung from the ceiling. My luggage lightly brushed against it as I walked inside. The entire partition shook and several panels came undone. A staff member hurried over and began carefully reassembling the panels. (Thank goodness nothing broke.) I apologized profusely. 'Don't worry,' she replied, 'This happens all the time.'" An airport lounge is a heavy-traffic area. People are always moving in and out. Ron Kaufman keeps asking, "What were the interior designers thinking? Who were they designing it for?"

"I am regularly amazed," declared Kaufman, "by brand new facilities that are obviously user 'unfriendly'! Huge investments of time and money . . . but who are they designing it for? What were the architects thinking about? Size? Grandeur? Physical exercise? Who were they designing it for?" He draws the following key learning point: "It's easy to get caught up in designing new things that are 'cool' or 'elegant' or 'hot.' But if you don't keep your customer in mind throughout, you could end up with an investment that's not."[35]

Alain d'Astous explored environmental aspects that irritate shoppers. His findings highlighted the following problems:

- *Ambient conditions* (ordered by severity of irritation):
  - Store is not clean
  - Too hot inside the store or the shopping center

Whether a certain type of background enhances consumer responses depends on the ambient scent of the service environment. Using a field experiment, Anna Mattila and Jochen Wirtz manipulated two types of pleasant music and pleasant scent in a gift store, which differed in their arousing qualities. Consumer impulse purchasing and satisfaction were measured for the various music and scent conditions.

The experiment used two compact discs from the Tune Your Brain™ series by Elizabeth Miles, an ethnomusicologist. The low-arousal music was the *Relaxing Collection*, featuring slow-tempo music, while the high-arousal music consisted of the *Energizing Collection*, featuring fast-tempo music. Similarly, scent was manipulated to have high or low arousal quality. Lavender was used for the low-arousal scent because of its relaxing and calming properties. Grapefruit was used for the high-arousal scent because of its stimulating properties, which can refresh, revive, and improve mental clarity and alertness, and can even enhance physical strength and energy.

The results of this experiment showed that when the arousal qualities of music and ambient scent were matched, consumers responded more favorably. The figures below show these effects clearly. For instance, scenting the store with low-arousal scent (lavender) combined with slow-tempo music led to higher satisfaction and more impulse purchases than using that scent with high-arousal music. Playing fast-tempo music had a more positive effect when the store was scented with grapefruit (high-arousal scent) rather than with lavender. This study showed that when environmental stimuli act together to provide a coherent atmosphere, consumers in that environment will respond more positively.

These findings suggest that bookstores might induce people to linger longer and buy more by playing slow-tempo music combined with a relaxing scent, or event managers might consider using arousing scents to enhance excitement.

Figure 10.A The Effect of Scent and Music on Satisfaction

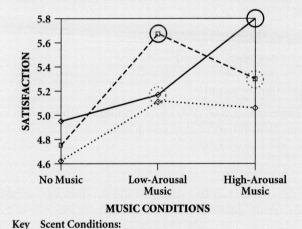

Figure 10.B The Effect of Scent and Music on Impulse Purchases

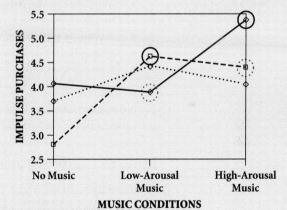

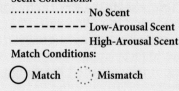

Note: Both charts are on a scale from 1 to 7, with 7 being the extreme positive response. The solid-line circles show the match conditions, in which both music and scent are either stimulating or relaxing, and the intermittent-line circles show the mismatch conditions, in which one stimulus is relaxing and the other is stimulating (i.e., relaxing music and stimulating scent, or stimulating music and relaxing scent).

Source: Adapted from Anna S. Mattila and Jochen Wirtz, "Congruency of Scent and Music as a Driver of In-Store Evaluations and Behavior," *Journal of Retailing* 77 (2001): 273–289.

Walt Disney was one of the undisputed champions of designing service environments. His tradition of amazingly careful and detailed planning has become one of his company's hallmarks, and is visible everywhere in its theme parks. For example, Main Street is angled to make it seem longer upon entry into the Magic Kingdom than it actually is. With myriad facilities and attractions strategically inclined and located at each side of the street, this makes people look forward to the relatively long journey to the Castle. However, looking down the slope from the Castle back toward the entrance makes Main Street appear shorter than it really is, relieving exhaustion and rejuvenating guests. It encourages strolling, which minimizes the number of people who take buses and so eliminates the threatening problem of traffic congestion.

Meandering sidewalks with multiple attractions keep guests feeling entertained by both the planned activities and also by watching other guests; trash bins are plentiful and always in sight, to convey the message that littering is prohibited; and repainting of facilities is a routine procedure that signals a high level of maintenance and cleanliness.

Disney's servicescape design and upkeep help to script customer experiences and create pleasure and satisfaction for guests, not only in its theme parks but also in its cruise ships and hotels.

Sources: Lewis P. Carbone and Stephen H. Haeckel, "Engineering Customer Experiences." *Marketing Management,* 3, no. 3 (Winter 1994): 10–11; Kathy Merlock Jackson, *Walt Disney, A Bio-Bibliography.* Westport, CT: Greenwood Press, 1993, pp. 36–39; Andrew Lainsbury, *Once Upon an American Dream: The Story of Euro Disneyland.* Lawrence, KS: University Press of Kansas, 2000, pp. 64–72.

- Music inside the store too loud
- Bad smell in the store
- *Environmental design variables:*
  - No mirror in the dressing room
  - Unable to find what one needs
  - Directions within the store are inadequate
  - Arrangement of store items has been changed
  - Store is too small
  - Finding the way in a large shopping center[36]

Now, contrast Kaufman's experiences and d'Astou's findings with the Disney example in Best Practice in Action 10.3. What conclusions do you draw?

Tools to Guide Servicescape Design

As a manager, how might you determine which aspects of the servicescape irritate customers and which they like? Among the tools that you can use are the following.

- *Keen observation* of customers' behavior and responses to the service environment by management, supervisors, branch managers, and front-line staff.
- *Feedback and ideas from front-line staff and customers,* using a broad array of research tools ranging from suggestion boxes to focus groups and surveys. (The latter are often called environmental surveys if they focus on the design of the service environment.)
- *Field experiments,* which can be used to manipulate specific dimensions in an environment so that the effects can be observed. For instance, you might experiment with the use of various types of music and scents, and then measure the time and money customers spend in the environment, and their level of satisfaction. Laboratory experiments, using slides or videos or other ways to simulate real-world service environments (such as computer-simulated virtual tours), can be used effectively to examine the effect of changes in design elements that cannot easily be manipulated in a field experiment. Examples include testing of alternative color schemes, spatial layouts, or styles of furnishing.

- *Blueprinting* or service mapping (described in Chapter 8) can be extended to include the physical evidence in the environment. Design elements and tangible cues can be documented as the customer moves through each step of the service delivery process. Photos and videos can supplement the map to make it more vivid.

Table 10.4 shows an analysis of a customer's visit to a movie theater, identifying how different environmental elements at each step exceeded or failed to meet expectations. The service process was broken up into increments, steps, decisions, duties, and activities, all designed to take the customer through the entire service encounter. The more a service company can see, understand, and experience the same things as its customers, the better equipped it will be to realize errors in the design of its environment, and to further improve what is already functioning well.

Table 10.4
A Visit to the Movies: The Service Environment as Perceived by the Customer

Steps in the Service Encounter	Design of the Service Environment	
	Exceeds Expectations	Fails Expectations
Locate a parking lot	Ample room in a bright place near the entrance, with a security officer protecting your valuables	Insufficient parking spaces, so patrons have to park in another lot
Queuing up to obtain tickets	Strategic placement of mirrors, posters of upcoming movies, and entertainment news to ease perception of long wait, if any; movies and time slots easily seen; ticket availability clearly communicated	A long queue and having to wait for a long while; difficult to see quickly what movies are being shown at what time slots and whether tickets are still available
Checking of tickets to enter the theater	A very well maintained lobby with clear directions to the theater and posters of the movie to enhance patrons' experience	A dirty lobby with rubbish strewn and unclear or misleading directions to the movie theater
Go to the restroom before the movie starts	Sparkling clean, spacious, brightly lit, dry floors, well stocked, nice decor, clear mirrors wiped regularly	Dirty, with an unbearable odor; broken toilets; no hand towels, soap, or toilet paper; overcrowded; dusty and dirty mirrors
Enter the theater and locate your seat	Spotless theater; well designed with no bad seats; sufficient lighting to locate your seat; spacious, comfortable chairs, with drink and popcorn holders on each seat; and a suitable temperature	Rubbish on the floor, broken seats, sticky floors, gloomy and insufficient lighting, burned-out exit signs
Watch the movie	Excellent sound system and film quality, nice audience, an enjoyable and memorable entertainment experience overall	Substandard sound and movie equipment, uncooperative audience that talks and smokes because of lack of "No Smoking" and other signs; a disturbing and unenjoyable entertainment experience overall
Leave the theater and return to the car	Friendly service staff greet patrons as they leave; an easy exit through a brightly lit and safe parking area back to the car with the help of clear lot signs	A difficult trip, as patrons squeeze through a narrow exit, unable to find the car because of no or insufficient lighting

Source: Adapted from Steven Albrecht, "See Things from the Customer's Point of View—How to Use the 'Cycles of Service' to Understand What the Customer Goes Through to Do Business with You." *World's Executive Digest* (December 1996): 53–58.

CONCLUSION

The service environment plays a major part in shaping customers' perception of a firm's image and positioning. As service quality is often difficult to assess objectively, customers frequently use the service environment as an important quality signal. A well-designed service environment makes customers feel good and boosts their satisfaction, while enhancing the productivity of the service operation.

The theoretical underpinnings for understanding the effects of service environments on customers come from the environmental psychology literature. The Mehrabian-Russell stimulus–response model holds that environments influence peoples' affective state (or feelings), which in turn drives their behavior in that environment. Affect can be modeled with the two key dimensions of pleasure and arousal, which together determine whether people approach, spend time and money in an environment, or avoid it. The servicescape concept, which was built on these theories, represents a comprehensive framework that explains how customers and service staff respond to service environments.

The main dimensions of service environments are ambient conditions (including music, scents, and colors), spatial layout and functionality, and signs, symbols, and artifacts. Each dimension can have important effects on customer responses. Because environments are perceived holistically, no individual aspect can be optimized without considering everything else. Designing service environments is an art. Professional designers tend to specialize in one or more specific types of environment, such as hotel lobbies, restaurants, clubs, cafés and bistros, retail outlets, health care facilities, and so on. Beyond esthetic considerations, the best service environments must be designed with the needs of the customer in mind if they are to achieve the goal of guiding these customers smoothly through the service process.

REVIEW QUESTIONS

1. Compare and contrast the strategic and functional roles of service environments within a service organization.
2. What are affective expectations? What is their role in driving customer satisfaction with service encounters?
3. What is the relationship or link between the Russell model of affect and Bitner's servicescape model?
4. Why is it likely that different customers and service staff respond differently to the same service environment?
5. Select a bad and a good waiting experience and contrast the situations with respect to the esthetics of the surrounding, diversions, people waiting, and attitude of servers.
6. Explain the dimensions of ambient conditions and how each can influence customer responses to the service environment.
7. What are the roles of signs, symbols, and artifacts?
8. What are the implications of the fact that environments are perceived holistically?
9. What tools are available for aiding our understanding of customer responses, and for guiding the design and improvements of service environments?

APPLICATION EXERCISES

1. Identify firms from three different service sectors in which the service environment is a crucial part of the overall value proposition. Analyze and explain in detail the value that is being delivered by the service environment.
2. Visit a service environment, and have a careful look around. Experience the environment and try and feel how the various design parameters shape what you feel and how you behave in that setting.
3. Visit a self-service environment and analyze how the design dimensions guide you thorough the service process. What do you find most effective for yourself, and what seems least effective? How could that environment be improved to further ease the "way-finding" for self-service customers?

ENDNOTES

1. The term *servicescape* was coined by Mary Jo Bitner in "Servicescapes: The Impact of Physical Surroundings on Customers and Employees." *Journal of Marketing,* 56 (1992): 57–71.
2. Julie Baker, Dhruv Grewal, and A. Parasuraman, "The Influence of Store Environment on Quality Inferences and Store Image." *Journal of the Academy of Marketing Science,* 22, no. 4 (1994): 328–339.
3. Véronique Aubert-Gamet, "Twisting Servicescapes: Diversion of the Physical Environment in a Reappropriation Process." *International Journal of Service Industry Management,* 8, no. 1 (1997): 26–41.
4. Madeleine E. Pullman and Michael A. Gross, "Ability of Experience Design Elements to Elicit Emotions and Loyalty Behaviors." *Decision Sciences,* 35, no. 1 (2004): 551–578.
5. Lisa Takeuchi Cullen, "Is Luxury the Ticket?" *Time,* August 22, 2005, pp. 38–39.
6. Richard B. Chase and Douglas M. Stewart, "Making Your Service Fail-Safe." *Sloan Management Review,* 35 (1994): 35–44.

7. Robert J. Donovan and John R. Rossiter, "Store Atmosphere: An Environmental Psychology Approach." *Journal of Retailing*, 58, no. 1 (1982): 34–57.

8. James A. Russell, "A Circumplex Model of Affect." *Journal of Personality and Social Psychology*, 39, no. 6 (1980): 1161–1178.

9. Jochen Wirtz and John E. G. Bateson, "Consumer Satisfaction with Services: Integrating the Environmental Perspective in Services Marketing into the Traditional Disconfirmation Paradigm." *Journal of Business Research*, 44, no. 1 (1999): 55–66.

10. Jochen Wirtz, Anna S. Mattila, and Rachel L. P. Tan, "The Moderating Role of Target-Arousal on the Impact of Affect on Satisfaction—An Examination in the Context of Service Experiences." *Journal of Retailing*, 76, no. 3 (2000): 347–365.

11. Barry J. Babin and Jill S. Attaway, "Atmospheric Affect as a Tool for Creating Value and Gaining Share of Customer." *Journal of Business Research*, 49 (2000): 91–99.

12. Mary Jo Bitner, "Service Environments: The Impact of Physical Surroundings on Customers and Employees." *Journal of Marketing*, 56 (April 1992): 57–71.

13. For a comprehensive review of experimental studies on the atmospheric effects, see L. W. Turley and Ronald E. Milliman, "Atmospheric Effects on Shopping Behavior: A Review of the Experimental Literature." *Journal of Business Research*, 49 (2000): 193–211.

14. Patrick M. Dunne, Robert F. Lusch, and David A. Griffith, *Retailing*, 4th ed. Orlando, FL: Harcourt, 2002, p. 518.

15. Barry Davies and Philippa Ward, *Managing Retail Consumption*. West Sussex, UK: John Wiley & Sons, 2002, p. 179.

16. Steve Oakes, "The Influence of the Musicscape Within Service Environments." *Journal of Services Marketing*, 14, no. 7 (2000): 539–556.

17. Morris B. Holbrook and Punam Anand, "Effects of Tempo and Situational Arousal on the Listener's Perceptual and Affective Responses to Music." *Psychology of Music*, 18 (1990): 150–162; S. J. Rohner and R. Miller, "Degrees of Familiar and Affective Music and Their Effects on State Anxiety." *Journal of Music Therapy*, 17, no. 1 (1980): 2–15.

18. Patrick M. Dunne, Robert F. Lusch, and David A. Griffith, *Retailing*, p. 520.

19. Alan R. Hirsch, *Dr. Hirsch's Guide to Scentsational Weight Loss*. UK: Harper Collins, 1997, pp. 12–15.

20. Alan R. Hirsch, "Effects of Ambient Odors on Slot Machine Usage in a Las Vegas Casino." *Psychology and Marketing*, 12, no. 7 (1995): 585–594.

21. Alan R. Hirsch and S. E. Gay, "Effect on Ambient Olfactory Stimuli on the Evaluation of a Common Consumer Product." *Chemical Senses*, 16 (1991): 535.

22. Linda Holtzschuhe, *Understanding Color—An Introduction for Designers*, 2nd ed. New York: John Wiley & Sons, 2002, p. 1.

23. Gerald J Gorn, Amitava Chattopadhyay, Tracey Yi, and Darren Dahl, "Effects of Color as an Executional Cue in Advertising: They're in the Shade." *Management Science*, 43, no. 10 (1997): 1387–1400; Ayn E. Crowley, "The Two-Dimensional Impact of Color on Shopping." *Marketing Letters*, 4, no. 1 (1993): 59–69; Gerald J. Gorn, Amitava Chattopadhyay, Jaideep Sengupta, and Shashank Tripathi, "Waiting for the Web: How Screen Color Affects Time Perception." *Journal of Marketing Research*, XLI (May 2004): 215–225; Iris Vilnai-Yavetz and Anat Rafaeli, "Aesthetics and Professionalism of Virtual Servicescapes." *Journal of Service Research* (2006, forthcoming).

24. Albert Henry Munsell, *A Munsell Color Product*. New York: Kollmorgen Corporation, 1996.

25. Linda Holtzschuhe, *Understanding Color—An Introduction for Designers*, p. 51.

26. Heinrich Zollinger, *Color: A Multidisciplinary Approach*. Zurich: Verlag Helvetica Chimica Acta (VHCA)–Weinheim: Wiley-VCH, 1999, pp. 71–79.

27. Joseph A. Bellizzi, Ayn E. Crowley, and Ronald W. Hasty, "The Effects of Color in Store Design." *Journal of Retailing*, 59, no. 1 (1983): 21–45.

28. John E. G. Bateson and K. Douglas Hoffman, *Managing Services Marketing*, 4th ed. Orlando, FL: The Dryden Press, 1999, p. 143.

29. Anat Rafaeli and Iris Vilnai-Yavetz, "Discerning Organizational Boundaries Through Physical Artifacts." In N. Paulsen and T. Hernes, eds., *Managing Boundaries in Organizations: Multiple Perspectives*. Basingstoke, Hampshire, UK: Macmillan, 2003; Anat Rafaeli and Iris Vilnai-Yavetz, "Emotion as a Connection of Physical Artifacts and Organizations." *Organization Science*, 15, no 6 (2004): 671–686; Anat Rafaeli and Iris Vilnai-Yavetz, "Managing Organizational Artifacts to Avoid Artifact Myopia." In A. Rafaeli and M. Pratt, eds., *Artifacts and Organization: Beyond Mere Symbolism*. Mahwah, NJ: Lawrence Erlbaum Associates, 2005, pp. 9–21.

30. Sara O. Marberry and Laurie Zagon, *The Power of Color—Creating Healthy Interior Spaces*. New York: John Wiley & Sons, 1995, p. 38.

31. Lewis P. Carbone and Stephen H. Haeckel, "Engineering Customer Experiences." *Marketing Management*, 3, no. 3 (Winter 1994): 9–18.

32. Dennis Nickson, Chris Warhurst, and Eli Dutton, "The Importance of Attitude and Appearance in the Service Encounter in Retail and Hospitality." *Managing Service Quality*, 2 (2005): 195–208.

33. Anna S. Mattila and Jochen Wirtz, "Congruency of Scent and Music as a Driver of In-Store Evaluations and Behavior." *Journal of Retailing*, 77 (2001): 273–289.

34. Christine M. Piotrowski and Elizabeth A. Rogers, *Designing Commercial Interiors*. New York: John Wiley & Sons, 1999; Martin M. Pegler, *Cafes & Bistros*. New York: Retail Reporting Corporation, 1998; Paco Asensio, *Bars & Restaurants*. New York: HarperCollins International, 2002; Bethan Ryder, *Bar and Club Design*. London: Laurence King Publishing, 2002.

35. Ron Kaufman, "Service Power: Who Were They Designing It For?" Newsletter, May 2001, http://Ron Kaufman.com.

36. Alan d'Astous, "Irritating Aspects of the Shopping Environment." *Journal of Business Research*, 49 (2000): 149–156. See also K. Douglas Hoffman, Scott W. Kelly, and Beth C. Chung, "A CIT Investigation of Servicscape Failures and Associated Recovery Strategies." *Journal of Services Marketing*, 17, no. 4 (2003): 322–340.

Chapter 11

Managing People for
Service Advantage

Among the most demanding jobs in service businesses are those in front-line positions. Employees working in these customer-facing jobs span the boundary between inside and outside the organization. They are expected to be fast and efficient in executing operational tasks, as well as courteous and helpful in dealing with customers. Unless operations and marketing managers can reach agreement on how to balance these two sets of objectives, employees may find themselves needlessly stressed by conflicting demands

Front-line employees, often working together in teams, are a key input to delivering service excellence and competitive advantage. In high-contact services, employees are a highly visible part of the product each and every time a customer uses it. In low-contact services, employees—most commonly reached by phone, mail, or email—are rarely seen but play a vital role in building (or destroying) customer confidence on those occasions when they are contacted to handle special requests or resolve problems. These are the reasons why the *People* element forms such an important part of the 8 Ps services marketing mix. It is this element that most closely links the marketing, operations, and human resource functions in the effort to create an effective value exchange between the organization and its customers.

Behind most of today's successful service organizations stands a firm commitment to effective management of human resources (HR), including recruitment, selection, training, motivation, and retention of employees. Organizations that display this commitment understand the economic payoff from investing in their people. These firms are also characterized by a distinctive culture of service leadership and role modeling by top management. It is probably harder for competitors to duplicate high-performance human assets than any other corporate resource.

In this chapter, we focus on the people side of service management and explore the following questions:

1. Why is the front line so crucially important to the success of a service firm?
2. Why is the work of service employees so demanding, challenging, and often difficult?
3. What are the cycles of failure, mediocrity, and success in HR for service firms?
4. How do we get it right? How are we to attract, select, train, motivate, and retain outstanding front-line employees?
5. What is the role of teams in service delivery, and how should they be created and managed?
6. What part do service culture and service leadership play in sustaining service excellence?

SERVICE EMPLOYEES ARE CRUCIALLY IMPORTANT

Almost everybody can recount some horror story of a dreadful experience with a service business. If pressed, many of these same people can also recount a really good service experience. Service personnel usually feature prominently in such dramas. They are either in roles as uncaring, incompetent, mean-spirited villains, or in roles as heroes who went out of their way to help customers by anticipating their needs and resolving problems in a helpful and empathetic manner. You probably have your own set of favorite stories, featuring both villains and heroes—and if you're like most people, you probably talk more about the former than the latter. From the firm's perspective, service staff are crucially important, as they can be a key determinant of customer loyalty (or defections), and therefore play a significant role in creating long-term profits for the firm.

Service Personnel as a Source of Customer Loyalty and Competitive Advantage

From a customer's perspective, the encounter with service staff is probably the most important aspect of a service. From the firm's perspective, the service levels and the way service is delivered by front-line personnel can be an important source of differentiation as well as competitive advantage. In addition, the strength of the customer–front-line employee relationship is often an important driver of customer loyalty.[1] Among the reasons why service employees are so important to customers and the firm's competitive positioning are that the front line

- *Is a core part of the product.* Often, service employees are the most visible element of the service, deliver the service, and significantly determine service quality.
- *Is the service firm.* Front-line employees represent the service firm, and from a customer's perspective, they are the firm.
- *Is the brand.* Front-line employees and the service they provide are often a core part of the brand. It is the employees who determine whether the brand promise is delivered.

Furthermore, front-line employees play a key role in anticipating customers' needs, customizing service delivery, and building personalized relationships with customers. Effective performance of these activities should ultimately result in customer loyalty. How attentive employees can be in anticipating customers' needs is shown in the following example. Steve Posner, a veteran room-service waiter at Ritz-Carlton, says that he constantly tries to anticipate what guests might want. He puts extra silverware on the table: "This may be for a child, so I also bring a small spoon for the soup." He includes A1 steak sauce with hamburger orders: "They may not even have thought they wanted it, but they're happy to find it there." He puts a plate of lemon wedges next to a Coke: "Always bring more than you think people need." The aim isn't to lay out a table in some fussily proper way, but to make sure that guests' "unexpressed wishes and needs" are met. "As a waiter, you're the pre-guest. You have to try to think the way a guest would."[2]

This and many other success stories of employees showing discretionary efforts that made a difference have reinforced the truism that highly motivated people are at the core of service excellence.[3] They are increasingly a key variable for creating and maintaining competitive positioning and advantage.

The intuitive importance of the effect of service employees on customer loyalty was integrated and formalized by James Heskett and his colleagues in their pioneering research on what they call the *service–profit chain*, which demonstrates the chain of relationships among (1) employee satisfaction, retention, and productivity; (2) service value; (3) customer satisfaction and loyalty; and (4) revenue growth and profitability for the firm.[4] They develop these themes further in their book, *The Value Profit Chain: Treat Employees Like Customers and Customers Like Employees*.[5] Unlike manufacturing, "shop-floor workers" in services (i.e., front-line staff) are in constant contact with customers, and there is solid evidence showing that employee satisfaction and customer satisfaction are highly correlated.[6] This chapter focuses on how to have satisfied, loyal, and productive service employees.

The Front Line in Low-Contact Services

Most research in service management and many of the best-practice examples featured in this chapter relate to high-contact services. This is not entirely surprising, of course, because the people in these jobs are so visible. They are the actors who appear front-stage in the service drama when they serve the customer. So it is obvious why the front line is crucially important to customers, and therefore also to the competitive positioning of the firm. However, there's a growing trend across virtually all types of services toward low-contact delivery channels such as call centers and self-service options. Many routine transactions are now being conducted without involving front-line staff at all. Examples include the many types of services that are provided via web sites, automatic teller machines (ATMs), and interactive voice-response (IVR) systems. In the light of these trends, is the front line really that important, especially when more and more routine transactions are being shifted to low- or no-contact channels?

Although the quality of the technology and self-service interface (i.e., the web site, the ATM network, and the IVRs) is becoming the core engine for service delivery and its importance has been elevated drastically, the quality of front-line employees remains crucially important. Most people do not call the service hotline or visit the service center of their mobile phone service operator or their credit card company more than once or twice a year. However, these occasional service encounters are absolutely critical—they are the "moments of truth" that drive a customer's perceptions of the service firm (see Figure 11.1). Also, it is likely that these interactions are not about routine transactions, but are about service problems and special requests. These very few contacts determine whether a customer thinks, "Customer service is excellent. When I need help, I can call you, and this is one important reason why I bank with you"; or "Your service stinks. I don't like interacting with you, and I am going to spread the word about how bad your service is."

Figure 11.1
A Friendly Employee at a San Diego Bank Delivering a "Moment of Truth."

Research by McKinsey & Co. in both Europe and the United States confirms the importance of focusing on moments of truth when customers have an unusual amount of emotional energy invested in the outcome. "Many companies," say consultants Marc Beaujean, Jonathan Davidson, and Stacey Madge, "make the mistake of overinvesting in humdrum transactions but fail to differentiate themselves in the customer transactions that really matter."[7] Given that technology is relatively commoditized, the service delivered by the front line, whether it is face to face, "ear to ear," or via email, is highly visible and important to customers, and therefore a critical component of marketing strategy.

FRONT-LINE WORK IS DIFFICULT AND STRESSFUL

The service–profit chain requires high-performing, satisfied employees to achieve service excellence and customer loyalty. However, these customer-facing employees work in some of the most demanding jobs in service firms. Perhaps you have worked in one or more such jobs, which are particularly common in the health care, hospitality, retailing, and travel industries. Let's discuss the main reasons these jobs are so demanding (and you can relate these to your own experience, while recognizing that there may be differences between working part-time for short periods and full-time as a career).

Boundary Spanning

The organizational behavior literature refers to front-line service employees as *boundary spanners*. They link the inside of an organization to the outside world, operating at the boundary of the company. Because of the position they occupy, boundary spanners often have conflicting roles. In particular, customer contact personnel must attend to both operational and marketing goals. To illustrate, service staff are expected to delight customers, and at the same time be fast and efficient in executing operational tasks. On top of that, they are often expected to do selling, cross-selling, and up-selling as well—for instance, "Now would be a good time to open a separate account to save for your children's education"; or "For only $25 more per night, you can upgrade to the executive floor." Finally, sometimes they are even responsible for enforcing rate integrity and pricing schedules that might be in direct conflict with customer satisfaction (e.g., "I'm sorry, we don't serve ice water in this restaurant, but we have an excellent selection of still and carbonated mineral waters"; or "I'm sorry, but we cannot waive the fee for the bounced check for the third time this quarter)."

In short, front-line staff may perform triple roles, creating service quality, improving productivity, and making sales. This multiplicity of roles in service jobs often leads to role conflict and role stress among employees,[8] which we discuss next.

Sources of Conflict

Role stress in front-line positions has three main causes: person/role, organization/client, and interclient conflicts.

Person/Role Conflict

Service staff may have conflicts between what their job requires and their own personality, self-perception, and beliefs. For example, the job may require staff to smile and be friendly to rude customers, even jaycustomers (as described in Chapter 8). V. S. Mahesh and Anand Kasturi note from their consulting work with service organizations around the world that thousands of front-line staff, when asked, consistently tend to describe customers with a pronounced negative flavor—frequently using phrases such as "overdemanding," "unreasonable," "refuse to listen," "always want everything their way, immediately," and even "arrogant."[9]

Providing quality service requires an independent, warm, and friendly personality. These traits are more likely to be found in people with higher self-esteem. However, many front-line jobs are perceived as low-level jobs, which require little education, offer low pay, and often lack prospects for advancement. If an organization is not able to "professionalize" its front-line jobs and move them away from this image, these jobs may be inconsistent with the staff's self-perception and lead to person/role conflicts.

Organization/Client Conflict

Service employees frequently face the dilemma of whether they should follow the company's rules or satisfy customer demands. This conflict is also called the two-bosses dilemma and arises when customers request services, extras, or exceptions that violate organizational rules. The problem is especially acute in organizations that are not customer-oriented. In these cases, staff frequently has to deal with conflicting customer needs and requests, as well as organizational rules, procedures, and productivity requirements.

Interclient Conflict

Conflicts between customers are not uncommon (e.g., smoking in a nonsmoking section, cutting into a line, talking on a cell phone in a movie theater, or being excessively noisy in a restaurant), and it is usually the service staff that is summoned to call the offending customer to order. This is a stressful and unpleasant task, as it is difficult and often impossible to satisfy both sides.

Emotional Labor

The term *emotional labor* was coined by Arlie Hochschild in her book, *The Managed Heart*.[10] Emotional labor arises when there is a discrepancy between the way front-line staff feel inside and the emotions that management requires them to show in front of customers. Front-line staff are expected to have a cheerful disposition, be genial, compassionate, sincere, or even self-effacing—emotions that can be conveyed through facial expressions, gestures, tone of voice, and words. Although some service firms make an effort to recruit employees with such characteristics, there will inevitably be situations when employees do not feel such positive emotions, yet are required to suppress their true feelings in order to conform to customer expectations. As Pannikkos Constanti and Paul Gibbs point out, "the power axis for emotional labor tends to favor both the management and the customer, with the front line employee . . . being subordinate," thus creating a potentially exploitative situation.[11]

The stress of emotional labor is nicely illustrated in the following, probably apocryphal story: A flight attendant was approached by a passenger with "Let's have a smile." She replied with "Okay. I'll tell you what, first you smile and then I'll smile, okay?" He smiled. "Good," she said. "Now hold that for 15 hours," and walked away.[12]

Companies are now taking steps to help employees deal with the problem of emotional labor. For example, because of Singapore Airlines' reputation for service excellence, its customers tend to have very high expectations and can be very demanding. This puts considerable pressure on its front-line employees. The commercial training manager of Singapore Airlines (SIA) explained:

> We have recently undertaken an external survey and it appears that more of the 'demanding customers' choose to fly with SIA. So the staff are really under a lot of pressure. We have a motto: 'If SIA can't do it for you, no other airline can.' So we encourage staff to try to sort things out, and to do as much as they can for the customer. Although they are very proud, and indeed protective of the company, we need to help them deal with the emotional turmoil of having to handle their customers well, and at the same time, feel they're not being taking advantage of. The challenge is to help our staff deal with difficult situations and take the brickbats. This will be the next thrust of our training programs.[13]

Firms need to be aware of ongoing emotional stress among their employees and to devise ways of alleviating it, which should include training on how to deal with such stress and how to cope with pressure from customers. Figure 11.2 captures emotional labor with humor.

Service Sweat Shops?

Rapid developments in information technology are permitting service businesses to make radical improvements in business processes and even completely reengineer their operations. These developments sometimes result in wrenching changes in the nature of work for existing employees. In instances where face-to-face contact has been

Figure 11.2
Dilbert Encounters Emotional Labor at the Bank

DILBERT: © Scott Adams/Dist. by permission of United Syndicate, Inc.

Figure 11.3
Work in Customer
Contact Centers Is
Intense, but How
Customer Service
Representatives
Perform Often
Determines How a
Firm's Service Quality
Is Perceived by
Customers

replaced by use of the Internet or call center-provided services, firms have redefined and relocated jobs, created new employee profiles for recruiting purposes, and sought to hire employees with a different set of qualifications.

As a result of the growing shift from high-contact to low-contact services, a large and increasing number of customer contact employees work by telephone or email, never meeting customers face to face.[14] For example, a remarkable 3 percent-plus of the total U.S. workforce is now employed in call centers as "customer service representatives" or CSRs.

At best, when they are well designed, such jobs can be rewarding, and often offer parents and students flexible working hours and part-time jobs (some 50 percent of call center workers are single mothers or students). In fact, it has been shown that part-time workers are more satisfied with their work as CSRs than are full-time staff, and perform just as well.[15] At worst, these jobs place employees in an electronic equivalent of the old-fashioned sweatshop. Even in the best-managed call centers (also often called *customer contact centers*), the work is intense (see Figure 11.3), with CSRs expected to deal with up to two calls a minute (including trips to the toilet and breaks) and under a high level of monitoring. There is also significant stress from customers themselves, because many are irate at the time of contact. Mahesh and Anand's research on call centers found that intrinsically motivated agents suffered less customer stress.[16] As we will discuss in this chapter, some of the keys to success in this area involve screening applicants to make sure they already know how to present themselves well on the telephone and have the potential to learn additional skills, training them carefully, and giving them a well-designed working environment.[17] For an in-depth discussion of call center management, see the reading, "Getting More from Call Centers," by Keith A. Gibson and Deepak K. Khandelwal (pp. 346–351).

CYCLES OF FAILURE, MEDIOCRITY, AND SUCCESS

All too often, poor working environments translate into dreadful service, with employees treating customers the way their managers treat them. Businesses with high employee turnover are frequently stuck in a *cycle of failure*. Others, which offer job security but little scope for personal initiative, may suffer from an equally unde-

Figure 11.4
The Cycle of Failure

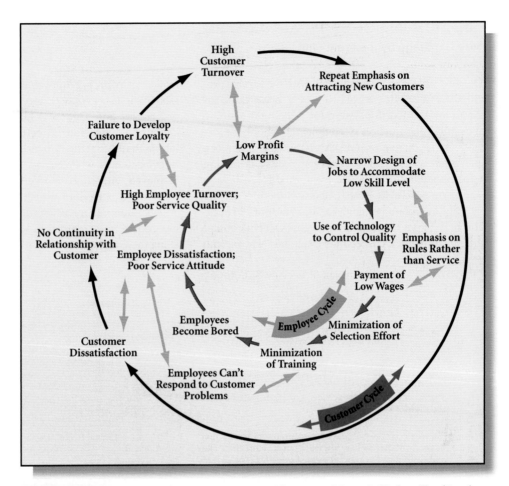

sirable *cycle of mediocrity*. However, if the working environment is managed well, there is potential for a virtuous cycle in service employment, a *cycle of success*.[18]

The Cycle of Failure

In many service industries, the search for productivity is being carried out with a vengeance. One solution takes the form of simplifying work routines and hiring workers as cheaply as possible to perform repetitive work tasks that require little or no training. Among consumer services, department stores, fast-food restaurants and call center operations are often cited as examples in which this problem abounds (although there are notable exceptions). The cycle of failure captures the implications of such a strategy, with its two concentric but interactive cycles: one involving failures with employees and the second, with customers (Figure 11.4).

The *employee cycle of failure* begins with a narrow design of jobs to accommodate low skill levels, an emphasis on rules rather than service, and the use of technology to control quality. A strategy of low wages is accompanied by minimal effort in selection or training. Consequences include bored employees who lack the ability to respond to customer problems, who become dissatisfied, and who develop a poor service attitude. Outcomes for the firm are low service quality and high employee turnover. Because of weak profit margins, the cycle repeats itself, with the hiring of more low-paid employees to work in this unrewarding atmosphere. Some service firms can reach such low levels of employee morale that front-line staff become hostile toward customers and may even engage in "service sabotage," as described in Research Insights 11.1.[19]

The next time you are dissatisfied with the service provided by a service employee—in a restaurant, for example—it's worth pausing for a moment to think about the consequences of complaining about the service. You might just become the unknowing victim of a malicious case of service sabotage, such as having something unhygienic added to your food.

There is actually a fairly high incidence of service sabotage by front-line employees. In a study of 182 front-line staff, Lloyd Harris and Emmanuel Ogbonna found that 90 percent of them accepted front-line behavior with malicious intent to reduce or spoil the service—service sabotage is an everyday occurrence in their organizations.

Harris and Ogbonna classify service sabotage along two dimensions: covert–overt, and routinized–intermittent behaviors. Covert behaviors are concealed from customers, whereas overt actions are purposefully displayed, often to co-workers and also to customers. Routinized behaviors are ingrained in the culture, whereas intermittent actions are sporadic and less common. Some true examples of service sabotage classified along these two dimensions appear in Figure 11.A.

Figure 11.A Examples of Service Sabotage

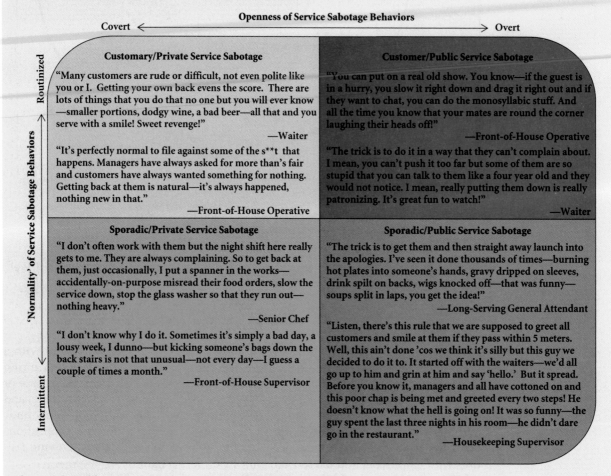

Source: Adapted from Lloyd C. Harris and Emmanuel Ogbonna, "Exploring Service Sabotage: The Antecedents, Types, and Consequences of Front-Line, Deviant, Antiservice Behaviors." *Journal of Service Research,* 4, no. 3 (2002): 163–183. Copyright © 2002 by Sage Publications, Inc. Reprinted by permission of Sage Publications, Inc.

The *customer cycle of failure* begins with heavy organizational emphasis on attracting new customers, who become dissatisfied with employee performance and the lack of continuity implicit in continually changing faces. These customers fail to develop any loyalty to the supplier, and turn over as rapidly as the staff. This situation requires an ongoing search for new customers to maintain sales volume. The departure of discontented customers is especially worrying in the light of what we now know about the greater profitability of a loyal customer base.

Managers' excuses and justifications for perpetuating the cycle of failure tend to focus on employees:

- "You just can't get good people nowadays."
- "People today just don't want to work."
- "To get good people would cost too much, and you can't pass these cost increases on to customers."
- "It's not worth training our front-line people when they leave so quickly."
- "High turnover is simply an inevitable part of our business. You've got to learn to live with it."[20]

Too many managers make short-sighted assumptions about the financial implications of low-pay/high-turnover human resource strategies. James Heskett, Earl Sasser, and Leonard Schlesinger argue that companies need to measure employee lifetime value, just as they seek to calculate customer lifetime value.[21] Part of the problem is failure to measure all relevant costs.

Three key cost variables are often omitted: (1) the cost of continually recruiting, hiring, and training (which is as much a time cost for managers as a financial cost); (2) the lower productivity of inexperienced new workers; and (3) the costs of constantly having to attract new customers (which requires extensive advertising and promotional discounts). Also ignored are two revenue variables: (4) future revenue streams that might have continued for years but are lost when unhappy customers take their business elsewhere; and (5) the potential income lost from prospective customers who are turned off by negative word of mouth. Finally, there are less easily quantifiable costs and opportunities for revenue enhancement. On the negative side are disruptions to service while a job remains unfilled, and loss of the departing employee's knowledge of the business (and its customers); on the positive side is the value of new product and service ideas generated by experienced employees who are committed to the success of the business.

The Cycle of Mediocrity

The cycle of mediocrity is another potentially vicious employment cycle (Figure 11.5). You're most likely to find it in large, bureaucratic organizations. These are often typified by state monopolies, industrial cartels, or regulated oligopolies, in which there's little incentive to improve performance, especially from more agile competitors, and in which fear of entrenched unions may discourage management from adopting more innovative labor practices.

In such environments, service delivery standards tend to be prescribed by rigid rulebooks, oriented toward standardized service, operational efficiencies, and prevention of both employee fraud and favoritism toward specific customers. Job responsibilities tend to be narrowly and unimaginatively defined, tightly categorized by grade and scope of responsibilities, and further rigidified by union work rules. Salary increases and promotions are based largely on longevity. Successful performance in a job is often measured by absence of mistakes, rather than by high productivity or outstanding customer service. Training focuses on learning the rules and the technical aspects of the job, not on improving human interactions with customers and co-workers. Because there is minimal allowance for flexibility or employee initiative, jobs tend to be boring and repetitive. However, in contrast to the cycle of failure, most positions provide adequate pay and often good benefits, combined with high job security. Thus, employees are reluctant to leave. This lack of mobility is compounded by an absence of marketable skills that would be valued by organizations in other fields of endeavor.

Customers find such organizations frustrating to deal with. Faced with bureaucratic hassles, lack of service flexibility, and the unwillingness of employees to make an effort to serve them well, customers can become resentful. It's not surprising that dissatisfied customers sometimes display hostility toward service employees who

Figure 11.5
The Cycle of
Mediocrity

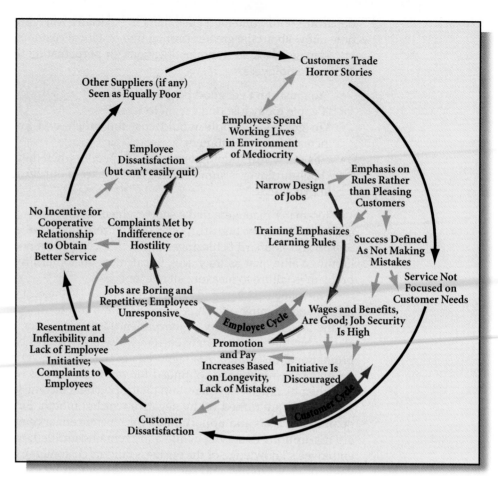

Source: Christopher Lovelock, "Managing Services: The Human Factor" in *Understanding Service Management,* ed. W.J. Glynn and J.G. Barnes (Chichester, UK John Wiley, 1995), 228.

feel trapped in their jobs and who are powerless to improve the situation. Perhaps you've been provoked by bad service and poor attitudes into reacting this way yourself. However, they often continue to be "held hostage" by the organization because there's nowhere else for them to go, either because the service provider holds a monopoly, or because all other available players are perceived as being equally bad or worse.

Employees may protect themselves through such mechanisms as withdrawal into indifference, playing overtly by the rulebook, or countering rudeness with rudeness. The net result is a vicious cycle of mediocrity in which unhappy customers continually complain to sullen employees (and also to other customers) about poor service and bad attitudes, generating greater defensiveness and lack of caring on the part of the staff. Under such circumstances, there's little incentive for customers to cooperate with the organization to achieve better service.

The Cycle of Success

Some firms reject the assumptions underlying the cycles of failure and mediocrity. Instead, they take a longer-term view of financial performance, seeking to prosper by investing in their people in order to create a cycle of success (Figure 11.6).

As with failure or mediocrity, success applies to both employees and customers. Attractive compensation packages are used to attract good-quality staff. Broadened job descriptions are accompanied by training and empowerment practices that allow front-line staff to control quality. With more focused recruitment, intensive training, and better wages, employees are likely to be happier in their work and to provide higher-quality, customer-pleasing service. Regular customers also appreciate the continuity in service relationships resulting from lower turnover, and so are more likely to remain loyal. Profit margins tend to be higher, and the organization is free to focus

Figure 11.6
The Cycle of Success

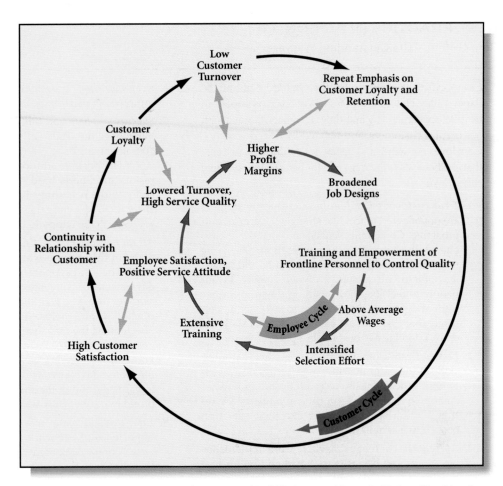

Low
Customer
Turnover

Repeat Emphasis on
Customer Loyalty and
Retention

Customer
Loyalty

Higher
Profit
Margins

Broadened
Job Designs

Lowered Turnover,
High Service Quality

Continuity in
Relationship with
Customer

Training and Empowerment of
Frontline Personnel to Control Quality

Employee Satisfaction,
Positive Service Attitude

Employee Cycle

Above Average
Wages

Extensive
Training

Intensified
Selection Effort

High Customer
Satisfaction

Customer Cycle

Reprinted from The Cycle of Success from Leonard L. Schlesinger and James L. Heskett "Breaking the Cycle of Failure in Services," *Sloan Management Review* 31 (Spring 1991): pp. 17–28, by permission of the publisher. Copyright © 2003 by Massachussetts Institute of Technology. All rights reserved.

its marketing efforts on reinforcing customer loyalty through customer-retention strategies. These strategies are usually much more profitable than strategies for attracting new customers. Public service organizations in many countries are increasingly working toward cycles of success, too, and offer their users good-quality service at a lower cost to the public.[22]

A powerful demonstration of a front-line employee working in the cycle of success is waitress Cora Griffith (featured in Best Practice in Action 11.1). Many of the themes in her nine rules of success are the result of good HR strategies for service firms, which we will discuss next.

HUMAN RESOURES MANAGEMENT—HOW TO GET IT RIGHT

Any rational manager would like to operate in the cycle of success. In this section we'll discuss HR strategies that can help service firms move toward that goal. Specifically, we'll discuss how firms can hire, motivate, and retain engaged service employees who are willing and able to perform along the three common dimensions of their jobs: delivering service excellence/customer satisfaction, productivity, and often sales as well. Figure 11.7 summarizes our main recommendations for successful HR strategies in service firms.

Also, it's naïve to think that it's sufficient to satisfy employees. Employee satisfaction should be seen as necessary but not sufficient for having high-performing

BEST PRACTICE IN ACTION 11.1
Cora Griffith—The Outstanding Waitress

Cora Griffith, a waitress for the Orchard Café at the Paper Valley Hotel in Appleton, Wisconsin, is superb in her role, appreciated by first-time customers, famous with her regular customers, and revered by her co-workers. Cora loves her work, and it shows. Comfortable in a role that she believes is the right one for her, she follows nine rules for success:

1. *Treat customers like family.* First-time customers are not allowed to feel like strangers. Cheerful and proactive, Cora smiles, chats, and includes everyone at the table in the conversation. She is as respectful to children as she is to adults and makes it a point to learn and use everyone's name. "I want people to feel like they're sitting down to dinner right at my house. I want them to feel they're welcome, that they can get comfortable, that they can relax. I don't just serve people, I pamper them."

2. *Listen first.* Cora has developed her listening skills to the point that she rarely writes down customers' orders. She listens carefully and provides a customized service: "Are they in a hurry? Or do they have a special diet or like their selection cooked in a certain way?"

3. *Anticipate customers' wants.* Cora replenishes beverages and brings extra bread and butter in a timely manner. One regular customer, for example, who likes honey with her coffee, gets it without having to ask. "I don't want my customers to have to ask for anything, so I always try to anticipate what they might need."

4. *Simple things make the difference.* She manages the details of her service, monitoring the cleanliness of the utensils and their correct placement. The fold of napkins must be just right. She inspects each plate in the kitchen before taking it to the table. She provides crayons for small children to draw pictures while waiting for the meal. "It's the little things that please the customer."

5. *Work smart.* Cora scans all her tables at once, looking for opportunities to combine tasks. "Never do just one thing at a time. And never go from the kitchen to the dining room empty-handed. Take coffee or iced tea or water with you." When she refills one water glass, she refills others. When clearing one plate, she clears others. "You have to be organized, and you have to keep in touch with the big picture."

6. *Keep learning.* Cora makes an ongoing effort to improve her existing skills and learn new ones.

7. *Success is where you find it.* Cora is content with her work. She finds satisfaction in pleasing her customers, and she enjoys helping other people enjoy. Her positive attitude is a positive force in the restaurant. She is hard to ignore. "If customers come to the restaurant in a bad mood, I'll try to cheer them up before they leave." Her definition of success: "To be happy in life."

8. *All for one, one for all.* Cora has been working with many of the same co-workers for more than eight years. The team supports one another on the crazy days when 300 conventioneers come to the restaurant for breakfast at the same time. Everyone pitches in and helps. The wait staff cover for one another, the managers bus the tables, the chefs garnish the plates. "We are like a little family. We know each other very well and we help each other out. If we have a crazy day, I'll go in the kitchen towards the end of the shift and say, 'Man, I'm just proud of us. We really worked hard today.'"

9. *Take pride in your work.* Cora believes in the importance of her work and in the need to do it well. "I don't think of myself as 'just a waitress.' . . . I've chosen to be a waitress. I'm doing this to my full potential, and I give it my best. I tell anyone who's starting out: Take pride in what you do. You're never just an anything, no matter what you do. You give it your all . . . and you do it with pride."

Cora Griffith is a success story. She is loyal to her employer and dedicated to her customers and co-workers. A perfectionist who seeks continuous improvement, Cora's enthusiasm for her work and unflagging spirit creates an energy that radiates through the restaurant. She is proud of being a waitress, proud of "touching lives." Says Cora: "I have always wanted to do my best. However, the owners really are the ones who taught me how important it is to take care of the customer and who gave me the freedom to do it. The company always has listened to my concerns and followed up. Had I not worked for the Orchard Café, I would have been a good waitress, but I would not have been the same waitress."

Source: Leonard L. Berry, *Discovering the Soul of Service—The Nine Drivers of Sustainable Business Success.* New York: The Free Press, 1999, pp. 156–159.

staff. For instance, a recent study showed that employee effort was a strong driver of customer satisfaction, over and above employee satisfaction.[23] As Jim Collins said, "The old adage, 'People are your most important asset,' is wrong. The *right* people are your most important asset." We would like to add to this: ". . . and the wrong people are a liability that is often difficult to get rid of." Getting it right starts with hiring the right people.

Figure 11.7 Wheel of Successful HR in Service Firms

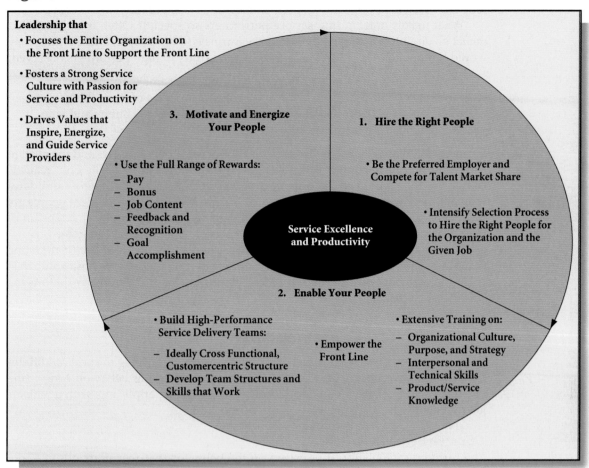

Hiring the Right People

Hiring the right people includes competing for applications from the best employees in the labor market, then selecting from this pool the best candidates for the specific jobs to be filled.

Be the Preferred Employer

To be able to select and hire the best people, they first have to apply for a job with you and then accept your job offer over others (the best people tend to be selected by several firms). That means a firm has to compete first for talent market share,[24] engaging in, as McKinsey & Company call it, "the war for talent."[25] Competing in the labor market means having an attractive value proposition for prospective employees, and includes factors such having a good image as a place to work, as well as delivering high-quality products and services that make employees proud to be part of the team.

Furthermore, the compensation package cannot be below average—top people expect above-average packages. In our experience, it takes a salary in the range of the 65th to 80th percentile of market wages for a particular type of position to attract top performers to top companies. However, a firm does not have to be a top paymaster, if other important aspects of the value proposition are attractive. In short, understand the needs of your target employees and get your value proposition right.

Select the Right People

There's no such thing as the perfect employee. Different positions are often best filled by people with different skill sets, styles, and personalities. For example, The Walt Disney Company assesses prospective employees in terms of their potential for on-stage or backstage work. On-stage workers, known as cast members, are assigned to those roles for which their appearance, personalities, and skills provide the best match.

What makes outstanding service performers so special? Often it is things that *cannot* be taught. It is the qualities that are intrinsic to the people, and qualities they would bring with them to any employer. As one study of high performers observed:

> Energy . . . cannot be taught, it has to be hired. The same is true for charm, for detail orientation, for work ethic, for neatness. Some of these things can be enhanced with on-the-job training . . . or incentives. . . . But by and large, such qualities are instilled early on.[26]

Also, HR managers have discovered that whereas good manners and the need to smile and make eye contact can be taught, warmth itself cannot. The only realistic solution is to ensure that the organization's recruitment criteria favors candidates with naturally warm personalities. Jim Collins emphasizes that "The right people are those who would exhibit the desired behaviors anyway, as a natural extension of their character and attitude, regardless of any control and incentive system."[27]

The logical conclusion is that service firms should devote great care to attracting and hiring the right candidates. Best Practice in Action 11.2 shows how Southwest Airlines goes about hiring staff with the right attitude and a personality that fits the Southwest culture.

How to Identify the Best Candidates

Excellent service firms use a number of approaches to identifying the best candidates in their applicant pool. These approaches include observing behavior, conducting personality tests, interviewing applicants, and providing applicants with a realistic job preview.[28]

Observe Behavior

The hiring decision should be based on the behavior that recruiters observe, not the words they hear. As John Wooden said, "Show me what you can do, don't tell me what you can do. Too often, the big talkers are the little doers."[29] Behavior can be observed directly or indirectly, by using behavioral simulations or assessment center tests, which use standardized situations in which applicants can be observed to see whether they display the kind of behaviors the firms' clients expect. Also, past behavior is the best predictor of future behavior: Hire the person who has won service excellence awards, received many complimentary letters, and has great references from past employers.

Conduct Personality Tests

Use personality tests that are relevant for a particular job. For example, willingness to treat customers and colleagues with courtesy, consideration, and tact, perceptiveness of customer needs, and ability to communicate accurately and pleasantly are traits that can be measured. Hiring decisions based on such tests tend to be accurate.

For example, the Ritz-Carlton Hotels Group uses personality profiles on all job applicants. Staff are selected for their natural predisposition for working in a service context. Inherent traits such as a ready smile, a willingness to help others, and an affinity for multitasking enable them to go beyond learned skills. An applicant to Ritz-Carlton shared her experience of going through the personality test for a job as a junior-level concierge at the Ritz-Carlton Millenia Singapore. Her best advice: Tell the truth. These are experts; they will know if you are lying. "On the big day, they asked if I liked helping people, if I was an organized person and if I liked to smile a lot." Yes, yes and yes, I said. But I had to support it with real life examples. This, at times, felt rather intrusive. To answer the first question for instance, I had to say a bit about the person I had helped—why she needed help, for example. The test forced me to recall even insignificant things I had done, like learning how to say hello in different languages which helped to get a fix on my character."[30] It's better to hire

BEST PRACTICE IN ACTION 11.2
Hiring at Southwest Airlines

Southwest hires people with the right attitude and with a personality that matches its corporate personality. Humor is the key. Herb Kelleher, Southwest's legendary former CEO and now chairman, said, "I want flying to be a helluva lot of fun!" "We look for attitudes; people with a sense of humor who don't take themselves too seriously. We'll train you on whatever it is you have to do, but the one thing Southwest cannot change in people is inherent attitudes." Southwest has one fundamental, consistent principle—hire people with the right spirit. Southwest looks for people with other-oriented, outgoing personalities, individuals who become part of an extended family of people who work hard and have fun at the same time.

Southwest's painstaking approach to interviewing continues to evolve in the light of experience. It is perhaps at its most innovative in the selection of flight attendants. A day-long visit to the company usually begins with applicants gathered in a group. Recruiters watch how well they interact with each other (another chance for such observation will come at lunchtime).

Then comes a series of personal interviews. Each candidate has three one-on-one "behavioral-type" interviews during the course of the day. Based on input from supervisors and peers in a given job category, interviewers target eight to ten dimensions for each position. For a flight attendant, these might include a willingness to take initiative, compassion, flexibility, sensitivity to people, sincerity, a customer service orientation, and a predisposition to be a team player. Even humor is "tested": Prospective employees are typically asked, "Tell me how you recently used your sense of humor in a work environment. Tell me how you have used humor to defuse a difficult situation."

Southwest describes the ideal interview as "a conversation," in which the goal is to make candidates comfortable. "The first interview of the day tends to be a bit stiff, the second is more comfortable, and by the third they tell us a whole lot more. It's really hard to fake it under those circumstances." The three interviewers don't discuss candidates during the day but compare notes afterward, to reduce the risk of bias.

To help select people with the right attitude, Southwest invites supervisors and peers (with whom future candidates will be working) to participate in the in-depth interviewing and selection process. In this way, existing employees buy into the recruitment process and feel a sense of responsibility for mentoring new recruits and helping them to become successful in the job (rather than wondering, as an interviewer put it, "who hired this turkey?"). More unusually, Southwest invites its own frequent flyers to participate in the initial interviews for flight attendants and to tell the candidates what they, the passengers, value.

The interviewing team asks a group of potential employees to prepare a five-minute presentation about themselves, and gives them plenty of time to prepare. As the presentations are delivered, the interviewers don't watch just the speakers. They watch the audience to see which applicants are using their time to work on their own presentations and which are enthusiastically cheering on and supporting their potential co-workers. Unselfish people who will support their teammates are the ones who catch Southwest's eyes, not the applicants who are tempted to polish their own presentations while others are speaking.

By hiring the right attitude, the company is able to foster the so-called Southwest spirit—an intangible quality in people that causes them to want to do whatever it takes and to want to go that extra mile whenever they need to. Southwest itself goes the extra mile for its employees and has never laid anyone off, even after it decided to close reservations centers in three cities in 2004 to cut costs. Management knows that the airline's culture is a key competitive advantage.

Sources: Kevin and Jackie Freiberg, *Nuts! Southwest Airlines' Crazy Recipe for Business and Personal Success.* New York: Broadway Books, 1997, pp. 64–69; Christopher Lovelock, *Product Plus.* New York: McGraw-Hill, 1994, pp. 323–326; Barney Gimbel, "Southwest's New Flight Plan." *Fortune,* May 16, 2005, pp. 93–98.

---

upbeat and happy people, because customers report higher satisfaction when being served by more satisfied staff.[31]

Apart from intensive interview-based psychological tests, cost-effective Internet-based testing kits are available. In these, applicants enter their test responses to a Web-based questionnaire, and the prospective employer receives the analysis, an appraisal of the candidate's suitability, and a hiring recommendation. Developing and administering such tests has become a significant service industry in its own right. The leading global supplier of assessment products, SHL Group, serves some 5,500 clients in 30 languages in more than 40 countries.

Employ Multiple, Structured Interviews

To improve hiring decisions, successful recruiters like to employ structured interviews built around job requirements, and to use more than one interviewer. People tend to be more careful in their judgments when they know that another individual is also evaluating the same applicant. Another advantage of using two or more interviewers is that it reduces the risk of "similar to me" biases—we all like people who are similar to ourselves.

Give Applicants a Realistic Preview of the Job

During the recruitment process, service companies should let candidates know the reality of the job,[32] thereby giving them a chance to "try on the job" and assess whether it's a good fit. At the same time, recruiters can observe how candidates respond to the job's realities. This approach allows some candidates to withdraw if they determine that the job is not suitable for them. At the same time, the company can manage new employees' expectations of their job. Many service companies adopt this approach. For example, Au Bon Pain, a chain of French bakery cafés, lets applicants work for two paid days in a café prior to the final selection interview. Managers can observe candidates in action, and candidates can assess whether they like the job and the work environment.[33]

Train Service Employees Actively

If a firm has good people, investments in training can yield outstanding results. Service champions show a strong commitment to training, in words, dollars, and action. As Benjamin Schneider and David Bowen put it, "The combination of attracting a diverse and competent applicant pool, utilizing effective techniques for hiring the most appropriate people from that pool, and then training the heck out of them would be gangbusters in any market."[34] Service employees need to learn:

- *The organizational culture, purpose, and strategy.* Start strong with new hires, and focus on getting emotional commitment to the firm's core strategy. Promote core values such as commitment to service excellence, responsiveness, team spirit, mutual respect, honesty, and integrity. Use managers to teach, and focus on "what," "why," and "how" rather than on the specifics of the job.[35] For example, new recruits at Disneyland attend the Disney University Orientation. The program starts with a detailed discussion of the company's history and philosophy, the service standards expected of cast members, and a comprehensive tour of Disneyland's operations.
- *Interpersonal and technical skills.* Interpersonal skills tend to be generic across service jobs, and include visual communications skills such as making eye contact, attentive listening, body language, and even facial expressions. Technical skills encompass all the required knowledge related to processes (e.g., how to handle a merchandized return), machines (e.g., how to operate the terminal, or cash machine), and rules and regulations related to customer service processes. Both technical and interpersonal skills are *necessary*, but neither alone is *sufficient* for optimal job performance.[36]
- *Product/service knowledge.* Knowledgeable staff are a key aspect of service quality. They must be able to explain product features effectively and also position the product correctly. For instance, in Best Practice in Action 11.3, Jennifer Grassano of Dial-A-Mattress coaches individual staff members on how to paint pictures in the customer's mind.

Of course, training has to result in tangible changes in behavior. If staff do not apply what they have learned, the investment is wasted. Learning is not only about becoming smarter, it is also about changing behaviors and improving decision making. To achieve this, practice and reinforcement are needed. Supervisors can play a crucial role by following up regularly on learning objectives, for

Coaching is a common method employed by services leaders to train and develop staff. Dial-A-Mattress's Jennifer Grassano is a bedding consultant (BC) three days a week, and a coach to other BCs one day a week. She focuses on staff whose productivity and sales performance are slumping.

Grassano's first step is to listen in on the BCs telephone calls with customers. She listens for about an hour and takes detailed notes on each call. The BCs understand that their calls may be monitored, but they receive no advance notice; that would defeat the purpose.

Next, Grassano conducts a coaching session with the staff member, in which strengths and areas for improvements are reviewed. She knows how difficult it is to maintain a high energy level and convey enthusiasm when handling some 60 calls per shift. She likes to suggest new tactics and phrasings "to spark up their presentation." One BC was not responding effectively when customers asked why one mattress was more expensive than another. Here, she stressed the need to paint a picture in the customer's mind:

"Customers are at our mercy when buying bedding. They don't know the difference between one coil system and another. It is just like buying a carburetor for my car. I don't even know what a carburetor looks like. We have to use very descriptive words to help bedding customers make the decision that is right for them. Tell the customer that the more costly mattress has richer, finer padding with a blend of silk and wool. Don't just say the mattress has more layers of padding."

About two months after the initial coaching session, Grassano conducts a follow-up monitoring session with that BC. She then compares the BC's performance before and after the coaching session to assess the effectiveness of the training.

Grassano's experience and productivity as a BC give her the credibility as a coach. "If I am not doing well as a BC, then who am I to be a coach? I have to lead by example. I would be much less effective if I was a full-time trainer." She clearly relishes the opportunity to share her knowledge and pass on her craft.

Source: Leonard L. Berry, *Discovering the Soul of Service—The Nine Drivers of Sustainable Business Success.* New York: The Free Press, 1999, pp. 171–172.

instance, meeting with staff to reinforce key lessons from recent complaints and compliments (Figure 11.8).

Training and learning professionalizes the front line, moving these individuals away from the common (self)-image of being in low-end jobs that have no significance. Well-trained employees are and feel like professionals. A waiter who knows

Figure 11.8
Morning Briefings by a Supervisor Offer Effective Training Opportunities

about food, cooking, wines, dining etiquette, and how to interact effectively with customers (even complaining ones) feels professional, has higher self-esteem, and is respected by his customers. Training is therefore extremely effective in reducing person/role stress.

Empower the Front Line

Virtually all breakthrough service firms have legendary stories of employees who recovered failed service transactions, or walked, the extra mile to make a customer's day, or avoid some kind of disaster for that client (for an example, see Best Practice in Action 11.4—Empowerment at Nordstrom).[37] To allow this to happen, employees have to be empowered. Nordstrom trains and trusts its employees to do the right thing and empowers them to do so. Its employee handbook has only one rule: "Use good judgment in all situations." Employee self-direction has become increasingly important, especially in service firms, because front-line staff frequently operate on their own, face to face with their customers, and it tends to be difficult for managers to monitor their behavior closely.[38] Research has also linked high empowerment to higher customer satisfaction.[39]

For many services, providing employees with greater discretion (and training in how to use their judgment) enables them to provide superior service on the spot, rather than taking time to get permission from supervisors. Empowerment looks to front-line staff to find solutions to service problems, and to make appropriate decisions about customizing service delivery.

Is Empowerment Always Appropriate?

Advocates claim that the empowerment approach is more likely to yield motivated employees and satisfied customers than the "production-line" alternative, in which management designs a relatively standardized system and expects workers to execute tasks within narrow guidelines. However, David Bowen and Edward Lawler

BEST PRACTICE IN ACTION 11.4
Empowerment at Nordstrom

Van Mensah, a men's apparel sales associate at Nordstrom, received a disturbing letter from one of his loyal customers. The gentleman had purchased some $2,000 worth of shirts and ties from Mensah, and mistakenly washed the shirts in hot water. They all shrank. He was writing to ask Mensah's professional advice on how he should deal with his predicament (the gentleman did not complain and readily conceded the mistake was his).

Mensah immediately called the customer and offered to replace those shirts with new ones at no charge. He asked the customer to mail the other shirts back to Nordstrom—at Nordstrom's expense. "I didn't have to ask for anyone's permission to do what I did for that customer," said Mensah. "Nordstrom would rather leave it up to me to decide what's best.

Middlemas, a Nordstrom's veteran, said to employees, "You will never be criticized for doing too much for a customer, you will only be criticized for doing too little. If you're ever in doubt as to what to do

in a situation, always make a decision that favors the customer before the company." Nordstrom's Employee Handbook confirms this. It reads:

Welcome to Nordstrom

We're glad to have you with our Company.

Our number one goal is to provide outstanding customer service.

Set both your personal and professional goals high. We have great confidence in your ability to achieve them.

Nordstrom Rules:

Rule #1: Use your good judgment in all situations. There will be no additional rules.

Please feel free to ask your department manager, store manager, or division general manager any question at any time.

Source: Adapted from Robert Spector and Patrick D. McCarthy, *The Nordstrom Way.* New York: John Wiley & Sons, 2000, pp. 15–16, 95.

suggest that different situations may require different solutions, declaring that "both the empowerment and production-line approaches have their advantages . . . and . . . each fits certain situations. The key is to choose the management approach that best meets the needs of both employees and customers." Not all employees are necessarily eager to be empowered, and many employees do not seek personal growth within their jobs and prefer to work to specific directions rather than to use their own initiative. Research has shown that a strategy of empowerment is most likely to be appropriate when most of the following factors are present within the organization and its environment:

- The firm's business strategy is based on competitive differentiation, and on offering personalized, customized service.
- The approach to customers is based on extended relationships rather than on short-term transactions.
- The organization uses technologies that are complex and nonroutine in nature.
- The business environment is unpredictable and surprises are to be expected.
- Existing managers are comfortable letting employees work independently for the benefit of both the organization and its customers.
- Employees have a strong need to grow and deepen their skills in the work environment, are interested in working with others, and have good interpersonal and group process skills.[40]

Control Versus Involvement

The production-line approach to managing people is based on the well-established *control* model of organization design and management. There are clearly defined roles, top-down control systems, hierarchical pyramid structures, and an assumption that the management knows best. Empowerment, by contrast, is based on the *involvement* (or *commitment*) model, which assumes that employees can make good decisions, and produce good ideas for operating the business, if they are properly socialized, trained, and informed. This model also assumes that employees can be internally motivated to perform effectively and that they are capable of self-control and self-direction.

Schneider and Bowen emphasize that "empowerment isn't just 'setting the front-line free' or 'throwing away the policy manuals.' It requires systematically redistributing four key ingredients throughout the organization, from the top downwards."[41] The four features are

- *Power* to make decisions that influence work procedures and organizational direction (e.g., through quality circles and self-managing teams)
- *Information* about organizational performance (e.g., operating results and measures of competitive performance)
- *Rewards* based on organizational performance, such as bonuses, profit sharing, and stock options
- *Knowledge* that enables employees to understand and contribute to organizational performance (e.g., problem-solving skills)

In the control model, the four features are concentrated at the top of the organization, whereas in the involvement model these features are pushed down through the organization.

Levels of Employee Involvement

The empowerment and production-line approaches are at opposite ends of a spectrum that reflects increasing levels of employee involvement as additional knowledge, information, power, and rewards are pushed down to the front line. Empowerment can take place at several levels:

- *Suggestion involvement* empowers employees to make recommendations through formalized programs. McDonald's, often portrayed as an archetype of the production-line approach, listens closely to its front line. Did you know that innovations ranging from Egg McMuffin to methods of wrapping burgers without leaving a thumbprint on the bun were invented by employees?

- *Job involvement* represents a dramatic opening up of job content. Jobs are redesigned to allow employees to use a wider array of skills. In complex service organizations such as airlines and hospitals, in which individual employees cannot offer all facets of a service, job involvement is often accomplished through the use of teams. To cope with the added demands accompanying this form of empowerment, employees require training, and supervisors need to be reoriented from directing the group to facilitating its performance in supportive ways.
- *High involvement* gives even the lowest-level employees a sense of involvement in the company's overall performance. Information is shared. Employees develop skills in teamwork, problem solving, and business operations, and they participate in work-unit management decisions. There is profit sharing, often in the form of bonuses.

Southwest Airlines illustrates a high-involvement company, promoting common sense and flexibility. It trusts its employees and gives them the latitude, discretion, and authority they need to do their jobs. The airline has eliminated inflexible work rules and rigid job descriptions so its people can assume ownership for getting the job done and enabling flights to leave on time, regardless of whose "official" responsibility it is. This gives employees the flexibility to help each other when needed. As a result, they adopt a "whatever it takes" mentality.

Southwest mechanics and pilots feel free to help ramp agents load bags. When a flight is running late, it's not uncommon to see pilots helping passengers in wheelchairs board the aircraft, assisting operations agents by taking boarding passes, or helping flight attendants clean the cabin between flights. All of these actions are their way of adapting to the situation and taking ownership for getting customers on board more quickly. In addition, Southwest employees apply common sense, not rules, when it's in the best interest of the customer.

Rod Jones, assistant chief pilot, recalls a captain who left the gate with a senior citizen who had boarded the wrong plane. The customer was confused and very upset. Southwest asks pilots not to go back to the gate with an incorrectly boarded customer. In this case, the captain was concerned about this individual's well-being. "So, he adapted to the situation," says Jones. "He came back in to the gate, deplaned the customer, pushed back out, and gave us an irregularity report. Even though he broke the rules, he used his judgment and did what he thought was best. And we said, 'Attaboy!'"[42]

Build High-Performance Service Delivery Teams

The nature of many services requires people to work in teams, often across functions, in order to offer seamless customer service processes. Traditionally, many firms were organized by functional structures, under which, for example, one department is in charge of consulting and selling (e.g., selling a cell phone with a subscription contract), another is in charge of customer service (e.g., activation of value-added services, changes of subscription plans), and still a third is in charge of billing. This structure prevents internal service teams from viewing end customers as their own, and this structure can also mean poorer teamwork across functions, slower service, and more errors between functions. When customers have service problems, they easily fall between the cracks.

Empirical research has confirmed that front-line staff themselves regard lack of interdepartmental support as an important factor in hindering them from satisfying their customers.[43] Because of these problems, service organizations in many industries need to create cross-functional teams with the authority and responsibility to serve customers from the beginning of the service encounter to the end. Such teams are also called self-managed teams.[44]

The Power of Teamwork in Services

Jon Katzenbach and Douglas Smith define a team as "a small number of people with complementary skills who are committed to a common purpose, set of performance

Singapore Airlines (SIA) understands the importance of teamwork in the delivery of service excellence, and has always worked hard to create *esprit de corps* among its cabin crew. This is made more difficult by the fact that many crew members are scattered around the world. SIA's answer is the "team concept."

Choo Poh Leong, Senior Manager Cabin Crew Performance, explained: "In order to effectively manage our 6,600 crew, we divide them into teams, small units, with a team leader in charge of about 13 people. We will roster them to fly together as much as we can. Flying together, as a unit, allows them to build up camaraderie, and crew members feel like they are part of a team, not just a member. The team leader will get to know them well, their strengths and weaknesses, and will become their mentor and their counsel, and someone to whom they can turn if they need help or advice. The "check trainers" oversee 12 or 13 teams and fly with them whenever possible, not only to inspect their performance, but also to help their team develop."

"The interaction within each of the teams is very strong. As a result, when a team leader does a staff appraisal they really know the staff. You would be amazed how meticulous and detailed each staff record is. So, in this way, we have good control, and through the control, we can ensure that the crew delivers the promise. They know that they're being constantly monitored and so they deliver. If there are problems, we will know about them and we can send them for re-training. Those who are good will be selected for promotion."

According to Toh Giam Ming, Senior Manger Crew Performance, "What is good about the team concept is that despite the huge number of crew, people can relate to a team and have a sense of belonging. 'This is my team.' And they are put together for 1-2 years and they are rostered together for about 60-70 percent of the time, so they do fly together quite a fair bit. . . . So especially for the new people, I think they find that they have less problems adjusting to the flying career, no matter what their background is. Because once you get familiar with the team, there is support and guidance on how to do things." Choo Poh Leong adds: "The individual, you see, is not a digit or a staff number, because if you don't have team-flying, you have 6000 odd people, it can be difficult for you to really know a particular person."

SIA also has a lot of seemingly unrelated activities in the cabin crew division. For example, there is a committee called the Performing Arts Circle, made up of talented employees with an interest in the arts. During a recent biennial Cabin Crew Gala Dinner, members of SIA raised over half a million dollars for charity. In addition to the Performing Arts Circle, SIA also has a gourmet circle, language circles (such as German- and French-speaking groups), and even sports circles (such as football and tennis teams). As mentioned by Sim Kay Wee, "SIA believes that all these things really encourage camaraderie and teamwork."

Sources: Jochen Wirtz and Robert Johnston, "Singapore Airlines: What It Takes to Sustain Service Excellence—A Senior Management Perspective." *Managing Service Quality,* 13, no.1 (2003): 10–19; Loizos Heracleous, Jochen Wirtz, and Nitin Pangarkar, *Flying High in Competitive Industry: Cost-Effective Service Excellence at Singapore Airlines.* Singapore: McGraw-Hill, 2006, pp. 145–173.

goals, and approach for which they hold themselves mutually accountable."[45] Teams, training, and empowerment go hand in hand. Teams facilitate communication among team members and the sharing of knowledge. By operating like a small, independent unit, service teams take on more responsibility and require less supervision than more traditional, functionally organized customer service units. Furthermore, teams often set higher performance targets for themselves than supervisors would. Within a good team, pressure to perform is high.[46] Best Practice in Action 11.5 shows not only how Singapore Airlines uses teams to provide emotional support and to mentor its cabin crew, but also how the company assesses, rewards, and promotes staff effectively.

Some academics even feel that too much emphasis is often put on hiring "individual stars," and too little attention is paid to hiring staff with good team abilities and motivation to work cooperatively. Stanford Professors Charles O'Reilly and Jeffrey Pfeffer emphasize that how well people work in teams is often as important as how good people are, and that stars can be outperformed by others through superior teamwork.[47]

Figure 11.9
Surgical Teams Work
Under Particularly
Demanding
Conditions

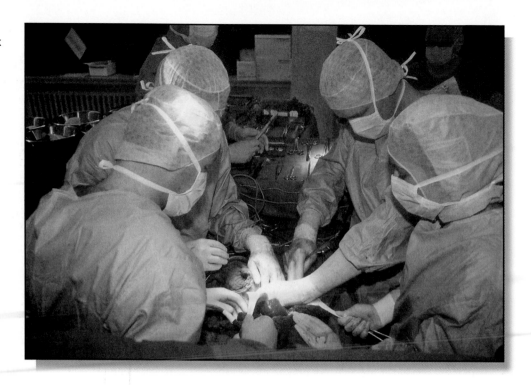

At Customer Research Inc. (CRI), a progressive and successful marketing research firm, team members' feelings are illustrated in the following quotes:

- "I like being on the team. You feel like you belong. Everyone knows what's going on."
- "We take ownership. Everyone accepts responsibility and jumps in to help."
- "When a client needs something in an hour, we work together to solve the problem."
- "There are no slugs. Everyone pulls their weight."[48]

Team ability and motivation are crucial for effective delivery of many types of services, especially those involving individuals who are each playing specialist roles. Health care services depend heavily on effective teamwork (see Figure 11.9).

Creating Successful Service Delivery Teams

It's not easy to make teams function well. If people are not prepared for team work, and the team structure isn't set up right, a firm risks having initially enthusiastic volunteers who lack the competencies that teamwork requires. The skills needed include not only cooperation, listening to others, coaching and encouraging one another, but also an understanding of how to air differences, tell one another hard truths, and ask tough questions. All these require training.[49] Management also needs to set up a structure that will steer the teams toward success. A good example is American Express Latin America, which developed the following rules for making its teams work:

- Each team has an "owner"—a person who owns the team's problems.
- Each team has a leader who monitors team progress and team process. Team leaders are selected for their strong business knowledge and people skills.
- Each team has a quality facilitator—someone who knows how to make teams work and who can remove barriers to progress and train others to work together effectively.[50]

Motivate and Energize People

Once a firm has hired the right people, trained them well, empowered them, and organized them into service delivery teams, how can it ensure that they will deliver service excellence? Staff performance is a function of ability and motivation.[51] Effective hiring, training, empowerment, and teams give a firm able people; reward systems, meantime, are the key to motivation. Service staff must get the message that providing quality service holds the key for them to be rewarded. Motivating and rewarding strong service performers are some of the most effective ways of retaining them. Staff pick up quickly whether those who get promoted are the truly outstanding service providers, and whether those who get fired are those who haven't delivered at the customer level.

A major way in which service businesses fail is not utilizing the full range of available rewards effectively. Many firms think in terms of money as reward, but it does not pass the test of an effective reward. Receiving a fair salary is a hygiene factor rather than a motivating factor. Paying more than what is seen as fair has only short-term motivating effects, and wears off quickly. On the other hand, bonuses that are contingent on performance have to be earned again and again, and therefore tend to be more lasting in their effectiveness. Other, more lasting rewards are the job content itself, recognition and feedback, and goal accomplishment.

Job Content

People are motivated and satisfied simply by knowing that they are doing a good job. They feel good about themselves, and they like to reinforce that feeling. This is true especially if the job also offers a variety of different activities, requires the completion of "whole" and identifiable pieces of work, is seen as significant in the sense that it has an impact on the lives of others, comes with autonomy, and if performing the job itself has a source of direct and clear feedback about how well employees did their work (e.g., grateful customers, and sales).

Feedback and Recognition

Humans are social beings, and they derive a sense of identity, and belonging to an organization, from the recognition and feedback they receive from the people around them—their customers, colleagues, and bosses. If employees are recognized and thanked for service excellence, they will desire to deliver it. We will discuss how to measure and use customer feedback in detail in Chapter 13.

Goal Accomplishment

Goals focus people's energy. Goals that are specific, difficult but attainable, and accepted by the staff are strong motivators and yield higher performance than no goals, or vague goals (e.g., "Do your best"), or goals that are impossible to achieve.[52] In short, goals are effective motivators.

The following are important points to note for effective goal setting:

- When goals are seen as important, achieving the goals is a reward in itself.
- Goal accomplishment can be used as a basis for giving rewards, including pay, feedback, and recognition. Feedback and recognition from peers can be given faster, more cheaply, and more effectively than pay, and have the additional benefit of gratifying an employee's self-esteem.
- Service employee goals that are specific and difficult must be set publicly to be accepted. Although goals must be specific, they can be something intangible such as improved employee courtesy ratings.
- Progress reports about goal accomplishment (feedback), and goal accomplishment itself, must be public events (recognition), if they are to gratify employees' esteem need.
- It's not usually necessary to specify the means to achieve goals. Feedback on progress while pursuing the goal serves as a corrective function. As long as the goal is specific, difficult but achievable, and accepted, goal pursuit will result in goal accomplishment, even in the absence of other rewards.

Successful firms recognize that people issues are complex. Hewitt Associates, a professional firm delivering human capital management services, captures the

Figure 11.10 "People Issues Are Complex: Managing Them Doesn't Have to Be,"
Declares Hewitt Associates

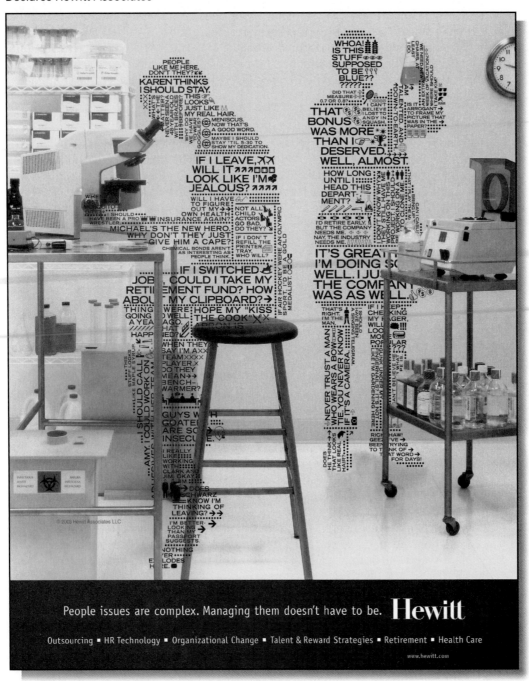

challenge of employee complexity in its advertising (Figure 11.10). Charles
O'Reilly and Jeffrey Pfeffer conducted in-depth research on why some companies
can succeed over long periods of time in highly competitive industries without
having the usual sources of competitive advantage such as barriers to entry or proprietary technology. They concluded that these firms did not succeed by winning
the war for talent (although these firms were hiring extremely carefully for fit),
"but by fully using the talent and unlocking the motivation of the people" they
already had in their organizations.[53]

The Role of Labor Unions

Labor unions and service excellence are sometimes seen as incompatible. The power of organized labor is widely cited as an excuse for not adopting new approaches in both service and manufacturing businesses. "We'd never get it past the unions," managers say, wringing their hands and muttering darkly about restrictive work practices. Unions are often portrayed as villains in the press, especially when high-profile strikes inconvenience millions. Many managers seem to be rather antagonistic toward unions.

Jeffrey Pfeffer has observed wryly that "the subject of unions and collective bargaining is . . . one that causes otherwise sensible people to lose their objectivity."[54] He urges a pragmatic approach to this issue, emphasizing that "the effects of unions depend very much on what *management* does." The higher wages, lower turnover, clearly established grievance procedures, and improved working conditions often found in highly unionized organizations can yield positive benefits in a well-managed service organization.

Contrary to the negative view presented above, many of the world's most successful service businesses are, in fact, highly unionized—Southwest Airlines is one example. The presence of unions in a service company is not an automatic barrier to high performance and innovation, unless there is a long history of mistrust, acrimonious relationships, and confrontation. However, management consultation and negotiation with union representatives are essential if employees are to accept new ideas (conditions that are equally valid in nonunionized firms). The challenge is to work jointly with unions, to reduce conflict and to create a climate for service.[55]

SERVICE LEADERSHIP AND CULTURE

So far, we have discussed the key strategies that can help to move an organization toward service excellence. However, to truly get there, we need a strong service culture that is continuously reinforced and developed by management to achieve alignment with the firm's strategy.[56] *Charismatic leadership*, also called *transformational leadership*, fundamentally changes the values, goals, and aspirations of the front line to be consistent with that of the firm. With this kind of leadership, staff are more likely to perform their best and, above and beyond the call of duty, because it is consistent with their own values, beliefs, and attitudes.[57]

Leonard Berry advocates a value-driven leadership that inspires and guides service providers. Leadership should bring out the passion for serving. It should also tap the creativity of service providers, nourish their energy and commitment, and give them a fulfilled working life. Some of the core values Berry found in excellent service firms included excellence, innovation, joy, teamwork, respect, integrity, and social profit.[58] These values are part of the firm's culture. A *service culture* can be defined as

- Shared perceptions of *what* is important in an organization, and
- Shared values and beliefs of *why* those things are important.[59]

Employees rely heavily on their perceptions of what is important by noting what the company and their leaders do, not so much what they say. Employees gain their understanding of what is important through the daily experiences they have with the firm's human resource, operations, and marketing practices and procedures.

A strong service culture is one in which the entire organization focuses on the front line, understanding that it is the lifeline of the business. The organization understands that today's as well as tomorrow's revenues are driven largely by what happens at the service encounter. Figure 11.11 shows the inverted pyramid, which highlights the importance of the front line, and that the role of top management and

Figure 11.11
The Traditional
Organizational
Pyramid versus The
Inverted Pyramid with
a Customer and
Frontline Focus

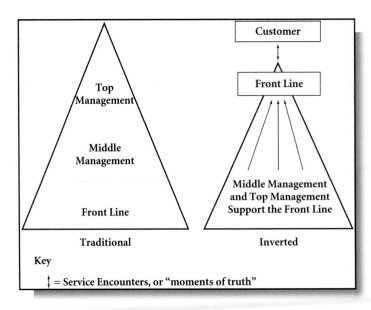

middle management is to support the front line in their task of delivering service excellence to their customers.

In firms with a passion for service, top management shows by their actions that what happens at the front line is crucially important to them, by being informed and actively involved. They achieve this by regularly talking to and working with front-line staff and customers. Many actually spend significant amounts of time at the front line, serving customers. For example, Disney World's management spends two weeks every year in front-line staff jobs such as sweeping streets, selling ice cream, or working as ride attendants, to gain a better appreciation and understanding of what really happens on the ground.[60]

Service leaders are interested not only in the big picture, they focus on the details of service, they see opportunities in nuances that competitors might consider trivial, and they believe that the way the firm handles little things sets the tone for how it handles everything else.

Internal Marketing

In addition to having strong leadership that focuses on the front line, it takes a strong communications effort to shape the culture and get the message to the troops. Service leaders use multiple tools to build their service culture, ranging from internal marketing and training to core principles, and to company events and celebrations.

Internal communications from senior managers to their employees play a vital role in maintaining and nurturing a corporate culture founded on specific service values. Well-planned internal marketing efforts are especially necessary in large service businesses that operate in widely dispersed sites, sometimes around the world. Even when employees are working far from the head office in the home country, they still need to be kept informed of new policies, changes in service features, and new quality initiatives. Communications may also be needed to nurture team spirit and support common corporate goals across national frontiers. Consider the challenge of maintaining a unified sense of purpose at the overseas offices of companies such as Citibank, Air Canada, Marriott, or Starbucks, where people from different cultures who speak different languages must work together to create consistent levels of service.

Effective internal communications can help ensure efficient and satisfactory service delivery, achieve productive and harmonious working relationships, and build employee trust, respect, and loyalty. Commonly used media include internal newsletters and magazines, videotapes, private corporate television networks such as those owned by FedEx and Merrill Lynch, intranets (private networks of web sites

THREE STEPS OF SERVICE

1
A warm and sincere greeting. Use the guest name, if and when possible.

2
Anticipation and compliance with guest needs.

3
Fond farewell. Give them a warm good-bye and use their names, if and when possible.

"We Are Ladies and Gentlemen Serving Ladies and Gentlemen"

THE EMPLOYEE PROMISE

At The Ritz-Carlton, our Ladies and Gentlemen are the most important resource in our service commitment to our guests.

By applying the principles of trust, honesty, respect, integrity and commitment, we nurture and maximize talent to the benefit of each individual and the company.

The Ritz-Carlton fosters a work environment where diversity is valued, quality of life is enhanced, individual aspirations are fulfilled, and The Ritz-Carlton mystique is strengthened.

CREDO

The Ritz-Carlton Hotel is a place where the genuine care and comfort of our guests is our highest mission.

We pledge to provide the finest personal service and facilities for our guests who will always enjoy a warm, relaxed yet refined ambience.

The Ritz-Carlton experience enlivens the senses, instills well-being, and fulfills even the unexpressed wishes and needs of our guests.

THE RITZ-CARLTON® BASICS

1. The Credo is the principal belief of our Company. It must be known, owned and energized by all.

2. Our Motto is: "We Are Ladies and Gentlemen serving Ladies and Gentlemen." As service professionals, we treat our guests and each other with respect and dignity.

3. The Three Steps of Service are the foundation of Ritz-Carlton hospitality. These steps must be used in every interaction to ensure satisfaction, retention and loyalty.

4. The Employee Promise is the basis for our Ritz-Carlton work environment. It will be honored by all employees.

5. All employees will successfully complete annual Training Certification for their position.

6. Company objectives are communicated to all employees. It is everyone's responsibility to support them.

7. To create pride and joy in the workplace, all employees have the right to be involved in the planning of the work that affects them.

8. Each employee will continuously identify defects (M.R. B.I.V.) throughout the Hotel.

9. It is the responsibility of each employee to create a work environment of teamwork and lateral service so that the needs of our guests and each other are met.

10. Each employee is empowered. For example, when a guest has a problem or needs something special, you should break away from your regular duties to address and resolve the issue.

11. Uncompromising levels of cleanliness are the responsibility of every employee.

12. To provide the finest personal service for our guests, each employee is responsible for identifying and recording individual guest preferences.

13. Never lose a guest. Instant guest pacification is the responsibility of each employee. Whoever receives a complaint will own it, resolve it to the guest's satisfaction and record it.

14. "Smile – We are on stage." Always maintain positive eye contact. Use the proper vocabulary with our guests and each other. (Use words like – "Good Morning," "Certainly," "I'll be happy to" and "My pleasure.")

15. Be an ambassador of your Hotel in and outside of the workplace. Always speak positively. Communicate any concerns to the appropriate person.

16. Escort guests rather than pointing out directions to another area of the Hotel.

17. Use Ritz-Carlton telephone etiquette. Answer within three rings with a "smile." Use the guest's name when possible. When necessary, ask the caller "May I place you on hold?"

Do not screen calls. Eliminate call transfers whenever possible. Adhere to voice mail standards.

18. Take pride in and care of your personal appearance. Everyone is responsible for conveying a professional image by adhering to Ritz-Carlton clothing and grooming standards.

19. Think safety first. Each employee is responsible for creating a safe, secure and accident free environment for all guests and each other. Be aware of all fire and safety emergency procedures and report any security risks immediately.

20. Protecting the assets of a Ritz-Carlton hotel is the responsibility of every employee. Conserve energy, properly maintain our Hotels and protect the environment.

Source: The Ritz-Carlton Hotel Company, LLC. Reprinted with permission.

and email that are inaccessible to the general public), face-to-face briefings, and promotional campaigns using displays, prizes, and recognition programs.

For example, Ritz-Carlton translated the key product and service requirements of its customers into the Ritz-Carlton Gold Standards, which include a credo, motto, three steps of service, and 20 "Ritz-Carlton Basics" (see Best Practice in Action 11.6). Tim Kirkpatrick, director of training and development of Ritz-Carlton's Boston Common Hotel, said, "The Gold Standards are part of our uniform, just like your name tag. But remember, it's just a laminated card until you put it into action."[61] To reinforce these standards, every morning briefing includes a discussion of one of the standards. The aim of rotating these discussions is to keep the Ritz-Carlton philosophy at the center of its employees' minds.

Another great example of a firm with a strong culture is Southwest Airlines, which uses continuously new and creative ways to strengthen its culture. Southwest's Culture Committee members are zealots when it comes to the continuation of Southwest's family feel. The committee represents everyone from flight attendants and reservationists to top executives; as one participant observed: "The Culture Committee is not made up of Big Shots; it is a committee of Big Hearts." Culture Committee members are not out to gain power. They use the power of the

Southwest spirit to better connect people to the cultural foundations of the company. The committee works behind the scenes to foster Southwest's commitment to its core values. Following are examples of events held to reinforce Southwest's cultures.

- *Walk a Mile in My Shoes.* The Walk a Mile in My Shoes program helped Southwest employees gain an appreciation for other people's jobs. Employees were asked to visit a different department on their day off and to spend a minimum of six hours on the "walk." These participants were rewarded not only with transferable round-trip passes, but also with goodwill and increased morale.
- *A Day in the Field.* This activity is practiced throughout the company, all year long. Barri Tucker, then a senior communications representative in the executive office, for example, once joined three flight attendants working a three-day trip. Tucker gained by experiencing the company from a new angle and by hearing directly from customers. She was able to see how important it was for corporate headquarters to support Southwest's front-line employees.
- *Helping Hands.* Southwest sent out volunteers from around the system to lighten the load of employees in the cities where Southwest was in direct competition with United's Shuttle. This not only built momentum and strengthened the troops for the battle with United, it also helped rekindle the fighting spirit of Southwest employees.[62]

Empirical research in the hotel industry demonstrates why it is so important for management to "walk the talk." Judi McLean Park and Tony Simons conducted a study of 6,500 employees at 76 Holiday Inn hotels to determine whether workers perceived that hotel managers showed behavioral integrity, using measures such as "My manager delivers on promises," and "My manager practices what he preaches." These statements were correlated with employee responses to questions such as "I am proud to tell others I am part of this hotel," and "My co-workers go out of the way to accommodate guests' special requests," and then to revenues and profitability.

The results were stunning. They showed that the behavioral integrity of a hotel's manager was highly correlated to employees' trust, commitment, and willingness to go the extra mile. Furthermore, of all manager behaviors measured, it was the single most important factor driving profitability. In fact, a mere one-eighth point increase in a hotel's overall behavioral integrity score on a five-point scale was associated with a 2.5 percent increase in revenue, and a $250,000 increase in profits per year per hotel.[63]

CONCLUSION

The quality of a service firm's people—especially those working in customer-facing positions—plays a crucial role in determining market success and financial performance. That's why the *People* element of the 8 Ps is so important. Successful service organizations are committed to effective management of human resources and work closely with marketing and operations managers to balance what might otherwise prove to be conflicting goals. They recognize the value of investing in HR and understand the costs resulting from high levels of turnover. In the long run, offering better wages and benefits may be a more financially viable strategy than paying less to employees who have no loyalty and soon defect.

Best-practice HR strategies start with recognition that in many industries the labor market is highly competitive. Competing for talent by being the preferred employer requires a marketing perspective. Careful selection is important, too, to ensure that new employees fit both job requirements and the organization's culture. Next come the tasks of painstaking training and creating policies that will empower staff, who will then have the authority and self-confidence to use their own initiative in delivering service excellence. Other tasks for both HR and line managers in marketing and operations include effective use of service delivery teams, and energizing and motivating the front line with a full set of rewards, ranging from pay, satisfying job content, recognition, and feedback to goal accomplishment.

Top and middle managers, including front-line supervisors, need to continuously reinforce a strong culture that emphasizes service excellence and productivity. Once employees understand and support the goals of an organization, a value-driven leadership will inspire and guide these service providers, bring their passion for serving to the full, and give them a fulfilled working life.

The market and financial results of managing people effectively for service advantage can be phenomenal. Good HR strategies allied with strong management leadership at all levels often lead to a sustainable competitive advantage. It is probably harder to duplicate high-performance human assets than any other corporate resource.

REVIEW QUESTIONS

1. Discuss the role that service personnel play in creating or destroying customer loyalty.
2. What is emotional labor? Explain the ways in which it may cause stress for employees in specific jobs. Illustrate with suitable examples.
3. What are the key barriers for firms to break the cycle of failure and move into the cycle of success? And how should an organization trapped in the cycle of mediocrity proceed?
4. List five ways in which investment in hiring and selection, training, and ongoing motivation of employees will pay dividends in customer satisfaction for such organizations as (a) a restaurant, (b) an airline, (c) a hospital, and (d) a consulting firm.
5. Identify the factors that favor a strategy of employee empowerment.
6. Define what is meant by the control and involvement models of management.
7. Identify the factors needed to make service teams successful in (a) a hotel and (b) a restaurant.
8. How can a service firm build a strong service culture that emphasizes service excellence and productivity?

APPLICATION EXERCISES

1. An airline runs a recruiting advertisement for cabin crew that shows a picture of a small boy sitting in an airline seat and clutching a teddy bear. The headline reads: "His mom told him not to talk to strangers. So what's he having for lunch?" Describe the types of personalities that you think would be (a) attracted to apply for the job by that ad and (b) discouraged from applying.
2. Consider the following jobs: emergency department nurse, bill collector, computer repair technician, supermarket cashier, dentist, kindergarten teacher, prosecuting attorney, server in a family restaurant, server in an expensive French restaurant, stockbroker, and undertaker. What type of emotions would you expect each of them to display to customers in the course of doing their job? What drives your expectations?
3. As a human resources manager, which issues do you see as most likely to create boundary-spanning problems for customer contact employees in a customer call center at a major Internet service provider? Select four issues and indicate how you would mediate between operations and marketing to create a satisfactory outcome for all three groups.

ENDNOTES

1. Liliana L. Bove and Lester W. Johnson, "Customer Relationships with Service Personnel: Do We Measure Closeness, Quality or Strength?" *Journal of Business Research*, 54 (2001): 189–197.
2. Paul Hemp, "My Week as a Room-Service Waiter at the Ritz." *Harvard Business Review*, 80 (June 2002): 8–11.
3. Recent research established the link between extra-role effort and customer satisfaction; e.g., Carmen Barroso Castro, Enrique Martín Armario, and David Martín Ruiz, "The Influence of Employee Organizational Citizenship Behavior on Customer Loyalty." *International Journal of Service Industry Management*, 15, no. 1 (2004): 27–53.
4. James L. Heskett, Thomas O. Jones, Gary W. Loveman, W. Earl Sasser, Jr., and Leonard A. Schlesinger, "Putting the Service Profit Chain to Work." *Harvard Business Review*, 72 (March–April 1994): 164–174; James L. Heskett, W. Earl Sasser, Jr., and Leonard L. Schlesinger, *The Service Profit Chain*. New York: The Free Press, 1997.
5. James L. Heskett, W. Earl Sasser, Jr., and Leonard L. Schlesinger, *The Value Profit Chain: Treat Employees Like Customers and Customers Like Employees*. New York: The Free Press, 2003.
6. Benjamin Schneider and David E. Bowen, "The Service Organization: Human Resources Management Is Crucial." *Organizational Dynamics*, 21, no. 4 (Spring 1993): 39–52.
7. Marc Beaujean, Jonathan Davidson, and Stacey Madge, "The 'Moment of Truth' in Customer Service." *The McKinsey Quarterly*, no. 21 (2006): 62–73.
8. David E. Bowen and Benjamin Schneider, "Boundary-Spanning Role Employees and the Service Encounter: Some Guidelines for Management and Research." In J. A. Czepiel, M. R. Solomon, and C. F. Surprenant, eds., *The Service Encounter*. Lexington, MA: Lexington Books, 1985, pp. 127–148.
9. Vaikakalathur Shankar Mashesh and Anand Kasturi, "Improving Call Centre Agent Performance: A UK-India Study Based on the Agents' Point of View." *International Journal of Service Industry Management*, 17, no. 2 (2006): 136–157.
10. Arlie R. Hochschild, *The Managed Heart: Commercialization of Human Feeling*. Berkeley: University of California Press, 1983.
11. Panikkos Constanti and Paul Gibbs, "Emotional labor and Surplus Value: The Case of Holiday 'Reps.'" *The Service Industries Journal*, 25 (January 2005): 103–116.

12. Arlie Hochschild, "Emotional Labor in the Friendly Skies." *Psychology Today* (June 1982): 13–15, cited in Valarie A. Zeithaml, Mary Jo Bitner, and Dwayne D. Gremler, *Services Marketing: Integrating Customer Focus Across the Firm*, 4th ed. New York: McGraw-Hill, 2006, p. 359. See also Aviad E. Raz, "The Slanted Smile Factory: Emotion Management in Tokyo Disneyland." *Studies in Symbolic Interaction*, 21 (1997): 201–217.

13. Jochen Wirtz and Robert Johnston, "Singapore Airlines: What It Takes to Sustain Service Excellence—A Senior Management Perspective." *Managing Service Quality*, 13, no.1 (2003): 10–19; Loizos Heracleous, Jochen Wirtz, and Nitin Pangarkar, *Flying High in Competitive Industry: Cost-Effective Service Excellence at Singapore Airlines.* Singapore: McGraw-Hill, 2006, p 155.

14. "The Bangalore Paradox." *The Economist*, April 23, 2005, pp. 67–69.

15. Dan Moshavi and James R. Terbord, "The Job Satisfaction and Performance of Contingent and Regular Customer Service Representatives—A Human Capital Perspective." *International Journal of Service Industry Management*, 13, no. 4 (2002): 333–347.

16. Mahesh and Anand, "Improving Call Centre Agent Performance."

17. Ibid.

18. The terms *cycle of failure* and *cycle of success* were coined by Leonard L. Schlesinger and James L. Heskett, "Breaking the Cycle of Failure in Services." *Sloan Management Review*, 32 (Spring 1991): 17–28. The term *cycle of mediocrity* comes from Christopher H. Lovelock, "Managing Services: The Human Factor." In W. J. Glynn and J. G. Barnes, eds., *Understanding Services Management.* Chichester, UK: John Wiley & Sons, 1995, p. 228.

19. Lloyd C. Harris and Emmanuel Ogbonna, "Exploring Service Sabotage: The Antecedents, Types, and Consequences of Front-Line, Deviant, Antiservice Behaviors." *Journal of Service Research*, 4, no. 3 (2002): 163–183. See also Lorna Douget, "Service Provider Hostility and Service Quality." *Academy of Management Journal*, 47, no. 5 (2004): 761–771.

20. Schlesinger and Heskett, "Breaking the Cycle of Failure in Services."

21. Heskett, Sasser, and Schlesinger, *The Value Profit Chain*, pp. 75–94.

22. Reg Price and Roderick J. Brodie, "Transforming a Public Service Organization from Inside out to Outside in." *Journal of Service Research*, 4, no. 1 (2001): 50–59.

23. Mahn Hee Yoon, "The Effect of Work Climate on Critical Employee and Customer Outcomes." *International Journal of Service Industry Management*, 12, no. 5 (2001): 500–521.

24. Leonard L. Berry and A. Parasuraman, *Marketing Services—Competing Through Quality.* New York: The Free Press, 1991, pp. 151–152.

25. Charles A. O'Reilly III and Jeffrey Pfeffer, *Hidden Value—How Great Companies Achieve Extraordinary Results with Ordinary People.* Boston: Harvard Business School Press, 2000, p. 1.

26. Bill Fromm and Len Schlesinger, *The Real Heroes of Business.* New York: Currency Doubleday, 1994, pp. 315–316.

27. Jim Collins, "Turning Goals into Results: The Power of Catalytic Mechanisms." *Harvard Business Review*, 77 (July–August 1999): 77.

28. This section was adapted from Benjamin Schneider and David E. Bowen, *Winning the Service Game.* (Boston: Harvard Business School Press, 1995), pp. 115–126.

29. John Wooden, *A Lifetime of Observations and Reflections On and Off the Court.* Chicago: Lincolnwood, 1997, p. 66.

30. Serene Goh, "All the Right Staff," and Arlina Arshad, "Putting Your Personality to the Test," *The Straits Times*, September 5, 2001, p. H1.

31. For a review of this literature, see Benjamin Schneider, "Service Quality and Profits: Can You Have Your Cake and Eat It, Too?" *Human Resource Planning*, 14, no. 2 (1991): 151–157.

32. This section was adapted from Leonard L. Berry, *On Great Service—A Framework for Action.* New York: The Free Press, 1995, pp. 181–182.

33. Schlesinger and Heskett, "Breaking the Cycle of Failure in Services," p. 26.

34. Benjamin Schneider and David E. Bowen, *Winning the Service Game.* Boston: Harvard Business School Press, 1995, p. 131.

35. Leonard L. Berry, *Discovering the Soul of Service—The Nine Drivers of Sustainable Business Success.* New York: The Free Press, 1999, p. 161.

36. David A. Tansik, "Managing Human Resource Issues for High Contact Service Personnel." In D. E. Bowen, R. B. Chase, T. G. Cummings, and Associates, eds., *Service Management Efectiveness.* San Francisco: Jossey-Bass, 1990, pp. 152–176.

37. Parts of this section are based on David E. Bowen and Edward E. Lawler, III, "The Empowerment of Service Workers: What, Why, How and When." *Sloan Management Review*, 33 (Spring 1992): 32–39.

38. Dana Yagil, "The Relationship of Customer Satisfaction and Service Workers' Perceived Control—Examination of Three Models." *International Journal of Service Industry Management*, 13, no. 4 (2002): 382–398.

39. Graham L. Bradley and Beverley A. Sparks, "Customer Reactions to Staff Empowerment: Mediators and Moderators." *Journal of Applied Social Psychology*, 30, no. 5 (2000): 991–1012.

40. Bowen and Lawler, "The Empowerment of Service Workers: What, Why, How and When."

41. Schneider and Bowen, *Winning the Service Game*, p. 250.

42. This paragraph is based on Kevin Freiberg and Jackie Freiberg, *Nuts! Southwest Airlines' Crazy Recipe for Business and Personal Success.* New York: Broadway Books, 1997, pp. 87–88.

43. Andrew Sergeant and Stephen Frenkel, "When Do Customer Contact Employees Satisfy Customers?" *Journal of Service Research*, 3, no. 1 (August 2000): 18–34.

44. For a recent study of self-managed team performance, see Ad de Jong, Ko de Ruyter, and Jos Lemmink, "Antecedents and Consequences of the Service Climate in Boundary-Spanning Self-Managing Service Teams." *Journal of Marketing*, 68 (April 2004): 18–35.

45. Jon R. Katzenbach and Douglas K. Smith, "The Discipline of Teams." *Harvard Business Review*, 71 (March–April, 1993): 112.

46. Berry, *On Great Service—A Framework for Action*, p. 131.

47. Charles A. O'Reilly III and Jeffrey Pfeffer, *Hidden Value—How Great Companies Achieve Extraordinary Results with Ordinary People*, p. 9.

48. Berry, *Discovering the Soul of Service*, p. 189.

49. Schneider and Bowen, *Winning the Service Game*, p. 141; Berry, *On Great Service*, p. 225.

50. Ron Zemke, "Experience Shows Intuition Isn't the Best Guide to Teamwork." *The Service Edge*, 7, no. 1 (January 1994): 5.

51. This section is based on Schneider and Bowen, *Winning the Service Game*, pp. 145–173.

52. A good summary of goal setting and motivation at work can be found in Edwin A. Locke and Gary Latham, *A Theory of Goal Setting and Task Performance*. Englewood Cliffs, NJ: Prentice Hall, 1990.

53. O'Reilly and Pfeffer, *Hidden Value—How Great Companies Achieve Extraordinary Results with Ordinary People*, p. 232.

54. Jeffrey Pfeffer, *Competitive Advantage Through People*. Boston: Harvard Business School Press, 1994, pp. 160–163.

55. Jody Hoffer Gittell, Andrew von Nordenflycht, and Thomas A. Kochan, "Mutual Gains for Zero Sum? Labor Relations and Firm Performance in the Airline Industry." *Industrial and Labor Relations Review*, 57, no. 2 (2004): 163–180.

56. The authors of the following paper emphasize the role of alignment among tradition, culture, and strategy that together form the basis for the firm's HR practices: Benjamin Schneider, Seth C. Hayes, Beng-Chong Lim, Jana L. Raver, Ellen G. Godfrey, Mina Huang, Lisa H. Nishii, and Jonathan C. Ziegert, "The Human Side of Strategy: Employee Experiences of a Strategic Alignment in a Service Organization." *Organizational Dynamics*, 32, no. 2 (2003): 122–141.

57. Scott B. MacKenzie, Philip M. Podsakoff, and Gregory A. Rich, "Transformational and Transactional Leadership and Salesperson Performance." *Journal of the Academy of Marketing Science*, 29, no. 2 (2001): 115–134.

58. Berry, *On Great Service*, pp. 236–237. The following study emphasized the importance of the perceived ethical climate in driving service commitment of service employees: Charles H. Schwepker, Jr., and Michael D. Hartline, "Managing the Ethical Climate of Customer-Contact Service Employees." *Journal of Service Research*, 7, no. 4 (2005): 377–397.

59. Schneider and Bowen, Winning the Service Game, p. 240.

60. Catherine DeVrye, *Good Service Is Good Business*. Upper Saddle River, NJ: Prentice Hall, 2000, p. 11.

61. Hemp, "My Week as a Room-Service Waiter at the Ritz."

62. Adapted from Freiberg and Freiberg, *Nuts! Southwest Airlines' Crazy Recipe for Business and Personal Success*, pp. 165–168.

63. Tony Simons, "The High Cost of Lost Trust." *Harvard Business Review*, 80 (September 2002): 2–3.

Readings

Kung-Fu Service Development at Singapore Airlines

Loizos Heracleous, Jochen Wirtz,
and Robert Johnston

How should firms approach the task of new service development? The lesson from Singapore Airlines (SIA) is that, to succeed as a serial innovator, a company requires both a "hard," formalized approach employing a centralized department and a "soft," flexible process in which service delivery teams surface and implement new ideas. SIA's product development department conceives new ideas from many sources and takes selected ones through to commercial application. Meantime, the airline's culture encourages a stream of ideas for service enhancement and implementation from its various functions, including both in-flight and ground services and also loyalty marketing.

The highest state of attainment in the martial art of kung-fu is the ability to seamlessly combine the hard and the soft. Speed and flexibility derive from being soft and fluid while penetrating attacks derive from applying hard energy at the right time to specific, targeted points. This winning combination of soft and hard does not come naturally; it needs to be ceaselessly practised.

In competitive, threatening situations, people—and organisations—unwittingly tend to tense and seize up. In so doing, they reduce their adaptive ability and diminish their chances of responding effectively. The only way to enter the realm of the kung-fu master is to drill this soft/hard orientation into one's sub-conscious through continuous practice, so that it becomes second nature.

This martial arts metaphor sheds light on how Singapore Airlines (SIA) has become the recognised master of innovation in the airline industry and has consistently outperformed the industry for decades. SIA has never incurred a loss on an annual basis and has shown healthy returns since its founding in 1972 (see Tables 1 and 2 for SIA's relative performance during 1992–2004), In contrast, the airline industry as a whole has suffered from a cyclical pattern of bubble, crash, stabilisation and recovery, with nearly half the years in the last two and a half decades marked by heavy losses.

BOOKING THE COOKS

SIA's success is built on its ability to be a serial innovator, introducing many firsts in the airline industry, and sustaining this over the decades in the face of intense cost pressures, industry crises, and trends towards commoditisation. SIA is known worldwide as a paragon of in-flight service and continuous innovation, and is continuously rewarded with prestigious industry awards that confirm its status as the airline that others seek to emulate. In addition to regularly introducing discontinuous, substantial innovations (such as the launch of the first on-demand in-flight entertainment system in all classes, the first non-stop flight to the US which only has two classes of travel, business class and "executive economy", or its current uses of biometric technology), SIA seems to have the ability to churn out a large quantity of incremental, cost-effective innovations across all its operating units (such as internet check-in, SMS check in or the "Book the Cook" service for passengers who like to order specific dishes in advance).

SIA's approach to innovation appears to deviate from the standard, linear, normative models of new service development (NSD) as propagated in many text books. It involves the seamless combination of both hard, structured, rigorous, centralised innovation, with soft, emergent, distributed, but equally significant, innovation.

The hard aspect is enshrined in a centralised product innovation department that tends to undertake major, discontinuous innovations, such as "LeaderShip", the first non-stop service between Singapore and Los Angeles with upgraded business and executive economy classes. SIA will be the first airline to fly the A380 super-jumbo plane and is currently working on designing the new services to be offered on it. The potential of biometrics is also currently being considered by SIA. The company has already identified 113 potential uses of biometrics and is looking at which ones would add value to the customer and to the

Business Strategy Review (Winter 2005): 26, 28–31.

Table 1 SIA vs Top 20 Airlines Net Profit Margin Performance 1992–2004

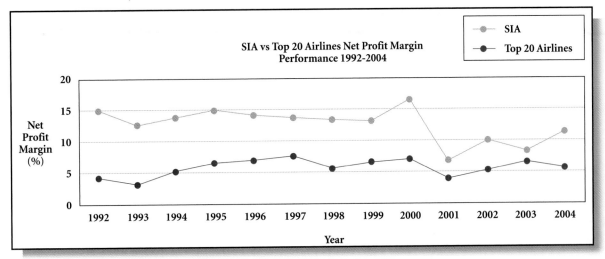

Table 2 SIA vs Top 20 Airlines ROA Performance 1992–2004

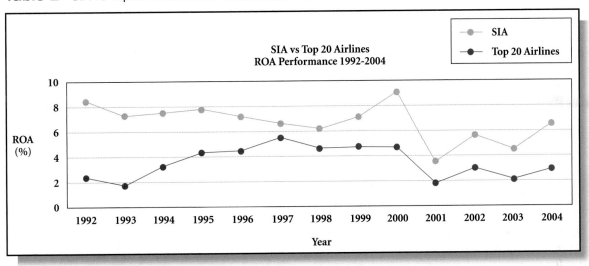

Note: The performance comparisons compare Singapore Airlines' performance in terms of net profit margin and return on assets against the weighted average for the top 20 airlines by market capitalisation (as at 15 May 2004), for the period 1992–2004. The 20 airlines are Southwest Airlines, Singapore Airlines, Cathay Pacific, Japan Airlines, Lufthansa, British Airways, All Nippon Airways, Quantas, Air France, Ryanair, JetBlue Airways, China Southern Airlines (A shares), China Eastern Airlines (A shares), Thai Airways, American Airlines, Malaysian Airlines, SAS AB, China Airlines, WestJet Airlines, and Alitalia.

company, and provide strategic differentiation while simultaneously improving efficiency. Its breakthrough pilot project where passengers use their biometrically-coded cards at a separate gateway to clear immigration and police checks and check in within around one minute has been ongoing since November 2004. This is expected not only to provide higher security and reduce costs, but also to significantly improve the customer experience, reinforcing SIA's image as a serial innovator and a paragon of service excellence.

There is a well-defined innovation framework guiding activities in the airline's product innovation department. This involves a sequential process of having inspirations or making discoveries; capturing them on the e-log, an elec-

tronic storage space of innovative ideas; having "war cabinet" meetings to explore feasibility and flesh out the details; preliminary endorsement of the idea by senior vice presidents; the holding of a user conference where SIA frequent flyers are invited to debate the idea and give their inputs; development of a robust business case with detailed cost and revenue projections; approval by senior management; and further refinement and implementation. Yap Kim Wah, SIA's senior vice president responsible for product and service explained: "SIA is a profit-generating organisation. We are not an institute of technology and whatever we do must make business sense and that is the guiding principle. To support the guiding principle we have to make a profit and customers must want to return."

Figure 1 The Hard and Soft Approach

NSD Process	NSD Organisational Activity	
	Centralised PD Department	Distributed Functional Departments
Hard highly structured NSD process	Well-defined and structured innovation framework, with a number of fixed points, focusing on major and usually high cost innovations.	Major NSD permitted within their areas of control; but subject to the same key fixed points. Structured assessment of customer feedback and rewards for innovation.
Soft flexible, unstructured, emerging process	Flexible process allowing individuals to pursue less orthodox ideas before being fed into the formal NSD process, or being handed over for development to the operational units.	Primarily an unstructured, emergent process that focuses on continuous improvements. Often, budget is absorbed in operating expenses.

The Product Development (PD) department in SIA is made up of a small number of people who eat, drink, sleep and breathe innovation. Their sole task is to conceive of innovative ideas and take selected ones through the development cycle to commercial introduction. There are several sources of ideas, including customer feedback, ideas from service staff, or competitor benchmarking. The most interesting ideas, however, are stumbled upon while panning for gold. The product development team surf the internet and read magazines in search of good ideas or existing technologies that can be adapted for airline use, such as biometrics.

The most interesting ideas are stumbled upon while panning for gold.

SIA's strategic partners are always companies with a robust brand image. Its in-flight Dolby sound for example was initially developed by a company called Lake. While SIA was interested in the technology, it wanted Lake to find a partner with a robust brand before it became involved. Lake invited Dolby to enter the alliance, which paved the way for SIA's support of further development and a two-year exclusivity agreement.

FLUID ONLY

SIA's service research and development involves a soft and flexible process. Although there are a few key fixed points, such as senior vice president endorsement, costing and approval, the other stages are quite fluid. For example, some innovations are developed in great detail, even tested, before seeking senior vice president endorsement; others are simply at the idea stage. There is also flexibility to allow individuals in the product development department to pursue less orthodox ideas and let them simmer and potentially feed at a later point into the formal NSD process, or hand them over to operational units for development.

In SIA there is a breed of softer emergent new service development which can best be described as distributed innovation, Dr Yeoh Teng Kwong, SIA's former senior manager of product innovation, explained: "I would not consider my department as the central product development unit as this would give the impression that we drive all new developments in SIA. Far from it, the culture of innovation is so pervasive in the company that most functional departments have the innovation objective as part of their mission. SIA strives to excel in a multitude of areas so that our competitors find it a near insurmountable task to try to rival us."

The culture of innovation is so pervasive in the company that most functional departments have the innovation objective as part of their mission.

SIA's culture encourages a stream of new ideas from its various functions, such as in-flight services, ground services and loyalty marketing. These ideas are developed and implemented by people in those functions in a decentralised, distributed manner, using department budgets at least for the initial stages of development. One example is the recently developed internet check-in, building on customer acceptance and high utilisation of telephone and SMS check-in, which was conceptualised, developed and implemented by the ground services department. This fluid process enables and encourages "live", continuously fine-tuned, innovations that are owned by specific departments which continuously monitor and develop them further, based on staff and customer feedback. Continuous enhancements to the SMS check-in process, for example, were made to improve functionality without sacrificing ease of use. Other improvements which have resulted from distributed innovation include the now commonly available ability to choose one's seat online or through SMS, or the unique service where business and first class passengers can order their favourite dish beforehand, and it is delivered to them on their flight.

This distributed innovation capability also guards against the company blindly following technological fads, because it engages the people who are close to the actual processes involved and can see hype for what it is. For example, the ground services department made a conscious decision, at the height of the hype about WAP, that it did not want to follow this technology, and that it would instead focus on SMS check-in because it was more user-friendly and the infrastructure was more widely available.

In addition, the influence and direct involvement of operations on the innovation process means that the ability to consistently and seamlessly deliver, a cornerstone of SIA's success, is not compromised by the introduction of innovations that sound good but cannot be delivered reliably. One example was the proposed idea of passengers ordering in-flight drinks through SIA's in-flight entertainment system, Krisflyer. It was decided not to pursue this, since the ability to deliver the drinks to passengers within a reasonable time frame and with the necessary level of customisation would be compromised. This operational ownership of innovations is crucial for SIA, reinforcing its key competency of the operational ability to deliver consistent and reliable service every time, in every customer transaction.

THE HARD SIDE

This soft distributed innovation process also has a hard edge. While minor adjustments can be made by almost anyone at any time, the more expensive and significant changes are subject to the key fixed points process also adhered to by the PD department: senior vice president endorsement, costing and approval. These developments are carried out totally independently of the PD department, but are still overseen by the senior vice president responsible for product and service innovation.

Other harder, structural and process-related aspects of SIA's organisational context support the development of this capability for distributed innovation. For example, the high importance given to customer feedback, means that any inputs by customers to boundary, front-line workers, such as the famous Singapore Girl, are duly recorded and swiftly transferred to the relevant departments for deliberation. Flexible rewards based on company performance give every incentive to employees to think innovatively, even though they are not part of the centralised PD department. SIA's team concept, where the in-flight teams composed of the same individuals remain the same for years, further reinforces the feeling

that personal fortunes are tied with company fortunes, and introduce peer pressure to perform. Job rotation of everyone from junior manager level upwards further enables company-wide rather than myopic, department-based thinking. Cultural values encouraging continuous improvement, change and innovation also support unlearning, the removal of legacy processes that may inhibit further innovations. For example, developing internet check-in meant having to challenge and reconstitute long-standing airport security and check-in procedures, which was duly implemented.

This hard/soft kung-fu approach to innovation is drilled into SIA's sub-conscious through conscious design, ceaseless practice and cultural reinforcement. As a result SIA is capable of deploying kung-fu tactics effortlessly even when the odds are stacked against it. During 2002–2003 when the global airline industry felt the devastating effects of the 9/11 terrorist attacks and then SARS, some airlines tensed up so much their business collapsed. SIA also had to cut costs, but it did so without compromising service levels and innovation, the cornerstones of its success. Costs were cut, for example, by imposing substantial salary cuts on senior management, encouraging employees to take unpaid leave, and temporarily suspending recruitment. At the same time, however, SIA continued its soft, fluid but penetrating attacks by continuously developing its people's innovative skills, investing in brand new planes, upgrading its facilities (such as by introducing the lie-flat "space-bed" seat in business class), and ultimately sustaining its competitive success and exceptional performance.

RESOURCES

Costa, P. R., Harnet, R. S, and Lunquist, J. T. (2002), "Rethinking the aviation industry," *McKinsey Quarterly, Special edition: Risk and resilience.*

Heracleous, L. & Wirtz, J. (2005), "Biometrics meets services," *Harvard Business Review,* "Breakthrough ideas for 2005", February: 48.

Heracleous, L., Wirtz, J. and Johnston, R. (2004), "Effective service excellence: Lessons from Singapore Airlines," *Business Strategy Review,* 15, 1,

Heracleous, L., Wirtz, J. & Pangarkar, N. (2006), *Flying High in Competitive industries: Cost effective service excellence at Singapore Airlines,* McGraw-Hill.

Staw, B., Sanderlands, L. & Dutton, J. (1981), "Threat-rigidity effects in organisational behaviour: A multi-level analysis," *Administrative Science Quarterly,* 21.

Wirtz, J. and Johnston, R. (2003), "Singapore Airlines: What it takes to sustain service excellence," *Managing Service Quality,* 13, 1.

Getting More from Call Centers

Used Properly, They Can Be Strategic Assets

KEITH A. GILSON AND DEEPAK K. KHANDELWAL

Today all Fortune 500 companies have at least one call center and employ an average of 4,500 agents across their sites. More than $300 billion is spent annually on call centers around the world, and yet they are among the most underused of all corporate assets. How can managers generate the best return from these centers? McKinsey consultants Gilson and Khandelwal argue that high-performing organizations balance costs, revenues generated, and quality to provide a competitive advantage and promote profitable growth. To deliver such a strategy, successful firms make judicious use of outsourcing and technology. And they ensure that agents offer high-quality service to customers in productive ways by investing time and money in both coaching and performance-management systems.

Call centers have become essential to the marketing and customer care strategies of many businesses over the past 30 years. But our experience shows that most of these facilities don't maximize their usefulness. No one can argue with the need to keep a firm grip on costs, but indiscriminately moving customer traffic to a company's Web site or haphazardly outsourcing call centers can make them less rather than more effective. The key is to develop a customer service strategy that successfully balances costs, revenues generated, and quality. Only then can companies transform their call centers into strategic assets that provide a competitive advantage and promote growth.

Companies that get the most from their call centers act on three imperatives. They define a customer service strategy that goes beyond merely providing good service at low cost. To deliver their strategy, they put in place an infrastructure that uses outsourcing and technology in a judicious way. And they ensure the best possible execution by their agents in all interactions with customers by investing time and money in coaching and in performance-management systems. These companies can reap big benefits: increasing revenue from call centers by 20 to 35 percent, cutting costs by 15 to 25 percent, and improving the quality of service.

DEFINING A CUSTOMER SERVICE STRATEGY

Call centers were born of a basic need: to answer customers' questions. In 1972 Continental Airlines asked the Rockwell Collins division of Rockwell International (now Rockwell Automation) to develop the first automated call distributor, thus launching the call-center industry. Initially, little thought was given to the use of call centers to acquire and retain business—they were there just to deal with inquiries. The change came in the 1990s, with the advent of software-based routing and customer-relationship-management applications, which increased the marketing possibilities of call centers.

Today all Fortune 500 companies have at least one call center. They employ an average of 4,500 agents across their sites. More than $300 billion is spent annually on call centers around the world.[1] This growth will almost certainly continue, despite the controversies that outsourcing and offshoring have generated in recent years. Although the number of call-center jobs in North America—2.9 million agents employed at 55,000 facilities—is expected to remain stable, the number of agents in the rest of the world is predicted to increase by 10 percent a year from its current level of 3 million. By 2007, domestic and foreign outsourcers are expected to employ about 12 percent of all call-center agents serving North America, and offshoring to foreign markets will account for 7 percent of the total number of positions.

But many companies fail to gain maximum value from the call centers they use. To do so, they must first develop a customer service strategy.

Don't Overmanage Costs

Running call centers is costly. But while creating a lean operation by raising their efficiency is vital, given the size of the cost base that call centers represent for many companies, an undue focus on curbing expenses and improving efficiency could have unintended secondary effects. Conversely, a number of companies, particularly in the financial, telecommunications, cable TV, and Internet industries, have shown that call centers can be a highly effective revenue-generating channel without requiring excessive increases in "average handle time"—that is, the time employees spend on the telephone with customers.

Average handle time—essentially a measure of the agents' productivity—is closely monitored by executives. Yet one North American telecom company found that squeezing it diminished returns and hurt the agents' ability to sell products and services: agents focused on limiting the time they spent on each call and, if they feared exceeding their target, would choose not to sell at all. In addition, even though many agents had similar average handle times, revenue per call varied widely. This company responded by using targeted sales training and coaching to raise the overall performance of its agents to the levels of revenue per call and average handle times that its top people achieved. It found that improved revenues per call created two and a half times more value than the same level of improvement in average handle times, so that a 10 percent increase in the former could justify a 25 percent increase in the latter.

Integrate Call Centers with the Organization

Poor integration between call centers and the rest of the organization can mean countless missed opportunities to drive sales and productivity. One travel-related company had more than 100 different promotions aimed at a variety of customer segments, including members of auto clubs and frequent-flier programs. Call-center agents, however, were not adequately briefed on the components of each promotion or trained to sell them. Callers asking about the "Disneyland special" would find themselves put on hold for several minutes while the agent found out that they were referring to the Disneyland vacation package offered through one of the company's club associations.

The best companies avoid such confusion by integrating their call centers with important departments. Banks, for example, link centers closely with product lines such as credit cards and mortgages, thereby keeping agents fully informed on the latest offers and using immediate feedback to refine them. Banks also link call centers with support resources, such as billing and the processing of payments, so that agents can answer questions quickly and know how to solve periodic billing glitches that might affect large numbers of customers.

Segment Customers

A sales call from a new customer is clearly more valuable than a routine billing inquiry. Successful companies therefore segment inbound calls and direct each to an appropriate agent. Sometimes this approach involves setting up a matrix—measuring, on one axis, the value of a customer segment (from low to high, through demographics or revenue generated) and, on the other, the value of each type of call. The result could be specialized queues for different customer segments or types of calls (sales, billing, service) or both (Exhibit 1). Companies using this and other tools at their disposal (including benchmarking their service performance against that of competitors and of service leaders in other industries) determine the right level of service for each segment and type of call.

EXHIBIT 1 Calling for Service
Segmentation strategy for inbound calls, telecom example

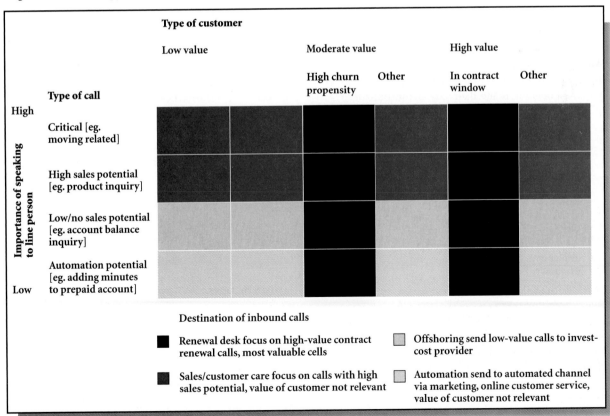

In the telecom industry, this approach works particularly well with customers who move to new homes and call to set up services there. Such customers generally are open to new offerings—high-speed Internet access, for example. Indeed, our experience shows that during this first call, they order products and services accounting for 50 to 70 percent of their lifetime value to the company. A North American telecom company, which understood such things, set up a special calling queue with agents who handle nothing but moving-related calls. That decision alone increased revenue from the call-center channel by 10 to 15 percent.

CHOOSING THE RIGHT INFRASTRUCTURE

A strategy is only as good as the infrastructure that delivers it. Winning companies put in place an optimal network of call centers, outsourcing when appropriate and using technology wisely.

Pause Before Outsourcing

To achieve this optimal network, a company must put its call centers in the right geographic locations; offer consistent service, whatever the day or time, with minimal disruptions from political, labor, or other factors; and maintain a scale sufficient to maximize the quality of service and to keep costs in line with revenues. In setting out to accomplish all of these goals, some companies think about outsourcing or offshoring—a hot topic among call-center executives and a contentious political issue in Europe and North America. Before companies make such a move, however, they should answer some specific questions about their current operations and their aims in outsourcing.

First, they should look at their current call-center network and determine its best possible cost and revenue position. This analysis involves working out what the network would cost to run and how much revenue it would generate if it were operating at best practice. Such benchmarking helps in two ways: it can tell companies whether staying in house and improving the operation would make more sense than outsourcing, and if outsourcing seems preferable it ensures that they understand their goals and don't leave money on the table when they negotiate an outsourcing contract.

Before making the final decision, companies should ask themselves several more questions about the value and complexity of their call-center interactions, their current capabilities, and how quickly they could implement an outsourcing arrangement. The relevance of these questions and the answers to them will vary according to the type of business (Exhibit 2).

Once a company decides to outsource its call centers, selecting the right partner and structuring a contract that achieves all of its objectives become crucial. A North American telecom company, hoping to cut its costs, entered into a multiyear contract to outsource its call centers, but the cost reductions came at the expense of opportunities to generate revenue. The long-term contract didn't properly balance the company's cost, revenue, and quality objectives—to be sure, a difficult feat at the best of times. As a result of these misaligned objectives, the vendor looked after its own best interest rather than the company's. Considerable management attention was needed to address the problem, and eventually the partnership ended.

Use Technology with Care

Companies striving to improve their call-center operations should be skeptical of hardware and software vendors promising big returns from expensive new technologies

EXHIBIT 2 Is Outsourcing the Answer?

QUESTION	KEEP IN HOUSE	OUTSOURCE	THIS QUESTION IS MOST RELEVANT . . .
How does keeping call center in house at best possible cost/revenue position compare with outsourcing it?	Better	Worse	. . . to stable, mature business
How valuable is speedy, customized implementation and ability to ramp up/down	Low in value	High in value	. . . to cyclical/seasonal business; new business
How financially valuable is interaction?	High in value	Low in value	. . . when call center is most important channel
How unstable is environment; how high is value of capturing knowledge?	High instability; high in value	Low instability; low in value	. . . when using new business model
How do internal capabilities compare with those of vendor?	Stronger	Weaker	. . . to new call center
How complex is customer interaction?	Highly complex	Not complex	. . . when experience and knowlege are critical

and should concentrate instead on getting the basic technologies right. These include the channel platform (automated voice systems and call routing to agents), the agent desktops (the screens that agents view), operational-system linkages (for entering orders and scheduling installations), and workforce-management software. The efficiency that the last of these systems can bring to the coordination of work schedules, vacations, breaks, and related matters in call centers with upward of 150 employees more than justifies the investment. Even smaller operations can now afford such software.

After the basic tools come technology investments targeted to specific needs, such as data feeds and the improvement of agent desktops. Companies should consider only cost-effective tools and determine which situations call for enhanced human intervention.

But no matter how good the software is, many companies fail to exploit it fully. Often the problem lies not with the software but rather with the corporate rules that guide its use. A leading financial institution couldn't raise its agents' utilization of software tools to best-in-class levels until it discovered that inflexible staffing was the root of the difficulty. The company then employed more part-time workers and changed its human-resources policies on work schedules by adding new ones, including workweeks with four ten-hour shifts, split shifts, and staggered start times. Moves of this sort helped to increase the tools' utilization by 10 percent and saved the company $25 million a year.

ENSURING EXECUTION

Beyond having a clear strategy and a strong infrastructure, companies should see to it that their call centers execute consistently. To do so, it will be necessary to make the right investments in people—by ensuring, for example, that agents receive effective coaching when they need it and by instituting performance-management systems embodying metrics and financial incentives that can encourage all employees to pull in the same direction.

Develop Effective Coaches

Of all the people necessary to extract value from a call center, the frontline supervisor has the most important role: coaching agents. It isn't easy to be a good coach given the administrative burdens that go with the job and the fact that coaching tends to receive less emphasis than it should. Companies commonly fail to give supervisors enough time on the floor to coach, for example, and supervisors often are responsible for too many agents.

Ideally, supervisors should spend 70 percent of their time coaching, and the number of agents they monitor should reflect the team's role, so that, say, a general-service queue would be supported by a 1:18 coach-to-agent ratio, while a vital sales or support queue that needed more coaching would enjoy a 1:14 ratio. Coaches should com-

bine side-by-side training with remote listening (in which the agent is unaware of being monitored) and should provide immediate feedback in both cases. The coach is also responsible for sharing best practices with agents.

In the experience of a North American telecom company, the more time supervisors spend on training, the more revenue per call their teams generate. The company therefore cut the number of compulsory meetings during peak hours and asked supervisors to carry out administrative tasks, including voice mail and e-mail, at the beginning and end of the day.

Of course, the quality of training is as crucial as the quantity. Supervisors must go beyond priming agents in elementary matters such as products (which they should already understand) and the use of systems and instead teach new skills: how to increase the efficiency of a call, to probe for the customer's needs, and to close a sale. Successful companies make coaching skills a criterion for promotion to supervisor and invest in the brightest stars. Rather than offering only a short orientation session on how to coach, these companies put supervisors through role-playing exercises and show what an employee-development plan looks like and how to devise one.

Manage Performance

Sometimes, performance-management programs can encourage the wrong kind of behavior. Using total revenue per month as a measure of sales performance, for example, can lead to "call churning," with the result that agents fail to extract full value from all customers (Exhibit 3).

The best policy is to strive for an integrated performance-management system that tracks the correct metrics—emphasizing costs, revenues, or quality, depending on corporate goals. A company can use these metrics to hold its agents accountable on a daily basis, balance its metrics to account for the fact that they sometimes influence one another, ensure that they are simple and easy to understand, and link them to financial incentives that encourage consistent behavior all the way from senior management to the front line.

Balancing metrics and incentives can be tricky. A North American telecom company thought it had balanced its agent-incentive system by including metrics on costs, quality, and revenues. But the targets for each metric were independent of one another, so if agents exceeded their target in one, the targets for the rest remained unaffected. As a result, when agents hit their revenue target for the month, they would stop selling, in an effort to bring down their monthly average handle time. To curb this tendency, the company created a trade-off between conversion rates and handle times. As an agent's conversion rate went up, so did the average-handle-time target (Exhibit 4).

Agents found the new scorecard to be fairer. Just as important, it had a negligible impact on overall handle-time costs and removed a barrier to the company's goal of raising sales through the service channel by at least 50 percent.

EXHIBIT 3 The Right Stuff

North American telecom call-center example

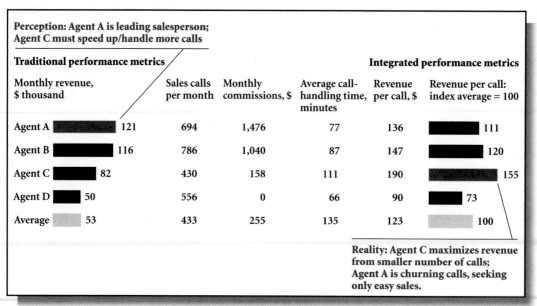

Perception: Agent A is leading salesperson;
Agent C must speed up/handle more calls

Traditional performance metrics						Integrated performance metrics	
Monthly revenue, $ thousand		Sales calls per month	Monthly commissions, $	Average call-handling time, minutes	Revenue per call, $	Revenue per call: index average = 100	
Agent A	121	694	1,476	77	136		111
Agent B	116	786	1,040	87	147		120
Agent C	82	430	158	111	190		155
Agent D	50	556	0	66	90		73
Average	53	433	255	135	123		100

Reality: Agent C maximizes revenue
from smaller number of calls;
Agent A is churning calls, seeking
only easy sales.

Reduce Employee Turnover

In most call centers, the turnover of agents is high. Often it is considered simply a cost of doing business. But with average attrition levels of 33 percent a year, and with the cost of hiring and training a new person averaging $15,000, attrition at even a small center of 200 agents could cost $1 million a year. Some turnover is to be expected given the often challenging nature of the job and the demographics of the workforce. Yet managing attrition actively will yield not only direct cost savings but also higher productivity from an increasingly experienced staff.

The highest rates of attrition come during the first year, often in the first few months. Executives tend to blame poor pay for high turnover—usually with reason. But as well as addressing pay, they need to motivate agents to stay by recognizing effort and offering good work conditions and career opportunities.

EXHIBIT 4 Balancing the Scorecard

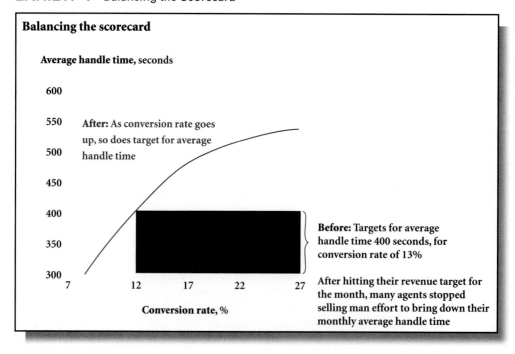

Balancing the scorecard

Average handle time, seconds

After: As conversion rate goes up, so does target for average handle time

Before: Targets for average handle time 400 seconds, for conversion rate of 13%

After hitting their revenue target for the month, many agents stopped selling man effort to bring down their monthly average handle time

Conversion rate, %

There is no quick way to create these conditions. Many things have to be done well across seven dimensions—recruitment, training and development, compensation incentives, career advancement, operations design, site selection, and culture. Certain steps can help a company to ensure, quickly, that it hires the right candidates: requiring senior coaches to conduct interviews, using predictive models to develop agent profiles, recruiting through referrals (which have a lower attrition rate), and hiring only with the site director's approval.

As a result of attitudes stemming from the days when call centers were considered little more than a cost to be minimized, they are among the most underused of all corporate assets. High-performing companies, though, understand the strategic value of a call center. They define a customer service strategy that balances cost cutting with revenue generation, integrates the centers with the organization, and offers segmented service b the value of each call. To realize this strategy, they u sourcing and technology in appropriate ways to crea diversified infrastructure. And they ensure that agents perform well by giving them careful coaching and integrating the relevant performance metrics and incentives. Companies that have acted on these imperatives are already generating higher revenues and providing better service—at a lower cost.

NOTES

1. The annual operating budget of a 200-agent center is more than $10 million.

How to Lead the Customer Experience

STEPHAN H. HAECKEL, LEWIS P. CARBONE,
AND LEONARD L. BERRY

Customers always have an experience when they interact with a firm. The question for managers is whether the firm is prepared to systematically manage the customers' experience or simply hope for the best. The customers' overall experience—influenced by sensory and emotional clues—evokes a value perception that determines brand preference. Through experience management principles, a firm can design a composite of clues that resonate with customers and earn their loyalty.

Business strategies centered on the holistic design and delivery of total customer experiences consistently create superior customer value. Holistic expériences begin and end long before and after actual transactions. They incorporate functional and affective attributes. They are orchestrated to deliver both intrinsic and extrinsic values. And they result in stronger, more sustainable customer preference than do independently managed communication, process, and service-centric strategies.

By "total experience" we mean the feelings customers take away from their interaction with a firm's goods, services, and "atmospheric" stimuli. Companies that interact with customers can't avoid giving them a total experience. They can, however, avoid managing it in a systematic way, and almost all do. Organizations that simply tweak design elements or focus on the customer experience in isolated pockets of their business will be disappointed in the results.

A number of organizations are starting to systematically apply customer experience management principles to strengthen customer preference and improve business outcomes. Unlike many goods or service enhancements, the holistic nature of these experiential designs makes it very difficult for competitors to copy them. Customer value creation is moving into a new arena—one that encompasses goods and service quality, but is a broader concept.

The customer's total experience directly affects perceptions of value, word-of-mouth endorsement, and repatronage intentions. A well-prepared, well-served meal consumed in a noisy restaurant with uncomfortable chairs is one experience for customers. The same food served the same way in a comfortable and relaxing environment is a completely different experience. The meal and the atmosphere are inextricably linked; both are part of the customer's overall restaurant experience. The facility design; servers' skills, attitudes, body language, choice of words, tone, inflection, and dress; pace of service; presentation and taste of the food; noise level; smell; texture of tableware; spacing, height, and shape of tables; and a multitude of other stimuli all coalesce into a positive, neutral, or negative experience.

The problem-solving properties of goods and services provide functional benefits. Managers must recognize two realities, however. First, competing goods and services often are quite similar in functionality. Second, customers desire more than functionality. They are emotional beings who also want intangible values such as a sense of control, fun, aesthetic pleasure, and enhanced self-esteem.

Companies compete best when they combine functional and emotional benefits in their market offer. Firms that make customers feel good are formidable competitors because customers like to feel good and few companies make them feel that way. Emotional bonds between firms and customers are difficult for competitors to penetrate.

CREATING CLUES

Customers always have an experience when they interact with an organization. They consciously and unconsciously filter a barrage of "clues" and organize them into a set of impressions, both rational and emotional. Anything perceived or sensed (or recognized by its absence) is an experience clue. If you can see, smell, taste, or hear it, it's a clue. Goods and services emit clues, as does the physical environment in which they're offered. The employees are another source of experience clues. Each clue carries a message; the composite of clues creates the total experience.

Effectively managing the customers' experience involves presenting an integrated series of clues that collectively meet or exceed customers' expectations. One category of clues concerns the actual functioning of the good or service. Did the key issued at the front desk open the hotel room door? Did the room's television set work? Was the wake-up call made as promised? These goods and service clues strictly concern functionality and are interpreted primarily by the conscious and logical circuitry of the brain.

A second category of clues stimulates the brain's emotional circuitry and evokes affective responses. The smell and feel of leather upholstery, the sound and smell of a steak on the grill, and the laugh, phrasing, and tone of voice of the person answering the customer service call line are clues that envelop the functionality of a good or service. Two types of clues affect customers' emotional perceptions: mechanics (clues emitted by things) and humanics (clues emitted by people).

"How to Lead the Customer Experience" by Stephan H. Haeckel, Lewis P. Carbone and Leonard L. Berry. *Marketing Management* January/February 2003.

The distinction between functional service clues and humanics clues is subtle. A retail salesperson who answers a customer's question about what other stores might carry an out-of-stock item is producing a functional service clue. The salesperson's choice of words, tone, and body language produce humanics clues. One salesperson may offer the information grudgingly or disinterestedly. Another may offer the information enthusiastically. The information is accurate in both cases, but the customer's emotional response to the two salespeople is quite different.

In the August 2000 issue of *Travel & Leisure*, Peter John Lindberg reported on Singapore Airlines, which is consistently rated by travelers as one of the world's best airlines. It invests heavily to orchestrate in-flight service mechanics and humanics clues, including fresh orchids in first- and business-class bathrooms, galley carts scrubbed before every flight, and female flight attendants who wear designer dresses and receive intensive training in body posture, grooming, and voice tone. One veteran flight attendant believes the dresses reduce air-rage incidents: "It's hard to be nasty to a girl in a sarong kebaya. Put them in pants, and passengers think they can take more abuse."

Functional, mechanics, and humanics clues are synergistic rather than additive; they must be melded from creation to execution. To fully leverage experience as a customer value proposition, organizations must understand and manage the emotional component of experiences with the same rigor they bring to managing manufactured product and service functionality.

THE CUSTOMER EXPERIENCE

Customer experience management focuses different parts of an organization on the common goal of creating an integrated, aligned customer feeling. It provides a means for breaking down organizational barriers. We have identified three fundamental principles that provide a foundation for creating distinctive customer value through experiences. Each requires a cross-functional organizational perspective.

Principle 1: Fuse experiential breadth and depth

Experiential breadth refers to the sequence of experience customers have in interacting with an organization. These experiences may begin well before customers pass through the firm's doors. For example, hotel guests' experiences begin before they walk into the lobby. Was the reservations agent competent and courteous? Was the hotel easy to find and access? And, even further back in the experience journey, was the promotional packet the hotel sent about its loyalty program well-designed and informative? Imagine the opportunity for a hotel company in defining the full breadth of the customers' experience, becoming attuned to the hundreds of clues along the way and seeking to manage these clues to evoke positive perceptions.

Whereas breadth refers to identifiable stages customers undergo in the experience, depth refers to the number and diversity of sensory clues at each stage. The more layers of multi-sensory clues that reinforce the targeted impression, the more successful an organization will be in anchoring and sustaining that impression in the customer's perception. Consider the depth of reinforcing clues embedded in the room experience at a Ritz-Carlton hotel. They typically include plush carpet, distinctive furniture and rich fabrics; the smell of fresh flowers; a complimentary refreshment stocked in the room; a welcome call from the concierge offering assistance; an iron and ironing board; a robe, thick towels, and distinctively scented "Ritz-Carlton" shampoos; a leather-bound television viewing guide with a bookmark on the current day; room service 24 hours a day; turn-down service; and *The New York Times* and *Wall Street Journal* delivered outside one's door in the morning.

Congruence or fusion of clues within and among experience stages is critical. Incongruent clues convey an incongruent message with customers likely to recall facets of the experience most salient to their needs. This is why a spacious, well-furnished hotel lobby can't make up for a cramped, poorly furnished hotel room. Guests don't live in the lobby. However, if lobby clues fuse with guest room clues, then one part of the experience reinforces another.

Principle 2: Use mechanics and humanics to improve function

In some cases, humanics and mechanics clues can be introduced to enhance goods or service functionality. Customers process these different types of clues holistically, so firms should manage them as such. Stimuli that envelop goods or services can affect customers' perceptions of functional quality. Mechanics and humanics must be simultaneously addressed and blended with the functional clues of the offering into reciprocally supported experience clues.

Roger Ulrich, a landscape architect with Texas A&M University, has done considerable research documenting how environmental factors in a hospital can affect patients' medical outcomes. For example, Ulrich has found that surgery patients with a bedside window overlooking trees had more favorable recovery courses than patients overlooking a brick wall. Based on accumulating research in environmental psychophysiology, Ulrich recommends designing hospital environments that foster patient control (including their privacy), encourage social support from family and friends, and provide access to nature and other positive distractions. The field of environmental psychophysiology has developed from the fundamental idea that environment affects function.

Principle 3: Connect emotionally

Organizations with effective experience management systems understand and respond to the emotional needs of their customers. They orchestrate a series of clues designed to provoke positive emotional reactions, such as joy, awe, interest, affection, and trust. They integrate emotional value into the total experience because consumers are not Spock-like Vulcans who make purchases on the basis of cold logic.

Managing customers' experiences requires awareness of all of their senses throughout the experience. Sight, motion, sound, smell, taste, and touch are direct pathways to customers' emotions. Connecting with customers in a sensory way is crucial to managing positive emotional elements of the experience.

The sensory-loaded experience of buying and consuming Krispy Kreme doughnuts illustrates the power of emotional connections with customers. At a time when consumers are inundated with information on healthy eating, Krispy Kreme's fried doughnut oozing with glaze enticed more than 3,000 people to wait in a Denver line extending for three city blocks on opening day. Even the name connects on a sensory level. Everything conspires to evoke a feeling of "delicious decadence."

No logical reason compels a person to stand in a long line for hours to buy a doughnut. But an experience so effectively choreographed and integrated with the product is hard to resist. The performance includes the counter person going into the production area, which is in full view, to box up the customer's dozen "original glazed" doughnuts hot off the line. A neon sign in the window lights up only when "HOT Donuts" are actually coming off the line, further heightening the anticipation. The light almost creates a Pavlovian response that, combined with the tempting smell that's pumped outside, brings customers in off the street like cartoon characters hypnotized by a pleasurable wafting scent. The customer walks out with a warm box, still another sensory clue. With its multisensory managed experience, Krispy Kreme makes customers feel good about indulging and forgetting their diets. And yes, the doughnuts taste very good.

MANAGEMENT TOOLS

More than anything else, customer experience management requires customer empathy—seeing what the customer sees, feeling what the customer feels. Organizations don't develop experience management competency overnight. They need to apply specialized tools in the context of a systematic methodology.

An experience audit is used to thoroughly analyze the current customer experience and to illuminate customers' emotional responses to specific clues. Videotape and digital photographs document actual customer experiences and provide the raw data for comprehensive study and categorization of clues. Hours of video are generated—some (with appropriate notification and approval) from pinhole cameras imbedded in wrist-watches, handbags, coats, or hats. Additionally, in-depth interviews with customers and employees reveal their feelings about different aspects of an experience and the emotional associations it generates.

Emotional strands are defined during an experience audit. An emotional strand is a charting of the emotional highs and lows customers commonly experience in a specific setting or situation. For example, female apparel customers commonly move from an emotional high when spotting a great-looking dress in a store to an emotional low if the dress doesn't fit. A goal of experience management is anticipating customers' emotional highs and lows and designing clues to support customers in their emotional strand.

An experience motif is developed based on findings from the experience audit and the organization's core values and branding strategy. Captured in a few words, the motif becomes the North Star—the foundation and filter for integrating and reconciling all elements of the experience. The motif is the unifying element for every clue in the experience design. One financial institution wanted its customers to feel "recognized, reassured, and engaged," terminology formalized into a motif. Subsequently, only clues that reinforced these three motif watchwords were incorporated into the experience design.

Based on the experience motif and other experience design criteria, clues are developed and translated into a blueprint. Mechanics clues are represented graphically in drawings on the blueprint, and humanics clues are described in employee role performance narratives. These narratives, which capture the tone and texture of desired performance, augment existing job descriptions that typically concern job functions rather than performance of a role. The blueprint and narratives become a critical part of an organization's roadmap for communicating, implementing, monitoring, and measuring the outcomes of an experience management system.

CASE STUDY

The Health and Wellness Center by Doylestown Hospital (Doylestown, Penn.) is a one-of-a-kind healthcare model: a combination clinic, health club, and spa with interactive health design services. Patrons just as frequently visit the center for their daily workout or to browse the bookstore as they do for outpatient surgery, a diabetes check, or their annual mammogram.

Construction of the Health and Wellness Center was completed in spring 2001 and expanded the hospital's market into a nearby, rapidly growing community. Beyond the business motivation was management's deepseated determination to make a positive difference in serving the community's modern healthcare needs. This legacy of community service dates from the turn of the century when an inspired women's group, the Village Improvement Association (VIA), founded Doylestown Hospital, which it still owns and oversees. It remains the only women's club in the United States to own and operate a community hospital.

The mandate for the new Center was to create a distinctive healthcare experience integrating traditional medical services with specialized retail, wellness, and fitness services. This means incorporating medical specialties like cardiology, orthopedics, dentistry, day surgery, and women's diagnostics with a full spa and fitness center, an interactive learning center, a restaurant, and a bookstore.

During the construction phase, senior hospital staff began applying experience management techniques. The resulting experience design became central to the planning and development of the facility. The services provided are related through a distinctive architectural and landscape design.

Connecting Emotionally

An experience audit provided deep insights into the basic emotions that surface in patients while on their health and wellness experience journey. Patients shared their feeling that medical process generally predominates over staff empathy for their personal situation. The experience audit, along with internal strategy sessions, produced an experience motif centered on patrons feeling understood, strengthened, and renewed through every interaction with the Health and Wellness Center.

The Center included only clues that reinforce understanding, strengthening, and renewal in the experience design. For example, in addition to standard amenities, the spa and fitness center are capable of downloading patient profiles sent from physicians and health design services—a clue that signals a unique understanding of that person's needs. Spa personnel will have information that an MS patient's whirlpool cannot exceed a certain temperature. In the fitness center, they will be aware of certain parameters for someone just coming out of cardiac rehab. In women's diagnostics, completion of a mammogram is rewarded with a coupon for the restaurant or bookstore—a strengthening and renewing clue. The meticulous building design adheres to the principles of Feng Shui that focus on energy and revitalization.

Integrating Clues

The center's experience management design specified more than 200 clues derived from the experience motif:

- Seasonal healing gardens surrounding the building, complete with meditation benches, music, and a labyrinth walk
- A 25-foot interior waterfall and pond
- A unique stone and wood atrium surrounding the waterfall that serves as a central and communal gathering point
- Internet hookups, overstuffed chairs, and library-style newspaper and magazine racks throughout the atrium
- A fitness center and spa that provide support to cardiac and orthopedic rehab patients as well as the public
- Health design nurses whose sole role is to help consumers create a customized health plan and then mentor and monitor their journey
- Numerous seminars and community events built around health and wellness

- Mammograms and blood pressure checks available without an appointment
- Beepers allowing clients to wait for appointments or test results in any area of the facility
- A bookstore and lending library centered on wellness and linked to the leading recommended Web sites on disease management and wellness strategies
- Distinguishing staff behaviors ranging from voice inflection to gestures to reinforce the motif

Customizing Healthcare

A key element of the differentiated experience is the Health Design Center, which provides customized, coordinated health and wellness plans. Studies show people place great value in coordinated healthcare and the perceived benefit expands dramatically when a person must deal with multiple conditions. The Health Design Center, available to anyone who desires the experience, provides an effective way of delivering a sense of unity and completeness.

The Health Design Center opened with one nurse and has expanded to three in a year's time. While most of the health design services are on a fee basis and not covered by insurance, customized health designs have become a popular service, with more than 200 generated per month.

No single clue at the Health and Wellness Center provides the magic for a distinctive, preferred experience. The benefit comes in the integrated design and layering of clues that support the Center's experience motif. It's the cumulative effect of the customer's take-away feeling from the experience.

The Center is making a difference. Benchmarked against other high-performing health facilities in the nation, it ranked third out of 357 facilities in its first participation in the national Press Ganey patient satisfaction survey. The Center scored in the 98th percentile in overall satisfaction and in the 99th percentile for "sensitivity to patient needs" and "explanations given by staff."

DELIVERING THE BRAND

An increasing number of experience-oriented executives will soon be changing their understanding of what their brand should be in the future. In fact, they will be changing their very understanding of what "brand" means. Rather than creating a set of messages and images that associate a company and its products with emotional values, experience pioneers will be focused on creating a business that delivers the brand as an experience incorporating these values. And this, we assert, is the real transformation, the real meaning, and the real potential of becoming a customer-centric business.[1]

NOTES

1. *Authors' note:* The authors acknowledge the contribution of Suzie Goan, experience director of Experience Engineering Inc. in Minneapolis.

Part  IV

Implementing Profitable Service Strategies

Part IV focuses on four key issues in implementation. First, we recognize that achieving profitability requires creating relationships with customers from the right segments and then finding ways to build and reinforce their loyalty. Second, developing a strategy for effective complaint handling and service recovery often determines whether a firm can build a loyal customer base or has to watch its customers take their business elsewhere.

Third, productivity and quality are both necessary and related ingredients for financial success in services. Productivity is concerned with bringing down costs, and quality increases revenues as a result of greater customer satisfaction.

The final chapter addresses the challenge of how organizations can remain competitive and forward-looking. A firm must be prepared to make ongoing, proactive changes not only in its marketing but also in its operations and human resources stategies. The caliber of managerial leadership determines whether a firm can be a service leader in its industry.

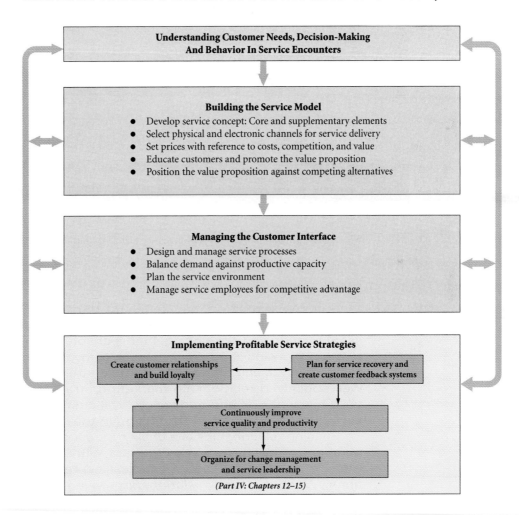

Understanding Customer Needs, Decision-Making And Behavior In Service Encounters

Building the Service Model
- Develop service concept: Core and supplementary elements
- Select physical and electronic channels for service delivery
- Set prices with reference to costs, competition, and value
- Educate customers and promote the value proposition
- Position the value proposition against competing alternatives

Managing the Customer Interface
- Design and manage service processes
- Balance demand against productive capacity
- Plan the service environment
- Manage service employees for competitive advantage

Implementing Profitable Service Strategies

Create customer relationships and build loyalty

Plan for service recovery and create customer feedback systems

Continuously improve service quality and productivity

Organize for change management and service leadership

(Part IV: Chapters 12–15)

Chapter 12

Managing Relationships and Building Loyalty

> *The first step in managing a loyalty-based business system is finding and acquiring the right customers.*

FREDERICK F. REICHHELD

> *Strategy first, then CRM.*

STEVEN S. RAMSEY

Targeting, acquiring, and retaining the "right" customers is at the core of many successful service firms. In Chapter 7 we discussed segmentation and positioning. In this chapter, we emphasize the importance of focusing carefully on desirable, loyal customers within the chosen segments, and then taking pains to strengthen their loyalty through well-conceived relationship marketing strategies. The objective is to build relationships and to develop loyal customers who will do a growing volume of business with the firm in the future.

Building relationships is a challenge, especially when a firm has vast numbers of customers who interact with the firm in many different ways, from email and web sites to call centers and face-to-face interactions. When *customer relationship management* (CRM) systems are implemented well, they provide managers with the tools to understand their customers and tailor their service, cross-selling, and retention efforts, often on a one-on-one basis.

In this chapter, we explore the following questions:

1. Why is customer loyalty an important driver of profitability for service firms?
2. Why is it so important for service firms to target the "right" customers?
3. How can a firm calculate the lifetime value of its customers?

4. What strategies are associated with the concept of relationship marketing and the wheel of loyalty?

5. How can tiering of service, loyalty bonds, and membership programs help in building customer loyalty?

6. What is the role of CRM systems in delivering customized services and building loyalty?

THE SEARCH FOR CUSTOMER LOYALTY

Loyalty is an old-fashioned word that has traditionally been used to describe fidelity and enthusiastic devotion to a country, a cause, or an individual. More recently, it has been used in a business context to describe a customer's willingness to continue patronizing a firm over the long term, preferably on an exclusive basis, and recommending the firm's products to friends and associates. Customer loyalty extends beyond behavior and includes preference, liking, and future intentions. Ask yourself: What service companies are you loyal to? And in what industries are they?

"Few companies think of customers as annuities," says Frederick Reichheld, author of *The Loyalty Effect*, and a major researcher in this field.[1] And yet that is precisely what a loyal customer can mean to a firm—a consistent source of revenue over a period of many years. The active management of the customer base and customer loyalty is also referred to as *customer asset management*.[2]

"Defector" is a nasty word during wartime. It describes disloyal people who sell out their own side and go over to the enemy. Even when they defect toward "our" side, rather than away from it, they're still suspect. Today, in a marketing context, the term *defection* is used to describe customers who drop off a company's radar screen and transfer their brand loyalty to another supplier. Reichheld and Sasser popularized the term *zero defections*, which they describe as keeping every customer the company can serve profitably.[3] Not only does a rising defection rate indicate that something is wrong with quality (or that competitors offer better value), it may also be a leading indicator signaling a fall in profits. Big customers don't necessarily disappear overnight; they often signal their mounting dissatisfaction by reducing their purchases and shifting part of their business elsewhere.

Why Is Customer Loyalty Important to a Firm's Profitability?

How much is a loyal customer worth in terms of profits? In a classic study, Reichheld and Sasser analyzed the profit per customer in various service businesses, as categorized by the number of years that a customer had been with the firm.[4] They found that customers became more profitable the longer they remained with a firm in each of these industries. Annual profits per customer, which have been indexed over a five-year period for easier comparison, are summarized in Figure 12.1. The industries studied (with average profits from a first-year customer shown in parentheses) were credit cards ($30), industrial laundry ($144), industrial distribution ($45), and automobile servicing ($25). A study of Internet sales showed similar loyalty effects; typically, it took more than a year to recoup acquisition costs, but profits increased as customers stayed longer with the firm.[5]

Underlying this profit growth, say Reichheld and Sasser, are four factors that work to the supplier's advantage to create incremental profits. In order of magnitude at the end of seven years, these factors are:

1. *Profit derived from increased purchases (or, in a credit card or banking environment, higher account balances).* Over time, business customers often grow larger and so need to purchase in greater quantities. Individuals may also purchase more as their families grow or as they become more affluent. Both types of customers may be willing to consolidate their purchases with a single supplier who provides high-quality service.

Figure 12.1 How Much Profit a Customer Generates over Time

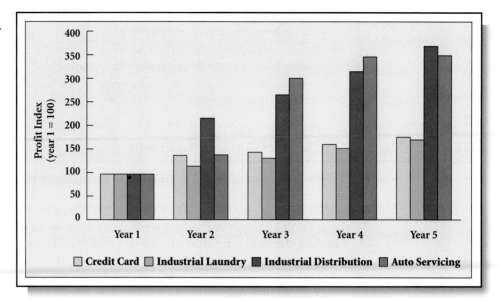

Source: Based on reanalysis of data from Frederick R. Reichheld and W. Earl Sasser, Jr., "Zero Defections: Quality Comes to Services," *Harvard Business Review* 68 (Sep.–Oct. 1990), 105–111.

2. *Profit from reduced operating costs.* As customers become more experienced, they make fewer demands on the supplier (for instance, they have less need for information and assistance). They may also make fewer mistakes when involved in operational processes, thus contributing to greater productivity.

3. *Profit from referrals of other customers.* Positive word-of-mouth recommendations are like free selling and advertising, saving the firm from having to invest as much money in these activities.

4. *Profit from price premium.* New customers often benefit from introductory promotional discounts, whereas long-term customers are more likely to pay regular prices, and when they are highly satisfied they are even willing to pay a price premium.[6] Moreover, customers who trust a supplier may be more willing to pay higher prices at peak periods or for express work.

Figure 12.2 shows the relative contribution of each of these different factors over a seven-year period, based on an analysis of 19 different product categories (both

Figure 12.2 Why Customers Are More Profitable over Time

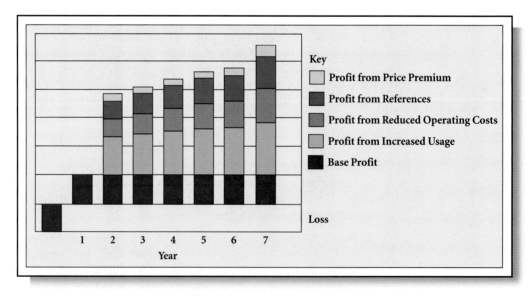

Source: Why Customers Are More Profitable Over Time from Frederick J. Reichheld and W. Earl Sasser Jr. "Zero Defections: Quality Comes to Services," *Harvard Business Review* 73 (Sep.–Oct. 1990): p. 108. Reprinted by permission of Harvard Business School.

goods and services). Reichheld argues that the economic benefits of customer loyalty noted above often explain why one firm is more profitable than a competitor. Furthermore, the up-front costs of attracting these buyers can be amortized over many years.

Assessing the Value of a Loyal Customer

It's a mistake to assume that loyal customers are always more profitable than those who make one-time purchases.[7] On the cost side, not all types of services incur heavy promotional expenditures to attract new customers. Sometimes it is more important to invest in a good retail location that will attract walk-in traffic. Unlike banks, insurance companies, and other "membership" organizations that incur costs for review of applications and account setup, many service firms face no such costs when a new customer first seeks to make a purchase. On the revenue side, loyal customers may not necessarily spend more than one-time buyers, and in some instances they may even expect price discounts.

Finally, revenue does not necessarily increase with time for all types of customers.[8] In most mass market business-to-customer (B2C) services such as banking, mobile phone services, or hospitality, customers can't negotiate prices. However, in many business-to-business (B2B) contexts, large customers have significant bargaining power and therefore will nearly always try to negotiate lower prices when contracts come up for renewal, which forces suppliers to share the cost savings resulting from doing business with a large, loyal customer. DHL has found that although each of its major accounts generates significant business, it yields below-average margins. In contrast, DHL's smaller, less powerful accounts provide significantly higher profitability.[9]

Recent work has also shown that the profit impact of a customer can vary dramatically depending on the stage of the service products life cycle. For instance, referrals by satisfied customers and negative word of mouth by defected customers have a much greater effect on profit in the early stages of the service product's life cycle than in later stages.[10]

One of the challenges that you will probably face in your work is to determine the costs and revenues associated with serving customers in different market segments at different points in their customer life cycles, and to predict future profitability. For insights on how to calculate customer value, see the box, "Worksheet for Calculating Customer Lifetime Value."[11]

The Gap Between Actual and Potential Customer Value

For profit-seeking firms, the potential profitability of a customer should be a key driver in marketing strategy. As Alan Grant and Leonard Schlesinger declare, "Achieving the full profit potential of each customer relationship should be the fundamental goal of every business. . . . Even using conservative estimates, the gap between most companies' current and full potential performance is enormous."[12] They suggest analysis of the following gaps between the actual and potential value of customers.

- What is the current purchasing behavior of customers in each target segment? What would be the effect on sales and profits if they exhibited the ideal behavior profile of (1) buying all services offered by the firm, (2) using these to the exclusion of any purchases from competitors, and (3) paying full price?
- How long, on average, do customers remain with the firm? What effect would it have if they remained customers for life?

As we showed earlier, the profitability of a customer often increases over time. Management's task is to design and implement marketing programs that increase loyalty, including share-of-wallet, upselling, cross-selling, and to identify the reasons why customers defect and then take corrective action.

Calculating customer value is an inexact science that is subject to a variety of assumptions. You may want to try varying these assumptions to see how it affects the final figures. Generally speaking, revenues per customer are easier to track on an individualized basis than are the associated costs of serving a customer, unless (1) no individual records are kept and/or (2) the accounts served are very large and all account-related costs are individually documented and assigned.

Acquisition Revenues Less Costs

If individual account records are kept, the initial application fee paid and initial purchase (if relevant) should be found in these records. Costs, by contrast, may have to be based on average data. For instance, the marketing cost of acquiring a new client can be calculated by dividing the total marketing costs (advertising, promotions, selling, etc.) devoted toward acquiring new customers by the total number of new customers acquired during the same period. If each acquisition takes place over an extended period of time, you may want to build in a lagged effect between when marketing expenditures are incurred and when new customers come on board. The cost of credit checks—where relevant—must be divided by the number of new customers, not the total number of applicants, because some applicants will probably fail this hurdle. Account set-up costs will also be an average figure in most organizations.

Annual Revenues and Costs

If annual sales, account fees, and service fees are documented on an individual-account basis, account revenue streams (except referrals) can be easily identified. The first priority is to segment your customer base by the length of its relationship with your firm. Depending on the sophistication and precision of your firm's records, annual costs in each category may be directly assigned to an individual account holder or averaged for all account holders in that age category.

Value of Referrals

Computing the value of referrals requires a variety of assumptions. To get started, you may need to conduct surveys to determine (1) what percentage of new customers claim that they were influenced by a recommendation from another customer and (2) what other marketing activities also drew the firm to that individual's attention. From these two items, estimates can be made of what percentage of the credit for all new customers should be assigned to referrals. Additional research may be needed to clarify whether "older" customers are more likely to be effective recommenders than "younger" ones.

Net Present Value

Calculating net present value (NPV) from a future profit stream will require choice of an appropriate annual discount figure. (This could reflect estimates of future inflation rates.) It also requires assessment of how long the average relationship lasts. The NPV of a customer, then, is the sum of the anticipated annual profit on each customer for the projected relationship lifetime, suitably discounted each year into the future.

ACQUISITION			YEAR 1	YEAR 2	YEAR 3	YEAR n
Initial Revenue		*Annual Revenues*				
Application fee[a]	____	Annual account fee[a]	____	____	____	____
Initial purchase[a]	____	Sales	____	____	____	____
		Service fees[a]	____	____	____	____
		Value of referrals[b]	____	____	____	____
Total Revenues	____		____	____	____	____
Initial Costs		*Annual Costs*				
Marketing	____	Account management	____	____	____	____
Credit check[a]	____	Cost of sales	____	____	____	____
Account setup[a]	____	Write-offs (e.g., bad debts)	____	____	____	____
Less total costs	____		____	____	____	____
Net Profit (Loss)	____		____	____	____	____

[a]If applicable.

[b]Anticipated profits from each new customer referred (could be limited to the first year or expressed as the net present value of the estimated future stream of profits through year n); this value could be negative if an unhappy customer starts to spread negative word of mouth that causes existing customers to defect.

Understanding the Customer–Firm Relationship

There's a fundamental distinction between strategies intended to produce a single transaction and those designed to create extended relationships with customers. Repeated transactions form the necessary basis for a relationship between customer and supplier, although we shouldn't assume that every customer who uses a service with some frequency seeks an active relationship.

Relationship Marketing

The term *relationship marketing* has been widely used, but until recently it was only loosely defined. Research by Nicole Coviello, Rod Brodie, and Hugh Munro suggest that there are, in fact, four distinct types of marketing: *transactional marketing* and three categories of what they call relational marketing: *database marketing, interaction marketing,* and *network marketing*.[13]

Transactional Marketing

A *transaction* is an event during which an exchange of value takes place between two parties. One transaction or even a series of transactions don't necessarily constitute a relationship, which requires mutual recognition and knowledge between the parties. When each transaction between a customer and a supplier is essentially discrete and anonymous, with no long-term record kept of a customer's purchasing history, and little or no mutual recognition between the customer and employees, then no meaningful marketing relationship can be said to exist. This is true for many services, ranging from passenger transport to food service or visits to a movie theater, in which each purchase and use is a separate event.

Database Marketing

In database marketing the focus is still on the market transaction, but now it includes information exchange. Marketers rely on information technology, usually in the form of a database, to form a relationship with targeted customers and retain their patronage over time. However, the nature of these relationships is often not a close one, with communication being driven and managed by the seller. Technology is used to (1) identify and build a database of current and potential customers, (2) deliver differentiated messages based on consumers' characteristics and preferences, and (3) track each relationship to monitor the cost of acquiring the consumer and the lifetime value of the resulting purchases.[14] Although technology can be used to personalize the relationship, relations remain somewhat distant. Utility services such as electricity, gas, and cable TV are good examples.

Interaction Marketing

A closer relationship often exists in situations where there is face-to-face interaction between customers and representatives of the supplier (or "ear-to-ear" interaction by phone). Although the service itself remains important, value is added by people and social processes. Interactions may include negotiations and sharing of insights in both directions. This type of relationship exists in many local service markets, ranging from community banks to dentistry, in which buyer and seller know and trust each other. It is also commonly found in many B2B services. Both the firm and the customer are prepared to invest resources to develop a mutually beneficial relationship. This investment may include time spent sharing and recording information.

As service companies grow larger and make increasing use of technologies such as interactive web sites and self-service technology, maintaining meaningful relationships with customers becomes a significant marketing challenge. Firms with large customer bases find it increasingly difficult to build and maintain meaningful relationships through call centers, web sites and other mass delivery channels (Figure 12.3).

Figure 12.3
Building and
Maintaining
Relationships
Through Call Centers
Is a Challenge

Network Marketing

We often say that someone is a "good networker" because he or she is able to put individuals in touch with others who have a mutual interest. In a B2B context, marketers work to develop networks of relationships with customers, distributors, suppliers, the media, consultants, trade associations, government agencies, competitors, and even the customers of their customers. Often, a team of individuals within the supplier's firm collaborates to provide effective service to a parallel team within the customer's organization.

The four types of marketing described above are not necessarily mutually exclusive. A firm may have transactions with some customers who have neither the desire nor the need to make future purchases, while working hard to move others up the loyalty ladder.[15] Evert Gummesson identifies no fewer than 30 types of relationships. He advocates *total relationship marketing,* describing it as

> . . . marketing based on relationships, networks, and interaction, recognizing that marketing is embedded in the total management of the networks of the selling organization, the market, and society. It is directed to long-term, win–win relationships with individual customers, and value is jointly created between the parties involved.[16]

Creating "Membership" Relationships

Ideally, we would like to create ongoing relationships with our customers. This is easier when customers receive service on a continuing basis. However, even where the transactions are themselves discrete, there may still be an opportunity to create an ongoing relationship, as we will discuss later in the chapter in the context of loyalty reward programs.

The nature of the current relationship can be analyzed by asking, first: Does the supplier enters into a formal "membership" relationship with customers, as with telephone subscriptions, banking, and the family doctor. Or is there no defined relationship? Second, is the service delivered on a continuous basis, as in insurance, broadcasting, and police protection? Or is each transaction recorded and charged separately? Table 12.1 shows a matrix resulting from this categorization, with examples in each category.

Table 12.1
Relationships with
Customers

NATURE OF SERVICE DELIVERY	TYPE OF RELATIONSHIP BETWEEN THE SERVICE ORGANIZATION AND ITS CUSTOMERS	
	MEMBERSHIP RELATIONSHIP	NO FORMAL RELATIONSHIP
Continuous delivery of service	Insurance	Radio station
	Cable TV subscription	Police protection
	College enrollment	Lighthouse
	Banking	Public highway
Discrete transactions	Long-distance calls from subscriber phone	Car rental
	Theater series subscription	Mail service
	Travel on commuter ticket	Toll highway
	Repair under warranty	Pay phone
	Health treatment for HMO member	Movie theater
		Public transportation
		Restaurant

A *membership relationship* is a formalized relationship between the firm and an identifiable customer, which may offer special benefits to both parties. Services involving discrete transactions can be transformed into membership relationships either by selling the service in bulk (for instance, a theater series subscription or a commuter ticket on public transport) or by offering extra benefits to customers who choose to register with the firm (loyalty programs for hotels, airlines, and car rental firms fall into this category). The advantage to the service organization of having membership relationships is that it knows who its current customers are and, usually, what use they make of the services offered. This can be valuable information for segmentation purposes if good records are kept and the data are readily accessible for analysis. Knowing the identities and addresses of current customers enables the organization to make effective use of direct mail (including e-mail), telephone selling, and personal sales calls—all highly targeted methods of marketing communication. In turn, members can be given access to special numbers or even designated account managers to facilitate their communications with the firm.

THE WHEEL OF LOYALTY

Building customer loyalty is difficult. Just try and think of all the service firms you yourself are loyal to. Most people cannot think of more than perhaps a handful of firms they truly like (i.e., give a high share of heart) and to whom they are committed to going back (i.e., give a high share-of-wallet). This shows that although firms put enormous amounts of money and effort into loyalty initiatives, they often are not successful in building true customer loyalty. We use the *wheel of loyalty* shown in Figure 12.4 as an organizing framework for thinking about how to build customer loyalty. It comprises three sequential strategies.

First, the firm needs a solid foundation for creating customer loyalty, which includes having the right portfolio of customer segments, attracting the right customers, tiering the service, and delivering high levels of satisfaction.

Second, to truly build loyalty, a firm needs to develop close bonds with its customers, which either deepen the relation ship through cross-selling and bundling, or add value to the customer through loyalty rewards and higher-level bonds.

Third, the firm needs to identify and eliminate factors that result in "churn"—the loss of existing customers and the need to replace them with new ones.

We discuss each of the components of the wheel of loyalty in the following sections.

Figure 12.4 The Wheel of Loyalty

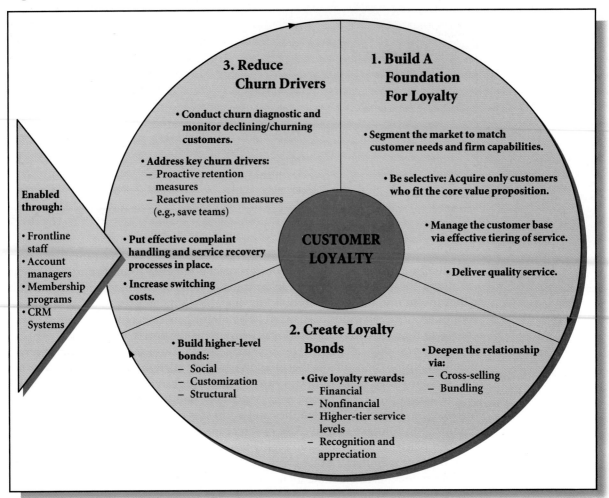

BUILDING A FOUNDATION FOR LOYALTY

Many elements are involved in creating long-term customer relationships and loyalty. In Chapter 7 we discussed segmentation and positioning. In this section, we emphasize the importance of focusing on desirable customers, and then taking pains to build their loyalty through well-conceived relationship marketing strategies, including delivery of quality service.

Good Relationships Start with a Good Fit Between Customer Needs and Company Capabilities

The process starts with identifying and targeting the right customers. "Who should we be serving?" is a question that every service business needs to raise periodically. Customers often differ widely in terms of needs. They also differ in terms of the value that they can contribute to a company. Not all customers offer a good fit with the organization's capabilities, delivery technologies, and strategic direction.

Companies need to be selective about the segments they target if they want to build successful customer relationships. In this section, we emphasize the importance of choosing to serve a portfolio of several carefully chosen target segments and taking pains to build and maintain their loyalty.

Matching customers to the firm's capabilities is vital. Managers must think carefully about how customer needs relate to such operational elements as speed and quality, the times when service is available, the firm's capacity to serve many customers simultaneously, and the physical features and appearance of service facilities. They also need to consider how well their service personnel can meet the expectations of specific types of customers, in terms of both personal style and technical competence.[17] Finally, they need to ask themselves whether their company can match or exceed competing services that are directed at the same types of customers.

The result of carefully targeting customers by matching the company capabilities and strengths with customer needs should be a superior service offering in the eyes of those customers who value what the firm has to offer. As Frederick Reichheld said, "the result should be a win–win situation, where profits are earned through the success and satisfaction of customers, and not at their expense."[18]

Searching for Value, Not Just Volume

Too many service firms still focus on the *number* of customers they serve, without giving sufficient attention to the *value* of each customer. Generally speaking, heavy users who buy more frequently and in larger volumes are more profitable than occasional users. Roger Hallowell makes this point nicely in a discussion of banking:

> A bank's population of customers undoubtedly contains individuals who either cannot be satisfied, given the service levels and pricing the bank is capable of offering, or will never be profitable, given their banking activity (their use of resources relative to the revenue they supply). Any bank would be wise to target and serve only those customers whose needs it can meet better than its competitors in a profitable manner. These are the customers who are most likely to remain with that bank for long periods, who will purchase multiple products and services, who will recommend that bank to their friends and relations, and who may be the source of superior returns to the bank's shareholders.[19]

Relationship customers are by definition not buying commodity services. Service customers who buy strictly based on lowest price (a minority in most markets) are not good target customers for relationship marketing in the first place. They are deal-prone, and continuously seek the lowest price on offer.

Loyalty leaders are picky about acquiring only the right customers, which are those for whom their firms have been designed to deliver truly special value. Acquiring the right customers can bring in long-term revenues, continued growth from referrals, and enhanced satisfaction from employees whose daily jobs are improved when they can deal with appreciative customers. Attracting the wrong customers typically results in costly churn, a diminished company reputation, and disillusioned employees. Ironically, it is often the firms that are highly focused and selective in their acquisition rather than those that focus on unbridled acquisition that are growing fast over long periods.[20] Best Practice in Action 12.1 shows how Vanguard Group, a leader in the mutual funds industry, designed its products and pricing to attract and retain the right customers for its business model.

Managers shouldn't assume that the "right customers" are always big spenders. Depending on the service business model, the right customers may come from a large group of people that no other supplier is doing a good job of serving. Many firms have built successful strategies on serving customers segments that had been neglected by established players, which didn't perceive them as being sufficiently "valuable." Examples include Enterprise Rent-A-Car, which targets customers who need a temporary replacement car, avoiding the more traditional segment of business travelers who are pursued by its principal competitors; Charles Schwab, which focuses on retail stock buyers; and Paychex, which provides small businesses with payroll and human resources services.[21]

Different segments offer different value for a service firm. Like investments, some types of customers may be more profitable than others in the short term, but others may have greater potential for long-term growth. Similarly, the spending patterns of

BEST PRACTICE IN ACTION 12.1
Vanguard Discourages the Acquisition of "Wrong" Customers

The Vanguard Group is a growth leader in the mutual fund industry that built its $850 billion in managed assets by painstakingly targeting the right customers for its business model. Its share of new sales, which was around 25 percent, reflected its share of assets or market share. However, it had a far lower share of redemptions, which gave it a market share of net cash flows of 55 percent (new sales minus redemptions), and made it the fastest-growing mutual fund in its industry.

How did Vanguard achieve such low redemption rates? The secret was its careful acquisitions, and its product and pricing strategies, which encouraged the acquisition of the "right" customers.

John Bogle, Vanguard's founder, believed in the superiority of index funds and that their lower management fees would lead to higher returns over the long run. He offered Vanguard's clients unparalleled low management fees through a policy of not trading (its index funds hold the market they are designed to track), not having a sales force, and spending only a fraction of what its competitors did on advertising. Another important part of keeping its costs low was its aim to discourage the acquisition of customers who were not long-term index holders.

John Bogle attributes the high customer loyalty Vanguard has achieved to a great deal of focus on customer redemptions, which are defections in the fund context. "I watched them like a hawk," he explained, and analyzed them more carefully than new sales to ensure that Vanguard's customer acquisition strategy was on course. Low redemption rates meant that the firm was attracting the right kind of loyal, long-term investors. The inherent stability of its loyal customer base was key to Vanguard's cost advantage. Bogle's pickiness became legendary. He scrutinized individual redemptions with a fine-tooth comb to see who let the wrong kind of customers on board. When an institutional investor redeemed $25 million from an index fund bought only nine months earlier, he regarded the acquisition of this customer as a failure of the system. He explained, "We don't want short-term investors.

They muck up the game at the expense of the long-term investor." At the end of his chairman's letter to the Vanguard Index Trust, Bogle reiterated: "We urge them [short-term investors] to look elsewhere for their investment opportunities."

This care and attention to acquiring the right customers became legendary. For example, Vanguard turned away an institutional investor who wanted to invest $40 million because Vanguard suspected that the customer would churn the investment within the next few weeks, creating extra costs for existing customers. The potential customer complained to Vanguard's CEO, who not only supported the decision but also used it as an opportunity to reinforce to his teams why they needed to be selective about the customers they accepted.

Furthermore, Vanguard introduced a number of changes to industry practices that discouraged active traders from buying its funds. For example, Vanguard did not allow telephone transfers for index funds, redemption fees were added to some funds, and the standard practice of subsidizing new accounts at the expense of existing customers was rejected, because the practice was considered disloyal to its core investor base. These product and pricing policies in effect turned away heavy traders, but made the fund unequivocally attractive for the long-term investor.

Finally, Vanguard's pricing was set up to reward loyal customers. For many of its funds, investors pay a one-time fee upfront, which goes into the funds themselves to compensate all current investors for the administrative costs of selling new shares. In essence, this fee subsidizes long-term investors and penalizes short-term investors. Another novel pricing approach was the creation of its Admiral shares for loyal investors, which carried an expense fee one-third less than that of ordinary shares (0.12 percent per year instead of 0.18 percent).

Source: Adapted from Frederick F. Reichheld, *Loyalty Rules! How Today's Leaders Build Lasting Relationships.* Boston: Harvard Business School Press, 2001, pp. 24–29, 84–87, 144–145; www.vanguard.com, accessed January 19, 2006.

some customers may be stable over time, while those of others may be more cyclical, spending heavily in boom times but cutting back sharply in recessions. A wise marketer seeks a mix of segments in order to reduce the risks associated with volatility.[22]

In many cases, as David Maister emphasizes, marketing is about getting *better* business, not just *more* business.[23] For instance, the caliber of a professional firm is measured by the type of clients it serves and the nature of the tasks on which it works. Volume alone is no measure of excellence, sustainability, or profitability. In professional services, such as consulting firms or legal partnerships, the mix of business attracted may play an important role in both defining the firm and providing a suitable mix of assignments for staff members at different levels in the organization.

Managing the Customer Base Through Effective Tiering of Services

Marketers should adopt a strategic approach to retaining, upgrading, and even terminating customers. Customer retention involves developing long-term, cost-effective links with customers for the mutual benefit of both parties, but these efforts need not necessarily target all customers with the same level of intensity. Recent research has confirmed that most firms have different tiers of customers in terms of profitability, and these tiers often have quite different service expectations and needs. According to Valarie Zeithaml, Roland Rust, and Katharine Lemon, it's critical for service firms to understand the needs of customers within different profitability tiers and to adjust their service levels accordingly.[24]

Just as service product categories can be tiered to reflect the level of value included (see Chapter 7, pp. 190–191), so can groups of customers. In the latter instance, customer tiers can be developed around different levels of profit contribution, needs (including sensitivities to variables such as price, comfort, and speed), and identifiable personal profiles such as demographics. Zeithaml, Rust, and Lemon illustrate this principle through a four-level pyramid (Figure 12.5).

- *Platinum.* These customers constitute a very small percentage of a firm's customer base, but they are heavy users and contribute a large share of the firm's profits. Typically, this segment is less price-sensitive but expects highest service levels, and it is likely to be willing to invest in and try new services.
- *Gold.* The gold tier includes a larger percentage of customers than the platinum tier, but individual customers contribute less profit than platinum customers. They tend to be slightly more price-sensitive and less committed to the firm.
- *Iron.* These customers provide the bulk of the customer base. Their numbers give the firm economies of scale. Hence, they are often important so that a firm can build and maintain a certain capacity level and infrastructure, which is often needed to serve gold and platinum customers well. However, iron customers in themselves are often only marginally profitable. Their level of business is not sufficient to warrant special treatment.
- *Lead.* Customers in this tier tend to generate low revenues for a firm, but often require the same level of service as iron customers, which turns them into a loss-making segment from the firm's perspective.

Figure 12.5 The Customer Pyramid

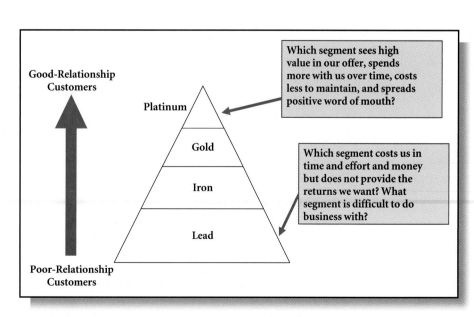

Source: Copyright © 2001, by The Regents of the University of California. Reprinted from the *California Management Review.* Vol. 43, No. 4. By permission of The Regents.

Tiering its clients helped a leading U.S. market research agency understand its customers better. The agency defined *platinum clients* as large accounts that were not only willing to plan a certain amount of research work during the year, but were also able to commit to the timing, scope, and nature of their projects, which made capacity management and project planning much easier for the research firm. The acquisition costs for projects sold to these clients were only 2 to 5 percent of project values (as compared to as much as 25 percent for clients who required extensive proposal work and project-by-project bidding). Platinum accounts were also more willing to try new services, and to buy a wider range of services from their preferred provider. These customers were generally very satisfied with the research agency's work and were willing to act as references for potential new clients.

Gold accounts had a similar profile to platinum clients, except that they were more price-sensitive, and were more inclined to spread their budgets across several firms. Although these accounts had been clients for many years, they were not willing to commit their research work for a year in advance even though the research firm would have been able to offer them better quality and priority in capacity allocation.

Iron accounts spent moderate amounts on research, and commissioned work on a project basis. Selling costs were high, as these firms tended to send out requests for proposals (RFPs) to a number of firms for all their projects. They sought the lowest price, and often did not allow sufficient time for the research firm to perform a good-quality job.

Lead accounts sought only isolated, low-cost projects, which tended be "quick and dirty" in nature, with little opportunity for the research firm to add value or to apply its skill sets appropriately. Sales costs were high as the client typically invited several firms to quote. Furthermore, because these firms were inexperienced in conducting research and in working with research agencies, selling a project often took several meetings and required multiple revisions to the proposal. Lead accounts also tended to be high-maintenance because they did not understand research work well; they often changed project parameters, scope, and deliverables midstream and then expected the research agency to absorb the cost of any rework, thus further reducing the profitability of the engagement.

Source: Adapted from Valarie A. Zeithaml, Roland T. Rust, and Katharine N. Lemon, "The Customer Pyramid: Creating and Serving Profitable Customers." *California Management Review*, 43, no. 4 (Summer 2001): 127–128.

The precise characteristics of customer tiers vary, of course, from one type of business to another and even from one firm to another. Service Perspective 12.1 provides an illustration from the marketing research industry.

Customer tiers are typically based on profitability and service needs. Rather than providing the same level of service to all customers, each segment receives a service level that is customized based on its requirements and value to the firm. For example, the platinum tier is provided some exclusive benefits that are not available to other segments. The benefit levels for platinum and gold customers are often designed with retention in mind, because these customers are the ones competitors would like to entice to switch.

Marketing efforts can be used to encourage an increased volume of purchases, upgrading the type of service used, or cross-selling additional services to any of the four tiers. However, these efforts have different thrusts for the different tiers, as their needs, usage behaviors, and spending patterns are usually very different. Among segments for which the firm already has a high share-of-wallet, the focus should be on nurturing, defending, and retaining these customers, possibly by use of loyalty programs.[25]

For lead-tier customers, the options are to either migrate them to the iron segment or to terminate them. Migration can be achieved via a combination of strategies, including base fees and price increases. Imposing a minimum fee that is waived when a certain level of revenue is generated may encourage customers who use several suppliers to consolidate their transactions with a single provider.

There may be opportunities to cut service costs to those customers. Customer behavior can be shaped in ways that reduces the cost of serving them; for instance, transaction charges for electronic channels may be priced lower than for people-intensive channels. Another option is to create an attractively priced, low-cost platform. In the cellular telephone industry, for example, low-use mobile users are directed to prepaid packages that do not require the firm to send out bills and collect payments, which also eliminates the risk of bad debts on such accounts.

Terminating customers comes as a logical consequence of the realization that not all existing customer relationships are worth keeping. Some relationships may no longer be profitable for the firm, because they may cost more to maintain than the revenues they generate. Some customers no longer fit the firm's strategy, either because that strategy has changed or because the customers' behavior and needs have changed. Just as investors need to dispose of poor investments and banks may have to write off bad loans, each service firm needs to evaluate its customer portfolio regularly and consider terminating unsuccessful relationships. Legal and ethical considerations, of course, will determine whether it is proper to take such action.

Occasionally, customers are "fired" outright (although concern for due process is still important). ING Direct is the fast-food model of consumer banking: It is about as no-frills as it gets. It has only a handful of basic products, and it lures low-maintenance customers with high interest rates (its Orange savings account paid 3.8 percent in January 2006, which was several times the industry average). To offset that generosity, its business model pushes its customers toward online transactions, and the bank routinely fires customers who don't fit its business model. When a customer calls too often (the average customer phone call costs the bank $5.25 to handle), or wants too many exceptions to the rule, the banks sales associates basically say,: "Look, this doesn't fit you. You need to go back to your community bank and get the kind of contact you're comfortable with." As a result, ING Direct's cost per account is only one-third of the industry average.[26]

Other examples of customers being fired include students who are caught cheating on examinations, or country club members who consistently abuse the facilities or other people. In some instances, termination may be less confrontational. Banks wishing to divest themselves of certain types of accounts that no longer fit with corporate priorities have been known to sell them to other banks (one example is credit card holders who receive a letter in the mail telling them that their account has been transferred to another card issuer).

Customer Satisfaction and Service Quality Are Prerequisites for Loyalty

The foundation for true loyalty lies in customer satisfaction, for which service quality is a key input. Highly satisfied or even delighted customers are more likely to become loyal apostles of a firm,[27] consolidate their buying with one suppler, and spread positive word of mouth. Dissatisfaction, in contrast, drives customers away and is a key factor in switching behavior. Recent research has even demonstrated that increases in customer satisfaction lead to increases in stock prices—see Research Insights 12.1.

The satisfaction–loyalty relationship can be divided into three main zones: Defection, indifference, and affection (Figure 12.7). The *zone of defection* occurs at low satisfaction levels. Customers will switch unless switching costs are high or there are no viable or convenient alternatives. Extremely dissatisfied customers can turn into "terrorists," providing an abundance of negative word of mouth for the service provider.[28] The *zone of indifference* is found at intermediate satisfaction levels. Here, customers are willing to switch if they find a better alternative. Finally, the *zone of affection* is located at very high satisfaction levels, where customers may have such high attitudinal loyalty that they do not look for alternative service providers. Customers who praise the firm in public and refer others to the firm are described as "apostles."

Does a firm's customer satisfaction level have anything to do with its stock price? This was the intriguing research question that Claes Fornell and his colleagues wanted to answer. More specifically, they examined whether investments in customer satisfaction lead to higher stock returns (see Figure 12.6), and if so, whether these returns were associated with higher risks, as would be predicted by finance theory. The researchers built two stock portfolios and then measured the return and risks of the firms in those portfolios compared to the firm's American Customer Satisfaction Index (ACSI) scores.

Their findings are striking for managers and investors alike. Fornell and his colleagues discovered that the ACSI was significantly related to the stock prices of the individual firms. However, simply publishing the latest data on the ACSI did not immediately move share prices, as efficient market theory would have predicted. Rather, share prices seemed to adjust slowly over time as firms published other results (perhaps earnings data or other "hard" facts that may lag customer satisfaction), and excess stock returns were generated as a result. This result represents a stock market imperfection, but it is consistent with research in marketing, which holds that satisfied customers improve the level and the stability of cash flow.

For marketing managers, this study's findings confirm that investments (or "expenses" if you talk to accountants) into managing customer relationships and the cash flows they produce are fundamental to the firm's, and therefore shareholders', value creation.

Although the results are convincing, be careful should you want to exploit this apparent market inefficiency and invest in firms that show high increases in customer satisfaction in future ACSI releases—your finance friends will tell you that efficient markets learn fast! You will know this has happened when you see stock prices move as a response to ACSI releases. You can learn more about the ACSI at www.theacsi.org.

Source: Claes Fornell, Sunil Mithas, Forrest V. Morgeson III, and M. S. Krishnan, "Customer Satisfaction and Stock Prices: High Returns, Low Risk." *Journal of Marketing,* 70 (January 2006): 3–14.

Figure 12.6 Can Customer Satisfaction Data Help to Outperform the Market?

Figure 12.7 The Customer Satisfaction/Loyalty Relationship

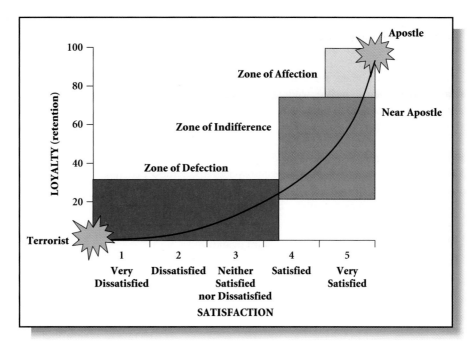

Source: The Customer Satisfaction-Loyalty Relationship from Thomas O. Jones and W. Earl Sasser, Jr., "Why Satisfied Customers Defect" *Harvard Business Review,* Nov.–Dec. 1995, p. 91. Reprinted by permission of Harvard Business School.

CREATING LOYALTY BONDS

What makes customers loyal to a firm, and how can marketers increase their loyalty? In this section, we first review the common loyalty drivers for customers, and then explore how firms can build or enhance such loyalty drivers.

How Do Customers See Relational Benefits?

Relationships create value for individual consumers through such factors as inspiring greater confidence, offering social benefits, and providing special treatment (see Research Insights 12.2). In a B2B service context, relationships depend largely on the quality of the interactions between individuals at each of the partnering firms, and service firms needs to take care to communicate the relevant benefits to the right people in the client organization, because purchasing decisions are often made jointly. As relationships strengthen over time, the service provider's employees often take on the role of an outsourced department and make critical decisions on behalf of their client.[29]

Strategies for Developing Loyalty Bonds with Customers

Having the right portfolio of customer segments, attracting the right customers, tiering the service, and delivering high levels of satisfaction are a solid foundation for creating customer loyalty, as shown in the wheel of loyalty in Figure 12.4. However, firms can do even more to bond more closely with their customers. Specific strategies include deepening the relationship through cross-selling and bundling, and creating loyalty rewards and higher-level bonds such as social, customization, and structural bonds.[30]

Deepening the Relationship
To tie customers more closely to the firm, deepening the relationship via bundling and/or cross-selling services is an effective strategy. For example, banks like to sell as many financial products to an account holder or household as possible. Once a family has a checking account, credit card, savings account, safe deposit box, car loan, mortgage, and so on, with the same bank, the relationship is so deep that switching

What benefits do customers see themselves receiving from an extended relationship with a service firm? Researchers seeking answers to this question conducted two studies. The first consisted of in-depth interviews with 21 respondents from a broad cross section of backgrounds. Respondents were asked to identify service providers that they used on a regular basis and invited to identify and discuss any benefits they received as a result of being a regular customer. Among the comments were

- "I like him [hair stylist]. . . . He's really funny and always has lots of good jokes. He's kind of like a friend now."

- "I know what I'm getting—I know that if I go to a restaurant that I regularly go to, rather than taking a chance on all of the new restaurants, the food will be good."

- "I often get price breaks. The little bakery that I go to in the morning, every once in a while, they'll give me a free muffin and say, 'You're a good customer, it's on us today.'"

- "You can get better service than drop-in customers. . . . We continue to go to the same automobile repair shop because we have gotten to know the owner on a kind of personal basis, and he . . . can always work us in."

- "Once people feel comfortable, they don't want to switch to another dentist. They don't want to train or break a new dentist in."

After evaluating and categorizing the comments, the researchers designed a second study in which they collected 299 survey questionnaires. The respondents were told to select a specific service provider with whom they had a strong, established relationship. Then the questionnaire asked them to assess the extent to which they received each of 21 benefits (derived from analysis of the first study) as a result of their relationship with the specific provider they had identified. Finally, they were asked to assess the importance of these benefits for them.

A factor analysis of the results showed that most of the benefits that customers derived from relationships could be grouped into three categories. The first, and most important, group involved what the researchers labeled confidence benefits, followed by social benefits and special treatment.

- *Confidence benefits* included feelings by customers that in an established relationship there was less risk of something going wrong, confidence in correct performance, ability to trust the provider, lowered anxiety when purchasing, knowing what to expect, and receipt of the firm's highest level of service.

- *Social benefits* embraced mutual recognition between customers and employees, being known by name, friendship with the service provider, and enjoyment of certain social aspects of the relationship.

- *Special treatment benefits* included better prices, discounts on special deals that were unavailable to most customers, extra services, higher priority when there was a wait, and faster service than most customers received.

Source: Kevin P. Gwinner, Dwayne D. Gremler, and Mary Jo Bitner, "Relational Benefits in Services Industries: The Customer's Perspective." *Journal of the Academy of Marketing Science,* 26, no. 2 (1998): 101–114.

becomes a major exercise and is unlikely, unless of course, the customer becomes extremely dissatisfied with the bank.

Customers can benefit from consolidating their purchasing of various services from the same provider through the added convenience of one-stop shopping and potentially higher service levels and/or higher service tiers because of the higher volume of business they bring to the firm.

Reward-Based Bonds

Within any competitive product category, managers recognize that few customers consistently buy only one brand, especially when service delivery involves discrete transactions (such as a car rental) rather than being continuous in nature (as with insurance coverage). In many instances, consumers are loyal to several brands while spurning others (sometimes described as "polygamous loyalty"). In such instances, the marketing goal becomes one of strengthening the customer's preference for one brand over the others, and well-designed loyalty programs can achieve increased loyalty and share-of-wallet.[31]

Incentives that offer rewards based on frequency of purchase, value of purchase, or a combination of both represent a basic level of customer bonding. Reward-based bonds can be financial or nonfinancial in nature. Financial bonds are built when loyal customers are rewarded with incentives that have a financial value, such as discounts on purchases and loyalty program rewards such as frequent flier miles or the cash-back programs provided by some credit card issuers. Nonfinancial rewards provide customers with benefits or value that cannot be translated directly into monetary terms. Examples include giving priority to loyalty program members for waitlists and queues in call centers, and access to special services. Some airlines provide benefits such as higher baggage allowances, priority upgrading, access to airport lounges, and the like to their frequent flyers, even when they are only flying in economy class. Informal loyalty rewards, sometimes found in small businesses, may take the form of periodically giving regular customers a small treat as a way of thanking them for their custom.

Important intangible rewards include special recognition and appreciation. Customers tend to value the extra attention given to their needs. They also appreciate the implicit service guarantee offered by high-tier memberships, including efforts to meet special requests. One objective of reward-based bonds is to motivate customers to consolidate their purchases with one provider or at least make it the most preferred provider. Tiered loyalty programs often provide direct incentives for customers to achieve the next higher level of membership. However, reward-based loyalty programs are relatively easy for other suppliers to copy and rarely provide a sustained competitive advantage. By contrast, the higher-level bonds that we discuss next tend to be more sustainable.

Social Bonds

Have you ever noticed how your favorite hairdresser addresses you by your name when you go for a haircut or how she asks why she hasn't seen you for a long time and hopes everything went well when you were away on a long business trip? Social bonds are typically based on personal relationships between providers and customers. Alternatively, they may reflect pride or satisfaction in holding membership in an organization. Although social bonds are more difficult to build than financial bonds and may require considerable time to achieve, for that same reason they are also harder for other suppliers to replicate for that same customer. A firm that has created social bonds with its customers has a better chance of retaining them for the long term. When social bonds extend to shared relationships or experiences between customers, such as in country clubs or educational settings, they can be a major loyalty driver for the organization.[32]

Customization Bonds

Customization bonds are built when the service provider succeeds in providing customized service to its loyal customers. For example, Starbucks' employees are encouraged to learn their regular customers' preferences and customize their service accordingly (Figure 12.8). One-to-one marketing is more specialized form of customization in which each individual is treated as a segment of its own.[33] Many large hotel chains capture the preferences of their customers through their loyalty program databases, so that when customers arrives at their hotel, they find that their individual needs have already been anticipated, from preferred drinks and snacks in the minibar to the kind of pillow they like and the newspaper they want to receive in the morning. When a customer becomes used to this special service, he or she may find it difficult to adjust to another service provider who is not able to customize the service (at least immediately, as it takes time for the new provider to learn about the customer's needs).

Structural Bonds

Structural bonds are seen mostly in B2B settings and aim to stimulate loyalty through structural relationships between the provider and the customer. Examples include joint investments in projects and sharing of information, processes, and equipment. Structural bonds can be created in a B2C environment, too. For instance, some airlines have introduced short message service (SMS) check-in, and SMS email alerts for flight arrival and departure times so that travelers do not have to waste time waiting at the airport in the case of delays. Some car rental companies offer travelers the

Figure 12.8
Starbucks' Employees Are Encouraged to Learn Their Customers' Preferences

opportunity to create customized pages on the firm's web site, where they can retrieve details of past trips including the types of cars, insurance coverage, and so forth. This simplifies and speeds the task of making new bookings. Once customers have integrated their way of doing things with the firm's processes, structural bonds are created that link the customers to the firm and make it more difficult for competition to draw them away.

Have you noticed that while all these bonds tie a customer closer to the firm, combined they also deliver the confidence, social, and special treatment benefits customers desire (refer back to Research Insights 12.1)? In general, bonds will not work well unless they also generate value for the customer.

Creation of Customer Bonds Through Membership Relationships and Loyalty Programs

Discrete transactions, in which each use involves a payment to the service supplier by an essentially "anonymous" consumer, are typical of services such as transport, restaurants, movie theaters, and shoe repairs. The problem for marketers of such services is that they tend to be less informed about who their customers are and what use each customer makes of the service, than their counterparts in membership-type organizations. Managers in businesses that sell discrete transactions have to work a little harder to establish relationships. In small businesses such as hair salons, frequent customers are (or should be) welcomed as "regulars" whose needs and preferences are remembered. Keeping formal records of customers' needs, preferences, and purchasing behavior is useful even for small firms, because it helps employees avoid having to ask the same questions on each service occasion, allows them to personalize the service given to each customer, and also enables the firm to anticipate future needs.

Transforming Discrete Transactions into Membership Relationships

In large companies with substantial customer bases, transactions can still be transformed into relationships by implementing loyalty reward programs, which require customers to apply for membership cards with which transactions can be captured and customers' preferences communicated to the front line. For transaction-type businesses, loyalty reward programs become a necessary enabler for implementing the strategies discussed in relation to the wheel of loyalty.

Besides airlines and hotels, more and more service firms ranging from retailers (such as department stores, supermarkets, book shops, and gas stations) to telecommunications providers, café chains, courier services and cinema chains have or are also launching similar reward programs in response to the increasing competitiveness of their markets. Although some provide their own rewards—such as free merchandise, vehicle upgrades, or free hotel rooms at vacation resorts—many firms denominate their awards in miles that can be credited to a selected frequent flyer program. In short, air miles have become a form of promotional currency in the service sector. Best Practice in Action 12.2 describes how British Airways has designed its Executive Club.

Customers may even get frustrated with a reward programs, so that rather than creating loyalty and goodwill, they actually breed dissatisfaction. Examples include when customers feel they are excluded from a reward program because of low balances or volume of business, if they cannot redeem their loyalty points because of blackout dates during high-demand periods, if the rewards are seen as having little or no value, and if redemption processes are cumbersome and time-consuming.[34]

Of course, even well-designed rewards programs by themselves will not suffice to retain a firm's most desirable customers. If you and other customers are dissatisfied with the quality of service, or believe that you can obtain better value from a less expensive service, you may quickly become disloyal. No service business that has instituted an awards program for frequent users can ever afford to lose sight of its broader goals of offering high service quality and good value relative to the price and other costs incurred by customers.[35]

One of the risks associated with a focus on strengthening relationships with high-value customers is that a firm may allow service to its other customers to deteriorate. In the reading, "Why Service Stinks" (pp. 471–477), Diane Brady explores the negative aspects of customer stratification.

How Customers Perceive Loyalty Reward Programs

Recent research in the credit card industry suggests that loyalty programs strengthen the customers' perception of the value proposition, and lead to increased revenues due to fewer defections and higher usage levels.[36] To assess the potential of a loyalty program to alter normal patterns of behavior, Grahame Dowling and Mark Uncles argue that marketers need to examine three psychological effects:[37]

- *Brand loyalty versus deal loyalty.* To what extent are customers loyal to the core service (or brand) rather than to the loyalty program itself? Marketers should focus on loyalty programs that directly support the value proposition and positioning of the product in question.
- *How buyers value rewards.* Several elements determine a loyalty program's value to customers: (1) the cash value of the redemption rewards (if customers had to purchase them); (2) the range of choice among rewards—for instance, a selection of gifts rather than just a single gift; (3) the aspirational value of the rewards—something exotic that the consumer would not normally purchase may have greater appeal than a cash-back offer; (4) whether the amount of usage required to obtain an award places it within the realm of possibility for any given consumer; (5) the ease of using the program and making claims for redemption; and (6) the psychological benefits of belonging to the program and accumulating points.
- *Timing.* How soon can benefits from participating in the rewards program be obtained by customers? Deferred gratification tends to weaken the appeal of a loyalty program. One solution is to send customers periodic statements of their account status, indicating progress toward reaching a particular milestone and promoting the rewards that might be forthcoming when that point is reached.

Unlike some frequent flyer programs, in which customer usage is measured simply in miles, British Airways' (BA's) Executive Club members receive both *air miles* toward redemption of air travel awards and *points* toward silver- or gold-tier status for travel on BA. With the creation of the OneWorld airline alliance with American Airlines, Qantas, Cathay Pacific, and other carriers, Executive Club members have been able to earn miles (and sometimes points) by flying these partner airlines, too.

As shown in Table 12.A, silver and gold cardholders are entitled to special benefits, such as priority reservations and a superior level of on-the-ground service. For instance, even if a gold cardholder is traveling in economy class, he or she will be entitled to first-class standards of treatment at check-in and in the airport lounges. However, whereas miles can be accumulated for up to three years (after which they expire), tier status is valid for only 12 months beyond the membership year in which it was earned. In short, the right to special privileges must be re-earned each year. The objective of awarding tier status (which is not unique to BA) is to encourage passengers who have a choice of airlines to concentrate their travel on British Airways, rather than to join several frequent flyer programs and collect mileage awards from all of them. Few passengers travel with such frequency that they will be able to obtain the benefits of gold-tier status (or its equivalent) on more than one airline. However, one of the rewards of that status may be the ability to use lounges and other amenities of airlines that belong to the same international alliance (such as OneWorld).

The assignment of points also varies according to the class of service. BA seeks to recognize higher ticket expenditures with proportionately higher awards. Longer trips earn more points than shorter ones (a domestic or short-haul European trip in economy class generates 15 points, a transatlantic trip 60 points, and a trip from the UK to Australia, 100 points.) However, tickets at deeply discounted prices may earn fewer miles and no points at all. To reward purchase of higher-priced tickets, passengers earn points at double the economy rate if they travel in club (business class), and at triple the rate in first class.

To encourage gold and silver cardholders to remain loyal, BA offers incentives for Executive Club members to retain their current tier status (or to move up from silver to gold). Silver cardholders receive a 25 percent bonus on all air miles, regardless of class of service, and gold cardholders receive a 50 percent bonus. In other words, it doesn't pay to spread the miles among several frequent flyer programs.

Although the airline makes no promises about complimentary upgrades, members of BA's Executive Club are more likely to receive such invitations than other passengers, with tier status being an important consideration. Unlike many airlines, BA tends to limit upgrades to situations in which a lower class of cabin is overbooked, rather than letting frequent travelers believe that they can plan on buying a less expensive ticket and then automatically receive an upgraded seat.

Table 12.A Benefits Offered by British Airways to Its Most Valued Passengers

BENEFIT	SILVER-TIER MEMBERS	GOLD-TIER MEMBERS
Reservations	Dedicated silver phone line	Dedicated gold phone line
Reservation assurance	If flight is full, guaranteed seat in economy class when booking full-fare ticket at least 24 hours in advance	If flight is full, guaranteed seat in economy class when booking full-fare ticket at least 24 hours in advance
Priority waitlist and standby	Higher priority	Highest priority
Advance notification of delays over 4 hours from U.S. or Canada	Yes	Yes
Check-in desk	Club (when traveling economy class)	First (when traveling club or economy class)
Lounge access	Club departure lounges for passenger and one guest regardless of class of travel	First-class departure lounge for passenger and one guest, regardless of travel class; use of arrivals lounges if traveling economy class; lounge access anytime, allowing use of lounges even when not flying BA intercontinental flights
Preferred boarding	Board aircraft at leisure	Board aircraft at leisure
Special services assistance		Problem solving beyond that accorded to other BA travelers
Bonus air miles	+25%	+50%
Upgrade for two		Free upgrade to next cabin for member and companion after earning 2,500 tier points in one year; another upgrade for two after 3,500 points in same year. Award someone else with a Silver Partner card on reaching 4,500 points within membership year

Source: British Airways Executive Club, www.britishairways.com/travel/ecbenftgold/public/en_us, accessed January 2006.

STRATEGIES FOR REDUCING CUSTOMER DEFECTIONS

So far, we have discussed drivers of loyalty and strategies to tie customers more closely to the firm. A complementary approach is to understand the drivers of customer defections, also called customer churn, and work on eliminating or reducing those drivers.

Analyze Customer Defections and Monitor Declining Accounts

The first step is to understand the reasons for customer switching. Susan Keaveney conducted a large-scale study across a range of services and found several key reasons why customers switch to another provider[38] (Figure 12.9). Core service failures were mentioned by 44 percent of respondents as a reason for switching; dissatisfactory service encounters by 34 percent; high, deceptive, or unfair pricing by 30 percent; inconvenience in terms of time, location, or delays by 21 percent; and poor response to service failure by 17 percent. Many respondents described a decision to switch as resulting from interrelated incidents, such as a service failure followed by an unsatisfactory service recovery.

In the mobile phone industry, players regularly conduct what is called *churn diagnostics*. This includes the analysis of data on churned and declining customers, exit interviews (call center staff often have a short set of questions they ask when a customer cancels an account, to gain a better understanding of why customers defect), and in-depth interviews of former customers by a third-party research agency, which typically yield a more detailed understanding of churn drivers.[39]

Many mobile phone service operations use *churn alert systems*, which monitor the activity in individual customer accounts with the objective of predicting impending customer switching. Accounts at risk are flagged and trigger proactive retention efforts such as sending a voucher and/or having a customer service representative call the customer to check on the health of the customer relationship and initiate corrective action if needed.

Figure 12.9
What Drives Customers to Switch Away from a Service Firm?

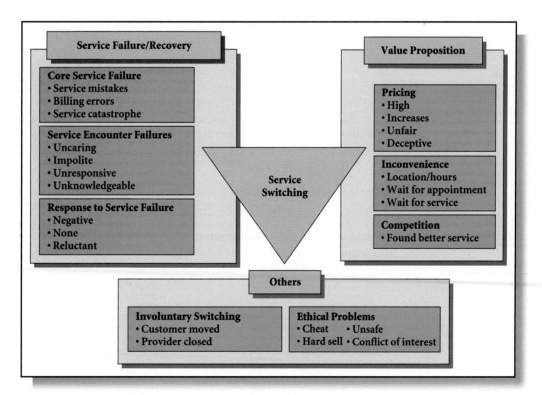

Source: Adapted from Susan M. Keaveney, "Customer Switching Behavior in Service Industries: An Exploratory Study," *Journal of Marketing* 59 (April 1995), 71–82.

America Online (AOL) agreed to pay $1.25 million in penalties and costs, and to change some of its customer service practices, to settle an investigation by the State of New York. In complaints filed with the office of the state attorney general, some 300 subscribers accused AOL of ignoring their demands to cancel the service and stop billing them.

What went wrong? AOL had been rewarding its call center employees for "saving" customers who called to cancel their service. Employees could earn high bonuses if they were able to dissuade half or more of such customers to stay with the firm. As claimed by the attorney general's office, this may have led AOL's employees to make it difficult to cancel service. As a response, AOL agreed in a settlement to record service cancellation requests and have them verified by a third-party monitor, and it agreed to provide up to four months' worth of refunds to all New York subscribers who claimed that their cancellation requests had been ignored (AOL did not admit to any wrongdoing in the settlement). Attorney General Eliot Spitzer said in a statement: "This agreement helps to ensure that AOL will strive to keep its customers through quality service, not stealth retention programs."

Source: Adapted from The Associated Press, "AOL to Pay $1.25M to Settle Spitzer Probe." *USA Today,* August 25, 2005, p. 5B.

Address Key Churn Drivers

Keaveney's findings underscore the importance of addressing some generic churn drivers by delivering quality service (see Chapter 14), minimizing inconvenience and other nonmonetary costs, and fair and transparent pricing (Chapter 5). In addition to these generic drivers, there are often industry-specific drivers as well. For example, handset replacement is a common reason for cellular phone service subscribers to discontinue an existing relationship, as new subscription plans typically come with heavily subsidized new handsets. To prevent handset-related churn, many providers now offer proactive handset replacement programs, in which their current subscribers are offered heavily discounted new handsets at regular intervals. Some providers even provide handsets free to high-value customers or against redemption of loyalty points.

In addition to such proactive retention measures, many firms use reactive measures as well. These include specially trained call center staff, so-called *save teams,* who deal with customers who intend to cancel their accounts. The main job of save team employees is to listen to customer needs and issues, and try to address them with the key focus of retaining the customer. However, you need to be careful about how you reward save teams—see Service Perspective 12.2.

Implement Effective Complaint-Handling and Service Recovery Procedures

Effective complaint handling and excellent service recovery are crucial to keeping unhappy customers from switching providers. That includes making it easy for customers to voice their problems with the firm, and then responding with strong service recovery. We will discuss in depth on how to do that effectively in Chapter 13.

Increase Switching Costs

Another way to reduce churn is to increase switching barriers. Many services have natural switching costs (e.g., it is a lot of work for customers to change their primary banking account, especially when many direct debits, credits, and other related banking services are tied to that account, plus many customers are reluctant to learn about the products and processes of a new provider).[40]

Switching costs can also be created by instituting contractual penalties for switching, such as the transfer fees levied by some brokerage firms for moving shares and bonds to another financial institution. However, firms need to be cautious that they are not perceived as holding their customers hostage. A firm with high switching barriers and poor service quality is likely to generate negative attitudes and bad word of mouth. "At some point, the last straw is reached and a previously inert customer will have had enough" and switch the service provider.[41]

CRM: Customer Relationship Management

Service marketers have understood for some time the power of customer relationship management, and certain industries have applied it for decades. Examples include the corner grocery store, the neighborhood car repair shop, and providers of banking services to high-net-worth clients. Mention the term *CRM*, however, and costly, complex IT systems and infrastructure, and CRM vendors such as SAP, Siebel Systems (Figure 12.10), and Oracle come immediately to mind. But CRM actually signifies the whole process by which relations with customers are built and maintained. It should be seen as an enabler of the successful implementation of the wheel of loyalty. Let us first look at CRM systems before we move to a more strategic perspective.

Common Objectives of CRM Systems

Many firms have large numbers of customers (sometimes millions), many different touch points (for instance, tellers, call center staff, self-service machines, and web sites), at multiple geographic locations. At a single large facility, it's unlikely that a customer will be served by the same front-line staff on two consecutive visits. In such situations, managers historically lacked the tools to practice relationship marketing. Today, however, CRM systems act as an enabler, capturing customer information and delivering it to the various touch points.

From a customer perspective, well-implemented CRM systems can offer a unified customer interface that delivers customization and personalization. This means that at each transaction, the relevant account details, knowledge of customer preferences and past transactions, or history of a service problem are at the fingertips of the person serving the customer. This can result in a vast service improvement and increased customer value.

From a company perspective, CRM systems allow the company to better understand, segment, and tier its customer base, better target promotions and cross-selling, and even implement churn alert systems that signal if a customer is in danger of defecting.[42] Service Perspective 12.3 highlights some common CRM applications.

What Does a Comprehensive CRM Strategy Encompass?

Rather than viewing CRM as a technology, we subscribe to a more strategic view of CRM that focuses on the profitable development and management of customer relationships. Figure 12.11 provides an integrated framework of five key processes involved in a CRM strategy:[43]

1. *Strategy development* involves the assessment of business strategy (including articulation of the company's vision, industry trends, and competition). The business strategy is typically the responsibility of top management. Once determined, the business strategy should be guiding the development of the customer strategy, including the choice of target segments, customer base tiering, the design of loyalty bonds, and churn management (as discussed in the wheel of loyalty, Figure 12.4).

- **Data collection.** The system captures customer data such as contact details, demographics, purchasing history, service preferences, and the like.

- **Data analysis.** The data captured are analyzed and categorized by the system according to criteria set by the firm. This information is then used to tier the customer base and tailor service delivery accordingly.

- **Sales force automation.** Sales leads, and cross-selling and up-selling opportunities, can be effectively identified and processed, and the entire sales cycle from lead generation to close of sales and after-sale service can be tracked and facilitated through the CRM system.

- **Marketing automation.** Mining of customer data enables the firm to target its market. A good CRM

system enables the firm to achieve one-to-one marketing and cost savings, often in the context of loyalty and retention programs. This results in increasing the return on its marketing expenditure. CRM systems also enable assessment of the effectiveness of marketing campaigns through the analysis of responses.

- **Call center automation.** Call center staff have customer information at their fingertips and can improve their service levels to all customers. Furthermore, caller ID and account numbers allow call centers to identify the customer tier to which the caller belongs, and to tailor the service accordingly. For example, platinum callers get priority in waiting queues.

Figure 12.10 An Integrated Framework for CRM Strategy

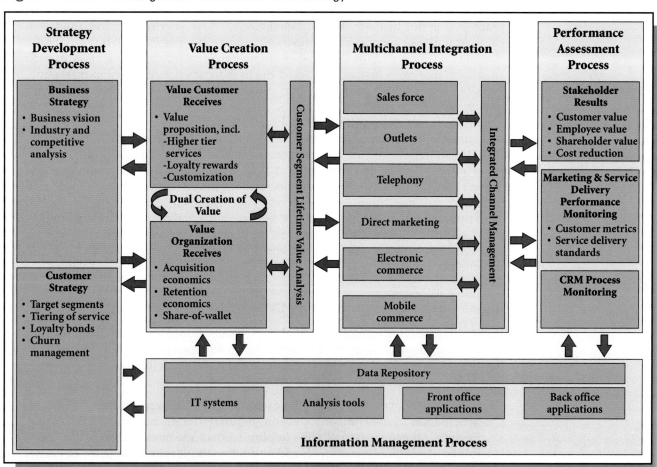

Source: Adapted from Adrian Payne and Pennie Frow, "A Strategic Framework for Customer Relationship Management," *Journal of Marketing* 69 (October 2005): 167–176.

2. *Value creation* translates the business and customer strategies into specific value propositions for customers and the firm. The value created for customers includes all the benefits that are delivered through priority tiered services, loyalty rewards, and customization and personalization. The value created for the firm needs to include reduced customer acquisition and retention costs, and increased share-of-wallet. Core of CRM is the concept of dual creation of value—customers need to participate in CRM (e.g., through volunteering information) so that they can reap value from the firm's CRM initiatives. For instance, only if my driver's license, billing address, credit card details, and car and insurance preferences are stored in a car rental's CRM system can I benefit from the increased convenience of not having to provide those data for each reservation. Firms can even create value through information drawn from one customer for others (e.g., Amazon's analysis of which other books customers with a profile similar to yours have bought, and customer ratings of books). CRM seems most successful when there is a win–win situation for the firm and its customers.[44]

3. *Multichannel integration:* Most service firms interact with their customers through a multitude of channels, and it has become a challenge to serve customers well across these many potential interfaces and offer a unified customer interface that delivers customization and personalization. CRM's channel integration addresses this challenge.

4. *Information management:* Service delivery across many channels relies on the firm's ability to collect customer information from all channels, integrate it with other relevant information, and make the relevant information available to the front line (or to the customer in a self-service context) at the various touch points. The information management process encompasses the data repository (which contains all the customer data), IT systems (which encompasses the IT hardware and software), analytical tools (which include data mining packages, and more specific application packages such as campaign management analysis, credit assessment, customer profiling, and churn alert systems), front-office applications (which support activities that involve direct customer contact, including sales force automation and call center management applications), and back-office applications (which support internal customer-related processes, including logistics, procurement, and financial processing).

5. *Performance assessment* must address three critical questions. First, is the CRM strategy creating value for its key stakeholders (i.e., customers, employees, and shareholders)? Second, are the marketing objectives (ranging from customer acquisition, share-of-wallet, retention to customer satisfaction) and service delivery performance objectives (e.g., call center service standards such as call waiting, abortion, and first-time resolution rates) being achieved? Third, is the CRM process itself performing up to expectations (e.g., are the relevant strategies being set, is customer and firm value being created, is the information management process working effectively, and is integration across customer service channels being achieved effectively)? The performance assessment process should drive the continuous improvement of the CRM strategy itself.

Common Failures in CRM Implementation

Unfortunately, the majority of CRM implementations failed in the past. According to the Gartner Group, the implementation failure rate is 55 percent, and Accenture claims it to be around 60 percent. A key reason for this high failure rate is that firms often equate installing CRM systems with having a customer relationship strategy. They forget that the system is just a tool to enhance the firm's customer servicing capabilities, and is not the strategy itself.

Furthermore, CRM cuts across many departments and functions (e.g., from customer contact centers, on-line services, and distribution to branch operations, employee training, and IT departments), programs (ranging from sales and loyalty programs to launching of new services, cross-selling, and upselling initiatives), and processes (e.g., from credit-line authorization all the way to complaint handling and service recovery). The wide-ranging scope of CRM implementation, and the unfortunate reality that it is often the weakest link that determines the success of an implementation, shows the challenge of getting it right. Common reasons for CRM failures include:[45]

- *Viewing CRM as a technology initiative.* It's easy to let the focus shift toward technology and its features, with the result that the IT department rather than top management or marketing takes the lead in devising CRM strategy. This often results in a lack of strategic direction and of understanding of customers and markets during implementation.
- *Lack of customer focus.* Many firms implement CRM without the ultimate goal to enable consistent service delivery for valued customers across all customer service processes and delivery channels.
- *Insufficient appreciation of customer lifetime value (LTV).* The marketing program of many firms is not sufficiently structured around the vastly different profitabilities of different customers. Furthermore, servicing costs for different customer segments are often not well captured (e.g., by using activity-based costing, as discussed in Chapter 5).
- *Inadequate support from top management.* Without ownership and active involvement of top management, the CRM strategic intent will not survive the implementation intact.
- *Failing to reengineer business processes.* It is virtually impossible to implement CRM successfully without redesigning customer service and back-office processes. Many implementations fail because CRM is being fitted into exiting processes, rather than redesigning the processes to fit a customer-centric CRM implementation. Redesigning also requires effective change management and employee engagement and support, which are often lacking.
- *Underestimating the challenges in data integration.* Firms frequently fail to integrate customer data, which are often scattered all over the organization. A key to unlocking the full potential of CRM is to make customer knowledge available in real time to all employees who need it.

In the long run, firms put their CRM strategies at substantial risk if customers believe that CRM is being used in a way that is detrimental to them. Examples include perceptions of not being treated fairly (including not being offered attractive pricing or promotions that are offered, for example, to new accounts, but not to existing customers), and potential privacy concerns (see Service Perspective 12.4). Being aware and actively avoiding these pitfalls is a first step toward successful CRM implementation.

How to Get CRM Implementation Right

In spite of the many horror stories of millions of dollars sunk into unsuccessful CRM projects, more and more firms are getting it right. "No longer a black hole, CMR is becoming a basic building block of corporate success," argue Darrell Rigby and Dianne Ledingham.[46] Even existing CRM systems that have have not yet shown results can be well positioned for future success. Seasoned McKinsey consultants recommend taking a step back and studying how to build customer loyalty, rather than focusing on the technology itself.[47] Rather than using CRM to transform entire businesses through the wholesale implementation of the CRM model advanced in Figure 12.11, successful implementations zero in on clearly defined problems within the firm's customer relationship cycle. These narrow CRM strategies often reveal additional opportunities for further improvements, which taken together, can evolve into broad CRM implementation extending across the entire company.

Operator: Thank you for calling Pizza Delight. Linda speaking, how may I help you?

Customer: Good evening, can I order. . . .

Operator: Sir, before taking your order, could I please have the number of your multipurpose smart card?

Customer: Hold on . . . it's . . . um . . . 4555-1000-9831-3213.

Operator: Thank you. Can I please confirm you're Mr. Thompson, calling from 10940 Wilford Boulevard? You are calling from your home number, 432-3876, your cellphone number is 992-4566, and your office number is 432-9377?

Customer: How in the world did you get my address and all my numbers?

Operator: Sir, we are connected to the Integrated Customer Intimacy System.

Customer: I would like to order a large seafood pizza. . . .

Operator: Sir, that's not a good idea.

Customer: Why not?

Operator: According to your medical records, you have very high blood pressure and a far too high cholesterol level, Sir.

Customer: What? . . . Then what do you recommend?

Operator: Try our Low Fat Soybean Yoghurt Pizza. You'll like it.

Customer: How do you know?

Operator: You borrowed the book, *Popular Soybean Dishes*, from the City Library last week, Sir.

Customer: OK, I give up. . . . Give me three large ones then. How much will that be?

Operator: That should be enough for your family of 8, Sir. The total is $47.97.

Customer: Can I pay by credit card?

Operator: I'm afraid you'll have to pay us cash, Sir. Your credit card is over your limit and your checking account has an overdue balance of $2,435.54. That's excluding the late-payment charges on your home equity loan, Sir.

Customer: I guess I'll have to run to the ATM and withdraw some cash before your guy arrives.

Operator: You can't do that, Sir. Based on the records, you've reached your daily machine withdrawals limit for today.

Customer: Never mind. Just send the pizzas. I'll have the cash ready. How long is it gonna take?

Operator: About 45 minutes, Sir, but if you don't want to wait you can always come and collect it on your Harley, registration number L.A.6468. . . .

Customer: #@$#@%^%%@.

Operator: Sir, please watch your language. Remember, on April 28th of last year you were convicted of using abusive language to a traffic warden. . . .

Customer: (Speechless)

Operator: Will there be anything else, Sir?

Source: This story was adapted from various sources, including www.lawdebt.com/gazette/nov2004/nov2004.pdf, accessed January 2006; and a video created by the American Civil Liberties Union (ACLU), available at www.aclu.org/pizza. This video aims to communicate the privacy threats that CRM poses to consumers. ACLU is a nonprofit organization that campaigns against government's and corporations' aggressive collection of information on people's personal lives and habits.

Rigby, Reichheld, and Schefter pose the question:

If your best customers knew that you planned to invest $130 million to increase their loyalty. . . , how would they tell you to spend it? Would they want you to create a loyalty card or would they ask you to open more cash registers and keep enough milk in stock? The answer depends on the kind of company you are and the kinds of relationships you and your customers want to have with one another.[48]

Among the key issues managers that should debate when defining their customer relationship strategy for a potential CRM system implementation are

1. How should our value proposition change to increase customer loyalty?
2. How much customization or one-to-one marketing and service delivery is appropriate and profitable?
3. What is the incremental profit potential of increasing the share-of-wallet with our current customers? How much does this vary by customer tier and/or segment?

4. How much time and resources can we allocate to CRM right now?
5. If we believe in customer relationship management, why haven't we taken more steps in that direction in the past? What can we do today to develop customer relationships without spending a lot on technology?

Answering these questions may lead to the conclusion that a CRM system may currently not be the best investment or highest priority, or that a scaled-down version may suffice to deliver the intended customer strategy. In any case, we emphasize that the system is merely a tool to drive the strategy, and must thus be tailored to deliver that strategy.

CONCLUSION

Many elements are involved in gaining market share, increasing share-of-wallet, cross-selling other products and services to existing customers, and creating long-term loyalty. We used the wheel of loyalty as an organizing framework, which starts with identifying and targeting the right customers, then learning about their needs, including their preferences for various forms of service delivery. Translating this knowledge into service delivery, tiered service levels, and customer relationship strategies are the key steps toward achieving customer loyalty.

Marketers need to pay special attention to those customers who offer the firm the greatest value, as they purchase its products with the greatest frequency and spend the most on premium services. Programs to reward frequent users—of which the most highly developed are the frequent flyer clubs created by the airlines—identify and provide rewards for high-value customers and facilitate tiered service delivery. These programs also enable marketers to track the behavior of high-value customers in terms of where and when they use the service, what service classes or types of product they buy, and how much they spend.

Customer relationship management is a key enabler for the strategies discussed in the wheel of loyalty and is often integrated with loyalty programs. From a customer perspective, CRM can result in a vast service improvement and increased customer value (e.g., through mass customization and increased convenience).

REVIEW QUESTIONS

1. Why is targeting the "right" customers so important for successful customer relationship management?
2. How can you estimate a customer's lifetime value (LTV)?
3. Explain what is meant by a customer portfolio. How should a firm decide what is the most appropriate mix of customers to have?
4. What criteria should a marketing manager use to decide which of several possible segments should be targeted by the firm?
5. What is tiering of services? Explain the rationale and strategic implications.
6. Identify some key measures that can be used to create customer bonds and encourage long-term relationships with customers.
7. What are the arguments for spending money to keep existing customers loyal?
8. How do the various strategies described in the wheel of loyalty relate to one another?
9. What is the role of CRM in delivering a customer relationship strategy?
10. Review the reading, "Why Service Stinks" (pp. 471–477). Do you agree with the author's view that loyalty programs result in poor service for less valuable customers? If so, what do you recommend should be done about this?

APPLICATION EXERCISES

1. Identify three service businesses that you patronize on a regular basis. Then, for each business, complete the following sentence: "I am loyal to this business because. . . ."
2. What conclusions do you draw about (a) yourself as a consumer and (b) the performance of each of the businesses in Exercise 1? Assess whether any of these businesses managed to develop a sustainable competitive advantage through the way it won your loyalty.
3. Identify two service businesses that you used several times but have now ceased to patronize (or plan to stop patronizing soon) because you were dissatisfied. Complete the sentence: "I stopped using (or will soon stop using) this organization as a customer because. . . ."

4. Again, what conclusions do you draw about yourself and the firms in Exercise 3? How could each of these firms potentially avoid your defection? What could each of these firms do to avoid defections in the future of customers with a profile similar to yours?

5. Evaluate the strengths and weaknesses of frequent user programs in different service industries.

6. Design a questionnaire and conduct a survey asking about two loyalty programs. The first should be a membership/loyalty program your classmates or their families like and keeps them loyal to that firm. The second should be about a loyalty program that is not well perceived, and does not seem to add value to the customer. Use open-ended questions, such as "What motivated you to sign up in the first place?"; "Why are you using this program?"; "Has participating in the program changed your purchasing/usage behavior in any way?"; "Has it made you less likely to use competing suppliers?"; "What do you think of the rewards available?"; "Did membership in the program lead to any immediate benefits in the use of the service?"; "What role does the loyalty program play in making you loyal?"; "What are the three things you like best about this loyalty/membership program?"; ". . .liked least"; and "Suggested improvements?" Analyze what features make loyalty/membership programs successful, and what features do not achieve the desired results. Use a framework such as the wheel of loyalty to guide your analysis and presentation.

7. Approach service employees in two or three firms that have implemented CRM systems. Ask the employees about their experience interfacing with these systems, and whether the CRM systems help them understand their customers better and whether this leads to improved service experiences for their customers. Do interview them about potential concerns and improvement suggestions they may have about their organization's CRM system.

ENDNOTES

1. Frederick F. Reichheld and Thomas Teal, *The Loyalty Effect*. Boston: Harvard Business School Press, 1996.

2. Ruth Bolton, Katherine N. Lemon, and Peter C. Verhoef, "The Theoretical Underpinnings of Customer Asset Management: A Framework and Propositions for Future Research." *Journal of the Academy of Marketing Science*, 32, no. 3 (2004): 271–292.

3. Frederick F. Reichheld and W. Earl Sasser, Jr., "Zero Defections: Quality Comes to Services." *Harvard Business Review*, 68 (October 1990): 105–111.

4. Ibid.

5. Frederick F. Reichheld and Phil Schefter, "E-Loyalty—Your Secret Weapon on the Web." *Harvard Business Review*, 80 (July–August 2002): 105–113.

6. Christian Homburg, Nicole Koschate, and Wayne D. Hoyer, "Do Satisfied Customers Really Pay More? A Study of the Relationship Between Customer Satisfaction and Willingness to Pay." *Journal of Marketing*, 69 (April 2005): 84–96.

7. Grahame R. Dowling and Mark Uncles, "Do Customer Loyalty Programs Really Work?" *Sloan Management Review*, 38 (Summer 1997): 71–81; Werner Reinartz and V. Kumar, "The Mismanagement of Customer Loyalty." *Harvard Business Review*, 80 (July 2002): 86–94.

8. Werner J. Reinartz and V. Kumar, "On the Profitability of Long-Life Customers in a Noncontractual Setting: An Empirical Investigation and Implications for Marketing." *Journal of Marketing*, 64 (October 2000): 17–35.

9. Jochen Wirtz, Indranil Sen, and Sanjay Singh, "Customer Asset Management at DHL in Asia." In Jochen Wirtz and Christopher Lovelock, eds., *Services Marketing in Asia—A Case Book*. Singapore: Prentice Hall, 2005, pp. 379–396.

10. John E. Hogan, Katherine N. Lemon, and Barak Libai, "What is the True Cost of a Lost Customer?" *Journal of Services Research*, 5, no. 3 (2003): 196–208.

11. For a discussion on how to evaluate the customer base of a firm, see Sunil Gupta, Donald R. Lehmann, and Jennifer Ames Stuart, "Valuing Customers." *Journal of Marketing Research*, 41, no. 1 (2004): 7–18.

12. Alan W. H. Grant and Leonard H. Schlesinger, "Realize Your Customer's Full Profit Potential." *Harvard Business Review*, 73 (September–October 1995): 59–75.

13. Nicole E. Coviello, Roderick J. Brodie, and Hugh J. Munro, "Understanding Contemporary Marketing: Development of a Classification Scheme." *Journal of Marketing Management*, 13, no. 6 (1995): 501–522.

14. J. R. Copulsky and M. J. Wolf, "Relationship Marketing: Positioning for the Future." *Journal of Business Strategy*, 11, no. 4 (1990): 16–20.

15. Johnson and Selnes proposed a typology of exchange relationships that included "strangers," "acquaintances," "friends," and "partners" and derived implications for customer portfolio management. For details, see Michael D. Johnson and Fred Selnes, "Customer Portfolio Management: Towards a Dynamic Theory of Exchange Relationships." *Journal of Marketing*, 68, no. 2 (2004): 1–17.

16. Evert Gummesson, *Total Relationship Marketing*. Oxford, UK: Butterworth-Heinemann, 1999, p. 24.

17. It has even been suggested to let "chronically dissatisfied customers go to allow front-line staff focus on satisfying the 'right' customers"; see Ka-shing Woo and Henry K. Y. Fock, "Retaining and Divesting Customers: An Exploratory Study of Right Customers, 'At-Risk' Right Customers, and Wrong Customers." *Journal of Services Marketing*, 18, no. 3 (2004): 187–197.

18. Frederick F. Reichheld, *Loyalty Rules—How Today's Leaders Build Lasting Relationships*. Boston: Harvard Business School Press, 2001, p. 45.

19. Roger Hallowell, "The Relationships of Customer Satisfaction, Customer Loyalty, and Profitability: An Empirical Study." *International Journal of Service Industry Management,* 7, no. 4 (1996): 27–42.

20. Reichheld, *Loyalty Rules—How Today's Leaders Build Lasting Relationships,* pp. 43, 84–85.

21. David Rosenblum, Doug Tomlinson, and Larry Scott, "Bottom-Feeding for Blockbuster Business." *Harvard Business Review,* 81 (March 2003): 52–59.

22. Ravi Dhar and Rashi Glazer, "Hedging Customers." *Harvard Business Review,* 81 (May 2003): 86–92.

23. David H. Maister, *True Professionalism.* New York: The Free Press, 1997 (see especially chap. 20).

24. Valarie A. Zeithaml, Roland T. Rust, and Katharine N. Lemon, "The Customer Pyramid: Creating and Serving Profitable Customers." *California Management Review,* 43, no. 4 (Summer 2001):118–142.

25. Werner J. Reinartz and V. Kumar, "The Impact of Customer Relationship Characteristics on Profitable Lifetime Duration." *Journal of Marketing,* 67, no. 1 (2003): 77–99.

26. Elizabeth Esfahani, "How to Get Tough with Bad Customers." *ING Direct,* October 2004, and http://home.ingdirect.com, accessed January 19, 2006.

27. Not only is there a positive relationship between satisfaction and share of wallet, the greatest positive impact is seen at the upper extreme levels of satisfaction. For details, see Timothy L. Keiningham, Tiffany Perkins-Munn, and Heather Evans, "The Impact of Customer Satisfaction on Share of Wallet in a Business-to-Business Environment." *Journal of Service Research,* 6, no. 1 (2003): 37–50.

28. Florian v. Wangenheim, "Postswitching Negative Word of Mouth." *Journal of Service Research,* 8, no. 1 (2005): 67–78.

29. Das Narayandas, "Building Loyalty in Business Markets." *Harvard Business Review,* 83 (September 2005): 131–139; Piyush Kumar, "The Impact of Long-Term Client Relationships on the Performance of Business Service Firms." *Journal of Service Research,* 2 (August 1999): 4–18.

30. Leonard L. Berry and A. Parasuraman, *Marketing Services—Competing Through Quality.* New York: The Free Press, 1991, pp. 136–142; Valarie A. Zeithaml, Mary Jo Bitner, and Dwayne D. Gremler, *Services Marketing,* 4th ed. New York: McGraw-Hill, 2006, pp. 196–201.

31. Michael Lewis, "The Influence of Loyalty Programs and Short-Term Promotions on Customer Retention." *Journal of Marketing Research,* 41 (August 2004): 281–292.

32. Mark S. Rosenbaum, Amy L. Ostrom, and Ronald Kuntze, "Loyalty Programs and a Sense of Community." *Journal of Services Marketing,* 19, no. 4 (2005): 222–233; Isabelle Szmigin, Louise Canning, and Alexander E. Reppel, "Online Community: Enhancing the Relationship Marketing Concept Through Customer Bonding." *International Journal of Service Industry Management,* 16, no. 5 (2005): 480–496; Inger Roos, Anders Gustafsson, and Bo Edvardsson, "The Role of Customer Clubs in Recent Telecom Relationships." *International Journal of Service Industry Management,* 16, no. 5 (2005): 436–454.

33. Don Peppers and Martha Rogers, *The One-to-One Manager.* New York: Currency/Doubleday, 1999.

34. Bernd Stauss, Maxie Schmidt, and Adreas Schoeler, "Customer Frustration in Loyalty Programs." *International Journal of Service Industry Management,* 16, no. 3 (2005): 229–252.

35. See, for example, Iselin Skogland and Judy Siguaw, "Are Your Satisfied Customers Loyal?" *Cornell Hotel and Restaurant Administration Quarterly,* 45, no. 3 (2004): 221–234.

36. Ruth N. Bolton, P. K. Kannan, and Matthew D. Bramlett, "Implications of Loyalty Program Membership and Service Experience for Customer Retention and Value." *Journal of the Academy of Marketing Science,* 28, no. 1 (2000): 95–108; Michael Lewis, "The Influence of Loyalty Programs and Short-Term Promotions on Customer Retention." *Journal of Marketing Research,* 41, no. 3 (2004): 281–292.

37. Dowling and Uncles, "Do Customer Loyalty Programs Really Work?"

38. Susan M. Keaveney, "Customer Switching Behavior in Service Industries: An Exploratory Study." *Journal of Marketing,* 59 (April 1995): 71–82.

39. For a more detailed discussion of situation-specific switching behavior, see Inger Roos, Bo Edvardsson, and Anders Gustafsson, "Customer Switching Patterns in Competitive and Noncompetitive Service Industries." *Journal of Service Research,* 6, no. 3 (2004): 256–271.

40. Shun Yin Lam, Venkatesh Shankar, M. Krishna Erramilli, and Bvsan Murthy, "Customer Value, Satisfaction, Loyalty, and Switching Costs: An Illustration from a Business-to-Business Service Context." *Journal of the Academy of Marketing Science,* 32, no. 3 (2004): 293–311; Moonkyu Lee and Lawrence F. Cunningham, "A Cost/Benefit Approach to Understanding Loyalty." *Journal of Services Marketing,* 15, no. 2 (2001): 113–130; Simon J. Bell, Seigyoung Auh, and Karen Smalley, "Customer Relationship Dynamics: Service Quality and Customer Loyalty in the Context of Varying Levels of Customer Expertise and Switching Costs." *Journal of the Academy of Marketing Science,* 33, no. 2 (2005): 169–183.

41. Lesley White and Venkat Yanamandram, "Why Customers Stay: Reasons and Consequences of Inertia in Financial Services." *International Journal of Service Industry Management,* 14, no. 3 (2004): 183–194.

42. V. Kumar and Werner J. Reinartz, *Customer Relationship Management: A Database Approach.* Hoboken, NJ: John Wiley & Sons, 2006; Kevin N. Quiring and Nancy K. Mullen, "More Than Data Warehousing: An Integrated View of the Customer." In John G. Freeland, ed., *The Ultimate CRM Handbook—Strategies & Concepts for Building Enduring Customer Loyalty & Profitability.* New York: McGraw-Hill, 2002, pp. 102–108.

43. This section is adapted from: Adrian Payne and Pennie Frow, "A Strategic Framework for Customer Relationship Management." *Journal of Marketing,* 69 (October 2005): 167–176.

44. William Boulding, Richard Staelin, Michael Ehret, and Wesley J. Johnston, "A Customer Relationship Management Roadmap: What Is Known, Potential Pitfalls, and Where to Go." *Journal of Marketing,* 69, no. 4 (2005): 155–166.

45. This section is based largely on: Sudhir H. Kale, "CRM Failure and the Seven Deadly Sins." *Marketing Management* (September/October 2004): 42–46.

46. Darrell K. Rigby and Dianne Ledingham, "CRM Done Right." *Harvard Business Review,* 82 (November 2004): 118–129.

47. Manuel Ebner, Arthur Hu, Daniel Levitt, and Jim McCrory, "How to Rescue CRM?" *The McKinsey Quarterly,* 4 (2002).

48. Darrell K. Rigby, Frederick F. Reichheld, and Phil Schefter, "Avoid the Four Perils of CRM." *Harvard Business Review,* 80 (February 2002): 108.

Chapter 13

Achieving Service Recovery and Obtaining Customer Feedback

> *One of the surest signs of a bad or declining relationship is the absence of complaints from the customer. Nobody is ever that satisfied, especially not over an extended period of time.*
>
> —THEODORE LEVITT

> *To err is human; to recover, divine.*
>
> —CHRISTOPHER HART, JAMES HESKETT, AND EARL SASSER
> (PARAPHRASING EIGHTEENTH-CENTURY POET ALEXANDER POPE)

The first law of service productivity and quality might be: Do it right the first time. But we can't ignore the fact that failures continue to occur, sometimes for reasons outside the organization's control. Many "moments of truth" in service encounters are vulnerable to breakdowns. Such distinctive service characteristics as real-time performance, customer involvement, and people as part of the product greatly increase the chance of service failures. How well a firm handles complaints and resolves problems may determine whether it builds customer loyalty or watches former customers take their business elsewhere.

However, developing effective service recovery strategies is not enough. Instituting service guarantees forces management to recognize the cost of service failures. In particular, management must learn from the firm's mistakes—as individual employees must learn from their own—so that action can be taken to eliminate those problems that can be controlled. Customer feedback systems play a key role in ensuring that information from complaints, compliments, market research, and other sources is systematically collected, analyzed, and disseminated in ways that will drive service improvements.

In this chapter, we explore the following questions:

1. Why do customers complain, and what do they expect from the firm?
2. How should an effective service recovery strategy be designed?
3. Under what circumstances should firms offer service guarantees, and is it wise to make them unconditional?
4. How should firms and their front-line staff respond to abusive and/or opportunistic customers?
5. How can organizations institutionalize systematic and continuous learning from customer feedback?

CUSTOMER COMPLAINING BEHAVIOR

The chances are high that you're not always satisfied with at least some of the services you receive. How do you respond to your dissatisfaction with these services? Do you complain informally to an employee, ask to speak to the manager, or file a complaint? Or, perhaps, do you just mutter darkly to yourself, grumble to your friends and family, and choose an alternative supplier the next time you need a similar type of service?

If you're among those who don't complain about poor service, you're not alone. Research around the globe has shown that most people fail to complain, especially if they think it will do no good.

Customer Response Options to Service Failures

Figure 13.1 depicts the courses of action a customer may take in response to a service failure. This model suggests at least three major courses of action:

1. Take some form of public action (including complaining to the firm or to a third party, such as a consumer advocacy group, a consumer affairs or regulatory agency, or even a civil or criminal court).

Figure 13.1
Customer Response Categories to Service Failures

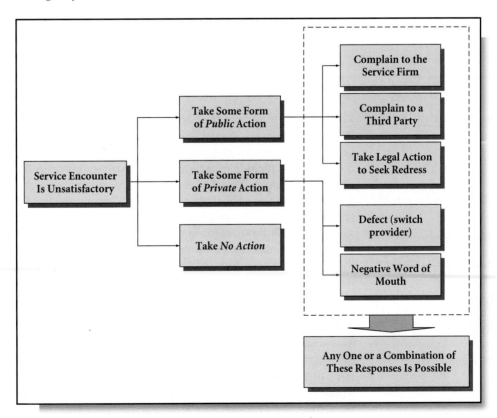

2. Take some form of private action (including abandoning the supplier).
3. Take no action.

It's important to remember that a customer can pursue any one or a combination of alternatives. Managers need to be aware that the impact of a defection can go far beyond the loss of a future revenue stream from that person. Angry customers often tell many other people about their problems.[1] The Internet allows unhappy customers to reach thousands of people by posting complaints on Internet-based bulletin boards or even setting up their own web sites to publicize their bad experiences with specific organizations.[2] A popular strategy in the past when creating such sites was to add a derogatory suffix (such as "sucks") to the name of the offending company.

Understanding Customer Responses to Service Failures

To be able to deal effectively with dissatisfied and complaining customers, managers need to understand key aspects of complaining behavior, starting with the questions posed below.

Why Do Customers Complain?

In general, studies of consumer complaining behavior have identified four main purposes for complaining.

1. *Obtain restitution or compensation.* Often, consumers complain to recover some economic loss by seeking a refund, compensation, and/or have the service performed again.[3]
2. *Vent their anger.* Some customers complain to rebuild self-esteem and/or to vent their anger and frustration. When service processes are bureaucratic and unreasonable, or when employees are rude, deliberately intimidating, or apparently uncaring, customers' self-esteem, self-worth, or sense of fairness can be negatively affected. They may become angry and emotional.
3. *Help to improve the service.* When customers are highly involved with a service (e.g., at a college, an alumni association, or their main banking connection), they give feedback to try and contribute toward service improvements.
4. *For altruistic reasons.* Finally, some customers are motivated by altruism. They want to spare other customers from experiencing the same shortcomings, and they may feel bad if they fail to draw attention to a problem that will cause difficulties for others if it remains uncorrected.

What Proportion of Unhappy Customers Complain?

Research shows that, on average, only 5 to 10 percent of customers who have been unhappy with a service actually complain.[4] Sometimes the percentage is far lower. A review of the records of a public bus company, showed that complaints occurred at the rate of about three for every million passenger trips. Assuming two trips a day, a person would need 1,370 years (roughly 27 lifetimes) to make a million trips. In other words, the rate of complaints was incredibly low, given that public bus companies are usually not known for service excellence. However, although generally only a minority of dissatisfied customers complain, there's evidence that consumers around the world are becoming better informed, more self-confident, and more assertive about seeking satisfactory outcomes for their complaints.

Why Don't Unhappy Customers Complain?

TARP Worldwide, a customer satisfaction and measurement firm, has identified a number of reasons why customers don't complain.[5] Customers may not want to take the time to write a letter, send an email, fill out a form, or make a phone call, particularly if they don't see the service as being important enough to be worth the effort. Many customers see the payoff as uncertain and believe that no one will care about their problem or be willing to resolve it. In some situations, people simply don't

Figure 13.2
Customers Often View
Complaining as
Difficult and
Unpleasant

Courtesy of Images.com.

know where to go or what to do. Also, many people feel that complaining is unpleasant (Figure 13.2). They may be afraid of confrontation, especially if the complaint involves someone whom the customer knows and may have to deal with again.

Complaining behavior can be influenced by role perceptions and social norms. Customers are less likely to voice complaints in service situations in which they perceive they have "low power" (ability to influence or control the transaction).[6] This is particularly true when the problem involves professional service providers, such as doctors, lawyers, or architects. Social norms tend to discourage customer criticism of such individuals, because of their perceived expertise.

Who Is Most Likely to Complain?

Research findings consistently show that people in higher socioeconomic circumstances are more likely to complain than those in lower levels. Their better education, higher income, and greater social involvement give them the confidence, knowledge, and motivation to speak up when they encounter problems.[7] Further, those who complain also tend to be more knowledgeable about the service products in question.

Where Do Customers Complain?

Studies show that the majority of complaints are made at the place where the service was received. One of the authors of this book recently completed a consulting project developing and implementing a customer feedback system and found that an astoundingly 99 percent-plus of customer feedback was given face to face or over the phone to customer service representatives. Less than 1 percent of all complaints were submitted via email, letters, faxes, or customer feedback cards. A survey of airline passengers found that only 3 percent of respondents who were unhappy with their meal actually complained about it, and they all complained to the flight attendant! None complained to the company's headquarters or to a consumer affairs office.[8] Also, customers tend to use noninteractive channels to complain (e.g., email or letters) when they mainly want to vent their anger and frustration, but resort to interactive channels such as face to face or the telephone when they want a problem to be fixed or redressed.[9] In practice, even when customers do complain, managers often don't hear about complaints made to front-line staff. Without a formal customer feedback system, only a small proportion of complaints may reach corporate headquarters.

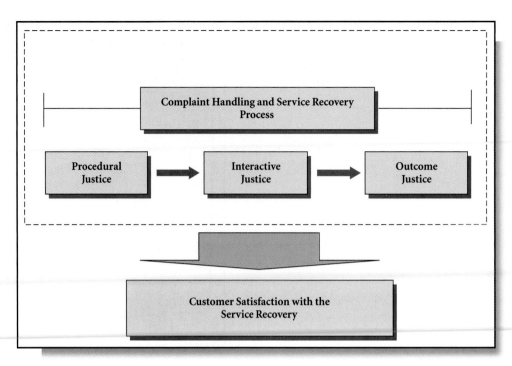

Source: Reprinted from Three Dimensions of Perceived Fairness in Service Recovery
Processes by Stephen S. Tax and Stephen W. Brown "Recovering and Learning from Service
Failure" *Sloan Management Review* 49, no. 1 (Fall 1998), pp. 75–88, by permission of publisher.
Copyright © 2003 by Massachussetts Institute of Technology. All rights reserved.

What Do Customers Expect Once They Have Made a Complaint?

Whenever a service failure occurs, people expect to be adequately compensated in a
fair manner. However, studies show that many customers feel that they have neither
been treated fairly nor received adequate recompense. When this happens, their
reactions tend to be immediate, emotional, and enduring.[10]

Stephen Tax and Stephen Brown found that as much as 85 percent of the variation in the satisfaction with a service recovery was determined by three dimensions
of fairness.[11] These are shown in Figure 13.3.

- *Procedural justice* concerns the policies and rules that any customer has to go
  through to seek fairness. Customers expect the firm to assume responsibility,
  which is the key to the start of a fair procedure, followed by a convenient and
  responsive recovery process. That includes flexibility of the system, and consideration of customer inputs into the recovery process.
- *Interactional justice* involves the employees of the firm who provide the service
  recovery and their behavior toward the customer. Giving an explanation for the
  failure and making an effort to resolve the problem are very important.
  However, the recovery effort must be perceived as genuine, honest, and polite.
- *Outcome justice* concerns the compensation that a customer receives as a result of
  the losses and inconveniences incurred because of a service failure. This includes
  compensation for not only the failure, but also the time, effort, and energy spent
  during the process of service recovery.[12]

CUSTOMER RESPONSES TO EFFECTIVE SERVICE RECOVERY

"Thank Heavens for Complainers" was the provocative title of an article about customer complaining behavior, which also featured a successful manager exclaiming,
"Thank goodness I've got a dissatisfied customer on the phone! The ones I worry
about are the ones I never hear from."[13] Customers who do complain give a firm the

chance to correct problems (including some the firm may not even know it has), restore relationships with the complainer, and improve future satisfaction for all.

Service recovery is an umbrella term for systematic efforts by a firm to correct a problem following a service failure and to retain a customer's goodwill. Service recovery efforts play a crucial role in achieving (or restoring) customer satisfaction.[14] In every organization, things may occur that have a negative impact on relationships with customers. The true test of a firm's commitment to satisfaction and service *quality* isn't in the advertising promises, but in the way it responds when things go wrong for the customer. Success in this area includes employee training and motivation. Simon Bell and James Luddington have found that although complaints tend, in general, to have a negative effect on service personnel's commitment to customer service, employees with a positive attitude toward service and their own jobs may be more likely to view complaints as a potential source of improvement and to explore additional ways in which they can help customers.[15]

Effective service recovery requires thoughtful procedures for resolving problems and handling disgruntled customers. It is critical for firms to have effective recovery strategies, because even a single service problem under the following conditions can destroy confidence in a firm:

- The failure is totally outrageous (e.g., blatant dishonesty on the part of the supplier).
- The problem fits into a pattern of failure rather than being an isolated incident.
- The recovery effort is weak, serving to compound the original problem rather than correct it.[16]

The risk of defection is high, especially when a variety of competing alternatives are available. One study of customer switching behavior in service industries found that close to 60 percent of all respondents who reported changing suppliers did so because of a service failure: 25 percent cited failures in the core service, 19 percent reported an unsatisfactory encounter with an employee, 10 percent reported an unsatisfactory response to a prior service failure, and 4 percent described unethical behavior on the part of the provider.[17]

Impact of Effective Service Recovery on Customer Loyalty

When complaints are resolved satisfactorily, there is a much higher chance that the customers involved will remain loyal. TARP research found that intentions to repurchase for different types of products ranged from 9 percent to 37 percent when customers were dissatisfied but did not complain. For a major complaint, the retention rate increased from 9 percent to 19 percent if the customer complained and the company offered a sympathetic ear but was unable to resolve the complaint to the satisfaction of the customer. If the complaint could be resolved to the satisfaction of the customer, the retention rate jumped to 54 percent. The highest retention rate, 82 percent, was achieved when problems were fixed quickly—typically, on the spot.[18]

The conclusion to be drawn is that complaint handling should be seen as a profit center and not a cost center. When a dissatisfied customer defects, the firm loses more than just the value of the next transaction. It may also lose a long-term stream of profits from that customer, and from anyone else who switches suppliers or is deterred from doing business with that firm because of negative comments from an unhappy friend. However, as can be seen in Service Perspective 13.1, many organizations have not yet bought into the concept that it pays to invest in service recovery to protect those long-term profits.

The Service Recovery Paradox

The *service recovery paradox* refers to the effect that customers who experience a service failure and then have it resolved to their full satisfaction are sometimes more

Here are some typical service recovery mistakes made by many organizations:

- **Managers disregard evidence that service recovery provides a significant financial return.** In recent years, many organizations have focused on cost cutting, paying only lip service to retaining their most profitable customers. On top of that, they have lost sight of the need to respect all their customers.

- **Companies do not invest enough in actions to prevent service failures.** Ideally, service planners address potential problems before they become customer problems. Although preventive measures don't eliminate the need for good service recovery systems, they greatly reduce the burden on both front-line staff and the service recovery system in its entirety.

- **Customer service employees fail to display good attitudes.** The three most important things in service recovery are attitude, attitude, and attitude. No matter how well designed and well planned the service recovery system is, it won't work well without the friendly and proverbial smile-in-the-voice attitude from front-line staff.

- **Organizations fail to make it easy for customers to complain or give feedback.** Although some improvements can be seen, such as hotels and restaurants offering comment cards, little is done to communicate their simplicity and value to customers. Research shows that a large proportion of customers are unaware of the existence of a proper feedback system that could help them get their problems solved.

Source: Adapted from Rod Stiefbold, "Dissatisfied Customers Requires Service Recovery Plans." *Marketing News*, 37, no. 22 (October 27, 2003): 44–45.

likely to make future purchases than are customers who have no problem in the first place. A study of repeated service failures in a retail banking context showed that the service recovery paradox held for the first service failure that was recovered to a customer's full satisfaction.[19] However, if a second service failure occurred, the paradox disappeared. It seems that customers may forgive a firm once, but become disillusioned if failures recur. Furthermore, the study also showed that customers' expectations were raised after they experienced a very good recovery; thus, excellent recovery becomes the standard they expect for dealing with future failures.

Some recent studies have challenged the existence of the service recovery paradox. For example, Tor Andreassen conducted a major study involving some 8,600 telephone interviews concerning a wide range of consumer services. The findings showed that after a service recovery, customers' intention to repurchase, and their perceptions of and attitudes toward the company, never surpassed the ratings of satisfied customers who did not experience a service problem in the first place. This was true even when the service recovery had gone very well and the customer expressed full satisfaction with the recovery.[20]

Whether a customer is delighted by service recovery may also depend on the severity and "recoverability" of the failure—no one can replace spoiled wedding photos or a ruined holiday, or eliminate the consequences of a debilitating injury caused by service equipment. In such situations, it's hard to imagine anyone being truly delighted even when a most professional service recovery is conducted. Contrast these examples with a lost hotel reservation, for which the recovery is often an upgrade to a suite. When poor service is recovered by delivery of a superior product, you're usually delighted and probably hope for another lost reservation in the future!

The best strategy, of course, is to do it right the first time. As Michael Hargrove puts it, "Service recovery is turning a service failure into an opportunity you wish you never had."[21] It's critical to insist that service recovery be well executed, but that failures cannot be tolerated. Unfortunately, empirical evidence shows that some 40 to 60 percent of customers report dissatisfaction with the service recovery process.[22]

PRINCIPLES OF EFFECTIVE SERVICE RECOVERY SYSTEMS

Recognizing that current customers are a valuable asset base, managers need to develop effective procedures for service recovery following unsatisfactory experiences. We discuss three guiding principles for how to do this well: Make it easy for customers to give feedback, enable effective service recovery, and establish appropriate compensation levels. The components of an effective service recovery system are shown in Figure 13.4.[23]

Make It Easy for Customers to Give Feedback

How can managers overcome unhappy customers' reluctance to complain about service failures? The best way is to address the reasons for their reluctance directly. Table 13.1 gives an overview of potential measures that can be taken to overcome those reasons we identified earlier in this chapter. Many companies have improved their complaint collection procedures by adding special toll-free phone lines, links on their web sites, prominently displayed customer comment cards in their branches, or even providing video terminals for recording complaints. In their customer newsletters, some companies feature service improvements that were the direct result of customer feedback under the title, "You told us, and we responded."

Enable Effective Service Recovery

Recovering from service failures takes more than just pious expressions of determination to resolve any problems that may occur. It requires commitment, planning, and clear guidelines. Specifically, effective service recovery procedures should be (1) proactive, (2) planned, (3) trained, and (4) empowered.

Service Recovery Should Be Proactive

Service recovery needs to be initiated on the spot—ideally, before customers have a chance to complain (see Best Practice in Action 13.1). Service personnel should

Figure 13.4
Components of an Effective Service Recovery System

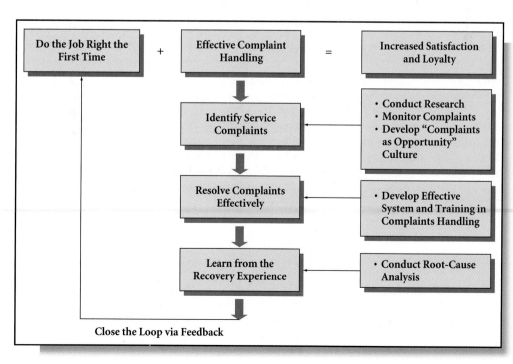

Source: Adapted from Christopher Lovelock, Paul Patterson, and Rhett Walker, *Services Marketing: An Asia-Pacific and Australian Perspective* (Melbourne: Prentice Hall Australia, 2004), p. 135.

Table 13.1 Strategies to Reduce Customer Complaint Barriers

COMPLAINT BARRIERS FOR DISSATISFIED CUSTOMERS	STRATEGIES TO REDUCE THESE BARRIERS
Inconvenience • Difficult to find the right complaint procedure • Effort, e.g., writing and mailing a letter	Make feedback easy and convenient: • Print customer service hotline numbers and email and postal addresses on all customer communications materials (letters, faxes, bills, brochures, phone book listing, yellow pages, etc.)
Doubtful payoff • Uncertain whether any or what action will be taken by the firm to address the issue the customer is unhappy with	Reassure customers that their feedback will be taken seriously and will pay off: • Have service recovery procedures in place and communicate this to customers, e.g., in customer newsletter and web site. • Feature service improvements that resulted from customer feedback.
Unpleasantness • Fear of being treated rudely • Fear of being hassled • Feeling embarrassed	Make providing feedback a positive experience: • Thank customers for their feedback (can be done publicly and in general by addressing the entire customer base). • Train the front line not to hassle and to make customers feel comfortable. • Allow for anonymous feedback.

BEST PRACTICE IN ACTION 13.1
Effective Service Recovery in Action

The lobby is almost deserted. It's not hard to overhear the conversation between the night manager at the Marriott Long Wharf Hotel in Boston and the late-arriving guest.

"Yes, Dr. Jones, we've been expecting you. I know you are scheduled to be here three nights. I'm sorry to tell you, sir, but we are booked solid tonight. A large number of guests we assumed were checking out did not. Where is your meeting tomorrow, sir?"

The doctor tells the clerk where it is.

"That's near the Omni Parker House. That's not very far from here. Let me call them and get you a room for the evening. I'll be right back."

A few minutes later the desk clerk returns with the good news.

"They're holding a room for you at the Omni Parker House, sir. And, of course, we'll pick up the tab. I'll forward any phone calls that come here for you. Here's a letter that will explain the situation and expedite your check-in, along with my business card so you can call me directly here at the front desk if you have any problems."

The doctor's mood is now turning from exasperation toward calm. But the desk clerk isn't finished. He reaches into the cash drawer. "Here are two $5 bills. That should more than cover your cab fare from here to the Parker House and back again in the morning. We don't have a problem tomorrow night, just tonight. And here's a coupon that will get you a complimentary continental breakfast on our concierge level on the fifth floor tomorrow morning . . . and again, I'm so sorry this happened."

As the doctor walks away, the night manager turns to the desk clerk. "Give him about 15 minutes and then call to make sure everything went okay."

A week later, when it is still a peak period for hotels in the city, the guest who had overheard the exchange is in a taxi, en route to the same hotel. Along the way, he tells his companion about the great service recovery episode he had witnessed the week before. The two travelers arrive at the hotel and make their way to the front desk, ready to check in.

They are greeted with unexpected news: "I'm so sorry, gentlemen. I know you were scheduled here for two nights. But we are booked solid tonight. Where is your meeting tomorrow?"

The would-be guests exchange a rueful glance as they tell the desk clerk their future plans. "That's near the Meridian. Let me call over there and see if I can get you a room. It won't take but a minute." As the clerk walks away, the tale teller says, "I'll bet he comes back with a letter and a business card."

Sure enough, the desk clerk returns to deliver the solution; it's not a robotic script, but all the elements from the previous week's show are on display. What the tale teller thought was pure desk-clerk initiative the previous week, he now realizes was planned, a spontaneous-feeling yet predetermined response to a specific category of customer problem.

Source: Ron Zemke and Chip R. Bell, *Knock Your Socks Off Service Recovery.* New York: AMACOM, 2000, pp. 59–60.

be sensitized to signs of dissatisfaction and ask whether customers might be experiencing a problem. For example, the waiter may ask a guest who has eaten only half of his dinner, "Is everything all right, sir?" The guest might say, "Yes, thank you, I'm not very hungry," or "The steak is well done but I asked for medium-rare; plus it's very salty." The latter response gives the waiter a chance to recover the service, rather than have an unhappy diner leave the restaurant and potentially not return.

Recovery Procedures Need to Be Planned

Contingency plans have to be developed for service failures, especially for those that can occur regularly and cannot be designed out of the system.[24] Revenue management practices in the travel and hospitality industries often result in overbooking, and travelers are denied boarding or hotel guests are "walked" even though they had confirmed seats or reservations. To simplify the task of front-line staff, firms should identify the most common service problems such as overbooking and develop predetermined solution sets for employees to follow.

Recovery Skills Must Be Taught

As a customer, you may quickly feel insecure at the point of service failure because things are not turning out as anticipated. So you look to an employee for assistance. But are they willing and able to help you? Effective training builds confidence and competence among front-line staff, enabling them to turn distress into delight.[25]

Recovery Requires Empowered Employees

Service recovery efforts should be flexible and employees should be empowered to use their judgment and communication skills to develop solutions that will satisfy complaining customers.[26] This is especially true for out-of-the-ordinary failures for which a firm may not have developed and trained potential solution sets. Employees need to have the authority to make decisions and spend money in order to resolve service problems promptly and recover customer goodwill.

How Generous Should Compensation Be?

Clearly, vastly different costs are associated with different recovery strategies. How much compensation should a firm offer when there has been a service failure? Or will an apology be sufficient? The following rules of thumb can help managers to answer these questions.

- *What is the positioning of our firm?* If it is known for service excellence, and charges a high premium for quality, then customers will expect service failures to be rare, so the firm should make a demonstrable effort to recover the few failures that do occur and be prepared to offer something of significant value. In a more downscale, mass market business, customers are likely to consider something quite modest, such as a free coffee or dessert, as fair compensation.
- *How severe was the service failure?* The general guideline is "Let the punishment fit the crime." Customers expect little for minor inconveniences, but much more significant compensation if major damage in terms of time, effort, annoyance, or anxiety, was created by the failure.
- *Who is the affected customer?* Long-term customers and those who spend heavily at a service provider expect more, and it is worth making an effort to save their business. One-time customers tend to be less demanding, and have less economic importance to the firm. Hence, compensation can be less, but should still be fair. There is always the possibility that a first-time user will become a repeat customer if he or she treated well. The overall rule of thumb for compensation for service

failures should be "well-dosed generosity." Being perceived as stingy adds insult to injury, and the firm will probably be better off simply apologizing than offering only minimal compensation.

Overly generous compensation is not only expensive, customers may even interpret such a response negatively, raising questions in their minds about the soundness of the business and leading them to become suspicious about the underlying motives. Customers may worry about the implications for the employee as well as for the business. Also, overgenerosity does not seem to result in higher repeat purchase rates than simply offering fair compensation.[27] There is a risk, too, that a reputation for overgenerosity may encourage dishonest jaycustomers to actively "seek" service failures.

Dealing with Complaining Customers

Both managers and front-line employees must be prepared to deal with distressed customers, including jaycustomers who become confrontational in unacceptable ways and sometimes behave insultingly toward service personnel who aren't at fault. Service Perspective 13.2 provides specific guidelines for effective problem resolution, designed to help calm upset customers and to deliver a resolution that they will see as fair and satisfying.

SERVICE GUARANTEES

A growing number of companies offer customers a service guarantee, promising that if service delivery fails to meet predefined standards, the customer will be entitled to one or more forms of compensation, such as an easy-to-claim replacement, refund, or credit. Some firms put conditions on these guarantees, others offer them unconditionally.

The Power of Service Guarantees

Christopher Hart declares that service guarantees are powerful tools for both promoting and achieving service quality, for the following reasons:[28]

1. Guarantees force firms to focus on what their customers want and expect in each element of the service.
2. Guarantees set clear standards, telling customers and employees alike what the company stands for. Payouts to compensate customers for poor service cause managers to take guarantees seriously, because they highlight the financial costs of quality failures.
3. Guarantees require the development of systems for generating meaningful customer feedback and acting on it.
4. Guarantees force service organizations to understand why they fail and encourage them to identify and overcome potential fail points.
5. Guarantees build "marketing muscle" by reducing the risk of the purchase decision and building long-term loyalty.

From the customer's perspective, the primary function of service guarantees is to lower the perceived risks associated with purchase.[29] The presence of a guarantee may also make it easier for customers to complain and more likely that they will do so, because they will anticipate that front-line employees will be prepared to resolve the problem and provide appropriate compensation. Sara Björlin Lidén and Per Skálén found that even when dissatisfied customers were unaware that a service guarantee existed before making their complaint, they were positively impressed to learn that the company had a preplanned procedure for handling failures and to find that their complaints were taken seriously.[30]

1. *Act fast.* If the complaint is made during service delivery, then time is of the essence to achieve a full recovery. When complaints are made after the fact, many companies have established policies of responding within 24 hours, or sooner. Even when full resolution is likely to take longer, fast acknowledgment remains very important.

2. *Acknowledge the customer's feelings.* Do this either tacitly or explicitly (for example, "I can understand why you're upset"). This action helps to build rapport, the first step in rebuilding a bruised relationship.

3. *Don't argue with the customer.* The goal should be to gather facts to reach a mutually acceptable solution, not to win a debate or prove that the customer is an idiot. Arguing gets in the way of listening and seldom diffuses anger.

4. *Show that you understand the problem from the customer's point of view.* Seeing situations through customers' eyes is the only way to understand what they think has gone wrong and why they're upset. Service personnel should avoid jumping to conclusions with their own interpretations.

5. *Clarify the truth and sort out the cause.* A failure may result from inefficiency of service, a misunderstanding by the customer, or the misbehavior of a third party. If you've done something wrong, apologize immediately. The more the customer can forgive you, the less he or she will expect to be compensated. Don't be defensive; acting defensively may suggest that the organization has something to hide or is reluctant to explore the situation fully.

6. *Give the customer the benefit of the doubt.* Not all customers are truthful, and not all complaints are justified. However, customers should be treated as though they have a valid complaint until clear evidence to the contrary emerges. If a lot of money is at stake (as in insurance claims or potential lawsuits), careful investigation is warranted. If the amount involved is small, it may not be worth haggling over a refund or other compensation. However, it's still a good idea to check records to see if there is a past history of dubious complaints by the same customer.

7. *Propose the steps needed to solve the problem.* When instant solutions aren't possible, telling the customer how the organization plans to proceed shows that corrective action is being taken. It also sets expectations about the time involved (so firms should be careful not to overpromise).

8. *Keep the customer informed of progress.* Nobody likes being left in the dark. Uncertainty breeds anxiety and stress. People tend to be more accepting of disruptions if they know what's going on and receive periodic progress reports.

9. *Consider compensation.* When customers do not receive the service outcome they believe they have paid for or have suffered serious inconvenience and/or loss of time and money because the service failed, either a monetary payment or an offer of equivalent service in kind is appropriate. This type of recovery strategy may also reduce the risk of legal action by an angry customer. Service guarantees often lay out in advance what such compensation will be, and the firm should ensure that all guarantees are met.

10. *Persevere to regain customer goodwill.* When customers have been disappointed, one of the biggest challenges is to restore their confidence and preserve the relationship for the future. Perseverance may be required to defuse customers' disappointment and even anger and to convince them that actions are being taken to avoid a recurrence of the problem. Truly exceptional recovery efforts can be extremely effective in building loyalty and referrals.

11. *Self-check the system and pursue eminence.* After the customer has left, you should check to determine whether the service failure was caused by an accident, a mistake, or a system defect. Take advantage of every complaint to perfect the whole service system. Even if the complaint is found to be a result of a misunderstanding by the customer, this implies that some part of your communication system is ineffective.

The benefits of service guarantees can be seen clearly in the case of Hampton Inn's "100% Hampton Guarantee" ("If you're not 100% satisfied, you don't pay"—see Figure 13.5), which has now been extended to Embassy Suites and Homewood Suites.[31] As a business-building program, Hampton's strategy of offering to refund the cost of the room to a guest who expresses dissatisfaction has attracted new customers and also served as a powerful retention device. People choose to stay at a Hampton Inn because they are confident they will be satisfied. At least as important, the guarantee has become a vital tool to help managers identify new opportunities for quality improvement.

Figure 13.5
Hampton Inn Includes
Its "100% Hampton
Guarantee" in Its
Advertising

Courtesy of Hilton.

In discussing the effect on staff and managers, the vice president—marketing of Hampton Inn stated: "Designing the guarantee made us understand what made guests satisfied, rather than what *we thought* made them satisfied." It became imperative that everyone from reservationists and front-line employees to general managers and personnel at corporate headquarters listen carefully to guests, anticipate their needs to the greatest extent possible, and remedy problems quickly so that guests were satisfied with the solution. Viewing a hotel's function in this customer-centric way had a profound effect on the way the firm conducted business.

The guarantee "turned up the pressure in the hose," as one manager put it, showing where "leaks" existed, and providing the financial incentive to plug them. As a result, the guarantee has had an important effect on product consistency and service delivery across the Hampton Inn chain. Finally, studies have shown a dramatically positive effect of the "100% Hampton Guarantee" on financial performance.

How to Design Service Guarantees

Some guarantees are simple and unconditional. Others appear to have been written by lawyers and contain many restrictions. Compare the examples in Service Perspective 13.3 and ask yourself which guarantees instill trust and confidence in you, and would make you like to do business with that supplier.

Both the L.L. Bean and BBBK guarantees are powerful, unconditional, and instill trust. The others are weakened by the many conditions. The USPS has added six new conditions in recent years! Hart argues that service guarantees should be designed to meet the following criteria:[32]

1. *Unconditional:* Whatever is promised in the guarantee must be totally unconditional and there should not be any element of surprise for the customer.

SERVICE PERSPECTIVES 13.3
Examples of Service Guarantees

United States Postal Service Express Mail Guarantee

Service Guarantee: *Express Mail international mailings are not covered by this service agreement. Military shipments delayed due to customs inspections are also excluded.* If the shipment is mailed at a designated USPS Express Mail facility on or before the specified deposit time for overnight delivery to the addressee, delivery to the addressee or agent will be attempted before the applicable guaranteed time. Signature of the addressee's agent, or delivery employee is required upon delivery. If a delivery attempt is not made by the guaranteed time and the mailer files a claim for a refund, the USPS will refund the postage unless the delay was caused by: proper retention for law enforcement purposes; strike or work stoppage; late deposit of shipment; forwarding, return, incorrect address, or incorrect ZIP code; delay or cancellation of flights; governmental action beyond the control of the Postal Service or air carriers; war, insurrection or civil disturbance; breakdowns of a substantial portion of the USPS transportation network resulting from events or factors outside the control of the Postal Service or Acts of God.

Source: Printed on back of Express Mail receipt, January 2006.

Excerpt from the "Quality Standard Guarantees" of an Office Services Company

- We guarantee 6-hour turnaround on documents of two pages or less . . . (does not include client subsequent changes or equipment failures).
- We guarantee that there will be a receptionist to greet you and your visitors during normal business hours . . . (short breaks of less than five minutes are not subject to this guarantee).

- You will not be obligated to pay rent for any day on which there is not a manager on site to assist you (lunch and reasonable breaks are expected and not subject to this guarantee).

Source: Reproduced in Eileen C. Shapiro, *Fad Surfing in the Boardroom.* Reading, MA: Addison-Wesley, 1995, p. 18.

The Bugs Burger Bug Killer (a Pest Control Company) Guarantee

- You don't owe us a penny until all the pests on your premises have been eradicated.
- If you're ever dissatisfied with the BBBK's service you will receive a refund for as much as 12 months of service—plus fees for another exterminator of your choice for the next year.
- If a guest spots a pest on your premises, the exterminator will pay for the guest's meal or room, send a letter of apology and pay for a future meal or stay.
- If your premises are closed down because of the presence of roaches or rodents, BBBK will pay any fines, as well as all lost profit, plus $5000.

Source: Reproduced in Christopher W. Hart, "The Power of Unconditional Service Guarantees." *Harvard Business Review* (July–August 1990).

L.L. Bean's Guarantee

Our Guarantee. Our products are guaranteed to give 100 percent satisfaction in every way. Return anything purchased from us at any time if it proves otherwise. We do not want you to have anything from L.L. Bean that is not completely satisfactory.

Source: Printed in all L.L. Bean catalogs and on the company's web site, www.llbean.com/customerService/aboutLLBean/guarantee.html, accessed June 2006.

2. *Easy to understand and communicate* to the customer so that he is clearly aware of the benefits that can be gained from the guarantee.
3. *Meaningful to the customer* in that the guarantee is on something important to the customer and the compensation should be more than adequate to cover the service failure.[33]
4. *Easy to invoke:* Less of the guarantee should be dependent on the customer and more on the service provider.
5. *Easy to collect:* If a service failure occurs, the customer should be able to collect on the guarantee easily, without any problems.
6. *Credible:* The guarantee should be believable.

Is Full Satisfaction the Best You Can Guarantee?

Full-satisfaction guarantees have generally been considered the best possible design. However, it has been suggested that the ambiguity associated with such guarantees can lead to discounting of their perceived value. Customers may raise questions such as "What does full satisfaction mean?" or "Can I invoke a guarantee when I am dissatisfied, although the fault does not lie with the service firm?"[34] The *combined guarantee* addresses this issue by combining the wide scope of a full-satisfaction guarantee with the low uncertainty of specific performance standards.[35] This type of guarantee has been shown to be superior to the pure full-satisfaction or attribute-specific guarantee designs. Specific performance standards are guaranteed (e.g., on-time delivery), but should the consumer be dissatisfied with any other element of the service, the full-satisfaction coverage of the combined guarantee applies. Table 13.2 shows examples of the various types of guarantees.

Table 13.2 Types of Service Guarantees

TERM	GUARANTEE SCOPE	EXAMPLE
Single attribute-specific guarantee	One key attribute of the service is covered by the guarantee.	"Any of three specified popular pizzas is guaranteed to be served within 10 minutes of ordering on working days between 12 A.M. and 2 P.M. If the pizza is late, the customer's next order is free."
Multiattribute-specific guarantee	A few important attributes of the service are covered by the guarantee.	Minneapolis Marriott's guarantee: "Our quality commitment to you is to provide: • A friendly, efficient check-in • A clean, comfortable room, where everything works • A friendly efficient check-out If we, in your opinion, do not deliver on this commitment, we will give you $20 in cash. No questions asked. It is your interpretation."
Full-satisfaction guarantee	All aspects of the service are covered by the guarantee. There are no exceptions.	Lands' End's guarantee: "If you are not completely satisfied with any item you buy from us, at any time during your use of it, return it and we will refund your full purchase price. We mean every word of it. Whatever. Whenever. Always. But to make sure this is perfectly clear, we've decided to simplify it further. GUARANTEED. Period."
Combined guarantee	All aspects of the service are covered by the full-satisfaction promise of the guarantee. Explicit minimum performance standards on important attributes are included in the guarantee to reduce uncertainty.	Datapro Information Services guarantees "to deliver the report on time, to high quality standards, and to the contents outlined in this proposal. Should we fail to deliver according to this guarantee, *or should you be dissatisfied with any aspect of our work,* you can deduct any amount from the final payment which is deemed as fair."

Source: Adapted from Jochen Wirtz and Doreen Kum, "Designing Service Guarantees—Is Full Satisfaction the Best You Can Guarantee?" *Journal of Services Marketing,* 15, no. 4 (2001): 282–299

Is It Always Appropriate to Introduce a Service Guarantee?

Managers should think carefully about their firm's strengths and weaknesses when deciding whether to introduce a service guarantee. In many instances, it may be inappropriate to do so. Companies that already have a strong reputation for service excellence may not need a guarantee. In fact, it might even be incongruent with their image to offer one, as it might even confuse the market.[36] By contrast, a firm whose service is currently poor must first work to improve quality to a level above that at which the guarantee might be invoked on a regular basis by most of their customers.

Service firms whose quality is truly uncontrollable because of external forces would be foolish to consider a guarantee. For example, when Amtrak realized that it was paying out substantial refunds because it lacked sufficient control over its railroad infrastructure, it was forced to drop a service guarantee that included reimbursement of fares in the event of unpunctual train service.

In a market in which consumers see little financial, personal, or physiological risk associated with purchasing and using a service, a guarantee adds little value but still costs money to design, implement, and manage. When little perceived difference in service quality exists among competing firms, the first company to institute a guarantee may be able to obtain a first-mover advantage and create a valued differentiation for its services. If more than one competitor already has a guarantee in place, offering a guarantee may become a qualifier for the industry, and the only real way to make an impact is to launch a highly distinctive guarantee beyond that already offered by competitors.[37]

DISCOURAGING ABUSE AND OPPORTUNISTIC BEHAVIOR

Throughout this chapter, we advocate that firms should welcome complaints and invocations of service guarantees and even encourage them. But how can this be done without inviting potential abuse by that undesirable group of people termed jaycustomers? (see Chapter 8).

Dealing with Consumer Fraud

Dishonest customers can take advantage of generous service recovery strategies, service guarantees, or simply a strong customer orientation in a number of ways. For example, they may steal from the firm, refuse to pay for a service, fake dissatisfaction, purposefully cause service failures to occur, or overstate losses resulting from genuine service failures. What steps can a firm take to protect itself against opportunistic customer behavior?

Treating customers with suspicion is likely to alienate them, especially in situations of service failure. The president of TARP notes:

> Our research has found that premeditated rip-offs represent 1 to 2 percent of the customer base in most organizations. However, most organizations defend themselves against unscrupulous customers by. . . treating the 98 percent of honest customers like crooks to catch the 2 percent who *are* crooks.[38]

Using this knowledge, the working assumption should be "If in doubt, believe the customer." However, as Service Perspective 13.4 shows, it's crucial to monitor invocations of service guarantees, or payments compensating for service failure, maintaining databases of all such cases, and monitoring repeated service payouts to the same customer. For example, one Asian airline found that the same customer lost his suitcase on three consecutive flights. The chances of this actually happening are probably lower than of winning the national lottery, so front-line staff were made aware of this individual. The next time he checked in his suitcase, the check-in staff

As part of its guarantee tracking system, Hampton Inn has developed ways to identify guests who appeared to be cheating—using aliases or various dissatisfaction problems to invoke the guarantee repeatedly in order to get the cost of their room refunded. Guests showing high invocation trends receive personalized attention and follow-up from the company's Guest Assistance Team. Wherever possible, senior managers telephone these guests to ask about their recent stays. The conversation might go as follows: "Hello, Mr. Jones. I'm the director of guest assistance at Hampton Inn, and I see that you've had some difficulty with the last four properties you've visited. Since we take our guarantee very seriously, I thought I'd give you a call and find out what the problems were."

The typical response is dead silence. Sometimes the silence is followed with questions of how head-quarters could possibly know about their problems. These calls have their humorous moments as well. One individual, who had invoked the guarantee 17 times in what appeared to be a trip that took him across the United States and back, was asked, innocuously, "Where do you like to stay when you travel?" "Hampton Inn," came the enthusiastic response. "But," said the executive making the call, "our records show that the last 17 times you stayed at a Hampton Inn, you have invoked the 100 percent satisfaction guarantee." "That's why I like them!" proclaimed the guest (who turned out to be a long-distance truck driver).

Source: Christopher W. Hart and Elizabeth Long, *Extraordinary Guarantees.* New York: AMACOM, 1997.

videotaped the suitcase almost from check-in to pickup in the baggage claim at the traveler's destination. It turned out that a companion collected the suitcase and took it away while the traveler again made his way to the lost-baggage counter to report his missing suitcase. This time, the police were waiting for him and his friend.

Recent research shows that the amount of a guarantee payout (e.g., whether it is a 10 percent or 100 percent money-back guarantee) had no effect on consumer cheating. However, repeat-purchase intention significantly reduced cheating intent. These findings suggest important managerial implications: (1) Managers can implement and thus reap the bigger marketing benefits of 100 percent money-back guarantees without worrying that the large payouts will increase cheating; and (2) guarantees can be offered to regular customers or as part of a membership program, because repeat customers are unlikely to cheat on service guarantees. A further finding was that customers were also reluctant to cheat if the service quality provided was truly high than when it was just satisfactory. This implied that truly excellent services firms have less to worry about than the average provider.[39]

LEARNING FROM CUSTOMER FEEDBACK

There are two ways of looking at complaints: first, as individual customer problems, each of which requires a resolution; and second, as a stream of information that can be used to measure quality and suggest improvements. So far in this chapter, we have taken the former perspective of the individual customer. In this section we discuss how customer feedback can be systematically collected, analyzed and disseminated[40] via an institutionalized customer feedback system (CFS) to achieve customer-driven learning.[41]

Key Objectives of Effective Customer Feedback Systems

"It is not the strongest species that survive, nor the most intelligent, but the ones most responsive to change," wrote Charles Darwin. Similarly, many strategists have concluded that in increasingly competitive markets, the ultimate competitive advantage for a firm is to learn and change faster than the competition.[42] Specific objectives of effective customer feedback systems typically fall into three main categories:

1. *Assessment and Benchmarking of Service Quality and Performance.* The objective is to answer the question, "How satisfied are our customers?" This objective includes learning about how well a firm has performed in comparison to its main competitor(s), how it has performed in comparison to the previous year (or quarter, or month), whether investments in certain service aspects have paid off in terms of customer satisfaction, and where the firm wants to be in the following period. Often, a key objective of comparison against other units (branches, teams, service products, competitors) is to motivate managers and service staff to improve performance, especially when the results are linked to compensation.

2. *Customer-Driven Learning and Improvements.* Here, the objective is to answer the questions, "What makes our customers happy or unhappy?" and "What are our strengths we need to maintain, and where and how do we need to improve?" For this, more specific or detailed information on processes and products is required to guide a firm's service improvement efforts, and to pinpoint areas with potentially high returns for quality investment. It is also about gaining an understanding of the things that other suppliers do well and those that make customers happy.

3. *Creating a Customer-Oriented Service Culture.* This objective is concerned with focusing the organization on customer needs and customer satisfaction, and rallying the entire organization toward a service quality culture.

Of these three objectives, firms seem to doing well on the first, but to be missing great opportunities in the other two. Neil Morgan, Eugene Anderson, and Vikas Mittal concluded in their research on customer satisfaction information usage (CSIU):

> Many of the firms in our sample do not appear to gain significant customer-focused learning benefits from their CS [customer satisfaction] systems, because they are designed to act primarily as a control mechanism [i.e., our assessment or benchmarking]. . . . [Firms] may be well served to reevaluate how they deploy their existing CSIU resources. The majority of CSIU resources . . . are consumed in CS data collection. This often leads to too few resources being allocated to the analysis, dissemination, and utilization of this information to realize fully the potential payback from the investment in data collection.[43]

Use a Mix of Customer Feedback Collection Tools

Renee Fleming, sorprano, "America's beautiful voice," once said, "We singers are unfortunately not able to hear ourselves sing. You sound entirely different to yourself. We need the ears of others—from outside. . . ." Likewise, firms need to listen to the voice of the customer. Table 13.3 gives an overview of typically used feedback tools and their ability to meet various requirements. Recognizing that different tools have different strengths and weaknesses, service marketers should select a mix of customer feedback collection tools that jointly deliver the needed information. As Leonard Berry and "Parsu" Parasuraman observe, "Combining approaches enables a firm to tap the strengths of each and compensate for weaknesses."[44]

Total Market Surveys, Annual Surveys, and Transactional Surveys

Total market surveys and *annual surveys* typically measure satisfaction with all major customer service processes and products.[45] The level of measurement is usually at a high level, with the objective of obtaining a global index or indicator of overall service satisfaction for the entire firm. This could be based on indexed (e.g., using various attribute ratings) and/or weighted data (e.g., weighted by core segments and/or products).

Table 13.3 Strengths and Weaknesses of Key Customer Feedback Collection Tools (meets requirements fully, ●; moderately, ◑; hardly/not at all, ○)

Collection Tools	Level of Measurement			Actionable	Representative, Reliable	Potential for Service Recovery	First-Hand Learning	Cost-Effectiveness
	Firm	Process	Transaction Specific					
Total market survey (including competitors)	●	○	○	○	●	○	○	○
Annual survey on overall satisfaction	●	◑	○	○	●	○	○	○
Transactional survey	●	●	◑	◑	●	○	○	○
Service feedback cards	◑	●	●	◑	◑	●	◑	●
Mystery shopping	○	◑	●	●	○	○	◑	○
Unsolicited feedback (e.g., complaints)	○	◑	●	●	○	●	◑	●
Focus group discussions	○	◑	●	●	○	◑	●	◑
Service reviews	○	◑	●	●	○	●	●	◑

Source: Adapted from Jochen Wirtz and Monica Tomlin, "Institutionalizing Customer-Driven Learning Through Fully Integrated Customer Feedback Systems." *Managing Service Quality,* 10, no. 4 (2000): 210.

Overall indices such as these tell how satisfied customers are, but not why they are happy or unhappy. There are limits to the number of questions that can be asked about each individual process or product. For example, a typical retail bank has some 30 to 50 key customer service processes (e.g., from car loan applications to cash deposits at the teller). Because of the sheer number of processes, many surveys have room for only one or two questions per process (e.g., how satisfied are you with our ATM services?) and cannot address issues in greater detail.

In contrast, *transactional surveys* are typically conducted after customers have completed a specific transaction (Figure 13.6). At this point, if time permit, they may be queried about this process in some depth. In the case of the bank, all key attributes and aspects of ATM services could be included in the survey, including some open-ended questions such as "liked best," "liked least," and "suggested improvements." Such feedback is more actionable, can tell the firm why customers are happy or unhappy with the process, and usually yield specific insights on how to improve customer satisfaction.

All three survey types are representative and reliable when designed properly. Representativeness and reliability are required for: (1) accurate assessments of where the company, a process, branch, or individual stands relative to quality goals (having a representative and reliable sample means that observed changes in quality scores are not the result of sample biases and/or random errors); and (2) evaluations of individuals, staff, teams, branches, and/or processes, especially when incentive schemes are linked to such measures. The methodology has to be watertight if staff are to trust and buy into the results, especially when surveys deliver bad news.

The potential for service recovery is important and should, if possible, be designed into feedback collection tools. However, many surveys promise anonymity, making it impossible to identify and respond to dissatisfied respondents. In personal encounters or telephone surveys, interviewers can be instructed to ask customers whether they would like the firm to get back to them on dissatisfying issues.

Service Feedback Cards

Service feedback cards are a powerful and inexpensive tool for evaluating customer response to service issues. Customers are given a feedback card following completion of each major service process and invited them to return it by mail or other means to a central customer feedback unit. For example, a feedback card can be attached to each housing loan approval letter or to each hospital invoice. Although these cards are a good indicator of process quality and yield specific feedback on what works well and what doesn't, the respondents tend not to be representative, being biased toward customers who are either very satisfied or very dissatisfied.

Mystery Shopping

Service businesses often use "mystery shoppers" to determine whether front-line staff are displaying desired behaviors. Banks, retailers, car rental firms, and hotels are among the industries that make active use of mystery shoppers. For example, the central reservation offices of a global hotel chain contracts for a large-scale monthly mystery caller survey to assess the skills of individual associates in relation to the phone sales process. Such actions as correctly positioning the various products, up-selling and cross-selling, and closing the deal are measured. The survey also assesses the quality of the phone conversation on such dimensions as "a warm and friendly greeting" and "establishing rapport with the caller." Mystery shopping gives highly actionable and in-depth insights for coaching, training, and performance evaluation.

Because the number of mystery calls or visits is typically small, no individual survey is reliable or representative. However, if a particular staff member performs well (or poorly) month after month, managers can infer with reasonable confidence that this person's performance is good (or poor).

Unsolicited Customer Feedback

Customer complaints, compliments, and suggestions can be transformed into a stream of information that can be used to help monitor quality, and highlight improvements needed to the service design and delivery. Complaints and compliments are rich sources of detailed feedback on what drives customers nuts and what delights them.

Like feedback cards, unsolicited feedback is not a reliable measure of overall customer satisfaction, but it is a good source of ideas for improvement. If the objective of collecting feedback is mainly to get feedback on what to improve (rather than for benchmarking and/or assessing staff), reliability and representativeness are not needed, and more qualitative tools such as complaints/compliments or focus groups generally suffice.

Detailed customer complaint and compliment letters, recorded telephone conversations, and direct feedback from employees can serve as an excellent tool for communicating internally what customers want, and enable employees and managers at all levels to "listen" to customers first-hand. This first-hand learning is much more powerful for shaping the thinking and customer orientation of service staff than using "clinical" statistics and reports.

For example, Singapore Airlines prints complaint and compliment letters in its monthly employee magazine, *Outlook*. Southwest Airlines shows staff videotapes containing footage of customers providing feedback. Seeing actual customers giving comments about their service leaves a much deeper and lasting impression on staff and motivates them to improve further.

Focus Group Discussions and Service Reviews

Both focus group discussions and service reviews give great specific insights on potential service improvements and ideas. Typically, focus groups are organized by key customer segments or user groups, to drill down on the needs of these users. Service reviews are in-depth, one-on-one interviews, usually conducted once a year with a firm's most valuable customers. Usually, a senior executive of the firm visits the customers and discusses issues such as how well the firm performed the previous year and what should be maintained or changed. That senior person then goes back to the organization and discusses the feedback with his or her account managers, and then both write a letter back to the client detailing how the firm will respond to that customer's service needs and how the account will be managed the following year.

Apart from providing an excellent learning opportunity (especially when the reviews across all customers are compiled and analyzed), service reviews focus on retention of the most valuable customers and get high marks for service recovery potential.

As we noted earlier, there are advantages to using a mix of feedback tools. Best Practice in Action 13.2 features FedEx's excellent customer feedback system, which combines various customer feedback collection tools with a detailed process performance measurement system.

Capturing Unsolicited Customer Feedback

For complaints, suggestions, and inquiries to be useful as research input, they have to be funneled into a central collection point, logged, categorized, and analyzed.[46] That requires a system for capturing customer feedback where it is made, and then reporting it to a central unit. Some firms use a simple intranet site to record all feedback received by any staff member. Coordinating such activities is not a simple matter, because of the many entry points, including the following:

- The firm's own front-line employees, who may be in contact with customers face to face, by telephone, or via mail or email
- Intermediary organizations acting on behalf of the original supplier
- Managers who normally work backstage, but who are contacted by a customer seeking higher authority
- Suggestion or complaint cards mailed, emailed, pasted on the firm's web site, or placed in a special box
- Complaints to third parties—consumer advocate groups, legislative agencies, trade organizations, and other customers

"We believe that service quality must be mathematically measured," declares Frederick W. Smith, chairman, president, and CEO of Federal Express Corporation. The company has a commitment to clear, frequently repeated quality goals, followed up with continuous measurement of progress against those goals. This practice forms the foundation for its approach to quality.

FedEx initially set two ambitious quality goals: 100 percent customer satisfaction for every interaction and transaction; and 100 percent service performance on every package handled. Customer satisfaction was measured by the percentage of on-time deliveries, which referred to the number of packages delivered on time as a percentage of total package volume. However, as things turned out, percentage of on-time delivery was an internal standard that was not synonymous with customer satisfaction.

Because FedEx had systematically cataloged customer complaints, it was able to develop what CEO Smith calls the "Hierarchy of Horrors," which referred to the eight most common complaints by customers: (1) wrong-day delivery, (2) right-day, late delivery, (3) pick-up not made, (4) lost package, (5) customer misinformed by FedEx, (6) billing and paperwork mistakes, (7) employee performance failures, and (8) damaged packages. This list was the foundation on which FedEx built its customer feedback system.

FedEx refined the list of "horrors" and developed the Service Quality Indicator (SQI), a 12-item measure of satisfaction and service quality from the customer's viewpoint. Weights were assigned to each item based on its relative importance in determining overall customer satisfaction. All items are tracked daily, so that a continuous index can be computed.

In addition to the SQI, which has been modified over time to reflect changes in procedures, services, and customer priorities, FedEx uses a variety of other ways to capture feedback:

Customer Satisfaction Survey This telephone survey is conducted on a quarterly basis with several thousand randomly selected customers, stratified by FedEx's key segments. The results are relayed to senior management on a quarterly basis.

Targeted Customer Satisfaction Survey This survey covers specific customer service processes and is conducted on a semiannual basis with clients who have experienced one of the specific FedEx processes within the last three months.

FedEx Center Comment Cards Comment cards are collected from each FedEx store-front business center. The results are tabulated twice a year and relayed to managers in charge of the centers.

Online Customer Feedback Surveys FedEx has commissioned regular studies to get feedback for its online services (e.g., package tracking) as well as *ad hoc* studies on new products.

The information from these various customer feedback measures has helped FedEx to maintain a leadership role in its industry and played an important role in enabling it to receive the prestigious Malcolm Baldrige National Quality Award.

Sources: "Blueprints for Service Quality: The Federal Express Approach." In *AMA Management Briefing*. New York: American Management Association, 1991, pp. 51–64; Linda Rosencrance, "BetaSphere Delivers FedEx Some Customer Feedback." *Computerworld*, 14, no. 14 (2000): 36.

Analysis, Reporting, and Dissemination of Customer Feedback

Choosing the relevant feedback tools and collecting customer feedback is meaningless if the company is unable to disseminate the information to the relevant parties to take action. Hence, to drive continuous improvement and learning, a reporting system needs to deliver feedback and its analysis to front-line staff, process owners, branch or department managers, and top management. The feedback loop to the front line should be immediate for complaints and compliments, as is practised in a number of service businesses in which complaints, compliments, and suggestions are discussed with staff during a daily morning briefing. In addition, we recommend three types of service performance reports to provide the information necessary for service management and team learning:

1. A monthly Service Performance Update provides process owners with timely feedback on customer comments and operational process performance. Here, the verbatim feedback is provided to the process manager, who can in turn discuss them with his or her service staff.

2. A quarterly Service Performance Review provides process owners and branch or department managers with trends in process performance and service quality.
3. An annual Service Performance Report gives top management a representative assessment of the status and long-term trends relating to customer satisfaction with the firm's services.

The reports should be short and reader-friendly, focusing on key indicators and providing an easily understood commentary.

CONCLUSION

Collecting customer feedback via complaints, suggestions, and compliments provides a means of increasing customer satisfaction. It's an opportunity to get into the hearts and minds of the customer. In all but the worst instances, complaining customers are indicating that they want to continue their relationship with the firm, but they are also indicating that all is not well and that they expect the company to make things right.

Service firms need to develop effective strategies to recover from service failures so that they can maintain customer goodwill, which is vital for the long-term success of the company. Even the best recovery strategy is not as good as being treated right the first time. Well-designed unconditional service guarantees have proved to be a powerful tool for identifying and justifying needed improvements, as well as creating a culture in which employees take proactive steps to ensure that customers will be satisfied.

Finally, a service firm and its staff must also learn from mistakes and work to eliminate the causes of known problems. Customer feedback systems should ensure that information originating from complaints, compliments, and other feedback tools is systematically collected, analyzed, and disseminated to drive service improvements. The ultimate objective of an effective customer feedback system is to institutionalize systematic and continuous customer-driven learning.

REVIEW QUESTIONS

1. Why don't many unhappy customers complain? And what do customers expect of a firm once they do file a complaint?
2. Why would a firm prefer its unhappy customers to come forward and complain?
3. What is the service recovery paradox? Under what conditions is this paradox most likely to hold? Why is it best to deliver the service as planned, even the paradox does hold in a specific context?
4. How can a firm make it easy for dissatisfied customers to complain?
5. Why should a service recovery strategy be proactive, planned, trained, and empowered?
6. How generous should compensations related to service recovery be? What are the economic costs to the firm of the typical types of compensation that service businesses offer?
7. How should service guarantees be designed? What are the benefits of service guarantees over and above a good complaint-handling and service recovery system?
8. What are the main objectives of customer feedback systems?
9. What customer feedback collection tools do you know, and what are the strengths and weaknesses of each of these tools?

APPLICATION EXERCISES

1. Think about the last time you experienced a less-than-satisfactory service experience. Did you complain? Why? If you did not complain, explain why not.
2. When was the last time you were truly satisfied with an organization's response to your complaint. Describe in detail what happened and what made you satisfied.
3. What would be an appropriate service recovery policy for a wrongly bounced check for (a) your local savings bank, (b) a major national bank, (c) a high-end private bank for high-net-worth individuals. Explain your rationale, and also compute the economic costs of the alternative service recovery policies.
4. Design a highly effective service guarantee for a service with high perceived risk. Explain why and how your guarantee would reduce perceived risk of potential customers, and why current customers would appreciate being offered this guarantee although they are already customers of that firm and therefore are likely to perceive lower levels of risk.

5. Collect a few customer feedback forms and tools (e.g., customer feedback cards, questionnaires, and online forms) and assess how the information gathered in those tools can be used to achieve the three main objectives of an effective customer feedback system.

6. How generous should compensation be? Review the following incident and comment. Then evaluate the available options, comment on each, select the one you recommend, and defend your decision.

"The shrimp cocktail was half-frozen. The waitress apologized and didn't charge me for any of my dinner," was the response of a very satisfied customer about the service recovery he received.

Consider the following range of service recovery policies a restaurant chain could set:

Option 1: Smile and apologize, defrost the shrimp cocktail, return it, smile and apologize again.

Option 2: Smile and apologize, replace the shrimp cocktail with a new one, and smile and apologize again.

Option 3: Smile, apologize, replace the shrimp cocktail, and offer a free coffee or dessert.

Option 4: Smile, apologize, replace the shrimp cocktail, and waive the bill of $80 for the entire meal.

Option 5: Smile, apologize, replace the shrimp cocktail, waive the bill for the entire dinner, and offer a free bottle of champagne.

Option 6: Smile, apologize, replace the shrimp cocktail, waive the bill for the entire dinner, offer a free bottle of champagne, and give a voucher valid for another dinner, to be redeemed within three months.

Try to establish the costs for each policy. Some data are provided in the endnotes (see Ref. 47), but before peeking at these data, think about the costs yourself.

ENDNOTES

1. Roger Bougie, Rik Pieters, and Marcel Zeelenberg, "Angry Customers Don't Come Back, They Get Back: The Experience and Behavioral Implications of Anger and Dissatisfaction in Service." *Journal of the Academy of Marketing Science,* 31, no. 4 (2003): 377–393; Florian v. Wangenheim, "Postswitching Negative Word of Mouth." *Journal of Service Research,* 8, no. 1 (2005): 67–78.

2. Bernd Stauss, "Global Word of Mouth." *Marketing Management* (Fall 1997): 28–30.

3. For research on cognitive and affective drivers of complaining behavior, see Jean-Charles Chebat, Moshe Davidow, and Isabelle Codjovi, "Silent Voices: Why Some Dissatisfied Consumers Fail to Complain." *Journal of Service Research,* 7, no. 4 (2005): 328–342.

4. Stephen S. Tax and Stephen W. Brown "Recovering and Learning from Service Failure." *Sloan Management Review,* 49, no. 1 (Fall 1998): 75–88.

5. Technical Assistance Research Programs Institute (TARP), *Consumer Complaint Handling in America; An Update Study, Part II.* Washington, DC: TARP and U.S. Office of Consumer Affairs, April 1986; Nancy Stephens and Kevin P. Gwinner, "Why Don't Some People Complain? A Cognitive-Emotive Process Model of Consumer Complaining Behavior." *Journal of the Academy of Marketing Science,* 26, no. 3 (1998): 172–189.

6. Cathy Goodwin and B. J. Verhage, "Role Perceptions of Services: A Cross-Cultural Comparison with Behavioral Implications." *Journal of Economic Psychology,* 10 (1990): 543–558.

7. Nancy Stephens, "Complaining." In Teresa A. Swartz and Dawn Iacobucci, eds., *Handbook of Services Marketing and Management.* Thousand Oaks, CA: Sage Publications, 2000, p. 291.

8. John Goodman, "Basic Facts on Customer Complaint Behavior and the Impact of Service on the Bottom Line." *Competitive Advantage* (June 1999): 1–5.

9. Anna Mattila and Jochen Wirtz, "Consumer Complaining to Firms: The Determinants of Channel Choice." *Journal of Services Marketing,* 18, no 2 (2004): 147–155; Kaisa Snellman and Tiina Vihtkari, "Customer Complaining Behavior in Technology-based Service Encounters." *International Journal of Service Industry Management,* 14, no. 2 (2003): 217–231; Terri Shapiro and Jennifer Nieman-Gonder, "Effect of Communication Mode in Justice-Based Service Recovery." *Managing Service Quality,* 16, no. 2 (2006): 124–144. .

10. Kathleen Seiders and Leonard L Berry, "Service Fairness: What It Is and Why It Matters." *Academy of Management Executive,* 12, no. 2 (1990): 8–20.

11. Tax and Brown, "Recovering and Learning from Service Failure."

12. Stephen S. Tax and Stephen W. Brown, "Service Recovery: Research, Insight and Practice." In Swartz and Iacobucci, *Handbook of Services Marketing and Management,* p. 277; Tor Wallin Andreassen, "Antecedents of Service Recovery." *European Journal of Marketing,* 34, no. 1–2 (2000): 156–175; Ko de Ruyter and Martin Wetzel, "Customer Equity Considerations in Service Recovery." *International Journal of Service Industry Management,* 13, no. 1 (2002): 91–108; Janet R. McColl-Kennedy and Beverley A. Sparks, "Application of Fairness Theory to Service Failures and Service Recovery." *Journal of Service Research,* 5, no. 3 (2003): 251–266; Jochen Wirtz and Anna Mattila, "Consumer Responses to Compensation, Speed of Recovery and Apology After a Service Failure." *International Journal of Service Industry Management,* 15, no. 2 (2004): 150–166.

13. Oren Harari, "Thank Heavens for Complainers." *Management Review* (March 1997): 25–29.

14. Clyde A. Warden, Tsung-Chi Liu, Chi-Tsun Huang, and Chi-Hsun Lee, "Service Failures Away from Home: Benefits in Intercultural Service Encounters." *International Journal of Service Industry Management,* 14, no. 4 (2003): 436–457; Anna S. Mattila and Paul G.

Patterson, "Service Recovery and Fairness Perceptions in Collectivist and Individualist Contexts." *Journal of Service Research*, 6, no. 4 (2004): 336–346.

15. Simon J. Bell and James A. Luddington, "Coping with Customer Complaints." *Journal of Service Research*, 8, no. 3 (February 2006): 221–233.

16. Leonard L. Berry, *On Great Service: A Framework for Action*. New York: The Free Press, 1995, p. 94.

17. Susan M. Keaveney, "Customer Switching Behavior in Service Industries: An Exploratory Study." *Journal of Marketing*, 59 (April 1995): 71–82.

18. TARP, *Consumer Complaint Handling in America*.

19. Stefan Michel, "Analyzing Service Failures and Recoveries: A Process Approach." *International Journal of Service Industry Management*, 12, no. 1 (2001): 20–33; James G. Maxham III and Richard G. Netemeyer, "A Longitudinal Study of Complaining Customers' Evaluations of Multiple Service Failures and Recovery Efforts." *Journal of Marketing*, 66, no. 4 (2002): 57–72.

20. Tor Wallin Andreassen, "From Disgust to Delight: Do Customers Hold a Grudge?" *Journal of Service Research*, 4, no. 1 (2001): 39–49. Other studies also confirmed that the service recovery paradox does not hold universally; e.g., Michael A. McCollough, Leonard L. Berry, and Manjit S. Yadav, "An Empirical Investigation of Customer Satisfaction After Service Failure and Recovery." *Journal of Service Research*, 3, no. 2 (2000): 121–137; and James G. Maxhamm III, "Service Recovery's Influence on Consumer Satisfaction, Positive Word-of-Mouth, and Purchase Intentions." *Journal of Business Research*, 54 (2001): 11–24.

21. Michael Hargrove, cited in Ron Kaufman, *Up Your Service!* Singapore: Ron Kaufman Plc. Ltd., 2005, p. 225.

22. Tax and Brown, "Recovering and Learning from Service Failure"; Stephen S. Tax, Stephen W. Brown, and Murali Chandrashekaran, "Customer Evaluation of Service Complaint Experiences: Implications for Relationship Marketing." *Journal of Marketing*, 62, no. 2 (Spring 1998): 60–76; Betsy B. Holloway and Sharon E. Beatty, "Service Failure in Online Retailing: A Recovery Opportunity." *Journal of Service Research*, 6, no. 1 (2003): 92–105.

23. For how to quantify complaint management profitability, see Bernd Stauss and Andreas Schoeler, "Complaint Management Profitability: What do Complaint Managers Know?" *Managing Service Quality*, 14, no.2/3 (2004): 147–156; and for a comprehensive treatment of all aspects, see Bernd Stauss and Wolfgang Seidel, *Complaint Management: The Heart of CRM*. Mason, OH: Thomson, 2004.

24. Christian Homburg and Andreas Fürst, "How Organizatonal Complaint Handling Drives Customer Loyalty: An Analysis of the Mechanistic and the Organic Approach." *Journal of Marketing*, 69 (July 2005): 95–114.

25. Ron Zemke and Chip R. Bell, *Knock Your Socks Off Service Recovery*. New York: AMACOM, 2000, p. 60.

26. Barbara R. Lewis, "Customer Care in Services." In W. J. Glynn and J. G. Barnes, eds., *Understanding Services Management*. Chichester, UK: John Wiley & Sons, 1995, pp. 57–89. Prior rapport between employees and customers has also been shown to improve service recovery satisfaction; see Tom DeWitt and Michael K. Brady, "Rethinking Service Recovery Strategies: The Effect of Rapport on Customer Responses to Service Failure." *Journal of Service Research*, 6, no. 2 (2003): 193–207.

27. Estelami Hooman and Peter De Maeyer, "Customer Reactions to Service Provider Overgenerosity." *Journal of Service Research*, 4, no. 3 (2002): 205–217; Rhonda Mack, Rene Mueller, John Crotts, and Amanda Broderick, "Perceptions, Corrections and Defections: Implications for Service Recovery in the Restaurant Industry." *Managing Service Quality*, 10, no. 6 (2000): 339–346.

28. Christopher W. L. Hart, "The Power of Unconditional Service Guarantees." *Harvard Business Review*, 68 (July–August 1990): 54–62.

29. L. A. Tucci and J. Talaga, "Service Guarantees and Consumers' Evaluation of Services." *Journal of Services Marketing*, 11, no. 1 (1997): 10–18; Amy Ostrom and Dawn Iacobucci, "The Effect of Guarantees on Consumers' Evaluation of Services." *Journal of Services Marketing*, 12, no. 5 (1998): 362–378.

30. Sara Björlin Lidén and Per Skålén, "The Effect of Service Guarantees on Service Recovery." *International Journal of Service Industry Management*, 14, no. 1 (2003): 36–58.

31. Christopher W. Hart and Elizabeth Long, *Extraordinary Guarantees*. New York: AMACOM, 1997.

32. Hart, "The Power of Unconditional Service Guarantees."

33. For a scientific discussion on the optimal guarantee payout amount, see Tim Baker and David A. Collier, "The Economic Payout Model for Service Guarantees." *Decision Sciences* 36, no. 2 (2005): 197–220).

34. McDougall, Gordon H., Terence Levesque, and Peter VanderPlaat, "Designing the Service Guarantee: Unconditional or Specific?" *Journal of Services Marketing*, 12, no. 4 (1998): 278–293; Jochen Wirtz, "Development of a Service Guarantee Model." *Asia Pacific Journal of Management*, 15, no. 1 (1998): 51–75.

35. Jochen Wirtz and Doreen Kum, "Designing Service Guarantees—Is Full Satisfaction the Best You Can Guarantee?" *Journal of Services Marketing*, 15, no. 4 (2001): 282–299.

36. Amy L. Ostrom and Christopher Hart, "Service Guarantee: Research and Practice." In Schwartz and Iacobucci, *Handbook of Services Marketing and Management*, pp. 299–316; Jochen Wirtz, Doreen Kum, and Khai Sheang Lee, "Should a Firm with a Reputation for Outstanding Service Quality Offer a Service Guarantee?" *Journal of Services Marketing*, 14, no. 6 (2000): 502–512.

37. For a decision support model and whether to have a service guarantee, and if yes, on how to design and implement it, see Louis Fabien, "Design and Implementation of a Service Guarantee." *Journal of Services Marketing*, 19, no. 1 (2005): 33–38.

38. John Goodman, quoted in "Improving Service Doesn't Always Require Big Investment." *The Service Edge* (July–August, 1990): 3.

39. Jochen Wirtz and Doreen Kum, "Consumer Cheating on Service Guarantees." *Journal of the Academy of Marketing Science*, 32, no. 2 (2004): 159–175.

40. This section is based partly on Jochen Wirtz and Monica Tomlin, "Institutionalizing Customer-Driven Learning Through Fully Integrated Customer Feedback Systems." *Managing Service Quality,* 10, no. 4 (2000): 205–215.

41. Customer listening practices have been shown to affect service performance, growth, and profitability; see William J. Glynn, Sean de Burca, Teresa Brannick, Brian Fynes, and Sean Ennis, "Listening Practices and Performance in Service Organizations." *International Journal of Service Industry Management,* 14, no. 3 (2003): 310–330.

42. W. E. Baker and J. M. Sinkula, "The Synergistic Effect of Market Orientation and Learning Orientation on Organizational Performance." *Journal of the Academy of Marketing Science,* 27, no. 4 (1999): 411–427.

43. Neil A. Morgan, Eugene W. Anderson, and Vikas Mittal, "Understanding Firms' Customer Satisfaction Information Usage." *Journal of Marketing,* 69 (July 2005): 131–151.

44. Leonard L. Berry and A. Parasuraman, "Listening to the Customer—The Concept of a Service Quality Information System." *Sloan Management Review,* 48 (Spring 1997): 65–76.

45. Jochen Wirtz and Lee Meng Chung, "An Examination of the Quality and Context-Specific Applicability of Commonly Used Customer Satisfaction Measures." *Journal of Service Research,* 5 (May 2003): 345–355.

46. Robert Johnston and Sandy Mehra, "Best-Practice Complaint Management." *Academy of Management Executive,* 16, no. 4 (2002): 145–154.

47. Data for calculation of recovery costs in Application Exercise 6: Option 1 has no direct costs, merely extra time for the employees. Option 2: Add the material costs of the shrimp cocktail, typically about one-third of the $8–$10 cost charged in a good restaurant. Option 3: Add the extra costs of the free coffee or dessert—material costs only if the diner would not otherwise have ordered these items, but full costs (say, $6 and $3) if the diner would otherwise have ordered and paid for these items. What probability would you assign to these alternatives? Option 4: Costs are for Option 1 plus $80, because that is the revenue actually foregone. Option 5: As for Option 4, plus the costs of the bottle of champagne, which needs to be computed using the probabilities of incremental and substitutional consumption and their respective costs. Option 6: As for Option 5, plus the costs of the voucher. The latter cost depends on the probability of its actually being used and whether the customer is using the voucher to pay for a meal he would otherwise have had at this restaurant and paid for himself or whether this is an incremental meal.

Chapter 14

Improving Service Quality and Productivity

> *Not everything that counts can be counted, and not everything that can be counted, counts.*

ALBERT EINSTEIN

> *Our mission remains inviolable: Offer the customer the best service we can provide; cut our costs to the bones; and generate a surplus to continue the unending process of renewal.*

JOSEPH PILLAY, FORMER CHAIRMAN, SINGAPORE AIRLINES

*P*roductivity has been a managerial imperative since the 1970s. During the 1980s and early 1990s, improving quality became a priority. In a service context, this strategy entails creating better service processes and outcomes to improve customer satisfaction. At the beginning of the twenty-first century, we're seeing growing emphasis on linking these two strategies in order to create better value for both customers and the firm.

Both quality and productivity have historically been seen as issues for operations managers. When improvements in these areas required better employee selection, training and supervision—or renegotiation of labor agreements relating to job assignments and work rules—then human resource managers were also expected to get involved. It was not until service quality was linked explicitly to customer satisfaction that marketers, too, were seen as having an important role to play.

Broadly defined, the task of value enhancement requires quality improvement programs to deliver and continuously enhance the benefits desired by customers. At the same time, productivity improvement efforts must seek to reduce the associated costs. The challenge is to ensure that these two programs are mutually reinforcing in achieving common goals, rather than operating at loggerheads with each other in pursuit of conflicting goals.

In this chapter, we review the challenges involved in improving both productivity and quality, key ingredients of the 8 Ps, and explore the following questions:

1. What is meant by *quality* and *productivity* in a service context, and why should the two be linked when formulating marketing strategy?
2. How can the Gaps model be used to diagnose and address service quality problems?
3. What are the key tools for measuring and improving service productivity?
4. How do concepts such as TQM, ISO 9000, the Malcolm Baldrige Approach, and Six Sigma relate to managing and improving productivity and service quality?

INTEGRATING SERVICE QUALITY AND PRODUCTIVITY STRATEGIES

A key theme of this book is that, where services are concerned, marketing cannot operate in isolation from other functional areas. Tasks that might be considered the sole preserve of operations in a manufacturing environment must involve marketers, because customers are often exposed to—even actively involved in—service processes. Making service processes more efficient does not necessarily result in a better quality experience for customers, nor does it always lead to improved benefits for them. Likewise, getting service employees to work faster may sometimes be welcomed by customers, but at other times it may make them feel rushed and unwanted. Thus, marketing, operations, and human resource managers should collaborate to ensure that they can deliver quality experiences more efficiently. If you go to work in a service business, you may find yourself working in a cross-functional team to achieve such goals.

Similarly, implementing marketing strategies that are designed to improve customer satisfaction can prove costly and disruptive if the implications for operations and human resources have not been carefully thought through. The bottom line: Quality and productivity improvement strategies must be considered jointly rather than in isolation.

Service Quality, Productivity, and Marketing

Marketing's interest in service quality is obvious when one thinks about it: Poor quality places a firm at a competitive disadvantage, potentially driving away dissatisfied customers. Recent years have witnessed a veritable explosion of discontent with service quality at a time when the quality of many manufacturers have been improving. The 2005 American Customer Satisfaction Index (ACSI) aggregate results for manufactured products, private-sector services, and government services in the United States shows clearly that the service sector lags significantly behind manufacturing in terms of quality provided. Surprisingly, as shown in Figure 14.1, private-sector services had only marginally higher scores than federal government services. Claes Fornell concluded: "Citizens have generally low expectations of public sector services, much lower than their expectations with the private sector. The reason behind this is difficult to determine, but possibly emanates from American's general skepticism towards government."[1] These findings show that there is much scope for improving service quality for both private- and public-sector services.

Improving productivity is important to marketers for several reasons. First, it helps to keep costs down. Lower costs either mean higher profits or the ability to hold down prices. The company with the lowest costs in an industry has the option to position itself as the low-price leader—usually a significant advantage among price-sensitive market segments. Second, firms with lower costs also generate higher

Figure 14.1
Services Have Lower Quality than Manufactured Goods

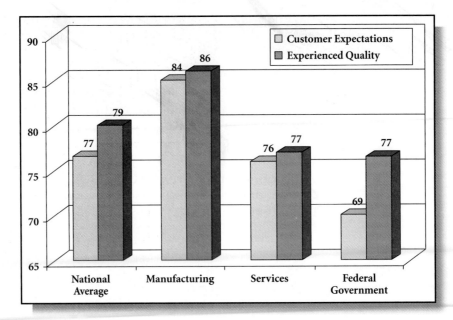

Source: Claes Fornell, "ACSI Commentary: Federal Government Scores," *Special Report: Government Satisfaction Scores,* Michigan: CFI Group, December 15, 2005, published on www.theacsi.com, accessed on 21 January 2006.

margins, giving them the option of spending more than the competition in marketing activities, improved customer service, and supplementary services. Such firms may also be able to offer higher margins to attract and reward the best distributors and intermediaries. Third is the opportunity to secure the firm's long-term future through investments in new service technologies and in research to create superior new services, improved features, and innovative delivery systems. Finally, efforts to improve productivity often affect customers. Marketers are responsible for ensuring that negative effects are avoided or minimized and that new procedures are carefully presented to customers. Positive effects can be promoted as a new advantage.

Historically, services lagged manufacturing in productivity growth, but research by the McKinsey Global Institute shows that five of the seven largest contributors to labor productivity growth in the United States since 2000 have been service industries, including retail and wholesale trade, finance and insurance, administrative support, and scientific and technical services.[2]

Quality and productivity are twin paths to creating value for both customers and companies. In broad terms, quality focuses on the benefits created for the customer's side of the equation and productivity addresses the financial costs incurred by the firm. Carefully integrating quality and productivity improvement programs will improve the long-term profitability of the firm.

WHAT IS SERVICE QUALITY?

What do we mean when we speak of service quality? Company personnel need a common understanding in order to be able to address issues such as the measurement of service quality, the identification of causes of service quality shortfalls, and the design and implement of corrective actions. As suggested humorously by the restaurant illustration in Figure 14.2, service quality can be difficult to manage, even when failures are tangible in nature.

Different Perspectives of Service Quality

The word *quality* means different things to people, according to the context. David Garvin identifies five perspectives on quality.[3]

Figure 14.2
Service Quality Is
Difficult to Manage

1. *The transcendent view* of quality is synonymous with innate excellence: a mark of uncompromising standards and high achievement. This viewpoint is often applied to the performing and visual arts. It argues that people learn to recognize quality only through the experience gained from repeated exposure. From a practical standpoint, however, suggesting that managers or customers will know quality when they see it is not very helpful.

2. *The product-based approach* sees quality as a precise and measurable variable. Differences in quality, it argues, reflect differences in the amount of an ingredient or attribute possessed by the product. Because this view is totally objective, it fails to account for differences in the tastes, needs, and preferences of individual customers (or even entire market segments).

3. *User-based definitions* start with the premise that quality lies in the eyes of the beholder. These definitions equate quality with maximum satisfaction. This subjective, demand-oriented perspective recognizes that different customers have different wants and needs.

4. *The manufacturing-based approach*, is supply-based, and is concerned primarily with engineering and manufacturing practices. (In services, we would say that quality is operations-driven.) It focuses on conformance to internally developed specifications, which are often driven by productivity and cost-containment goals.

5. *Value-based definitions* define quality in terms of value and price. By considering the trade-off between performance (or conformance) and price, quality comes to be defined as "affordable excellence."

Garvin suggests that these alternative views of quality help to explain the conflicts that sometimes arise between managers in different functional departments.

Manufacturing-Based Components of Quality

To incorporate the different perspectives, Garvin developed the following components of quality that may be useful as a framework for analysis and strategic planning: (1) performance (primary operating characteristics), (2) features (bells and whistles), (3) reliability (probability of malfunction or failure), (4) conformance (ability to meet specifications), (5) durability (how long the product continues to provide value to the customer), (6) serviceability (speed, courtesy, competence, and ease of having problems fixed), (7) esthetics (how the product appeals to any or all of the user's five senses), and (8) perceived quality (associations such as the reputation of the company or brand name). Note that these categories were developed from a manufacturing perspective, but they do address the notion of "serviceability" of a physical good.

Service-Based Components of Quality

Researchers argue that the nature of services requires a distinctive approach to defining and measuring service quality. The intangible, multifaceted nature of many services makes it harder to evaluate the quality of a service compared to a good. Because customers are often involved in service production, a distinction needs to be drawn between the *process* of service delivery (what Christian Grönroos calls functional quality) and the actual *output* (or outcome) of the service—what he calls technical quality.[4] Grönroos and others also suggest that the perceived quality of a service is the result of an evaluation process in which customers compare their perceptions of service delivery and its outcome to what they expect.

From focus group research, Valarie Zeithaml, Leonard Berry, and A. Parasuraman identified 10 criteria used by consumers in evaluating service quality (Table 14.1). In subsequent research, they found a high degree of correlation between several of these variables and so consolidated them into five broad dimensions:

- *Tangibles* (appearance of physical elements)
- *Reliability* (dependable, accurate performance)
- *Responsiveness* (promptness and helpfulness)
- *Assurance* (competence, courtesy, credibility, and security)
- *Empathy* (easy access, good communications, and customer understanding)[5]

Only one of these five dimensions, reliability, has a direct parallel to findings from Garvin's research on manufacturing quality.

Capturing the Customer's Perspective of Service Quality

To measure customer satisfaction with various aspects of service quality, Valarie Zeithaml and her colleagues developed a survey research instrument called SERVQUAL.[6] It's based on the premise that customers can evaluate a firm's service quality by comparing their perceptions of its service with their own expectations. SERVQUAL is seen as a generic measurement tool that can be applied across a broad spectrum of service industries. In its basic form, the scale contains 22 perception items and a series of expectation items, reflecting the five dimensions of service quality described earlier (Table 14.2). Respondents complete a series of scales that measure their expectations of companies in a particular industry on a wide array of specific service characteristics. Subsequently, they are asked to record their perceptions of a specific company whose services they have used. When perceived performance ratings are lower than expectations, this is a sign of poor quality. The reverse indicates good quality.

Limitations of SERVQUAL

Although SERVQUAL has been widely used by service companies, doubts have been expressed about both its conceptual foundation and methodological limitations.[7] For example, Anne Smith notes that the majority of researchers using SERVQUAL have omitted from, added to, or altered the list of statements purporting to measure service quality.[8] To evaluate the stability of the five underlying dimensions when applied to a variety of different service industries, Gerhard Mels, Christo Boshoff, and Denon Nel analyzed datasets from banks, insurance brokers, vehicle repair firms, electrical repair firms, and life insurance companies. Their findings suggest that, in reality, SERVQUAL scores measure only two factors: intrinsic service quality (resembling what Grönroos termed functional quality) and extrinsic service quality (which refers to the tangible aspects of service delivery and "resembles to some extent what Grönroos refers to as technical quality")[9].

These findings don't undermine the value of Zeithaml, Berry, and Parasuraman's achievement in identifying some of the key underlying constructs in service quality, but they do highlight the difficulty of measuring customer perceptions of quality, and the need to customize dimensions and measures to the research context.

Table 14.1
Generic Dimensions Customers Used by Customers to Evaluate Service Quality

DIMENSION	DEFINITION	EXAMPLES OF CUSTOMERS' QUESTIONS
Credibility	Trustworthiness, believability, honesty of the service provider	Does the hospital have a good reputation? Does my stockbroker refrain from pressuring me to buy? Does the repair firm guarantee its work?
Security	Freedom from danger, risk, or doubt	Is it safe for me to use the bank's ATMs at night? Is my credit card protected against unauthorized use? Can I be sure that my insurance policy provides complete coverage?
Access	Approachability and ease of contact	How easy is it for me to talk to a supervisor when I have a problem? Does the airline have a 24-hour toll-free phone number? Is the hotel conveniently located?
Communication	Listening to customers and keeping them informed in language they can understand	When I have a complaint, is the manager willing to listen to me? Does my doctor avoid using technical jargon? Does the electrician call when he or she is unable to keep a scheduled appointment?
Understanding the customer	Making the effort to know customers and their needs	Does someone in the hotel recognize me as a regular customer? Does my stockbroker try to determine my specific financial objectives? Is the moving company willing to accommodate my schedule?
Tangibles	Appearance of physical facilities, equipment, personnel, and communication materials	Are the hotel's facilities attractive? Is my accountant dressed appropriately? Is my bank statement easy to understand?
Reliability	Ability to perform the promised service dependably and accurately	Does my lawyer call me back when promised? Is my telephone bill free of errors? Is my TV repaired right the first time?
Responsiveness	Willingness to help customers and provide prompt service	When there's a problem, does the firm resolve it quickly? Is my stockbroker willing to answer my questions? Is the cable TV company willing to give me a specific time when the installer will show up?
Competence	Possession of the skills and knowledge required to perform the service	Can the bank teller process my transaction without fumbling around? Is my travel agent able to obtain the information I need when I call? Does the dentist appear to be competent?
Courtesy	Politeness, respect, consideration, and friendliness of contact personnel	Does the flight attendant have a pleasant demeanor? Are the telephone operators consistently polite when answering my calls? Does the plumber take off muddy shoes before stepping on my carpet?

Source: Adapted from Valarie A. Zeithaml, A. Parasuraman, and Leonard L. Berry, *Delivering Quality Service: Balancing Customer Perceptions and Expectations.* New York: The Free Press, 1990.

Table 14.2
The SERVQUAL Scale

The SERVQUAL scale includes five dimensions: tangibles, reliability, responsiveness, assurance, and empathy. Within each dimension, several items are measured on a 7-point scale, from *strongly agree* to *strongly disagree*, for a total of 21 items.

SERVQUAL Questions

Note: For actual survey respondents, instructions are also included, and each statement is accompanied by a seven-point scale ranging from "strongly agree = 7" to "strongly disagree = 1." Only the end points of the scale are labeled; there are no words above the numbers 2 through 6.

Tangibles
- Excellent banks (refer to cable TV companies, hospitals, or the appropriate service business throughout the questionnaire) will have modern-looking equipment.
- The physical facilities at excellent banks will be visually appealing.
- Employees at excellent banks will be neat in appearance.
- Materials (e.g., brochures or statements) associated with the service will be visually appealing in an excellent bank.

Reliability
- When excellent banks promise to do something by a certain time, they will do so.
- When customers have a problem, excellent banks will show a sincere interest in solving it.
- Excellent banks will perform the service right the first time.
- Excellent banks will provide their services at the time they promise to do so.
- Excellent banks will insist on error-free records.

Responsiveness
- Employees of excellent banks will tell customers exactly when service will be performed.
- Employees of excellent banks will give prompt service to customers.
- Employees of excellent banks will always be willing to help customers.
- Employees of excellent banks will never be too busy to respond to customer requests.

Assurance
- The behavior of employees of excellent banks will instill confidence in customers.
- Customers of excellent banks will feel safe in their transactions.
- Employees of excellent banks will be consistently courteous with customers.
- Employees of excellent banks will have the knowledge to answer customer questions.

Empathy
- Excellent banks will give customers individual attention.
- Excellent banks will have operating hours convenient to all their customers.
- Excellent banks will have employees who give customers personal attention.
- The employees of excellent banks will understand the specific needs of their customers.

Source: Adapted from A. Parasuraman, Valarie A. Zeithaml, and Leonard Berry, "SERVQUAL: A Multiple Item Scale for Measuring Consumer Perceptions of Service Quality." *Journal of Retailing,* 64 (1988): 12–40.

Measuring Service Quality in Online Environments

SERVQUAL was developed primarily in the context of face-to-face encounters. In the modern online environment, different service quality dimensions with new measurement items become relevant. To measure electronic service quality on web sites, Parasuraman, Zeithaml, and Malhotra created a 22-item scale called E-S-QUAL, reflecting the four key dimensions of *efficiency* (i.e., navigation is easy, transactions can be completed quickly, and the web site loads quickly), *system availability* (i.e., the site is always available, it launches right away, and it is stable and doesn't crash), *fulfillment* (i.e., orders are delivered as promised, and offerings are described truthfully), and *privacy* (i.e., information privacy is protected and personal information is not shared with other sites).[10] Research Insights 14.1, "New Thinking on Defining and Measuring E-Service Quality," offers the latest perspectives on this topic and addresses the challenge of integrating service quality measures across both virtual and physical channels.

"To managers of companies with a Web presence," say Joel Collier and Carol Bienstock, "an awareness of how customers perceive service quality is essential to understanding what [they] value in an online-service transaction." E-service quality involves more than just interactions with a web site, described as *process quality*, and extends to *outcome quality* and *recovery quality*. And each must be measured. The separation of customers from providers during online transactions highlights the importance of evaluating how well a firm handles customers' questions, concerns, and frustrations when problems arise.

- *Process Quality* Customers initially evaluate their experiences with an e-retailing web site against five process quality dimensions: *privacy, design, information, ease of use,* and *functionality*. This last construct refers to quick page loads, links that don't dead-end, payment options, accurate execution of customer commands, and ability to appeal to a universal audience (including the disabled and those who speak other languages).

- *Outcome Quality* Customers' evaluations of process quality have a significant effect on their evaluation of outcome quality, made up of *order timeliness, order accuracy,* and *order condition*.

- *Recovery Quality* In the event of a problem, customers evaluate the recovery process against *interactive fairness* (ability to locate and interact with technology support for a web site, including

telephone-based assistance), *procedural fairness* (policies, procedures, and responsiveness in the complaint process), and *outcome fairness*. How the company responds has a significant effect on the customer's satisfaction level and future intentions.

Multichannel Issues

Going one step further, Rui Sousa and Christopher Voss note that many services offer customers a choice of both virtual and physical delivery channels. Customers' evaluations of service quality are formed across all points of contact they have with the firm. In a multichannel setting, researchers must measure *physical quality, virtual quality,* and *integration quality*—the ability to provide customers with a seamless service experience across multiple channels. Achieving consistency across such interactions is particularly relevant when a firm adds new virtual channels, accompanied by specialist support systems that are often poorly integrated with existing systems. To avoid such fragmentation and achieve consistent service quality, Sousa and Voss call for explicit links between the firm's marketing and operations functions.

Source: Joel E. Collier and Carol C. Bienstock, "Measuring Service Quality in E-Retailing." *Journal of Service Research,* 8 (February 2006): 260–275; Rui Sousa and Christopher A. Voss, "Service Quality in Multichannel Services Employing Virtual Channels." *Journal of Service Research,* 8 (May 2006): 356–371.

Other Considerations in Service Quality Measurement

Comparing performance to expectations works well in reasonably competitive markets in which customers have sufficient knowledge to choose a service that meets their needs and wants. However, in uncompetitive markets or in situations in which customers do not have free choice (e.g., because switching costs would be prohibitive, or because of time or location constraints), there are risks to defining service quality primarily in terms of customers' satisfaction with outcomes relative to their prior expectations. If customers' expectations are low and actual service delivery proves to be marginally better than the dismal level that had been expected, we can hardly claim that customers are receiving good-quality service. In such situations, it is better to use needs or wants as comparison standards, and to define good service quality as meeting or exceeding customer wants and needs rather than expectations.[11]

Satisfaction-based research into quality assumes that customers are dealing with services that are high in search or experience characteristics (see Chapter 2). However, a problem arises when they're asked to evaluate the quality of services that are high in *credence* characteristics, such as complex legal cases or medical treatments, which they find difficult to evaluate even after delivery is completed. In short, customers may be unsure what to expect in advance and may not know for years—if ever—how good a job the professional actually did. A natural tendency in such situations is for clients or patients to use process factors and tangible cues as proxies to evaluate quality.

Process factors include customers' feelings about the personal style of individual providers and satisfaction levels with those supplementary elements they feel competent to evaluate (e.g., the tastiness of hospital meals or the clarity of bills for legal services). As a result, customers' perceptions of core service quality may be strongly influenced by their evaluation of process attributes and tangible elements of the service—a halo effect.[12] In order to obtain credible measures of professional performance quality, it may be necessary to include peer reviews of both process and outcomes as these relate to service execution on the core product.

THE GAPS MODEL—A CONCEPTUAL TOOL TO IDENTIFY AND CORRECT SERVICE QUALITY PROBLEMS

If one accepts the view that quality entails consistently meeting or exceeding customers' expectations, the manager's task is to balance customer expectations and perceptions and to close any gaps between the two.

Gaps in Service Design and Delivery

Zeithaml, Berry, and Parasuraman identify four potential gaps within the service organization that may lead to a fifth and most serious final gap—the difference between what customers expected and what they perceived was delivered.[13] Figure 14.3 extends and refines their framework to identify a total of seven types of gaps that can occur at different points during the design and delivery of a service performance. Let's look at each in turn.

1. The *knowledge gap* is the difference between what service providers believe customers expect and customers' actual needs and expectations.
2. The *standards gap* is the difference between management's perceptions of customer expectations and the quality standards established for service delivery.
3. The *delivery gap* is the difference between specified delivery standards and the service provider's actual performance on these standards.
4. The *internal communications gap* is the difference between what the company's advertising and sales personnel think are the product's features, performance, and service quality level and what the company is actually able to deliver.
5. The *perceptions gap* is the difference between what is, in fact, delivered and what customers perceive they received (because they are unable to evaluate service quality accurately).
6. The *interpretation gap* is the difference between what a service provider's communication efforts (in advance of service delivery) actually promise and what a customer thinks was promised by these communications.
7. The *service gap* is the difference between what customers expect to receive and their perceptions of the service that is actually delivered.

Gaps 1, 5, 6, and 7 represent external gaps between the customer and the organization. Gaps 2, 3, and 4 are internal gaps that occur between various functions and departments within the organization.

Gaps at any point in service design and delivery can damage relationships with customers. The service gap (no. 7) is the most critical; hence the ultimate goal in improving service quality is to close or narrow this gap as much as possible. However, to achieve this, service organizations usually need to work on closing the other six gaps depicted in Figure 14.3. Improving service quality requires identifying the specific causes of all the gaps and then developing strategies to close them.

Figure 14.3
Seven Service Quality
Gaps

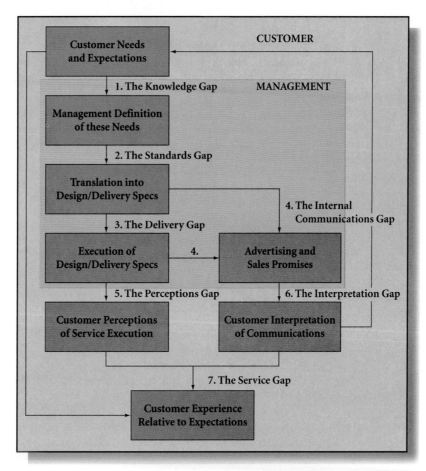

Source: The 7-gaps model by Christopher Lovelock, *Product Plus* (New York: McGraw-Hill, 1994: 112), with further refinement by Lauren Wright, adapts and expands the original 5-gaps model created by A. Parasuraman, Valarie A. Zeithaml, and Leonard L. Berry, "A Conceptual Model of Service Quality and Its Implications for Future Research," *Journal of Marketing* 49, Fall 1985, 41–50.

Core Strategies to Address Service Quality Gaps

The strength of the gap model is that it offers generic insights and solutions that can be applied across industries. We summarize a series of generic prescriptions for closing the seven quality gaps in Table 14.3. These prescriptions are a good starting point to think about how to close specific gaps in an organization. Of course, each firm must develop its own customized approach to ensure that service quality becomes and remains a key objective.

MEASURING AND IMPROVING SERVICE QUALITY

It is commonly said that what is not measured is not managed. Without measurement, you can't be sure whether service quality gaps exist, let alone what types of gaps, where they exist, and what potential corrective actions should be taken. And, of course, measurement is needed to determine whether goals for improvement are being met after changes have been implemented.

Table 14.3
Prescriptions for
Closing the Seven
Service Quality Gaps

Gap 1—The Knowledge Gap

Prescription: Learn What Customers Expect

- Sharpen market research procedures, including questionnaire and interview design, sampling, and field implementation, and repeat research studies periodically.
- Implement an effective customer feedback system that includes satisfaction research, complaint content analysis, and customer panels.
- Increase interactions between managers (middle and top management) and customers.
- Facilitate and encourage communication between front-line employees and management.

Gap 2—The Standards Gap

Prescription: Establish the Right Service Processes and Specify Standards

- Get the customer service processes right:
  - Use a rigorous, systematic, and customer-centric process for designing and redesigning customer service processes.
  - Standardize repetitive work tasks to ensure consistency and reliability by substituting hard technology for human contact and improving work methods (soft technology).
- Set, communicate, and reinforce measurable customer-oriented service standards for all work units:
  - Establish for each step in service delivery a set of clear service quality goals that are challenging, realistic, and explicitly designed to meet customer expectations.
  - Ensure that employees understand and accept goals, standards, and priorities.

Gap 3—The Delivery Gap

Prescription: Ensure That Performance Meets Standards

- Ensure that customer service teams are motivated and able to meet service standards:
  - Improve recruitment with a focus on employee–job fit; select employees for the abilities and skills needed to perform their job well.
  - Train employees on the technical and soft skills needed to perform their assigned tasks effectively, including interpersonal skills, especially for dealing with customers under stressful conditions.
  - Clarify employee roles and ensure that employees understand how their jobs contribute to customer satisfaction; teach them about customer expectations, perceptions, and problems.
  - Build cross-functional service teams that can offer customer-centric service delivery and problem resolution.
  - Empower managers and employees in the field by pushing decision-making power down the organization.
  - Measure performance, provide regular feedback, and reward customer service team performance as well as individual employees and managers for attaining quality goals.
- Install the right technology, equipment, support processes, and capacity:
  - Select the most appropriate technology and equipment for enhanced performance.
  - Ensure that employees working on internal support jobs provide good service to their own internal customers, the front-line personnel.
  - Balance demand against productive capacity.
- Manage customers for service quality:
  - Educate customers so that they can perform their roles and responsibilities in service delivery effectively.

Soft and Hard Service Quality Measures

Customer-defined standards and measures of service quality can be grouped into two broad categories: soft and hard. *Soft measures* cannot easily be observed and must be collected by talking to customers, employees, or others. As noted by Valarie Zeithaml and Mary Jo Bitner, "Soft standards provide direction, guidance and feedback to employees on ways to achieve customer satisfaction and can be quantified by measuring customer perceptions and beliefs."[14] SERVQUAL is an example of a soft measurement system.

Hard measures, in contrast, are characteristics and activities that can be counted, timed, or measured through audits. Such measures might include how many telephone calls were abandoned while the customer was on hold, how many minutes customers had to wait in line at a particular stage in the service delivery, the time required to complete a specific task, the temperature of a particular food item, how many trains arrived late, how many bags were lost, how many patients made a complete recovery

- Educate, control, or terminate jaycustomers who negatively affect other customers, employees, service processes, or facilities.

Gap 4—The Internal Communications Gap

Prescription: Ensure That Communications Promises Are Realistic

- Educate managers responsible for sales and marketing communications about operational capabilities:
  - Seek inputs from front-line employees and operations personnel when new communications programs are being developed.
  - Let service providers preview advertisements and other communications before customers are exposed to them.
  - Get sales staff to involve operations staff in face-to-face meetings with customers.
  - Develop internal educational and motivational advertising campaigns to strengthen understanding and integration among the marketing, operations, and human resource functions, and to standardize service delivery across different locations.
- Ensure that communications content sets realistic customer expectations.

Gap 5—The Perceptions Gap

Prescription: Tangibilize and Communicate the Service Quality Delivered

- Develop service environments and physical evidence cues that are consistent with the level of service provided.
- For complex and credence services, keep customers informed during service delivery on what is being done, and give debriefings after the delivery so that customers can appreciate the quality of service they received.
- Provide physical evidence (e.g., for repairs, show customers the damaged components that were removed).

Gap 6—The Interpretation Gap

Prescription: Be Specific with Promises and Manage Customers' Understanding of Communication Content

- Pretest all advertising, brochures, telephone scripts, and web site content prior to external release, to determine if the target audience interprets them as the firm intends (if not, revise and retest):
  - Ensure that advertising content accurately reflects those service characteristics that are most important to customers.
  - Let customers know what is and is not possible—and the reasons why.
- Offer customers different levels of service at different prices, explaining the distinctions.
- Identify and explain in real time the reasons for shortcomings in service performance, highlighting those that cannot be controlled by the firm.
- Document precisely:
  - Upfront, what tasks and performance guarantees are included in an agreement or contract.
  - Afterward, what work was performed in relation to a specific billing statement.

Gap 7—The Service Gap

Prescription: Close Gaps 1 to 6 to Meet Customer Expectations Consistently

- Gap 7 is the accumulated outcome of all preceding open gaps. It will be closed when Gaps 1 through 6 have been addressed.

Source: Prescriptions for Gaps 1 through 4 were distilled from Valarie A Zeithaml, A. Parasuraman, and Leonard L. Berry, *Delivering Service Quality: Balancing Customer Perceptions and Expectations.* New York: The Free Press, 1990, chaps. 4–7; and Valarie A. Zeithaml, Mary Jo Bitner, and Dwayne Gremler, *Services Marketing: Integrating Customer Focus Across the Firm,* 4th ed. New York: McGraw-Hill, 2006, chap. 2. The remaining prescriptions were developed by the authors.

following a specific type of operation, and how many orders were filled correctly. Standards are often set with reference to the percentage of occasions on which a particular measure is achieved. The challenge for service marketers is to ensure that operational measures of service quality reflect customer input.

Organizations that are known for excellent service make use of both soft and hard measures. These organizations are good at listening to both their customers and their customer contact employees. The larger the organization, the more important it is to create formalized feedback programs using a variety of professionally designed and implemented research procedures.

Soft Measures of Service Quality

How can companies measure their performance against soft standards of service quality? According to Leonard Berry and A. Parasuraman:

> [C]ompanies need to establish ongoing listening systems using multiple methods among different customer groups. A single service quality study is a snapshot taken at a point in time and from a particular angle. Deeper insight and more informed decision making come from a continuing series of snapshots taken from various angles and through different lenses, which form the essence of systematic listening.[15]

Berry and Parasuraman recommend that ongoing research be conducted through a portfolio of research approaches. Key customer-centric service quality measures include total market surveys, annual surveys, transactional surveys, service feedback cards, mystery shopping, analysis of unsolicited feedback, focus group discussions, and service reviews (which we discussed in Chapter 12). Other soft measures include *customer advisory panels* to offer feedback and advice on service performance; and *employee surveys and panels* to determine perceptions of the quality of service delivered to customers on specific dimensions, barriers to better service, and suggestions for improvement.

Designing and implementing a large-scale customer survey to measure service across a wide array of attributes is no simple task. Line managers sometimes view the findings as threatening when direct comparisons are made of the performance of different departments or branches.

Hard Measures of Service Quality

Hard measures typically refer to operational processes or outcomes and include such data as uptime, service response times, failure rates, and delivery costs. In a complex service operation, multiple measures of service quality will be recorded at many different points. In low-contact services, in which customers are not deeply involved in the service delivery process, many operational measures apply to backstage activities that have only a second-order effect on customers.

FedEx was one of the first service companies to understand the need for a firm-wide index of service quality that embraced all the key activities that affect customers. By publishing a single, composite index on a frequent basis, senior managers hoped that all FedEx employees would work toward improving quality. The firm recognized the danger of using percentages as targets, because they might lead to complacency. In an organization as large as FedEx, which ships millions of packages a day, even delivering 99 percent of packages on time or having 99.9 percent of flights arrive safely would lead to horrendous problems. Instead, the company decided to approach quality measurement from the baseline of zero failures. As noted by one senior executive:

> It's only when you examine the types of failures, the number that occur of each type, and the reasons why, that you begin to improve the quality of your service. For us the trick was to express quality failures in absolute numbers. That led us to develop the Service Quality Index or SQI [pronounced "sky"], which takes each of 12 different events that occur every day, takes the numbers of those events and multiplies them by a weight . . . based on the amount of aggravation caused to customers—as evidenced by their tendency to write to Federal Express and complain about them.[16]

This design of this "hard" index reflected the findings of extensive "soft" customer research. Looking at service failures from the customer's perspective, the SQI measures daily the occurrence of 12 different activities that are likely to lead to customer dissatisfaction. The index is compiled by taking the raw number of each event and multiplying it by a weighting—which highlights the seriousness of that event for customers—to give a point score for each item. The points are then used to generate that day's index (Table 14.4). Like a golf score, the lower the index, the better the

Table 14.4
Composition of FedEx's Service Quality Index (SQI)

FAILURE TYPE	WEIGHTING FACTOR × NO. OF INCIDENTS = DAILY POINTS		
Late delivery—right day	1		
Late delivery—wrong day	5		
Tracing requests unanswered	1		
Complaints reopened	5		
Missing proofs of delivery	1		
Invoice adjustments	1		
Missed pickups	10		
Lost packages	10		
Damaged packages	10		
Aircraft delays (minutes)	5		
Overgoods (packages missing labels)	5		
Abandoned calls	1		
Total failure points (SQI)	XXX,XXX		

Source: Christopher Lovelock, *Product Plus.* New York: McGraw-Hill, 1994, p. 131.

performance. However, unlike golf, the SQI involves substantial numbers—typically six figures—reflecting the huge number of packages shipped daily. An annual goal is set for the average daily SQI, based on reducing the occurrence of failures over the previous year's total. To ensure a continuing focus on each separate component of the SQI, FedEx established 12 Quality Action Teams, one for each component. The teams were charged with understanding and correcting the root causes underlying the observed problems. In the light of new research insights, the SQI components and their weights have been modified slightly over time from the version shown here.

Control charts offer a simple method of displaying performance on hard measures over time against specific quality standards. The charts can be used to monitor and communicate individual variables or an overall index. Because they are visual, trends are easily identified. Figure 14.4 shows an airline's performance on the important hard standard of on-time departures. The trends displayed suggest that this issue needs to be addressed by management, because performance is erratic and not very satisfactory. Of course, control charts are only as good as the data on which they are based.

Tools to Analyze and Address Service Quality Problems

When a problem is caused by controllable, internal forces, there's no excuse for allowing it to recur. In fact, maintaining customers' goodwill after a service failure

Figure 14.4
Control Chart for Departure Delays Showing Percentage of Flights Departing Within 15 Minutes of Schedule

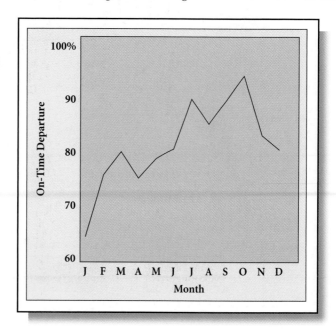

depends on keeping promises made to the effect that "we're taking steps to ensure that it doesn't happen again." With prevention as a goal, let's look briefly at some tools for determining the root causes of specific service quality problems.

Root-Cause Analysis: The Fishbone Diagram

Cause-and-effect analysis employs a technique first developed by the Japanese quality expert, Kaoru Ishikawa. Groups of managers and staff brainstorm all the possible reasons that might cause a specific problem. The resulting factors are then categorized into one of five groupings—equipment, manpower (or people), material, procedures, and other—on a cause-and-effect chart, popularly known as a *fishbone diagram* because of its shape. This technique has been used for many years in manufacturing and, more recently, also in services.

To sharpen the value of the analysis for use in service organizations, we show an extended framework that comprises eight rather than five groupings.[17] "People" has been broken down into front-stage personnel and backstage personnel, to highlight the fact that front-stage service problems are often experienced directly by customers, whereas backstage failures tend to show up more obliquely, through a ripple effect. "Information" has been split out from "Procedures," recognizing that many service problems result from information failures, often failures by front-stage personnel to tell customers what to do and when. In manufacturing, customers have little effect on day-to-day operational processes, but in a high-contact service they are involved in front-stage operations. If they don't play their own roles correctly, they may reduce service productivity and cause quality problems for themselves and other customers. For instance, an aircraft can be delayed if a passenger tries to board at the last minute with an oversized suitcase that then has to be loaded into the cargo hold. An example of the extended fishbone is shown in Figure 14.5, displaying 27 possible reasons for late departures of passenger aircraft.[18]

Figure 14.5 Cause-and-Effect Chart for Flight Departure Delays

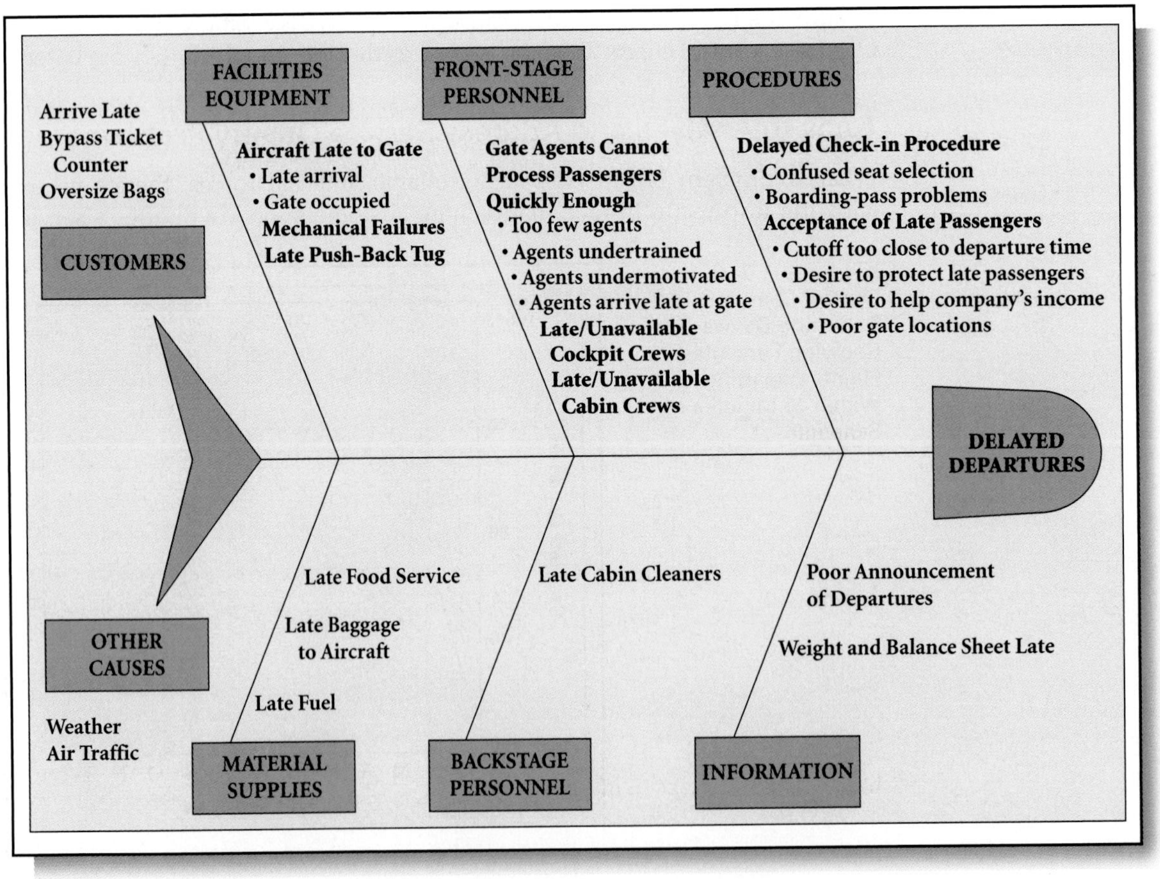

Once all the main potential causes for flight delays have been identified, it's necessary to assess how much impact each cause has on actual delays.

Pareto analysis (named after the Italian economist who first developed it) seeks to identify the principal causes of observed outcomes. This type of analysis underlies the so-called 80/20 rule, because it often reveals that around 80 percent of the value of one variable (in this instance, the number of service failures) is accounted for by only 20 percent of the causal variable (i.e., the number of possible causes).

In the airline example, analysis showed that 88 percent of the company's late-departing flights from the airports it served were caused by only four (15 percent) of all the possible factors. In fact, more than half the delays were caused by a single factor: acceptance of late passengers (when the staff held a flight for one more passenger who was checking in after the official cutoff time).

On such occasions, the airline made a friend of that late passenger—possibly encouraging a repeat of this undesirable action on a future occasion—but risked alienating all the other passengers who were already onboard, waiting for the aircraft to depart. Other major causes of delays included waiting for pushback (a special vehicle must push the aircraft away from the gate), waiting for fueling, and delays in signing the weight and balance sheet (a safety requirement relating to the distribution of the aircraft's load, which the captain must record for each flight). Further analysis, however, showed some significant variations in reasons from one airport to another (see Figure 14.6).

Combining the Fishbone diagram and Pareto analysis serves to highlight the main causes of service failure.

Blueprinting—A Powerful Tool for Identifying Fail Points
As described in Chapter 8, a well-constructed blueprint enables us to visualize the process of service delivery by depicting the sequence of front-stage interactions that customers experience as they encounter service providers, facilities, and equipment,

Figure 14.6
Analysis of Causes of
Flight Departure Delays

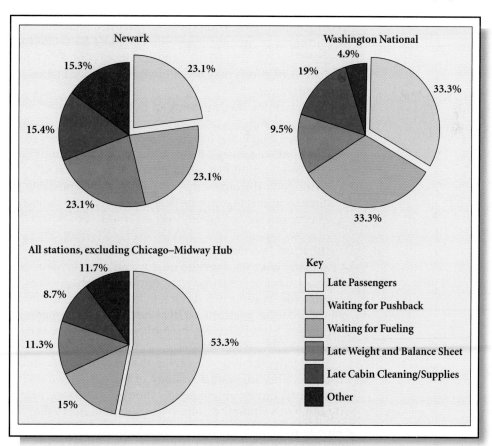

Source: Based on D. Daryl Wyckoff, "New Tools for Achieving Service Quality," *Cornell Hotel and Restaurant Administration Quarterly* 42 (August–September 2001), 25–38.

together with supporting backstage activities, which are hidden from the customers and are not part of their service experience.

Blueprints can be used to identify potential *fail points,* at which failures are most likely to occur. Blueprints help us to understand how failures at one point (such as incorrect entry of an appointment date) may have a ripple effect later in the process (the customer arrives at the doctor's office and is told that the doctor is unavailable). Using frequency counts, managers can identify the specific types of failures that occur most frequently and thus need urgent attention. One desirable solution is to design fail points out of the system (see Chapter 8, p. 242, for a discussion of the poka-yoke technique on how to approach this). In the case of failures that cannot easily be designed out of a process or are not easily prevented (such as problems related to weather or the public infrastructure), solutions may revolve around development of contingency plans and service recovery guidelines. Knowing what can go wrong and where is an important first step in preventing service quality problems.

Return on Quality

Despite the attention paid to improving service quality, some companies have been disappointed by the results. Even firms that have been recognized for service quality efforts have sometimes run into financial difficulties, in part because they spent too lavishly on quality improvements. In other instances, such outcomes reflect poor or incomplete execution of the quality program itself.

Assess Costs and Benefits of Quality Initiatives

Roland Rust, Anthony Zahonik, and Timothy Keiningham argue for a "return on quality" (ROQ) approach, based on the assumptions that (1) quality is an investment, (2) quality efforts must be financially accountable, (3) it is possible to spend too much on quality, and (4) not all quality expenditures are equally valid.[19] Hence expenditures on quality improvement must be related to anticipated increases in profitability. An important implication of the ROQ perspective is that quality improvement efforts may benefit from being coordinated with productivity improvement programs.

To determine the feasibility of new quality improvement efforts, they must be carefully costed in advance and then related to anticipated customer response. Will the program enable the firm to attract more customers (e.g., through word of mouth from current customers), increase share-of-wallet, and/or reduce defections? And if so, how much additional net income will be generated?

With good documentation, it is sometimes possible for a firm that operates in multiple locations to examine past experience and determine whether a relationship exists between service quality and revenues. (See Research Insights 14.2).

Determine the Optimal Level of Reliability

A company with poor service quality can often achieve big jumps in reliability with relatively modest investments in improvements. As illustrated in Figure 14.7, initial investments in reducing service failure often bring dramatic results, but at some point diminishing returns set in as further improvements require increasing levels of investment, even becoming prohibitively expensive. What level of reliability should we target?

Typically, the cost of service recovery is lower than the cost of an unhappy customer. This suggests a strategy of increasing reliability up to the point that the incremental improvement equals the cost of service recovery or the cost of failure. Although this strategy results in a service that is less than 100 percent failure-free, the firm can still aim to satisfy 100 percent of its target customers by ensuring that either they receive the service as planned or, if a failure occurs, they obtain a satisfying service recovery (see Chapter 13).

To determine the relationship between product quality and financial performance in a hotel context, Sheryl Kimes analyzed three years of quality and operational performance data from 1,135 franchised Holiday Inn hotels in the United States and Canada.

Indicators of product quality came from the franchisor's quality assurance reports. These reports were based on unannounced, semiannual inspections by trained quality auditors who were rotated among different regions and who spent most of a day inspecting and rating 19 different areas of each hotel. Twelve of these areas were included in the study: two relating to the guest rooms (bedroom and bathroom) and 10 relating to so-called commercial areas (e.g., exterior, lobby, public restrooms, dining facilities, lounge facilities, corridors, meeting areas, recreation areas, kitchen, back of house). Each area typically included 10 to 12 individual items that could be passed or failed. The inspector noted the number of defects for each area and the total number for the entire hotel.

Holiday Inn Worldwide also provided data on revenue per available room (RevPAR) at each hotel. To adjust for differences in local conditions, Kimes analyzed sales and revenue statistics obtained from thousands of U.S. and Canadian hotels and reported in the monthly Smith Travel Accommodation Reports (a widely used service in the travel industry). These data enabled Kimes to calculate the RevPAR for the immediate mid-scale competitors of each Holiday Inn hotel.

The resulting information was then used to normalize the RevPARs for all Holiday Inns in the sample so that they were now truly comparable. The average daily room rate at the time was about $50.

The analysis was conducted using six-month intervals over a three year period. For the purposes of the research, if a hotel had failed at least one item in an area, it was considered "defective" in that area. A comparison was then made, on an area-by-area basis, of the average normalized RevPAR for hotels that were defective in an area against those that were "nondefective."

The findings showed that as the number of defects in a hotel increased, the RevPAR decreased. Hotel areas that had a particularly strong effect on RevPAR were the exterior, the guest rooms, and the guest bathrooms. Even a single deficiency resulted in a statistically significant reduction in RevPAR, but the combination of deficiencies in all three areas showed an even larger effect on RevPAR over time. Kimes calculated that the average annual revenue impact on a defective hotel was $204,400.

Using a return-on-quality perspective, the implication was that the primary focus of increased expenditures on housekeeping and preventive maintenance should be the hotel exterior, the guest bedrooms, and guest bathrooms.

Source: Adapted from Sheryl E. Kimes, "The Relationship Between Product Quality and Revenue per Available Room at Holiday Inn." *Journal of Service Research*, 2 (November 1999): 138–144.

DEFINING AND MEASURING PRODUCTIVITY

Simply defined, productivity measures the amount of output produced relative to the amount of inputs used. Hence, improvements in productivity require an increase in the ratio of outputs to inputs. An improvement in this ratio might be achieved by cutting the resources required to create a given volume of output or by increasing the output obtained from a given level of inputs.

Defining Productivity in a Service Context

What do we mean by "input" in a service context? Input varies according to the nature of the business, but may include labor (both physical and intellectual), materials, energy, and capital (consisting of land, buildings, equipment, information systems, and financial assets). The intangible nature of service performances makes it more difficult to measure the productivity of service industries than that of manufacturing. The problem is especially acute for information-based services.

Measuring productivity is difficult in services for which the output is difficult to define. In a people processing service, such as a hospital, we can look at the number

Figure 14.7   When Does Improving Service Reliability Become Uneconomical?

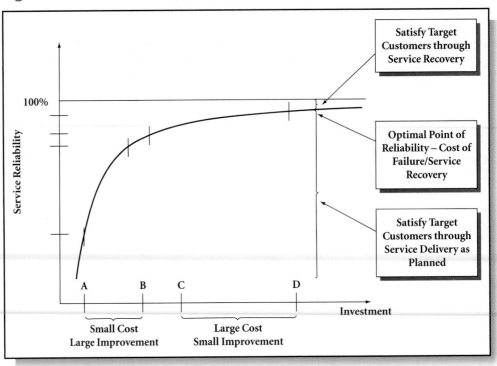

of patients treated in the course of a year and at the hospital's "census" or average bed occupancy. But how do we account for the various types of interventions performed, such as removal of cancerous tumors, treatment of diabetes, or setting of broken bones? What about differences between patients? How do we evaluate the inevitable differences in outcomes? Some patients get better, some develop complications, and sadly, some even die. Relatively few standard medical procedures offer highly predictable outcomes.

The measurement task is perhaps simpler in possession processing services, because many are quasi-manufacturing organizations, performing routine tasks with easily measurable inputs and outputs. Examples include garages that change a car's oil and rotate its tires and fast-food restaurants that offer limited and simple menus. However, the task gets more complicated when the garage mechanic has to find and repair a water leak, or when we are dealing with a French restaurant known for its varied and exceptional cuisine. What about information-based services? How should we define the output of a bank or a consulting firm? And how does the latter's output compare to that of a law firm?

Service Efficiency, Productivity, and Effectiveness

We need to distinguish among efficiency, productivity, and effectiveness.[20] *Efficiency* involves comparison to a standard, which is usually time-based—such as how long it takes for an employee to perform a particular task relative to a predefined standard. *Productivity*, however, involves financial valuation of outputs to inputs. *Effectiveness*, by contrast, can be defined as the degree to which an organization is meeting its goals.

A major problem in measuring service productivity concerns variability. As James Heskett points out, traditional measures of service output tend to ignore variations in the quality or value of service. In freight transport, for instance, a ton-mile of output for freight that is delivered late is treated the same for productivity purposes as a similar shipment delivered on time.[21]

Another approach—counting the number of customers served per unit of time—suffers from the same shortcoming. What happens when an increase in customer throughput is achieved at the expense of perceived service quality? Suppose a hairdresser serves three customers per hour and finds she can increase her output to one every 15 minutes by using a faster but noisier hairdryer, reducing conversation with the customer, and rushing her customers. Even if the haircut itself is just as good, the delivery process may be perceived as functionally inferior, leading customers to rate the overall service experience less positively.

Classical techniques of productivity measurement focus on outputs rather than *outcomes*, stressing efficiency but neglecting effectiveness. In the long run, organizations that are more effective in consistently delivering outcomes desired by customers should be able to command higher prices for their output. The need to emphasize effectiveness and outcomes suggests that issues of productivity cannot be divorced from those of quality and value. Loyal customers who remain with a firm tend to become more profitable over time, an indication of the payback to be obtained from providing quality service.

IMPROVING SERVICE PRODUCTIVITY

Intensive competition in many service sectors pushes firms to continually seek ways to improve their productivity.[22] This section discusses various potential approaches to and sources of productivity gains.

Generic Productivity Improvement Strategies

The task of improving service productivity has traditionally been assigned to operations managers, whose approach has typically centered on such actions as

- Careful control of costs at every step in the process
- Efforts to reduce wasteful use of materials or labor
- Matching productive capacity to average levels of demand rather than peak levels, so that workers and equipment are not underemployed for extended periods
- Replacing workers by automated machines
- Providing employees with equipment and databases that enable them to work faster and/or to a higher level of quality
- Teaching employees how to work more productively (faster is not necessarily better if it leads to mistakes or unsatisfactory work that has to be redone)
- Broadening the array of tasks that a service worker can perform (which may require revised labor agreements) eliminates bottlenecks and wasteful downtime by allowing managers to deploy workers wherever they are most needed
- Installing expert systems that allow paraprofessionals to take on work previously performed by professionals who earn higher salaries

Although improving productivity can be approached incrementally, major gains often require redesigning entire processes. For example, it's time for service process redesign when customers face unbearably long waiting times, as happens all too often in health care (Figure 14.8). We discussed service process redesign in depth in Chapter 8.

Customer-Driven Approaches to Improve Productivity

In situations in which customers are deeply involved in the service production process (typically, people processing services), operations managers should be examining how customer inputs can be made more productive. Marketing managers should be thinking about what marketing strategies should be used to influence

Figure 14.8
Long Waiting Times
Often Indicate a Need
for Service Process
Redesign

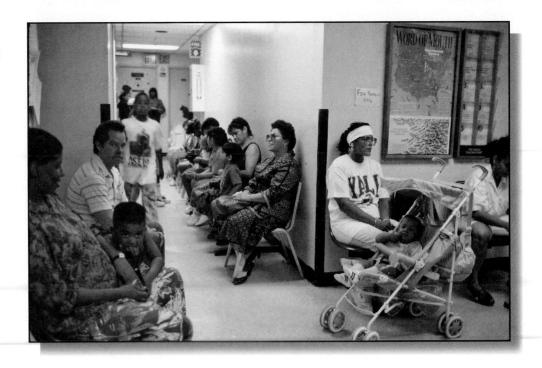

customers to behave in more productive ways. We review three strategies: changing the timing of customer demand, involving customers more actively in the production process, and asking customers to use third parties.

Changing the Timing of Customer Demand

Managing demand in capacity-constrained service businesses has been a recurring theme in this book (see especially Chapters 6 and 9). Customers often complain that the services they use are crowded and congested, reflecting time-of-day, seasonal, or other cyclical peaks in demand. During the off-peak periods in those same cycles, managers often worry that there are too few customers and that their facilities and staff are not fully productive. By encouraging customers to use a service outside peak periods and even offering them incentives to do so, managers can make better use of their firm's productive assets and provide better service. Offering access through alternative channels, such as the Internet and voice or text telephone, can facilitate demand management by reducing the pressure on employees and certain types of physical facilities at peak hours.

Involve Customers More in Production

Customers who assume a more active role in the service production and delivery process can take over some labor tasks from the service organization. Benefits for both parties may result when customers perform self-service.

Many technological innovations are designed to get customers to perform tasks previously undertaken by service employees (e.g., see Figure 14.9). The Internet has become a vital tool in productivity improvement. Increasing numbers of customers are using the Web (instead of telephoning or visiting a firm in person) to perform an array of self-service tasks that might previously have required employee assistance. Text messaging, too, is now substituting for some personal interactions.

Even five-star hotels with traditionally high levels of personal service have been asking their guests to do more of the work. For example, in-room safe deposit boxes and voice-mail systems in guestroom telephones have been implemented in most hotels. In the past, these services were provided by a service counter or concierge. However, despite the reduction in personal service, this innovation has

Figure 14.9 Self-Service Pumps with Credit Card Readers Have Increased Gas Station Productivity

been positioned as a benefit that is actually more convenient for guests. They can have fast and easy access to their in-room safe deposit boxes, and can easily see from a blinking light on the phone whether there is a voice mail waiting for them, rather than having to contact the operator.

Some customers may be more willing than others to serve themselves. In fact, research suggests that this predisposition may be a useful segmentation variable. A large-scale study presented respondents with the choice of a do-it-yourself option versus traditional delivery systems at gas stations, banks, restaurants, hotels, airports, and travel services.[23] For each service, a particular scenario was outlined, because earlier interviews had determined that decisions to choose self-service options are likely to be situation-specific. Analysis showed some overlap of preferences for self-service (or for being served) across the different services.

Quality and productivity improvements often depend on customers' willingness to learn new procedures, follow instructions, and interact cooperatively with employees and other people. Customers who arrive at the service encounter with a set of preexisting norms, values, and role definitions may resist change. Cathy Goodwin suggests that insights from research on socialization can help service marketers redesign the nature of the service encounter in ways that increase the chances of gaining customer cooperation.[24] In particular, she argues that customers will need help to learn new skills, form a new self-image ("I can do it myself"), develop new relationships with providers and fellow customers, and acquire new values.

Ask Customers to Use Third Parties

In some instances, managers may be able to improve service productivity by delegating one or more marketing support functions to third parties. The purchase process often breaks down into four components: information, reservation, payment, and consumption. When consumption of the core product takes place at a location not easily accessible from customers' homes or workplaces (e.g., an airport, theater, stadium, or a hotel in a distant city), it makes sense to delegate delivery of supplementary service elements to intermediary organizations.

Specialist intermediaries may enjoy economies of scale, enabling them to perform the task more cheaply than the core service provider, allowing the latter to focus on quality and productivity in its own area of expertise. Some intermediaries are identifiable local organizations, such as insurance brokers or travel agencies, which customers can visit in person. Others, such as call centers, often subjugate their own identity to that of the client service company.

How Productivity Improvements Affect Quality and Value

Managers would do well to examine productivity from the broader perspective of the business processes used to transform resource inputs into the outcomes desired by customers—processes that not only cross departmental and sometimes geographic boundaries, but also link the backstage and front-stage areas of the service operation.

How Backstage Changes May Affect Customers

The marketing implications of backstage changes depend on whether they affect or are noticed by customers. If airline mechanics develop a procedure for servicing jet engines more quickly, without incurring increased wage rates or material costs, the airline has obtained a productivity improvement that has no effect on the customer's service experience.

Other backstage changes, however, may have a ripple effect that extends front-stage and affects customers. Marketers should keep abreast of proposed backstage changes, not only to identify such ripples but also to prepare customers for them. At a bank, for instance, the decision to install new computers and printer peripherals may be driven by plans to improve internal quality controls and reduce the cost of preparing monthly statements. However, this new equipment may change the appearance of bank statements and the time of the month when they are posted. If customers are likely to notice such changes, an explanation may be warranted. If the new statements are easier to read and understand, the change may be worth promoting as a service enhancement.

Front-Stage Efforts to Improve Productivity

In high-contact services, many productivity enhancements are quite visible. Some changes simply require passive acceptance by customers; others require customers to adopt new patterns of behavior in their dealings with the organization. If substantial changes are proposed, then it makes sense to conduct market research first to determine how customers may respond. Failure to think through effects on customers may result in a loss of business and cancel out anticipated productivity gains. Service Perspective 14.1 identifies ways of addressing customer resistance to change, particularly when the innovation is a radical one. Once the nature of the changes has been decided, marketing communication can help prepare customers for the change, explaining the rationale, the benefits, and what customers will need to do differently in the future.

A Caution on Cost-Reduction Strategies

In the absence of new technology, most attempts to improve service productivity tend to center on efforts to eliminate waste and reduce labor costs. Cutbacks in front-stage staffing mean either that the remaining employees have to work harder and faster, or that there are insufficient personnel to serve customers promptly at busy times. Although employees may be able to work faster for a brief period of time, few can maintain a rapid pace for extended periods: They become

Customer resistance to changes in familiar environments and long-established behavior patterns can thwart attempts to improve productivity and even quality. Failure to examine proposed changes from the customer's perspective my spur resistance. The following six steps can help smooth the path of change.

1. *Develop Customer Trust.* It's more difficult to introduce productivity-related changes when people are basically distrustful of the initiator, as they often are in the case of large, seemingly impersonal institutions. Customers' willingness to accept change may be closely related to the degree of goodwill they bear toward the organization.

2. *Understand Customers' Habits and Expectations.* People often get into a routine in using a particular service, with certain steps being taken in a specific sequence. In effect, they have their own individual flowchart in mind. Innovations that disrupt ingrained routines are likely to face resistance unless consumers are carefully briefed as to what changes to expect.

3. *Pretest New Procedures and Equipment.* To determine probable customer response to new procedures and equipment, marketing researchers can employ concept and laboratory testing and/or field testing. If service personnel are going to be replaced by automatic equipment, it's essential to create designs that customers of almost all types and backgrounds will find easy to use. Even the phrasing of instructions needs careful thought. Ambiguous, complex, or authoritarian instructions may discourage customers with poor reading skills, as well as those used to personal courtesies from the service personnel whom the machine replaces.

4. *Publicize the Benefits.* Introduction of self-service equipment or procedures requires consumers to perform part of the task themselves. Although this additional "work" may be associated with such benefits as extended service hours, time savings, and (in some instances) monetary savings, these benefits are not necessarily obvious—they have to be promoted. Useful strategies may include use of mass media advertising, on-site posters and signage, and personal communications to inform people of the innovation, arouse their interest in it, and clarify the specific benefits to customers of changing their behavior and using new delivery systems.

5. *Teach Customers to Use Innovations and Promote Trial.* Assigning service personnel to demonstrate new equipment and answer questions—providing reassurance as well as educational assistance—is a key element in gaining acceptance of new procedures and technology. The costs of such demonstration programs can be spread across multiple outlets by moving staff members from one site to another if the innovation is rolled out sequentially across the various locations. For Web-based innovations, it's important to provide access to email, chat, or even telephone-based assistance. Promotional incentives and price discounts may also serve to stimulate initial trial. Once customers have tried a self-service option (particularly an electronically based one) and found that it works well, they will be more likely to use it regularly in the future.

6. *Monitor Performance and Continue to Seek Improvements.* Introducing quality and productivity improvements is an ongoing process. The competitive edge provided by productivity improvements may quickly be erased as other firms adopt similar or better procedures. Service managers have to work hard to keep up the momentum so that programs achieve their full potential and are not allowed to flag. If customers are displeased by new procedures, they may revert to their previous behavior, so it's important to continue monitoring utilization over time.

---

exhausted, make mistakes, and treat customers in a cursory manner. Workers who are trying to do two or three things at once—serving a customer face to face while simultaneously answering the telephone and sorting papers, for example—may do a poor job of each task. Excessive pressure breeds discontent and frustration, especially among customer contact personnel who are caught between trying to meet customer needs and attempting to achieve management's productivity goals.

A better way is to search for service process redesign opportunities that lead to drastic improvements in productivity and at the same time increase service quality. Biometrics is set to become a new technology that may allow both—see Service Perspective 14.2.

Intense competitive pressures and razor-thin margins in service industries do not allow firms the luxury of increasing costs to improve quality. Rather, the trick is to constantly seek ways to simultaneously achieve leaps in service quality as well as efficiency, something Heracleous, Wirtz, and their co-authors termed *cost-effective service excellence*. The Internet has in the past allowed many firms to do just that, and has redefined industries including financial services, book and music retailing, and travel agencies. Biometrics may be the next major technology driving further service and productivity enhancements.

Biometrics is the authentication or identification of individuals based on a physical characteristic or trait. Physical characteristics include fingerprints, facial recognition, hand geometry, and iris configuration, and traits include signature formation, keystroke patterns, and voice recognition. Biometrics, as something you are, is both more convenient and more secure than something you know (passwords or pieces of personal information) or something you have (card keys, smart cards, or tokens). There is no risk of forgetting, losing, copying, loaning, or having your biometrics stolen (Figure 14.10).

Applications of biometrics range from controlling access to service facilities (used by Disneyworld to provide access to season-pass holders), voice recognition at call centers (used by the Home Shopping Network and Charles Schwab to enable fast and hassle-free client authentication), self-service access to safe deposit vaults at banks (used by the Bank of Hawaii and First Tennessee Bank), and cashing checks in supermarkets (used by Kroger, Food 4 Less, and BI-LO).

Singapore Airlines (SIA) and the Civil Aviation Authority of Singapore, which operates Changi Airport, arguably one of the best airports in the world, are planning to use biometric technologies to offer every traveler's dream when it comes to airport procedures: the ability to breeze through airline check-in, security checks, as well as immigration checks in less than one minute, all within a context of enhanced travel security. A pilot test of Fully Automated Seamless Travel, as the process is called, integrated three processes: airline check-in, preimmigration security checks, and immigration clearance, whereas most other biometrics-based trials elsewhere focus primarily on improving security. This initiative at Changi Airport is a world's first of integrating these processes with the clear objective of driving service excellence at airport operations and SIA's ground services, while at the same time driving efficiency and improving security.

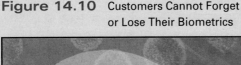

Figure 14.10 Customers Cannot Forget
or Lose Their Biometrics

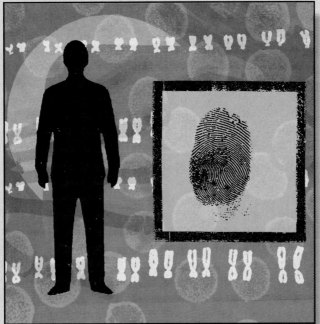

The pilot phase involved 9,000 of SIA's frequent flyers who are Singapore citizens, and was implemented at Terminal 2 at Changi Airport. Participants signed up first at an enrollment station of the Immigration and Checkpoints Authority, where their biometric information (fingerprints and facial features) were captured on a smart card called SVIP (Smart Visa for Identification with Passport). When traveling, these registered users can simply walk through a separate gateway at immigration, where they can do a self-service check-in at a computerized service station. Here, they tap their card onto a reader, have their fingerprint scanned, and use a touch screen to check in while their face is being scanned by a camera. The system identifies the card holder, clears security checks and immigration, at the same time recommends a seat based on the known preferences of the traveler, and upon acceptance by the traveler, prints a boarding pass. If the traveler is happy with the suggested seat, the entire process takes less than 60 seconds (or some three minutes if a passenger wishes to change his or her seat up to three times). The pilot test does not handle passengers with check-in baggage, but a separate process, the "baggage drop-off" concept, is being considered for that. Hand luggage is taken on board as usual.

SIA believes that in the not too distant future most international travelers will be carrying a passport, visa, or smartcard that will contain selected biometric information about its owner. In response to this opportunity, a task force in SIA identified an astounding 113 potential biometrics applications in a recent retreat, and is currently exploring which ones would provide simultaneous strategic differentiation through service excellence, while improving productivity as well as security.

Sources: Loizos Heracleous, Jochen Wirtz, and Nitin Pangarkar, *Flying High in a Competitive Industry—Cost-Effective Service Excellence at Singapore Airlines.* Singapore: McGraw-Hill, 2006, pp. 104–112; Jochen Wirtz and Loizos Heracleous, "Biometrics Meets Services." *Harvard Business Review,* 83 (February 2005): 48–49; Loizos Heracleous and Jochen Wirtz, "Biometrics— The Next Frontier in Service Excellence, Productivity and Security in the Service Sector." *Managing Service Quality,* 16, no. 1 (2006): 12–22.

CONCLUSION

Enhancing service quality and improving service productivity are often two sides of the same coin, offering powerful potential to improve value for both customers and the firm. A key challenge for any service business is to deliver satisfactory outcomes to its customers in ways that are cost-effective for the company. If customers are dissatisfied with the quality of a service, they won't be willing to pay very much for it, or even to buy it at all if competitors offer better quality. Low sales volumes and/or low prices mean less productive assets.

It's a widely accepted notion that customers are the best judges of the quality of a service process and its outcome. When the customer is seen as the final arbiter of quality, then marketing managers come to play a key role in defining expectations and in measuring customer satisfaction. However, service marketers need to work closely with other management functions in service design and implementation.

This chapter presented a number of frameworks and tools for defining, measuring, managing, and improving service quality, including research programs to identify quality gaps, and various analytical tools to identify and improve fail points.

Service process redesign is an important tool to increase service productivity. Marketing managers should be included in productivity improvement programs whenever these efforts are likely to have an effect on customers. Because customers are often involved in the service production process, marketers should keep their eyes open for opportunities to reshape customer behavior in ways that may help the service firm to become more productive. Possibilities for cooperative behavior include adopting self-service options, changing the timing of customer demand to less busy periods, and making use of third-party suppliers of supplementary services.

In summary, value, quality, and productivity are all of great concern to senior management, as they relate directly to an organization's profitability and survival in the competitive marketplace. Strategies designed to enhance value are dependent in large measure on continuous improvement in service quality (as defined by customers) and productivity that reinforce rather than counteract customer satisfaction. The marketing function has much to offer in reshaping our thinking about these issues, as well as in helping to achieve significant improvements in all of them.

REVIEW QUESTIONS

1. Explain the relationships among service quality, productivity, and marketing.
2. Identify the gaps that can occur in service quality and the steps that service marketers can take to prevent them.
3. Why are both soft and hard measures of service quality needed?
4. What are the main tools that service firms can use to analyze and address service quality problems?

5. Why is productivity a more difficult issue for service firms than for manufacturers?
6. What are the key tools for improving service productivity?
7. How do concepts such as TQM, ISO 9000, the Malcolm-Baldrige model, and Six Sigma (see the Appendix to this chapter) relate to managing and improving productivity and service quality?

APPLICATION EXERCISES

1. Review the five dimensions of service quality. What do they mean in the context of (a) an industrial repair shop, (b) a retail bank, (c) a Big 4 accounting firm?
2. How would you define "excellent service quality" for an enquiry/information service provided by your phone or electricity company? Call a service organization and go through a service experience, then evaluate it against your definition of "excellence."
3. Consider your own recent experiences as a service consumer. On which dimensions of service quality have you most often experienced a large gap between your expectations and your perceptions of the service performance? What do you think the underlying causes might be? What steps should management take to improve quality?
4. In what ways can you, as a consumer, help to improve productivity for at least three service organizations that you patronize? What distinctive characteristics of each service make some of these actions possible?
5. What key measures could be used for monitoring service quality, productivity and profitability for a large pizza restaurant chain? Specifically, what measures would you recommend to such a firm to use, taking administration costs into consideration? Who should receive what type of feedback on the results and why? On which measures would you base a part of the salary scheme of branch level staff and why?
6. (Refer to the Appendix to this chapter.) Undertake a literature search and identify the critical factors for a successful implementation of ISO 9000, the Malcolm-Baldrige model, and Six Sigma in service firms. Contrast the success factors suggested in the literature.

Appendix

Systematic Approaches to Productivity and Quality Improvement and to Process Standardization

Many of the thinking, tools, and concepts introduced in this chapter originate from Total Quality Management (TQM), ISO 9000, Six Sigma, and the Malcom-Baldrige model. This appendix provides a brief overview of each approach.

Total Quality Management

Total Quality Management (TQM) concepts, originally developed in Japan and widely used in manufacturing, are now being used by many service firms. Some concepts and tools of TQM can be applied directly to services. TQM tools such as control charts, flowcharts, and fishbone diagrams have helped service firms firms monitor service quality and determining the root causes of specific problems.

Sureshchander, Rajendran, and Anantharaman identified 12 critical dimensions for successful implementation of TQM in a service context: (1) top management commitment and visionary leadership; (2) human resource management; (3) technical system, including service process design and process management; (4) information and analysis system; (5) benchmarking; (6) continuous improvement; (7) customer focus; (8) employee satisfaction; (9) union intervention and employee relations; (10) social responsibility; (11) servicescapes; and (12) service culture.[25]

ISO 9000 Certification

More than 90 countries are members of ISO (the International Organization for Standardization, based in Geneva, Switzerland), which promotes standardization and quality to facilitate international trade. ISO 9000 comprises requirements, definitions, guidelines, and related standards to provide an independent assessment and certification of a firm's quality management system. The official ISO 9000 definition of quality is "The totality of features and characteristics of a product or service that bear on its ability to satisfy a stated or implied need. Simply stated, quality is about meeting or exceeding your customer's needs and requirements." To ensure quality, ISO 9000 uses many TQM tools and routinizes their use in participating firms. By adopting ISO 9000 standards, service firms, especially small ones, can not only ensure that their services conform to customer expectations but also achieve improvements in internal productivity.

As in other quality initiatives, such as TQM and Six Sigma, service firms were later than manufacturers in adopting the ISO 9000 standards.[26] Major service sectors achieving ISO 9000 certification now include wholesale and retail firms, information technology service providers, health care providers, consultancy firms, and educational institutions.

The Malcolm-Baldrige Model Applied to Services

The Malcolm-Baldrige National Quality Award (MBNQA) was developed by the National Institute of Standards and Technology (NIST) with the goal of promoting best practices in quality management, and recognizing and publicizing quality achievements among U.S. firms.

While the framework is generic and does not distinguish between manufacturing and service organizations, the award has a specific service category, and the model can be used to create a culture of ongoing service improvements. Major services firms that have won the award include Ritz-Carlton, FedEx, and AT&T. Research has confirmed that employing this framework can improve organizational performance.[27]

The Baldrige model assesses firms on seven areas: (1) leadership commitment to a service quality cultures; (2) planning priorities for improvement, including service standards, performance targets and measurement of customer satisfaction, defects, cycle-time, and productivity; (3) information and analysis that will aid the organization to collect, measure, analyze, and report strategic and operational indicators; (4) human resources management that enables the firm to deliver service excellence, ranging from hiring the right people, to involvement, empowerment, and motivation; (5) process management, including monitoring, continuous improvement, and process redesign; (6) customer and market focus that allows the firm to determine customer requirements and expectations; and finally, (7) business results.[28]

Six Sigma Applied to Service Organizations

The Six Sigma approach was originally developed by Motorola engineers in the mid-1980s to address the issue of increasing number of complaints from its field sales force regarding warranty claims and was soon adopted by other manufacturing firms to reduce defects in a variety of areas.

Subsequently, service firms embraced various Six Sigma strategies to reduce defects, reduce cycle times, and improve productivity.[29] As early as 1990, GE Capital applied Six Sigma methodology to reduce the back-room costs of selling consumer loans, credit card insurance, and payment protection. Its president and COO Denis Nayden said:

> Although Six Sigma was originally designed for manufacturing, it can be applied to transactional services.

One obvious example is in making sure the millions of credit card and other bills GE sends to customer are correct, which drives down our costs of making adjustments. One of our biggest costs in the financial business is winning new customers. If we treat them well, they will stay with us, reducing our customer-origination costs.[30]

Statistically, Six Sigma means achieving a quality level of only 3.4 defects per million opportunities (DPMO). To understand how stringent this target is, consider mail deliveries. If a mail service delivers with 99 percent accuracy, it misses 3,000 items in 300,000 deliveries. But if it achieves a Six Sigma performance level, only one item of this total will go astray!

Over time, Six Sigma has evolved from a defect-reduction approach to an overall business improvement approach. As defined by Pande, Neuman, and Cavanagh,

> Six Sigma is a comprehensive and flexible system for achieving, sustaining and maximizing business success. Six sigma is uniquely driven by close understanding of customer needs, disciplined use of facts, data and statistical analysis, and diligent attention to managing, improving, and reinventing business processes.[31]

Two strategies, process improvement and process design/redesign, form the cornerstone of the Six Sigma approach. Process improvement strategies aim at identifying and eliminating the root causes of service delivery problems, thereby improving service quality. Process design/redesign strategies act as a supplementary strategy to improvement strategy. If a root cause can't be identified or effectively eliminated within the existing processes, either new processes are *designed* or existing process are *redesigned* to fully or partially address the problem.

The most popular Six Sigma improvement model for analyzing and improving business processes is the DMAIC model, shown in Table 14.5. DMAIC stands for *Define* the opportunities, *Measure* key steps/inputs, *Analyze* to identify root causes, *Improve* performance, and *Control* to maintain performance.

Which Methodology Should a Firm Adopt?

As there are various approaches to systematically improving a service firm's service quality and productivity, the question arises: Which approach should we adopt—TQM, ISO 9000, the Malcolm-Baldrige model, or Six Sigma? Some firms have even implemented more than one program. TQM can be applied at differing levels of sophistication. Basic tools such as flowcharting, frequency charts, and fishbone diagrams can be usefully adopted by almost any type of service firm. ISO 9000 seems to offer the next level of commitment and complexity, followed by the Malcolm-Baldrige model, and finally, Six Sigma.

It's clear that in fact any one of these approaches can offer a useful framework for understanding customer

Table 14.5 Applying the DMAIC Model to Process Improvement and Redesign

	SIX SIGMA METHODOLOGY TO IMPROVE AND REDESIGN PROCESSES	
	PROCESS IMPROVEMENT	PROCESS DESIGN/REDESIGN
Define	Identify the problem Define requirements Set goals	Identify specific or broad problems Define goal/change vision Clarify scope and customer requirements
Measure	Validate problem/process Refine problem/goal Measure key steps/inputs	Measure performance to requirements Gather process efficiency data
Analyze	Develop causal hypothesis Identify "vital few" root causes Validate hypothesis	Identify best practices Assess process design • Value/non–value-adding • Bottlenecks/disconnects • Alternative paths Refine requirements
Improve	Develop ideas to remove root causes Test solutions Standardize solution/measure results	Design new process • Challenge assumptions • Apply creativity • Workflow principles Implement new process, structures, systems
Control	Establish standard measures to maintain performance Correct problems as needed	Establish measures and reviews to maintain performance Correct problems as needed

Source: Reproduced from Peter Pande, Robert P. Neuman, and Ronald R. Cavanagh, *The Six Sigma Way*. New York: McGraw-Hill, 2000.

needs, analyzing processes, and improving service quality and productivity. Each program has its own merits, and firms can adopt more than one. For example, the ISO 9000 program can be used for standardizing the procedures and process documentation, which can lead to reduction in variability. Six Sigma and Malcolm-Baldrige programs can be used to improve processes and to focus on performance improvement across the organization.

Success will depend on how well a specific improvement program is integrated with the overall business strategy. Firms that adopt a program because of peer pressure or just as a marketing tool are less likely to succeed than firms that view these programs as useful development tools.[32]

Service champions make best practices in service quality management a core part of their organizational culture.[33]

The National Institute of Standards and Technology, which organizes the Malcolm-Baldrige Award program, tracked a hypothetical stock index called the "Baldrige Index" of award winners and observed that winners consistently outperformed the S&P 500 index.[34] Ironically, the two-time winner of the award, and Six Sigma pioneer, Motorola had been suffering financially and losing market share, in part through failure to keep up with new technology. Success cannot be taken for granted, and implementation, commitment, and constant adaptation to changing markets, technologies, and environments are the keys to sustained success.

ENDNOTES

1. Claes Fornell, "ACSI Commentary: Federal Government Scores." Special Report: Government Satisfaction Scores, Ann Arbor, Michigan: CFI Group, December 15, 2005; www.theacsi.com, accessed January 21, 2006.
2. Martin Neil Baily, Diana Farrell, and Jaana Remes, "Where US Productivity is Growing." *The McKinsey Quarterly*, no. 2 (2006): 10–12.
3. David A. Garvin, *Managing Quality*. New York: The Free Press, 1988, especially chap. 3.
4. Christian Grönroos, *Service Management and Marketing*, 2nd ed. Chichester, UK: John Wiley & Sons, 2000.
5. Valarie A. Zeithaml, A. Parasuraman, and Leonard L. Berry, *Delivering Quality Service*. New York: The Free Press, 1990.
6. A. Parasuraman, Valarie A. Zeithaml, and Leonard Berry, "SERVQUAL: A Multiple Item Scale for Measuring Consumer Perceptions of Service Quality." *Journal of Retailing*, 64 (1988): 12–40.
7. See, for instance, Francis Buttle, "SERVQUAL: Review, Critique, Research Agenda." *European Journal of Marketing*, 30, no. 1 (1996): 8–32; Simon S. K. Lam and Ka Shing Woo, "Measuring Service Quality: A Test-Retest Reliability Investigation of SERVQUAL." *Journal of the Market Research Society*, 39 (April 1997): 381–393; Terrence H. Witkowski, and Mary F. Wolfinbarger, "Comparative Service Quality: German and American Ratings Across Service Settings." *Journal of Business Research*, 55 (2002): 875–881; Lisa J. Morrison Coulthard, "Measuring Service Quality: A Review and

Critique of Research Using SERVQUAL." *International Journal of Market Research,* 46 (Quarter 4, 2004): 479–497.

8. Anne M. Smith, "Measuring Service Quality: Is SERVQUAL Now Redundant?" *Journal of Marketing Management,* 11 (January/February/April 1995): 257–276.

9. Gerhard Mels, Christo Boshoff, and Denon Nel, "The Dimensions of Service Quality: The Original European Perspective Revisited." *The Service Industries Journal,* 17 (January 1997): 173–189.

10. A. Parasuraman, Valarie A. Zeithaml, and Arvind Malhotra, "E-S-QUAL: A Multiple-Item Scale for Assessing Electronic Service Quality." *Journal of Service Research,* 7, no. 3 (2005): 213–233.

11. Jochen Wirtz and Anna S. Mattila, "Exploring the Role of Alternative Perceived Performance Measures and Needs-Congruency in the Consumer Satisfaction Process." *Journal of Consumer Psychology,* 11, no. 3 (2001): 181–192.

12. Jochen Wirtz, "Halo in Customer Satisfaction Measures— The Role of Purpose of Rating, Number of Attributes, and Customer Involvement." *International Journal of Service Industry Management,* 14, no. 1 (2003): 96–119.

13. A. Parasuraman, Valarie A. Zeithaml, and Leonard L. Berry, "A Conceptual Model of Service Quality and Its Implications for Future Research." *Journal of Marketing,* 49, (Fall 1985): 41–50; Valarie A. Zeithaml, Leonard L. Berry, and A. Parasuraman, "Communication and Control Processes in the Delivery of Services." *Journal of Marketing,* 52 (April 1988): 36–58.

14. Valarie A. Zeithaml, Mary Jo Bitner, and Dwayne D. Gremler, *Services Marketing,* 4th ed. New York: McGraw-Hill, 2006, p. 292.

15. Leonard L. Berry and A. Parasuraman, "Listening to the Customer—The Concept of a Service Quality Information System." *Sloan Management Review,* 38 (Spring 1997): 65–76.

16. Comments by Thomas R. Oliver, then senior vice president, sales and customer service, Federal Express; reported in Christopher H. Lovelock, *Federal Express: Quality Improvement Program.* Lausanne, Switzerland: International Institute for Management Development, 1990.

17. Christopher Lovelock, *Product Plus: How Product + Service = Competitive Advantage.* New York: McGraw-Hill, 1994, p. 218.

18. These categories and the research data that follow have been adapted from information in D. Daryl Wyckoff, "New Tools for Achieving Service Quality." *Cornell Hotel and Restaurant Administration Quarterly,* 42 (August–September 2001): 25–38.

19. Roland T. Rust, Anthony J. Zahonik, and Timothy L. Keiningham, "Return on Quality (ROQ): Making Service Quality Financially Accountable." *Journal of Marketing,* 59 (April 1995): 58–70; Roland T. Rust, Christine Moorman, and Peter R. Dickson, "Getting Return on Quality: Revenue Expansion, Cost Reduction, or Both?" *Journal of Marketing,* 66 (October 2002): 7–24.

20. Kenneth J. Klassen, Randolph M. Russell, and James J. Chrisman, "Efficiency and Productivity Measures for High Contact Services." *The Service Industries Journal,* 18 (October 1998): 1–18.

21. James L. Heskett, *Managing in the Service Economy.* New York: The Free Press, 1986.

22. For an in-depth discussion of service productivity, see Cynthia Karen Swank, "The Lean Service Machine." *Harvard Business Review,* 81, no. 10 (2003): 123–129.

23. Eric Langeard, John E. G. Bateson, Christopher H. Lovelock, and Pierre Eiglier, *Services Marketing: New Insights from Consumers and Managers.* Cambridge, MA: Marketing Science Institute, 1981, esp. chap. 2. A good summary of this research is provided in J. E. G. Bateson, "Self-Service Consumer: An Exploratory Study." *Journal of Retailing,* 51 (Fall 1985): 49–76.

24. Cathy Goodwin, "I Can Do It Myself: Training the Service Consumer to Contribute to Service Productivity." *Journal of Services Marketing,* 2 (Fall 1988): 71–78.

25. G. S. Sureshchandar, Chandrasekharan Rajendran, and R. N. Anantharaman, "A Holistic Model for Total Service Quality." *International Journal of Service Industry Management,* 12, no. 4 (2001): 378–412.

26. *ISO (2001), The ISO Survey of ISO 9000 and ISO 14000 Certificates (Eleventh Cycle).* Geneva: International Organization for Standards, 2001.

27. Susan Meyer Goldstein and Sharon B. Schweikhart, "Empirical Support for the Baldrige Award Framework in U.S. Hospitals." *Health Care Management Review,* 27, no. 1 (2002): 62–75.

28. Allan Shirks, William B. Weeks, and Annie Stein, "Baldrige-Based Quality Awards: Veterans Health Administration's 3-Year Experience." *Quality Management in Health Care,* 10, no. 3 (2002): 47–54; National Institute of Standards and Technology, "Baldrige FAQs," www.nist.gov./public_affairs/factsheet/ baldfaqs.htm, accessed January 11, 2006.

29. Jim Biolos, "Six Sigma Meets the Service Economy." *Harvard Business Review,* 80 (November 2002): 3–5.

30. Mikel Harry and Richard Schroeder, *Six Sigma—The Breakthrough Management Strategy Revolutionizing the World's Top Corporations.* New York: Currency. 2000, p. 232.

31. Peter S. Pande, Robert P. Neuman, and Ronald R. Cavanagh, *The Six Sigma Way: How GE, Motorola, and Other Top Companies Are Honing Their Performance.* New York: McGraw-Hill, 2000.

32. Gavin Dick, Kevin Gallimore, and Jane C. Brown, "ISO9000 and Quality Emphasis: An Empirical Study of Front-Room and Back Room Dominated Service Industries." *International Journal of Service Industry Management,* 12, no. 2 (2001): 114–136; Adrian Hughes and David N. Halsall, "Comparison of the 14 Deadly Diseases and the Business Excellence Model." *Total Quality Management,* 13, no. 2 (2002): 255–263.

33. Cathy A. Enz and Judy A. Siguaw, "Best Practices in Service Quality." *Cornell Hotel and Restaurant Administration Quarterly,* 41 (October 2000): 20–29.

34. *Eighth NIST Stock Investment Study.* Gaithersburg, MD: National Institute of Standards and Technology, 2002.

Chapter 15

Organizing for Change Management and Service Leadership

> *Marketing is so basic that it cannot be considered a separate function. . . . It is the whole business seen from the point of view of its final result, that is, from the customer's point of view. Concern and responsibility for marketing must, therefore, permeate all areas of the enterprise.*
>
> PETER DRUCKER

> *[T]he more short-term a company's focus becomes, the more likely the firm will be to engage in behavior that actually destroys value.*
>
> DON PEPPERS AND MARTHA ROGERS

Throughout this book, we've examined how to manage service businesses to achieve customer satisfaction and profitable performance. Our focus has been on marketing, the only function that actually generates operating revenues for a business. However, we've consistently emphasized that the array of marketing activities in service organizations, embracing each element of the 8 Ps, extends beyond the responsibilities assigned to a traditional marketing department. Hence both planning and implementation of service marketing strategies require active collaboration with operations and human resources management.

We've shown that marketing itself can be viewed in several ways: as a strategic and competitive thrust pursued by senior management, as a set of functional activities performed by line managers, or as a customer-driven orientation for the entire organization. In fact, all three perspectives are necessary to develop strategies for service success.

Service organizations that are already successful cannot afford to rest on their laurels. They must continuously evolve to take advantage of new or developing markets, meet new customer needs, counter competitors, and exploit new technologies. By contrast, underperforming or dysfunctional organizations require a turnaround strategy if they are to survive and prosper. As we'll see in this chapter, both situations involve change management.

However, it's very difficult for a firm to achieve and maintain leadership in a service industry if it lacks human leaders who can articulate the necessary vision and help bring it to fruition. The emphasis could include defining the terms on which the company seeks to compete, creating an outstanding work environment, ensuring that customers receive good value, initiating important innovations, implementing new technologies for competitive advantage, setting the standards for service quality, or a combination. of any of these strategic elements.

We now draw together themes and insights from earlier chapters, particularly those on managing employees, building customer loyalty, and improving service quality, as we examine the challenging task of leading a service business that seeks to be both customer-focused and market-oriented. In particular, this chapter explores the following questions:

1. What are the implications of the service profit chain for service management?

2. What actions are required to move a service firm from a reactive position, merely being available for service, toward the status of world-class service delivery? How should management set priorities?

3. Why do the marketing, operations, and human resource management functions need to be closely coordinated and integrated in service businesses? And what are the barriers to achieving this?

4. What is the distinction between evolutionary change and turnaround when seeking to transform a service business? For each case, what role should the CEO play?

5. What roles do leaders play in fostering success at all levels within their organization?

EFFECTIVE MARKETING LIES AT THE HEART OF VALUE CREATION

"Businesses succeed by getting, keeping, and growing customers," state respected consultants and authors Don Peppers and Martha Rogers.[1] Arguing that Wall Street's ongoing obsession with current-period revenue and earnings can actually destroy value, they declare:

> Investors today want executives to demonstrate that their companies can make money and grow, the old-fashioned way—by earning it from the value proposition they offer customers. They want a firm's customers to buy more, to buy more often, and to stay loyal longer. They want a firm to show that it can go out and get more customers. . . .
>
> Growth fuels innovation and creativity, generating new ideas and initiatives, and stimulating managers in all areas to "think outside the box." Growth keeps a company vibrant and alive, making it a good place to work—a place that provides employees with economic benefits and opportunities for advancement.[2]

The Service–Profit Chain

James Heskett and his colleagues at Harvard argue that when service companies put employees and customers first, a radical shift occurs in the way they manage and measure success. They relate profitability, customer loyalty, and customer satisfaction to the value created by satisfied, loyal, and productive employees.

> Top-level executives of outstanding service organizations spend little time setting profit goals or focusing on market share. . . . Instead they understand that in the new economics of service, frontline workers and customers need to be the center of management concern. Successful service managers pay attention to the factors that drive profitability . . . investment in people, technology that supports frontline workers, revamped recruiting and training practices, and compensation linked to performance for employees at every level. . . .
>
> The service–profit chain, developed from analyses of successful service organizations, puts "hard" values on "soft" measures. It helps managers target new investments to develop service and satisfaction levels for maximum competitive impact, widening the gap between service leaders and their merely good competitors.[3]

The service–profit chain, shown in Figure 15.1, displays a series of hypothesized links in a managerial process that can lead to success in service businesses.

Table 15.1 provides a useful summary, highlighting the behaviors required of service leaders in order to manage their organizations effectively. Working backwards from the desired end results of revenue growth and profitability, links 1 and 2 focus on customers and include an emphasis on identifying and understanding customer needs, investments to ensure customer retention, and a commitment to adopting new performance measures that track such variables as satisfaction and loyalty among both customers and employees. Link 3 focuses on the value for customers created by the service concept and highlights the need for investments to continually improve both service quality and productivity.

Figure 15.1 The Service–Profit Chain

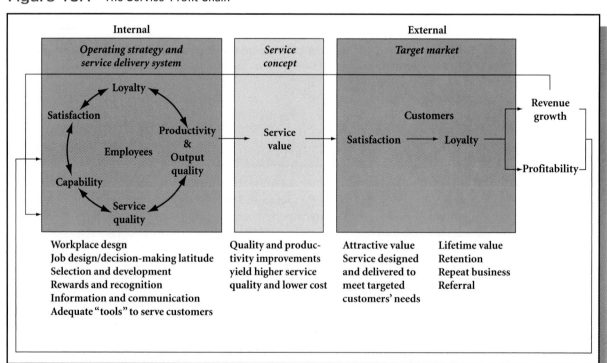

Source: "Putting the Service Profit Chain to Work" by James L. Heskett, Thomas O. Jones, Gary W. Loveman, W. Earl Sasser Jr., and Leonard A. Schlesinger. March–April 1994, p. 166. Reprinted by permission of Harvard Business School.

Table 15.1
Links in the
Service–Profit Chain

1. Customer loyalty drives profitability and growth.
2. Customer satisfaction drives customer loyalty.
3. Value drives customer satisfaction.
4. Quality and productivity drive value.
5. Employee loyalty drives service quality and productivity.
6. Employee satisfaction drives employee loyalty.
7. Internal quality drives employee satisfaction.
8. Top management leadership underlies the chain's success.

Sources: James L. Heskett et al., "Putting the Service Profit Chain to Work." *Harvard Business Review* (March April 1994); James L. Heskett, W. Earl Sasser, and Leonard L. Schlesinger, *The Service Profit Chain.* Boston: Harvard Business School Press, 1997.

Another set of service leadership behaviors (links 4–7) relates to employees and include organizational focus on the front line, supporting the design of jobs that offer greater latitude for employees, and investing in the development of promising managers. Also included in this category is the concept that paying higher wages actually decreases labor costs after reduced turnover, higher productivity, and higher quality are taken into account. Underlying the chain's success (link 8) is top management leadership.

What Qualities Are Associated with Service Leaders?

The themes and relationships underlying the service–profit chain illustrate compellingly the mutual dependency among marketing, operations, and human resources. An organization that is recognized as a service leader offers its customers superior value and quality. It has marketing strategies that beat the competition, yet is viewed as a trustworthy organization that does business in ethical ways. It is seen a leader in operations, too—respected for its superior operational processes and innovative use of technology. Finally, it is recognized as an outstanding place to work, leading its industry in human resource management (HRM) practices and staffed by loyal, productive, and customer-oriented employees. Clearly, implementation of the service–profit chain requires a thorough understanding of how marketing, operations, and human resources each relate to a company's broader strategic concerns and jointly contribute to creation of value.

Attaining service leadership requires a coherent vision of what it takes to succeed, with the resulting strategy defined and driven by a strong, effective leadership team. Implementation of that strategy involves careful coordination among marketing (which, broadly defined, includes all aspects of customer service), operations (which includes management of technology), and human resources. As we've emphasized throughout this book, the marketing function in service businesses cannot easily be separated from other management activities, and the marketing function is typically much broader than the work performed by the marketing department.

Ideally, service firms should be organized in ways that enable the three functions of marketing, operations, and human resources to work closely together so that the organization can be responsive to its various stakeholders and achieve success in its chosen markets. For firms that do it right, that success is ultimately rewarded by an increase in the value attached to the organization itself, expressed for public companies by their stock price. As demonstrated by American Customer Satisfaction Index (ACSI) research, most service industries demonstrate a strong relationship between customer satisfaction—what everyone in the firm should be working to achieve—and shareholder value (Figure 15.2). An important distinction between service leaders and firms in other categories is how they approach value creation. The former seek to create value through customer satisfaction and its antecedents, whereas the others often aim to boost shareholder value through tactical measures to increase sales, short-term cost cutting, unlocking asset value through selected sell-offs, and taking advantage of financial market dynamics.

Figure 15.2 Customer Satisfaction Is Closely Linked to Shareholder Value in Most Service Industries

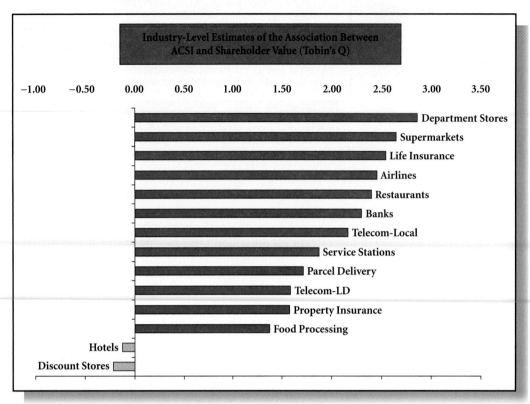

Source: Claes Fornell with David Van Amburg, Forrest Morgeson, Eugene V. Anderson, Barbara Everitt Bryant, and Michael D. Johnson, *The American Customer Satisfaction Index at Ten Years.* Ann Arbor. MI: ACSI, 2005, p. 42 (service industry data extracted from larger table).

INTEGRATING MARKETING, OPERATIONS, AND HUMAN RESOURCES

Although there's a long tradition of functional specialization in business, narrow perspectives get in the way of effective service management. One of the challenges facing senior managers in any type of organization is to avoid creating what are sometimes referred to as "functional silos" in which each function exists in isolation from the others, jealously guarding its independence.

Why is it so important in service firms to integrate the activities performed by the marketing, operations, and human resource functions? As we've seen, many service enterprises—especially those involving people processing services—are literally "factories in the field" that customers enter whenever they need the service in question. When customers are actively involved in production and the service output is consumed as it is produced, active engagement between production (operations) and consumers should be mandatory. Despite the rise of self-service technologies, contact between operations personnel and customers remains the rule rather than the exception in many industries—although its extent varies according to the nature of the service. The net result is that the services marketing function can't avoid being entwined with—and dependent on—the procedures, personnel, and facilities managed by operations. In a high-contact service, competitive outcomes may live or die on the basis of the caliber of service personnel recruited and trained by the human resources department. Nowadays, service organizations can't afford to have HR specialists who don't understand customers.

In many service businesses, in fact, the caliber and commitment of the labor force have become a major source of competitive advantage:[4] Think Marriott and Southwest Airlines, or McKinsey and Goldman Sachs. As a consumer, you can and do differentiate among competing firms on the basis of their employees. A strong commitment by top management to human resources is a feature of many successful service firms.[5] For HRM to succeed, argues Terri Kabachnick, "it must be a business-driven function with a thorough understanding of the organization's big picture. It must be viewed as a strategic consulting partner, providing innovative solutions and influencing key decisions and policies."[6] To the extent that employees understand and support the goals of their organization, have the skills and training needed to succeed in their jobs, and recognize the importance of creating and maintaining customer satisfaction, both marketing and operations activities should be easier to manage.

Reducing Interfunctional Conflict

As service firms place more emphasis on developing a strong market orientation and serving customers well, there's increased potential for conflict among the three functions, especially between marketing and operations. How comfortably can the three functions coexist in a service business, and how are their relative roles perceived? Sandra Vandermerwe makes the point that high-value-creating enterprises should be thinking in term of *activities*, not functions.[7] Yet in many firms, we still find individuals from marketing and operations backgrounds at odds with each other. Marketers may see their role as one of continually adding value to the product offering, enhancing its appeal to customers and stimulating sales. Operations managers, by contrast, may see their job as paring back "extras" to reflect the reality of service constraints—such as staff and equipment—and the need for cost containment. After all, they may argue, no value will be created if we operate at a loss. Conflicts may also occur between human resources and the other two functions, especially where employees are in boundary-spanning roles that require them to balance customer satisfaction against operational efficiency.

Changing traditional organizational perspectives doesn't come readily to managers who have been comfortable with established approaches. However, as long as a service business continues to be organized along functional lines (and many are), achieving the necessary coordination and strategic synergy requires that top management establish clear imperatives for each function. Each imperative should relate to customers and define how a specific function contributes to the overall mission. Part of the challenge of service management is to ensure that each of these three functional imperatives is compatible with the others and that all are mutually reinforcing. Although a firm will need to phrase each imperative in ways that are specific to its own business, we can express them generically as follows.

- *The marketing imperative:* To target specific types of customers whom the firm is well equipped to serve and create ongoing relationships with them by delivering a carefully defined service product package in return for a price that offers value to customers and the potential for profits to the firm. Customers will recognize this value proposition as being one of consistent quality that delivers solutions to their needs and is superior to competing alternatives.
- *The operations imperative:* To create and deliver the specified service package to targeted customers by selecting those operational techniques that allow the firm to consistently meet customer-driven cost, schedule, and quality goals and also enable the business to reduce its costs through continuing improvements in productivity. The chosen operational methods will match skills that employees and intermediaries or contractors currently possess or can be trained to develop. The firm will have the resources to support these operations with the necessary facilities, equipment, and technology while avoiding negative effects on employees and the broader community.
- *The human resources imperative:* To recruit, train, and motivate front-line employees, service delivery team leaders, and managers and who can work well together in return for realistic compensation and benefits to balance the twin goals of customer satisfaction and operational effectiveness. Employees will

want to stay with the firm and to enhance their own skills because they value the working environment, appreciate the opportunities it presents, and take pride in the services they help create and deliver.

CREATING A LEADING SERVICE ORGANIZATION

In your own life as a consumer, you've probably encountered an assortment of service organizations, ranging from those you can always trust to deliver excellent service to those that consistently deliver bad service and mistreat their customers. Why are some service organizations so much better than others? What separates the sheep from the goats?

From Losers to Leaders: Four Levels of Service Performance

Service leadership is not based on outstanding performance within a single dimension. Rather, it reflects excellence across multiple dimensions. In an effort to capture this performance spectrum, we need to evaluate an organization within each of the three functional areas described earlier—marketing, operations, and human resources. Table 15.2 modifies and extends an operations-oriented framework proposed by Richard Chase and Robert Hayes.[8] It categorizes service performers into one of four levels: loser, nonentity, professional, and leader. For each level, there is a brief description of a typical organization across 12 dimensions.

Under the marketing function, we look at the role of marketing, competitive appeal, customer profile, and service quality. Under the operations function, we consider the role of operations, service delivery (front stage), backstage operations, productivity, and introduction of new technology. Finally, under the human resources function, we consider the role of human resources management, the workforce, and front-line management. Obviously, there are overlaps between these dimensions and across functions. Additionally, there may be variations in the relative importance of some dimensions in different industries and across different delivery systems. For instance, human resource management tends to play a more prominent strategic role in high contact services. The goal of this overall service performance framework is to generate insights into how service leaders perform so well and what needs to be changed in organizations that are not performing as well as they might.

If you want to do an in-depth appraisal of a company in a specific industry, you may find it useful to view Table 15.2 as a point of departure, modifying some of the elements to create a customized framework for analysis.

Service Losers

Service losers are at the bottom of the barrel from both customer and managerial perspectives, getting failing grades in marketing, operations, and HRM. Customers patronize them for reasons other than performance—typically, because there is no viable alternative, which is one reason why service losers continue to survive. Managers of such organizations may even see service delivery as a necessary evil. New technology is introduced only under duress, and the uncaring workforce is a negative constraint on performance. The cycle of failure presented in Chapter 11 (see Figure 11.4) describes how such organizations behave in relation to employees and what the consequences are for customers.

Service Nonentities

Although their performance still leaves much to be desired, service nonentities have eliminated the worst features of losers. As shown in Table 15.2, nonentities are dominated by a traditional operations mindset, typically based on achieving cost savings through standardization. Their marketing strategies are unsophisticated, and the roles of human resources and operations might be summed up, respectively, by the philosophies

Figure 15.3 Dilbert's Boss Loses Focus—and His Audience

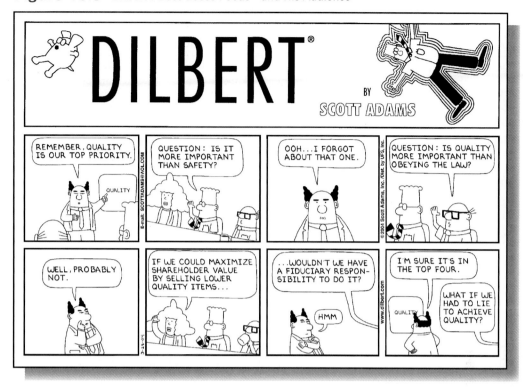

DILBERT: © Scott Adams/Dist. by permission of United Syndicate, Inc.

"adequate is good enough" and "if it ain't broke, don't fix it." Consumers neither seek out nor avoid such organizations. Managers may spout platitudes about improving quality and other goals, but they are unable to set clear priorities, chart a clear course, or command the respect and commitment of their subordinates (Figure 15.3). Several such firms can often be found competing in lackluster fashion within a given marketplace, and you might have difficulty distinguishing one from the others. Periodic price discounts tend to be the primary means of trying to attract new customers. The cycle of mediocrity (see Chapter 11, Figure 11.5) portrays the human resources environment of many such organizations and the consequences for customers.

Service Professionals

Service professionals are in a different league from nonentities and have a clear market positioning strategy. Customers within the target segments seek out these firms based on their sustained reputation for meeting expectations. Marketing is more sophisticated, using targeted communications and pricing based on value to the customer. Research is used to measure customer satisfaction and obtain ideas for service enhancement. Operations and marketing work together to introduce new delivery systems and recognize the trade-off between productivity and customer-defined quality. There are explicit links between backstage and front-stage activities and a much more proactive, investment-oriented approach to HRM than is found among nonentities. The cycle of success (see Figure 11.6) highlights the HR strategies that lead to a high level of performance by most employees of organizations in the service professionals category (and by all who work for service leaders), together with its positive impact on customer satisfaction and loyalty.

Service Leaders

Service leaders are the *crème de la crème* of their respective industries. Whereas service professionals are good, service leaders are outstanding. Their company names are synonymous with excellence and an ability to delight customers. Service leaders

Table 15.2   Four Levels of Service Performance

LEVEL	1. LOSER	2. NONENTITY
Marketing Function		
Role of marketing	Tactical role only; advertising and promotions lack focus; no involvement in product or pricing decision	Uses mix of selling and mass communication, using simple segmentation strategy; makes selective use of price discounts and promotions; conducts and tabulates basic satisfaction surveys
Competitive appeal	Customers patronize firm for reasons other than performance	Customers neither seek out nor avoid the firm
Customer profile	Unspecified; a mass market to be served at a minimum cost	One or more segments whose basic needs are understood
Service quality	Highly variable, usually unsatisfactory. Subservient to operations priorities	Meets some customer expectations; consistent on one or two key dimensions, but not all
Operations Function		
Role of operations	Reactive; cost oriented	The principal line management function: Creates and delivers product, focuses on standardization as key to productivity, defines quality from internal perspective
Service delivery (front-stage)	A necessary evil. Locations and schedules are unrelated to preferences of customers, who are routinely ignored	Sticklers for tradition; "If it ain't broke, don't fix it"; tight rules for customers; each step in delivery run independently
Backstage operations	Divorced from front-stage; cogs in a machine	Contributes to individual front-stage delivery steps but organized separately; unfamiliar with customers
Productivity	Undefined; managers are punished for failing to stick within budget	Based on standardization; rewarded for keeping costs below budget
Introduction of new technology	Late adopter, under duress, when necessary for survival	Follows the crowd when justified by cost savings
Human Resources Function		
Role of human resources	Supplies low-cost employees who meet minimum skill requirements for the job	Recruits and trains employees who can perform competently
Workforce	Negative constraint: poor performers, don't care, disloyal	Adequate resource, follows procedures but uninspired; turnover often high
Frontline management	Controls workers	Controls the process

Note: This framework was inspired by–and expands upon–work in service operations management by Richard Chase and Robert Hayes.

(Continued)

Table 15.2   Four Levels of Service Performance (*continued*)

Marketing Function

3. Professional	4. Leader
Has clear positioning strategy against competition; uses focused communications with distinctive appeals to clarify promises and educate customers; pricing is based on value; monitors customer usage and operates loyalty programs; uses a variety of research techniques to measure customer satisfaction and obtain ideas for service enhancements; works with operations to introduce new delivery systems	Innovative leader in chosen segments, known for marketing skills; brands at product/process level; conducts sophisticated analysis of relational databases as inputs to one-to-one marketing and proactive account management; uses state-of-the art research techniques; uses concept testing, observation, and use of lead customers as inputs to new-product development; close to operations/HR
Customers seek out the firm, based on its sustained reputation for meeting customer expectations	Company name is synonymous with service excellence; its ability to delight customers raises expectations to levels that competitors can't meet
Groups of individuals whose variation in needs and value to the firm are clearly understood	Individuals are selected and retained based on their future value to the firm, including their potential for new service opportunities and their ability to stimulate innovation.
Consistently meets or exceeds customer expectations across multiple dimensions	Raises customer expectations to new levels; improves continuously

Operations Function

3. Professional	4. Leader
Plays a strategic role in competitive strategy; recognizes tradeoff between productivity and customer-defined quality; willing to outsource; monitors competing operations for ideas, threats	Recognized for innovation, focus, and excellence; an equal partner with marketing and HR management; has in-house research capability and academic contacts; continually experimenting
Driven by customer satisfaction, not tradition; willing to customize, embrace new approaches; emphasis on speed, convenience, and comfort	Delivery is a seamless process organized around the customer; employees know whom they are serving; focuses on continuous improvement
Process is explicitly linked to front-stage activities; sees role as serving "internal customers," who in turn serve external customers	Closely integrated with front-stage delivery, even when geographically far apart; understands how own role relates to overall process of serving external customers; continuing dialogue
Focuses on reengineering backstage processes; avoids productivity improvements that will degrade customers' service experience; continually refining processes for efficiency	Understands concept of return on quality; actively seeks customer involvement in productivity improvement; ongoing testing of new processes and technologies
An early adopter when IT promises to enhance service for customers and provide a competitive edge	Works with technology leaders to develop new applications that create first-mover advantage; seeks to perform at levels competitors can't match

Human Resources Function

3. Professional	4. Leader
Invests in selective recruiting, ongoing training; keeps close to employees, promotes upward mobility; strives to enhance quality of working life	Sees quality of employees as strategic advantage; firm is recognized as outstanding place to work; HR helps top management to nurture culture
Motivated, hard working, allowed some discretion in choice of procedures, offers suggestions	Innovative and empowered; very loyal, committed to firm's values and goals; creates procedures
Listens to customers; coaches and facilitates workers	Source of new ideas for top management; mentors workers to enhance career growth, value to firm

are recognized for their innovation in each functional area of management as well as for their superior internal communications and coordination among these three functions—often the result of a relatively flat organizational structure and extensive use of teams. As a result, service delivery is a seamless process organized around the customer.

Marketing efforts by service leaders make extensive use of customer relationship (CRM) systems that offer strategic insights about customers, who are often addressed on a one-to-one basis. Concept testing, observation, and contacts with lead customers are employed in the development of new, breakthrough services that respond to previously unrecognized needs. Operations specialists work with technology leaders around the world to develop new applications that will create a first-mover advantage and enable the firm to perform at levels that competitors cannot hope to reach for a long period of time. Senior executives see quality of employees as a strategic advantage. HRM works with them to develop and maintain a service-oriented culture and to create an outstanding working environment that simplifies the task of attracting and retaining the best people.[9] The employees themselves are committed to the firm's values and goals. Because they are engaged, empowered, and quick to embrace change, they are an ongoing source of new ideas.

Moving to a Higher Level of Performance

Firms can move either up or down the performance ladder. Once-stellar performers can become complacent and sluggish. Organizations that are devoted to satisfying their current customers may miss important shifts in the marketplace and find themselves turning into has-beens. These businesses may continue to serve a loyal but dwindling band of conservative customers, but they are unable to attract demanding new consumers with different expectations. Companies whose original success was based on mastery of a specific technological process may find that, in defending their control of that process, they have encouraged competitors to find higher-performing alternatives. And organizations whose management has worked for years to build up a loyal workforce with a strong service ethic may find that such a culture can be quickly destroyed as a result of a merger or acquisition that brings in new leaders who emphasize short-term profits. Unfortunately, senior managers sometimes delude themselves into thinking that their company has achieved a superior level of performance when, in fact, the foundations of that success are crumbling.

In most markets, we can also find companies that are moving up the performance ladder through conscious efforts to coordinate their marketing, operations, and HRM functions to establish more favorable competitive positions and better satisfy their customers. Best Practice in Action 15.1 describes how Stena Line, a Swedish ferry company, successfully enhanced the performance level of a newly acquired subsidiary that had earlier been state-owned.

IN SEARCH OF HUMAN LEADERSHIP

Service leaders are organizations that stand out in their market and industry, but it still requires human leaders to take them in the right direction, set the right strategic priorities, and ensure that the relevant strategies are implemented throughout the organization. Much of the literature on leadership is concerned with turnarounds and transformation. It's easy to see why poorly performing organizations may require a major transformation of their culture and operating procedures to make them more competitive. In times of rapid change, however, even high-performing firms need to evolve on a continuing basis, transforming themselves in evolutionary fashion.

Leading a Service Organization

John Kotter, perhaps the best-known authority on leadership, argues that in most successful change management processes, those in leadership roles must navigate through eight complicated and often time-consuming stages:[10]

1. Creating a sense of urgency to develop the impetus for change
2. Putting together a strong enough team to direct the process
3. Creating an appropriate vision of where the organization needs to go
4. Communicating that new vision broadly
5. Empowering employees to act on that vision
6. Producing sufficient short-term results to create credibility and counter cynicism
7. Building momentum and using that to tackle the tougher change problems
8. Anchoring the new behaviors in the organizational culture

Leadership Versus Management

The primary force behind successful change is *leadership*, which is concerned with the development of vision and strategies, and the empowerment of people to overcome obstacles and make the vision happen. *Management*, by contrast, involves keeping the current situation operating through planning, budgeting, organizing, staffing, controlling, and problem solving. Warren Bennis and Bert Nanus distinguish between leaders who emphasize the emotional and even spiritual resources of an organization and managers who stress its physical resources, such as raw materials, technology, and capital.[11] Says Kotter:

> Leadership works through people and culture. It's soft and hot. Management works through hierarchy and systems. It's harder and cooler. . . . The fundamental purpose of management is to keep the current system functioning. The fundamental purpose of leadership is to produce useful change, especially nonincremental change. It's possible to have too much or too little of either. Strong leadership with no management risks chaos; the organization might walk right off a cliff. Strong management with no leadership tends to entrench an organization in deadly bureaucracy.[12]

Leadership is an essential and growing aspect of managerial work because the rate of change has been increasing. Reflecting both competition and technological advances, new services or service features are being introduced at a faster rate and tend to have shorter life cycles. Meantime, the competitive environment shifts continually as a result of international firms entering new geographic markets, mergers and acquisitions, and the exit of former competitors. The process of service delivery itself has speeded up, with customers demanding faster service and quicker responses when things go wrong. As a result, declares Kotter, effective top executives may now spend up to 80 percent of their time leading, double the amount required not that long ago. Even those at the bottom of the management hierarchy may spend at least 20 percent of their time on leadership.

Setting Direction Is Different from Planning

People often confuse the activities of planning and setting direction. *Planning*, according to Kotter, is a management process, designed to produce orderly results, not change. *Setting a direction*, by contrast, is more inductive than deductive. Leaders look for patterns, relationships, and linkages that help to explain things and suggest future trends. Direction setting creates visions and strategies that describe a business, technology, or corporate culture in terms of what it should become over the long term and that articulate a feasible way of achieving this goal. Effective leaders have a talent for simplicity in communicating with others who may not share their background or knowledge; they know their audiences and are able to distill their messages, conveying even complicated concepts in just a few phrases.[13]

When Stena Line purchased Sealink British Ferries (whose routes linked Britain to Ireland and several European countries), the Swedish company more than doubled in size to become one of the world's largest car-ferry operators. Stena boasted a whole department dedicated to monitoring quality improvements. By contrast, this philosophy was described as "alien" to Sealink's culture, which reflected a top-down, military-style structure that focused on the operational aspects of ship movements. The quality of customers' experiences received only secondary consideration.

Managerial weaknesses included lack of attention to growing competition from other companies, whose new, high-speed ferries offered customers a faster and more comfortable ride. Sealink's top management exercised tight control, issuing directives and applying company-wide standards across all divisions, rather than customizing policies to the needs of individual routes. All decisions were subject to head-office review. Divisional managers were separated by two management levels from the functional teams engaged in the actual operation. This organizational structure led to conflicts, slow decision making, and inability to respond quickly to market changes.

Stena's philosophy was very different. It operated a decentralized structure, believing that each management function should be responsible for its own activities and accountable for the results. Stena wanted management decisions in the British subsidiary to be taken by people close to the market who understood local competition and demand. Some central functions were moved out to the divisions, including much responsibility for marketing activities. New skills and perspectives came from retraining, transfers, and outside hiring.

Before the merger, no priority had been given to either punctual or reliable operations. Ferries were often late, but standard excuses were used in reports, customer complaints were ignored, and there was little pressure from customer service managers to improve the situation. After the takeover, things started to change. The challenge of late departures and arrivals was resolved through concentration on individual problem areas. On one route, for instance, the port manager involved all operational staff and gave each person "ownership" of a specific aspect of the improvement process. They kept detailed records of each sailing, together with reasons for late departures, as well as monitoring competitors' performance. This participative approach created close liaison between staff members in different job positions and also helped customer service staff to learn from experience. Within two years, the Stena ferries on this route were operating at close to 100 percent punctuality.

On-board service was another area singled out for improvement. Historically, customer service managers did what was convenient for staff rather than customers, including scheduling meal breaks at times when customer demand for service was greatest. As one observer noted, "customers were ignored during the first and last half hour on board, when facilities were closed. . . . Customers were left to find their own way around [the ship]. . . . Staff only responded to customers when [they] initiated a direct request and made some effort to attract their attention." So Stena required personnel from each on-board functional area to choose a specific area for improvement and to work in small groups to achieve this. Initially, some teams were more successful than others, resulting in inconsistent levels of service and customer orientation from one ship to another. Subsequently, managers shared ideas, reviewed experiences, and made adaptations for individual ships. Key changes during the first two years (Table 15.A) contributed to eventual success in achieving consistent service levels on all sailings and all ferries.

By 2006, Stena Line had 34 ships sailing on 18 routes (of which seven served UK ports), carrying some 17 million passengers and 3 million vehicles annually. They included three of the world's largest fast ferries. A leader in all its markets, Stena emphasizes constant service and product improvement. Says the company's web site:

> The phrase Making Good Time summarises the core of the Stena Line business in three words: fast, enjoyable and efficient sea travel. Today's customers are looking for more. Basic factors such as punctuality, safety, clean and well-equipped ferries with good service are now taken for granted, so at Stena Line we're trying even harder to give guests that little extra so they'll want to travel with us again. A way of meeting these new demands is to develop new products and services, and to further customise our offers to suit different requirements. Our ambition is that everyone should find a travel offer in our selection that they like.

Sources: Adapted from Audrey Gilmore, "Services Marketing Management Competencies: A Ferry Company Example." *International Journal of Service Industry Management*, 9, no. 1 (1998): 74–92; www.stenaline.com, accessed June 2006.

Table 15.A Changing Contexts, Competencies, and Performance Following the Takeover

	INHERITED SITUATION	SITUATION AFTER TWO YEARS
External Context	Inactive competition—"share" market with one competitor	Aggressive competitive activity (two competitors, one operating new, high-speed ferries)
	Static market demand	Growing market
Internal Context	Centralized organization	Decentralized organization
	Centralized decision making	Delegation to specialized decision-making units
	Top management directives	Key manager responsible for each unit team
Managerial Competencies		
Knowledge	General to industry rather than specific to local markets	Understand both industry and local market
Experience	Operational and tactical	Operational and decision making
	General, industry-based	Functional management responsibility
	Noncompetitive environment	Exposed to competitive environment
Expertise	Vague approach to judging situations	Diagnostic judgmental capabilities
	Short-term focus	Longer-term focus
	Generalist competencies	Specific skills for functional tasks
Marketing Decision Making		
Planning	React to internal circumstances and external threats	Proactive identification of problems
	Minimal information search or evaluation of alternatives	Collect information, consider options
	Focus on tactical issues	Choose among several options
	Inconsistent with other marketing activities	Consistent with other marketing activities
Actions	Follow top management directives	Delegation of responsibility
	Look to next in line for responsibility	Responsibility and ownership for activity
	Minimal or intermittent communication between functions	Liaison between functions
Marketing Efforts		
Prepurchase	Mostly media advertising	Advertising plus promotions and informational materials
Service delivery	Slow, manual booking system	New, computerized reservation system
	Focus on tangible aspects of on-board customer service (e.g., seating, cabins, food, bar)	Better tangibles, sharply improved staff/customer interactions
	Little pressure on operations to improve poor punctuality	Highly reliable, punctual service
	Poor communications at ports and on board ships	Much improved signage, printed guides, electronic message boards, public announcements
	Reactive approach to problem solving	Proactive approach to welcoming customers and solving their problems

Many of the best visions and strategies are not brilliantly innovative; rather, they combine some basic insights and translate them into a realistic competitive strategy that serves the interests of customers, employees, and stockholders. Some visions, however, fall into the category that Gary Hamel and C. K. Pralahad describe as "stretch"—a challenge to attain new levels of performance and competitive advantage that might at first seem to be beyond the organization's reach.[14] Stretching to achieve such bold goals requires creative reappraisal of traditional ways of doing business and leverage of existing resources through partnerships (see Service Perspective 15.1). It also requires creating the energy and the will among managers and employees alike to perform at higher levels than they believe themselves able to do.

Leonard Berry and his colleagues emphasize that executives who seek to develop strategies based on service innovation must concentrate on the tasks that determine success or failure, and recognize that innovation starts with culture and requires a

Who would have believed in the mid-1980s that Le Club des Talons Hauts (The High Heels Club), a small band of French-speaking street performers who walked on stilts and lived in a youth hostel near Quebec City, Canada, would one day become the world-famous *Cirque du Soleil*? With its unique mix of music, dance, and acrobatics—but no animals—the *Cirque du Soleil* (Circus of the Sun) has created a new category of live entertainment, packaged in a variety of distinctive shows, attended by millions around the world (Figure 15.4). "People said we reinvented the circus—we didn't reinvent the circus," declares President Guy Laliberté:

Figure 15.4   *Cirque du Soleil* Advertises Its *Mystère* Show in Las Vegas

Courtesy Cirque du Soleil Inc.

We repackaged a way of presenting the circus show in a much more modern way. . . . We took an art form that was known, that had a lot of dust on it, where people had forgotten it could be something other than what they knew, and we organized for ourselves a new creative platform.

To achieve its present eminence, featuring six touring shows and six permanent shows in conjunction with partnering resorts—five with Las Vegas casino hotels and one at Walt DisneyWorld resort in Florida—the *Cirque* has had to face and resolve financial, managerial, and artistic challenges. For the well-paid performers, who include many former Olympic athletes, the notion of stretch (both physically and metaphorically) is central to their professional lives. "Creative people always need new challenges," says COO Daniel Lamarre. Organizations, by contrast, sometimes find it easier to rest on their laurels. However, such an approach could contain the seeds of failure for the *Cirque*.

Cirque du Soleil faces new competitors today, including two that have emerged from its home turf, *Cirque Éloize* and *Cirque Éos*, both spawned by the growing supply of graduates from two recently formed circus schools in Quebec. *Cirque* copycats have also sprung up in France and Argentina. An even greater challenge comes from a U.S. company, Feld Enterprises, which owns the famous Ringling Bros. and Barnum & Bailey Circus. Feld has created a new production, Barnum's Kaleidoscope, that replaces the traditional circus performers with a mix of acrobatic performers and live music at much higher admission prices.

Cirque du Soleil has grown in recent years by adding new shows with new partner resorts. In 2006 it launched *Love*, a show based on the music of the Beatles, making the Mirage casino its fifth partner in Las Vegas. However, a key question for *Cirque* is where future growth will come from as its core market becomes more crowded. Not only is new competition driving up the cost of finding and retaining top performers, it is unclear how much longer the privately held Canadian company can continue filling 1,000-seat theaters at high admission prices with what some critics view as essentially variations on the same product. Continued evolution will be required.

Sources: Robert J. David and Amir Motamedi, "*Cirque du Soleil:* Can It Burn Brighter?" *Journal of Strategic Management Education,* 1, no. 2 (2004): 369–382; http://www.cirquedusoleil. com, accessed June 2006.

champion.[15] Their research (reprinted in the reading, "Creating New Markets Through Service Innovation," pp. 478–484) identifies nine success drivers, including comprehensive customer-experience management, investment in employee performance, brand differentiation, and a superior customer benefit. Planning follows and complements direction setting, serving as a useful reality check and a road map for strategic execution. A good plan provides an action agenda for accomplishing the mission, using existing resources or identifying potential new sources.

Individual Leadership Qualities

Many commentators have written on the topic of leadership. It has even been described as a service in its own right.[16] The late Sam Walton, founder of the Wal-Mart retail chain, highlighted the role of managers as "servant leaders."[17]

Leonard Berry argues that service leadership requires a special perspective. "Regardless of the target markets, the specific services, or the pricing strategy, service leaders visualize quality of service as the foundation for competing."[18] Recognizing the key role of employees in delivering service, he emphasizes that service leaders need to believe in the people who work for them and make communicating with employees a priority. Love of the business is another service leadership characteristic he highlights, to the extent that it combines natural enthusiasm with the right setting in which to express it. Such enthusiasm motivates individuals to teach the business to others and to pass on to them the nuances, secrets, and craft of operating it. Berry also stresses the importance for leaders of being driven by a set of core values that they infuse into the organization, arguing that "A critical role of values-driven leaders is cultivating the leadership qualities of others in the organization." And he notes that "values-driven leaders rely on their values to navigate their companies through difficult periods."[19]

Rakesh Karma warns against excessive emphasis on charisma in selecting CEOs, arguing that it leads to unrealistic expectations.[20] He notes that unethical behavior may occur when charismatic but unprincipled leaders induce blind obedience in their followers, and cites the illegal activities stimulated by the leadership of Enron, which eventually led to the company's collapse. Jim Collins concludes that a leader does not require a larger-than-life personality. Leaders who aspire to take a company to greatness, he says, need to have personal humility blended with intensive professional will, ferocious resolve, and a willingness to give credit to others while taking the blame to themselves.[21]

In hierarchical organizations, structured on a military model, it's often assumed that leadership at the top is sufficient. However, as Sandra Vandermerwe points out, forward-looking service businesses need to be more flexible. Today's greater emphasis on using teams within service businesses means that

> [L]eaders are everywhere, disseminated throughout the teams. They are found especially in the customer facing and interfacing jobs in order that decision-making will lead to long-lasting relationships with customers … leaders are customer and project champions who energize the group by virtue of their enthusiasm, interest, and know-how.[22]

CHANGE MANAGEMENT

There are important distinctions between leading a successful organization that is functioning well, redirecting a firm into new areas of activity, and trying to turn around a dysfunctional organization. In the case of Wal-Mart, Sam Walton created both the company and the culture, so his task was to preserve that culture as the company grew and to select a successor who would maintain an appropriate culture as the company continued to grow. Herb Kelleher, a lawyer by training and one of the founders of Southwest Airlines, used his legal skills in his initial role as the company's general counsel. After he was appointed CEO some years later, he deployed his considerable human relations skills to shape and reinforce the company's distinctive culture as it evolved into one of the largest domestic air operations in the United States. Meg Whitman, who had both consulting and managerial experience, was recruited as CEO of eBay when it became clear to the founders that the fledgling Internet start-up needed leadership from someone possessing the insights and discipline of an experienced marketer.

Evolution Versus Turnaround

Transformation of an organization can take place in two different ways: evolution or turnaround. *Evolution* in a business context involves continual mutations designed to ensure the survival of the fittest. Top management must proactively evolve the focus and strategy of the firm to take advantage of changing conditions and the advent of new technologies. Without a continuing series of mutations, it's unlikely that a firm can remain successful in a dynamic marketplace.

A different type of transformation occurs in *turnaround* situations, in which leaders (usually new ones) seek to bring distressed organizations back from the brink of failure and set them on a healthier course. Such an approach is exemplified by the experience of American Express, which has undergone several transformations during its more than 150-year history (Service Perspective 15.2).

According to noted author Rosabeth Moss Kanter, it can be advantageous in turnaround situations to bring in a new CEO from outside the organization.[23] Such individuals, she argues, are better able to disentangle system dynamics because they were not previously caught up in them, and to voice problems and change habits. New CEOs may also have more credibility in representing and respecting customers. Exemplary turnaround leaders, she says, understand the powerful, unifying effect of focusing on customers. This focus can facilitate the difficult task of obtaining collaboration across departments and divisions. In addition to breaking down barriers between marketing, operations, and human resources, or between various product or geographic divisions, turnaround CEOs

"Frankly, you can't be a jerk in the service business and be successful for a long period of time," says Kenneth Chenault, CEO of American Express. "When you're in the service business, reputation is everything." However, he also cautions: "Sometimes when you are very successful, you become arrogant, and what I've tried to instill [here] is a very strong sense of customer needs [and] respect for your colleagues."

American Express, best known today as an icon in travel and financial services, has evolved through what it describes as "150 years of reinvention and customer service." Established in 1850 in New York, it was among the first and most successful express delivery firms created during the westward expansion of the United States. Intrepid expressmen, typically on horseback or driving stagecoaches, transported letters, parcels, freight, gold, and currency from Eastern cities to the Western Frontier. The largest and most consistent clients were banks. Delivering their small parcels—stock certificates, notes, currency, and other financial instruments—was much more profitable than transporting larger freight. As the railroads grew, the company scaled down its delivery business in favor of creating and selling its own financial products, launching money orders in 1882 and the world's first traveler's cheques in 1891. The American Express name became increasingly visible overseas, and offices were opened in Europe.

From the 1920s on, the company focused on travel services, supported by selling traveler's cheques and money orders (and profits from investing the substantial float on these products). The first American Express charge card was issued in 1958. This business grew rapidly and included both individual and corporate cardholders. Gold and platinum cards followed, offering extra features and privileges in return for a higher annual fee.

In an effort to diversify, American Express sought to create a "financial supermarket" through acquisition of other financial service firms. However, the anticipated synergies were never realized and the company stumbled in the early 1990s. Meantime, its card business faced intense competition from Visa and MasterCard, on which merchants paid lower fees.

In 1991, a group of Boston restauranteurs, upset about high rates, staged a revolt nicknamed the Boston Fee Party, and refused to accept American Express cards. Other merchants joined them, both at home and abroad. Chenault, then a rising young executive, headed the successful effort to achieve reconciliation and to reduce rates. Promoted to president and COO, he broadened the cards' appeal by offering new features and loyalty programs, creating new types of cards, and signing up mass market retailers, including Wal-Mart. Spending through American Express cards, once dominated by travel and entertainment, is today led by retail and everyday purchases, including office expenditures by small-business cardholders.

Soon after being named CEO in 2001, Chenault faced the daunting challenge of helping the company recover from both the human trauma of seeing the World Trade Center destroyed across the street from the firm's headquarters and the sharp decline in travel that followed 9/11. Widely praised for his leadership, Chenault offered a road map designed to make the company leaner and able to respond faster to business opportunities as the economy recovered. By 2005 he had completed the dismantling of the "financial supermarket" and refocused the business on its core activities of card services and travel, with operations in 130 countries.

Chenault looks back at 2001 as "critical and fundamental to our company's success. It tested our management in incredible ways." Asked by a reporter to describe his leadership philosophy, he responded: "The role of a leader is to define reality and give hope."

Sources: Nelson D. Schwartz, "What's in the Cards for Amex?" *Fortune,* January 22, 2001, pp. 58–70; Greg Farrell, "A CEO and a Gentleman." *USA Today,* April 25, 2005, pp. 1B, 3B; "Our History. Becoming American Express: 150+ Years of Reinvention and Customer Service." http://home3.americanexpress.com/corp/os/history/circle.aspm, accessed June 2006.

may also need to reorient financial priorities to enable collaborative groups to tackle new business opportunities.

Chan Kim and Renée Mauborgne, both professors at INSEAD, have identified four hurdles that leaders face in reorienting and formulating strategy.[24]

- *Cognitive hurdles* are present when people cannot agree on the causes of current problems and the need for change.
- *Resource hurdles* exist when the organization is constrained by limited funds.

- *Motivational hurdles* prevent a strategy's rapid execution when employees are reluctant to make needed changes.
- *Political hurdles* take the form of organized resistance from powerful vested interests seeking to protect their positions.

Turning around an organization that has limited resources requires concentrating those resources where the need and the likely payoffs are greatest. As an example of effective leadership under such conditions, Kim and Mauborgne highlight the work of William Bratton, who achieved fame during a 20-year police career in Boston and New York. Bratton believed in putting his key managers face to face with the problems that were of greatest concern to the public. When he became chief of the New York Transit Police, Bratton found that none of the senior staff officers rode the subway. So he required all transit police officials, including himself, to ride the subway to work and to meetings, even at night, instead of traveling in cars provided by the city. In that way, senior officials were exposed to the reality of the problems faced by millions of ordinary citizens and by police officers who strove to keep order.

Bratton's predecessors had lobbied for money to increase the number of subway cops, believing that the only way to stop muggers was to have officers ride every subway line and patrol each of the system's 700 exits and entrances. Bratton, in contrast, had his staff analyze where subway crimes were being committed. Finding that the vast majority occurred at only a few stations and on a couple of lines, the chief redeployed his officers to focus on the problem areas and shifted a number of uniformed officers into plain clothes. Coupled with time-saving innovations in arrest-processing procedures, this dramatic reallocation of resources resulted in a significant reduction in subway crime without new investments..

A firm's search for growth often involves expansion—even diversification— into new lines of business. Many manufacturing businesses have transformed themselves by expanding into services. However, if they are marketed under the company's corporate brand, the challenge of transformation extends to shifting the market's perception of that company's capabilities. The further removed the new services are from the original physical product, the greater the challenge. Consider IBM. It's one thing to persuade existing users of its computers that it can offer them value with new or expanded services relating to equipment installation, maintenance, upgrades, networking, or security. But how should the company build awareness and credibility for an international management consulting subsidiary called IBM Business Consulting? The company developed an advertising campaign headlined "The Other IBM," raising a series of strategic questions to which it promises to "find the answers with an altogether different kind of thinking." To succeed, it must, of course, deliver on that promise.

Role Modeling Desired Behavior

One of the traits of successful leaders is their ability to role model the behavior they expect of managers and other employees. Often, this requires the approach known as "management by walking around," popularized by Thomas Peters and Robert Waterman in their classic book, *In Search of Excellence*.[25] Walking around involves regular visits, sometimes unannounced, to various areas of the company's operation. This approach provides insights into both backstage and front-stage operations, the ability to observe and meet both employees and customers, and an opportunity to see how corporate strategy is implemented on the front line. When Herb Kelleher was CEO of Southwest Airlines, no one was surprised to see him turn up at a Southwest maintenance hanger at 2 o'clock in the morning or even to encounter him working an occasional stint as a flight attendant.

Periodically, this approach may lead to a recognition that changes are needed in that strategy. For employees, encountering the CEO on such a visit can be motivating. It also provides the latter with an opportunity for role modeling good service. Best Practice in Action 15.2 describes how the CEO of a major hospital learned the power of role modeling early in his tenure.

During his 30-year tenure as president of Boston's Beth Israel Hospital (now Beth Israel-Deaconess Medical Center), Mitchell T. Rabkin, MD, was known for regularly spending time making informal visits to all parts of the hospital. "You learn a lot from 'management by walking around,'" he said, "And you're also seen. When I visit another hospital and am given a tour by its CEO, I watch how that CEO interacts with other people, and what the body language is in each instance. It's very revealing. Even more, it's very important for role modeling." To reinforce that point, Dr. Rabkin likes to tell the following story.

> People learn to *do* as a result of the way they see you and others *behave*. An example from the Beth Israel that's now almost apocryphal—but *is* true—is the story of the bits of litter on the floor.
>
> One of our trustees, the late Max Feldberg, head of the Zayre Corporation, asked me one time to take a walk around the hospital with him and inquired, "Why do you think there are so many pieces of paper scattered on the floor of this patient care unit?"

"Well, it's because people don't pick them up," I replied.

He said, "Look, you're a scientist. We'll do an experiment. We'll walk down this floor and we'll pick up every other piece of paper. And then we'll go upstairs, there's another unit, same geography, statistically the same amount of paper, but we won't pick up anything."

So this 72-year-old man and I went picking up alternate bits of the litter on one floor and nothing on the other. When we came back 10 minutes later, virtually all the rest of the litter on the first floor had been removed and nothing, of course, had changed on the second.

And "Mr. Max" said to me, "You see, it's not because *people* don't pick them up, it's because *you* don't pick them up. If you're so fancy that you can't bend down and pick up a piece of paper, why should anybody else?"

Source: Christopher Lovelock, *Product Plus: How Product + Service = Competitive Advantage.* New York: McGraw-Hill, 1994.

There is a risk, of course, that prominent leaders may become too externally focused at the risk of their internal effectiveness. A CEO who enjoys an enormous income (often through exercise of huge stock options), maintains a princely lifestyle, and basks in widespread publicity may even turn off low-paid service workers at the bottom of the organization.

Evaluating Leadership Potential

The need for leadership in service organizations is not confined to chief executives or other top managers. Leadership traits are needed of everyone in a supervisory or managerial position, including those heading teams. FedEx believes this so strongly that it requires all employees interested in entering the ranks of first-line management to participate in its Leadership Evaluation and Awareness Process (LEAP).[26]

LEAP's first step involves participation in an introductory, one-day class that familiarizes candidates with managerial responsibilities. About one candidate in five concludes at this point that "management is not for me." The next step is a three- to six-month period during which the candidate's manager coaches him or her based on a series of leadership attributes identified by the company. A third step involves peer assessment by a number of the candidate's co-workers (selected by the manager). Finally, the candidate must present written and oral arguments regarding specific leadership scenarios to a group of managers trained in LEAP assessment; this panel compares its findings with those from the other sources above.

FedEx emphasizes leadership at every level through its Survey Feedback Action surveys, including the Leadership Index in which subordinates rate their managers along 10 dimensions. Unfortunately, not every company is equally thorough in addressing the role of leadership at all levels in the organization. In many firms, promotional decisions often appear haphazard or based on such criteria as duration of tenure in a previous position.

Leadership, Culture, and Climate

To close this chapter, we take a brief look at a theme that runs throughout the book:[27] the leader's role in nurturing an effective culture within the firm. *Organizational culture* can be defined as including:

- Shared perceptions or themes regarding what is important in the organization
- Shared values about what is right and wrong
- Shared understanding about what works and what doesn't work
- Shared beliefs, and assumptions about *why* these things are important
- Shared styles of working and relating to others

John Hamm believes that effective communication is a leader's most critical tool for doing the essential task of inspiring the organization to take responsibility for creating a better future. The most effective leaders, he says, ask themselves, "What needs to happen today to get where we want to go? What vague belief or notion can I clarify or debunk?" Those CEOs who can communicate precisely will best be able to align the organization's commitment and energy with a well-understood vision of the firm's real goals and opportunities.[28]

Transforming an organization to develop and nurture a new culture is no easy task for even the most gifted leader. It's doubly difficult when the organization is part of an industry that prides itself on deeply-rooted traditions, including many departments run by independent-minded professionals in different fields who are very attuned to how they are perceived by fellow professionals in the same field at other institutions. This situation is often found in such pillars of the nonprofit world as colleges and universities, major hospitals, and large museums. Service Perspective 15.3 describes the challenges faced by a new director in transforming Boston's Museum of Fine Arts at a low point in its history.

SERVICE PERSPECTIVES 15.3
Reversing Course at the Museum of Fine Arts, Boston

Boston's venerable Museum of Fine Arts (MFA), founded in 1870, had been going downhill for several years when the board recruited a new director in June 1994. Their choice was art historian Malcolm Rogers, then deputy director of the National Portrait Gallery in London. Upon arriving in Boston, Rogers found a dispirited institution. Reflecting financial difficulties and recent staff cutbacks, morale was low. Corporate memberships had slumped and attendance had declined.

One of the new director's first acts was to host a breakfast for the entire staff and introduce what would become a central theme:

> We are one museum, not a collection of departments. The museum consists of security guards, curators, technicians, benefactors, volunteers, public relations personnel. We all have our individual professional expertise. And by working cooperatively with colleagues, we all have areas that can be improved.

Rogers' "one museum" theme, repeated at frequent intervals, sent the message that the director's agenda took precedence over that of the traditionally independent curators who operated the museum's many different art departments and set priorities for acquisitions and exhibitions. One curator quickly resigned. While he was recognized for his good humor and friendly, outgoing manner, the new director showed that he could be blunt and decisive. He took a tough line with expenditures and began a program to cut staff size by 20 percent. However, his cutbacks did not extend to services for museum visitors. Instead, he set about creating a more welcoming environment. Said Rogers:

> I'm firmly committed to the idea that museums are here to serve the community, and that's going to be one of the keynotes of my work here in Boston—to encourage the MFA to turn out toward its public and to satisfy as broad a constituency as possible.

He soon reopened the main entrance on Huntington Avenue, which had been closed to save money, and reversed the trend of curtailing admission hours, another of his predecessor's cost-cutting initiatives. Daily schedules were extended and seven-day operations instituted. Three nights a week, the museum remained open until 10 P.M. On "Community Days," three Sundays a year, the MFA was open free of charge.

Each successive year, Rogers launched activities to improve the museum's facilities and image, including new exterior lighting to better display the MFA's imposing facade at night, extending the main restaurant, and opening a new roof-top terrace. Making the MFA an evening destination, especially for people living in or close to the city, was another objective. The broader variety of exhibitions (to encourage multiple visits per year), upgraded restaurants, and improved museum atmosphere all played a role. An ambitious $500 million capital campaign was launched, part of which would fund construction of a major building expansion.

Externally, Rogers enjoyed a much higher public profile than his predecessors. Said Pat Jacoby, then deputy director of marketing and development, "Malcolm personifies marketing: He's accessible, he's an advocate of PR, he cares about the visitors, and he believes the MFA can set the standard for other museums." Rogers declared:

Marketing is central to the life of a great museum that's trying to get its message out. It's part of our educational outreach, our social outreach. Unfortunately, certain people don't like the word "marketing." What I see out there—and also to a certain extent inside the museum—is a very conservative culture that cannot accept that institutions previously considered "elite" should actually be trying to attract a broader public and also listening to what the public is saying. But it's all to do with fulfilling your mission.

Clearly part of a museum's mission is guardianship of precious objects, but unless we're communicating those objects to people effectively and our visitors are enjoying them—and the ambiance of the setting in which they are displayed and interpreted—then we're only operating at 50% effectiveness or less. Having said this, I want to stress that the mission comes first and that marketing is absolutely the servant of our mission. We're not just in the business of finding out what people want and then giving it to them.

Rogers sought to pick a mix of exhibitions that combined high scholarly content with popular appeal. His view, shared by the senior staff and supported by the board, was that one show in five should be of a "blockbuster" nature, which meant hosting such an exhibition at least once every two years. He also sought to display art from the MFA's permanent collection to best advantage, including small revolving shows. Paintings in the 15 European galleries were rehung in innovative ways designed to stimulate the audience and engage them more actively. However, there was much criticism in the art community when 27 Impressionist paintings from the MFA's celebrated Monet collection were loaned (for a reported $1 million fee) to a gallery at the Bellagio casino in Las Vegas, where they were seen by 450,000 visitors.

In 2002, the MFA board adopted a long-term strategic plan, titled "One Museum—Great Museum—Your Museum." It was organized around 10 strategic goals (Table 15.B), each supported by a set of initiatives and over 200 detailed action plans.

By mid-2006, many of these initiatives were well underway. The fundraising drive for the new extension had passed the $335 million mark. Attendance had begun to grow again, after slumping nationwide following 9/11. The MFA continued its strategy of periodically exhibiting nontraditional art forms and art collections, including "Speed, Style and Beauty: Cars from the Ralph Lauren Collection," featuring 16 classic European cars owned by the fashion designer. Rogers argued that these vehicles were as much works of art as furniture, long an accepted component of many art museums' collections. Despite such criticisms as a *New York Times* review headlined, "Art with Lousy Mileage but Shiny Celebrity Gloss," attendance exceeded its goals and met an important objective of attracting a much higher proportion of male visitors than usually came to the museum.

Table 15.B Ten Strategic Goals for the MFA

Collections	1. Continue to improve quality of the collection.
	2. Improve management, care, and knowledge of the collection.
	3. Provide and promote worldwide electronic access to the collection.
Experiencing the Museum	4. Engage, educate, and delight visitors.
	5. Retain and expand audiences by understanding their needs.
	6. Schedule an exhibition program that meets a variety of objectives.
Facilities	7. Enlarge and improve the physical plant.
Financial	8. Pursue fundraising required by the Master Site plan and other strategic goals.
	9. Ensure fiscal stability.
Organization	10. Adopt an audience-aware, results-oriented experimental attitude and realign the organization to support these activities.

Sources: Christopher Lovelock, "Museum of Fine Arts, Boston." *Services Marketing*, 4th ed. Upper Saddle River, NJ: Prentice Hall, 2001, pp. 625–638; V. Kasturi Rangan and Marie Bell, "Museum of Fine Arts Boston." Harvard Business School Case 9-506-027; Museum of Fine Arts web site, www.mfa.org, accessed May 2006.

Organizational climate represents the tangible surface layer on top of the organization's underlying culture. Among six key factors that influence an organization's working environment are its *flexibility* (how free employees feel to innovate); their sense of *responsibility* to the organization; the level of *standards* that people set; the perceived aptness of *rewards*; the *clarity* people have about mission and values; and the level of *commitment* to a common purpose.[29] From an employee perspective, this climate is related directly to managerial policies and procedures, especially those associated with human resource management. In short, climate represents the shared perceptions of employees about the practices, procedures, and types of behaviors that get rewarded and supported in a particular setting.

Because multiple climates often exist simultaneously within a single organization, a climate must relate to something specific—for instance, service, support, innovation, or safety. A climate for service refers to employee perceptions of those practices, procedures, and behaviors that are expected with regard to customer service and service quality, and that get rewarded when performed well. Essential features of a service-oriented culture include clear marketing goals and a strong drive to be the best in delivering superior value or service quality.[30]

Leaders are responsible for creating cultures and the service climates that go along with them. Transformational leadership may require changing a culture that has become dysfunctional in the context of what it takes to be successful. Why are some leaders more effective than others in bringing about a desired change in climate? As presented in Research Insights 15.1, research suggests that it may be a matter of style.

Creating a new climate for service, based on an understanding of what is needed for market success, may require radical rethinking of human resource management activities, operational procedures, and the firm's reward and recognition policies. Newcomers to an organization must quickly familiarize themselves with the existing culture, otherwise they will find themselves being led by it, rather than leading through it and, if necessary, changing it.

RESEARCH INSIGHTS 15.1
The Effect of Leadership Style on Climate

Daniel Goleman, an applied psychologist at Rutgers University, is known for his work on emotional intelligence—the ability to manage ourselves and our relationships effectively. Having earlier identified six styles of leadership, he investigated how successful each style has proved to be in affecting climate or working atmosphere, based on a major study of the behavior and effect on their organizations of thousands of executives.

Coercive leaders demand immediate compliance ("Do what I tell you") and were found to have a negative effect on climate. Goleman comments that this controlling style, often highly confrontational, has value only in a crisis or in dealing with problem employees. *Pacesetting leaders* set high standards for performance and exemplify these through their own energetic behavior; this style can be summarized as "Do as I do, now." Somewhat surprisingly it, too, was found to have a negative effect on climate. In practice, the pacesetting leader may destroy morale by assuming too much, too soon, of subordinates—expecting them to know already what to do and how to do it. Finding others to be less capable than expected, the leader may lapse into obsessing over details and micromanaging. This style is likely to work only when seeking to get quick results from a highly motivated and competent team.

The research found that the most effective style for achieving a positive change in climate came from *authoritative leaders* who have the skills and personality to mobilize people toward a vision, building confidence and using a "Come with me" approach. The research also found that three other styles had quite positive effects on climate: *affiliative leaders* who believe that "People come first," seeking to create harmony and build emotional bonds; *democratic leaders* who forge consensus through participation ("What do you think?"); and *coaching leaders* who work to develop people for the future and whose style might be summarized as "Try this."

Source: Daniel Goleman, "Leadership That Gets Results." *Harvard Business Review, 78* (March–April 2000): 78–93.

CONCLUSION

As illustrated by the service–profit chain, service leadership in an industry requires high performance across a number of dimensions, including managing and motivating employees, continuously improving service quality and productivity, creating and delivering a value proposition that target customers will perceive as superior to competing offerings, managing customer relationships effectively, and developing strategies for building and sustaining customer loyalty. These tasks cross traditional functional boundaries. Ultimately, a company's ability to achieve and maintain profitability will hinge on top management's skills in integrating the activities of marketing, operations, and human resources. Failure to do so may doom the organization to the status of a service nonentity or even service loser.

No organization can hope to achieve enduring success without change. The primary force behind effective change management is human leadership, which is concerned with the development of vision and strategies, the empowerment of people to overcome obstacles, and the ability to make the vision happen. One of the challenges for top management is to create a culture for innovation that gives employees the confidence to take risks, share ideas, and be willing to try new approaches

Transformation of an organization can take place in two different ways: evolution or turnaround. *Evolution* in a business context involves continual changes and enhancements designed to ensure the survival of the fittest in often fiercely competitive markets. Top manage-

ment must proactively evolve the firm's focus and strategy to take advantage of such factors as changing customer needs, the growth and decline of different markets, and the advent of new technologies. New and evolving strategies should anticipate the entry of new competitors and the repositioning of existing ones. A different type of transformation occurs in *turnaround* situations, in which leaders (often new to the firm) seek to bring distressed organizations back from the brink of failure and set them on a healthier course.

Exemplary leaders understand the powerful, unifying effect of focusing on customers and creating a culture for service. In turnaround situations, especially, this focus can facilitate the difficult task of obtaining collaboration across departments and divisions. Among the traits of successful leaders is their ability to role model the behavior they expect of others. Turning around an organization that has limited resources requires concentrating those resources where the need and the likely payoffs are greatest. However, the need for leadership in service organizations is not confined to chief executives and other top managers. Leadership skills are required of everyone in a supervisory or managerial position, particularly those who head teams charged with key elements of the change management process.

In summary, transforming an organization to develop and nurture a new culture and its accompanying service climate is no easy task for even the most gifted leader. It's doubly difficult when the organization is part of an industry that prides itself on maintaining deeply rooted traditions.

REVIEW QUESTIONS

1. Supporters of the service–profit chain argue that there links connecting employee satisfaction and loyalty; service quality and productivity; value; and customer satisfaction and loyalty. Do you think these same relationships would prevail in a low-contact environment in which customers use self-service technology? Why (or why not)?
2. What are the causes of tension among the marketing, operations, and human resource functions? Provide specific examples of how these tensions might vary from one service industry to another.
3. How are the four levels of service performance defined? Based on your own service experiences, provide an example of a company for each category.
4. What is the difference between leadership and management? Illustrate with examples.
5. What is meant by transformational leadership? Explain how the challenges differ between an organization that is undergoing evolutionary change and one that requires a turnaround.
6. "Exemplary turnaround leaders understand the powerful, unifying effect of focusing on customers." Comment on this statement. Is focusing on customers more likely to have a unifying effect within a company under turnaround conditions than at other times?
7. What is the relationship among leadership, climate, and culture?

APPLICATION EXERCISES

1. Contrast the roles of marketing, operations, and human resources in (a) a gas station chain, (b) a Web-based brokerage firm, and (c) an insurance company.
2. Select a company that you know well and obtain additional information from a literature review, web site, company publications, and so on. Evaluate the company on as many dimensions of service performance as you can, identifying where you believe it fits on the service performance spectrum shown in Table 15.2.
3. Profile an individual whose leadership skills have played a significant role in the success of a service organization, identifying personal characteristics that you consider important.

1. Don Peppers and Martha Rogers, *Return on Customer.* New York: Currency Doubleday, 2005, p. 1.

2. Ibid., pp. 7–8.

3. James L. Heskett., Thomas O. Jones, Gary W. Loveman, W. Earl Sasser, Jr., and Leonard A. Schlesinger, "Putting the Service Profit Chain to Work." *Harvard Business Review,* 72 (March/April 1994): 164–174; and James L. Heskett, W. Earl Sasser, Jr., and Leonard A. Schlesinger, *The Service Profit Chain.* New York: The Free Press, 1997.

4. See, for example, Jeffrey Pfeffer, *Competitive Advantage Through People.* Boston: Harvard Business School Press, 1994.

5. See, for example, Benjamin Schneider and David E. Bowen, *Winning the Service Game.* Boston: Harvard Business School Press, 1995; Leonard L. Berry, *On Great Service: A Framework for Action.* New York: The Free Press, 1995, chaps. 8–10.

6. Terri Kabachnick, "The Strategic Role of Human Resources." *Arthur Andersen Retailing Issues Letter,* 11, no. 1 (January 1999): 3.

7. Sandra Vandermerwe, *From Tin Soldiers to Russian Dolls,* Oxford, UK: Butterworth-Heinemann, 1993, p. 82.

8. Richard B. Chase and Robert H. Hayes, "Beefing up Operations in Service Firms." *Sloan Management Review,* 32 (Fall 1991): 15–26.

9. Claudia H. Deutsch, "Management: Companies Scramble to Fill Shoes at the Top." nytimes.com, November 1, 2000.

10. John P. Kotter, *What Leaders Really Do.* Boston: Harvard Business School Press, 1999, pp. 10–11.

11. Warren Bennis and Burt Nanus, *Leaders: The Strategies for Taking Charge.* New York: Harper & Row, 1985, p. 92.

12. Kotter, *What Leaders Really Do,* pp. 10–11.

13. Deborah Blagg and Susan Young, "What Makes a Leader?" *Harvard Business School Bulletin* (February 2001): 31–36.

14. Gary Hamel and C. K. Prahlahad, *Competing for the Future.* Boston: Harvard Business School Press, 1994.

15. Leonard L. Berry, Venkatesh Shankar, Janet Turner Parish, Susan Cadwallader, and Thomas Dotzel, "Creating New Markets Through Service Innovation. *MIT Sloan Management Review,* 47 (Winter 2006): 56–63.

16. See, for instance, the special issue on "Leadership as a Service" (Celeste Wilderom, guest editor), *International Journal of Service Industry Management,* 3, no. 2 (1992).

17. Heskett, Sasser, and Schlesinger, *The Service Profit Chain,* p. 236.

18. Berry, *On Great Service,* p. 9.

19. Leonard L. Berry, *Discovering the Soul of Service.* New York,: The Free Press, 1999, pp. 44, 47. See also D. Micheal Abrashoff, "Retention Through Redemption." *Harvard Business Review,* 79 (February 2001): 136–141, which provides a fascinating example on successful leadership in the U.S. Navy.

20. Rakesh Karma, "The Curse of the Superstar CEO." *Harvard Business Review,* 80 (September 2002): 60–66.

21. Jim Collins, "Level 5 Leadership: The Triumph of Humility and Fierce Resolve." *Harvard Business Review,* 79 (January 2001): 66–76.

22. Vandermerwe, *From Tin Soldiers to Russian Dolls,* p. 129.

23. Rosabeth Moss Kanter, "Leadership and the Psychology of Turnaround." *Harvard Business Review,* 81 (June 2003): 58–67.

24. W. Chan Kim and Renée Mauborgne, "Tipping Point Leadership." *Harvard Business Review,* 81 (April 2003): 61–69.

25. Thomas J. Peters and Robert H. Waterman, *In Search of Excellence.* New York: Harper & Row, 1982, p. 122.

26. Christopher Lovelock, "Federal Express: Quality Improvement Program," IMD case. Cranfield, UK: European Case Clearing House, 1990.

27. This section is based, in part, on Benjamin Schneider and David E. Bowen, *Winning the Service Game.* Boston: Harvard Business School Press, 1995; and David E. Bowen, Benjamin Schneider, and Sandra S. Kim, "Shaping Service Cultures Through Strategic Human Resource Management." In T. Schwartz and D. Iacobucci, eds., *Handbook of Services Marketing and Management.* Thousand Oaks, CA: Sage, 2000, pp. 439–454.

28. John Hamm, "The Five Messages Leaders Must Manage." *Harvard Business Review,* 84 (May 2006).

29. Daniel Goleman, "Leadership That Gets Results." *Harvard Business Review,* 78 (March–April, 2000): 78–93.

30. Hans Kasper, "Culture and Leadership in Market-Oriented Service Organisations." *European Journal of Marketing,* 36, no. 9/10 (2002): 1047–1057.

Readings

Why Service Stinks

DIANE BRADY

The essence of relationship management is that the best customers get the most attention and are encouraged to remain loyal through rewards and special treatment. However, there's a downside to loyalty strategies that group customers into tiers based on their profitability for the firm. The evidence from industries as diverse as financial services, utilities, telecommunications, airlines, and hotels is that top-tier customers are getting unprecedented attention while those who spend less and use a service infrequently are being treated poorly and forced into self-service options if they want customer service. Tiering may seem logical, but it poses some drawbacks for marketers. Most programs tend to measure only the current value of a customer, based on past transactions, not his or her potential value. Another concern is that the segmentation of service, based on a wealth of personal information, raises troubling questions about privacy and what constitutes appropriate use of customer data drawn from many different sources.

Companies know just how good a customer you are—and unless you are a high roller, they would rather lose you than take the time to fix your problem.

When Tom Unger of New Haven started banking at First Union Corp. several years ago, he knew he wasn't top of the heap. But Unger didn't realize just how dispensable he was until mysterious service charges started showing up on his account. He called the bank's toll-free number, only to reach a bored service representative who brushed him off. Then he wrote two letters, neither of which received a response. A First Union spokeswoman, Mary Eshet, says the bank doesn't discuss individual accounts but notes that customer service has been steadily improving. Not for Unger. He left. "They wouldn't even give me the courtesy of listening to my complaint," he says.

And Unger ought to know bad service when he sees it. He works as a customer-service representative at an electric utility where the top 350 business clients are served by six people. The next tier of 700 are handled by six more, and 30,000 others get Unger and one other rep to serve their needs. Meanwhile, the 300,000 residential customers at the lowest end are left with an 800 number. As Unger explains: "We don't ignore anyone, but our biggest customers certainly get more attention than the rest."

As time goes on, that service gap is only growing wider. Studies by groups ranging from the Council of Better Business Bureaus Inc. to the University of Michigan vividly detail what consumers already know: Good service is increasingly rare (see Figures A and B). From passengers languishing in airport queues to bank clients caught in voice-mail hell, most consumers feel they're getting squeezed by Corporate America's push for profits

Figure A

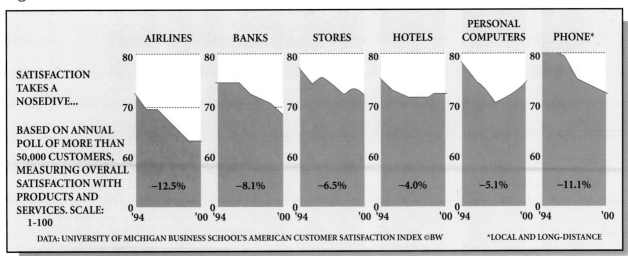

SATISFACTION TAKES A NOSEDIVE...

BASED ON ANNUAL POLL OF MORE THAN 50,000 CUSTOMERS, MEASURING OVERALL SATISFACTION WITH PRODUCTS AND SERVICES. SCALE: 1-100

AIRLINES −12.5% | BANKS −8.1% | STORES −6.5% | HOTELS −4.0% | PERSONAL COMPUTERS −5.1% | PHONE* −11.1%

DATA: UNIVERSITY OF MICHIGAN BUSINESS SCHOOL'S AMERICAN CUSTOMER SATISFACTION INDEX ©BW   *LOCAL AND LONG-DISTANCE

Figure B

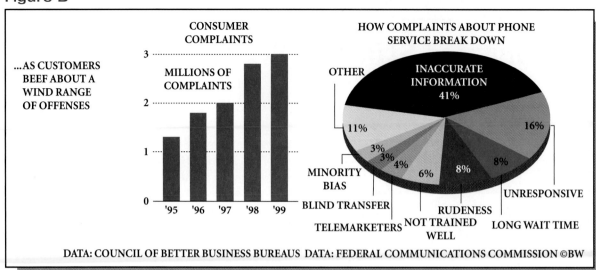

CONSUMER COMPLAINTS

...AS CUSTOMERS BEEF ABOUT A WIND RANGE OF OFFENSES

MILLIONS OF COMPLAINTS

HOW COMPLAINTS ABOUT PHONE SERVICE BREAK DOWN

OTHER

INACCURATE INFORMATION 41%

11%

16%

3%
3%
4%
6%
8%
8%

MINORITY BIAS

BLIND TRANSFER

TELEMARKETERS

NOT TRAINED WELL

RUDENESS

UNRESPONSIVE

LONG WAIT TIME

'95 '96 '97 '98 '99

DATA: COUNCIL OF BETTER BUSINESS BUREAUS DATA: FEDERAL COMMUNICATIONS COMMISSION ©BW

and productivity. The result is more efficiencies for companies—and more frustration for their less valuable customers. "Time saved for them is not time saved for us," says Claes Fornell, a University of Michigan professor who created the [American Customer] Satisfaction Index, which shows broad declines across an array of industries. Fornell points to slight improvements in areas like autos and computers.

Andrew Chan's experience with Ikea is typical. The Manhattan artist recently hauled a table home from an Ikea store in New Jersey only to discover that all the screws and brackets were missing. When he called to complain, the giant furniture retailer refused to send out the missing items and insisted he come back to pick them up himself, even though he doesn't own a car. Maybe he just reached the wrong guy, says Tom Cox, customer-service manager for Ikea North America, noting that the usual procedure is to mail small items out within a couple of days.

NO ELEPHANT?

Life isn't so tough for everyone, though. Roy Sharda, a Chicago Internet executive and road warrior is a "platinum" customer of Starwood Hotels & Resorts Worldwide. When he wanted to propose to his girlfriend, Starwood's Sheraton Agra in India arranged entry to the Taj Mahal after hours so he could pop the question in private. Starwood also threw in a horse-drawn carriage, flowers, a personalized meal, upgrades to the presidential suite, and a cheering reception line led by the general manager. It's no wonder Sharda feels he was "treated like true royalty."

Welcome to the new consumer apartheid. Those long lines and frustrating telephone trees aren't always the result of companies simply not caring about pleasing the customer anymore. Increasingly, companies have made a deliberate decision to give some people skimpy service because that's all their business is worth. Call it the dark side of the technology boom, where marketers can amass a mountain of data that gives them an almost Orwellian view of each buyer. Consumers have become commodities to pamper, squeeze, or toss away, according to Leonard L. Berry, marketing professor at Texas A&M University. He sees "a decline in the level of respect given to customers and their experiences."

More importantly, technology is creating a radical new business model that alters the whole dynamic of customer service. For the first time, companies can truly measure exactly what such service costs on an individual level and assess the return on each dollar. They can know exactly how much business someone generates, what he is likely to buy, and how much it costs to answer the phone. That allows them to deliver a level of service based on each person's potential to produce a profit—and not a single phone call more.

The result could be a whole new stratification of consumer society. The top tier may enjoy an unprecedented level of personal attention. But those who fall below a certain level of profitability for too long may find themselves bounced from the customer rolls altogether or facing fees that all but usher them out the door. A few years ago, GE Capital decided to charge $25 a year to GE Rewards MasterCard holders who didn't rack up at least that much in annual interest charges. The message was clear: Those who pay their bills in full each month don't boost the bottom line. GE has since sold its credit-card business to First USA. Others are charging extra for things like deliveries and repairs or reducing service staff in stores and call centers.

Instead of providing premium service across the board, companies may offer to move people to the front of the line for a fee. "There has been a fundamental shift in how companies assess customer value and apply their resources," says Cincinnati marketing consultant Richard G. Barlow. He argues that managers increasingly treat top clients with kid gloves and cast the masses "into a labyrinth of low-cost customer service where, if they complain, you just live with it."

Companies have always known that some people don't pay their way. Ravi Dhar, an associate professor at Yale University, cites the old rule that 80 percent of profits come from 20 percent of customers. "The rest nag you, call you, and don't add much revenue," he says. But technology changed everything. To start, it has become much easier to track and measure individual transactions across businesses. Second, the Web has also opened up options. People can now serve themselves at their convenience at a negligible cost, but they have to accept little or no human contact in return. Such huge savings in service costs have proven irresistible to marketers, who are doing everything possible to push their customers—especially low-margin ones—toward self-service.

FRONT-LOADING ELITE

That's a far cry from the days when the customer was king. In the data-rich new millennium, sales staff no longer let you return goods without question while rushing to shake your hand. And they don't particularly want to hear from you again unless you're worth the effort. How they define that top tier can vary a lot by industry. Airlines and hotels love those who buy premier offerings again and again. Financial institutions, on the other hand, salivate over day traders and the plastic-addicted who pay heavy interest charges because they cover only the minimum on their monthly credit-card bills.

Almost everyone is doing it (see Table A). Charles Schwab Corp.'s top-rated Signature clients—who start with at least $100,000 in assets or trade 12 times a year—never wait longer than 15 seconds to get a call answered, while other customers can wait 10 minutes or more. At Sears, Roebuck & Co., big spenders on the company's credit card get to choose a preferred two-hour time slot for repair calls while regular patrons are given a four-hour slot. Maytag Corp. provides premium service to people who buy pricey products such as its front-loading Neptune washing machines, which sell for about $1,000, twice the cost of a top-loading washer. This group gets a dedicated staff of "product experts," an exclusive toll-free number, and speedy service on repairs. When people are paying this much, "they not only want more service; they deserve it," says Dale Reeder, Maytag's general manager of customer service.

Of course, while some companies gloat about the growing attention to their top tier, most hate to admit that the bottom rungs are getting less. GE Capital would not talk. Sprint Corp. and WorldCom Inc. declined repeated requests to speak about service divisions. Off the record, one company official explains that customers don't like to know they're being treated differently.

Obviously, taking service away from the low spenders doesn't generate much positive press for companies. Look at AT&T, which recently agreed to remove its minimum usage charges on the 28 million residential customers in its lowest-level basic plan, many of whom don't make enough calls to turn a profit. "To a lot of people, it's not important that a company make money," says AT&T Senior Vice-President Howard E. McNally, who argues that AT&T is still treated by regulators and the public as a carrier of last resort. Now, it's trying to push up profits by giving top callers everything from better rates to free premium cable channels.

Table A How You Can Get Stiffed

Flying
Canceled flight? No problem. With top status, you're whisked past the queue, handed a ticket for the next flight, and driven to the first-class lounge.

Billing
Big spenders can expect special discounts, promotional offers, and other goodies when they open their bills. The rest might get higher fees, stripped-down service, and a machine to answer their questions.

Banking
There's nothing like a big bank account to get those complaints answered and service charges waived every time. Get pegged as a money-loser, and your negotiating clout vanishes.

Lodging
Another day, another upgrade for frequent guests. Sip champagne before the chef prepares your meal. First-time guest? So sorry. Your room is up three flights and to the left.

Retailing
Welcome to an after-hours preview for key customers where great sales abound and staff await your every need. Out in the aisles, it's back to self-service.

SERIAL CALLERS

Is this service divide fair? That depends on your perspective. In an era when labor costs are rising while prices have come under pressure, U.S. companies insist they simply can't afford to spend big bucks giving every customer the hands-on service of yesteryear (see Table B). Adrian J. Slywotzky, a partner with Mercer Management Consulting Inc., estimates that gross margins in many industries have shrunk an average of 5 to 10 percentage points over the past decade because of competition. "Customers used to be more profitable 10 years ago, and they're becoming more different than similar" in how they want to be served, he says.

The new ability to segment customers into ever finer categories doesn't have to be bad news for consumers. In many cases, the trade-off in service means lower prices. Susanne D. Lyons, chief marketing officer at Charles Schwab, points out that the commission charged on Schwab stock trades has dropped by two-thirds over the past five years. Costs to Schwab, meanwhile, vary from a few cents for Web deals to several dollars per live interaction. And companies note that they're delivering a much wider range of products and services than ever before—as well as more ways to handle transactions. Thanks to the Internet, for example, consumers have far better tools to conveniently serve themselves.

Look at a company like Fidelity Investments, which not only has a mind-boggling menu of fund options but now lets people do research and manipulate their accounts without an intermediary. Ten years ago, the company got 97,000 calls a day, of which half were automated. It now gets about 550,000 Web site visits a day and more than 700,000 daily calls, about three-quarters of which go to automated systems that cost the company less than a buck each, including development and research costs. The rest are handled by human beings,

which costs about $13 per call. No wonder Fidelity last year contacted 25,000 high-cost "serial" callers and told them they must use the Web or automated calls for simple account and price information. Each name was flagged and routed to a special representative who would direct callers back to automated services—and tell them how to use it. "If all our customers chose to go through live reps, it would be cost-prohibitive," says a Fidelity spokeswoman.

ENTITLED?

Segmenting is one way to manage those costs efficiently. Bass Hotels & Resorts, owners of such brands as Holiday Inn and Inter-Continental Hotels, knows so much about individual response rates to its promotions that it no longer bothers sending deals to those who did not bite in the past. The result: 50 percent slashed off mailing costs but a 20 percent jump in response rates. "As information becomes more sophisticated, the whole area of customer service is becoming much more complex," says Chief Marketing Officer Ravi Saligram.

Consumers themselves have cast a vote against high-quality service by increasingly choosing price, choice, and convenience over all else. Not that convenience always takes the sting out of rotten service—witness Priceline.com Inc., the ultimate self-service site that lets customers name their own price for plane tickets, hotels, and other goods. Many consumers didn't fully understand the trade-offs, such as being forced to stop over on flights, take whatever brand was handed to them, and forgo the right to any refund. And when things went wrong, critics say, no one was around to help. The result: a slew of complaints that has prompted at least one state investigation. Priceline.com responds that it's revamping the Web site and intensifying efforts

---

Table B "We're Sorry, All of Our Agents Are Busy with More Valuable Customers"

Companies have become sophisticated about figuring out if you're worth pampering—or whether to just let the phone keep ringing. Here are some of their techniques:

Coding
Some companies grade customers based on how profitable their business is. They give each account a code with instructions to service staff on how to handle each category.

Routing
Based on the customer's code, call centers route customers to different queues. Big spenders are whisked to high-level problem solvers. Others may never speak to a live person at all.

Targeting
Choice customers have fees waived and get other hidden discounts based on the value of their business. Less valuable customers may never even know the promotions exist.

Sharing
Companies sell data about your transaction history to outsiders. You can be slotted before you even walk in the door, since your buying potential has already been measured.

Table C Making the Grade: How to Get Better Service

Consolidate Your Activities
Few things elevate status and trim costs like spending big in one place. Be on the lookout for packages or programs that reward loyal behavior.

Protect Your Privacy
Avoid surveys and be frugal with releasing credit-card or Social Security information. The less companies know, the less they can slot you.

Jump the Phone Queue
If you want to reach a live human, don't admit to having a touch-tone phone at the prompt. Or listen for options that are less likely to be handled automatically.

Fight Back
If you feel badly treated, complain. Make sure management knows just how much business you represent and that you're willing to take it elsewhere.

to improve customer service. While many consumers refuse to pay more for service, they're clearly dismayed when service is taken away. "People have higher expectations now than two or three years ago because we have all this information at our fingertips," says Jupiter Communications Inc. analyst David Daniels.

Indeed, marketers point to what they call a growing culture of entitlement, where consumers are much more demanding about getting what they want. One reason is the explosion of choices, with everything from hundreds of cable channels to new players emerging from deregulated industries like airlines and telecom companies. Meanwhile, years of rewards programs such as frequent-flier miles have contributed to the new mind-set. Those who know their worth expect special privileges that reflect it. Says Bonnie S. Reitz, senior vice-president for marketing, sales, and distribution at Continental Airlines Inc.: "We've got a hugely educated, informed, and more experienced consumer out there now."

For top-dollar clients, all this technology allows corporations to feign an almost small-town intimacy. Marketers can know your name, your spending habits, and even details of your personal life. Centura Banks Inc. of Raleigh, N.C., now rates its 2 million customers on a profitability scale from 1 to 5. The real moneymakers get calls from service reps several times a year for what Controller Terry Earley calls "a friendly chat" and even an annual call from the CEO to wish them happy holidays. No wonder attrition in this group is down by 50 percent since 1996, while the percentage of unprofitable customers has slipped to 21 percent from 27 percent. Even for the lower tier, companies insist that this intense focus on data is leading to service that's better than ever. To start with, it's more customized. And while executives admit to pushing self-help instead of staff, they contend that such service is often preferable. After all, many banking customers prefer using automated teller machines to standing in line at their local branch. American Airlines Inc., the pioneer of customer segmentation with its two-decade-old

loyalty program, says it's not ignoring those in the cheap seats, pointing to the airline's recent move to add more legroom in economy class. Says Elizabeth S. Crandall, managing director of personalized marketing: "We're just putting more of our energies into rewarding our best customers."

MARKED MAN

This segmentation of sales, marketing, and service, based on a wealth of personal information, raises some troubling questions about privacy. It threatens to become an intensely personal form of "redlining"—the controversial practice of identifying and avoiding unprofitable neighborhoods or types of people. Unlike traditional loyalty programs, the new tiers are not only highly individualized but they are often invisible. You don't know when you're being directed to a different telephone queue or sales promotion. You don't hear about the benefits you're missing. You don't realize your power to negotiate with everyone from gate agents to bank employees is predetermined by the code that pops up next to your name on a computer screen.

When the curtain is pulled back on such sophisticated tiering, it can reveal some uses of customer information that are downright disturbing. Steve Reed, a West Coast sales executive, was shocked when a United Airlines Inc. ticketing agent told him: "Wow, somebody doesn't like you." Not only did she have access to his Premier Executive account information but there was a nasty note about an argument he had had with a gate agent in San Francisco several months earlier. In retrospect, he feels that explained why staff seemed less accommodating following the incident. Now, Reed refuses to give more than his name for fear "of being coded and marked for repercussions." United spokesman Joe Hopkins says such notes give agents a more complete picture of passengers. "It's not always negative information," says Hopkins, adding that the practice is common throughout the industry.

Those who don't make the top tier have no idea how good things can be for the free-spending few. American Express Co. has a new Centurion concierge service that promises to get members almost anything from anywhere in the world. The program, with an annual fee of $1,000, is open by invitation only. "We're seeing a lot of people who value service more than price," says Alfred F. Kelly Jr., AmEx group president for consumer and small-business services. Dean Burri, a Rock Hill (S.C.) insurance executive, found out how the other half lives when he joined their ranks. Once he became a platinum customer of Starwood Hotels, it seemed there was nothing the hotel operator wouldn't do for him. When the Four Points Hotel in Lubbock, Tex., was completely booked for Texas Tech freshman orientation in August, it bumped a lower-status guest to get Burri a last-minute room. Starwood says that's part of the platinum policy, noting that ejected customers are put elsewhere and compensated for inconvenience. With the right status, says Burri, "you get completely different treatment."

The distinctions in customer status are getting sliced ever finer. Continental Airlines Inc. has started rolling out a Customer Information System where every one of its 43,000 gate, reservation, and service agents will immediately know the history and value of each customer. A so-called intelligent engine not only mines data on status but also suggests remedies and perks, from automatic coupons for service delays to priority for upgrades, giving the carrier more consistency in staff behavior and service delivery. The technology will even allow Continental staff to note details about the preferences of top customers so the airline can offer them extra services. As Vice-President Reitz puts it: "We even know if they put their eyeshades on and go to sleep." Such tiering pays off. Thanks to its heavy emphasis on top-tier clients, about 47 percent of Continental's customers now pay higher-cost, unrestricted fares, up from 38 percent in 1995.

Elsewhere, the selectivity is more subtle. At All First Bank in Baltimore, only those slotted as top customers get the option to click on a Web icon that directs them to a live service agent for a phone conversation. The rest never see it. First Union meanwhile, codes its credit-card customers with tiny colored squares that flash when service reps call up an account on their computer screens. Green means the person is a profitable customer and should be granted waivers or otherwise given white-glove treatment. Reds are the money losers who have almost no negotiating power, and yellow is a more discretionary category in between. "The information helps our people make decisions on fees and rates," explains First Union spokeswoman Mary Eshet.

Banks are especially motivated to take such steps because they have one of the widest gaps in profitability. Market Line Associates, an Atlanta financial consultancy, estimates that the top 20 percent of customers at a typical commercial bank generate up to six times as much revenue as they cost, while the bottom fifth cost three to four times more than they make for the company. Gartner Group Inc. recently found that, among banks with deposits of more than $4 billion, 68 percent are segmenting customers into profitability tranches while many more have plans to do so.

Tiering, however, poses some drawbacks for marketers. For one thing, most programs fail to measure the potential value of a customer. Most companies can still measure only past transactions—and some find it tough to combine information from different business units. The problem, of course, is that what someone spends today is not always a good predictor of what they'll spend tomorrow. Life situations and spending habits can change. In some cases, low activity may be a direct result of the consumer's dissatisfaction with current offerings. "We have to be careful not to make judgments based on a person's interaction with us," cautions Steven P. Young, vice-president for worldwide customer care at Compaq Computer Corp.'s consumer-products group. "It may not reflect their intentions or future behavior."

PAY NOT TO WAIT?

Already, innovative players are striving to use their treasure trove of information to move customers up the value chain instead of letting them walk out the door. Capital One Financial Corp. of Falls Church, Va., is an acknowledged master of tiering, offering more than 6,000 credit cards and up to 20,000 permutations of other products, from phone cards to insurance. That range lets the company match clients with someone who has appropriate expertise. "We look at every single customer contact as an opportunity to make an unprofitable customer profitable or make a profitable customer more profitable," says Marge Connelly, senior vice-president for domestic card operations.

In the future, therefore, the service divide may become much more transparent. The trade-off between price and service could be explicit, and customers will be able to choose where they want to fall on that continuum. In essence, customer service will become just another product for sale. Walker Digital, the research lab run by priceline.com founder Jay S. Walker, has patented a "value-based queuing" of phone calls that allows companies to prioritize calls according to what each person will pay. As Walker Digital CEO Vikas Kapoor argues, customers can say: "I don't want to wait in line—I'll pay to reduce my wait time."

For consumers, though, the reality is that service as we've known it has changed forever. As Roger S. Siboni, chief executive of customer-service software provider E. piphany Inc., points out, not all customers are the same.

Even if you're not a big spender, there are ways to improve your standing with companies in order to command better service. The key is to recognize that your spending habits, payment history, and any information you volunteer can be used for or against you. What's more, if you do think you're being pegged at a low tier, there are ways to get the recognition you feel you deserve.

The first step in fighting segmentation is to be stingy with the information you give out—especially if it's unlikely to help your status. Don't fill out surveys, sweepstakes forms, or applications if you're not comfortable with how the information might be used. Be wary when a company asks if it can alert you to other products and services. A yes may permit them to sell data that you don't want distributed.

Pigeonholing

The Consumers Union (CU) points out that it's unnecessary to fill out surveys with warranty cards. Just send in a proof of purchase with your name and address. "Protecting your privacy is a significant tool to prevent yourself from being pigeonholed as undesirable," says Gene Kimmelman, Washington co-director for the CU. It's equally important to recognize what kind of information companies are looking for. If you don't live in an upmarket Zip Code, consider using your work address for correspondence. Be optimistic when estimating your income or spending: The better the numbers look, the better you'll be treated.

Still, it's tough to keep personal information to yourself, especially when companies are compiling data on the business they do with you. A critical concern for all consumers is their actual payment record. Donna Fluss, a vice-president at the technology consultants Gartner Group Inc., advises pulling your credit history at least once a year to check if there are any liens or mistakes. "You may discover that you're listed as having missed a payment that you thought you made on time," she says. The three main reporting bureaus—Experian, Trans Union, and Equifax—charge a small fee for a copy of your credit history. If, however you have recently been denied credit, employment, or insurance, such a report is free from all three companies. The largest bureau is Equifax, which has data on 190 million Americans, but all three may have slightly different records based on who reports to them.

Multiple credit cards can be a mistake, especially if they're the no-frills variety that are frequently offered to less desirable candidates. Not only can they drain the credit you might need for other activities, but they're also unlikely to propel you into a higher category. Using a spouse's card or account is also to be avoided, because it robs you of a chance to build your own credit history. If a mistake is made on your account, fight it.

Pros disagree on tactics for bypassing the service maze. One customer representative argues that when calling a service center it's better to punch in no account number if you're a low-value customer. The reason? Without proper identification, he says, a live person has to get on the line. "Pretend you're calling from a rotary phone," he advises. But another tactic may be to punch zero or choose an option that's likely to get immediate attention.

In the end, resistance may be futile, and the best strategy for beating the system may be to join it. Shop around for the best company, and try to consolidate your business there. These days, the best way to ensure good service is to make yourself look like a high-value, free-spending customer.

"Some you want to absolutely retain and throw rose petals at their feet," Siboni says. "Others will never be profitable." Armed with detailed data on who's who, companies are learning that it makes financial sense to serve people based on what they're worth. The rest can serve themselves or simply go away.

Creating New Markets Through Service Innovation

Leonard L. Berry, Venkatesh Shankar,
Janet Turner Parish, Susan Cadwallader,
and Thomas Dotzel

Many companies make incremental improvements to their service offerings, but few succeed in creating service innovations that generate new markets or reshape existing ones. To move in that direction, executives must understand the different types of market-creating service innovations as well as the nine factors that enable these innovations.

For decades, the importance of services to the global economy has grown steadily while the importance of goods has declined. In fact, services now dominate, making up about 70% of the aggregate production and employment in the Organization for Economic Cooperation and Development (OECD) nations and contributing about 75% of the GDP in the United States.[1] It's only natural, then, that companies are constantly seeking to provide better services, regardless of whether they are in a "pure" service business or in a manufacturing industry that must increasingly rely on its service operations for continued profitability.

However, most improvements to service activities are incremental. Stores stay open longer; product makers establish Web sites with e-commerce functions; airlines, casinos and supermarket chains enhance loyalty card programs. These improvements are useful and indeed necessary, but they are limited in the kind of returns they can produce. Only rarely does a company develop a service that creates an entirely new market or so reshapes a market that the company enjoys unforeseen profits for a considerable length of time.

One such organization is Enterprise Rent-A-Car Company. Enterprise has been strikingly successful: In an industry long led by The Hertz Corp. and Avis Rent-A-Car System Inc., it exploited a new idea to overtake them both. Founded by Jack Taylor in St. Louis in 1957 as a car leasing business, Enterprise added a rental division in 1962 when Taylor's customers began telling him that they often needed a car when theirs was in the shop for repair. While other rental car companies targeted travelers at airports, Enterprise focused on local customers who needed a replacement vehicle temporarily. This strategy required Enterprise to locate its offices close to where people live

and work, and encouraged the company to develop such innovations as its "We'll pick you up" service. Today, Enterprise's revenues exceed $8 billion, and the company boasts the largest fleet size and the most rental locations in the United States.[2] Ninety percent of the U.S. population lives within a 15-mile drive of one of Enterprise's offices.[3]

In effect, Enterprise's innovative view created a new market for car rentals in the same way that FedEx Corp. redefined the package delivery market. Both companies exemplify "market-creating service innovation," which we define as an idea for a performance enhancement that customers perceive as offering a new benefit of sufficient appeal that it dramatically influences their behavior, as well as the behavior of competing companies.

Market-creating service innovation promises far greater upside potential than imitative or incrementally improved service offerings. Consider, for example, that market creators Google (incorporated in 1998) and eBay Inc. (started in 1996) have market capitalizations of approximately $110 billion and $60 billion respectively, placing them in the top ranks of U.S. companies.

Service innovation differs from product innovation in important ways. First, for labor-intensive, interactive services, the actual providers—the service delivery staff—are part of the customer experience and thus part of the innovation. Second, services requiring the physical presence of the customer necessitate "local" decentralized production capacity. (Customers will drive only so far to eat at a restaurant, no matter how innovative it may be.) Third, service innovators usually do not have a tangible product to carry a brand name.

Over the past year, we have conducted research on service innovation and have developed a matrix that offers a different way of thinking strategically about service innovations that can create new markets. Our research has helped us to better understand how service innovation differs from product innovation, and to envision the central drivers of success in a service innovation effort. Executives who develop an understanding of these issues will be better prepared to lead effective initiatives in service innovation. (See "About the Research.")

Leonard L. Berry, Venkatesh Shankar, Janet Turner Parish, Susan Cadwallader, and Thomas Dotzel, "Creating New Markets Through Service Innovation." *MIT Sloan Management Review*, 47, no. 2 (Winter 2006): 56–63. Copyright © Massachusetts Institute of Technology, 2006. All rights reserved.

ABOUT THE RESEARCH

Our research involved several steps spanning one year. First, we developed and refined a working definition of market-creating service innovations. Then, based on reviews of published materials, we developed a list of services that created entirely new markets. Building on the service management literature, we developed a matrix to classify market-creating service innovations. Next, we analyzed each innovation to answer such questions as: What need did it address? What factors contributed to its performance? Our sources included books, articles, annual reports, Web sites and interviews with company executives. We also identified several market-creating product innovations and collected information on these innovations in a similar manner. Then we compared our analyses of both types of market-creating innovations and developed a list of success drivers for each. Finally, we presented our analysis, results and insights to several academicians and executives involved in service management and innovation management and made refinements as a result of their feedback.

ARRIVING AT A TAXONOMY OF SERVICE INNOVATIONS

Service innovations that create new markets differ from each other along two primary dimensions: the type of benefit offered and the degree of service "separability." On the first dimension, businesses can innovate by offering an important new core benefit or a new delivery benefit that revolutionizes customers' access to the core benefit. For example, Cirque du Soleil created a new market for live entertainment—a core benefit—by offering a show that is neither a circus nor a dance performance but a hybrid of the two.[4] The unique shows are a phenomenal success, selling 97% of available seats.[5] The delivery of the service, however, is standard: Customers buy tickets in advance and see the performance in a theater. Conversely, the University of Phoenix Inc. enables students to receive an established core benefit—a college degree—by a new delivery system: the Internet. The University of Phoenix has become America's largest institution of higher education in just a few years.

The second dimension concerns whether the service must be produced and consumed simultaneously. Health care has traditionally been an "inseparable" service: The doctor must be in the room with the patient. Although patients, for the most part, continue to go to a clinic or hospital when they need health care, the delivery of "separable" care is growing. Doctors and nurses can advise patients via privacy-protected e-mail or voice mail and can monitor patients' health through telemedicine.[6] Technology has transformed many formerly inseparable services into services that can be consumed at any time or place. Customers who want to plan a trip no longer have to check their watches to see if the local travel agency is open.

Combining the dimensions of separability and type of benefit creates a two-by-two matrix that can help managers see where their companies fit and how they may seek to innovate. (See "The Four Types of Market-Creating Service Innovations.") For instance, executives from IBM Corp.—which has identified service science as the next frontier discipline after computer and information sciences—believe they can use this type of matrix to facilitate strategic thinking about market-creating service innovation. Like many large companies today, IBM is betting on new services for its future growth.

Each cell in the matrix offers a way to imagine a particular approach to market-creating service innovation. It is useful for managers to identify the cell in which they are targeting innovation and to understand the cell's dynamics and leverage points. A failure to do so may lead to lost growth opportunities. Consider Amazon.com Inc.'s creation of the online market for book retailing—a highly innovative separable service. An analysis of the matrix in 1999 might have tempted Amazon's management, flush with capital, to try to acquire the Borders Group Inc.'s Borders bookstore chain, which, at the time, had a minimal online presence. By combining "clicks with bricks," Amazon could have extended its reach into a second

The Four Types of Market-Creating Service Innovations

These innovations can be characterized on two dimensions: (1) whether they offer a new core benefit or new way of delivering a core benefit, and (2) whether the service must be consumed where and when it is produced or can be consumed separately from its production.

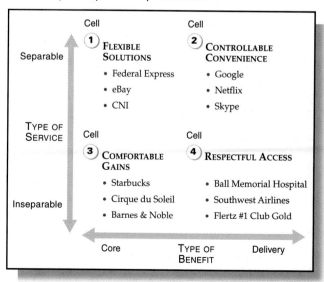

(inseparable) cell and created synergies between the two. But the company chose not to do so. Notwithstanding Amazon's bookselling prowess today, this was a lost opportunity for an even larger market impact. What follows is a breakdown of the characteristics of each cell.

Cell 1: Flexible Solutions

This cell describes service innovations that offer a new core benefit *and* that can be consumed apart from where and when they are produced. These innovations allow their users to break free of the constraints of time and place.

An early pioneer of this type of innovation was FedEx. The idea for the business was born in 1965, when Frederick W. Smith wrote a college term paper about shortcomings of airfreight shippers using passenger route systems for moving deadline-critical items.[7] At first glance, it might seem that FedEx was simply offering a new delivery benefit. But FedEx didn't invent the idea of delivering documents and packages by air. The company created a new market for the core benefit: the rapid, reliable delivery of time-sensitive materials. Combining speed and reliability has made FedEx a trusted deadline-beater and productivity booster for many businesses. In fact, executives from Merrill Lynch & Co. Inc. once learned that their employees were using FedEx to deliver documents between floors of its Manhattan headquarters building. FedEx's service was faster and more reliable than interoffice mail![8] FedEx has become synonymous with dependable just-in-time delivery. Its results justify its status: A share of FedEx stock purchased in 1978 for $31.36 was worth more than $2,600 by July 2005.

Other examples in this cell include Time Warner Inc.'s CNN, the television network that for the first time allowed viewers around the world to watch updated news 24 hours a day, and eBay, the online marketplace that allows buyers and sellers to transact business day or night, weekday or weekend. CNN's business model brought a new core benefit for viewers who couldn't tune in at 6:00 p.m. or 11:00 p.m.; eBay created the first never-closed worldwide garage sale.

FedEx, CNN and eBay offer a valuable lesson to managers. By focusing on a fundamental service benefit that can be experienced separately from the service provider, executives can turn unsolved customer problems into service innovation opportunities that spawn new markets.

Cell 2: Controllable Convenience

Innovations that create markets on the basis of new delivery benefits offer controllable convenience. As with flexible solutions, customers can enjoy the service benefits in this cell at any time and place.

Consider the changes in information delivery created by Google. Of course, Google didn't invent the core benefit of providing information, but its market-creating service innovation is the availability of relevant and rapid Web searches for information on virtually any subject. Paid for by advertising revenue, Google offers free access to an index comprising more than 8 billion URLs. In effect, Google is an information department store available where and whenever it is needed.

Founders Larry Page and Sergey Brin led two crucial innovations that positioned the company for dominance. First, they developed search algorithms that interpret hypertext links to Web pages as votes of importance; the more links, the higher the site rises to the top of the list that searchers see. This approach proved superior to that of competitors, whose search engines operated primarily by looking for keywords and tallying their frequency. Second, Google developed its own serving infrastructure—rejecting conventional, larger server configurations that slow under peak loads—by employing linked computers to quickly find each query's answer. These innovations reshaped the world of Internet searching, and Google now averages more than 80 million users per month. The company's share price more than tripled within a year of its 2004 initial public offering.

Other companies offering controllable convenience include Netflix Inc. and Skype Technologies SA. Netflix offers a familiar core benefit—movie rentals—through a delivery system that combines the Internet and regular mail. Its customers don't have to race back to the store at 10:59 p.m. to return their rentals and avoid late fees. Skype, the peer-to-peer telephone company, offers free calling between Skype members over the Internet (for a small fee, members can connect to any traditional phone worldwide). The company thus uses a delivery innovation to offer the benefit of global telecommunications. Launched in August 2003, Skype had more than 60 million registered customers by late 2005.[9] In October 2005, eBay acquired the company for $2.6 billion, promising additional payments if performance targets are met.[10]

Companies should look for innovative ways to put customers in control of how they access a desired service. Creative service system design and technology application can enable customers to reach and use a service more easily—and can open up untapped markets.

Cell 3: Comfortable Gains

This cell refers to service innovations that offer a new core benefit consumed at the time and place of production. These innovations provide comfortable gains—substantially new experiences with direct benefits to customers' emotional or physical comfort.

The Starbucks sign has become ubiquitous—so much so that it may be hard to remember life before the coffee retailer became a feature of urban street corners. Coffee shops existed in abundance before Starbucks Corp. came along, to be sure, but the quality of both the coffee and the customer experience were inconsistent. Since 1987, when Howard Schultz bought the original Starbucks and began its transformation, the company has worked to offer an improved experience for coffee lovers. First, it has brewed coffee of uniform quality and pioneered the development of premium-priced drinks. Second, it has emphasized a relaxing atmosphere. Tables are purposely spaced apart so private conversations can take place or customers can be alone with their thoughts (or their laptops). Even the decision to use round tables is deliberate, since research indicates that a customer can be alone at a round table without feeling isolated or uncomfortable.[11] In Starbucks' first 12 years as a public company, its stock value increased by more than 3,000%.

Cirque du Soleil also fits into this cell, as does Barnes & Noble Inc. The United States was populated with bookstores before Barnes & Noble developed its superstores. Barnes & Noble, however, created a new market nationwide based on the idea that Americans of all stripes would respond positively to a radically enhanced core benefit. Thus, its bookstores came to be known for their large stocks of books on an array of topics, easy chairs for reading and co-located Starbucks coffee bars.

Managers of services that are produced and experienced in the same location need to look for creative ways by which the service experience can be made more comfortable, distinctive, enjoyable or memorable. Service innovations in this cell allow customers to benefit from a distinctive experience.

Cell 4: Respectful Access

In this cell, service innovators offer a new delivery benefit, and the production and consumption of the service are inseparable. Companies that create new markets in this space are granting their customers respectful access: They're demonstrating respect for their customers' time and physical presence in using the service. (See "Lowering Stress in the ER.")

Walgreen Co.'s Walgreens, America's largest and fastest-growing drugstore chain, with 2005 sales of $42 billion, opened its 5,000th store in October 2005. It is the only Fortune 500 company other than Wal-Mart Stores Inc. to achieve sales and earnings gains for 30 years in a row.[12] Walgreens makes its stores easy to get to and easy to get through. Its market-creating innovation is in fact an array of innovations geared to shoppers who place a premium on saving time and effort. Walgreens' strategy is to blanket its markets with freestanding stores that are easily accessible—stores on the corner of "Main and Main." Ample parking, drive-through pharmacy windows, 24-hour stores, wide aisles, low shelves, excellent in-store signage, one-hour photo departments, telephone prescription refills and auto-

---

LOWERING STRESS IN THE ER

Few experiences are dreaded more than a trip to a hospital emergency room. Such trips are usually notable for the anxiety and pain associated with the illness or injury, for the impersonal and crowded waiting area and for long waits for treatment. But one hospital now offers far superior service, reshaping the market for emergency health care in its region and potentially influencing emergency departments throughout the country. The hospital found an innovative way to demonstrate respect for patients in their access to emergency medical services.

Ball Memorial Hospital Inc., in Muncie, Indiana, had been offering a typical ER experience when growth forced construction of a larger facility. The CEO of the hospital's parent, Cardinal Health System Inc., challenged the staff and the architects of the new facility "to think differently about the patient and family experience—to look at [the] service in terms of the patient and not what was most convenient for the staff."[1]

The result was the nation's first hospital emergency department with no waiting room. The walk-in area is similar to a small hotel lobby. An arriving patient gives basic information at a triage desk, receives an account number and is escorted (with any accompanying family members) to a private room that has a TV and telephone. A nurse records the patient's vital signs and gathers other health information; a physician arrives within 30 minutes. Patient registration is completed electronically at the bedside.

Ball Memorial's delivery-benefit innovation was the conversion of a soulless, stressful public space into a calm and comforting private space for patients and family. The service process was re-engineered to remove bottlenecks. An electronic board keeps track of all patients. The staff communicates with one another via wireless phones. The department has its own radiology and CT scanner services, which minimize delays in receiving test results. Every patient room has a locked, electronically controlled medical supply cabinet with automated inventory control and billing.

The results, to date, are encouraging. Previously, Ball Memorial received patient satisfaction scores below the 50th percentile in a national database; in the year after the new facility opened, the scores topped the 80th percentile, while a patient's length of stay dropped by 30 minutes. Local residents are more willing to consider Ball Memorial first when they need immediate medical attention. Although the area's population is shrinking. Ball Memorial's new emergency department saw 17% growth in patient volume from start-up in 2003 to the middle of 2005—a crucial metric given that 47% of the hospital's admissions come through its emergency department.[2]

1. "Want to Keep Patients Flowing Out of the Waiting Room? Don't Have Chairs," ED Management (January 2005):2.
2. K. Kirby, administrative director of emergency services, Ball Memorial Hospital, interviews with authors, July 7 and Nov. 7, 2005.

mated queuing of prescriptions to reduce customer waiting time are all part of Walgreens' strategy of superior access.

Other companies that have created new markets through respectful access include Southwest Airlines Co. and The Hertz Corp. Southwest successfully created a market for affordable, reliable short-haul air transportation, in part by abandoning the hub-and-spoke strategy of its larger competitors. The company flies passengers directly to their destination rather than first taking them to a hub airport. Hertz was the first to create a membership program, Hertz #1 Club Gold, which gave frequent users faster and easier access to the company's core benefit—the temporary use of a car.

By fundamentally enhancing the ease with which customers can experience a service, companies can attract new customers and even create new markets. In the case of inseparable services, a company's greatest opportunity to win is at the service location. The key is to respect the customer's presence and time.

SUCCESS DRIVERS OF MARKET-CREATING SERVICE INNOVATIONS

Executives who attempt to create a new market through service innovation must concentrate on the tasks that determine success or failure. Our research identified nine success drivers behind such innovations, some of which will be familiar to readers. But the key insight is that the cases studied featured all these drivers, with slight variations in emphasis depending on the specific cell in question. (See "The Nine Drivers of Successful Service Innovations.") In other words, the best service innovators take a holistic approach to market leadership. Close examination of the nine drivers reveals how each contributes to successful innovation.

1. A Scalable Business Model

The path to scalability for a product innovation is relatively straightforward. When The Gillette Company comes out with a new razor, for example, it can achieve scale through production economies and distribution benefits. However, many service innovations are people-intensive and thus harder to scale. This is especially true in the cells where service usage is inseparable from production. In these businesses, employees are both the primary cost center and customer-value creator, so their productivity is critical to long-term profitability.[13]

Service providers can consider a variety of strategies to strengthen their business models. One option is to become more capital-intensive. For example, eBay invests in its auction trading platform's features and security technologies, minimizing the need to add large numbers of new employees to serve an expanding market. Another options is to encourage customers to perform more of the service themselves. Hertz #1 Club Gold members can go directly to their rental cars, bypassing the customer service counter. A variable compensation plan that rewards

employee productivity is another way to encourage profit growth in labor-intensive businesses. Enterprise Rent-A-Car emphasizes variable pay for its office managers; the more profitable a rental office, the more the manager earns.

Yet another alternative is to create a separable version of the service to extend the market while reducing labor intensity. For most of its history, tax preparation company H&R Block Inc. expanded primarily by opening new retail offices with its own dedicated staff. But it has recently been able to scale the business substantially by creating TaxCut, online and software tax preparation versions of its services.

2. Comprehensive Customer-experience Management

Services generally involve many more customer "touch-points," or discrete experiences, than do manufactured goods. These experiences hinge upon "experience clues" in three forms: *functional clues*, those that point to the technical quality of the offering; *mechanical clues*, relating to nonhuman elements such as the design of the facility; and *human clues*, coming from the behavior and appearance of employees.[14] The clues converge to create a total experience that directly influences the customer's assessment of quality and value.

Customer experience management is relevant to some degree for all market-creating innovations, but it is critical to the success of inseparable services because customers visit the service "factory" and directly experience what occurs there. Starbucks' success, for example, depends on an excellent product (functional), a pleasing physical environment (mechanical) and service-minded employees (the human component). To implement its core strategy, Starbucks must excel in managing all the categories of customer experience clues.

The Nine Drivers of Successful Service Innovations

There are nine success drivers behind market-creating service innovations. Some are more important for service innovations; others apply to all innovations. The most innovative companies exploit all these drivers.

MARKET-CREATING
INNOVATIONS

1. A scalable business model
2. Comprehensive customer experience management
3. Investment in employee performance
4. Continuous operational innovation
5. Brand differentiation
6. An innovation champion
7. A superior customer benefit
8. Affordability
9. Continuous strategic innovation

MARKET-CREATING
SERVICE
INNOVATIONS

---

3. Investment in Employee Performance

The more important, personal and enduring the service, the more pronounced the human effects of the customer-provider interaction. Customers' perceptions of employee effort in delivering service have an especially strong impact on customer satisfaction and switching behavior.[15]

Successful service innovators invest in their employees' willingness and capability to perform at consistently high levels. These investments commonly include careful hiring, initial and ongoing training and education, information sharing, performance-based compensation and internal branding (that is, teaching, selling and reinforcing the desired brand image to employees). Cirque du Soleil has more than 30 individuals in its casting department who travel the world looking for talent. About three-fourths of Cirque du Soleil's onstage performers are former athletes; some have competed in the Olympics. Prospective cast members complete a rigorous 16-week training program in Montreal, receiving instruction in acting, movement, voice and makeup application, in addition to acrobatic and athletic skills. They are paid and housed during the training phase.[16]

The importance of investing in employee performance is not limited to companies offering inseparable services. Services are performances, and well-managed companies invest in their performers regardless of whether they are "onstage" or "offstage." A good example is Google, which depends on cutting-edge technology to stay ahead and vies aggressively for technical talent, sometimes even raiding its competitors.

4. Continuous Operational Innovation

Service businesses are operations-intensive regardless of whether their offerings are separable or inseparable, or whether they provide a core or delivery benefit. It is difficult for imitators to catch up with service innovators that are continually improving operations.

FedEx has been particularly innovative in this area. When it was established in 1973, customers had to call the company to initiate service. FedEx's introduction of drop boxes in 1975 led the company to consider the need to allow customers to track their shipments. As Frederick W. Smith put it, "It was not acceptable . . . that customers should be willing to take goods that were very valuable to them into this big anonymous transportation system and hope they came out the other end."[17] In 1984, FedEx began providing free computers and proprietary software to key customers, enabling them to monitor their shipments. In 1994, the company launched fedex.com, the first transportation Web site that offered online shipment tracking.

Starbucks, in addition to serving sit-down coffee drinkers, serves another big market segment: takeout customers who want fast service. In 2005, a Starbucks customer spent about three minutes on average from getting in line to receiving an order, a wait time reduced by about 30 seconds from that of five years earlier. Among the company's timesaving innovations are eliminating credit card signatures for purchases under $25, inventing a more efficient ice scoop for cold beverages and creating a new position in which an employee "floats" to where he or she is needed most to shorten overall service time.[18]

5. Brand Differentiation

This success driver is important for market-creating product innovators, but may be even more so for service innovators. Because services are performances, there are no "tires to kick" prior to purchasing. A trusted brand reduces perceived risk. Distinctively communicating a consistent message, performing core services reliably and finding ways to connect emotionally with customers—these factors help build strong, trusted brands.

A strong brand is vital for service innovations in Cell 1: Flexible Solutions. Customers face increased risk with innovations in this cell because they have to evaluate an unfamiliar core benefit and cannot control or observe when or how the benefit is produced. FedEx has invested heavily in keeping its brand positioning promise of on-time delivery by solving problems before they reach customers. Each night, some of the company's aircraft start out empty or partially full so they can be diverted to airports where they are needed because of overload, mechanical or other problems. Also, on-call aircraft and crews (called "hot spares") are on standby each night.[19]

6. An Innovation Champion

Market-creating innovations of all kinds require a champion—a mobilizer of resources, a master persuader and doer, someone who can imagine the possibilities embedded in an idea and lead the transformation of the idea into a market reality. The stories of successful major innovations typically begin with the story of a person: Edwin Land at Polaroid Corp., Ted Turner at CNN or Ray Kroc at McDonald's Corp.

7. A Superior Customer Benefit

Innovations can create new markets only if they offer a clear and better solution to a problem of sufficient importance to stimulate customers to try the product or service—and then to repeat the action and give the product or service favorable word of mouth. Saving customers time and effort is a common benefit of market-creating innovations. In product categories, consider the microwave oven, the videocassette recorder and the cellular telephone; for services, the bank ATM, the online bookstore and the Internet search engine.

8. Affordability

Creating a market requires that customers not only are willing to change their behavior (for a superior benefit), but also have the means to do so. Cost-structure innovation is a common path to customer affordability. Southwest Airlines was designed to compete on price with automobile and bus travel. The entire operating model—including the use of a single type of aircraft to minimize training and servicing costs, fast airport turnarounds so planes spend more time in the air and no seat assignments—emphasizes cost efficiency.

9. Continuous Strategic Innovation

Neither service businesses nor their manufacturing counterparts can neglect strategic innovation. Google maintains its strategic edge by allowing technical staff to devote one day a week to work on new business ideas called "Googlettes," and by sponsoring an online "Ideas List," open office hours with managers and periodic brainstorming sessions for employees to pitch ideas on new technologies and businesses.[20] Netflix is teaming with TiVo Inc. to develop a video-on-demand service that will make movies available over the Internet.

SERVICE INNOVATION STARTS WITH CULTURE

The success drivers discussed above require an organizational culture that supports human performance and innovation. For companies operating in the inseparable cells, the quality of employees' interactions with customers is critical. Competitors can more easily imitate the infrastructure and technology of an innovator like Netflix than they can re-create the employee culture of Starbucks or Southwest Airlines. These companies have invested considerable time, effort and money to build work cultures that amount to a form of competitive advantage. For companies operating in the separable cells, it's especially important to use continuous innovation to stay ahead of the competition, because these businesses place greater reliance on factors that can easily be replicated.

In addition to fostering a corporate culture that builds human capital, companies seeking to create new markets with services must create a culture for innovation—a "style of corporate behavior that is comfortable with, even aggressive about, new ideas, change, risk and failure."[21] Employees must have the confidence to take risks and to freely share thoughts and suggestions with anyone in the organization. They must care enough and trust enough to try to create something new.

Companies that successfully create cultures that value human capital and innovation will see a steady stream of incremental improvements that help the bottom line. But when leaders understand the types of innovations that lead to new markets and work to implement the drivers of success, they also can build new businesses that position their companies for sustained growth and profitability. By thinking about a service in terms of its core benefits and the separability of its use from its production, managers can more easily determine how to out-innovate their competitors.

REFERENCES

1. A. Wölfl, "The Service Economy in OECD Countries," working paper 2005/3, OECD—Directorate for Science, Technology and Industry, Feb. 11, 2005; and Office of the U.S. Trade Representative, "U.S. Submits Revised Services Offer to the WTO," press release (Washington, D.C.: Executive Office of the President, May 31, 2005).
2. "Enterprise Rent-A-Car Revenue Exceeds $8 Billion: Records Set in Revenues, Fleet Size and Locations," September 21, 2005, www.enterprise.com; and "Car Rental in the United States—Industry Profile," October 2004, www.datamonitor.com.
3. "Rental Car Industry Expansion into Neighborhoods Fuels and Fills Americans' Appetites," Enterprise Rent-A-Car press release, May 18, 2005.
4. W.C. Kim and R. Mauborgne, "Blue Ocean Strategy," Harvard Business Review 82 (October 2004): 76-84.
5. G. Keighley, "The Phantasmagoria Factory," Business 2.0 (February 2004): 103-107.
6. L.L. Berry, K. Seiders and S.S. Wilder, "Innovations in Access to Care: A Patient-Centered Approach," Annals of internal Medicine 139, no. 7 (2003): 568-574.
7. "FedEx Corporate History," accessed October 30, 2005, www.fedex.com.
8. D. Foust, "Frederick W. Smith: No Overnight Success," Business Week, Sept. 20, 2004, 18.
9. "Skype Gives Small Businesses Market Advantage," Skype press release, Oct. 25, 2005.
10. "Change in Assets: Item 2.01 Completion of Acquisition or Disposition of Assets," SEC Filings for eBay, Form 8-K for eBay Inc., Oct. 18, 2005.
11. M. Krauss, "Starbucks 'architect' explains brand design," Marketing News 39, no. 8 (May 1, 2005): 19-20.
12. M. Boyle, "Drug Wars," Fortune, June 13, 2005, 79.
13. F. F. Barber and R. Strack, "The Surprising Economics of 'People Business'," Harvard Business Review (June 2005): 80-90.
14. L.L. Berry, L.P. Carbone and S.H. Haeckel, "Managing the Total Customer Experience," MIT Sloan Management Review 43, no. 3 (spring 2002): 85-89.
15. S.M. Keaveney, "Customer Switching Behavior in Service Industries: An Exploratory Study," Journal of Marketing 59 (April 1995): 71-82; and L.A. Mohr and M.J. Bitner, "The Role of Employee Effort in Satisfaction with Service Transactions," Journal of Business Research 32, no. 3 (March 1995): 239-252.
16. B. DeSimone, "Cirque's Siren Call to Athletes," USA Today, July 7, 2005, sec. C, p. 1.
17. D. Joachim, "FedEx Delivers on CEO's IT Vision," Oct. 25, 1999, www.internetweek.com.
18. S. Gray, "Coffee on the Double," Wall Street Journal, Apr. 12, 2005, B1.
19. S. Munoz, media relations manager, FedEx, interview with authors, July 8, 2005.
20. B. Elgin, "Managing Google's Idea Factory," Business Week, Oct. 3, 2005, 88-90.
21. B. O'Reilly, "The Secrets of America's Most Admired Corporations: New Ideas, New Products," Fortune, March 3, 1997, 60-64.

The One Number You Need to Grow

FREDERICK F. REICHHELD

> *If growth is what you're after, you won't learn much from complex measurements of customer satisfaction or retention. You simply need to know what your customers tell their friends about you.*

The CEOs in the room knew all about the power of loyalty. They had already transformed their companies into industry leaders, largely by building intensely loyal relationships with customers and employees. Now the chief executives—from Vanguard, Chick-fil-A, State Farm, and a half-dozen other leading companies—had gathered at a daylong forum to swap insights that would help them further enhance their loyalty efforts. And what they were hearing from Andy Taylor, the CEO of Enterprise Rent-A-Car, was riveting.

Taylor and his senior team had figured out a way to measure and manage customer loyalty without the complexity of traditional customer surveys. Every month, Enterprise polled its customers using just two simple questions, one about the quality of their rental experience and the other about the likelihood that they would rent from the company again. Because the process was so simple, it was fast. That allowed the company to publish ranked results for its 5,000 U.S. branches within days, giving the offices real-time feedback on how they were doing and the opportunity to learn from successful peers.

The survey was different in another important way. In ranking the branches, the company counted only the customers who gave the experience the highest possible rating. That narrow focus on enthusiastic customers surprised the CEOs in the room. Hands shot up. What about the rest of Enterprise's customers, the marginally satisfied who continued to rent from Enterprise and were necessary to its business? Wouldn't it be better to track, in a more sophisticated way, mean or median statistics? No, Taylor said. By concentrating solely on those most enthusiastic about their rental experience, the company could focus on a key driver of profitable growth: customers who not only return to rent again but also recommend Enterprise to their friends.

Enterprise's approach surprised me, too. Most customer satisfaction surveys aren't very useful. They tend to be long and complicated, yielding low response rates and ambiguous implications that are difficult for operating managers to act on. Furthermore, they are rarely challenged or audited because most senior executives, board members, and investors don't take them very seriously. That's because their results don't correlate tightly with profits or growth.

But Enterprise's method—and its ability to generate profitable growth through what appeared to be quite a simple tool—got me thinking that the company might be on to something. Could you get similar results in other industries—including those seemingly more complex than car rentals—by focusing only on customers who provided the most enthusiastic responses to a short list of questions designed to assess their loyalty to a company? Could the list be reduced to a single question? If so, what would that question be?

It took me two years of research to figure that out, research that linked survey responses with actual customer behavior—purchasing patterns and referrals—and ultimately with company growth. The results were clear yet counterintuitive. It turned out that a single survey question can, in fact, serve as a useful predictor of growth. But that question isn't about customer satisfaction or even loyalty—at least in so many words. Rather, it's about customers' willingness to recommend a product or service to someone else. In fact, in most of the industries that I studied, the percentage of customers who were enthusiastic enough to refer a friend or colleague—perhaps the strongest sign of customer loyalty—correlated directly with differences in growth rates among competitors.

Certainly, other factors besides customer loyalty play a role in driving a company's growth—economic or industry expansion, innovation, and so on. And I don't want to overstate the findings: Although the "would recommend" question generally proved to be the most effective in determining loyalty and predicting growth, that wasn't the case in every single industry. But evangelistic customer loyalty is clearly one of the most important drivers of growth. While it doesn't guarantee growth, in general profitable growth can't be achieved without it.

Furthermore, these findings point to an entirely new approach to customer surveys, one based on simplicity that directly links to a company's results. By substituting a single question—blunt tool though it may appear to be—for the complex black box of the typical customer satisfaction survey, companies can actually put consumer survey results to use and focus employees on the task of stimulating growth.

> *By substituting a single question for the complex black box of the typical customer satisfaction survey, companies can actually put consumer survey results to use and focus employees on the task of stimulating growth.*

Loyalty and Growth

Before I describe my research and the results from a number of industries, let's briefly look at the concept of loyalty and some of the mistakes companies make when trying to measure it. First, a definition. Loyalty is the willingness of someone—a customer, an employee, a friend—to make an investment or personal sacrifice in order to strengthen a relationship. For a customer, that can mean sticking with a supplier who treats him well and gives him good value in the long term even if the supplier does not offer the best price in a particular transaction.

Consequently, customer loyalty is about much more than repeat purchases. Indeed, even someone who buys again and again from the same company may not necessarily be loyal to that company but instead may be trapped by inertia, indifference, or exit barriers erected by the company or circumstance. (Someone may regularly take the same airline to a city only because it offers the most flights there.) Conversely, a loyal customer may not make frequent repeat purchases because of a reduced need for a product or service. (Someone may buy a new car less often as he gets older and drives less.)

True loyalty clearly affects profitability. While regular customers aren't always profitable, their choice to stick with a product or service typically reduces a company's customer acquisition costs. Loyalty also drives top-line growth. Obviously, no company can grow if its customer bucket is leaky, and loyalty helps eliminate this outflow. Indeed, loyal customers can raise the water level in the bucket: Customers who are truly loyal tend to buy more over time, as their incomes grow or they devote a larger share of their wallets to a company they feel good about.

And loyal customers talk up a company to their friends, family, and colleagues. In fact, such a recommendation is one of the best indicators of loyalty because of the customer's sacrifice, if you will, in making the recommendation. When customers act as references, they do more than indicate that they've received good economic value from a company; they put their own reputations on the line. And they will risk their reputations only if they feel intense loyalty. (Note that here, too, loyalty may have little to do with repeat purchases. As someone's income increases, she may move up the automotive ladder from the Hondas she has bought for years. But if she is loyal to the company, she will enthusiastically recommend a Honda to, say, a nephew who is buying his first car.)

The tendency of loyal customers to bring in new customers—at no charge to the company—is particularly beneficial as a company grows, especially if it operates in a mature industry. In such a case, the tremendous marketing costs of acquiring each new customer through advertising and other promotions make it hard to grow profitably. In fact, the only path to profitable growth may lie in a company's ability to get its loyal customers to become, in effect, its marketing department.

> *The only path to profitable growth may lie in a company's ability to get its loyal customers to become, in effect, its marketing department.*

The Wrong Yardsticks

Because loyalty is so important to profitable growth, measuring and managing it make good sense. Unfortunately, existing approaches haven't proved very effective. Not only does their complexity make them practically useless to line managers, but they also often yield flawed results.

The best companies have tended to focus on customer retention rates, but that measurement is merely the best of a mediocre lot. Retention rates provide, in many industries, a valuable link to profitability, but their relationship to growth is tenuous. That's because they basically track customer defections—the degree to which a bucket is emptying rather filling up. Furthermore, as I have noted, retention rates are a poor indication of customer loyalty in situations where customers are held hostage by high switching costs or other barriers, or where customers naturally outgrow a product because of their aging, increased income, or other factors. You'd want a stronger connection between retention and growth before you went ahead and invested significant money based only on data about retention.

An even less reliable means of gauging loyalty is through conventional customer-satisfaction measures. Our research indicates that satisfaction lacks a consistently demonstrable connection to actual customer behavior and growth. This finding is borne out by the short shrift that investors give to such reports as the American Consumer Satisfaction Index. The ACSI, published quarterly in the *Wall Street Journal*, reflects the customer satisfaction ratings of some 200 U.S. companies. In general, it is difficult to discern a strong correlation between high customer satisfaction scores and outstanding sales growth. Indeed, in some cases, there is an inverse relationship; at Kmart, for example, a significant increase in the company's ACSI rating was accompanied by a sharp decrease in sales as it slid into bankruptcy.

Even the most sophisticated satisfaction measurement systems have serious flaws. I saw this firsthand at one of the Big Three car manufacturers. The marketing executive at the company wanted to understand why, after the firm had spent millions of dollars on customer satisfaction surveys, satisfaction ratings for individual dealers did not relate very closely to dealer profits or growth. When I interviewed dealers, they agreed that customer satisfaction seemed like a reasonable goal. But they also pointed out that other factors were far more important to their profits and growth, such as keeping pressure on salespeople to close a high percentage of leads, filling showrooms with prospects through aggressive advertising, and charging customers the highest possible price for a car.

In most cases, dealers told me, the satisfaction survey is a charade that they play along with to remain in the good graces of the manufacturer and to ensure generous allocations of the hottest-selling models. The pressure they put on salespeople to boost scores often results in postsale pleading with customers to provide top ratings—even if they must offer something like free floor mats or oil changes in return. Dealers are usually complicit with salespeople in this process, a circumstance that further degrades the integrity of these scores. Indeed, some savvy customers negotiate a low price—and then offer to sell the dealer a set of top satisfaction survey ratings for another $500 off the price.

Figuring out a way to accurately measure customer loyalty and satisfaction is extremely important. Companies won't realize the fruits of loyalty until usable measurement systems enable firms to measure their performance against clear loyalty goals—just as they now do in the case of profitability and quality goals. For a while, it seemed as though information technology would provide a means to accurately measure loyalty. Sophisticated customer-relationship-management systems promised to help firms track customer behavior in real time. But the successes thus far have been limited to select industries, such as credit cards or grocery stores, where purchases are so frequent that changes in customer loyalty can be quickly spotted and acted on.

GETTING THE FACTS

So what would be a useful metric for gauging customer loyalty? To find out, I needed to do something rarely undertaken with customer surveys: Match survey responses from individual customers to their actual behavior—repeat purchases and referral patterns—over time. I sought the assistance of Satmetrix, a company that develops software to gather and analyze real-time customer feedback—and on whose board of directors I serve. Teams from Bain also helped with the project.

We started with the roughly 20 questions on the Loyalty Acid Test, a survey that I designed four years ago with Bain colleagues, which does a pretty good job of establishing the state of relations between a company and its customers. (The complete test can be found at http://www.loyaltyrules.com/loyaltyrules/acid_test_customer.html.) We administered the test to thousands of customers recruited from public lists in six industries: financial services, cable and telephony, personal computers, e-commerce, auto insurance, and Internet service providers.

We then obtained a purchase history for each person surveyed and asked those people to name specific instances in which they had referred someone else to the company in question. When this information wasn't immediately available, we waited six to 12 months and gathered information on subsequent purchases and referrals from those individuals. With information from more than 4,000 customers, we were able to build 14 case studies—that is, cases in which we had sufficient sample sizes to measure the link between survey responses of individual customers of a company and those individuals' actual referral and purchase behavior.

The data allowed us to determine which survey questions had the strongest statistical correlation with repeat purchases or referrals. We hoped that we would find at least one question for each industry that effectively predicted such behaviors, which can drive growth. We found something more: One question was best for *most* industries. "How likely is it that you would recommend [company X] to a friend or colleague?" ranked first or second in 11 of the 14 cases studies. And in two of the three other cases, "would recommend" ranked so close behind the top two predictors that the surveys would be nearly as accurate by relying on results of this single question. (For a ranking of the best-scoring questions, see the sidebar "Ask the Right Question.")

These findings surprised me. My personal bet for the top question (probably reflecting the focus of my research on employee loyalty in recent years) would have been "How strongly do you agree that [company X] deserves your loyalty?" Clearly, though, the abstract concept of loyalty was less compelling to customers than what may be the ultimate act of loyalty, a recommendation to a friend. I also expected that "How strongly do you agree that [company X] sets the standard for excellence in its industry?"—with its implications of offering customers both economic benefit and fair treatment—would prove more predictive than it did. One result did not startle me at all. The question "How satisfied are you with [company X's] overall performance?" while relevant in certain industries, would prove to be a relatively weak predictor of growth.

So my colleagues and I had the right question—"How likely is it that you would recommend [company X] to a friend or colleague?"—and now we needed to develop a scale to score the responses. This may seem somewhat trivial, but, as statisticians know, it's not. Making customer loyalty a strategic goal that managers can work toward requires a scale as simple and unambiguous as the question itself. The right one will effectively divide customers into practical groups deserving different attention and organizational responses. It must be intuitive to customers when they assign grades and to employees and partners responsible for interpreting the results and taking action. Ideally, the scale would be so easy to understand that even outsiders, such as investors, regulators, and journalists, would grasp the basic messages without needing a handbook and a statistical abstract.

For these reasons, we settled on a scale where ten means "extremely likely" to recommend, five means neutral, and zero means "not at all likely." When we examined customer referral and repurchase behaviors along this scale, we found three logical clusters. "Promoters," the customers with the highest rates of repurchase and referral, gave ratings of nine or ten to the question. The "passively satisfied" logged a seven or an eight, and "detractors" scored from zero to six.

By limiting the promoter designation to only the most enthusiastic customers, we avoided the "grade inflation" that often infects traditional customer-satisfaction assessments, in which someone a molecule north of neutral is considered "satisfied." (This was the danger that Enterprise Rent-A-Car avoided when it decided to focus on its most enthusiastic customers.) And not only did clustering customers into three categories—promoters, the passively satisfied, and detractors—turn out to provide the simplest, most intuitive, and best predictor of customer behavior; it also made sense to frontline managers, who could relate to the goal of increasing the number of promoters and reducing the number of detractors more readily than increasing the mean of their satisfaction index by one standard deviation.

THE GROWTH CONNECTION

All of our analysis to this point had focused on customer survey responses and how well those linked to customers' referral and repurchase behavior at 14 companies in six industries. But the real test would be how well this approach explained relative growth rates for all competitors in an industry—and across a broader range of industry sectors.

In the first quarter of 2001, Satmetrix began tracking the "would recommend" scores of a new universe of customers, many thousands of them from more than 400 companies in more than a dozen industries. In each subsequent quarter, they then gathered 10,000 to 15,000 responses to a very brief e-mail survey that asked respondents (drawn again from public sources, not Satmetrix's internal client customer lists) to rate one or two companies with which they were familiar. Where we could obtain comparable and reliable revenue-growth data for a range of competitors, and where there were sufficient consumer responses, we plotted each firm's net promoters—the percentage of promoters minus the percentage of detractors—against the company's revenue growth rate.

The results were striking. In airlines, for example, a strong correlation existed between net-promoter figures and a company's average growth rate over the three-year period from 1999 to 2002. Remarkably, this one simple statistic seemed to explain the relative growth rates across the entire industry; that is, no airline has found a way to increase growth without improving its ratio of promoters to detractors. That result was reflected, to a greater or lesser degree, in most of the industries we examined—including rental cars, where Enterprise enjoys both the highest rate of growth and the highest net-promoter percentage among its competitors. (See the exhibit "Growth by Word of Mouth.")

The "would recommend" question wasn't the best predictor of growth in every case. In a few situations, it was simply irrelevant. In database software or computer systems, for instance, senior executives select vendors, and top managers typically didn't appear on the public e-mail lists we used to sample customers. Asking users of the system whether they would recommend the system to a friend or colleague seemed a little abstract, as they had no choice in the matter. In these cases, we found that the "sets the standard of excellence" or "deserves your loyalty" questions were more predictive.

Not surprisingly, "would recommend" also didn't predict relative growth in industries dominated by monopolies

Growth by Word of Mouth

Research shows that, in most industries, there is a strong correlation between a company's growth rate and the percentage of its customers who are promoters"—that is, those who say they are extremely likely to recommend the company to a friend or colleague (The net-promoter figure is calculated by subtracting the percentage of customers who say they are unlikely to make a recommendation from the percentage who say they are extremely likely to do so.) It's worth noting that the size of companies has no relationship to their net-promoter status.

and near monopolies, where consumers have little choice. For example, in the local telephone and cable TV businesses, population growth and economic expansion in the region determine growth rates, not how well customers are treated by their suppliers. And in certain cases, we found small niche companies that were growing faster than their net-promoter percentages would imply. But for most companies in most industries, getting customers enthusiastic enough to recommend a company appears to be crucial to growth. (To calculate your own net-promoter number, see the sidebar "A Net-Promoter Primer.")

Airlines

Internet Service Providers

Car Rentals

THE DANGERS OF DETRACTORS

The battle for growth among Internet service providers AOL, MSN, and EarthLink brings to life our findings. For years, market leader AOL aggressively focused on new customer acquisition. Through those efforts, AOL more than offset a substantial number of defections. But the company paid much less attention to converting these new customers into intensely loyal promoters. Customer service lapsed, to the point where customers couldn't even find a phone number to contact company representatives to answer questions or resolve problems.

Today, AOL is struggling to grow. Even though AOL's customer count surged to an eventual peak of 35 million, its deteriorating mix of promoters and detractors eventually choked off expansion. The fire hose of new customer flow—filled with people attracted to free trial promotions—couldn't keep up with the leaks in AOL's customer bucket. Defection rates exceeded 200,000 customers per month in 2003. Marketing costs were ratcheted up to stem the tide, and those expenditures, along with the collapse of online advertising, contributed to declines in cash flow of almost 40% between 2001 and 2003.

By 2002, our research found, 42% of the company's customers were detractors, while only 32% were promoters, giving the company a net-promoter percentage of -10%. The current management team is working on the problem, but it's a challenging one because disappointed customers are undoubtedly spreading their opinions about AOL to family, friends, colleagues, and acquaintances.

AOL's dial-up competitors have done a better job in building promoters, and it shows in their relative rates of growth. MSN invested $500 million in R&D to upgrade its service with functional improvements such as improved parental controls and spam filters. By 2003, MSN's promoter population reached 41% of its customer base, compared with a detractor population of 32%,

Tracking net promoters—the percentage of customers who are promoters of a brand or company minus the percentage who are detractors—offers organizations a powerful way to measure and manage customer loyalty. Firms with the highest net-promoter scores consistently garner the lion's share of industry growth. So how can companies get started?

Survey a statistically valid sample of your customers with the following question: "How likely is it that you would recommend [brand or company X] to a friend or colleague?" It's critical to provide a consistent scale for responses that range from zero to ten, where zero means not at all likely, five means neutral, and ten means extremely likely.

Resist the urge to let survey questions multiply; more questions diminish response rates along with the reliability of your sample. You need only one question to determine the status—promoter, passively satisfied, or detractor—of a customer. (Follow-up questions can help unearth the reasons for customers' feelings and point to profitable remedies. But such questions should be tailored to the three categories of customers. Learning how to turn a passively satisfied customer into a promoter requires a very different line of questioning from learning how to resolve the problems of a detractor.)

Calculate the percentage of customers who respond with nine or ten (promoters) and the percentage who respond with zero through six (detractors). Subtract the percentage of detractors from the percentage of promoters to arrive at your net-promoter score. Don't be surprised if your score is lower than you expect. The median net-promoter score of more than 400 companies in 28 industries (based on some 130,000 customer survey responses gathered over the past two-plus years by Satmetrix, a maker of software for managing real-time customer feedback) was just 16%.

Compare net-promoter scores from specific regions, branches, service or sales reps, and customer segments. This often reveals root causes of differences as well as best practices that can be shared. What really counts, of course, is how your company compares with direct competitors. Have your market researchers survey your competitors' customers using the same method. You can then determine how your company stacks up within your industry and whether your current net-promoter number is a competitive asset or a liability.

Improve your score. The companies with the most enthusiastic customer referrals, including eBay, Amazon, and USAA, receive net-promoter scores of 75% to more than 80%. For companies aiming to garner world-class loyalty—and the growth that comes with it—this should be the target.

giving the company a net-promoter percentage of 9%. EarthLink managed to nearly match MSN's net-promoter score over this period by continuing to invest in the reliability of its dial-up connections (minimizing the irritation of busy signals and dropped connections) and by making phone support readily available.

AOL's experience vividly illustrates the folly of seeking growth through shortcuts such as massive price cuts or other incentives rather than through building true loyalty. It also illustrates the detrimental effect that detractors' word-of-mouth communications can have on a business—the flip side of customers' recommendations to their friends. Countering a damaged reputation requires a company to create tremendously appealing incentives that will persuade skeptical customers to give a product or service a try, and the incentives drive up already significant customer acquisition costs.

Furthermore, detractors—and even customers who are only passively satisfied but not enthusiastically loyal—typically take a toll on employees and increase service costs. Finally, every detractor represents a missed opportunity to add a promoter to the customer population, one more unpaid salesperson to market your product or service and generate growth.

KEEP IT SIMPLE

One of the main takeaways from our research is that companies can keep customer surveys simple. The most basic surveys—employing the right questions—can allow companies to report timely data that are easy to act on. Too many of today's satisfaction survey processes yield complex information that's months out of date by the time it reaches frontline managers. Good luck to the branch manager who tries to help an employee interpret a score resulting from a complex weighting algorithm based on feedback from anonymous customers, many of whom were surveyed before the employee had his current job.

Contrast that scenario with one in which a manager presents employees with numbers from the previous week (or day) showing the percentages (and names) of a branch office's customers who are promoters, passively satisfied, and detractors—and then issues the managerial charge, "We need more promoters and fewer detractors in order to grow." The goal is clear-cut, actionable, and motivating.

In short, a customer feedback program should be viewed not as "market research" but as an operating management tool. Again, consider Enterprise Rent-A-Car. The first step in the development of Enterprise's current system was to devise a way to track loyalty by measuring service quality from the customer's perspective. The initial effort yielded a long, unwieldy research questionnaire, one that included the pet questions of everyone involved in drafting the survey. It only captured average service quality on a regional basis—interesting, but useless, since managers needed to see scores for each individual branch to establish clear accountability. Over time, the sample was expanded to provide this information. And the number of questions on the survey was sharply reduced; this simplified the collating of answers and allowed the company to post monthly branch-level results almost as soon as they were collected.

The company then began examining the relationships between customer responses and actual purchases and referrals. This is when Enterprise learned the value of enthusiasts. Customers who gave the highest rating to their rental experience were three times more likely to rent again than those who gave Enterprise the second-highest grade. When a customer reported a neutral or negative experience, marking him a potential detractor, the interviewer requested permission to immediately forward this information to the branch manager, who was trained how to apologize, identify the root cause of the problem, and resolve it.

The measurement system cost more than $4 million per year, but the company made such significant progress in building customer loyalty that the company's management considers it one of the company's best investments. And the new system had definitely started to get employees' attention. In fact, a few branch managers (perhaps taking a cue from car dealers) attempted to manipulate the system to their benefit. Enterprise responded with a process for spotting—for example, by ensuring that the phone numbers of dissatisfied respondents hadn't been changed, making it difficult to follow up—and punishing "gamers."

Despite the system's success, CEO Andy Taylor felt something was missing. Branch scores were not improving quickly enough, and a big gap continued to separate the worst- and best-performing regions. Taylor's assessment: "We needed a greater a sense of urgency." So the management team decided that field managers would not be eligible for promotion unless their branch or group of branches matched or exceeded the company's average scores. That's a pretty radical idea when you think about it: giving customers, in effect, veto power over managerial pay raises and promotions.

The rigorous implementation of this simple customer feedback system had a clear impact on business. As the survey scores rose, so did Enterprise's growth relative to its competition. Taylor cites the linking of customer feedback to employee rewards as one of the most important reasons that Enterprise has continued to grow, even as the business became bigger and, arguably, more mature. (For more on Enterprise's customer survey program, see "Driving Customer Satisfaction," HBR July 2002.)

CONVERTING CUSTOMERS INTO PROMOTERS

If collecting and applying customer feedback is this simple, why don't companies already do it this way? I don't want to be too cynical, but perhaps the research firms that administer current customer surveys know there is very little profit margin for them in something as bare-bones as this. Complex loyalty indexes, based on a dozen or more proprietary questions and weighted with a black-box scaling function, simply generate more business for survey firms.

The market research firms have an even deeper fear. With the advent of e-mail and analytical software, leading-edge companies can now bypass the research firms entirely, cutting costs and improving the quality and timeliness of feedback. These new tools enable companies to gather customer feedback and report results in real time, funneling it directly to frontline employees and managers. This can also threaten in-house market research departments, which typically have built their power base through controlling and interpreting customer survey data. Marketing departments understandably focus surveys on the areas they can control, such as brand image, pricing, and product features. But a customer's willingness to recommend to a friend results from how well the customer is treated by frontline employees, which in turn is determined by all the functional areas that contribute to a customer's experience.

For a measure to be practical, operational, and reliable—that is, for it to determine the percentage of net promoters among customers and allow managers to act on it—the process and the results need to be owned and accepted by all of the business functions. And all the people in the organization must know which customers they are responsible for. Overseeing such a process is a more appropriate task for the CFO, or for the general manager of the business unit, than for the marketing department. Indeed, it is too important (and politically charged) to delegate to any one function.

The path to sustainable, profitable growth begins with creating more promoters and fewer detractors and making your net-promoter number transparent throughout your organization. This number is the one number you need to grow. It's that simple and that profound.

Cases

Case 1   *Susan Munro, Service Consumer*

In the course of a single day, a busy young woman makes use of a wide array of services.

Susan Munro, a final-year business student, had worked late the night before on a big paper and overslept the following morning in the apartment she shared with three other students. Her roommates, who had early classes, had already left when she got up. After showering, she dressed hurriedly, then made a quick cup of coffee. But she skipped her usual bowl of cereal, figuring she could pick up a bagel at school.

Noticing that the weather outside looked ominous, she clicked onto the Internet to check the local weather forecast. It predicted rain, so she grabbed an umbrella before leaving the apartment and walking to the bus stop for her daily ride to the university. On the way, she dropped a letter in a mailbox. The bus arrived on schedule. It was the usual driver, who recognized her and gave a cheerful greeting as she showed her monthly pass. The bus was quite full, carrying a mix of students and office workers, so she had to stand.

Arriving at her destination, Susan left the bus and walked to the School of Business. Feeling hungry, she entered the main lobby and headed to the small, cheerfully decorated food stand in the far corner. "Sorry," said the attendant in answer to her question. "We just sold the last of the bagels and are waiting for more French Roast. Would you like decaf?" Susan sighed. It wasn't the first time this had happened. But the class was about to start and she couldn't wait.

Joining a crowd of other students, she took a seat in the large classroom where her finance class was held. The professor lectured in a near monotone for 75 minutes, occasionally projecting charts on a large screen to illustrate certain calculations. It didn't help that she was still feeling sleepy. Susan reflected that it would be just as effective—and far more convenient—if the course were transmitted over the Web or recorded on DVDs that students could watch at their leisure. She much preferred the marketing course that followed because this professor was a very dynamic individual who believed in having an active dialogue with the students. Susan made several contributions to the discussion and felt that she learned a lot from listening to others' analyses and opinions.

She and three friends ate lunch at the recently modernized Student Union. The old cafeteria, a gloomy place that served unappetizing food at high prices, had been replaced by a well-lit and colorfully painted new food court, featuring a variety of options. These included both local suppliers and brand-name fast-food chains, which offered choices of sandwiches, as well as ethnic foods, salads, and a variety of desserts. Although she had wanted a sandwich, the line of waiting customers at the sandwich shop was rather long, so Susan joined her friends at Burger King and then splurged on a caffe latte from the adjacent Hav-a-Java coffee stand. The food court was unusually crowded today, perhaps because of the rain now pouring down outside. When they finally found a table, they had to clear off the dirty trays. "Lazy slobs!" commented her friend Mark, referring to the previous customers.

After lunch, Susan stopped at an ATM, inserted her card, and withdrew some money. Remembering that she had a job interview at the end of the week, she telephoned her hairdresser and counted herself lucky to be able to make an appointment for later in the day because of a cancellation by another client. Leaving the Student Union, she ran across the rain-soaked plaza to the Language Department. In preparation for her next class, Business Spanish, she spent an hour in the language lab, watching an engaging video of customers making purchases at different types of stores, then repeating key phrases and listening to her own recorded voice. "My accent's definitely getting better!" she said to herself.

With her last class over and Spanish phrases filling her head, Susan headed off to visit the hairdresser. She liked the store, which had a bright, trendy decor and well-groomed, friendly staff. Unfortunately, the cutter was running late and Susan had to wait 20 minutes, which she used to review a chapter for tomorrow's human resources course. Some of the other waiting customers were reading magazines provided by the store. Eventually, it was time for a shampoo, after which the cutter proposed a slightly different cut. Susan agreed, although she drew the line at the suggestion to lighten her hair color. She sat very still, watching the process in the mirror and turning her head when requested. She was pleased with the result and complimented the cutter on her work. Including the shampoo, the process had lasted about 40 minutes. She tipped the cutter and paid at the reception desk.

The rain had stopped and the sun was shining as Susan left the store, so she walked home, stopping to pick up clothes from the cleaners. This store was rather gloomy,

---

© 2007 Christopher H. Lovelock

492

smelled of cleaning solvents, and badly needed repainting. She was annoyed to find that although her silk blouse was ready as promised, the suit she would need for her interview was not. The assistant, who had dirty fingernails, mumbled an apology in an insincere tone without making eye contact. Although the store was convenient and the quality of work quite good, Susan considered the employees unfriendly and not very helpful.

Back at her apartment building, she opened the mailbox in the lobby and collected the mail for herself and her roommates. Her own mail, which was rather dull, included a quarterly bill from her insurance company, which required no action since she had signed an agreement to deduct the funds automatically from her bank account. There was also a postcard from her optometrist, reminding her that it was time to schedule a new eye exam. Susan made a mental note to call for an appointment, anticipating that she might need a revised prescription for her contact lenses. She was about to discard the junk mail when she noticed a flyer promoting a new dry-cleaning store and including a coupon for a discount. She decided to try the new firm and pocketed the coupon.

Since it was her turn to cook dinner, she wandered into the kitchen, turned on the light, and started looking in the refrigerator and then the cupboards to see what was available. Susan sighed—there wasn't much in there. Maybe she would make a salad and call for home delivery of a large pizza.

STUDY QUESTIONS

1. *Identify each of the services that Susan Munro has used or is planning to use. Categorize them according to the nature of the underlying process.*
2. *What needs is she attempting to satisfy in each instance?*
3. *What proportion of these services (a) involve self-service, (b) some degree of customer involvement with the production process, (c) dependence on the service provider. Where do you see more potential for self-service, and what would be the implications for customer and supplier?*
4. *What similarities and differences are there between the dry-cleaning store and the hair salon? What could each learn from studying the other?*

Case 2   *Four Customers in Search of Solutions*

CHRISTOPHER LOVELOCK

Four telephone subscribers from suburban Toronto call their telephone company to complain about a variety of problems. How should the company respond in each instance?

Among the many customers of Bell Canada in Toronto, Ontario, are four individuals living on Willow Street in a middle-class suburb of the city. Each of them has a telephone-related problem and decides to call the company about it.

Winston Chen

Winston Chen grumbles constantly about the amount of his home telephone bill (which is, in fact, in the top 2% of all household phone bills in Ontario). There are many calls to countries in Southeast Asia on weekday evenings, almost daily calls to Kingston (a smaller city not far from Toronto) around mid-day, and calls to Vancouver, British Columbia, most weekends. One day, Mr. Chen receives a telephone bill which is even larger than usual. On reviewing the bill, he is convinced that he has been overcharged, so he calls the phone company to complain and request an adjustment.

Marie Portillo

Marie Portillo has missed several important calls recently because the caller received a busy signal. She phones the customer service department to determine possible solutions to this problem. Ms. Portillo's telephone bill is at the median level for a household subscriber. (The median is the point at which 50% of all bills are higher and 50% are lower.) Most of the calls from her house are local, but there are occasional international calls to Mexico or to countries in South America. She does not subscribe to any value-added services.

Eleanor Vanderbilt

During the past several weeks, Mrs. Vanderbilt has been distressed to receive a series of obscene telephone calls. It sounds like the same person each time. She calls the telephone company to see if they can put a stop to this harassment. Her phone bill is in the bottom 10% of all household subscriber bills and almost all calls are local.

Richard Robbins

For more than a week, the phone line at Rich Robbins' house has been making strange humming and crackling noises, making it difficult to hear what the other person is saying. After two of his friends comment on these distracting noises, Mr. Robbins calls to report the problem. His guess is that it is being caused by the answering machine, which is getting old and sometimes loses messages. Mr. Robbins' phone bill is at the 75th percentile for a household subscriber. Most calls are made to locations within Canada, usually at evenings and weekends, although there are a few calls to the U.S., too.

STUDY QUESTIONS

1. *Based strictly on the information in the case, how many possibilities do you see to segment the telecommunications market?*
2. *As a customer service rep, how would you address each of the problems and complaints reported?*
3. *As a marketing manager, do you see any marketing opportunities for the telephone company in these complaints?*

© 2007 Christopher H. Lovelock

494

Case 3   Dr. Beckett's Dental Office

LAUREN K. WRIGHT

A dentist seeks to differentiate her practice on the basis of quality. She constructs a new office and redesigns the practice to deliver high quality to her patients and to improve productivity through increased efficiency. However, it's not always easy to convince patients that her superior service justifies higher fees that are not always covered by insurance.

"I just hope the quality differences are visible to our patients," mused Dr. Barbro Beckett as she surveyed the office that housed her well-established dental practice. She had recently moved to her current location from an office she felt was too cramped to allow her staff to work efficiently—a factor that was becoming increasingly important as the costs of providing dental care continued to rise. While Dr. Beckett realized that productivity gains were necessary, she did not want to compromise the quality of service her patients received.

MANAGEMENT COMES TO DENTISTRY

The classes Dr. Beckett took in dental school taught her a lot about the technical side of dentistry but nothing about the business side. She received no formal training in the mechanics of running a business or understanding customer needs. In fact, professional guidelines discouraged marketing or advertising of any kind. That had not been a major problem 22 years earlier, when Dr. Beckett started her practice, for profit margins had been good then. However, the dental care industry had changed dramatically. Costs rose as a result of labor laws, malpractice insurance, and the constant need to invest in new equipment and staff training as new technologies were introduced. Dr. Beckett's overhead was now between 70–80% of revenues before accounting for her wages or office rental.

At the same time as provider overhead was rising, there was a movement in the United States to reduce health care costs to insurance companies, employers and patients by offering "managed health care" through large health maintenance organizations (HMOs). The HMOs set the prices for various services by putting an upper limit on the amount that their doctors and dentists could charge for various procedures. The advantage to patients was that their health insurance covered virtually all costs. But the price limitations meant that HMO doctors and dentists would not be able to offer certain services that might provide better quality care but were too expensive. Dr. Beckett had decided not to become an HMO provider because the reimbursement rate was only 80–85% of what she normally charged for treatment. She felt that she could not provide high-quality care to patients at these rates.

These changes presented some significant challenges to Dr. Beckett, who wanted to offer the highest level of dental care rather than being a low-cost provider. With the help of a consultant, she decided that her top priority was differentiating the practice on the basis of quality. She and her staff developed an internal mission statement that reflected this goal.

The mission statement (prominently displayed in the back office) read, in part: *"It is our goal to provide superior dentistry in an efficient, profitable manner within the confines of a caring, quality environment."*

Since higher quality care was more costly, Dr. Beckett's patients sometimes had to pay fees for costs that were not covered by their insurance policies. If the quality differences weren't substantial, these patients might decide to switch to an HMO dentist or another lower-cost provider.

REDESIGNING THE SERVICE DELIVERY SYSTEM

The move to a new office gave Dr. Beckett a unique opportunity to rethink almost every aspect of her service. She wanted the work environment to reflect her own personality and values as well as providing a pleasant place for her staff to work.

Facilities and Equipment

Dr. Beckett first looked into the office spaces that were available in the Northern California town where she practiced. She didn't find anything she liked, so she hired an architect from San Francisco to design a contemporary office building with lots of light and space. This increased the building costs by $100,000 but Dr. Beckett felt that it would be a critical factor in differentiating her service.

Dr. Beckett's new office was Scandinavian in design (reflecting her Swedish heritage and attention to detail.) The waiting room and reception area were filled with modern furniture in muted shades of brown, grey, green and purple. Live plants and flowers were abundant, and the walls were covered with art. Classical music played softly in the background. Patients could enjoy a cup of coffee or tea and browse through the large selection of current magazines while they waited for their appointments.

The treatment areas were both functional and appealing. There was a small conference room with toys for children and a VCR that was used to show patients educational films about different dental procedures. Literature was available here to explain what patients needed to do to maximize the benefits of their treatment outcomes.

The chairs in the examining rooms were covered in leather and very comfortable. Each room had a large window that allowed patients to watch birds eating at the feeders that were filled each day. There were also attractive mobiles hanging from the ceiling to distract patients from the unfamiliar sounds and sensations they might be experiencing. Headphones were available with a wide selection of music.

The entire "back office" staff (including Dr. Beckett) wore uniforms in cheerful shades of pink, purple and blue that matched the office décor. All the technical equipment looked very modern and was spotlessly clean. State-of-the-art computerized machinery was used for some procedures. Dr. Beckett's dental degrees were prominently displayed in her office, along with certificates from various programs that she and her staff had attended to update their technical skills.

Service Personnel

There were eight employees in the dental practice, including Dr. Beckett (the only dentist.) The seven staff members were separated by job function into "front office" and "back office" workers. Front office duties (covered by two employees) included receptionist and secretarial tasks and financial/budgeting work. The back office was divided into hygienists and chair side assistants.

The three chair side assistants helped the hygienists and Dr. Beckett with treatment procedures. They had specialized training for their jobs but did not need a college degree. The two hygienists handled routine exams and teeth cleaning plus some treatment procedures. In many dental offices, hygienists had a tendency to act like "prima donnas" because of their education (a bachelor's degree plus specialized training) and experience. According to Dr. Beckett, such an attitude could destroy any possibility of team work among the office staff. She felt very fortunate that her hygienists viewed themselves as part of a larger team that worked together to provide quality care to patients.

Dr. Beckett valued her friendships with staff members and also understood that they were a vital part of the service delivery. "90% of patients' perceptions of quality comes from their interactions with the front desk and the other employees—not from the staff's technical skills," she stated. When the dentist began to redesign her practice, she discussed her goals with the staff and involved them in the decision-making process. The changes meant new expectations and routines for most employees, and some were not willing to adapt. There was some staff

turnover (mostly voluntary) as the new office procedures were implemented. The current group worked very well as a team.

Dr. Beckett and her staff met briefly each morning to discuss the day's schedule and patients. They also had longer meetings every other week to discuss more strategic issues and resolve any problems that might have developed. During these meetings, employees made suggestions about how to improve patient care. Some of the most successful staff suggestions include: "thank-you" cards to patients who referred other patients; follow-up calls to patients after major procedures; a "goodie box" for patients including toothbrush, toothpaste, mouthwash and floss; buckwheat pillows and blankets for patient comfort during long procedures; coffee and tea in the waiting area; and a photo album in the waiting area with pictures of staff and their families.

The expectations for staff performance (in terms of both technical competence and patient interactions) were very high. But Dr. Beckett provided her employees with many opportunities to update their skills by attending classes and workshops. She also rewarded their hard work by giving monthly bonuses if business had been good. Since she shared the financial data with her staff, they could see the difference in revenues if the schedule was slow or patients were dissatisfied. This provided an extra incentive to improve service delivery. The entire office also went on trips together once a year (paid for by Dr. Beckett); spouses were welcome to participate but had to cover their own trip expenses. Past destinations for these excursions had included Hawaii and Washington, D.C.

Procedures and Patients

With the help of a consultant, all the office systems (including billing, ordering, lab work and patient treatment) were redesigned. One of the main goals was to standardize some of the routine procedures so that error was reduced and all patients would receive the same level of care. Specific times were allotted for each procedure and the staff worked very hard to see that these times were met. Office policy specified that patients should be kept waiting no longer than 20 minutes without being given the option to reschedule, and employees often called patients in advance if they knew there would be a delay. They also attempted to fill in cancellations to make sure office capacity was maximized. Staff members would substitute for each other when necessary or help with tasks that were not specifically in their job descriptions in order to make things run more smoothly.

Dr. Beckett's practice included about 2000 "active" patients and many more who came infrequently. They were mostly white collar workers with professional jobs (university employees, health care workers and managers/owners of local establishments.) She did no advertising—all of her new business came from positive word of mouth by current patients.

The dentist believed that referrals were a real advantage because new patients didn't come in "cold." She did not have to sell herself because they had already been told about her service by friends or family. All new patients were required to have an initial exam so that Dr. Beckett could do a needs assessment and educate them about her service. She believed this was the first indication to patients that her practice was different from others they might have experienced. Patients might sometimes have to wait another 3–4 months for a routine cleaning and exam because the schedule was so busy, but they did not seem to mind.

THE BIGGEST CHALLENGE

"Redesigning the business was the easy part," Dr. Beckett sighed. "Demonstrating the high level of quality to patients is the hard job." She said this task was especially difficult since most people disliked going to the dentist or felt that it was an inconvenience and so came in with a negative attitude. Dr. Beckett tried to reinforce the idea that quality dental care depended on a positive long-term relationship between patients and the dental team. This philosophy was reflected in a section of the patient mission statement hanging in the waiting area: *"We are a caring, professional dental team serving motivated, quality-oriented patients interested in keeping healthy smiles for a lifetime. Our goal is to offer a progressive and educational environment. Your concerns are our focus."*

Although Dr. Beckett enjoyed her work, she admitted it could be difficult to maintain a positive attitude. The job required precision and attention to detail, and the procedures were often painful for patients. She often felt as though she were "walking on eggshells" because she knew patients were anxious and uncomfortable, which made them more critical of her service delivery. It was not uncommon for patients to say negative things to Dr. Beckett even before treatment began (such as, "I really hate going to the dentist—it's not you, but I just don't want to be here!"). When this happened, she reminded herself that she was providing quality service whether patients appreciated it or not. "The person will usually have to have the dental work done anyway," she remarked, "So I just do the best job I can and make them as comfortable as possible." Even though patients seldom expressed appreciation for her services, she hoped that she had made a positive difference in their health or appearance that would benefit them in the long run.

STUDY QUESTIONS

1. Which of the eight elements of the services marketing mix are addressed in this case? Give examples of each "P" you identify.
2. Why do people dislike going to the dentist? Do you feel Dr. Beckett has addressed this problem effectively?
3. How do Dr. Beckett and her staff educate patients about the service they are receiving? What else could they do?
4. What supplementary services are offered? How do they enhance service delivery?
5. Contrast your own dental care experiences with those offered by Dr. Beckett's practice. What differences do you see? Based on your review of this case, what advice would you give (a) to your current or former dentist, and (b) to Dr. Beckett?

Case 4   Starbucks: Delivering Customer Service

YOUNGME MOON AND JOHN QUELCH

Starbucks, the dominant specialty-coffee brand in North America, must respond to recent market research indicating that the company is not meeting customer expectations in terms of service. To increase customer satisfaction, the company is debating a plan that would increase the amount of labor in its stores and theoretically increase speed-of-service. However, the impact of the plan (which would cost $40 million annually) on the company's bottom line is unclear.

In mid-2002, Christine Day, Starbucks' senior vice president of administration in North America, sat in the seventh-floor conference room of Starbucks' Seattle headquarters and reached for her second cup of *toffee nut latte*. The handcrafted beverage—a buttery, toffee-nut flavored espresso concoction topped with whipped cream and toffee sprinkles—had become a regular afternoon indulgence for Day ever since its introduction earlier that year.

As she waited for her colleagues to join her, Day reflected on the company's recent performance. While other retailers were still reeling from the post-9/11 recession, Starbucks was enjoying its 11th consecutive year of 5% or higher comparable store sales growth, prompting its founder and chairman, Howard Schultz, to declare: "I think we've demonstrated that we are close to a recession-proof product."[1]

Day, however, was not feeling nearly as sanguine, in part because Starbucks' most recent market research had revealed some unexpected findings. "We've always taken great pride in our retail service," said Day, "but according to the data, we're not always meeting our customers' expectations in the area of customer satisfaction."

As a result of these concerns, Day and her associates had come up with a plan to invest an additional $40 million annually in the company's 4,500 stores, which would allow each store to add the equivalent of 20 hours of labor a week. "The idea is to improve speed-of-service and thereby increase customer satisfaction," said Day.

In two days, Day was due to make a final recommendation to both Schultz and Orin Smith, Starbucks' CEO, about whether the company should move forward with the plan. "The investment is the EPS [earnings per share] equivalent of almost seven cents a share," said Day. In preparation for her meeting with Schultz and Smith, Day had asked one of her associates to help her think through the implications of the plan. Day noted, "The real question is, do we believe what our customers are telling us about what constitutes 'excellent' customer service? And if we deliver it, what will the impact be on our sales and profitability?"

COMPANY BACKGROUND

The story of how Howard Schultz managed to transform a commodity into an upscale cultural phenomenon had become the stuff of legends. In 1971, three coffee fanatics—Gerald Baldwin, Gordon Bowker, and Ziev Siegl—opened a small coffee shop in Seattle's Pike Place Market. The shop specialized in selling whole arabica beans to a niche market of coffee purists.

In 1982, Schultz joined the Starbucks marketing team; shortly thereafter, he traveled to Italy, where he became fascinated with Milan's coffee culture, in particular, the role the neighborhood espresso bars played in Italians' everyday social lives. Upon his return, the inspired Schultz convinced the company to set up an espresso bar in the corner of its only downtown Seattle shop. As Schultz explained, the bar became the prototype for his long-term vision:

> The idea was to create a chain of coffeehouses that would become America's "third place." At the time, most Americans had two places in their lives—home and work. But I believed that people needed another place, a place where they could go to relax and enjoy others, or just be by themselves. I envisioned a place that would be separate from home or work, a place that would mean different things to different people.

A few years later, Schultz got his chance when Starbucks' founders agreed to sell him the company. As soon as Schultz took over, he immediately began opening new stores. The stores sold whole beans and premium-priced coffee beverages by the cup and catered primarily to affluent, well-educated, white-collar patrons (skewed female) between the ages of 25 and 44. By 1992, the company had 140 such stores in the Northwest and Chicago and was successfully competing against other small-scale

Professors Youngme Moon and John Quetch prepared this case. HBS cases are developed solely as the basis for class discussion. Cases are not intended to serve as endorsements, sources of primary data, or illustrations of effective or ineffective management. Copyright © 2003 President and Fellows of Harvard College. To order copies or request permission to reproduce materials, call 1-800-545-7685, write Harvard Business School Publishing, Boston, MA 02163, or go to http://www.hbsp.harvard.edu. No part of this publication may be reproduced, stored in a retrieval system, used in a spreadsheet, or transmitted in any form or by any means—electronic, mechanical, photocopying, recording, or otherwise—without the permission of Harvard Business School. Copying or posting is an infringement of copyright. Permissions@hbsp.harvard.edu or 617-783-7860.

coffee chains such as Gloria Jean's Coffee Bean and Barnie's Coffee & Tea.

That same year, Schultz decided to take the company public. As he recalled, many Wall Street types were dubious about the idea: "They'd say, 'You mean, you're going to sell coffee for a dollar in a paper cup, with Italian names that no one in America can say? At a time in America when no one's drinking coffee? And I can get coffee at the local coffee shop or doughnut shop for 50 cents? Are you kidding me?'"[2]

Ignoring the skeptics, Schultz forged ahead with the public offering, raising $25 million in the process. The proceeds allowed Starbucks to open more stores across the nation.

By mid-2002, Schultz had unequivocally established Starbucks as the dominant specialty-coffee brand in North America. Sales had climbed at a compound annual growth rate (CAGR) of 40% since the company had gone public, and net earnings had risen at a CAGR of 50%. The company was now serving 20 million unique customers in well over 5,000 stores around the globe and was opening on average three new stores a day. (See **Exhibits 1–3** for company financials and store growth over time.)

What made Starbucks' success even more impressive was that the company had spent almost nothing on advertising to achieve it. North American marketing primarily consisted of point-of-sale materials and local-store marketing and was far less than the industry average. (Most fast-food chains had marketing budgets in the 3%–6% range.)

For his part, Schultz remained as chairman and chief global strategist in control of the company, handing over day-to-day operations in 2002 to CEO Orin Smith, a Harvard MBA (1967) who had joined the company in 1990.

THE STARBUCKS VALUE PROPOSITION

Starbucks' brand strategy was best captured by its "live coffee" mantra, a phrase that reflected the importance the company attached to keeping the national coffee culture alive. From a retail perspective, this meant creating an "experience" around the consumption of coffee, an experience that people could weave into the fabric of their everyday lives.

There were three components to this experiential branding strategy. The first component was the coffee itself. Starbucks prided itself on offering what it believed to be the highest-quality coffee in the world, sourced from the Africa, Central and South America, and Asia-Pacific regions. To enforce its exacting coffee standards, Starbucks controlled as much of the supply chain as possible—it worked directly with growers in various countries of origin to purchase green coffee beans, it oversaw the custom-roasting process for the company's various blends and single-origin coffees, and it controlled distribution to retail stores around the world.

EXHIBIT 1 Starbucks' Financials, FY 1998 to FY 2002 ($ in millions)

	FY 1998	FY 1999	FY 2000	FY 2001	FY 2002
Revenue					
Co-Owned North American	1,076.8	1,375.0	1,734.9	2,086.4	2,583.8
Co-Owned Int'l (UK, Thailand, Australia)	25.8	48.4	88.7	143.2	209.1
Total Company-Operated Retail	1,102.6	1,423.4	1,823.6	2,229.6	2,792.9
Specialty Operations	206.1	263.4	354.0	419.4	496.0
Net Revenues	**1,308.7**	**1,686.8**	**2,177.6**	**2,649.0**	**3,288.9**
Cost of Goods Sold	578.5	747.6	961.9	1,112.8	1,350.0
Gross Profit	**730.2**	**939.2**	**1,215.7**	**1,536.2**	**1,938.9**
Joint-Venture Income[a]	1.0	3.2	20.3	28.6	35.8
Expenses:					
Store Operating Expense	418.5	543.6	704.9	875.5	1,121.1
Other Operating Expense	44.5	54.6	78.4	93.3	127.2
Depreciation & Amortization Expense	72.5	97.8	130.2	163.5	205.6
General & Admin Expense	77.6	89.7	110.2	151.4	202.1
Operating Expenses	**613.1**	**785.7**	**1,023.8**	**1,283.7**	**1,656.0**
Operating Profit	**109.2**	**156.7**	**212.3**	**281.1**	**310.0**
Net Income	**68.4**	**101.7**	**94.5**	**181.2**	**215.1**
% Change in Monthly Comparable Store Sales[b]					
North America	5%	6%	9%	5%	7%
Consolidated	5%	6%	9%	5%	6%

Source: Adapted from company reports and Lehman Brothers, November 5, 2002.

[a]Includes income from various joint ventures, including Starbucks' partnership with the Pepsi-Cola Company to develop and distribute Frappuccino and with Dreyer's Grand Ice Cream to develop and distribute premium ice creams.

[b]Includes only company-operated stores open 13 months or longer.

EXHIBIT 2   Starbucks' Store Growth

	FY 1998	FY 1999	FY 2000	FY 2001	FY 2002
Total North America	**1,755**	**2,217**	**2,976**	**3,780**	**4,574**
Company-Operated	1,622	2,038	2,446	2,971	3,496
Licensed Stores[a]	133	179	530	809	1,078
Total International	**131**	**281**	**525**	**929**	**1,312**
Company-Operated	66	97	173	295	384
Licensed Stores	65	184	352	634	928
Total Stores	**1,886**	**2,498**	**3,501**	**4,709**	**5,886**

Source: Company reports.

[a]Includes kiosks located in grocery stores, bookstores, hotels, airports, and so on.

The second brand component was service, or what the company sometimes referred to as "customer intimacy." "Our goal is to create an uplifting experience every time you walk through our door," explained Jim Alling, Starbucks' senior vice president of North American retail. "Our most loyal customers visit us as often as 18 times a month, so it could be something as simple as recognizing you and knowing your drink or customizing your drink just the way you like it."

The third brand component was atmosphere. "People come for the coffee," explained Day, "but the ambience is what makes them want to stay." For that reason, most Starbucks had seating areas to encourage lounging and layouts that were designed to provide an upscale yet inviting environment for those who wanted to linger. "What we have built has universal appeal," remarked Schultz. "It's based on the human spirit, it's based on a sense of community, the need for people to come together."[3]

Channels of Distribution

Almost all of Starbucks' locations in North America were company-operated stores located in high-traffic, high-visibility settings such as retail centers, office buildings, and university campuses.[4] In addition to selling whole-bean coffees, these stores sold rich-brewed coffees, Italian-style espresso drinks, cold-blended beverages, and premium teas. Product mixes tended to vary depending on a store's size and location, but most stores offered a variety of pastries, sodas, and juices, along with coffee-related accessories and equipment, music CDs, games, and seasonal novelty items. (About 500 stores even carried a selection of sandwiches and salads.)

Beverages accounted for the largest percentage of sales in these stores (77%); this represented a change from 10 years earlier, when about half of store revenues had come from sales of whole-bean coffees. (See **Exhibit 4** for retail sales mix by product type; see **Exhibit 5** for a typical menu board and price list.)

Starbucks also sold coffee products through non-company-operated retail channels; these so-called "Specialty Operations" accounted for 15% of net revenues. About 27% of these revenues came from North American food-service accounts, that is, sales of whole-bean and ground coffees to hotels, airlines, restaurants, and the like. Another 18% came from domestic retail store licenses that, in North America, were only granted when there was no other way to achieve access to desirable retail space (e.g., in airports).

The remaining 55% of specialty revenues came from a variety of sources, including international licensed stores, grocery stores and warehouse clubs (Kraft Foods handled marketing and distribution for Starbucks in this channel), and online and mail-order sales. Starbucks also had a joint venture with Pepsi-Cola to distribute bottled Frappuccino beverages in North America, as well as a partnership with Dreyer's Grand Ice Cream to develop and distribute a line of premium ice creams.

EXHIBIT 3   Additional Data, North American Company-Operated Stores (FY2002)

	AVERAGE
Average hourly rate with shift supervisors and hourly partners	$ 9.00
Total labor hours per week, average store	360
Average weekly store volume	$15,400
Average ticket	$3.85
Average daily customer count, per store	570

Source: Company reports.

EXHIBIT 4   Product Mix, North American Company-Operated Stores (FY2002)

	PERCENT OF SALES
Retail Product Mix	
Coffee Beverages	77%
Food Items	13%
Whole-Bean Coffees	6%
Equipment & Accessories	4%

Source: Company reports.

Espresso Traditions Classic Favorites	Tall	Grande	Venti
Toffee Nut Latte	2.95	3.50	3.80
Vanilla Latte	2.85	3.40	3.70
Caffe Latte	2.55	3.10	3.40
Cappuccino	2.55	3.10	3.40
Caramel Macchiato	2.80	3.40	3.65
White Chocolate Mocha	3.20	3.75	4.00
Caffe Mocha	2.75	3.30	3.55
Caffe Americano	1.75	2.05	2.40

Espresso	Solo		Doppio
Espresso	1.45		1.75

Extras			
Additional Espresso Shot			.55
Add flavored syrup			.30
Organic milk & soy available upon request			

Frappuccino Ice Blended Beverages	Tall	Grande	Venti
Coffee	2.65	3.15	3.65
Mocha	2.90	3.40	3.90
Caramel Frappuccino	3.15	3.65	4.15
Mocha Coconut (limited offering)	3.15	3.65	4.15

Crème Frappuccino Ice Blended Crème	Tall	Grande	Venti
Toffee Nut Crème	3.15	3.65	4.15
Vanilla Crème	2.65	3.15	3.65
Coconut Crème	3.15	3.65	4.15

Tazo Tea Frappuccino Ice Blended Teas	Tall	Grande	Venti
Tazo Citrus	2.90	3.40	3.90
Tazoberry	2.90	3.40	3.90
Tazo Chai Crème	3.15	3.65	4.15

Brewed Coffee	Tall	Grande	Venti
Coffee of the Day	1.40	1.60	1.70
Decaf of the Day	1.40	1.60	1.70

Cold Beverages	Tall	Grande	Venti
Iced Caffe Latte	2.55	3.10	3.50
Iced Caramel Macchiato	2.80	3.40	3.80
Iced Caffe Americano	1.75	2.05	3.40

Coffee Alternatives	Tall	Grande	Venti
Toffee Nut Crème	2.45	2.70	2.95
Vanilla Crème	2.20	2.45	2.70
Caramel Apple Cider	2.45	2.70	2.95
Hot Chocolate	2.20	2.45	2.70
Tazo Hot Tea	1.15	1.65	1.65
Tazo Chai	2.70	3.10	3.35

Whole Beans: Bold Our most intriguing and exotic coffees	1/2 lb	1 lb
Gold Coast Blend	5.70	10.95
French Roast	5.20	9.95
Sumatra	5.30	10.15
Decaf Sumatra	5.60	10.65
Ethiopia Sidame	5.20	9.95
Arabian Mocha Sanani	8.30	15.95
Kenya	5.30	10.15
Italian Roast	5.20	9.95
Sulawesi	6.10	11.65

Whole Beans: Smooth Richer, more flavorful coffees	1/2 lb	1 lb
Espresso Roast	5.20	9.95
Decaf Espresso Roast	5.60	10.65
Yukon Blend	5.20	9.95
Café Verona	5.20	9.95
Guatemala Antigua	5.30	10.15
Arabian Mocha Java	6.30	11.95
Decaf Mocha Java/SWP	6.50	12.45

Whole Beans: Mild The perfect introduction to Starbucks coffees	1/2 lb	1 lb
Breakfast Blend	5.20	9.95
Lightnote Blend	5.20	9.95
Decaf Lightnote Blend	5.60	10.65
Colombia Narino	5.50	10.45
House Blend	5.20	9.95
Decaf House Blend	5.60	10.65
Fair Trade Coffee	5.95	11.45

Source: Starbucks location: Harvard Square, Cambridge, Massachusetts, February 2003.

Day explained the company's broad distribution strategy:

Our philosophy is pretty straightforward—we want to reach customers where they work, travel, shop, and dine. In order to do this, we sometimes have to establish relationships with third parties that share our values and commitment to quality. This is a particularly effective way to reach newcomers with our brand. It's a lot less intimidating to buy Starbucks at a grocery store than it is to walk into one of our coffeehouses for the first time. In fact, about 40% of our new coffeehouse customers have already tried the Starbucks brand before they walk through our doors. Even something like ice cream has become an important trial vehicle for us.

Starbucks Partners

All Starbucks employees were called "partners." The company employed 60,000 partners worldwide, about 50,000 in North America. Most were hourly-wage employees (called *baristas*) who worked in Starbucks retail stores. Alling remarked, "From day one, Howard has made clear his belief that partner satisfaction leads to customer satisfaction. This belief is part of Howard's DNA, and because it's been pounded into each and every one of us, it's become part of our DNA too."

The company had a generous policy of giving health insurance and stock options to even the most entry-level partners, most of whom were between the ages of 17 and 23. Partly as a result of this, Starbucks' partner satisfaction rate consistently hovered in the 80% to 90% range, well above the industry norm,[5] and the company had recently been ranked 47th in the *Fortune* magazine list of best places to work, quite an accomplishment for a company with so many hourly-wage workers.

In addition, Starbucks had one of the lowest employee turnover rates in the industry—just 70%, compared with fast-food industry averages as high as 300%. The rate was even lower for managers, and as Alling noted, the company was always looking for ways to bring turnover down further: "Whenever we have a problem store, we almost always find either an inexperienced store manager or inexperienced baristas. Manager stability is key—it not only decreases partner turnover, but it also enables the store to do a much better job of recognizing regular customers and providing personalized service. So our goal is to make the position a lifetime job."

To this end, the company encouraged promotion from within its own ranks. About 70% of the company's store managers were ex-baristas, and about 60% of its district managers were ex-store managers. In fact, upon being hired, all senior executives had to train and succeed as baristas before being allowed to assume their positions in corporate headquarters.

DELIVERING ON SERVICE

When a partner was hired to work in one of Starbucks' North American retail stores, he or she had to undergo two types of training. The first type focused on "hard skills" such as learning how to use the cash register and learning how to mix drinks. Most Starbucks beverages were handcrafted, and to ensure product quality, there was a prespecified process associated with each drink. Making an espresso beverage, for example, required seven specific steps.

The other type of training focused on "soft skills." Alling explained:

> In our training manual, we explicitly teach partners to connect with customers—to enthusiastically welcome them to the store, to establish eye contact, to smile, and to try to remember their names and orders if they're regulars. We also encourage partners to create conversations with customers using questions that require more than a yes or no answer. So for example, "I noticed you were looking at the menu board—what types of beverages do you typically enjoy?" is a good question for a partner to ask.

Starbucks' "Just Say Yes" policy empowered partners to provide the best service possible, even if it required going beyond company rules. "This means that if a customer spills a drink and asks for a refill, we'll give it to him," said Day. "Or if a customer doesn't have cash and wants to pay with a check (which we aren't supposed to accept), then we'll give her a sample drink for free. The last thing we want to do is win the argument and lose the customer."

Most barista turnover occurred within the first 90 days of employment; if a barista lasted beyond that, there was a high probability that he or she would stay for three years or more. "Our training ends up being a self-selection process," Alling said. Indeed, the ability to balance hard and soft skills required a particular type of person, and Alling believed the challenges had only grown over time:

> Back in the days when we sold mostly beans, every customer who walked in the door was a coffee connoisseur, and it was easy for baristas to engage in chitchat while ringing up a bag. Those days are long gone. Today, almost every customer orders a handcrafted beverage. If the line is stretching out the door and everyone's clamoring for their coffee fix, it's not that easy to strike up a conversation with a customer.

The complexity of the barista's job had also increased over time; making a *venti tazoberry and crème*, for instance, required 10 different steps. "It used to be that a barista could make every variation of drink we offered in half a day," Day observed. "Nowadays, given our product proliferation, it would take 16 days of eight-hour shifts. There are literally hundreds of combinations of drinks in our portfolio."

This job complexity was compounded by the fact that almost half of Starbucks' customers customized their drinks. According to Day, this created a tension between product quality and customer focus for Starbucks:

> On the one hand, we train baristas to make beverages to our preestablished quality standards—this means enforcing a consistent process that baristas can master. On the other hand, if a customer comes in and wants it their way—extra vanilla, for instance—what should we do? Our heaviest users are always the most demanding. Of course, every time we customize, we slow down the service for everyone else. We also put a lot of strain on our baristas, who are already dealing with an extraordinary number of sophisticated drinks.

One obvious solution to the problem was to hire more baristas to share the workload; however, the company had been extremely reluctant to do this in recent years, particularly given the economic downturn. Labor was already the company's largest expense item in North America (see **Exhibit 3**), and Starbucks stores tended to be located in urban areas with high wage rates. Instead, the company had focused on increasing barista efficiency by removing all non-value-added tasks, simplifying the beverage production process, and tinkering with the facility design to eliminate bottlenecks.

In addition, the company had recently begun installing automated espresso machines in its North American cafés. The *verismo* machines, which decreased the number of steps required to make an espresso beverage, reduced waste, improved consistency, and had generated an overwhelmingly positive customer and barista response.

Measuring Service Performance

Starbucks tracked service performance using a variety of metrics, including monthly status reports and self-reported checklists. The company's most prominent measurement tool was a mystery shopper program called the "Customer Snapshot." Under this program, every store was visited by an anonymous mystery shopper three times a quarter. Upon completing the visit, the shopper would rate the store on four "Basic Service" criteria:

- **Service**—Did the register partner verbally greet the customer? Did the barista and register partner make eye contact with the customer? Say thank you?
- **Cleanliness**—Was the store clean? The counters? The tables? The restrooms?
- **Product quality**—Was the order filled accurately? Was the temperature of the drink within range? Was the beverage properly presented?
- **Speed of service**—How long did the customer have to wait? The company's goal was to serve a customer within three minutes, from back-of-the-line to drink-in-hand. This benchmark was based on market research which indicated that the three-minute standard was a key component in how current Starbucks customers defined "excellent service."

In addition to Basic Service, stores were also rated on "Legendary Service," which was defined as "behavior that created a memorable experience for a customer, that inspired a customer to return often and tell a friend." Legendary Service scores were based on secret shopper observations of service attributes such as partners initiating conversations with customers, partners recognizing customers by name or drink order, and partners being responsive to service problems.

During 2002, the company's Customer Snapshot scores had increased across all stores (see **Exhibit 7**), leading Day to comment, "The Snapshot is not a perfect measurement tool, but we believe it does a good job of measuring trends over the course of a quarter. In order for a store to do well on the Snapshot, it needs to have sustainable processes in place that create a well-established pattern of doing things right so that it gets 'caught' doing things right."

COMPETITION

In the United States, Starbucks competed against a variety of small-scale specialty coffee chains, most of which were regionally concentrated. Each tried to differentiate itself from Starbucks in a different way. For example, Minneapolis-based Caribou Coffee, which operated more than 200 stores in nine states, differentiated itself on store environment. Rather than offer an upscale, pseudo-European atmosphere, its strategy was to simulate the look and feel of an Alaskan lodge, with knotty-pine cabinetry, fireplaces, and soft seating. Another example was California-based Peet's Coffee & Tea, which operated about 70 stores in five states. More than 60% of Peet's revenues came from the sale of whole beans. Peet's strategy was to build a super-premium brand by offering the freshest coffee on the market. One of the ways it delivered on this promise was by "roasting to order," that is, by hand roasting small batches of coffee at its California plant and making sure that all of its coffee shipped within 24 hours of roasting.

Starbucks also competed against thousands of independent specialty coffee shops. Some of these independent coffee shops offered a wide range of food and beverages, including beer, wine, and liquor; others offered satellite televisions or Internet-connected computers. Still others differentiated themselves by delivering highly personalized service to an eclectic clientele.

Finally, Starbucks competed against donut and bagel chains such as Dunkin Donuts, which operated over 3,700 stores in 38 states. Dunkin Donuts attributed half of its sales to coffee and in recent years had begun offering flavored coffee and noncoffee alternatives, such as Dunkaccino (a coffee and chocolate combination available with various toppings) and Vanilla Chai (a combination of tea, vanilla, honey, and spices).

CAFFEINATING THE WORLD

The company's overall objective was to establish Starbucks as the "most recognized and respected brand in the world."[6] This ambitious goal required an aggressive growth strategy, and in 2002, the two biggest drivers of company growth were retail expansion and product innovation.

Retail Expansion

Starbucks already owned close to one-third of America's coffee bars, more than its next five biggest competitors combined. (By comparison, the U.S.'s second-largest player, Diedrich Coffee, operated fewer than 400 stores.) However, the company had plans to open 525 company-operated and 225 licensed North American stores in 2003, and Schultz believed that there was no reason North

America could not eventually expand to at least 10,000 stores. As he put it, "These are still the early days of the company's growth."[7]

The company's optimistic growth plans were based on a number of considerations:

- First, coffee consumption was on the rise in the United States, following years of decline. More than 109 million people (about half of the U.S. population) now drank coffee every day, and an additional 52 million drank it on occasion. The market's biggest growth appeared to be among drinkers of specialty coffee,[8] and it was estimated that about one-third of all U.S. coffee consumption took place outside of the home, in places such as offices, restaurants, and coffee shops. (See **Exhibit 6**.)
- Second, there were still eight states in the United States without a single company-operated Starbucks; in fact, the company was only in 150 of the roughly 300 metropolitan statistical areas in the nation.
- Third, the company believed it was far from reaching saturation levels in many existing markets. In the Southeast, for example, there was only one store for every 110,000 people (compared with one

store for every 20,000 people in the Pacific Northwest). More generally, only seven states had more than 100 Starbucks locations.

Starbucks' strategy for expanding its retail business was to open stores in new markets while geographically clustering stores in existing markets. Although the latter often resulted in significant cannibalization, the company believed that this was more than offset by the total incremental sales associated with the increased store concentration. As Schultz readily conceded, "We self-cannibalize at least a third of our stores every day."[9]

When it came to selecting new retail sites, the company considered a number of criteria, including the extent to which the demographics of the area matched the profile of the typical Starbucks drinker, the level of coffee consumption in the area, the nature and intensity of competition in the local market, and the availability of attractive real estate. Once a decision was made to move forward with a site, the company was capable of designing, permitting, constructing, and opening a new store within 16 weeks. A new store typically averaged about $610,000 in sales during its first year; same-store sales (comps) were

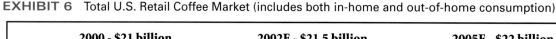

EXHIBIT 6   Total U.S. Retail Coffee Market (includes both in-home and out-of-home consumption)

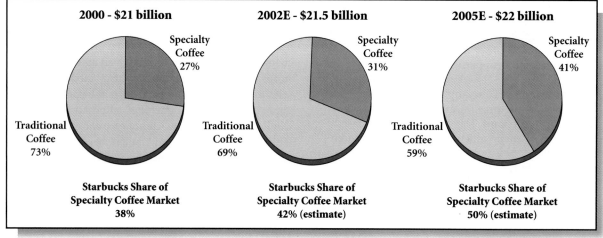

Other estimates[a] for the U.S. retail coffee market in 2002:

- In the home, specialty coffee[b] was estimated to be a $3.2 billion business, of which Starbucks was estimated to have a 4% share.
- In the food-service channel, specialty coffee was estimated to be a $5 billion business, of which Starbucks was estimated to have a 5% share.
- In grocery stores, Starbucks was estimated to have a 7.3% share in the ground-coffee category and a 21.7% share in the whole-beans category.
- It was estimated that over the next several years, the overall retail market would grow less than 1% per annum, but growth in the specialty-coffee category would be strong, with compound annual growth rate (CAGR) of 9% to 10%.
- Starbucks' U.S. business was projected to grow at a CAGR of approximately 20% top-line revenue growth.

Source: Adapted from company reports and Lehman Brothers, November 5, 2002.

[a]The value of the retail coffee market was difficult to estimate given the highly fragmented and loosely monitored nature of the market (i.e., specialty coffeehouses, restaurants, delis, kiosks, street carts, grocery and convenience stores, vending machines, etc.).

[b]Specialty coffee includes espresso, cappuccino, latte, café mocha, iced/ice-blended coffee, gourmet coffee (premium whole bean or ground), and blended coffee.

EXHIBIT 7 Customer Snapshot Scores (North American stores)

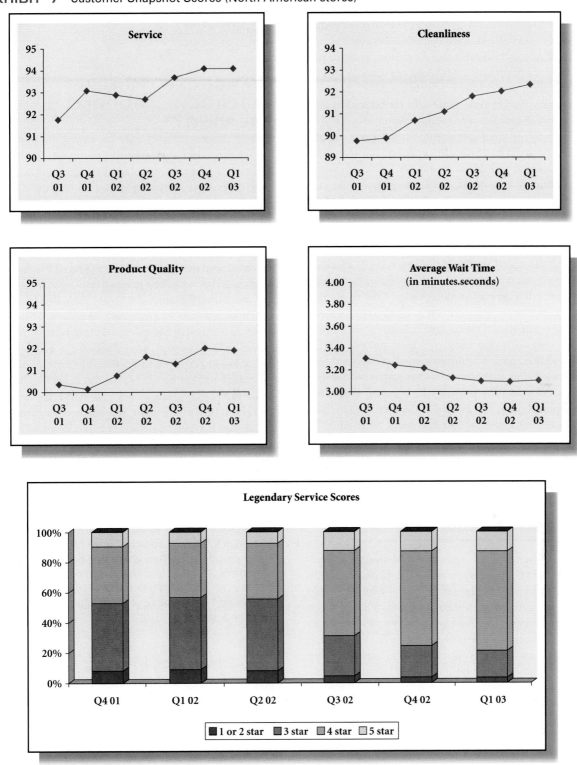

Source: Company information.

strongest in the first three years and then continued to comp positively, consistent with the company average.

Starbucks' international expansion plans were equally ambitious. Starbucks already operated over 300 company-owned stores in the United Kingdom, Australia, and Thailand, in addition to about 900 licensed stores in various countries in Asia, Europe, the Middle East, Africa, and Latin America. (Its largest international market was Japan, with close to 400 stores.) The company's goal was to ultimately have 15,000 international stores.

Product Innovation

The second big driver of company growth was product innovation. Internally, this was considered one of the most significant factors in comparable store sales growth, particularly since Starbucks' prices had remained relatively stable in recent years. New products were launched on a regular basis; for example, Starbucks introduced at least one new hot beverage every holiday season.

The new product development process generally operated on a 12- to 18-month cycle, during which the internal research and development (R&D) team tinkered with product formulations, ran focus groups, and conducted in-store experiments and market tests. Aside from consumer acceptance, whether a product made it to market depended on a number of factors, including the extent to which the drink fit into the "ergonomic flow" of operations and the speed with which the beverage could be handcrafted. Most importantly, the success of a new beverage depended on partner acceptance. "We've learned that no matter how great a drink it is, if our partners aren't excited about it, it won't sell," said Alling.

In recent years, the company's most successful innovation had been the 1995 introduction of a coffee and non-coffee-based line of Frappuccino beverages, which had driven same-store sales primarily by boosting traffic during nonpeak hours. The bottled version of the beverage (distributed by PepsiCo) had become a $400 million[10] franchise; it had managed to capture 90% of the ready-to-drink coffee category, in large part due to its appeal to non-coffee-drinking 20-somethings.

SERVICE INNOVATION

In terms of nonproduct innovation, Starbucks' stored-value card (SVC) had been launched in November 2001. This prepaid, swipeable smart card—which Schultz referred to as "the most significant product introduction since Frappuccino"[11]—could be used to pay for transactions in any company-operated store in North America. Early indications of the SVC's appeal were very positive: After less than one year on the market, about 6 million cards had been issued, and initial activations and reloads had already reached $160 million in sales. In surveys, the company had learned that cardholders tended to visit Starbucks twice as often as cash customers and tended to experience reduced transaction times.

Day remarked, "We've found that a lot of the cards are being given away as gifts, and many of those gift recipients are being introduced to our brand for the first time. Not to mention the fact that the cards allow us to collect all kinds of customer-transaction data, data that we haven't even begun to do anything with yet."

The company's latest service innovation was its T-Mobile HotSpot wireless Internet service, which it planned to introduce in August 2002. The service would offer high-speed access to the Internet in 2,000 Starbucks stores in the United States and Europe, starting at $49.99 a month.

STARBUCKS' MARKET RESEARCH: TROUBLE BREWING?

Interestingly, although Starbucks was considered one of the world's most effective marketing organizations, it lacked a strategic marketing group. In fact, the company had no chief marketing officer, and its marketing department functioned as three separate groups—a market research group that gathered and analyzed market data requested by the various business units, a category group that developed new products and managed the menu and margins, and a marketing group that developed the quarterly promotional plans.

This organizational structure forced all of Starbucks' senior executives to assume marketing-related responsibilities. As Day pointed out, "Marketing is everywhere at Starbucks—it just doesn't necessarily show up in a line item called 'marketing.' Everyone has to get involved in a collaborative marketing effort." However, the organizational structure also meant that market- and customer-related trends could sometimes be overlooked. "We tend to be great at measuring things, at collecting market data," Day noted, "but we are not very disciplined when it comes to using this data to drive decision making." She continued:

> This is exactly what started to happen a few years ago. We had evidence coming in from market research that contradicted some of the fundamental assumptions we had about our brand and our customers. The problem was that this evidence was all over the place—no one was really looking at the "big picture." As a result, it took awhile before we started to take notice.

Starbucks' Brand Meaning

Once the team did take notice, it discovered several things. First, despite Starbucks' overwhelming presence and convenience, there was very little image or product differentiation between Starbucks and the smaller coffee chains (other than Starbucks' ubiquity) in the minds of specialty coffeehouse customers. There *was* significant differentiation, however, between Starbucks and the independent specialty coffeehouses (see **Table A** below).

More generally, the market research team discovered that Starbucks' brand image had some rough edges. The number of respondents who strongly agreed with the statement "Starbucks cares primarily about making money" was up from 53% in 2000 to 61% in 2001, while the number of respondents who strongly

Table A Qualitative Brand Meaning: Independents vs. Starbucks

Independents:
- Social and inclusive
- Diverse and intellectual
- Artsy and funky
- Liberal and free-spirited
- Lingering encouraged
- Particularly appealing to younger coffeehouse customers
- Somewhat intimidating to older, more mainstream coffeehouse customers

Starbucks:
- Everywhere—the trend
- Good coffee on the run
- Place to meet and move on
- Convenience oriented; on the way to work
- Accessible and consistent

Source: Starbucks, based on qualitative interviews with specialty-coffeehouse customers.

Table B The Top Five Attributes Consumers Associate with the Starbucks Brand

- Known for specialty/gourmet coffee (54% strongly agree)
- Widely available (43% strongly agree)
- Corporate (42% strongly agree)
- Trendy (41% strongly agree)
- Always feel welcome at Starbucks (39% strongly agree)

Source: Starbucks, based on 2002 survey.

agreed with the statement "Starbucks cares primarily about building more stores" was up from 48% to 55%. Day noted, "It's become apparent that we need to ask ourselves, 'Are we focusing on the right things? Are we clearly communicating our value and values to our customers, instead of just our growth plans?'" (see **Table B** below).

The Changing Customer

The market research team also discovered that Starbucks' customer base was evolving. Starbucks' newer customers tended to be younger, less well-educated, and in a lower income bracket than Starbucks' more established customers. In addition, they visited the stores less frequently and had very different perceptions of the Starbucks brand compared to more established customers (see **Exhibit 8**).

Furthermore, the team learned that Starbucks' historical customer profile—the affluent, well-educated, white-collar female between the ages of 24 and 44—had

EXHIBIT 8 Starbucks' Customer Retention Information

% OF STARBUCKS' CUSTOMERS WHO FIRST STARTED VISITING STARBUCKS . . .	
In the past year	27%
1–2 years ago	20%
2–5 years ago	30%
5 or more years ago	23%

Source: Starbucks, 2002. Based on a sample of Starbucks' 2002 customer base.

	NEW CUSTOMERS (FIRST VISITED IN PAST YEAR)	ESTABLISHED CUSTOMERS (FIRST VISITED 5 + YEARS AGO)
Percent female	45%	49%
Average Age	36	40
Percent with College Degree +	37%	63%
Average income	$65,000	$81,000
Average # cups of coffee/week (includes at home and away from home)	15	19
Attitudes toward Starbucks:		
High-quality brand	34%	51%
Brand I trust	30%	50%
For someone like me	15%	40%
Worth paying more for	8%	32%
Known for specialty coffee	44%	60%
Known as the coffee expert	31%	45%
Best-tasting coffee	20%	31%
Highest-quality coffee	26%	41%
Overall opinion of Starbucks	**25%**	**44%**

Source: Starbucks, 2002. "Attitudes toward Starbucks" measured according to the percent of customers who agreed with the above statements.

Figure A Customer Visit Frequency

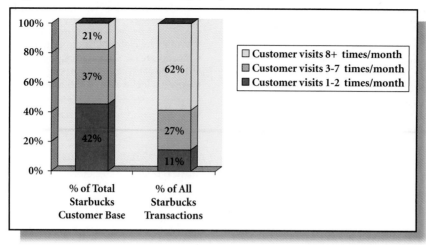

Source: Starbucks, 2002.

expanded. For example, about half of the stores in southern California had large numbers of Hispanic customers. In Florida, the company had stores that catered primarily to Cuban-Americans.

Customer Behavior

With respect to customer behavior, the market research team discovered that, regardless of the market—urban versus rural, new versus established—customers tended to use the stores the same way. The team also learned that, although the company's most frequent customers averaged 18 visits a month, the typical customer visited just five times a month (see **Figure A**).

Measuring and Driving Customer Satisfaction

Finally, the team discovered that, despite its high Customer Snapshot scores, Starbucks was not meeting expectations in terms of customer satisfaction. The satisfaction scores were considered critical because the team also had evidence of a direct link between satisfaction level and customer loyalty (see **Exhibit 9** for customer satisfaction data).

While customer satisfaction was driven by a number of different factors (see **Exhibit 10**), Day believed that the customer satisfaction gap could primarily be attributed to a *service gap* between Starbucks scores on key attributes and customer expectations. When Starbucks had polled its customers to determine what it could do to make them feel more like valued customers, "improvements to service"—in particular, speed-of-service—had been mentioned most frequently (see **Exhibit 11** for more information).

REDISCOVERING THE STARBUCKS CUSTOMER

Responding to the market research findings posed a difficult management challenge. The most controversial proposal was the one on the table before Day—it involved relaxing the labor-hour controls in the stores to add an additional 20 hours of labor, per week, per store, at a cost of an extra $40 million per year. Not surprisingly, the plan was being met with significant internal resistance. "Our CFO is understandably concerned about the potential impact on our bottom line," said Day. "Each $6 million in profit contribution translates into a penny a share. But my argument is that if we

EXHIBIT 9 Starbucks' Customer Behavior, by Satisfaction Level

	UNSATISFIED CUSTOMER	SATISFIED CUSTOMER	HIGHLY SATISFIED CUSTOMER
Number of Starbucks Visits/Month	3.9	4.3	7.2
Average Ticket Size/Visit	$3.88	$4.06	$4.42
Average Customer Life (Years)	1.1	4.4	8.3

Source: Self-reported customer activity from Starbucks survey, 2002.

EXHIBIT 10   Importance Rankings of Key Attributes in Creating Customer Satisfaction

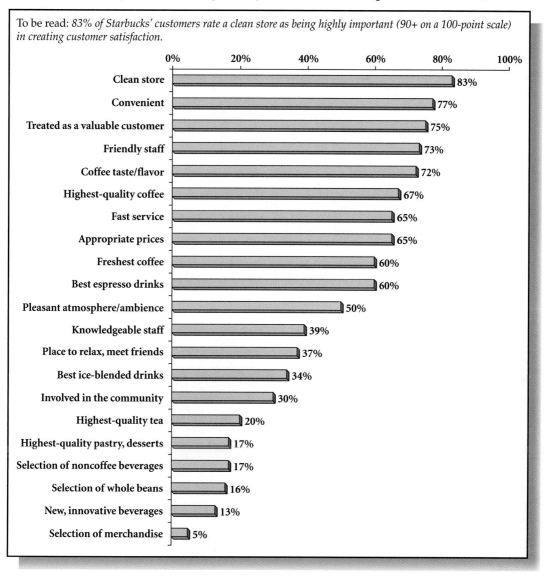

To be read: *83% of Starbucks' customers rate a clean store as being highly important (90+ on a 100-point scale) in creating customer satisfaction.*

Attribute	Percentage
Clean store	83%
Convenient	77%
Treated as a valuable customer	75%
Friendly staff	73%
Coffee taste/flavor	72%
Highest-quality coffee	67%
Fast service	65%
Appropriate prices	65%
Freshest coffee	60%
Best espresso drinks	60%
Pleasant atmosphere/ambience	50%
Knowledgeable staff	39%
Place to relax, meet friends	37%
Best ice-blended drinks	34%
Involved in the community	30%
Highest-quality tea	20%
Highest-quality pastry, desserts	17%
Selection of noncoffee beverages	17%
Selection of whole beans	16%
New, innovative beverages	13%
Selection of merchandise	5%

Source: Self-reported customer activity from Starbucks survey, 2002.

move away from seeing labor as an expense to seeing it as a customer-oriented investment, we'll see a positive return." She continued:

> We need to bring service time down to the three-minute level in all of our stores, regardless of the time of day. If we do this, we'll not only increase customer satisfaction and build stronger long-term relationships with our customers, we'll also improve our customer throughput. The goal is to move each store closer to the $20,000 level in terms of weekly sales, and I think that this plan will help us get there.

In two days, Day was scheduled to make a final recommendation to Howard Schultz and Orin Smith about whether the company should roll out the $40 million plan in October 2002. In preparation for this meeting, Day had asked Alling to help her think through the implications of the plan one final time. She mused:

> We've been operating with the assumption that we do customer service well. But the reality is, we've started to lose sight of the consumer. It's amazing that this could happen to a company like us—after all, we've become one of the most prominent consumer brands in the world. For all of our focus on building the brand and introducing new products, we've simply stopped talking about the customer. We've lost the connection between satisfying our customers and growing the business.

Alling's response was simple: "We know that both Howard and Orin are totally committed to satisfying our retail customers. Our challenge is to tie customer satisfaction to the bottom line. What evidence do we have?"

EXHIBIT 11   Factors Driving "Valued Customer" Perceptions

How could Starbucks make you feel more like a valued customer?	% Responses
Improvements to Service (total)	**34%**
Friendlier, more attentive staff	19%
Faster, more efficient service	10%
Personal treatment (remember my name, remember my order)	4%
More knowledgeable staff	4%
Better service	2%
Offer Better Prices/Incentive Programs (total)	**31%**
Free cup after X number of visits	19%
Reduce prices	11%
Offer promotions, specials	3%
Other (total)	**21%**
Better quality/Variety of products	9%
Improve atmosphere	8%
Community outreach/Charity	2%
More stores/More convenient locations	2%
Don't Know/Already Satisfied	**28%**

Source: Starbucks, 2002. Based on a survey of Starbucks' 2002 customer base, including highly satisfied, satisfied, and unsatisfied customers.

ENDNOTES

1. Jake Batsell, "A Grande Decade for Starbucks," *The Seattle Times*, June 26, 2002.
2. Batsell.
3. Batsell.
4. Starbucks had recently begun experimenting with drive-throughs. Less than 10% of its stores had drive-throughs, but in these stores, the drive-throughs accounted for 50% of all business.
5. Industrywide, employee satisfaction rates tended to be in the 50% to 60% range. Source: Starbucks, 2000.
6. Starbucks 2002 Annual Report.
7. Dina ElBoghdady, "Pouring It On: The Starbucks Strategy? Locations, Locations, Locations," *The Washington Post*, August 25, 2002.
8. National Coffee Association.
9. ElBoghdady.
10. Refers to sales at retail. Actual revenue contribution was much lower due to the joint-venture structure.
11. Stanley Holmes, "Starbucks' Card Smarts," *BusinessWeek*, March 18, 2002.

STUDY QUESTIONS

1. *What factors accounted for Starbucks' success in the early 1990s and what was so compelling about its value proposition? What brand image did Starbucks develop during this period?*
2. *Why have Starbucks' customer satisfaction scores declined? Has the company's service declined or is it simply measuring satisfaction the wrong way?*
3. *How has Starbucks changed since its early days?*
4. *Describe the ideal Starbucks customer from a profitability standpoint. What would it take to ensure that this customer is highly satisfied? How valuable to Starbucks is a highly satisfied customer?*
5. *Should Starbucks make the $40 million investment in labor in the stores? What's the goal of this investment? Is it possible for a mega-brand to deliver customer intimacy?*

Case 5   Giordano: Positioning for International Expansion

Jochen Wirtz

> To make people "feel good" and "look great."—Giordano's Corporate Mission

As it looks to the future, a successful Asian retailer of casual apparel must decide whether to maintain its existing positioning strategy. Management wonders what factors will be critical to success and whether the firm's competitive strengths in merchandise selection and service are readily transferable to new international markets.

In early 2006, Giordano, a Hong Kong-based retailer of casual clothes targeted at men, women and children through its four company brands, Giordano, Giordano

Ladies, Giordano Junior and Blue Star Exchange, was operating over 1,600 retail stores and counters in some 31 markets in the Asia-Pacific and Middle-East region. Its main markets were Mainland China, Hong Kong, Japan, Korea, Singapore, and Taiwan. Other countries in which it had a presence were Australia, Indonesia, Malaysia and the Middle East. In its main markets there were 1478 Giordano and Giordano Junior stores, 27 Giordano Ladies stores, and 132 Blue Star Exchange stores. Sales had grown to HK$4,003 million (US$517 million) by 2004 (see **Exhibit 1**). Giordano stores were located in retail shopping districts

EXHIBIT 1   Giordano Financial Highlights

	2004	2003	2002	2001	2000	1999	1998	1997	1996	1995	1994
Turnover (million HK$)	4,003	3,389	3,588	3,479	3,431	3,092	2,609	3,014	3,522	3,482	2,864
Turnover increase (percent)	18.1	(5.5)	3.1	1.4	11.0	18.5	(13.4)	(14.4)	1.1	21.5	22.7
Profit after tax and minority interests (million HK$)	393	266	328	377	416	360	76	68	261	250	195
Profit after tax and minority interests increase over previous year (percent)	47.7	(18.9)	(13.0)	(9.4)	15.3	373.7	11.8	(73.9)	4.4	28.2	41.9
Shareholders' fund (million HK$)	1,954	1,799	1,794	1,695	1,558	1,449	1,135	1,069	1,220	976	593
Working capital (million HK$)	1,004	961	861	798	1,014	960	725	655	752	560	410
Total debt to equity ratio	0.35	0.4	0.3	0.4	0.3	0.3	0.3	0.3	0.4	0.7	0.9
Inventory turnover on sales (days)	30	24	26	30	32	28	44	48	58	55	53
Return on total assets (percent)	14.9	10.7	13.7	16.8	20.7	21.5	5.3	4.5	16.8	19.5	20.9
Return on average equity (percent)	20.9	14.8	18.8	23.2	27.7	27.9	6.9	5.9	23.8	31.8	35.8
Return on sales (percent)	9.8	7.8	9.1	10.8	12.1	11.6	2.9	2.3	7.4	7.2	6.8
Earning per share (cents)	27.20	18.50	22.80	26.30	29.30	25.65	5.40	4.80	18.45	19.40	15.45
Cash dividend per share (cents)	23.00	21.00	19.00	14.00	15.25	17.25	2.25	2.50	8.00	6.75	5.50

Source: Annual Report 2004, Giordano International.

© 2007 Jochen Wirtz.

This case is based on published information and quotes from a wide array of sources. The generous help and feedback provided by Alison Law, former Assistant to Chairman, Giordano International Ltd, to earlier versions of this case are gratefully acknowledged. The author thanks Zhaohui Chen for his excellent research assistance.

511

EXHIBIT 2   Typical Giordano Storefront

with good foot traffic. Views of a typical storefront and store interior are shown in **Exhibit 2**. In most geographic markets serviced by Giordano, the retail clothing business was deemed to be extremely competitive.

The board and top management team were eager to maintain Giordano's success in existing markets and to enter new markets in Asia and beyond. Several issues were under discussion. First, in what ways, if at all, should Giordano change its current positioning in the marketplace? Second, would the factors that had contributed to Giordano's success in the past remain equally critical over the coming years or were new key success factors emerging? Finally, as Giordano sought to enter new markets around the world, were its competitive strengths readily transferable to other markets?

COMPANY BACKGROUND

Giordano was founded in Hong Kong in 1980 by Jimmy Lai. In 1981, it opened its first retail store in Hong Kong and also began to expand its market by distributing Giordano merchandise in Taiwan through a joint venture. In 1985, it opened its first retail outlet in Singapore.

Responding to slow sales, Giordano changed its positioning strategy in 1987. Until 1987, it had sold exclusively men's casual apparel. When Lai and his colleagues realized that an increasing number of female customers were attracted to its stores, he repositioned the chain as a retailer of value-for-money merchandise, selling discounted casual unisex apparel, with the goal of maximizing unit sales instead of margins. This shift in strategy was successful, leading to a substantial increase in turnover. In 1994, Peter Lau Kwok Kuen succeeded Lai and became Chairman.

Management Values and Style

A willingness to try new and unconventional ways of doing business and to learn from past errors was part of Lai's management philosophy and soon became an integral part of Giordano's culture. Lai saw the occasional failure as a current limitation that indirectly pointed management to the right decision in the future. To demonstrate his commitment to this philosophy, Lai took the lead by being a role model for his employees, adding, ". . . Like in a meeting, I say, look, I have made this mistake. I'm sorry for that. I hope everybody learns from this. If I can make mistakes, who . . . do you think you are that you can't make mistakes?" He also believed strongly that empowerment would minimize mistakes—that if everyone was allowed to contribute and participate, mistakes could be minimized.

Another factor that contributed to the firm's success was its dedicated, ever-smiling sales staff of over 8000. Giordano considered front-line workers to be its customer-service heroes. Charles Fung, executive director and chief operations officer (Southeast Asia), remarked:

> Even the most sophisticated training program won't guarantee the best customer service. People are the key. They make exceptional service possible. Training is merely a skeleton of a customer service program. It's the people who deliver that give it form and meaning.

Giordano had instituted stringent selection procedures to make sure that the candidates selected matched the desired employee profile. Selection continued into its training workshops, which tested the service orientation and character of a new employee.

Giordano's philosophy of quality service could be observed not only in Hong Kong but also in its overseas outlets. The company had been honored by numerous service awards over the years (see **Exhibit 3**). Fung described its obsession with providing excellent customer service in the following terms:

> The only way to keep abreast with stiff competition in the retail market is to know the customers' needs and serve them well. Customers pay our pay checks; they are our bosses. . . . Giordano considers service to be a very important element [in trying to draw customers]; . . . service is in the blood of every member of our staff.

Giordano believed and invested heavily in employee training and had been recognized for its commitment to training and developing its staff by such awards as the Hong Kong Management Association Certificate of Merit for Excellence in Training and the People Developer Award from Singapore, among others.

> Training is important. However, what is more important is the transfer of learning to the store. When there is a transfer of learning, each dollar invested in training yields a high return. We try to encourage this [transfer of learning] by cultivating a culture and by providing positive reinforcement, rewarding those who practice what they learned.

Giordano offered what Fung claimed was "an attractive package in an industry where employee turnover is high." Giordano motivated its people through a base salary that probably was below market average, but added attractive performance-related bonuses. These initiatives and Giordano's emphasis on training had resulted in a lower staff turnover rate.

Managing its vital human resources (HR) became a challenge to Giordano when it decided to expand into global markets. To replicate its high-service-quality positioning, Giordano needed to consider the HR issues involved in setting up retail outlets in unfamiliar territory. For example, the recruitment, selection and training of local employees could require modifications to its formula for success in its current markets, owing to differences in the culture, education and technology of the new countries. Labor regulations could also affect such HR policies

EXHIBIT 3 Selected Awards Giordano Received over the Years

AWARD	AWARDING ORGANIZATION	CATEGORY	YEAR(S)
American Service Excellence Award	American Express	Fashion/Apparel	1995
Ear Award	Radio Corporation of Singapore	Listeners' Choice & Creative Merits	1996
Excellent Service Award	Singapore Productivity and Standards Board	—	1996, 1997, 1998
People Developer Award	Singapore Productivity and Standards Board	—	1998
HKRMA Customer Service Award	Hong Kong Retail Management Association	—	1999
The Fourth Hong Kong Awards for Services	Hong Kong Trade Development Council	Export Marketing & Customer Service	2000
Grand Award (Giordano International)	Hong Kong Trade Development Council	Export Marketing	2002
Grand Award (Giordano Ladies)	Hong Kong Retail Management Association	—	2002
Business-to-Consumer Service Supplier Award	Middle East Economic Digest (MEED)	—	2002
Dubai Services Excellence Scheme Award	Dubai Department of Economic Development Customer Service	Customer Service	2003
Hong Kong Superbrands(TM) Award	Hong Kong Superbrands Council	—	2004
Top Service Award	Next Magazine	Chain Stores of Fashion & Accessories	2004

as compensation and welfare benefits. Finally, management needed to consider expatriate policies for staff members who had been seconded to help run Giordano outside their home countries, as well as the management practices themselves in those countries.

Focusing Giordano's Organizational Structure on Simplicity and Speed

Giordano maintained a flat organizational structure. The company's decentralized management style empowered line managers, and at the same time encouraged fast and close communication and coordination. For example, top management and staff had desks located next to each other, separated only by shoulder panels. This closeness allowed easy communication, efficient project management and speedy decision making, which were all seen as critical ingredients to success amid fast-changing consumer tastes and fashion trends. This kept Giordano's product development cycle short. The firm made similar demands on its suppliers.

Service

Giordano's commitment to service began with its major Customer Service Campaign in 1989. In that campaign, yellow badges bearing the words "Giordano Means Service" were worn by every Giordano employee, and its service philosophy had three tenets: "We welcome unlimited try-ons; we exchange—no questions asked; and we serve with a smile." As a result, the firm started receiving its numerous service-related awards over the years. It had also been ranked number one for eight consecutive years by the *Far Eastern Economic Review* for being innovative in responding to customers' needs.

Management had launched several creative, customer-focused campaigns and promotions to extend its service orientation. For instance, in Singapore, Giordano asked its customers what they thought would be the fairest price to charge for a pair of jeans and charged each customer the price that they were willing to pay. This one-month campaign was immensely successful, with some 3,000 pairs of jeans sold every day during the promotion. In another service-related campaign, over 10,000 free T-shirts were given to customers for giving feedback and criticizing Giordano's services.

To ensure customer service excellence, performance evaluations were conducted frequently at the store level, as well as for individual employees. Internal competitions were designed to motivate employees and store teams to do their best in serving customers. Every month, Giordano awarded the "Service Star" to individual employees, based on nominations provided by shoppers. In addition, every Giordano store was evaluated every month by mystery shoppers. Based on the combined results of these evaluations, the "Best Service Shop" award was given to the top store. Customer feedback cards were available at all stores, and were collected and posted at the office for further action. Increasingly, customers were providing feedback via the firm's corporate Web site.

Value for Money

Lai explained the rationale for Giordano's value-for-money policy.

> Consumers are learning a lot better about what value is. So we always ask ourselves how can we sell it cheaper, make it more convenient for the consumer to buy and deliver faster today than [we did] yesterday. That is all value, because convenience is value for the consumer. Time is value for the customer.

Giordano was able to sell value-for-money merchandise consistently through careful selection of suppliers, strict cost control and by resisting the temptation to increase retail prices unnecessarily. For instance, to provide greater shopping convenience to customers, Giordano started to open kiosks in subway and train stations in 2003 aimed at providing their customers with a "grab and go" service.

Inventory Control

In order to maximize use of store space for sales opportunities, a central distribution center replaced the function of a back storeroom in its outlets. Information technology (IT) was used to facilitate inventory management and demand forecasting. When an item was sold, the barcode information—identifying size, color, style and price—was recorded by the point-of-sale cash register and transmitted to the company's main computer. At the end of each day, the information was compiled at the store level and sent to the sales department and the distribution center. The compiled sales information became the store's order for the following day. Orders were filled during the night and were ready for delivery by early morning, ensuring that before a Giordano store opened for business, new inventory was already on the shelves.

Another advantage of its IT system was that information was disseminated to production facilities in real time. Such information allowed customers' purchase patterns to be understood, and this provided valuable input to its manufacturing operations, resulting in less problems and costs related to slow-moving inventory. The use of IT also afforded more efficient inventory holding. Giordano's inventory turnover on sales was reduced from 58 days in 1996 to merely 30 days in 2004. Its excellent inventory management reduced costs and allowed reasonable margins, while still allowing Giordano to reinforce its value-for-money philosophy. All in all, despite the relatively lower margins as compared to its peers, Giordano was still able to post healthy profits. Such efficiency became a crucial factor when periodic price wars were encountered.

PRODUCT POSITIONING

Fung recognized the importance of limiting the firm's expansion and focusing on one specific area. Simplicity and focus were reflected in the way Giordano merchandised its goods. Its stores featured no more than 100 variants of 17 core items, whereas competing retailers might feature 200 to 300 items. He believed that merchandising a wide range of products made it difficult to react quickly to market changes.

Giordano's willingness to experiment with new ideas and its perseverance despite past failures could also be seen in its introduction of new product lines. It ventured into mid-priced women's fashion with the label "Gio Ladies"—featuring a line of smart blouses, dress pants and skirts—targeted at executive women. Reflecting retailer practices for such clothing, Giordano enjoyed higher margins on upscale women's clothing—typically 50 to 60 percent of selling price as compared to 40 percent for casual wear.

Here, however, Giordano ran into some difficulties as it found itself competing with more than a dozen seasoned players in the retail clothing business, including Theme and Esprit. Initially, the firm failed to differentiate its new Giordano Ladies line from its mainstream product line, and even sold both through the same outlets. In 1999, however, Giordano took advantage of the financial troubles facing rivals such as Theme, as well as the boom that followed the Asian currency crisis in many parts of Asia, to aggressively re-launch its "Giordano Ladies" line, which subsequently met with great success. As of January 2006, the reinforced "Giordano Ladies" focused on a select segment, with 27 "Giordano Ladies" shops in Hong Kong, Taiwan, Singapore and China, offering personalized service. Among other things, the staff were trained to memorize names of regular customers and recall their past purchases.

Differentiation and Repositioning

During the late 1990s, Giordano had begun to reposition its brand, by emphasizing differentiated, functionally value-added products clothes and broadening its appeal by improving on visual merchandising and apparel. A typical storefront and store layout are shown in **Exhibit 2** and **Exhibit 4**. Giordano's relatively mid-priced positioning worked well—inexpensive, yet contemporary-looking outfits appealed to Asia's frugal customers, especially during a period of economic slowdown. However, over time, this positioning became inconsistent with the brand image that Giordano had tried hard to build over the years. As one senior executive remarked, "The feeling went from 'this is nice and good value' to 'this is cheap.'"

Giordano gradually remarketed its core brand in ways that sort to create the image of a trendier label. To continue meeting the needs of customers who favored its value-for-money positioning, Giordano launched several

EXHIBIT 4   A Typical Store Layout

promotions. Among its successes was the "Simply Khakis" promotion, launched in April 1999, which emphasized basic, street-culture style that "mixed and matched," and thus fitted all occasions. Within days of its launch in Singapore, the new line sold out and had to be re-launched two weeks later. By October 1999, over a million pairs of khaki trousers and shorts had been sold. The firm's skills in executing innovative and effective promotional strategies helped the retailer to reduce the impact of the Asian crisis on its sales and to take advantage of the slight recovery seen in early 1999.

In 1999, the firm launched a new brand of casual clothing, Blue Star Exchange (BSE), following successful prototyping in Hong Kong and Taiwan. In 2002, the first Blue Star Exchange store was set up in Southern China. The strong market response to this new brand led the company to expand the number of stores branded as Blue Star Exchange to 132 by 2005. The Group was also evaluating the possibility of launching the Blue Star chain in its other markets.

In June 2003, right after the SARS (severe acute respiratory syndrome) health crisis, which discouraged shopping and consumer spending, Giordano launched the "Yoga Collection" which used a moisture-managed fabric, Dry-Tech™. It was an instant big hit, allowing Giordano to recover nicely from the SARS crisis in Hong Kong and enabling its new brand to stand out from competing offerings.

Giordano's Competitors

To beat the intense competition prevalent in Asia—especially in Hong Kong—founder Jimmy Lai believed that Giordano had to develop a distinctive competitive advantage. So he benchmarked Giordano against best-practice organizations in four key areas: (1) computerization (from The Limited), (2) a tightly controlled menu (from McDonald's), (3) frugality (from Wal-Mart), and (4) value pricing (as implemented at the British retail chain Marks & Spencer). The emphasis on service and the value-for-money concept had proven to be successful.

Giordano's main competitors in the value-for-money segment had been Hang Ten, Bossini, and Baleno, and at the higher end, Esprit. **Exhibit 5** shows the relative positioning of Giordano and its competitors: The Gap, Bossini, Hang Ten, Baleno, and Esprit.

Hang Ten and Bossini were generally positioned as low-price retailers offering reasonable quality and service. The clothes emphasized versatility and simplicity. But while Hang Ten and Baleno were more popular among teenagers and young adults, Bossini had a more general appeal. Their distribution strategies were somewhat similar, but they focused on different markets. For instance, while Hang Ten was mainly strong in Taiwan, Baleno increasingly penetrated Mainland China and Taiwan. On the other hand, Bossini was very strong in Hong Kong and relatively strong in China. The company planned to make its business in China into the group's largest turnover and profit contributor. The geographic areas in which Giordano, The Gap, Espirit, Bossini, Baleno, and Hang Ten operate are shown in **Exhibit 6**.

Esprit was an international fashion lifestyle brand. Esprit promoted a "lifestyle" image and its products were strategically positioned as good quality and value for money—a position that Giordano was occupying. By 2005, Esprit had a distribution network of over 10,000 stores and outlets in 40 countries in Europe, Asia, America, Middle East and Australia. The main markets were in Europe, which accounted for approximately 65 percent sales. The Esprit brand products were principally sold via directly managed retail outlets, wholesale customers (including department stores, specialty stores and franchisees), and by licensees for products manufactured under license, principally through the licensees' own distribution networks.

Theme International Holdings Limited was founded in Hong Kong in 1986 by Chairman and CEO Kenneth Lai. He identified a niche in the local market, for high-quality, fashionable ladies' businesswear, although the firm subsequently expanded into casual wear. The Theme label and chain were in direct competition with "Giordano Ladies." From the first store in 1986 to a chain comprising over 130

EXHIBIT 5   Market Positioning of Giordano and Principal Competitors

FIRMS	POSITIONING	TARGET MARKET
Giordano (www.giordano.com.hk)	Value for money Mid-priced but trendy fashion	Unisex casual wear for all ages (under different brands)
The Gap (www.gap.com)	Value for money Mid-priced but trendy fashion	Unisex casual wear for all ages (under different brands)
Esprit (www.esprit-intl.com)	More up-market than Giordano Stylish, trendy	Ladies' casual, but also other specialized lines for children and men
Bossini (www.bossini.com)	Value for money (comparable to Giordano)	Unisex, casual wear, both young and old (above 30s)
Baleno (www.baleno.com.hk)	Value for money Trendy, young age casual wear	Unisex appeal, young adults
Hang Ten (www.hangten.com)	Value for money Sporty lifestyle	Casual wear and sports wear, teens and young adults

EXHIBIT 6 Geographic Presence of Giordano and Its Principal Competitors

COUNTRY	GIORDANO	THE GAP	ESPRIT	BOSSINI	BALENO	HANG TEN
Asia						
Hong Kong/Macau	X	—	X	X	X	X
Singapore	X	—	X	X	X	X
South Korea	X	—	X	—	—	X
Taiwan	X	—	X	X	X	X
China	X	—	X	X	X	X
Malaysia	X	—	X	—	X	—
Indonesia	X	—	X	X	—	—
Philippines	X	—	X	X	—	X
Thailand	X	—	X	X	—	—
World						
U.S. and Canada	—	X	X	X	—	X
Europe	—	X	X	—	—	X
Japan	X	X	—	—	—	X
Australia	X	—	X	—	—	X
Total	1,585	3,117	9,751	827	1,160	NA

Note: "X" indicates presence in the country/region; "—" indicates no presence.

Sources: Annual Report 2004, Giordano International; *Gap Inc.,* retrieved June 23, 2004, from http://www.gapinc.com/about/realestate/storecount.htm; Annual Report 2004/5, *Esprit; Financial Report 2004/5,* Bossini International Holdings Limited; *Baleno,* Retrieved December 12, 2005, from http://www.baleno.com.hk/EN/stores_list.asp?area=cn; Hang Ten, retrieved December 12, 2005, from http://www.hangten.com.

outlets in Hong Kong, Mainland China, Macau, Taiwan, Singapore, Malaysia, Indonesia, the Philippines, the phenomenal growth of Theme was built on a vertically integrated corporate structure and advanced management system. However, its ambitious expansion proved to be costly. In 1999, the company announced a HK$106.1 million net loss for the six months up to September 30, 1998, and was subsequently acquired by High Fashion International, a Hong Kong-based fashion retailer specializing in up-market, trendy apparel. Theme was then focusing on expansion in China, after having fortified its image as a sophisticated and high-end smart-causal fashion for career women.

Although each of these firms had slightly different positioning strategies, they competed in a number of areas. For example, all firms heavily emphasized advertising and sales promotion—selling fashionable clothes at attractive prices. Almost all stores were also located primarily in good ground-floor areas, drawing high-volume traffic and facilitating shopping, browsing and impulse buying. However, none had been able to match the great customer value offered by Giordano.

A threat from U.S.-based The Gap was also looming. The Gap had already entered Japan. After 2005, when garment quotas were largely abolished, imports into the region had become more cost effective for this U.S. competitor.

Financial data for Giordano, Esprit, The Gap, Bossini, and Theme are shown in **Exhibit 7**.

EXHIBIT 7 Competitive Financial Data for Giordano, The Gap, Esprit, Bossini and Theme

	GIORDANO	THE GAP	ESPRIT	BOSSINI	THEME
Turnover (US$ million)	517	16,267	2,662	260	26
Profit after tax and minority interests (US$ million)	51	1,150	431	23	(1)
Return on total assets (percent)	14.9	11.1	36.2	24.9	(7.3)
Return on average equity (percent)	20.9	24	53.6	36.2	NA
Return on sales (percent)	9.8	7.1	20.6	13.5	(3.2)
Number of employees	9,000	152,000	7,720	3,963	2,500
Sales per employee (US$ '000)	57.44	107.02	344.82	65.61	10.4

Note: The Gap reports its earnings in US$. All reported figures have been converted into US$ at the following exchange rate (as of January 2006): US$1 = HK$7.75.

Sources: Annual Report 2004, Giordano International; *Annual Report 2004,* The Gap; *Financial Highlights 2004/5,* Esprit International; *Financial Report 2004/5,* Bossini International Holdings Limited; *Annual Report 2004,* Theme Holdings; Reuters, Retrieved December 12, 2005, from www.knowledge.reuters.com.

GIORDANO'S GROWTH STRATEGY

Early in its existence, Giordano's management had realized that regional expansion was required to achieve substantial growth and economies of scale. By 2006, Giordano had over 1,600 stores in 31 markets. **Exhibit 8** shows the growth achieved across a number of dimensions from 1994 to 2004.

Driven in part by its desire for growth and in part by the need to reduce its dependence on Asia in the wake of the 1998 economic meltdown, Giordano set its sights on markets outside Asia. Australia was an early target and the number of retail outlets increased from four in 1999 to 46 in 2006. In Japan, Giordano opened 21 outlets from 2001 to 2006. Although the Asian financial crisis had caused Giordano to rethink its regional strategy, it was still determined to enter and further penetrate new Asian markets. This determination led to successful expansion in Mainland China (see **Exhibit 9**), where the number of retail outlets grew from 253 in 1999 to 644 by 2006. Giordano's management foresaw both challenges and opportunities arising from the People's Republic of China's accession to the World Trade Organization.

Giordano opened more stores in Indonesia, bringing its total in that country to 39 stores. In Malaysia, Giordano planned to refurnish its outlets and intensify its local promotional campaigns to consolidate its leadership position in the Malaysian market. To improve store profitability, Giordano had already converted some of its franchised Malaysian stores into company-owned stores.

The senior management team knew that Giordano's future success in such markets would depend on a detailed understanding of consumer tastes and preferences for fabrics, colors and advertising. In the past, the firm had relied on maintaining a consistent strategy across different countries, including such elements as positioning, service levels, information systems, logistics, and human resource policies. However, implementation of such tactical elements as promotional campaigns was usually left mostly to local managers. A country's overall performance in terms of sales, contribution, service levels and customer feedback was monitored by regional headquarters (for instance, Singapore for Southeast Asia) and the head office in Hong Kong. Weekly performance reports were distributed to all managers.

As the organization expanded beyond Asia, it was becoming clear that different strategies had to be developed for different regions or countries. For instance, to enhance profitability in Mainland China, the company recognized that better sourcing was needed to enhance price competitiveness. Turning around the Taiwan operation required refocusing on basic designs, streamlining product portfolio, and implementing their micromarketing strategy more aggressively. The company was continuing to explore the market in Japan and planned to open a few more stores in the second half of 2006. In Europe, it was investigating a variety of distribution channels, including a wholesale-based business model.

Decisions Facing the Senior Management Team

Although Giordano had been extremely successful, it faced a number of challenges. A key issue was how the Giordano brand should be positioned against the com-

EXHIBIT 8 Operational Highlights for Giordano's Retail and Distribution Division

	2004	2003	2002	2001	2000	1999	1998	1997	1996	1995	1994
Number of retail outlets											
—Managed directly by the group	811	550	473	456	367	317	308	324	294	280	283
—Franchised	774	813	783	703	553	423	370	316	221	171	77
Total number of retail outlets	1,585	1,363	1,256	1,159	920	740	678	640	515	451	360
Retail floor area managed directly by the group (in '000 sq. ft.)	846	650	599	597	465	301	358	313	295	286	282
Sales per square foot (HK$)	4,300	4,200	4,500	5,100	7,400	8,400	6,800	8,000	9,900	10,500	10,600
Number of employees	9,000	7,900	8,000	8,287	7,166	6,237	6,319	8,175	10,004	10,348	6,863
Comparable store sales: increase/(decrease) (percent)	7	(9)	(2)	(4)	4	21	(13)	(11)	(6)	8	(9)
Number of sales associates	NA	3,200	2,900	2,603	2,417	2,026	1,681	1,929	1,958	2,069	1,928

Source: Annual Report 2004, Giordano International.

EXHIBIT 9 Giordano's Flagship Store in Shanghai

petition in both new and existing markets. Was a repositioning required in existing markets and would it be necessary to follow different positioning strategies for different markets (e.g., Hong Kong versus Southeast Asia)?

A second issue was the sustainability of Giordano's key success factors. Giordano had to carefully explore how its core competencies and the pillars of its success were likely to develop over the coming years. Which of its competitive advantages were likely to be sustainable and which ones were likely to be eroded?

A third issue was Giordano's growth strategy in Asia as well as across continents. Would Giordano's competitive strengths be readily transferable to other markets? Would strategic adaptations to its strategy and marketing mix be required, or would tactical moves suffice?

STUDY QUESTIONS

1. Describe and evaluate Giordano's product, business and corporate strategies.
2. Describe and evaluate Giordano's current positioning strategy. Should Giordano reposition itself against its competitors in its current and new markets, and should it have different positioning strategies for different geographic markets?
3. What are Giordano's key success factors and sources of competitive advantage? Are its competitive advantages sustainable, and how would they develop in the future?
4. Could Giordano transfer its key success factors to new markets as it expands both in Asia and in other parts of the world?
5. How do you think Giordano had/would have to adapt its marketing and operations strategies and tactics when entering and penetrating your country?
6. What general lessons can major clothing retailers in your country learn from Giordano?

Case 6   *Aussie Pooch Mobile*

CHRISTOPHER LOVELOCK AND LORELLE FRAZER

After creating a mobile service that washes dogs outside their owners' homes, a young entrepreneur has successfully franchised the concept. Her firm now has more than 100 franchises in many parts of Australia, as well as a few in other countries. She and her management team are debating how best to plan future expansion.

Elaine and Paul Beal drew up in their 4 × 4 outside 22 Ferndale Avenue, towing a bright blue trailer with red and white lettering. As Aussie Pooch Mobile franchisees whose territory covered four suburbs of Brisbane, Australia, they were having a busy day. It was only 1:00 p.m. and they had already washed and groomed 16 dogs at 12 different houses. Now they were at their last appointment—a 'pooch party' of ten dogs at number 22, where five other residents of the street had arranged to have their dogs washed on a fortnightly basis.

Prior to their arrival outside the house, there had been ferocious growling and snarling from a fierce-looking Rottweiler. But when the animal caught sight of the brightly-colored trailer, he and two other dogs in the yard bounded forward eagerly to the chain link fence, in a flurry of barking and wagging tails.

Throughout residential areas of Brisbane and in a number of other Australian cities, dogs of all shapes and sizes were being washed and groomed by Aussie Pooch Mobile franchisees. By early 2002, the company had grown to over 100 franchisees and claimed to be "Australia's largest mobile dog wash and care company." A key issue facing its managing director, Christine Taylor, and members of the management team was how to plan and shape future expansion.

COMPANY BACKGROUND

Located in Burpengary, Queensland, just north of Brisbane, Aussie Pooch Mobile Pty. Ltd. (APM) was founded in 1991 by Christine Taylor, then aged 22. Taylor had learned customer service early, working in her parents' bait and tackle shop from the age of 8. Growing up in an environment with dogs and horses as pets, she knew she wanted to work with animals and learned dog grooming skills from working in a local salon. At 16, Chris left school and began her own grooming business on a part-time basis, using a bathtub in the family garage. Since she was still too young to drive, her parents would take her to pick up the dogs from their owners. She washed and groomed the animals at home and then returned them.

Once Taylor had learned to drive and bought her own car, she decided to take her service to the customers. So she went mobile, creating a trailer in which the dogs could be washed outside their owners' homes and naming the fledgling venture The Aussie Pooch Mobile. Soon, it became a full-time job. Eventually, she found she had more business than she could handle alone, so hired assistants. The next step was to add a second trailer. Newly married, she and her husband, David McNamara, ploughed their profits into the purchase of additional trailers and gradually expanded until they had six mobile units.

The idea of franchising came to Taylor when she found herself physically constrained by a difficult pregnancy:

> David would go bike riding or head to the coast and have fun with the jet ski and I was stuck at home and felt like I was going nuts, because I'm a really active person. I was hungry for information on how to expand the business, so I started researching other companies and reading heaps of books and came up with franchising as the best way to go, since it would provide capital and also allow a dedicated group of small business people to help expand the business further.

As existing units were converted from employees to franchisee operations, Taylor noticed that they quickly became about 20% more profitable. Initially, APM focused on Brisbane and the surrounding region of southeast Queensland. Subsequently, it expanded into New South Wales and South Australia in 1995, into Canberra, Australian Capital Territory (ACT), in 1999, and into Victoria in 2000 (**Exhibit 1**). Expansion into Western Australia was expected in mid 2002. In 1996, a New Zealand division of the firm was launched in Tauranga, a small city some 200 km southeast of Auckland, under the name Kiwi Pooch Mobile. In 2001 Aussie Pooch Mobile launched into the United Kingdom, beginning with a town in northern England. Soon, there were four operators under a master franchisee. The following year saw the official launch of The Pooch Mobile Malaysia, also under a master franchisee.

By early 2002, the company had 125 mobile units in Australia, of which 55 were located in Queensland, 42 in New South Wales, 8 in ACT, 12 in South Australia and 8 in Victoria. In addition, representatives operated another six company-owned units. The company bathed more than

---

© 2003 Christopher H. Lovelock and Lorelle Frazer.

520

EXHIBIT 1   Map of Australia

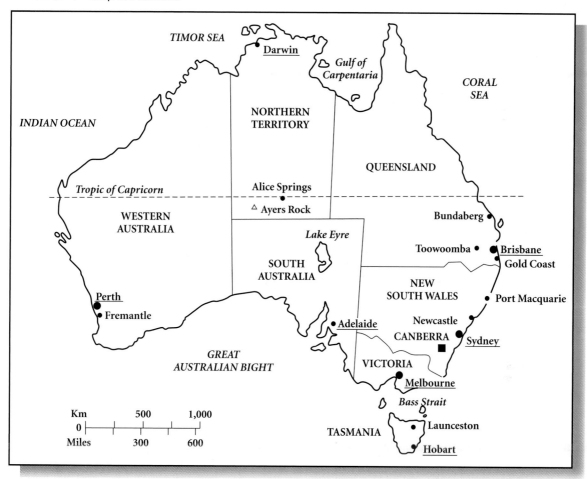

20,000 dogs each month and had an annual turnover of some $3 million. (Financial data are in Australian dollars. Exchange rates at this time were A$1.00 = US$0.57 = €0.58.) APM was a member of the Franchise Council of Australia and complied with the Franchising Code of Conduct. The management team consisted of Chris Taylor as managing director and David McNamara as director responsible for overseeing trailer design and systems support. Each state had its own manager and training team. The central support office also housed staff who provided further assistance to managers and franchisees.

Expansion had benefitted from the leverage provided by several master franchisees, who had obtained the rights to work a large territory and sell franchises within it. Said Taylor:

> I look at the business as if it's my first child. I see it now starting to get into those early teens where it wants to go alone, but it still needs me to hold its hand a little bit, whereas initially it needed me there the whole time. With the support staff we have in place, the business is now gaining the support structure it needs to work without me; this is what I am aiming towards. I appreciate that a team of people can achieve much more than one person alone.

The Service Concept

Aussie Pooch Mobile specialized in bringing its dog washing services to customers' homes. Dogs were washed in a hydrobath installed in a specially-designed trailer, which was parked in the street. The trailer had partly open sides and a roof to provide protection from sun and rain (**Exhibit 2**). Apart from flea control products and a few grooming aids, APM did not attempt to sell dog food and other pet supplies. The company had resisted the temptation to diversify into other fields. "Our niche is in the dog bathing industry," declared Chris Taylor:

> I don't want us to be a jack of all trades because you'll never be good at anything. We now have an exclusive range of products that customer demand has driven us to providing, but we still work closely with vets and pet shops and are by no means a pet shop on wheels.

In contrast to retail pet service stores, where customers brought their animals to the store or kennel, APM brought the service to customers' homes, with the trailer being parked outside on the street. The use of hydrobath equipment, in which warm, pressurized water was pumped through a shower head, enabled operators to

EXHIBIT 2 The Aussie Pooch Mobile Trailer

The rear door of the trailer has been swung open and the franchisee is washing a dog inside.

clean dogs more thoroughly than would be possible with a garden hose. The bath was designed to rid the dog of fleas and ticks and improve its skin condition as well as to clean its coat and eliminate smells. Customers supplied water and electrical power.

The fee paid by customers varied from $15–$30 per dog, depending on breed and size, condition of coat and skin, behavior, and geographic location, with discounts for multiple animals at the same address. On average, regular customers paid a fee of $25 for one dog, $47 for two, and $66 for three. At "pooch parties," a concept developed at APM, the homeowner acting as host typically received one complimentary dogwash at the discretion of the operator. Additional services, for which an extra fee was charged, included the recently introduced aromatherapy bath ($2.50) and blow drying of the animal's coat for $5–10 (on average, $8). Blow drying was especially recommended in cool weather to prevent the animal from getting cold.

Operators also offered free advice to customers about their dogs' diet and health care, including such issues as ticks and skin problems. They encouraged customers to have their dogs bathed on a regular basis. The most commonly scheduled frequencies were once every two or four weeks.

A Satisfied User

The process of bathing a dog involved a sequence of carefully coordinated actions, as exemplified by Elaine Beal's treatment of Zak, the Rottweiler. "Hello my darling, who's a good boy?" crooned Elaine as she patted the enthusiastic dog, placed him on a leash and led him out through the gate to the footpath on this warm, sunny day. Paul busied himself connecting hoses and electrical cords to the house, while Elaine began back-combing Zak's coat in order to set it up for the water to get underneath. She then led the now placid dog to the hydrobath inside the trailer, where he sat patiently while she removed his leash and clipped him to a special collar in the bath for security. Meanwhile the water had been heating to the desired temperature.

Over the next few minutes Elaine bathed the dog, applied a medicated herbal shampoo to his coat and rinsed him thoroughly with the pressure driven hose (**Exhibit 3**). After releasing Zak from the special collar and reattaching his leash, she led him out of the hydrobath and onto the footpath, where she wrapped him in a chamois cloth and dried him. Next, she cleaned the dog's ears and eyes with disposable baby wipes, all the time continuing to talk soothingly to him. She checked his coat and skin to ensure that there were no ticks or skin problems, gave his nails a quick clip, and sprayed a herbal conditioner and deodoriser onto Zak's now gleaming coat and brushed it in. Returning Zak to the yard and removing the leash, Elaine patted him and gave him a large biscuit, specially formulated to protect the animal's teeth.

THE AUSTRALIAN MARKET

Australia's population of 19.3 million in 2001 was small in
relation to the country's vast land area of 7.7 million km^2
(almost three million square miles). By contrast, the United
States had a population 15 times that of Australia on a land
area, including Alaska and Hawaii, of 9.2 million km^2. A
federal nation, Australia was divided into six states—New
South Wales (NSW), Victoria, Queensland, South Australia,
Western Australia, and the island of Tasmania—plus two
territories: the large but thinly populated Northern
Territory and the small Australian Capital Territory (ACT)
which contained the federal capital, Canberra, and its suburbs and was an enclave within NSW. The average annual
earnings for employed persons were $35,000.

With much of the interior of the continent uninhabit-
able and many other areas inhospitable to permanent settlement, most of the Australian population was concentrated in a narrow coastal band running clockwise from
Brisbane on the southeast coast through Sydney and
Melbourne to Adelaide, the capital of South Australia.
Some 2700 km (1600 miles) to the west lay Perth, known as
the most isolated city in the world. A breakdown of the
population by state and territory is shown in **Exhibit 4**. The
northern half of the country was in the tropics, Brisbane
and Perth enjoyed a subtropical climate, and the remaining
major cities had a temperate climate (**Exhibit 5**). Melbourne
was known for its sharp fluctuations in temperature.

There were about four million domestic dogs in the
country and approximately 42% of the nation's 7.4 million
households owned at least one. Ownership rates were

EXHIBIT 4 Population of Australia by State and
Territory, June 2001

STATE/TERRITORY	POPULATION (000)
New South Wales	6,533
Victoria	4,829
Queensland	3,628
South Australia	1,502
Western Australia	1,910
Tasmania	470
Australian Capital Territory	314
Northern Territory	198
Australia Total	*19,387*

Source: Australian Bureau of Statistics 2001.

EXHIBIT 5 Average Temperatures for Principal Australian Cities (in degrees Celsius)*

	JULY (WINTER)		JANUARY (SUMMER)	
	HIGH	LOW	HIGH	LOW
Adelaide, SA	14.9	6.9	27.9	15.7
Brisbane, Qld	20.6	9.5	29.1	20.9
Canberra, ACT	11.5	0.0	28.5	13.6
Darwin, NT	30.7	19.7	32.4	25.2
Hobart, Tas	12.3	4.0	22.3	11.9
Melbourne, Vic	12.9	5.2	26.0	13.5
Perth, WA	17.7	8.1	31.5	16.9
Sydney, NSW	16.9	6.9	26.3	18.6

Source: Australian Bureau of Meteorology, http://www.bom.gov.au.

*Celsius to Fahrenheit Conversion: 0°C = 32°F, 10°C = 50°F, 20°C = 68°F, 30°C = 86°F.

slightly above average in Tasmania, the Northern Territory and Queensland, and somewhat below average in Victoria and the ACT. In 1995, it was estimated that Australians spent an estimated $1.3 billion on dog-related goods and services, of which 46% went to dog food, 22% to veterinary services, 12% to dog products and equipment, and 11% to other services, including washing and grooming (**Exhibit 6**).

Franchising in Australia

By the beginning of the 21st Century, the Australian franchising sector had reached a stage of early maturity. McDonald's, KFC and Pizza Hut opened their first outlets in Australia in the 1970s. These imported systems were followed by many home-grown business format franchises such as Just Cuts (hairdressing), Snap Printing, Eagle Boys Pizza, and VIP Home Services, all of which grew into large domestic systems and then expanded internationally, principally to New Zealand and Southeast Asia.

In 2002, Australia boasted approximately 700 business format franchise systems holding over 50,000 outlets. Although the United States had many more systems and outlets, Australia had more franchisors per capita, reflecting the relative ease of entry into franchising in this country. Most of the growth in franchising had occurred in business format franchising as opposed to product franchising.

EXHIBIT 6 Distribution of Consumer Expenditures on Dog-Related Goods and Services, 1995

PRODUCT/SERVICE	ALLOCATION
Dog food	46%
Vet charges	21%
Dog products	10%
Dog equipment	2%
Dog services	11%
Pet purchases	5%
Other expenses	4%
Total dog-related expenditures	*$1.3 billion*

Source: BIS Shrapnell Survey 1995.

Business format franchises provided franchisees with a full business system and the rights to operate under the franchisor's brand name, whereas product franchises merely allowed independent operators to supply a manufacturer's product, such as car dealerships or soft-drink bottlers. Typically, franchisees were required to pay an upfront franchise fee (averaging $30,000 in service industries and $40,000 in retailing) for the right to operate under the franchise system within a defined geographic area. This initial fee was included in the total start-up cost of the business (ranging from around $60,000 in the service sector to more than $200,000 in the retail industry). In addition, franchisees paid a royalty on all sales and an ongoing contribution towards advertising and promotional activities that were designed to build brand awareness and preference. Would-be franchisees who lacked sufficient capital might be able to obtain bank financing against personal assets such as property or an acceptable guarantor.

Franchising Trends

The rapid growth of franchising in Australia had been stimulated in part by demographic trends, including the increase in dual-income families, which had led to greater demand for outsourcing of household services such as lawn mowing, house cleaning and pet grooming. Some franchise systems offered multiple concepts under a single corporate brand name. For instance, VIP Home Services had separate franchises available in lawn mowing, cleaning, car washing and rubbish removal. Additional growth came from conversion of existing individual businesses to a franchise format. For instance, Eagle Boys Pizza had often approached local pizza operators and offered them the opportunity to join this franchise.

Almost half the franchise systems in Australia were in retail trade (32% non-food and 14% food). Another large and growing industry was the property and business services sector (20%), as shown in **Exhibit 7**. Most franchisees were ex-white collar workers or blue collar supervisors who craved independence and a lifestyle change.

INDUSTRY	PERCENTAGE
Retail trade—non-food	31
Property and business services	20
Retail trade—food	14
Personal and other services	7
Construction and trade services	6
Accommodation, cafes and restaurants	4
Education	4
Cultural and recreation services	4
Unclassified	3
Manufacturing and printing	3
Finance and insurance	2
Transport and storage	1
Communication services	1
Total—all industries	*100%*

Source: Lorelle Frazer and Colin McCosker, *Franchising Australia 1999,* Franchise Council of Australia/University of Southern Queensland, Toowoomba, 1999, p. 39.

Over the years, Australia's franchising sector had experienced a myriad of regulatory regimes. Finally in 1998, in response to perceived problems in many franchising systems, the federal government introduced a mandatory Franchising Code of Conduct, administered under the Trade Practices Act. Among other things, the Code required that potential franchisees be given full disclosure about the franchisor's background and operations prior to signing a franchise agreement. In contrast, the franchising sector in the United States faced a patchwork of regulations that varied from one state to another. Yet in the United Kingdom, there were no specific franchising regulations beyond those applying to all corporations operating in designated industries.

Master franchising arrangements had become common in Australian franchise systems. Under master franchising, a local entrepreneur was awarded the rights to sub-franchise the system within a specific geographic area, such as an entire state. Because of Australia's vast geographic size it was difficult for a franchisor to monitor franchisees who were located far from the head office. The solution was to delegate to master franchisees many of the tasks normally handled by the franchisor itself, making them responsible for recruiting, selecting, training and monitoring franchisees in their territories, as well as overseeing marketing and operations.

Not all franchisees proved successful and individual outlets periodically failed. The main reasons for failure appeared to be poor choice of location or territory and a franchisee's own shortcomings. In addition to the obvious technical skills required in a given field, success often hinged on possession of sales and communication abilities. Disputes in franchising were not uncommon, but could usually be resolved internally without recourse to legal action. The causes of conflict most frequently cited by franchisees related to franchise fees and alleged misrepresentations made by the franchisor. By contrast, franchisors cited conflicts based on lack of adherence to the system by franchisees.

Australia was home to a number of internationally-known franchise operators, including Hertz Rent-a-Car, Avis, McDonald's, KFC, Pizza Hut, Subway, Kwik Kopy and Snap-on Tools. By contrast, most Burger King outlets operated under the name Hungry Jack's, an acquired Australian chain with significant brand equity.

Jim's Group

Among Australia's best-known, locally developed franchisors was Melbourne-based Jim's Group, which described itself as one of the world's largest home service franchise organizations. The company had originated with a mowing service started by Jim Penman in Melbourne in 1982 when he abandoned ideas of an academic career after his PhD thesis was rejected. In 1989, Penman began franchising the service, now known as Jim's Mowing, as a way to facilitate expansion. The business grew rapidly, using master franchisees in different regions to recruit and manage individual franchisees. The company's dark green trucks, displaying a larger-than-life logo of Penman himself, bearded and wearing a hat, soon became a familiar sight on suburban streets around Melbourne. Before long, the franchise expanded to other parts of Victoria and then to other states.

Over the following years, an array of other home-related services was launched under the Jim's brand, including Jim's Trees, Jim's Paving, Jim's Cleaning, Jim's Appliance Repair, and Jim's Floors. Each service featured the well-recognized logo of Jim Penman's face on a different colored background. Jim's Dogwash made its debut in 1996, employing a bright red, fully enclosed trailer, emblazoned by a logo that had been amended to show Jim with a dog. By early 2002, Jim's Group comprised more than two dozen different service divisions, over ninety master franchisees, and some 1,900 individual franchisees. In many instances, master franchisees were responsible for two or more different service divisions within their regions. Jim's Group's philosophy was to price franchises according to local market conditions. If work in a prospective territory were easy to find but franchisees hard to attract, the price might be lowered somewhat, but not too much, otherwise the company felt there would be insufficient commitment.

In recent years, Jim's Group had expanded overseas. In New Zealand, it had six master franchisees and 232 franchisees and offered mowing, tree work, cleaning, and dogwashing services. It had also established a significant presence for Jim's Mowing in the Canadian province of British Columbia. But attempts to launch Jim's Mowing in the United States had failed due to difficulty in finding good operators.

Jim's Dogwash had over 60 franchises operating in Australia (primarily in Victoria) and New Zealand. This firm's experience had shown that growth was hampered by the shortage of suitable franchisees, since operators needed to be dog lovers with a background in dog care.

FRANCHISING STRATEGY AT AUSSIE POOCH MOBILE

New APM franchisees were recruited through newspaper advertisements and "advertorials" (**Exhibit 8**) as well as by word of mouth. The concept appealed to individuals who sought to become self-employed but wanted the security of a proven business system rather than striking out entirely on their own. Interested individuals were invited to meet with a representative of the company to learn more. If they wished to proceed further, they had to complete an application form and submit a deposit of $250 to hold a particular area for a maximum of four weeks, during which the applicant could further investigate the characteristics and prospects of the designated territory. This fee was credited to the purchase cost of the franchise if the applicant decided to proceed or returned if the applicant withdrew. A new franchise cost $24,000 (up from $19,500 in 1999). An additional 10% had to be added to this fee to pay the recently introduced federal goods and services tax (GST). **Exhibit 9** identifies how APM costed out the different elements.

Selection Requirements for Prospective Franchisees

The company had set a minimum educational requirement of passing Year 10 of high school (or equivalent). Taylor noted that successful applicants tended to be outdoor people who shared four characteristics:

> They are self motivated and outgoing. They love dogs and they want to work for themselves. Obviously, being great with dogs is one part of the business—our franchisees understand that the dog's even an extended member of the customer's family—but it's really important that they can handle the bookwork side of the business as well, because that's basically where your bread and butter is made.

EXHIBIT 8   Examples of Franchisee Recruitment Advertisements and Promotional Materials

EXHIBIT 9   Aussie Pooch Mobile: Breakdown of Franchise Purchase Cost, 2002 vs. 1999

ITEM	1999		2002	
	$	$	$	$
Initial training		2,200.00		2,200.00
Initial franchise fee		4,021.50		6,173.00
Guaranteed income		5,000.00		N/A
Exclusive territory plus trailer registration		N/A		6,600.00
Fixtures, fittings, stock, insurance etc:				
Aussie Pooch Mobile trailer and hydrobath	4,860.00		5,340.00	
Consumables (shampoo, conditioner, etc.)	160.00		230.00	
Trade equipment and uniforms	920.00		881.65	
Insurance	338.50	6,278.50	575.35	7,027.00
Initial advertising		2,000.00		2,000.00
*Total franchise cost**		$19,500.00		$24,000.00

*Total franchise costs excludes 10% GST, introduced in July 2000.

Other desirable characteristics included people skills and patience, plus a good telephone manner. Would-be franchisees also had to have a valid driver's license, access to a vehicle that was capable of towing a trailer, and the ability to do this type of driving in an urban setting. Originally, Taylor had expected that most franchisees would be relatively young, with parents being willing to buy their children a franchise and set them up with a job, but in fact only about half of all franchisees were aged 21–30; 40% were aged 31–40 and 10% were in their forties or fifties. About 60% were female.

Potential franchisees were offered a trial work period with an operator to see if they liked the job and were suited to the business, including not only skills with both animals and people but also sufficient physical fitness.

In return for the franchise fee, successful applicants received the rights to a geographically defined franchise, typically comprising about 12,000 homes. Franchisees also obtained an APM trailer with all necessary products and solutions to service the first one hundred dogs, plus red uniform shirts and cap, advertising material, and stationery. The trailer was built to industrial grade standards and its design included many refinements developed by APM in consultation with franchisees to simplify the process of dog washing and enhance the experience for the animal. Operators were required to travel with a mobile phone, which they had to pay for themselves.

In addition to franchised territories, APM had six company-owned outlets. These were operated by representatives, who leased the territory and equipment and in return paid APM 25% of the gross weekly revenues (including GST). Taylor had no plans to increase the number of representatives. The reps were generally individuals who either could not currently afford the start-up cost or who were being evaluated by the company for their suitability as franchisees. Typically, reps either became franchisees within about six months or left the company.

Assisting New Franchisees

The franchisor provided two weeks' pre-opening training for all new franchisees and representatives also spent about 10 hours with each one to help them open their new territories. Training topics included operational and business procedures, effective use of the telephone, hydrobathing techniques, dog grooming techniques, and information on dog health and behavior. Franchisees were given a detailed operations manual containing 104 pages of instructions on running the business in accordance with company standards.

To help new franchisees get started, APM placed advertisements in local newspapers for a period of 20 weeks. It also prepared human interest stories for distribution to these newspapers. Other promotional activities at the time of launch included distributing pamphlets in the territory and writing to local vets and pet shops to inform them of the business. APM guaranteed new franchisees a weekly income of $600 for the first ten weeks and paid for a package of insurance policies for six months, after which the franchisee became responsible for the coverage.

Fees and Services

Ongoing support by the franchisor included marketing efforts, monthly newsletters, a telephone hotline service for advice, an insurance package, regular (but brief) field visits, and additional training. If a franchisee fell sick or wished to take a vacation, APM would offer advice on how to best deal with this situation, in many cases being able to organise a trained person to help out. It also organized periodic meetings for franchisees in the major metropolitan areas at which guest presenters spoke on topics relating to franchise operations. Previous guest speakers had included veterinarians, natural therapists, pharmacists, and accountants. More

EXPENSE	1999 $	2002 $
Consumable products	3,552	2,880
Car registration	430	430
Car insurance	500	500
Fuel	2,400	3,360
Insurances	642	1,151
Repairs and maintenance	1,104	1,104
Phones, stationery, etc.	1,440	1,920
Communication levy	624	624
Franchise royalties	4,416	5,583
Advertising levy	1,104	1,395
Total	$16,212	$18,947

recently, APM had offered one-day seminars, providing more team support and generating greater motivation than the traditional meeting style.

In return for these services, franchisees paid a royalty fee of 10% of their gross weekly income, plus an advertising levy of an additional 2.5%. Income was reported on a weekly basis and fees had to be paid weekly. In addition to these fees, operating costs for a franchisee included car-related expenses, purchase of consumable products such as shampoo, insurance, telephone, and stationery. **Exhibit 10** shows the average weekly costs that a typical franchisee might expect to incur.

Franchisees included several couples, like the Beals, but Taylor believed that having two operators work together was not really efficient, although it could be companionable. Paul Beal, a retired advertising executive, had other interests and did not always accompany Elaine. Some couples split the work, with one operating three days a week and the other three or even four days. All franchisees were required to be substantially involved in the hands-on running of the business; some had more than one territory and employed additional operators to help them.

To further support individual franchisees, APM had formed a Franchise Advisory Council, composed of a group of experienced franchisees who had volunteered their time to help other franchisees and the system as a whole. Each franchisee was assigned to a team leader, who was a member of the FAC. The Council facilitated communications between franchisees and the support office, meeting with the managers every three months to discuss different issues within the company.

MARKETING AND COMPETITION

The company advertised Aussie Pooch Mobile service in the Yellow Pages as well as paying for listings in the White Pages of local phone directories. It promoted a single tele-

phone number nationwide in Australia, staffed by an answering service 24 hours a day, seven days a week. Customers paid only a local call charge of 25 cents to access this number. They could leave their name and telephone number, which would then be electronically sorted and forwarded via alphanumeric pagers to the appropriate franchisee, who would then return the call to arrange a convenient appointment time. APM also offered expert advice on local advertising and promotions, and made promotional products and advertising templates available to franchisees. Other corporate communications activities included maintaining the web site (www.hydrobath.com), distributing public relations releases to the media, and controlling all aspects of corporate identity such as trailer design, business cards, and uniforms.

"I try to hold the reins pretty tightly on advertising matters," said Taylor, noting that the franchise agreement required individual franchisees to submit their plans for promotional activities for corporate approval. She shook her head as she remembered an early disaster, involving an unauthorized campaign by a franchisee who had placed an offer of a free dog wash in a widely distributed coupon book. Unfortunately, this promotion had set no expiration date or geographic restriction, with the result that customers were still presenting the coupon more than a year later across several different franchise territories.

With APM's approval, some franchisees had developed additional promotional ideas. For example, Elaine and Paul Beal wrote informative articles and human interest stories about dogs for their local newspaper. When a client's dog died, Elaine sent a sympathy card and presented the owner with a small tree to plant in memory of the pet.

Developing a Territory

Obtaining new customers and retaining existing ones was an important aspect of each franchisee's work. The brightly colored trailer often attracted questions from passers-by and presented a useful opportunity to promote the service. Operators could ask satisfied customers to recommend the service to their friends and neighbors. Encouraging owners to increase the frequency of washing their dogs was another way to build business. Knowing that a dog might become lonely when its owner was absent and was liable to develop behavior problems, Elaine Beal sometimes recommended the acquisition of a "companion pet." As Paul remarked, "Having two dogs is not twice the trouble, it halves the problem!"

However, to maximize profitability, franchisees also had to operate as efficiently as possible, minimizing time spent in non-revenue producing activities such as travel, set up, and socializing. As business grew, some franchisees employed additional operators to handle the excess workload, so that the trailer might be in service extended hours, seven days a week. Eventually, a busy territory might be split, with a portion being sold off to a new franchisee.

APM encouraged this practice. The company had found that franchisees reached a comfort zone at about 80 dogs a week and then their business stopped growing because they could not physically wash any more dogs. Franchisees could set their own price when selling all or part of a territory and APM helped them to coordinate the sale. When a territory was split, a franchisee was usually motivated to rebuild the remaining half to its maximum potential.

Competition

Although many dog owners had traditionally washed their animals themselves (or had not even bothered), there was a growing trend towards paying a third party to handle this task. Dog washing services fell into two broad groups. One consisted of fixed-site operations to which dog owners brought their animals for bathing. The location of these businesses included retail sites in suburban shopping areas, kennels, and service providers' own homes or garages. The second type of competition, which had grown in popularity in recent years, consisted of mobile operations that traveled to customers' homes.

With few barriers to entry, there were numerous dog washing services in most major metropolitan areas; many of these services included the word "hydrobath" in their names. In Brisbane, for example, the Yellow Pages listed 19 mobile suppliers in addition to APM and 26 fixed-site suppliers, a few of which also washed other types of animals (**Exhibit 11**). The majority of dog washing services in Australia were believed to be stand-alone operations, but there were other franchisors in addition to Aussie Pooch Mobile. Of these, the most significant appeared to be Jim's Dogwash and Hydrodog.

Jim's Dogwash (part of Melbourne-based Jim's Group) had nine master franchisees and 52 franchises in Australia and four masters and nine franchisees in New Zealand (**Exhibit 12**). Jim's expansion strategy had been achieved in part by creating smaller territories than APM and pricing them relatively inexpensively, in order to stimulate recruitment of new franchisees. A territory, typically encompassing about 2,000 homes, currently sold for $10,000 (comprising an initial franchise fee of $6,000, $3000 for the trailer, and $1000 for other equipment) plus 10% GST. Jim's fee for washing a dog, including blow drying, ranged from $28 to $38. However, the firm did not offer aromatherapy or anything similar.

Another franchised dogwashing operation was Hydrodog, based on the Gold Coast in Queensland with 49 units in Queensland, 9 in New South Wales, 8 in Western Australia and one each in Victoria, South Australia, and the Northern Territory. Hydrodog began franchising in 1994. By 2002, a new franchise unit cost

$24,950 (including GST), of which $10,800 was accounted for by the initial franchise fee for a 10,000-home territory. In addition to their dog grooming services, which included blowdrying and ranged in price from $15 to $40, Hydrodog franchisees sold dog food products, including dry biscuits and cooked or raw meats (chicken, beef or kangaroo). They did not offer aromatherapy.

DEVELOPING A STRATEGY FOR THE FUTURE

Managing continued expansion presented an ongoing challenge to the directors of Aussie Pooch Mobile. However, as Chris Taylor pointed out, "You can be the largest but you may not be the best. Our focus is on doing a good job and making our franchisees successful."

To facilitate expansion outside its original base of southeast Queensland, APM had appointed a franchise sales manager in Sydney for the New South Wales market and another in Melbourne for both Victoria and South Australia. One question was whether to adopt a formal strategy of appointing master franchisees. Currently, there were master franchises on the Gold Coast (a fast-growing resort and residential area southeast of Brisbane), in the ACT, and in the regional cities of Toowoomba and Bundaberg in Queensland, and in Newcastle and Port Macquarie in New South Wales.

For some years, Taylor had been attracted by the idea of expanding internationally. In 1996, the company had licensed a franchisee in New Zealand to operate a subsidiary named Kiwi Pooch Mobile. However, there was only one unit operating by early 2002 and she wondered how best to increase this number. Another subsidiary had been established as a master franchise in the French province of New Caledonia, a large island northeast of Australia. Launched in late 2000 under the name of La Pooch Mobile; it had one unit. Another master franchise territory had been established in Malaysia in late 2001 and there were two units operating in 2002.

In 2001, APM had granted exclusive rights for operation in the United Kingdom to a British entrepreneur, who operated under the name The Pooch Mobile. Thus far, four units were operating in the English county of Lincolnshire, some 200 km (125 miles) north of London. This individual noted that English people traditionally washed their dogs very infrequently, often as little as once every two to three years, but once they had tried The Pooch Mobile, they quickly converted to becoming monthly clients, primarily for the hygiene benefits.

As the company grew, the directors knew it was likely to face increased competition from other providers of dogwashing services. But as one successful franchisee remarked: "Competition keeps us on our toes. It's hard being in the lead and maintaining the lead if you haven't got anybody on your tail."

EXHIBIT 11   Competing Dog Washing Services in the Greater Brisbane Area, 2002

(A) Services including the word "mobile" in their names

A & Jane's Mobile Dog Wash

A Spotless Dog Mobile Hydrobath

Akleena K9 Mobile Hydrobath

Alan's Mobile Dog and Cat Wash

Fancy Tails Mobile Hydrobath

Fido's Mobile Dog Wash and Clipping

Go-Go's Mobile Pet Parlour

Happy Pets Mobile Hydrobath

Itch-Eeze Mobile Dog Grooming and Hydrobath Service

James' Mobile Pet Grooming and Hydrobath

My Pets Mobile Hydrobath

Paw Prints Mobile Dog Grooming

Preen A Pooch-Mobile

Rainbow Mobile Dog Wash

Redlands Mobile Pet Grooming and Hydrobath

Sallie's Mobile Dogwash

Scrappy Doo's Mobile Hydrobath

Superdog Mobile Hydrobath

Western Suburbs Mobile Dog Bath

(B) Other listings containing the words "bath," "wash," hydro," or similar allusions

Aussie Dog Hydrobath

Budget K9 Baths

Conmurra Hydrobaths

Dandy Dog Hydrobath

Dial A Dogwash

Doggy Dunk

Flush-Puppy

Heavenly Hydropet

Helen's Hydrobath

Herbal Dog Wash

Home Hydrobath Service

Hydro-Hound

Jo's Hydrowash

K9 Aquatics

K9 Kleeners

Keep Em Kleen

Maggie's Shampooch

Nome's Turbo Pet Wash

P.R. Turbo Pet Wash

Paws n More Hydrobath and Pet Care Services

Puppy Paws Dog Wash

Splish Splash Hydrobath

Scrubba Dub Dog

Soapy Dog

Super Clean Professional Dog Wash

Tidy Tim's Hydrobath

Source: Yellow Pages Online, March 2002 under "Dog & Cat Clipping & Grooming" (excludes services delivered only to cats).

EXHIBIT 12   Profile of Jim's Group Franchisees

Location	All Master Franchisees	Master Dogwash Franchisees	Individual Dogwash Franchisees
Victoria	41	6	36
New South Wales + ACT	8	1	7
Queensland	13	—	—
South Australia	6	1	4
Western Australia	13	—	3
Tasmania	1	—	—
Northern Territory	1	1	2
Australia	83	9	52
New Zealand	6	4	9
Canada	1	—	—
Grand Total	90	13	61

Source: Jim's Group website, www.jims.net, January 2002.

STUDY QUESTIONS

1. How did Christine Taylor succeed in evolving the local dogwashing service she developed as a teenager into an international franchise business?
2. Compare and contrast the tasks involved in recruiting new customers and recruiting new franchisees.
3. From a franchisee's perspective, what are the key benefits of belonging to the APM franchise in (a) the first year and (b) the third and subsequent years?
4. In planning for future expansion, what strategy should Taylor adopt for APM and why?

Case 7   *Jollibee Foods Corporation*

Leonardo R. Garcia, Jr.,
Christopher Lovelock, and Jochen Wirtz

The Philippines' leading food service company has grown both organically and through acquisitions. Ranked among Asia's top companies, it now dominates the fast-food market in its home country, where it offers four separate fast-food concepts under separate brand identities, led by the original Jollibee stores. However, despite international aspirations, it has made only modest progress overseas, where recent growth has come primarily from purchase of the Yonghe King chain in China.

Around the world, when someone says "fast-food restaurant" the chances are high that the first name that comes to mind will be McDonald's, the world's largest quick-service restaurant chain. In 2005, McDonald's held a 20 percent share of the U.S. fast-food market, triple that of its nearest competitor Burger King. This was not the case, however, in the Philippines where, for more than two decades, fast-food had been synonymous with the name Jollibee. In the global business arena, Jollibee Foods Corporation (JFC) was not exactly a household name. But in its niche, the Philippines, where it controlled four brands—Jollibee, Delifrance, Greenwich Pizza, and Chowking—it dominated the market.

During the 1990s, JFC extended its sights overseas, opening a small number of restaurants in several Asian and Middle Eastern locations. The company's chairman and CEO, Tony Tan Caktiong, observed:

> Internationalization remains a key component of our business strategy, even as we continue to reinforce our domestic network of stores. Our goals of continued growth, profitability and market leadership, as well as our contribution to the development of our country, may lie not just in continuing to expand aggressively at home but also in becoming a truly multinational Filipino corporation.

By June 2005, the total number of stores worldwide in the JFC Group had grown to 1,200, of which 1,079 were located in the Philippines and the balance in several other countries, led by the recently acquired Yonghe King chain in China. Jollibee had recently beaten 31 other entrepreneurs from around the world to win the 2004 World Entrepreneur of the Year award, sponsored by Ernst and Young, one of the world's top accounting firms.

JOLLIBEE: THE EARLY YEARS

Humble Beginnings

In 1975, Tony Tan Caktiong, a Filipino of Chinese ancestry, and his brothers opened two ice-cream parlors in Manila's commercial districts of Cubao and Quiapo. These ice-cream parlors were an instant hit among food-loving Filipinos, who came to associate the stores with special occasions such as birthdays and holidays. In no time the Tan brothers had decided to expand their menu and began offering other quick-meals such as hot sandwiches, spaghetti and burgers. After its second year of operations, the Tan brothers noted that the store was actually earning more from the side orders, specifically their burgers, than from the ice-cream.

Following the taste and feel of the market, the Tan brothers decided to develop their own unique brand by coming up with a menu that would appeal to the Filipino palate. Jollibee was conceived as a fast-food outlet of high-quality but reasonably-priced food products tailored especially for Filipinos, who were served by a jolly, "busy-as-a-bee" restaurant crew. Hence the birth of the bright red and yellow "Jolly Bee" mascot, which had since become a favorite among Filipino children. In response to the growing popularity of their sweet homemade burgers—made from their mother's secret recipe—and the other hot meals, Tony Tan and his brothers formed Jollibee Foods Corporation (JFC) in 1978 to exploit the possibilities of a hamburger concept more fully. By that time the firm had seven outlets.

When McDonald's entered the Philippine market in 1981 and began opening stores in Manila, some industry observers questioned whether the little 11-store local chain could survive. However, Jollibee's management team decided to see this as an opportunity that would allow them to benchmark the American giant's operations and then bring their own chain up to world-class standards. In particular, they focused on learning about the sophisticated operating systems that enabled McDonald's to control its quality, costs, and service at the store level—an area of weakness in the local firm that had constrained its further expansion. As Tony Tan gained a better understanding of McDonald's business model, he recognized not only strengths but also specific

© 2007 Leonardo R, Garcia, Jr., Christopher H. Lovelock, and Jochen Wirtz.

The authors gratefully acknowledge the assistance of Kristine Abante.

This case is based on published sources, student research, and personal experience. It was prepared solely for use as a learning tool and is not intended to serve as an endorsement, source of primary data, or illustration of effective or ineffective management. Financial data are in Philippine pesos (exchange rates in mid-2004 were PHP 1 = US$0.018, or US$1 = PHP 56).

areas of weakness in the latter's strategy, reflecting its standardized product line and a U.S.-dominated decision processes.

Capturing Filipinos' Taste buds

In the Philippines, people love to eat and are used to doing so up to five times daily, enjoying snacks in between meals and a comfortable place to chat with friends and loved ones. As a result the nation had become an attractive market for global players such as McDonald's, KFC, Wendy's, Burger King, and Pizza Hut. Yet despite growing competition, Jollibee had managed to maintain its dominant position as the leading fast-food chain in the Philippines with a menu tailored specifically to the Filipinos' preferences.

Jollibee's keen insight and understanding of the Filipino psyche had brought to everyone's lips the promise of *langhap-sara* (freely translated, this means "smells good so it must taste good"). In addition to meals with fries, Jollibee offered rice or spaghetti with its entrees. Its moist burger patties and spicy sauces were so distinctly Filipino that Jollibee's burgers were often likened to what a Filipino mother would cook at home. This strong understanding of Filipinos' taste and preferences set Jollibee apart from its competitors.

Although long-time favorites like Chickenjoy, Spaghetti Special, Jolly Hotdog, French fries and Yumburgers still continued to hold their appeal, over time Jollibee had broadened its product range to create more excitement and variety. The enlarged menu included more rice-based products like Honey Beef Rice and Shanghai Rolls; a variety of burger choices from mushroom to garlic and cheese, a variety of chicken dishes, more flavorful desserts like the Ice Craze in *Buko pandan* (coconut and jelly) and *mais con yelo* (sweet corn) served with milk and crushed ice; traditional Filipino breakfast rice meals, and options such as the Tuna Pie and Pies-to-Go. Never before had Filipinos—children, families,

and adults from all walks of life—been offered so much in a single location.

Addition of New Brands

By 1989, Jollibee had become the first Philippine fast-food chain to break the one billion peso sales mark. In 1993, Jollibee Food Corporation (JFC) went public on the Philippine Stock Exchange to broaden its capital base, laying the groundwork for expansion both within and beyond Philippine shores. Over the years, the size, geographic expanse and breadth of the company's operations had continued to grow. In addition to the original chain of Jollibee burger restaurants, several new brands had been added through acquisition.

Even as the Jollibee brand achieved market dominance, the firm was also pursuing a strategy of diversification as a hedge against both competition and downturns in specific market niches. Reaching out to other segments, Jollibee Foods Corporation had acquired a portfolio of other fast food concepts, to which it applied its carefully honed operational and marketing skills. In 1994 it purchased Greenwich Pizza, the Philippines' leading pizza and pasta chain. The following year, seeking to cater to the changing taste preferences of the Filipinos, JFC acquired the right to operate the Philippine's franchise of Délifrance, an international chain of French bakery-cafés headquartered in France. In 2000, JFC bought Chowking Foods Corporation, which operated the Philippines' top chain serving Chinese fast-food.

Although Chowking had reported excellent sales and performance since its purchase, it took time before Greenwich Pizza was able to establish a strong position in the market. By the end of 2003, JFC was the Philippines market leader in three segments. In the hamburger and chicken segment, Jollibee had 467 outlets to only 240 for its nearest rival, McDonald's. In Chinese fast-food, there

EXHIBIT 1 Trends in Number of Stores by Brand, 1998–2005

		DECEMBER 31						
	JUNE 2005	2004	2003	2002	2001	2000	1999	1998
Philippines								
Jollibee	508	499	467	436	408	374	350	302
Greenwich	228	232	213	191	194	193	191	169
Chowking	310	303	245	216	194	164	159	142
Delifrance	33	31	30	28	24	13	6	4
Subtotal	1,079	1,065	955	871	832	744	712	617
International								
Jollibee	22	22	21	21	23	22	21	n.a.
Chowking	11	10	9	8	7	6	6	n.a.
Tomi's Teriyaki	—	—	3	2	1	—	—	n.a.
Yonghe King	88	88	—	—	—	—	—	n.a.
Subtotal	121	120	33	31	31	29	27	n.a.
TOTAL	1,200	1,185	988	902	863	772	739	n.a.

Source: Fourth quarter reports, 1998–2004.

EXHIBIT 2 Jollibee Foods Corporation: Selected Annual Financial and Operational Data, 1998–2004*

	2004	2003	2002	2001	2000	1999	1998
Consolidated Systemwide Sales	35.5	28.9	26.8	24.1	20.3	18.1	16.7
Gross Revenues	26.2	21.6	20.3	18.8	15.7	14.1	12.9
Income from Operations	2.0	1.4	1.5	0.8	1.1	0.9	1.2
Net Income	1.6	1.3	1.0	0.5	0.9	0.6	0.8
Number of Personnel (000)	26.5	21.6	22.0	21.8	20.6	14.2	13.9

*All financial data in billions of pesos.

Source: Annual Reports, Jollibee Foods Corporation, 1998–2004.

were 245 Chowking restaurants, compared to 136 for its nearest competitor, Luk Yuen. And finally, JFC's pizza and pasta outlet, Greenwich, had 213 stores as compared to 113 for its nearest rival, Pizza Hut.[1] **Exhibit 1** shows trends in the number of stores by brand between the end of 1998 and September 2004.

By that time, Jollibee had become had become an international brand that, as management declared, made Filipinos proud. *Forbes, Far Eastern Economic Review,* and *Asian Business* had all ranked JFC among Asia's top companies. It was recognized as the number one food company in Asia by *Euromoney* and as the best-managed company in the Philippines by *Asiamoney,* and was consistently ranked among Asia's best employers in the *Far Eastern Economic Review's* annual survey. In 2004, Jollibee Foods Corporation topped the "Asia's Most Admired Company" (AMAC) survey, conducted by Hong Kong-based *Asian Business Magazine.* **Exhibit 2** shows annual financial and operational data for JFC from 1998 to 2004. **Exhibit 3** reproduces the company's values, vision, and mission.

Twenty-nine years after Jollibee was founded, JFC controlled about 55% of the quick-service restaurant market in the Philippines based on "visit shares" and held 70% of the burger-based meals market. One million customers ate at JFC stores daily, averaging a per capita spending of about 40 pesos (US$0.71). Each day, JFC bought or produced 40,000 packs of chicken (with eight pieces in each pack), 320,000 pieces of burger, and 44,250 eggs. With more than one thousand stores across the Philippines, JFC's four brands enjoyed substantial economies of scale, gaining leverage in terms of retail site selection and operations, procurement, manufacturing, distribution and marketing at levels unavailable to most industry players. Despite a recent economic slowdown in the Philippines and unfavorable business conditions, JFC had continued to deliver same-store sales growth. **Exhibit 4** shows a modern Jollibee store.

MARKETING, OPERATIONS, AND HUMAN RESOURCES

Jollibee's 'FSC' Commitment

The acronym FSC, described by the company on its website as "a byword in all of Jollibee," represented its commitment to meeting high standards in three key areas:

Every Food (F) item served to the public must meet the company's excellent standards or it will not be served at all; the Service (S) must be fast and courte-

EXHIBIT 3 Jollibee Food Corporation: Values—Mission—Vision

Values
- Always put customer first
- Excellence through teamwork
- Spirit of family and fun
- Frugality, Honesty and Integrity
- Humility to listen and learn

Mission
We bring great taste and happiness to everyone

Vision
Become the most dominant and best tasting QSR . . . . The most endearing brand that has ever been.
We will be within reach of every Filipino . . .
We will lead in product taste at all times
We will provide FSC excellence in every encounter . . . Happiness in every moment

Source: www.jollibee.com.ph, accessed July 2004.

EXHIBIT 4   Typical Jollibee Outlet in the Philippines

ous; and Cleanliness (C) from sidewalk to kitchen, from uniforms to utensils, must be maintained at all times.

The company recognized that maintaining high standards required that employees be committed to FSC. Jollibee Foods Corporation paid the highest compensation and benefits package in the Philippine fast foods industry. All employees underwent comprehensive training programs based on the underlying standards. In addition, managers received ongoing training in the latest operations systems and in people-management skills. Opportunities existed for qualified crew members to pursue a career path into management positions.

Marketing Strategy

JFC's marketing philosophy was based on being closer to Filipino families than its competitors. There was wide awareness that Jollibee was a local Filipino service business establishment that had captured the unique Filipino taste, so it appealed to patriotic or "pam-Pinoy" instincts. The chain also appealed to a broad cross-section of the population that felt comfortable and very much at home

in an environment where the crew talked to them in the local language, unlike other outlets where the crew spoke in English and where the atmosphere might be perceived by some as projecting an elitist appeal.

The Jollibee chain had tailored its marketing strategies to suit the Filipino culture and lifestyle. "What happens in the normal Filipino family is that weekends are reserved especially for children," noted a Filipino business analyst, "and parents try to ask their children where they want to eat." Jollibee appealed to children with in-store play activities and a cast of captivating characters. Its hamburger-headed Champ, complete with boxing gloves, went head-to-head against McDonald's Hamburglar. Industry observers reported that Jollibee's giant smiling red and yellow bee and a blond spaghetti-haired girl named Hetti (a mascot for Jollibee restaurants) were better known and loved in the Philippines than Ronald McDonald. Jollibee endeavored to maintain its dominance in the children's segment by promoting its Jolly Kiddie Meals and offering a choice of Regular Yum, Spaghetti Special or Chickenjoy. Having an advertising strategy that was deeply rooted in the traditional values of family, with a tinge of national pride, allowed Jollibee to position itself as the destination for family outings.

The DLSU Survey

A survey conducted by advertising management students from De La Salle University in Manila in mid-2004 contrasted Jollibee's value proposition against that of McDonald's operations in the Philippines (**Exhibit 5**) and revealed the main rational and emotional factors that drove Filipino consumers' choices in fast food restaurants.

Rational Attributes

Of the top ten rational attributes underlying selection of a fast food restaurant, the most significant, cited by 90 percent of respondents, was for it to be "affordable and/or cheap." Next came "faster service" (cited by 78 percent), followed by "accessibility," (70 percent). Other attributes mentioned were "tasty," "variety of food," "accommodating personnel," "delivery services," "promotional items are useful," "frequent and effective ads," and "offers seasonal products" (**Exhibit 6**). Among Jollibee's patrons, affordable/cheaper prices was ranked top, with 94 percent mentioning this attribute, followed by accessibility/many outlets (72 percent) and tastier (66 percent). However, only 44 percent of respondents cited "faster" as a desired attribute.

Emotional Attributes

For fast-foods in general, the three most dominant attributes were friendly atmosphere (76 percent), family-oriented *pampamilya* (74 percent), and hang out or *tambayan* (66 percent). (**Exhibit 7**). The other emotional attributes considered by respondents were mass appeal,

	VALUE PROPOSITION	
TARGET MARKET	JOLLIBEE FAMILIES & CHILDREN	MCDONALD'S FAMILIES & CHILDREN
Business Operations	To provide high quality food, fast and friendly service in a clean and comfortable environment.	To provide outstanding quality, service, cleanliness and value.
Menu	Tailored to the Filipino palate. E.g., peach-mango pie, meals with spaghetti or rice.	Standardized Fare E.g., meals with fries.*
Promotions	• Langhap Sarap Value Meals • Jolly Kiddie Meal (with premium items and toys) • *Eats for Free* purchase rewards program • Bestsellers Campaign (20 percent discounts on various combinations of the popular Langhap Sarap Value Meals)	• Extra Value Meal • Happy Meal (with premium items and toys)
No. of Stores in the Philippines (mid-2004)	472	241
Mode of International Expansion	Franchising	Franchising

*McDonald's subsequently bowed to the pressure of conforming to Filipino taste preferences by introducing menu items such as McSpaghetti and McDo, a heavily seasoned burger.

Source: DLSU student research project, 2004.

better environment for kids, patriotic or *pam-Pinoy* or *lasang Pinoy*, "brings you closer to home," "likeable Filipiso selections" or "putaheng Pinoy"/"sangkap Pinoy," "use of Filipino language" particularly by the service crew, and the use of "wholesome" or "cute" endorsers. Broadly similar ratings of these attributes were achieved for Jollibees, although "family-oriented" was ranked first and "friendly," second.

Organizational Structure

By concentrating on a country market with distinct preferences, Jollibee had been able to tailor its menu and marketing strategies to better reach and satisfy the customers. While global players like McDonald's and KFC chose to spread their resources among their fast-food chains worldwide, for many years Jollibee focused its efforts only in the Philippines. During the 1980s, when political instability hit the Philippines, McDonald's had to curtail its expansion process. Jollibee, on the other hand, continued with its strategic plans of expansion. By the time the country was back on track, Jollibee had already gained the upper hand in terms of store locations, thus leaving the global giant trailing behind.

The unique geographical structure of the Philippines with its many islands made it a challenging market for fast-food companies. Among all the fast-food chains competing in the Philippines, Jollibee was the only one that operated nationwide. In some locations, it faced no competition from other fast-food chains.

EXHIBIT 6   Rational Attributes Filipinos Look for in Fast-Food Restaurants/Jollibee

	FAST-FOOD MARKET OVERALL		JOLLIBEE	
RANK	ATTRIBUTE	PERCENT	ATTRIBUTE	PERCENT
1	Affordable/Cheaper	90	Affordable/Cheaper	94
2	Faster Service	78	Accessibility/Many outlets	72
3	Accessibility/"Maraming" (many) outlets	70	Tastier	66
4	Tastier	68	Frequent and Effective Ads	56
5	Variety of food chains	60	Variety of food chains	50
6	Accommodating personnel	34	Faster service	44
7	Delivery Services	42	Promotional items are useful	40
8	Promotional items are useful	38	Accommodating personnel	38
9	Frequent and effective ads	34	Delivery Services	38
10	Offers seasonal products	28	Offers seasonal products	36
	Total N = 50	100		100

Source: DLSU student research project, 2004.

EXHIBIT 7 Emotional Attributes Filipinos Look for in Fast-Foods/Jollibee

	FAST-FOOD MARKET				JOLLIBEE		
RANK	ATTRIBUTE	N	PERCENT	RANK	ATTRIBUTE	N	PERCENT
1	Friendly Atmosphere	38	76	1	Family togetherness ("Pampamilya")	39	78
2	Family togetherness ("Pampamilya")	37	74	2	Friendly atmosphere	32	64
3	Hang-out ("Tambayan")	33	66	3	Patriotic, "Pam-Pinoy," "Lasang Pinoy"	30	60
4	Mass Appeal	27	54	4	Mass Appeal	30	60
5	Better environment for kids	27	54	5	Likeable Filipino selections, "Putaheng Pinoy," "Sangkap Pinoy"	28	56
6	Patriotic ("Pam-Pinoy"/ "Lasang Pinoy")	22	44	6	Better environment for kids	28	56
7	Brings you closer to home selections	17	34	7	Use of Filipino language	20	40
8	Likeable Filipino selections ("Putaheng Pinoy"/ "Sangkap-Pinoy")	16	32	8	Wholesome/"cute" endorsers	13	26
9	Use of Filipino language	13	26	9	Hang-out/"Tambayan"	12	24
10	Wholesome/"cute" endorsers N:50	8	16	10	Brings you closer to home N:50	11	22

Source: DLSU student research project, 2004.

JFC's strategy included a focus on achieving operational efficiency in its commissary and hiring the right candidates to manage its operations and strategy planning. To meet the challenges of a more intensely competitive market and to manage business more effectively, the company had undertaken a major initiative in 2000 to re-align the structure of Jollibee Philippines, decentralizing the organization into four autonomous Regional Business Units (RBUs) that corresponded to the country's major geographic markets: Mega Manila, Luzon, South Luzon, and Visayas-Mindanao. This structure ensured a more manageable business size and span of control. Key support functions like human resources and administration, finance and network development were transferred to the RBUs for greater efficiency in the delivery of products and services, quicker coordination, and more timely decision-making.

The Head Office/Corporate Services functions (Marketing, Finance, Restaurant Systems, Engineering) were re-aligned as a Support Center to provide corporate-level direction and continuing assistance to the RBUs. Top management believed that the new structure had resulted in better execution of programs and renewed enthusiasm and commitment from JFC's managers and employees.

The continuing growth in the number of Jollibee, Chowking, and Greenwich restaurants obscured the fact that each year some stores were closed, either because they were underperforming or because they were being replaced by newer and larger stores in better locations. Over time, a higher percentage of stores were being operated by franchisees instead of company-owned.

INTERNATIONAL OPERATIONS

Building on its success in the Philippines, Jollibee turned its sights overseas. Initially, the company focused on reaching communities with a large Filipino population to capitalize on its brand awareness, targeting markets where there were substantial numbers of "OFWs" (Overseas Filipino Workers). By the early 1990s, Jollibee restaurants were operating in Hong Kong, Saipan and Guam (both islands in the NW Pacific), Vietnam, Brunei, Indonesia, Dubai, and Kuwait.

In 1998, the firm entered one of the most demanding fast-food markets in the world, the United States, which had at that time an estimated two million Filipino immigrants. But aside from Jollibee's popularity among Filipinos, the brand also sought to appeal to other ethnic groups in its U.S. outlets. Other immigrants from Asia came with their families to eat at Jollibee's. One African-American customer stated that the chicken is "excellent, almost like my mother's Southern fried chicken!" And white Americans enjoyed delicacies not offered by competitors, such as Peach Mango Pie.

The company's international expansion strategy focused on markets where management believed it "could successfully develop the Jollibee brand and put up the supply chain to support the critical mass of stores in these selected markets." In the U.S., the first state targeted was California, with plans to expand into Nevada, Hawaii, and New York in future years. By adopting a franchise mode in the U.S., JFC was able to draw on local capital and entrepreneurial drive. In 2001, the firm purchased a

EXHIBIT 8 Location of JFC Group Stores by Brand, June 2005

	JOLLIBEE	GREENWICH	CHOWKING	DÉLIFRANCE*	YONGHE KING	TOTAL
Philippines						
Co-owned	207	122	99	29	—	457
Franchised	301	106	211	4	—	622
Subtotal	508	228	310	33	—	1,079
Hong Kong	1	—	—	—	—	1
U.S.A.	10	—	8	—	—	18
China						
Co-owned	—	—	—	—	82	82
Franchised	—	—	—	—	6	6
Others	11	—	3	—	—	14
TOTAL	530	228	321	33	88	1,200

*JFC was a master franchisee for Délifrance, a French-owned franchise, in the Philippines but not in other countries.

majority interest in Tokyo Teriyaki House, a Japanese restaurant in California, with the objective of expanding into the Japanese QSR segment and developing it into another major chain; it renamed the restaurant Tomi's Teriyaki House.

The annual report for 2002 noted that the overseas stores were providing the company "the experience in the know-how that we need in gearing up to the realities of international competition and in reorienting ourselves to the global environment."

JFC had identified several markets in Asia for its expansion activities. In 2004, the company was looking at the possibility of expanding its three-store network in Vietnam. There were also plans to introduce the Chowking brand to Indonesia, responding to the growing market for Chinese food in that nation. Despite an earlier, unsuccessful experience operating a now-closed Jollibee's store in Xiamen, eastern China, JFC saw huge potential in the People's Republic. In March 2004, the company signed an agreement to purchase 85 percent ownership in the Shanghai-based Yonghe King chain, which offered Chinese style fast-food in ten cities. The number of Yonghe King stores grew from 77 at the end of 2003 to 89 by the end of the third quarter of 2004, by which point this brand accounted for 6 percent of JFC's system-wide sales and was more profitable than the domestic operation, which had been hit by rising costs. The strategy for Yonghe King was to open 20 new stores a year in each of the next three years, increasing to another 50 in year four and 100 additional stores in year five.

In May 2004, Mr. Ysmael V. Baysa, the company's chief finance officer, announced that during the first quarter of the year JFC had opened 21 new stores but closed 13, of which seven were in foreign locations. It closed all three Chowking stores in Dubai, one Jollibee store in the US, and shuttered its 3-store Tomi's Teriyaki operation in the US. Said Mr Baysa: "Tomi's Teriyaki business did not grow according to expectations. Its basic concept is sound, but there is still much work to be done to turn it into a strong brand. We are keeping the brand trademark and the recipes for possible future use. In the meantime, management is placing its priority on brand development of Yonghe King in China."

Over the course of the following 12 months, most of JFC's growth came from within the Philippines, led by the Jollibee and Chowking brands, both of which were dominated by franchisee-operated units (**Exhibit 8**). The number of Yonghe King stores in China had remained almost unchanged, but was expected to increase to over 100 stores by early 2006.

Summarizing the company's strategy, the chairman, Mr. Tan, noted:

> There are still major challenges to address to ensure the long-term soundness of the business—we have to improve our cost structure particularly in the support groups, we have to sustain positive growth in same store sales, and we have to win big in foreign operations if we are to become a truly World Class Business.

REFERENCES

[1]"Jollibee beats McDonald's at its own game," *PJI Journal*, www.journal.com.ph, accessed January 17, 2005.
Additional sources consulted for this case include: Jollibee Foods Corporation Website (www.jollibee.com.ph).

Christopher A. Bartlett and Sumantra Ghoshal, "Going Global: Lessons from Late Movers," *Harvard Business Review* 78 (March–April 2001) 132–145.

STUDY QUESTIONS

1. Evaluate Jollibee Food Corporation's performance in the Philippines. What are the secrets of its success in terms of marketing, operations, and human resource strategies?

2. In what ways does JFC's strategy of adding new brands leverage or dilute the strengths of the original Jollibee concept?

3. What rational and emotional attributes do you look for in a fast-food restaurant? Do these attributes fit your favorite food establishment in your country?

4. Evaluate JFC's performance overseas. To what extent can the company transfer its core competency to its international operations? Should it modify its consumer-driven strategies to suit foreign markets, even if that means Jollibee becomes much less 'Philippine' in nature?

5. Should Jollibee continue in its efforts to go international or concentrate on expanding and consolidating its foothold in the Philippines only? Why?

Case 8   *The Accra Beach Hotel*

Block Booking of Capacity During a Peak Period

SHERYL KIMES, JOCHEN WIRTZ,
AND CHRISTOPHER LOVELOCK

The sales manager for a Caribbean hotel wonders whether to accept a large block booking at a discount rate from a group participating in an international sporting event. Do the promised publicity benefits justify the risk of turning away guests from higher-paying segments?

Cherita Howard, sales manager for the Accra Beach Hotel, a 141-room hotel on the Caribbean island of Barbados, was debating what to do about a request from the West Indies Cricket Board. The Board wanted to book a large block of rooms more than six months ahead during several of the hotel's busiest times and was asking for a discount. In return, it promised to promote the Accra Beach in all advertising materials and television broadcasts as the host hotel for the upcoming West Indies Cricket Series, an important international sporting event.

THE HOTEL

The Accra Beach Hotel and Resort had a prime beach-front location on the south coast of Barbados, just a short distance from the airport and the capital city of Bridgetown. Located on 3½ acres (1.4 ha) of tropical landscape and fronting one of the best beaches on Barbados, the hotel featured rooms offering panoramic views of the ocean, pool or island.

The centerpiece of its lush gardens was the large swimming pool, which had a shallow bank for lounging plus a swim-up bar. In addition, there was a squash court and a fully equipped gym. Golf was also available only 15 minutes away at the Barbados Golf Club, with which the hotel was affiliated.

The Accra Beach had two restaurants and two bars, as well as extensive banquet and conference facilities. It offered state-of-the-art conference facilities to local, regional and international corporate clientele and had hosted a number of summits in recent years. Three conference rooms, which could be configured in a number of ways, served as the setting for large corporate meetings, training seminars, product displays, dinners, and wedding receptions. A business center provided guests with Internet access, faxing capabilities, and photocopying services.

The hotel's 122 standard rooms were categorized into three groups—Island View, Pool View, and Ocean View—and there were also 13 Island View Junior Suites, and 6 Penthouse Suites, each decorated in tropical pastel prints and handcrafted furniture. All rooms were equipped with cable/satellite TV, air-conditioning, ceiling fans, hairdryer, coffee percolator, direct-dial telephone, bathtub/shower and a balcony.

Standard rooms were configured with either a king-size bed or two twin beds in the Island and Ocean View

categories, while the Pool Views had two double beds. The six Penthouse Suites, which all offered ocean views, contained all the features listed for the standard rooms plus added comforts. They were built on two levels, featuring a living room with a bar area on the third floor of the hotel and a bedroom accessed by an internal stairway on the fourth floor. These suites also had a bathroom containing a Jacuzzi, shower stall, double vanity basin and a skylight.

The thirteen Junior Suites were fitted with either a double bed or two twin beds, plus a living room area with a sofa that converted to another bed.

HOTEL PERFORMANCE

The Accra Beach enjoyed a relatively high occupancy rate, with the highest occupancy achieved from January through March and the lowest generally during the summer (**Exhibit 1**). The hotel's average room rates followed a similar pattern, with the highest rates (US$150–$170) being achieved from December through March but relatively low rates (US $120) during the summer months (**Exhibit 2**). The hotel's RevPAR (revenue per available room—a product of the occupancy rate times the average room rate) showed even more variation, with RevPARs exceeding $140 from January through March but falling

EXHIBIT 1 Accra Beach Hotel: Monthly Occupancy Rate

YEAR	MONTH	OCCUPANCY
2 Years Ago	January	87.7%
2 Years Ago	February	94.1%
2 Years Ago	March	91.9%
2 Years Ago	April	78.7%
2 Years Ago	May	76.7%
2 Years Ago	June	70.7%
2 Years Ago	July	82.0%
2 Years Ago	August	84.9%
2 Years Ago	September	64.7%
2 Years Ago	October	82.0%
2 Years Ago	November	83.8%
2 Years Ago	December	66.1%
Last Year	January	87.6%
Last Year	February	88.8%
Last Year	March	90.3%
Last Year	April	82.0%
Last Year	May	74.7%
Last Year	June	69.1%
Last Year	July	76.7%
Last Year	August	70.5%
Last Year	September	64.7%
Last Year	October	71.3%
Last Year	November	81.7%
Last Year	December	72.1%

EXHIBIT 2 Accra Beach Hotel: Average Daily Room Rate (ADR)

YEAR	MONTH	AVERAGE DAILY ROOM RATE (ADR) (IN US$)
2 Years Ago	January	$159.05
2 Years Ago	February	$153.73
2 Years Ago	March	$157.00
2 Years Ago	April	$153.70
2 Years Ago	May	$144.00
2 Years Ago	June	$136.69
2 Years Ago	July	$122.13
2 Years Ago	August	$121.03
2 Years Ago	September	$123.45
2 Years Ago	October	$129.03
2 Years Ago	November	$141.03
2 Years Ago	December	$152.87
Last Year	January	$162.04
Last Year	February	$167.50
Last Year	March	$158.44
Last Year	April	$150.15
Last Year	May	$141.79
Last Year	June	$136.46
Last Year	July	$128.49
Last Year	August	$128.49
Last Year	September	$127.11
Last Year	October	$132.76
Last Year	November	$141.86
Last Year	December	$151.59

Note: Average daily room rate (ADR) is inclusive of VAT.

EXHIBIT 3 Accra Beach Hotel: Revenue per Available Room (RevPAR)

YEAR	MONTH	REVENUE PER AVAILABLE ROOM (IN US$)
2 Years Ago	January	$139.49
2 Years Ago	February	$144.66
2 Years Ago	March	$144.28
2 Years Ago	April	$120.96
2 Years Ago	May	$110.45
2 Years Ago	June	$96.64
2 Years Ago	July	$100.15
2 Years Ago	August	$102.75
2 Years Ago	September	$79.87
2 Years Ago	October	$105.80
2 Years Ago	November	$118.18
2 Years Ago	December	$101.05
Last Year	January	$141.90
Last Year	February	$148.67
Last Year	March	$143.02
Last Year	April	$123.12
Last Year	May	$105.87
Last Year	June	$94.23
Last Year	July	$98.55
Last Year	August	$90.59
Last Year	September	$82.24
Last Year	October	$94.62
Last Year	November	$115.89
Last Year	December	$109.24

Note: RevPAR refers to revenue per available room and is computed by multiplying the room occupancy rate (see **Exhibit 1**) with the average room rate (**Exhibit 2**). Revenue per available room is inclusive of VAT.

to less than $100 from June through October (**Exhibit 3**). The rates on the Penthouse suites ranged from $310 to $395, while those on the junior suites ranged from $195 to $235. Guests had to pay Barbados value-added tax (VAT) of 7.5 percent on room charges and 15 percent on meals.

The Accra Beach had traditionally promoted itself as a resort destination, but in the last few years, it had been promoting its convenient location and had attracted many business customers. Cherita worked extensively with tour operators and corporate travel managers. The majority of hotel guests were corporate clients from companies such as Barbados Cable & Wireless, and the Caribbean International Banking Corporation (**Exhibit 4**). The composition of hotel guests had changed drastically over the past few years. Traditionally, the hotel's clientele had been dominated by tourists from the UK and Canada, but during the past few years, the percentage of corporate customers had increased dramatically. The majority of corporate customers come for business meetings with local companies.

Sometimes, guests who were on vacation (particularly during the winter months) felt uncomfortable finding themselves surrounded by business people. As one vacationer put it, "There's just something weird about being on vacation and going to the beach and then seeing suit-clad business people chatting on their cell phones." However, the hotel achieved a higher average room rate from business guests than vacationers and management had found the volume of corporate business to be much more stable than that from tour operators and individual guests.

EXHIBIT 4   Accra Beach Hotel: Market Segments 2002

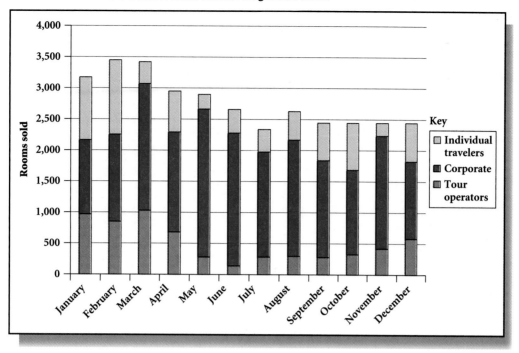

THE WEST INDIES CRICKET BOARD

Cherita Howard, the hotel's sales manager, had been approached by the West Indies Cricket Board (WICB) about the possibility of the Accra Beach Hotel serving as the host hotel for the following spring's West Indies Cricket Home Series, an important international sporting event among cricket-loving nations. The location of this event rotated among several different Caribbean nations and Barbados would be hosting the next one, which would feature visiting teams from India and New Zealand.

Cherita and Jon Martineau, general manager of the hotel, both thought that the marketing exposure associated with hosting the teams would be very beneficial for the hotel but were concerned about accepting the business because they knew from past experience that many of the desired dates were usually very busy days for the hotel. They were sure that the rate that the WICB was willing to pay would be lower than the average rate of US$140–$150 (including VAT) they normally achieved during these times. In contrast to regular guests, who could usually be counted upon to have a number of meals at the hotel, team members and officials would probably be less likely to dine at the hotel because they would be on a per diem budget. On average, both corporate customers and vacationers spent $8 per person for breakfast and $25 per person for dinner (per person, including VAT). The margin on food and beverage was approximately 30%. About 80% of all guests had breakfast at the hotel and approximately 30% of all guests dined at the hotel (there were many other attractive restaurant options nearby). Jon Martineau thought that only about 25% of the cricket group would have breakfast at the hotel and maybe only about 10% would dine at the hotel. Also, they worried about how the hotel's other guests might react to the presence of the cricket teams. Still, the marketing potential for the hotel was substantial. The WICB had promised to list the Accra Beach as the host hotel in all promotional materials and during the televised matches.

The West Indies Home Series was divided into three parts, and each would require bookings at the Accra Beach Hotel. The first part pitted the West Indies team against the Indian team and would run from April 24 to May 7. The second part featured the same two teams and would run from May 27 to May 30. The final part showcased the West Indies against New Zealand and would run from June 17 to June 26.

The WICB wanted 50 rooms (including two suites at no additional cost) for the duration of each part and was willing to pay US$130 per night per room. Both breakfast and VAT (value-added tax) were included in this price and each team had to be housed on a single floor of the hotel. In addition, the WICB insisted that laundry service for team uniforms (cricket teams typically wear all-white clothing) and practice gear be provided at no additional charge for all team members. Cherita estimated that it would cost the hotel about $20 per day if they could do the laundry in-house, but about $200 per day if they had to send it to an outside source.

Cherita called Ferne Armstrong, the Reservations Manager of the hotel, and asked her what she thought. Like Cherita, Ferne was concerned about the possible displacement of higher-paying customers, but offered to do further investigation into the expected room sales and

EXHIBIT 5   Room Sales and Average Daily Room Rates for Same Periods in Previous Year

DATE OF WICB HOME SERIES	ROOMS SOLD IN LAST YEAR DURING THE SAME PERIOD	AVERAGE DAILY ROOM RATE (ADR) IN US$
Part I		
4/24	141	$138.68
4/25	138	$129.00
4/26	135	$137.60
4/27	134	$145.13
4/28	123	$142.98
4/29	128	$133.30
4/30	141	$127.93
5/1	141	$133.30
5/2	141	$103.08
5/3	139	$131.15
5/4	112	$126.85
5/5	78	$135.45
5/6	95	$139.75
5/7	113	$148.35
Part II		
5/27	99	$140.83
5/28	114	$141.90
5/29	114	$146.20
5/30	125	$146.20
Part III		
6/17	124	$134.38
6/18	119	$131.15
6/19	112	$135.45
6/20	119	$119.33
6/21	125	$118.25
6/22	116	$112.88
6/23	130	$113.95
6/24	141	$108.58
6/25	141	$118.25
6/26	125	$123.63

Note: ADR includes VAT of 7.5 percent.

associated room rates for the desired dates. Since the dates were over six months in the future, Ferne had not yet developed forecasts. But she was able to provide data on room sales and average room rates from the same days of the previous year (**Exhibit 5**).

Soon after Cherita returned to her office to analyze the data, she was interrupted by a phone call from the head of the WICB wanting to know the status of his request. She promised to have an answer for him before the end of the day. As soon as she hung up, Jon Martineau called and chatted about the huge marketing potential of being the host hotel.

Cherita shook her head and wondered, "What should I do?"

STUDY QUESTIONS

1. *What factors lead to variations in demand for rooms at a hotel such as the Accra Beach?*
2. *Identify the various market segments currently served by the hotel. What are the pros and cons of seeking to serve customers from several segments?*
3. *What are the key considerations facing the hotel as it reviews the booking requests from the West Indies Cricket Board?*
4. *What action should Cherita Howard take and why?*

Case 9   *Sullivan Ford Auto World*

CHRISTOPHER LOVELOCK

A young health care manager unexpectedly finds herself running a family-owned car dealership that is in financial trouble. She is very concerned about the poor performance of the service department and wonders whether a turnaround is possible.

Viewed from Wilson Avenue, the dealership presented a festive sight. Flags waved and strings of triangular pennants in red, white, and blue fluttered gaily in the late afternoon breeze. Rows of new-model cars and trucks gleamed and winked in the sunlight. Geraniums graced the flowerbeds outside the showroom entrance. A huge rotating sign at the corner of Wilson Avenue and Route 78 sported the Ford logo and identified the business as Sullivan Ford Auto World. Banners below urged "Let's Make a Deal!"

Inside the handsome, high-ceilinged showroom, four of the new model Fords were on display—a silver Escape hybrid SUV, a blue Mustang convertible, a black Five Hundred sedan, and a red Ranger pickup truck. Each vehicle was polished to a high sheen. Two groups of customers were chatting with salespeople, and a middle-aged man sat in the driver's seat of the Mustang, studying the controls.

Upstairs in the comfortably furnished general manager's office, Carol Sullivan-Diaz finished running another spreadsheet analysis on her laptop. She felt tired and depressed. Her father, Walter Sullivan, had died four weeks earlier at the age of 56 of a sudden heart attack. As executor of his estate, the bank had asked her to temporarily assume the position of general manager of the dealership. The only visible change that she had made to her father's office was installing an all-in-one laser printer, scanner, copier, and fax, but she had been very busy analyzing the current position of the business.

Sullivan-Diaz did not like the look of the numbers on the printout. Auto World's financial situation had been deteriorating for 18 months, and it had been running in the red for the first half of the current year. New car sales had declined, dampened in part by rising interest rates. Margins had been squeezed by promotions and other efforts to move new cars off the lot. Reflecting rising fuel prices, industry forecasts of future sales were discouraging, and so were her own financial projections for Auto World's sales department. Service revenues, which were below average for a dealership of this size, had also declined, although the service department still made a small surplus.

Had she had made a mistake last week, Carol wondered, in turning down Bill Froelich's offer to buy the business? Admittedly, the amount was substantially below the offer from Froelich that her father had rejected two years earlier, but the business had been more profitable then.

THE SULLIVAN FAMILY

Walter Sullivan had purchased a small Ford dealership in 1983, renaming it Sullivan's Auto World, and had built it up to become one of the best known in the metropolitan area. In 1999, he had borrowed heavily to purchase the current site at a major suburban highway intersection, in an area of town with many new housing developments.

There had been a dealership on the site, but the buildings were 30 years old. Sullivan had retained the service and repair bays, but torn down the showroom in front of them, and replaced it by an attractive modern facility. On moving to the new location, which was substantially larger than the old one, he had renamed his business Sullivan Ford Auto World.

Everybody had seemed to know Walt Sullivan. He had been a consummate showman and entrepreneur, appearing in his own radio and television commercials and active in community affairs. His approach to car sales had emphasized promotions, discounts, and deals in order to maintain volume. He was never happier than when making a sale.

Carol Sullivan-Diaz, aged 28, was the eldest of Walter and Carmen Sullivan's three daughters. After obtaining a bachelor's degree in economics, she had gone on to take an MBA degree and had then embarked on a career in health care management. She was married to Dr. Roberto Diaz, a surgeon at St. Luke's Hospital. Her 20-year old twin sisters, Gail and Joanne, who were students at the state university, lived with their mother.

In her own student days, Sullivan-Diaz had worked part-time in her father's business on secretarial and bookkeeping tasks, and also as a service writer in the service department; so she was quite familiar with the operations of the dealership. At business school, she had decided on a career in health care management. After graduation, she had worked as an executive assistant to the president of St. Luke's, a large teaching hospital. Two years later, she joined Metropolitan Health Plan as assistant director of marketing, a position she had now held for almost three years. Her responsibilities included attracting new members, complaint handling, market research, and member retention programs.

Carol's employer had given her a six-week leave of absence to put her father's affairs in order. She doubted that she could extend that leave much beyond the two weeks still remaining. Neither she nor other family members were interested in making a career of running the dealership. However, she was prepared to take time out from her health care career to work on a turnaround if that seemed a viable proposition. She had been successful in her present job and believed it would not be difficult to find another health management position in the future.

THE DEALERSHIP

Like other car dealerships, Sullivan Ford Auto World operated both sales and service departments, often referred to in the trade as "front end" and "back end," respectively. Both new and used vehicles were sold, since a high proportion of new car and van purchases involved trading in the purchaser's existing vehicle. Auto World would also buy well-maintained used cars at auction for resale. Purchasers who decided that they could not afford a new car would often buy a "preowned" vehicle instead, while shoppers who came in looking for a used car could sometimes be persuaded to buy a new one. Before being put on sale, used vehicles were carefully serviced, with parts being replaced as needed. They were then thoroughly cleaned by a detailer whose services were hired as needed. Dents and other blemishes were removed at a nearby body shop and occasionally the vehicle's paintwork was resprayed, too.

The front end of the dealership employed a sales manager, seven salespeople, an office manager, and a secretary. One of the salespeople had given notice and would be leaving at the end of the following week. The service department, when fully staffed, consisted of a service manager, a parts supervisor, nine mechanics, and two service writers. The Sullivan twins often worked part-time as service writers, filling in at busy periods, when one of the other writers was sick or on vacation, or when—as currently—there was an unfilled vacancy. The job entailed scheduling appointments for repairs and maintenance, writing up each work order, calling customers with repair estimates, and assisting customers when they returned to pick up the cars and pay for the work that had been done.

Sullivan-Diaz knew from her own experience as a service writer that it could be a stressful job. Few people liked to be without their car, even for a day. When a car broke down or was having problems, the owner was often nervous about how long it would take to get it fixed and, if the warranty had expired, how much the labor and parts would cost. Customers were quite unforgiving when a problem was not fixed completely on the first attempt and they had to return their vehicle for further work.

Major mechanical failures were not usually difficult to repair, although the parts replacement costs might be expensive. It was often the "little" things like water leaks and wiring problems that were the hardest to diagnose and correct, and it might be necessary for the customer to return two or three times before such a problem was resolved. In these situations, parts and materials costs were relatively low, but labor costs mounted up quickly, being charged out at $45 an hour. Customers could sometimes be quite abusive, yelling at service writers over the phone or arguing with service writers, mechanics, and the service manager in person.

Turnover in the service writer job was high, which was one reason why Carol—and more recently her sisters—had often been pressed into service by their father to "hold the fort" as he described it. More than once, she had seen an exasperated service writer respond sharply to a complaining customer or hang up on one who was being abusive over the telephone. Gail and Joanne were currently taking turns to cover the vacant position, but there were times when both of them had classes and the dealership had only one service writer on duty.

By national standards, Sullivan Ford Auto World stood toward the lower end of medium-sized dealerships, selling around 1,100 cars a year, equally divided between new and used vehicles. In the most recent year, its revenues totaled $26.6 million from new and used car sales and $2.9 million from service and parts—down from $30.5 million and $3.6 million, respectively, in the previous year. Although the unit value of car sales was high, the margins were quite low, with margins for new cars being substantially lower than for used ones. Industry guidelines suggested that the contribution margin (known as the departmental selling gross) from car sales should be about 5.5 percent of sales revenues, and from service, around 25 percent of revenues. In a typical dealership, 60 percent of the selling gross had traditionally come from sales and 40 percent from service, but the balance was shifting from sales to service. The selling gross was then applied to fixed expenses, such as administrative salaries, rent or mortgage payments, and utilities.

For the most recent 12 months at Auto World, Sullivan-Diaz had determined that the selling gross figures were 4.6 percent and 24 percent, respectively, both of them lower than in the previous year and insufficient to cover the dealership's fixed expenses. Her father had made no mention of financial difficulties and she had been shocked to learn from the bank after his death that Auto World had been two months behind in mortgage payments on the property. Further analysis showed that accounts payable had risen sharply in the previous six months. Fortunately, the dealership held a large insurance policy on Sullivan's life, and the proceeds from this had been more than sufficient to bring mortgage payments up to date, pay down all overdue accounts, and leave some funds for future contingencies.

OUTLOOK

The opportunities for expanding new car sales did not appear promising, given declining consumer confidence and recent layoffs at several local plants that were expected to hurt the local economy. However, promotional incentives had reduced the inventory to manageable levels. From discussions with Larry Winters, Auto World's sales manager, Sullivan-Diaz had concluded that costs could be cut by not replacing the departing sales rep, maintaining inventory at its current reduced level, and trying to make more efficient use of advertising and promotion. Although Winters did not have Walter's exuberant personality, he had been Auto World's leading sales rep before being promoted, and had shown strong managerial capabilities in his current position.

As she reviewed the figures for the service department, Sullivan-Diaz wondered what potential might exist for improving its sales volume and selling gross. Her father had never been very interested in the parts and service business, seeing it simply as a necessary adjunct of the dealership. "Customers always seem to be miserable back there," he had once remarked to her. "But here in the front end, everybody's happy when someone buys a new car." The service facility was not easily visible from the main highway, being hidden behind the showroom. Although the building looked old and greasy, the equipment itself was modern and well maintained. There was sufficient capacity to handle more repair work, but a higher volume would require hiring one or more new mechanics.

Customers were required to bring cars in for servicing before 8:30 A.M. After parking their cars, customers entered the service building by a side door and waited their turn to see the service writers, who occupied a cramped room with peeling paint and an interior window overlooking the service bays. Customers stood while work orders for their cars were prepared. Ringing telephones frequently interrupted the process. Filing cabinets containing customer records and other documents lined the far wall of the room.

If the work were of a routine nature, such as an oil change or tune up, the customer was given an estimate immediately. For more complex jobs, they would be called with an estimate later in the morning once the car had been examined. Customers were required to pick up their cars by 6:00 P.M. on the day the work was completed. On several occasions, Carol had urged her father to computerize the service work order process, but he had never acted on her suggestions, so all orders continued to be handwritten on large yellow sheets, with carbon copies below.

The service manager, Rick Obert, who was in his late forties, had held the position since Auto World opened at its current location. The Sullivan family considered him to be technically skilled, and he managed the mechanics effectively. However, his manner with customers could be gruff and argumentative.

CUSTOMER SURVEY RESULTS

Another set of data that Sullivan-Diaz had studied carefully were the results of the customer satisfaction surveys that were mailed to the dealership monthly by a research firm retained by the Ford Motor Company.

Purchasers of all new Ford cars were sent a questionnaire by mail within 30 days of making the purchase and asked to use a five-point scale to rate their satisfaction with the dealership sales department, vehicle preparation, and the characteristics of the vehicle itself. The questionnaire asked how likely the purchaser would be to recommend the dealership, the salesperson, and the manufacturer to someone else. Other questions asked if the customers had been introduced to the dealer's service department and been given explanations on what to do if their cars needed service. Finally, there were some classification questions relating to customer demographics.

A second survey was sent to new car purchasers nine months after they had bought their cars. This questionnaire began by asking about satisfaction with the vehicle and then asked customers if they had taken their vehicles to the selling dealer for service of any kind. If so, respondents were then asked to rate the service department on 14 different attributes—ranging from the attitudes of service personnel to the quality of the work performed—and then to rate their overall satisfaction with service from the dealer.

Customers were also asked about where they would go in the future for maintenance service, minor mechanical and electrical repairs, major repairs in those same categories, and bodywork. The options listed for service were selling dealer, another Ford dealer, "some other place," or "do-it-yourself." Finally, there were questions about overall satisfaction with the dealer sales department and the dealership in general, as well as the likelihood of their purchasing another Ford Motor Company product and buying it from the same dealership.

Dealers received monthly reports summarizing customer ratings of their dealership for the most recent month and for several previous months. To provide a comparison with how other Ford dealerships performed, the reports also included regional and national rating averages. After analysis, completed questionnaires were returned to the dealership; since these included each customer's name, a dealer could see which customers were satisfied and which were not.

In the 30-day survey of new purchasers, Auto World achieved better than average ratings on most dimensions. One finding which puzzled Carol was that almost 90 percent of respondents answered "yes" when asked if someone from Auto World had explained what to do if they needed service, but less than a third said that they had been introduced to someone in the service department. She resolved to ask Larry Winters about this discrepancy.

The nine-month survey findings disturbed her. Although vehicle ratings were in line with national averages, the overall level of satisfaction with service at Auto World was consistently low, placing it in the bottom 25 percent of all Ford dealerships.

The worst ratings for service concerned promptness of writing up orders, convenience of scheduling the work, convenience of service hours, and appearance of the service department. On length of time to complete the work, availability of needed parts, and quality of work done ("was it fixed right?"), Auto World's rating was close to the average. For interpersonal variables such as attitude of service department personnel, politeness, understanding of customer problems, and explanation of work performed, its ratings were relatively poor.

When Sullivan-Diaz reviewed the individual questionnaires, she found that there was a wide degree of variation between customers' responses on these interpersonal variables, ranging all the way across a 5-point scale from "completely satisfied" to "very dissatisfied." Curious, she had gone to the service files and examined the records for several dozen customers who had recently completed the nine-month surveys. At least part of the ratings could be explained by which service writers the customer had dealt with. Those who had been served two or more times by her sisters, for instance, gave much better ratings than those who had dealt primarily with Jim Fiskell, the service writer who had recently quit.

Perhaps the most worrying responses were those relating to customers' likely use of Auto World's service department in the future. More than half indicated that they would use another Ford dealer or "some other place" for maintenance service (such as oil change, lubrication, or tune-up) or for minor mechanical and electrical repairs. About 30 percent would use another source for major repairs. The rating for overall satisfaction with the selling dealer after nine months was below average and the customer's likelihood of purchasing from the same dealership again was a full point below that of buying another Ford product.

OPTIONS

Sullivan-Diaz pushed aside the spreadsheets she had printed out and shut down her laptop. It was time to go home for dinner. She saw the options for the dealership as basically twofold: either prepare the business for an early sale at what would amount to a distress price, or take a year or two to try to turn it around financially. In the latter instance, if the turnaround succeeded, the business could subsequently be sold at a higher price than it presently commanded, or the family could install a general manager to run the dealership for them.

Bill Froelich, owner of another nearby dealership plus three more in nearby cities, had offered to buy Auto World for a price that represented a fair valuation of the net assets, according to Auto World's accountants, plus $250,000 in goodwill. However, the rule of thumb when the auto industry was enjoying good times was that goodwill should be valued at $1,200 per vehicle sold each year. Carol knew that Froelich was eager to develop a network of dealerships in order to achieve economies of scale. His prices on new cars were very competitive and his nearest dealership clustered several franchises—Ford, Lincoln-Mercury, Volvo, and Jaguar—on a single large property.

AN UNWELCOME DISTURBANCE

As Carol left her office, she spotted the sales manager coming up the stairs leading from the showroom floor. "Larry," she said, "I've got a question for you."

"Fire away!" replied the sales manager.

"I've been looking at the customer satisfaction surveys. Why aren't our sales reps introducing new customers to the folks in the Service Department? It's supposedly part of our sales protocol, but it only seems to be happening about one-third of the time!"

Larry Winters shuffled his feet. "Well, Carol, basically I leave it to their discretion. We tell them about service, of course, but some of the folks on the floor feel a bit uncomfortable taking people over to the service bays after they've been in here. It's quite a contrast, if you know what I mean."

Suddenly, the sound of shouting arose from the floor below. A man of about 40, wearing a windbreaker and jeans, was standing in the doorway yelling at one of the salespeople. The two managers could catch snatches of what he was saying, in between various obscenities:

". . . three visits. . . still not fixed right. . . service stinks. . . who's in charge here?" Everybody else in the showroom had stopped what they were doing and had turned to look at the newcomer.

Winters looked at his young employer and rolled his eyes. "If there was something your dad couldn't stand, it was guys like that, yelling and screaming in the showroom and asking for the boss. Walt would go hide out in his office! Don't worry, Tom'll take care of that fellow and get him out of here. What a jerk!"

"No," said Sullivan-Diaz, firmly. "I'll deal with him! One thing I learned when I worked at St. Luke's was that you don't let people yell about their problems in front of everybody else. You take them off somewhere, calm them down, and find out what's bugging them."

She stepped quickly down the stairs, wondering to herself, "What else have I learned in health care that I can apply to this business?"

EXHIBIT 1   CompuMentor Mission Statement

"Many organizations are serving the needs of low-income, underserved populations and creating positive social change. We believe these organizations could have even greater impact through the appropriate use of technology. This requires access to technology—resources, tools, and information—as well as assistance with planning and implementation. Every day, through our broad range of technology programs, we're working behind the scenes to provide this kind of support.

'Appropriate' Technology
We believe technology solutions must be appropriate for each organization. The solution must fill the technology need. But the organization must also be able to afford it, manage it themselves, and sustain it over time.

Our broad range of services is designed with this in mind. Organizations can choose the type of assistance that's appropriate for them at any given time. Our hands-on consulting services provide deeper, project-based assistance typically for a fee. With our online resources, all found on TechSoup.org, nonprofits help themselves to ready answers, information, and tools like software and worksheets. Organizations can use both forms of assistance together, as they move through their technology lifecycle.

Our Staff
A key to CompuMentor's success is its unique staff. We hire individuals with highly developed technical and organizational skills who want to devote these skills to public service. To attract and retain staff, CompuMentor is committed to maintaining an equitable, actively collaborative internal environment, emphasizing fair compensation, continual learning and skill enhancement."

---

expenses budgeted at $8.19 million, up from revenues of $4.85 million and expenses of $4.60 million in FY 2002. Historically, the principal sources of revenue had been grant and foundation support, software handling, and IT consulting services, but earned income from DiscounTech was expected to assume increasing significance.

TechSoup

In 2000, CompuMentor launched TechSoup to leverage its 13 years of technology assistance experience. TechSoup created an IT information portal and online community where nonprofits could read about and discuss technology issues relevant to their own operations at no charge. It provided unbiased product information, reviews, tools, checklists, and resources to a community of more than one million nonprofit technology users. TechSoup also provided customers with its weekly e-newsletter, *By the Cup*. To build this community, it even featured actual soup recipes submitted by users. During each of its first two years, TechSoup was ranked number one by the British organization IT for Charities who declared, "If you want to find out about IT information or resources for charities, then this is the place to go on the Web."

Technology Product Philanthropy

Ben-Horin believed that technology product philanthropy—offering hardware and software free or at deeply discounted prices—was the key to helping nonprofits capitalize on the use of technology in their operations. Although many technology companies donated products to nonprofits, they often found that running in-house product donation programs was costly and difficult. Similarly, many nonprofits had found the process of obtaining donations directly from companies to be time-consuming and awkward.

Several factors made it hard for nonprofits to obtain technology products through traditional product donation programs. A nonprofit would need to:

- Understand that it needed a technology product/service.
- Determine that the only way to meet this need was via a donation or negotiated discount.
- Identify which firms offered this option.
- Request an application to the donation program.
- Meet the requirements and complete the application forms—usually comprising dozens of paper pages, supported by numerous copies of required documentation.
- Perform each of these tasks for each vendor of each product.

As a result, the application process for donated products could take anywhere from weeks to months, during which time the nonprofit would have no idea of the status of its request. These difficulties were compounded by the fact that each item was donated separately and there were few if any consolidated product offerings available for nonprofit technology customers.

This situation gave Ben-Horin and executive director Phil Ferrante-Roseberry the idea of creating a subsidiary organization that would generate income for CompuMentor by providing a distribution channel for technology suppliers to donate their products to nonprofits simply and inexpensively, while simultaneously providing nonprofits with easy access to a both a consolidated array of related products and adequate support services. This new earned-income venture, launched in January 2002, was named DiscounTech.

Ben-Horin and Ferrante-Roseberry were pleased with DiscounTech's progress and ambitious for its future financial success. They had emphasized to Masisak and the board the importance of generating a growing and dependable level of earned income that would enable CompuMentor to expand, thereby insulating it from the risk of cutbacks in grants and foundation support.

THE NONPROFIT MARKET

There were more than 1.6 million nonprofit corporations across the United States, collectively employing some 10.6 million paid employees. Nonprofits contributed 6.7% of the U.S. gross domestic product, ahead of banking, technology, and the federal government. Independent Sector estimated that 82,000 new entities were formed each year. Although the nonprofit market was growing at an annual rate in excess of 5%, faster than the 3.1% rate of the gross domestic product, it represented one of the largest underserved business markets in the United States.

The nonprofit market could be segmented by budget size, sub-sector, and geography. Based on data from GuideStar, the national database of nonprofit organizations, nonprofits could be grouped by size of budget into three segments. Some 92% had annual budgets of less than $1 million, 5.7% had budgets from $1 million to $5 million, and only 1.9% had budgets in excess of $5 million. According to a survey of one million IRS-recognized nonprofit organizations, four sub-sectors—Human services, education, public/societal, and health services—encompassed 41.3% of all nonprofits. Finally, there were two forms of geographic segmentation, by region and by type of location, such as urban or rural. The states with the most nonprofits included California, Texas, Illinois, Michigan, Ohio, Pennsylvania and New York.

Research suggested that most nonprofits were wired, willing, and ready to adopt information technology. Some 77% of nonprofits in the field of human services provided Internet access to their staffs and 80% of their executives saw information technology as a timesaving and production-enhancing tool. However, nonprofits were constrained by funding, limited time, and lack of expertise when it came to making technology-related decisions. Factors influencing the extent and selection of their technology purchases often reflected the number of technology-dedicated staff, the nature of the existing technology infrastructure, and where the organization stood in its technology lifecycle.

Nonprofit Ventures in the United States

Because the income derived from programmatic activities rarely covered the full costs of running such organizations, nonprofits were forced to rely on funding from donors and grantors, including corporations, government entities, foundations, or individuals. In recent years, there had been growing interest among nonprofits categorized as tax-exempt under Section 501(c)(3) of the Internal Revenue Code (**Exhibit 2**) in creating "nonprofit ventures," defined

EXHIBIT 2   Internal Revenue Code Section 501(c)(3)

Corporations, and any community chest, fund, or foundation, organized and operated exclusively for religious, charitable, scientific, testing for public safety, literary, or educational purposes, or to foster national or international amateur sports competition (but only if no part of its activities involve the provision of athletic facilities or equipment), or for the prevention of cruelty to children or animals, no part of the net earnings of which inures to the benefit of any private shareholder or individual, no substantial part of the activities of which is carrying on propaganda, or otherwise attempting, to influence legislation (except as otherwise provided in subsection (h)), and which does not participate in, or intervene in (including the publishing or distributing of statements), any political campaign on behalf of (or in opposition to) any candidate for public office.

as for-profit subsidiary businesses that would serve as additional sources of earned income. This income stream was seen as particularly attractive because it could be used to cross-subsidize the social mission of the organization without the restrictions commonly attached to grants and donations.

There were two broad types of ventures: commercial and semi-commercial. In both instances, organizations had to pay income taxes on ventures unrelated to the nonprofit mission. A *commercial venture* was defined as one that could survive based solely on profit-making criteria, such as a restaurant run by an art museum. Although it might enhance the visitor experience, the restaurant did not contribute directly to the institutional mission of exposing the public to the visual arts. However, its after-tax profits could be used to help fund museum activities. A *semi-commercial venture* might earn profits but its existence was justified by the parent nonprofit's social mission. For instance, a venture in which a theater decided to rent its costumes to other theaters or schools could be seen as meeting the nonprofit's mission to share quality theater with society. If the revenues raised from this venture proved insignificant, a case could be made to the IRS that the rental shop existed solely to serve the mission of the theater.

DISCOUNTECH

DiscounTech's donation-distribution model was based on a prior software distribution program that CompuMentor had operated as early as 1989. At that time, staff rented trucks, collected review copies of software from journalists, and distributed them to nonprofit clients during consulting engagements. In 1995, CompuMentor had formed tentative product distribution partnerships with Microsoft and Lotus. This fledgling program enabled CompuMentor to forge the key corporate relationships that would later make the DiscounTech venture possible. Once the first few suppliers made agreements with DiscounTech, others became more interested.

Service Concept

DiscounTech employed a web-based service that offered donated and discounted technology products and services (plus support) at a very low price to nonprofits across the U.S. It operated as a centralized location where corporations could donate products and nonprofits could order them. By aligning its product distribution and services to complement the information distributed by TechSoup, DiscounTech and TechSoup jointly enabled nonprofits to obtain general technology information; make good choices on acquisition of needed hardware, software, and services; obtain support; and keep up-to-date with new developments. In its first year of operation, FY 2002, DiscounTech had saved customers over $20 million relative to the retail price for the same products. The following year, savings reached $120 million.

Other than warehousing of certain products, there was virtually no cost of goods sold, since DiscounTech was not acting as a reseller. Nonprofit customers ordered the products online much as they might order from amazon.com or other e-commerce websites, thus avoiding the need to deal with a complex web of suppliers. DiscounTech generated earned income by charging customers an administrative fee for each item, usually ranging from 5% to 10% of retail price. Operating costs were minimized by directing nearly all marketing and customer transactions toward one Web-based point of sale and by sharing support resources with CompuMentor.

Similarly, a supplier of donated and discounted hardware, software, and services could access a central resource that operated a platform to publicize and promote the donor's giving programs to nonprofits; provided no-cost outsourcing of product donation, distribution, and administration in line with the donor's own specific guidelines; and supplemented donations with the information and resources found on TechSoup. As Masisak observed:

In most donor firms, philanthropic work is managed by someone in the HR, marketing, or corporate philanthropy departments. At Microsoft, the community affairs office handles the work, and at Cisco, corporate philanthropy does. At some other firms, individual people are philanthropically oriented, but there is no philanthropy group within the company. That's a different mindset. Those that are more philanthropically oriented want the program to grow, they just don't want to spend lots of time or money on it, so we help. It doesn't conflict with the interests of the sales group and saves their resources to focus on their own for-profit business. We will work with any type, as long as it benefits our customers and donors.

Operations

DiscounTech was located in a 4,800-square foot warehouse facility in San Francisco, around the corner from CompuMentor's offices. Approximately 25% of this space was reserved for secure product storage. The general manager, Rebecca Masisak, who held an MBA from Columbia, had previously been senior vice president of strategy and operations for the largest private Internet and local telecom service provider in the U.S. Reporting to Ferrante-Roseberry (**Exhibit 3**), Masisak managed a staff of 17, organized into four groups: operations; project management; inventory/reporting and analysis; and systems analysis and administration. The staff verified prospective customers' tax-exempt status and vendor specific eligibility, provided customer service, processed and fulfilled orders, managed inventory, and worked with donors to launch new products on the site.

Customers could use DiscounTech's website to order products in a similar fashion to many other e-commerce sites. The following chart illustrates the process.

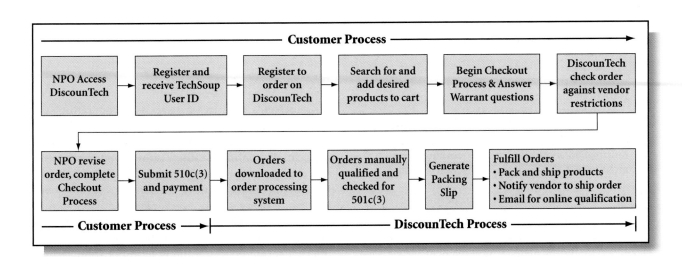

EXHIBIT 3 CompuMentor Organization Structure

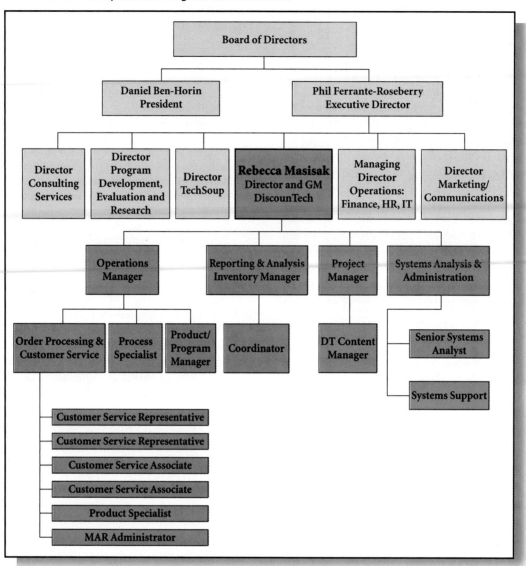

Delivery procedures varied according to the nature of the product and supplier preferences.

- **Downloadable products:** DiscounTech sent the customer an email with instructions on how to download the software, and sent a validation email to the donor.
- **Products warehoused by DiscounTech:** Staff would pick products such as full-packaged software from the storage area, then pack, and ship them to customers (**Exhibit 4**).
- **Products Warehoused by donors:** Some donating firms warehoused and shipped items, such as refurbished computers and networking equipment, directly to customers. DiscounTech staff qualified customer orders and sent them, in spreadsheet form, to the vendor partner for fulfillment.

Nonprofits could contact DiscounTech by phone or email. Service representatives were ready to answer their questions and could direct them to online, print, or other resources for further technology information. Over 80 emails a day reached the office, and the number was expected to increase as the service grew. Staff could run quarterly or monthly sales reports by vendor.

Products and Markets

DiscounTech's product range included operating systems, office applications, networking equipment, website tools, media and design tools, hosted and database applications, online training, refurbished computers, and credit card processing hardware. Specialized software applications included accounting, development and fundraising. There were plans to expand into services such as payroll processing, broadband communications and training programs, accessible via the Internet through subscriptions to application service

providers (ASPs). Most products were new and donated by firms such as Microsoft, Cisco Systems, Symantec, and Intuit. DiscounTech typically charged 5–10% of the retail price, offering the lowest available prices to nonprofits. Its top-selling products were currently Microsoft Office and operating system tools, Symantec anti-virus software, and Micromedia Studio web-production software.

General product offerings, such as printers or operating systems, were targeted at the entire nonprofit market. However, within this market, specific segments might have distinctive product needs and be reached through specific channels. Budget size was known to be correlated with the type of products needed, and whether or not there was likely to be a dedicated technology decision maker. For example, a larger budget in a mature organization would indicate the need for server-based products and more sophisticated networking and licensing solutions.

Rural and urban nonprofits had different requirements for technology infrastructure and tools, as well as for support and advice. The lack of infrastructure in many rural areas necessitated wireless connectivity. Some market sub-sectors required unique products and solutions. For example, community health clinics shared a common need for electronic medical records software that was compliant with the Health Insurance Portability and Accountability Act (HIPAA) of 1996. In general, DiscounTech targeted nonprofits with operating budgets of less than $2 million. They had a wide range of social missions, no line item in their budgets for technology, and no in-house IT personnel. Remarked Masisak: "They often have ten employees or less and in most, no one knows technology."

According to GuideStar, only about one percent of tax-exempt organizations listed a top technology position on their IRS Form 990. In the absence of a technology specialist, decisions about the use of technology were taken by "accidental techies" or the senior management team, most often the executive director. Reaching people in each category required different modes and channels of communication. "Accidental techies"—staff members or volunteers who possessed some computer knowledge and supported an organization's technology infrastructure in addition to their primary assignments—were seen as particularly important decision makers.

Customer Acquisition

At the end of FY 2003, DiscounTech had 11,989 active customers, of whom 70% were classified as *new* (acquired during that year) and 30% as *existing* (acquired previously). The annual costs associated with retaining existing customers amounted to $4 each.

New customers were further subdivided by method of acquisition. *New/Paid* customers were those attracted to DiscounTech through paid outreach channels; at the end of FY 2003, they accounted for 42% of all active customers and had an average acquisition cost of $28 each. Reflecting growing advertising expenditures, Masisak forecast that this cost would reach $35 in FY 2004. *New/Referral* customers, representing 28% of the customer base, were acquired through referral programs, such as tag-on messages to emails and newsletters encouraging recipients to tell their contacts about DiscounTech, at an average cost of only $3 each.

The most common sources of awareness of DiscounTech were word-of-mouth from friends and colleagues (26%) and the CompuMentor website (26%). Another 14% became aware of DiscounTech through TechSoup, whose communication channels included the website itself, an email newsletter, special product announcement emails, and targeted emails to customers who had expressed interest in new product offerings in the past. Unfortunately, DiscounTech's lack of marketing information systems limited its ability to realize the full potential of referrals and promotions. A major systems project to develop a new customer relationship management system had been initiated in October 2003, but was running significantly behind schedule.

Advertising was the primary promotional strategy employed in FY 2004, with expenditures budgeted at $258,794, a 31% increase over the previous year. The goal was to attract a certain number of new visitors each month to the DiscounTech web site and then convert a proportion of these into paying customers. To get a prospective purchaser to visit the site, DiscounTech marketed to prospects through online advertising, through donated and paid Google keyword ads, on partner websites, at events, and by word of mouth. For online advertising, the objective was to get the prospect to click on a small banner ad displayed on another organization's website. DiscounTech's average click-through rate (CTR) was 0.6%, as compared to an industry average of 0.3%. (For a glossary of terminology used in online advertising, see **Appendix A**.)

The next step was to convert the visitor to customer status by placing an order. Lacking the tracking tools to follow specific visitors, categorize them as new visitors, returning visitors, or existing customers, and see what actions they took, DiscounTech was limited to calculating an average conversion rate across all types of visitors. This was based on the simple expedient of dividing the number of orders placed during a specified period of time by the number of visitors during that period. In FY 2002, the conversion rate was only 1.6% but it rose to 3.3% in FY 2003 and Masisak's goal was to achieve a rate of 5% in FY 2004 and 7% in FY 2005.

Communicating with prospective customers was complicated by the highly fragmented nature of the nonprofit market. With few targeted channels available, DiscounTech had been forced to use channels directed at a broad cross-section of nonprofit organizations (collectively described as "nonprofit-facing media"). Building on an initial donated banner ad campaign in FY 2002, DiscounTech's online advertising continued to appear largely in such media as the websites of *Nonprofit Times, Chronicle of Philanthropy, Philanthropy Journal,* and *Charity Channel.* Creative elements included banner ads, e-newsletters, and direct emails.

After saturating those vehicles, DiscounTech expanded into general-audience online media, seeking to reach nonprofit decision makers or influencers with specific lifestyles and psychographics (opinions and values). These media included some focused on technology (for instance, CNET, *Information Week*); on-line newspapers emphasizing topics such as education and politics; and some media that focused on social change, such as *Mother Jones* and About.com's environmental section. Banners had also been placed on the websites of such general news media as *The New York Times, Los Angeles Times,* and *Washington Post.*

Banner ad messages were necessarily simple. One promoted "The Software You Know—Donated Just for Nonprofits", flashed the names of Microsoft and several other well-known brand names, and added "Get it at DiscounTech.org." Another showed a dollar sign morphing into the message: "Stretch Your Budget. Software and More. Donated and Discounted Just for Nonprofits. Available at DiscounTech.org. Made possible by Generous Corporate Donations."

Paid advertising was one way in which traffic was attracted to the DiscounTech site, accounting for 14% of the 69,659 visits recorded in February 2004 (**Exhibit 5**). TechSoup.org, with its large online community, was the largest single traffic source that month at 41%, with another 2% traced to its weekly newsletter, *By the Cup* ("BTC"), and 1% from Compumentor.org ("CM.org"). Other sources included online chat-rooms such as Connections for Tomorrow and WIN-TAP—sites that helped small nonprofits share information regarding grants, product offers, and new products. However, no specific referral source could be identified for 22% of all traffic.

Relationships with Suppliers

To create a new donor or discounter relationship, the DiscounTech staff analyzed market information, obtained in-house expert feedback, created financial projections,

EXHIBIT 5 Sources of Referrals to DiscounTech, FY 2004

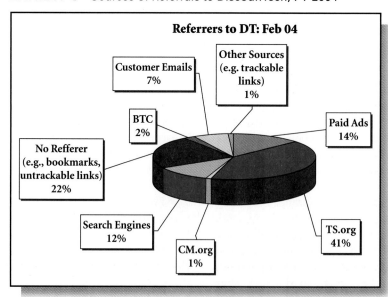

and carefully explored how the donation might meet program goals. Prior to accepting a specific product, staff members assessed factors such as the hardware or software's importance to the nonprofit sector, number and description of items being donated, specific guidelines and terms concerning the donation, and DiscounTech's ability to provide support and implementation guidance.

"Setting up suppliers really starts with building relationships with them," Masisak observed:

> Suppliers are not all the same. Some are very philanthropic, while some are very interested in marketing benefits, and they see DiscounTech as a channel for marketing to nonprofits. We will work with any vendor, as long as it's beneficial to the nonprofits we serve. You can't assume ones that are more philanthropic are similar; you need to work with each firm's unique needs and interests.

If both parties agreed, DiscounTech created a memorandum of understanding to define the offering and the relationship. The donor usually determined the guidelines, including the right to reduce or even withdraw donations depending upon its financial status. Each donor could specify the types of nonprofits that qualified for its products, as well as the number of products that might be obtained over a given time period. For example, Microsoft's new program allowed any 501(c)(3) nonprofit that was not a religious organization to order one each of up to six different products and up to 50 licenses per product during a two-year period. DiscounTech's website recorded these rules so that an organization's order history and status could be reviewed online to determine if it had been qualified in the past and was now eligible to order.

DiscounTech then created a product content for its website, set up order qualifying and fulfillment processes, and trained staff in the new process and the new product itself. The Marketing Communications department considered when and how to announce the new product to customers. Staff forecasted sales volumes, plus initial inventory levels in the case of warehoused products. The final step was to establish administrative fees.

Most donors had regular product donation cycles, but fulfillment delays sometimes occurred when they gave priority to fulfilling profit-generating orders first. In some cases, a donor supplied products through such non-typical channels as a refurbished products group or corporate philanthropy department. These practices could also result in delays, thus complicating DiscounTech's ability to manage lead times and product availability. In general, however, donors did their best to maintain a steady supply.

Many donors had expanded their programs over time. Said Masisak:

> Once we have some kind of 'starter' donation with most of our partners, they like their experience in the program. They have also been willing to listen to

feedback on customer needs and have often expanded either their product line, the scope of who is eligible, or have allowed us to streamline our process to qualify organizations and fulfill donation requests.

For instance, Microsoft's Community Affairs group had worked with CompuMentor for several years and had grown their product donations substantially. While other suppliers could offer Microsoft products at an 80% to 90% discount through the MS Charity Program, DiscounTech was the only licensed distributor of donated Microsoft products in the United States. Microsoft projected that the annual retail value of products distributed through DiscounTech would increase from $35 million in FY 2002 to approximately $125 million in 2004. Although Microsoft donations dominated DiscounTech orders and revenues, increased offerings from other suppliers meant that the proportion of total derived from Microsoft products was expected to slip from over 90% in FY 2002 to slightly less than 70% in FY 2004.

Many suppliers had told DiscounTech staff how much they appreciated the time and cost savings obtained by using its services, as well as expressing support for the social benefits achieved. However, staff members reported that some donors had expressed dislike for the name DiscounTech, arguing that it was too commercial and did not represent their philanthropic intentions. In particular, they seemed frustrated that their greater contributions—products donated free of charge—were being presented equally alongside those that were merely discounted. Masisak wondered if the name might also lead nonprofits to assume that the products themselves were not of the same quality as those sold through regular retail channels. An internal debate had developed on whether to rebrand the organization.

Pricing Strategy

Masisak noted that it was important that nonprofits should pay something for the donated products they obtained from DiscounTech.

> We don't want nonprofits to order things just because they are free or dirt cheap. And besides, we want the impact of donations to DiscounTech to be spread around as much as possible. Our goal will always be to provide technology with the knowledge, training, and guidance to use it well. Making nonprofits take technology seriously through a small financial commitment is part of that process. Feedback shows that this financial aspect not only motivates recipients to use a donated product but also gives them a very real and tangible understanding of its value to their organization.

Accordingly, DiscounTech set administrative fees for each new product with reference to the costs of program implementation and operations. Operational costs included creating website content, order function programming, advertising, and any warehousing. The fees set by DiscounTech for donated products ranged from 3% to 35% of retail price, but rarely exceeded $200. Discounted products accounted for only a very small percentage of all items and typically sold for about 5% less than a nonprofit would pay if it applied directly to the supplier.

Competition

A variety of other sources offered free or discounted technology products to nonprofits:

- *Gifts in Kind International* (GIKI), itself a nonprofit, provided discounted and donated office supplies, building supplies, education/recreation, and consumer products to nonprofits. Serving ten countries, it had good name recognition. Its tech offerings included hardware from 3Com, Nortel, PowerQuest, and used laptops from IBM. GIKI did not provide technical assistance and users had to pay a $250 registration fee in order to access most GIKI offerings. Its lowest administration fee was $15.
- *Consistent Computer Bargains* (CCB) was a for-profit, charity-pricing reseller. Its CCBNonprofits division targeted nonprofits exclusively and offered both software and hardware, but emphasized software products, on which it enjoyed much better margins. It currently offered Microsoft software as a charity reseller, Macromedia (academic pricing only), Corel, MacAfee, Computer Associates, Cisco, and some smaller companies via their reseller channel. Hardware discounts were lower than competitors' since CCB was a pass-through for Compaq, Gateway, and Acer. It charged a $5 handling fee on all purchases under $500, plus $4.95 for all license orders. Discounts ranged from 5% to 20% off retail.

- *TechMarketplace* was a project of the TechFoundation. This for-profit service provided very specialized discounted and donated product offerings specifically for nonprofits. Current product offerings included WebEvent, WebEx, Mission Maestro, and Awards, among others. An online ordering platform had been listed as coming soon, but was not yet in place. The size of the discounts depended upon the vendor contract.
- *Charity Licensing Resellers* were a group of for-profit online agents offering technology products specially discounted for non-profits. "Charity pricing" was higher than the cost of donated products. Microsoft and Symantec had the most publicized programs and allowed verified nonprofits to receive software at 80–90% off retail pricing. There were specific rules regarding how this software could be acquired, and strong dictates that products received under these rules could not be re-sold or used by for-profit entities.
- *Other commercial retailers* of technology products included Office Depot, CompUSA, or local computer stores. These retailers could provide discounts, but the amount was constrained by the wholesale prices they paid for each product. Costs were linked to the vendor-pricing program. No additional price savings came from the retailer.
- *Dell, HP and other manufacturers:* These firms provided personal computers, printers, and other hardware through discount programs to nonprofits. This hardware was often bundled with an operating system and office management software. Increasingly, these firms saw large nonprofits as an important market.

DiscounTech offered products from a broader array of suppliers than competing organizations (**Exhibit 6**).

EXHIBIT 6 Supplier Offerings Comparison

DISCOUNTECH	GIKI	TECHMARKETPLACE	CONSISTENT COMPUTER BARGAINS
Akiva	Citrix	Altrue	Acer
B2P	Dell (recycled printers)	Broadleaf Services	Adobe
BAVC	IBM	CDW	Corel
BEA	Microsoft	Dell	Dell
Cisco	Office Depot	Easeweb	Gateway
ClickTime		Everon IT	HP
eTapestry		Intranet	IBM
GrantStation		Kaseya	Lexmark
Groundspring		Microsoft (Charity)	McAfee
Intuit		PC Connection	Microsoft (Charity)
Lotus		Qurb	Symantec
Macromedia		Telosa	Toshiba
Mailshell			Xerox
Microsoft			
Ontero			
PayCycle			
Symantec			
Telosa			
Ulead			
VeriFone/NPC			
WebGecko			

Some competitors had attempted to position themselves as a central order point for discounted software, a business model most recently been attempted by 501click, a for-profit business. However, 501click had found that relying on discounted merchandise alone was insufficient to bring nonprofits to their site, and was eventually forced to exit the market. Surviving entities combined either an extensive array of choices at low prices, or donations/discounts with additional resources.

FUTURE PLANS THROUGH FY 2005

For the fiscal year ending June 30, 2004, DiscounTech projected a net income of $571,762. (**Exhibit 7**). With the exception of some small grants from foundations, usually tied to specific projects such as enhancing back-end systems to accommodate the requirements of a new donor, almost all of DiscounTech's projected FY 2004 revenues of $6.12 million were earned income derived from administrative fees charged to nonprofit customers. About 1% of this revenue would be shared with certain discount partners whose products were sold through DiscounTech's own warehouse, while 42% would be shared with CompuMentor to cover costs associated with consulting services, TechSoup support, and emerging programs. The balance of $3.66 million represented gross income before expenses of $3.09 million, including advertising and salaries.

Now that DiscounTech was both established and profitable, Masisak sought to maintain an appropriate image and service level for donors and customers, as well as to reinforce customers' relationships with CompuMentor and TechSoup. With the board's approval, ambitious goals had been set. Masisak and her team aimed to generate a net income of more than $1.9 million in FY 2005. Achieving this goal would require attracting significant numbers of new customers in addition to retention of existing customers. One issue was whether it would be realistic to try to increase average spending levels per customer.

Masisak was debating what role paid marketing communications should play in future strategy and how to budget advertising and related communications expenditures most effectively. Could a case be made for employing offline media, particularly print? If so, what types of nonprofits should be targeted and how might the messages be differentiated from those in the banner ads and e-news items that DiscounTech had emphasized to date?

As inputs to these decisions, she planned to undertake an in-depth analysis of recent experience with different channels (**Exhibit 8**) and also to re-examine the findings of an online survey of DiscounTech customers that had been

EXHIBIT 7 DiscounTech Pro Forma Statement of Activities, FY 2002–FY 2005

	FY 2002[1] ACTUAL		FY 2003 ACTUAL		FY 2004 FORECAST		FY 2005 FORECAST	
Income								
Contribution Revenue								
Foundation Contributions	–		60,000		70,000		80,000	
Total	–		60,000	1%	70,000	1%	80,000	1%
Earned Revenue								
Product Distribution	1,251,315		4,006,575		6,053,531		8,252,882	
Total Earned Revenue	1,251,315		4,006,575	99%	6,053,531	99%	8,252,882	99%
Total income	1,251,315	100%	4,066,575	100%	6,123,531	100%	8,332,882	100%
Revenue Sharing								
Partners	–		51,663	1%	67,123	1%	85,000	1%
Compumentor Programs								
Consulting Services	355,818		764,801		1,118,078		1,278,039	
Emerging Programs	250,526		127,962		163,854		187,262	
TechSoup	610,946		801,108		1,116,152		1,267,031	
Total Compumentor Programs	1,217,290	97%	1,693,871	42%	2,398,084	39%	2,732,332	33%
Total Revenue Sharing	1,217,290	97%	1,745,534	43%	2,465,207	40%	2,817,332	34%
Gross Income	34,025	3%	2,321,041	57%	3,658,324	60%	5,515,550	66%
Expenses								
Advertising	482	0%	196,931	5%	258,794	4%	237,686	3%
Salaries	224,666	18%	1,460,365	36%	1,819,710	30%	2,246,941	27%
Other expenses	122,151	10%	1,291,428	32%	1,525,646	25%	1,569,964	19%
Total Expenses	346,335	27.7%	2,554,862	62.8%	3,086,562	50.4%	3,579,219	43.0%
Net Income	(312,310)	–25.0%	(233,821)	–5.7%	571,762	9.3%	1,936,331	23.2%
Capital Investment	–		15,000		22,587		30,737	
Net Increase to CompuMentor Reserves	(312,310)		(248,822)		549,174		1,905,595	

Fiscal year runs from July 1 to June 30

EXHIBIT 8 Summary of Representative Monthly Advertising Results, FY 2004

CHANNEL	AD TYPE	TARGETING	IMP	VISITS	CTR	COST
Assoc. of Fundraising Professionals	e-news	NP-facing	26,000	86	0.33%	$750.00
Assoc. of Fundraising Professionals	banners	NP-facing	300,000	68	0.02%	$1,167.00
Charity Channel	e-news	NP-facing	22,000	29	0.13%	$217.00
Chronicle of Philanthropy	e-news	NP-facing	20,000	96	0.48%	$960.00
Chronicle of Philanthropy	banners	NP-facing	11,323	52	0.46%	$900.00
The Foundation Center	e-news	NP-facing	52,800	358	0.68%	$418.00
The Foundation Center	e-news	NP-facing - regional (DC, NY)	32,000	200	0.63%	$315.00
Los Angeles Times	banners	general - news	1,095,481	1,002	0.09%	$4,733.00
Mother Jones	e-news	general - social issues	30,000	161	0.54%	$1,125.00
Mother Jones	banners	general - social issues	80,194	439	0.55%	$1,604.00
The Nation	e-news	general - politics	220,000	212	0.10%	$1,000.00
The Nation	banners	general - politics	814,022	1,575	0.19%	$2,333.00
Nat. Center for Family Philanthropy	e-news	NP-facing	7,000	51	0.73%	$500.00
The New Republic	e-news	general - social issues	20,000	100	0.50%	$1,000.00
Nonprofit Times	e-news	NP-facing	14,900	8	0.05%	$975.00
New York Times	e-news	general - news	400,000	983	0.25%	$2,900.00
New York Times	banners	general - news	191,553	2,073	1.08%	$2,492.00
Philanthropy Journal	banners	NP-facing	33,434	5	0.01%	$475.00
PNN	e-news	NP-facing	10,000	14	0.14%	$240.00
Sprinks	keywords pay-per-click	general - keywords	n/a	4,398	n/a	$1,724.00
Washington Post	banners	general - news	453,459	400	0.09%	$8,180.00
Previously run ads				598		
TOTALS			**3,834,166**	**12,908**	**0.34%**	**$34,008.00**

Key
Imp = Impressions
CTR = Click-through rate

conducted eighteen months earlier (key findings are reproduced in **Appendix B**).

Although CompuMentor's board and management team welcomed the prospect of increasing financial contributions from DiscounTech, some wondered how continued expansion of this earned-income venture might eventually affect the culture and priorities of the parent nonprofit.

Glossary of Commonly-Used Terms in On-Line Advertising

Click-through Click-through (**CT**) is generated when a user clicks on an online advertisement in order to visit the advertiser's Web site.

Click-through Rate The response rate of an online advertisement, typically expressed as a percentage and calculated by taking the number of click-throughs the ad received, dividing that number by the number of impressions and multiplying by 100 to obtain a percentage: Example: 20 clicks/1,000 impressions = .02 × 100 = 2% **CTR.**

Cost-per-Impression Percentage of impressions measured against total spend on a given advertisement. Abbreviated as **CPI.**

Cost-per-Click Percentage of click-through made measured against total spend on a given advertisement. Abbreviated as **CPC.**

Conversion Rate Percentage of web visitors who complete a desired action (e.g., register and become a paying customer) measured against total click-throughs. Abbreviated as **CV.**

Impressions The number of times an ad is viewed.

Page View The number of times a web page is requested.

Visit A visit is a user entering a Web site at some page for the first time that day (or some other specified period). The number of visits is roughly equivalent to the number of different people that visit a site. This term is ambiguous since it could mean a user session or it could mean a unique visitor that day.

Unique Visitor A unique visitor is someone with a unique address who is entering a Web site for the first time that day (or some other specified period). Thus, a visitor that returns within the same day is not counted twice. A unique visitor count tells you how many different people there are in your audience during the time period.

Findings from Online Survey
of DiscounTech Users

September 2002*

Figure A   Source of Awareness of DiscounTech

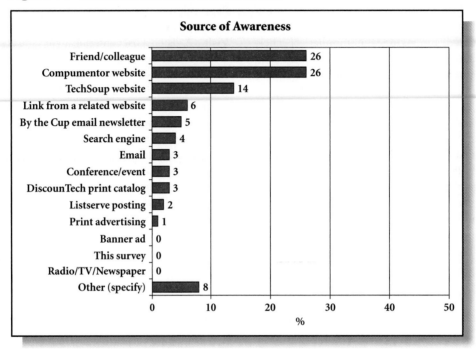

*Note: A total of 4,569 registered users were contacted and 831 responded. Of these respondents, 88% were buyers, while 12% were registered but had not yet purchased.

Figure B User Agreement on DiscounTech's Service

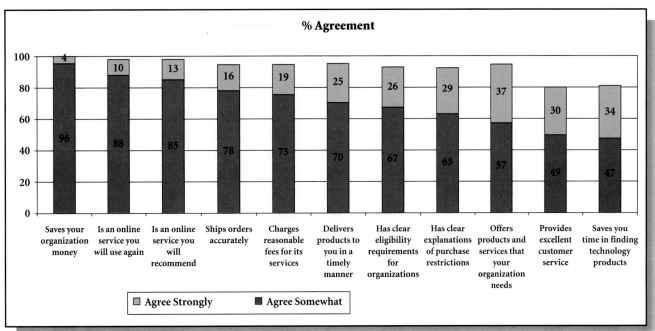

Figure C Methods of Finding Out About New Products

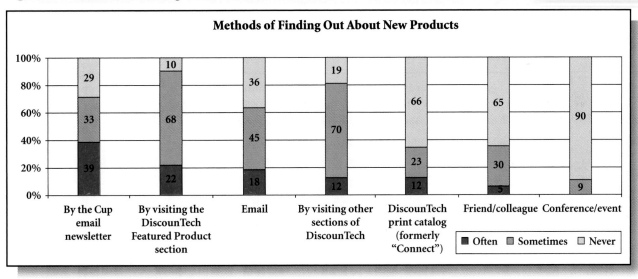

Figure D Importance of DiscounTech Features

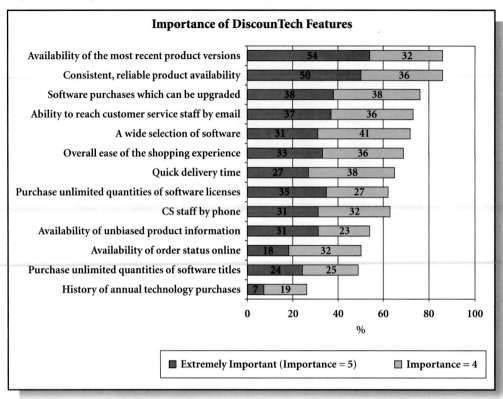

Figure E Technology Sources

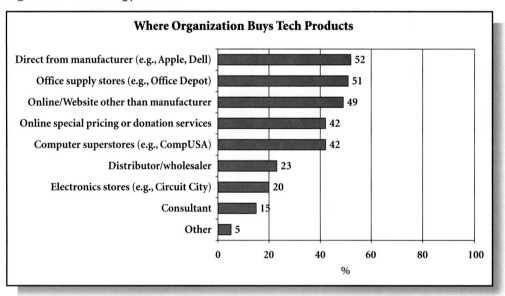

Figure F Products Customers Would Buy if Offered on DiscounTech

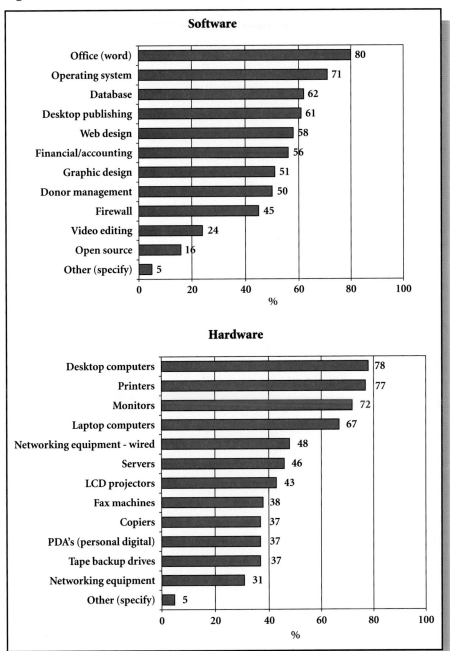

Table 1 User Ratings of Attributes, with Corresponding Performance Rating

Most Important Attributes	Extremely Important	Very Important	DiscounTech Performance
Availability of the most recent product versions	54%	32%	+
Consistent, reliable product availability	50	36	+
Software purchases which can be upgraded	38	38	–
Ability to reach customer service staff by email	37	36	–
Overall ease of the shopping experience	33	36	NA
A wide selection of software	31	41	–
Quick delivery time	27	38	+
Ability to reach customer service staff by phone	31	32	–

Table 2 Reasons for Not Purchasing

For the 12% of registered users who have not made a purchase yet, the primary reasons were lack of need and the limited product selection.

No need for products	24%
Don't have what I needed	24
Haven't yet but intend to	16
Not eligible	10
Not familiar enough/just learned about it	8
No funding	4
Customer service comments	4
Found alternative source	3
Still in planning stages	3

STUDY QUESTIONS

1. *What do you see as the pros and cons for nonprofits of engaging in large-scale earned-income ventures?*
2. *What do you see as the missions of CompuMentor and DiscounTech, respectively? Are the two compatible? Why or why not?*
3. *Evaluate DiscounTech's service concept and business model. What role does effective marketing planning and execution play in ensuring continued success? What could go wrong with plans to expand sales volume and profits?*
4. *How effective is DiscounTech's current communications strategy? Where does it seem to be getting the most and least bang for its buck?*
5. *What actions should Rebecca Masisak take, and why?*

Case 11   Dr. Mahalee Goes to London

CHRISTOPHER LOVELOCK

A senior account officer at an international bank is about to meet a wealthy Asian businessman who seeks funding for a buyout of his company. The prospective client has already visited a competing bank.

It was a Friday in mid-February and Dr. Kadir Mahalee, a wealthy businessman from the southeast Asian nation of Tailesia, was visiting London on a trip that combined business and pleasure. Mahalee, who held a doctorate from the London School of Economics and had earlier been a professor of international trade and government trade negotiator, was the founder of Eximsa, a major export company in Tailesia. Business brought him to London every two to three months. These trips provided him with the opportunity to visit his daughter, Leona, the eldest of his four children, who lived in London. Several of his ten grandchildren were attending college in Britain and he was especially proud of his grandson, Anson, who was a student at the Royal Academy of Music. In fact, he had scheduled this trip to coincide with a violin recital by Anson at _00 P.M. on this day.

The primary purpose of Mahalee's visit was to resolve a delicate matter regarding his company. He had decided to retire and wished to make arrangements for the company's future. His son, Victor, was involved in the business and ran Eximsa's trading office in Europe. However, Victor was in poor health and unable to take over the firm. Mahalee believed that a group of loyal employees were interested in buying his company if the necessary credit could be arranged.

Before leaving Tailesia, Mahalee had discussed the possibility of a buyout with his trusted financial adviser, Li Sieuw Meng, who recommended that he talk to several banks in London because of the potential complexity of the business deal:

> The London banks are experienced in buyouts. Also, you need a bank that can handle the credit for the interested buyers in New York and London, as well as Asia. Once the buyout takes place, you'll have significant cash to invest. This would be a good time to review your estate plans as well.

Referring Mahalee to two competitors, The Trust Company and Global Private Bank, Li added:

> I've met an account officer from Global who called on me several times. Here's his business card; his name is Miguel Kim. I've never done any business with him, but he did seem quite competent. Unfortunately, I don't know anyone at the Trust Company, but here's their address in London.

After checking into the Savoy Hotel in London the following Wednesday, Mahalee telephoned Kim's office. Since Kim was out, Mahalee spoke to the account officer's secretary, described himself briefly, and arranged to stop by Global's Lombard Street office around mid-morning on Friday.

On Thursday, Mahalee visited The Trust Company. The two people he met were extremely pleasant and had spent some time in Tailesia. They seemed very knowledgeable about managing estates and gave him some good recommendations about handling his complex family affairs. However, they were clearly less experienced in handling business credit, his most urgent need.

The next morning, Mahalee had breakfast with Leona. As they parted, she said, "I'll meet you at 1:30 P.M. in the lobby of the Savoy, and we'll go to the recital together. We mustn't be late if we want to get front-row seats."

On his way to Global Private Bank, Mahalee stopped at Mappin & Webb's jewelry store to buy his wife a present for their anniversary. His shopping was pleasant and leisurely; he purchased a beautiful emerald necklace that he knew his wife would like. When he emerged from the jewelry store, he was caught in an unexpected snow flurry. He had difficulty finding a taxi and his arthritis started acting up, making walking to the nearest Tube station out of the question. At last he caught a taxi and arrived at the Lombard Street location of Global Bancorp about noon. After going into the street-level branch of Global Retail Bank, he was redirected by a security guard to the Private Bank offices on the second floor.

He arrived at the Private Bank's nicely appointed reception area at 12:15 P.M. The receptionist greeted him and contacted Miguel Kim's secretary, who came out promptly to see Mahalee, and declared:

> Mr. Kim was disappointed that he couldn't be here to welcome you, Dr. Mahalee, but he had a lunch appointment with one of his clients that was scheduled over a month ago. He expects to return at about 1:30. In the meantime, he has asked another senior account officer, Sophia Costa, to assist you.

Sophia Costa, 41, was a vice president of the bank and had worked for Global Bancorp for 14 years (two years longer than Miguel Kim). She had visited Tailesia once, but had not met Mahalee's financial adviser nor any member of the Mahalee family. An experienced relationship manager, Costa was knowledgeable about offshore investment management and fiduciary services. Miguel Kim had looked into her office at 11:45 A.M. and asked her if she would cover for him in case a prospective client, a Dr. Mahalee, whom he had expected to see earlier, should happen to arrive. He told Costa that Mahalee was a successful Tailesian businessman planning for his retirement, but that he had never met the prospect personally, then rushed off to lunch.

The phone rang in Costa's office and she reached across the desk to pick it up. It was Kim's secretary. "Dr. Mahalee is in reception, Ms. Costa."

STUDY QUESTIONS

1. Prepare a flowchart of Dr. Mahalee's service encounters.
2. Putting yourself in Mahalee's shoes, how do you feel (both physically and mentally) after speaking with the receptionist at Global? What are your priorities right now?
3. As Sophia Costa, what action would you take in your first five minutes with Mahalee?
4. What would constitute a good outcome of the meeting for both the client and the bank? How should Costa try to bring about such an outcome?

Case 12   *Menton Bank*

CHRISTOPHER LOVELOCK

Problems arise when a large bank, attempting to develop a stronger customer service orientation, enlarges the tellers' responsibilities to include selling activities.

"I'm concerned about Karen," said Margaret Costanzo to David Reeves. The two bank officers were seated in the former's office at Menton Bank. Costanzo was a vice president of the bank and manager of the Victory Square branch, the third largest in Menton's large branch network. She and Reeves, the branch's customer service director, were having an employee appraisal meeting. Reeves was responsible for the customer service department, which coordinated the activities of the customer service representatives (CSRs, formerly known as tellers) and the customer assistance representatives (CARs, formerly known as new accounts assistants).

Costanzo and Reeves were discussing Karen Mitchell, a 24-year-old customer service rep, who had applied for the soon-to-be-vacant position of head CSR. Mitchell had been with the bank for three and a half years. She had applied for the position of what had then been called head teller a year earlier, but the job had gone to a candidate with more seniority. Now that individual was leaving—his wife had been transferred to a new job in another city—and the position was once again open. Two other candidates had also applied for the job.

Both Costanzo and Reeves were agreed that, against all criteria used in the past, Karen Mitchell would have been the obvious choice for head teller. She was both fast and accurate in her work, presented a smart and professional appearance, and was well liked by customers and her fellow CSRs. However, the nature of the teller's job had been significantly revised nine months earlier to add a stronger marketing component. CSRs were now expected to offer polite suggestions that customers use automated teller machines (ATMs) for simple transactions. They were also required to stimulate customer interest in the broadening array of financial services offered by the bank. "The problem with Karen," as Reeves put it, "is that she simply refuses to sell."

THE NEW FOCUS ON CUSTOMER SERVICE AT MENTON BANK

Although it was the largest bank in the region, Menton had historically focused on corporate business and its share of the retail consumer banking business had declined in the face of aggressive competition from other financial institutions. Three years earlier, the Board of Directors had appointed a new chief executive officer (CEO) and given him the mandate of developing a stronger consumer orientation at the retail level. The goal was to seize the initiative in marketing the ever-increasing array of financial services now available to retail customers. The CEO's strategy, after putting in a new management team, was to begin by ordering an expansion and speed-up of Menton's investment in electronic delivery systems, which had fallen behind the competition. To achieve this strategy, a new banking technology team had been created.

During the past eighteen months, the bank had tripled the number of automated teller machines (ATMs) located inside its branches, replacing older ATMs by the latest models featuring color touch screens and capable of a broader array of transactions in multiple languages. Menton was already a member of a several ATM networks, giving its customers access to freestanding 24-hour booths in shopping centers, airports, and other high-traffic locations. The installation of new ATMs was coupled with a branch renovation program, designed to improve the physical appearance of the branches. A pilot program to test the impact of these "new look" branches was already underway. Longer term, top management intended to redesign the interior of each branch. As more customers switched to electronic banking from remote locations, the bank planned to close a number of its smaller branches.

Another important move had been to introduce automated telephone banking, which allowed customers to check account balances and to move funds from one account to another by touching specific keys on their phone in response to the instructions of a computerized voice. This service was available 24/7 and utilization was rising steadily. Customers could also call a central customer service office to speak with a bank representative concerning service questions or problems with their accounts, as well as to request new account applications or new checkbooks, which would be sent by mail. This office currently operated on weekdays from 8:00 A.M. to 8:00 P.M. and on Saturdays from 8:00 A.M. to 2:00 P.M., but Menton was evaluating the possibility of expanding the operation to include a broad array of retail bank services, offered on a 24-hour basis.

The technology team had completely redesigned the bank's web site to make it possible to offer what were described as the region's most "user-friendly" Internet banking services. Customers had online access to their

---

accounts and could also obtain information about bank services, branch locations and service hours, location of ATMs, as well as answers to commonly asked questions. Menton was also testing the use of Web-enabled services for customers who had digital cell phones with Internet access.

Finally, the bank had recently started issuing new credit cards containing chips imbued with radio-frequency identification (RFID), which speeded transactions by allowing customers to wave their cards close to a special reader rather than having to swipe them in the traditional way. All these actions seemed to be bearing fruit. In the most recent six months, Menton had seen a significant increase in the number of new accounts opened, as compared to the same period of the previous year. And quarterly survey data showed that Menton Bank was steadily increasing its share of new deposits in the region.

CUSTOMER SERVICE ISSUES

New financial products had been introduced at a rapid rate. But the bank found that many existing "platform" staff—known as new accounts assistants—were ill equipped to sell these services because of lack of product knowledge and inadequate training in selling skills. As Costanzo recalled:

> The problem was that they were so used to sitting at their desks waiting for a customer to approach them with a specific request, such as a mortgage or car loan, that it was hard to get them to take a more positive approach that involved actively probing for customer needs. Their whole job seemed to revolve around filling out forms or responding to prompts on their computer screens. We were way behind most other banks in this respect.

As the automation program proceeded, the mix of activities performed by the tellers started to change. A growing number of customers were using the ATMs, the web site, and automated telephone banking for a broad array of transactions, including cash withdrawals and deposits (from the ATMs), transfers of funds between accounts, and requesting account balances. The ATMs at the Victory Square branch had the highest utilization of any of Menton's branches, reflecting the large number of students and young professionals served at that location. Costanzo noted that customers who were older or less well-educated seemed to prefer being served by "a real person, rather than a machine." They were particularly reluctant to make deposits via an ATM.

A year earlier, the head office had selected three branches, including Victory Square, as test sites for a new customer service program, which included a radical redesign of the branch interior. The Victory Square branch was in a busy urban location, about one mile from the central business district and less than 10-minutes' walk from the campus of a large university. The branch was surrounded by retail stores and close to commercial and professional offices. The other test branches were among the bank's larger suburban offices in two different metropolitan areas and were located in a shopping mall and next to a big hospital, respectively.

As part of the branch renovation program, each of these three branches had previously been remodeled to include no fewer than four ATMs (Victory Square had six), which could be closed off from the rest of the branch so that they would remain accessible to customers 24 hours a day. Further remodeling was then undertaken to locate a customer service desk near the entrance; close to each desk were two electronic information terminals, featuring color touch screens that customers could activate to obtain information on a variety of bank services. The teller stations were redesigned to provide two levels of service: an express station for simple deposits and for cashing of approved checks, and regular stations for the full array of services provided by tellers. The number of stations open at a given time was varied to reflect the volume of anticipated business and staffing arrangements were changed to ensure that more tellers were on hand to serve customers during the busiest periods. Finally, the platform area in each branch was reconstructed to create what the architect described as "a friendly, yet professional appearance."

HUMAN RESOURCES

With the new environment came new training programs for the staff of these three branches and new job descriptions and job titles: customer assistance representatives (for the platform staff), customer service representatives (for the tellers), and customer service director (instead of assistant branch manager). The head teller position was renamed head CSR. Details of the new job descriptions are shown in the Appendix. The training programs for each group included sessions designed to develop improved knowledge of both new and existing retail products. (CARs received more extensive training in this area than did CSRs.) The CARs also attended a 15-hour course, offered in three separate sessions, on basic selling skills. This program covered key steps in the sales process, including building a relationship, exploring customer needs, determining a solution, and overcoming objections.

The sales training program for CSRs, by contrast, consisted of just two 2-hour sessions designed to develop skills in recognizing and probing customer needs, presenting product features and benefits, overcoming objections, and referring customers to CARs. All staff members in customer service positions participated in sessions designed to improve their communication skills and professional image: clothing and personal grooming and interactions with customers were all discussed. Said the trainer, "Remember, people's money is too important to entrust someone who doesn't look and act the part!"

CARs were instructed to rise from their seats and shake hands with customers. Both CARs and CSRs were given exercises designed to improve their listening skills and their powers of observation. All employees working where they could be seen by customers were ordered to refrain from drinking soda and chewing gum on the job. (Smoking by both employees and customers had been banned some years earlier under the bank's smoke-free office policy.)

Although Menton Bank's management anticipated that most of the increased emphasis on selling would fall to the CARs, they also foresaw a limited selling role for the customer service reps, who would be expected to mention various products and facilities offered by the bank as they served customers at the teller windows. For instance, if a customer happened to say something about an upcoming vacation, the CSR was supposed to mention traveler's checks; if the customer complained about bounced checks, the CSR should suggest speaking to a CAR about opening a personal line of credit that would provide an automatic overdraft protection; if the customer mentioned investments, the CSR was expected to refer him or her to a CAR who could provide information on money market accounts, certificates of deposit, or Menton's discount brokerage service. All CSRs were supplied with their own business cards. When making a referral, they were expected to write the customer's name and the product of interest on the back of a card, give it to the customer and send that individual to the customer assistance desks.

In an effort to motivate CSRs at the three branches to sell specific financial products, the bank experimented with various incentive programs. The first involved cash bonuses for referrals to CARs that resulted in sale of specific products. During a one-month period, CSRs were offered a $50 bonus for each referral leading to a customer's opening a personal line of credit account; the CARs received a $20 bonus for each account they opened, regardless of whether or not it came as a referral or simply a walk-in. Eight such bonuses were paid to CSRs at Victory Square, with three each going to just two of the full-time CSRs, Jean Warshawski and Bruce Greenfield. Karen Mitchell was not among the recipients. However, this program was not renewed, since it was felt that there were other, more cost-effective means of marketing this product. In addition, Reeves, the customer service director, had reason to believe that Greenfield had colluded with one of the CARs, his girlfriend, to claim referrals which he had not, in fact, made. Another test branch reported similar suspicions of two of its CSRs

A second promotion followed and was based on allocating credits to the CSRs for successful referrals. The value of the credit varied according to the nature of the product—for instance, a debit card was worth 500 credits—and accumulated credits could be exchanged for merchandise gifts. This program was deemed ineffective and discontinued after three months. The basic problem seemed to be that the value of the gifts was seen as too low in relation to the amount of effort required. Other problems with these promotional schemes included lack of product knowledge on the part of the CSRs and time pressures when many customers were waiting in line to be served.

The bank had next turned to an approach which, in David Reeves' words, "used the stick rather than the carrot." All CSRs had traditionally been evaluated half-yearly on a variety of criteria, including accuracy, speed, quality of interactions with customers, punctuality of arrival for work, job attitudes, cooperation with other employees, and professional image. The evaluation process assigned a number of points to each criterion, with accuracy and speed being the most heavily weighted. In addition to appraisals by the customer service director and the branch manager, with input from the head CSR, Menton had recently instituted a program of anonymous visits by what was popularly known as the "mystery client." Each CSR was visited at least once a quarter by a professional evaluator posing as a customer. This individual's appraisal of the CSR's appearance, performance, and attitude was included in the overall evaluation. The number of points scored by each CSR had a direct impact on merit pay raises and on selection for promotion to the head CSR position or to platform jobs.

To encourage improved product knowledge and "consultative selling" by CSRs, the evaluation process was revised to include points assigned for each individual's success in sales referrals. Under the new evaluation scheme, the maximum number of points assignable for effectiveness in making sales—directly or through referrals to CARs—amounted to 30 percent of the potential total score. Although CSR-initiated sales had risen significantly in the most recent half-year, Reeves sensed that morale had dropped among this group, in contrast to the CARs, whose enthusiasm and commitment had risen significantly. He had also noticed an increase in CSR errors. One CSR had quit, complaining about too much pressure.

Karen Mitchell

Under the old scoring system, Karen Mitchell had been the highest-scoring teller/CSR for four consecutive half-years. But after two half-years under the new system, her ranking had dropped to fourth out of the seven full-time tellers. The top-ranking CSR, Mary Bell, had been with Menton Bank for sixteen years, but had declined repeated invitations to apply for a head teller position, saying that she was happy where she was, earning at the top of the CSR scale, and did not want "the extra worry and responsibility." Mitchell ranked first on all but one of the operationally related criteria (interactions with customers, where she ranked second), but sixth on selling effectiveness (**Exhibit 1**).

Costanzo and Reeves had spoken to Mitchell about her performance and expressed disappointment. Mitchell had informed them, respectfully but firmly, that she saw

CSR Name[3]	Length of Full-Time Bank Service	Operational Criteria[1] (Max.: 70 Points)		Selling Effectiveness[2] (Max.: 30 Points)		Total Score	
		1st Half	2nd Half	1st Half	2nd Half	1st Half	2nd Half
Mary Bell	16 years, 10 months	65	64	16	20	81	84
Scott Dubois	2 years, 3 months	63	61	15	19	78	80
Bruce Greenfield	12 months	48	42	20	26	68	68
Karen Mitchell	3 years, 7 months	67	67	13	12	80	79
Sharon Rubin	1 year, 4 months	53	55	8	9	61	64
Swee Hoon Chen	7 months	—	50	—	22	—	72
Jean Warshawski	2 years, 1 month	57	55	21	28	79	83

[1]Totals based on sum of ratings points against various criteria, including accuracy, work production, attendance and punctuality, personal appearance, organization of work, initiative, cooperation with others, problem-solving ability, and quality of interaction with customers.

[2]Points awarded for both direct sales by CSR (e.g., traveler's checks) and referral selling by CSR to CAR (e.g., debit card, certificates of deposit, personal line of credit).

[3]Full-time CSRs only (part-time CSRs were evaluated separately).

the most important aspect of her job as giving customers fast, accurate, and courteous service, telling the two bank officers:

> I did try this selling thing but it just seemed to annoy people. Some said they were in a hurry and couldn't talk now; others looked at me as if I were slightly crazy to bring up the subject of a different bank service than the one they were currently transacting. And then, when you got the odd person who seemed interested, you could hear the other customers in the line grumbling about the slow service.
>
> Really, the last straw was when I noticed on the computer screen that this woman had several thousand in her savings account so I suggested to her, just as the trainer had told us, that she could earn more interest if she opened a money market account. Well, she told me it was none of my business what she did with her money, and stomped off. Don't get me wrong, I love being able to help customers, and if they ask for my advice, I'll gladly tell them about what the bank has to offer.

Selecting a New Head CSR

Two weeks after this meeting, it was announced that the head CSR was leaving. The job entailed some supervision of the work of the other CSRs (including allocation of work assignments and scheduling part-time CSRs at busy periods or during employ vacations), consultation on—and, where possible, resolution of—any problems occurring at the teller stations, and handling of large cash deposits and withdrawals by local retailers (see position description in the Appendix). When not engaged on such tasks, the head CSR was expected to operate a regular teller window.

The pay scale for a head CSR ranged from $8.60 to $14.50 per hour, depending on qualifications, seniority, and branch size, as compared to a range $6.70 to $11.10 per hour for CSRs. The pay scale for CARs ranged from $7.70 to $13.00. Full-time employees (who were not unionized) worked a 40-hour week, including some evenings until 6:00 P.M. and certain Saturday mornings. Costanzo indicated that the pay scales were typical for banks in the region, although the average CSR at Menton was better qualified than those at smaller banks and therefore higher on the scale. Karen Mitchell was currently earning $9.80 per hour, reflecting her education, which included an associate's degree in business administration from the local community college, three-and-a-half years' experience, and significant past merit increases. If promoted to head CSR, she would qualify for an initial rate of $11.80 an hour. When applications for the positions closed, Mitchell was one of three candidates. The other two candidates were Jean Warshawski, 42, another CSR at the Victory Square branch; and Curtis Richter, 24, the head CSR at one of Menton Bank's small suburban branches, who was seeking more responsibility.

Warshawski was married with two sons in school. She had started working as a part-time teller at Victory Square some three years previously, switching to full-time work a year later in order, as she said, to put away some money for her boys' college education. Warshawski was a cheerful woman with a jolly laugh. She had a wonderful memory for people's names and Reeves had often seen her greeting customers on the street or in a restaurant during her lunch hour. Reviewing her evaluations over the previous three years, Reeves noted that she had initially performed poorly on accuracy and at one point, when she was still a part-timer, had been put on probation because of frequent inaccuracies in the balance in her cash drawer at the end of the day. Although Reeves considered her much improved on this score, he still saw room for improvement. The customer service director had also had occasion to reprimand her for tardiness during the past year. Warshawski attributed this to health problems with her elder son who, she said, was now responding to treatment.

Both Reeves and Costanzo had observed Warshawski at work and agreed that her interactions with customers were exceptionally good, although she tended to be overly chatty and was not as fast as Karen Mitchell. She seemed to have a natural ability to size up customers and to decide which ones were good prospects for a quick sales pitch on a specific financial product. Although slightly untidy in her personal appearance, she was very well organized in her work and was quick to help her fellow CSRs, especially new hires. She was currently earning $8.90 per hour as a CSR and would qualify for a rate of $11.20 as head CSR. In the most recent six months, Warshawski had ranked ahead of Mitchell as a result of being very successful in consultative selling (**Exhibit 1**).

Richter, the third candidate, was not working in one of the three test branches, so had not been exposed to the consultative selling program and its corresponding evaluation scheme. However, he had received excellent evaluations for his work in Menton's small Longmeadow branch, where he had been employed for three years. A move to Victory Square would increase his earnings from $9.40 to $10.40 per hour. Reeves and Costanzo had interviewed Richter and considered him intelligent and personable. He had joined the bank after dropping out of college midway through his third year, but had recently started taking evening courses in order to complete his degree. The Longmeadow branch was located in an older part of town, where commercial and retail activity were rather stagnant. This branch (which was rumored to be under consideration for closure) had not yet been renovated and had no ATMs, although there was an ATM accessible to Menton customers one block away. Richter supervised three CSRs and reported directly to the branch manager, who spoke very highly of him. Since there were no CARs in this branch, Richter and another experienced CSR took turns to handle new accounts and loan or mortgage applications.

Costanzo and Reeves were troubled by the decision that faced them. Prior to the bank's shift in focus, Mitchell would have been the natural choice for the head CSR job which, in turn, could be a stepping stone to further promotions, including customer assistance representative, customer service director, and, eventually, manager of a small branch or a management position in the head office. Mitchell had told her superiors that she was interested in making a career in banking and that she was eager to take on further responsibilities.

Compounding the problem was the fact that the three branches testing the improved branch design and new customer service program had just completed a full year of the test. Costanzo knew that sales and profits were up significantly at all three branches, relative to the bank's performance as a whole. She anticipated that top management would want to extend the program systemwide after making any modifications that seemed desirable.

Menton Bank: Job Descriptions for Customer Service Staff in Branches

Previous Job Description for Teller

FUNCTION: Provides customer services by receiving, paying out, and keeping accurate records of all moneys involved in paying and receiving transactions. Promotes the bank's services.

RESPONSIBILITIES

1. Serves customers:
   - Accepts deposits, verifies cash and endorsements, and gives customers their receipts.
   - Cashes checks within the limits assigned or refers customers to supervisor for authorization.
   - Accepts savings deposits and withdrawals, verifies signatures, and posts interest and balances as necessary.
   - Accepts loan, credit card, utility, and other payments.
   - Issues money orders, cashier's checks, traveler's checks, and foreign currency
   - Reconciles customer statements and confers with bookkeeping personnel regarding discrepancies in balances or other problems.
   - Issues credit card advances.
2. Prepares individual daily settlement of teller cash and proof transactions.
3. Prepares branch daily journal and general ledger.
4. Promotes the bank's services:
   - Cross-sells other bank services appropriate to customer's needs.
   - Answers inquiries regarding bank matters.
   - Directs customers to other departments for specialized services.
5. Assists with other branch duties:
   - Receipts night and mail deposits.
   - Reconciles ATM transactions.
   - Provides safe deposit services.
   - Performs secretarial duties.

New Job Description for Customer Service Representative

FUNCTION: Provides customers with the highest-quality services, with special emphasis on recognizing customer need and cross-selling appropriate bank services. Plays an active role in developing and maintaining good relations.

RESPONSIBILITIES

1. Presents and communicates the best possible customer service:
   - Greets all customers with a courteous, friendly attitude.
   - Provides fast, accurate, friendly service.
   - Uses customer's name whenever possible.
2. Sells bank services and maintains customer relations:
   - Cross-sells retail services by identifying and referring valid prospects to a customer assistance representative or customer service director. When time permits (no other customers waiting in line), should actively cross-sell retail services.
   - Develops new business by acquainting noncustomers with bank services and existing customers with additional services that they are not currently using.
3. Provides a prompt and efficient operation on a professional level:
   - Receives cash and/or checks for checking accounts, savings accounts, taxes withheld, loan payments, Mastercard and Visa, mortgage payments, money orders, traveler's checks, cashier's checks.
   - Verifies amount of cash and/or checks received, being alert to counterfeit or fraudulent items.
   - Cashes checks in accordance with bank policy. Watches for stop payments and holds funds per bank policy.
   - Receives payment of collection items, safe deposit rentals, and other miscellaneous items.
   - Confers with head CSR or customer service director on nonroutine situations.
   - Sells traveler's checks, money orders, monthly transit passes, and cashier's checks and may redeem coupons and sell or redeem foreign currency.
   - Prepares coin and currency orders as necessary.
   - Services, maintains, and settles ATMs as required.
   - Ensures only minimum cash exposure necessary for efficient operation is kept in cash drawer; removes excess cash immediately to secured location.
   - Prepares accurate and timely daily settlement of work.
   - Performs bookkeeping and operational functions as assigned by customer service director.

New Job Description for Head Customer Service Representative

FUNCTION: Supervises all customer service representatives in the designated branch office, ensuring efficient operation and the highest-quality service to customers. Plays an active role in developing and maintaining good customer relations. Assists other branch personnel on request.

RESPONSIBILITIES

1. Supervises the CSRs in the branch:
   - Allocates work, coordinates work flow, reviews and revises work procedures.
   - Ensures teller area is adequately and efficiently staffed with well-trained, qualified personnel. Assists CSRs with more complex transactions.
   - Resolves routine personnel problems, referring more complex situations to customer service director.
   - Participates in decisions concerning performance appraisal, promotions, wage changes, transfers, and termination of subordinate CSR staff.

2. Assumes responsibility for CSRs' money:
   - Buys and sells money in the vault, ensuring adequacy of branch currency and coin supply.
   - Ensures that CSRs and cash sheets are in balance.
   - Maintains necessary records, including daily branch journal and general ledger.

3. Accepts deposits and withdrawals by business customers at the commercial window.

4. Operates teller window to provide services to retail customers (see Responsibilities for CSRs).

New Job Description for Customer Assistance Representative

FUNCTION: Provides services and guidance to customers/prospects seeking banking relationships or related information. Promotes and sells needed products and responds to special requests by existing customers.

RESPONSIBILITIES

1. Provides prompt, efficient, and friendly service to all customers and prospective customers:
   - Describes and sells bank services to customers/prospects who approach them directly or via referral from customer service reps or other bank personnel.
   - Answers customers' questions regarding bank services, hours, etc.

2. Identifies and responds to customers' needs:
   - Promotes and sells retail services and identifies any existing cross-sell opportunities.
   - Opens new accounts for individuals, businesses, and private organizations.
   - Prepares temporary checks and deposit slips for new checking/NOW accounts.
   - Sells checks and deposit slips.
   - Interviews and takes applications for and pays out on installment/charge card accounts and other credit-related products.
   - Certifies checks.
   - Handles stop payment requests.
   - Responds to telephone mail inquiries from customers or bank personnel.
   - Receives notification of name or address changes and takes necessary action.
   - Takes action on notification of lost passbooks, credit cards, ATM cards, collateral, and other lost or stolen items.
   - Demonstrates ATMs to customers and assists with problems.
   - Coordinates closing of accounts and ascertains reasons.

3. Sells and services all retail products:
   - Advises customers and processes applications for all products covered in CAR training programs (and updates).
   - Initiates referrals to the appropriate department when a trust or corporate business need is identified.

New Job Description for Customer Service Director

FUNCTION: Supervises customer service representatives, customer assistance representatives, and other staff as assigned to provide the most effective and profitable retail banking delivery system in the local marketplace. Supervises sales efforts and provides feedback to management concerning response to products and services by current and prospective banking customers. Communicates goals and results to those supervised and ensures operational standards are met in order to achieve outstanding customer service.

RESPONSIBILITIES

1. Supervises effective delivery of retail products:
   - Selects, trains, and manages CSRs and CARs.
   - Assigns duties and work schedules.
   - Completes performance reviews.

2. Personally, and through those supervised, renders the highest level of professional and efficient customer service available in the local marketplace:
   - Provides high level of service while implementing most efficient and customer-sensitive staffing schedules.
   - Supervises all on-the-job programs within office.
   - Ensures that outstanding customer service standards are achieved.
   - Directs remedial programs for CSRs and CARs as necessary.

3. Develops retail sales effectiveness to the degree necessary to achieve market share objectives:
   - Ensures that all CSRs and CARs possess comprehensive product knowledge.
   - Directs coordinated cross-sell program within office at all times.
   - Reports staff training needs to branch manager and/or regional training director.

4. Ensures adherence to operational standards:
   - Oversees preparation of daily and monthly operational and sales reports.
   - Estimates, approves, and coordinates branch cash needs in advance.
   - Oversees ATM processing function.
   - Handles or consults with CSRs/CARs on more complex transactions.
   - Ensures clean and businesslike appearance of the branch facility.

5. Informs branch manager of customer response to products:
   - Reports customer complaints and types of sales resistance encountered.
   - Describes and summarizes reasons for account closings.
6. Communicates effectively the goals and results of the bank to those under supervision:
   - Reduces office goals into format which translates to goals for each CSR or CAR.

- Reports sales and cross-sell results to all CSRs and CARs.
- Conducts sales- and service-oriented staff meetings with CSRs/CARs on a regular basis.
- Attends all scheduled customer service management meetings organized by regional office.

STUDY QUESTIONS

1. *Identify the steps taken by Menton Bank to develop a stronger customer orientation in its retail branches.*
2. *Compare and contrast the jobs of CAR and CSR. How important is each (a) to bank operations and (b) to customer satisfaction?*
3. *Evaluate the strengths and weaknesses of Karen Mitchell and other candidates for head CSR.*
4. *What action do you recommend for filling the head CSR position?*

Case 13   Red Lobster

CHRISTOHER LOVELOCK

A peer review panel of managers and service workers from a restaurant chain must decide whether or not a waitress has been unfairly fired from her job.

"It felt like a knife going through me!" declared Mary Campbell, 53, after she was fired from her waitressing job at a restaurant in the Red Lobster chain. But instead of suing for what she considered unfair dismissal after 19 years of service, Campbell called for a peer review, seeking to recover her job and three weeks of lost wages.

Three weeks after the firing, a panel of employees from different Red Lobster restaurants was reviewing the evidence and trying to determine whether the server had, in fact, been unjustly fired for allegedly stealing a guest comment card completed by a couple of customers whom she had served.

PEER REVIEW AT DARDEN INDUSTRIES

Red Lobster was owned by Darden Industries, which also owned a second large restaurant chain known as Olive Garden. The company, which had a total of 110,000 employees, had adopted a policy of encouraging peer review of disputed employee firings and disciplinary actions several years earlier. The company's key objectives were to limit worker lawsuits and ease workplace tensions.

Advocates of the peer review approach, which had been adopted at several other companies, believed that it was a very effective way of channeling constructively the pain and anger that employees felt after being fired or disciplined by their managers. By reducing the incidence of lawsuits, a company could also save on legal expenses.

A Darden spokesperson stated that the peer review program had been "tremendously successful" in keeping valuable employees from unfair dismissal. Each year, about 100 disputes ended up in peer review, with only 10 subsequently resulting in lawsuits. Red Lobster managers and many employees also credited peer review with reducing racial tensions. Ms. Campbell, who said she had received dozens of calls of support, chose peer review over a lawsuit not only because it was much cheaper, but "I also liked the idea of being judged by people who know how things work in a little restaurant."

THE EVIDENCE

The review panel included a general manager, an assistant manager, a server, a hostess, and a bartender, who had all volunteered to review the circumstances of Mary Campbell's firing. Each panelist had received peer review training and was receiving regular wages plus travel expenses. The instructions to panelists were simply to do what they felt was fair.

Campbell had been fired by Jean Larimer, the general manager of the Red Lobster in Marston, where the former worked as a restaurant server. The reason given for the firing was that Campbell had asked the restaurant's hostess, Eve Taunton, for the key to the guest comment box and stolen a card from it. The card had been completed by a couple of guests whom Campbell had served and who seemed dissatisfied with their experience at the restaurant. Subsequently, the guests learned that their comment card, which complained that their prime rib of beef was too rare and their waitress was "uncooperative," had been removed from the box.

Jean Larimer's Testimony

Larimer, who supervised 100 full- and part-time employees, testified that she had dismissed Campbell after one of the two customers complained angrily to her and her supervisor. "She [the guest] felt violated," declared the manager, "because her card was taken from the box and her complaint about the food was ignored." Larimer drew the panel's attention to the company rule book, pointing out that Campbell had violated the policy that forbade removal of company property.

Mary Campbell's Testimony

Campbell testified that the female customer had requested that her prime rib be cooked "well done" and then subsequently complained that it was fatty and undercooked. The waitress told the panel that she had politely suggested that "prime rib always has fat on it," but arranged to have the meat cooked some more. However, the woman still seemed unhappy; she poured some steak sauce over the meat, but then pushed away her plate without eating all the food. When the customer remained displeased, Cambell offered her a free dessert. But the guests decided to leave, paid the bill, filled out the guest comment card, and dropped it in the guest comment box.

Admitting that she was consumed by curiosity, Campbell asked Eve Taunton, the restaurant's hostess, for the key to the box. After removing and reading the card, she pocketed it. Her intent, she declared, was to show the card to Ms. Larimer, who had been concerned earlier that the prime rib served at the restaurant was overcooked, not undercooked. However, she forgot about the card and later, accidentally, threw it out.

Eve Taunton's Testimony
At the time of the firing, Taunton, a 17-year-old student, was working at Red Lobster for the summer. "I didn't think it was a big deal to give her [Campbell] the key," she said. "A lot of people would come up to me to get it."

THE PANEL DELIBERATES

Having heard the testimony, the members of the review panel had to decide whether Ms. Larimer had been justified in firing Ms. Campbell. The panelists' initial reactions to the situation were split by rank, with the hourly workers supporting Campbell and the managers supporting Larimer. But then the debate began in earnest in an effort to reach consensus.

STUDY QUESTIONS

1. What are the marketing implications of this situation?
2. Evaluate the concept of peer review. What are its strengths and weaknesses? What type of environment is required to make it work well?
3. Review the evidence. Do you believe the testimony presented?
4. What decision would you make and why?

Case 14   Hilton HHonors Worldwide: Loyalty Wars

JOHN DEIGHTON AND STOWE SHOEMAKER

Hilton Hotels regards frequent guest programs as the lodging industry's most important marketing tool, serving to direct promotional and customer service efforts at the heavy user. How should management of Hilton's international guest rewards program respond when Starwood, a competing hotel group operating several brands, ups the ante in the loyalty stakes?

Jeff Diskin, head of Hilton HHonors® (Hilton's guest reward program), opened *The Wall Street Journal* on February 2, 1999, and read the headline, "Hotels Raise the Ante in Business-Travel Game." The story read, "Starwood Hotels and Resorts Worldwide Inc. is expected to unveil tomorrow an aggressive frequent-guest program that it hopes will help lure more business travelers to its Sheraton, Westin and other hotels. Accompanied by a $50 million ad campaign, the program ratchets up the stakes in the loyalty-program game that big corporate hotel companies, including Starwood and its rivals at Marriott, Hilton and Hyatt are playing."[1]

Diskin did not hide his concern: "These guys are raising their costs, and they're probably raising mine too. They are reducing the cost-effectiveness of the industry's most important marketing tool by deficit spending against their program. Loyalty programs have been at the core of how we attract and retain our best customers for over a decade. But they are only as cost-effective as our competitors let them be."

LOYALTY MARKETING PROGRAMS

The idea of rewarding loyalty had its origins in coupons and trading stamps. First in the 1900s and again in the 1950s, America experienced episodes of trading-stamp frenzy that became so intense that congressional investigations were mounted. Retailers would give customers small adhesive stamps in proportion to the amount of their purchases, to be pasted into books and eventually redeemed for merchandise. The best-known operator had been the S&H Green Stamp Company. Both episodes had lasted about 20 years, declining as the consumer passion for collecting abated and vendors came to the conclusion that any advantage they might once have held had been competed away by emulators.

Loyalty marketing in its modern form was born in 1981 when American Airlines introduced the AAdvantage frequent-flyer program, giving "miles" in proportion to the miles traveled, redeemable for free travel. It did so in response to the competitive pressure that followed airline deregulation. The American Airlines program had no need of stamps, because it took advantage of the data-warehousing capabilities of computers. Soon program administrators realized that they had a tool that did not merely reward loyalty but identified by name and address the people who accounted for most of aviation's revenues and made a one-to-one relationship possible.

Competing airlines launched their own programs, but, unlike stamp programs, frequent-flyer programs seemed to survive emulation. By 1990, almost all airlines offered them. In the late 1990s, Delta Air Lines and United Airlines linked their programs together, as did American and US Airways in the United States. Internationally, United Airlines and Lufthansa combined with 11 other airlines to form Star Alliance, and American, British Airways, and four others formed an alliance called Oneworld. In these alliances, qualifying flights on any of the member airlines could be credited to the frequent-flyer club of the flyer's choice.

As the decade ended, computer-based frequency programs were common in many service industries, including car rentals, department stores, video and book retailing, credit cards, movie theaters, and the hotel industry.

THE HOTEL INDUSTRY

Chain brands were a major factor in the global hotel market of 13.6 million rooms.[2] The chains supplied reservation services, field sales operations, loyalty program administration,

---

and the management of hotel properties under well-recognized names such as Hilton and Marriott. (See **Exhibit 1** for details of the seven largest U.S. hotel chains competing in the business-class hotel segment.)

While the brands stood for quality, there was less standardization of operations in hotel chains than in many other services. The reason was that behind a consumer's experience of a hotel brand might lie any of many methods of control. A branded hotel might be owned and managed by the chain, but it might be owned by a third party and managed by the chain, or owned by the chain and managed by a franchisee, or, in some cases, owned and managed by the franchisee. Occasionally chains managed one another's brands, because one chain could be another's franchisee. Starwood, for example, ran hotels under the Hilton brand as Hilton's franchisee. Information about competitors' operating procedures therefore circulated quite freely in the industry.

Consumers

For most Americans, a stay in a hotel was a relatively rare event. Of the 74% of Americans who traveled overnight in a year, only 41% used a hotel, motel, or resort. The market in which Hilton competed was smaller still, defined by price point and trip purpose and divided among business, convention, and leisure segments.

The **business** segment accounted for one-third of all room nights in the market that Hilton served. About two-thirds of these stays were at rates negotiated between the guest's employer and the chain, but since most corporations negotiated rates with two and sometimes three hotel chains, business travelers had some discretion to choose where they would stay. About one-third of business travelers did not have access to negotiated corporate rates and had full discretion to choose their hotel.

The **convention** segment, comprising convention, conference, and other meeting-related travel, accounted for another third of room nights in Hilton's competitive set. The choice of hotel in this instance was in the hands of a small number of professional conference organizers, typically employees of professional associations and major corporations.

The **leisure** segment accounted for the final third. Leisure guests were price sensitive, often making their selections from among packages of airlines, cars, tours, and hotels assembled by a small group of wholesalers and tour organizers at rates discounted below business rates.

EXHIBIT 1   The U.S. Lodging Industry

	COUNTRIES	PROPERTIES	ROOMS	OWNED PROPERTIES	FRANCHISED PROPERTIES	MANAGEMENT CONTRACTS
Marriott International[a]	53	1,764	339,200	49	936	776
Bass Hotels and Resorts[b]	90	2,700	447,967	76	2,439	185
Hilton Hotels Corp.[c]	11	272	91,060	39	207	16
Starwood Hotels and Resorts Worldwide, Inc.[d]	72	695	212,950	171	291	233
Hyatt[e]	45	246	93,729	NA	NA	NA
Carlson[f]	50	581	112,089	1	542	38
Hilton International[g]	50	224	62,941	154	0	70
Promus[h]	11	1,398	198,526	160	1,059	179

[a]Includes Marriott Hotels, Resorts and Suites; Courtyard, Residence Inn, TownePlace Suites, Fairfield Inn, SpringHill Suites, Marriott Vacation Club International; Conference Centers, Marriott Executive Residences, Ritz-Carlton, Renaissance, Ramada International.

[b]Includes Inter-Continental, Forum, Crowne Plaza, Holiday Inn, Holiday Inn Express, Staybridge.

[c]Includes Hilton Hotels, Hilton Garden Inns, Hilton Suites, Hilton Grand Vacation Clubs, and Conrad International.

[d]Includes St. Regis, Westin Hotels and Resorts, Sheraton Hotels and Resorts, Four Points, Sheraton Inns, The W Hotels. Does not include other Starwood-owned hotels, flagged under other brands (93 properties for 29,322 rooms).

[e]Includes Hyatt Hotels, Hyatt International, and Southern Pacific Hotel Corporation (SPHC). Because it is a privately held corporation, it will not divulge the breakdown of rooms between ownership, franchise, and management contract.

[f]Includes Radisson Hotels Worldwide, Regent International Hotels, Country Inns and Suites.

[g]A wholly owned subsidiary of what was once known as the Ladbroke Group. In spring 1999, Ladbroke changed their name to Hilton Group PLC to reflect the emphasis on hotels.

[h]Includes such brands as Doubletree, Red Lion, Hampton Inn, Hampton Inn & Suites, Embassy Suites, and Homewood Suites.

Source: World Trade Organization and company information.

Although the chains as a whole experienced demand from all segments, individual properties tended to draw disproportionately from one segment or another. Resort hotels served leisure travelers and some conventioneers, convention hotels depended on group and business travel, and hotels near airports were patronized by guests on business, for example. These segmentation schemes, however, obscured the fact that the individuals in segments differentiated by trip purpose and price point were often the same people. Frequent travelers patronized hotels of various kinds and price segments, depending, for example, on whether a stay was a reimbursable business expense, a vacation, or a personal expense.

Competition

Four large global brands dominated the business-class hotel market (**Table A**). Each competed at more than one price point. (**Exhibit 2** shows the price points in the industry, and **Exhibit 3** shows the distribution of brands across price points.)

Starwood

Beginning in 1991, Barry Sternlicht built Starwood Hotels and Resorts Worldwide from a base in a real estate investment trust. In January 1998, Starwood bought Westin Hotels and Resorts, and a month later it bought ITT

Table A

Marriott International	339,200 rooms
Starwood Hotels and Resorts	212,900 rooms
Hyatt Hotels	93,700 rooms
Hilton Hotels	91,100 rooms
Hilton International	62,900 rooms

Source: Company records.

Corporation, which included Sheraton Hotels and Resorts, after a well-publicized battle with Hilton Hotels Corporation. By year-end, Starwood had under unified management the Westin, Sheraton, St. Regis, Four Points, and Caesar's Palace brands. Starwood had recently announced plans to create a new brand, W, aimed at younger professionals.

Marriott

Marriott International operated and franchised hotels under the Marriott, Ritz-Carlton, Renaissance, Residence Inn, Courtyard, TownePlace Suites, Fairfield Inn, SpringHill Suites, and Ramada International brands. It also operated conference centers and provided furnished corporate housing. A real estate investment trust, Host Marriott, owned some of the properties operated by Marriott International, as well as some Hyatt, Four Season, and Swissotel properties.

EXHIBIT 2   Price Segments in the Lodging Industry

- Luxury: Average rack rate over $125, full-service hotels with deluxe amenities for leisure travelers and special amenities for business and meeting markets. Chains in this segment include Four Seasons, Hilton, Hyatt, Inter-Continental (a Bass Hotels and Resorts brand), Marriott Hotels and Resorts, Renaissance (a Marriott International brand), Ritz-Carlton (also a Marriott International brand), Sheraton (a Starwood Hotels and Resorts brand), and Westin (also a Starwood Hotels and Resorts brand).
- Upscale: Average rack rate between $100 and $125, full-service hotels with standard amenities. Includes most all-suite, non-extended-stay brands. Crowne Plaza (a Bass Hotels and Resorts brand), Doubletree Guest Suites (a Promus Hotel Corp. brand), Embassy Suites (also a Promus Hotel Corp. brand), Radisson (a Carlson Worldwide Hospitality brand), Hilton Inn, and Clarion (a Choice Hotels brand) are all examples of chains in this segment.
- Midmarket with food and beverage (F&B): Average rack rate between $60 and $90, full-service hotels with lower service levels and amenities than the upscale segment. Examples include Best Western, Courtyard (a Marriott International brand), Garden Inn (a Hilton brand), Holiday Inn (a Bass Hotels and Resorts brand), and Howard Johnson (a Cendant brand).
- Midmarket without F&B: Average rack rate between $45 and $70, with limited-service and comparable amenities to the midmarket with F&B segment. Examples of chains in this segment include Hampton Inns (a Promus brand), Holiday Inn Express (a Bass Hotels and Resorts brand), and Comfort Inn (a Choice Hotels brand).
- Economy: Average rack rate between $40 and $65, with limited service and few amenities. Fairfield Inn (a Marriott International brand), Red Roof Inn, Travelodge, and Days Inn of America (a Cendant brand) are examples of economy chains.
- Budget: Average rack rate between $30 and $60, with limited service and basic amenities. Motel 6, Super 8, and Econo Lodge are the best-known chains in this segment.
- Extended stay: Average rack rate between $60 and $90, targeted to extended-stay market and designed for extended length of stay. Marriott International has the following two brands in this market: Residence Inn by Marriott and TownePlace Suites. Other chains include Homewood Suites (a Bass Hotels and Resorts brand), Summerfield Suites, and Extended Stay America.

Source: U.S. lodging chains segmented by RealTime Hotel Reports Inc., authors of the 1998 Lodging Survey.

EXHIBIT 3 Segments Served by the Major Chains

	LUXURY	UPSCALE	MID-MARKET WITH FOOD AND BEVERAGE	MID-MARKET WITHOUT FOOD AND BEVERAGE	ECONOMY	BUDGET	EXTENDED STAY
Hilton	X	X	X	X			
Hyatt	X						
Marriott	X	X	X		X		X
Starwood	X	X	X				X

Source: Company records.

Hyatt

The Pritzker family of Chicago owned Hyatt Corporation, the only privately owned major hotel chain. Hyatt comprised Hyatt Hotels, operating hotels and resorts in the United States, Canada, and the Caribbean; and Hyatt International, operating overseas. Hyatt also owned Southern Pacific Hotel Group, a three- and four-star hotel chain based primarily in Australia. Although the companies operated independently, they ran joint marketing programs.

The 1990s had been a time of consolidation and rationalization in the lodging industry, partly due to application of information technologies to reservation systems and control of operations. Diskin reflected on the trend: "Historically, bigger has been better because it has led to economies of scale and bigger and better brands to leverage. Historically, big players could win even if they did not do a particularly good job on service, performance, or programs. Now [after the Starwood deal] there's another big player. It would have been nice if it had been Hilton that was the largest hotel chain in the world, but biggest is not the only way to be best."

MARKETING THE HILTON BRAND

The Hilton brand was controlled by two entirely unrelated corporations, Hilton Hotels Corporation (HHC), based in Beverley Hills, California, and Hilton International (HIC), headquartered near London, England. In 1997, however, HHC and HIC agreed to reunify the Hilton brand worldwide. They agreed to cooperate on sales and marketing, standardize operations, and run the Hilton HHonors loyalty program across all HHC and HIC hotels. At the end of 1998, HHC divested itself of casino interests and announced "a new era as a dedicated hotel company."

The exit from gaming, the reunification of Hilton's worldwide marketing, and the extension of the brand into the middle market under the Hilton Garden Inns name were initiatives that followed the appointment in 1997 of Stephen F. Bollenbach as president and chief executive officer of Hilton. Bollenbach had served as chief financial officer of Marriott and most recently as chief financial officer of Disney, and he brought to Hilton a passion for branding. To some members of the Hilton management team, the focus on brand development was a welcome one. "Hilton's advantage has been a well-recognized name, but a potentially limiting factor has been a widely varying product and the challenge of managing customer expectation with such a variety of product offerings. Since Hilton includes everything from world-renowned properties like The Waldorf-Astoria and Hilton Hawaiian Village to the smaller middle-market Hilton Garden Inns, it's important to give consumers a clear sense of what to expect from the various types of hotels," observed one manager.

In mid-1999, the properties branded as Hilton hotels comprised:

1. 39 owned or partly owned by HHC in the United States
2. 207 franchised by HHC to third-party managers in the United States
3. 16 managed by HHC in the United States on behalf of third-party owners
4. 10 managed internationally under HHC's Conrad International brand
5. 220 managed by HIC in over 50 countries excluding the U.S.

The executives at Hilton HHonors worked for these 492 hotels and their 154,000 rooms. The previous year had been successful. Revenues had been in the region of $158 per night per guest, and occupancy had exceeded break-even. Hotels like Hilton's tended to cover fixed costs at about 68% occupancy, and 80% of all revenue at higher occupancy levels flowed to the bottom line. Advertising, selling, and other marketing costs (a component of fixed costs) for this group of hotels were not published, but industry norms ran at about $750 per room per year.[3]

Hilton HHonors Program

Hilton HHonors was the name Hilton gave to its program designed to build loyalty to the Hilton brand worldwide. Hilton HHonors Worldwide (HHW) operated the program, not as a profit center but as a service

EXHIBIT 4 Hilton HHonors Worldwide: 1998 Income Statement

(While these data are broadly reflective of the economic situation, certain competitively sensitive information has been masked.)

	$ (THOUSANDS)	
Revenue		
Contributions from hotels		
Domestic	$39,755	
International	$10,100	
Strategic partner contributions	$18,841	
Membership fees[a]	$1,141	
Total		**$69,837**
Expense		
Redemptions		
Cash payments to hotels	$12,654	
Deferred liability[b]	$9,436	
Airline miles purchases	$17,851	
Member acquisition expenses	$7,273	
Member communication expenses	4,236	
Program administration expenses	$17,988	
Total		**$69,438**
Net Income		**$399**

[a]From members of the Hilton Senior HHonors program only. The Senior HHonors program invited people over 60 to receive discounted stays in exchange for a membership fee. Regular HHonors members do not pay a membership fee.

[b]More points were issued than redeemed. From the outstanding balance a deferred liability was charged to HHW's income statement, based on estimating the proportion of points that would ultimately be redeemed.

Source: Company records (masked). For purposes of consistency in calculation among class members, assume an average nightly revenue of $158 per room. Assume that airline miles are purchased from the airline by Hilton at 1 cent per mile.

to its two parents, HHC and HIC. It was required to break even each year and to measure its effectiveness through a complex set of program metrics. Diskin ran the limited liability corporation with a staff of 30, with one vice president overseeing the program's marketing efforts and one with operational and customer service oversight. (**Exhibit 4** shows the income statement for HHW.)

Membership in the Hilton HHonors program was open to anyone who applied, at no charge. Members earned points toward their Hilton HHonors account whenever they stayed at HHC or HIC hotels. When Hilton HHonors members accumulated enough points in the program, they could redeem them for stays at HHonors hotels, use them to buy products and services from partner companies, or convert them to miles in airline frequent-flyer programs. (**Exhibit 5** shows how points in the program flowed among participants in the program, as detailed in the text that follows.)

There were four tiers of membership—Blue, Silver, Gold, and Diamond. The program worked as follows at the **Blue** level in 1998.

- When a member stayed at a Hilton hotel and paid a so-called business rate,[4] the hotel typically paid HHW 4.5 cents per dollar of the guest's folio (folio is the total charge by the guest before taxes). HHW credited the guest's Hilton HHonors account with 10 points per eligible dollar of folio.

- Hilton guests could earn mileage in partner airline frequent-flyer programs for the same stay that earned them HHonors points, a practice known as Double Dipping. (Hilton was the only hotel chain to offer double dipping; other chains with frequency programs required guests to choose between points in the hotel program or miles in the airline program.) If the member chose to double-dip, HHW bought miles from the relevant airline and credited the guest's airline frequent-flyer account at 500 miles per stay.

- If the guest used points to pay for a stay, HHW reimbursed the hosting hotel at more than the costs incremental to the cost of leaving the room empty but less than the revenue from a paying guest. The points needed to earn a stay depended on the class of hotel and fell when occupancy was low. As illustration, redemption rates ranged from 5,000 points to get 50% off the $128 cost of a weekend at the Hilton Albuquerque, to 25,000 points for a free weekend night at the $239 per night Hilton Boston Back Bay. A number of exotic rewards were offered, such as a two-person, seven-night diving adventure in the Red Sea for 350,000 points, including hotel and airfare.

- Members earned points by renting a car, flying with a partner airline, using the Hilton Credit Card from American Express, or buying products promoted in mailings by partners such as FTD Florists and Mrs. Field's Cookies. Members could buy

EXHIBIT 5   How the Hilton HHonors Program Works

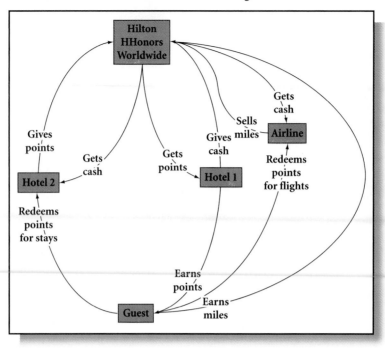

Source: Company.

points at $10 per thousand for up to 20% of the points needed for a reward.

- Members had other benefits besides free stays. They had a priority-reservation telephone number. Check-in went faster because information on preferences was on file. Members were favored over nonmembers when they asked for late checkout. If members were dissatisfied, they were guaranteed a room upgrade certificate in exchange for a letter explaining their dissatisfaction. Points could be exchanged for airline miles and vice versa and to buy partner products such as airline tickets, flowers, Mrs. Field's Cookies products, Cannondale bicycles, AAA membership, Princess Cruises trips, and car rentals.

Members were awarded **Silver VIP** status if they stayed at HHonors hotels four times in a year. They earned a 15% bonus on base points, received a 5,000-point bonus after seven stays in a quarter, and received a 10,000-point discount when they claimed a reward costing 100,000 points. They were given a certificate for an upgrade to the best room in the hotel after every fifth stay.

Members were awarded **Gold VIP** status if they stayed at HHonors hotels 16 times or for 36 nights in a year. They earned a 25% bonus on base points, received a 5,000-point bonus after seven stays in a quarter, and received a 20,000-point discount when they claimed a reward costing 100,000 points. They were given a certificate for an upgrade to the best room in the hotel after every fifth stay and were upgraded to best available room at time of check-in.

The top 1% of members were given **Diamond VIP** status. This level was not mentioned in promotional material, and no benefits were promised. Diskin explained, "Our goal at the time was to underpromise and overdeliver. If you stay a lot, we say thank you, and as a reward we want to give you Diamond VIP status. We get a lot more bang, more affinity, more vesting from the customer if we do something unexpected. As an industry, we should never overpromise. It leads the public to decide that this is all smoke and mirrors, and it makes it harder for us to deliver genuine value." **Table B** shows HHW's member activity in 1998.

A further 712,000 stays averaging 2.4 nights were recorded in 1998 for which no Hilton HHonors membership card was presented but instead airline miles were claimed and airline membership numbers were captured, so that the guest could be given a unique identifier in the Hilton database. Spending on these stays totaled $327 million.

Guests identified by their HHonors or airline membership numbers occupied 22.5% of all the rooms occupied in the Hilton Hotels and Hilton International network in a year. They were a much smaller proportion of all the guests who stayed with Hilton in a year because they tended to be frequent travelers. Hilton's research found that Hilton HHonors members spent about $4.6 billion on accommodation per year, not all of which was with Hilton. The industry estimated that members of the frequent-stayer programs of all the major hotel chains represented a market worth $11.1 billion and that the average member belonged to 3.5 programs.

Table B Members' Paid Activity in 1998

	Members (000)	Members Active in 1998 (000)	Stays for Which Members Paid (000)	Nights for Which They Paid (000)	Spending on Which They Earned Points ($000)	Stays per Active Member in 1998	Nights per Active Member in 1998	Reward Claimed by Member
Diamond	24	20	310	521	$62,000	15.5	26.1	27,000
Gold	220	84	1,110	1,916	$266,000	13.2	22.8	34,200
Silver	694	324	1,023	1,999	$341,000	3.2	6.2	70,200
Blue	1,712	992	1,121	2,579	$439,000	1.1	2.6	48,600
Total	2,650	1,420	3,564	7,015	$1,108,000	2.5	4.9	180,000

Source: Company records (certain competitively sensitive information has been masked).

Rationales for the Program

1. Revenue and Yield Management

Hotel profitability was acutely sensitive to revenue. A trend in the industry was to appoint a "revenue manager" to each property to oversee the day-to-day decisions that affected hotel revenue. Yield management models were probabilistic algorithms that helped this manager set reservations policy. He or she used past history and other statistical data to make continuously updated recommendations regarding hotel booking patterns and what price to offer a particular guest. Simulation studies had shown that when booking was guided by a good yield management model, a company's revenue increased by 20% over a simple "first come, first served, fixed price" policy.

In the hotel industry, effectively managing yield meant utilizing a model to predict that a room was highly likely to come available due to cancellation or no-show, as well as driving business to higher-paying or longer-staying guests. Variable pricing meant that the rate charged for a room depended not only on its size and fittings but also on the day of booking, the day of occupation, the length of stay, and customer characteristics. Of these factors, customer characteristics were the most problematic.

Customer characteristics were needed by the model to estimate "walking cost," the cost of turning a customer away. That cost in turn depended on the customer's future lifetime value to the chain, a function of their willingness to pay, and past loyalty to the chain. These were considered "soft" variables, notoriously difficult to estimate. The better the historical information on a customer, however, the better the estimate. As Adam Burke, HHonors' senior director of marketing for North America, put it, "Who gets the room—the person paying $20 more that you may never see again, or the guy spending thousands of dollars in the system? If we have the right data, the model can be smart enough to know the difference." Some in the hotel industry argued that a benefit of a frequent-guest program was to let the reservations system make those distinctions.

2. Collaborating with Partners

HHW partnered with 25 airlines, three car rental firms, and a number of other firms. Burke explained, "Why is Mrs. Field's Cookies in the program? We have several objectives—regional relevance to consumers, access to partners' customers, making it easier for members to attain rewards. A franchisee may say, 'Why are we doing something with FTD Florists?' We point out that their investment keeps costs down and gives a broader range of rewards to our members."

Burke explained why Hilton offered double dipping: "We have 2.5 million members. The airline frequent-flyer programs have 20, 30, 40 million members who aren't HHonors members and do travel a lot. Airlines don't mind us talking to their members because—through double dipping—we don't compete with their programs. In fact, we complement them by allowing our joint customers to earn both currencies."

3. Working with Franchisees

The Hilton HHonors program was a strong factor in persuading hotel owners to become Hilton franchisees or give Hilton a management contract to run their property. Franchisees tended to be smaller hotels, more dependent on "road warrior" business than many of Hilton's convention hotels, resort hotels, and flagship properties. They saw value in a frequent-guest program to attract business, and HHW's program cost was comparable with or lower than its competitors'. The program's ability to drive business, however, remained its biggest selling point. Diskin elaborated, "Seven or eight years ago some operators were concerned about the cost of the program. We took a bunch of the most vocal, critical guys and we put them in a room for two days with us to discuss the importance of building long-term customer loyalty, and they came out saying, 'We need to spend more money on the program!'"

4. Relations with Guests

The program let the most valuable guests be recognized on-property. Diskin explained:

> In a sense, the loyalty program is a safe haven for the guest. If there is a problem and it is not taken care of

at the property level, the guest can contact our customer service team. It's a mechanism to make sure we hear about those problems. We also do outbound after-visit calling, and we call HHonors members because they're the best database and the most critical guests we have. They have the most experience and the highest expectations. We do feedback groups with members in addition to focus groups and quantitative research. We invite a bunch of members in the hotel down for dinner, and we say we want to talk about a subject. I get calls from people that are lifelong loyalists, not because of any changes we've made, but because once we invited them and asked them their opinion. People care about organizations that care about them.

Hilton customized a guest's hotel experience. Diskin explained, "We build guest profiles that keep track of preferences, enabling the hotel to provide customized services. For instance, consider the guest that always wants a room that is for nonsmokers and has a double bed. This information can be stored as part of the member's record so that when she or he makes a reservation, the guest will receive this type of room without having to ask, no matter where the guest is staying."

HHW used direct mail to cultivate the relationship between members and the Hilton brand. Diskin explained, "Certainly you want to focus much of your effort on your highest-revenue guests, but there are also opportunities to reach out and try to target other customer segments. For example, we worked with a nontravel partner to overlay data from their customer files onto our total membership base and identified segments that might like vacation ownership, others who would be great for the casinos, and some that might like the business and teleconferencing services we offer."

Diskin was concerned that some travelers spread their hotel patronage among several chains and did not receive the service to which their total expenditure entitled them. He noted, "Our research suggests that a quarter of the frequent travelers are members of loyalty programs but don't have true loyalty to any one brand. They never get to enjoy the benefits of elite-program status because they don't consolidate their business with one chain. They typically don't see the value in any of the loyalty schemes because they haven't changed their stay behavior to see the benefits."

5. Helping Travel Managers Gain Compliance

A significant proportion of Hilton's business came from contracts with large corporate clients. Hilton offered discounted rates if the corporation delivered enough stays. Burke explained:

If you are a corporate travel manager, you want employees to comply with the corporate travel policy. You negotiated a rate by promising a volume of stays. While some travel managers can tell employees that they have to follow the company policy if they want to get reimbursed, many others can only recommend. What if someone is a very loyal Marriott customer, yet Marriott is not one of that company's preferred vendors? A travel office is going to have a real hard time getting that guy to stay at Hilton if they can't mandate it.

We respond with a roster of offerings to give that Marriott traveler a personal incentive to use us, the preferred vendor. Our overall objective is to use the program as a tool that can help the travel manager with compliance to their overall travel policy.

Member Attitudes

HHW made extensive use of conjoint analysis to measure what members wanted from the Hilton HHonors program. Burke explained:

Members come in for an hour-and-a-half interview. They're asked to trade off program elements, including services and amenities in the hotel, based on the value they place on those attributes relative to their cost. The results help us determine the appropriate priorities for modifying the program. We find that different people have different needs. Some people are service oriented. No amount of miles or points is ever going to replace a warm welcome and being recognized by the hotel as a loyal customer. Other people are games players. They go after free stays, and they know the rules as well as we do. We've been in feedback groups where these people will educate us on how our program works! And, of course, many people are a combination of both.

Using a sample that was broadly representative of the program's upper-tier membership categories, program research found that Hilton HHonors members had an average of over 30 stays in all hotel chains per year, staying 4.2 nights per stay. Between 1997 and 1998, Hilton experienced a 17.5% increase in member utilization of HHonors hotels globally. Despite this improvement, more than half of HHonors member stays went to competing chains annually—this was primarily attributable to Hilton's relatively limited network size and distribution. The conjoint analysis suggested that roughly one in five HHonors member stays were solely attributable to their membership in the program—making these stays purely incremental.

The study found that the most important features of a hotel program were room upgrades and airline miles, followed by free hotel stays and a variety of on-property benefits and services. Members wanted a streamlined reward-redemption process and points that did not expire. These findings led to refinements in the terms of membership for 1999, but Diskin was exploring more innovative approaches to the rewards program.

Diskin recognized that in their market research studies, consumers tended to describe an ideal program that was simply a version of the programs with which they were familiar. He was looking for more radical innovation:

> Hilton and Marriott tend to attract "games players." We want to compete effectively on the reward elements but also introduce them to the more high-touch, high-feel kind of guest experience as well. The customer base that we have accumulated comprises games players primarily. So we've got to deliver that benefit but still go further.
>
> We've been on a mission to dramatically improve the stay experience for members of the upper-tier ranks of the program. That is the key to competitive distinctiveness. That's not something that anybody can imitate. We want our best customers to feel that when they go to Hilton, they know Hilton knows they're the best customer and they're treated special. We want them to think, "I'm going to have the kind of room I want, I'm going to have the kind of stay I like, and if I have a problem, they're going to take care of it." We want the staff to know who's coming in each day and make sure that these guests get a personal welcome. Our new customer reservation system will get more information down to the hotel. We'll know a lot more about our incoming guests. We will have a guest manager in the hotel whose job it is to make you feel special and to address any concerns you may have.

THE STARWOOD ANNOUNCEMENT

The Wall Street Journal of February 2, 1999, announced the birth of the Starwood Preferred Guest Program, covering Westin Hotels Resorts, Sheraton Hotels Resorts, The Luxury Collection, Four Points, Caesar's, and Starwood's new W brand hotels, representing more than 550 participating properties worldwide. It became clear that Starwood was adding program features that might be expensive to match. Four features in particular were of concern.

No blackout dates	All frequent guest and airline programs until now had ruled that members could not claim free travel during the very height of seasonal demand and when local events guaranteed a hotel full occupancy. Starwood was saying that if there was a room to rent, points were as good as money.
No capacity control	Programs until now had let hotel properties limit the number of rooms for free stays. Starwood was telling hotels that all unreserved rooms should be available to guests paying with points.
Paperless rewards	Guests had had previously to exchange points for a certificate and then use the certificate to pay for an authorized stay. Under Starwood's system, individual properties would be able to accept points to pay for a stay.
Hotel reimbursement	Now that blackout dates were abolished, a property, particularly an attractive vacation destination, might have to contend with many more points-paying guests than before. Starwood therefore raised the rate at which it reimbursed hotels for these stays. To meet the cost, it charged participating hotels 20%–100% more than its competitors on paid stays.

Starwood was pledging to invest $50 million in advertising to publicize the program—significantly more than HHW had historically spent on program communications. (**Exhibit 6** compares the loyalty programs of the four major business-class hotel chains after the Starwood announcement.)

Diskin's Dilemma

Without any doubt, Starwood had raised the ante in the competition for customer loyalty. Diskin had to decide whether to match or pass. He mused:

> Do we have to compete point for point? Or do we want to take a different positioning and hold on to our loyal members and differentiate HHonors from Starwood and other competitors? We're in a cycle where for 10 years the cost to our hotels of our frequent-guest program as a percent of the folio has been cycling down. Yet activation, retention, and member spend per visit all have improved. If we can deliver the same amount of business to the Hilton brand and it costs less, Hilton makes more margin. That attracts investors, franchise ownership, new builders. That's another reason why they buy the Hilton flag.

As Diskin saw it, Starwood's Preferred Guest announcement was a solution to a problem Hilton did not have, arising from its recent purchases of the Sheraton and Westin chains:

> They are trying to develop the Starwood brand with the Starwood Preferred Guest Program. They are targeting the most lucrative part of the business, the individual business traveler, where Sheraton and Westin independently have never been as effective as Marriott, Hyatt, and Hilton. Sheraton's frequent-guest program wasn't very effective. They changed it every few years; they used to have members pay for it. Westin never had enough critical mass of properties for it to be important for enough people. So now, together they can address Westin's critical-mass problem and Sheraton's relevance.

EXHIBIT 6   Membership Offerings of the Four Major Business-Class Hotel Chains in 1998

CHAIN	MEMBERSHIP RESTRICTIONS[a]	POINT VALUE	ELIGIBLE CHARGES	NEW MEMBER BONUS	AIRLINE MILEAGE ACCRUAL
Starwood	One stay per year to remain active—basic; 10 stays or 25 room nights per year—medium; 25 stays or 50 room nights	2 Starpoints = $1 basic; 3 Starpoints = $1 medium or premium	Room rate, F&B, laundry/valet, phone, in-room movies	Periodically	Starpoints earned can be converted to miles 1:1; cannot earn both points and miles for the same stay
Hilton	One stay per year to remain active—Blue; 4 stays per year or 10 nights—medium; 16 stays per year or 36 nights—premium; 28 stays or 60 nights—top	10 pts. = $1—Blue; +15% bonus on points earned—medium; +25% bonus on points earned—premium; +50% bonus on points earned—top	Room rate, F&B, laundry, phone	Periodically	500 miles per qualifying stay in addition to point earnings
Hyatt	One stay per year to remain active—basic; 5 stays or 15 nights per year—medium; 25 stays or 50 nights per year—premium	5 pts. = $1; +15% bonus on points earned—medium; +30% bonus on points earned—premium	Room rate, F&B, laundry, phone	Periodically	500 miles per stay; not available if earning points
Marriott	No requirements for basic; 15 nights per year—medium; 50 nights per year—premium	10 pts. = $1; +20% bonus on points earned—medium; +25% bonus on points earned—premium	Room rate, F&B, laundry, phone	Double points first 120 days	3 miles per dollar spent at full-service hotels; 1 mile per dollar spent at other hotels; not available if earning points

[a]Most programs run three tiers. For ease of comparison, the three levels are named basic, medium, and premium. HHonors has four tiers.

But if frequent-guest programs were a good idea, perhaps bigger programs were an even better idea. Diskin reflected: "Hotel properties routinely pay 10% commission to a travel agent to bring them a guest. Yet they continually scrutinize the cost of these programs. Of course, they're justified in doing so, but the return on investment clearly justifies the expenditure. And our competitors certainly seem to see a value in increasing their investment in their programs."

Diskin tried to predict Hyatt's and Marriott's response to the Starwood announcement. The industry was quite competitive enough. He thought back to his early years at United Airlines and recalled the damage that price wars had done to that industry.

EXHIBIT 6 (Continued)

CHAIN	AFFINITY CREDIT CARD POINT ACCRUAL	POINT PURCHASE	BONUS THRESHOLD REWARD	EXCHANGE HOTEL POINTS FOR AIRLINE MILES	HOTEL REWARDS
Starwood	1,000 hotel pts. first card use; 1 hotel pt. = $1 spent; 4 hotel points = $1 spent at Starwood hotels	NA	NA	1:1 conversion except JAL, KLM, Ansett, Qantas, Air New Zealand; 5,000 bonus miles when you convert 20,000 hotel points; minimum 2,000 Starpoints—basic; minimum 15,000—medium; no minimum for premium	5 categories; 1 free night category 1 is 3,000 Starpoints; 1 free night category 5 is 12,000 Starpoints
Hilton	5,000 hotel pts. for application; 2,500 hotel points first card use; 2 hotel pts. = $1 spent; 3 hotel pts. = $1 spent at HHonors Hotels	$10 = 1,000 pts. up to 20% of the total points of the reward	2,000 pts. = 4 stays per quarter	10,000 pts. = 1,500 miles; 20,000 pts. = 3,500 miles; 50,000 pts. = 10,000 miles; minimum 10,000 hotel points exchange, can also exchange airline miles for hotel points	5 categories: free weekend night 10,000 lowest; 35,000 highest
Hyatt	None	$10 = 500 pts. up to 10% of the total points of the reward	None basic	3 pts. = 1 mile; minimum 9,000-point exchange	Weekend night no category: 8,000 pts.; if premium time there is an additional 5,000 pts.; come with partner awards
Marriott	5,000 hotel pts. first card use; 1 hotel pt. = $1 spent; 3 hotel points = $1 spent at Marriott Rewards hotels	$10 = 1,000 pts. up to 10% of the total points of the reward	None basic	10,000 pts. = 2,000 miles; 20,000 pts. = 5,000 miles; 30,000 pts. = 10,000 miles; minimum = 10,000 hotel point exchange	2 categories: 20,000 free weekend low category, and 30,000 high category

Source: Assembled by the casewriters from the promotional materials of each hotel chain in 1999.

ENDNOTES

1. *The Wall Street Journal*, February 2, 1999, p. B1.
2. World Trade Organization.
3. For the purpose of consistency in calculation among class members, assume an occupancy of 70%. The information in this paragraph has been masked. No data of this kind are publicly available, and these data are not to be interpreted as indicative of information private to either HHC or HIC.

4. Hilton distinguished three kinds of rate. "Business rates" were higher than "leisure rates," which in turn were higher than "ineligible rates," which referred to group tour wholesale rates, airline crew rates, and other deeply discounted rates.

STUDY QUESTIONS

1. What are the strengths and weaknesses of the Hilton HHonors program from the standpoints of:
   a. Hilton Hotels Corp and Hilton International
   b. member properties (franchised hotels)
   c. guests
   d. corporate travel departments

2. How does the value generated to Hilton by the program compare to its cost?
3. What is Starwood attempting to do and how should Jeff Diskin respond?

Case 15   The Accellion Service Guarantee

JOCHEN WIRTZ AND JILL KLEIN

A high-technology company introduces what it considers to be a bold service quality guarantee to communicate its commitment to service excellence to customers, prospects, and its own employees.

Accellion was a young high-technology firm with leading-edge technology in the distributed file storage, management and delivery market space. Still new to the industry, the firm aimed to become the global backbone for the next generation of Internet-based applications.

Accellion's main value proposition to the world's largest enterprises ("the Global 2000"), as well as to Internet-based providers of premium content, was to allow them to serve their users faster, increase operational efficiencies, and lower total costs. Specifically, Accellion customers could improve the access time for downloading and uploading files by more than 200 percent. This performance improvement was achieved by locating an intelligent storage and file management system at the "edges of the Internet" and thereby delivering content from regions located closer to the end-user. The typical time-consuming routing through many servers and hubs could be avoided using Accellion's infrastructure.

The need for an Internet infrastructure to deliver high bandwidth content to end-users had never been greater. There was a trend towards multimedia and personalized Web content, all of which could not be delivered efficiently by existing infrastructure, which routed data through the congested network of servers that form the backbone of the Internet. This prompted Accellion to develop and launch a new service: distributed file storage, management and delivery. Accellion provided an applications platform that resided on independent servers, which were directly connected to the users' Internet Service Providers (ISPs), thereby avoiding the congested "centers" of the Internet. This decreased access time and allowed Accellion to distribute specialized content and applications more efficiently.

To effectively market Accellion's value proposition, Warren J. Kaplan, Accellion's CEO, and S. Mohan, its Chief Strategist, felt that in addition to its leading-edge technology, key success factors for Accellion's aggressive growth strategy were excellence in service delivery and high customer satisfaction. They envisioned that customers would prefer to leverage Accellion's technology and partnerships instead of having to manage the details of deploying, maintaining and upgrading their own storage infrastructure for distributed Internet applications. To build a customer-driven culture and to communicate service excellence credibly to the market, Accellion aimed to harness the power of service guarantees.

Cost-effective services for improving performance and reliability were becoming critical as the widespread use of multimedia and other large files increased exponentially. The value proposition was clearly attractive, but how could Accellion convince prospective clients that its technology and service actually could deliver what they promised?

Mohan felt that a Quality of Service (QoS) Guarantee would be a powerful tool to make its promises credible and, at the same time, push his team to deliver what has been promised. Mark Ranford, Accellion's Director for Product Management, and Mohan spearheaded the development of the QoS Guarantee. They finally launched the QoS Guarantee (shown in **Exhibit 1**) stating that "it is a revolutionary statement of our commitment to the customer to do whatever it takes to ensure satisfaction." The official launch of the guarantee was announced to all staff by email (**Exhibit 2**)

Their QoS Guarantee, however, was just part of Accellion's push for operational excellence. Many factors worked together to keep the company focused on its clients and providing the best possible service, so that the staff could create a large and loyal customer base for their innovative product. Thus, it was very important to raise awareness for Accellion's unique value proposition and convince the early adopters of the advantages.

Accellion's customers reacted positively. One customer stated, "Hey look at this. I haven't seen anything like it. No one offers 100 percent availability. That's tremendous." Another customer exclaimed, "You must really be confident in your service. This really is risk free now, isn't it?" Accellion was committed to its guarantee and strongly believed that having the best network and technology partners would enable it to deliver on its promise.

This case is an updated version of a case previously in the INSEAD case series. The authors gratefully acknowledge the invaluable support by S. Mohan, Accellion's Chief Strategist, for his assistance and feedback to earlier versions of this case.

EXHIBIT 1 Accellion's Service Guarantee

QUALITY OF SERVICE GUARANTEE

The Accellion Quality of Service Guarantee defines Accellion's assurance and commitment to providing the Customer with value-added Service and is incorporated into Accellion's Customer Contract. The definition of terms used herein is the same as those found in the Customer Contract.

1. **Performance Guarantee**

   Accellion guarantees that the performance of the Network in uploading and downloading content, as a result of using the Accellion Service, will be no less than 200 percent of that which is achieved by a benchmark origin site being accessed from the edges of the Internet. For all purposes herein, performance measurement tests will be conducted by Accellion.

2. **Availability Guarantee**

   Accellion guarantees 100 percent Service availability, excluding *Force Majeure* and Scheduled Maintenance for Customers who have opted for our replication services.

3. **Customer Service Guarantee**

   Should Accellion fail to meet the service levels set out in Sections 1 and 2 above, Accellion will credit the Customer's account with one (1) month's service fee for the month affected when the failure(s) occurred, provided the Customer gives written notice to Accellion of such failure within five (5) days from the date such failure occurred. The Customer's failure to comply with this requirement will forfeit the Customer's right to receive such credit.

   Accellion will notify the Customer no less than 48 hours (2 days) in advance of Scheduled Maintenance. If the Service becomes unavailable for any other reason, Accellion will promptly notify the Customer and take all necessary action to restore the Service.

   Accellion maintains a 24-hour support center and will provide the Customer with a response to any inquiry in relation to the Service no more than 2 hours from the time of receipt of such query by customer service.

4. **Security and Privacy Policy**

   Accellion has complete respect for the Customer's privacy and that of any Customer data stored in Accellion servers. The Accellion Service does not require Customers to provide any end-user private details for the data being stored on the servers. All information provided to Accellion by the Customer is stored for the Customer's sole benefit. Accellion will not share, disclose or sell any personally identifiable information to which it may have access and will ensure that the Customer's information and data [are] kept secure.

   Disclosure of Customer's information or data in Accellion's possession shall only be made where such disclosure is necessary for compliance with a court order, to protect the rights or property of Accellion and to enforce the terms of use of the Service as provided in the Contract.

   Accellion will ensure that the Customer's information and data [are] kept secure and protected from unauthorized access or improper use, which includes taking all reasonable steps to verify the Customer's identity before granting access.

EXHIBIT 2 Email to All Accellion Staff Announcing the Launch of the QoS Guarantee

Dear Team,

I am pleased to forward to everyone our industry's leading Quality of Service guarantee (QoS). Please read it over very carefully. You will find it to be very aggressive, and it puts the ownership on everyone in this company to deliver. Customers don't want a Service Level Agreement (SLA); they just want their network up and running all the time. That is why we have created this no questions asked guarantee. This type of guarantee has proven successful in other industries where service is key to success (e.g., Industry Leaders such as Gartner Group, LL Bean, Nordstrom, etc.).

As a member of the Accellion team, you are key to our client's satisfaction.

Thanks in advance for your support in making our clients and ourselves successful.

STUDY QUESTIONS

1. *What is the marketing impact of a well-designed service guarantee?*
2. *Evaluate the design of Accellion's guarantee shown in* **Exhibit 1.** *How effective will it be in communicating service excellence to potential and current customers? Would you recommend any changes to its design or implementation?*
3. *Will the guarantee be successful in creating a culture for service excellence within Accellion? What else may be needed for achieving such a culture?*
4. *Do you think customers might take advantage of this guarantee and "stage" service failures to invoke the guarantee? If yes, how could Accellion minimize potential cheating on its guarantee?*

Case 16   *Shouldice Hospital Limited (Abridged)*

JAMES HESKETT AND ROGER HALLOWELL

A Canadian hospital specializing in hernia operations is considering whether and how to expand the reach of its services, including expansion into other specialty areas. Various proposals have been advanced to increase the capacity of the hospital without demotivating the staff or losing control over service quality, which, in addition to achieving excellent medical outcomes, has created a very devoted base of patient "alumni." Options include adding Saturday surgical operations, building an extension, and constructing a new hospital in another location, perhaps in the United States.

Two shadowy figures, enrobed and in slippers, walked slowly down the semi-darkened hall of the Shouldice Hospital. They didn't notice Alan O'Dell, the hospital's managing director, and his guest. Once they were out of earshot, O'Dell remarked good naturedly, "By the way they act, you'd think our patients own this place. And while they're here, in a way they do." Following a visit to the five operating rooms, O'Dell and his visitor once again encountered the same pair of patients still engrossed in discussing their hernia operations, which had been performed the previous morning.

HISTORY

An attractive brochure that was recently printed, although neither dated nor distributed to prospective patients, described Dr. Earle Shouldice, the founder of the hospital:

> Dr. Shouldice's interest in early ambulation stemmed, in part, from an operation he performed in 1932 to remove the appendix from a seven-year-old girl and the girl's subsequent refusal to stay quietly in bed. In spite of her activity, no harm was done, and the experience recalled to the doctor the postoperative actions of animals upon which he had performed surgery. They had all moved about freely with no ill effects.

By 1940, Shouldice had given extensive thought to several factors that contributed to early ambulation following surgery. Among them were the use of a local anesthetic, the nature of the surgical procedure itself, the

design of a facility to encourage movement without unnecessarily causing discomfort, and the postoperative regimen. With these things in mind, he began to develop a surgical technique for repairing hernias[1] that was superior to others; word of his early success generated demand.

Dr. Shouldice's medical license permitted him to operate anywhere, even on a kitchen table. However, as more and more patients requested operations, Dr. Shouldice created new facilities by buying a rambling 130-acre estate with a 17,000-square foot main house in the Toronto suburb of Thornhill. After some years of planning, a large wing was added to provide a total capacity of 89 beds.

Dr. Shouldice died in 1965. At that time, Shouldice Hospital Limited was formed to operate both the hospital and clinical facilities under the surgical direction of Dr. Nicholas Obney. In 1999, Dr. Casim Degani, an internationally-recognized authority, became surgeon-in-chief. By 2004, 7,600 operations were performed per year.

THE SHOULDICE METHOD

Only external (vs. internal) abdominal hernias were repaired at Shouldice Hospital. Thus most first-time repairs, "primaries," were straightforward operations requiring about 45 minutes. The remaining procedures involved patients suffering recurrences of hernias previously repaired elsewhere.[2] Many of the recurrences and very difficult hernia repairs required 90 minutes or more.

In the Shouldice method, the muscles of the abdominal wall were arranged in three distinct layers, and the opening was repaired—each layer in turn—by overlapping its margins as the edges of a coat might be overlapped when buttoned. The end result reinforced the muscular wall of the abdomen with six rows of sutures (stitches) under the skin cover, which was then closed with clamps that were later removed. (Other methods might not separate muscle layers, often involved fewer rows of sutures, and sometimes involved the insertion of screens or meshes under the skin.)

Copyright © 2004 President and Fellows of Harvard College. To order copies or request permission to reproduce materials, call 1-800-545-7685, write Harvard Business School Publishing, Boston, MA 02163, or go to http://www.hbsp.harvard.edu. No part of this publication may be reproduced, stored in a retrieval system, used in a spreadsheet, or transmitted in any form or by any means—electronic, mechanical, photocopying, recording, or otherwise—without the permission of Harvard Business School.

Professor James Heskett prepared the original version of this case, "Shouldice Hospital Limited," HBS No. 683-068. This version was prepared jointly by Professor James Heskett and Roger Hallowell (MBA 1989, DBA 1997). HBS cases are developed solely as the basis for class discussion. Cases are not intended to serve as endorsements, sources of primary data, or illustrations of effective or ineffective management.

A typical first-time repair could be completed with the use of preoperative sedation (sleeping pill) and analgesic (pain killer) plus a local anesthetic, an injection of Novocain in the region of the incision. This allowed immediate post-operative patient ambulation and facilitated rapid recovery.

THE PATIENTS' EXPERIENCE

Most potential Shouldice patients learned about the hospital from previous Shouldice patients. Although thousands of doctors had referred patients, doctors were less likely to recommend Shouldice because of the generally regarded simplicity of the surgery, often considered a "bread and butter" operation. Typically, many patients had their problem diagnosed by a personal physician and then contacted Shouldice directly. Many more made this diagnosis themselves.

The process experienced by Shouldice patients depended on whether or not they lived close enough to the hospital to visit the facility to obtain a diagnosis. Approximately 10% of Shouldice patients came from outside the province of Ontario, most of these from the United States. Another 60% of patients lived beyond the Toronto area. These out-of-own patients often were diagnosed by mail using the Medical Information Questionnaire shown in **Exhibit 1**. Based on information in the questionnaire, a Shouldice surgeon would determine the type of hernia the respondent had and whether there were signs that some risk might be associated with surgery (for example, an overweight or heart condition, or a patient who had suffered a heart attack or a stroke in the past six months to a year, or whether a general or local anesthetic was required). At this point, a patient was given a operating date and sent a brochure describing the hospital and the Shouldice method. If necessary, a sheet outlining a weight-loss program prior to surgery was also sent. A small proportion was refused treatment, either because they were overweight, represented an undue medical risk, or because it was determined that they did not have a hernia.

Arriving at the clinic between 1:00 P.M. and 3:00 P.M. the day before the operation, a patient joined other patients in the waiting room. He or she was soon examined in one of six examination rooms staffed by surgeons who had completed their operating schedules for the day. This examination required no more than 20 minutes, unless the patient needed reassurance. (Patients typically exhibited a moderate level of anxiety until their operation was completed.) At this point it occasionally was discovered that a patient had not corrected his or her weight problem; others might be found not to have a hernia at all. In either case, the patient was sent home.

After checking administrative details, about an hour after arriving at the hospital, a patient was directed to the room number shown on his or her wrist band. Throughout

the process, patients were asked to keep their luggage (usually light) with them.

All patient rooms at the hospital were semiprivate, containing two beds. Patients with similar jobs, backgrounds, or interests were assigned to the same room to the extent possible. Upon reaching their rooms, patients busied themselves unpacking, getting acquainted with roommates, shaving themselves in the area of the operation, and changing into pajamas.

At 4:30 P.M., a nurse's orientation provided the group of incoming patients with information about what to expect, including the need for exercise after the operation and the daily routine. According to Alan O'Dell, "Half are so nervous they don't remember much." Dinner was then served, followed by further recreation, and tea and cookies at 9:00 P.M. Nurses emphasized the importance of attendance at that time because it provided an opportunity for preoperative patients to talk with those whose operations had been completed earlier that same day.

Patients to be operated on early were awakened at 5:30 A.M. to be given preop sedation. An attempt was made to schedule operations for roommates at approximately the same time. Patients were taken to the preoperating room where the circulating nurse administered Demerol, an analgesic, 45 minutes before surgery. A few minutes prior to the first operation at 7:30 A.M., the surgeon assigned to each patient administered Novocain, a local anesthetic, in the operating room. This was in contrast to the typical hospital procedure in which patients were sedated in their rooms prior to being taken to the operating rooms.

Upon the completion of their operation, during which a few patients were "chatty" and fully aware of what was going on, patients were invited to get off the operating table and walk to the post-operating room with the help of their surgeons. According to the director of nursing:

> Ninety-nine percent accept the surgeon's invitation. While we use wheelchairs to return them to their rooms, the walk from the operating table is for psychological as well as physiological [blood pressure, respiratory] reasons. Patients prove to themselves that they can do it, and they start their all-important exercise immediately.

Throughout the day after their operation, patients were encouraged to exercise by nurses and housekeepers alike. By 9:00 P.M. on the day of their operations, all patients were ready and able to walk down to the dining room for tea and cookies, even if it meant climbing stairs, to help indoctrinate the new "class" admitted that day. On the fourth morning, patients were ready for discharge.

During their stay, patients were encouraged to take advantage of the opportunity to explore the premises and make new friends. Some members of the staff felt that the patients and their attitudes were the most important

EXHIBIT 1   Medical Information Questionnaire

SHOULDICE HOSPITAL

7750 Bayview Avenue
Box 379, Thornhill, Ontario L3T 4A3 Canada
Phone (418) 889-1125

(Thornhill - One Mile North Metro Toronto)

MEDICAL
INFORMATION

Patients who live at a distance often prefer their examination, admission and operation to be arranged all on a single visit — to save making two lengthy journeys. The whole purpose of this questionnaire is to make such arrangements possible, although, of course, it cannot replace the examination in any way. Its completion and return will not put you under any obligation.

Please be sure to fill in both sides.

This information will be treated as confidential.

(continued on next page)

FAMILY NAME (Last Name)	FIRST NAME	MIDDLE NAME

STREET & NUMBER (or Rural Route or P.O. Box)	Town/City	Province/State

County	Township	Zip or Postal Code	Birthdate: Month	Day	Year

| | | | Married or Single | Religion | |

Telephone
Home _____ if none, give
Work _____ neighbour's number _____

NEXT OF KIN: Name _____   Address _____   Telephone # _____

Date form completed _____

INSURANCE INFORMATION: Please give name of Insurance Company and Numbers.

HOSPITAL INSURANCE: (Please bring hospital certificates)   OTHER HOSPITAL INSURANCE

O.H.I.P.
Number _____   BLUE CROSS
Number _____

Company Name _____
Policy Number _____

SURGICAL INSURANCE: (Please bring insurance certificates)   OTHER SURGICAL INSURANCE

O.H.I.P.
Number _____   BLUE SHIELD
Number _____

Company Name _____
Policy Number _____

WORKMEN'S COMPENSATION BOARD

	Approved	Social Insurance (Security) Number

Claim No. _____   Yes ____ No ____

Occupation _____   Name of Business _____   Are you the owner? If Retired – Former Occupation _____   Yes ____ No ____

How did you hear about Shouldice Hospital? (If referred by a doctor, give name & address) _____

Are you a former patient of Shouldice Hospital?   Yes ____ No ____   Do you smoke?   Yes ____ No ____

Have you ever written to Shouldice Hospital in the past?   Yes ____ No ____

What is your preferred admission date? (Please give as much advance notice as possible) _____
No admissions Friday, Saturday or Sunday.

FOR OFFICE USE ONLY

Date Received	Type of Hernia	Weight Loss
		lbs.

Special Instructions _____   Approved _____

Consent to Operate ☐
Heart Report ☐

Refering Doctor Notified _____   Operation Date _____

594

EXHIBIT 1 (Continued)

THIS CHART IS FOR EXPLANATION ONLY

Ordinary hernias are mostly either
at the navel ("belly-button") - or just above it

or down in the groin area on either side

An "Incisional hernia" is one that bulges through
the scar of any other surgical operation that has
failed to hold - wherever it may be.

THIS IS YOUR CHART – PLEASE MARK IT!

(MARK THE POSITION OF EACH HERNIA
YOU WANT REPAIRED WITH AN "X")

APPROXIMATE SIZE...
Walnut (or less)
Hen's Egg or Lemon
Grapefruit (or more)

ESSENTIAL EXTRA INFORMATION
Use only the sections that apply to your hernias and put a ✓ in each
box that seems appropriate.

NAVEL AREA (AND JUST ABOVE NAVEL) ONLY
Is this navel (bellybutton) hernia your FIRST one?   Yes ☐   No ☐

If it's NOT your first, how many repair attempts so far?   ☐

GROIN HERNIAS ONLY

	RIGHT GROIN		LEFT GROIN	
	Yes	No	Yes	No
Is this your FIRST GROIN HERNIA ON THIS SIDE?	☐	☐	☐	☐

How many hernia operations in this groin already?   Right ☐   Left ☐

DATE OF LAST OPERATION

INCISIONAL HERNIAS ONLY (the ones bulging through previous operation scars)
Was the original operation for your Appendix? ☐ , or Gallbladder? ☐ ,
or Stomach? ☐ , or Prostate? ☐ , or Hysterectomy? ☐ , or Other? ☐ ,

How many attempts to repair the hernias have been made so far? ☐

PLEASE BE ACCURATE!: Misleading figures, when checked on a
admission day, could mean postponement of your operation till your weight
is suitable.

HEIGHT.........ft.........ins.   WEIGHT.........lbs. Nude   Recent gain?.........lbs.
                                  or just pyjamas   Recent loss?.........lbs.

Waist (muscles relaxed).........ins.   Chest (not expanded).........ins.

GENERAL HEALTH

Age.........years   is your health now GOOD ☐ ,   FAIR ☐ ,   or POOR ☐

Please mention briefly any severe past illness – such as a
"heart attack" or a "stroke", for example, from which you
have now recovered (and its approximate date).........

We need to know about any other present conditions, even though your admission is
NOT likely to be refused because of them.

Please tick ✓ any condition
for which you are having regular
treatment:

Blood Pressure   ☐
Excess body fluids   ☐
Chest pain ("angina")   ☐
Irregular Heartbeat   ☐
Diabetes   ☐
Asthma & Bronchitis   ☐
Ulcers   ☐
Anticoagulants   ☐
(to delay blood-clotting
or to "thin the blood")

Other.........

Name of any prescribed
pills, tablets or capsules you
take regularly -

Did you remember to MARK AN "X" on your body chart to show us where
each of your hernias is located?

element of the Shouldice program. According to Dr. Byrnes Shouldice, son of the founder, a surgeon on the staff, and a 50% owner of the hospital:

> Patients sometimes ask to stay an extra day. Why? Well, think about it. They are basically well to begin with. But they arrive with a problem and a certain amount of nervousness, tension, and anxiety about their surgery. Their first morning here they're operated on and experience a sense of relief from something that's been bothering them for a long time. They are immediately able to get around, and they've got a three-day holiday ahead of them with a perfectly good reason to be away from work with no sense of guilt. They share experiences with other patients, make friends easily, and have the run of the hospital. In summer, the most common after-effect from the surgery is sunburn.

THE NURSES' EXPERIENCE

34 full-time-equivalent nurses staffed Shouldice each 24 hour period. However, during non-operating hours, only six full-time-equivalent nurses were on the premises at any given time. While the Canadian acute-care hospital average ratio of nurses to patients was 1:4, at Shouldice the ratio was 1:15. Shouldice nurses spent an unusually large proportion of their time in counseling activities. As one supervisor commented, "We don't use bedpans." According to a manager, "Shouldice has a waiting list of nurses wanting to be hired, while other hospitals in Toronto are short-staffed and perpetually recruiting."

THE DOCTORS' EXPERIENCE

The hospital employed 10 full-time surgeons and 8 part-time assistant surgeons. Two anesthetists were also on site. The anesthetists floated among cases except when general anesthesia was in use. Each operating team required a surgeon, an assistant surgeon, a scrub nurse, and a circulating nurse. The operating load varied from 30 to 36 operations per day. As a result, each surgeon typically performed three or four operations each day.

A typical surgeon's day started with a *scrubbing* shortly before the first scheduled operation at 7:30 A.M. If the first operation was routine, it usually was completed by 8:15 A.M. At its conclusion, the surgical team helped the patient walk from the room and summoned the next patient. After scrubbing, the surgeon could be ready to operate again at 8:30 A.M. Surgeons were advised to take a coffee break after their second or third operation. Even so, a surgeon could complete three routine operations and a fourth involving a recurrence and

still be finished in time for a 12:30 P.M. lunch in the staff dining room.

Upon finishing lunch, surgeons not scheduled to operate in the afternoon examined incoming patients. A surgeon's day ended by 4:00 P.M. In addition, a surgeon could expect to be on call one weekday night in ten and one weekend in ten. Alan O'Dell commented that the position appealed to doctors who "want to watch their children grow up. A doctor on call is rarely called to the hospital and has regular hours." According to Dr. Obney:

> When I interview prospective surgeons, I look for experience and a good education. I try to gain some insight into their domestic situation and personal interests and habits. I also try to find out why a surgeon wants to switch positions. And I try to determine if he's willing to perform the repair exactly as he's told. This is no place for prima donnas.

Dr. Shouldice added:

> Traditionally a hernia is often the first operation that a junior resident in surgery performs. Hernia repair is regarded as a relatively simple operation compared to other major operations. This is quite wrong, as is borne out by the resulting high recurrence rate. It is a tricky anatomical area and occasionally very complicated, especially to the novice or those doing very few hernia repairs each year. But at Shouldice Hospital a surgeon learns the Shouldice technique over a period of several months. He learns when he can go fast and when he must go slow. He develops a pace and a touch. If he encounters something unusual, he is encouraged to consult immediately with other surgeons. We teach each other and try to encourage a group effort. And he learns not to take risks to achieve absolute perfection. Excellence is the enemy of good.

Chief Surgeon Degani assigned surgeons to an operating room on a daily basis by noon of the preceding day. This allowed surgeons to examine the specific patients that they were to operate on. Surgeons and assistants were rotated every few days. Cases were assigned to give doctors a non-routine operation (often involving a recurrence) several times a week. More complex procedures were assigned to more senior and experienced members of the staff. Dr. Obney commented:

> If something goes wrong, we want to make sure that we have an experienced surgeon in charge. Experience is most important. The typical general surgeon may perform 25 to 50 hernia operations per year. Ours perform 750 or more.

The 10 full-time surgeons were paid a straight salary, typically $144,000.[3] In addition, bonuses to doctors were distributed monthly. These depended on profit, individual productivity, and performance. The total bonus pool paid to the surgeons in a recent year was approximately $400,000. Total surgeon compensation (including benefits) was approximately 15% more than the average income for a surgeon in Ontario.

Training in the Shouldice technique was important because the procedure could not be varied. It was accomplished through direct supervision by one or more of the senior surgeons. The rotation of teams and frequent consultations allowed for an ongoing opportunity to appraise performance and take corrective action. Where possible, former Shouldice patients suffering recurrences were assigned to the doctor who performed the first operation "to allow the doctor to learn from his mistake." Dr. Obney commented on being a Shouldice surgeon:

> A doctor must decide after several years whether he wants to do this for the rest of his life because, just as in other specialties—for example, radiology—he loses touch with other medical disciplines. If he stays for five years, he doesn't leave. Even among younger doctors, few elect to leave.

THE FACILITY

The Shouldice Hospital contained two facilities in one building—the hospital and the clinic. On its first-level, the hospital contained the kitchen and dining rooms. The second level contained a large, open lounge area, the admissions offices, patient rooms, and a spacious glass-covered Florida room. The third level had additional patient rooms and recreational areas. Patients could be seen visiting in each others' rooms, walking up and down hallways, lounging in the sunroom, and making use of light recreational facilities ranging from a pool table to an exercycle. Alan O'Dell pointed out some of the features of the hospital:

> The rooms contain no telephone or television sets. If a patient needs to make a call or wants to watch television, he or she has to take a walk. The steps are designed specially with a small rise to allow patients recently operated on to negotiate the stairs without undue discomfort. Every square foot of the hospital is carpeted to reduce the hospital feeling and the possibility of a fall. Carpeting also gives the place a smell other than that of disinfectant.
>
> This facility was designed by an architect with input from Dr. Byrnes Shouldice and Mrs. W. H. Urquhart (the daughter of the founder). The facility was discussed for years and many changes in the plans were made before the first concrete was poured. A number of unique policies were also instituted. For example, parents accompanying children here for an operation stay free. You may wonder why we can do it, but we learned that we save more in nursing costs than we spend for the parent's room and board.

Patients and staff were served food prepared in the same kitchen, and staff members picked up food from a cafeteria line placed in the very center of the kitchen. This provided an opportunity for everyone to chat with the kitchen staff several times a day, and the hospital staff to eat together. According to O'Dell, "We use all fresh ingredients and prepare the food from scratch in the kitchen."

The director of housekeeping pointed out:

> I have only three on my housekeeping staff for the entire facility. One of the reasons for so few housekeepers is that we don't need to change linens during a patient's four-day stay. Also, the medical staff doesn't want the patients in bed all day. They want the nurses to encourage the patients to be up socializing, comparing notes [for confidence], encouraging each other, and walking around, getting exercise. Of course, we're in the rooms straightening up throughout the day. This gives the housekeepers a chance to josh with the patients and to encourage them to exercise.

The clinic housed five operating rooms, a laboratory, and the patient-recovery room. In total, the estimated cost to furnish an operating room was $30,000. This was considerably less than for other hospitals requiring a bank of equipment with which to administer anesthetics for each room. At Shouldice, two mobile units were used by the anesthetists when needed. In addition, the complex had one "crash cart" per floor for use if a patient should suffer a heart attack or stroke.

ADMINISTRATION

Alan O'Dell described his job:

> We try to meet people's needs and make this as good a place to work as possible. There is a strong concern for employees here. Nobody is fired. [This was later reinforced by Dr. Shouldice, who described a situation involving two employees who confessed to theft in the hospital. They agreed to seek psychiatric help and were allowed to remain on the job.] As a result, turnover is low.
>
> Our administrative and support staff are non-union, but we try to maintain a pay scale higher than the union scale for comparable jobs in the area. We have a profit-sharing plan that is separate from the doctors'. Last year the administrative and support staff divided up $60,000.
>
> If work needs to be done, people pitch in to help each other. A unique aspect of our administration is that I insist that each secretary is trained to do another's work and in an emergency is able to switch to another function immediately. We don't have an organization chart. A chart tends to make people think they're boxed in jobs.[4] I try to stay one night a week, having dinner and listening to the patients, to find out how things are really going around here.

Operating Costs

The 2004 budgets for the hospital and clinic were close to $8.5 million[5] and $3.5 million, respectively.[6]

EXHIBIT 2 Organization Chart

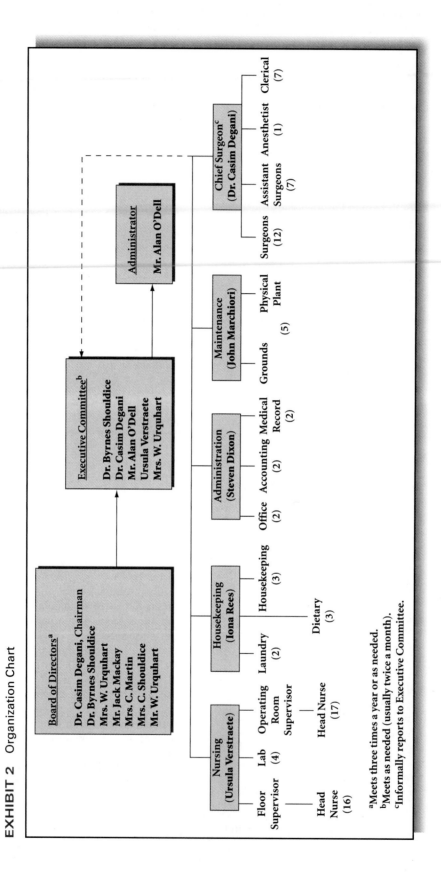

THE MARKET

Hernia operations were among the most common performed on males. In 2000 an estimated 1,000,000 such operations were performed in the United States alone. According to Dr. Shouldice:

> When our backlog of scheduled operations gets too large, we wonder how many people decide instead to have their local doctor perform the operation. Every time we've expanded our capacity, the backlog has declined briefly, only to climb once again. Right now, at 2,400, it is larger than it has ever been and is growing by 100 every six months.

The hospital relied entirely on word-of-mouth advertising, the importance of which was suggested by the results of a poll carried out by students of DePaul University as part of a project (**Exhibit 3** shows a portion of these results). Although little systematic data about patients had been collected, Alan O'Dell remarked that "if we had to rely on wealthy patients only, our practice would be much smaller."

Patients were attracted to the hospital, in part, by its reasonable rates. Charges for a typical operation were four days of hospital stay at $320 per day, and a $650 surgical fee for a primary inguinal (the most common hernia). An additional fee of $300 was assessed if general anesthesia was required (in about 20% of cases). These charges compared to an average charge of $5,240 for operations performed elsewhere.

Round-trip fares for travel to Toronto from various major cities on the North American continent ranged from roughly $200 to $600.

The hospital also provided annual checkups to alumni, free of charge. Many occurred at the time of the patient reunion. The most recent reunion, featuring dinner and a floor show, was held at a first-class hotel in downtown Toronto and was attended by 1,000 former patients, many from outside Canada.

PROBLEMS AND PLANS

When asked about major questions confronting the management of the hospital, Dr. Shouldice cited a desire to seek ways of increasing the hospital's capacity while at the same time maintaining control over the quality of service delivered, the future role of government in the operations of the hospital, and the use of the Shouldice name by potential competitors. As Dr. Shouldice put it:

> I'm a doctor first and an entrepreneur second. For example, we could refuse permission to other doctors who want to visit the hospital. They may copy our technique and misapply it or misinform their patients about the use of it. This results in failure, and we are concerned that the technique will be blamed. But

EXHIBIT 3 Shouldice Hospital Annual Patient Reunion Data

Direction: For each question, please place a check mark as it applies to you.

1. Sex Male 41 95.34%
   Female 2 4.65%

2. Age 20 or less
   21–40 4 9.30%
   41–60 17 39.54%
   61 or more 22 51.16%

3. Nationality

   Directions: Please place a check mark in nation you represent and please write in your province, state or country where it applies.

   Canada 38 Province 88.37%
   America 5 State 11.63%
   Europe Country
   Other

4. Education level

   Elementary 5 11.63%
   High School 18 41.86%
   College 1980 30.23%
   Graduate work 7 16.28%

5. Occupation _____

6. Have you been overnight in a hospital other than Shouldice before your operation? Yes 31 No 12

7. What brought Shouldice Hospital to your attention?

   Friend 23 Doctor 9 Relative 7 Article ____ Other 4
   53.49% 20.93% 16.28% (Please explain) 9.30%

8. Did you have a single 25 or double 18 hernia operation?
   58.14% 41.86%

9. Is this your first Annual Reunion? Yes 20 No 23
   46.51% 53.49%
   If no, how many reunions have you attended? ____

   2–5 reunions – 11 47.63%
   6–10 reunions – 5 21.73%
   11–20 reunions – 4 12.39%
   21–36 reunions – 3 13.05%

10. Do you feel that Shouldice Hospital cared for you as a person?

    Most definitely 37 Definitely 6 Very little ____ Not at all ____
    86.05% 13.95%

EXHIBIT 3   (Continued)

11.   What impressed you the most about your stay at Shouldice? Please
      check one answer for each of the following.

A.   Fees charged for operation and hospital stay

Very Important	10	Important	3	Somewhat Important	6	Not Important	24

B.   Operation Procedure

| Very Important | 33 | Important | 9 | Somewhat Important | 1 | Not Important | |
| | 76.74% | | 20.93% | | 2.33% | | |

C.   Physician's Care

| Very Important | 31 | Important | 12 | Somewhat Important | - | Not Important | - |
| | 72.10% | | 27.90% | | | | |

D.   Nursing Care

| Very Important | 28 | Important | 14 | Somewhat Important | 1 | Not Important | |
| | 65.12% | | 32.56% | | 2.32% | | |

E.   Food Service

| Very Important | 23 | Important | 11 | Somewhat Important | 7 | Not Important | 2 |
| | 53.48% | | 25.59% | | 16.28% | | 4.65% |

F.   Shortness of Hospital Stay

| Very Important | 17 | Important | 15 | Somewhat Important | 8 | Not Important | 3 |
| | 39.53% | | 34.88% | | 18.60% | | 6.98% |

G.   Exercise; Recreational Activities

| Very Important | 17 | Important | 14 | Somewhat Important | 12 | Not Important | - |
| | 39.53% | | 32.56% | | 27.91% | | |

H.   Friendships with Patients

| Very Important | 25 | Important | 10 | Somewhat Important | 5 | Not Important | 3 |
| | 58.15% | | 23.25% | | 11.63% | | 6.98% |

I.   "Shouldice Hospital hardly seemed like a hospital at all."

| Very Important | 25 | Important | 13 | Somewhat Important | 5 | Not Important | |
| | 58.14% | | 30.23% | | 11.63% | | |

12.   In a few words, give the MAIN REASON why you returned for this annual
      reunion.

---

we're doctors, and it is our obligation to help other surgeons learn. On the other hand, it's quite clear that others are trying to emulate us. Look at this ad. [The advertisement is shown in **Exhibit 4**.]

This makes me believe that we should add to our capacity, either here or elsewhere. Here, we could go to Saturday operations and increase our capacity by 20%. Throughout the year, no operations are scheduled for Saturdays or Sundays, although patients whose operations are scheduled late in the week remain in the hospital over the weekend. Or, with an investment of perhaps $4 million in new space, we could expand our number of beds by 50%, and schedule the operating rooms more heavily.

On the other hand, given government regulation, do we want to invest more in Toronto? Or should we establish another hospital with similar design, perhaps in the United States? There is also the possibility that we could diversify into other specialties offering similar opportunities such as eye surgery, varicose veins, or diagnostic services (e.g., colonoscopies).

For now, we're also beginning the process of grooming someone to succeed Dr. Degani when he retires. He's in his early 60s, but at some point we'll have to address this issue. And for good reason, he's resisted changing certain successful procedures that I think we could improve on. We had quite a time changing the schedule for the administration of Demerol to patients to increase their comfort level during the operation. Dr. Degani has opposed a Saturday operating program on the premise that he won't be here and won't be able to maintain proper control.

Alan O'Dell added his own concerns:

How should we be marketing our services? Right now, we don't advertise directly to patients. We're even afraid to send out this new brochure we've put together, unless a potential patient specifically requests it, for fear it will generate too much demand. Our records show that just under 1% of our

EXHIBIT 4   Advertisement by a Shouldice Competitor

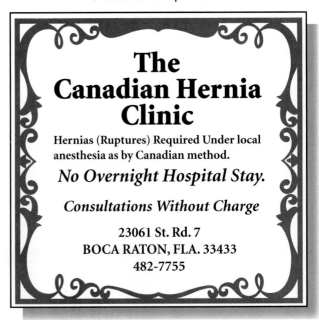

patients are medical doctors, a significantly high percentage. How should we capitalize on that? I'm also concerned about this talk of Saturday operations. We are already getting good utilization of this facility. And if we expand further, it will be very difficult to maintain the same kind of working relationships and attitudes. Already there are rumors floating around among the staff about it. And the staff is not pleased.

The matter of Saturday operations had been a topic of conversation among the doctors as well. Four of the older doctors were opposed to it. While most of the younger doctors were indifferent or supportive, at least two who had been at the hospital for some time were particularly concerned about the possibility that the issue would drive a wedge between the two groups. As one put it, "I'd hate to see the practice split over the issue."

ENDNOTES

1. Most hernias, knows as external abdominal hernias, are protrusions of some part of the abdominal contents through a hole or slit in the muscular layers of the abdominal wall which is supposed to contain them. Well over 90% of these hernias occur in the groin area. Of these, by far the most common are inguinal hernias, many of which are caused by a slight weakness in the muscle layers brought about by the passage of the testicles in male babies through the groin area shortly before birth. Aging also contributes to the development of inguinal hernias. Because of the cause of the affliction, 85% of all hernias occur in males.
2. Based on tracking of patients over more than 30 years, the gross recurrence rate for all operations performed

at Shouldice was 0.8%. Recurrence rates reported in the literature for these types of hernia varied greatly. However, one text stated, "In the United States the gross rate of recurrence for groin hernias approaches 10%."
3. All monetary references in the case are to Canadian dollars. $1 US equaled $1.33 Canadian on February 23, 2004.
4. The chart in **Exhibit 2** was prepared by the casewriter, based on conversations with hospital personnel.
5. This figure included a provincially mandated return on investment.
6. The latter figure included the bonus pool for doctors.

STUDY QUESTIONS

1. *What is the market for this service? How successful is Shouldice Hospital?*
2. *Define the service model for Shouldice. How does each of its elements contribute to the hospital's success?*
3. *As Dr. Shouldice, what actions, if any, would you take to expand the hospital's capacity and how would you implement such changes?*

Case 17   Massachusetts Audubon Society

CHRISTOPHER LOVELOCK

We embrace a vision of Massachusetts in which people appreciate and understand native plants and animals and their habitats and work together to ensure that they are truly protected.

From the barrier beaches, heathlands, and salt marshes of the coast; to the vernal pools, red maple swamps, and forests of the interior; all the way to the fens and mountaintops of the Berkshire highlands, the Commonwealth's natural splendor encompasses an abundance of scenic and ecological treasures. But unless and until the public develops a conservation ethic that incorporates a love and respect for nature with a willingness to act on its behalf, we are in danger of losing this natural wealth forever.

FROM THE STRATEGIC PLAN 2000–2010

A nonprofit environmental organization that operates more than 40 wildlife sanctuaries seeks to develop a strategy to increase the loyalty and involvement of its current members. A task force is focusing on developing a communications strategy for the existing membership, with the primary objective being to increase member value. Findings from a survey of its members may offer some insights.

Several pairs of cardinals were fluttering around the bird feeder outside the Audubon Shop at Drumlin Farm Wildlife Sanctuary; the scarlet and crimson plumage of the males stood out vividly against the bare trees. Nearby, under the watchful eyes of their teachers and a sanctuary naturalist, a group of schoolchildren were chattering excitedly as they walked down the path toward the enclosure where the farm animals were located.

Despite the chill in the air on this November day, several people were lined up in the reception area to gain admission to the sanctuary. The staff member on duty was explaining sympathetically to two visitors from New York that their membership in the National Audubon Society did not, unfortunately, entitle them to free admission at Massachusetts Audubon Society sanctuaries, since the two organizations had no formal relationship.

Steven Solomon and Susannah Caffry watched the bright red birds from the warm interior of the shop as they put on their jackets. Solomon was vice president of Mass Audubon's resources division and Caffry was director of marketing and communication. They had been meeting with the store manager and were now about to return to the nearby mansion that served as the Society's headquarters. Both were scheduled to participate in a task force discussion of how to develop a new communications strategy targeted at existing members. "The key to success," Solomon told Caffry as they stepped outside, "lies in finding ways to engage our members more actively in Mass Audubon."

HISTORY OF THE AUDUBON MOVEMENT

In the late 19th century, there were no laws in the United States to control the hunting of birds and animals. Entire species went into decline and two birds, the great auk and Carolina parakeet, were exterminated. Migratory fowl were killed in immense numbers, with hunters traveling to the coastal marshes of Massachusetts from as far away as Ohio.

Among those who spoke up against this slaughter was George Bird Grinnell, editor of the magazine *Forest and Stream*. In 1886, he created the nation's first bird preservation organization, which he named the Audubon Society after the great American naturalist and wildlife painter, John James Audubon (1785–1851). Within three months, more than 38,000 people had joined the society. But Grinnell was unable to cater to such a large, geographically dispersed group and had to disband the society after a couple of years.

The Audubon Societies

In 1896, two socially prominent cousins from Boston's Back Bay, Harriet Hemenway and Minna Hall, galvanized public support and formed the Massachusetts Audubon Society, which soon had 900 members. Refusing to wear hats and clothing decorated with plumes or other bird parts, they lobbied politicians and newspaper editors for protection of birds. Several months later, the Pennsylvania Audubon Society was founded, and by 1899 another 15 states had established Audubon societies.

In 1901, several local Audubon Societies for med the National Association of Audubon Societies for the Protection of Wild Birds and Animals. Both this association and local societies worked for passage of bird protection laws. An early priority included state bans on selling the plumes of native birds. National legislation included the Federal Migratory Bird Treaty Act of 1918 and creation of a National

---

Wildlife Refuge system where birds would be safe from hunters. Over the years, additional state societies affiliated or merged with the National Association (later renamed the National Audubon Society). By 2001, the Massachusetts Audubon Society was one of only a handful of state societies remaining unaffiliated with the national society.

Other Players in the Environmental Movement

There were literally hundreds of environmental organizations in the U.S., with most being local or regional in nature. Some pursued a broad agenda; others focused on a specific goal, such as the Rails-to-Trails Conservancy, which sought to convert thousands of miles of unused railroad corridors into trails for recreation and nature appreciation.

National players included Friends of the Earth, National Audubon Society, Sierra Club, The Nature Conservancy, and the Wilderness Society. Several of these organizations had chapters or offices in Massachusetts. The Appalachian Mountain Club was regional, with chapters throughout the Northeast U.S. By contrast, Mass Audubon, the Trustees of Reservations and MASSPIRG confined their activities to Massachusetts. (See the **Appendix** for brief profiles.)

Although organizations sometimes worked in coalitions to advocate specific political agenda, they also competed for funding and, to some extent, for members. On occasion, some of them had even competed for the same piece of environmentally sensitive property. The Nature Conservancy protected 17,000 acres (70 km^2) in the state, Mass Audubon held 29,000 acres (120 km^2), and The Trustees of Reservations had more than 45,000 acres (180 km^2). Many other nonprofit organizations operated individual sanctuaries and nature centers or preserved land from development through land trusts.

In the public sector, preservation and conservation agencies included the National Park Service, which was best known in Massachusetts for the 43,600-acre (176-km^2) Cape Cod National Seashore. The Commonwealth of Massachusetts preserved land for recreational purposes through a number of state parks, and many towns and cities had parks and conservation land trusts of their own. The motivations ranged from keeping attractive vistas and recreational areas out of the hands of developers to preserving habitats for threatened animal and plant species and protecting local water supplies.

EVOLUTION OF MASS AUDUBON

From its initial focus on bird protection, the Massachusetts Audubon Society (MAS) embraced a variety of conservation issues, including the protection of land and habitat, especially wetlands. In 1916, it created America's first private wildlife sanctuary at Moose Hill, 20 miles (32 km)

southwest of Boston, later adding many other sanctuaries. It became known for its lectures, guided nature walks, and educational programs for children. MAS created the first environmental summer camp for children and one of the first natural history travel programs to offer guided nature tours and birding trips overseas. It also opened one of the first stores to focus on natural history merchandise.

In 1952, Louise Ayer Hathaway bequeathed to MAS her Drumlin Farm estate in Lincoln, 15 miles north of Boston. Her will stipulated that this working New England farm was to serve as a sanctuary for wildlife and as a model farm to show young city dwellers how food was grown. The accompanying mansion became the Society's new headquarters.

Under the presidency of Gerard Bertrand (1980–1998), MAS acquired many threatened locations through gift or purchase. It also helped landowners to obtain conservation restrictions that offered tax benefits and then assumed management of their properties. These strategies were made possible by active fundraising and a growing membership.

Bertrand also re-emphasized the Society's historical commitment to the study, observation, and protection of birds. Like the renowned ornithologist, Roger Tory Peterson, he recognized that birds were an "ecological litmus paper." Because of their rapid metabolism and wide geographic range, bird populations were quick to reflect changes in the environment. Hence a documented decline in bird numbers provided an early warning of environmental deterioration. Key initiatives during this period included plans for two urban sanctuaries to better serve the needs of city dwellers, especially urban children. Completion of the new Boston Nature Center, constructed on the 67-acre grounds of a former state mental hospital, was scheduled for fall 2002.

Membership grew from 26,600 in 1980 to 67,000 in 1998, while the area of land protected by the Society rose from 11,600 to 28,000 acres (**Exhibit 1**). The number of research studies and educational programs also increased substantially. Following the Centennial celebrations of 1996 and completion of a $34 million capital campaign, Bertrand left to chair Bird Life International; later he was also named vice chairman of the National Audubon Society's board of directors.

New Leadership

Although proud of the amount of wildlife habitat now protected by the Society, some board members and staff were concerned by the absence of a comprehensive plan to guide future direction. They worried that years of rapid growth were affecting Mass Audubon's ability to do the best possible job of managing the many properties it had acquired. As Bancroft Poor, VP–Operations, recalled: "The Society was really stretched by the years of expansion and some of the infrastructure was near the breaking point."

EXHIBIT 1 Massachusetts Audubon Society: Key Statistics, 1980–2001

Year	# Members (000)	# Acres Protected[1] (000)	Operating Revenue ($000)	Operating Gifts/Grants ($000)	Endowment[2] ($ million)
1980	26.6	11.6	2,529	362	10.9
1985	31.0	12.4	4,180	490	22.8
1990	48.0	18.1	6,955	1,017	35.2
1995	55.1	23.9	9,042	1,486	57.1
2000	67.6	28.6	13,791	2,584	92.3
2001	65.4	29.1	14,113	2,863	89.2

[1]1,000 acres = approximately 400 hectares (ha) or 4 square kilometers (km^2).

[2]Endowment is shown at market value except for land, which is valued at either its original purchase price or at $1 if donated as a gift (based on the Society's intention never to sell).

Source: MAS records

In January 1999, the board appointed Laura Johnson as the Society's new president. Johnson came to MAS from a 16-year career with The Nature Conservancy (TNC), an international environmental organization that maintained the largest private system of nature sanctuaries in the world. A native of Massachusetts and a lawyer by training, Johnson had initially worked on legal issues for TNC but soon switched over to management, eventually being placed in charge of 12 states as eastern regional director. Reflecting on her time with TNC, she noted that it was a very focused organization with a culture of measurement. In particular, she said, the Conservancy offered a clear and compelling message about its goal of identifying important landscapes for protection, purchasing them, and protecting them. People could readily understand that their donations made a difference and thus feel a part of the enterprise.

A key motivation for Johnson was to be involved in creating an overall conservation ethic in Massachusetts, a task that she believed MAS performed better than any other organization. She was very concerned that modern lifestyles tended to separate people, especially children, from the natural environment. "Kids today are not outside, they're indoors playing on their computers," she said, "Or if they are outside, it's to play in a soccer game. Parents are afraid to let them wander." In Johnson's view, simply protecting land would be insufficient if in the future people forgot why the land in question was important, did not feel connected to it, and had no stake in it.

Johnson soon articulated a need to sharpen the Society's focus and develop a clear sense of direction. Despite a strong "feel good" sentiment towards the organization, relatively few members, she discovered, had a sense of the array of activities in which it was engaged and made assumptions that tended to mirror how they had come to join the organization. For instance, birders thought MAS was about birds, young families from the Boston area thought in terms of Drumlin Farm, and individuals who cared about public policy perceived the Society in terms of lobbying activities on Beacon Hill, site of the Massachusetts state government. So the first question Johnson asked was: "What are we and what do we want to be?"

Developing a Strategic Plan for 2000–2010

Over a six-month period in 1999, Johnson led and guided a comprehensive strategic planning effort. Its goals were to assess MAS strengths and resources, to evaluate the status of the Massachusetts environment and the impact of widespread changes, and to clearly define critical conservation issues. This assessment would enable MAS to define its own specific role relative to other conservation organizations. McKinsey & Co., the international consulting firm, gave pro bono support to the project.

A strong consensus emerged that biological conservation—that is, maintaining sustainable populations of the state's native biological diversity—lay at the heart of the Society's work. In looking toward the future, staff, the board, volunteers, and members reaffirmed their belief, passionately in many cases, that all of the Society's efforts should be directed toward protecting the nature of Massachusetts. From this belief emerged a common vision (reproduced at the beginning of this case) and a specific role for the Society:

> The Massachusetts Audubon Society serves both as a leader and as a catalyst for conservation, by acting directly to protect the nature of Massachusetts and by stimulating individual and institutional action through education, advocacy, and habitat protection.

The phrase, "Protecting the Nature of Massachusetts," which had been used sporadically up to this point, was adopted as the organization's signature and appeared beneath the Society's name on publications and stationery.

The strategic plan identified five major threats to biodiversity: loss of habitat to development; fragmentation of wildlife habitat; disruption of natural ecological cycles and processes through human alterations; the crowding out of native plants and animals by invasive species; and incompatible land use, such as using open space for recreational activities that damaged plants and threatened wildlife.

Following board approval of the plan, Johnson launched an in-depth examination of educational activities at MAS. In addition, the board directed a science review committee, composed of distinguished educators and scientists, to examine scientific activities at Mass Audubon. It also commissioned a study of information technology needs.

Education Plan

Discussions with staff members revealed that existing education programs, while high quality and well respected, lacked a common focus and connection to Mass Audubon themes and mission. Johnson acknowledged that the biggest challenge was to identify the most effective ways to use education to stimulate conservation action:

> We needed to find the best way to leverage our unique strengths—our sanctuary system, our scientific expertise, our advocacy capability, and our tremendously passionate staff—so that Mass Audubon could be a catalyst for conservation. We do thousands of programs, so there's plenty of activity to measure and we could say great things in terms of the number of programs held and the number of school-children involved. But none of those measures would identify what the activities accomplished in terms of making a difference.
>
> Our teacher naturalists do a wonderful job with our programs, but it's a very expensive business

model. And not every visitor to our sanctuaries wants to enroll in a program for a day or even a couple of hours. So we decided to explore an array of activities to get the message across. Our education director said at one point that we have this cultural bias at Mass Audubon that if we can just open up people's heads and dump into their heads what we know, they'll become just like us! But it doesn't work that way. We now have this paradigm from "caring to knowledge to action." When people act, that's the impact.

The education master plan emphasized the importance of creating significant outdoor experiences that might bring about transformations in people's environmental attitudes and values. Research showed that among children, shared family experiences in nature had the greatest influence in forming their attitudes as adults. To meet varied learning styles, the plan called for a mix of live programs, nature center exhibits, and self-guided trails at sanctuaries, plus opportunities for learning through publications, audiovisual media, interactive pages on the MAS web site, and articles in local newspapers.

ORGANIZATION

By this time, MAS was operating 58 wildlife sanctuaries across the Commonwealth, of which 41 were open to the public and 23 were staffed (**Exhibit 2**). They ranged in size from the 4-acre (1.5-ha) Nahant Thicket, a magnet for migrating songbirds on an otherwise rocky peninsula, to

EXHIBIT 2   Map of Massachusetts Showing Location of Sanctuaries

There's a Massachusetts Audubon Wildlife Sanctuary near you...

Berkshires
1 Canoe Meadows (Pittsfield)
2 Pleasant Valley (Lenox)

Connecticut River Valley
3 High Ledges (Shelburne)
4 Road's End (Worthington)
5 Arcadia (Easthampton)
6 Laughing Brook (Hampden)

Central Massachusetts
7 Lake Wampanoag (Gardner)
8 Flat Rock (Fitchburg)
9 Lincoln Woods (Leominster)
10 Wachusett Meadow (Princeton)
11 Cook's Canyon (Barre)
12 Broad Meadow Brook (Worcester)
13 Pierpont Meadow (Dudley)

Source: MAS records

South of Boston
14 Waseeka (Hopkinton)
15 Stony Brook (Norfolk)
16 Moose Hill (Sharon)
17 North River (Marshfield)
18 Daniel Webster (Marshfield)
19 North Hill Marsh (Duxbury)
20 Oak Knoll (Attleboro)
21 Allens Pond (Dartmouth)

Cape Cod and the Islands
22 Ashumet Holly (Falmouth)
23 Skunknett River (Barnstable)
24 Wellfleet Bay (Wellfleet)
25 Felix Neck (Edgartown)
26 Sesachacha Healthlands (Nantucket)
27 Long Pasture (Barnstable)
28 Sampson's Island (Barnstable)

North of Boston
29 Joppa Flats (Newburyport)
30 Ipswich River (Topsfield)
31 Endicott (Wenham)
32 Eastern Point (Gloucester)
33 Marblehead Neck (Marblehead)
34 Nahant Thicket (Nahant)
35 Nashoba Brook (Westford)

Greater Boston
36 Drumlin Farm (Lincoln)
37 Habitat Education Center (Belmont)
38 Boston Nature Center (Mattapan)
39 Broadmoor (Natick)
40 Blue Hills Trailside Museum (Milton)
41 Visual Arts Center (Canton)

Source: MAS records

Ipswich River which comprised 2,265 acres (917 ha) of forests, meadows, and wetlands. There were 511,000 visits to the sanctuaries in the most recent year, including some 145,000 schoolchildren. The five most popular sanctuaries—Blue Hills Trailside Museum on the western edge of Greater Boston, Daniel Webster and North River on the South Shore, Wellfleet Bay on Cape Cod, and Drumlin Farm in Lincoln—jointly accounted for 70% of all visitation.

Historically, some sanctuaries had operated with a high degree of independence from MAS headquarters, targeting local residents, schools, and vacationers. Their directors were often well known in the communities they served. Sanctuaries were under considerable pressure to increase program revenues each year to help balance the budget. However, the result was often what one director described as "a hodgepodge of programs, many of which have little to do with the society's mission."

MAS was one of only two environmental organizations that monitored the Massachusetts state government and promoted a specific environmental agenda. Although some members were invested in these statewide advocacy efforts, others saw Mass Audubon simply in terms of their local sanctuary. Declared one staff member, "In our members' eyes, we can be as big as a major advocacy issue or as small as a favorite trail."

For the most recent fiscal year, MAS had an operating income of $14.6 million and generated a small surplus—as it had done for the past three years. Gifts, grants and unrestricted bequests totaled $3.3 million and membership dues, $2.7 million; income from programs and investments each amounted to $4.2 million; and revenues from all other sources, including profits from the Audubon shop, a Mass Audubon credit card, and the Society's Natural History Travel program came to $0.2 million (**Exhibit 3**). Salaries and benefits accounted for more than 70% of all expenses.

Restructuring

MAS was governed by a 27-member board of directors, who elected from among their number a chair, three vice-chairs, and a treasurer. Providing additional expertise and support was a board-appointed council, whose 75 members were

EXHIBIT 3 Massachusetts Audubon Society: Income and Expenditures for Year Ending June 30, 2001

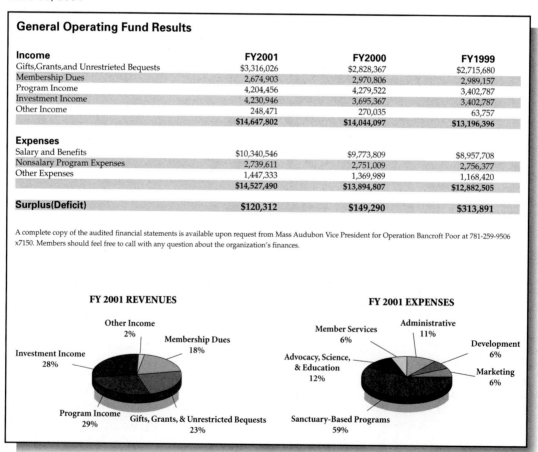

General Operating Fund Results

Income	FY2001	FY2000	FY1999
Gifts, Grants, and Unrestricted Bequests	$3,316,026	$2,828,367	$2,715,680
Membership Dues	2,674,903	2,970,806	2,989,157
Program Income	4,204,456	4,279,522	3,402,787
Investment Income	4,230,946	3,695,367	3,402,787
Other Income	248,471	270,035	63,757
	$14,647,802	**$14,044,097**	**$13,196,396**
Expenses			
Salary and Benefits	$10,340,546	$9,773,809	$8,957,708
Nonsalary Program Expenses	2,739,611	2,751,009	2,756,377
Other Expenses	1,447,333	1,369,989	1,168,420
	$14,527,490	**$13,894,807**	**$12,882,505**
Surplus (Deficit)	**$120,312**	**$149,290**	**$313,891**

A complete copy of the audited financial statements is available upon request from Mass Audubon Vice President for Operation Bancroft Poor at 781-259-9506 x7150. Members should feel free to call with any question about the organization's finances.

FY 2001 REVENUES

Other Income 2%
Membership Dues 18%
Investment Income 28%
Program Income 29%
Gifts, Grants, & Unrestricted Bequests 23%

FY 2001 EXPENSES

Member Services 6%
Administrative 11%
Advocacy, Science, & Education 12%
Development 6%
Marketing 6%
Sanctuary-Based Programs 59%

Source: MAS records

EXHIBIT 4 Organization Chart

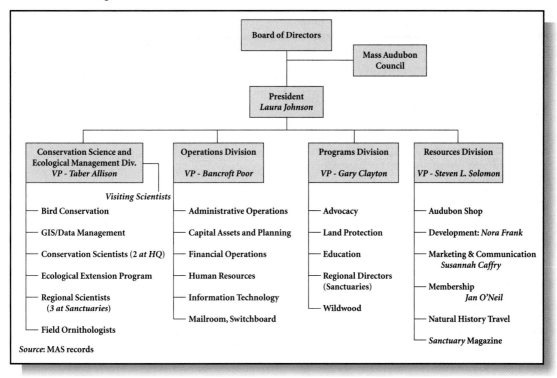

Source: MAS records

Source: MAS records

drawn from across the state, often being recommended by staff members at HQ or the sanctuaries. This governance structure, adopted in 1999, replaced an unwieldy 80-member board with different categories of directors, which lacked clear roles and expectations for its members and had no term limits.

One outcome of the strategic planning process was changes to the design of the MAS organization. The revised structure in place in 2001 consisted of four divisions, each of which was each headed by a vice president reporting to Laura Johnson (**Exhibit 4**).

Conservation Science and Ecological Management was formerly within Programs, but in response to the findings of the Science Review Committee was established as a separate division in order to sharpen its focus and raise its stature. It included a bird conservation department, GIS/data management, and employed five scientists with responsibilities for each of the three regions, the education department, and advocacy.

Operations was headed by Bancroft Poor, chief financial officer (CFO), whose responsibilities included administrative and financial operations, capital assets and planning, human resources, and information technology. The *Programs* division incorporated advocacy, education, land protection, the sanctuaries, and the Society's overnight summer camp. Finally, the *Resources* division was created to integrate fundraising, membership, and marketing activities and to raise their visibility.

THE RESOURCES DIVISION

To head the new Resources Division, Johnson hired Steven L. Solomon, previously vice president of resources at the Museum of Science in Boston. Earlier, he had also worked for the Boston Symphony Orchestra and the Museum of Fine Arts, as well as Harvard's Graduate School of Design. Solomon was attracted by the changes that were taking place at MAS and shared Johnson's belief that development and marketing should be linked: He declared:

> There are a lot of organizations that have separate marketing and development divisions, but in fact they have so many interlocking elements that they need to work closely together. When you're working in development at the level we are, it's based almost entirely on relationships. We want to be like Britain's RSBP [Royal Society for the Protection of Birds], which has a very clearly defined philosophy: "Membership is everybody's job."

The new division included the directors of development, marketing and communication, and membership; the editor of *Sanctuary*, the Society's bimonthly magazine; the manager of Natural History Travel, which organized naturalist-led tours (particularly for birders) to destinations around the world; and the manager of the Audubon Shop.

Development

Development activities embraced an annual fund to raise unrestricted gifts and capital campaigns to finance specific projects. All members were urged to contribute to the annual appeal; most were contacted by mail although major donors might be solicited personally. Capital campaigns ran over a period of several years. They usually involved intensive advance planning and early solicitation of major gifts. Several campaigns were currently in progress: $4 million for new facilities at the Wellfleet sanctuary; $2 million for new information technology; $6 million for Drumlin Farm; and $1.2 million for Wildwood, the new residential summer camp

Nora Frank, director of development, had joined Mass Audubon as manager of major gifts after working in admissions, development, and marketing for a residential school. She believed strongly in the need to keep donors and members involved and informed:

> One way to engage people is to let them know what we are doing and what their money is supporting. Right now, we don't have any common vehicle outside of solicitation that tells people what we are doing with their money, applauds them for helping to make a difference, and tells them how they can get further involved. Money comes in every time we use *Sanctuary* to highlight a specific need, even when we don't specifically ask for it. People do want to get involved but we haven't been letting them know what's happening.

Membership

Jan O'Neil had joined Mass Audubon 18 months earlier as director of membership. "Coming to Mass Audubon was a great opportunity to transition from dealing with many different organizations to focusing on one that I'd been a member of almost my whole life," remarked O'Neil. Her prior experience included 12 years with the New Boston Group, a telemarketing firm that made fundraising calls for nonprofits, many of them in the environmental area. She then spent two years working for Target Analysis Group, which performed detailed analytical studies for nonprofit clients.

O'Neil was a strong proponent of employing reliable data as the basis for planning and evaluating membership and fundraising strategies. As she examined Mass Audubon's membership program, she found there was insufficient information in the database to enable her to create detailed profiles of the membership. The lack of reliable benchmark data meant that it was hard to document what was going on. One of her initial tasks was to find ways to validate which membership strategies worked and which didn't, rather than simply continuing past practices or relying on conjecture. At her previous job, she remarked with a smile, they had a saying, "The plural of anecdote is not data."

As part of the $2 million technology initiative, some $400,000 was being invested in new membership and development software, together with associated installation and training. The new software would have extremely robust data storage and reporting capabilities, greatly enhancing the membership department's ability to profile and track members.

Between 1997 and 1999, MAS membership had surged from 54,400 to 67,400 households, spurred by the $34 million Centennial fundraising campaign, which included a $400,000 advertising campaign involving radio, billboards, and press. But it had since fallen back to around 65,000 household members. Like many nonprofits, MAS experienced churn in its membership, with about 20% turning over each year. Although that was less than in most organizations, there was still a continuing need to recruit new members. Although regular household membership cost $47 ($37 for individuals), new members could join initially for only $25. Forty-five percent of new members were recruited at the sanctuaries and 42% through direct mail solicitation. The balance joined as a result of visiting Mass Audubon's website, word-of-mouth recommendations, or other encounters.

Admission charges to the sanctuaries for non-members ranged from $3 for adults and $2 for children up to $6/$4 at Drumlin Farm. As one aspect of their pitch, admissions staff were trained to point out the savings associated with joining immediately and then being able to make this and future visits for the next year free of charge. It had proved a particularly compelling sell for families.

Direct mail solicitation involved purchase of mailing lists from brokers or swapping of membership lists with other nonprofits. Some 500,000–700,000 letters were mailed each year, at an average cost of $0.39 each, and typically yielded a response rate of around 1%. A recent mailing came in a colorful envelope bearing the slogan "Coming soon to a neighborhood near you" and a picture of a bird standing on a for-sale sign in open countryside. The letter inside was headed "Massachusetts Is Disappearing!" and warned that every day the state lost 44 acres of land to development. It then described Mass Audubon's conservation, education, and advocacy efforts and promoted the benefits of membership. New members received a welcome package of materials. The unit cost to MAS was about $3.25, exclusive of any premiums offered as inducements.

O'Neil noted that only 55% of first-year members would renew their membership, but this figure compared favorably to comparable national organizations, where renewal rates were typically only 30–35%. The estimated annual printing and mailing costs for renewals was $195,000. Although some members remained loyal for life, a board member with expertise in marketing estimated that the average duration of a member relationship that was renewed after the first year was eight years. In general, said O'Neil, "The longer someone has been a member, the more likely they are to stay a member." Added Solomon: "Members who are happily engaged are much more likely to renew."

At renewal time, members were encouraged to migrate to higher levels of membership: Supporting ($60), Defender ($75), Donor ($100), Protector ($150), Sponsor ($250), Patron ($500), and Leadership Friend ($1,250). Dues for the last-named category had been raised from $1,000 the previous year. Members of this group received a number of benefits, including invitations to exclusive events, meetings with Mass Audubon scientists and sanctuary directors, and special outings such as naturalist-led hikes or canoe trips. A small fee was sometimes charged for outings in order to preserve the full tax deductibility of the membership contribution. O'Neil and her colleagues in the Resources Division had been discussing the possibility of developing supplementary benefits for members enrolled in some of the other levels.

In addition to free admission to the sanctuaries, all members received six issues of *Sanctuary* magazine each year, discounts on MAS courses, lectures, programs, and day camps, and savings on purchases from the sanctuary shops. Depending on location, they might also receive newsletters from their nearest sanctuary. O'Neil estimated the annual printing and mailing costs associated with serving members at $330,000. This did not include the cost of staff time.

Premiums, such as day packs or tote bags bearing the Mass Audubon logo, were often used as inducements to renew at a higher level. The unit cost of purchasing and mailing such a premium was about $5. Former members were contacted for up to ten years in an effort to get them to rejoin. **Exhibit 5** shows the division of membership between the different levels at the end of the 2000–2001 fiscal year. About 70% of members renewed at the same rate, 20% upgraded, and 10% downgraded.

Marketing and Communication

Susannah Caffry had worked for Mass Audubon for two years. After leaving college, she entered the telecommunications industry, but found the work increasingly unrewarding. A keen outdoorswoman, she took a three-month sabbatical during which she went on an intensive canoeing trip with Outward Bound. Her experience convinced her that she wanted to work in the nonprofit sector and she accepted an offer from Outward Bound to join their Boston operation as director of admissions, later being promoted to vice president of marketing and public relations. In addition to communications, her work included recommendations on design, scheduling, and pricing of courses and programs.

MAS had earlier employed a director of marketing to manage communication activities associated with the Society's Centennial. As these activities wound down, the position was expanded to include development activities, but the attention given to marketing dwindled due to the more pressing needs of fundraising. The incumbent left at the same time the Resources Division was created and Caffry was recruited by Steve Solomon for the newly defined position of director of marketing and communication.

Caffry said she was attracted to Mass Audubon by the commitment to marketing among the leadership, but had found that not everyone in the organization understood or appreciated the value of a marketing perspective. More than once, she admitted, somebody had told her, "We don't like the M-word!" An important task involved marketing Wildwood, the Society's new summer camp for children. Because some staff members assumed that marketing activities only involved communication tasks such as signage and development of brochures, it took her some time, she admitted, to become involved in decisions on scheduling, pricing, and service features at the camp, all of which she saw as critical to success.

Caffry spent her first few months gathering information and learning how people on the staff, board, and council felt about marketing-related issues at Mass Audubon. She encountered passionately held views that were often widely divergent. There were, for instance, those who loved *Sanctuary* magazine because they saw it as "pure" and free from overt marketing and promotion of Mass Audubon's programs and agenda. Others, by contrast, regarded it as "elitist" and "arrogant," noting that the stories presupposed a level of technical understanding of the environment beyond that held by nonspecialists. Similar variations in viewpoint surrounded the newsletters published by the individual sanctuaries and also the web site. Summarizing the situation, Caffry remarked:

> There was no holistic approach as to how we were communicating. We had many different vehicles but they weren't held to any consistent message. I found a lot of conflicting opinions concerning the objectives of Mass Audubon's different communications activities. For instance there was no consensus at all as to what the purpose of *Sanctuary* magazine was. I also discovered that our annual report was not meeting the needs of our development office. This is a fundamental, critical communication effort for nonprofits.

EXHIBIT 5 MAS Membership by Contribution Level, June 30, 2001

LEVEL	DUES	NUMBER
Introductory	$25	12,093
Student	$20	460
Individual	$37	9,224
Family	$47	28,908
Supporting	$60	6,366
Defender	$75	2,152
Donor	$100	3,335
Protector	$150	1,092
Sponsor	$250	433
Patron	$500	205
Leadership Friend	$1,000	584
Complimentary		520
TOTAL		**65,372**

Source: MAS Membership Department

I see our overall objective as bringing together the communications activities without undermining the strengths of the organization—an important one being the commitment and feeling of ownership demonstrated by the sanctuary directors and other program staff.

COMMUNICATION STRATEGY TASK FORCE

Prior to Solomon's arrival, there had been no explicit strategy for coordinating all the Society's communications efforts. As a board member, Alfred (Appy) Chandler had long been concerned about the fragmentation of communication efforts, with each group, such as advocacy, attending to its own portfolio and operating relatively independently of the others. *Sanctuary* magazine, the Society's primary periodical for members, was started, he declared, "not as a mouthpiece of Mass Audubon but almost as an independent journal that would carry articles about the Society's mission as opposed to stories about Mass Audubon itself."

In addition to an in-house publishing effort that produced books and field guides, a variety of staff members across the organization wrote press releases, and there were various public relations efforts by the development office, such as staffing a booth at a flower show or other event. Many of the individual sanctuaries published their own newsletters, but they lacked a coordinated formatting and often failed to convey any real sense of being part of a larger, statewide organization. Chandler promoted the need for an integrated communication strategy to pull all the pieces together, so that the Society could speak with a single voice.

As president, Laura Johnson facilitated a meeting of MAS Council members to define the challenges that the Society faced with regard to its communications strategy. Among the key themes that emerged were a need for greater clarity in terms of "what, why, when, and to whom?" and a sense that the Society was not doing a good enough job of telling the MAS story to either its members or the general public. Break-out reports emphasized the need to find ways to strengthen the "brand" and to understand members and their preferences better. A range of opinions was expressed about *Sanctuary;* while most agreed that it was a high-quality magazine, many argued that it needed to clarify its purpose.

The following month, the board approved creation of a communication strategy task force to work with a consulting firm and MAS staff. Its purpose was to "oversee a review and analysis of current external communication activities and preparation of a communication plan for the Society, including recommendations for long-term strategy." Its scope extended to membership, education, public relations, advocacy, marketing, sanctuary activities, and publications. The task force was composed of board and council members who either had marketing and communications expertise or who represented a consumer point of view.

Chandler was named as chair. Commenting on the role of the consultant, EMI Strategic Marketing, Caffry observed:

> The consultant was very useful. There were so many sacred cows at Mass Audubon, so many personal feelings, and so many emotions that the consultant could ask questions that I, frankly, could not. There's a certain amount of skepticism in some quarters about the work related to communications and marketing. Not everybody is eager to see change and we have joked that there's a great deal of "anticipoint-ment" related to the communication plan.

Focus and Objectives

After some debate, the task force decided to focus on developing a communications strategy for the existing membership, with the primary objective being to increase member value. This would be achieved through better education of members about Mass Audubon's mission, by engaging them actively in "protecting the nature of Massachusetts, increasing their support for MAS programs, and growing their financial contributions."

Additional objectives were (1) to reinforce MAS's role and positioning as the leader in conservation, environmental education, and advocacy within Massachusetts, thus differentiating it from other environmental organizations; (2) to establish a clear, distinctive, contemporary image for the Society, portraying it as dynamic, current, and important; and (3) to communicate more cost effectively through better use of all available media and channels. The work of the task force included reviewing Mass Audubon's existing communications, undertaking a competitive audit of those organizations whose activities and appeal overlapped MAS in some measure (see the **Appendix**), and conducting a detailed survey.

Member Survey

Recognizing that existing knowledge of members' interests and perceptions was largely anecdotal, the task force decided to conduct a large-scale survey of members. It sought to identify channels for future communications, understand how members perceived MAS, and determine the relative importance they placed on its mission and programs. Additional goals included gauging the degree of membership overlap between MAS and other organizations, and determining whether there were meaningful differences between demographic groups in their reactions to MAS communications and content.

Working with the consultant, the task force developed a mail questionnaire that was bound around the cover of an issue of *Sanctuary* magazine and mailed to 62,000 members. More than 8,000 completed questionnaires were returned and promptly reviewed to gather any handwritten comments. Work on manually keying, coding, and cleaning the quantitative data concluded after 4,448 questionnaires, which was viewed as more than enough responses for the proposed statistical analysis.

Following a review of the preliminary tabulations (**Exhibit 6**), cross-tabs were run to determine how member views and priorities related to member characteristics on a wide array of segmentation variables. One aspect of this analysis involved segmenting members according to their most important reason for joining Mass Audubon. The top three reasons, accounting for 90% of respondents, were "believe in the organization and mission" (34%), "to protect the environment" (30%), and "to visit the sanctuaries" (26%).

Analysis showed that, compared to the first two groups, those who joined primarily to visit the sanctuaries tended to be younger and were more likely to have children under 18 in their households. Over 90% had visited a sanctuary within the past year, compared to about three-fourths of those in the other segments. They were somewhat less likely to have made a gift to the Society and a higher proportion of them belonged at the $47 (or lower) membership levels. Although they were less likely to read *Sanctuary* magazine in depth, they expressed more interest than the other groups in receiving a newsletter that listed MAS programs, classes, and events.

CREATING A NEW COMMUNICATIONS PROGRAM

After returning to the headquarters building from their visit to the Audubon Shop, Solomon and Caffry joined other members of the task force in the board room. The topic for discussion involved drawing some preliminary conclusions from the survey results and the competitive audit, and relating these insights to current communication efforts. Within the next few weeks, the task force was expected to present the board with recommendations for a new communications program.

EXHIBIT 6   Responses to Selected Questions on Member Survey, September 2001 (N = 4,448)

Why did you become a member of Mass Audubon? Please rank importance:

	#1	#2	#3
Believe in organization and mission	34%	35%	12%
Protect the environment	30	29	15
Visit the sanctuaries	26	21	25
Participate in programs, classes, events	6	8	10
Participate in birding related events, seminars	3	3	5
Get *Sanctuary* magazine	1	4	9

How important are the following aspects of Mass Audubon's mission to you?
(5-point scale: 5 = extremely important, 4 = very important)

	5	4
Protecting the environment for wildlife	81%	14%
Saving land from development	75	15
Providing nature preserves to walk/hike, enjoy birds/wildlife	60	29
Educating kids about the natural world/environment	60	27
Being an advocate for legal actions to protect environment	55	24

How often have you visited a Mass Audubon sanctuary or site in the past year?

Not visited	21%
1 visit	17
2–3 visits	24
>3 visits	38

What do you know about the relationship between National Audubon and Mass Audubon?

Same group	1%
MA is local branch	21
Separate organizations	48
Don't know	30

Do you read *Sanctuary* magazine?
Yes: 96%   No: 4%

If yes, how frequently?
Always: 43%   Frequently: 27%   Sometimes: 18%   Skim: 12%

Do you read the newsletter from your local sanctuary?
Yes: 78%   No: 16%   No response: 6%

If yes, how frequently?
Always: 50%   Frequently: 26%   Sometimes: 14%   Skim: 10%

How interested would you be in a newsletter that listed MA programs, classes, and events across the state?
Extremely: 9%   Very: 20%   Somewhat: 51%   Not at all: 20%

If interested, how often would you want to receive this listing?
Bimonthly: 15%   Quarterly: 56%   Two times per year: 29%

(*Continued*)

EXHIBIT 6   (Continued)

Do you have an e-mail address for personal mail?
Yes: 74%   No: 26%

If yes, would you be interested in learning about MA events by e-mail?
Yes: 46%   No: 54%

If yes, how often would you like to receive e-mails?
Weekly: 12%   Monthly: 61%   Quarterly: 27%

What types of things would you like to be informed about via e-mail?

Calendars of events at sanctuaries	72%
News about important public legislation/policy in Mass.	58
Mass Audubon activities to protect the nature of Mass.	57
Environment-related events in Mass.	55
News about the sanctuaries	48
News about your local sanctuary only	24

Have you ever visited our Web site?
Yes: 18%   No: 82%

Have you ever visited other environmental Web sites?
Yes: 38%   No: 62%

If yes, how often do you visit environmental Web sites in a month?
Once: 53%   2–3 times: 29%   4–10 times: 13%   11 or more: 5% (Mean = 2.8)

Would you come to the Mass Audubon Web site to sign up for events?
Yes: 63%   No: 37%

Would you go to interesting Mass Audubon events more than 20 miles from home?
Yes: 63%   No: 37%

If yes, how many miles would you travel?
20 miles: 5%   30 miles: 28%   50 miles: 49%   100+ miles: 18%

To which environmental organizations do you belong? Are you a member of any of these?

Mass Audubon	100%	PBS/WGBH	83%
The Nature Conservancy	38	Museum of Fine Arts	42
Trustees of Reservations	27	WBUR	36
Appalachian Mountain Club	18	Museum of Science	25
World Wildlife	15	New England Aquarium	15
National Audubon	15	Franklin Park Zoo	8
Other	27		

Source: MAS records. Note that certain data have been disguised.

Profiles of Selected Environmental Organizations

Appalachian Mountain Club (www.outdoors.org)

Founded in 1876 and headquartered in Boston, the AMC had some 94,000 members and described itself as "America's oldest conservation and recreation organization." Membership cost $40 for an individual and $65 for a family. AMC's mission statement emphasized "protection, enjoyment, and wise use of the mountains, rivers, and trails of the Northeast." Its 125th Anniversary Capital Campaign had a target of $30 million. AMC had 12 chapters extending from Maine to Washington, DC, including four in Massachusetts that collectively accounted for some 32,000 members. The Club's active publication program included *AMC Outdoors,* an award-winning monthly member magazine dedicated to recreation and conservation in the Northeast; *Appalachia,* described as "America's longest-running journal of mountaineering and conservation"; many trail and field guides; and a variety of recreation-oriented "how-to" books. AMC offered environmental education programs and sought to develop the skills and understanding needed to enjoy, protect, and advocate for the backcountry. Outdoor recreation services included group trips, trail maintenance, and provision of a network of camps, campgrounds, lodges, and cabins, plus a chain of high-mountain huts for hikers and climbers along the New Hampshire segments of the Appalachian Mountain Trail.

Friends of the Earth (www.foe.org)

FoE was founded in 1972 by a former president of the Sierra Club, who felt that the latter organization was insufficiently vigorous in its defense of the environment. Based in Washington, DC, it was a national nonprofit advocacy organization with affiliates in 66 countries, "dedicated to protecting the planet from environmental degradation; preserving biological, cultural, and ethnic diversity; and empowering citizens to have an influential voice in decisions affecting the quality of the environment—and their lives." In the U.S., FoE worked to preserve clean air and water, advocate public health protection, and examine the root causes of environmental degradation. It researched government policies and tax programs, and engaged in lobbying and legal action. FoE's "Economics for the Earth" program focused on the economics of protecting the environment and included the "Green Scissors" campaign—an alliance of environmentalists and conservative taxpayer organizations dedicated to cutting government subsidies that resulted in environmental damage. Its legal program to ensure enforcement of, and compliance with, U.S. environmental laws was located in FoE's Northeast office in Burlington, Vermont. Membership could be obtained for a donation of $25 or more. Members received a quarterly newsletter, *EarthFocus,* and the biweekly *EarthFocus Online.* They were also entitled to discounts on FoE publications and merchandise.

National Audubon Society (www.audubon.org)

Based in New York, NAS boasted 550,000 members, 508 chapters, and 100 sanctuaries and nature centers from coast to coast, including eight in Connecticut and two in Maine, but none in Massachusetts. Dedicated to the preservation of birds, other wildlife, and habitat, it employed more than 300 staff members and had assets of some $170 million. Expenses in 2000 totaled $58 million, of which $8.7 million was devoted to marketing and communications and $23 million to field operations. Membership cost $35, but new members could enroll for only $20. Benefits included membership in the local chapter (which usually organized a variety of activities) and receipt of the widely praised bimonthly magazine *Audubon,* which had won many awards in fields such as nature photography, essays, and design. NAS's 1995 strategic plan committed it to decentralize activities, with a goal of moving from nine regional offices to, ultimately, 50 state programs. In pursuit of this goal, the president had actively encouraged independent state Audubon societies to join or affiliate themselves with NAS. By 2001, the only states in which NAS lacked offices or chapters were Massachusetts, New Hampshire, and Rhode Island, each of which had its own state society. NAS lobbied actively in Washington on issues that were central to its mission, including improved funding of the National Wildlife Refuge system. Chapters worked at the state and local levels. Seeking to protect migratory birds, NAS was also active in Bermuda, the U.S. Virgin Islands, many Central American countries, and parts of South America. The Society was actively engaged in a major rebranding program, including a revised logo, and was now promoting itself simply as "Audubon."

Sierra Club (www.sierraclub.org)

Based in San Francisco, the Sierra Club took its name from California's Sierra Nevada range and was founded in 1892 by the famous naturalist, writer, and conservationist John Muir. From its early days, it combined organization of group excursions in the mountains with political activity to create national parks and forest reserves. Over subsequent decades it was often successful in fighting proposals for damming of wild and scenic rivers across large areas of the western United States. It gradually evolved into a national organization, with a strong presence in Washington, using education, lobbying, and litigation to achieve its environmental goals. From the 1970s onwards, it broadened its emphasis to fight for clean air and water and extended its anti-dam crusade to other countries, including Canada and Brazil. Its mission emphasized enjoyment, exploration and preservation of the "wild places of the earth," promoting responsible use of resources, and education to protect and restore the quality of both the natural and human environment. By 2001, it had some 700,000 members and chapters in many states, including Massachusetts. The club organized more than 300 national and international outings in addition to the numerous outings organized by local chapters. Members received a monthly environmental newsletter, *The Planet,* and an attractive glossy bimonthly magazine, *Sierra.*

The Trustees of Reservations (www.thetrustees.org)

Founded in 1891, this Massachusetts organization maintained 91 reservations representing many of the state's most scenic, ecologically rich, and historically important landscapes. Its landholdings, which also included several historic buildings, protected some 45,000 acres (180 km^2) through ownership or conservation restrictions. Collectively, the reservations provided a wide range of recreational opportunities. The organization also offered function rentals at the large Crane Estate in Ipswich and bed-and-breakfast accommodation at this and one other property. Basic membership cost $40 for individuals or $60 for couples and families. Benefits included a free guidebook, a 50% discount off admission charges at TTOR reservations, discounts in its shops, and receipt of a quarterly newsletter.

MASSPIRG (www.masspirg.org)

The Massachusetts Public Interest Research Group was one of 26 independent, state-based research groups advocating for the public interest in their home states. In 1983, an alliance of state-based PIRGs created US PIRG (www.uspirg.org) to share ideas and resources and, where appropriate, coordinate regional or national efforts. MASSPIRG sought to uncover threats to public health or well-being and fight to end them, using investigative research, media exposés, grassroots organizing, advocacy, and litigation. Its stated goal was to deliver persistent, results-oriented, public interest activism that protected the environment, encouraged a fair and sustainable economy, and fostered responsive, democratic government. Among the six programs it was pursuing in Massachusetts were the environment (open space, recycling, clean water, and toxics), energy (efficiency and clean, renewable power), and transportation (efficient and environmentally sound). Each program director worked with many different constituencies in support of specific goals. Located in Boston close to the Massachusetts State House, the organization had a full-time attorney on its staff. Members received MASSPIRG MASSCITIZEN, a quarterly report of activities.

The Nature Conservancy (www.nature.org)

Founded in 1951, TNC defined its mission as preserving "the plants, animals, and natural communities that represent the diversity of life on Earth by protecting the lands and waters they need to survive." Its approach was to protect carefully chosen portfolios of land and water within scientifically defined ecoregions, in order to ensure the survival of each region's biological diversity. TNC had a reputation as a very focused organization that used a non-confrontational approach to achieve its goals. By 2002, it had successfully protected 12.6 million acres (50,000 km^2) in the United States and an additional 80.2 million acres (325,000 km^2) across Canada, the Asia-Pacific Region, the Caribbean, and Latin America. It had 1,400 preserves, one million members, and had launched a $1 billion campaign—the largest private conservation campaign ever undertaken—to save 200 of the world's "Last Great Places." TNC's approaches employed outright purchase and management of land under partnerships or conservation easements. A few of its properties, principally in the western U.S., offered accommodation and excursions, but none of those in Massachusetts did. TNC was based in Arlington, Virginia, and published *Nature News,* an interactive newsletter for members sent once or twice monthly by email, as well as *Nature Conservancy* magazine, which had recently been revamped and was offered free of charge to members enrolled at the $50 or higher level. Basic membership was $25 a year.

The Wilderness Society (www.wilderness.org)

Founded in 1935, TWS worked to develop a nationwide network of wild lands through public education, scientific analysis, and advocacy. Its goal was "to ensure that future generations will enjoy the clean air and water, wildlife, beauty, and opportunities for recreation, and renewal that pristine forests, rivers, deserts, and mountains provide." Headquartered in Washington, TWS had eight regional offices across the country, including one in Boston. The activities of the northeast region focused on the Great Northern Forest—"the largest and last continuous wild forest east of the Mississippi River"—which stretched from northern New York state, across the northern Green and White Mountains, to the remote wetlands of eastern Maine. In return for a contribution of $30 or more, members received the Society's annual full-color publication *Wilderness Year,* a quarterly color newsletter, and member alerts.

STUDY QUESTIONS

1. How is MAS currently positioned against other environmental organizations in Massachusetts?

2. What is a new member potentially worth to MAS? (Hint: Use customer lifetime value analysis.) Beyond the financial issue, why is membership important to MAS?

3. What approaches should MAS use to retain members and to persuade them to upgrade their membership levels?

4. As a participant in the Task Force on Member Communications Strategy, what actions would you recommend to the board?

Case 18   *TLContact: CarePages Service (A)*

CHRISTOPHER LOVELOCK

An Internet start-up company has successfully developed a Web-based service that enables hospital patients to stay in touch with family and friends through the medium of individualized home pages. Three years after launch, the company is finally becoming profitable and the founder and CEO is reviewing strategies for future growth.

Eric Langshur, CEO of TLContact, Inc. (TLC), was pleased as he drafted the company's latest quarterly activity update.. The news was encouraging on almost all fronts.

TLC's primary product, CarePages, was a Web-based service that enabled patients to stay in touch with family members and friends through the medium of individualized home pages. Utilization of CarePages was accelerating among existing customers, primarily acute care hospitals in the United States and Canada, and the company continued its record of 100% renewals. New sales were up dramatically, individual users continued to be delighted with the service, and new enhancements had been well received. Press coverage and word-of-mouth had been phenomenal; the latest Google search of "tlcontact" had yielded more than 400 entries. Meanwhile, competitors were stumbling and one had just shut down. Eric predicted that consolidated annual revenues would reach about $3 million, up sharply over the previous year.

Then he shook his head as he looked again at the $3 million figure. Fifteen years earlier, at age 25 and fresh out of an MBA program, he had been running a $25 million business. And prior to launching TLContact in 2000 with his wife, Sharon, a physician, he had been president of a large division of a multinational aerospace company. Were challenge and reward directly proportional to scale? He didn't think so.

The activity update on which he was working would make pleasant reading, he reflected, for the firm's board of directors in advance of their upcoming meeting. But Eric wanted to avoid any sense of complacency, because the firm's very success could still attract viable competition. Despite having some prestigious clients, TLC had only penetrated a small percentage of what was potentially a very large market. The firm offered a trusted and valued access to hospital patients, with potential for hospitals and other sponsors to use it as a customized communication channel. Yet TLC also offered access to a vastly larger audience of health-oriented consumers. Might other sponsors, in addition to hospitals, be interested in the potential synergies?

THE COMPANY

Located in Chicago and created at the height of the dot.com boom, TLC was among the small percentage of Internet start-ups that had survived after the bubble burst. The management team consisted of Eric Langshur, CEO; Charlyn Slade, RNC, president; Raul Vasquez, chief technical officer; Lindsay Paul, VP–business development–healthcare; JoAnne Resnic, VP–health care services; and Sharon Langshur, MD, medical director. In addition, the company employed a technical team of four consisting of a graphic designer, a customer service manager, and two software engineers. The Sales and Business Development team comprised Slade and Resnic, both former nurse administrators, and Paul, a Harvard MBA with an extensive background in healthcare consulting.

During 2002, TLC had a net loss of $0.7 million. The company was privately held by the founders and 20 private investors. Initial financing had involved an initial investment in 2000 of $3 million by what Eric described as "angel" investors, and an additional investment of $900,000 plus $1.7 million of convertible loans, again from private investors in 2002. At the end of the first quarter of 2003, monthly revenues were meeting operational expenses.

The TLC Service Concept

On behalf of sponsoring hospitals and other in-patient healthcare facilities in North America, TLC created personalized homepages for patients that linked them to family and friends during hospitalization and extended care, including maternity. Typically, the homepage, which TLC branded as a CarePage, was accessed through the healthcare organization's own website, but TLC also offered the option of access through the company's website. In both instances, all hosting took place on TLC's servers. The CarePage enabled family and friends to stay up to date on the patient's condition and to communicate messages of support (for an example, see **Exhibit 1**).

A CarePage was usually created when a patient was first admitted, although maternity patients often requested it be set up before their due dates. In most instances, a friend or family member agreed to act as CarePage manager and was provided with simple procedures for creating a page and updating content. The manager then informed the patient's family and friends of the address and the password required for access. Two levels of security were offered, with the higher

EXHIBIT 1 Sample CarePage

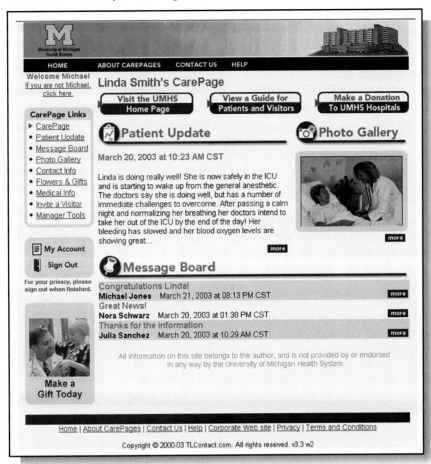

level requiring additional screening to ensure that only specified visitors could gain access. Visitors, known as "members," could leave short messages on the site for all to read.

The service was offered free to patients and visitors, being presented as an added benefit of patronizing the sponsoring healthcare organization. The fee paid by the sponsor varied according the size of the institution, level of use, and premium options selected, but in 2003 averaged about $20,000 a year. TLC was exploring an alternative business model in which a third-party corporate sponsor paid the fee on behalf of the institution and received co-branding recognition on the CarePages.

The basic offering included such features as sending automatic email notification of an update on the patient's condition to all registered visitors to a specific CarePage, the ability to order gifts and flowers, and a guestbook tracking all visitors to the site, plus the options of posting photos and creating links to relevant background medical information.

TLC was currently testing a new feature that enabled visitors to make a donation to the healthcare institution serving the patient. For an additional fee, sponsors could also obtain feedback on usage patterns, conduct surveys of visitors, post a hospital CEO welcome message, link to

the hospital gift shop, and feature a customized inbox. Spanish-language CarePages were also available for an extra fee. The company had documented different patterns of CarePage use, showing that it varied according to the nature of the patient's situation. On average, a CarePage remained "up" for 85 days and attracted 50 members, each of whom visited 15 times. However, the average hospital stay in the United States, across all categories, was only 5.2 days.

TLC's procedures ensured privacy protection, meeting the provisions of the Health Information Privacy and Accountability Act (HIPAA). Its website displayed the TRUSTe Privacy Seal, a consumer branded symbol certifying that the site met stringent requirements of notice, choice, access, security, and redress.

Operations

TLContact's service operated on three company-owned servers positioned at a remote facility, an arrangement termed co-location. These servers were connected to TLC's offices across a high-speed T1 line, which allowed almost all administrative and backup tasks to be achieved remotely.

TLC had invested heavily in technology, primarily its custom-built software, as part of a continuing effort to improve the usability of the service. This process benefited considerably from having a development team that, by necessity of the company's small size, spent part of their time providing customer support. Direct contact with users' problems and questions provided a constant stream of ideas for improvements to the site. In general, a new version of the software was released every six to eight weeks, incorporating newly developed ideas as well as the needs of new customers.

HISTORY: GENESIS OF AN IDEA

In February 1998, Eric and Sharon Langshur were looking forward to the birth of their first child. Like any young couple, they anticipated that this event would change their lives but had no inkling of the changes that would result in their careers, especially Eric's.

Eric, then 35, had enjoyed a meteoric career, developing an enviable record for his skills in both start-up and turnaround management. Born in Canada, he grew up in Montreal and graduated from the University of New Brunswick with a degree in finance and information systems. Later, he obtained an MBA from Columbia and began a fast-paced progression through many different divisions of United Technologies Corporation in the space of just nine years. As he later recalled,

> When I was 25, UTC gave me a chance to run a "little" $25 million entity in southern California, which was my first opportunity to develop a quantifiable track record. I was fresh out of business school. I had to learn a great deal about managing people, which was definitely beneficial so early in my career.
>
> I did well in that job and was put in charge of a series of increasingly larger and more challenging businesses. Then I became vice president and general manager of UTC's Hamilton Standard propeller systems business that manufactures props for most of the commercial aircraft in the world. My last job was as president of ONSI, UTC's fuel cell business, the world's largest. In 1997, I received an offer to be president of the aerospace services division at Bombardier. It was a dream job.

Sharon, also a native of Canada, had graduated from McGill University in 1986 and entered the field of human genetics. Initially she worked as a researcher and then, following completion of an MS at Sarah Lawrence College, as a genetic counselor in clinical human genetics. Deciding to pursue a career in medicine, she enrolled in medical school at the University of Connecticut and received her MD in 1997, achieving honors in all clinical rotations and serving as class valedictorian. During her pregnancy, she continued her one-year academic fellowship in anatomic pathology.

Eric's new job with Bombardier—a prominent Canadian manufacturer whose products included aircraft, rail transit systems, and recreational vehicles—involved a move from Connecticut to Chicago in September 1997. The plan was for him to commute for several months while Sharon remained in Hartford to await the birth of their baby.

On February 25, Sharon gave birth to a son, whom they named Matthew. But complications became evident almost immediately and within days, a pediatric cardiologist had diagnosed the baby's heart as missing a left ventricle, a potentially fatal condition that would have been untreatable only a decade earlier. Facing the prospect of a series of complex operations on Matthew's heart, involving surgical procedures that only a handful of hospitals in the nation were qualified to perform, the Langshurs decided to complete their move to Chicago and have the baby treated at the University of Michigan Medical Center in Ann Arbor. The first surgery took place five days later.

It was a desperately worrying time for everyone. "When Sharon was pregnant," Eric remembered, "I wanted our child to be smart, handsome, athletic, outgoing, and with all the social graces. After he was diagnosed, I just wanted him to live." The couple's extended family and large circle of friends were deeply concerned and anxious for news.

Out on the West Coast, Sharon's younger brother, Mark Day, was completing his PhD in mechanical engineering at Stanford. Feeling isolated, knowing nothing about the heart, and wanting to do something useful, Mark turned to the Internet, which was just beginning to hit its stride. His search turned up a lot of information from the American Heart Association and an array of medical sources. Within a few weeks, he had created a simple website that family and friends could access. He edited the information he had gathered and loaded it on the site, together with bulletins on Matthew's condition and how the baby was responding to treatment. Sharon sent him regular updates on Matthew's progress and additional medical information. "It was a very simple site," Mark declared later. "If I had paid somebody else to do it for me, it probably wouldn't have cost more than a few hundred dollars." To minimize the need for emailing, Mark added a bulletin board so that people could send messages to Sharon and Eric.

To everyone's surprise, the site proved exceptionally popular. News spread by word-of-mouth and the site recorded hundreds of daily visitors, with more than 200 different people leaving messages for the family. People who had never before used the Internet found a way to access the site, follow Matthew's progress, and send messages.

The Langshurs were overwhelmed by this outpouring of support but also deeply grateful for the way in which the website enabled them to avoid having to spend massive amounts of time responding to phone calls and repeating the same information time and time again. The site remained up for two years, during which time

Matthew successfully underwent three surgeries to repair his heart and eventually developed into a happy, healthy toddler.

Creation of TLContact.com

The success of Matthew's website convinced the Langshurs that there was a market opportunity for an Internet-based company to deliver similar information services for patients and their families, potentially on a national basis. They were inspired not only by the business opportunities this venture presented, but also by a desire to help other families enjoy the same benefits that they had received.

In late 1999, Eric and Sharon made the decision to quit their jobs (Sharon was a pediatric resident at Children's Memorial Hospital) and start their own company. "It was the height of the Internet boom," Eric recalled, "and a very heady time when millions of dollars could be raised on the basis of a short business plan." The Langshurs soon succeeded in raising $3 million from several "angel" investors.

Meantime, Mark was enjoying a long-planned hiking and climbing tour of several countries in Asia and Africa. Having recently obtained his PhD, he had decided against pursuing an academic career and was debating what to do next. He and a group of friends celebrated New Year's Eve by climbing Mount Kilimanjaro, a dramatic extinct volcano in Kenya and, at 19,340 feet (5,896 m), the highest mountain in Africa. When the party returned to civilization, Mark found a message waiting for him from his sister and brother-in-law: Would he like to join their new start-up as chief technology officer?

Mark flew into Chicago on the day of the Super Bowl, the freezing temperatures of the upper Midwest contrasting sharply with the tropical heat of Kenya. But it was an intoxicating atmosphere for dot.com entrepreneurs and investors. Business news stories that day described the huge amounts of money that an array of Internet-based companies were spending on TV advertising during the Super Bowl broadcast.

The business model for the new venture followed the b2c approach that dominated most Internet start-ups. The goal was to market directly to patients' families and to prospective parents, charging a fee per page. The company needed a name and, in keeping with its consumer orientation, the Langshurs wanted to call it 4U.com, which they saw as simple and memorable. However, a search revealed that this domain name, although not in use, was already registered. Eric laughed as he recalled what happened next.

> When we contacted the owner, he indicated that he was willing to sell the rights to the URL for $2 million. The lunacy of the times was further highlighted when one of our early investors urged us to just go ahead and buy it! But we didn't think that was a prudent use of $2 million.

Instead, they selected the name TLContact.com, a play on the common abbreviation of "tender loving care." Each patient site was named a "CarePage," and procedures were devised to control access and ensure patient confidentiality.

Initial Start-Up

In addition to Eric as CEO, Sharon as director of medical services, and Mark as CTO, the team was expanded to include a president with an extensive healthcare operations background, a VP–business development, and a VP–health care services, as well as administrative support staff. Mark began to build a technology team to create the website and its supporting systems. Meantime, an advisory board was formed to help shape the new company's strategy, monitor progress, and provide an objective perspective. TLC also benefited from advice provided by Sharon's father, George Day, an internationally recognized marketing professor at the Wharton School of the University of Pennsylvania. She noted that he had taught them the importance of listening to the market, understanding the needs of target customers, and finding ways to avoid or circumvent strategic obstacles.

Eric found himself making a sharp transition in his professional lifestyle, moving from the president's office of a multimillion business to a second-floor office above a storefront. At Bombardier's aerospace division, and prior to that at UTC, he had had thousands of employees. After a few months, TLC's payroll (including himself, Sharon, Mark, and technical staff) was up to $50,000 per month. However, he conceded that this situation did not prevent him from continuing to think big. There were 6,000 acute-care hospitals in the U.S., 17,000 nursing homes, and over 3,000 hospices. The number of patients treated each year was estimated at 40 million. Everyone was convinced that huge rewards awaited the firm that could move quickly to penetrate this market.

Quickly recognizing the difficulties and expense of trying to market directly to individual patients, TLC soon shifted its sales focus to a hospital-based approach. With competition between hospitals becoming increasingly heated, enhancing patient satisfaction had become a strategic imperative at many institutions. Offering patients access to TLC seemed like a logical service enhancement to its proponents. But, despite early support from the pediatric cardiology group at the University of Michigan Medical Center (where Matthew had been treated), selling to hospitals proved much more difficult than expected.

TLC's original business model anticipated being in hundreds of hospitals within a year or so. The company was in a hurry to build a strong market base before competitors could do so. Already, there were a number of competing organizations, all of them quite small and each started by individuals who had created a website to keep family and friends informed of developments relating to somebody's health. They included Baby Press Conference, targeted at prospective parents; TheStatus, run as a sideline of a Web design company in Anchorage, Alaska; VisitingOurs, a rather basic service that oursourced the Web technology; and another rather basic service called CaringBridge, operated by a nonprofit organization.

To their dismay, the Langshurs and their colleagues soon realized that selling to hospitals was going to be a slow and difficult task. Sharon observed:

> We found the difficulties of selling to hospitals to be myriad. Based on my experience as a physician, we initially felt that we could sell to docs on the basis of helping them to enhance the quality of the patient experience. We knew they cared about patients and wanted to do the best for them. But after several months of barking up that tree, we realized that physicians didn't have the time to listen or the budget to purchase and were usually just too busy with delivery of medical care.
>
> So after six months or so, we shifted our efforts to PR and marketing departments, which did have a budget and were more likely to be able to see the advantages for their hospitals in terms of increased patient satisfaction.

However, hospital administrators didn't like the idea of having to ask their patients to pay for the service—after all, there were no charges for television and other non-medical services designed to enhance satisfaction—so the discussion then shifted to the possibility of the hospital itself purchasing the basic service and making the option available to all patients who requested it. Yet many administrators failed to grasp the appeal of the service for patients or the advantages to the hospital of offering it. So TLC had to adopt a missionary approach, pointing out that advantages for the hospital included not only more satisfied patients but also fewer demands on hospital staff as families and friends replaced telephone requests for information by a simple search of the website.

In its sales efforts, TLC also cited the findings of a national study on patient satisfaction by the Picker Institute, which found that when asked about problems encountered during their hospital stays, 27% of the 23,763 patients surveyed reported lack of emotional support, 28% cited inadequate information and education, and 23% complained about insufficient involvement of family and friends. The survey data showed that patients receiving inadequate emotional support during their hospital stay were up to ten times more likely to say that they would not return to that hospital or recommend it.

Meantime, Mark and his technology team were hard at work on systems design. He emphasized that this task was vastly different in cost and complexity from the simple website that he had designed earlier for his nephew.

> A key question at the outset had been whether to contract with someone to build the website or do it ourselves. It wasn't entirely clear whether it was worth the extra cost of outsourcing to gain the advantage of speed, although we were under tremendous pressure to move quickly since there was a level of paranoia about the risk that competitors might get a jump on us and dominate what was seen as a very lucrative market. On the other hand, if we did it ourselves, we would retain the intellectual capital and would find it easier to undertake future updates and expansions. Having had the experience of creating the initial website and seen its functionality, I had a very clear idea of how I wanted this thing built, which gave us a running start.
>
> In February 2000, the dot.com boom was just about at its peak and outsourcing was wildly expensive—we were quoted $400,000 for just a scoping study! So we hired some consultants who could really help us set up the initial architecture and help achieve some of our key goals, especially flexibility. During the same period, I hired several people full time. We took a deliberate approach to hire very skilled people. After a couple of months we had a technical team of about 10, including a programming group, a graphic design team, and a support group whose work included content design. The total cost was in the range of four to five hundred thousand dollars to achieve a functioning website.
>
> It's very difficult to create a piece of software that's really user friendly. It takes an incredible amount of skill, effort, and time to develop something that's usable, functional, and scalable—meaning that it can be expanded and built upon without failing. For enterprise-wide applications you have to support the server with an operating system. We chose to go open source, which significantly reduced the cost because the source code is freely available. We launched in early August.

An additional round of "angel" financing was obtained during the summer of 2000, which enabled TLC to enhance the functionality of the service and add optional features. By late 2000, TLC had completed proof-of-concept prototype and alpha testing of the service. It had secured launch customers in three targeted market segments: acute care, long-term care, and hospice. Recognizing two distinct needs, it had created two distinct products, Acute CarePage and Baby CarePage. The latter was targeted at parents who were expecting a baby.

AN EVOLVING MARKETING STRATEGY

TLC's market strategy evolved into a threefold thrust. The first strategic component was to continue offering a stand-alone service, positioned as an e-business patient satisfaction solution that offered important benefits for hospitals and health systems. Among patients and their families, TLC planned to rely on a "viral" marketing effect through word-of-mouth referrals, thus limiting the need for mass media advertising. Although the number of users was still small, feedback had been exceptionally positive. The second component involved outsourcing direct sales to a national distribution partner that had established relationships with hospitals and health facilities. The third component involved licensing TLC software and its functionality to trusted third-party vendors and consultants. These partners could then bundle TLC's service as a "feature" to enhance their own product offerings, in return for royalties and other payments.

Sales Activities

By early 2001, sales discussions were in progress at more than two dozen hospitals and health systems. Despite validation of TLC service by a number of leading healthcare providers, the sales process was proving very slow. Hospital acceptance required the buy-in of numerous constituents, including administration, marketing, patient services, IT, legal, and physicians. But some could still not see the value of the service. As Sharon put it, "They had difficulty thinking outside the box." Budgetary constraints were a major reason for saying no. A few large hospitals with significant endowments declined on the grounds that they might want to develop their own services in house.

However, TLC met its sales target for the first quarter by signing contracts with the University of Michigan Health System, New York Presbyterian Hospital, and Children's Memorial Hospital in Chicago. The first two hospitals specified that CarePages had to be fully branded under their own names and employ their own distinctive color schemes, although the tag line, "Powered by TLContact" would appear as a subscript.

Each branded product required the customization of over 70 Web pages and 400 images, but TLC soon developed this capability, which it believed offered a significant competitive advantage. Other enhancements included an option for user feedback, addition of an email notification tool to announce updated news on a CarePage, and inclusion of software logic to automatically fix common mistakes that visitors might make in CarePage names, thereby reducing the volume of customer service enquires.

Eric had always been very cost conscious, so planning at TLC had emphasized the need to rush toward cash flow positive status. However, with the dot.com bubble now burst and sales progress proving sluggish, the Langshurs realized that TLC had to slow its burn rate by making significant cutbacks in staff numbers. It was a painful decision.

TLC continued to refine its sales approach so that it could address the specific concerns of the different decision makers at a hospital. It also refined its pricing policy, which Eric admitted had been rather unsophisticated, and began customizing it to the characteristics and needs of individual hospitals. On average, hospitals paid about $20,000 a year for the service. One encouraging development was that the lead time for concluding a sales agreement with a hospital was getting shorter, dropping from an average of nine months in early 2001 to only three months by the end of 2002. Eric remarked:

> We've learned a great deal about how to communicate our value proposition succinctly and to simplify our sales process. Most importantly, with every new account we sign, market acceptance of the product grows and the sales cycle shortens.

An important contributing factor was the exceptionally positive nature of the feedback received from CarePage users (see **Exhibit 2** for a representative sample). Competitors, however, did not seem to be faring as well. BabyPressConference had shut down in 2002. TLC considered purchasing its assets but decided that this would not be a worthwhile investment. None of the remaining three appeared as active in the marketplace.

Although continuing to add individual hospitals to its client base and target new ones, TLC now recognized that prospects for significant sales growth centered on achieving distribution agreements with large systems. Its first success in what was seen as a long-lead-time sale came with a distribution agreement with CHCA, a buying consortium for 38 leading children's hospitals. A direct-to-hospice co-marketing initiative was launched with the National Hospice and Palliative Care Organization, which represented 2,100 of the nation's 3,140 hospices. Subsequently, the firm began a paid pilot program with Tenet Corporation, operator of 116 acute-care hospitals.

Continued innovation in CarePages functionality included creation of a Spanish-language option, developed in collaboration with a Mexican hospital system, which would be offered to U.S. hospitals for an extra fee. Also under development was refinement of procedures for surveying members after they had completed a certain number of visits. Other new features in development included a Nurses Hall of Fame, allowing members to pay tribute to exceptional healthcare workers, thereby improving nursing hiring and retention; a Message Inbox, allowing hospitals to deliver targeted messages to members; and a "Send a Prayer" feature which provided a functional link to a faith-based prayer group. Eric believed that each of these features demonstrated that the product had great acceptance as a trusted channel to the healthcare consumer.

In June 2002, Mark Day left the company to enroll in the MBA program at Wharton. Having transitioned from a technical role to one more deeply involved with marketing, sales, and fund raising, Mark now sought to build a more fundamental understanding of these areas through his MBA studies.

Research Insights

Working with researchers and a sponsoring institution, TLC had conducted a survey of CarePages visitors and managers. In September 2002, it added a new feature to the Children's Hospital Boston site, an online survey capability.

EXHIBIT 2 Recent Feedback

- "TLContact has been the lifeline of many of the families on my unit and keeps the support network of family and friends alive and thriving. I cannot stress enough how important this website is to families in crisis or enduring a chronic illness. Thank you. Thank you. Thank you!" (Theresa, Child Life Specialist, C.S. Mott Children's Hospital)
- "This is a prime example of why Children's [Hospital] has the world-class reputation it does. Thanks for caring enough about your patients and their families to continually strive to keep Children's 'a cut above.'"
- "What a wonderful service to provide to your patients and their families. . . . This can only help to enhance the patient's rate of recovery and help everyone cope with the hospitalization experience."
- "I cannot express what an incredible blessing this website was. We could update everyone at the same time without anything getting misconstrued. To go to the site and see so many folks sending well wishes and prayers and was so uplifting and helpful. We received so many comments from family and friends that the site was fabulous! Please keep this service!"
- "I want you to know that this is a brilliant idea. It helps immeasurably to humanize the difficulties of communication surrounding hospitalization."
- "What a great concept! For someone that is not a family member, but a close friend, this is a great way to communicate on the schedule of the patient's family. I'm really impressed. . . . I'm going to forward this link to my pastor, I'm sure he will find it useful."
- "My daughter's illness was sudden and life threatening. We were transferred from one hospital to a children's hospital. Everyone had thought the worst when they couldn't find us in our hometown hospital. Our only connection was your service. It saved me, mom, from intense stress as everyone wanted to know hour-by-hour updates. In some cases it was the ONLY information our families received. Your service is a godsend for the patients and the families. Because of your service churches around the US gathered to pray for our little girl. Those prayers wouldn't have happened if we didn't have the internet connection that you and the hospital gave to us. Now we celebrate that our little girl made it and people like you helped us."
- "Excellent service, and such a help at such a stressful time in our lives. Not having to make multiple phone calls, and everyone hearing information 'firsthand.' is such a huge help. We've often logged on in the middle of the night, from the ICU, in the middle of our stressful life-and-death dance as the baby fights to live, to read all the kind words of encouragement our family & friends have left for us. The baby's been in and out of the hospital many times now in his short 6 months so far, and words cannot express what a difference it makes, to know that everyone's out there pulling for us, and praying for us. Thanks so much!"
- "This web service is perfect for our situation. My 19-year-old son suffered a severe head injury. The hospital he was transferred to is 3 hours from our home. We live in a very small, tight community. We have lots and lots of concerned family and friends. Our son will have ongoing treatment and progress that our family & friends want to stay informed of. It's a wonderful tool and I have had nothing but positive feedback from the users. Thank you."
- "You have a truly done a wonderful thing with this CarePage, and the pictures, updates, and message board help friends and family all keep in contact, all at the same place—it's just remarkable! Thank you so much for providing this service. It's great for those of us who cannot afford to be there in person, but whose hearts are there to support our friends and family. It's people like you who make a difference in this world! May God Richly Bless You All in your continued efforts to help those in need!"

This was tested during a two-week period in the pediatric cardiology unit. One version was offered to CarePages managers, who were automatically presented with the survey at their fifth log-in, and another to CarePages visitors who first saw the survey at their third log-in. During a two-week period, 27 managers (90%) and 636 visitors (79%) responded. A majority (63%) of all respondents were female. The results, presented in **Exhibit 3,** showed that the service was highly valued. The majority of users reported that the service improved their opinion of the Children's Hospital, made them more likely to recommend it, led them to visit the hospital's website, and increased their likelihood of donating to the hospital foundation.

A second project involved the launch of pilot donation programs at C.S. Mott Children's Hospital in Michigan and Children's Memorial Hospital in Chicago. When visitors were asked about their willingness to make a donation, 11% stated that they were willing to make a donation immediately and another 22% requested the opportunity to do so later.

Eric was very excited about this finding, since it suggested that TLC could be presented to nonprofit hospitals as a self-financing service. But he recognized the importance of continuing to employ what some experts had described as "permission marketing."

> We're a mission-driven organization. We created this company to serve patients, their families, and their support networks. We understand the importance of the contract that we make with our members and we like to think of it as a moral contract. However, we recognize that the service we deliver to our members doesn't provide sufficient revenue to our customers, the hospitals. Added value items are what persuade hospitals to buy. So in certain respects we've commercialized the reach that we offer to the hospitals, but we try to do it in a way that we regard as "noble."

> We wouldn't do anything that would adversely impact the integrity of our service delivery. So we ask permission from our users to give their names to the hospital foundation for mailing—they can choose to opt in. If a hospital's CarePages service is sponsored by a third party, then a similar, permission-based approach might be used to give members the opportunity to receive information from that sponsor.

EXHIBIT 3   Executive Summary: Children's Hospital Boston Online Survey Results

In September 2002, TLContact added a new feature to the Children's Hospital Boston branded site: an online survey, with one version offered to CarePage Managers (who are first presented with the survey at their 5th log-in) and another to CarePages Visitors (who first see the survey after their 3rd log-in).

The TLContact Online Survey garnered an outstanding response rate. The initial test period ran from August 29 to September 13, 2002, and was targeted at patient families of the 50- bed cardiovascular unit of CHB. During the initial test period, surveys were completed by 27/30 (90%) of Managers and 636/806 (79%) of Visitors. There were a total of 663 respondents, most (63%) of whom were female. As detailed in the following section, virtually all Managers and Visitors highly value the CarePages service. Moreover, the majority of people who used the service report that it improved their opinion of the hospital, made them more likely to recommend the hospital, led them to visit the hospital's website, and increased their likelihood of donating to the hospital foundation.

Questions Asked of Both Managers and Visitors (27 Managers + 636 Visitors = 663 total)

	NUMBER OF RESPONSES	PERCENT
1. How are you related to the patient?		
I am a friend:	466	72%
I am a family member or guardian:	169	26%
I am a caregiver or care provider:	14	2%
I am the patient:	2	0%
2. Would you recommend the CarePage service to other people?		
Yes:	641	99%
No:	5	1%
3. Do you think that CarePages are an important service for hospitals to offer?		
Yes:	643	99%
No:	6	1%

4. Did your experience with Children's Hospital Boston's CarePage service. . .

	# YES	% YES
Improve your opinion of the hospital?	528	91%
Make you more likely to recommend this hospital?	503	86%
Cause you to visit Children's Boston Web site?	319	55%
Make you more likely to make a charitable gift to the hospital foundation?	298	53%

The questions that were asked only of Managers indicated that most learned of the CarePages service via hospital materials. The item in which Managers rated hospital service (see #2 below) indicates the value of increasing adoption of the CarePages service, perhaps though personal messages from hospital staff. These "real-time" service ratings offer clear and significant opportunities for improving service and satisfaction.

Questions Asked Only of Managers (27 total)

1. How did you learn about the CarePage service?

	NUMBER OF RESPONSES	PERCENT
Materials in the hospital	11	46%
Hospital staff member	7	29%
Friend or family member	6	25%
Hospital physician	0	0%
The Internet	0	0%
Ad or story in the media	0	0%

2. Please rate the following. . .

	POOR	FAIR	GOOD	VERY GOOD	EXCELLENT
	(% BASED ON 21 RESPONSES TO THIS ITEM)				
Overall quality of patient care:	0%	0%	0%	14%	86%
Doctor courtesy and attentiveness:	0%	5%	5%	19%	71%
Staff courtesy and attentiveness:	0%	0%	0%	33%	67%
Communication about patient care:	0%	0%	5%	43%	52%
Admissions process:	5%	5%	20%	30%	40%
Cleanliness of room:	0%	10%	14%	38%	38%
Food:	5%	10%	29%	38%	19%

(Continued)

EXHIBIT 3 (Continued)

Questions Asked Only of Visitors (442 Responses of 636 Total)

1. Please rate your overall impression of Children's Hospital Boston. . .

	% N/A	% POOR	% GOOD	% EXCELLENT
Quality of care:	55%	0%	9%	36%
Commitment to patient satisfaction:	51%	0%	11%	38%
Staff courtesy and attention:	60%	0%	9%	31%

Valid Percent (based on responses other than N/A)

Quality of care:	0%	20%	80%
Commitment to patient satisfaction:	0%	22%	78%
Staff courtesy and attention:	0%	23%	77%

2. Which of the following areas of health education are of interest to you?

	NUMBER OF RESPONSES	PERCENT OF RESPONDENTS*
Heart disease	153	47%
Cancer screening and treatment	120	37%
Women's health issues	122	37%
Health and fitness	121	37%
Weight control and obesity	96	29%
Common aging concerns	84	26%
Allergies and asthma	77	24%
Depression	75	23%
Diabetes	69	21%
Pain management	58	18%
Growth and development	51	16%
Behavioral problems	45	14%
Common childhood illnesses	41	13%
Clinical trials	21	6%
Immunization	17	5%
"Other"	28	9%

*The total percentage for all items is greater than 100% because the 326 people who answered this question offered multiple responses (i.e., they were interested in more than one area).

Responses to the Visitors' question regarding hospital service reflect what they hear from the CarePage Managers, as well as general impressions and personal experience. The item regarding interest in health education provides a sense of topics about which respondents desire more information, suggesting an opportunity for TLContact's partners.

The Current Situation

The first quarter of 2003 saw a rapid acceleration of revenues as more hospitals signed up for TLC service, existing customers renewed their contracts, and the number of CarePages at each institution continued to grow. Unlike new sales, renewals involved almost no additional cost for TLC and increasing utilization generated higher revenues from existing customers. TLC now served 40 hospitals; they were predominantly academic medical centers and included several of the most prestigious institutions in the United States and Canada. There were additional prospects in the sales pipeline. However, the company did not yet have any customers among nursing homes and hospices.

Existing competitors no longer seemed to pose a threat. VisitingOurs had recently shut down, and a comparison of the service features offered by TLC and the two remaining players, TheStatus and CaringBridge, showed that TLC's CarePages service had substantial advantages (**Exhibit 4**). Moreover, the prospect that some hospitals might attempt to create their own service offerings appeared increasingly unlikely. A large, well-endowed children's hospital, which had previously declared its intention to develop a similar service in-house, had recently decided to adopt TLC instead, admitting that internal analysis had revealed that going it alone would be not only be very time consuming but also prohibitively expensive.

PLANNING THE AGENDA FOR THE BOARD MEETING

Having completed the quarterly activity update, Eric turned to the task of creating an agenda for the upcoming board meeting. He started to rough out some thoughts. Under FUTURE GROWTH, he jotted down: "How fast? What directions? Key targets as selling priorities? Opportunities for revenues from new added-value services? Launch stripped-down version of TLC service at much lower price?"

The next heading was COMPETITION. He wrote "VisitingOurs folds. Comparison chart of TLC vs TheStatus, Caring Bridge. Future threats??" Eric paused, holding his pen in the air. He recognized that at some point a major player in the trillion-dollar healthcare market might be

EXHIBIT 4 Patient Communication Service Feature Comparison

	TLCONTACT	THESTATUS	CARINGBRIDGE
Customer Service			
Toll-free phone support	✓	✓	
Email support	✓	✓	✓
Spanish-language support	✓		
Comprehensive online help	✓	✓	
Features for Healthcare Facilities			
Custom Services			
Welcome message	✓		
Active survey system	✓		
Active donation system	✓		
Custom links to hospital's web site	✓	✓	
Unit specification	✓		
Spanish-language version	✓		
Baby-specific version	✓	✓	✓
Detailed usage reports	✓	✓	
Branding			
Co-branded patient page	✓	✓	✓
Entire web site co-branded	✓		
Customized colors and graphics	✓		
Features for Patients			
Patient Updates/News	✓	✓	✓
Email notification	✓		
Ability to edit	✓	✓	
Adjustable time zones	✓	✓	
Sorting and paging	✓		
Printer-friendly version	✓	✓	
Message Board	✓	✓	✓
Ability to reply to messages	✓		
Printer-friendly version	✓	✓	

tempted to replicate TLC's CarePages technology and service features. However, he was reassured that it would require an extensive investment of money and time. A further barrier to competition was patent protection. Ultimately, however, strategic partnerships, continued growth, product enhancements, and maintenance of exceptional customer satisfaction levels constituted the most complete defense. Lowering the pen to paper, he added: "Would competition hurt us? Can we competition-proof TLC?"

An important issue for the board to discuss concerned the role of future partnerships between TLC and other industry players. Recently, one large supplier of medical equipment and services had expressed interest in taking a minority financial stake in the company. POSSIBLE FINANCIAL PARTNERSHIP, he wrote, and below it: "Finance for accelerated growth? Market leverage? Pros and cons? Timing—now vs. later?"

Eric smiled. With an agenda like this, he anticipated a stimulating discussion at the board meeting. Then his face took on a more serious look. "WE ARE A MISSION-DRIVEN ORGANIZATION" he printed carefully, and underlined it twice.

STUDY QUESTIONS

1. *Evaluate the evolution of TLC and identify the key decisions that kept it afloat and underpinned its subsequent success.*
2. *How does TLC create value for (a) patients and (b) hospitals?*

3. *Review the four topics on Eric Langshur's draft of the agenda for the board meeting. As a board member, what position would you take on each topic and why?*

Glossary of Service Marketing and Management Terms

This glossary defines key terms used in this book and more generally in service marketing and management. For a broader coverage of marketing terms, see the glossaries in marketing management texts such as Philip Kotler and Kevin Lane Keller, *Marketing Management*, 12/e (Upper Saddle River, NJ: Prentice Hall, 2006) or consult the American Marketing Association's online *Dictionary of Marketing Terms* (www.marketingpower.com/mg-dictionary.php).

You should be aware that not everyone attaches precisely the same meaning to the same term. That's why it's important that you know and can clarify your own understanding when using a particular word or phrase. As often happens in an evolving field, the same terms are sometimes defined and used in different ways by academics and practitioners and among managers in different industries. Even individual companies may attach distinctive meanings to specific terms.

Words and phrases may also mean entirely different things when applied in nonmanagerial contexts. This situation, is of course, typical of language in general. For example, the 3,750-page, two-volume *Shorter Oxford English Dictionary*, 5/e (Oxford, UK, and New York: Oxford University Press, 2003) contains no less than 31 definitions of the word "service," embracing applications from domestic work, waiting in restaurants, and military duty to tennis, legal procedures, and the breeding of farm animals!

A

activity-based costing (ABC): an approach to costing based on identifying the activities being performed and then determining the resources that each consumes.

adequate service: minimum level of service that a customer will accept without being dissatisfied.

advertising: any paid form of nonpersonal communication by a marketer to inform, educate, or persuade members of target audiences.

arm's-length transactions: interactions between customers and service suppliers in which mail or telecommunications minimize the need to meet face to face.

attitude: A person's consistently favorable or unfavorable evaluations, feelings, and action tendencies toward an object or idea.

auction: a selling procedure managed by a specialist intermediary in which the price is set by allowing prospective purchasers to bid against each other for a product offered by a seller.

augmented product: a core product (a good or a service) plus supplementary elements that add value for customers (*see also* **flower of service**).

B

backstage (or technical core): those aspects of service operations that are hidden from customers.

balking: a decision by a customer not to join a queue because the wait appears too long.

banner ads: small, rectangular boxes on web sites that contain text and perhaps a picture to support a brand.

benchmarking: comparing an organization's products and processes to those of competitors or leading firms in the same or other industries to find ways to improve performance, quality, and cost effectiveness.

benefit: an advantage or gain that customers obtain from performance of a service or use of a physical good.

benefit-driven pricing: strategy of relating price to that aspect of the service that directly creates benefits for customers.

blog: a publicly accessible "web log" containing frequently updated pages in the form of journals, diaries, news listings, etc.; authors—known as bloggers—typically focus on specific topics.

blueprint: a visual map of the sequence of activities required for service delivery that specifies front-stage and backstage elements and the linkages between them.

boundary-spanning positions: jobs that straddle the boundary between the external environment, where customers are encountered, and the internal operations of the organization.

brand: a name, phrase, design, symbol, or some combination of these elements that identifies a company's services and differentiates it from competitors.

business model: means by which an organization generates income from sales and other sources through choice of pricing mechanisms and payors (e.g, user, advertiser or sponsor, other third parties), ideally sufficient to cover costs and create value for its owners. (*Note:* For nonprofits and public agencies, donations and designated tax revenues may be an integral part of the model.)

C

chain stores: two or more outlets under common ownership and control, and selling similar goods and services.

chase demand strategy: adjusting the level of capacity to meet the level of demand at any given time.

churn: loss of existing customer accounts and the need to replace them with new ones.

clicks and mortar: a strategy of offering service through both physical stores and virtual storefronts via web sites on the Internet.

competition-based pricing: setting prices relative to those charged by competitors.

competitive advantage: a firm's ability to perform in ways that competitors cannot or will not match.

complaint: a formal expression of dissatisfaction with any aspect of a service experience.

complaint log: a detailed record of all customer complaints received by a service provider.

conjoint analysis: a research method for determining the utility values that consumers attach to varying levels of a product's attributes.

consumption: purchase and use of a service or good.

control chart: a chart that graphs quantitative changes in service performance on a specific variable relative to a predefined standard.

control model of management: an approach based on clearly defined roles, top-down control systems, a hierarchical organizational structure, and the assumption that management knows best.

core competency: a capability that is a source of competitive advantage.

corporate culture: shared beliefs, norms, experiences, and stories that characterize an organization.

corporate design: consistent application of distinctive colors, symbols, and lettering to give a firm an easily recognizable identity.

cost leader: a firm that bases its pricing strategy on achieving the lowest costs in its industry.

cost-based pricing: relating the price to be charged for a product to the costs associated with producing, delivering, and marketing it.

credence attributes: product characteristics that customers may not be able to evaluate even after purchase and consumption.

critical incident: a specific encounter between customer and service provider in which the outcome has proved especially satisfying or dissatisfying for one or both parties.

critical incident technique (CIT): a methodology for collecting, categorizing, and analyzing critical incidents that have occurred between customers and service providers.

CRM system: information technology (IT) systems and infrastructure that support the implementation and delivery of a customer-relationship management strategy.

customer contact personnel: service employees who interact directly with individual customers, either in person or through mail and telecommunications.

customer equity: total combined customer lifetime value (*see definition*) of the company's entire customer base.

customer interface: all points at which customers interact with a service organization.

customer lifetime value (CLV): net present value of the stream of future contributions or profits expected over each customer's purchases during his or her anticipated lifetime as a customer of a specific organization.

customer relationship management (CRM): overall process of building and maintaining profitable customer relationships by delivering superior customer value and satisfaction.

customer satisfaction: a short-term emotional reaction to a specific service performance.

customer training: training programs offered by service firms to teach customers about complex service products.

customization: tailoring service characteristics to meet each customer's specific needs and preferences.

cyberspace: a virtual reality without physical existence, in which electronic transactions or communications occur.

D

data mining: extracting useful information about individuals, trends, and segments from often massive amounts of customer data.

data warehouse: a comprehensive database containing customer information and transaction data.

database marketing: building, maintaining, and using customer databases and other databases for contacting, selling, cross-selling, up-selling, and building customer relationships.

defection: a customer's decision to transfer brand loyalty from a current service provider to a competitor.

delivery channels: physical and electronic means by which a service firm (sometimes assisted by intermediaries) delivers one or more product elements to its customers.

demand curve: A curve that shows the number of units the market will buy at different prices.

demand cycle: a period of time during which the level of demand for a service will increase and decrease in a somewhat predictable way before repeating itself.

demographic segmentation: dividing the market into groups based on demographic variables such as age, gender, family life cycle, family size, income, occupation, education, religion, or ethnic group.

desired service: the "wished for" level of service quality that a customer believes can and should be delivered.

discounting: a strategy of reducing the price of an item below the normal level.

dynamic pricing: a technique, employed primarily by e-tailers, to charge different customers different prices for the same products, based on information collected about their purchase history, preferences, and price sensitivity.

E

e-commerce: buying, selling, and other marketing processes supported by the Internet (*see also* **e-tailing**).

eight (8) Ps: eight strategic elements, each beginning with P, in the services marketing mix, representing the key ingredients required to create viable strategies for meeting customer needs profitably in a competitive marketplace.

emotional labor: expressing socially appropriate (but sometimes false) emotions toward customers during service transactions.

empowerment: authorizing employees to find solutions to service problems and make appropriate decisions about responding to customer concerns without having to obtain a supervisor's approval.

enablement: providing employees with the skills, tools, and resources they need to use their own discretion confidently and effectively.

enhancing supplementary services: supplementary services that may add extra value for customers.

e-tailing: retailing through the Internet instead of through physical stores.

excess capacity: an organization's capacity to create service output that is not fully utilized.

excess demand: demand for a service at a given time that exceeds the organization's ability to meet customer needs.

expectations: internal standards that customers use to judge the quality of a service experience.

experience attributes: product performance features that customers can evaluate only during service delivery.

expert systems: interactive computer programs that mimic a human expert's reasoning to draw conclusions from data, solve problems, and give customized advice.

F

facilitating supplementary services: supplementary services that aid in the use of the core product or are required for service delivery.

fail point: a point in a process at which there is a significant risk of problems that can damage service quality (sometimes referred to humorously as an OTSU, short for "opportunity to screw up").

financial outlays: all monetary expenditures incurred by customers in purchasing and consuming a service.

fishbone diagram: a chart-based technique that relates specific service problems to different categories of underlying causes (also known as a cause-and-effect chart).

fixed costs: costs that do not vary with production or sales revenue.

flat-rate pricing: quoting a fixed price for a service in advance of delivery.

flowchart: a visual representation of the steps involved in delivering service to customers (*see also* **blueprint**).

flower of service: a visual framework for understanding the supplementary service elements that surround and add value to the product core (*see also* **augmented product**).

focus group: a group, typically consisting of six to eight people and carefully preselected on certain characteristics (e.g., demographics, psychographics, or product ownership), who are convened by researchers for indepth, moderator-led discussion of specific topics.

franchise: A contractual association between a franchiser (typically a manufacturer, wholesaler, or service organization) and independent businesspeople (franchisees), who buy the right to own and operate one or more units in the franchise system.

frequency program (FPs): a program designed to reward customers who buy frequently and in substantial amounts.

front stage: those aspects of service operations and delivery that are visible or otherwise apparent to customers.

G

geographic segmentation: dividing a market into geographic units such as countries, regions, or cities.

goods: physical objects or devices that provide benefits for customers through ownership or use.

H

halo effect: tendency for consumer ratings of one prominent product characteristic to influence ratings for many other attributes of that same product.

high-contact services: services that involve significant interaction among customers, service personnel, and equipment and facilities.

human resource management (HRM): coordination of tasks related to job design, employee recruitment, selection, training, and motivation; also includes planning and administering other employee-related activities.

I

image: a set of beliefs, ideas, and impressions held regarding an object.

impersonal communications: one-way communications directed at target audiences who are not in personal contact with the message source (including advertising, promotions, and public relations).

information processing: intangible actions directed at customers' assets.

information-based services: all services in which the principal value comes from the transmission of data to customers; also includes mental stimulus processing and information processing (*see definitions*).

in-process wait: a wait that occurs during service delivery.

inputs: all resources (labor, materials, energy, and capital) required to create service offerings.

intangibility: (*see* **mental intangibility** *and* **physical intangibility**).

intangible: something that is experienced and that cannot be touched or preserved.

integrated marketing communications (IMC): a concept under which an organization carefully integrates and coordinates its many communications channels to deliver a clear, consistent, and compelling message about the organization and its products

internal communications: all forms of communication from management to employees within an organization.

internal customers: employees who receive services from an internal supplier (another employee or department) as a necessary input to performing their own jobs.

internal marketing: marketing activities directed internally to employees to train and motivate them and instill a customer focus.

internal services: service elements within any type of business that facilitate creation of, or add value to, its final output.

Internet: a large public web of computer networks that connects users from around the world to each other and to a vast information repository.

inventory: for *manufacturing*, physical output stockpiled after production for sale at a later date; for *services*, future output that has not yet been reserved in advance, such as the number of hotel rooms still available for sale on a given day.

involvement model of management: an approach based on the assumption that employees are capable of self-direction and, if properly trained, motivated, and informed, can make good decisions concerning service operations and delivery.

iTV: (interactive television) procedures that allow viewers to alter the viewing experience by controlling TV program delivery (e.g., TiVo, video on demand) and/or content.

J

jaycustomer: a customer who acts in a thoughtless or abusive way, causing problems for the firm, its employees, and other customers.

L

levels of customer contact: extent to which customers interact physically with the service organization.

low-contact services: services that require minimal or no direct contact between customers and the service organization.

loyalty: a customer's commitment to continue patronizing a specific firm over an extended period of time.

M

market focus: extent to which a firm serves few or many markets.

market segmentation: process of dividing a market into distinct groups within each of which all customers share relevant characteristics that distinguish them from customers in other segments, and respond in similar ways to a given set of marketing efforts.

marketing communications mix: full set of communication tools (both paid and unpaid) available to marketers, including advertising, sales promotion, events, public relations and publicity, direct marketing, and personal selling.

marketing implementation: process that turns marketing plans into projects and ensures that such projects are executed in a way that accomplishes the plan's stated objectives.

marketing research: systematic design, collection, analysis, and reporting of customer and competitor data and findings relevant to a specific marketing situation facing an organization.

marketplace: a location in physical space or cyberspace (*see definition*) where suppliers and customers meet to do business.

mass customization: offering a service with some individualized product elements to a large number of customers at a relatively low price.

maximum capacity: upper limit to a firm's ability to meet customer demand at a particular time.

medium-contact services: services that involve only a limited amount of contact between customers and elements of the service organization.

membership relationship: a formalized relationship between the firm and a specified customer that may offer special benefits to both parties.

mental intangibility: difficulty for customers in visualizing an experience in advance of purchase and understanding the process and even the nature of the outcome (*see also* **physical intangibility**).

mental stimulus processing: intangible actions directed at people's minds.

mission statement: succinct description of what the organization does, its standards and values, whom it serves, and what it intends to accomplish.

molecular model: a framework that uses a chemical analogy to describe the structure of service offerings.

moment of truth: a point in service delivery at which customers interact with service employees or self-service equipment and the outcome may affect perceptions of service quality.

mystery shopping: a research technique that employs individuals posing as ordinary customers to obtain feedback on the service environment and customer–employee interactions.

N

needs: subconscious, deeply felt desires that often concern long-term existence and identity issues.

net value: the sum of all perceived benefits (gross value) minus the sum of all perceived outlays.

nonfinancial outlays: time expenditures, physical and mental effort, and unwanted sensory experiences associated with searching for, buying, and using a service.

nonmonetary costs: (*see* **nonfinancial outlays**).

O

opportunity cost: potential value of income or other benefits foregone as a result of choosing one course of action instead of other alternatives.

optimum capacity: point beyond which a firm's efforts to serve additional customers will lead to a perceived decline in service quality.

organizational climate: employees' shared perceptions of the practices, procedures, and types of behaviors that are rewarded and supported in a particular setting.

organizational culture: shared values, beliefs, and work styles that are based on an understanding of what is important to the organization and why.

OTSU ("opportunity to screw up"): (*see* **fail point**).

outputs: final outcome of the service delivery process as perceived and valued by customers.

P

Pareto analysis: an analytical procedure to identify what proportion of problem events is caused by each of several different factors.

people: customers and employees who are involved in service production.

people processing: services that involve tangible actions to people's bodies.

perception: process by which individuals select, organize, and interpret information to form a meaningful picture of the world.

perceptual map: a visual illustration of how customers perceive competing services.

permission marketing: a marketing communication strategy that encourages customers to volunteer permission to a company to communicate with them through specified channels so they may learn more about its products and continue to receive useful information or something else of value to them.

personal communications: direct communications between marketers and individual customers that involve two-way dialog (including face-to-face conversations, phone calls, and email).

personal selling: two-way communications between service employees and customers designed to influence the purchase process directly.

physical effort: undesired consequences to a customer's body resulting from involvement in the service delivery process.

physical evidence: visual or other tangible clues that provide evidence of service quality.

physical intangibility: service elements that are not accessible to examination by any of the five senses; (*more narrowly*) elements that cannot be touched or preserved by customers.

place and time: management decisions about when, where, and how to deliver services to customers.

positioning: establishing a distinctive place in the minds of customers relative to the attributes possessed by or absent from competing products.

possession processing: tangible actions to goods and other physical possessions belonging to customers.

postprocess wait: a wait that occurs after service delivery has been completed.

post-encounter stage: final stage in the service purchase process, in which customers evaluate the service experienced, form their satisfaction/dissatisfaction judgment with the service outcome, and establish future intentions.

post-transaction survey: a technique to measure customer satisfaction and perceptions of service quality while a specific service experience is still fresh in the customer's mind.

predicted service: level of service quality a customer believes a firm will actually deliver.

preprocess wait: a wait before service delivery begins.

prepurchase stage: first stage in the service purchase process, in which customers identify alternatives, weigh benefits and risks, and make a purchase decision.

price and other user outlays: expenditures of money, time, and effort that customers incur in purchasing and consuming services.

price bucket: an allocation of service capacity (e.g., seats) for sale at a particular price.

price bundling: charging a base price for a core service plus additional fees for optional supplementary elements.

price elasticity: extent to which a change in price leads to a corresponding change in demand in the opposite direction. (Demand is described as *price inelastic* when changes in price have little or no effect on demand.)

price leader: a firm that takes the initiative on price changes in its market area and is copied by others.

process: a particular method of operations or series of actions, typically involving steps that need to occur in a defined sequence.

product: the core output (either a service or a manufactured good) produced by a firm.

product attributes: all features (both tangible and intangible) of a good or service that can be evaluated by customers.

product elements: all components of the service performance that create value for customers.

productive capacity: amount of facilities, equipment, labor, infrastructure, and other assets available to a firm to create output for its customers.

productivity: how efficiently service inputs are transformed into outputs that add value for customers.

promotion and education: all communication activities and incentives designed to build customer preference for a specific service or service provider.

psychographic segmentation: dividing a market into different groups based on personality characteristics, social class, or lifestyle.

psychological burdens: undesired mental or emotional states experienced by customers as a result of the service delivery process.

public relations: efforts to stimulate positive interest in a company and its products by sending out news releases, holding press conferences, staging special events, and sponsoring newsworthy activities put on by third parties.

purchase process: the stages a customer goes through in choosing, consuming, and evaluating a service.

Q

quality: the degree to which a service satisfies customers by consistently meeting their needs, wants, and expectations.

queue: a line of people, vehicles, other physical objects, or intangible items waiting their turn to be served or processed.

queue configuration: the way in which a waiting line is organized.

R

rate fences: techniques for separating customers so that segments for whom the service offers high value are unable to take advantage of lower-priced offers.

reciprocal marketing: a marketing communication tactic in which an online retailer allows paying customers to receive promotions for another online retailer and vice versa, at no upfront cost to either party.

reengineering: analysis and redesign of business processes to create dramatic performance improvements in such areas as cost, quality, speed, and customers' service experiences.

relationship marketing: activities aimed at developing long-term, cost-effective links between an organization and its customers for the mutual benefit of both parties.

reneging: a decision by a customer to leave a queue before reaching its end because the wait is longer or more burdensome than originally anticipated.

repositioning: changing the position a firm holds in a consumer's mind relative to competing services.

retail displays: presentations in store windows and other locations of merchandise, service experiences, and benefits.

retail gravity model: a mathematical approach to retail site selection that involves calculating the geographic center of gravity for the target population and then locating a facility to optimize customers' ease of access.

return on quality: financial return obtained from investing in service quality improvements.

revenue management: a pricing and product design strategy based on charging different prices to different segments at different times to maximize the revenue that can be derived from a firm's available capacity during a specific time frame (also known as *yield management*).

role: a combination of social cues that guides behavior in a specific setting or context.

role congruence: extent to which both customers and employees act out their prescribed roles during a service encounter.

S

sales promotion: a short-term incentive offered to customers and intermediaries to stimulate faster or larger purchase.

satisfaction: a person's feelings of pleasure or disappointment resulting from a consumption experience when comparing a product's perceived performance or outcome in relation to his or her expectations.

script: a learned sequence of behaviors obtained through personal experience or communication with others.

search attributes: product characteristics that consumers can readily evaluate prior to purchase.

segment: a group of current or prospective customers who share common characteristics, needs, purchasing behavior, or consumption patterns.

sensory burdens: negative sensations experienced through a customer's five senses during the service delivery process.

service: an economic activity offered by one party to another, typically without transfer of ownership, creating value from rental of, or access to, goods, labor, professional skills, facilities, networks, or systems, singly or in combination.

service blueprint: (*see* **blueprint, flowchart**).

service concept: what the firm offers, to whom, and through what processes.

service delivery system: that part of the total service system during which final "assembly" of the elements takes place and the product is delivered to the customer; it includes the visible elements of the service operation.

service encounter: a period of time during which customers interact directly with a service.

service encounter stage: the second stage in the service purchase process, in which the required service is delivered through interactions between customers and the service provider.

service factory: a physical site where service operations take place.

service failure: a perception by customers that one or more specific aspects of service delivery have not met their expectations.

service focus: extent to which a firm offers few or many services.

service guarantee: a promise that if service delivery fails to meet predefined standards, the customer is entitled to one or more forms of compensation.

service marketing system: that part of the total service system in which the firm has any form of contact with its customers, from advertising to billing; it includes contacts made at the point of delivery.

service model: an integrative statement that specifies the nature of the service concept (what the firm offers, to whom, and through what processes), the service blueprint (how the concept is delivered to target customers), and the accompanying business model (how revenues will be generated sufficient to cover costs and ensure financial viability).

service operations system: that part of the total service system in which inputs are processed and the elements of the service product are created.

service preview: a demonstration of how a service works, to educate customers about the roles they are expected to perform in service delivery.

service quality: customers' long term, cognitive evaluations of a firm's service delivery.

service quality information system: an ongoing service research process that provides timely, useful data to managers about customer satisfaction, expectations, and perceptions of quality.

service recovery: systematic efforts by a firm after a service failure to correct a problem and retain a customer's goodwill.

service sector: the portion of a nation's economy represented by services of all kinds, including those offered by public and nonprofit organizations.

service–profit chain: a strategic framework that links employee satisfaction to performance on service attributes to customer satisfaction, then to customer retention, and finally to profits.

services marketing mix (*see* **eight (8) Ps**).

servicescape: the design of any physical location where customers come to place orders and obtain service delivery.

SERVQUAL: a pair of standardized 22-item scales that measure customers' expectations and perceptions concerning five dimensions of service quality.

standardization: reducing variation in service operations and delivery.

stickiness: a web site's ability to encourage repeat visits and purchases by providing users with easy navigation, problem-free execution of tasks, and keeping its audience engaged with interactive communication presented in an appealing fashion.

sustainable competitive advantage: a position in the marketplace that can't be taken away or minimized by competitors in the short run.

T

tangible: capable of being touched, held, or preserved in physical form over time.

target market: A part of the qualified available market with common needs or characteristics that a company decides to serve.

target segments: segments selected because their needs and other characteristics fit well with a specific firm's goals and capabilities.

time expenditures: time spent by customers during all aspects of the service delivery process.

three-stage model of service consumption: a framework depicting how consumers move from a prepurchase stage (in which they recognize their needs, search for and evaluate alternative solutions, and make a decision), to a service encounter search (in which they obtain service delivery), and thence a post-encounter stage (in which they evaluate service performance against expectations).

third-party payments: Payments to cover all or part of the cost of a service or good made by a party other than the user (who may or may not have made the actual purchase decision).

total costs: The sum of the fixed and variable costs for any given level of production.

transaction: an event during which an exchange of value takes place between two parties.

U

undesirable demand: requests for service that conflict with the organization's mission, priorities, or capabilities.

V

value chain: The series of departments within a firm or external partners and subcontractors that carry out value-creating activities to design, produce, market, deliver, and support a product or service offering.

value exchange: transfer of the benefits and solutions offered by a seller in return for financial and other value offered by a purchaser.

value net (*or* value network): a system of partnerships and alliances that a firm creates to source, augment, and deliver its service offering.

value proposition: a specified package of benefits and solutions that a company intends to offer and how it proposes to deliver them to customers, emphasizing key points of difference relative to competing alternatives.

value-based pricing: the practice of setting prices based on what customers are willing to pay for the value they believe they will receive.

variability: a lack of consistency in inputs and outputs during the service production process.

variable costs: costs that depend directly on the volume of production or service transactions.

viral marketing: using the Internet to create word-of-mouth effects to support marketing efforts.

W

wheel of loyalty: a systematic and integrated approach to targeting, acquiring, developing, and retaining a valuable customer base.

word of mouth: positive or negative comments about a service made by one individual (usually a current or former customer) to another.

Y

yield: the average revenue received per unit of capacity offered for sale.

yield management: (*see* **revenue management**).

Z

zone of tolerance: the range within which customers are willing to accept variations in service delivery.

Credits

Chapter 1, p. 8: Cunard Line Limited; p 19: Jerome Tisne, Getty Images, Inc.–Taxi; p. 22: Courtesy of Progressive Insurance; p. 23: Recreational Equipment, Inc. (REI). Kent, Washington.

Chapter 2, p. 37: Reprinted by permission of Boston Symphony Orchestra and Michael J. Lutch; p. 41: Courtesy of Masterfile Corporation; p. 43: Jeff Greenberg, PhotoEdit Inc.; p. 46: 2003–2004 XL Capital Ltd. All rights reserved; p. 58: Andrew Ward, Getty Images, Inc.–Photodisc.

Reading for Part I, p. 64: "In a Dizzying World, One Way to Keep Up," by Nick Wingfield, *The Wall Street Journal,* October 17, 2005, p. A1. Copyright 2005 by Dow Jones & Company, Inc. Reproduced with permission of Dow Jones & Company, Inc.

Chapter 3, p. 75: Sepp Seitz, Camp Woodfin & Associates; p. 79: Courtesy of Your Credit Card Companies; p. 92: Reprinted Courtesy of Caterpillar, Inc.

Chapter 4, p. 108: Courtesy of Swissôtel; p. 111: Shawn G. Henry; p. 113: Courtesy WilmerHale; p. 118: DHL Systems, Inc. Reprinted with permission of DHL International Ltd.

Chapter 5, p. 133: © King Features Syndicate; p. 150: Courtesy JP Morgan Chase & Company.

Chapter 6, p. 156: Courtesy of Wausau Insurance; p. 158: Courtesy of Accenture; p. 160: "What Did Your Consultants Leave Behind?" Copyright A. T. Kearney. All rights reserved. Reprinted with permission; p. 161: Courtesy of DHL Express Singapore; p. 178: www.easyjet.com/EN/Abut/photgallery.html. © easyJet airline company limited.

Chapter 7, p. 194: Courtesy Grant Thornton, LLP.

Readings for Part II, p. 207: "The Health Travellers," by Prosenjit Datta and Gina S. Krishnan, *Business World,* www.businessworldindia.com/Dec2203/coverstory02.asp. Reprinted with permission; p. 211: "The Strategic Levers of Yield Management," by Sheryl E. Kimes and Richard B. Chase, *Journal of Service Research,* 1, no. 2 (November 1998): 156–166. Sponsored by Center for Service Marketing, Owen Graduate School of Management, Vanderbilt University. Copyright © 1998 by Sage Publications, Inc. Reprinted by permission of Sage Publications, Inc.; p. 220: "FEES! FEES! FEES!" by Emily Thornton. Reprinted from 09/23/03 issue of *Business Week* by special permission, Copyright © 2003 by The McGraw-Hill Companies, Inc.; p. 225: "Best Practice: Defensive Marketing—How a Strong Incumbent Can Protect Its Position," by John H. Roberts, Harvard Business Review, November 2005. Reprinted by permission of Harvard Business School. © HBSP. All rights reserved.

Chapter 8, p. 247: Courtesy HSBC; p. 253: Richard Hutchings, PhotoEdit Inc.

Chapter 9, p. 265: David K. Crow, PhotoEdit Inc.; p. 272: Intrawest Corporation. Courtesy of Intrawest Corporation. Photo by Randy Links; p. 274: © 2003 The Hertz Corporation. All rights reserved; p. 282: Alexander Walter, Getty Images, Inc.–Taxi. Getty Images, Inc.

Chapter 10, p. 290 (top): Orbit Hotel & Hostel. Courtesy of ORBIT Hotel & Hostel in Los Angeles, orbithotel. com; (bottom): Starwood Hotels & Resorts, Worldwide, Inc.; p. 295: The Servicescapes Model from Mary J. Bitner, "Servicescapes: The Impact of Physical Surroundings on Customers and Employees," *Journal of Marketing* 56 (April 1992): 57–71; p. 298: Getty Images/Digital Vision; p. 301: Malaysia Tourism Promotion Board; p. 302: Iean-Leo Dugast, Panos Pictures; p. 303 (top): Gordon, Larry Dale, Getty Images, Inc.–Image Bank. (bottom): Angus Oborn, Rough Guides; Dorling Kindersley; Angus Oborn © Rough Guides; p. 305: The Impact of Scent and Music on Satisfaction and The Impact of Scent and Music on Impulse Purchases from Anna S. Mattila and Jochen Wirtz, "Congruency of Scent and Music as a Driver of In-Store Evaluations and Behavior," *Journal of Retailing* 77 (2001): 273–289.

Chapter 11, p. 313: Spencer Grant, Photo Researchers, Inc.; p. 315: DILBERT reprinted by permission of United Syndicate, Inc.; p. 316: Jagadeesh, Corbis/Reuters America. LLC. © Jagadeesh/Reuters/CORBIS. All rights reserved; p. 317: Reprinted from The Cycle of Failure from Leonard L. Schlesinger and James L. Heskett, "Breaking the Cycle of Failure in Services," *MIT Sloan Management Review* 31 (Spring 1991): 17–28, by permission of the publisher. Copyright © 2003 by Massachusetts Institute of Technology. All rights reserved; p. 318: Adapted from Lloyd C. Harris and Emmanuel Ogbonna, "Exploring Service Sabotage: The Antecedents, Types, and Consequences of Front-Line, Deviant, Antiservice Behaviors." *Journal of Service Research,* 4, no. 3 (2002): 163–183. Copyright © 2002 by Sage Publications, Inc. Reprinted by permission of Sage Publications, Inc.; p. 321: Reprinted from The Cycle of Success from Leonard L. Schlesinger and James L. Heskett, "Breaking the Cycle of Failure in Services," *MIT Sloan Management Review*

31 (Spring 1991): 17–28, by permission of the publisher. Copyright © 2003 by Massachusetts Institute of Technology. All rights reserved; p. 327: Spencer Grant, PhotoEdit Inc.; p. 332: Markus Matzel/Das. Peter Arnold, Inc.; p. 334: Copyright © 2003 Hewitt Associates LLC; p. 337: Reprinted with permission of The Ritz–Carlton Hotel Company, LLC.

Readings for Part III, p. 342: "Kung-Fu Service Development at Singapore Airlines," by Loizos Heracleous, Jochen Wirtz, and Robert Johnston from *Business Strategy Review* (Winter 2005): 26, 28–31; p. 346: "Getting More from Call Centers: Used Properly, They Can Be Strategic Assets," by Keith A. Gibson and Deepak K. Khandelwal from *The McKinsey Quarterly* (www.mckinseyquarterly.com). Copyright © 2005 McKinsey & Company. All rights reserved. Reprinted by permission; "How to Lead the Customer Experience," by Stephan H. Haeckel, Lewis P. Carbone, and Leonard L. Berry from *Marketing Management* January/February 2003.

Chapter 12, p. 360 (top): How Much Profit a Customer Generates over Time, based on reanalysis of data from Frederick J. Reichheld and W. Earl Sasser Jr., "Zero Defections: Quality Comes to Services," *Harvard Business Review* 73 (Sep–Oct 1990), 106–107. Reprinted by permission of Harvard Business School; p. 360 (bottom): Why Customers Are More Profitable over Time, based on reanalysis of data from Frederick J. Reichheld and W. Earl Sasser Jr., "Zero Defections: Quality Comes to Services," *Harvard Business Review* 73 (Sep–Oct 1990), 108. Reprinted by permission of Harvard Business School; p. 364: Corbis RF; p. 372: AP Wide World Photos; p. 372: Copyright © 2001, by The Regents of the University of California. Reprinted from the California Management Review 43, no. 4. By permission of The Regents; p. 373: The Customer Satisfaction–Loyalty Relationship, from Thomas O. Jones and W. Earl Sasser Jr., "Why Satisfied Customers Defect." *Harvard Business Review*, Nov–Dec 1995, p. 91. Reprinted by permission of Harvard Business School; p. 376: AP Wide World Photos; p. 379: Adapted from Susan M. Keaveney, "Customer Switching Behavior in Service Industries: An Exploratory Study," *Journal of Marketing* 59 (April 1995): 71–82.

Chapter 13, p. 393: Images.com; p. 394: Reprinted from Three Dimensions of Perceived Fairness in Service Recovery Processes, by Stephen S. Tax and Stephen W. Brown, "Recovering and Learning from Service Failure," *Sloan Management Review* 49, no. 1 (Fall 1998), pp. 75–88, by permission of the publisher. Copyright © 2003 by Massachusetts Institute of Technology. All rights reserved; p. 397: Adapted from Christopher Lovelock, Paul Patterson, and Rhett Walker, *Services Marketing: An Asia–Pacific and Australian Perspective* (Melbourne: Prentice Hall Australia, 2004) p. 135; p. 402: "Hampton Inn 100% Satisfaction Guarantee, Research Justifying the Guarantee." Used with permission of the Hilton Family. All rights reserved; p. 409: Bob Daemmrich, The Image Works.

Chapter 14, p. 418: Claes Fornell, "ASCI Commentary: Federal Government Scores," Special Report: Government Satisfaction Scores, Michigan: CFI Group, December 15, 2005, published on www.theacsi.com, accessed 21 Jan. 2006; p. 419: Betsie Van der Meer, Getty Images. Inc.– Stone Allstock; p. 425: The 7-gaps model, by Christopher Lovelock, *Product Plus* (New York: McGraw-Hill, 1994: 112), with further refinement by Lauren Wright, adapts and expands the 5-gaps model created by A. Parasuraman, Valarie A. Zeithaml, and Leonard L. Berry, "A Conceptual Model of Service Quality and Its Implications for Future Research," *Journal of Marketing* 49, Fall 1985, 41–50; p. 429: Christopher Lovelock, *Product Plus*, New York: McGraw-Hill, 1994, p. 131; p. 436: Getty Images, Inc.–Photodisc. Alex Williamson/Photodisc/Getty Images; p. 437: Andersen Ross, Getty Images–Digital Vision; p. 440: Randy Matusow; p. 444: Reproduced from Peter Pande, Robert P. Neuman, and Ronald R. Cavanagh, *The Six Sigma Way*, New York: McGraw-Hill, 2000.

Chapter 15, p. 448: *Putting the Service–Profit Chain to Work*, James L. Heskett, Thomas O. Jones, Gary W. Loverman, W. Earl Sasser Jr., and Leonard A. Schlesinger. March–April 1994, p. 166. Reprinted by permission of Harvard Business School; p. 450: Claes Fornell with David Van Amburg, Forrest Morgeson, Eugene V. Anderson, Barbara Everitt Bryant, and Michael C. Johnson, The American Customer Satisfaction Index at Ten Years. Ann Arbor, MI: ACSI, 2005, p. 45; p. 453: DILBERT reprinted by permission of United Syndicate, Inc.; p. 460: Courtesy Cirque du Soleil, Inc.

Readings for Part IV, p. 471: "Why Service Stinks," by Diane Brady, *Business Week*, October 23, 2000; p. 478: "Creating New Markets Through Service Innovation," by Leonard L. Berry, Venkatesh Shankar, Janet Turner Parish, Susan Cadwallader, and Thomas Dotzel, MIT Sloan Management Review, 47, no. 2 (Winter 2006): 56–63. Copyright © Massachusetts Institute of Technology, 2006. All rights reserved; p. 485: "The One Number You Need to Grow" by Frederick F. Reichheld. December 2003, p. 1. Reprinted by permission of Harvard Business School.

Cases, *p. 492:* "Susan Munro, Service Consumer," by Christopher Lovelock. Copyright © 2007 Christopher H. Lovelock; *p. 494:* "Four Customers in Search of Solutions," by Christopher

NAME INDEX

SUBJECT INDEX

A

Abstractness, 157
Access fees, 147
Account management programs, 168
Accounting firms, 193–194, 233–234
Activity-based costing (ABC), 128
Adequate service level, 47, 48
Advertising. *See also* Communications
  airline industry and, 162
  consumer resistance to, 169
  contribution of service personnel, 163
  defensive marketing and, 225, 227
  imagery and, 192, 194, 195
  intangibility and, 157–159
  Internet, 176–179, 561
  metaphors, 159–161
  pop-ups, 166
  repositioning and, 204
  service benefits, 45–46
  types of, 169–170
  visualization and, 159
Affect, drivers of, 293–294
Air rage, 253, 254, 353
Airline industry
  advertising and, 162
  airport location, 104–105
  biometrics and, 440–441
  branding and, 88
  check-in service, 263, 265, 279, 375
  customer loyalty and, 485–491
  determinant attributes, 189–190
  employee involvement in, 330
  fees, 220, 223
  flexible capacity and, 265
  flight departure delays and, 430–431
  hospitality and, 83
  international trade barriers and, 116–117
  Internet information and, 21
  job applicants, 324
  molecular model of, 69–70
  new service development in, 342–345
  organizational culture and, 337–338
  passenger behavior and, 251, 253, 254, 353
  pricing in, 133, 217, 270–271, 483–484
  revenue management and, 137, 138
  rewards program in, 377, 378
  service employees and, 315
  Southwest Airlines, 325
  team concept in, 331
  terminals, 105–106
  tiering in, 190–191, 471, 473, 475–476
  yield management in, 212–213
Alternative delivery methods, 91
Ambient conditions, effect of, 295–300, 304–306
American Customer Satisfaction Index (ACSI), 59, 60, 372, 417, 449, 486
America's Cup, 171
Annual surveys, 407–408
Aromatherapy, 298–299
Arousal, 292–294, 305
Arrival uncertainty, 215
Artifacts, 301–302
ATMs, 21, 57, 84, 105

B

Auctions, 133, 134
Augmented product, 69–70
Automobile industry, 16
  customer satisfaction and, 486–487
  Sullivan Ford (case), 545–549

Backstage, 133, 233, 240, 241, 438
Bank statements, 81
Banking industry
  ATMs, 21, 57, 84, 105
  Banco Azteca, 189
  bounce protection, 144
  call centers, 347
  electronic, 108, 109, 176
  fees and penalties, 143–144, 220–224
  front-line staff, 167
  global, 115
  ING Direct, 371
  Long Island Trust, 204
  Menton Bank, 569–576
  Royal Bank of Canada, 188
  service delivery system and, 108, 109, 112
  tiering in, 471, 473, 475, 476
  waiting time and, 275, 276
Banner advertising, 177–178
Barriers to entry, 116–117, 119, 334
Bartered services, 265
Behavior. *See* Customer behavior
Belligerent jaycustomer, 252–253
Benefit-driven pricing, 131
Billing, 77, 80–81, 85
Biometrics, 440–441
Blogs, 172–174
Blueprinting
  developing, 233–234
  fail points, identifying, 234, 240, 431–432
  failure proofing, 241–242
  of restaurant experience, 234–241
  script for employees and customers, 234
  for service environment design, 307
  setting service standards, 241
Bounce protection, 144
Boundary spanning, 313–314
Branded house, 87
Brands
  differentiation, 483
  hotel industry, 87
  positioning, 192–195
  shaping customer's experience of, 88–89
Break-even analysis, 128, 129
Bundling, 86, 144, 148, 244
Business model, 27, 66–67
  defined, 125

C

Call centers, 315–316
  maintaining relationships through, 363, 364
  as strategic assets, 346–351

Capacity, 149
  -constrained firms, 262–265, 283
  chasing demand, 264
  demand and, 261–262
  demand management strategies, 162–163
  flexible, 265
  productive defined, 262–263
  reservations system, 277–278, 281–284
  reserving for high-yield customers, 113
  stretching and shrinking, 264
  waiting time and, 275
Car rental industry
  customer loyalty and, 485, 488–491
  fees, 142, 223
  front-line staff, 167
  redesign and, 243
  service innovation in, 375–376, 478, 482
  tiering in, 190–191
Cause-and-effect analysis, 430
Cellular phone service pricing, 142, 143, 151, 371
Changeover time reduction, 216
Channel preferences, service delivery system, 103
Charismatic leadership, 335, 461–462
Chase demand strategy, 264
Check-in service, at airports, 263, 265, 279, 375
Child care centers, 192, 193
Churn, 365, 366, 379–380
Clicks and mortar, 90
Climate, organizational, 468
Co-branding, 195
Color, 299–300
Communications, 154–183. *See also* Advertising
  blogs, 172–174
  challenges and opportunities, 156–163
  changes in, 11
  corporate design, role of, 175–176
  direct marketing, 170
  editorial coverage, 174
  ethical issues in, 174–175
  integrated strategy, 179–180
  internal, 164, 336–338
  Internet marketing, 176–179
  marketing mix, 164–175
  originating sources of, 165–167
  public relations (PR), 171
  role in marketing, 155–156
  sales promotion, 170–172
  setting objectives, 163–164
  word of mouth, 172, 485, 486, 488, 489
Compensation, service recovery and, 399–400
Compensation package, 323
Competition drivers, 117, 118, 121
Competition-based pricing, 125, 130
Competitive advantage, 12
  service employees as source of, 311–312
Competitive markets, 10–11
Competitive positioning. *See* Positioning strategy

M

Malcolm-Baldrige model, 442–444
Management, leadership versus, 457
Market analysis, 196–197
Market drivers, 117–118, 121
Market entry, international, 114–115
Market focus, 186
Market niches, 114
Market research, 95, 491
Market segment
    defined, 187
    demand and, 267–268
Market segmentation, 114, 187–188, 279
Market size, 129
Market synergy, 95
Marketing
    communications (see communications)
    defensive, 225–229
    integration with other functions, 25–26,
      450–452
    internal, 336–337
    new perspectives on, 4–29
    permission, 170
    relationship marketing strategies, 168,
      363–365
    role of positioning in, 195–196
    services, challenges of, 16–22
    at Stena Line, 456, 458
Marketing communications mix, 164–175
Marketing mix, 22
    4 Ps of, 22
    8 Ps of services marketing, 22–25
Mass customization, 187
Master franchising, 111
Maximum capacity, 129
Medical travelers, 207–210
Mediocrity, cycle of, 317, 319–320
Mehrabian-Russell Stimulus-Response
    model, 292
Membership relationships, 364–365,
    376–377
Mental impalpability, 158
Mental processing services, 115
Mental stimulus processing, 34, 36, 37, 71,
    75–76
Mercosur, 116
Metaphors, advertising and, 159–161
Micro-segmentation strategies, 187, 188
Ministores, 105
Mobile telephony, 108, 109
Moment of truth, 50, 312, 313, 390
Motivation, 332–334
Multiculturalism, 112, 114
Multipurpose facilities, 105–106
Munsell system, 299
Music, 296–298, 305
Mystery shopping, 408, 409

N

NAFTA (North American Free Trade
    Agreement), 115
NAICS (North American Industry
    Classification System), 8, 9, 15
NAPCS (North American Product
    Classification System), 9
Needs, 11–12, 40–42
Negotiation flow, 99, 108
Net value, 131, 136
Network marketing, 363, 364
New service development
    in airline industry, 342–345
    hierarchy of, 89–90

physical goods as source of ideas,
    91–93
reengineering service processes,
    90–91
research in design of, 93
success in, 93–94
Nongovernmental organizations
    (NGOs), 6
Nonmonetary costs, 133, 134–136
Nonownership, distinction between
    ownership and, 12–14
Nonphysical rate fences, 141, 217
Nonprofit organizations
    earned-income venture (case), 550–566
    Massachusetts Audubon Society (case),
      602–615
Nonsearchability, 157

O

Online auction services, 89, 480, 482
Online banking, 108, 109
Online shopping, 110, 169
Operating hours, extended, 106–107
Operations, 52
    integration with marketing/human
      resources, 25–26, 450–452
    interfunctional conflict, 451–452
    at Stena Line, 456, 458
Order taking, 77, 78–80
Organizational climate, 468
Organizational culture, 326, 335–338,
    466–467, 484
OTSU (opportunity to screw up), 240
Outcome justice, 394
Outputs, 20–21
Outsourcing, 5, 10, 118, 129, 198, 199, 348
Overbooking, 146, 215
Overdraft protection, 143, 144
Ownership, benefits without, 12–14

P

Package delivery industry, 89, 103, 118,
    127, 160, 162, 175, 223, 478, 480, 483
Pacto Andino, 116
Parallel waiting lines, 275–276, 277
Pareto analysis, 431
Parity strategy, 226
Pass-along emails, 172, 173
Payment, 77, 81, 85
    collection of, 148
    forms of, 149–150
    prepayments, 149
PDAs (personal digital assistants), 108
Pedestrian counts, 101
Penalties, 143–145
People, 25, 310. See also Service employees
People processing services, 34, 35, 71,
    74–75, 85
    impact of globalization drivers on, 121
    international market entry and,
      114–115
    internationalization opportunities of,
      119–120
Perceived risk, 43–44
Perceptual mapping, 199–203
Permission marketing, 170
Personal communications, 165
Personal selling, 168
Personality tests, 324–325
Personalized pricing, 134
Physical costs, 134–136

Physical environment, 25. See also Service
    environment
Physical equipment and facilities,
    productive capacity and, 262
Physical rate fences, 141, 217
Place, 23–24. See also Service delivery
    system
Planning, 86–89, 457
Platinum-tier customers, 369, 370
Pleasure, 292–294
Podcasting, 166, 170
Poka-yoke technique, 241–242, 432
Pop-ups, 166, 170
Position statement, 197
Positioning maps, 199–203
Positioning strategy, 66, 78, 184–206
    across multiple services, 198
    for brand distinguishment, 191–196
    changing, 204
    child care centers, 192, 193
    copy versus product positioning,
      192–195
    evolutionary, 199
    focus for competitive advantage,
      185–187
    in general, 184
    Giordano (case), 511–519
    internal, market, and competitor
      analyses, 196–199
    market segmentation for, 187–188
    positioning maps, 199–203
    service attributes and levels, 188–191
Positive strategy, 226
Possession processing services, 34, 35–36,
    71, 75, 85–86
    impact of globalization drivers on, 121
    international market entry and, 115
    internationalization opportunities of,
      120
Post-encounter stage of service
    consumption, 38, 40, 58–60, 164
Postconsumption costs (aftercosts), 135
Predicted service levels, 47–48
Prepayments, 149
Prepurchase stage of service
    consumption, 39–40, 164
Price bucket, 137, 141
Price bundling, 48, 144
Price customization, 140–141
Price discrimination, 134
Price elasticity, 139–140
Price leadership, 130
Price sensitivity, 129, 136
Price/quality relationship, 47
Pricing, 24
    activity-based, 128
    benefit-driven, 131
    cellular phone service, 142, 143, 151
    competition-based, 125, 130
    complexity in, 142–144
    cost-based, 125, 128–130
    defensive marketing and, 226–228
    demand and, 269, 270–271
    differential, 216–218
    discounting, 127, 132, 144, 148, 162
    dynamic, 133, 134
    effective, 125–127
    ethical concerns and, 142–146
    flat-rate, 132
    hotel positioning maps and, 199–203
    objectives, 126–127
    proper price mix, 217
    putting into practice, 146–151
    revenue management, 136–142
    specific basis for, 146–147